MANAGING
PROTECTED
AREAS
A GLOBAL GUIDE

MANAGING PROTECTED AREAS

A GLOBAL GUIDE

Edited by Michael Lockwood, Graeme L. Worboys and Ashish Kothari

The World Conservation Union

WORLD COMMISSION ON PROTECTED AREAS

FROM THE AMERICAN PEOPLE

Ministero dell'Ambiente e della Tutela del Territorio

DIREZIONE GENERALE PER LA PROTEZIONE DELLA NATURA

GLOBAL ENVIRONMENT FACILITY

UNEP

London • Sterling, VA

First published by Earthscan in the UK and USA in 2006

ISBN: 1-84407-303-3   paperback
        978-1-84407-303-0   paperback
        1-84407-302-5   hardback
        978-1-84407-302-3   hardback

Typesetting by FiSH Books, Enfield
Printed and bound in the UK by Cromwell Press, Trowbridge
Cover design by Andrew Corbett

For a full list of publications please contact:

Earthscan
8–12 Camden High Street
London, NW1 0JH, UK
Tel: +44 (0)20 7387 8558
Fax: +44 (0)20 7387 8998
Email: earthinfo@earthscan.co.uk
Web: www.earthscan.co.uk

22883 Quicksilver Drive, Sterling, VA 20166-2012, USA

Earthscan is an imprint of James and James (Science Publishers) Ltd and publishes in association with the
International Institute for Environment and Development

A catalogue record for this book is available from the British Library

Library of Congress Cataloging-in-Publication Data

Protected areas management: a global guide/edited by Michael Lockwood,
Graeme L. Worboys and Ashish Kothari.
       p. cm.
    Includes bibliographical references.
    ISBN-13: 978-1-84407-303-0 (pbk. : alk. paper)
    ISBN-10: 1-84407-303-3 (pbk. : alk. paper)
    ISBN-13: 978-1-84407-302-3 (hardback : alk. paper)
    ISBN-10: 1-84407-302-5 (hardback : alk. paper)
  1. Protected areas–Management. I. Lockwood, Michael, 1955– II. Worboys,
Graeme L. III. Kothari, Ashish, 1961–
    S944.5.P78P76 2006
    333.72–dc22

                                                    2006029025

Cover photographs by Graeme L. Worboys, from top left Wolong Nature Reserve, China; Sequoia National
Park, US; Niagara Falls, Canada; Gannet Colony, New Zealand; Yellowstone National Park, US; Aboriginal
paintings, Australia; Grass trees, Kosciuszko National Park, Australia.

The paper used for the text of this book if FSC certified.
FSC (the Forest Stewardship Council) is an international network to
promote responsible management of the world's forests.

Printed on elemental chlorine-free paper

Mixed Sources
Product group from well-managed
forests and other controlled sources
www.fsc.org Cert no. TT-TOC-2082
© 1996 Forest Stewardship Council
FSC

Contents

List of Plates, Figures and Tables

Plates

Figures

Tables

List of Boxes and Case Studies

Boxes

Case studies

Acknowledgements

This book is a result of a collective effort by many people from around the world.

Editors

The compilers and editors of the book were:

- Michael Lockwood, senior lecturer at the School of Geography and Environmental Studies, University of Tasmania, Australia;
- Graeme L. Worboys, the World Conservation Union (IUCN) World Commission on Protected Areas (WCPA), vice chair for the Mountains Biome, Australia;
- Ashish Kothari, IUCN WCPA Commission on Environmental, Economic and Social Policy (CEESP), vice chair of Theme on Indigenous and Local Communities, Equity and Protected Areas (TILCEPA), India.

Executive editorial team

The work was guided by input from the IUCN Executive Editorial Team, comprising:

- Adrian Phillips, IUCN WCPA, Cardiff;
- Peter Shadie, IUCN Programme on Protected Areas, Switzerland;
- Elaine Shaughnessy, IUCN Publications, Cambridge;
- David Sheppard, IUCN Programme on Protected Areas, Switzerland.

Special thanks go to Peter Shadie for his extensive liaison and coordination work, as well as for his compilation of Appendices 3 and 4.

Vth IUCN World Parks Congress workshop and theme leaders

This book draws heavily on the knowledge compiled for, and generated at, the 2003 Vth IUCN World Parks Congress in Durban, South Africa. In recognition of all contributors to that congress, we acknowledge as their representatives the leaders of the seven workshop streams and three cross-cutting themes:

- Mohamed I. Bakarr and Gustavo da Fonseca, 'Building Comprehensive Protected Area Systems';
- Peter Bridgewater, 'Linkages in the Landscape and Seascape';
- Julia Carabias, 'Developing the Capacity to Manage Protected Areas';
- Charles Ehler and Peter Cochrane, 'Marine Protected Areas';
- Marc Hockings, 'Evaluating Management Effectiveness';
- Natarajan Ishwaran and Adrian Phillips, 'World Heritage';
- Jim Johnston and Grazia Borrini-Feyerabend, 'Governance of Protected Areas: New Ways of Working Together';
- Ashish Kothari, 'Communities and Equity'.
- Jeffrey A. McNeely, 'Building Broader Support for Protected Areas';
- Carlos E. Quintela and Lee Thomas, 'Building a Secure Financial Future'.

Chapter authors

The editors have had the pleasure of working with a group of dedicated chapter authors from each continent (with the exception of Antarctica!). Apart from the editors, these authors were:

- Mohammed I. Bakkar, director of projects, Conservation International, US;
- Grazia Borrini-Feyerabend, IUCN CEESP vice chair (governance, equity and rights) and WCPA vice chair (governance, equity and livelihoods), Italy;
- Juliet Chapman, honorary research associate, School of Geography and Environmental Studies, University of Tasmania, Australia;
- Jon Day, director of conservation, heritage and indigenous partnerships, Great Barrier Reef Marine Park Authority, Australia;
- Terry De Lacy, chief executive, Sustainable Tourism Cooperative Research Centre, Australia;
- Marc Hockings, leader of IUCN WCPA Science and Management, and senior lecturer at the School of Natural and Rural Systems Management, University of Queensland, Australia;
- John Hough, leader of IUCN WCPA Capacity-Building and Awareness-Raising, and principal technical adviser in biodiversity at the Global Environment Facility (GEF), US;
- Robyn James, senior conservation officer, Queensland Parks and Wildlife Service, Australia;
- Jim Johnston, Cooperative Programmes Branch, Parks Canada, Canada;
- Kevin Kiernan, lecturer at the School of Geography and Environmental Studies, University of Tasmania, Australia;
- Jamie Kirkpatrick, professor at the School of Geography and Environmental Studies, University of Tasmania, Australia;
- Jane Lennon, councillor at the Australian Heritage Council, Australia;
- Fiona Leverington, Team Leader in planning and interpretation, Queensland Parks and Wildlife Service, Australia;

- Jeffrey A. McNeely, chief scientist at the IUCN, Switzerland;
- Diane Pansky, associate director of the Michoacan Reforestation Fund, US;
- Carlos E. Quintela, IUCN WCPA vice chair of Sustainable Financing of Protected Areas, Bolivia; and director of the Conservation Finance Program, Wildlife Conservation Society, US;
- Trevor Sandwith, deputy chair for WCPA and project coordinator at Cape Action for People and the Environment, South Africa;
- Michelle Whitmore, research associate at the Cooperative Research Centre for Sustainable Tourism, Australia;
- Colin Winkler, honorary research associate at the School of Geography and Environmental Studies, University of Tasmania, Australia.

Case study contributors

This book is illustrated by numerous case studies that illustrate examples of good protected area management practice around the world. Some of these studies have been drawn from published sources, while others, importantly, are original contributions to the book by the following authors:

- María J. Andrade-Nuñez, CID/Karumbe and Facultad de Ciencias de la Universidad de la República Oriental del Uruguay, Uraguay;
- Linus Bagley, Binna Burra Mountain Lodge, Australia;
- Grant Baker, Department of Conservation, Wellington, New Zealand;
- Tom Barrett, Parks and Wildlife Division, New South Wales, Australia;
- Marco Bassi, University of Bologna, Italy;
- Rosemary Black, Charles Sturt University, Australia;
- Rob Buffler, Yellowstone to Yukon Conservation Initiative, US;
- Robyn Bushell, University of Western Sydney, Australia;
- Bruno Carpinetti, Administración de Parques Nacionales, Argentina;
- Oscar Castillo, Wildlife Conservation Society, Bolivia;
- Jessica Castro-Prieto, CID/Karumbe and

Facultad de Ciencias de la Universidad de la República Oriental del Uruguay, Uraguay;
- Vanessa Coverdale, Queensland Parks and Wildlife Service (QPWS), Australia;
- Pam Cromarty, New Zealand Department of Conservation, New Zealand;
- Jon Day, Great Barrier Reef Marine Park Authority, Australia;
- Susan Downing, Griffith University, Australia;
- Sylvain Dromzee, Parc National de Port-Cros, France;
- Joanna Durbin, Durrell Wildlife Conservation Trust, Madagascar;
- Christo Fabricius, Rhodes University, South Africa;
- Murray Ferguson, Cairngorms National Park Authority, UK;
- Peter Fearnhead, South African National Parks, South Africa;
- Percy FitzPatrick, Institute of Ornithology, University of Cape Town, South Africa;
- Peter Fredman, European Tourism Research Institute, Sweden;
- Chachu Ganya, Pastoralist Integrated Support Programme, Kenya;
- Catherine Gillies, Parks and Wildlife Division, New South Wales Department of Environment and Conservation, Australia;
- Jim Johnston, Parks Canada, Canada;
- Kumi Kato, School of Language and Comparative Culture, University of Queensland, Australia;
- Ashish Kothari, co-chair, TILCEPA;
- Pramod Krishnan, Periyar Tiger Reserve, India;
- Charles Lawson, Griffith University, Australia;
- Fung Mei Sarah Li, Murdoch University, Western Australia;
- Carolyn Littlefair, Griffith University, Australia;
- Martha West Lyman, Quebec-Labrador Foundation, Atlantic Center for the Environment, US;
- Ian McFadden, New Zealand Department of Conservation, New Zealand;
- Pedro da Cunha e Menezes, Brazilian Ministry of External Relations, Brazil;
- Tobgay S. Namgyal, Bhutan Trust Fund for Environmental Conservation, Bhutan;
- Andrew Noss, Wildlife Conservation Society, Bolivia;

- Chief Edwin Ogar, Ekuri community, Nigeria;
- Gonzalo Oviedo, IUCN, Ecuador;
- Sanjeeva Pandey, Great Himalayan National Park, India;
- Alberto Paniagua, Peruvian Trust Fund for National Parks and Protected Areas, Peru;
- Neema Pathak, Kalpavriksh, India;
- Catherine Pickering, Griffith University, Australia;
- Damien Pierce, Department for Environment and Heritage, South Australia, Australia;
- Mark Poll, Tasmania Parks and Wildlife Service, Australia;
- David Priddel, New South Wales Department of Environment and Conservation, Parks and Wildlife Division, Australia;
- Floyd Robinson, Partners in Community Development, Fiji;
- Allison Rossetto, James Cook University, Australia;
- Roy Morgan Research, Australia;
- Steve Sallans, Tasmanian Parks and Wildlife Service, Australia;
- Margaret Sandwith, Institute of Ornithology, University of Cape Town, South Africa;
- Trevor Sandwith, IUCN/WCPA Task Force on Transboundary Protected Areas, South Africa;
- Marcelo Segalerba, Amazon Conservation Team, Brazil;
- Peter Shadie, IUCN Programme on Protected Areas, Switzerland;
- Jim Sharp, Department of Conservation and Land Management, Western Australia, Australia;
- David Singh, Iwokrama International Centre, Guyana;
- Irynej Skira, formerly Tasmania Parks and Wildlife Service, Australia;
- Dermot Smyth, James Cook University, Australia;
- Vivienne Solís Rivera, General Manager of CoopeSoliDar RL, Costa Rica;
- Penny Spoelder, New South Wales Department of Environment and Conservation, Australia;
- Erica Stanciu, Scientific Council, Retezat National Park, Romania;

- Karma Tshering, Nature Conservation Division, Ministry of Agriculture, Bhutan
- Stephanie Tuxill, Quebec–Labrador Foundation (QLF), Atlantic Center for the Environment, US;
- Christopher Vaughan, Department for International and Rural Development, University of Reading, UK;
- John Watson, Western Australia Department of Conservation and Land Management, Australia;
- Agathe Wegner, Murdoch University, Western Australia;
- Andy Wilson, North York Moors National Park, UK;
- Amanda Younge, development consultant, South Africa.

Reviewers

The text has benefited considerably from the constructive comments and criticisms made by a number of reviewers.

A draft of the whole manuscript was reviewed by:

- David Harmon, WCPA regional vice chair for North America and executive director at the George Wright Society, US;
- Cristi Nozawa, IUCN WCPA regional vice chair for South-East Asia, and partner development officer at Birdlife International, the Philippines.

We particularly thank Cristi and Dave for their dedicated and detailed work on such a large volume of material.

Each chapter has been subject to scrutiny by at least one reviewer, and their suggestions and corrections have been addressed by the editors and chapter authors. We thank the following reviewers for their efforts:

- Janis Alcorn, independent consultant, US;
- Tasneem Balasinorwala, Kalpavriksh and IUCN WCPA–CEESP TILCEPA, India;
- Grazia Borrini-Feyerabend, IUCN WCPA–CEESP, 'Governance Equity and Livelihoods';
- Jessica Campese, IUCN WCPA–CEESP

Theme on Governance, Equity and Rights (TGER), US;
- Nigel Dudley, 'Equilibrium', UK;
- Lorne Kriwoken, University of Tasmania, Australia;
- Leonardo Lacerda, Protected Areas Initiative, World Wildlife Fund (WWF) International, Switzerland;
- Jeffrey Langholz, Monterey Institute of International Studies, US;
- Nikita Lopoukhine, IUCN WCPA, Canada;
- Jeffrey A. McNeely, IUCN, Switzerland;
- Adrian Phillips, Cardiff University, UK;
- Simon Rietbergen, IUCN Ecosystem Management Programme, Switzerland;
- Robbie Robinson, consultant, South Africa;
- Trevor Sandwith, IUCN/WCPA Task Force on Transboundary Protected Areas, South Africa;
- Gilles Seutin, national coordinator with Parks Canada, Canada;
- Peter Shadie, IUCN Programme on Protected Areas, Switzerland;
- David Sheppard, IUCN Programme on Protected Areas, Switzerland;
- Lee Thomas, IUCN/WCPA Task Force on Sustainable Financing, Australia;
- Simon Woodley, S&J Woodley Party Ltd, Australia.

Numerous people also provided helpful comments on specific sections, including Andrea Athanas (IUCN), Mark Botha (Botanical Society of South Africa), Stuart Chape (United Nations Environment Programme (UNEP)–World Conservation Monitoring Centre (WCMC)), Andrew Parsons, International Council on Mining and Metals (ICMM)) and Charles Taylor (BHP Billiton).

Publishing and production

Our special thanks are extended to Rob West, Camille Adamson, Mike Fell and other staff of Earthscan.

We also sincerely thank:

- Hélène Annonier for her French translation;
- Juliet Chapman for her extensive administrative support;
- Ian Charles, Charles Walsh Nature Tourism

Services Party Ltd, for his prompt and high-quality work in preparing the figures for publication;

- Terry De Lacy, for his assistance in managing the financial support;
- Alicia Held and Sarah Gindre for their assistance in accessing images from the IUCN photo library;
- Debra James, Oxford University Press Australia, for her assistance in securing permission to use material from Protected Area Management: Principles and Practice (Worboys et al, 2005);
- Laura Macleod, Higher Education Division, Oxford University Press Canada, for her comments on an early proposal for this book;
- Jim Thorsell for permission to use his photographs;
- Cesar Tovar for his administrative support;
- Lynda White, business manager, Cooperative Research Centre for Sustainable Tourism, for her administrative support;
- Colin Winkler for compiling the data for Appendices 5 and 6;
- project facilitation by UNEP and IUCN.

Financial support

Preparation and publication of this book has been made possible by the financial support of:

- US Agency for International Development (USAID);
- Ministry of Environment and Protection of the Territory, Nature Conservation Service, Government of Italy;
- Environment Australia, Australian Department of the Environment and Heritage, Australia;
- UNEP Division of Global Environment Facility Coordination (UNEP DGEF);
- host organizations that supported all of the above editors, authors and contributors.

Copyright permissions

Material in several chapters has been reproduced by permission of Oxford University Press Australia from *Protected Area Management Second Edition* by Worboys, Lockwood and De Lacy, 2005 © Oxford University Press, www.oup.com.au.

Every effort has been made to trace the original source of copyright material contained in this book. The publisher would be pleased to hear from copyright holders to rectify any errors and omissions.

Foreword

The book you hold in your hands represents a first. Never before has such a compilation and synthesis on protected area management been attempted. *Managing Protected Areas: A Global Guide* brings together state-of-the-art thinking from around the world on the complex business of managing protected areas.

There are many fine books celebrating the beauty and uniqueness of the world's protected areas, but fewer on how to manage these special places. This book synthesizes contributions of renowned specialists from different countries; diverse environments; vastly variable resourcing and capacity levels; and many different cultural contexts. The result is a cohesive set of issue-driven chapters that offer the reader the latest thinking on the intricacies of contemporary protected area management.

Today's protected area manager needs a broad range of skills and personal attributes to manage effectively. Beyond the core knowledge of an area's natural, cultural and other assets, he or she needs a far deeper understanding of the landscape, both physical and metaphorical, within which protected areas must operate in the 21st century. It is only through understanding the driving ecological, social and economic processes which impact on a protected area that one can address the conditions which are necessary for a protected area to flourish. Today's protected area manager needs to be part ecologist, historian, economist, sociologist, diplomat, negotiator and marketer to name but a few!

This book was conceived during the course of the highly successful Vth World Conservation Union (IUCN) World Parks Congress held in Durban, South Africa, in 2003. Its content draws heavily on the rich deliberations in Durban and the many experts and stakeholders who gathered to chart a global agenda for protected areas as we enter the new millennium. The congress produced the Durban Accord, a passionate collective statement that spells out the principles by which protected areas should be managed to ensure a prosperous future. In a sense, *Managing Protected Areas: A Global Guide* offers a detailed elaboration of the principles of the Durban Accord: a handbook for managers and others to translate these high-level principles into practical management action.

The contribution of each of the learned authors drawing on extensive input from IUCN's global network of protected area expertise, most particularly the World Commission on Protected Areas (WCPA), strengthens our understanding of the intricacies of protected area management, ensuring that we have robust systems of protected areas with well-informed managers at their helm. Whatever your interests in protected areas, I am sure you will find this book an invaluable reference, a source book of ideas, models, case studies and approaches from around the world.

Nikita Lopoukhine
Chair, IUCN World Commission on Protected Areas
March 2006
Gatineau, Quebec, Canada

Introduction

Michael Lockwood, Graeme L. Worboys and Ashish Kothari

One of the greatest land-use and sea-use transformations occurred at the end of the 20th century and continues into the start of the 21st century. Nearly all nations on Earth contributed to the establishment of national parks and other protected areas, so that in just 40 years a few hundred formally declared protected areas have grown to more than 100,000 protected areas worldwide. Recognition is also starting to be given to community conserved areas, many of which have for a much longer time provided protection to natural and cultural values. With 188 nations participating as parties to the Convention on Biological Diversity (CBD), there is almost universal agreement that protected areas are among the most important tools for the conservation of biodiversity in a rapidly developing and more populous world. As such, they play a critical role for life on Earth, including the health and well-being of humans.

Protected areas are therefore one of the Earth's most significant land- and sea-use designations. They incorporate a wide range of sites, from those established and managed by governments, to those managed by indigenous people, local communities, non-governmental organizations (NGOs), and private companies and individuals. They are essential to conserve wild nature and the cultural aspects associated with it. They help to sustain life on Earth. They safeguard the varied landscapes and rich biodiversity that are valuable for their own sakes, and for the many benefits they provide to humans – local communities, indigenous peoples and the many non-locals who care about and have an interest in them:

> *Protected areas, together with conservation, sustainable use and restoration initiatives in the wider land and seascape, are essential components in national and global biodiversity conservation strategies. They provide a range of goods and ecological services while preserving natural and cultural heritage. They can contribute to poverty alleviation by providing employment opportunities and livelihoods to people living in and around them. In addition, they also provide opportunities for research, including for adaptive measures to cope with climate change, environmental education, recreation and tourism. (CBD, 2003, p349)*

The growth of protected areas will continue during the 21st century, and so will the need for their effective management. The act of reservation does not in itself ensure that these values and benefits are maintained in the long term. Protected areas must be actively managed to meet the objectives for which they were established. Plants, animals, landscapes, seascapes and ecosystems face numerous threats to their health and integrity. Such threats, ranging from unsustainable development processes and projects to over-extraction of resources, the introduction of invasive species and – the latest of them all – climate change, need to be understood and countered effectively. The needs, rights and responsibilities of local communities and indigenous peoples must be addressed. Tourists need to be hosted safely and sustainably.

Effective handling of such matters requires an understanding of managerial, administrative, operational, planning and evaluative processes. It must incorporate knowledge of natural and cultural systems, their components, and threats to their integrity and health.

Protected areas also need the support of citizens, governments, local communities and indigenous peoples. Individuals, NGOs, corporations, nations and the international community must continue and extend their substantial efforts and investments in protected areas. Their special values must become as much a part of people's aspirations and world views as security, health and education.

If they are to achieve this 'mainstreaming', protected areas must be understood and managed as part of the complex social, economic and biophysical matrix in which they are located. Their management must be linked to the surrounding land and seascape. They must be governed in ways that recognize the rights, needs and aspirations of local communities and indigenous peoples, as well as the values ascribed to them by people from around the world. Sustainable use of resources from some types of protected areas, and exclusion of such uses from others, is an important part of this mix.

In this book, contributors from all continents, with varied backgrounds and experiences, address the social, cultural, economic, scientific and managerial aspects of protected areas. In compiling the contributions, we have taken care to produce a seamlessly edited and integrated text, rather than a collection of discrete papers. While there is certainly a range of views among our contributors about what protected areas should be and how they should be managed, we have tried to give expression to a consistent and clear message about good-practice protected area management. The central task in doing this has been to maintain nature conservation as an essential core mission of protected areas, while recognizing that this must be achieved alongside community development, good governance, participatory decision-making, poverty alleviation and equitable sharing of the costs and benefits of protection.

This integrated and balanced approach is consistent with a maturing international effort that is both professional and community based. An internationally significant expression of this maturing was evident at the Vth IUCN World Parks Congress that was held in 2003 in Durban, South Africa. This book is in large measure an outcome of that event. It attempts to incorporate and encapsulate the knowledge and understandings generated at the congress, along with other information and experience from around the world. Some chapters, to a greater or lesser degree, also draw on an Australian book on protected area management (Worboys et al, 2005), in which two of us were heavily involved.

It is, of course, an immense challenge to even begin to portray the incredible richness and diversity of protected area practice and experience. We have attempted to provide a balanced view across continents, nations and environments. In part, this is achieved through a selection of illustrative case studies, some drawn from the literature and others specially commissioned for this volume. We do not, however, pretend that these cases are fully representative of the enormous diversity of situations on the ground.

In the first seven chapters, we consider the core context of protected areas: natural heritage; the social dimension; major protected area types and supporting institutions; values and benefits; governance modes; management processes; and capacity development. Commencing with their establishment, the next 18 chapters cover the essential practice of protected area management. Each of these chapters concludes with a set of principles that have been distilled from the text. In the final chapter we offer a view on the future of protected areas on a global scale. The book is supported by appendices that give a short chronologies of the Earth's evolutionary development and of protected areas, summarize the outputs from the Vth IUCN World Parks Congress and the Convention on Biological Diversity Protected Area Programme of Work, and give data on the extent and distribution of the world's national and international protected areas.

While the term 'protected areas' in this book is meant to incorporate both those managed by governments and those managed by other actors, it must also be acknowledged that the recognition of the latter (such as community conserved areas and private protected areas) is relatively recent in formal conservation circles. Hence, the experience reflected in some sections of this text may be biased towards government-designated and managed protected areas. To counteract this, several chapters have a particular focus on other types of protected area governance.

The book is intended to assist current and future protected area managers, and other rights holders and stakeholders, from around the world. More specifically, this includes protected area professionals such as rangers and other field staff, scientists, planners and middle managers; government and policy staff; private-sector organizations and consultants; NGOs; community and indigenous managers of protected areas; university students; and community and stakeholder groups. In addressing this wide range of audiences, we recognize that sections will be well known to some readers; but we hope that there is something new here for everyone, as well as a compendium of material that has not been hitherto available at a global scale in a single volume.

List of Acronyms and Abbreviations

AHTEG	Convention on Biological Diversity Ad Hoc Technical Expert Group
AIDS	acquired immune deficiency syndrome
AIIMS	Australian Inter-service Incident Management System
ANAM	Panama's National Environmental Agency
APEC	Asia-Pacific Economic Cooperation
ARPA	Amazon Region Protected Areas
ASEAN	Association of South-East Asian Nations
ASMA	Antarctic specially managed area
ASPA	Antarctic specially protected area
BBQ	barbeque
BCA	benefit–cost analysis
BiodCS	Biodiversity Conservation Society (India)
BTF	Bhutan Trust Fund
°C	degrees Celsius
CABI	Capitanía de Alto y Bajo Isoso (Bolivia)
CALM	Department of Conservation and Land Management (Western Australia)
CAPAS	Central American Protected Area System
C.A.P.E.	Cape Action for People and the Environment (South Africa)
CATIE	Central American Tropical Agricultural Centre for Research and Education
CBD	Convention on Biological Diversity
CBNRM	Community-based Natural Resource Management
CCA	community conserved area
CEASPA	Centro de Estudios y Accion Social Panameno
CEESP	Commission on Environmental, Economic and Social Policy (*of the* IUCN Commission on Protected Areas)
CEO	chief executive officer
CERP	Comprehensive Everglades Restoration Plan
CFR	Cape Floristic Region (South Africa)
CI	Conservation International
CITES	Convention on International Trade in Endangered Species of Wild Flora and Fauna
CMAP	collaborative management area plan
CMPA	collaboratively managed protected area
CMS	Convention on the Conservation of Migratory Species of Animals
CMT	customary marine tenure
CONANP	Mexican Commission for Protected Areas
CoopeSoli-Dar R	Cooperativa Autogestionaria de Servicios Profesionales para la Solidaridad Social RL
COP	Conference of the Parties
C-Plan	Conservation-Plan
CRC	Sustainable Tourism Cooperative Research Centre
CSIRO	Commonwealth Scientific and Industrial Research Organisation

DDT	dichloro-diphenyl-trichloroethane			of the Preservation and Restoration of Cultural Property in Rome
D&Es	directions and expectations		ICIMOD	International Centre for Mountain Research and Development
EEZ	exclusive economic zone			
EIA	environmental impact assessment		ICMM	International Council on Mining and Metals
EIS	environmental impact statement			
EMC	environmental management charge		ICOM	International Council of Museums
EMS	environmental management system(s)		ICOMOS	International Council on Monuments and Sites
EPBC Act	Environment Protection and Biodiversity Conservation Act (Australia)		ICS	incident control system
			ICSU	International Council for Science
EU	European Union		ICZM	integrated coastal zone management
FAO	United Nations Food and Agriculture Organization		IGCP	International Gorilla Conservation Programme
FKNMS	Florida Keys National Marine Sanctuary		ILO	International Labour Organization
			IMA	inter-institutional management authority
FNP	Fulufjället National Park (Sweden)			
FRNP	Fitzgerald River National Park (Australia)		IMO	International Maritime Organization
G7	Group of 7 industrialized nations (Canada, France, Germany, Italy, Japan, the UK and the US)		INMAN	Inversiones La Manguera Sociedad Anonima (Costa Rica)
			INSULA	International Scientific Council for Island Development
GBRMP	Great Barrier Reef Marine Park			
GBRMPA	Great Barrier Reef Marine Park Authority		I–O	input–output
			IPA	indigenous protected area
GDP	gross domestic product		IPCC	Intergovernmental Panel on Climate Change
GEF	Global Environment Facility (US)			
GELOSE	Gestion Localisée Securisée law (Secure Local Management law)		ISC	independent scientific committee
			ISO	International Organization for Standardization
GHNP	Great Himalayan National Park (India)		IT	information technology
GIS	geographic information systems		IUCN	World Conservation Union (*formerly* the International Union for the Conservation of Nature)
GLCA	Great Limpopo Conservation Area			
GLTP	Great Limpopo Transfrontier Park			
GNP	Galapagos National Park		JMB	joint management board
GPS	global positioning systems		KBA	key biodiversity area
GTB	Gas Transboliviano SA		kg	kilogramme
HDI	Human Development Index		KIF	Kaa-Iya Foundation (Bolivia)
HIPC	Highly Indebted Poor Country		KINP	Kaa-Iya del Gran Chaco National Park (Bolivia)
HR	human resource			
IABIN	Inter-American Biodiversity Information Network		km	kilometre
			km²	square kilometre
IADB	Inter-American Development Bank		KTP	Kgalagadi Transfrontier Park
IAS	International Accounting Standards		kW	kilowatt
IBD	Inter-American Development Bank		kWh	kilowatt hour
IBRA	Interim Biogeographic Regionalization for Australia		LAC	limits of acceptable change
			m	metre
ICC	International Chamber of Commerce		MAB	Man and the Biosphere programme
ICCROM	International Centre for the Study		MCA	multi-criteria analysis

MCL	Monteverde Conservation League (Costa Rica)	PROARCA	Programa Ambiental Regional para Centroamaerica
MCPA	marine and coastal protected area	PROFO-NANPE	Peruvian Trust Fund for National Parks and Protected Areas
MDG	Millennium Development Goal	PSSA	particularly sensitive sea area
MDSP	Ministerio de Desarrollo Sostenible y Planificación	PV	present value
MET	Namibian Ministry of Environment and Tourism	PWS	Parks and Wildlife Service (Tasmania)
mm	millimetre	QLF	Quebec–Labrador Foundation
MOST	Management of Social Transformations Programme (*of* UNESCO)	QPWS	Queensland Parks and Wildlife Service
MPA	marine protected area	RADAM	Rada na Amazônia
MPRU	Marine Parks and Reserves Unit (Tanzania)	RAP	Representative Areas Programme (Australia)
MWh	megawatt hour	RAPPAM	Rapid Assessment and Prioritization of Protected Areas Management
NGO	non-governmental organizations	REF	review of environmental factors
NIIMS	National Interagency Incident Management Systems	RNP	regional nature park
NIPAP	National Protected Area Programme (the Philippines)	RNPA	Retezat National Park Administration (Romania)
NOAA	National Oceanic and Atmospheric Administration (US)	RO	reverse osmosis
NPV	Net Present Value	ROS	Recreation Opportunity Spectrum
NPWS	National Parks and Wildlife Service (New South Wales)	RSF	Reserves Standards Framework
NRM	natural resource management	SAHARA	Society for Advancement of Hill and Rural Areas (India)
NRS	National Reserve System (Australia)	SANParks	South African National Parks
NSW	New South Wales	SCOPE	Scientific Committee on Problems of the Environment (*of* ICSU)
NTFP	non-timber forest product	SERNAP	Servicio Nacional de Areas Protegidas
NUFFIC/IK	The Netherlands Organization for International Cooperation in Higher Education/Indigenous Knowledge	SIA	social and cultural impact assessment
		SINAP	El Sistema Nacional de Áreas Protegidas de Panamá (Panama)
ODA	Overseas Development Agency	SLNP	South Luangwa National Park (Zambia)
OECD	Organisation for Economic Co-operation and Development	SMART	specific, measurable, appropriate, realistic and time bound
PAAF	permit application assessment fee	SNH	Scottish Natural Heritage
PACOS	Partners of Community Organizations (Malaysia)	SNP	Sapo National Park (Liberia)
PAD	personnel and administration department	SPA	specially protected area
		SPAW Protocol	Protocol Concerning Specially Protected Areas and Wildlife
PALNet	Protected Areas Learning Network	SPNN	National Natural Parks System (Colombia)
PAN	Protected Area Network of Parks		
PCD	Partners in Community Development (Fiji)	STCRC	Sustainable Tourism Cooperative Research Centre (Australia)
PFB	Programme for Belize	SWOT	strengths, weaknesses, opportunities and threats
PIMS	Parks and Wildlife Service Information Management System (Tasmania)		
PMB	participatory management board	TBPA	transboundary protected area

TCM	travel cost method	US	United States
TCO	Tierra Comunitaria de Origen (Bolivia)	USAID	US Agency for International Development
TCZCDP	Tanga Coastal Zone Conservation and Development Programme	USSR	United Soviet Socialist Republic
TGER	IUCN Theme on Governance, Equity and Rights	VAMP	Visitor Activity Management Programme
TILCEPA	IUCN Theme on Indigenous and Local Communities, Equity and Protected Areas	VERP	visitor experience and resource protection
		VIM	visitor impact management
TOMM	Tourism Optimization Management Model	WA	Western Australia
		WBCSD	World Business Council for Sustainable Development
TNC	The Nature Conservancy	WCC	World Conservation Congress
TPA	terrestrial protected area	WCED	World Commission on Environment and Development
TRIPS	Trade Related Aspects of Intellectual Property Rights Agreement (*of the* WTO)	WCI	Wildlife Conservation International
		WCMC	World Conservation Monitoring Centre
TTF	Tourism and Transport Forum Australia	WCPA	World Commission on Protected Areas
UAESPNC	Special Administrative Unit for the National Parks System of Colombia	WCS	Wildlife Conservation Society
UK	United Kingdom	WDPA	World Database on Protected Areas
UN	United Nations	WHC	World Heritage Convention
UNCED	United Nations Conference on Environment and Development	WILD	Wildlife in Livelihoods Diversification project
UNCLOS	United Nations Convention on the Law of the Sea	WPC	World Parks Congress
		WSCG	Women's Savings and Credit Group (India)
UNDP	United Nations Development Programme	WSSD	World Summit on Sustainable Development
UNEP	United Nations Environment Programme	WTO	World Tourism Organization
		WTO	World Trade Organization
UNESCO	United Nations Educational, Scientific and Cultural Organization	WTP	willingness to pay
		WTTC	World Travel and Tourism Council
UNFCCC	United Nations Framework Convention on Climate Change	WWF	World Wide Fund for Nature
UNHCR	United Nations High Commission on Refugees	Y2Y	Yellowstone to Yukon Conservation Initiative

Part I

Setting the Context

1

Natural Heritage

Graeme L. Worboys and Colin Winkler

The nature of planet Earth is for many of us a source of inspiration, wonder and knowledge. Photographs of the planet taken from space dramatically show our brown and green continents, blue oceans, and frozen images of cloud patterns and weather systems in motion. They also show how finite the planet is in an immensity of space, and emphasize the precious and fragile nature of life on Earth. This life is supported by a number of interacting components, including the geosphere, atmosphere, hydrosphere and biosphere. It is rich, diverse and has developed through millennia of evolutionary processes. These global life-support systems cannot be taken for granted if life on Earth is to be sustained.

Protected areas are a critical land-use type for the future of life on Earth. At the beginning of the 21st century, in one of the greatest land- and sea-use transformations in human history, nations of Earth had reserved over 12 per cent of the Earth's terrestrial surface and 0.5 per cent of its marine systems as protected areas. These lands and seas are typically the finest representative examples of natural and cultural heritage, and are often critical for the survival of key species. They are also critical for their contribution to maintaining the life-support systems of Earth. This land-use transformation is unfinished, as many important ecosystems, species and environments are currently poorly represented in protected area systems (see Chapter 8).

In this chapter, we introduce the natural heritage of Earth, and provide a biogeographical context for the establishment and management of protected areas throughout the world. We describe the evolution of the world's environments and illustrate this with selected World Heritage protected area examples. Aspects of Earth's abiotic environments, including geology, landforms, geodiversity, soils and climate, are described for their intrinsic qualities as well as to provide background for a description of biological diversity. The world's flora, fauna, fungi and other organisms are introduced to provide an account of the richness of the planet's biodiversity. Biogeographical realms and the global biomes are used to illustrate the major habitat types and ecosystems of the world. The World Wide Fund for Nature's (WWF) Global 200 and Conservation International's biodiversity hotspots are also described. Stepping into detail from this global view, we also highlight the critical role that protected area managers play in managing and conserving at the individual protected area level. This individual effort directly contributes to the bigger picture of protecting life and life-support systems on Earth. For managers, this opportunity to help conserve parts of the finest natural heritage of this remarkable planet is a special privilege and an enormous challenge.

The evolution of global environments

One of the challenges for protected area managers is to comprehend the vast time scale of the natural heritage they are conserving. The geological time scale covers a vast period of over 4500 million years. To illustrate the magnitude of this time scale, the first hominids evolved just 4 million years ago and modern humans have probably evolved only in the past 100,000 years (Gore, 1997).

Every protected area exhibits a part of the planet's evolutionary history, and some of them contain outstanding examples of geological evolution (see Appendix 1 and Case Studies 1.1–1.3). Such geological heritage warrants conservation, no less than do contemporary life forms and landforms. It provides a context for understanding and managing our current environments. It is a rich source of information for scientific enquiry, and its preservation within protected areas is essential if we are to educate current and future generations about the richness of our heritage and its possible futures. We live on a dynamic planet where geological forces, bio-sphere life support and evolutionary processes continue, despite direct and indirect human interventions. Significant samples of the world's geological heritage have been permanently protected within the reserve system of various countries. Interpreting the past through this record allows us to prepare and manage for the future and involves, among other things, understanding the nature of climate change and species extinctions over time. Protected area managers need to have a very clear idea of this context when they set management goals.

The physical environment

In this section we give an overview of the richness and importance of the Earth's geodiversity. This diversity includes variation in rocks, landforms and soil types. The Earth's atmosphere and, more particularly, climate and climatic change are also discussed.

Case Study **1.1**

World Heritage fossil mammal sites, Riversleigh and Naracoorte, Australia

Riversleigh is part of Lawn Hill National Park, 200km north-west of Mount Isa in Queensland. It is one of the most significant fossil sites in the world and 10,000ha of the park were inscribed as a World Heritage property in 1994. The fossil sites meet the World Heritage criteria as 'outstanding examples representing major stages of the Earth's evolutionary history' and as 'outstanding examples representing significant ongoing ecological and biological evolution'. The Riversleigh fossils preserve the remains of a wide cross-section of vertebrate animals. It is one of the world's richest Oligocene–Miocene mammal records, linking the period of 15 million to 25 million years ago. The fossils confirm that there was once a tropical rainforest over the Riversleigh site 25 million years ago; but the sequence continues and shows the profound effects on fauna when Australia's rainforests largely vanished. The fossils include marsupial lions, carnivorous kangaroos, diprotodonts, 7m pythons, early ancestors of the now extinct Tasmanian tiger or thylacine (*Thylacinus cynocephalus*), and primitive platypuses. Evidence from Riversleigh shows that the fauna of the lowland rainforests of 20 million to 15 million years ago became the progenitors for almost all of Australia's living animals. Riversleigh tells us that Australia's surviving rainforests are more than just beautiful remnants of a once green continent. They contain many of the descendants of the 'seminal' creatures that spawned thousands of new species to rapidly fill a continent that had become 44 per cent arid.

The Naracoorte Caves are found in the south-east of South Australia and feature 300ha of land inscribed in 1994 as World Heritage property within the Naracoorte Caves National Park. The fossil site found here complements the Riversleigh fossil site. The fossils in the caves illustrate faunal change spanning several ice ages and highlight the impacts of climate change and the influence of humans on Australia's mammals from at least 350,000 years before present. Some 99 vertebrate species have been discovered, including exceptionally well-preserved examples of the ice age megafauna, as well as a host of modern species such as the Tasmanian devil, thylacine and others.

Sources: adapted from Archer et al (1994) and DEH (2004)

Riversleigh fossil site, Queensland, Australia

Source: IUCN Photo Library © Jim Thorsell

Case Study **1.2**

Dorset and East Devon Coast World Heritage Area, UK

The Dorset and East Devon Coast (often referred to as the Jurassic Coast) displays a remarkable combination of internationally renowned geological features and is considered one of the most significant Earth science sites in the world. It was inscribed as a World Heritage property in 2001, and comprises a near-continuous sequence of Triassic, Jurassic and Cretaceous rock exposures that represents almost the entire Mesozoic era – 190 million years of Earth history. The Triassic succession records span over 50 million years, including a global sea-level rise and flooding of a desert landscape. The succession of Jurassic rocks is considered to be one of the best sections of marine origin anywhere in the world and includes important vertebrate fossils. For most of the Jurassic, tropical seas covered Dorset and marine life flourished. Exceptionally well-preserved remains of a late Jurassic fossil forest estimated to be over 140 million years old have been found and these are considered to be one of the most complete fossil forests of any age. Many of the trees are preserved *in situ* with soils and pollen and display well-preserved growth rings. Folds and faults buckle and cut through the Jurassic and Cretaceous strata to form spectacular features, and dome-shaped folds and fractures within the rocks have created oil traps, including Britain's largest onshore source of oil. Additionally, the coast contains an exceptional diversity of modern geomorphological features, landforms and processes that are considered the finest 'text-book' examples of their kind.

Source: adapted from Gray (2004)

Case Study **1.3**

Rocky Mountain Parks World Heritage Area (Burgess Shale), Canada

The Canadian Rocky Mountain Parks include the Yoho National Park, within which the Burgess Shale is an exceptional fossil locality of Middle Cambrian age (about 540 million years ago). It was inscribed as a World Heritage property in 1984. The Burgess Shale is special because of the preservation of a wide diversity of soft-bodied fossil invertebrate animals and has been intensely studied since its discovery in 1909 by Charles Walcott. At the time of deposition, the Burgess Shale area was near the equator and was the continental margin of North America. A 100m high near-vertical cliff of limestone occurred at the edge of the shelf. The Burgess Shale was deposited at the base of this cliff, probably in anoxic conditions, as indicated by the lack of burrows and trackways and the abundance of pyrite. All of the organisms within the Burgess Shale have been transported to this location, probably by small mudflows. Among the inclusions are *Anomalocaris* sp. (a large 60cm arthropod-like predator); *Marrella splendens* (a small arthropod somewhat reminiscent of a trilobite); *Olenoides serratus* (the largest of several species of trilobites found in the burgess shale); the sponge *Vauxia gracilenta*; *Tuzoia*, a bivalved crustacean; and *Ottoia*, a priapulid worm.

Source: adapted from MacRae (1995)

Geodiversity

Geodiversity is a term that came into use during the 1990s to describe variety within abiotic nature. It has been defined by Gray (2004, p8) as:

> ... *the natural range (diversity) of geological (rocks, minerals, fossils), geomorphological (landform processes) and soil features. It includes their assemblages, relationships, properties, interpretations and systems.*

The Earth's geodiversity is important to society for the economic value of physical resources such as fossil fuels; minerals, including gold, iron and diamonds; and essential minerals for development, such as limestone, clay and sand (Wilson, 1994). It also has especially significant, intrinsic, aesthetic, cultural and social heritage values and many geoheritage sites are permanently protected. These include the Giant's Causeway of Northern Ireland, important for its intrinsic qualities and in folklore; Uluru (Ayers Rock) in Australia for its intrinsic qualities and importance for spirituality; the archaeological and historical interest of houses carved in cliffs at Petra in Jordan; and the Grand Canyon in US for its intrinsic qualities and importance to tourism and recreation.

Structural geological features

The Earth is a dynamic planet. Plate tectonics, a consequence of the inner dynamics of the Earth at work, are causing the continents to slowly spread across the planet's surface, as they have done for millennia. Faulting, folding and structural deformation are part of this dynamic, as are the processes of volcanism and igneous emplacement. The development of mountain ranges and the subduction of marine sediments are part of this process. External impacts have also affected Earth. Meteorites and other space matter have created impact craters and astroblemes on the Earth's surface. Many parts of the world display evidence of such geological structures and their part in the evolution of the Earth. Many such sites are permanently protected.

Landforms

Just as there are processes creating new land or changing its nature, there are also the forces of wind, temperature, rain, ice and water and organisms all acting on the Earth's rocks and strata. Such weathering and erosion forces help to shape and mould landscapes, help to create and develop soils, and help to develop landscapes such as deltas, sandy deserts, glacial moraines and solitary rock mountains.

The world's landforms have evolved from a complexity of geological processes typically including one or more of the forces of tectonism, volcanism, sedimentary processes, erosion and weathering. Many of the world's protected areas

Uluru Kata Tjuta National Park, Australia

Source: IUCN Photo Library © Jim Thorsell

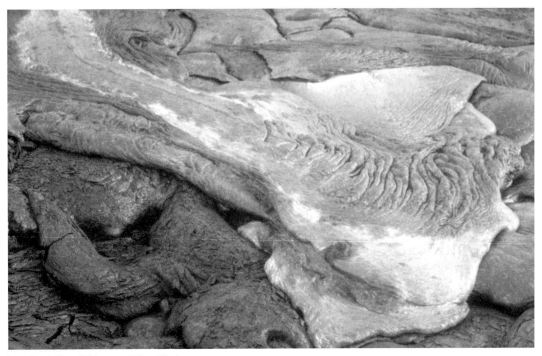

Lava flow in Hawaii Volcanoes National Park

Source: IUCN Photo Library © Jim Thorsell

Grand Canyon, US, formed during the last 6 million years by river erosion

Source: IUCN Photo Library © Jim Thorsell

have been established to protect outstanding examples of landforms for their superlative aesthetic and often cultural and spiritual values. Some of these outstanding global landform types are presented in Table 1.1 along with notes about their characteristics.

Rock types

Rocks are remarkably variable in their origins and makeup. Igneous plutonic rocks derived from slowly cooled deep-seated melts of the Earth's crust and mantle material are typically coarsely crystalline, but vary remarkably from the silica-rich (acidic) granites and granodiorites to the dark-coloured and basic gabbros depending upon the source of the melt and its mix. These differences in chemistry account for a wide variety of landforms and soil developments on the surface of the Earth. Some of these melts actually reach the surface and are erupted as quickly cooled and fine-grained volcanic rocks, tuffs and other ejecta. Such volcanic rocks also vary in composition from acidic (rhyolite) to basic (basalt), with a range of intermediate compositions, including rhyodacite, dacite and andesite. Rocks are not always erupted and can be cooled quickly in vents, sills and dykes

Mount Everest, Sagarmatha National Park, Nepal

Source: IUCN Photo Library © Jim Thorsell

Table 1.1   Descriptions of some of Earth's outstanding landforms

Dominant landform process	World Heritage area example	Notes
Mountain-building	Sagarmatha National Park, Nepal, includes Mount Everest – the highest (measured from sea level) mountain on Earth at 8850m.	Mountain-building occurred at the beginning of the Pleistocene with the upthrust of the Tibetan plateau. This was followed by a second more limited upthrust that created the highest mountain range on Earth, the Himalayas.
Volcanism	Yellowstone National Park, US, includes the world's largest volcanic caldera.	Volcanic activity has occurred at Yellowstone for more than 50 million years. It was the site of one of the world's most powerful volcanic explosions 2 million years ago, and today the site is famous for its hot springs and geysers.
Volcanism	The volcanoes of Kamchatka, Russian Federation, are one of the most outstanding examples of a volcanic region in the world.	This volcanically active region is located on the circum-pacific volcanic belt. The site contains a high density of active volcanoes, a variety of different types, and a wide range of volcanic features.
Faulting and folding	Lake Malawi National Park in the Great Rift Valley, Malawi, is the fourth deepest and 11th largest lake in the world.	The lake is very old, between 1 million and 2 million years, and is part of the Great Rift Valley, a major tectonic geological structure of Africa.
Meteorite impact	The Vredefort Dome, south-west of Johannesburg, South Africa, is the world's largest and oldest astrobleme (meteorite impact structure); circular-shaped hills at the site outline the effects of the impact.	The Vredefort Dome meteorite impact structure was created 2023 million years ago by a meteor about 12km in diameter travelling at 20m a second when it hit Earth. The radius of impact effect was 190km. It is the single greatest explosive event known for Earth.
River erosion	Grand Canyon National Park, US, is one of the world's largest canyons at 443km long, 1.5km deep and 30km wide.	The canyon was formed in the last 6 million years by the eroding Colorado River and exposes rock sequences from the Precambrian through to the Cenozoic era, revealing five different life zones.
River erosion	Examples are Victoria Falls National Park and Zambezi National Park in Zimbabwe; Mosi-oa-Tunya National Park in Zambia features the world's largest curtain of falling water.	It is estimated for the Zambezi River during flood that 500 million litres of water flow over Victoria Falls every minute, and that a plume of spray extends 500m into the air. Three national parks covering 65,200ha in two countries protect the site.
Coastal erosion	The Giant's Causeway and Causeway Coast in Northern Ireland, UK, feature the best and most accessible example of basaltic columnar jointing in the world.	Perfectly formed polygonal jointed basalt columns are exposed on a promontory at the county of Antrim, Northern Ireland. Volcanism during the early Tertiary was the source of these columnar basalts.
Weathering and erosion	Uluru (Ayers Rock) in Uluru–Kata Tjuta National Park, Northern Territory, Australia is an inselberg; it is the second largest monolith in the world at 9.4km in circumference and 348m above the surrounding plain.	Uluru is a single rock formation. It is sedimentary in origin and composed of arkose, a type of sandstone rich in feldspar. It was formed when folding of sedimentary sequences produced steeply dipping beds that have subsequently been partly exposed by erosion.

Table 1.1   Continued

Dominant landform process	World Heritage area example	Notes
Chemical weathering and erosion	The Škojan Caves, Socialist Republic of Slovenia, is one of the most beautiful speleological sites in the world – a remarkably well-preserved example of subterranean karst formation.	This 40ha site includes four deep chasms, a system of underground passages created by the River Reka, including one of the largest subterranean canyons in the world. The length of the cave system is over 5km and has a depth of 230m.
Glaciation	Los Glaciers National Park, Argentina, includes the Patagonian ice field, one of the largest ice mantles in the world.	This 445,900ha national park includes a 350km (between 40km to 70km wide) stretch of glaciers. There are 47 glaciers within the park.
Chemical deposition	The Jiuzhaigou Valley, Sichuan Province, China, is famous for its ensemble of mountains, waterfalls, lakes, pools and forests and travertine lakes grouped around the base of a tufa gully.	The 72,000ha Jiuzhaigou Valley site is found between 2140m and 4588m. It features rocks that are the result of severe seismic activity, glaciation and recent tufa deposition. There are 18 travertine lakes within the valley.
Reef-building and islands	The Great Barrier Reef Marine Park, Queensland, Australia, is the world's largest expanse of living coral reefs.	The 34.87 million hectare Great Barrier Reef Marine Park extends 2000km along the eastern coast of Queensland. It comprises 2500 individual reefs interspersed with 71 coral cays.

Sources: Twidale (1968); Swadling (1995); Dolce (2003)

as medium-grained volcanic rocks such as dolerite. Sedimentary rocks reflect constant weathering, erosion and deposition processes on the surface of the Earth, as well as limestone deposits from marine animals. Such rocks include conglomerates, sandstones, siltstones, mudstones, shales and limestones, many of which are fossiliferous. Often such sedimentary rocks are contact metamorphosed by intruding plutonic rocks or by regional metamorphism from the heat of the mantle. This results in a suite of non-melted rocks affected by heat and pressure, including marble, quartzite, hornfels, slate, phyllites schists and gneiss. Many very different rocks also occur, such as rare belts of serpentinite and other ultramafic (mantle-derived) rocks. Unusual minerals may be deposited at deep sea hydrothermal vents, and igneous hydrothermal waters interacting with limestones and other country rock may generate unusual mineral deposits (Gray, 2004).

Protected area managers need to be aware of this variation. Managing active volcanic protected areas is very different for more acidic and potentially explosive volcanic melts, such as Indonesia's Anak Krakatau, than it is for less explosive basic melts, such as at Hawaii Volcanoes National Park. Constructing walking trails in schists in steep terrain is very different from construction in steep sandstone terrain, and road gravel sourced from one granite stock is highly likely to be very different for an immediately adjacent (different) granite stock. Importantly, there are special conservation and heritage education responsibilities for rare and unusual rocks or outcrops, such as ultramafic rocks, skarns and fossils.

Soils

Soils are made up of weathered rock material and organic matter and are produced by interactions between geologic (rock and hydrologic cycles) and biological processes. The formation of soil is affected primarily by climate and topography,

One of the 47 glaciers in Los Glaciares National Park, Argentina

Source: IUCN Photo Library © Jim Thorsell

with parent material, time and biological activity as important secondary factors. Despite soils being derived from rocks, the distribution of soils does not always match the distribution of rocks, principally because of climatic differences. Soils are described by many types of classification systems. The United Nations Food and Agriculture Organization (FAO) developed a World Soil Classification that provided useful generalizations about soil genesis in relation to the main soil-forming factors. This system has been adapted by many countries. The classification includes 26 world classes, made up of 106 soil units (such as chernozems, fluvisols and podzols), which are mapped as soil associations. These associations are designated by the dominant soil unit with soil phases (soil properties, such as saline, lithic or stony); three textural classes (coarse, medium and fine); and three slopes classes (level to gently undulating, rolling to hilly, and steeply dissected to mountainous) superimposed. The FAO soil classi-

fication system is intended for mapping soils at a continental scale. At national or provincial scales, protected area managers may need to apply more detailed systems specific to such areas.

Climate

The Earth's climate is like a giant solar-powered engine (White, 1990). It is a global circulation of hot rising air and cooling and descending air that is complicated by the effects of a tilted and rotating planet, the location of continents, a varied terrain, oceans and currents, and day and night differences. There is also a dynamic and an evolutionary aspect to the atmosphere, which is directly linked to the Earth's remarkable biosphere. Life on Earth has helped to create the atmosphere as we know it today. It helps to maintain it and is dependent upon it (White, 2003) (see Box 1.1). Satellite images of the Earth illustrate the interconnectedness of our atmosphere and its weather patterns, and reinforce a need to respond to our climate management responsibilities. At a global scale, a widely used classification system developed by the geographer Köppen recognizes five broad climatic types:

1   *tropical climates*, where average annual temperatures are above 18 degrees Celsius (°C);
2   *dry climates*, where potential evaporation exceeds precipitation on the average throughout the year;
3   *warm temperate climates*, where the coldest month is below 18°C but above −3°C;
4   *snow climates*, where the coldest month average temperatures are below −3°C and the average warmest month is above 10°C; and
5   *ice climates*, where the average warmest month is below 10°C (Strahler, 1969; Strahler and Strahler, 1992).

Subgroups within the five major groups are recognized and include steppe climate, desert climate, moist climate, dry season in winter, dry season in summer and rainforest (Strahler and Strahler, 1992).

Biological diversity

The term biological diversity (or biodiversity) refers to the variety of all living things: the plants, fungi, animals and micro-organisms; the genetic information they contain; and the ecosystems they form. It was defined by the United Nations Convention on Biological Diversity (CBD) Article 2 (CBD, 2005) as the:

> … *variability among living organisms from all sources including, inter alia, terrestrial, marine and other aquatic ecosystems and the ecological complexes of which they are part; this includes diversity within species, between species and of ecosystems.*

There are an estimated 14 million species, of which some 11 per cent have been described (see Table 1.2). In the global distribution of species, the overall abundance of species increases in total and per unit area from polar regions to temperate regions to the tropics. This applies as an overall principle, as well as within most of the individual taxa and within most similar habitats.

This rich global biological diversity is supported by an interconnected global biosphere that has evolved over geologic time and is essential for life on Earth. The biosphere is the envelope around the Earth's surface that contains all living organisms and the elements they exchange with the non-living environment. It is estimated to be 20km thick. The top is the top of the atmosphere, and its bottom is continental rock and ocean depths (White, 2003). The world's weather is found within it and sunlight provides the energy that maintains the biosphere. It is used by micro-organisms, algae and plants to produce organic molecules by photosynthesis. The net primary production includes organic material synthesized by photosynthetic organisms and the amount of energy-rich material left to sustain all other life on Earth (Groombridge and Jenkins, 2000).

The biosphere is an intricately interconnected system. It works on cause and effect and action and reaction, and ultimately sets the rules for the survival of species of all sorts, including humans (White, 2003). It is the interconnectedness of everything within this system that has influenced the evolution of species and, thus, of the biosphere itself over billions of years. The biosphere is alive and metabolizing, and everything is forever changing, renewing and evolving. The interconnectedness and symbiotic functioning of living matter at all levels in the biosphere maintains the checks and balances essential for life (White, 2003).

Life on Earth: Archaea, bacteria and eukarya

Life on Earth can be assigned to three basic forms of life or domains: archaea, bacteria and eukarya. Viruses are also a life form, but they are not cells or assemblages of cells. They exist on the very boundaries of most definitions of life. Archaeans, like bacteria, have their genetic material free within the cell, while for eukaryotes the genetic material is linked to proteins and organized into chromosomes that are packed within a membrane-surrounded cell nucleus (Groombridge and Jenkins, 2002). Archaeans are commonly known as extremophiles or life forms living under conditions of extreme heat or salt; but they are also known from less extreme environments and 175 archaean species have been described. Bacteria

Box 1.1 Life on Earth: Changes to the Earth's atmosphere and five major extinctions

Important 'stages' in the development of the Earth's atmosphere are described in Appendix 1. Life on land on our planet has not always been possible. It took until the late Silurian for photosynthesis on Earth to build up sufficient atmospheric oxygen to create a thick ozone layer. This was needed to filter out harmful radiation before life on land was possible (White, 1990). Throughout geological time, five great extinctions of species have been recognized and have most likely been caused by changes to the atmosphere and biosphere:

1   late Ordovician extinctions, probably caused by the cooling and warming of the Earth, marine transgressions and regressions, and anoxia;
2   late Devonian extinctions, probably caused by marine transgressions and anoxia;
3   end of Permian extinctions due to volcanism, warming, marine transgression and anoxia;
4   end of Triassic extinctions due to marine transgression; and
5   end of the Cretaceous mass extinction due to the impact of a large meteor, volcanism, cooling and marine regression (Groombridge and Jenkins, 2002).

Other perturbations to the biosphere have occurred. During the Palaeocene (55 million years ago) a phenomenon believed to have been linked to a sudden, widespread release of methane from sediments caused rapid global warming that took tens of thousands of years to regain equilibrium (White, 2003). Ice cores from Greenland reveal a 5°C to 10°C warming for a 20-year period just 12,000 years ago.

Humans are now introducing major changes to the biosphere, including the atmosphere. It has been estimated that in less than 1000 years, between 2 and 4 gigatonnes of carbon have been added to the atmosphere by humans, causing non-natural increases in temperatures and global warming (White, 2003).

Reduction in the thickness of the protective ozone layer over Antarctica occurred slowly from the 1950s to the 1970s, with a rapid decline during the mid-1990s. There was a 60 per cent loss in ozone (Gifford, 2003). Chlorofluorocarbon and methyl bromide pollution of the upper atmosphere caused this problem. The area of the 'ozone hole' over the Antarctic was near its maximum size in 2001 (Gifford, 2003), which caused ultra-violet stressed phytoplankton over Antarctica (White, 2003). Urgent global responses have halted impacts; however, full ozone layer recovery to pre-1970 levels is unlikely to occur before 2050 (Manins et al, 2001; Gifford, 2003).

reproduce asexually by cell splitting or by producing genetic recombinants by accepting genes from other bacteria or from the fluid medium. About 10,000 species of bacteria have been described (Groombridge and Jenkins, 2000, 2002) but well over 1 million may exist. Fungi, plants and animals and protoctists (a diverse microscopic collection of eukaryotes) make up the eukarya. The management of protected areas typically focuses on the conservation of biodiversity, which includes all life. Emphasis in this book will be centred on the three kingdoms of eukarya: fungi, plantae and animalia (see Table 1.2).

Fungi

Fungi are not plants. Their structure differs from that of plants, with the walls of the mycelium and individual hyphae (the body of the fungi) constructed of a type of chitin (this compares with the cellulose of plants). The fruiting body of larger fungi (such as mushrooms, toadstools or other structures) is used to produce spores that are then dispersed by air, water, animals and themselves. Generally, the spores contain a single living cell (Young, 2005). Fungi have representatives in almost every available habitat on Earth. They provide a food source for animals, including insects, reptiles and mammals, and often there is a symbiotic relationship between fungi, animals and plants (Claridge et al, 1996; Young, 2005). Fungi play a prominent role in the decomposition and breakdown of dead plant material to allow the recycling of nutrients, and therefore play a critical part of the functioning of ecosystems (Recher et al, 1986).

Table 1.2   Estimated numbers of described species and possible global total

Domain	Eukaryote kingdoms	Number of described species*	Estimated total
Archaea		175	Unknown
Bacteria		10,000	Unknown
Eukarya	Animalia		
	Craniata (vertebrates), total	52,500	55,000
	Mammals	4630	
	Birds	9750	
	Reptiles	8002	
	Amphibians	4950	
	Fishes	25,000	
	Mandibulata (insects and myriapods)	963,000	8,000,000
	Chelicerata (arachnids, etc.)	75,000	750,000
	Mollusca	70,000	200,000
	Crustacea	40,000	150,000
	Nemotoda	25,000	400,000
	Fungi	72,000	1,500,000
	Plantae	270,000	320,000
	Protoctista	80,000	600,000
Total		1,750,000	At least 14,000,000

Note: * Estimates of global species numbers vary between literature sources reflecting the difficulties of taxonomic classification and global variation in the data available.

Source: Groombridge and Jenkins (2002)

Plants

Over 400,000 species of terrestrial plants are known for Earth and include many species from ancient plant life forms. The plant kingdom is divided into four major phyla:

1   thallophytes (algae, seaweed, diatoms and dinoflagellates);
2   bryophytes (liverworts and mosses);
3   pteridophytes (vascular plants that reproduce by spores, ferns, psilophytes or horsetails); and

4   spermatophytes (vascular plants that reproduce by seed) (White, 1990).

Green plants (those with chlorophyll) are fundamental for life on Earth. They have the capacity to convert sunlight through photosynthesis into sugars that are, in turn, used to fuel the life-support processes of the planet. Plants are consumed by herbivores and this forms the basis of food chains (Marinelli, 2004). During photosynthesis, plants provide the critical role in the production of oxygen for the atmosphere and the sequestering of carbon dioxide. They provide cover and protection for watersheds and prevent soil erosion, and they provide food, shelter, medicines and raw materials for multiple species, including humans. Angiosperms (flowering plants) have the planet's greatest number of species.

The pattern and distribution of species across the Earth's diversity of habitats are described in 'Biogeographical realms', with a more detailed description of the dominant biomes (ecosystem types and habitats) given in 'Global terrestrial biomes'. Nations and some individual protected areas that include particular concentrations of plant diversity have special responsibilities for the conservation of species.

Animals

The earliest forms of life developed on the planet 3.5 billion years ago and helped to contribute oxygen to the Earth's early atmosphere. By the Silurian they and their subsequent more evolved counterparts gradually helped to develop atmospheric conditions suitable for animal life outside of oceans (see Appendix 1). Life in the oceans and on land has evolved since then and has survived five mass extinction events. In geologically recent times, life has adapted to occupy a remarkable diversity of habitats. The nature and distribution of species on Earth has been shaped by continental drift, geographic isolation, animal adaptation and speciation. Convergence has occurred, as has symbiotic partnerships between species. Currently on Earth, there are approximately 1.5 million animals that have been identified (Burnie, 2004). For the Kingdom Animalia, the Linnaean classification system differentiates 11 major phyla occupying a wide variety of terrestrial and aquatic habitats:

1   Porifera (sponges);
2   Coelenterata (jelly fish and corals);
3   Platyhelminthes and Nemertinia (worms);
4   Mollusca (gastropods, mollusks and squids);
5   Annelida (segmented worms);
6   Onychophora (peripatus);
7   Arthropoda (spiders, scorpions, ticks, lobsters, insects, ants, bees and butterflies);
8   Ectoprocta (moss animals);

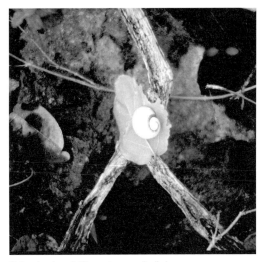

Cuban land snail (*Caracolus marginellus*)
Source: IUCN Photo Library © Jim Thorsell

9   Brachiopoda (lampshells);
10 Echinodermata (starfish sea urchins); and
11 Chordata (fish, amphibians, reptiles, birds and mammals) (White, 1990).

Like plants, the pattern of animal life is not uniform, with the greatest concentrations of animal species being found in the tropics, especially in Asia, South America and Africa (see Figure 1.1).

Migratory species

Many species migrate over medium to large distances of the Earth and between biogeographic realms and biomes. Some birds migrate by walking, including migrations on the African plains by ostriches (*Struthio camelus*), and in Antarctica, emperor penguins (*Aptenodytes forsteri*) trek over ice to their breeding grounds. Some birds fly short-distance seasonal migrations between coast and mountains, while many undertake long-distance migrations, such as between the northern hemisphere and southern hemisphere (Elphick, 1995). Some special natural sites around the world provide staging posts for migratory bird species. Many of these are protected areas, and their managers are aware of their special international conservation responsibilities (see Figure 1.2).

Many mammals migrate over long distances, both in marine and terrestrial environments.

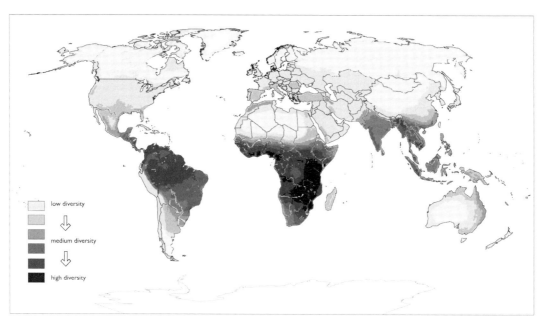

Figure 1.1   Terrestrial vertebrate family density

Source: Groombridge and Jenkins (2002, p100)

Some mammal migrations include the movement of baleen whales from the Krill-rich summer waters of the Arctic (and Antarctic) to tropical waters in winter, where they give birth, mate again immediately and then return slowly to the summer feeding grounds (Burnie, 2004). Gray whales (*Eschrichtius robustus*) migrate an estimated 20,000km each year, further than any other mammal species (Burnie, 2004). The caribou or reindeer (*Rangifer tarundus*) of North America and Northern Europe may migrate up to 1200km twice yearly to their calving grounds in spring (see Case Study 1.4). The wildebeest (*Connochaetes taurinus*) band into large herds and migrate hundreds of kilometres in Southern and Eastern Africa in search of seasonal grazing (Burnie, 2004).

Fish, such as the bluefin tuna (*Thunnus thynnus*), undertake major journeys within the world's oceans. Other fish, including the European eel (*Anguilla anguilla*), the European sturgeon (*Acipenser sturio*) and the sockeye salmon (*Oncorhynchus nerka*), migrate hundreds of kilometres up rivers from the sea and return to the sea at different stages of their life cycle. Reptiles such as the green turtle (*Chelonia mydas*) migrate over large distances and return to the same beaches annually to lay their eggs. Some green turtles, for example, feed off the coast of Brazil and nest on Ascension Island, 4500km away in the eastern Atlantic (Burnie, 2004).

Insects also migrate. The monarch butterfly (*Danaus plexippus*) migrates up to 4000km from Canada and the eastern US to winter in warmer roosting sites in California and Mexico (Burnie, 2004). In Australia, the bogong moth (*Agrotis infusa*) migrates hundreds of kilometres from western New South Wales to the Australian Alps every summer.

Governments and protected area managers may need to enter into special arrangements to ensure that the habitats needed for such migratory species, as well as the core habitat areas, are conserved.

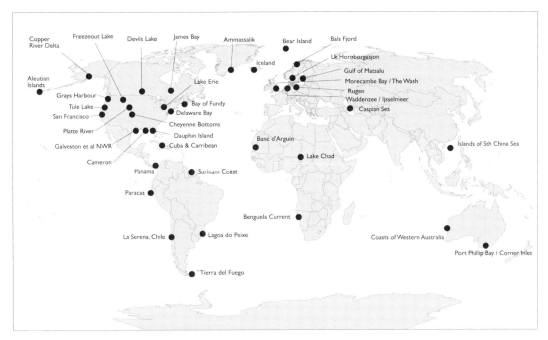

Figure 1.2   Global habitats used as stopovers by migratory bird species

Source: Elphick (1995)

Wildebeest in Maasai Mara National Reserve, Kenya

Source: IUCN Photo Library © Jim Thorsell

Case Study **1.4**

Caribou migrations and calving grounds

The annual return of caribou (*Rangifer tarundus*) to their traditional calving grounds is one of the best examples of migratory phenomena. Throughout northern Canada and Alaska, free-roaming caribou are an important subsistence food for aboriginal peoples. In Russia, another important site for caribou, or reindeer, many populations are semi-domesticated and managed by local people. There are 15 major caribou herds in Canada, each with different spring migration routes. The Eastern Canadian Shield Taiga ecoregion is home to the George River herd, the single largest caribou herd in the world. The Northwest Territories contain an additional 1.6 million caribou. In Alaska, 25 caribou herds totalling approximately 1 million animals annually stream between wintering and calving grounds. Caribou range across virtually all of Alaska's ecoregions. Caribou cows, especially when they have newborn calves, are highly sensitive to human activities. Not only do cows and calves need protection but the calving ground habitat itself needs to be safeguarded. Mining and mineral exploration pose serious threats.

Source: adapted from Rickets et al (1999)

Marine life

The world's oceans cover 71 per cent of the surface area of the planet. They are constantly in motion, and such large-scale circulation plays a critical role in influencing world climates and ocean ecosystems. Latitudinal temperature variations and marine upwellings on the western boundaries of continents influence life in the oceans. In addition, major marine zones such as the shallower continental shelf waters, the deep sea with its pelagic zone (the water column) and the variable abyssal zone (ocean floor with its large plains, sea mounts and deep trenches) influences the distribution and abundance of marine life. Some 64 large marine ecosystems have been defined. They are vast and some are 200,000 square kilometres or larger. There is a great diversity of life in the oceans. Of the approximately 82 Eukaryote phyla recognized, 60 have marine representatives. The representation is even higher with animals (36 of 37 phyla). Some of the phyla (23) are only found in marine environments (Groombridge and Jenkins, 2002). Marine algae, fish, corals, reptiles, birds, mammals, mangroves, salt marshes, rocky shores, seagrasses and coral reefs are just some of the important life forms and habitats of the world's oceans. With less than 1 per cent of the ocean's surface permanently protected at the start of the 21st century, it is the area requiring greatest effort for conservation by the nations of the world. Marine environments are considered in more detail in Chapter 23.

Biogeographical realms

Life on Earth, as has been shown, is rich, variable, dynamic and interdependent with global life-support processes. This immediately introduces a complexity for communicating about biodiversity and for its conservation and management. For protected area managers, it is useful to understand the biogeographical context within which they are managing. If they are aware, for example, that their protected area is one of the few for a major biogeographical realm, it will influence the development of plans and priority conservation actions. To assist in dealing with such complexity in a systematic way Professor Miklos Udvardy was commissioned by the IUCN during the 1970s to bring forward a classification system of biogeographical provinces for the world.

The Udvardy system recognizes eight biogeographical realms that classify continent or subcontinent-sized terrestrial areas according to unifying features of geography, fauna and flora (Udvardy 1975, see Figure 1.3). The 193 biogeographical provinces are ecosystematic or biotic subdivisions of biogeographical realms. The classification also recognizes 14 biomes for the world, but only 1 element of the hydrosphere: lakes. Descriptions of the biogeographic realms are

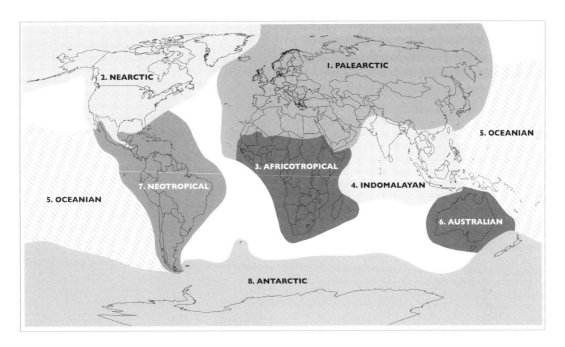

Figure 1.3   Udvardy's eight biogeographical realms

Source: Udvardy (1975)

provided here, based on Bramwell (1973), Udvardy (1975), Owen (1993), Hare (1994), Groombridge and Jenkins (2002), Mackay (2002), Burnie (2004) and Marinelli (2004). Today, the Udvardy classification is often used in combination with the WWF's Global 200 and Conservation International's biodiversity 'hotspots'. WWF's Global 200 (see p34) recognizes Udvardy's eight biogeographical realms, but expands the number of biomes to 30 and recognizes 867 ecoregions.

Palearctic realm
Geography

The Palearctic is the largest biogeographical realm and includes Europe, Asia north of the Himalayas, Northern Africa, and the northern and central parts of the Arabian Peninsula. There are many mountain ranges, with the Himalayan Mountains forming the boundary between the Palearctic and Indomalayan realm. The Caucasus Mountains, which run between the Black Sea and the Caspian Sea, incorporate important temperate

forests (see Case Study 1.5). The Palearctic contains significant freshwater areas, including the rivers of Europe and Russia, which flow into the Arctic, Baltic, Black and Caspian seas, and Siberia's Lake Baikal, the oldest and deepest lake on Earth. The Palearctic includes many protected areas, and 0.72 per cent of its area has been inscribed as World Heritage (see Table 1.3).

Flora

From north to south, natural lands include tundra; the boreal, or taiga (a belt of predominantly conifers extending from Scandinavia to the Sea of Okhotsk); the temperate deciduous forests of Europe (extending across the British Isles, northern Spain, Central Europe and Russia); Mediterranean shrublands; grasslands, or steppes; and the desert lands of Central Asia. The Mediterranean shrublands are home to 13,000 endemic species. Central Asia and the Iranian plateau are home to grasslands and desert basins, with montane forests and grasslands in the region's high mountains and plateaux. The Far

East and Japan are dominated by broadleaf forests. In the subtropical southern parts of China and Japan, the Palearctic temperate forests transition to the subtropical and tropical forests of the Indomalayan realm, creating habitat for a rich and diverse mix of plant and animal species.

Fauna

The Palearctic supports a wide range of fauna, including:

- in great northern taiga forests, brown bear (*Ursus arctos*), elk (*Alces alces*), altai red deer (*Cervus elaphus asiaticus*), sable (*Martes zibellina*), wolverine (*Gulo gulo*) and osprey (*Pandion haliaetus*);
- in temperate mixed woodlands of Europe, red fox (*Vulpes vulpes*), hedgehog (*Erinaceus europaeus*), great tit (*Parus major*), green woodpecker (*Picus viridis*), wild boar (*Sus scrofa*), red deer (*Cervus elaphus*) and badger (*Meles meles*);
- in grasslands of Northern Asia, Przewalski's horse (*Equus przewalskii*), saiga (*Saiga tatarica*), steppe lemming (*Lagurus lagurus*), Bobac marmot (*Marmota bobac*) and marbled polecat (*Vormela peregusna*);
- in cold deserts from the Caspian Sea to Mongolia, desert monitor (*Varanus griseus*), Bactrian camel (*Camelus bactrianus*), goitered gazelle (*Gazella subgutturosa*) and Asian wild ass (*Equus hemonius*);
- in mountains of Central Asia, snow leopard (*Panthera uncia*), ibex (*Capra ibex*), argali (*Ovis ammon*), yak (*Bos grunniens*) and Tibetan gazelle (*Procapra piticaudata*);
- in mountains of Eastern Asia, giant panda (*Ailuropoda melanoleuca*), red panda (*Ailurus fulgens*), takin (*Budorcas taxicolor*), serow (*Capricornis crispus*), Chinese monal (*Lophophorus lhuysii*) and musk deer (*Moschus* sp.);
- in the Far East and Japan, Siberian tiger (*Panthera tigris altaica*), Mandarin duck (*Aix galericulata*), Japanese crane (*Grus japonensis*), Japanese macaque (*Macaca fuscata*) and Korean hamster (*Cricetulus triton*) (Bramwell, 1973; Burnie, 2004).

Giant panda, Palearctic realm, China

Source: IUCN Photo Library © IUCN/David Sheppard

Nearctic realm
Geography

The Nearctic covers most of North America, including Greenland and the highlands of Mexico (see Figure 1.3). It was separated from South America for tens of millions of years, and evolved very different plant and animal lineages. A former land bridge across the Bering Strait between Asia and North America allowed many plants and animals to move between these continents, and the Nearctic shares many plants and animals with the Palearctic. Major mountain chains are found (the Appalachians and the Rockies), along with major freshwater lake systems (the Great Lakes) and wetlands such as the Everglades. Many of the outstanding natural areas of the Nearctic are protected areas and 0.92 per cent of its area is inscribed as World Heritage (see Table 1.3).

Case Study **1.5**

The Western Caucasus World Heritage Area, Russian Federation

The Western Caucasus extend over 275,000ha of the extreme western end of the Caucasus Mountains and are located 50km north-east of the Black Sea in the Russian Federation. The area was inscribed as a World Heritage property in 1999. It is one of the few large mountain areas of Europe that has not experienced significant human impact. Its sub-alpine and alpine pastures have only been grazed by wild animals, and its extensive tracts of undisturbed mountain forests, extending from the lowlands to the sub-alpine zone, are unique in Europe. The site has a great diversity of ecosystems, with important endemic plants. It has 1580 vascular plants, including 967 in the high mountain zone. There are over 700 species of fungi. It has 384 vertebrate species, and the mammal species include bear (*Ursus arctos*), lynx (*Felis lynx*) and wild boar (*Sus scrofa*). There are 246 species of birds and about 2500 species of insects recorded. The Western Caucasus has a remarkable diversity of geology, ecosystems and species. It is of global significance as a centre of plant diversity.

Source: adapted from UNESCO (2005a)

Maligne Lake, Jasper National Park, Nearctic realm

Source: IUCN Photo Library © Jim Thorsell

Flora

Major natural plant communities of the Nearctic from north to south include the tundra, boreal and montane forests, broadleaf woodlands, interior grasslands and dry and desert lands.

Fauna

The Nearctic includes a rich diversity of fauna. Some of its species include:

- in montane and boreal forests and rivers, moose (*Alces alces*), grey wolf (*Canis lupis*), red squirrel (*Tamiasciurus hudsonicus*), spruce grouse (*Canachites canadensis*) and salmon (*Onchorhyncus* sp.);
- in broadleafed forests, white-tailed deer (*Odocoileus virginianus*), striped skunk (*Mephitus mephitus*) and blue jay (*Cyanocitta cristata*);
- in protected natural grasslands of the interior, bison (*Bison bison*), black-tailed jack rabbit (*Lepus californicus*), prairie falcon (*Falco mexicanus*) and coyote (*Canis latrans*);
- in dry lands and deserts, western rattle snake (*Crotalus viridis*) and Gila woodpecker (*Centurus uropygialis*); and
- in mountain lands, brown bear (*Ursus arctos*), black bear (*Ursus americanus*), American bighorn sheep (*Ovis canadensis*) and bald eagle (*Haliaeetus leucocephalus*) (Bramwell, 1973; Burnie, 2004).

Africotropical realm
Geography

The Africotropical realm comprises Africa south of the Sahara desert, with Madagascar and neighbouring islands forming a distinctive sub-region.

Table 1.3   World Heritage by biogeographical realm

Biogeographical realm	Number of World Heritage sites	Land area (km²)	Area of World Heritage sites (km²)	Percentage realm in World Heritage sites
Palearctic	53	54,137,007	387,627	0.72
Nearctic	18	22,895,770	210,068	0.92
Africotropical	32	22,156,119	285,454	1.29
Indomalayan	16	7,533,958	12,052	0.16
Oceanian	5	1,035,302	16,934	1.64
Australian	12	7,704,909	69,786	0.91
Neotropical	33	18,975,799	243,531	1.28
Antarctic	6	285,806	25,021	8.75

Source: UNEP–WCMC (2005)

Madagascar and the Seychelles are old pieces of the ancient supercontinent of Gondwana, which broke away from Africa millions of years ago. The realm includes large freshwater lake systems; large areas of wetlands such as the upper Nile; a large tectonic geological feature, the Great Rift Valley; high mountains such as Mount Kilimanjaro (5595m) and Mount Kenya (5200m); and high mountain ranges such as the Mountains of the Moon and the Drakensbergs. The Africotropical realm includes many protected areas, and 1.29 per cent of its area has been inscribed as World Heritage (see Table 1.3).

Flora

From north to south and commencing at the southern limits of the Sahara, the Africotropical realm includes savannah grasslands, tropical rain-forest, dry open woodland, thorn forests, desert communities (the Kalahari and the Namib) and Mediterranean shrublands. At Africa's southern tip is a Mediterranean climate area that is home to a significant number of endemic taxa, as well as to plant families such as the proteas (*Proteaceae*). The Africotropical realm is home to a number of endemic plant families, including *Oliniaceae*, *Heteropyxidaceae*, *Penaeaceae*, *Psiloxlaceae* and *Rhynchocalycaceae* (order Myrtales), and *Sarcolaenaceae* (order Malvales).

Cloud forest, Rwenzori Mountains National Park, Africotropical realm, western Uganda

Source: IUCN Photo Library © Jim Thorsell

Fauna

The Africotropical realm is famous for its diversity of fauna. Some species found there include:

- in the rich central African rainforests and forested lands, western gorilla (*Gorilla gorilla*), chimpanzee (*Pan troglodytes*), small spotted genet (*Genetta genetta*), bongo (*Tragelaphus euryceros*), yellow-casqued hornbill (*Ceratogymna elata*) and congo peafowl (*Afropavo congensis*);
- in the highly productive perennial grasslands, a wide variety of herbivores, including elephant (*Loxodonta africana*), giraffe (*Giraffa camelopardalis*), wildebeest (*Connochaetes taurinus*), Thomson's gazelle (*Gazella thomsonii*), and Burchell's zebra (*Equus burchelli*); and a wide range of predators and scavengers, including lion (*Panthera leo*), leopard (*Panthera pardus*), spotted hyena (*Crocuta crocuta*) and African white-backed vulture (*Gyps africanus*);
- in wetlands, Nile crocodile (*Crocodylus niloticus*), saddlebilled stork (*Ephippiorhynchus senegalensis*), malachite kingfisher (*Alcado cristata*) herald snake (*Crotaphopeltis hotamboeia*) and hippopotamus (*Hippopotamus amphibius*);
- in the alkaline lakes of the Great Rift Valley, lesser flamingo (*Phoeniconaias minor*) and greater flamingo (*Phoenicopterus ruber*);
- in desert lands between the Atlantic and the Red Sea, addax (*Addax nasomaculatis*), fennec fox (*Fennecus zerda*), desert hedgehog (*Erinaceus* sp.), lanner falcon (*Falco biarmicus*) and pin-tailed sandgrouse (*Pterocles alchata*);
- in the Namib and Kalahari deserts, klipspringer (*Oreotragus oreotragus*) and brown hyena (*Parahyaena brunnea*);
- in the equatorial highlands, Verreaux's eagle (*Aquila verreauxii*), gelada baboon (*Theropithecus gelada*), walia ibex (*Capra walie*) and malachite sunbird (*Nectarinia famosa*); and
- in Madagascar, ting-tailed lemur (*Lemur catta*), Oustalet's charmeleon (*Furcifer oustaleti*) and Madagascar egret (*Egretta dimorpha*) (Bramwell, 1973; Burnie, 2004).

Indomalayan realm
Geography

The Indomalayan realm extends from the Hindu Kush range of Afghanistan through the Indian subcontinent and South-East Asia to southern China, and through Indonesia as far as Java, Bali, and Borneo. It also includes the Philippines and Japan's Ryukyu Islands. East of Borneo is the Wallace line that separates the Indomalayan realm from the Australasian realm. The Indomalayan realm has the highest mountains on Earth immediately to its north, and includes major rivers such as the Ganges and the Brahmaputra, volcanic landscapes, rainforests, mangrove forests, and coral reef systems. The Indomalayan realm includes numerous protected areas, and 0.16 per cent of its area has been inscribed as World Heritage (Table 1.3).

Flora

From north to south, the Indomalayan realm includes the flora of the southern side of the high Himalayan Mountains, temperate mixed forests, semi-deciduous forests, tropical deciduous forests, tropical rainforests and some savannah. The flora of the Indomalayan realm blends elements from Laurasia and Gondwana (see Appendix 1 and Case Study 1.6). Gondwana elements were first introduced by India that detached from Gondwana approximately 90 million years ago. Later, as Australia–New Guinea drifted north, the collision of the Australian and Asian plates allowed an exchange between Indomalayan and Australian floras. The tropical forests of the Indomalayan realm are dominated by trees of the dipterocarp family (*Dipterocarpaceae*).

Fauna

Lying west of the Wallace line, the Indomalayan realm shares its fauna with mainland Asia and species from Africa to the west and Asian fauna to the east, including:

- on the Indian subcontinent, tiger (*Panthera tigris*), wild boar (*Sus scrofa*), Indian rhinoceros (*Rhinoceros unicornis*), Asian water buffalo (*Bubalus bubalis*), palm civet (*Paradoxurus hermaphroditus*), sloth bear (*Melursus ursinus*), striped hyena (*Hyaena hyena*), Indian cobra (*Naja naja*) and rhesus monkey (*Macaca mulatta*);
- in South-East Asia tropical forests, Lar gibbon (*Hylobates lar*), Bornean orangutan (*Pongo pygmaeus*), Malay tapir (*Tapirus indicus*), Javan rhinoceros (*Rhinoceros sondaicus*) and Wallace's flying frog (*Rhacophorus nigropalmatus*); and

Case Study **1.6**

Kinabalu Park World Heritage Area, Malaysia

Kinabalu Park, in the state of Sabah on the northern end of the island of Borneo, is dominated by Mount Kinabalu (4095m), the highest mountain between the Himalayas and New Guinea. The area was inscribed as a World Heritage property in 2000. It has a very wide range of habitats, from rich tropical lowland and hill rainforest to tropical mountain forest, sub-alpine forest and scrub on the higher elevations. It has been designated as a centre of plant diversity for South-East Asia and is exceptionally rich in species, with examples of flora from the Himalayas, China, Australia and Malaysia, as well as pan-tropical flora. The site has a diverse biota and high endemism. The altitudinal and climatic gradient from tropical forest to alpine conditions combines with precipitous topography, diverse geology and frequent climate oscillations to provide conditions that are ideal for the development of new species. The park contains high biodiversity with representatives from more than half the families of all flowering plants. The majority of Borneo's mammals, birds, amphibians and invertebrates occur in the park.

Source: adapted from UNESCO (2005b)

- in mangroves, probiscus monkey (*Nasalis larvatus*), and mangrove snake (*Boiga dendrophila*) (Bramwell, 1973; Burnie, 2004).

Oceanian realm
Geography

This is the smallest and youngest in geological terms of the world's terrestrial realms. The realm includes the Pacific Ocean islands of Micronesia, the Fijian Islands and most of Polynesia, with the exception of New Zealand, New Guinea and the eastern part of the Indonesian archipelago, as well as several Pacific island groups, including the Bismarck Archipelago, Vanuatu, the Solomon Islands and New Caledonia. The realm includes high mountains in Indonesia and New Guinea. It is unique in not including any continental land mass. The Oceanian realm is composed mostly of volcanic, island arc or coral island groups. They range from tiny coral atolls to large mountainous islands, such as Hawaii. It includes many protected areas, and 1.64 per cent of its area has been designated as World Heritage property (see Table 1.3).

Flora

The climate of Oceanian islands is tropical or subtropical, and ranges from humid to seasonally dry. Wetter parts of islands are covered by tropical and subtropical humid forests, while drier parts are covered by tropical and subtropical dry forests, grasslands and savannahs. Land plants colonized the islands from wind-blown spores and seeds, floating seeds (such as coconuts) and by migrating birds.

Fauna

Dispersal across the ocean is difficult for most land animals, and Oceania has relatively few indigenous land animals. Birds are relatively diverse and abundant and include many sea birds and some species of land birds whose ancestors may have been blown out to sea by storms. Many island bird species have adapted to occupy the different niches available. Some (such as rails) have become flightless. A number of islands have indigenous lizards, including geckoes and skinks, whose ancestors probably arrived on floating rafts of vegetation washed out to sea by storms. With the exception of bats, which live on most of the island groups, there are few if any indigenous mammal species in Oceania.

Australian realm
Geography

This realm is dominated by Australia. The Great Dividing Range of Eastern Australia provides steep upland environments in comparison to the larger expanses of flat terrain in Central Australia. During the ice ages, sea levels were lower, exposing the continental shelf that links Australia to New Guinea and some of the islands of Asia, allowing land animal transfers. The largest coral

Kauai Is, Hawaii, Oceanian realm

Source: IUCN Photo Library © Jim Thorsell

reef system in the world is found off the east coast of Queensland. The Australian realm includes many protected areas, and 0.91 per cent of its area has been inscribed as World Heritage (see Table 1.3).

Flora

From north to south, the Australian realm includes tropical rainforest, tall grass savannah, eucalypt woodland, short grass savannah, subtropical and tropical rainforest, desert communities, mallee, eucalyptus forest and cool temperate rainforest, including beech and conifer forests. The Australian mainland is dominated by drought- and fire-tolerant flora, including *Eucalyptus*, *Casuarina* and *Acacia*, and by grasses and shrubs where rainfall is low. It is also home to rainforest species and flora descended from southern Gondwana, including the species of southern beech (*Nothofagus*), hakea, telopea and grevillea, coniferous podocarps and *Araucaria* pines. It includes Mediterranean shrublands in south-west Western Australia.

Fauna

Australia is distinguished by its large population of marsupials. The rich diversity of fauna includes:

- in tropical Queensland, cassowary (*Casuarius casuarius*), cuscus (*Phalanger maculatus*), Lumholz's tree kangaroo (*Dendrolagus lumholzi*), green turtle (*Chelonia mydas*) and a bird of paradise the trumpet manucode (*Manucodia keraudrenii*);
- in the arid interior, red kangaroo (*Macropus rufus*), frilled lizard (*Chlamydosaurus kingii*), bilby (*Macrotis lagotis*), budgerigar (*Melopsittacus undulatus*) and emu (*Dromaius novaehollandiae*);
- in south-west Western Australia, numbat (*Myrmecobius fasciatus*), quokka (*Settonix brachyurus*), honey possum (*Tarsipes rostratus*) and New Holland honeyeater (*Phylidonyris novae-hollandiae*); and
- in the temperate south-east, koala (*Phascolarctos cinereus*), eastern grey kangaroo (*Macropus giganteus*), brush-tailed rock wallaby

Temperate eucalypt forest, Blue Mountains World Heritage Area, Australia

Source: IUCN Photo Library © Jim Thorsell

(*Petrogale penicillata*), platypus (*Ornithoryhnchus anatinus*) and lyrebird (*Menura novaehollandiae*). (Bramwell, 1973; Dawson and Lucas, 2000; Menkhorst and Knight, 2001; Pizzey and Knight, 2003; Burnie, 2004).

Neotropical realm
Geography

The Neotropical realm includes South America, Central America (including the Mexican lowlands and Florida) and the Caribbean. The dominant mountain spine, the Andes, extends north–south from the northern hemisphere almost to Antarctica, and includes high mountains, volcanoes and large ice fields. The realm includes one of the great rivers of the world, the Amazon. South America was originally part of Gondwana and shares many plant and animal lineages with Gondwanan continents, including marsupials and the Antarctic flora. The Neotropical realm includes many protected areas, and 1.28 per cent of its area has been inscribed as World Heritage (see Table 1.3).

Flora

The flora varies considerably from north to south. Rainforest dominates the north, and the Neotropical realm includes more tropical and subtropical forest than any other. These forests extend from southern Mexico through Central America and northern South America to southern Brazil and include the vast Amazon rainforest. The flora also includes montane grass and shrubs, tall grass galleria forests, semi-deciduous forests, *Araucaria* forests, tall grasslands, desert communities and beech and cedar forests. The temperate forest areas of south-western South America are a refuge for the ancient Antarctic flora, which includes trees such as southern beech (*Nothofagus*), podocarps, alerce (*Fitzroya cupressoides*) and pines such as the monkey-puzzle tree (*Araucaria araucana*). Important food plant species originating in the Neotropics include the potato (*Solanum tuberosum*) and the cacao tree (*Theobroma cacao*).

Fauna

The Neotropical realm is rich in terrestrial mammal species (nearly 600) with the greatest number being bats (140) and rodents (360). It has few large herbivores. Some species include:

- in the Amazon, giant otter (*Pteroneura brasiliensis*), spectacled caiman (*Caiman crocodilus*), capybara (*Hydrochaerus hydrocharis*) and Arapaima fish (*Arapaima gigas*);
- in rainforest communities, Lime's two-toed sloth (*Choloepus didactylus*), black spider monkey (*Ateles chamek*), hyacinth macaw (*Anodorynchus hyacinthinus*), toco toucon (*Rhamphastos toco*) and southern anteater (*Tamandua tetradactyla*);
- in the chaco, pampas and steppe, pampas fox (*Dusicyon gymnocercus*), giant anteater (*Myrmecophaga tridactyla*), mara (*Dolichotis patagonum*), plains viscacha (*Lagostomas maximus*) and scarlet-headed blackbird (*Amblyramphus holosericeus*);
- in the Andes Mountain chain, Andean spectacled bear (*Tremarctus ornatus*), alpaca (*Lama pacos*), llama (*Lama glama*), vicuna (*Vicugna vicugna*), guanaco (*Lama guanicoe*) and torrent duck (*Merganetta armata*); and

Riverine forest in the Neotropical Amazon, Jau National Park, Brazil

Source: IUCN Photo Library © Jim Thorsell

- in the west coast deserts, green iguana (*Iguana iguana*) and Andean condor (*Vultur gryphus*) (Bramwell, 1973; Burnie, 2004).

Antarctic realm
Geography

This realm includes New Zealand, Antarctica and several island groups in the South Atlantic and Indian Oceans. Several Antarctic island groups are considered part of Antarctica, including the Scotia Sea Islands tundra of South Georgia and the South Sandwich Islands, the South Orkney Islands, the South Shetland Islands and Bouvet Island; and the Southern Indian Ocean islands tundra of the Crozet Islands, the Prince Edward Islands, Heard Island, the Kerguelen Islands and the McDonald Islands. The Antarctic realm includes some protected areas, and 8.75 per cent of its area has been inscribed as World Heritage (see Table 1.3). This includes the World Heritage areas of Heard and McDonald Islands, Macquarie Island and Gough Island.

Flora

In New Zealand, the native forest flora is dominated in the North Island by conifer (*Podocarp*) – broad leaf forest, and in the South Island by southern beech (*Nothofagus*) forest. The islands include grasslands and alpine regions.

The Antarctic continent flora consists primarily of lichens, mosses, liverworts and algal species that live on the areas of exposed rock and soil around the shore of the continent. Antarctica's two flowering plant species, the Antarctic hair grass (*Deschampsia antarctica*) and the Antarctic pearlwort (*Colobanthus quitensis*), are found on the milder northern and western parts of the Antarctic Peninsula. The remaining tundra comprise the Marielandia Antarctic tundra, including the Antarctic Peninsula, and the Maudlandia Antarctic desert of eastern Antarctica.

Fauna

Few animal species are present on the Antarctic Peninsula, with some insects present; otherwise, animals are restricted to the coastal zone. Antarctic species include:

- in the coastal zone, Ross seal (*Ommatophoca rossii*), Weddel seal (*Leptonychotes weddelli*), leopard seal (*Hydrurga leptonyx*) and emperor penguin (*Aptenodytes forsteri*); and
- in the Antarctic sub-polar zone, wandering albatross (*Diomedia exulans*) and southern elephant seal (*Mirounga leonina*) (Bramwell, 1973; Burnie, 2004).

In New Zealand, the island setting and its long isolation have led to the evolution of a range of species including tuatara (*Sphenodon punctatus*), brown kiwi (*Apteryx australis*), kakapo (*Strigops habroptilus*) and Hochstetter's frog (*Leiopelma hochstetteri*).

Global terrestrial biomes

Udvardy's 1975 classification recognizes 14 biome types: 11 correspond to major ecosystem groups, 2 (mountains and islands) are composites of several vegetational zones and their biota, and 1 includes large or ancient lakes that may warrant special consideration as biogeographic provinces. They are:

- tropical humid forests;
- subtropical and temperate rainforests or woodlands;
- temperate needle-leaf forests or woodlands;
- tropical dry or deciduous forests (including monsoon forests) or woodlands;
- temperate broadleaf forests or woodlands and sub-polar deciduous thickets;
- evergreen sclerophyllous forests, scrubs or woodlands;
- warm deserts and semi-deserts;
- cold winter (continental) deserts and semi-deserts;
- tundra communities and barren arctic desert;
- tropical grasslands and savannahs;
- temperate grasslands;
- mixed mountain and highland systems with complex zonation;
- mixed island systems; and
- lake systems.

While biogeographic realms provide a geographical regional subdivision that respects fauna and flora elements important for conservation, a geographical catalogue of the ecosystems present in each realm is also needed. Biomes provide such a classification of the chief ecosystems (biomes) of the world (Udvardy, 1975). The following material is based on Udvardy (1975) and draws on Bramwell (1973), Owen (1993), Hare (1994), Groombridge and Jenkins (2002), Mackay (2002), Burnie (2004) and Marinelli (2004). The biomes described are presented in the order offered by Udvardy. Additional biomes have been described in WWF's Global 200, and these are presented separately (see p34).

Tropical humid forests

These forests, also known as tropical rainforests, are found in a belt around the equator and in the humid subtropics and are characterized by warm climates with high rainfall. The forests are common in parts of the Africotropical, Indomalayan, Neotropical, Australasian and Oceanian realms. Rainforests cover less than 6 per cent of Earth's land surface, produce 40 per cent of Earth's oxygen and host more than half of the world's plant and animal species. Biodiversity is generally focused in the forest canopy, although five layers typify the forest structure: the over-storey canopy with emergent crowns, a medium layer of canopy, lower canopy, shrub level and an understorey. A perpetually warm, wet climate promotes explosive plant growth. The canopy is home to many forest animals, including, in some biogeographic realms, apes and monkeys. All levels of these forests contain a rich diversity of invertebrate species.

Subtropical and temperate rainforests or woodlands

The structural form of 'closed forest' or rainforest extends from the tropics to cool temperate climates wherever conditions are favourable. Differences in the characteristics of rainforest occur away from the equator as latitude increases and temperatures decrease, or with altitude. The east coast of Australia, for example, includes tropical, subtropical, warm temperate and cool temperate rainforest areas over 3000km in extent from Cairns to Tasmania. Rainforests typically occur as discrete patches, with species diversity and structural complexity of the rainforest decreasing as latitude increases (Adam, 1994; Specht and Specht, 1999). The cool temperate rainforests of South-East Australia have similarities in floristics and structure with New Zealand and the southern Andes and with montane communities of New Guinea (Adam, 1994). Cool temperate rainforests are also found in southern Japan, south-eastern US and in the Azores and Canary Islands (Strahler, 1969).

Temperate needle-leaf forests or woodlands

In most temperate coniferous forests, evergreen conifers predominate, while some are a mix of conifers and broadleaf evergreen trees and/or broadleaf deciduous trees. The temperate coniferous rainforests sustain the highest levels of biomass in any terrestrial ecosystem and are notable for trees of massive proportions, including the giant sequoia (*Sequoiadendron giganteum*), Douglas fir (*Pseudotsuga menziesii*), Sitka spruce (*Picea sitchensis*), alerce (*Fitzroya cupressoides*) and kauri (*Agathis australis*). These forests occur in small areas of western North America, south-western South America and the North Island of New Zealand (see Case Study 1.7).

Tropical dry or deciduous forests (including monsoon forests) or woodlands

These forests are found in southern Mexico, Central America, South-East Africa, the Lesser Sundas, central India, Indochina, Madagascar, New Caledonia, eastern Bolivia, central Brazil, the Caribbean, the northern Andes, and along the coasts of Ecuador and Peru (see Case Study 1.8). Although these forests occur in consistently warm climates and receive several hundred centimetres of rain per year, they also cope with long dry seasons that last several months and vary with geographic location. These seasonal droughts have a great impact on all living things in the forest. Deciduous trees dominate these forests, and during the drought a leafless period occurs, which varies with species type. The tropical dry forests are home to a wide variety of wildlife, including monkeys, large cats, parrots, various rodents and ground-dwelling birds. The most diverse dry forests in the world occur in southern Mexico and in the Bolivian lowlands. The dry forests of the Pacific Coast of north-western South America support a wealth of unique species due to their isolation. The dry forests of central India and Indochina are notable for their diverse large vertebrate fauna, while the dry forests of Madagascar and New Caledonia display pronounced endemism and a large number of relict taxa.

Case Study 1.7

Redwood National Park, California, US

Redwood National Park comprises a region of coastal mountains bordering the Pacific Ocean north of San Francisco. The area was inscribed as a World Heritage property in 1980. The dominant vegetation type is coastal redwood forest with *Sequoia sempervirens*. There are 15,776ha of old-growth redwood, 20,800ha of post-harvest regrowth and the balance (5034ha) comprises other vegetation types, some 856 flora species having been noted, 699 of which are native. The redwoods are surviving remnants of the forest type that was once found throughout many of the world's moist temperate regions, but are now confined to wet regions on the west coast of North America. The park contains the tallest known tree in the world at 112.1m. The animal life is equally remarkable, with 75 mammal and 400 bird species, and 168 invertebrate species found in the intertidal zone.

Source: adapted from UNESCO (2005c)

Case Study 1.8

Manu National Park, Peru

This 1.5 million hectare park has successive tiers of vegetation rising from 150m to 4200m above sea level. The area was inscribed as a World Heritage property in 1987. The tropical forest in the lower tiers is home to an unrivalled variety of animal and plant species. Some 850 species of birds have been identified and rare species such as the giant otter and the giant armadillo also find refuge there. Jaguar (*Panthera onca*) are often sighted in the park.

Source: adapted from UNESCO (2005d)

Temperate broadleaf forests or woodlands and sub-polar deciduous thickets

These occur in areas where rainfall is broadly distributed throughout the year and deciduous trees mix with species of evergreens. Species such as oak (*Quercus* spp.), beech (*Fagus* spp.), birch (*Betula* spp.) and maple (*Acer* spp.) typify the composition of this biome. Structurally, these forests are characterized by four layers: a canopy composed of mature full-sized dominant species; a slightly lower layer of mature trees; a shrub layer; and an understorey layer of grasses and other herbaceous plants. Most of the biodiversity is concentrated close to the forest floor. These forests are richest and most distinctive in central China and eastern North America, but are also found in the Caucasus, the Himalayas, Southern Europe and the Russian Far East. Temperate broadleaf forests exhibit typically fertile soils and a profusion of animals, including many mammals, birds, reptiles, insects and arachnids.

Evergreen sclerophyllous forests, scrubs or woodlands

Sclerophyllous woodlands and chaparral usually occur in mild climates with moderate winter precipitation, but long, usually hot dry summers (Brown and Lomino 1998). Globally rare, there are five regions that manifest these conditions, all of which occur on the west coast of continents in the mid latitudes: the Mediterranean basin; South-Central and South-Western Australia; the Fynbos in the Cape Province of South Africa; central Chile; and parts of California in the US. Between them, these regions contain 20 per cent of the Earth's plant species. The scrubs feature an extraordinary biodiversity of animal and plant species that are uniquely adapted to the stresses of long, hot summers with little rain. They are typically low, woody, sclerophyllous and fire adapted. They are known by names such as maquis, chaparral, Fynbos (see Case Study 1.9), and mallee. The hot, dry summers make much of the region prone to fires, and lightning-caused fires occur with some frequency. Many of the plants depend upon fire for reproduction, recycling of nutrients, and the removal of dead or senescent vegetation.

Warm deserts and semi-deserts

This biome receives little precipitation and often harbours a wealth of life that may remain hidden in daylight to preserve moisture. Desert landscapes have certain common features. There is minimal soil development and soils are composed mostly of sand; sand dunes may be present; exposures of rocky terrain are typical; and there is a sparseness of vegetation. Aeolian (wind-driven) processes are major factors in shaping desert landscapes. Some classifications of deserts rely on some combination of rainfall, temperature and humidity, while others utilize geographical location and dominant weather pattern. There is a range of types of deserts recognized, including trade wind, mid latitude, rain shadow, coastal and monsoon deserts (see Case Study 1.10). Most desert plants are drought or salt tolerant, and some store water in their leaves, roots and stems. Other desert plants have long tap roots that penetrate the water table, anchor the soil and control erosion. Although cacti are often thought of as characteristic desert plants, other types of plants have also adapted well to the arid environment.

Case Study **1.9**

Cape Floral Region protected areas, South Africa

The Cape Floral Region is a serial World Heritage site in Cape Province, South Africa. It is made up of eight protected areas covering 553,000ha. The area was inscribed as a World Heritage property in 2004. The Cape Floral Region is one of the richest areas for plants in the world. It represents less than 0.5 per cent of the area of Africa, but is home to nearly 20 per cent of the continent's flora. The site displays outstanding ecological and biological processes associated with the Fynbos (meaning 'fine bush') shrubland, which is unique to the region. The outstanding diversity, density and endemism of the flora are among the highest worldwide. It displays the highest levels of endemism at 31.9 per cent and it has been identified as one of the world's 18 biodiversity hotspots (see p37).

Source: adapted from UNESCO (2005e)

Aïr and Ténéré Natural Reserves, Niger

Source: IUCN Photo Library © Jim Thorsell

Cold winter (continental) deserts and semi-deserts

Deserts sometimes occur deep in the heart of continents in areas where moisture-laden winds never reach them. Where there are high mountain areas with a permanently dry climate, these deserts can be very cold, with, for example, Gobi Desert temperatures plunging to −20°C. Cold deserts have grasses and shrubs as the dominant vegetation.

Tundra communities and barren arctic desert

Tundra is an area where tree growth is hindered by low temperatures and short growing seasons. There are three types of tundra: arctic, antarctic and alpine (discussed under the mountain biome; see 'Mixed mountain and highland systems with complex zonation'). In all of these types, the dominant vegetation comprises grasses, mosses and lichens. Tundra is species poor when compared with forested ecosystems. Tundra ecoregions have seasonal concentrations of breeding waterfowl and shorebirds, as well as migrating species such as caribou (*Rangifer tarandus*). The varied habitats are critical for the survival of such species, as are their migration corridors for these allow the large-scale seasonal movements.

Arctic tundra

This occurs in the far northern hemisphere and includes large areas of northern Russia and Canada. The subsurface of arctic tundra is permanently frozen (permafrost). Notable animals in the arctic tundra include caribou, musk ox (*Ovibos moschatus*), polar bear (*Ursus maritimus*) and brown lemming (*Lemmus sibericus*). The arctic tundra is home to several peoples who maintain a relatively traditional lifestyle that includes hunting and

Case Study **1.10**

Aïr and Ténéré Natural Reserves, Niger

Aïr and Ténéré Natural Reserves, inscribed as a World Heritage property in 1991, combine to be the largest protected area in Africa, covering some 7.7 million hectares, of which one sixth constitutes a protected sanctuary. It includes the volcanic rock mass of the Aïr, a small Sahelian pocket, isolated with regard to its climate and flora and fauna, and situated in the Saharan desert of Ténéré. The reserves possess an exceptional natural assemblage of landscapes, vegetation and wildlife unsurpassed in the Saharo–Sahelian region and are the last stronghold of Saharo–Sahelian wildlife in Niger. The interaction of human activity and ecological processes has created a unique and spectacular environment. The area has been settled for over 30,000 years, and the many archaeological sites present are of great historic and cultural value. Owing to the remoteness of the Aïr and the low intensity of settlement over the past 2000 years, much of the wildlife that has been eliminated elsewhere in the Sahara and Sahel survives. The mountain massifs have been likened to biological islands in a sea of sand, a Sahelian enclave in the Sahara. The reserve harbours internationally important populations of five species of threatened fauna: Dorcas gazelle (*Gazella dorcas*), Dama gazelle (*Gazella dama*), addax (*Addax nasomaculatus*), aoudad (*Ammotragus lervia*) and ostrich (*Struthio camelus*).

Source: adapted from UNESCO (2005f)

reindeer (caribou) herding. There are many protected areas established in the Arctic by Greenland, Canada, the US, Russia, Finland, Norway and Sweden.

Antarctic tundra

Antarctic tundra occurs on Antarctica and on several antarctic and sub-antarctic islands, including South Georgia and the South Sandwich Islands and the Kerguelen Islands. Antarctica is mostly too cold and dry to support vegetation, and most of the continent is covered by ice fields. The Antarctic tundra lacks a large mammal fauna, mostly due to its physical isolation from the other continents. Animals present include sea mammals and sea birds, including whales, seals and penguins that inhabit areas near the shore. Special protected areas have been established in the UK's South Orkney Islands (protecting sea birds, fur seals and flora) and at sites in Antarctica (protecting sea birds; flora and fauna; rare mosses and liverworts; and petrel-breeding colonies and emperor penguin-breeding colonies).

Tropical grasslands and savannahs

Tropical and subtropical grasslands and savannahs are large expanses of land where there is insufficient rainfall to support extensive tree cover. They are characterized by rainfall levels between 90cm and 150cm per year; however, there may be great variability in soil moisture throughout the year. Grasses dominate, although scattered trees may be common. Large mammals that have evolved to take advantage of the ample forage typify the biodiversity associated with these habitats, and are at their highest diversity and density in African savannahs and grasslands. In Africa, large-scale migration of tropical savannah herbivores, such as wildebeest (*Connochaetes taurinus*) and plains zebra (*Equus quagga*), occur. The tropical savannahs of Northern Australia and southern New Guinea exhibit distinct species of fauna.

Temperate grasslands

This biome is characterized by grasses and other erect herbs, usually without trees or shrubs. Temperate grasslands occur naturally in the dry, temperate interiors of continents. The nomenclature for temperate grasslands varies and includes the prairies of North America, the pampas of South America, the veldt of Southern Africa and the steppe of Asia. Temperate grasslands differ from tropical and subtropical grasslands in the annual temperature regime, as well as the types of species found. Some trees may be found as riparian or gallery forests associated with streams and rivers. However, some areas do support savannah conditions characterized by interspersed individuals or

King penguin (*Aptenodytes patagonicus*), Macquarie Island National Park, Australia

Source: IUCN Photo Library © Jim Thorsell

clusters of trees. The vast expanses of grass in North America and Eurasia once sustained immense migrations of large vertebrates such as bison (*Bison bison*), Asian water buffalo (*Bubalus bubalis*), saiga (*Saiga tatarica*), Tibetan antelope (*Pantholops hodgsonii*) and onager (*Equus hemionus*).

Mixed mountain and highland systems with complex zonation

Mountains are defined as being conspicuous steep features having altitudinal plant zonation, and at least 700m in relative relief (Hamilton, 2002). This is a biome that includes high elevation grasslands and shrublands, including the puna and paramo in South America, sub-alpine heath in New Guinea and East Africa, and the Tibetan steppes. Temperature is the major influence on species distribution. Because temperatures decline with altitude as well as latitude, similar biomes exist on mountains even when they are at low latitudes. As a rule of thumb, flora and fauna change over 300m in altitude in a manner similar to that found over 1000km of increased latitude. Mountains occupy about 23 per cent of the surface of the

Earth, and major mountain regions of the world include the Himalayas, the Andes, the Rocky Mountains and the European Alps (Hamilton et al, 2003). As a single great landscape type, reaching almost from pole to pole, they encompass an extensive array of topographic, soil, climatic, faunal, floral and cultural differentiation.

Alpine tundra occurs at high enough altitude at any latitude on Earth. Alpine tundra lacks trees, but does not usually have permafrost, and alpine soils are generally better drained than permafrost soils. Alpine tundra transitions to sub-alpine forests or montane grasslands below the tree line. Some alpine tundra fauna include Kea parrot (*Nestor notabilis*), marmots (genus *Marmota*) and various mountain goats.

Mixed island systems

Islands typically have fewer species than an equivalent area on the mainland. They can also, because of isolation and an absence of predators, develop distinctive fauna and flora. Darwin's observations on finch diversity in the Galapagos Islands, the giant Komodo dragon (*Varanus komodoensis*) of

Indonesia, the flightless species of Lord Howe Island (Lord Howe Island Wood hen, *Gallirallus sylvestris*) and New Zealand (the kiwi and kakapo) provide examples of the effects of species isolation on islands.

Lake systems

Because lakes are generally separated from one another, they are home to few animal and plant species. While lakes can exist for centuries, other inland bodies of water, such as ponds, tend to dry up periodically. Lakes and ponds are divided into separate zones (littoral, limnetic and profundal zones) that are defined by their distance from the shore. The warmer littoral zone (closest to the shore) is especially important as a host to a wide variety of species. Various species of invertebrates, crustaceans, plants and amphibians thrive here and, in turn, provide food for predators such as birds, reptiles and other creatures inhabiting the shoreline. Because freshwater biomes are inland, they are more subject to seasonal changes.

WWF ecoregions and Global 200

WWF's Conservation Science Programme sought to strategically target the loss of biodiversity affecting the planet. This was hindered, however, by the absence of a suitable global biodiversity status map. The work of geographers Dasmann and Udvardy during the 1970s was not sufficiently detailed, and did not include marine or all freshwater systems. WWF's response was to develop a detailed map of the world's ecoregions (Olson et al, 2001; WWF, 2005a, 2005b, 2005c, 2005d). This has enabled the identification of areas of outstanding biodiversity and representative communities. Ecoregions were defined as:

> ... *relatively large units of land containing a distinct assemblage of natural communities and species, with boundaries that approximate the original extent of natural communities prior to major land-use change (Olson et al, 2001, p933).*

Elaborated with further detail, ecoregions are:

> *a large area of land or water that contains a geographically distinct assemblage of natural communities that:*

> • *share a large majority of their species and ecological dynamics;*
> • *share similar environmental conditions; and*
> • *interact ecologically in ways that that are critical for their long-term persistence (Olson and Dinerstein, 2002, p200).*

Ecoregions are regional-scale units of biodiversity. The researchers identified 30 biomes and within these 867 ecoregions (Olson et al, 2001; Olson and Dinerstein, 2002). The ecoregions may be ranked by the distinctiveness of their biodiversity features and by threats. They form the basis of global priority-setting analyses such as the WWF Global 200 (Olson et al, 2000) and Conservation International's hotspots (Myers et al, 2000). The larger ecoregions provide a basis for conservation assessment by nations and global organizations.

The Global 200 programme identified priority ecoregions. Of the 867 ecoregions, WWF identified 238 critical ones whose biodiversity and representation values are outstanding or globally significant. This was the first attempt to identify a set of ecoregions whose conservation would achieve the goal of saving a broad diversity of the Earth's ecosystems (WWF, 2005a). These critical eco-regions were identified within terrestrial, freshwater and marine 'realms' and 'biomes' (see Table 1.4) that differ from those considered in 'Biogeographical realms' and 'Global terrestrial biomes'. Fifty-three per cent of the terrestrial ecoregions were considered to be in a critical or endangered condition, 27 per cent (39 ecoregions) vulnerable, and 20 per cent (28 ecoregions) were relatively stable or intact. For freshwater ecoregions, 58 per cent (31 ecoregions) were critical or endangered and for marine environments, 29 per cent (12 ecoregions) were considered critical or endangered (Olson and Dinerstein, 2002).

The Udvardy system did not include freshwater (other than lakes) and marine biomes, and this shortcoming was addressed by WWF's Global 200 system (which describes them as realms). WWF advises, however, that their classification work for marine ecoregions is not complete:

Table 1.4   WWF Global 200 realms, biomes and ecoregions

WWF Global 200 realm	WWF Global 200 biome	Number of WWF Global 200 ecoregions	Notes
Terrestrial	Tropical and subtropical moist forests	50	The number of ecoregions reflects the biological richness and complexity of these forests.
	Tropical and subtropical dry forests	10	The most diverse dry forests of the world are found in southern Mexico and in the Bolivian lowlands.
	Tropical and subtropical coniferous forests	3	Mexico has the world's richest and most complex subtropical coniferous forests.
	Temperate broadleaf and mixed forests	8	These forests are richest in central China and eastern North America.
	Temperate coniferous forests	9	Forests dominated by huge trees are only found in western North America, south-western South America and in Australia and northern New Zealand.
	Boreal forests and taiga	5	Large-scale migrations of caribou occur in the northern boreal forests of Canada.
	Tropical and subtropical grasslands, savannahs and shrublands	8	Natural large-scale migrations of wildebeest and zebra are now only found in East Africa, the central Zambezian region and in the Sudd region (Uganda knob).
	Temperate grasslands, savannahs and shrublands	3	These environments have largely been converted to agriculture; the Patagonian steppe and grasslands include important mammals.
	Flooded grasslands and savannahs	5	These are found in the Everglades, Pantanal, Sahelain-flooded savannahs, Zambezian-flooded savannahs (including the Okavango) and the Mamberamo River inland delta in New Guinea.
	Montane grasslands and shrublands	11	The paramos (northern Andes) are the most extensive example of this ecoregion.
	Tundra	5	These areas have large seasonal concentrations of breeding waterfowl, shorebirds and caribou.
	Deserts and xeric shrublands	11	The Namib–Karoo deserts of South-West Africa are the world's richest desert flora.
	Mediterranean forests, woodlands and scrub	6	Collectively, these communities harbour 20 per cent of the Earth's plant species; the Fynbos is considered a separate floral kingdom by some.
	Mangroves	8	The mangrove swamps and forests of the Indomalayan and Australasian realms are the world's most extensive; the Sundarbans are the largest contiguous mangrove forest in the world.

Table 1.4   Continued

WWF Global 200 realm	WWF Global 200 biome	Number of WWF Global 200 ecoregions	Notes
Freshwater	Large rivers	7	The Mekong, Congo, Parana and Amazon–Orinoco rivers (see Case Study 1.11) harbour the four great large tropical river faunas.
	Large river headwaters	5	The most diverse vertebrate assemblages on Earth occur in freshwater communities of the Amazon and the Orinoco River basins.
	Large river deltas	6	Africa's most extensive delta, the Niger, has a high species richness.
	Small river basins	21	The Mississippi River embayment, the Mobile River basin and coastal streams of south-eastern North America support one of the richest temperate freshwater biotas.
	Large lakes	4	Notable lake biotas include the African Rift lakes, Lake Tana (Ethiopia), Lake Baikal (south-east Siberia), Lake Biwa (Japan), the high-altitude lakes of the Andes, and the highland lakes of Mexico.
	Small lakes	7	These include Lakes Kutubu and Sentani (New Guinea), the Yunnan lakes and streams in the Mexican Highlands, the Cameroon Crater lakes, Lake Lanao (the Philippines), Lake Inle (Myanmar) and the central Sulawesi lakes.
	Xeric basins	3	The Cuatro Ciénegas spring and pool complex in the Chihuahuan Desert is globally unique (high species richness and extreme endemism).
Marine	Polar	3	Productive and diverse ecoregions for Antarctic and Arctic waters.
	Temperate shelf and seas	9	Some of the most productive marine ecosystems are found in the Grand Banks and New Zealand, as well as the Patagonian ecoregions.
	Temperate upwelling	4	Highly productive upwellings occur along the west coast of North America and the south-west coast of Africa.
	Tropical upwelling	5	Upwellings along the west coast of South America and the west coast of Africa support highly productive marine systems.
	Tropical coral	22	South-East Asian seas support more than 450 species of hard corals (West Indian Ocean – 200 species; Caribbean – 50 species; see Case Study 1.12). The Great Barrier Reef is the largest barrier reef in the world.
Total	Ecoregions	438	

Source: Olson and Dinerstein (2002)

Case Study 1.11

Central Amazon Conservation Complex, Brazil

The Central Amazon Conservation Complex makes up the largest protected area in the Amazon Basin (over 6 million hectares) and is one of the planet's richest regions in terms of biodiversity. The area was first inscribed as a World Heritage property in 2000 and extended in 2003. It also includes an important sample of *varzea* ecosystems and *igapó* forests, lakes and channels which take the form of a constantly evolving aquatic mosaic that is home to the largest array of electric fish in the world. The site protects key threatened species, including giant arapaima fish (*Arapaima gigas*), the black caiman (*Caiman* sp.) and two species of river dolphin. The *varzea* and *igapó* forests, lakes, rivers and islands together constitute physical and biological formations and demonstrate ongoing ecological processes in the development of terrestrial and freshwater ecosystems. They include a constantly changing and evolving mosaic of river channels, lakes and landforms. The area is one of the endemic bird areas of the world and is considered one of the WWF's 200 priority ecoregions for conservation. It is also a centre of plant diversity.

Source: adapted from UNESCO (2005g)

We categorized the marine realm into ten biomes. Pelagic (trades and westerlies), abyssal, and hadal biomes, however, were not assessed for the Global 200 marine analysis because of the large scale of those units compared to other Global 200 eco-regions, the lack of consensus on their classification and the limited biodiversity information for these ecosystems (Olson and Dinerstein, 2002).

Several centres of endemism for the marine realm were identified by WWF and included the southern coast of Australia, New Caledonia, Lord Howe and Norfolk Islands, the northern coast of South America, the Yellow and East China Seas, the Red Sea, the Mediterranean Sea, the Sea of Cortez, the Great Barrier Reef and tropical pacific islands (such as Hawaii).

Conservation International's biodiversity hotspots

Conservation International has identified 34 regions worldwide where 75 per cent of the planet's most threatened animal species (mammals, birds and amphibians) survive within habitat that covers just 2.3 per cent of Earth (see Table 1.5). These same areas host an estimated 50 per cent of the Earth's vascular plants and 42 per cent of its terrestrial vertebrates (CI, 2005a). Conservation International has called these areas 'biodiversity hotspots' and they serve as a means for the global prioritization of conservation investment and effort (CI, 2005b). Conservation International defines conservation outcomes for their hotspots according to extinctions avoided, areas protected and connectivity corridors consolidated.

To qualify as a hotspot, an area must contain at least 1500 species of vascular plants and to have

Case Study 1.12

Barrier Reef Reserve System, Belize

The coastal area of Belize is an outstanding natural system consisting of the largest barrier reef in the northern hemisphere, offshore atolls, sand cays, mangrove forests, coastal lagoons and estuaries. The area was inscribed as a World Heritage property in 1996. The system's seven sites illustrate the evolutionary history of reef development and are a significant habitat for threatened species, including marine turtles, manatees and the American marine crocodile. The system includes examples of fringing, barrier and atoll reef types.

Source: adapted from UNESCO (2005h)

Table 1.5   Conservation International's 34 global biodiversity hotspots

Biodiversity hotspot	Area (km²)	Habitat left IUCN Category I–IV (km²) (percentage of original area)	Endemic plants	Endemic mammals	Endemic birds	Endemic reptiles	Endemic amphibians
Atlantic forest	99,944	22,782 (1.8)	135	12	23	8	15
California Floristic Province	73,451	30,002 (10.2)	52	0	0	0	0
Cape Floristic Tegion	15,711	10,154 (12.9)	160	0	0	0	2
Caribbean Islands	22,955	16,306 (7.1)	205	15	36	8	1
Caucasus	143,818	35,538 (6.7)	17	1	0	0	1
Cerrado	438,910	28,736 (1.4)	Unknown	4	1	0	0
Chilean winter rainfall – Valdivian forests	119,143	44,388 (11.2)	Unknown	5	2	0	5
Coastal forests, East Africa	29,125	11,343 (3.9)	28	0	0	1	0
East Melanesian Islands	29,815	0 (0)	Unknown	3	7	6	4
Eastern Afromontane	106,870	59,191 (5.8)	44	12	8	1	9
Guinean forests, West Africa	93,047	18,880 (3.0)	Unknown	7	7	1	6
Himalayas	185,427	77,739 (10.5)	Unknown	1	1	1	0
Horn of Africa	82,968	51,229 (3.1)	60	5	1	6	1
Indo–Burma	118,653	132,283 (5.6)	Unknown	7	5	13	3

Table 1.5   Continued

Biodiversity hotspot (km²)	Habitat left Area IUCN Category I–IV (km²) (percentage of original area)	Endemic plants	Endemic mammals	Endemic birds	Endemic reptiles	Endemic amphibians
Irano–Anatolian	134,966	25,783 (2.9)	Unknown	0	0	0	0
Japan	74,698	21,918 (5.9)	20	6	2	0	1
Madagascar and Indian Ocean islands	60,046	14,664 (2.4)	310	40	42	49	22
Madrean pine, oak woodlands	92,253	8900 (1.9)	Unknown	2	3	1	0
Maputaland, Pondoland, Albany	67,163	20,332 (7.4)	39	0	0	2	2
Mediterranean Basin	98,009	28,751 (1.4)	Unknown	0	0	4	1
Mesoamerica	226,004	63,902 (5.7)	65	3	22	10	11
Mountains of Central Asia	172,672	58,605 (6.8)	64	0	0	0	0
Mountains of south-west China	20,996	4273 (1.6)	20	0	0	0	0
New Caledonia	5,122	497 (2.6)	107	0	3	11	0
New Zealand	59,443	59,794 (22.1)	35	2	17	5	1
The Philippines	20,803	18,060 (6.1)	26	23	9	6	0
Polynesia–Micronesia	10,015	2088 (4.4)	63	0	27	2	0
South-west Australia	107,015	38,258 (10.7)	87	3	0	2	4
Succulent Karoo	29,780	1890 (1.8)	80	0	0	0	0

Table 1.5   Continued

Biodiversity hotspot	(km²)	Habitat left Area IUCN Category I–IV (km²) (percentage of original area)	Endemic plants	Endemic mammals	Endemic birds	Endemic reptiles	Endemic amphibians
Sundaland	100,571	77,408 (5.2)	117	17	13	24	7
Tropical Andes	385,661	121,650 (7.9)	330	5	63	3	8
Tumbes, Chocó, Magdalena	65,903	18,814 (6.9)	Unknown	1	14	5	0
Wallacea	50,774	19,702 (5.8)	12	22	29	3	0
Western Ghats and Sri Lanka	43,611	21,259 (11.2)	81	4	0	22	6

Sources: CI (2005c, 2005d, 2005e)

lost at least 70 per cent of its original vegetation (Barber, 2004). As a whole, the biodiversity hotspots contain:

- 150,000 plants endemic to the hotspots (50 per cent of the world total);
- 11,980 terrestrial vertebrate species endemic to the hotspots (42 per cent of the world total);
- 22,022 terrestrial vertebrate species (77 per cent of the world total); and
- an average area of 5 per cent conserved as Category I–IV (see Chapter 3, p82) protected areas (CI, 2005b, 2005c).

The hotspot approach has had some critics. Concerns have been expressed about:

- the use of plants as the primary area determinant;
- the use of habitat destruction as the principal threat;
- a need for conservation resources to be used for maintaining functioning ecosystems throughout the world;

- a need to recognize the importance of ecosystem services; and
- the conservation of wilderness also serves important purposes (Barber, 2004).

Nonetheless, they remain an important tool for setting conservation priorities.

Further reading

Baille, J .E. M., Hilton-Taylor, C. and Stuart, S. M. (eds) (2004) *2004 Red List of Threatened Species: A Global Species Assessment*, IUCN Species Survival Commission, Gland

Barber, C.V. (2004) 'Designing protected area systems for a changing world', in Barber, C.V., Miller, K. R. and Boness, M. (eds) *Securing Protected Areas in the Face of Global Change: Issues and Strategies*, IUCN, Gland and Cambridge

Burnie, D. (ed) (2004) *Animal*, Dorling Kindersley, London

Groombridge, B. and Jenkins, M. D. (2002) *World Atlas of Biodiversity: Earth's Living Resources in the 21st Century*, University of California Press, Berkeley, and UNEP–WCMC, Cambridge

Marinelli, J. (ed) (2004) *Plant*, Dorling Kindersley, London

2

Social Context

Michael Lockwood and Ashish Kothari

Managing protected areas is essentially a social process. It takes place within communities of place and interest that are, in part, formed (and reformed) by their histories, cultures, institutions, economic circumstances and politics. Managers and policy-makers must grasp the broader context in which their work is embedded. Since formally designated protected areas reach beyond 12 per cent of the Earth's terrestrial surface, and as more and more community managed conservation sites also gain recognition as protected areas, their roles will continue to deepen and diversify (Eagles, 2003). The meanings, purposes and management of protected areas are not static, but develop in conjunction with wider social, historical, economic and cultural influences. Cultural and socio-economic diversity give rise to a range of views about how we should relate to the natural world, why we should protect natural environments, and how we should manage and use them. Managers must recognize and meet responsibilities concerning local communities and indigenous peoples. To relate effectively to tourists and visitors, managers must understand how an individual's cultural background can cause him or her to hold certain views or to act in certain ways. When devising policies and strategies a manager must take into account politics, the legal system, the internal dynamics of institutions, and the broad social and political structures of society.

Since the 1980s, sustainable development has become widely established as a guiding policy framework at all scales, although there are concerns that despite the rhetoric much of the world continues to practise 'business as usual'. The world's population continues to grow. People aspire to improve their standard of living, placing increasing demands on the world's natural resources. Over-consumption is particularly evident in affluent countries and is increasing in others that are now industrializing. However, a majority of the world's population still needs to attain basic food and water security, as well as meet fundamental housing, health and education needs. Addressing poverty and affluence has been recognized as being a precondition for establishing sustainable environmental management at a global scale.

Economic, cultural and religious tensions continue to produce political instability and erupt into armed conflict. As well as destroying life and property, such upheavals damage protected areas and prevent effective management. These security concerns are dominating world agendas, and are likely to continue to do so for some time. At the same time, world leaders continue to pursue economic and community development, often within the rhetoric of 'sustainability'. Protected areas can tend to be dwarfed by such concerns; but as we will show in this book, they are a vital part of securing human prosperity and quality of life. Human well-being requires basic resources for a good life, freedom and choice, health, good social relations, and security. Poverty is a pronounced deprivation of well-being. Healthy ecosystems are essential for human well-being,

Jiuzhaigou Valley, China

Source: IUCN Photo Library © Jim Thorsell

and protected areas play a central role in their long-term maintenance (Millennium Ecosystem Assessment Board, 2003, 2005).

Globalization of financial, economic and political systems, and the unprecedented degree of international connectivity and integration that has emerged from innovations in communication technology are changing relations between peoples and the pressures they place on natural environments. Transformation of power and the extent of government action in relation to markets and the private sector has reduced the capacity of governments to act, while at the same time extending the range of policy instruments that are being used to tackle environmental problems. These wider economic and political changes influence the establishment, governance and management of protected areas.

In this chapter we consider these topics, with particular reference to protected area management. We also explore the emergence of a new

paradigm in protected area management that is largely a consequence of and response to these factors. This serves to frame the more specific considerations of protected area management that are covered in subsequent chapters.

Throughout the book, we will need to discuss countries in relation to their development status. Commonly used classifications include 'developed/developing' and 'North/South'. We have chosen not to use such terminology in this book because we find the former too narrowly defined according to economic criteria and the latter misleading because some southern hemisphere countries, such as Australia, have more in common with northern hemisphere countries, such as Canada, whereas northern hemisphere countries such as Bangladesh have more in common with southern hemisphere countries such as Namibia. Instead, we have adopted the United Nations Development Programme (UNDP) Human Development Index (HDI), and will refer to high, medium and low HDI countries (see Box 2.1). This, too, is not an entirely satisfactory way of differentiating countries, particularly since it does not adequately build in a number of environmental and cultural factors. However, for our purposes it is the most appropriate of the widely accepted international classifications available.

Socio-cultural context
Philosophies, worldviews and attitudes

Worldviews, aspirations, values and attitudes are important factors that shape human behaviour. They influence the ways in which we relate to and treat natural environments. They affect our capacity to work effectively towards finding and implementing solutions to environmental problems. Understanding people's values and attitudes can inform the design of protected area plans and projects. Such understanding is also an essential ingredient of effective protected area governance (see Chapter 5), particularly with respect to community based or co-management of these areas (see Chapters 20 and 21).

In Western countries where the modern conception of protected areas originated, human attitudes to nature have been profoundly influenced by the Enlightenment (1650–1850) and 'the project of modernity' (Taylor, 1998).

Box 2.1 Human Development Index

Human development is a process of enlarging people's choices. The United Nations Development Programme's (UNDP's) Human Development Index (HDI) combines three components that reflect key aspects of human development:

1   *Longevity.* A long life is considered of value in itself, but also indicates adequate nutrition and healthcare. The indicator used to measure this variable is life expectancy at birth.
2   *Acquiring knowledge.* Literacy levels and enrolment in primary education are used as indicators of access to education. Literacy is considered the first step to acquiring knowledge needed to operate productively in modern society.
3   *Access to resources needed for a decent standard of living.* This component could be measured by indicators such as access to land, credit, income and other resources; but such data are not readily available on a global scale. Purchasing power gives a good indication of people's relative command over resources and therefore their capacity to achieve an improved standard of living. By using the logarithm of real gross domestic product (GDP) this indicator also reflects the fact that initial investments in building personal capacity tend to yield high returns; but as capacity increases, the marginal return per unit investment declines.

The index has three categories: low HDI, medium HDI and high HDI. All countries measured fall into one of these three categories. Table 2.1 gives examples of the composite indicators and country rankings. The HDI uses national averages so that disparities within national populations are not revealed.

Sources: UNDP (1990, 2004)

Table 2.1   Examples of Human Development Index (HDI) rankings

HDI rank	Life expectancy index	Education index	Gross domestic product (GDP) index	HDI value
High				
1 Norway	0.90	0.99	0.99	0.956
27 Slovenia	0.85	0.96	0.87	0.895
55 Antigua and Barbuda	0.82	0.80	0.78	0.80
Medium				
56 Bulgaria	0.77	0.91	0.71	0.796
101 Islamic Republic of Iran	0.75	0.74	0.7	0.732
141 Cameroon	0.34	0.64	0.5	0.501
Low				
142 Pakistan	0.6	0.4	0.49	0.497
156 Eritrea	0.46	0.49	0.36	0.439
177 Sierra Leone	0.16	0.39	0.28	0.273

Source: UNDP (2004)

Modernity is characterized by a reductionist scientific worldview; belief in progress, especially that afforded by technological advances; and a preference for order and classification. The Enlightenment also elevated the importance, rights and responsibilities of individuals as apart from, or even above, the traditional authority of the church. Democracy and trade based on competitive profit-seeking organizations, together with the technical, economic and social transformations of the Industrial Revolution, are other key aspects of modernity (Friedmann, 1987). In the modern world, technical capacity and a belief that knowledge generated by rational scientific enquiry is universal and objective truth enabled humans to maintain the illusion that environments are separate entities that can be fully understood, predicted and controlled. Traditional protected management grew up during the last phases of modernity, and as such many of its concepts and methods were also modernist in character. Despite this, political influences and resource limitations mean that Western science is under-utilized in many protected area management systems.

We are now moving into post-modern times in which the old 'certainties' and confidence of modernism are being superseded by more complex, diverse and dynamic understandings and behaviours. The post-modern sensibility is relativistic rather than absolute, pluralistic rather than segregated, richly chaotic rather than ordered. Knowledge belongs to particular social and historical contexts, and as such is relative and subjective (Allmendinger, 2002). Post-modernists reject the possibility of a monolithic 'public interest', replacing it with a plurality of voices and interests (Campbell and Fainstein, 2003). Given that one of the traditional roles for protected area management is to serve 'the public interest', such thinking poses significant challenges to the role and place of protected areas in society. The new protected area paradigm (see p67) is a way of meeting such challenges.

Increasingly, it is recognized that protected areas cannot be seen in isolation from the communities that have inhabited or used their resources, nor can many of them be seen only as wildlife conservation sites, given that these communities may perceive the same areas as cultural landscapes or areas for essential survival. Various sections of society may value the same area differently, and there is no single 'right' way to achieve conservation. Indeed, many have powerfully argued that if humanity has to find its peace with Earth and all of its living creatures, then industrial society must learn from the cultures and indigenous worldviews that still exist amid natural ecosystems (Knudtson and Suzuki, 1992).

Indigenous and traditional communities incorporate their natural surrounds within their cultural systems. Many do not separate culture from nature – one is considered part of the other (Posey, 1999). The Asheninka and the Arakmbut of Peru, for example, see no duality between nature and culture – all living beings and the physical world are considered part of one's social relations (Gray, 1999). Awareness of such understandings is critical for protected area professionals and advocates since it forms a basis for questioning the assumption of much protected area history: that humans have to be separated from nature to protect the latter. Many indigenous peoples and traditional communities have pointed out that the landscapes and seascapes which are considered to be 'wild' by conservationists are, in fact, 'lived-in' by human societies. Even more important, they are partly shaped by the activities of these societies. The savannahs of Africa, the forests of the Amazon, the prairies of North America, the 'outback' of Australia, even the relatively inhospitable tundra and polar regions of Northern Europe have all been influenced by humans for centuries, if not millennia (Posey, 1999). Communities living in these and other natural areas do not consider their surrounds as being separate from their own societies; the entire landscape (or seascape) is thought of as a cultural landscape.

While it must be reconceptualized to acknowledge pervasive or subtle human presence and influence, the notion of 'wilderness' remains a powerful motivator of conservation action worldwide. Large areas of land and seascape that have not been subjected to modernist methods of resource extraction, or broached by infrastructure such as roads and pipelines, continue to inspire and be a focus for protection efforts. Notable outcomes from the Eighth World Wilderness Congress included the formation of the Native Lands and Wilderness Council by native people from 25 nations to demonstrate that they are an important part of conserving wildlands globally, as well as additional pressure on the US to prohibit oil exploration and development in the biological heart of the Arctic National Wildlife Refuge, and to designate this area as wilderness under the 1964 Wilderness Act (International Wilderness Leadership Foundation, 2005).

Deep and significant attitudinal changes have occurred in many countries over the past 40 years or so. Notions of environmental protection, biodiversity conservation and sustainable development have gained international support. A survey in The Netherlands identified the top three values and functions of nature as the value for human health, intrinsic value and the value for future generations (Van den Born et al, 2001). In a global survey of values conducted in 2000, 76 per cent of respondents believed that human beings should 'coexist with nature', while only 19 per cent said they should 'master nature' (Leiserowitz et al, 2005). The general public in Europe and the US have strong recognition of the right of nature to exist even if not useful to humans in any way. A large majority would agree to an increase in taxes if the extra money was used to prevent environmental damage, and there is also widespread global support for stronger environmental protection laws and regulations (Leiserowitz et al, 2004). Another survey conducted by GlobeScan in 2000 found that 83 per cent of respondents were concerned about environmental problems, with large majorities worldwide indicating that water pollution, destruction of rainforests, depletion of natural resources, and species loss were very serious issues (Leiserowitz et al, 2004). Results of a 2004 poll show that the majority of people in the 20 countries surveyed (that included low, medium and high HDI countries) believed that failure to address species loss within 20 years would imperil the Earth's ability to sustain life (GlobeScan, 2004). Many respondents also reported having practical, experiential and spiritual values for nature. Majorities in all countries surveyed, ranging from 62 per cent in Turkey to 94 per cent in Canada, agreed that 'experiencing nature and wildlife is one of the best experiences [they] can have' (GlobeScan, 2004). Such values and attitudes support the democratic legitimacy of protected area establishment and management.

History

The first areas to be protected by humans for their natural or spiritual values were established in various parts of the world by indigenous peoples and local communities – examples include sacred sites of Australian aboriginal peoples, *tapu* areas in the Pacific and sacred places in Africa, such as the Itshyanya sanctuary in Rwanda, and thousands of sacred sites in India (Harroy et al, 1974; Gokhale et al, 1997; Ramakrishnan et al, 1998; Phillips et al, 2003). Indigenous peoples and local communities in many parts of the world have long given certain places a special significance and meaning that demanded their protection. This is often derived from nature-based cosmologies and spirituality. Relationship with nature is fundamental to survival:

> From the beginning, wherever they lived, indigenous peoples have considered the Earth sacred. She gives us life and is the fundamental element of our worldview. Because of this we respect and venerate her. Far from attempting to subjugate nature as if we were her owners, we have inherited from our ancestors a form of harmonious coexistence with nature.
>
> The Earth is the root and source of our culture, and we must return to her daily to renew ourselves. She contains our memory, she shelters our ancestors, and for this she requires that we honour her and respectfully give back the goods she provides for us.
>
> We must watch over and care for Mother Earth so that our children and grandchildren will also experience the bounty she provides. If the world doesn't learn to respect nature now, what future will there be for the generations to come? (Menchu, 2001)

Over centuries and, in some cases, millennia, indigenous people and local communities have evolved a lifestyle that integrates with the land they inhabit and developed customary laws that regulate their use of natural resources (Posey, 1999). Diverse cultures perceive this relationship in different ways and institutionalize various rules of behaviour (taboos) with regard to the sacred space and its elements. Taboos are placed, for example, on particular species or are expressed as rules about when plants, animals, fish and birds can be harvested, which ones to take and how much. Protected sites include burial grounds, meeting places and particular mountains, rivers, forests and deserts that are homes of gods or ancestors. For example, India has thousands of sacred groves that are believed to contain elements of the divine. These are segments of the landscape that are delimited and protected in a relatively undisturbed state. Keeping them intact expresses a relationship with the divine (Malhotra et al, 2001).

Prior to the late 19th century, there were also many private reserves set up for providing royalty and wealthy landowners with amenity values and hunting opportunities (though there are significant exceptions, such as the protection given to wildlife by Emperor Ashoka as a matter of ethical concern during 3rd century BC in India). For example, the Gran Paradiso area in Italy was declared as a hunting zone in 1836 and then a royal hunting reserve in 1856, before being declared a national park in 1922 (Harroy et al, 1974). New thinking about nature emerged during the 19th century in Europe and North America from nature poets such as William Wordsworth and writers such as Henry David Thoreau and George Perkins Marsh. Published in New York in 1864, Marsh's *Man and Nature* argued that humanity's dominant role over the natural world was having significant, unrecognized and largely destructive consequences. It was a radical position at the time (Powell, 1976) and was as significant a book as Rachael Carson's *Silent Spring* a century later (Hutton and Connors, 1999).

In Western countries, naturalists, struck by the uniqueness of many ecosystems, began to appreciate their vulnerability and were among the first to call for the protection of areas and species. They conducted their campaigns through various scientific societies. During the 19th century, the moral principle behind the conservation movement's thinking was conservation for future exploitation. They argued for the economic utility of protecting birds, the efficiency in terms of timber production for preserving native forests and the

recreational value of public parks (Hutton and Connors, 1999).

The first 'modern' state-designated protected areas were established in the US and Australia during the 1860s and 1870s. A reserve at Yosemite was declared in 1864, and the US Congress dedicated Yellowstone, the world's first national park, in 1872. The idea of national parks as a land use spread to Australia, with the establishment in 1879 of The National Park (later called Royal National Park) near Sydney. The concept of a national park gradually spread to other continents and countries. Many early parks were established to provide for human uses, such as recreation and hunting. In Africa, the first reserves were created in remote areas that were unsuitable for agriculture, primarily for the protection of large mammals whose populations were in decline due to over-hunting and disease. Over time, this purpose has widened to embrace, from the 1930s, the provision of public aesthetic and recreation benefits; from the 1970s, biodiversity conservation; and most recently a focus on economic and social benefits (Cumming, 2004). For example, Sabie Game Reserve in South Africa, declared in 1898 to protect game animals for hunting by visiting Europeans, became the basis of the Kruger National Park in 1926 when the National Parks Act was passed in South Africa. Earlier, the St Lucia Wetland Area was declared a game reserve in 1895. In 1999 the Greater St Lucia Wetland Area was designated as a World Heritage area. Kilimanjaro National Park was a game reserve in the 1890s, a forest reserve in 1921 and then Tanganyika National Park in 1957.

From the 1870s, the growth in number and extent of protected areas was slow, though steady, with 1823 sites covering 217 million hectares declared by 1972. By this time, a range of other types of protected area had been identified, and in 1978 the IUCN published a categorization system that recognized scientific reserves, natural monument/national landmarks, nature conservation reserves and protected landscapes, as well as national parks. During the past 30 years the rate of reservation of such areas has escalated (see Figure 2.1). By 2005, there were 113,707 protected areas covering 19.6 million square kilometres recorded in the World Database on Protected Areas. This

Travertine terraces, Mammoth Hot Springs, Yellowstone National Park, US

Source: Graeme L. Worboys

initiatives helped to shape the direction of conservation activity. In 1980, the IUCN launched the influential World Conservation Strategy, and subsequently many governments have developed their own national strategies. Other important initiatives are discussed in Chapter 3 (p79). Here we will highlight a major driver of international protected area thinking – the World Parks Congresses (WPCs) organized by the IUCN. These congresses have been held about every ten years since the first in Seattle, US, in 1962. Discourses over the 50-year span of the congresses have helped to evolve several key strategies and philosophies of protected area management (Whitehouse, 1992). An overview of the major themes discussed at the congresses is given in Box 2.2.

figure might jump dramatically as countries act on the new acceptance of community conserved areas (CCAs) as protected areas (see Chapter 21). Some of the major developments in protected area history are listed in Appendix 2.

Internationally, a series of conferences and

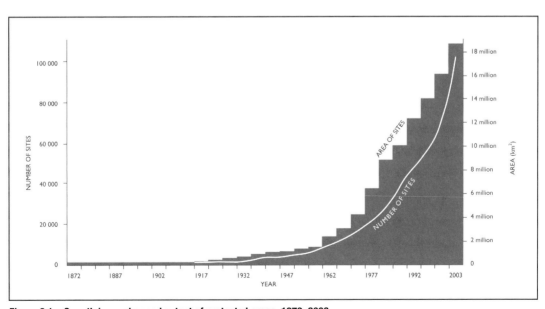

Figure 2.1   Growth in number and extent of protected areas, 1873–2003

Source: Chape et al (2005, p450)

Box 2.2 IUCN World Park Congresses, 1962–2003

Five World Parks conferences have been held under the auspices of the IUCN over the past 50 years, the most recent in Durban, South Africa, in 2003.

The Ist World Conference on National Parks, held in Seattle in 1962, was the first wide-ranging parks forum that included contributors from all over the world. Issues discussed included the effects of humans on wildlife; species extinction; the religious significance and aesthetic meaning of certain parks and wilderness; international supervision of boundary parks; the economic benefits of tourism; the role of national parks in scientific studies; and the practical problems of park management. There was consensus that national parks were of international significance.

The IInd World Conference on National Parks was held in Yellowstone, US, in 1972 to coincide with the centenary of the world's first national park. One hundred years on, there were 1200 national parks worldwide. Issues discussed included effective park planning and management; the effects of tourism on parks; communicating park values to visitors and raising environmental awareness; providing international training opportunities; and expanding the global park and reserve system.

The IIIrd World National Parks Congress was held in Bali, Indonesia, in 1982 and focused on the role of protected areas in sustaining society. Ten major areas of concern were recognized by the congress. A key element was the need to expand the world network of protected areas in all biomes. Recommendations promoted developing a system of consistent categories for protected areas; linking protected areas to sustainable development; capacity-building for protected area management; promoting the true value of protected areas using economic tools, such as cost-benefit analysis; monitoring to ensure effective management and that the needs of society are met; and creating a global programme for protected areas using the IUCN network.

The IVth World Congress on National Parks and Protected Areas was held in Caracas, Venezuela, in 1992. There were 2500 participants, a massive increase from the Bali event that had 500 attendees. Messages from the congress were that communities wanted to be involved in decision-making and the management of protected areas. Political, social, economic and cultural issues were understood to be central to protected area concerns, not peripheral. Mutual respect between cultures was also acknowledged as an essential component of sound protected area management. Other major themes included addressing the bioregional context of protected areas and habitat fragmentation, and securing the investment needed for effective protected area management.

The Caracas Action Plan, an output from the congress, provided strategic action over the decade between 1992 and 2002 for protected area professionals in four areas:

1   integrating protected areas within larger planning frameworks;
2   expanding support for protected areas by involving local communities and other interest groups;
3   strengthening the capacity to manage protected areas; and
4   expanding international cooperation in finance, management and development for protected areas.

The Vth World Parks Congress (WPC) was held in Durban, South Africa, in 2003. The congress was organized around seven workshop streams with three cross-cutting themes. The workshop streams were:

- linkages in the landscape/seascape;
- mainstreaming protected areas – building awareness and support;
- governance – new ways of working together;
- capacity-building – building the capacity to manage;
- management effectiveness – maintaining protected areas for now and the future;
- finances and resources – building a secure financial future; and
- comprehensive global systems – building a comprehensive protected area system; gaps in the system.

The cross-cutting themes were world heritage, marine protected areas and communities and equity.

The congress delivered the Durban Accord, a declaration for the future of protected areas; an action plan, which has specific outcomes and targets for the next decade; a set of recommendations; and a Message to the Meeting of the Convention on Biological Diversity. The Durban Accord is a declaration of celebration and intent by the 3000 participants from

Box 2.2 continued

154 countries, including scientists, civil servants, resource managers, industry leaders, non-governmental organization (NGO) leaders, indigenous peoples, mobile peoples and local communities. The *Durban Action Plan* is the mechanism to realize the goals of the Durban Accord and requires action from the many stakeholders involved in and around protected areas and for people to work together in a committed way at global, regional, national and local levels. These congress outputs are summarized in Appendix 3.

Source: IUCN (2003c)

Cultural diversity and identity

Protected areas are a cultural construct in so far as they reflect the attitudes and beliefs of local, national and/or international society. This is manifested from the earliest times when indigenous peoples designated sites or species for protection or regulated use, or established customary rules for the use of elements of the landscape. It has carried on to modern societies that are allocating sites for nature protection on the basis of ethical, scientific, aesthetic or recreational concerns related to nature.

Human beings have through much of their history displayed an incredible level of cultural diversity. As one indicator (considered by many as the best available indicator for cultural diversity), there are approximately 7000 languages (mostly oral) used across the world, the vast majority of these developed by indigenous peoples and other traditional communities. The correlation of biological and cultural diversity is striking. Harmon (1996) showed, for instance, that 10 of the 12 most mega-diverse countries (from a biodiversity perspective) identified by McNeely et al (1990) were also on the list of the 25 countries with the highest number of endemic languages. The correlation is vividly demonstrated at the micro level, where even within the same broad societal groups, significant linguistic (and other cultural) diversity seems to mirror high levels of biological diversity (Maffi, 1999).

The link between cultural and biological diversity is not coincidental. Harmon (1996) points out that mega-diverse countries are characterized by a diversity of terrains and landscapes and climatic conditions, or are islands, leading to a high incidence of relatively isolated evolution and

human development. Human cultures have developed in response to diverse ecological and physical living conditions, and in turn have shaped these conditions. This has also led to diversity of aspects of culture other than language: cuisine, dress, modes of shelter, social institutions, occupations and so on. From hunting-gathering to fishing, nomadic and settled pastoralism, shifting and settled agriculture, and urban occupations, human societies have for thousands of years displayed a remarkable degree of diverse modes of existence.

The historical inability or refusal of dominant agricultural or industrial societies to respect traditional cultures and their worldviews, the global spread of colonialism and with it the dominance of 'Western' cultures and economies, and finally, during the last few decades, the drive towards a homogenous notion of economic growth and development across the world have led to a massive erosion of traditional cultures. Approximately 90 per cent of the world's languages may become extinct or nearly extinct within this century; several hundred are already nearing extinction (Maffi, 1999). The loss of a language is not only a loss of the means to communicate (for in most cases it is likely to be replaced by another more dominant language); more importantly, it signifies the loss of knowledge that is embedded in that language. This includes knowledge relating to biodiversity and its uses, ways of surviving in different environments, and other aspects of the culture–nature link. This is both a serious human rights issue and a matter of significant concern for the future of conservation, for the world is losing critical perspectives, insights and knowledge.

Knowledge and science

Protected area management has been, in part, motivated by understandings of natural processes developed by ecological science. The natural sciences (in particular, botany, zoology, ecology, geology, geomorphology and conservation biology) continue to inform protected area management practices. Science underpins efforts as diverse as the control of introduced plants and animals, fire management, sustainable wildlife harvesting and identification of representative reserve networks.

Protected area managers also make extensive use of technology, ranging from helicopters for fire control through to satellite imagery to monitor environmental change and the internet for information-gathering and dissemination. The US government launched the first Landsat satellite in 1972. Since then, a massive amount of data has been collected on environmental conditions across the planet. In 1993, the World Wide Web had only 50 pages – this had exploded to 50 million by the end of the decade, enhancing both the production and availability of knowledge, as well as facilitating cooperation and joint action (UNEP, 2002). And, of course, personal computers are now a fundamental support to all of these activities and many others, including the writing of this book. Information and communication technology continues to expand and advance rapidly, offering opportunities for further improvements to protected area management capability.

The benefits of such technologies are unevenly distributed. In 2004, 79 per cent of internet users lived in the high HDI Organisation for Economic Co-operation and Development (OECD) countries, which then contained only 14 per cent of the world's population. Nonetheless, low and medium HDI countries are also experiencing a dramatic increase in internet use — for example, in Asia, close to 258 million people, or 7.1 per cent of the population, are online. This accounts for 31.7 per cent of the total online population in the world (European Travel Commission, 2005).

In the past, managers of state-managed protected areas and protected area systems designers mostly ignored and sidestepped the enormous depth of knowledge regarding biodiversity that indigenous peoples and other traditional communities hold. Even where used, such knowledge has been seen more in an instrumental manner, rather than as an integral component of community identity and existence. This is changing. Increasingly, managers are recognizing the importance of respecting the value of traditional knowledge, and are experimenting with synergistic ways of combining it with modern knowledge and practices. As community conserved areas gain increasing recognition as protected areas, the importance of such knowledge to conservation becomes even more visible. These trends are explored further in Chapters 20 and 21. Additionally, this recognition and mutually beneficial relationship is also being promoted through international forums, such as the Convention on Biological Diversity (CBD).

Population and demographics

Demographic factors influence protected area management in many ways. Protected area visitor needs, demands and impacts can change according to factors such as income, age distribution and ethnic background. Population size and consumption patterns are correlated with resource demand. Unless tempered by changing management and technologies, growing populations or changing lifestyles among stable populations increase the pressure to modify natural areas through resource extraction and clearing for agriculture, settlement, industry and infrastructure. Forced population movements – for example, as a result of natural disasters, or when inappropriate development projects displace people from their homes – can cause disruption of natural ecosystems when not accompanied by sensitive resettlement and rehabilitation. This can make the establishment of new protected areas more difficult, as well as threaten values in existing protected areas.

The world's population increased from about 3.8 billion people in 1972 to 6.4 billion in mid 2004. It is projected that this will increase to 7.9 billion by 2025 and to 9.3 billion by 2050 (PRB, 2004). Most of the projected growth from now until 2025 is concentrated in Asia (58.7 per cent) and Africa (28.5 per cent). Six countries account for nearly half of the projected growth: India (18.0 per cent); China (11.4 per cent); Pakistan (4.5 per cent); Nigeria (4.4 per cent); Bangladesh (4.1 per cent); and Indonesia (3.7 per cent) (UNEP, 2002; PRB, 2004).

As discussed in the following section on 'Economic context', protected area management should be considered part of the wider sustainability concerns. Environmental sustainability is closely linked to social and economic sustainability, including adequate food, housing, sanitation, health and education services for the world's human population. Rapidly growing populations can make it more difficult to achieve these aims (UNEP, 2002). Population growth exceeds food production in many low HDI countries, particularly in Africa (UNFPA, 2001; UNEP 2002). Nearly 50 per cent of humans currently live in the 12 countries that are mega-diverse and where the population growth rate is expected to exceed the global average (Millennium Ecosystem Assessment Board, 2003).

Socio-demographic variables such as age, gender, residential location and wealth may be correlated with individuals' attitudes and values for natural environments. For example, research in the southern US with respect to forest environments suggested that older people are more likely to favour uses such as wood production, whereas younger people tend to place more importance on intrinsic forest values (Cordell and Tarrant, 2002). The ageing population in high HDI countries means that there will also be significant demand shifts in what activities, settings and experiences visitors seek from parks areas (Eagles, 2003). Women tend to have stronger pro-environmental attitudes than men (Steel et al, 1994; Dietz et al, 1998; Cordell and Tarrant, 2002). In a survey of people in The Netherlands, younger and more highly educated respondents gave more importance to the intrinsic value of nature compared with utilitarian values (Van den Born et al, 2001). It seems that in some high HDI countries, urban residents have been more concerned about the environment than rural residents (Jones and Dunlap, 1992). Although relationships between socio-demographic variables and environmentalism are sometimes weak, Gebhardt and Lindsey (1995) concluded that at a broad social level there

is evidence supporting the typical environmentalist in industrial countries as being young, well educated and living in an urban environment. On the other hand, Dietz et al (1998) and Schultz and Zelezny (1999) found no consistent pattern associating environmental values and ethnic background.

The location of populations is also important since it affects consumption patterns and resource demands (food, water, energy and so on), as well as production of waste and pollution. As people move from rural to urban areas, their lifestyle changes, as do their environmental needs and impacts. Forty-eight per cent of the world's population live in cities; the proportion is highest for the high HDI regions: Europe (74 per cent) and North America (79 per cent) (PRB, 2004). However, while the ratio of urban to rural dwellers increased in most high HDI and some medium HDI countries between 1960 and 1995, the absolute number of rural dwellers increased in low HDI countries, with the total rural population of Africa increasing by 68 per cent over this period. Populations in coastal areas around the world are increasing rapidly. More than half of the world's population live within 200km of a coast, and by 2025 it is estimated that 6.3 billion people will live in such areas (Barber et al, 2004). This is causing particular pressures on fragile ecosystems such as dunes, heaths, saltmarshes, estuaries and mangroves, and exposes a much greater percentage of the world's population to catastrophic events such as tsunamis.

Economic context
Globalization

Over the past 30 years or so there has been a substantial shift in the structures and institutions that support global economic activity. Major aspects of globalization include:

- the internationalization of capital and markets through the development of an international financial sector;
- the expansion of free trade agreements;
- the expansion of petroleum-fuelled transportation infrastructure;
- the emergence of powerful transnational corporations (with a relative decline of the

power of national governments as a consequence); and

- the development of power blocs based on economic association, such as the European Union (EU) and the Asia Pacific Economic Community.

The internationalization of communications and the media through technologies such as satellites and the internet has reinforced this economic restructuring, increasing connections and interdependencies between people in most parts of the world. Yet, at the same time, television and print media outlets are concentrated in fewer and fewer hands.

Global economic, cultural and technological integration is having both positive and negative impacts on human and environmental welfare. While global connectivity can foster international understanding and cooperation, it can also serve to heighten ethnic and religious tensions and exacerbate political instability. Immigration pressures can also be elevated as people suffering under poverty and conflict become more aware of opportunities for security and economic advancement afforded by the higher HDI countries.

Economic globalization has had enormous environmental consequences (Hines, 2000). Wealthy consumers can now access natural resources from anywhere in the world, with little regard for the consequences at the sites of extraction, or on the routes of their transportation. High HDI countries are exporting their wastes. Countries without a major industrial base export natural resources such as timber, fishery products and minerals in a bid to earn foreign exchange for the goods they want to purchase. Low HDI countries may also relax their environmental and social regulations to allow direct investments by powerful multinational corporations, many of which employ lower standards in these countries than in their own parent countries. Such factors increase the pressure to exploit natural resources within protected areas and add to the challenge of establishing new strictly protected areas of land or sea.

The mobility of people has increased dramatically with the development of the airline industry. Travelling to different countries for holidays, education, business and conferences has become commonplace for many people in high HDI countries and for some medium HDI countries. It is also rapidly increasing for a numerically significant (if proportionally small) segment of low HDI countries. This has provided opportunities for tourism to develop in many countries, and protected areas are often key destinations.

Deregulation and the removal of trade barriers can open up new opportunities for economic development; but at the same time there is strong evidence that power and wealth are becoming even more concentrated in the hands of an elite minority. The centrality of markets in the process of globalization has meant that these opportunities, and the benefits that arise from them, are not equitably distributed (UNDP, 1999). Some sections of society, it is argued, are being systematically disadvantaged, and environmental quality is also facing new pressures. While there will be employment benefits in some countries arising from increased economic activity, concerns have been raised about the increasing gap between rich and poor. High-income countries, with about 20 per cent of the world's population, capture 86 per cent of global gross domestic product (GDP) – a measure of the total market value of final goods and services produced within a country – 82 per cent of export markets and 68 per cent of direct foreign investment, while the poorest 20 per cent have about 1 per cent in each of these categories (UNDP, 1999):

> In the developing world, governments desperate for investment funds are accepting the prescription of globalization and direct private sector investment, without necessarily being totally convinced of the benefits for their people. Many in developing countries fear these investments as neo-colonization that will exploit the natural resources and labour markets, leaving behind even more impoverished lands and peoples (McNeely and Schutyser, 2003, p12).

Such polarization, if left unchecked, is likely to lead to further deteriorations in world security through immigration pressures, increasing numbers of economic and environmental refugees, escalation of regional tensions and terrorism. In high HDI countries, people concerned with equity of opportunity, labour rights and environmental values have made their opposition known through protests at major gatherings, such as the regular meetings of Group of 7 (G7: Canada, France, Germany, Italy, Japan, the UK and the US) finance ministers and central bank governors. However, globalization has already irreversibly changed human institutions and understandings. Effective and cohesive governance is now crucial so that as many people as possible can gain benefits from the complex new economic, social and cultural situations that have arisen, as well as securing environmental outcomes at international, national, regional and local levels. Protected areas can contribute to improving security and equity outcomes through good governance (see Chapter 5) and transboundary initiatives (see Chapter 22).

Economic development and resource utilization

Economic development involves the production, distribution and consumption of goods and services through investment of human and financial capital. One manifestation of globalization is the increasing degree of integration and connection across product, financial and labour markets that is being facilitated by deregulation, including the reduction of trade barriers and quantum advances in communication and information technology (UNEP, 2002). Economic growth is widely considered to be a key factor in improving human welfare and alleviating poverty, though many critics have justifiably pointed out that growth *per se*

is not as important as distribution of what is produced and empowerment to control such production and distribution. The United Nations (UN, 2000) estimated that 3.5 billion people in low-income countries earn less than 20 per cent of the world's income, while the 1 billion people living in developed countries earn 60 per cent. There are similar inequalities in resource consumption. It has been estimated that the richest 20 per cent of the world's population account for 86 per cent of total private consumption expenditure, consume 58 per cent of the world's energy, and own 87 per cent of cars and 74 per cent per cent of telephones, while the poorest 20 per cent consume 5 per cent or less of these goods and services (UNEP, 2002).

A standard economic growth indicator is change in GDP. Gross world GDP grew from US$17 trillion in 1950 to over US$107 trillion in 2000 (Barber et al, 2004). Growth, as measured by change in GDP, was strongest, on average, in high-income countries during the 1980s, with regions such as Latin America and sub-Saharan Africa experiencing economic decline over this period. During the 1990s, there was little difference in average growth rates between high-income countries and the rest of the world, although considerable regional variation was again evident, with East Asia and Pacific economies growing strongly while sub-Saharan Africa still experienced economic decline (see Table 2.2 and Figure 2.2). Growth in high HDI countries has been

Table 2.2 Percentage annual average gross domestic product (GDP) growth rates based on constant 1995 US$

	1980s	1990s	Forecast 2001–2005	Forecast 2006–2015
World	1.3	1.2	1.0	2.2
High-income countries	2.5	1.8	1.4	2.5
Developing countries	0.7	1.7	2.7	3.4
East Asia and Pacific	5.6	6.4	5.4	5.4
Latin American and Caribbean	−0.9	1.7	0.3	2.5
Sub-Saharan Africa	−1.1	−0.2	1.0	1.6

Source: World Bank (2003)

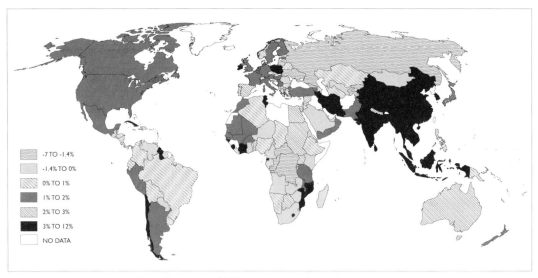

Figure 2.2   Per capita gross domestic product (GDP) average annual growth, 1990–2003

Source: Millennium Ecosystem Assessment Board (2005)

relatively slow during the first few years of this century, with stronger growth being evident in economies such as China and India (World Bank, 2003). In the longer term, it is forecast that economic growth will be more evenly distributed between regions (see Table 2.2).

It is important to note that these GDP figures do not take into account the considerable 'free' contribution that un-priced natural area goods and services make to the local, national and global economy. It is also important to note that despite better than average rates of economic growth, low HDI countries are coming from a very low base, and many are struggling under high levels of foreign debt, political instability, poorly developed infrastructure, underdeveloped labour markets and low levels of education and literacy.

Furthermore, apparent increases in wealth can be shown to be spurious when economic losses associated with the depletion of natural resources are taken into account, especially for countries heavily dependent upon natural resources. In 2001, in 39 countries out of the 122 countries for which sufficient data were available, net national savings were reduced by at least 5 per cent when costs associated with the depletion of natural resources and damage from carbon emissions were

included. Some countries such as Ecuador, Kazakhstan and Venezuela that had positive growth in net savings in 2001 actually experienced a loss in net savings when natural resource depletion was taken into account (Millennium Ecosystem Assessment Board, 2005). In recognition of such concerns, Bhutan is pursuing a more holistic development philosophy (see Case Study 2.1).

Economic growth generates surplus wealth that can be used, among other things, to establish and manage protected areas. High-income countries typically have greater capacity to effectively manage protected areas. Non-governmental organizations (NGOs) funded by private donors in these countries also play a major role in supporting protected areas in low HDI countries.

On the other hand, the location of protected areas is influenced by economic growth imperatives and pressures to develop natural resources. The consumerism of the world's rich is a major factor in ecological degradation in virtually every part of the world. Some (probably significant) portion of global resource degradation is also being driven by population growth and the needs of impoverished people. Waste products from production and consumption activities

Case Study **2.1**

Bhutan's development philosophy: Gross national happiness

Karma Tshering, Nature Conservation Division, Ministry of Agriculture, Bhutan

Bhutan, a small Buddhist kingdom located in the eastern Himalayas, has remained in a self-imposed isolation for several centuries. Although this seclusion prevented the country from experiencing some of the benefits of medical, technical and scientific advances, it has also shielded us from many of the detrimental side effects of poorly planned or haphazard development. As a result, the country has emerged into the 21st century with an intact natural environment of rich flora and fauna existing in a relatively harmonious relationship with its people. However, Bhutan faces some daunting development challenges. The Bhutan government under the visionary leadership of His Majesty King Jigme Singye Wangchuck, and with the overwhelming support of the people, is taking a cautious approach to development needs. Being a Buddhist country, respect for all living things has led to the adoption of environmentally informed policies and strategies.

Historically, as per international norms, economic development has been measured according to gross domestic product (GDP). However, King Wangchuck, ever since he ascended the throne in 1974, has strongly believed in a development path that involves pursuing values that are in harmony with Bhutan's vibrant culture, institutions and spiritual values, rather than by externally determined factors. This reflection led to His Majesty's enunciation of the development philosophy that 'Gross national happiness is much more important than the gross national product.' This approach recognizes that economic development, while necessary, should be driven by gross national happiness, and not become an end in itself.

The government and people of Bhutan recognize the need to follow a middle path that is committed to pursuing economic growth without undermining the integrity of the natural resource base or the country's unique cultural heritage. This development philosophy of gross national happiness is based on four government-endorsed pillars: conservation and sustainable use of the natural environment; preservation and promotion of cultural heritage; equitable economic development; and good governance. The country is currently working on identifying indicators that can allow measurement of progress in relation to these four pillars, thereby tracking development in terms of gross national happiness as an alternative to the traditional GDP measure.

outside protected areas alter and degrade ecosystems within protected areas (see Chapter 9, p228). Forest, wetland, riverine, coastal and marine ecosystems have suffered particularly severe impacts. By the early 21st century, human activities such as agriculture, forestry and energy production appropriated about 40 per cent of the net global primary production arising from plants converting solar energy through photosynthesis (Barber et al, 2004). The desire of forestry, fisheries, mining and agricultural industry stakeholders to maximize access to natural resources constrains opportunities to establish new protected areas. During the 1990s, the global forest area was reduced by approximately 2.4 per cent (94 million hectares). Along with clearing for agriculture, forests were being destroyed by unsustainable logging, fuelwood collection and overgrazing. Clearing in the biologically diverse tropical rainforests has been

of particular concern. Over 60 per cent of Asia's mangrove areas have been cleared for aquaculture (UNEP, 2002). These examples illustrate the critical importance of establishing a comprehensive, representative and well-managed global network of protected areas, both for biodiversity conservation and for maintaining the ecosystems upon which all economic activity ultimately depends.

Poverty

Over the last 20 to 30 years the status of human development has improved. Fewer people are living in poverty, life expectancy has increased and education levels have improved (UNEP, 2002). However, poverty and deprivation from basic services remain widespread. It is estimated that some 840 million people (over 13 per cent of the world's population) go hungry every day (UNEP, 2005a). Parts of Africa and Asia, in particular, have

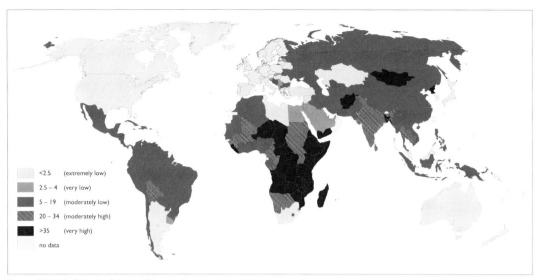

Figure 2.3   Under-nourishment by country

Source: UNEP (2002)

high levels of under-nourishment (see Figure 2.3). Many also lack clean water and adequate housing. It has also been estimated that one quarter of the world's urban population lives below the poverty line and that female-headed households are disproportionately affected (UNEP, 2002). Over 1 billion people, 18 per cent of the world's population, live on less than US$1 a day, and nearly half the world's population live on less than US$2 a day (UNDP, 2001). A high proportion of people living in extreme poverty are from rural areas (IFAD, 2001), with the majority being women. Poverty is also evident in high HDI countries. Over 12 per cent of the population (38.5 million people) in the US are income poor (UNDP, 2001).

Poverty, however, is not only a function of lack of money. More broadly, it can be seen as deprivation from the resources that are needed for dignified survival and secure livelihoods. In the case of tens of millions of people who are directly dependent upon natural resources for water, energy, food, shelter, clothing and medicine, poverty could mean lack of access to these resources. In this sense, individuals and communities who continue to have secure access to such resources but may not be earning much money may not be considered 'poor'. Conversely, individuals and communities who are now earning more money, but have been deprived of these resources that they cannot replace through what is available in the market, may be considered 'poor'. Environmental degradation can increase poverty by reducing resource access; in turn, poverty can cause ecological damage if the affected communities have to turn to desperate survival and livelihood measures.

Conservation policies, in general, and protected areas, in particular, have also increased poverty by denying or reducing community access to resources traditionally used for survival and livelihoods. This negative impact has increasingly been recognized in international conservation circles and was the subject of intense discussion at the Vth World Parks Congress in 2003. In turn, it has long been recognized that absolute poverty can lead local populations to damage protected area values in a desperate bid to survive. The implications of this and our earlier comments on consumerism are clear – effective protected area management at a global scale cannot be achieved without simultaneously addressing issues of poverty and over-consumption. Protected area establishment and effective management must therefore be part of the sustainable development agenda.

Sustainable development

During the 1970s and 1980s, the global community realized that supposedly renewable resources of wild stocks – for example, fish, whales and timber trees – were being pushed towards extinction. World consumption was increasingly depleting non-renewable resources. The consequences of exploitation, ecologically and socially, were becoming unacceptable. Development projects, including infrastructure, transportation, energy production and industrialization, were (and are) destroying or damaging critical ecosystems and ecological functions. Governments and NGOs have responded in a series of meetings and related policy initiatives. In 1972, the UN sponsored a conference held in Stockholm on the human environment. This event provided an international forum for expressing the growing environmental concern that had been building since the early 1960s. The Stockholm Conference produced a *Declaration of Principles* and an *Action Plan*, and set targets concerning commercial whaling, oil discharges into marine environments and energy use.

A decade later, the World Commission on Environment and Development (WCED) was established by the UN to address the apparent conflict between economic and environmental interests, and to propose strategies for sustainable development. Norwegian Prime Minister Gro Brundtland chaired the commission, and its report *Our Common Future*, published in 1987, was commonly known as the Brundtland Report. This landmark report helped to trigger a wide range of actions, and brought the concept of sustainable development to public attention. This report described sustainable development as 'development which meets the needs of the present without compromising the ability of future generations to meet their own needs'. Sustainable development is based on three broad goals: environmental integrity, economic efficiency and equity between and within present and future generations. Sustainability has emerged as a unifying aspiration for future development.

However, progress towards sustainability is being hampered by widespread poverty, on the one hand, and excessive consumption and affluence, on the other, in turn brought about by global inequities in decision-making and power, and the unwillingness of many high HDI countries to curb their production and consumption. The consumerism of the world's rich is a major factor in ecological degradation in virtually every part of the world. One measure of this is the 'ecological footprint' of such people or of the world's wealthy countries. The global consequences are alarming: if all of the world's 7 billion people were to consume at these levels, we would need ten worlds to meet the demand (Salim, 1994). Other impediments to environmental, social and economic sustainability include the debt burden of low HDI countries, inadequate governance structures and insufficient funding for the environment (UNEP, 2002).

Following on from the Brundtland Report, the United Nations Conference on Environment and Development (UNCED), also known as the Earth Summit, was held in Rio de Janeiro, Brazil, in June 1992. The conference stimulated debate and action, both nationally and internationally. Two major outcomes were the *Rio Declaration* and *Agenda 21*.

The *Rio Declaration on the Environment and Development* is a set of 27 principles designed to guide the economic and environmental behaviour of both nations and individuals. *Agenda 21* is an action plan that draws on these principles and addresses the social and economic aspects of the conservation and management of resources. It contains sections covering social and economic dimensions, conservation and management of resources for development, strengthening the role of major groups, and means of implementation. *Agenda 21* required each nation state to develop their own national sustainable development strategy, and this led to a succession of national, local and industry-based versions of *Agenda 21* (Stunden, 2002).

A special session of the United Nations General Assembly was called in 1997 to assess progress five years on from the Earth Summit. This was followed by another special session in 2000 called the Millennium Summit. This meeting, held in New York, discussed how to strengthen the role of the UN in the 21st century. Environmental and human development issues were prominent. In a report to the meeting, UN Secretary-General Kofi Annan stated that the international community was failing to provide for future generations and that 'we have been plundering our children's future heritage to pay for environmentally unsustainable practices in the present' (UN, 2000). One of the outcomes of the Millennium Summit were the Millennium Development Goals (MDGs). These are targets aimed at reducing poverty and promoting sustainable development.

The World Summit on Sustainable Development was held in Johannesburg in 2002 to identify issues that were impeding implementation of *Agenda 21*. This summit reaffirmed commitment to *Agenda 21* and the MDGs (UN, 2003). The main official outcomes of the summit were a political statement and an implementation plan. There were new targets and commitments under the MDGs – for example, the creation of a representative network of marine protected areas by 2012; but there was very little about how these would be achieved. For many people, the summit fell far short of expectations (Bigg, 2003). Such slow and insubstantial progress reinforces concerns held by many in the environmental community regarding the token or ineffectual nature of much sustainability policy, and despite the rhetoric, widespread pursuit of 'business as usual' practices.

The Vth IUCN World Parks Congress was a turning point for placing protected areas on the sustainable development agenda. Its theme 'Benefits beyond Boundaries' recognized the importance of protected areas for communities and the economic activities in and around them. Protected areas already contribute, and can be managed to contribute more fully, to the social, economic and environmental components of sustainable development. They supply safe drinking water and contribute to integrated management of watersheds and marine resources. Indigenous peoples and poor rural communities who have least access to health, education and other services live in and around protected areas, making them integral to poverty alleviation and sustainable resource use. Protected area managers and advocates provide leadership, expertise and policy support to sustainability initiatives. One of the major outputs from the congress, the *Durban Action Plan* (see Appendix 3), indicated that wider recognition is needed that protected areas are an essential component of the environmental, social and economic agendas agreed at the Rio Earth Summit and further developed at the World Summit on Sustainable Development.

Community development

The traditional view of protected areas as isolated repositories for natural and cultural heritage ignores the interactions between protected areas and indigenous and local communities. For the values of a protected area to be maintained, it must not be divorced from local and regional land uses (Machlis and Field, 2000a). Most exist in a matrix of multiple-use public, communal and private lands devoted to agriculture, forestry, human settlement and other uses (see Case Study 2.2). Regional growth or decline will affect management.

Increasing recognition is being given to the importance of protected areas in furthering community development. This is prompted partly by concerns that reduced access to resources such as timber and grazing adversely affects regional economies and communities. Protected area managers have a responsibility to explain the local and regional benefits that protected areas provide, as well as engaging more fully with local communities to minimize costs and maximize the flow of these benefits.

Protected areas may require transportation routes, energy grids, water supply and waste disposal systems. They can create employment, housing needs and business opportunities, particularly those related to supply of the goods and services needed to support visitor activities. These needs and opportunities, in turn, trigger development requirements within a region for infrastructure, waste disposal and natural resources such as water (Machlis and Field, 2000a). Management issues ranging from fire protection and prevention to the spread of introduced species can arise from such development activity.

This implies that management policies for protected areas should be integrated within the broader context of community sustainability. Strategic planning is required to integrate those

Hill tribe settlement in Chiang Mai, Thailand, where the forest is integral to daily life

Source: IUCN Photo Library © Jim Thorsell

concerns within the boundaries of the protected area network (biodiversity conservation, visitor service provision and environmental protection) with wider environmental, economic and social sustainability. Machlis and Field (2000b) advocate that protected area managers should:

- take responsibility to influence development in rural areas, and aggressively seek to maintain the viability of communities that surround protected areas;
- promote a sense of local identity that allows people to determine their own destinies;
- create allies among local citizens, especially local leaders, to develop a management capability at a landscape scale;
- emphasize the local and regional benefits of protected areas;
- adopt a collaborative approach to planning, with citizen participation understood as being crucial to the development of leadership and capacity for sustainable development;

- contribute to preserving or enhancing the overall character and lifestyle adjacent to protected areas while maintaining opportunities for planned growth;
- give technical assistance to rural and gateway regions, train staff in rural development and collaboration skills, and asses progress in achieving sustainable rural development; and
- ensure that conservation priorities are met and protected areas staff are not diverted to other activities.

Roles of governments and markets

The social, economic, and political structures of most countries include public and private sectors. The public sector, also called 'the state', comprises governments and parliaments, their associated departments and agencies, as well as the court system, police and defence forces. Governments usually provide public goods or services (see Box 2.3) through funding social services, education and protected area agencies. Governments or their

Case Study 2.2

Livelihoods and conservation in Namibia's communal areas

Christopher Vaughan, Department for International Rural Development, University of Reading, UK

The Namibian community-based natural resources management programme is one of a few conservation programmes credited with supporting the rural poor and providing for the devolution of community rights to new local institutions. Central to the programme's sustainability is its capacity to support the natural resource-dependent livelihood priorities of the rural poor in Namibia's communal areas. This is particularly critical to communities living with or adjacent to high wildlife populations, such as those bordering Etosha National Park.

The livelihood priorities of the poor in Namibia's communal land areas focus on income, food security, and reducing vulnerability and livestock and cropping, along with natural resource use, a reliance on pensions and remittances from kin, and access to informal employment. Residents of communal areas are constrained by a lack of alternative employment opportunities, with households critically dependent upon access to a variety of natural resources for fuelwood, grazing and especially wildlife for economic, social and cultural needs.

Incomes to conservancies from consumptive and non-consumptive tourism (for example, community harvesting, sales to trophy hunters and live sales) provide urgently needed financial resources for local communities to develop and manage their own wildlife management institutions and for local distribution. Aggregate conservancy incomes generated through consumptive and non-consumptive tourism have been significant. In 2000, the estimated total income for conservancies was just under 3.5 million Namibian dollars. In 2003, the income quadrupled to approximately 14.5 million Namibian dollars. In a number of cases, collective revenues are used for conservancy running costs. In 2003, conservancy incomes ranged from 65,000 to over 1.8 million Namibian dollars. The bulk of income comes from community-based tourism enterprises, such as campsites, which accounted for 36 per cent of all income in 2003. Access to cash income is critical for livelihood security, providing money for food security, education and healthcare, and farming activities. The distribution of collective conservancy income has taken place in six conservancies since 1998. For example, in Kunene region the Torra conservancy payout of 630 Namibian dollars to registered members in 2003 amounted to 8 per cent of the average annual household incomes for the region. The income was predominantly used to pay school costs. While one-off well-targeted cash payments help at crucial times of household financial need, many community members are interested in the development of long-term social enterprises that provide the communities with long-term benefits. There is no single way to improve and provide livelihood support; rather, a suite of small-scale interventions and a broader programmatic focus on livelihood priorities is needed in order to achieve conservation and development objectives.

agencies can directly produce goods such as electricity, or they can assist the private sector to provide goods and services through subsidies. The private sector comprises individuals, companies and the mechanisms for exchanging goods and services. These enable people, within the limits of their economic means, to acquire the necessities of life and to achieve the standard of living they desire. A defining component of the private sector is the market (see Box 2.3).

How much power should the public and private sectors have? How should they relate to each other? Answers to these questions are crucially important to protected area managers. They influence, among other things:

- who has responsibility for managing protected areas;
- what resources are allocated for managing protected areas;
- who pays for these resources;
- who has the power to make decisions; and
- how decisions are made.

The appropriate balance of powers and responsibilities between the public and private sectors has long been a matter for philosophical, political and economic debate. Over the past few decades, policy questions about the role of governments relative to the freedom of individuals to further their own interests have been heavily influenced by economic rationalism. This doctrine essentially

Box 2.3 Markets, market failure and the role of governments

A market is a set of rules and institutions that facilitates the orderly exchange of goods to the benefits of both the buyers (consumers) and sellers (producers). In theory, perfect markets will tend to be efficient in that goods will be bought and sold until the point is reached where everyone involved in the market can gain no additional benefit from further exchange – that is, economic benefits have been maximized. Therefore, economic rationalists argue, we should strive to create perfect markets for as many goods and services as possible.

An ideal market requires:

- perfect competition between the actors in the market;
- availability of full information in relation to the goods being traded and the mechanisms of trade; and
- allocation of property rights for all goods in the market:
  - that are transferable and secure;
  - for which use entitlements are known and enforced;
  - that are excludable – benefits and costs accrue only to the holder.

When one or more of these conditions does not apply, market failure occurs. Without effective property rights, for example, some people may chose to 'free ride' on the payments of others. A free-rider is someone who cannot be excluded from enjoying the benefits of a project but who pays nothing (or pays a disproportionately small amount) to cover its costs. While one may devise means of determining preferences for public goods, it is difficult to extract payment on the basis of these preferences without encountering free-riding behaviour.

Three sorts of market failure are of particular interest in relation to environmental issues:

1 The excessive production of unwanted 'externalities' can impose costs on other people. For example, clearing native vegetation in one area can cause hydrological changes that salinize soils and thereby decrease the productivity of another area some distance away. Pollution is another example of an externality that imposes large costs on society. In this case, market failure is due to the fact that there is no 'ownership' of the externality. Furthermore, given that there is generally no market price for the externality, there are no incentives to optimize the level of emissions.

2 The private sector economy will not produce enough public goods. Public goods and services contribute to the general welfare of society, but cannot be 'owned' by individuals – for example, health, education, defence and parklands. The private sector is not able to efficiently provide these goods and services because they cannot recover all the costs of producing them.

3 Depletion of common property goods occurs due to a lack of any incentive for those extracting the resource to take account of its sustainability – if one user takes less, then there is more available for a competitor. This so-called 'tragedy of the commons' occurs when all users take as much as they can so that the resource is degraded for all. Such unsustainable exploitation has occurred, for example, with respect to commons grazing and fish stocks. In some places, this tragedy has arisen because of the breakdown of traditional common property governance and management regimes.

Furthermore, markets do not guarantee that resources will be used in a sustainable fashion. It can be economically rational to exploit resources in the short to medium term, rather than preserving opportunities for future generations.

Table 2.3 shows that, in general, there are four types of good, which are defined according to whether or not they possess the properties of rivalry and exclusivity. A good is 'rival' when one person's use of it automatically precludes others from using it. A good is exclusive when, once the good is provided, only those who pay for it are able to use it. A mixed good is one that has at least two different types of values that are in different categories. For example, a forest is a mixed good that provides private goods such as timber and public goods such as wildlife habitat.

Table 2.3   An economic classification of goods

	Rival	Non-rival
Exclusive	Car, house, commercial recreation tour	Road toll way with no delays due to excess traffic
	Private goods	*Toll goods*
Non-exclusive	Fishery, crowded park with unrestricted access	Uncrowded park with unrestricted access
	Common property goods	*Public goods*

advocates maximizing the market's role in determining how resources are produced and allocated. However, the trend to privatize has also been criticized for being insensitive to many 'public good' activities. In countries such as the UK, governments have undertaken extensive privatization programmes that have significantly increased the use of markets as a mechanism to facilitate the production, exchange and consumption of goods and services such as water and transport. Markets are also increasingly being used to address problems such as pollution, global warming and even biodiversity conservation. More of the revenue to support protected area management is being generated from visitors and other park users who are increasingly being charged for the benefits they enjoy, and NGOs raise large sums of money from private donors to support protected area management.

In this context, it is important to make a distinction between private, public and common property goods (see Box 2.3). Markets are very effective at providing an efficient supply of private goods, but often not at maintaining public goods and services, and they are usually problematic in relation to managing common property resources. Public goods such as biodiversity conservation are generally 'produced' by governments through mechanisms such as establishing protected areas. Common property goods such as fisheries may require government intervention in the form of regulation and/or allocation of property rights to ensure sustainable management of the resource. Another option is for local communities or industries to be self-regulating, using customary law or formal agreements to ensure sustainable use of the

resource. Externalities (unintended 'by-products' of economic activity, such as pollution) have traditionally been addressed by governments through regulation; but increasingly economic measures such as emission taxes are being used. Social measures such as community sanctions are also being encouraged.

The once clear-cut differentiation between markets and governments is also becoming somewhat blurred. Public and private sectors are no longer so clearly separable, but are increasingly embedded in each other through public–private partnerships, corporatization of public sector agencies, pro-competition policies and the like. Autonomous public authorities are increasingly acting like hybrids between a public agency and a private firm. Public sector planners use tools developed in the private sector such as strategic planning, as well as market-based analysis such as cost-benefit analysis. Also being blurred to some extent is the distinction between government and local community as political decentralization gains ground (see the following section on 'Political context'). Rather than being the exclusive province of governments, as discussed in many places throughout this book, many key questions of environmental policy now revolve around deciding on the most effective form of governance, and selection of the most appropriate policy instruments, including market-based instruments.

Political context
Governance

Governance refers to actions, processes, traditions and institutions by which authority is exercised.

While often associated with national, provincial and local governments, it also encompasses institutions such as the UN, corporations and civil society institutions such as NGOs and community organizations. The United Nations Environment Programme (UNEP) considers that good governance is essential for environmental sustainability:

The political will and vision of governments and other authorities determine, above all else, whether environmentally sustainable development comes within reach worldwide. Where strong institutions for environmental governance are absent … or afforded a lower status than other institutions … improvements in environmental conditions are less likely to occur. As the range of concerns traverses the local to the global, so must these institutions. Furthermore, as all sectors of society are, in some way, both responsible for and impacted by the status of natural and human systems, these institutions must reach across these sectors. Thus, not only formal governments, but also business, NGOs and other elements of civil society must play a role, individually and in partnership, in establishing and maintaining these institutions (UNEP, 2002, pp396–397).

The past 50 years have seen major changes in governance at all levels. Many countries in Africa, Asia and the Pacific that were colonized by European powers have achieved independence. Apartheid has ended in South Africa. Communist regimes in the former Soviet Union and Eastern Europe have been replaced by more democratic systems. During the 1990s, more than 100 low and medium HDI countries replaced military or single-party governance with democratic institutions (UNDP, 2001; UNEP, 2002). From an environmental perspective, most governments now have ministries and departments to assist the development and implementation of environmental policies, including those related to protected areas. The governance of protected areas has also been changing, and we devote Chapter 5 to this topic.

NGOs are now a major international force, particularly in relation to alleviating poverty, responding to natural disasters and working for biodiversity conservation. Internationally, for example, the World Wide Fund for Nature

(WWF), The Nature Conservancy and Conservation International (CI) and others are investing hundreds of millions of dollars annually in protected area establishment and management (McNeely and Schutyser, 2003). Thousands of national and local NGOs have also been contributing to meeting national or local environment and development needs in most countries for the past 20 years. The ease and speed of communication afforded by information technology and enhanced transport infrastructure has also supported the development of extensive networks and partnerships between organizations.

Despite such advances, various elements of good governance (see Chapter 5) are still weak or absent in most countries. Of particular concern is the slow movement towards empowering citizens in decision-making processes related to conservation and development, lack of transparency in state or corporate institutions, and widespread corruption. For example, 14 African countries recently scored less than five out of ten on a corruption index, with four scoring less than two (UNEP, 2002). Corruption in high HDI countries is also evident, as witnessed by recent exposures of corporate crime and political bribery in the US and Japan. Some state agencies have also been unduly influenced by powerful special interest groups. Such distortions of legitimate governance threaten the integrity and effective management of protected areas through decision-making processes biased towards exploitation and activities such as illegal logging.

Public policy instruments and the environment

Protected area management is heavily influenced by the policies developed by governments and the instruments that they use to deliver these policies. Public policy involves the intentions of governments with respect to public issues, as well as the activities that are associated with these intentions. There is a suite of policy instruments that governments can use to achieve environmental or welfare policy objectives. Broadly, these can be classified into six categories: regulations; economic (market-based) instruments; non-economic voluntary measures; framework strategies and policy statements; institutional reform; and education. Within these categories, some instruments are well established (such as regulations to prevent trade in endangered species), while others are still being developed (such as markets for ecosystem services).

Regulatory instruments are often referred to as 'command-and-control' measures, and have traditionally been favoured by governments to carry out policy. Community environmental concern, particularly from the 1970s on, has led many governments to develop extensive bodies of environmental regulation. Such regulations are often established through legislation. Regulations can attempt to:

- prohibit or regulate action (such as stopping or restricting resource extraction from some categories of protected area);
- require action (such as environmental impact assessment of development proposals);
- establish processes (such as public participation in the preparation of park management plans);
- establish the structure, powers and responsibilities of institutions and their employees (many public protected area management agencies are established through legislation);
- set standards (such as extraction rates for renewable resources that are based on sustainable yield); and
- establish land tenure (the boundaries and governance of public protected areas are generally established through legislation).

Economic instruments, which act through market processes and other financial mechanisms, can create incentives for rational resource use and protection. Economic instruments include creating markets for natural resources such as water, or for trading the rights to produce externalities such as greenhouse gases; offering incentives for reducing environmental degradation; and placing financial burdens on resource users.

Non-economic voluntary measures such as self-regulation are used in some industries to achieve professional, safety, legal, social or environmental objectives. A common method of self-regulation is the use of codes of practice, through which an industry strives to achieve best practice. Such codes are most effective when they incorporate incentives to encourage compliance.

Framework strategies and programmes provide guidance and set direction. They do not require compliance, as is the case with many regulatory instruments. Rather, their adoption relies on widespread support and good will on the part of individuals and institutions. *Agenda 21* is an international example of a framework strategy.

Institutional reform can involve the modification of an existing organization, or the establishment of a new institution where there is currently no capacity to serve an identified need. A current trend in institutional reform is to reshape public conservation agencies by structuring and managing them more like private sector corporations, as well as exposing them to market-based mechanisms through contracting out of services and competitive tendering. This approach is largely founded on a belief that non-governmental or private sector efficiency and competition are answers to the many perceived problems of government bureaucracy, waste and overspending. As noted above, public agencies are also increasingly relying on NGOs and the private sector to perform environmental functions. Many new NGOs have emerged as a result – for example, the Caribbean Coastal Area Management Foundation (manager of the Portland Bight Protected Area), the Shimshal Nature Trust in Pakistan and the Tagbanwa Foundation of Coron Island in the Philippines. The two latter organizations are indigenous communities who have organized themselves into NGOs to gain greater bargaining power and input into decision-making over protection and use of traditional lands and practices (Ali and Butz, 2003; Ferrari and De Vera, 2003). The creation of co-management institutions for protected areas is another global trend (see Chapter 20).

Education is used to enhance awareness of environmental values and problems, as well as informing about potential solutions and appropriate courses of action. People are more likely to act in an environmentally responsible manner if they have an understanding of the importance of protecting environmental quality and how this might be achieved. In some cases, education also seeks to modify values and attitudes or change behaviour. There has been considerable investment of resources over the past two or three decades in awareness-raising and education programmes. This topic is addressed in relation to protected area management in 'Communication' in Chapter 10.

Decentralization of power and citizen participation

Citizen involvement is a central component in most, if not all, statements of sustainability principles. This is a consequence of widespread discontent with the legitimacy and efficacy of representative democratic government – in particular, the failure of representative democratic institutions, on their own, to represent and give expression to citizens' interests and aspirations. A number of countries have moved at a policy and legislative level to devolve power to local bodies. Uganda, South Africa, India and a number of other countries have made radical shifts towards political decentralization (although in many cases achieving this on the ground is proving to be more difficult than enacting policies and laws). The precise impacts on conservation have not been systematically studied; but it is clear that decentralization enhances the conditions for participation of local people in conservation. A number of other factors, however, need to be in place for this potential to be utilized (see Chapters 5, 20 and 21).

Growing demands for democratic forms of government translate into increased public participation and collaboration in protected area planning and management (Eagles, 2003). Citizen involvement in environmental decision-making, including that related to protected areas, is manifested in two related approaches.

Participatory approaches involve a shift from representative to participative democracy, in which citizens are actively engaged with the processes of policy development and implementation. Participative methods range from formal enquiries and opportunities to make written submissions, to informal consultation via face-to-face discussions with participants, through to actual participation in decision-making. Such public engagement can improve the legitimacy of representative democracy by supporting political

equality and the rights of citizens to be involved in decisions that affect them, reducing citizen alienation and increasing government accountability, as well as clarifying and representing the diversity of citizen interests and values concerning sustainability policy (Webler and Renn, 1995; Selin et al, 2000; Barham, 2001). It can improve the efficacy of government policy development and implementation by reducing failure; increasing acceptance; reducing delays; using local knowledge; managing competing interests and mediating conflict; and enhancing public ownership and commitment to solutions (Pimbert and Pretty, 1997; Curtis and Lockwood, 1998; Shindler and Brunson, 1999; Wondolleck and Yaffee, 2000).

Guidelines for effective participation processes include encouragement of all stakeholders to contribute; opportunities for participation in a manner that best suits the particular understandings, needs and contributions of each participant; and ensuring that participants have access to all relevant information (O'Riorden and O'Riorden, 1993; Moote et al, 1997). The 'information revolution' has greatly increased the availability of information, enabling citizens, communities and institutions to participate more meaningfully in protected area decisions and actions. This, coupled with a growing demand for a right to information, has led many countries to enact legislation that guarantees citizens access to most kinds of information.

Participation is often marketed by government as a mechanism for giving participants power to influence policy outcomes. However, despite some participatory processes offering opportunities for citizens to express views, and perhaps have an influence at the margin, the core policy agenda and framework may often largely remain under the control of governments.

More extensive are deliberative democratic processes that provide for collective decision-making through discussion, examination of relevant information and critical analysis of options. Attempts are made to eliminate the power and advantage afforded by political or economic position so that participants regard one another as equals, defend and criticize positions in a reasonable manner and accept the outcomes of

Participants in the First Joint White Volta Basin Communities Consultative Forum, Burkina Faso, September 2005

Source: IUCN Photo Library © IUCN/Jean-Jacques Nduita

such discussions (Dryzek, 1997). Deliberative methods include citizen juries, deliberative polls and consensus conferences. Deliberative democracy is seen by its proponents as more effectively recognizing citizens' interests than the more limited participative approaches (Dryzek and Braithwaite, 2000).

Collaborative approaches constitute a more radical model of participation, which attempts to construct consensus policy decisions in which citizens have a central, not marginal, influence. Collaborative planning, as articulated by leading proponents such as Healey (1997), draws on the theory of communicative rationality, according to which judgements are made about the quality of communication using criteria such as honesty, clarity and sincerity, as well as lack of distortion, manipulation and deception. With communicative rationality, decisions and actions are valid only if they arise from circumstances where all actors have been able to express themselves without inhibition or constraint, and where outcomes are unconditionally and freely accepted by all parties.

In practice, these conditions are almost impossible to achieve in full, and collaborative participation sometimes remains an ideal rather than a reality. Some commentators have also argued that even in apparently well-functioning collaborative processes, it is inevitable that some people will exert undue power and influence (Flyvberg and Richardson, 2002).

Citizen engagement in relation to protected area decisions generally follows a participatory approach, although at a local community level collaborative participation may be practicable. In either case, it is incumbent on protected area managers to work towards making such processes as accessible, equitable and inclusive as possible.

Political instability, armed conflict and terrorism

The world continues to be rife with conflicts that destroy lives, irreparably affect survivors, inflict barely imaginable levels of suffering and misery, and damage many, many important natural areas. Such conflicts also divert massive levels of human and financial resources away from creative endeavours, such as provision of health and education services and environmental protection. The environmental toll of such conflict increases the already difficult tasks of rebuilding war-ravaged lives. Such problems as polluted soils, river and groundwater resources create a major health risk (UNEP, 2005a). Radioactive contamination is also a problem, as are landmines in some protected areas in regions such as the Balkans. People's lives are at risk long after the war has stopped.

Evident motivations driving the high level of global conflict include ideological beliefs, personal ambition and greed, ethnic and religious differences, and competition for natural resources (UNEP, 2002). It is also increasingly being recognized that poverty and inequity are fundamentally implicated. This provides another reason why environmental sustainability, including biodiversity conservation and other protected area goals, cannot be achieved without concurrently addressing the economic and social sustainability of human communities.

Protected areas and 'the new paradigm'

As noted earlier in 'Socio-cultural context', p42, the modern designation of protected areas is generally considered to have begun in 1872 with the declaration of the Yellowstone National Park in the US. Such parks were defended against hunters, loggers and miners, as well as from the activities of indigenous peoples and local communities (Anderson and James, 2001b). Through much of the 20th century, centralized, state-based 'top-down' governance remained the dominant mode for protected area management, particularly in high HDI countries. Towards the end of the 20th century, voices against the exclusionary model of protected area management became more prominent. Factors driving the change include:

- greater scientific understanding of the role of humans in shaping environments and landscapes;
- cultural and social awareness of local and indigenous communities;

- acknowledgement of human rights, especially of indigenous people and local communities to their environments, as well as the rights of women and minorities;
- recognition of multicultural perspectives of protected areas and their management;
- recognition of the rights of people to have a say in decisions that affect them;
- democratization and devolution of central government power; and
- economic forces leading to more business-like approaches to protected area management (Phillips, 2003).

Three views have emerged.

Landscape ecologists point out that natural processes and organisms do not respect anthropogenic land-use boundaries, and the connectivity between protected areas and other regional land uses must be recognized (see Chapter 22).

Second, from a pragmatic perspective, managers and supporters of protected areas note that some state-run protected areas in some parts of the world suffer from ineffective management (objectives not being achieved); inadequate allocation of resources; lack of local support; and incursions from local communities, including poaching and sabotage, that are very difficult to counter (Stevens, 1997b; Brechin et al, 2002; McLean and Straede, 2003; Mutebi, 2003). In Namibia, for example, local people have been prohibited from traditional uses of wildlife, and the resulting illegal exploitation led to declines in wildlife numbers (Jones and Murphree, 2001). Low HDI countries have little capacity to fund protected areas through national treasuries, as is the norm with centralized governance, to the extent that attempts to translate the Yellowstone model to such countries have frequently been to the detriment of local communities and, in some cases, to conservation outcomes as well (Anderson and James, 2001b). Poaching is chronic – for example, in Malawi's Nyika National Park – and game species populations are in decline. Tourists come, in part, to see these species, and reduced numbers will further undermine the finance available to deal with the problems (Hess, 2001).

The third perspective is an ethical one. Protected area establishment and management have caused unjust suffering and disadvantage to some people, particularly indigenous and local communities (Ghimire and Pimbert, 1997; Hess, 2001; Brechin et al, 2002; Phillips, 2003). Yellowstone and many other sites have a disturbing history of indigenous peoples and local communities being forcibly removed from their lands. Such concerns were very evident at the 2003 World Parks Congress in Durban, expressed informally in discussions, through formal presentations such as Ali (2003) and Mutebi (2003), and throughout the cross-cut theme sessions on communities and equity. In Latin America and sub-Saharan Africa, for example, over 85 per cent of all protected area establishments were associated with state expropriation of customary tribal lands, dismantling of villages and exiling communities (Hess, 2001).

These three views, together with the wider trends and influences outlined in the previous section on 'Political context', have contributed to the emergence of new thinking about the role and management of parks. Many people now conceive protected areas as a long-term societal endeavour that goes well beyond the original Yellowstone vision of what a national park should be. Important elements of this endeavour are building a wide constituency that supports protected areas, locating protected areas within the wider agenda of sustainable development, and responding to calls from indigenous peoples and local communities for more recognition of their rights, needs and cultures. In sum, these constitute a 'paradigm shift' in thinking about protected areas. The separation of humans from nature implied by the conventional national parks paradigm is now maturing into a view in which humans both engage with and show respect for the natural world, together with the values that it affords and embodies.

This shift is summarized in Box 2.4, where Phillips (2003) characterizes the old and new paradigms according to factors such as the objectives of protected areas, their governance, attitudes towards local people, and management.

However, support for this new approach is not unanimous. Critics argue that the central purpose of protected areas, to conserve biodiversity and protect wild nature, is being marginalized within, and compromised by, the wider agenda:

> *Wild biodiversity will not be well served by adoption of this new paradigm, which will devalue conservation biology, undermine the creation of more strictly protected reserves, inflate the amount of area in reserves and place people at the centre of the protected area agenda at the expense of wild biodiversity (Locke and Dearden, 2005, p1).*

Furthermore, community-based approaches to natural resource management that are one feature of the new paradigm have often failed to deliver sustainable resource use, economic benefits or biodiversity protection (Kellert et al, 2000). In some areas, loss of traditional knowledge, increase in population, lifestyle changes, adoption of new technologies, breakdown of traditional norms, generational change and increased consumerism are eroding the willingness and capacity of some communities to maintain sustainable practices (Alcorn, 1993; Soulé, 1995; Dearden et al, 1998; Terborgh, 1999). Advocates of more top-down management have also questioned decentralized approaches on the grounds that locals are often divided, poorly organized and may not possess a conservation ethic (Brandon et al, 1998). The capacity of remaining natural ecosystems to absorb human use without loss of integrity has also been reduced as the extent of natural areas has declined through clearing for agriculture, forestry and human settlement (Bennett, 2003). While recognizing social and economic needs alongside conservation imperatives, some critics of the new paradigm suggest that protected areas cannot be expected to simultaneously accommodate all interests and should therefore focus on a core biodiversity conservation mission (Schelhas, 2001; Terborgh, 2004).

While some of the more extreme expressions of the new paradigm may tend to marginalize the role of conservation biology in protected area management, this is not our view of the way forward – both people and wild biodiversity must be jointly at the centre of the protected area agenda. We argue in this book for a range of situations that helps to conserve biodiversity, cultural diversity and the conditions for secure livelihoods.

Box 2.4 Traditional and emerging protected area paradigms

Traditional paradigm

Objectives:

- Protected areas are 'set aside' for conservation in the sense that the land (or water) is seen as taken out of productive use.
- They are established mainly for scenic protection and spectacular wildlife, with a major emphasis on how things look rather than how natural systems function.
- They are managed mainly for visitors and tourists, whose interests normally prevail over those of local people.
- A high value is placed on wilderness – that is, areas believed to be free of human influence.
- Protected areas are about protection of existing natural and landscape assets – not about the restoration of lost values.

Governance:

- Protected areas are run by central government, or at the very least set up at the instigation only of central government.

Local people:

- Protected areas are planned and managed against the impact of people (except for visitors), and especially to exclude local people.
- They are managed with little regard to the local community, who are rarely consulted on management intentions and might not even be informed of them.

The wider context:

- Protected areas are developed separately – that is, planned one by one, in an *ad hoc* manner.
- They are also managed as 'islands' – managed without regard to the areas around them.

Perceptions:

- Protected areas are viewed primarily as a national asset, with national considerations prevailing over local ones.
- They are also viewed exclusively as a national concern, with little or no regard to international obligations.

Management technique:

- Management of protected areas is treated as an essentially technocratic exercise, with little regard to political considerations.
- Protected areas are managed reactively within a short time scale, with little regard to the need to learn from experience.

Finance:

- Protected areas are paid for by the taxpayer.

Management skills:

- Protected areas are managed by natural scientists or natural resource experts.
- Management is expert led.

Emerging paradigm

Objectives:

- Protected areas are run with social and economic objectives, as well as conservation and recreation ones.
- They are often set up for scientific, economic and cultural reasons – the rationale for establishing protected areas therefore becoming much more sophisticated.

Box 2.4 Continued

- They are managed to help meet the needs of local people, who are increasingly seen as essential beneficiaries of protected area policy, economically and culturally.
- So-called wilderness areas are recognized as often being culturally important places.
- Objectives are about restoration and rehabilitation, as well as protection, so that lost or eroded values can be recovered.

Governance:

- Protected areas are run by many partners; thus, different tiers of government, local communities, indigenous groups, the private sector, non-governmental organizations (NGOs) and others are all engaged in protected areas management.

Local people:

- Protected areas are run with, for and, in some cases, by local people – that is, local people are no longer seen as passive recipients of protected areas policy, but as active partners, even initiators and leaders in some cases.
- They are managed to help meet the needs of local people, who are increasingly seen as essential beneficiaries of protected area policy, economically and culturally.

The wider context:

- Protected areas are planned as part of national, regional and international systems, with protected areas developed as part of a family of sites. The Convention on Biological Diversity (CBD) makes the development of national protected area systems a requirement.
- They are also developed as 'networks' – that is, with strictly protected areas, which are buffered and linked by green corridors, and integrated within surrounding land that is managed sustainably by communities.

Perceptions:

- Protected areas are viewed as a community asset, balancing the idea of a national heritage.
- Management is guided by international responsibilities and duties, as well as national and local concerns. The result is transboundary protected areas and international protected area systems.

Management technique:

- Protected areas are managed adaptively according to a long-term perspective, with management being a learning process.
- Selection, planning and management are viewed as essentially a political exercise, requiring sensitivity, consultations and astute judgement.

Finance:

- Protected areas are paid for through a variety of means to supplement – or replace – government subsidy.

Management skills:

- Protected areas are managed by people with a range of skills, especially people-related skills.
- Management values and draws on the knowledge of local people.

Source: adapted from Phillips (2003)

This view is consistent with the tone and contents of the key outputs from the Durban Congress: the Durban Accord, Action Plan, Recommendations and the Message to the Convention on Biological Diversity. It is also one of the central tenets of the Convention on Biological Diversity Programme of Work on Protected Areas (see Appendix 4).

We acknowledge that community-based

approaches can fail to deliver sustainable resource use and biodiversity conservation, but have also noted the predominance of 'paper parks' that have been created under the old paradigm. Recognition of such realities does not obviate appreciation of the rights, achievements and continued conservation relevance of traditional management practices (Stevens, 1997b). We also note that Hess (2001) cites numerous examples of the sustainability of local and indigenous land-use practices. Better governance and alleviating poverty are the two keys to making community-based approaches work more effectively. In part, this can be done by establishing robust partnerships among governments, NGOs and communities, as illustrated by the examples in Case Study 2.3 and Chapter 20, and by supporting community-initiated or managed efforts, as described in Chapter 21.

There is also a fear that in the future newly declared parks will tend to be less strictly protected, relegating biodiversity conservation to a subsidiary objective. The political reality is that some people have an interest in using the new paradigm and the opportunities it may provide to focus on protected area types where resource extraction is permitted. In other words, establishing large areas of less strictly protected parks could be used as a mechanism to avoid a more comprehensive network of strictly protected areas. It is up to protected area managers and supporters worldwide to ensure that the new paradigm is not distorted in this fashion. Care needs to be taken that in the rush to remedy past wrongs, important protected area values are not compromised and opportunities for establishing new strictly protected areas are not diminished. Centralized governance is often better able to represent the wider public good values of protected areas, and may also be better placed to efficiently mobilize resources and establish long-term and consistent management direction. Strictly protected reserves must remain a core part of the global biodiversity conservation effort; as discussed in Chapter 8, many more such areas need to be established before a comprehensive, adequate and representative network of protected areas is secured.

Such areas must be part of a network that also

Case Study 2.3

Protected area partnerships: Community-managed marine protected areas in the Pacific

A combination of community–government–non-governmental organization (NGO) partnerships and acceptance of customary marine tenure and local governance systems has contributed to the success of marine protected areas in several Pacific island nations.

In Fiji and the Cook Islands, traditional leaders have been the driving force behind reserve establishment and management, with support from the World Wide Fund for Nature (WWF) and government fisheries departments. In Samoa, protected area establishment and management were initiated by the government fisheries division, with the help of outside donor funding, and traditional leaders have been supporting the process by approving and endorsing plans and applying sanctions. In Vanuatu, the fisheries division initiated marine protection and management programmes, which have now been passed on to local communities under traditional leadership. In Fiji and Samoa, there have been additional measures to ensure co-management so that the national authorities can assist communities in managing the resources in the face of illegal fishing from those outside the village. All areas informally recognize customary marine tenure (CMT), making it easier to implement closed or reserve areas. Fiji and Vanuatu give legal recognition to CMT.

In most cases, local communities are able to enforce compliance with park regulations on community members by using traditional sanctions, which are strengthened by outside legitimization through co-management with government. In Samoa, some village by-laws are recognized by the Fisheries Act, allowing government fisheries officers and police to enforce local rules. In the Cook Islands, respect for traditional systems and community leaders engenders compliance even among non-community members. In Vanuatu, education of villagers is leading to village-enforced compliance of national laws.

Source: adapted from MacKay (2005)

makes space for a large range of protected areas that are under human use, and furthermore that all forms of protected areas, including strictly protected ones, can be under various governance models. Today's social and political contexts demand such a nuanced approach if conservation is to succeed. While there is no 'one size fits all' solution, it is likely that effective protected area governance will require democratic and mutually supportive central and local governance institutions. Contemporary experience suggests that this is difficult to achieve, and in many parts of the world integrated democratic governance capacity needs to be enhanced at both the national and local levels (Ribot, 2002, 2003).

Constituency-building is a global trend that involves establishing broadly based coalitions and partnerships directed towards sustainable environmental management, including conservation through various forms of protected area. Long-term conservation across the landscape scale requires genuine support and commitment from a wide range of constituencies. At the Durban Congress and elsewhere, representatives of indigenous and mobile peoples and local communities have declared themselves ready to collaborate with others for achieving conservation outcomes, and in turn have asked the global community to respect their rights, traditions and practices. Protected area managers must secure widespread trust and community support, both to legitimize their work and to secure the support necessary to expand and strengthen their activities. It is widely acknowledged that achieving satisfactory conservation outcomes will require considerable expenditure of funds – funds that will only be raised if there is community understanding of and support for protected area management objectives. But no matter how much funding is made available, protected area management will not be successful in the long term unless it is accepted as a core part of a wider social, cultural, economic and political agenda. Protected areas are already widely supported, and not just among those people who might be identified as 'green'. However, they need to become more 'mainstreamed' into popular consciousness and acceptance so that they are recognized as a key element in people's quality of life and linked to their personal and communal identity and aspirations.

Further reading

Anderson, T. L. and James, A. (eds) (2001) *The Politics and Economics of Park Management*, Rowman and Littlefield, Lanham

Barber, C.V., Miller, K. R. and Boness, M. (eds) (2004) *Securing Protected Areas in the Face of Global Change: Issues and Strategies*, IUCN, Gland and Cambridge

Brandon, K., Redford K. H. and Sanderson S. E. (eds) (1998) *Parks in Peril: People, Politics and Protected Areas*, Island Press, Washington, DC

Child, G. (ed) (2004) *Parks in Transition: Biodiversity, Rural Development and the Bottom Line*, Earthscan, London

Ghimire, K. B. and Pimbert, M. P. (eds) (1997) *Social Change and Conservation: Environmental Politics and Impacts of National Parks and Protected Areas*, Earthscan, London

IUCN (2005) *Benefits beyond Boundaries: Proceedings of the Vth IUCN World Parks Congress, Durban, South Africa*, IUCN, Gland and Cambridge

Jaireth, H. and Smyth, D. (eds) (2003) *Innovative Governance: Indigenous Peoples, Local Communities and Protected Areas*, Ane Books, New Delhi

McNeely, J. A. and Schutyser, F. (2003) *Protected Areas in 2023: Scenarios for an Uncertain Future*, IUCN, Gland and Cambridge

Millennium Ecosystem Assessment Board (2005) *Millennium Ecosystem Assessment Synthesis Report*, Island Press, Washington, DC

Stevens, S. (ed) (1997) *Conservation through Cultural Survival: Indigenous Peoples and Protected Areas*, Island Press, Washington, DC

UNEP (2002) *Global Environment Outlook 3*, Earthscan, London

3

Global Protected Area Framework

Michael Lockwood

Protected area management is supported and delivered by a wide range of institutions, agreements and processes. This chapter focuses on major international institutions, and briefly considers typical organizations operating at national and local scales. Such institutions work within a framework provided by international conventions, national laws and local regimes that may be based on formal regulation, contractual arrangements or customary law. The chapter outlines the major international conventions and treaties and offers a sketch of national, provincial and local regimes. A key component of the global protected area framework is the IUCN system for categorizing protected areas. In this chapter the main features of this system are outlined and a summary of the extent of the world's protected areas is presented.

Institutions working for protected areas

Protected area management is supported and delivered by a wide range of governments, NGOs, communities and private companies, as well as partnerships between such institutions. Some work globally or at a continental scale. Others act primarily at national, provincial or local levels. This section describes the nature and function of some typical protected area institutions across these types and scales.

International institutions

International protected area organizations and programmes play a central role in developing best practice standards and strategies for conserving nature. International efforts have also increased national governments' awareness of the need for protected areas. Sharing successes and difficulties experienced by various national programmes through established communication networks has been beneficial. International congresses, publications and reports are major fora for discussion and dissemination of information. The significant outcome of such discourse on protected areas has been several major international institutions, conventions and agreements that have assisted in developing worldwide conservation efforts.

United Nations

In 1945 the United Nations (UN) was established to deliver peace and security along with global social and economic development. Early partnerships between nations to protect species, and the first international conservation organizations, appeared around this time. The UN has initiated international policies, strategies, conventions and programmes for conserving and managing environments. Since the UN holds a key position in international politics, it has taken an important role in promoting environmental policies. Several UN agencies are relevant to protected areas:

- The United Nations Educational, Scientific and Cultural Organization (UNESCO) was formed in 1945. Its main objective is to bring 'peace and security in the world by promoting collaboration among nations through education, science, culture and communication'. UNESCO negotiated the World Heritage Convention (WHC) in 1972 and administers the Man and the Biosphere programme, which are considered in more detail in the following sections on 'Conventions' and 'Types of protected areas'. The International Council on Monuments and Sites (ICOMOS) is an international organization linked to UNESCO. It brings together people concerned with the conservation and study of places of cultural significance.

- The United Nations Environment Programme (UNEP), formed in 1972, now has major offices in Africa, Europe, North America, Asia and the Pacific, Latin America and the Caribbean, and West Asia. Major divisions within UNEP address matters including environmental policy and law; regional cooperation; environmental conventions; scientific and technical advice; and education (UNEP, 2005b). UNEP is also one of the three implementing agencies of the Global Environment Facility (GEF). In 1979 the IUCN established a centre in Cambridge, England, to monitor endangered species. In partnership with the World Wide Fund for Nature (WWF) and UNEP, this centre evolved in 1988 into the World Conservation Monitoring Centre (WCMC). Since 2000, the WCMC has been part of UNEP and functions as the world's primary biodiversity information and assessment centre. Global-scale data is compiled on species and habitats; forest, marine, mountain and freshwater environments; and protected areas.
- WCMC has a major international role in identifying and compiling information on the world's protected areas. The World Database on Protected Areas is a collaborative initiative between WCMC and the IUCN World Commission on Protected Areas (WCPA), supported by several NGOs and most national and provincial protected area management agencies, as well as the secretariats of international conventions and programmes. A central

part of the database is a list of the world's protected areas, including their location, size and type (UNEP-WCMC, 2005). This database is also linked to the *United Nations List of Protected Areas*.

- The United Nations Development Programme (UNDP) was established in 1965 to focus resources on meeting a series of objectives central to sustainable human development: poverty eradication; environmental regeneration; job creation; and the advancement of women. One of its focus areas of work concerns energy and environment practice, including the conservation and sustainable use of biodiversity. The UNDP helps countries and communities to maintain and benefit from biodiversity and supports a pro-poor approach to conservation and protected areas.
- The GEF, established in 1991, serves as a funding mechanism for international cooperation. The GEF raises funds from donor countries and then provides grants and low-interest loans for environmental projects that address issues such as biodiversity, climate change and land degradation, with a particular focus on low and medium Human Development Index (HDI) countries. GEF projects are managed by three implementing agencies: the UNEP, the UNDP and the World Bank (GEF, 2005).

IUCN

IUCN, formerly the International Union for the Conservation of Nature, was established in 1947. It is the world's largest and most important conservation network, bringing together (as of 2005) over 100 nations and government agencies, more than 800 NGOs, and tens of thousands of scientists and practitioners from over 180 countries. The IUCN has several programmes and commissions, including the Programme on Protected Areas that supports the work of the WCPA. WCPA membership is by invitation and includes managers of protected areas; experts in relation to the fields of WCPA's interests; academic specialists in areas relating to protected areas, resource economics, biogeography, wildlife management, marine conservation and other related fields; officials from relevant NGOs involved with protected areas; and members from key partner organizations. The WCPA seeks to promote the establishment and effective management of a worldwide representative network of terrestrial and marine protected areas. The four goals of the WCPA are to:

1   strengthen the capacity and effectiveness of protected area managers through provision of management guidelines, tools and information;
2   integrate protected areas with sustainable development and biodiversity conservation by provision of strategic advice to policy-makers;
3   increase investment in protected areas by persuading public and corporate sources of their value; and
4   strengthen the capacity of the WCPA to implement its programme through collaboration with IUCN and partner (IUCN, 2005a).

The WCPA has some 1300 members from more than 140 countries and is coordinated by a steer-ing committee. It is organized geographically, thematically and functionally into:

•   15 regions: Australia/New Zealand; Brazil; Caribbean; Central America; East Asia; Eastern and Southern Africa; Europe; North Africa/ Middle East; North America; North Eurasia; Pacific; South America; South Asia; South-East Asia; and Western and Central Africa;
•   two biomes: mountains and marine; and
•   six themes: 'Building the Global System'; 'Understand and Prepare for Global Change'; 'Improving the Effectiveness of Protected Area Management'; 'Equity and People'; 'Developing the Capacity to Manage'; and 'Sustainable Financing of Protected Areas'.

The WCPA publishes a *Best Practice Protected Area Guidelines* series (see Table 3.1) and, once every ten years, hosts a World Parks Congress (WPC) (see Box 2.2 in Chapter 2), with the most recent held in 2003 (see Box 3.1). Further detail on IUCN's work related to protected areas is given in Box 3.2.

IUCN Headquarters, Gland, Switzerland

Source: IUCN Photo Library © Peter Shadie

Table 3.1   IUCN Best Practice Protected Area Guidelines

Title and publication date	Related chapter in this book
National System Planning for Protected Areas (Davey, 1998)	Chapter 8, 'Establishing Protected Areas'
Economic Values of Protected Areas: Guidelines for Protected Area Managers (IUCN, 1998)	Chapter 4, 'Values and Benefits'; Chapter 12, 'Finance and Economics'
Guidelines for Marine Protected Areas (Kelleher, 1999)	Chapter 23, 'Marine Protected Areas'
Indigenous and Traditional Peoples and Protected Areas: Principles, Guidelines and Case Studies (Beltrán, 2000)	Chapter 20, 'Collaboratively Managed Protected Areas'; Chapter 21, 'Community Conserved Areas'
Evaluating Effectiveness: A Framework for Assessing the Management of Protected Areas (Hockings et al, 2000)	Chapter 24, 'Evaluating Management Effectiveness'
Financing Protected Areas: Guidelines for Protected Area Managers (IUCN, 2000b)	Chapter 12, 'Finance and Economics'
Transboundary Protected Areas for Peace and Co-operation (Sandwith, 2001)	Chapter 22, 'Linking the Landscape'
Sustainable Tourism in Protected Areas: Guidelines for Planning and Management (Eagles et al, 2002)	Chapter 19, 'Tourism and Recreation'
Management Guidelines for IUCN Category V Protected Areas Protected Landscapes/Seascapes (Phillips, 2002)	Chapter 3, 'Global Protected Area Framework'
Guidelines for Management Planning of Protected Areas (Thomas and Middleton, 2003)	Chapter 11, 'Management Planning'
Indigenous and Local Communities and Protected Areas (Borrini-Feyerabend et al, 2004b)	Chapter 2, 'Social Context'; Chapter 20, 'Collaboratively Managed Protected Areas'; Chapter 21, 'Community Conserved Areas'
Forests and Protected Areas: Guidance on the Use of the IUCN Protected Area Categories (Dudley and Phillips, 2006)	Chapter 3, 'Global Protected Area Framework'
Sustainable Financing of Protected Areas: A Global Review of Challenges and Options (Emerton et al, 2006)	Chapter 12, 'Finance and Economics'

Other major international NGOs and networks

The World Wildlife Fund was established in 1961 to raise private sector funds for the IUCN and to promote conservation. It now operates independently. In 1986 the organization changed its name to the World Wide Fund for Nature, but kept the acronym WWF. It now operates in more than 100 countries, and in 2005 was funding about 2000 conservation projects and employing almost 4000 people around the world (WWF, 2005e). The role of WWF and other international organizations has been to push for conservation to be included on international political agendas, improve coordination between nations and assist in putting strategies into action. Primary mechanisms include:

- initiating international conferences and meetings that bring together experts from around the world;
- placing the issue of conservation in political and legal arenas by formulating and administering conventions, agreements and treaties;
- establishing commissions and working groups for collating information and research;
- monitoring the state of the global environment and disseminating the data;

Box 3.1 Vth IUCN World Parks Congress 2003

The Vth IUCN World Congress on Protected Areas, or World Parks Congress (WPC), was held in Durban, South Africa, from 8 to 17 September 2003. Some 3000 participants attended, representing governments and public agencies, international organizations, the private sector, academic and research institutions, NGOs, and community and indigenous organizations. The theme of the 2003 WPC was 'Benefits beyond Boundaries'.

The congress included seven workshop streams. 'Linkages in the Landscape and Seascape' examined ecological and socio-cultural linkages at different scales, and investigated the application of the ecosystem approach to protected area management and governance. 'Developing the Capacity to Manage' focused on the skills, attributes and support systems needed for protected area institutions, decision-makers and practitioners. 'Building Broader Support' addressed building cultural support for protected areas; working with neighbours and local communities; and building support from new constituencies. 'Evaluating Management Effectiveness' examined the status of tools for evaluating management effectiveness, including principles, methods and current issues. 'Governance' reviewed different protected area governance models, discussed key governance issues, evaluated good governance, and provided guidance for decision-makers. 'Building a Secure Financial Future' addressed a range of financial arrangements and options for generating revenue, with emphasis on the development of a business approach to protected area management and applications of sustainable protected area financing. 'Building Comprehensive Protected Area Systems' assessed the status of global protected area coverage, with a focus on poorly represented biomes; identified gaps in protected area systems and ways to address them; and addressed global change factors and best practice for protected area design.

There were also three 'cross-cutting' workshop themes. 'Marine Protected Areas' emphasized improving marine protected area management effectiveness; building resilient marine protected area networks; integrating marine protected areas within marine and coastal governance; and expanding marine protected areas in the high seas and exclusive economic zones. 'World Heritage' identified ways of capitalizing on these areas of outstanding value to build awareness and support, and assessed their characteristics, needs and potential. 'Communities and Equity' focused on indigenous and local communities' rights and responsibilities in protected area management.

The main congress outputs were the *Durban Accord* and *Action Plan*, consisting of a high-level vision statement for protected areas and an outline of implementation mechanisms; 32 recommendations approved by the workshop streams; and the *Message to the Convention on Biological Diversity* (see Appendix 3).

Source: adapted from IISD (2003)

- assisting national programmes directly and indirectly; and
- attracting funding for all these functions.

The Nature Conservancy, founded in 1951, is a leading international conservation NGO whose mission, to preserve the plants, animals and natural communities that represent the diversity of life on Earth by protecting the lands and waters they need to survive, is directly related to protected areas. As well as in its home base in the US, The Nature Conservancy works in 27 countries and has helped to protect more than 47 million hectares of land and 8000km of river around the world, as well as being involved in more than 100 marine conservation projects. Properties for acquisition are targeted based on science-based value analyses. The Nature Conservancy has about 1 million members and supporters, over 1500 volunteers and 3200 employees, 720 of whom are scientists (The Nature Conservancy, 2005).

As well as buying land and placing it into protection, The Nature Conservancy assists landowners to better manage their properties for conservation outcomes. The organization has adopted a collaborative approach and works in partnership with corporations, indigenous people and local traditional communities. It has been at the forefront of developing and promoting innovative approaches to conservation funding, including debt-for-nature swaps (see Chapter 12).

Conservation International (CI), founded in 1987, is also based in the US. CI works in more than 40 countries, and is particularly active in low

Box 3.2 The IUCN and protected areas

Peter Shadie, IUCN, Switzerland

The IUCN has consistently played an influential global role for protected areas. Protected areas have traditionally been an issue of interest for IUCN members, with an estimated 76 per cent directly or indirectly involved with protected area issues. A recent analysis of all IUCN member resolutions and recommendations found that close to 30 per cent are directly or indirectly related to protected areas, demonstrating the central place these areas play in achieving IUCN's vision and mission.

IUCN and the World Commission on Protected Areas (WCPA) invested considerably in the staging of the Vth IUCN World Parks Congress in 2003 (see Appendix 3). Following the congress, the IUCN and the WCPA played equally a central role in the Convention on Biological Diversity (CBD) processes, which culminated in the adoption of the Convention on Biological Diversity Programme of Work on Protected Areas (see Appendix 4). The *Durban Action Plan* and Programme of Work have been supported by IUCN's membership through a number of resolutions passed at the Third World Conservation Congress (WCC) in Bangkok in November 2004. Key is WCC Resolution 035, which endorses these two crucial documents as the essential blueprints for IUCN's future work on protected areas. Since the Third WCC, a new *Strategic Plan* has been prepared based on the key directions within the *Durban Accord*, the *Durban Action Plan* and the Programme of Work. The plan covers the period of 2005–2015 and aims to direct IUCN and WCPA's activities on protected areas over this period, which spans the period up to and including the next world parks congress.

The plan recognizes the 'sea change' in our approach to protected areas, which was articulated as the new paradigm (see Chapter 2, p67) within the *Durban Accord*. Under the plan, the IUCN, through the WCPA and its partners, strives to provide leadership on protected area issues to governments, NGOs, communities and other key stakeholders. Emphasizing its power to convene a diversity of actors, the IUCN works by bringing science, knowledge and experience to bear on decision-making in order to address the existing challenges, and on future issues and opportunities in order to realize a common vision:

> … that society fully recognizes and supports the importance of protected areas in the 21st Century by securing key places for biological and cultural diversity, promoting equity and justice, maintaining the quality of the environment, and ensuring the sustainable use of the natural resources for poverty reduction, food and water security, and the prevention of conflicts (WCPA, 2005).

To realize this vision the mission of the WCPA is to promote an effectively managed, representative system of marine and terrestrial protected areas as an integral part of IUCN mission.

The *Durban Action Plan* identifies four strategic directions that will guide its future work:

1   *Conservation and sustainable use of biodiversity.* Priorities include conservation of biodiversity through completion of systems of protected areas, particularly in the marine biome, as well as promotion of ecological networks and the ecosystem approach to enhance biodiversity conservation and, where appropriate, sustainable use of biodiversity.
2   *Knowledge, science and management of protected areas.* Priorities include knowledge generation and networking and the integration of conservation science, including traditional knowledge, in management decisions; conservation tools and mechanisms; protected area management categories; and the setting and maintenance of standards for protected areas.
3   *Capacity-building and awareness-raising.* Priorities include building awareness; promoting effective conservation education and building up practitioners' skills; developing strategies for sustainable financing; and generating and disseminating knowledge, including through the Protected Areas Learning Network (PALNet).
4   *Governance, equity and livelihoods.* Priorities include improved governance of protected areas; promotion of the full range of governance types for protected areas; increased participation of indigenous peoples and local communities; and promotion of contribution of protected areas to human well-being.

The plan emphasizes the importance of delivering the benefits of global protected area guidance and science at a regional level. It will be implemented through the IUCN's network of regional and country offices; through the WCPA's regional vice-chairs; and through its members and partners who operate throughout the world. The *IUCN Strategic Plan on Protected Areas 2005–2015* and more information on the IUCN's Programme on Protected Areas and the WCPA may be found at www.iucn.org/themes/wcpa.

Table 3.2 Types of national, provincial and local protected area management institutions

Scale	Governance type (see Chapter 5)	Key enabling mechanisms	Examples
National	Government	Statutory legislation	National Park Service, US Department of the Interior
	Co-management	Signed agreement (may be supported by legislation)	Richtersveld National Park, South Africa
Provincial	Government	Statutory legislation	Parks Victoria, Australia
	Co-management	Signed agreement (may be in conjunction with regulation)	Tanga Coastal Zone, Conservation and Development Programme, Tanzania
Local	Government	Statutory legislation and regulation (may be by delegation)	Fujairah Municipality, Wadi Wuraya Mountain Protected Area, United Arab Emirates
	Co-management	Signed agreement (may be in conjunction with regulation)	Retezat National Park Administration and Consultative Council, Romania
	Community conserved areas	Customary law; traditional authority (may be supported by legislation)	Life Reserve of Awa People, Ecuador
	NGO	Private title; legislation; delegation through agreement or regulation	Birdlife International, Cousin Island, Republic of Seychelles
	Private management	Title to land; covenant; delegation through agreement or regulation	Chumbe Island Coral Park Ltd, Chumbe Island Coral Park, Tanzania

HDI countries in Africa, the Asia-Pacific and the Americas, targeting areas of high biodiversity that are under particular threat. CI employs over 800 people, including biological scientists, economists and educators. Like The Nature Conservancy and WWF, CI places considerable emphasis on building partnerships with donors and funding agencies, governments and communities (CI, 2005).

A number of indigenous peoples' and local community networks are also active on protected area issues. An Indigenous People's Ad Hoc Working Group, set up to coordinate inputs to the World Parks Congress and the Convention on Biological Diversity Conference of the Parties during 2003–2004, has continued linking various indigenous peoples' groups. Via Campesina, a global network of peasants, has expressed interest in linking with protected area issues. International forums that bring together indigenous and local communities and support groups, such as the World Rainforest Movement, also play a significant role.

National, provincial and local management institutions

The vast diversity of legal, social, cultural and environmental traditions has given rise to an equally varied array of national, provincial and local institutions with protected area management responsibilities. It is, of course, impossible for us to give anything but the briefest indication of the nature of these institutions. Table 3.2 indicates the variation in broad governance types, related instruments and traditions used to formalize these governance arrangements, and a scatter of examples from around the world.

Conventions

International conventions form a framework for interactions between nations. They document the mutually agreed obligations to work towards common goals. Conventions are formulated through submissions from various interested parties. The final stages of their ratification are often controversial when underlying political issues such as equity are raised. Conventions are generally finalized at internationally convened meetings that are attended by representatives from interested nations and organizations. They are then put forward to be ratified by nations. They come into force when a specified number of nations have ratified them.

Recognizing that documents in themselves have limited value, conventions also establish administering bodies. These have a similar role to national bureaucracies. The Convention on Biological Diversity (CBD), for example, established a Conference of the Parties to make formal decisions; a secretariat for administrative functions; a Subsidiary Body on Scientific, Technical and Technological Advice to advise the Conference of the Parties; and a financial institution to distribute the funds. At the national and sub-national levels, governments are generally free to choose whether they enact legislation that pursues the principles and strategies of such conventions, although legally binding agreements such as the CBD do place such obligations on governments.

Given their overarching importance, this section considers the CBD and the Convention Concerning the Protection of the World Cultural and Natural Heritage (often simply called the World Heritage Convention) in detail. Other globally relevant international conventions that encourage reservation of protected areas or directly affect their management include:

• Convention on International Trade in Endangered Species of Wild Flora and Fauna (CITES);
• United Nations Convention on the Law of the Sea (UNCLOS) (see 'MPA governance' in Chapter 23);
• International Convention for the Regulation of Whaling;
• Convention on the Conservation of Migratory Species of Wild Animals (Bonn Convention); and

• Convention on Wetlands of International Importance especially as Waterfowl Habitat (Ramsar Convention; see the following section on 'Types of protected areas').

International conventions have also been developed between regional groupings of nations – for example, the *ASEAN Declaration on Heritage Parks and Reserves* that concerns protected areas across South-East Asia, the Barcelona Convention that addresses marine and coastal conservation issues in the Mediterranean, or the European Union's (EU's) Natura 2000. The Antarctic Treaty and the Madrid Protocol that provide international mechanisms to protect the Antarctic content are considered in 'Types of protected areas'.

Convention on Biological Diversity (CBD)

At the 1992 Rio Earth Summit, one of the agreements adopted was the Convention on Biological Diversity. The CBD came into force in 1993. It was the first global agreement on the conservation and sustainable use of biodiversity and serves as a blueprint for national action. The CBD establishes three main goals: the conservation of biological diversity, the sustainable use of its components, and the fair and equitable sharing of the benefits from the use of genetic resources. It also has a significant influence on the expenditure priorities of the GEF. Many biodiversity issues are addressed, including habitat preservation, intellectual property rights, bio-safety and indigenous peoples' rights. Article 8 of the CBD requires member states to 'establish a system of protected areas or areas where special measures need to be taken to conserve biological diversity' and to manage these areas effectively. The convention defines protected areas as 'a geographically defined area which is designated or regulated and managed to achieve specific conservation objectives'.

The convention stands as a landmark in international law, noted for its comprehensive ecosystems approach to biodiversity protection, and it has gained rapid and widespread acceptance (UNEP, 2002). As of early 2006, 188 countries were parties to the convention, with 168 of these being signatories.

The responsibility for achieving the goals of the convention rests largely with these individual countries, but requires the combined efforts of the world's nations if it is to be successful. The Conference of the Parties is the governing body of the CBD, and advances implementation of the convention through the decisions it takes at its periodic meetings. The Conference of the Parties held seven 'ordinary meetings' between 1994 and 2004. The major themes at the seventh meeting were mountain ecosystems, protected areas, and transfer of technology and technology cooperation. Decision VII/28 from this meeting specifically concerns protected areas. Part of this decision is a series of goals and related targets, together with a programme of work (see Appendix 3) comprising suggested activities for the parties and supporting activities for the executive secretary of the CBD. The overall objective of the programme of work is the establishment and maintenance, by 2010 for terrestrial and by 2012 for marine areas, of comprehensive, effectively managed and ecologically representative national and regional systems of protected areas that contribute to achieving the three objectives of the convention and the 2010 target to significantly reduce the current rate of biodiversity loss, as well as contributing to poverty reduction and the pursuit of sustainable development.

The Biodiversity Planning Support Programme, implemented by the UNDP and UNEP with core financing from the GEF, addresses the need to strengthen the capacity of nations to prepare and implement national biodiversity strategies and action plans, in compliance with Article 6 of the convention. Information on CBD biodiversity issues and planning are made available to national planning teams. Good practice guidelines and training modules are also developed during the course of plan preparation.

World Heritage Convention

The United Nations Conference on the Human Environment held at Stockholm in 1972 established the World Heritage Convention, which took effect in 1975. As the administering agency for the convention, UNESCO seeks to:

- encourage countries to sign the convention (and thereby become 'states parties' to the convention) – 180 states have signed the convention as of 31 March 2005;
- encourage states parties to nominate sites within their jurisdictions for inclusion on the *World Heritage List*;
- encourage states parties to establish management plans and set up reporting systems on the state of conservation of their World Heritage sites;
- provide emergency assistance for World Heritage sites in immediate danger; and
- support states parties' public awareness-building activities for World Heritage conservation (UNESCO, 2005k).

Areas with such outstanding natural and cultural values should be regarded as being part of the common heritage of all people now and in the future, so that everyone has rights with respect to their conservation (Spalding, 2002). The convention requires that states adopt management regimes to counteract threats, and defines the kind of natural or cultural sites that can be considered for inscription on the *World Heritage List*. For a site to merit being inscribed on the *World Heritage List*, it must have what the convention calls 'outstanding universal value'. Sites can be recognized for their natural value, cultural value or a combination of the two (mixed sites). Natural sites, for example, must:

- be outstanding examples representing major stages of the Earth's history, including the record of life, significant ongoing geological processes in the development of landforms, or significant geomorphic or physiographic features; or
- be outstanding examples representing significant ongoing ecological and biological processes in the evolution and development of terrestrial, freshwater, coastal and marine ecosystems and communities of plants and animals; or
- contain superlative natural phenomena or areas of exceptional natural beauty and aesthetic importance; or
- contain the most important and significant natural habitats for conservation of biological diversity, including those containing threatened species of outstanding universal value

from the point of view of science or conservation.

They must also be of sufficient size and disposition for the long-term conservation of the values they contain, as well as having adequate long-term legislative, regulatory, institutional or traditional protection (Spalding, 2002).

All states parties meet in a general assembly every two years to elect the World Heritage Committee and to decide on major policy issues. The World Heritage Committee, comprising representatives from 21 states parties that provide equitable representation of the world's regions and cultures, meets once a year. This committee makes decisions relating to the implementation of the convention and is responsible for the *World Heritage List*. The World Heritage Centre is a secretariat that supports the committee and implements meeting decisions (Spalding, 2002). The International Centre for the Study of the Preservation and Restoration of Cultural Property, ICOMOS and the IUCN have central advisory roles, and the IUCN is the key organization assessing natural site nominations.

The convention requires that states periodically report to the World Heritage Committee on the state of their World Heritage properties. Sites on the *World Heritage List* may also be included on a second list – a *List of World Heritage Sites in Danger* – if the values on which they were selected are threatened. Article 11(4) of the convention outlines the nature of threatening processes warranting concern:

> … *serious and specific dangers, such as the threat of disappearance caused by accelerated deterioration, large-scale public or private projects or rapid urban or tourist development projects; destruction caused by changes in the use or ownership of the land; major alterations due to unknown causes; abandonment for any reason whatsoever; the outbreak or the threat of an armed conflict; calamities and cataclysms; serious fires, earthquakes, landslides; volcanic eruptions; changes in water level, floods and tidal waves* (UNESCO, 1999).

Inscription on the *List of World Heritage Sites in Danger* requires the committee, in consultation with the relevant state party, to develop a programme of corrective measures and to monitor progress. If the site ultimately loses those values for which it was inscribed, the committee may remove it from the *World Heritage List*. The threat of removal from the *World Heritage List* has, in some cases, led to significantly enhanced efforts to prevent damage to sites (Spalding, 2002). As of 2006, 31 properties were listed as *World Heritage Sites in Danger*. The 'in danger' list includes such places as the Everglades National Park in the US, the Rio Platano Biosphere Reserve in Honduras, and the cultural landscape and archaeological remains of the Bamiyan Valley in Afghanistan.

In 1992 the World Heritage Committee recognized those cultural landscapes that provide outstanding examples of the joint evolution of human society and settlement and the natural environments where they are found. Examples include the Hortobágy National Park in Hungary, the Ouadi Qadisha (the Holy Valley) and the Forest of the Cedars of God (Horsh Arz el-Rab) in the Lebanon, and the Rice Terraces of the Philippine Cordilleras (Spalding, 2002).

Types of protected areas
IUCN protected area categories

At the IUCN General Assembly in New Delhi in 1969, a resolution was passed to define national parks as 'a relatively large area where one or several ecosystems are not materially altered by human exploitation and occupation'. Subsequently, a series of IUCN publications documented the growth in the number and extent of protected areas; but the collection and analysis of information about them had revealed confusion over the meaning of terms such as 'national park' and 'nature reserve'. In 1975, a decision was taken by the then Commission on National Parks and Protected Areas to develop a categories system for protected areas. The work was led by a committee chaired by Dr Kenton Miller, and its final report, published in 1978, proposed ten categories differentiated on the basis of management objectives. While this was a considerable advance, the system lacked a definition of 'protected area', so the scope of land uses covered by the categories was not evident. There was also some overlap evident between categories, and the system did not adequately incorporate marine protected areas (Bishop et al, 2004).

In response to these concerns, a protracted review of the system led, in 1994, to the publication of the *Guidelines for Protected Area Management Categories* (IUCN, 1994) that remains the basis for the international classification of protected areas. In these guidelines, a protected area is defined as:

> *An area of land and/or sea especially dedicated to the protection and maintenance of biological diversity, and of natural and associated cultural resources, and managed through legal or other effective means (IUCN 1994, p7).*

The IUCN guidelines then identify six categories of protected areas (see Box 3.3). A central principle of the guidelines for the selection and management of each category is that categories should be defined by the objectives of management, rather than the title of an area or the effectiveness of management in meeting those objectives (IUCN, 1994). For each category the IUCN guidelines indicate the following elements:

- a definition that outlines the broad biophysical and cultural characteristics and the overall management objectives for each category as distinct from the other five;
- management objectives that give more detail on specific management issues, such as indigenous and local use, resource use, public access and recreation; and
- guidance for selection that specifies the parameters that should be considered when designating a protected area to a category, such as size and naturalness.

All categories are important; but a gradation of human intervention is implied. Size is not a relevant factor in assigning the categories, although the area should be big enough to meet its objectives in the long term. Zoning within protected areas may allow for uses that would not be accepted throughout, but at least 75 per cent of the area should be managed for the primary purpose. Management responsibility may rest with the public, private, community or voluntary sectors, regardless of category. Ownership of land may similarly be in the public, private, community

or voluntary sectors, regardless of category. International designations (World Heritage and so on) are considered as quite separate from the categorization (Bishop et al, 2004).

Category I areas represent the most pristine natural environments. They are the most strictly protected class of protected area, with human intervention generally restricted to scientific research and low-intensity passive (non-motorized) recreation. Category II areas are the archetypal national park (although not as the term 'national park' is interpreted in Europe), and while they generally exhibit a high degree of 'naturalness', they often allow for higher levels of human use than Category I, particularly with respect to tourism and associated infrastructure and facilities. Categories III and IV are designed to protect a more specific, limited range of values than Categories I and II. Consistent with the conservation of these values, they may also allow for a greater degree of human intervention than Categories I and II.

Categories V and VI are less strictly protected areas that specifically cater for human use of, and interaction with, natural environments (see Box 3.4). They have consequently been the subject of considerable debate, with supporters advocating their key position within the protected area pantheon (see, for example, Phillips, 2002) as part of the 'new paradigm' (see Chapter 2, p67), while others have criticized their inclusion on the grounds that they do not give sufficient weight to nature conservation (see, for example, Locke and Dearden, 2005). In all classes, biodiversity conservation is a core goal of management.

The purposes of the categories as identified in the IUCN (1994) guidelines are to:

- alert governments to the importance of protected areas;
- encourage governments to develop systems of protected areas with management aims tailored to national and local circumstances;
- reduce the confusion that has arisen from the adoption of many different terms to describe different kinds of protected areas;
- provide international standards to help global and regional accounting and comparisons between countries;

- provide a framework for the collection, handling and dissemination of data about protected areas; and
- improve communication and understanding between all those engaged in conservation.

The IUCN designations facilitate uniform national reporting and inter-jurisdictional comparisons. They have also enabled some jurisdictions to rationalize their protected area categories. For example, in Tasmania, Australia, the Resource Planning and Development Commission utilized the IUCN categories to reduce 138 land-use categories down to 13:

In the commission's view, one of the most important features of the IUCN system is its non-hierarchical nature – it does not represent a gradation of conservation importance from categories I to VI… The difference between the categories lies in the application of their management objectives – these provide for a gradation of human intervention. The recommended Tasmanian system embodies the principle of non-hierarchical categories (Leaver, 1999).

Box 3.3 IUCN protected area categories

Category Ia: Strict nature reserve

Purpose: protected area managed mainly for science.

Definition: area of land and/or sea possessing some outstanding or representative ecosystems, geological or physiological features and/or species, available primarily for scientific research and/or environmental monitoring. There is a proposal to include cultural heritage as a management objective, which if approved would enable the inclusion of some community conserved areas, such as strictly protected sacred sites.

Example: Case Study 3.1.

Category Ib: Wilderness area

Purpose: protected area managed mainly for wilderness protection.
Definition: large area of unmodified or slightly modified land and/or sea, retaining its natural character and influence, without permanent or significant habitation, which is protected and managed in order to preserve its natural condition.

Example: Case Study 3.2.

Category II: National park

Purpose: protected area managed mainly for ecosystem protection and recreation.

Definition: natural area of land and/or sea, designated to:

- protect the ecological integrity of one or more ecosystems for this and future generations;
- exclude exploitation or occupation inimical to the purposes of designation of the area; and
- provide a foundation for spiritual, scientific, educational, recreational and visitor opportunities, all of which must be environmentally and culturally compatible.

Example: Case Study 3.3.

Category III: Natural monument

Purpose: protected area managed mainly for conservation of specific natural features.

Definition: area containing one or more specific natural/cultural feature that is of outstanding or unique value because of its inherent rarity, representative or aesthetic qualities, or cultural significance.

Example: Case Study 3.4.

Box 3.3 Continued

Category IV: Habitat/species management area

Purpose: protected area managed mainly for conservation through management intervention.

Definition: area of land and/or sea subject to active intervention for management purposes in order to ensure the mainte-nance of habitats and/or to meet the requirements of specific species.

Example: Case Study 3.5.

Category V: Protected landscape/seascape

Purpose: protected area managed mainly for landscape/seascape conservation and recreation.

Definition: an area of land, with coast and sea as appropriate, where the interaction of people and nature over time has produced an area of distinct character with significant aesthetic, ecological and/or cultural values, and often with high biolog-ical diversity. Safeguarding the integrity of this traditional interaction is vital to the protection, maintenance and evolution of such an area.

Example: Case Study 3.6.

Category VI: Managed resource protected areas

Purpose: protected areas managed mainly for the sustainable use of natural ecosystems.

Definition: area containing predominantly unmodified natural systems, managed to ensure long-term protection and mainte-nance of biological diversity, while at the same time providing a sustainable flow of natural products and services to meet community needs.

Example: Case Study 3.7.

Source: IUCN (1994)

Case Study **3.1**

Example of a Category Ia protected area: *Zapovedniks* in Russia

Zapovedniks, Russia's strictly protected state nature reserves, are a representative network of most of the country's ecosystems. Due to the foresight of the Congress of Russian Naturalists, these areas of land were being designated as early as 1916. Ecological research and monitoring has been carried out in the *zapovedniks* since the 1930s. Regulations forbid any kind of economic activity on their territory, and until the 1990s the only human activities were those required to manage the area and scientific research. During the early 1990s, education programmes and tourist excursions on designated routes or to specific sites were permitted. There are now over 100 *zapoved-niks* in Russia. The areas closest to densely populated areas are relatively small, (seven being under 10,000ha), while in the Arctic zone, Siberia and the Far East, vast tracts of land and water are allotted to *zapovedniks*. The largest is Bolshoi Arktichesky Zapovednik, situated on the Taimyr Peninsula and covering more than 4 million hectares.

Sources: Danilina (2001); Danilina and Boreyko (2003)

Geyser Valley in Kronotsky Zapovednik, Russian Federation

Source: IUCN Photo Library © IUCN/Peter Shadie

Case Study 3.2

Example of a Category Ib protected area: Noatak Wilderness, Alaska, US

The US Congress designated the Alaskan Noatak Wilderness in 1980 and it now has a total of 2,333,211ha. Together with neighbouring Gates of the Arctic Wilderness, Noatak National Preserve, managed by the US National Park Service, protects almost all of the Noatak River catchment, the largest undeveloped river basin in America. All of the wilderness area, except for an area around the village of Noatak, is included in the preserve. From glacial melt on Mount Igikpak in the Brooks Range (in Gates of the Arctic National Park), the Noatak River flows west for some 700km to Kotzebue Sound. Visitor activities include canoeing and walking. Fauna of the area include caribou (*Rangifer tarandus*), brown bear (*Ursus arctos*), gray wolf (*Canis lupus*), lynx (*Felis lynx*) and dall sheep (*Ovis dalli dalli*).

Source: Wilderness.net (2005)

Case Study 3.3

Example of a Category II protected area: Kaziranga National Park, India

Kaziranga National Park (also a World Heritage area) extends over 430 square kilometres of Brahmaputra River floodplains. The riverine habitat consists primarily of tall, dense grasslands interspersed with open forests, interconnecting streams and numerous small lakes or 'bheels'. Three-quarters or more of the area is submerged annually by floodwaters. Significant conservation values of Kaziranga National Park include:

- the largest undisturbed and representative area of Brahmaputra Valley floodplain grassland and forest with associated large herbivores, avifauna and wetland values;
- transitional and successional example of grassland to forest and floodplain, to hill evergreen forest communities;
- the world's largest population of Indian one-horned rhinoceros (*Rhinoceros unicornis*);
- high density of tiger (*Panthera tigris*);
- a significant population of Asiatic elephant (*Elephas maximus*); and
- a high diversity of avifauna (480 species recorded).

This rich array of animals and the relatively open nature of parts of the park make it a popular tourist destination. A management plan has been developed to manage conservation and World Heritage values more effectively and to deal with threats to the park, which include poaching, urban encroachment and inappropriate infrastructure development.

Source: Vasu (2002)

Bishop et al (2004) also noted several additional ways in which the category system is now being used, including determining appropriate activities in protected areas; establishing criteria to assess management effectiveness; advocacy in relation to protected areas; providing a basis for national protected area legislation and policy and international agreements; provision of quality standards; and as a tool for bioregional planning.

In a recent review, Bishop et al (2004) considered the appropriateness and effectiveness of the IUCN category system, and while recommend-ing that no changes be made to the system itself, identified a number of ways in which the interpretation and the application of this system could be improved. For example, a proposal was made at the Vth IUCN World Parks Congress to incorporate governance type within the system by adding a governance dimension. To this end, a draft matrix for detailing the governance of protected areas has been developed (see Chapter 5, p117). World Parks Congress Recommendation 19 supported the continued use of the IUCN protected area management categories

Case Study **3.4**

Example of a Category III protected area: Bosques Petrificados, Argentina

Bosques Petrificados in Argentina is a 13,700ha national monument that protects an important example of the petrifaction process. About 150 million years ago, the area currently occupied by the national monument supported tall forests featuring trees related to present-day araucarias, among others. During the Cretaceous period, volcanic eruptions buried vast areas of Patagonia. Many of the forests were covered by ash and became petrified. In prehistoric periods, the area was inhabited by hunter-gather populations. Evidence of these inhabitants can be found in the park in the form of *'picaderos'* – workshops where the araucarias' fossil wood was used to create stone tools.

Source: Administración de Parques Nacionales (2005)

Case Study **3.5**

Example of a Category IV protected area (with associated Category 1a area): Lord Howe Island Marine Park, Australia

The 300,510ha Lord Howe Island Marine Park (also part of a World Heritage area) is located 700km north-east of Sydney, Australia. About 70 per cent of the park is assigned to IUCN Category IV (Habitat Protection Zone), where multiple-use management is designed to protect marine biodiversity, habitats and ecological processes associated with the volcanic seamount system. The management arrangements for the park also ensure the long-term maintenance of the island's tourism industry and the traditions and lifestyle of the local community. Only island residents are permitted to fish by drop line; gear must be limited to 3 lines and 15 hooks per line; a radio beacon must be fitted to each line to prevent lines becoming lost and 'ghost fishing'; and fish can only be taken for consumption on the island. Charter and recreational hand lining, trolling and breath-held spear fishing are allowed within the Habitat Protection Zone provided that they are carried out in accordance with any relevant concessions and are consistent with legal lengths, catch limits, permitted gear and other relevant regulations. The remaining 30 per cent of the park has been assigned to IUCN Category Ia, with all forms of fishing and other extractive activity prohibited.

Source: DEH (2005)

Lord Howe Island World Heritage Area, Australia

Source: Graeme L. Worboys

Case Study 3.6

Example of a Category V protected area system: Les Parcs Naturels Régionaux, France

In France, the Category V Les Parcs Naturels Régionaux system was established in 1967. The first park, Saint Amand-Raismes, was created in 1969. There are now 44 such parks, including two – Martinique and Guyane – in overseas territories with developing country characteristics. They are created as a result of collaboration between a number of local communities (communes), working in close association with the central regional administration in which they are located. The objectives of the system are to conserve the natural and cultural heritage of the area; to improve employment and social opportunities; and to make more effective use of the educational and recreational assets of the area. Each park must prepare a charter detailing the management policies and priorities and their cost. Most parks are managed by an organization consisting of representatives from the communes, public bodies, chambers of trade and commerce, and various local social groups. This body is served by an advisory and administration team, the elected members of which are drawn from the communities and the public authorities.

Source: Phillips (2002)

Case Study 3.7

Example of a Category VI protected area: Nabq Managed Resource Protected Area, Egypt

The 600 square kilometre Nabq Managed Resource Protected Area is located on the eastern coast of the South Sinai Peninsula in the Gulf of Aqaba. The Nabq protected area incorporates both coast and inshore marine areas, and features fringing reefs, sea-grass meadows and the largest mangrove (*Avicennia marina*) stand on the Gulf of Aqaba. The area is managed by the Egyptian Environmental Affairs Agency in cooperation with local Bedouin people. Activities that may damage habitats or reduce their biodiversity are regulated by the agency. Bedouin are contracted by the agency as park rangers. Sustainable use by the Bedouin using traditional methods is permitted. This includes both grazing of camels and other livestock, and fishing by access from the shore or using non-mechanized vessels. In 1995, in collaboration with local Bedouin fishermen, five no-take fisheries reserves were established within the reserve.

Source: Galal et al (2002)

system, with the definition of a protected area as the overarching criterion, and recommends that IUCN, in collaboration with other stakeholders, develop a revised edition of the 1994 guidelines that, among other things:

- builds on the existing objectives set out for each category, including by improved summary definitions of the categories;
- includes a set of criteria and principles which should underpin the categories system and its application;
- explains how the categories relate to ecological networks and wider regional planning;
- considers removing generic names of protected areas from the category system since

these may have different meanings in different countries, and using only management objectives and numbers for each category;

- gives more emphasis to marine and freshwater protected areas;
- gives more consideration to the linkage between protected areas and sustainable livelihoods;
- gives greater recognition of cultural and spiritual values so that the full range of special qualities of each protected area is fully recognized;
- provides guidance on the inclusion, within the system, of private protected areas and of those managed by local and indigenous communities;

Box 3.4 Management of Category V and Category VI protected areas

Category V focuses on managing the interface between people and nature at a land/seascape scale. Category V land/seascapes arise from the interaction of people with their environments over time. Their protection requires that these interactions are maintained; unlike Categories I to IV, protected land/seascapes require an active human presence.

While landscape is always culturally influenced, it is often rich in biodiversity and other natural values. Many lived-in landscapes are important for nature conservation, with valuable habitats and rare species whose continued existence may depend upon the survival of traditional forms of land use. Some landscapes reflect specific techniques of sustainable land use or embody a particular spiritual relationship to nature. Protection of such landscapes, and of the way of life within them so that it can evolve in balance with natural systems, is therefore essential to maintain biological and cultural diversity. But landscapes can also bear the imprint of past exploitation: for example, in small island states of the Caribbean, the pre-colonial landscapes were replaced by those derived from an exploitative system of production using forcibly imported labour. Planning for landscape conservation needs to be sensitive to such history, taking into account that not all heritage conveys positive messages.

Category V shares with Category VI the idea of multiple use, and together they are often referred to as 'less strictly protected' categories. Whereas Category V protected areas are lived-in landscapes that have been extensively modified by people over time, the definition of Category VI speaks of an 'area of predominantly unmodified natural systems', which is to be managed so that at least two-thirds of it remain that way. Management in such places is thus generally for long-term protection and maintenance of biodiversity, while at the same time providing a sustainable flow of goods and services for community needs.

While Category V had it origins in Europe, and a relatively high proportion of the protected area estate in this region is classified under this category, there has been growing application of the concept in South and Central America and Asia. With its emphasis on the value of the interactions between people and nature over time, Category V designation can be particularly appropriate for lived-in landscapes in low Human Development Index (HDI) nations of the world. Compared with other categories, it may more readily accommodate and respect diverse management regimes, community demands and governance arrangements.

The people living within Category V protected areas should be supported in their role as stewards of the landscape. They are essentially the managers, ideally in partnership with professionals who are facilitators and negotiators. A more active role for management may also be required, not only in the protection but also in the restoration of natural or cultural values that have been eroded or lost.

The introduction of Category VI in the 1994 categorization was a response to a widely held concern among many low HDI country participants at the Caracas Congress that the system needed to recognize that there are many places where resources are conserved in essentially their natural condition as a basis for sustainable use. There was, however, some concern that the inclusion of this category might extend the concept of a protected area so far that it would include, for example, a commercially worked forest. For that reason the guidelines lay down some qualifying considerations to apply in the case of Category VI. As well as reaffirming that the overall definition of a protected area must apply, the 1994 IUCN guidelines state that a Category VI protected area must be managed for the long-term protection and maintenance of biodiversity, maintain at least two-thirds of the area in its natural state and exclude large commercial plantations.

Sources: adapted from Phillips (2002) and Bishop et al (2004)

- enables protected areas to have more than one category when zones within them have been legally defined for different management objectives; and
- suggests how protected areas, which are assigned to their category by primary management objectives, can also be described by reference to the organization responsible for their governance, the effectiveness of their management and the degree to which they retain their naturalness.

International designations

The major international protected area designations are World Heritage areas, Ramsar wetlands and UNESCO Man and the Biosphere (MAB) reserves. The level of protection and the style of management for these areas vary between jurisdictions. In addition, the special case of Antarctica is considered.

World Heritage areas

As indicated earlier in 'Conventions', World Heritage is perhaps the most significant recognition that can be given to a site's natural and/or cultural values. While many sites on the list are already protected under national legislation, listing engenders an international profile, fostering international scrutiny and providing cooperative mechanisms that support conservation management. World Heritage areas are designated over a range of land tenures. This does not change the ownership or application of national, provincial or local laws; but it does limit the scope of activities permitted in those areas – these must not threaten the universal, natural and cultural values of the area.

As of mid 2005, the *World Heritage List* includes 812 properties of outstanding cultural and natural value in 137 states – comprising 628 cultural, 160 natural and 24 mixed properties (see Figure 3.1). An example of a World Heritage property is given in Case Study 3.8.

Ramsar wetlands

Ramsar wetlands are established under the Ramsar Convention, which was initiated at the small Iranian town of Ramsar in 1971. The Ramsar Convention is an intergovernmental treaty that provides the framework for national action and international cooperation for the conservation and sustainable use of wetlands. Under Article 2 of the convention, a prospective contracting party is required to designate at least one wetland within its territory. Contracting parties designate wetlands on the *Ramsar List* 'to develop and maintain an international network of wetlands which are important for the conservation of global biological diversity and for sustaining human life through the ecological and hydrological functions they perform' (Taylor, 2002). The four main commitments for contracting parties are:

1 nominating suitable sites as wetlands of international importance and thereby ensuring that they are managed in order to maintain their ecological character;
2 formulating and implementing national land-use planning to include wetland conservation considerations and, as possible, to promote the wise use of all wetlands within their territory;
3 developing national systems of wetlands reserves, facilitating the exchange of data and publications, and to promote training in wetlands research and management; and
4 cooperating with other nations in promoting the wise use of wetlands, where wetlands and their resources, such as migratory birds, are shared.

A wetland is identified as being of international importance if it meets at least one of the criteria adopted by successive meetings of the Conference of the Parties to the convention, including sites:

- containing representative, rare or unique wetland types;
- of international importance for conserving biological diversity in that they support vulnerable, endangered or critically endangered species or threatened ecological communities;
- supporting populations of plant and/or animal species important for maintaining the biological diversity of a particular biogeographic region;
- supporting plant and/or animal species at a critical stage in their life cycles, or providing refuge during adverse conditions;
- regularly supporting 20,000 or more waterbirds;
- regularly supporting 1 per cent of the individuals in a population of one species or subspecies of waterbird;
- supporting a significant proportion of indigenous fish subspecies, species or families, life history stages, species interactions and/or populations that are representative of wetland benefits and/or values and thereby contributing to global biological diversity; or
- that are an important source of food for fishes, or that are spawning grounds, nursery and/or

Figure 3.1 Global distribution of natural and mixed World Heritage sites

Case Study **3.8**

Kluane/Wrangell–St Elias/Glacier Bay/Tatshenshini–Alsek World Heritage Area, Canada and the US

Kluane/Wrangell–St Elias/Glacier Bay/Tatshenshini–Alsek was the first bi-national World Heritage area listed (1979). After the addition of Glacier Bay National Park and Preserve (1992) and Tatshenshini–Alsek Provincial Park (1994), this World Heritage area now consists of four adjacent protected areas that cover 97,000 square kilometres in Alaska (US), the Yukon and British Columbia (Canada). Tatshenshini–Alsek Provincial Park in British Columbia is jointly managed with the Champagne and Aishihik First Nations. The area features outstanding examples of active natural processes (tectonic, volcanic, glacial, fluvial, aeolian, mass wasting, soil formation, plant succession and animal migration); a combination of marine, coastal, riverine and high mountain environments with an associated diversity of flora and fauna; and minimal human modification. The St Elias Mountains of Wrangell–St Elias National Park and Preserve include the largest group of high peaks on the continent, including the 5959m Mount Logan, the highest mountain in Canada. In the Wrangells, vegetation ranges from coastal and valley forests to alpine tundra, providing habitat for the largest concentration of dall sheep (*Ovis dalli dalli*) in the world. Tatshenshini–Alsek Park contains nearly 1 million hectares of glaciers and mountain peaks and unmodified river systems. As well as mountains, Glacier Bay National Park and Preserve has a wide range of coastal environments, including beaches, fjords, tidewater glaciers, coastal and estuarine waters, and freshwater lakes. These diverse land and seascapes host a mosaic of plant communities ranging from pioneer species in areas recently exposed by receding glaciers, to climax communities in older coastal and alpine ecosystems.

Sources: adapted from National Park Service (2005) and Parks Canada (2005)

Mount Steele Kluane National Park, part of Kluane/Wrangell–St Elias/Glacier Bay/Tatshenshini–Alsek World Heritage Area

Source: IUCN Photo Library © Jim Thorsell

migration paths upon which fish stocks, either within the wetland or elsewhere, depend.

The *Ramsar List* is maintained by the Ramsar Bureau. Recording and managing sites that are in danger of degradation is facilitated by the *Montreux Record*, which is maintained by the bureau in consultation with the relevant contracting party. As of mid 2005, there are 146 contracting parties to the convention, with 1458 wetland sites protected totalling 125.4 million hectares. Case Study 3.9 gives an example of a transboundary European Ramsar wetland.

UNESCO Man and the Biosphere reserves

Biosphere reserves are established under the UNESCO MAB programme. They are nominated by national governments and remain under their jurisdiction. Nominations are assessed by a UNESCO Advisory Committee for Biosphere Reserves for recommendation to the Intergovernmental Coordinating Council of the MAB programme. By early 2006, 482 biosphere reserves were listed in 102 countries. Individual countries propose sites within their territories that meet a given set of criteria for this designation.

Case Study **3.9**

Morava–Dyje Ramsar Wetland

The Morava–Dyje riverine landscape is one of the most valuable wetlands in Europe. A mosaic of meadows, river meanders and oxbow lakes, old hardwood floodplains, forests and reed beds, it is home to an extraordinary variety of wildlife. This area spans three countries: Austria, the Slovak Republic and the Czech Republic. Four NGOs – Daphne (Slovak Republic), Distelverein (Austria), Veronica (Czech Republic) and World Wide Fund for Nature (WWF) International Danube Carpathian Programme – work together to educate and raise awareness, to restore and rehabilitate degraded areas and to generate support for the ongoing cooperative management of these wetland sites. The existing adjacent Ramsar sites include the Danube–Morava floodplains on the Austrian side, the floodplain of the lower Dyje on the Czech side, and the Morava floodplains on the Slovak site, covering together 55,000ha. These four organizations won a Ramsar Evian Prize for the work that they have been carrying out for many years at the national level in each of the three countries, and at the international level to ensure sustainable use and conservation of the natural and cultural heritage of the floodplains of the Morava (March) and Dyje (Thaya) rivers. Their activities have led to the signature, by the ministries for the environment of the three countries, of a memorandum of understanding to implement the Ramsar Convention in the transboundary trilateral area of the Morava–Dyje Floodplains.

Source: Ramsar Convention Secretariat (2005)

Biosphere reserves have a conservation objective supported by research, monitoring and training activities, as well as involving the cooperation and interests of the local populations. Biosphere reserves are thus a potentially valuable operational tool to further sustainable development (Bridgewater, 2002). Biosphere reserves serve to combine three functions:

1 a conservation function to preserve genetic resources, species, ecosystems and landscapes;
2 a development function to foster sustainable economic and human development; and
3 a logistic support function to support demonstration projects, environmental education and training, and research and monitoring related to local, national and global issues of conservation and sustainable development.

To qualify for designation as a biosphere reserve, an area should normally:

- be representative of a major biogeographic region, including a gradation of human intervention in these systems;
- contain landscapes, ecosystems, animal and plant species, or varieties which need to be conserved;
- provide an opportunity to explore and demonstrate approaches to sustainable development within the larger region where they are located;

- be of an appropriate size to serve the three functions of biosphere reserves mentioned above; and
- have an appropriate zoning system, with a legally constituted core area (or areas) devoted to long-term protection, a clearly identified buffer zone (or zones) and an outer transition area.

Biosphere reserves emphasize the integration of human and natural systems. Physically, each biosphere reserve should contain three elements: one or more legally protected core area devoted to long-term conservation of nature; a buffer zone in which activities compatible with the conservation objectives may occur; and an outer transition area devoted to the promotion and practice of sustainable development (see Case Study 3.10). The reserve as a whole may contain a variety of agricultural activities, settlements or other activities. In many cases, the buffer zone is in community or private ownership, and this is also generally the case for the transition area. In practice, this zonation is applied in many different ways in order to accommodate geographical conditions, socio-cultural settings, available legal protection measures and local constraints. A number of biosphere reserves simultaneously encompass areas protected under other systems (such as national parks or nature reserves) and other internationally recognized sites (such as World Heritage sites or Ramsar wetland sites).

Case Study 3.10

Somiedo Biosphere Reserve, Spain

The Somiedo Biosphere Reserve in Spain ranges from the Alpine systems on the peaks (up to 2100m) and high ridges of the Cantabrican range, through slopes covered by beech woods, green oak or Pyrenean oak, depending upon the aspect and soil, to swift flowing streams in the meadows lining the bottom of the U-shaped glacial valleys. The beech woods are home to capercaillie (*Tetrao urogallus*), and the woodlands support many animals species, including a substantial population of brown bear (*Ursus arctos*), lynx (*Felis lynx*), chamois (*Rupicapra rupicapra*) and a number of species of amphibians and reptiles restricted to the north of the Iberian Peninsula. From the point of view of a biosphere reserve, the key feature is the integration of human populations, still practising a form of transhumance by taking herds of cattle up to the higher meadows during spring and summer, with this special natural environment. There are concentrations of traditional *Braña*, or cattle/people homes, still maintained by the local *Vaqueiros de alzeda*, or mountain cowboys. The *Vaqueiros* use the *Braña* not only to shelter cattle, but to live in themselves. The *Braña* are thatched with broom (*Cytisus*), brought down by the *Vaqueiros* from the higher slopes. The cattle are a special local breed, which have been kept as a separate race (called *Vaca roxa* by the *Vaqueiros*) and are well adapted to the environment and the transhumance activity. The reserve has substantial woodland and high montane habitats in the core area and buffer zone. The *Vaqueiros* areas in the buffer zone and transition area also include a number of small and very typical cantabrican villages, of which the largest is Pola de Somiedo. Villages have a number of buildings of architectural interest, including some of the churches. Local mayors support sustainable development activities, balancing the needs of the population with demands for conservation.

Source: UNESCO (2005i)

Antarctica

Argentina, Australia, Belgium, Chile, France, Japan, New Zealand, Norway, South Africa, the Union of Soviet Socialist Republics, the UK and the US signed the Antarctic Treaty in December 1959, and it entered into force in June 1961. The treaty applies to the entire area south of 60° South, including ice shelves, and has the dual purpose of ensuring that activities in the Antarctic region are dedicated to peaceful purposes and facilitating freedom of scientific investigation and cooperation. Currently, 45 states are signatories to the treaty, 28 of which are Antarctic Treaty Consultative Parties – that is, states which have full voting rights as a result of being original signatories to the treaty, or through conducting substantial research activity. The other 17 signatories to the treaty are known as acceding states, which do not have voting rights.

The treaty does not explicitly address the notion of environmental protection. Antarctic protected areas have been addressed under subsequent agreements developed by Antarctic Treaty Consultative Parties. The earliest of these was the Agreed Measures for the Conservation of Antarctic Fauna and Flora, adopted in 1964. Under the agreed measures, the entire Antarctic Treaty Area was designated a Special Conservation Area where the 'killing, wounding, capturing or molesting of any native mammal or native bird, or any attempt at any such act, except in accordance with a permit' was prohibited. The agreed measures also provided for the designation of specially protected areas (SPAs). With subsequent amendments, criteria for SPA designation include:

- representative samples of the major Antarctic land and freshwater ecological systems;
- areas with unique complexes of species;
- areas that are the type locality (that is, the populations that were used to establish scientific descriptions of species) or only known habitat of any plant or invertebrate species;
- areas that contain specially interesting breeding colonies of birds or mammals; and
- areas that should be kept inviolate so that in the future they may be used for purposes of comparison with localities that have been disturbed by humans (Felix, 2005).

Other categories of reserve provided protection for sites of exceptional scientific interest, historic sites and monuments, and areas of outstanding geological, glaciological, geomorphological, aesthetic, scenic or wilderness value.

The Protocol on Environmental Protection to the Antarctic Treaty (the Madrid Protocol), which entered into force in 1998, designated the entire treaty area as 'a natural reserve, devoted to peace and science'. An Annex to the Protocol on Area Protection and Management (Annex V) was added and ratified in 2002. Prior to the signing of the Madrid Protocol, the mechanisms for area protection in the Antarctic did not result in protection of significant portions of the continent, or in the systematic designation and management of protected areas. The absence of an overall protected areas framework meant that the protected area system had developed in an *ad hoc* fashion, with individual protected areas established by individual countries or scientists, and based mainly on convenience (proximity to stations) or a desire to conduct scientific research in a particular area. Annex V laid the legal and practical foundation for a more comprehensive network of protected areas in Antarctica. Annex V also acknowledged the need to standardize protected area designation and management, and the existing range of protected area categories were simplified into two new designations: Antarctic specially protected areas (ASPAs) and Antarctic specially managed areas (ASMAs) (Felix, 2005).

Any area (including marine areas) can be designated as an ASPA by treaty parties to protect 'outstanding environmental, scientific, historic, aesthetic or wilderness values, any combination of those values or ongoing or planned scientific research' (Madrid Protocol, Article 3, paragraph 1). Entry into an ASPA is prohibited without a permit. Existing specially protected areas and other reserves were re-designated as ASPAs. Currently, there are 62 ASPAs in the treaty area.

National designations

National protected area systems have developed uniquely according to their individual socio-political histories. There is a great variety in the terminology used to identify various types of reserve, the type and amount of human activities

El Vizcaino Biosphere Reserve, Mexico

Source: IUCN Photo Library © Jim Thorsell

permitted, and the legal mechanisms of reservation and protection. Existing national conservation strategies vary widely in their effectiveness, and reserve nomenclature is not necessarily indicative of the protected status of an area. On paper, some parks may be afforded top-level protection. In reality, they may be threatened by a range of degrading processes, often because there is a lack of funding for proper management.

National or provincial designations may be overlaid by one or more in international designations. For example, the 82,000ha Hortobágy National Park in Hungary is also a World Heritage Cultural Landscape, a UNESCO biosphere reserve, and 30 per cent of it is a Ramsar wetland.

With national and provincial jurisdictions, nomenclature varies widely and can cause confusion when inconsistent with the IUCN terminology. Over 1000 different terms are used around the world (Chape et al, 2005). In general, protected area designations used by countries are not comparable. The same term can mean different things in different countries. For example, in the Republic of Korea, the term 'national park' is applied to areas classified as Category V under the IUCN system; Dipperu National Park in Australia is classified as Category I; Yozgat National Park in Turkey is classified as Category III; Pallas Ounastunturi National Park in Finland is classified as Category IV; and Snowdonia National Park in the UK is classified as Category V. Different labels are used for the same type of protected area. For example, national names used for Category V protected areas include potected landscape (Austria); environmental protection areas (Brazil); protection forest reserve (Colombia); conservation park (New Zealand); and protected landscape/seascape (the Philippines) (IUCN, 1998).

Environmental contexts

Protected areas are located within environmental contexts that can be characterized by varying degrees of development. Some are located within a wider region of relatively undisturbed environment. Many are surrounded by lands used for forestry and agriculture and seas used for fishing. Some smaller terrestrial protected areas exist as remnants of earlier landscapes that are now situated within predominantly agricultural or urban environments. Throughout this book, we deal with protected areas across all of these environments. However, there is little specific reference to protected areas located within urban areas. While many of the general points made in the book apply to urban protected areas, Case Study 3.11 indicates some of the particular management considerations that apply to these areas.

Extent of the world's protected areas

The World Database on Protected Areas (WDPA), maintained by the WCMC (see the section on 'Institutions working for protected areas') provides a comprehensive global inventory of the world's protected areas. Major updates are undertaken every three to five years and the results are published as the *United Nations List of Protected Areas*. The extent of the world's protected areas is summarized in Figure 3.2 (see plate section for colour version).

In 2005, the database recorded 113,707 protected areas covering 19.6 million square kilometres over 12 per cent of the planet's surface. The vast majority of protected areas are located on terrestrial environments. A recent analysis using MPA Global, a spatial database of marine protected areas, showed that approximately 0.5 to 1 per cent of marine habitats are protected globally, with the most located along coastlines (Wood et al, 2005). Table 3.3 summarizes the world's protected areas according to geopolitical region. The database recognizes specifically designated reserves in Antarctica, but does not count the entire continent, although this is given protection under the Madrid Protocol of the Antarctic Treaty (see 'Institutions working for protected areas') (Chape et al, 2005). More detail on the extent of national and international protected areas is given in Appendices 5 and 6.

Note that these figures do not include non-government designated protected areas that are not yet formally a part of official protected area systems. Once community conserved areas and private protected areas are added to official protected area systems, the figures may increase considerably. On the other hand, there appears to

Case Study **3.11**

Raising the priority of urban areas in protected area systems, Brazil

Pedro da Cunha e Menezes, Brazilian Ministry of External Relations

When, in a conversation between two friends, someone mentions that he or she would like to spend the weekend in a national park, what comes straight to mind is a remote natural area of astonishing beauty, where wildlife and vegetation are forever protected. The knowledgeable will immediately dream of Yellowstone, Chitwan, Serengeti, the Galapagos, the Great Barrier Reef or Iguaçu Falls. Most people will think of a protected area in a remote region within a 300km range of their homes. Very few will even remember the national parks that, more often than not, exist within the great metropolises of the world, at the doorstep of hundreds of millions of city dwellers. The past history of environmental protection, however, is intimately linked to the establishment of urban protected areas.

Let us take the Brazilian case as an example. One could say that the history of nature conservation in Brazil started in 1861 with the legal decree that established the Forest of Tijuca on the outskirts of Rio de Janeiro, then the national capital. Tijuca was created to protect the severely logged and degraded watersheds from which Rio sourced its drinking water. A vigorous expropriation of private lands was followed by a very successful reforestation scheme, which mostly utilized native species. In those times, management plans were still an unheard-of concept; but, in its first 30 years, Tijuca was so well managed that today, 150 years later, its early programmes of reforestation, environmental education, recreation and governance can still be successfully applied in any park, anywhere in the world. Tijuca was declared a national park in 1961, in a political gesture devised to commemorate the centenary of the beginning of the reforestation scheme that gave life to it.

Paradoxically, Tijuca's elevation to park status was detrimental to its users. The conservationist mainstream ideas of the time in Brazil induced a management that refused to recognize a complementarity between the park and its adjacent metropolis. Around that time, federal and state conservation agencies started to run their urban parks in a similar fashion to the way that they managed their more remote and less impacted upon protected areas. Recreation was perceived to be a serious environmental impact. There were even attempts to close off many highly used trails.

However, urban protected areas, while small and under heavy pressure, very often provide the only opportunity for contact with nature for a significant percentage of the population. In this sense, they are the representatives of the protected areas system. In the context of an increasingly urbanized world, urban protected areas should incorporate within their mission statements the task of serving as focal points for environmental education. Urban protected areas are the recipients of the overwhelming majority of visitors to protected areas throughout the planet. Each well-catered-for visitor, given the right programmes of environmental education, guided by intelligent signage and met by well-trained staff will almost certainly become an ally of the greater cause for protected areas. An urban protected area must be managed as a huge open classroom for environmental education.

Source: adapted from Cunha e Menezes (2005)

---

be some double counting in the data, and some areas are included that do not meet the IUCN definition. Compiling comprehensive and accurate data on the extent of the worlds' protected areas is an ongoing project.

IUCN management categories have been applied to about 60 per cent of sites. As is the case with their geopolitical distribution, there is considerable variation across IUCN categories and between regions (see Table 3.4). There are relatively few Category Ia and Ib sites, whereas Category III sites are numerous but make up only 1 per cent of the total protected area coverage. Categories II and VI cover large areas but comprise only 4 per cent of sites. Category II is dominant in North America, Category IV in South Asia and North Eurasia, Category V in Europe, and Category VI in North Africa–Middle East and Australia–New Zealand. In some cases, regional dominance of a particular category is due to a single large protected area, such as the 640,000 square kilometre Category VI Ar-Rub'al-Khali Wildlife Management Area in Saudi Arabia (Chape et al, 2005).

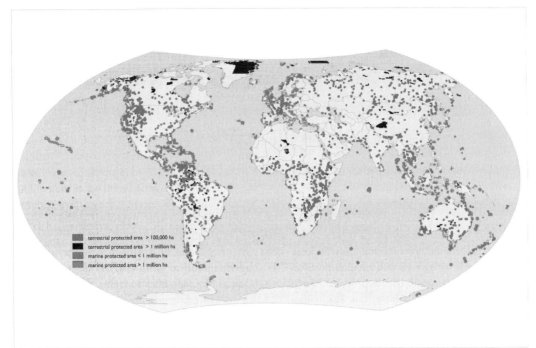

Figure 3.2 Extent of the world's protected areas

Source: Based on data from UNEP-WCMC

Further reading

Bishop, K., Dudley, N., Phillips, A. and Stolton, S. (2004) *Speaking a Common Language: The Uses and Performance of the IUCN System of Management Categories for Protected Areas*, Cardiff University, IUCN and UNEP–WCMC, Cardiff, Gland and Cambridge

Bridgewater, P. (2002) 'Biosphere reserves: A network for conservation and sustainability', *Parks*, vol 12, no 3, pp15–20

Chape, S., Blyth, S., Fish, L., Fox, P. and Spalding, M. (2003) *United Nations List of Protected Areas*, IUCN and UNEP–WCMC, Gland and Cambridge

Chape, S., Harrison, J., Spalding, M. and Lysenko, I. (2005) 'Measuring the extent and effectiveness of protected areas as an indicator for meeting global biodiversity targets', *Philosophical Transactions of the Royal Society B*, vol 360, pp443–455

Spalding, M. (2002) 'The World Heritage List: The best of all worlds?', *Parks*, vol 12, no 3, pp50–57

Taylor, D. (2002) 'The Ramsar Convention on Wetlands', *Parks*, vol 12, no 3, pp42–49

Websites

Conservation International (CI): www.conservation.org

Convention on Biological Diversity (CBD): www.biodiv.org

Global Environment Facility (GEF): www.gefweb.org

Man and the Biosphere (MAB) programme: www.unesco.org/mab/wnbr.htm

Ramsar Convention Secretariat: www.ramsar.org

The Nature Conservancy: www.nature.org

United Nations Educational, Scientific and Cultural Organization (UNESCO): www.unesco.org

United Nations Environment Programme (UNEP): www.unep.org

United Nations Environment Programme (UNEP) World Conservation: Monitoring Centre (WCMC): www.unep-wcmc.org

World Commission on Protected Areas (WCPA): www.iucn.org/themes/wcpa

World Conservation Union (IUCN): www.iucn.org

World Heritage Convention (WHC): www.whc.unesco.org

World Wide Fund for Nature (WWF): www.panda.org

Table 3.3 Global distribution of protected areas by geopolitical region

Region	Total sites	Total protected area (km²)	Total protected land area (km²)	Total land area (km²)	Percentage land area protected (km²)	Total number of marine sites (km²)	Total protected marine area
Central America	677	151,058	133,731	521,600	25.6	103	17,327
South America	1507	2,217,725	2,056,559	9,306,560	22.1	114	161,166
North America	13,414	4,450,119	4,231,839	23,724,226	17.8	754	218,280
East Asia	3265	1,930,651	1,904,342	11,799,212	16.1	285	26,309
South-East Asia	2674	791,681	715,218	4,480,990	16	390	76,463
Eastern and Southern Africa	4117	1,838,144	1,825,918	11,487,920	15.9	155	12,226
Caribbean	973	80,770	36,469	234,840	15.5	370	44,301
South America (Brazil)	1280	1,321,751	1,305,864	8,547,400	15.3	88	15,887
Europe	43,837	699,761	634,248	5,119,172	12.4	829	65,513
Australia/New Zealand	9550	1,400,292	831,420	8,011,930	10.4	422	568,872
Western and Central Africa	2583	1,302,812	1,293,206	12,804,860	10.1	43	9606
Pacific	404	418,641	54,949	553,058	9.9	240	363,692
North Africa and Middle East	1247	1,251,034	1,226,928	12,954,170	9.5	136	24,106
North Eurasia	17,719	2,006,914	1,789,006	22,110,050	8.1	82	217,908
South Asia	1478	344,248	339,058	4,487,510	7.6	184	5190
Antarctic	66	70,233	3470	14,024,832	0	59	66,763
World	104,791	20,275,834	18,378,755	150,168,330	12.2	4254	1,893,609

Source: Chape et al (2005, p448)

Table 3.4 Distribution of protected areas by IUCN category

Region		Ia	Ib	II	III	IV	V	VI	No catcgory
North America	Area (km²)	80,469	478,492	1,681,824	73,688	647,266	144,212	1,131,604	670,609
	Number of sites	845	701	1362	595	1338	2082	1287	5204
Caribbean	Area (km²)	168	90	24,087	460	31,221	3711	24,005	4666
	Number of sites	11	18	164	38	284	38	192	228
Central America	Area (km²)	9180	165	31,180	5475	13,628	1462	43,532	48,293
	Number of sites	16	1	95	49	198	5	100	213
South America (Brazil)	Area (km²)	82,769	–	159,742	2809	5091	134,233	183,251	866,172
	Number of sites	180	–	177	5	259	115 6	7	477
South America (Hispanic)	Area (km²)	11,833	1925	520,550	110,389	89,661	113,405	536,993	1,020,111
	Number of sites	58	28	222	80	154	164	254	691
Europe	Area (km²)	56,331	37,146	101,043	4344	74,994	293,411	21,924	148,673
	Number of sites	1465	508	265	3444	15,310	3010	203	19,453
Western and Central Africa	Area (km²)	17,801	11,384	3,342,195	4393	379,902	214	106,705	489,254
	Number of sites	19	7	90	5	124	1	46	2291
Eastern and Southern Africa	Area (km²)	2946	1260	509,651	155	272,038	15,558	530,362	620,976
	Number of sites	22	7	218	24	481	29	224	3087
North Africa and Middle East	Area (km²)	6652	48	229,808	12,448	101,624	108,881	776,049	67,537
	Number of sites	29	2	72	50	274	157	28	635
North Eurasia	Area (km²)	350,676	24	95,471	29,028	1,056,633	15,054	95,724	391,712
	Number of sites	195	–	66	11,324	5267	407	54	406
South Asia	Area (km²)	2672	201	72,294	–	179,368	4608	24,244	73,924
	Number of sites	31	1	139	–	658	11	11	627
East Asia	Area (km²)	63,908	46,449	105,900	20,323	5938	1,631,329	58,660	30,643
	Number of sites	43	34	78	34	121	2146	77	732
South-East Asia	Area (km²)	25,072	25,343	205,195	4035	138,877	26,806	197,908	203,584
	Number of sites	287	12	254	68	199	169	830	833
Australia/ New Zealand	Area (km²)	216,679	39,383	309,644	33,152	251,100	21,662	593,162	2,864
	Number of sites	2137	38	681	3948	1653	216	489	388
Pacific	Area (km²)	3524	576	6837	723	4368	11,089	346,600	45,553
	Number of sites	27	–	31	24	77	20	54	193
Antarctic	Area (km²)	67,735	–	599	–	365	–	-	1534
	Number of sites	88	–	3	2	23	5	1	4

Source: Chape et al (2005, p449)

4

Values and Benefits

Michael Lockwood

An understanding of the values and benefits of protected areas is of fundamental importance to their management. Values give meaning to protected areas – they provide the motivation for their creation, give direction to their management and allow evaluation of their effectiveness. More effective communication of protected areas benefits is essential to secure support for their establishment, as well as the necessary investment to ensure sound management.

There is often a range of views about whether a protected area should be established and what its management objectives should be. Once protected, people often place competing and sometimes incompatible demands on an area, seeking to gain benefits that may disadvantage others or have a negative effect on the area itself. An understanding of values can assist managers to negotiate an appropriate course through such issues.

It is important to recognize that values are not static. The values we place on natural environments are socially constructed and influenced by different cultures and experiences. Although they are influenced by and directed towards the objective condition of the world, they are essentially subjective (with the possible exception of intrinsic natural value; see p104). Our understanding and appreciation of natural and cultural values is significantly different from that of 50 years ago, of 100 years ago. No doubt, future generations will have different values than our own. One of the principles of sustainability is that the present generation has a responsibility to pass on the natural and cultural heritage to future generations so that they can enjoy their many benefits. Protected area managers also have a responsibility to current generations to ensure, as far as is within their power, that protected areas continue to provide benefits to humans, as well as conserving nature for its own sake.

This chapter describes the types of values and benefits associated with protected areas, and then considers the importance of each type, using examples from a wide range of protected areas.

Value language and classification

The word 'value' has a range of meanings, which can lead to imprecision and confusion. Value language is complex, with the word having three distinct grammatical forms – verb (to value), adjective (a valuable object) and noun (a value) (Gaus, 1990). Rokeach (1973, p5) defined value as 'an enduring belief that a specific mode of conduct or end state of existence is personally or socially preferable to an opposite or converse mode of conduct or end state of existence'. Following Najder (1975), there are three ways in which such value can be understood:

1 value as the worth of something, expressible in some measurable unit (as in 'this tree is worth US$500');
2 value as a property of a thing (as in 'this protected area has value in its own right' or 'the spectacular scenery of this protected area means that it has high recreation value'); and

3   value as an idea or feeling (as in 'this protected area has great spiritual value to me', or 'I feel satisfaction knowing that this area is protected').

In various places through this chapter, and in the rest of the book, 'value' will be used in each of these three senses.

'Value' and 'benefit' are very close in meaning and are often used interchangeably; but this chapter uses these terms in slightly different ways. 'Benefit' is used to indicate a situation that involves a recipient who gains in some way from the presence or ascription of value. Existence here is not confined to biophysical nature, but also includes human thought and emotion, as people ascribe value to the natural world. Thus, value is the more direct term, which may have physical, cognitive, affective or spiritual aspects, whereas benefit indicates a flow of value to a recipient. For example, the recreation value of some protected areas includes opportunities to engage in exercise, which leads to a flow of health benefits to the individuals taking part and, in turn, to the community.

Categorization of values can enable systematic elucidation of their key features, facilitate management of complexity, and avoid the confusion associated with comparing value types across classificatory boundaries. The range of possibilities, together with the complexity of value language, has meant that there are numerous different ways in which protected area values have been classified and described. Trying to express the full range of protected area values in a simple typology is challenging. Some of the most treasured and important values are difficult to conceptualize and express. Other values are multifaceted, and could be located within several categories. This section briefly indicates some approaches to protected area value classification and then describes the system and terminology that will be used in this book.

The environmental philosopher Rolston (1985) identified types of 'wildland' value as market value, life-support value, recreational value, scientific value, genetic diversity value, aesthetic value, cultural symbolization value, historical value, character-building value, therapeutic value, religious value and intrinsic natural value.

A widely used typology developed by environmental economists (see, for example, Pearce and Warford, 1993) identifies *direct-use* values (timber, fish and so on); *indirect-use* values that derive from ecological processes that form soil, recycle nutrients and clean water; *option* values that are potentials of natural systems that can be used in the future; *existence* values that are based upon the enjoyment people get from knowing that an area is being preserved, regardless of whether they will see it or directly use its resources; and *bequest* values derived from the belief that natural resources should be retained for future generations to appreciate and enjoy.

Putney (2003) presented the following typology of intangible protected area values developed by the World Commission on Protected Areas (WCPA) Cultural and Spiritual Values Taskforce: recreation values; spiritual values; cultural values; identity values; existence values; artistic values; aesthetic values; educational values; research and monitoring values; peace values; and therapeutic values.

Dearden and Rollins (2002) described 11 categories and offered an analogy for each category:

1   aesthetic (art gallery);
2   wildlife viewing (zoo);
3   historical (museum);
4   spiritual (cathedral);
5   recreation (playground);
6   tourism (factory);
7   education (schoolroom);
8   science (laboratory);
9   ecological capital (bank);
10 ecological processes (hospital); and
11 ecological benchmarks (museum).

Drawing on such sources, as well as Lockwood (1999), Harmon and Putney (2003) and Worboys et al (2005), this chapter uses the classification given in Table 4.1.

Note that the terms 'biodiversity value' or 'economic value' are specifically not included in this classification system. It is widely accepted that biodiversity and geodiversity provide the foundations that support protected area values. However, biodiversity and geodiversity are better regarded

Table 4.1 Classification of protected area values

Category	Examples
Intrinsic value	Fauna
	Flora
	Ecosystems
	Land and seascapes
On-site goods and services	Plant products
	Animal products
	Recreation and tourism
	Representations (such as films)
	Historic sites and artefacts
	Scientific knowledge and research
	Education
Off-site goods and services	Human life support
	Non-human life support
	Water quality and quantity
	Air quality and quantity
	Fishery protection
	Agriculture protection
	Protection of human settlements
Community value (non-material)	Culture
	Identity
	Spiritual meaning
	Social well-being
	Bequest for future generations
Individual value (non-material)	Satisfaction (existence)
	Satisfaction (experiential)
	Physical health
	Mental health
	Spiritual well-being

not as values in themselves, but as properties of the natural world, as conceptualized by humans, which are essential to maintain the many types of protected area values and related flows of benefits.

Economic benefits can flow from both on-site and off-site goods and services, and even non-material values can be exploited for economic gain (for example, spiritual retreats for which clients pay a fee to the organizer). Thus, this chapter does not identify economic value as a separate category, but treats it as one common way in which protected area values generate benefits for people. A value that is expressed and measured in economic terms can be traded off for something else of value. Money provides a common standard that enables the relative economic benefits associated with different values to be compared (timber is worth $X, recreation is worth $Y, and so on). The benefits associated with non-tradeable values cannot be expressed in economic terms. Some protected area values can thus have both economic and non-economic aspects. For example, an on-site value such as recreation generates a range of economic benefits, as well as having non-economic benefits associated with individual well-being. This chapter notes examples of where certain values give rise to particularly significant economic benefits – other aspects of protected area economics are considered in Chapter 12.

Historic sites and artefacts do not fit neatly into any category, but here they are placed alongside goods and services, while also allowing for the non-material benefits that communities gain from cultural heritage.

Intrinsic value

The basis of much ethical thought rests on the notion of intrinsic value. In traditional Western philosophy, rational nature (interpreted as human beings) is considered to have intrinsic value:

> … *everything has either a price or a dignity. If it has a price, something else can be put in its place as an equivalent … but that which constitutes the sole condition under which anything can be an end in itself has not merely a relative value – that is, a price – but has an intrinsic value – that is, dignity (Kant, 1956 [1785], p102).*

The notion that something has intrinsic value can consequently impose obligations in relation to it. The presence of intrinsic value implies moral considerability. The intrinsic value of humans leads to the well-known 'categorical imperative', an ethical prescription that one should:

> *Act in such a way that you always treat humanity, whether in your own person or in the person of any other, never simply as a means, but always at the same time as an end (Kant 1956 [1785], p96).*

From the middle of the 20th century, a more inclusive Western view of intrinsic value and related ethical duties emerged. An early influential example is Aldo Leopold's notion of a land ethic that extends moral consideration beyond humans into nature:

> *It is inconceivable to me that an ethical relation to land can exist without love, respect and admiration for land, and a high regard for its value. By value, I of course mean something far broader than mere economic value; I mean value in the philosophical sense… A thing is right when it tends to preserve the integrity, stability and beauty of the biotic community. It is wrong when it tends otherwise (Leopold, 1949, pp223, 224–225).*

Subsequently, philosophers such as Routley and Routley (1979) argued that nature is valuable

quite apart from any benefits that humans might gain from it. Natural areas, or parts thereof, can be conceived of as having intrinsic value – that is, value in their own right, regardless of humans. Of course, notions of intrinsic value in nature can also be found in many and much older non-Western philosophical and religious traditions. The presence of Brahman in all natural things is the Hindu basis of intrinsic value. The enlightened Buddhist is able to appreciate the intrinsic value of nature. Jains believe every living organism is inhabited by an immaterial soul, and adhere to a doctrine of non-harm to all living beings. In the Japanese Shinto religious tradition, aspects of nature with which the *kami* (gods) are associated are thought to have intrinsic value (Millennium Ecosystem Assessment, 2005). There are also diverse folk traditions, outside of the formal organized religions, which espouse and practise the view of nature as having intrinsic value. As noted by Callicott (1986, p140), the intrinsic value of non-human species is a 'widely shared intuition'.

Intrinsic value in nature means that we cannot simply treat nature as a resource to satisfy human wants and needs: 'things are not merely to be *valued for me and my kind* (as resources), not even as goods of *my kind* … but as *goods of their kind*' (Rolston, 1983, p191).

Such beliefs may concern animal species and, perhaps, plants as well – these views are termed *biocentric*. As ecological science has developed, so too has our appreciation of the significance of interactions between plants, animals and the physical environment: air, water and earth. This has led some people to believe that ecosystems have intrinsic value, apart from, or additional to, the intrinsic value of individual plants and animals that live within them. This is an *ecocentric* position. On whatever basis, intrinsic value has been attributed to various aspects of nature (genes, organisms, populations, species, evolutionarily significant units, biotic communities, ecosystems) and to nature as a whole (the biosphere) (Millennium Ecosystem Assessment, 2005).

Such views and how they might be applied have been debated extensively by environmental philosophers. Yet, in practice, acceptance of an intrinsic value in nature, and the obligations that

Garajonay National Park, Spain

Source: IUCN Photo Library © Jim Thorsell

such a belief imposes on humans, is widely acknowledged in international fora. The Convention on Biological Diversity (CBD) affirmed 'the intrinsic value of biodiversity'. The *United Nations World Charter for Nature*, signed by over 100 nations and adopted in 1982, stated:

> *Every form of life is unique, warranting respect regardless of its worth to man [sic], and, to accord other organisms such recognition, man [sic] must be guided by a moral code of action.*

In the context of protected areas, recognition of an intrinsic value in nature imposes a duty on managers to work for nature conservation out of recognition and respect for, to use Kant's terminology, the dignity of the natural world. Protected areas are one of the principal mechanisms by which we can fulfil this duty. The new thinking about the role of protected areas in contributing to human development must be complemented by this wider recognition of the relationship between human and non-human nature (see

Chapter 2, p67). Protected area governance and management objectives should give due recognition to both intrinsic and human-centred (anthropocentric) values.

On-site goods and services

Many valuable goods and services are derived directly from protected areas. IUCN Category V and VI protected areas (see Chapter 3) allow for sustainable extraction of natural resources. Activities may include grazing of livestock, fishing, hunting, harvesting of forest products and water extraction. Goods from coastal and marine protected areas can include seafood products, raw materials such as seaweed, medicinal treatments and products, live specimens for aquariums, and recreation (DEH, 2003b). An example of such renewable resource use is in the Danayiku Nature Park at Shan-Mei in Taiwan, where a once-depleted and unsustainably harvested stock of freshwater fish, Kooye minnow (*Varicorhinus barbatulus*), now supports a financially successful

Case Study **4.1**

Examples of the importance of direct-use values from protected areas for local and indigenous communities

The Kayan Mentarang National Park in the interior of East Kalimantan (Indonesian Borneo) is the largest protected area of rainforest in Borneo and one of the largest in South-East Asia. About 16,000 Dayak people live inside or near the park. Their use of natural resources is largely regulated by customary law. Traditional forest areas are given protection under strict management regimes. Important forest resources that are managed in this way include rattan (*Calamus* spp.), sang (*Licuala* sp.), hardwood for construction, fish and game, all of which have high use value for the local community.

The Gwaii Haanas National Park Reserve, located within the Queen Charlotte Islands off the coast of British Columbia, Canada, was established in 1986 under an agreement between Parks Canada and the Council of the Haida Nation. In the Haida language, *gwaii haanas* means 'islands of wonder and beauty'. The Haida themselves initiated the process after their land and culture started to disappear due to heavy logging in their traditional territories. The connection between land and culture is vital for the Haida, who are dependent upon natural resources for their livelihood through fishing, hunting and trapping, as well as for medicines and expression of their cultural identity through art. Employment opportunities have been created by the park, with more than 50 per cent of the park staff being Haida people. The establishment of the park has also promoted a shift in the local economy from logging to tourism.

The Kuhi are one of about 20 sub-tribes of the Shish Bayli tribe of the Qashqai nomadic pastoralists of southern Iran. The community-conserved Chartang-Kushkizar wetland, extending some 9km in length, is shared between the Kuhi and the Kolahli sub-tribes. The Kuhi obtain benefits from the wetland, including water, reeds for handicrafts, fish, medicinal plants and wildlife. In a controversial plan, the government designated part of the area to be divided up among households for agricultural use. The Kuhi believe that it is better to preserve this area as a *qorukh*, or local reserve. They have thus submitted a petition and a proposal to the government to declare the wetland and the surrounding rangelands as a community conserved area (CCA), with use rights being regulated by the sub-tribe elders. In terms of IUCN categories, the overall CCA, covering the Kuhi wintering and summering grounds, together with the access routes, could be considered as a Category V protected area, with the wetland portion as Category II.

Source: adapted from case studies presented in Borrini-Feyerbend et al (2004b)

sport fishing and ecotourism venture (Chape et al, 2003b).

Use of natural resources from IUCN Category V and VI protected areas is particularly important for local and indigenous communities (see Case Study 4.1). Many of the direct and indirect goods and services listed in Table 4.1 can make a contribution to alleviating poverty. While protected areas can impose significant costs on local communities through reduced access to natural resources, especially in relation to IUCN Categories I to IV, measures that can mitigate such effects include establishing agreed conditions for access to resources in a way that does not compromise other management objectives; providing alternative resources; offering employment; allocating a portion of protected area fees (for example, in Uganda 12 per cent of income generated by protected areas goes back to adjacent

communities); improving socio-economic conditions such as provision of education and health services; and providing compensation (Lewis, 1996).

Biodiversity has become increasingly relevant to agriculture and medicine. Stocks of native plants and animals can provide valuable genetic material and chemical compounds for developing disease-resistant strains of important agricultural crop species or new pharmaceuticals. For example, by the early 1990s, 3000 plants had been identified by the US National Cancer Institute as being active against cancer cells, of which 70 per cent came from rainforests, which are best preserved in protected areas (Bird, 1991) or in the territories of indigenous peoples.

Nature-based recreation is an important part of many people's lives, and protected areas provide the best opportunities for engaging in activities

Fishing on Lake Kosi St Lucia, South Africa

Source: IUCN Photo Library © Jim Thorsell

such as sightseeing, walking, camping, canoeing, bird watching, photography, skiing, rock climbing and many others. Tourism based on protected areas is a major international industry that provides experiential benefits to participants and economic benefits to local, provincial (see Case Study 4.2) and national economies. More detail on nature-based tourism and recreation, as well as the management of such activities, is given in Chapter 19.

An important part of a visit to a protected area is often aesthetic appreciation. Coral reefs, red desert plains, mountain landscapes, waterfalls and forests can move, inspire and delight. Books, photographs, films and paintings of such places are enjoyed by many people. For example, the work of the great American photographer Ansel Adams, and the protected areas he depicts, is a source of inspiration and awe for people throughout the world.

Many protected areas have significant cultural value. Examples include sacred sites and other sites of cultural significance, as well as past settlements,

access routes and so on. Even more important, many protected areas, including community conserved areas (CCAs), are 'bio-cultural' landscapes inhabited by indigenous peoples and local communities, and viewed through their particular cultural visions:

> *Cultural heritage is the term used to refer to qualities and attributes possessed by places that have aesthetic, historic, scientific or social value for past, present and future generations. These values may be seen in a place's physical features, but can also be associated with intangible qualities such as people's associations with, or feelings for, a place (Lennon et al, 1999, p8).*

To many people, the value of viewing, experiencing, appreciating and learning about such sites, and the cultures from which they derive, is an important reason for visiting. The historic sanctuary of Machu Picchu, inscribed on the *World Heritage List* for both its natural and its cultural values, draws hundreds of thousands of people

Case Study 4.2

Economic benefits associated with the recreation values of provincial parks in British Columbia, Canada

The Canadian province of British Columbia has 807 provincial protected areas covering more than 11.35 million hectares, or 11.8 per cent of the province's land area. These parks provide a wide range of benefits that contributes to the social, environmental and economic well-being of the province. The economic impacts associated with government and visitor expenditures benefits of the system have been quantified as follows:

- total expenditures related to provincial parks approximated Cdn$533 million in 1999;
- visitor expenditures on parks were estimated to represent over 90 per cent of total expenditures;
- for each dollar invested by government in the protected areas system, there were about Cdn$10 dollars in visitor expenditures;
- almost one third of visitor expenditures, Cdn$148 million, are made by out-of-province residents, making the parks equivalent to a significant export industry;
- economic activity generated by the park system sustains about 9100 direct and indirect person years of employment every year;
- overall, the park system is estimated to contribute about Cdn$521 million to the provincial gross domestic product (GDP);
- the economic benefits of parks are widely distributed across British Columbia's communities and regions; and
- the parks generate about Cdn$219 million in tax revenues for the federal and provincial governments.

Source: adapted from Ministry of Water, Land and Air Protection (2001)

every year into remote mountains to view the Incan ruins of what was probably a royal estate and religious retreat; the cultural landscape of Southern Öland in Sweden is recognized for its World Heritage values (see Case Study 4.3); and Kakadu National Park in Australia features internationally significant Aboriginal paintings. Protecting landscapes and seascapes where people and nature have interacted to produce areas of distinct character is an important function of protected areas, and is particularly relevant to IUCN Category V protected areas and also for cultural landscapes as defined under the World Heritage Convention. The value of such places to the particular societies and cultures with whom they are associated is considered in the later section on 'Community value (non-material)'. The wider significance and management of such sites is addressed in detail in Chapter 17.

Protected areas are important repositories of scientific knowledge and provide innumerable opportunities for research. Protected areas feature some of the best and most significant examples of the Earth's geological past, as well as currently active geomorphological processes. Such places further our understanding of natural processes of landscape formation and erosion. Many type localities of plants are situated in protected areas. Large protected areas provide the best opportunities for studying wild populations of animals. The protection afforded by protected areas to many cultural sites helps to ensure that the basis of our knowledge of past human activity and culture is maintained, and that opportunities for augmenting this knowledge are preserved.

Education is an important function of protected areas, and many protected areas have specific programmes designed to communicate knowledge about natural and cultural heritage (see Chapter 10, p279). For example, the Imbewu Youth Programme, a joint venture between South African National Parks and the Wilderness Foundation South Africa, takes groups of 8 to 16 young people into a national park for four-day bush camps. Participants identify and learn about species and their significance to local peoples through stories, conservation practices and traditions. The programme is followed up by the Junior Honorary Ranger Orientation Course – a six- to nine-month

Case Study **4.3**

Southern Öland cultural landscape, Sweden

The 1342 square kilometre Southern Öland is Sweden's second largest island and has about 25,000 inhabitants. Significant areas of Southern Öland are designated as landscape protection areas. The entire landscape reflects more than 5000 years of human habitation and the current farming systems have evolved to match the physical constraints and environmental values of the area. The Stora Alvaret on Southern Öland – a treeless 40km long steppe containing many rare plant species – is the largest actively farmed limestone pavement in the world. Öland also has southern Sweden's largest continuous deciduous forest. The area's high biodiversity and historic values are conserved through low-impact traditional farming practices, which respect the land's capabilities and the area's natural ecosystems and cultural heritage. A legally binding stewardship agreement between all farmers and the relevant management bodies ensures that an integrated approach to managing farmland is adopted throughout the area. The recognition by the farming community of their inter-generational responsibilities enables modern farming and economic development activities to be undertaken without compromising the area's traditional natural and cultural values. These relationships have created a distinctive landscape, the outstanding importance and uniqueness of which has been recognized as a Cultural Landscape of World Heritage status.

Source: Ogden (2003)

course involving a training package that includes an interactive workbook, workshop and group project (Makwaeba, 2004).

All of the above direct-use values also have a temporal dimension. We can choose to enjoy them in the current time period, or we can delay utilization to some future time. In some cases, simply having the option to enjoy a particular use in the future can be considered a value, even if that use never actually occurs. Many people value the option of visiting a protected area such as Kruger in South Africa, Sagamartha in Nepal, the Great Barrier Reef in Australia or Yosemite in the US, and of anticipating that they will find it in good condition, even if they never actually take up such an opportunity. It is likely that some protected areas contain resource potential that we are not even aware of. Protected areas, through conserving wild stocks of plants and animals, provide options for future development of new crops and pharmaceuticals (Chape et al, 2003b). Scientific discoveries in the future may indicate, for example, the medicinal value of a chemical found only in a rare plant species whose population has been conserved in a protected area. Such potential future use values provide yet another reason for establishing and maintaining a comprehensive network of protected areas.

Off-site goods and services

Every living organism relies upon a network of abiotic and biotic activities known as ecological processes. When forests are felled, wetlands filled in, watercourses altered and species are over-harvested, ecological processes are damaged or destroyed. As a result, many of nature's 'free' services to humanity are lost. *Ecosystem services* flow from natural assets (soil, biota, water systems and the atmosphere) to support human activities and lifestyles that are generated outside natural areas but are indirectly dependent upon them. For example, wetlands can help to remove pollutants from water, thereby ensuring that downstream flow can be extracted for domestic uses. The agricultural industry depends heavily upon many ecological processes, including soil formation and nutrient cycling. Common instances of agricultural failure after ecosystem alteration include soil salinization and soil loss after excessive tree removal, as well as population explosions of pest species once the habitat for their predators has been removed (Cork and Shelton, 2000). In general, terrestrial protected areas provide a number of ecosystem service benefits, including:

- climate regulation through carbon sequestration, regulation of albedo and other processes;

- hydrological benefits associated with controlling the timing and volume of water flows and maintaining or improving water quality for uses such as domestic, agricultural and industrial consumption, recreation and fisheries;
- protection of, and habitat for, useful predators, pollinators and dispersal agents;
- reducing sedimentation, thereby avoiding damage to downstream infrastructure such as reservoirs, hydroelectric power stations, irrigation pumps and canals (see Case Study 4.4);
- maintaining soil and land productivity; and
- disaster prevention through watershed protection, reducing the risk of flooding and landslides (Georgieva et al, 2003).

Services from coastal and marine protected areas include shoreline maintenance; flood and storm protection; disaster mitigation (for example, intact mangrove forests in protected areas helped to reduce the impact of the December 2004 Asian tsunami); sand production; nutrient cycling; waste assimilation and remediation; and water quality maintenance. Marine protected areas can provide benefits to surrounding fisheries, including protection of specific life stages (such as nursery grounds); protection of critical functions (feeding grounds, spawning grounds); provision of dispersion centres for the supply of larvae to a fishery; improved socio-economic outcomes for local communities; and support for fishery stability (DEH, 2003b). For example, five small marine reserves in St Lucia increased the productivity of adjacent fisheries by between 49 and 90 per cent (Roberts et al, 2001a).

The economic benefits flowing from three national parks in Cambodia, including on-site and off-site goods and services, are described in Case Study 4.5. At a global scale, Balmford et al (2002) estimated that the economic benefits of an effective global network of protected areas would yield goods and services with an annual value of between US$4400 billion and US$5200 billion – about 100 times the costs associated with such a system.

City water supply pipeline from Morne Trois Pitons National Park, Dominica

Source: IUCN Photo Library © Jim Thorsell

Case Study **4.4**

Ecosystem services and the Panama Canal

The functioning of the Panama Canal depends upon water from Gatún Lake, one of the largest artificial lakes in the world, created during construction of the canal. An adequate supply of water is essential for ensuring passage through the canal. During the drought winter of 1990–1991, lack of water forced canal operators to significantly reduce the number of lockages. Although Panama City is a major financial centre, some estimates suggest that the canal and its associated businesses contribute over 40 per cent of the nation's economy.

On forested slopes, water soaks into the ground and feeds slowly into streams and then into Gatún Lake. But deforested slopes cannot absorb heavy rains. Floodwaters drain rapidly into the lake, overflow Gatún Dam and run out to sea – useless for lockage. Eroded sediment also ends up on the lake bottom, reducing its storage capacity.

Cutting down the forest to build pasture peaked in the 1980s, and by 2000, 53 per cent of the forest had been cleared. At the urging of a scientific study group, Eric Arturo Delvalle, then the country's president, established Chagres National Park, which covers over 100,000 hectares, or about one third of the canal watershed. For a time, deforestation continued outside the park; but factors such as a decision by leading Panamanian bankers to stop financing cattle ranchers who cut down forest for pasture and expansion of protected watershed areas have dramatically reduced forest clearing. However, there are concerns that the management agencies do not have enough money or staff to patrol the parks as closely as they wish. There are constant threats on the park boundaries, so the canal authority and other agencies have also begun community efforts to educate rural Panamanians about the importance of preserving the forest landscape.

Source: adapted from Dean (2005)

Case Study **4.5**

Economic benefits of Bokor, Kirirom and Ream National Parks, Cambodia

People living in and around Bokor, Kirirom and Ream National Parks in Cambodia use a wide range of forest products, including firewood, wild foods, wild animals, plant-based medicines, materials for house construction, and fibres used for ropes, baskets and mats. The sale of medicinal plants, wild animals, timber, firewood and charcoal provides important household income. In Bokor National Park, adjacent communities use 46 plant species for non-timber forest products (NTFPs). The most important of these include fruits from sam rong (*Sterculia lychnophora*), vor romiet (*Coscinium usitatum*) and khos (*Castanopsis cambodiana*), and resin from *Shorea* sp. A wide range of fish and crustaceans is harvested from marine and mangrove areas in Ream and Kep national parks. However, not all of these resource uses are sustainable. The three parks also support tourism and recreation, with some of the benefits from these activities flowing to local people through the provision of employment and sale of goods and services.

The rivers that originate from Bokor and Kirirom National Parks provide domestic and industrial water supplies, and support irrigation developments, downstream fisheries and hydroelectric facilities in neighbouring Kampot and Kompong Speu provinces. Protection of the watersheds maintains the quality, quantity and seasonal flow of the rivers. Mangroves in Ream and Kep National Parks provide a wide range of ecosystems services. They are a breeding and nursery ground for fish and crustaceans; stabilize soil and slow down water flow, thereby decreasing coastal erosion and protecting against coastal storms and surges; filter out nutrients and toxins such as pesticides, industrial waste and human sewage; and help to mitigate global warming by acting as a sink for carbon.

Source: adapted from ICEM (2003a)

Community value (non-material)

Human society has always, through interaction with nature, forged identity, tradition, lifestyle and spirituality. For many communities, natural areas are closely associated with deeply held historical, national, ethical, religious and spiritual values. A particular mountain, forest or river may, for example, have been the site of an important event in their past, the home or shrine of a deity, the place of a moral transformation, or the embodiment of national ideals (Millennium Ecosystem Assessment, 2005). On a more pragmatic level, protected areas can contribute to bringing people together to work cooperatively. Involvement in recreation and volunteer management activities can reduce alienation, as well as facilitate bonding, reciprocity, understanding and sharing between people.

A sense of place is a positive emotional bond that develops between people and their environment. A sense of place arises from human interpretations of a setting that is constructed and given meaning through experience with the area. Thus, places encompass a physical setting, as well as human meaning and interpretation that are given to that setting (Stedman, 2003). While authors such as Greider and Garkovich (1994) assert that landscapes are wholly a reflection of cultural identity, so that any physical place has the potential to embody multiple landscapes, others such as Shields (1991) argue that the characteristics and quality of the physical space also strongly affect the human creation of place. This chapter agrees with the latter view, which implies that a change in the physical landscape may destroy or alter meanings (Stedman, 2003). Protected areas therefore have a key role in helping to maintain the community identity and cohesion associated with place attachment.

For many people, an important responsibility of contemporary society is to pass on natural and cultural heritage as a bequest to future generations. Appreciation of protected areas and commitment to their establishment to protect natural places from degradation have brought people together in organizations that operate at international (for example, Greenpeace and the International Alliance of Indigenous and Tribal Peoples of the Tropical Forests), national (for instance, the Society for the Protection of Nature in Israel and the Australian Conservation Foundation) and local scales (for example, the Flower Valley Conservation Trust in South Africa and the Ranapur Community Forestry Federation, consisting of 190 villages in the Orissa state of southern India).

Protected areas provide opportunities to keep alive or conserve community values that give a sense of identity, connection or meaning. For many communities, identity is, in part, formed by a connection with places, including protected areas. To people living in or around protected areas, such places often engender feelings of pride and belonging. Community histories are often ingrained with stories and memories in which such places are a central element.

Transboundary protected areas (see Chapter 22, p584) can contribute to regional peace and stability by providing a focus for cooperative management across land and sea borders between nations or provinces. Protected areas can also foster understanding between traditional and modern societies, or between distinct cultures (Putney, 2003).

As was noted in Chapter 2, the creation of the earliest protected areas – sacred groves – was explicitly motivated by spiritual values. Many mountains have spiritual meaning. Examples given by Hamilton (2000) include the following:

- mountain forests in the Yunnan prefecture of Xishuanbanna in China are largely intact because of the reverence that the Dai people have for these places, where the spirits of ancestors dwell;
- within Hawaii's Volcanoes National Park, the volcano goddess Pele, creator and destroyer by her lava flows, is both feared and loved; and
- the sacred peak of Gauri Shanker in Nepal depicts the lord Shankar and his consort Gauri.

Such sites provide spiritual connection between indigenous peoples and the wider universe, and are essential to the vitality and survival of traditional cultures (Acha, 2003; see Case Study 4.6).

Case Study **4.6**

Wixarika/Huichol sacred natural site, Mexico

The indigenous Huichol (Wixarika) people live in scattered small communities in valleys of the Mexican Sierra Madre Occidental. Outside their communal lands, the Huichol recognize five main sacred sites, one of which is Wirikuta, the final destination of the ancestors and the deities in the pilgrimage they undertook to witness the birth of the sun. A Huichol song speaks of this place:

> Flowers fly, flowers swirl,
> going around the Cerro Quemado
> and from the heart of our grandfather
> the deer and the hikuri are born:
> the gods are speaking.
> In Wirikuta there is a flower that talks
> and the arrow stuck in the jícuri's core
> understands the language of the gods.
> Who knows why the hills speak in Wirikuta.

Wirikuta is located in the Chihuahuan Desert in the province of San Luis Potosi. In 2001, a 140,211ha reserve was established as a sacred natural site, which is defined under San Luis Potosi law as an area which, in addition to having significant biodiversity, includes sacred spaces for indigenous peoples. The sacred natural site of Wirikuta features key biodiversity elements of the Chihuahuan Desert, including endemic and endangered cacti and relict forests. Although it encompasses only a fraction of 1 per cent of the desert, about 50 per cent of flora, 70 per cent of avifauna and 60 per cent of mammal species occur within the reserve.

Source: adapted from Acha (2003)

As well as providing a reason for reservation in the first instance, there are qualities of protected areas that can allow a visitor to experience reverence and to become aware of the sacred.

Individual value (non-material)

Protected areas contribute to personal development by providing opportunities for transformative experiences through connection with wild nature (see Case Study 4.7). Involvement in activities such as bushwalking can lead to the development of leadership skills, building of self-reliance and confidence, and acceptance of responsibility. Physical activity in natural settings gives rise to therapeutic values by creating a potential for healing and enhancing psychological well-being (a sense of wellness, stress management and the prevention and reduction of depression, anxiety and anger) and physical well-being (cardiovascular, weight, strength and increased life expectancy) (Shultis, 2003). Under the banner of 'Healthy Parks, Healthy People', the Australian

agency Parks Victoria has developed a strategy to communicate the benefits of a protected area system and its contribution to the health of individuals and society. The initiative, which has now also been taken up by several other Australian states, is based on evidence that shows:

* viewing nature is positive for health in terms of recovering from stress, improving concentration and productivity, and improving psychological state;
* people have a more positive outlook on life and higher life satisfaction when in proximity to nature;
* natural environments foster recovery from mental fatigue and are restorative;
* nature-based therapies have success in healing patients who previously had not responded to treatment;
* there are psychological and physiological benefits to health from the act of nurturing living things;

Tourists and seals, Galapagos Islands

Source: IUCN Photo Library © Jim Thorsell

- protected areas provide settings for contemplation, reflection and inspiration; invoke a sense of place; and facilitate feeling a connection to something beyond human concerns; and
- activities undertaken in protected areas are a fundamental health resource, particularly in terms of disease prevention (Maller et al, 2002).

Many artists and writers have found in protected areas qualities that inspired imagination and creative expression. William Wordsworth, in a famous poem composed a few miles above Tintern Abbey in south-east Wales, expressed his own profound experience of nature:

> … And I have felt
> A presence that disturbs me with the joy
> Of elevated thoughts; a sense sublime
> Of something far more deeply interfused,
> Whose dwelling is the light of setting suns,
> And the round ocean and the living air.

Philosophers have found inspiration in wild natural places as sources, as well as resources:

> *We pass the gate and pay the admission fee; we are inside the park's official boundaries. But politics and society soon fade, and the natural history commands the scene. And the first commandment is: survive. Adapt. Eat or be eaten. Life or death. Our first observation is: life goes on – protected in the parks but on its own, wild and free… Forests and soil, sunshine and rain, rivers and sky, the everlasting hills, the rolling prairies, the cycling seasons – these are superficially just pleasant scenes in which to recreate. At depth, they are surrounding creation that supports life. If one insists on the word, they are resources, but now it seems inadequate to call them recreation resources. They are the sources that define life (Rolston, 2003, pp104–105).*

Many people gain satisfaction from simply knowing that an area is being preserved, regardless of whether they will see it or directly use its resources. We feel enriched and fulfilled when we can be sure that such places are protected.

Case Study **4.7**

Testimonies of the personal significance of protected areas

Recalling his first visit to Yosemite in the US, which had a profound effect on him that lasted all of his life, Ansel Adams stated:

That first impression of the valley – white water, azaleas, cool fir caverns, tall pines and stolid oaks, cliffs rising to undreamed-of heights, the poignant sounds and smells of the Sierra ... was a culmination of experience so intense as to be almost painful. From that day in 1916 my life has been coloured and modulated by the great earth gesture of the Sierra. (Turnage, 1980)

Dave Green, a PhD student studying the soils of south-west Tasmania, recalled:

This is a relatively unexplored place. Nobody else has undertaken a survey of the soils here, except in the river valleys for dam feasibility. There is no general understanding of the soils of this area and its links to Gondwana. Already I am finding links to soils in Argentina and South Africa. It is exciting to be doing something that nobody else has done, finding a lot that is new, that hasn't been described.

Cynthia Roberts, who ran a successful ecotourism business for over ten years, took small groups of people into New Zealand's national parks:

Being in wild areas is a spiritual experience – uplifting, being elated, excited, refreshed and peaceful all at once. Different landscapes have different impacts. The forest is sensuous: the trees, the greenery and especially the smells. The experience is the joy of growth. The sea and coast are different. The sound is stimulating and the long distance views are restful to the eyes and mind. There is a sense of settling and being cleansed.

Ayuko worked in Tokyo and found the city stressful and boring. There were too many people and it was always noisy. Then a friend introduced her to mountaineering in national parks in Japan:

They are some of the few places where you can climb, where rich nature is still to be found. The mountains are quiet, beautiful [and] enable me to be in contact with nature and with god. I like to climb on my own to fully experience being with nature. Mountains are considered sacred in Japanese traditional custom. There are some mountains where women were not allowed to climb to the top. Through my experiences climbing, I started thinking about the issues and problems of parks and had ideas of wanting to conserve nature. I also started to find out more about Japanese traditional culture where nature conservation is strong.

Further reading

Balmford, A., Bruner, A., Cooper, P., Costanza, R., Farber, S., Green, R. E., Jenkins, M., Jefferiss, P., Jessamy, V., Madden, J., Munro, K., Myers, N., Naeem, S., Paavola, J., Rayment, M., Rosendo, S., Roughgarden, J., Trumper, K. and Turner, R. K. (2002) 'Economic reasons for conserving wild nature', *Science*, vol 297, pp950–953

DEH (Department of Environment and Heritage) (2003) *The Benefits of Marine Protected Areas*, Commonwealth of Australia, Canberra

Harmon, D. and Putney, A. (eds) (2003) *The Full Value of Parks: From Economics to the Intangible*, Rowman and Littlefield Publishers, Lanham

IUCN (1998) *Economic Values of Protected Areas: Guidelines for Protected Area Managers*, IUCN, Gland and Cambridge

IUCN (2005) *Benefits beyond Boundaries: Proceedings of the Vth IUCN World Parks Congress*, Durban, South Africa, 8–17 September 2003, IUCN, Gland and Cambridge

Lockwood, M. (1999) 'Humans valuing nature', *Environmental Values*, vol 8, pp381–401

5

Governance of Protected Areas

Grazia Borrini-Feyerabend, Jim Johnston and Diane Pansky

Governance is a relatively new and powerful concept that people concerned with protected areas should understand and clearly distinguish from 'management'. While 'management' addresses what is done about a given site or situation, 'governance' addresses who makes those decisions and how. Governance is about power, relationships, responsibility and accountability. It is about who has influence, who decides and how decision-makers are held accountable. Graham et al (2003, pp2–3) define governance as:

> … the interactions among structures, processes and traditions that determine how power is exercised, how decisions are taken on issues of public concern, and how citizens or other stakeholders have their say.

In other words, the governance setting of a given public concern is what a society enables – or at least is prepared to accept – in terms of the whos and hows of the relevant authority and responsibility.

'Government' and 'governance' have similar roots; but 'government' generally refers only to bodies and processes that are largely separate from citizens, the private sector and civil society. Governments are key players in governance, but are only one among the many possible players: 'equating governance with government [can] put blinders around the range of strategies that seem available' (Plumptre and Graham, 1999, p2). As affirmed by the United Nations Development Programme (UNDP, 1997):

> Governance includes the state, but transcends it by taking in the private sector and civil society. All three are critical for sustaining human development. The state creates a conducive political and legal environment. The private sector generates jobs and income. And civil society facilitates political and social interaction – mobilizing groups to participate in economic, social and political activities. Because each has weaknesses and strengths, a major objective of our support for good governance is to promote constructive interaction among all three.

There are many important decisions to be made about protected areas; related to those are specific powers and responsibilities. These include:

- determining where a protected area is needed, where it should be located and what type of status it should have;
- determining who is entitled to have a say about matters relevant to the protected area;
- creating rules about the land and resource uses allowed inside the protected area, and establishing zones for different levels of access and use;
- enforcing the agreed zoning and rules;
- deciding how financial and other resources will be spent to support specific conservation and sustainable development activities concerning the protected area;
- generating revenues – for example, by selling permits and generating fees, taxes and in-kind

contributions, and deciding how those are distributed and used; and

- entering into agreements with other parties to share or delegate some of the above powers or to decide about other matters relevant to the protected area (adapted from Graham et al, 2003).

Who takes on the above decisions, powers and responsibilities and how they do so – the governance setting of the protected area – determine whether the protected area achieves its management objectives (is it effective?), whether it is able to share fairly the relevant benefits and costs (is it equitable?), and whether it has the support of local communities, politicians and the broader society (is it sustainable?).

In turn, the governance setting depends in large part upon formal mandates, institutions, processes and relevant legal and customary rights. But it is a more complex and nuanced phenomenon than one may imagine, not easy to circumscribe. Regardless of formal authority, decisions may be influenced by history and culture (see Box 5.1), access to information, basic

economic outlook and many other factors. Any simple governance typology is necessarily crude.

In this chapter, we discuss the types of governance applicable to protected areas and present in some detail the various governance roles of protected area actors. We then consider issues of quality, awareness and innovation in relation to protected area governance.

Types of governance for protected areas

The first attempts at establishing a governance typology for protected areas were made by Borrini-Feyerabend et al (2002) and Graham et al (2003) in preparation for the Vth IUCN World Parks Congress (see 'Institutions working for protected areas' in Chapter 3). These attempts were discussed and refined at the congress, where delegates settled on a set of protected area governance categories based on answers to the following questions (Borrini-Feyerabend, 2003a): who holds the main decision-making authority for the protected area? Who is responsible and can be held accountable for it? Four main types of governance were thus identified:

Elders in the Biamo village still play the paramount role in natural resource management, northern Cameroon

Source: Grazia Borrini-Feyerabend

Box 5.1 Historical influences on protected area governance

Until recently, protected area advocates and managers have disregarded the widespread and significant contributions that local communities make towards conservation. This disregard can be traced back to colonial times (Murombedzi, 2003), when it helped to justify the exclusion of communities from the control of natural resources.

Colonization and colonialism are neither the first nor the only phenomenon at the historical roots of official protected areas. Earlier changes in land tenure systems and management practices that go under the name of 'enclosure of the commons' appropriated and partitioned previously communally held lands. This process started in England as early as the 13th century as a by-product of the monetization of feudal life, and it reached its climax in the late 18th and early 19th centuries. First the aristocracy, and later the state, removed land from customary common access and use and set it under their own management authority for the aim of financial profit and political power. The phenomenon slowly came to affect most countries in Europe and was exported all over the world through colonization and colonialism. Upon independence, most new national states maintained the land tenure regimes they had inherited.

The 'enclosure of the commons' has been so pervasive that, today, most land in the world formally belongs either to a state or to a private owner (individuals or corporations). Customary land rights vested in a community of people have become the exception. From the haciendas of South America (Burbach and Flynn, 1980) to the so-called wastelands of India and the immense expanses of the US, land has been appropriated by bureaucrats and experts, merchants and entrepreneurs. With that change of tenure came also a major intensification of use. Forests and wildlife habitats, for instance, have been replaced by cultivated land and infrastructure. This 'agricultural revolution' has provided the basis for the industrial revolution and for at least part of the growth of the world population. At the same time, it has prompted the intensive exploitation of natural resources that so threatens the world's biodiversity.

Throughout history, the appropriation of nature has gone hand in hand with racial segregation (in some parts of colonial Africa, Asia and the Caribbean, for example, only white people were allowed to hunt). And colonial force has been the primary means by which the new protectionist regimes for the 'conservation of nature' were established in many countries. Indeed, a state's first move following the establishment of a protected area has often been to force out the area's residents (Stevens, 1997b). The humanitarian consequences have been severe; in some cases, they have even reached genocidal proportion (Turnbull, 1972).

As noted in Chapter 2 (p42), a large proportion of the world's protected areas have been created in areas inhabited by indigenous and local communities. The challenge, then, if we are to overcome the untenable practices of the past, is not to remove people from nature but to find a way of ensuring that their interaction is the best possible to achieve both conservation aims and equity.

Regarding the rights of indigenous peoples and local communities (considered in more detail in Chapters 20 and 21), different world regions show similar histories of land dispossession but different emerging realities. While pastoral communities in East Africa are now locked in land conflicts with both sedentary agricultural communities and state conservation agencies (Bassi, 2003), the indigenous communities of the Andean region have made important progress in regaining formal rights to natural resources.

The critical factor in empowering communities remains the recognition and/or restoration of their entitlements to land and natural resources (Brockington, 2002; Bassi, 2003). Unfortunately, despite inspiring examples and policy achievements (see Case Study 21.7), even forced eviction practices are not yet a matter of the past (Cernea and Schmidt-Soltau, 2005). We are still far from achieving universally equitable treatment of indigenous and local communities in protected area establishment and management.

1 government protected areas (government agencies at various levels make and enforce decisions);

2 co-managed protected areas (various actors together make and enforce decisions);

3 private protected areas (private landowners make and enforce decisions); and

4 community conserved areas (CCAs) (indigenous peoples or local communities make and enforce decisions).

The fourth type uses the term 'conserved area' rather than 'protected area' as indigenous peoples and local communities have a unique way of understanding and relating to areas under their stewardship (see Chapter 21).

Government protected areas

Most people are familiar with this type of governance, in which a government body (such as a ministry or park agency reporting directly to the government) holds the authority, responsibility and accountability for managing the protected area, and determines its conservation objectives (such as the ones that distinguish the IUCN categories) and management rules. Most often, the government also owns the protected area's land, water and related resources. Reflecting the trend towards administrative decentralization, sub-national and municipal government bodies have become prominent in declaring and managing protected areas. In some cases, the state retains full landownership and/or control or oversight of protected areas, but delegates their management to a parastatal organization, NGO or even a private operator or community. The government may or may not have a legal obligation to inform or consult other identified stakeholders prior to setting up protected areas and making or enforcing management decisions.

Co-managed protected areas

This type of governance, which is discussed further in Chapter 20, is also becoming increasingly common, responding to the variety of interlocked entitlements recognized by democratic societies. Complex processes and institutional mechanisms are employed to share management authority and responsibility among a plurality of actors – from national to sub-national and local government authorities, from representatives of indigenous peoples and local communities (sedentary or mobile) to user associations, from private entrepreneurs to landowners. The actors recognize the legitimacy of their respective entitlements to manage the protected area and agree on subjecting it to a specific conservation objective (such as the ones that distinguish the IUCN categories). Distinct co-management subtypes may be identified.

In collaborative management, for instance, formal decision-making authority, responsibility and accountability may rest with one agency (often a national governmental agency), but the agency is required – by law or policy – to collaborate with other stakeholders. In its weak connotation, 'collaboration' means informing and consulting stakeholders. In its strong form, 'collaboration' means that a multi-stakeholder body has to develop and approve by consensus a number of technical proposals for protected area regulation and management, to be later submitted to the decision-making authority. In joint management decision-making authority, responsibility and accountability is shared in a formal way, with various actors entitled to one or more seats in a management body. Again, the requirements for joint management are made stronger if decision-making is carried out by consensus. When this is not the case, the balance of power reflected in the composition of the joint management body may *de facto* transform it into a different governance type (such as when government actors or private landowners hold an absolute majority of votes). Because of the various actors necessarily involved, some form of multi-stakeholder management is particularly suited to the needs of transboundary protected areas (Sandwith et al, 2001).

Private protected areas

Private governance has a relatively long history, as kings and aristocracies often preserved for themselves certain areas of land or the privilege to hunt wildlife. Such private reserves had important secondary conservation benefits. Today, private ownership is still an enormously important force in conservation. A private protected area refers to a land parcel owned by individuals, communities, corporations or NGOs and managed for biodiversity conservation with or without formal government recognition. Landowners can pursue conservation objectives because of their sense of respect for the land or their desire to maintain its beauty and ecological value. Utilitarian purposes, such as gaining revenue from ecotourism or reducing levies and taxes, can be additional incentives or even the main ultimate aim. In all cases, authority for managing the protected land and resources rests with the landowners, who are responsible for decision-making, determine a conservation objective and impose a conservation regime. While landowners are subject to applicable legislation and their freedom is restricted under terms agreed with their governments, their accountability to the larger society is quite limited. Some forms of accountability may be negotiated with the government in exchange for specific incentives (as in the case of easements and land trusts – see Case Study 5.2).

Community conserved areas

This governance type involves governance by indigenous peoples and local communities – including settled and mobile groups. This may be the oldest form of protected area governance and it is still widespread (see Chapter 21). Throughout the world and over thousands of years, human communities have shaped their lifestyles and livelihood strategies to respond to the opportunities and challenges presented by their surrounding land and natural resources. In so doing, they managed, modified and often conserved and even enriched their environments. In many cases, community interaction with the environment generated a sort of symbiosis, which some refer to as 'bio-cultural units' or 'cultural landscapes/ seascapes'. Much of this interaction happened not for the intentional conservation of biodiversity, but in pursuit of a variety of interlocked objectives and values (spiritual, religious, security related, survival related), which did, however, result in the conservation of ecosystems, species and ecosystem-related values. In this sense, CCAs comprise 'natural and modified ecosystems including significant biodiversity and ecological and cultural values voluntarily conserved by indigenous, mobile and local communities through customary laws or other effective means'.

In CCAs, authority and responsibility rest with the communities through a variety of forms of ethnic governance or locally agreed organizations and rules. These forms and rules of customary law can be very diverse and extremely complex. For instance, land and/or some resources may be community owned and managed, but other resources may be individually owned and managed, or managed on a clan basis (Baird and Dearden, 2003). Different communities may also have rights over the same lands at different times. In general, CCAs depend upon the willingness of governments to let communities manage their land (*de jure* or *de facto*). In this sense, the territorial reserves of indigenous peoples living in voluntary isolation represent a unique CCA example. In the Amazon, some indigenous groups still attempt to maintain their hunting and gathering nomadic existence in complete isolation from the outside world in some of the world's most biodiverse tropical forests. In these areas, biological diversity is conserved because governments decided to respect the will for extreme solitude of these communities.

Nearly every community has developed specific management regulations and organizations for its natural resources. In many parts of the world, national legal systems grant no ownership rights to communities over the lands and resources they collectively own and manage through customary law. This is particularly true in Africa, Asia and Europe. In a number of countries, however, and notably in Bolivia, Colombia, the Philippines, Australia and Indonesia, some indigenous and local communities have fought for and won legal title to their lands. In such cases, communities are private landowners, and the CCAs they have established are a form of private protected area. Indeed, achieving recognized legal title to their customarily held lands and resources is the surest step for communities to establish and manage their own reserves.

In CCAs, whether recognized through customary law and/or formal landownership (for example, by indigenous land councils or trusts), the community's accountability to the larger society remains usually limited, although it may be defined as part of broader negotiations with the national government and other partners. For example, a government may offer to acknowledge collective land rights and provide an economic development package if a community commits to maintaining its customary practices. Such negotiations may even result in a joint management arrangement among communities, government actors and other stakeholders (thus changing the governance type into a co-managed protected area).

Governance and the IUCN categories of protected area

Since governance is different from management, governance types are different from the IUCN/ World Commission on Protected Areas (WCPA) management categories, which, as explained in 'Types of protected areas' in Chapter 3, are based on the management objective of the protected area. The four governance types mentioned above and several sub-types are presented in Table 5.1, in combination with the IUCN/WCPA category system. The four main governance types are fully complementary to the IUCN categories (they are category neutral) in the sense that protected areas exist that fill each possible combination of IUCN category and governance type.

The IUCN protected area definition and associated management categories do not prescribe any type of ownership or authority – they are 'neutral' about these, so to speak. This means that protected areas in any of the six categories can be governed by communities, private parties, government authorities, NGOs or various combinations of these. In particular, private ownership and customary community rights can coexist with the status of a protected area, although an official declaration may impose some restrictions and obligations. As to a human presence in protected areas, whether as residents or resource users, the IUCN protected area Categories V and VI are conceived to be quite inclusive, and greater restrictions on human activities normally apply in Categories I to IV. Table 5.1 is an exceedingly useful tool to assist in the development of a viable system of protected areas.

Table 5.1 A matrix to characterize protected areas by both management objective and governance type

Governance type / IUCN category	Government-managed protected areas			Co-managed protected areas			Private protected areas			Community conserved areas (CCAs)	
	Federal or national ministry or agency in charge	Local/municipal ministry or agency in change	Government-delegated management (e.g. to an NGO)	Transboundary management	Collaborative management (various forms of pluralist influence)	Joint management (pluralist management board)	Declared and run by individual landowner	Declared and run by non-profit organizations (e.g. NGOs, universities)	Declared and run by for profit organizations (such as individual or corporate landowners)	Declared and run by indigenous peoples	Declared and run by local communities
I Strict nature reserve/ Wilderness area											
II National park											
III Natural monument											
IV Habitat/species management											
V Protected landscape/ seascape											
VI Managed resource											

Source: Borrini-Feyerabend et al (2004b)

Scale of governance settings

Scale is an important consideration in governance settings. Local governance arrangements are often dependent upon customary requirements and norms and need to engage a variety of local actors in discussing, developing and implementing regulations. They are well suited for protected areas of limited size and specific local value. Arrangements at ecosystem level, suited for larger protected areas of IUCN Category II or V, tend to engage actors from different background and values, and to require specific efforts at communication and conflict management. Arrangements at national or international levels are best indicated to understand and optimize the collective value of a system of protected areas. They are often developed by people who have indirect stakes in the matters decided. Governance settings at different levels are frequently 'nested bodies' and need to fit one another, presupposing compatible rules and smooth communication. In general, every protected area needs to take scale into account as it fits within a broader landscape or seascape.

Requirements to make protected areas safe from the negative impacts of activities outside their boundaries have played an important role in international instruments, starting with the concept of 'buffer zones', where activities affecting the protected area are prohibited. The biosphere reserve (see 'Types of protected areas' in Chapter 3) is an international soft law instrument that broadened and refined this approach, providing also for 'transition areas', which can include ecological corridors. A further step has been the requirement to regulate processes and activities occurring well outside a protected area, but still likely to affect it.

Overall, the necessity is apparent to move from the governance of single isolated areas to the governance of several sites, planned to be representatives of the biodiversity of a region and to promote the genetic diversity of species through good biological connectivity. There is also a growing trend to take into account more comprehensively the social and economic factors surrounding the protected areas, towards social acceptability, transparency and sustainable development. This includes:

- fine-tuning to ecological needs the prohibitions enforced within protected areas, and allowing all human activities compatible with conservation;
- evaluating economic growth and development processes in and around protected areas, especially those that threaten ecosystem integrity or wildlife populations;
- building the capacity of stakeholders, particularly local or indigenous communities;
- empowering local stakeholders to play an active role in governing protected areas and providing incentives through benefit-sharing; and
- providing sufficient support, including financial support, towards ecological and socio-economic goals.

Other legal principles, tools and techniques relevant for the governance of protected areas and related to issues of scale address:

- requirements to provide for procedural rights (right to information, public participation and access to justice);
- requirements to follow the precautionary approach, enabling states to also take restrictive measures in the absence of fully scientifically established threats;
- international common responsibilities with differentiated national requirements and funding;
- requirements for equitable sharing of benefits deriving from the use of genetic resources between those husbanding these resources and those manufacturing products protected by intellectual property rights;
- international requirements to subject projects, plans and programmes to an environmental impact assessment (EIA);
- accountability at the regional or international level, through periodic reports by individual parties to the Conferences of the Parties to international treaties; and
- transfrontier obligations, whenever action, or lack of action, in a particular state significantly affects the environment of another, and joint management obligation, when resources are shared.

Transboundary protected areas (see Chapter 22) present particular challenges and risks. On the one hand, they typically involve and affect many parties and thus require some form of co-management. If the relevant border is a state border, this involves at least the protected area agencies of two or more governments, but can also involve the foreign affairs, agriculture, fishery, minerals and forestry ministries of those governments; several state, provincial, district or local authorities; communities and private landowners; and international NGOs. Often there are multiple legal systems at play, and the laws of various national or sub-national political units may confer different sets of rights and obligations upon institutions and individuals (Guillett, 2005). On top of what may be an already complex political landscape, their establishment superimposes a new set of institutions and rules (Wolmer, 2005). Interestingly, the governance of transboundary protected areas may also offer a model for the co-management of high-sea protected areas beyond the jurisdiction of any one country.

Governance roles of different actors

One of the most remarkable innovations in governing protected areas is the recognition of the possible roles and valuable capacities and comparative advantages of social actors besides national governmental agencies. This can be seen as part of a broader acceptance of pluralism as a fundamental value in public life, with pluralism defined as 'the recognition of the value and legitimacy of the concerns, capacities and institutions of different social and ethnic groups and the facilitation of their coexistence and collaboration for the common good'. As we have seen, some of these actors – such as indigenous peoples, local communities and private landowners – are the most ancient and far from 'new' actors in the governance of protected areas. Yet, it is important to provide them with a formal and explicit recognition of their roles.

In most countries, state agencies continue to fulfil crucial governance roles. Over the past 30

Professional park manager, Finland

Source: Grazia Borrini-Feyerabend

years, these agencies have increasingly engaged with communities and stakeholders (local, indigenous, 'the general public', recreationists and so on) to secure legitimate, equitable and effective management outcomes – see, for example, the many cases presented in Pansky (2005). In some cases, these engagements have led to formal co-management arrangements. It is also worth noting that not all protected areas have a 'local community' – examples include Heard Island and McDonald Islands World Heritage Area in the Southern Ocean and Antarctic protected areas. For others the local community may be content to allow the state to manage areas on its behalf and in the interests of the wider public. Governments are also well placed to 'represent' and give voice to 'silent nature', thereby meeting what some people perceive as a moral obligation to protect the intrinsic value of plants, animals and natural systems (see Chapter 4).

National and sub-national government agencies

Most of the world's protected areas and the major systems of protected areas are managed by governments, notwithstanding the significant increase in the number of privately managed protected areas, the growing recognition of CCAs as vital to conserve biodiversity and sustain communities, and the importance of NGOs. Government protected area agencies derive their legitimacy from democratic processes and play a significant role in securing the ongoing provision of the public good benefits associated with protected areas. The 'government', however, is not a monolithic entity within a country. On the contrary, governments are made up of different ministries, agencies, administrative levels and actors that work in tension, as well as in coordination, with one another. Protected areas governed by agencies at various levels and under various delegation arrangements may be markedly different. In particular, local, regional, provincial and national governments have different agendas, sources of local legitimacy and capabilities to deliver conservation.

Many protected area governance issues revolve around the balance of responsibility between protected area agencies and other actors. There is a possible continuum, ranging from full control by

a state agency to full control by other actors (see Table 5.1). During the past decade, a shift towards more collaborative decision-making has occurred. Cooperative decision-making, joint decision-making and delegated decision-making are now more prevalent, and very few national or sub-national protected area agencies operate under a model where government is the sole decision-maker. In recent years, many countries have also encouraged greater attention to regional differences through decentralization of protected area agencies. More than one third of the respondents to a 2002 international survey of government protected area agencies (Dearden et al, 2005) suggested that their agency structure is less centralized than was the case a decade earlier. As a result, decision-making power has been, and is being, increasingly delegated to various levels of government and other stakeholder groups. Participatory management is legally required for more than half of the protected area agencies that responded to the survey.

A major aspect of protected area governance by governmental agencies is the accountability to the public that they represent. Accountability mechanisms are designed to ensure that tasks and objectives are completed on time and that public funds are spent for the purpose for which they are intended. During the last decade, a trend towards the increased use of such mechanisms is evident. Accountability measures designed to involve the local community, improve communication between protected area managers and the public, and make the process more inclusive for stakeholders have become increasingly popular. Currently, approaches such as state of protected area reports, annual reports, external audits, national advisory committees, stakeholder roundtables and parliamentary debates are more frequently used than they were just a decade ago. Funding is another critical component of effective governance. There is an indication that, during the past decade, the proportion of protected area funding provided by government agencies and private donors decreased, while the proportion provided by NGOs and user fees increased (Dearden et al, 2005).

In recent decades, protected areas established and managed at provincial, regional and local level have become increasingly common. They can be simpler to declare, more flexible in terms of arrangements and budgeting, and better suited to the interests and concerns of the local actors. In addition, they can be open to innovative governance arrangements that directly involve the representatives of civil society, as shown in Case Study 5.1.

Case Study 5.1

Creating a system of governance of national parks in Scotland

Murray Ferguson, Cairngorms National Park Authority

In 1997, shortly after the first steps had been taken to establish the Scottish Parliament, the government announced a proposal to create a new system of national parks for Scotland. The intention was that this new park system should complement the existing family of protected areas (which consisted of national nature reserves, sites of special scientific interest, etc.), and should integrate conservation, public enjoyment and sustainable economic and social development of the areas' communities and natural resources. The proposal led to a national debate about what form the new national parks should take. Two of the most critical issues to be decided were what would be the most appropriate institutional framework and who should have authority in each of the new parks.

Scottish Natural Heritage (SNH), the government's conservation adviser, was asked to lead the debate and to advise ministers. SNH undertook a number of research reviews and based its initial advice on two rounds of public consultation. Particular efforts were made to gain the views of those people who lived and worked within the two areas proposed for designation as parks, around Loch Lomond and in the Cairngorms.

SNH recommended that the system should comprise new primary legislation setting out the purpose and criteria for designation of all Scottish national parks. Each park should be designated by secondary legislation and managed by a separate new organization, the National Park Authority. SNH also recommended that each park authority should have the status of non-departmental public body, should be financed entirely by central government and should have a governing board supported by a professional staff (SNH, 1999).

Ministers largely accepted SNH's advice and the relevant primary legislation was passed in the form of the National Parks (Scotland) Act 2000 with unanimous cross-party support. The act confirmed that the parks should be managed by the relevant park authority within a framework of national guidance provided by ministers. The maximum number of places on the board of each park authority was set at 25.

The legislation contained a number of innovative approaches to meet the challenges of designing appropriate systems of governance. These are best examined by looking at the particular circumstances of the Cairngorms National Park that was designated in 2003.

Loch Morlich, Cairngorms National Park, Scotland

Source: David Gowans

During the early discussions about the proposed parks, all parties agreed that a strong degree of local support for the parks was essential. One way of achieving this was to ensure that there were people who lived and worked in the area appointed to the board. This was achieved through a new system of direct elections in which only people living within the boundary of the park could vote. In the Cairngorms, where the board was to have 25 places, five of the places were to be elected in this way.

Case Study **5.1** continued

There is no doubt that this system is relatively expensive. Five new electoral wards had to be drawn up and postal voting forms issued to every registered voter in the park. But the final outcome has been extremely encouraging. In each of the five new electoral wards there were between four and six candidates competing for election. And the turnout was, on average, around 60 per cent compared to an average turnout of only 49 per cent in local elections in Scotland (Highland Council Deputy Returning Officer, pers comm, 2005).

It is also interesting to review who was elected. When the system was first proposed there had been some concern expressed locally that nationally prominent conservationists from outside the area would stand for election and would be likely to be elected because of their prominence. In fact, this never happened. In the end, the successful candidates had a very good knowledge of the area and, perhaps more importantly, excellent social networks and a wide range of contacts. For example, they included a veterinary surgeon, a doctor (and farmer), a postmaster and a person who had worked for many years in a local bank (also from a farming family).

It is notable that these directly elected places on the board complement the ten places available for nominees from participating local authorities (while the remainder are directly appointed by ministers from a pool of people who have applied on the basis of public advertisement). These local authority-nominated places have been filled, to date, by the elected members (councillors) for the local area. Therefore, in the Cairngorms 15 out of 25 (or 60 per cent) board members have a very significant degree of local democratic support for their participation in managing the national park.

With only 25 places available on the board, it was always going to be challenging to provide a sufficient level of involvement by the very wide range of stakeholder and interest groups. One of the approaches taken through the legislation has been to move away from the idea of appointment to the board on the basis of 'representation' of particular interest groups. The preferred system has involved appointment on the basis of skills, knowledge and experience of the national park and the issues that it is to address. One particular advantage of this approach is that each individual on the board comes to the table with more than one 'hat' and multiple perspectives are contributed to the resolution of issues. Another technique used to involve people in the debates about managing the area has been the establishment of a number of advisory forums on issues such as outdoor access and integrated land management.

Even if protected areas can be declared and managed at the sub-national level, government agencies at the national level continue to have unique roles to play as policy-makers, coordinators of protected area systems (whereby a system must be much more than the sum of its component protected areas), monitors and evaluators of performance and guiding agencies for training, and distributors of resources. These roles remain indispensable and some national agencies may need to strengthen these capacities rather than focus only on direct protected area management.

Non-governmental organizations

International, national and local NGOs dealing with environmental concerns have dramatically risen in number and influence during the last 30 years (see Chapter 2, p63). As an example, approximately 3000 NGOs with consultative status were accredited to participate in the 2002 Johannesburg Summit compared to 134 in the 1972 Stockholm Conference on the Human Environment. Furthermore, more than US$7 billion in private and government aid to developing countries now flows through NGOs, compared to US$1 billion in 1970.

Environmental NGOs are frequently involved in governing protected areas. At times, they act on the delegation of national governments (such as the Audubon Society in Belize). In other cases, they provide technical advice to the government agencies in charge or influence them by offering or withholding supportive funds or services, and/or by affecting the opinion of potential donors. NGOs can also manage protected areas on their own, especially when they can pull together enough resources to purchase the land. They can also play invaluable roles as promoters of coalitions of private owners to set up their own protected areas through land-use trusts (see Case Study 5.2).

Case Study 5.2

NGOs as catalysers of conservation easements between private landowners and the government

Land trusts are a key force in land protection in the US and Canada (Mitchell and Brown, 1998). Basically, they involve a partnership among an environmentally oriented NGO, some local authorities, state authorities (when relevant) and a number of local landowners. The NGO, at times staffed by volunteers and endowed only with a tiny budget, mobilizes to respond in a timely manner to special conservation opportunities or risks. It contacts a number of landowners in adjacent lands and convinces them to agree to some sound management practices, sign a conservation easement and/or donate their land for conservation purposes. The landowners are motivated by conservation values and positive social pressure, but also by the tax advantages provided by local authorities and/or the state to those who enter into such a partnership.

At times, the agreement is simply a verbal statement between the landowner and the NGO, with technical assistance sometimes provided to the landowner. It may include restrictions to certain types of land development, assurance of keeping the land under appropriate use (such as forestry or agriculture) or assurance of using specific management practices (such as integrated pest management or run-off control devices). In other cases, full management plans are agreed upon by the landowners and the NGO and a conservation easement (deed restriction) is signed. The latter formally prohibits 'in perpetuity' certain land uses (for example, infrastructure developments and buildings) and allows only others (for example, traditional agriculture). In other words, landownership is retained with restriction of uses. For an easement to be effective, a specific legislation needs to be developed and approved, usually to provide tax incentives to the signatories of the easement. An extreme form of easement is one in which the landowners donate their property to the NGO, which assumes the responsibility to manage it. There are now over 1200 land trusts in the US (one third of them in New England) and many are also found along the Atlantic Coast of Canada. The basic outcome is more land dedicated to conservation while people retain their property rights and also save in terms of taxes.

Source: J. Brown, pers comm., 2000

With respect to co-managed protected areas, NGOs can be full partners, with a role at times enshrined in national law, or, even more frequently, can play invaluable roles in facilitating the development of co-management by state and community partners, by acting as communicators, trainers, conveners, mediators, conflict managers and providers of legal, technical and administrative support. Many NGOs have taken upon themselves to assist indigenous peoples and local communities in assessing their legal rights pertaining to existing protected areas and/or establishing and managing their own protected areas.

NGOs can also powerfully influence protected areas through policy since many play advisory roles in national and international policy-making, acting as advocates for specific provisions within national legislation and international protected area agreements, such as the Convention on Biological Diversity (CBD), the World Heritage Convention or the Ramsar Convention. NGOs are also known to play a vital role in forging supra-national protected area agreements and initiatives and holding governmental agencies accountable for their action or lack of action on protected areas.

Conservation by NGOs is prominent in rich countries. Notable examples include conservation NGOs buying land for conservation purposes in the UK, Australia and the US. In the US, The Nature Conservancy has a system of more than 1300 reserves protecting well over half a million hectares (The Nature Conservancy, 2005). The Australian Bush Heritage Fund manages 19 reserves around Australia, covering more than 347,000ha (Australian Bush Heritage Fund, 2005). Such NGOs typically have a public trust responsibility that derives from a government-recognized status as non-profit corporations, which usually confers tax exemptions and other benefits.

Private landowners

Private landowners – including individuals, corporations, NGOs and communities – who dedicate their own land to conservation have added a sizeable proportion of the worldwide total of land under a protected status. Langholz and Krug (2005) prepared an extensive review of the contributions of private owners to conservation for the 2003 World Parks Congress. Unless otherwise indicated, much of the information in this section is derived from that paper. As surveyed by Langholz and Krug, the amount of land under private conservation in Southern Africa is estimated to be more than 14 million hectares (Krug, 2001). In South Africa alone, the amount under private governance is larger than under the national government agency (Peterson, 2003; see Case Study 5.3). A study of 63 Latin American and sub-Saharan private reserves revealed that they cover approximately 1 million hectares (Alderman, 1994). Private landowners in Costa Rica have established protected areas that cover 1.2 per cent of the national territory, or the equivalent of 4.5 medium-sized Costa Rican national parks (Langholz, 2002). Private landowners in Colombia and Brazil have established hundreds of reserves, and Chile, which has a policy to promote private parks, is home to Pumalin, the largest private park in Latin America (270,000ha in extent) (Langholz and Krug, 2005). Corporations are also increasingly willing to devote a part of their lands to conservation. Some oil refineries in India, for instance, are protecting wetlands harbouring migratory waterfowl populations (TPCG and Kalpavriksh, 2005). Companies or individuals owning large tea, coffee or other tree plantations have also, in some cases, set aside natural forest patches inside their estates.

Landowners willing to manage their land for some conservation objective have shown the tendency to pull their land together to form collaborative reserves and conservancies over larger, and thus more effective, units. In South Africa and Namibia, such 'conservancies' are common to allow large habitats for wildlife and the setting-up of tourist enterprises. The trend started with individual landowners and was later pursued by community landowners as well. While individual or group landownership is retained, all the units are managed as a single entity. Landowners can also join forces in non-profit land trusts, often established through conservation easements (see Case Study 5.2). Partnerships are also occurring between private landowners and the governmental agencies managing adjacent national parks, as described in Case Study 5.3.

Calculating the total number of private protected areas worldwide would require a globally accepted definition that currently does not exist. One definition describes private protected areas as 'any lands of more than 20ha that are intentionally maintained in a mostly natural state and are not government owned' (Langholz and Lassoie, 2001). Like state protected areas, these lands vary dramatically in size and uses, and go by myriad labels ranging from 'preserves', 'reserves' and 'conservancies' to 'parks' and 'protected areas'. Extensive information is not yet available as to whether private landowners tend to protect lands smaller in size than other protected areas, although this may be plausible. If proven, this would suggest that private protected areas can supplement but hardly substitute a government protected area network. Interestingly, however, private protection is frequently a precursor to public protection. Private parks can be established in threatened lands until governments become willing or able to assume responsibility for protection. A private land conservancy, for example, conserved a large tract of rare habitat in the central US until the Tallgrass Prairie National Preserve Act 1994 made it a formal public park unit.

A governance advantage of private landowners is the fact that national legislations often assign to them a very broad set of powers. A major drawback is their frequent lack of formality and the reversibility of their protection status. To remedy that, some countries (such as Madagascar) are considering legislation that accepts as formal 'private protected areas' only areas that inscribe the protection vocation in their property deeds, placing obligations not only the present but also future owners. The *Wild Life (Protection) Act 2002* in India contains a category of protected area, community reserves, which includes private lands.

Governments and society as a whole benefit from the biodiversity gains achieved on private

Case Study **5.3**

Marakele National Park and Marakele Park, Ltd: A South African public–private partnership

In South Africa, national and provincial governments have set aside over 7 million hectares of land as national parks or other protected areas. Although impressive, this total represents only 5.8 per cent of the country's total landmass, far short of the 10 per cent target set by the IUCN. Private landowners are filling this conservation gap, now managing and conserving nearly 16 million additional hectares for hunting, ecotourism, game ranching and mixed live stock and game enterprises. In many cases, the national protected area agency, SANParks, and private landowners have collaborated to effectively extend the size of major national parks.

An example of such a public–private partnership has developed around Marakele National Park in the Waterburg region. During the mid 1980s, SANParks had the vision to secure a large portion of the Waterberg as a national park (originally named Kransberg, but later to become Marakele). Over the course of ten years, SANParks acquired close to 40,000ha through a process of land expropriation and acquisition from willing sellers. To achieve its objectives for Marakele, however, SANParks needed to acquire a further 20,000ha of ecologically valuable habitat to the north.

In 1994, the agency forged a cooperative agreement with a Dutch businessman and conservationist named Paul Van Vlissingen to create a large contractual national park adjacent to Marakele. The idea was that Van Vlissingen would purchase several marginal cattle and hunting farms, convert the land to conservation purposes in collaboration with SANParks, and that ecotourism concessions could be run in this newly created Marakele Contractual Park. Thousands of kilometres of internal fencing were thus removed, along with old farming structures and houses, 55km of overhead power lines and telephone lines, cattle kraals and water piping. An alien species clearing project was initiated, and bush was cleared to restore areas overgrazed by cattle.

A large-scale programme was then initiated between SANParks and Marakele Ltd to reintroduce all of the game indigenous to the region, including species that had been absent for nearly 100 years. The process was completed within three years and the newly extended Marakele National Park–Marakele Contractual Park complex was launched at a ceremony in 2003. A further public–private partnership that same year brought down the fence between Marakele National Park and its neighbour to the east, Welgevonden Private Game Reserve, a private protected area nearly as large as the park itself. Together, Marakele National Park, Marakele Contractual Park and the Welgevonden Reserve now constitute a 110,000ha jointly managed protected area in which animals roam freely across public and private lands.

Similar public–private partnerships on the western boundary of Kruger National Park have effectively increased the size of the greater Kruger National Park management area by close to 10 per cent, and more partnerships of a similar nature can be anticipated as a result of recently passed tax incentives designed to encourage private sector partnerships with national and provincial parks.

Source: adapted from Anderson (2003)

protected areas, and from an extension of their national protected area systems. Local communities may also reap benefits due to jobs or improved ecological conditions. At the same time, however, there are concerns about equity and fairness when private landowners establish and manage protected areas. Usually, only the wealthy individuals and groups in society can afford to establish protected areas on their land, and when they do so, the public oversight may be minimal. There may be little opportunity for participation in private protected area decision-making, including by the neighbouring communities, and little to no accountability to the government or the public at large.

The quality of private reserve management and impacts on other groups in society varies greatly. Landowners are generally free to establish their own management objectives, allowable activities and level of protection, all of which may or may not be stated in formal management plans. Some owners only wish to conserve biodiversity and be a good neighbour to local communities; but others prioritize financial gain over conservation or social justice, such as when tourism operators build a large number of cabins, roads and other infrastructure on their lands despite detrimental impacts on wildlife and neighbouring areas (for example, because of water pollution, excessive traffic and so on). Negligence in achieving conservation objectives as well as disregard of negative social impacts are of particular concern where private reserve owners benefit from a reduction in taxes or other payments that would otherwise fill the public coffers.

Some have expressed concern that private parks may contribute to the concentration of landownership by the wealthy. Indeed, as stated by Langholz and Krug (2005, p8), 'a major social pitfall of private parks is that they can become islands of elites – places where wealthy landowners host affluent tourists'. As ecotourism and private hunting reserves grow in popularity and profitability, the value of land that can support such enterprises goes up. Depending upon the legal and political context, communities living on or near such lands may be forced to move away, either by threat of force or by economic necessity, or they may stay but lose the right to access game, medicinal plants or other resources on land that

has been designated a reserve. As Langholz and Krug (2005) note, questions of equity become even more troubling where foreign ownership is involved. They point to a study by Alderman (1994) which found that one third of private reserves in Africa and one fifth of private reserves in Latin America were exclusively foreign owned.

As private landowners continue and enhance their involvement in protected areas, there is a need for them to build upon their strengths while improving their governance system as much as possible. They could, for instance, promote community involvement in their work, share benefits by offering employment, or assist communities to feel ownership and pride in the local environment and wildlife. At the same time, governments need to strengthen the legal framework for private land conservation, so that individuals and groups can more easily establish and manage protected areas though easements, concessions, conservation trusts or financial incentives. Governments can also play a proactive role in monitoring and evaluating the effectiveness and equity of the private conservation efforts.

Manu people, Manu National Park, Peru

Source: IUCN Photo Library © IUCN/Jeffrey McNeely

Chiefs of the community of Peruanito in Abinico del Pastaza wish their own conserved areas to be recognized by the government as 'communal reserves', Peru

Source: Linda Norgrove

Indigenous peoples, local communities and civil society

Indigenous peoples, local communities and civil society, in general, are possibly the latest to have become formally recognized as protected area managers, but they are the oldest in terms of historical experience. Over centuries, communities of hunter–gatherers, herders, fishing folks and agriculturalists have managed the natural resources they held in common property. The interaction between people and nature has been intimate and profound, affecting livelihoods but also the spiritual, religious, magic and symbolic values ascribed to nature, and the sense of cultural identity of the people themselves. Some have used the term 'ethnic governance' to describe the myriads of systems of organizations and rules that developed in particular socio-ecological contexts (Bassi, 2003). There are no general patterns for such systems, as they are tailored to the context and consist of interlocked beliefs, patterns of traditional behaviours and rules. Many such rules are also overlapping (for example, some resources are collectively owned and regulated; other resources are individually owned and managed, or managed on a clan basis; still others are managed together with other communities and groups) and have a tendency to vary with the climate and the seasons in order to accommodate the changing situations of communities.

A 'community' is a human group sharing a territory and involved in different but related aspects of livelihoods – such as managing natural resources, developing productive technologies and practices, and producing knowledge and culture. We speak of a local community when its members are likely to have face-to-face encounters and/or direct mutual influences in their daily life – whether they are permanently settled or mobile. Their identity and cultural characteristics are generally related to the 'ethnic governance' systems mentioned above, and they commonly evolve together.

While most people have an intuitive understanding of what a local community is, this is not the case for the term 'indigenous peoples'. The term is rich and nuanced, loaded with political implications and evolving in meaning. According to the International Labour Organization Convention 169, indigenous peoples include:

- tribal peoples in independent countries whose social, cultural and economic conditions distinguish them from other sections of the national community, and whose status is regulated wholly or partially by their own customs or traditions or by special laws or regulations; and
- peoples in independent countries who are regarded as indigenous on account of their descent from the populations that inhabited the country, or a geographical region to which the country belongs, at the time of conquest or colonization or the establishment of present state boundaries and who, irrespective of their legal status, retain some or all of their own social, economic, cultural and political institutions.

Also according to the convention, self-identification as indigenous or tribal will be regarded as a fundamental criterion for determining the groups to which the provisions of the convention apply. Among the criteria used by indigenous peoples to identify themselves as such are their own historical continuity with pre-colonial societies; the close relationship with the land and natural resources of their own territory; their peculiar socio-political system; their own language, culture, values and beliefs; and the fact of not belonging to the dominant sectors of their national society and seeing themselves as different from it.

Indigenous peoples and local communities have various advantages and limitations as managers and/or owners of protected areas, many of which relate to the collective nature of their perceived rights and to the complex and porous nature of their governance systems.

Most indigenous peoples and local communities advocate for collective rather than individual rights to their lands and resources, and such a collective approach has proven to be beneficial from a biodiversity conservation standpoint (Oviedo, 2003). This is because collective rights to land and natural resources are the basis for maintaining the integrity of a territory, avoiding ecological fragmentation and fostering long-term objectives – key requirements for biodiversity conservation. Collective rights also provide a strong basis for the building and functioning of community institutions, which are indispensable for sound long-term land and resource management. And, last but not least, collective rights strengthen the role of customary law and may provide the foundation for formal legal recognition of community landownership.

Besides being the repository of age-old knowledge and skills, carved on the specifics of given territories and resources, community-based forms of governance can also be flexible and responsive, bending around a variety of factors and responding to circumstances in ways that can be rapid and effective. The limitations are related to the fact that indigenous peoples and local communities may be required – as managers – to respond to the formal requirements of state governments, something they may find difficult to do for a variety of reasons. For instance, their forms of representations may not fit the national requirements or their skills in reporting, and accounting may be limited. In other cases, the sets of principles and values that regulate the traditional institutions may be at odds with the ones of the state. There is frequently also an inability to deal with external threats and challenges. In general, it is the interface between 'traditional' and 'modern' systems that is at stake. The advantages

and limitations of indigenous peoples and local communities as protected area managers and/or owners are important, and become even more so when one brings in the issue of socio-economic, cultural and environmental rights. For people whose livelihoods and cultural identity are intimately related with the natural resources of a protected territory, its governance can be much more important than for the rest of society.

Chapter 21 explores, in depth, CCAs – that is, those areas and resources where indigenous peoples and local communities play the principal governance role – while Chapter 20 discusses cases in which they more or less formally participate in governance partnerships with others. Both chapters contain a variety of specific examples in which indigenous peoples and local communities shape and affect the governance of protected areas. Other less clear-cut cases exist, however. These typically include situations in which 'civil society' is at stake.

Civil society refers to a variety of collective actors and initiatives – distinct from family, state and the market – that maintain a degree of autonomy, ensure space and nourishment for pluralism, and engage in critically constructive relationships with politics and public policy. In this sense, all sorts of spontaneous, voluntary and evolving associations attempting to influence decision-making in protected areas belong to civil society and represent a formidable potential for conservation. At times, however, they also represent a considerable source of instability and perceived problems. Associations created specifically to develop and exert that influence on a particular protected area are usually very influential. Such associations can challenge external threats to protected areas, but can also reject, and fight against, management decisions by government.

There exist infinite possible pathways by which lay actors and civil society can influence collective decisions. Those span all sorts of 'powers', from power of position to the power of unique knowledge; from personal, family or group influence to economic might; from political influence and legal expertise to violent coercion or non-violent civil disobedience. These powers can be brought to bear, more or less openly, upon official decision-makers. Because of the specific voluntary and evolving character of the initiatives by civil society, it is not easy to analyse them. A typical model is the one of the natural regional parks of France (see Case Study 3.6 in Chapter 3), where workshops, broad consultations and public deliberations are widely used to discuss and develop ideas that will later be transformed in management priorities and decisions. But there may be less fair pathways of influence. For instance, during a participatory evaluation of the co-management setting of the Galapagos Marine Reserve (Ecuador) participants noted that – beyond the official and relatively transparent ways by which power was shared among stakeholder groups and concurred to determine technical choices and decisions – it was much simpler and sometimes more effective to affect the top of the decision-making chain with a persuasive phone call! Some, in fact, are critical of the 'undemocratic' nature of the engagement of civil society since active engagement of a few, and not the counted votes of the majority of those having legitimate rights, appears as the key source of influence.

International governance institutions

There is increasing recognition of the value of multilateral legal instruments in strengthening conservation at the national level and in achieving global conservation goals. This is evidenced by the formidable list of international conventions relating to both natural and cultural conservation, with direct and indirect implications for protected areas, which has developed over the past 30 years. Such conventions are also viewed as a means of achieving intergenerational equity. International environmental law is expressed mostly as agreed obligations and duties of individual countries. These involve specific treaties and binding principles (hard law), but also non-binding resolutions and declarations (soft law). Overall, both have a powerful guiding influence, especially for those states that participated in the drafting of the relevant texts.

International governance of protected areas comprises a complex system of hard and soft laws. Jeffrey (2004) describes soft law initiatives, such as the United Nations Educational, Scientific and Cultural Organization's (UNESCO's) Man and the Biosphere (MAB) programme, and hard law treaties, such as the United Nations Convention on Biological Diversity (CBD) (see Chapter 3, p79). The latter includes an article addressing *in situ* conservation, which calls upon parties to establish a system of protected areas or areas where special measures are taken to conserve biological diversity. Protected area systems are to be established and managed in the context of the three goals of the convention:

1   conservation of biodiversity;
2   sustainable development; and
3   equitable access to, and benefit-sharing from, genetic resources.

In 2004, a specific Programme of Work on Protected Areas was adopted under the CBD (see Appendix 4).

Protected areas are recognized by both hard and soft laws as a critical tool for the conservation of biological diversity. Starting from early provisions, such as the 1940 Convention on Nature Protection and Wildlife Preservation in the Western Hemisphere, states are mandated to maintain existing protected areas and establish new ones. This general guidance became global in character with the adoption of the 1992 CBD, although the Programme of Work on Protected Areas mentioned above was adopted only in 2004 – one of the last programmes of work to be decided by the parties.

Concerted international action is called for to achieve conservation objectives at various geographic levels (local, national, regional and international). Early regional action was called for by the *Migratory Bird Convention Act 1916* between the US and Great Britain on behalf of Canada. This provided, among other matters, for the establishment of refuges. Global requirements started later with the Ramsar Convention, the World Heritage Convention, the Convention on Migratory Birds and the CBD. Through time, the standards for biodiversity conservation and the relevant strategies and techniques have also tended to become global. This, however, did not diminish the usefulness and benefits of regional governance arrangements (see Case Study 5.4).

Case Study **5.4**

Protocol Concerning Specially Protected Areas and Wildlife in the Wider Caribbean Region

The Protocol Concerning Specially Protected Areas and Wildlife (the SPAW Protocol) adopted under the Convention for the Protection and Development of the Marine Environment of the Wider Caribbean Region (Cartagena Convention) became international law in 2000. It is an example of a successful regional approach to protecting important ecosystem habitats and species. The SPAW Protocol preceded other multilateral environmental agreements in utilizing an ecosystem approach to conservation and addressing sustainable development objectives. The protocol deals with the establishment of protected areas and buffer zones for *in situ* conservation of wildlife, but also with national and regional measures for collaboration.

The United Nations Environment Programme (UNEP) provides the secretariat for the convention and its protocols in Kingston, Jamaica, and assists the governments of the region. In terms of authority, responsibility and accountability, the convention and the SPAW Protocol constitute a legal commitment by the countries of the region to protect, develop and manage their common coastal and marine resources individually and jointly. Countries that are parties to the protocol are thus accountable to their own citizens and to the wider region. As a means of achieving this, Article 19 of the protocol requires that parties report on the status of existing and newly established protected areas, buffer zones and protected species in areas over which they exercise sovereignty or sovereign rights or jurisdiction. They also have a duty to document any changes in the delimitation or legal status of protected areas, buffer zones and protected species.

Source: adapted from Vanzella-Khouri (2005)

Quality of protected area governance

The Durban Congress (see Appendix 3) and Convention on Biological Diversity Programme of Work on Protected Areas (see Appendix 4) stressed the need to recognize and support different types of protected area governance, but also encouraged improving the 'quality of governance', regardless of type. This is to be pursued by establishing criteria, principles and values to guide action – an area that, to date, still has to be systematically explored.

For some, governance is improved by curbing the power of the state, releasing a country's trade barriers and opening up as much as possible to the influence, values and working style of the private sector and markets (Rhodes, 1996). In some cases, this type of 'good governance' is utilized as a form of aid conditionality, meaning that the requirements of good governance may be an excellent means through which the perspectives of lending countries can be imposed on poorer governments.

For others, improving governance means highlighting pluralist debate, fair procedures, negotiation processes and the seeking of consensus among various actors as the best foundations for decision-making in society (deliberative processes and participatory democracy) (Borrini-Feyerabend et al, 2004a; Pimbert, 2004). By curbing the power of the state and favouring the appreciation of cultural differences, pluralistic governance would have a liberating value, and it might even usher the dissolving of uncritical certainties about the foundations of power, laws and knowledge in society.

For others still, good governance is the meeting point of performance and equity, an evolving process through which fundamental principles and values, including environmental rights and human rights, can percolate in society (UNDP, 1999, 2002). This is the position often advanced by some United Nations (UN) agencies and by professionals who believe that a fundamental tenet of good governance should be decent, fulfilling and sustainable livelihoods.

Other contrasting views are found with respect to the supposed relationship between governance of natural resources – protected areas in particular – and governance of a country's polity at large. Some believe that the good gover-

Participatory evaluation of the governance of Galapagos National Park, Ecuador

Source: Grazia Borrini-Feyerabend

nance in the realm of natural resources cannot happen without good governance in society at large. Others consider that improvements in the first can be an effective entry point to lift up governance standards in other sectors in society as well.

Inspiration can be taken from a variety of principles that have been discussed and already endorsed internationally. Considerable work towards establishing a set of principles of good governance has been done by the UN as part of both its overall work on human rights and the promotion of public involvement in environmental governance prompted since the 1992 United Nations Conference on Environment and Development (UNCED). In the UN discussions, it is generally understood that governance princi-

ples are to be interpreted within their particular context of application (history, culture, technology and economic conditions) and that complexities abound (indeed, 'the devil is in the detail'). Two volumes that were prepared for the Vth IUCN World Parks Congress take inspiration from the UN work and recommend that both protected area systems and individual protected areas engage in participatory governance evaluation processes (Abrams et al, 2003; Graham et al, 2003). This is probably the ideal way to proceed, as no one better than the relevant social actors (stakeholders) can understand and define what constitutes good governance in a given situation. Table 5.2 draws from all the documents cited above and takes the analysis forward to reflect upon the specific responsibilities of protected areas managers.

Table 5.2 Proposed governance principles for protected areas

Governance principles	The United Nations principles upon which the governance principles are based	Related governance responsibilities that can be taken on by the official protected area managers and fostered by various other actors
Legitimacy and voice	*Participation:* all men and women should have a voice in decision-making, either directly or through legitimate intermediate institutions that represent their intention. Such broad participation is built on freedom of association and speech, as well as capacities to participate constructively	Promoting the free expression of views, with no discrimination related to gender, ethnicity, social class and so on (yet, positive discrimination may be required in some situations to address historical injustices) Fostering dialogue and achieving collective agreements on management objectives and strategy, activities and tools to pursue them
	Consensus orientation: good governance mediates differing interests to reach a broad consensus on what is in the best interest of the group and, where possible, on policies and procedures	Fostering relations of trust among stakeholders Making sure that rules are respected because they are 'owned' by people and not solely because of fear of repression Promoting associations of citizens to deal with protected area issues and securing the role of an independent media.
	Subsidiarity: this is not a UN principle, but a principle of the European Union (EU), stating that decisions should be taken at the level closest to the issues at stake taking into account relevant capacities	If a new protected area is to be established, ensuring the participation and respect for the legal and customary rights of the relevant indigenous peoples, local communities and other stakeholders
Equity	*Fairness of opportunity:* all men and women have opportunities to improve or maintain their well-being	Making sure that conservation is undertaken with decency: without humiliation or harm to people Promoting participatory mechanisms for decision-making about the protected area
	Rule of law: legal frameworks are fair and enforced impartially, particularly the laws on human rights	Providing fair avenues for conflict management and, as needed, non-discriminatory recourse to justice, as well as for recognizing and dealing with past injustices resulting from the establishment of protected areas Ensuring that the governing mechanisms (such as laws, policies conflict-resolution forums, funding opportunities and so on) distribute equitably the costs and benefits deriving from conservation Ensuring public service promotions that are merit based and equitable human resource management practices for protected area staff Being consistent through time and impartial in enforcing the protected area laws and regulations

Table 5.2 Continued

Governance principles	The United Nations principles upon which the governance principles are based	Related governance responsibilities that can be taken on by the official protected area managers and fostered by various other actors
Direction	*Strategic vision:* leaders and the public have a broad and long-term perspective on good governance and human development, along with a sense of what is needed for such development *Embracing complexities:* the historical, cultural and social complexities in which the long-term perspective is grounded are understood and taken into account effectively	Listening to people, understanding their concerns, and fostering the generation and support of innovative ideas and processes Providing effective leadership by fostering and maintaining an inspiring and consistent vision for the long-term development of the protected area, mobilizing support for this vision and garnering the necessary resources to implement the relevant plans Clarifying specific objectives for the protected areas, as well as partnerships, and associated adaptive management initiatives Ensuring consistency with international conventions, national legislation and agreements, and traditional or 'modern' best practices Providing a model of good conduct Being consistent in what it is said and done
Performance	*Responsiveness:* institutions and processes try to serve all stakeholders *Effectiveness and efficiency:* processes and institutions produce results that meet needs while making the best use of resources	Making sure that there is sufficient and well-coordinated institutional and human capacity to carry out the required roles and assume the relevant responsibilities Making sure there is sufficient and timely material, financial ability and information capacity to undertake the required functions, as well as a competent administration, cost effective in achieving objectives Ensuring a management structure that is robust and resilient, and that is able to overcome a variety of threats or obstacles and come out strengthened from the experiences Dealing with complaints and criticism in a responsive and constructive manner Regularly engaging in monitoring and evaluation, and changing in response to findings as part of an adaptive management strategy

Table 5.2 Continued

Governance principles	The United Nations principles upon which the governance principles are based	Related governance responsibilities that can be taken on by the official protected area managers and fostered by various other actors
Accountability	*Accountability:* decision-makers are accountable to the public, as well as to institutional stakeholders. This accountability differs depending upon the organizations and whether the decision is internal or external	Making sure that stakeholders possess an adequate quantity and quality of knowledge regarding what is at stake in decision-making, who is responsible for what, how their performance can be evaluated, and how the responsible actors can be made accountable
		Making sure that the public avenues to demand accountability are accessible to all and are effective
	Transparency: transparency is built on the free flow of information. Processes, institutions and information are directly accessible to those concerned with them. Enough information is provided to understand and monitor institutions and their decision-making processes	Ensuring that accountability is not limited to verbal exchanges but linked to concrete and appropriate rewards and sanctions
		Making sure that the media is allowed to carry out rule-based investigative reporting, particularly about allegations of corruption

Source: modified from Borrini-Feyerabend et al (2004a)

Typically, national governments are responsible for their systems of protected areas and should be accountable for both management effectiveness (see Chapter 24) and good governance (see Case Study 5.5). For the first, governments have to develop and assign the relevant capacities and ensure the overall socio-political conditions within which protected areas can prosper. For the second, governments need to ensure fair and well-enforced legislation and rules, but also leave the necessary space for civil society to organize and take on autonomous or collaborating roles. In this sense, a growing number of conservation professionals are considering that the good governance of protected areas depends upon the overall power relations between civil society and government, the quality of government, and the quality of engagement of other actors. Respect for human rights of all parties, as well as for the intrinsic value of nature, is central.

The government is not the only actor that can foster improvements in the governance of protected areas. NGOs, in particular, have many roles to play. NGOs can foster good governance by serving as providers of information and innovative ideas, mobilizers of the public, promoters of associations and coalitions, providers of financial support, and facilitators of dialogues and negotiation processes (Alcorn et al, 2005a). NGOs can also provide technical support and training (in particular, for smaller and younger NGOs), monitor compliance of environmental law and policies, and serve as policy advocates and as proponents for a variety of improvements and concerns (for example, by creating demand for certified goods or assisting people to get to court).

Although NGOs can do much to improve governance of protected areas, Alcorn et al (2005a) caution that they also have limitations and can inadvertently have negative impacts. NGOs can overstep their roles, absorb all of the available resources or centralize upon themselves all technical issues, thereby disempowering the local actors. They can also become unduly enmeshed in local politics by selecting only certain local or national partners. International NGOs can weaken some stakeholders, strengthen others, create new conflicts or override local agendas and priorities. Inadequate attention to local decision-making, exacerbation of social inequality and inequitable distribution of benefits can increase tensions and threats to protected areas over the long term and cause a

Case Study 5.5

Accountability framework for Parks Canada

Parks Canada is one of the oldest government protected area organizations in the world and was originally established as a parks branch in 1911. Since then, it has been reorganized several times until, in 1998, it became an agency of the federal government through the Parks Canada Agency Act. Its mandate is to protect and present nationally significant examples of Canada's natural and cultural heritage, and to foster public understanding, appreciation and enjoyment in ways that ensure the ecological and commemorative integrity of these places for present and future generations.

Parks Canada reports to the minister of the environment who is, in turn, accountable to parliament and the broad Canadian electorate. Parks Canada is required by law to produce system plans and management plans, yearly reports and, every two years, a *State of Protected Heritage Areas Report*. This report assesses the ecological and commemorative integrity of Canada's heritage places, services offered to visitors and progress in establishing new sites. A sustainable development strategy is prepared every three years, outlining Parks Canada's efforts to integrate environmental, economic and social factors in its work.

As a further accountability measure, a citizens' roundtable is convened every two years to advise the minister on the performance by the agency. The minister must respond within 180 days to any written recommendations submitted by the roundtable. A further formal way for citizens to speak their mind is through the environmental petitions process managed by the auditor general of Canada. Federal ministers who receive petitions are compelled to provide a response within 120 days of receiving the petition.

backlash against conservation organizations. Foreign NGOs, in particular, need to take care not to implement programmes at the local level without explicit attention to governance issues, and without detailed knowledge of community history and dynamics. Finally, Alcorn et al (2005a) note that NGOs, unlike governments and community-based organizations, are not elected or otherwise dependent upon the support of the local or national citizenry. This means that they are not accountable to citizens for the results of their actions.

A third social actor that can take a major role in improving the governance of protected areas is indigenous peoples and local communities, who can be very effective with regard to the sites that they govern themselves or in partnership with others. Lessons from CCAs (see Chapter 21) can be important in resolving conflicts and achieving more effective management of government-designated and managed areas. The terms 'indigenous peoples' and 'local communities' may give the impression that these bodies are internally homogenous entities, whereas they may differ greatly along social (access to status), economic (access to resources) and political (access to power) lines. This

may result in a range of inequities internal to the communities. Thus, women are often disadvantaged compared to men, those without land compared to landowners, the young vis-à-vis the elders, the 'lower' castes relative to the 'higher' ones, and the poorer sections compared to the rich. In mixed communities, indigenous people may be weaker relative to non-indigenous ones. No such inequity is universally valid; but all of them are significant in many countries. Who can take remedial steps? The indigenous peoples and local communities themselves have major roles to play. So do outside actors, including government agencies and civil society organizations. Through joint analysis and dialogue with the people directly affected, remedial action can be devised, as well as efforts to prevent or diminish any inequity likely to be enhanced by conservation policies and practices. This may involve:

• providing decision-making opportunities to underprivileged groups – for example, by ensuring their representation on relevant conservation or management bodies;
• helping to improve the capacity of underprivileged groups; and

- ensuring that the benefits of conservation and resource-use initiatives accrue in fair proportion to economically or socially underprivileged sections of the community.

In general, conservation practices and human rights are linked in complex ways. Supporting human rights often has positive consequences for the environment; but there are cases in which human rights initiatives (such as provision of housing and shelters of refugees) have directly caused serious environmental problems. It may also be, on the other hand, that fear of infringing upon human rights may restrict conservationists from initiating needed measures to protect endangered ecosystems and species. Conversely, conservation understood as 'sustainable use' is essential to promote livelihood security and to fight against poverty – themes central to human rights. Yet, there are many known cases of conservation efforts carried out in ways that directly violate human rights, not least through forced resettlement, sedentarization and exclusion, and through the economic and cultural impoverishment of entire communities. Efforts to improve the governance of protected areas need to pay crucial attention to respecting and upholding human rights.

Governance awareness and innovations

It is important to ground our governance analysis in history, as history offers us a key to understand many current phenomena (see Box 5.1). In the last few decades, for instance, governments have increasingly experimented with models of protected areas that see actors other than the state as guarantors of conservation (Dearden et al, 2005). The concerns, capacities and resources of NGOs, the private sectors, research institutions, sub-national agencies and indigenous peoples and local communities have been better recognized in policy and also, at times, in practice. Protected landscapes have been explicitly valuing and upholding local knowledge and skills, and involving civil society in management functions (for example, throughout Europe and, increasingly, in South America). National legislations have allowed for large stretches of ecologically sensitive areas to be managed with regulations established in partnerships with local communities (for example, in the Annapurna Conservation Area of Nepal; King Mahendra Trust, 1994). Project-supported initiatives have pursued uneasy compromises between state agencies and local communities, as in the Amarakaeri Communal Reserve in Peru (Oviedo, 2003), the Ramsar site of Lake Alotra in Madagascar (Rakotoniaina and Durbin, 2004) or the Cardamom Mountain National Park in Cambodia (Appleton, 2004). In line with decentralization policies, more protected areas have also been created at sub-national level (as with the regional natural parks of France), by the private sector (as in South Africa) or assigned to be managed by NGOs (as in Belize).

The topic of governance of protected areas was a central focus at the 2003 World Parks Congress, and delegates from around the world gathered in its 'Governance Stream' to discuss, recognize, examine and celebrate a diversity of governance types and the meaning of 'good governance' in protected area contexts. Much of the new thinking that emerged was summarized in specific recommendations produced by the stream, as well as in the *Durban Accord* and *Action Plan* and in the *Congress Message to the Convention on Biological Diversity* (see Appendix 3). Just a few months after the congress, the parties to the CBD gathered at their seventh conference in Kuala Lumpur, Malaysia, and strengthened the innovations developed in Durban, identifying 'governance' as one of the key elements of their Programme of Work on Protected Areas (see Appendix 4). In the space of a few months, the concept had moved from relative obscurity to occupy an important place in the concerns of protected area managers. The most important international treaty on biodiversity had recognized that the concept could play a powerful and positive role for conservation and equity.

The relatively fast emergence of the concept of governance of a protected area may appear odd and promote scepticism. One has to consider, however, that this happened at the heart of a broad change in perspective on protected areas overall. On the one hand, this change was promoted by decentralization and structural adjustment policies, which tended to reduce the role of state governments in public affairs. These are eminently practical concerns, as conservation needs the support, concurrence and resources of the relevant communities and many other actors. On the other hand, change was promoted by the emerging awareness of the socio-economic impact of conservation.

In a climate committed to the eradication of poverty (see Chapter 2, p51), it makes no sense to set up poverty eradication programmes alongside conservation initiatives that result in greater poverty. Thus, governance considerations emerged hand in hand with ethical concerns. They also appeared to fit a growing awareness of the rights of indigenous peoples and local communities through the efforts of UN agencies and specific covenants and conventions.

Thus, it is within this broad climate of emerging concerns for efficiency and equity that we can best understand the new governance awareness about protected areas and the policy innovations that it introduced. Two topics appear central to such policy innovations: the 'type' and 'quality' of protected areas governance – in other words, new answers to the key questions of 'who?' and 'how?' about protected areas.

The governance typology introduced at the World Parks Congress drew inspiration from existing practices and, in turn, inspired specific countries to innovate. A case in point is Madagascar, which in 2005 adopted the matrix presented in Table 5.1 as a model to develop its new system of protected areas. The Malagasy Vision Durban Group – comprising the key governmental and non-governmental actors concerned with conservation policy – recognized that only by taking advantage of regional protected areas, co-management, CCAs and private protected areas would it have a chance of carrying out the ambitious conservation programme envisaged and announced by Madagascar's president at the congress (Borrini-Feyerabend and Dudley, 2005). For other countries, inspiration was provided to offer greater and stronger legitimacy to more participatory governance arrangements. With due cautions regarding final results, relevant innovative processes are proceeding in countries as diverse as Iran, Peru, Senegal, Cambodia, the Philippines and

Italy. In general, new actors are becoming better accepted as bearers of governance roles; as a consequence, new areas are being included in national protected area systems.

Why did the Durban Congress and Convention on Biological Diversity Programme of Work place such emphasis on understanding, and acting upon, the governance of protected areas? There would be no reason to complicate the field of conservation without real necessity and benefits. As mentioned, however, protected areas have progressively become more ambitious, enlarging their size and assuming more complex tasks in the environment, while irrevocable damages to the natural non-protected environment have progressed unabated. People are more conscious than ever about the need to establish comprehensive and effective conservation systems, and of the challenge that this implies. The challenge involves extending current protected area coverage to close the gaps that still exist about specific ecosystems and species, and to ensure the physical connectivity essential for their long-term survival. It also involves uplifting and dramatically improving the management of the protected areas that already exists. For both of these challenges, the concept of governance is crucial:

- Attention to governance types broadens the spectrum of the social actors recognized as legitimate protected area managers and the perspective on the estate that can be formally protected – essential for coverage and connectivity.
- Attention to governance types diversifies the social actors engaged in conservation, which is an important factor in resilience and sustainability.
- Attention to governance quality introduces considerations of principles and values, affecting what is considered as possible and desirable for protected areas, as well as the overall perception of civil society and its desire to be engaged and supportive.
- The possibility of utilizing a flexible and pluralist tool, such as the matrix of Table 5.1, can be central to developing a viable system of protected areas.

Coverage, connectivity and sustainability

Let us imagine that a government decides to officially recognize different governance types for protected areas. Under such a scenario, community conserved areas and areas set under protection regimes by their owners (individuals, corporations or NGOs) could acquire full legitimacy alongside government managed protected areas and co-managed protected areas. Surveys of the existing or planned conservation practices of local communities and individual, corporate or NGO landowners could be carried out as part of regional planning exercises to identify the candidates for official recognition. The opportunities to combine the conservation potential of diversely governed protected areas, to address gaps in the national system of protected areas, to improve connectivity and to optimize the protection of biodiversity would be greatly enhanced.

For example, where any form of protected area borders a government managed protected area (see Case Study 5.3), there is potential to manage the two in an integrated way in order to improve conservation outcomes. Private protected areas or CCAs that are biologically connected to government managed areas may contain crucial habitat or resources for threatened species. If the private landowners or communities and the government managers agree to remove fences and/or establish a shared management strategy for the entire habitats, the effective range available to wildlife is increased. It can also be argued that by incorporating a diversity of governance types, a system of protected areas becomes more resilient, responsive and adaptive since economic, social and ecological changes affect different types of protected areas in different ways. Wars and civil strife, for instance, may lead a government agency to withdraw from an area that it is managing; but local communities who own, manage or co-manage a protected area may remain in place and continue to carry out their conservation practices and enforce their rules. Also, in cases where urgent action is needed to avert an impending danger, a private individual, a community or an NGO may have more flexibility than a governmental agency to rapidly undertake the necessary actions. By combining different capacities to respond to both threats and opportunities, a protected area system that comprises various governance types would be more effective overall and more sustainable in the long run.

Given the size, complexity and impending global changes facing protected areas systems, it is increasingly recognized that many national governments confront an impossible task in attempting to ensure, alone, the accomplishment of all of their conservation objectives. Fortunately, an impressive wealth and diversity of conservation-relevant knowledge, skills, resources and institutions are also at the disposal of indigenous peoples and local communities, local governments, NGOs and the private sector.

The collective conservation potential represented by various types of governance of protected areas is thus enormous and most timely. National governments are aware of the potential represented by this 'governance variety' and have begun to harness it through appropriate forms of recognition, support and collaboration (see Case Study 5.6).

Attention to governance quality – that is, to principles such as participation, equity, direction, performance and accountability – is likely to prompt a variety of policy measures, from the recognition of customary rights to the provision of economic incentives for conservation. In turn, these tend to promote dialogue and collaboration with communities and landowners, enhancing public awareness and support for conservation, and strengthening the relationship between people and nature.

The acceptance and legitimization of a pluralist conservation system is also likely to promote relationships of mutual respect, communication and support between and among people managing protected areas under different governance types. This is bound to promote much needed exchanges and action research to explore governance principles, requirements and results. It is also bound to enhance capacities and promote management effectiveness, particularly through learning by doing. The IUCN is working towards an agreed-upon nomenclature of governance types and the incorporation of the governance matrix within a revision of the IUCN category

Case Study 5.6

An integrated approach to protected area governance, Colombia

Colombia is one country that is well on its way to formally recognizing a diversity of protected area governance types and incorporating them within the national protected areas system. The country's National Natural Parks System (SPNN) was established in 1968 as a traditional network of government-owned and managed protected areas; but, over the past decade, the system has embraced participatory approaches and granted formal recognition to co-managed, community managed and private protected areas. The result has been a significantly expanded and more effectively managed protected areas system.

The traditional SPNN is composed of 49 protected areas spanning more than 9 million hectares and accounting for 9 per cent of the nation's continental area. Given the high biodiversity rates of the country, however, the system is not complete in the sense that it does not cover all of the areas where valuable biodiverse resources are located. Moreover, for many years the SPNN operated with little regard for the social and economic conditions in and around protected areas, creating hostility and resistance in the local communities. Lack of budgetary funds, lack of accountability and lack of law enforcement were major issues.

Recognizing the limits inherent in its approach to protected areas, in 1998 the SPNN implemented a Policy for Social Participation in Conservation that has been striving towards the effective participation of local peasant communities, indigenous peoples and other local stakeholders in protected area management. An additional objective of the new policy is to increase the number of protected hectares in the nation by developing several smaller regional protected area systems, to be formed by regional and local reserves, private landowners and other landholders interested in conservation. The final result is a parks system with high levels of community participation in the management of each of the component parks, along with a decentralized protected area scheme that integrates national parks with regional and local parks, private reserves, community conserved areas (CCAs) and, in some cases, indigenous territories.

An important example of integrated governance in protected area management is the co-management of Cahuinari National Natural Park, which partially overlaps the Miraña indigenous reservation in the Colombian Amazon. The conservation strategy of the park has been developed by the Bora – Miraña indigenous communities – and the government management agency. The indigenous communities located within the protected area and the park administration have collaborated in several natural resource management initiatives, including programmes and specific commitments to regulate the use of threatened species such as the giant South American river turtle (*Podocnemis expansa*). National and international NGOs have been technically and financially involved in the projects, leading to a joint management setting between SPNN and the local indigenous peoples. The joint management plan is now being developed based on formal agreements signed by the Colombian minister of the environment and the leaders of the Miraña communities. In the agreement, both parties recognized each other as public authorities with conservation duties in the area where the Cahuinari National Natural Park and the Miraña reservation overlap. The agreement aims to coordinate activities by both authorities based on an intercultural perspective. Consequently, the park management plan aims to both conserve biodiversity and strengthen the indigenous cultural identity.

Source: adapted from Alcorn et al (2005b)

system, which would set the conditions for dialogue and create a foundation upon which to explore subtleties. Dialogues, exchanges and research are exactly what are needed to explore and diffuse, in all of its facets and complexities, the art of conservation.

Evaluating and improving governance: A process of social learning

Improving governance presupposes an analysis of the nature and scale of the organization in charge of the protected area and of its powers with respect to other bodies and levels. It also requires an understanding of where and why disputes and conflicts happen and how they can be solved. One of the likely outcomes of the analysis is that important efforts may be needed in terms of capacity-building. For instance, new skills may be needed for technical services, including for engaging in participatory diagnosis and planning, negotiating consensus solutions, managing resources and finances, and collecting and storing data. Enhanced capacities of local government institutions to interact with civil society may also be identified as an important help. Local communities and community-based organizations may need to be better informed about their rights and obligations with respect to the protected areas, which implies engaging them in intense social communication efforts. Resource user groups, the private sector and civil society are also likely to need better information on their rights and obligations, as well as improved participation avenues and skills. All social actors are likely to profit from improved vision and leadership skills.

Another possible outcome of the governance evaluation effort may be the recommendation that, in harmony with the subsidiarity principle (see Table 5.2), protected areas set up decentralized fiscal arrangements to raise their own resources and arrange for some of those resources to contribute to local processes of sustainable development. Only very few countries have so far devolved the responsibility for budgeting and revenue collection to sub-national institutions (state, district or municipality). The central authorities are generally reluctant to give up their power of raising and managing financial resources, and there may be good reasons to want to distribute revenues among highly 'popular' and 'unpopular', but equally needed, protected areas. Another often quoted reason to maintain centralization of revenue collection is that the local relevant capacities may be limited.

Social actors involved in analysing and attempting to improve governance in a protected area setting typically act as innovators, trying out, in practice, novel technical and institutional solutions to problems, which often demand a readjustment of their habitual ways of working. This adds to the always present need of dealing with the complex, uncertain and rapidly changing characteristics of environment and society. It is well known that the environment is currently responding to a variety of influences – from climate change to overexploitation and pollution – which alters its natural features, rhythms and cycles. Equally pervasive, socio-cultural and economic change has been sweeping across the planet. Today, even remote rural livelihoods are undergoing dynamic change, and all human communities increasingly express differentiated and evolving needs. In this context, adaptive governance – besides adaptive management – also seems a sensible approach.

Adaptive management emphasizes ongoing learning through iterative processes and fitting solutions to specific contexts. It is based on systematic experimentation and careful analysis of environmental and social feedback to policies and management interventions (see Chapter 11, p293). Embracing a similar 'adaptive governance' approach demands a process of participatory analysis and evaluation, and – after that – the political will to respond to its result. It also involves recognition that there is nothing sacred or immutable about a particular system of protected area governance. And that governance needs to integrate the evolving conditions and needs of environment and society.

As illustrated in this chapter, a variety of relatively new actors have important roles to play in protected area governance. Protected area systems are well advised to take advantage of their contributions and to promote improvements in governance type and quality. Analysis and action about governance of protected areas can prove a powerful and insightful process of social learning – a process that has all the chances of resulting in more effective and equitable conservation.

Further reading

Borrini-Feyerabend, G. (2004) 'Governance of protected areas, participation and equity', in *Biodiversity Issues for Consideration in the Planning, Establishment and Management of Protected Areas Sites and Networks*, Convention on Biological Diversity Technical Series 15, Secretariat of the Convention on Biological Diversity, Montreal

Borrini-Feyerabend, G., Pimbert, M., Farvar, M. T., Kothari, A. and Renard, Y. (2004a) *Sharing Power: Learning by Doing in Co-management of Natural Resources throughout the World*, IIED and IUCN/CEESP, Teheran, www.iucn.org/themes/ceesp/Publications/sharingpower

Borrini-Feyerabend, G., Kothari, A. and Oviedo, G. (2004b) *Indigenous and Local Communities and Protected Areas: Towards Equity and Enhanced Conservation*, WCPA Best Practice Series 11, IUCN, Gland and Cambridge

CEESP (Commission on Environment, Economic and Social Policy of the World Conservation Union) (2003) *Policy Matters 12: Special Issue on Community Empowerment for Conservation for the Vth*

World Parks Congress, www.iucn.org/themes/ceesp/Publications/newsletter/PM12.pdf

Dearden, P., Bennett, M. and Johnston, J. (2005) 'Trends in global protected area governance, 1992–2002', *Environmental Management*, vol 36, no 1, pp89–100

Graham, J., Amos, B. and Plumptre, T. (2003) 'Governance principles for protected areas in the 21st century', Paper prepared for the Vth IUCN World Parks Congress, Durban, South Africa, Institute of Governance, Ottawa

Langholz, J. and Krug, W. (2005) 'New forms of biodiversity governance: Non-state actors and the private protected area action plan', in Pansky, D. (ed) *Governance Stream of the Vth World Parks Congress*, Parks Canada and IUCN/WCPA, Ottawa

Pansky, D. (ed) (2005) *Governance Stream of the Vth World Parks Congress*, Parks Canada and IUCN/WCPA, Ottawa

Ribot, J. C. (2004) *Waiting for Democracy: The Politics of Choice in Natural Resource Decentralisation*, WRI, Washington, DC

UNDP (United Nations Development Programme) (1997) *Governance for Sustainable Human Development: A UNDP Policy Document*, UNDP, New York, www.magnet.undp.org/policy/default.htm

UNDP (2002) *Human Development Report: Deepening Democracy in a Fragmented World*, UNDP, New York

WRI (World Resources Institute) (2005) *The Wealth of the Poor: Managing Ecosystems to Fight Poverty*, WRI, Washington, DC

Websites

IUCN Theme on Governance, Equity and Rights (TGER), www.iucn.org/themes/ceesp/TGER.html

IUCN Theme on Indigenous and Local Communities, Equity and Protected Areas (TILCEPA), www.iucn.org/themes/ceesp/Wkg_grp/TILCEPA/TILCEPA.htm

6

Process of Management

Graeme L. Worboys and Colin Winkler

Protected areas need to be managed efficiently and effectively if the purposes for which they have been reserved are to be realized. Whether their status is as a community conserved area (CCA), a private protected area, a co-managed protected area or a government agency-managed protected area, there must be a management presence.

Establishing protected areas (see Chapter 8) is the start of the process for achieving the many purposes for which protected areas are reserved. There is a multiplicity of threats that need to be dealt with to maintain their integrity (see Chapter 9). The phenomenon of 'paper parks', where protected areas are designated but never managed, is recognized as a serious issue. Simply designating protected areas neither ensures their survival nor guarantees that social and economic benefits are derived from them (Chape et al, 2003b). Protected area values can be destroyed through the lack of any form of a management presence. Effective management is essential for the future of protected areas.

Management has been described by Follett (1949) as the art of getting things done through the actions of people. It is an activity concerned with the orchestration of people, resources, work and systems in the pursuit of organizational goals (Follett, 1949). Given that management is so important for protected areas, it is essential to provide an understanding of the process of management and some basic management principles. This chapter introduces the principles underlying the management of protected areas. It describes the process of management and basic management functions, as well as specific skills and knowledge needed by managers.

Management functions

A process of perspective is particularly useful in examining the work of managers in organizations that are responsible for protected areas. An orchestra provides a useful analogy. The manager is the orchestra's conductor, coaxing the best performance from the individual members and sections. The conductor's role is very different from the technical role of individual musicians on their various instruments. Without the musicians, there would be no orchestra; but without the conductor, the musicians would find it more difficult to coordinate their playing into a harmonious performance. The role of every manager is to orchestrate organizational effectiveness through the process of management. This process involves four related management functions: planning, organizing, leading and controlling (see Figure 6.1).

These functions are applicable irrespective of who has the primary governance responsibilities for a protected area; the type of organization, geographical location or ownership; or the level of the manager in the organization. However, there will be differences in emphasis, and there will be very different systems, processes and procedures, from the very flexible (as with a private land manager or small NGO), to the highly bureaucratic and institutionalized (as is often the case

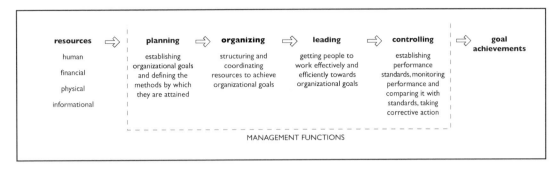

Figure 6.1 The four functions of management as part of the managerial process

Source: authors

with government agencies). While we tend to concentrate on a highly institutionalized environment in this chapter, the principles apply equally to all governance types.

In practice, a protected area manager is able to undertake all functions only if he or she has the necessary resources. This is a particular challenge in middle or low Human Development Index (HDI) countries. In this regard, advocacy (see Chapter 25), developing capacity (see Chapter 8) and sustainable financing (see Chapter 12) are crucial. Thus, protected area managers must also function externally to the management organization as communicators, advocates, trainers and fundraisers.

It is important to recognize that the proportion of time devoted to each function varies markedly between managerial levels in something resembling the pattern shown in Figure 6.2.

This is fundamental. Top-level managers are expected to provide strategic planning direction and policy for their organizations, while front-line staff are anticipated to spend more time on leadership issues.

Planning

Planning is one of the first management functions undertaken by any organization. First, the organization must determine its goals. Its planners should also look at the range of issues they may encounter and where strategic improvements can be made. Such planning is critical to achieving conservation goals. While this section deals briefly with planning in general, Chapter 8 examines the planning required to establish protected areas, and Chapter 11 considers in detail processes for preparing protected area management plans.

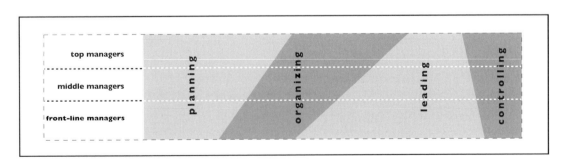

Figure 6.2 Relative amount of time that managers spend on the four managerial functions

Source: adapted from Mahoney et al (1965)

Three levels of planning

The function of planning is commonly undertaken at three levels of detail – strategic, tactical or operational – especially within larger organizations that deal with an entire system of protected areas. An organization cannot achieve its primary goal unless each level of management carries out the appropriate level of planning. Organizational goals are translated into a series of strategic plans that, as they pass down the hierarchy, are translated initially into a series of tactical and then operational plans, which are the plans required by front-line staff. Such a system can only work if each level in the agency clearly understands its role and is provided with the freedom to manage. Note that in 'informal' systems of management, as in the case of many CCAs, all of these elements may not exist, or may not be clearly distinguishable.

Strategic plans

To achieve its principal purpose, an organization identifies what major strategic goals must first be attained and the ways to achieve these goals. Such plans have ramifications for the whole of an organization and have a long-term time frame. In protected area management, examples of strategic planning include corporate planning; organizational policies; organizational planning, budget systems and business planning; management effectiveness evaluation systems, including monitoring; organizational baseline sustainable performance measures; and operational procedural systems and statements. Part of such strategic planning includes carefully assessing the operating environment of a protected area system (see also Chapter 11, p293).

All protected area managers should be aware that their organizations are subject to a variety of environmental influences, including those emanating from the socio-cultural, legal-political, technological, economic and international sectors. These are important inputs to the process of management and strategic planning. Some typical influences are illustrated in Figure 6.3.

Tactical plans

Tactical plans set tactical goals that help in implementing a strategic plan. They are typically associated with part of a protected area system and deal with multiple protected areas. They prescribe how parts of an organization's strategic plan are to be achieved. Tactical plans typically establish a set of steps to achieve each tactical goal. They are usually developed by middle-level managers and staff and have an intermediate time frame. They represent a critical level of planning. Good tactical planning ensures efficient and effective allocation of an organization's internal resources. A tactical plan, for instance, might deal with tourism and the sharing of the visitor load across a region, and might be developed cooperatively by a number of organizations.

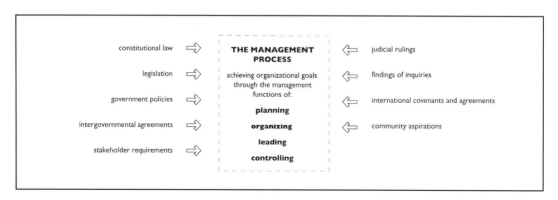

Figure 6.3   Some potential external influences on the process of management

Operational plans

Operational plans are directed towards actions and short-term goals derived from the strategic and tactical plans. They are usually implemented by an organization's front-line managers (managers who work at the 'delivery end' of an organization). Operational plans may be developed as a consequence of tactical plans. As such, they contribute to achieving tactical goals. A tactical plan for distributing the visitor load across a region, for example, could have as one of its operational plans to set up a staff training course that focuses on customer service for visitors.

Integrating planning, budgeting and operational systems

The project of developing a plan (at strategic, tactical or operational level) is no different from any other project. The relationships between various types of protected area plans are considered further in Chapter 11. Linking the planning, budgeting and operational systems within an organization into one unified system is quite critical. Unless this is achieved, plans cannot be implemented. The excellent system implemented by the Department of Conservation in New Zealand is described in Case Study 6.1.

Case Study **6.1**

New Zealand Department of Conservation strategic systems

Grant Baker, Department of Conservation, Wellington, New Zealand

The New Zealand Department of Conservation's annual business planning system is one of the core business systems of the department. It is integrated with other systems and has three phases: directions and expectations setting; business planning; and work planning. The purpose of the process is to allocate resources to departmental priorities and achieve conservation outcomes.

Directions and expectations

Annual business planning starts from setting directions and expectations (D&Es). This is a 'top-down' process. The D&Es outline the expected achievements for the coming year. They guide the department's business planning and work planning. The chief executive sets up the D&Es for the whole department at a high strategic and outcome level. The D&Es are then cascaded down to general managers and other managers who then interpret the chief executive's D&Es and set up their own D&Es for their divisions, units and staff. The D&Es' setting phase opens the discussion among managers at different levels about what the stakeholders, such as the minister and New Zealand public, expect the department to achieve; the department's performance, strategic risks, options and alternatives to meet the stakeholders' expectations; and the capability requirement. The D&Es' setting is supported by the department's environmental scan (see Chapter 11, p296) and department strategies and policies.

Business planning

During the business planning stage, the managers develop their business plans based on the D&Es of their managers to prioritize work, allocate resources such as staff time and financial resource, and set up performance target estimates. Business planning is a bottom-up process. Unit and divisional business plans are consolidated and reprioritized in order to best use the resources and achieve conservation outcomes. The business planning process is integrated within the government budgeting process, such as the budget bids process. It is supported by the department's performance measurement system, which covers the conservation outcomes, rationale for intervention and outputs. The result of the business planning process contributes to the department's statement of intent, the definitive planning document for the next three to five years, with a focus on the first year (see also Chapter 12, p328).

Work planning

Work planning starts after the department's budget and statement of intent have been approved by the government and signed off by the minister. The work planning sets up details of work programmes and projects, which include task, time, budget and performance targets. They identify work that will be carried out by staff day by day. During the year, business plans and work plans may be modified and performance targets may be re-forecasted based on the circumstance. The business plans and work plans provide the base for performance monitoring and reporting. It also provides the criteria for staff performance appraisal and remuneration.

Organizing

As a management function, organizing is concerned with how managers allocate and arrange human and other resources to enable plans to be implemented. It involves managers determining the range of tasks to be performed and allocating the available resources to obtain the best results most efficiently. Organizing is a process that never stops. In a fast-changing world, managers and staff are constantly refining how their organizations work towards required goals.

As to how organizations should be organized, there are many approaches, particularly in larger organizations. The way in which an organization is governed plays a large part in determining the nature of its organizational structure. An organizational structure can be thought of as the formal pattern of interactions and coordination designed to link the tasks of individuals and groups to achieve organizational goals. Usually, for large organizations, this is shown as an organizational chart that identifies the organization's major positions or departments and the reporting arrangements (chain of command) from top-level to front-line level. Such structures are organized into divisions, with units and individuals reporting in a systematic way. Organizational activities are usually coordinated both across and up and down the organization.

Demands on protected area organizations are different from those facing organizations that operate on the basis of a single-shift working day. There is a need to ensure that other public and private sector organizations are aware of these differences, and that 'standard' organizational models and systems are not inappropriately applied to protected areas. Some of the special characteristics of a protected area operating environment are as follows:

- Protected area managers have a public trust responsibility, and measures of success in operations, for example, are not as straightforward as in private sector organizations.
- Protected areas are a 24-hour-a-day, seven-days-a-week operation, with operational matters that arise on protected area lands or waters often needing a rapid response.

- Since protected areas exist within local communities and are often central to their human livelihoods and well-being, they must have a continuous operational capacity.
- Protected area lands and waters are dynamic living systems, and the dynamics of natural events are superimposed on a routine organizational timetable of events.
- Protected areas are managed in the context of dynamic, evolving groups of people, with often unpredictable behaviours.
- Protected areas are frequently rough, rugged and remote, giving rise to special management needs related to organizational time and resource allocation, as well as staff competencies and capacities.
- Protected areas are used by a wide range of resource consumers, recreational and other users, with peak-use periods often clashing with peak-incident periods.
- Incidents such as fires, search and rescues, wildlife incidents, and other events (see Chapter 18) will occur, and they may cut across an organization's timetabled events.
- The practical and experiential knowledge accumulated by protected area staff (including those from local communities) is crucial for effective protected area decision-making.
- In order to maintain consistent provision of ecosystem services, protected areas need responsible management investments that are uninterrupted and long term.

Organizing work

Protected area management organizations are typically under-funded and have too few staff for the work they need to do. Every staff position is vital. Every resource that will help an organization to achieve its goals is critical. How these resources are best organized is fundamental to an organization's success. This drive for more effective use of limited resources is often at the heart of organizational change processes. There is a constant need to deploy available staff, funding and resources in the best way to achieve goals. Adaptive management (see Chapter 11) practices mean that organizations will need to be designed for flexibility.

Yosemite National Park, US

Source: IUCN Photo Library © Jim Thorsell

Most agencies have mechanisms to ensure that all staff are aware of how they are contributing to their organization's primary goals. However, these mechanisms sometimes fail. Staff may not always appreciate the roles that their colleagues play in other parts of an organization. Grumbling that 'head office staff have it easy' or that 'rangers have a wonderful life working in paradise' reflects such ignorance. Other comments, such as 'the only real work for conservation is here in the park itself', reflect, at best, a misguided view of how organizations work and, at worst, a dangerously divisive attitude that could jeopardize the work of an organization. It may also give the wrong message to external stakeholders. Internal cohesiveness and teamwork are critical. Inequities of various kinds (gender, social, political and economic) can play a major role in management, and the organization of work has to be dynamic enough to tackle this. So, what do different levels of an organization do? Typically, there are three levels of management for

protected area organizations: top-level, middle-level and front-line staff.

Top-level managers

Top-level managers are ultimately responsible for the entire organization. The executive provides leadership for an organization, including long-term strategic planning, and the monitoring of the organization's performance. Although there is much variation around the world, typically there is a chief executive officer (CEO) and a small team of senior staff who, in terms of the four functions of management, will give planning and organizing about two-thirds of their time, the balance being more or less equally divided between leading and controlling (see Figure 6.2). Top-level managers usually have highly developed conceptual and human management skills, but fewer technical skills (see Figure 6.4). The CEO is important as a figurehead, as the person account-able for the organization's performance, as the lead

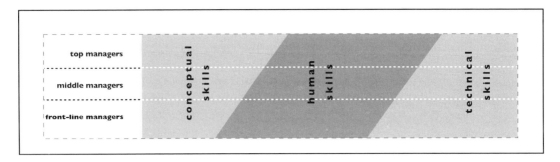

Figure 6.4   Skill distribution at various management levels

Source: adapted from Katz (1974)

spokesperson, and in leading top-level management in setting strategic directions. This level also devises, with input from staff, organizational restructures necessary to meet new strategic directions.

Middle-level managers

Middle-level managers and staff develop plans to advance corporate goals. For large organizations, there may be a number of layers of middle managers, depending upon needs. The trend of many organizations is to flatten structures in order to reduce the layers and number of middle managers. This may cut costs and streamline communication. However, if the cuts are too great, it may impact upon the organization's performance. The limit to such steps is usually governed by the effective span of control and by the volume, sensitivity and complexity of work. The common result of having fewer hierarchical layers is that the remaining middle management levels gain greater autonomy and responsibility. Typically, middle-level managers will have a balanced approach to dealing with the four functions of management, giving each function roughly the same attention, although leading may often occupy the greatest amount of time and controlling the least (see Figure 6.2). Technical skills, conceptual skills and people management skills are important for people in these positions. Middle-level managers are expected to be entrepreneurial and exhibit leadership in their roles.

Middle-level managers in a conservation agency may be responsible for functional tasks, such as human resource management, legal services, financial management, research, community relations and policy. Since protected area organizations are in the business of land or sea management, tasks may need to be delegated on a geographic basis. Middle-level managers lead such units. Considerable effort is needed by managers and staff to work horizontally or across an organization in order to achieve its goals, as well as managing up and managing down.

Front-line managers

Front-line managers and staff are at the operational level in the hierarchy. They ensure that the day-to-day operations of a protected area run smoothly (see Chapter 15). In undertaking the four functions of management, a front-line manager is typically involved in less planning and organizing and more in leading, which may absorb half of their time. Controlling is an important function, but at this level does not typically take up more than 10 per cent of their time, although again circumstances around the world can vary considerably. The position usually requires strong human and technical skills, with long-term strategic skills being less important (see Figure 6.4). Front-line managers are increasingly being involved with whole-of-organization tasks, as well as with increasingly sophisticated management control systems.

Organizing work vertically and horizontally

Typically, protected area organizations are spread across wide geographic areas. It is very easy for isolated units to work at variance with the primary goals of an organization. Even when organizational units are in the same building, strong-minded managers or poor systems of coordination may lead to problems such as units or individuals 'doing their own thing' or concentrating on lower priority tasks. Effective coordination of work effort is required up, down and across an organization. Some systems and techniques are available to achieve this and include preparing policies and procedures; providing effective delegations; a span of control that lets managers deal effectively with their responsibilities; and clear operational policies in relation to centralized accountabilities and decentralized responsibilities.

Organizing staff structures

There are many approaches to how organizations structure their staff, particularly in the public and private sectors. The most appropriate structure for an organization depends upon the particular balance between an organization's strategy, the environment in which it operates, the technology it employs, and the characteristics of its people. It is important that structure and strategy are compatible. If 'form follows function', then an organization's strategy should influence a particular structure, driven by considerations such as:

- the types of tasks that employees perform (highly technical tasks may require a matrix-type structure and high-labour content repetitive tasks, for example, may be better served by a network structure);
- the technology that is appropriate (as the number of managers, management levels and clerical and administrative staff increases, the technology systems increase in complexity); and
- a suitable task environment in which the organization functions (mechanistic structures tend to suit stable environments, while organic structures are more appropriate in turbulent environments).

An organization's operational environment, technological support and people skills also affect an organization's structure. Some considerations are as follows.

Change. The relative predictability of change in an organization's environment itself may impact upon the level of (de)centralization.

External environment. The complexity or heterogeneity of the environment can influence the degree of structural differentiation (Mintzberg, 1979; Perrow, 1986).

Competencies. The level of education and work involvement of people in an organization may have an influence on structure, as may increasing interest in employee participation in decision-making.

Decentralization is the degree to which decision-making authority is spread throughout the organization, as opposed to being concentrated (centralized) at the top.

Standardization is the extent to which work activities are described in detail and performed uniformly throughout the organization.

Task specialization is the degree to which work is divided into narrow tasks with extensive division of labour.

Complexity is the number of specialized job types, the number of hierarchical levels and the number of operating geographical locations.

Stratification. These are the status differences among individuals and groups.

Configuration is the number of hierarchical levels, spans of control and ratios such as managers to technical employees and support to operating employees.

Protected area agency structures

The act of structuring organizations is a continuous process to adjust to the changes in and affecting organizations over time. There are a number of structural alternatives that can be used (see Box 6.1).

Organizational structures for protected areas reflect the nature of the major governance types (see Chapter 5). In CCAs (see Chapter 21), authority and responsibility rest with the communities through a variety of forms of customary law or locally agreed organizations and rules. These rules can be diverse and complex, such as land and

Box 6.1 Organizational structural alternatives

Different organizational structural alternatives are described within this box. Each of the approaches reflects different uses of chain of command to define departmental groupings and reporting relationships along the hierarchy.

Functional or thematic structures place positions into units based on expertise, skill and similarity of work activity (such as operations, human resources and finance). Among the protected area agencies that fall into this category are the New Jersey Pinelands Commission in the US, the Peak National Park Authority in the UK and the Ngorongoro Conservation Area Authority in Tanzania.

Divisional structures group positions based on a common programme or geographic region (for the day-to-day management of the Great Barrier Reef Marine Park by the Queensland Parks and Wildlife Service, the reef is divided into various sections, such as the far northern and cairns sections).

Hybrid structures combine aspects of the functional and divisional forms, with some activities grouped by function and others by geography or some other criterion. This is exemplified by the Annapurna Conservation Area Project, which, operating under the auspices of the King Mahendra Trust for Nature Conservation, utilizes such functional areas as the Conservation Education and Extension Programme and Alternative Energy, as well as a two-level division by geography involving Northern and Southern programmes, within each of which smaller zones have been defined.

Matrix structures superimpose, or overlay, horizontal divisional reporting relationships over a hierarchical functional structure, creating a dual chain of command. This evolved as a way of improving horizontal coordination and information-sharing.

New approaches have emerged to meet organizational needs in a rapidly changing global environment. Of these new approaches, both the team-based and networked structures are worthy of attention. Team-based structures are where a series of teams has been created to accomplish specific tasks and to coordinate major departments. The vertical chain of command is a powerful means of control; but passing all decisions up the hierarchy takes too long and keeps responsibility at the top. Many organizations reorganize into permanent teams after re-engineering, which is the radical redesign of processes to achieve dramatic improvements in cost, quality, service and speed. Networked structures extend the idea of horizontal coordination and collaboration beyond the boundaries of the organization. The organization itself becomes a small, central hub linked to other organizations that perform vital functions. Departments are independent, contracting services to the central hub. This type of structure is also referred to as the virtual organization.

some resources being collectively owned and managed and other resources individually owned or managed on a clan basis (Borrini-Feyerabend et al, 2004b).

For private protected areas, authority for the management of land rests with the landowners. They determine the objectives of management within the bounds of law. This may include some agreements with government. The private property may be managed by an individual, a board of management, a trust or by some other mechanism. Co-managed protected areas are becoming increasingly common. Often, there are complex processes and institutional arrangements that are employed to share management authority

(see Chapter 20). A multi-stakeholder management group is a typical model for transboundary protected area management structures.

Government managed protected areas typically hold the authority, responsibility and accountability for managing protected areas. They usually report directly to the central or provincial government (Borrini-Feyerabend et al, 2004b). There are, however, variations on governmental involvement in protected area management, ranging from a single agency carrying responsibility for a protected area or cluster of areas, through integrating either legislation or agencies, through to a 'whole-of-government' approach (see Case Study 6.2).

Case Study 6.2

Examples of approaches to structuring government protected area management agencies

Integrating legislation

Reforming the contradictions and inconsistent overlaps in legislation involves streamlining and condensing the body of environmental regulations. New Zealand, by statute, integrated the management of land, air and water resources within one piece of legislation governed by a common purpose (sustainable management) and provided a consistent setting for policy-making, plan development, consent-giving and enforcement.

Integrating agencies

Some governments have combined the full range of environmental agencies (such as fisheries, forestry and protected areas) into a single agency responsible for the management of natural resources, including land identification and management; resource development; use and protection; and conservation and environmental management. In some cases, protected area agencies have been linked to tourism or development sectors. The potential advantages are improved coordination of efforts, more effective use of scarce resources, and potential to overcome existing interagency conflicts. The disadvantage is that it may simply internalize conflict and prevent examination of different perspectives in resource management. In addition, unless functions are integrated, there is no guarantee that one large agency will be more resource efficient and less bureaucratic than a number of smaller specialist agencies. There is also the risk that those parts of a large agency responsible for protected areas may become marginalized within a larger bureaucracy.

Whole-of-government responsibilities

A model for natural resource management for government is one that develops a system where relevant government agencies assume environmental responsibilities, without the system being 'owned' by any one agency. This essentially seeks to realign the way in which agencies operate. The whole-of-government model for sharing environmental responsibilities has been undertaken by the Canadian government in creating a commissioner of the environment and sustainable development within the Office of the Auditor General of Canada. This is responsible for ensuring that agencies 'green' their policies, operations and programmes. All agencies must have sustainable development strategies, an approach that is aimed at placing sustainable development among the mainstream operations of all agencies with minimal disruption.

Other organizational and structural considerations

Organizational structural arrangements may be supplemented and modified by a number of techniques. Contracting and tendering, purchaser provider and corporatization–privatization have been methods used by protected area organizations and are described briefly here.

Contracting out and competitive tendering

Contracting out relies on suppliers for goods or services that cannot be provided in-house, whereas competitive tendering is an extension of competition into areas previously undertaken solely by protected area organizational staff. In effect, this means that organizational divisions are expected to compete for contracts with other potential contractors.

Purchaser provider

This separates regulatory and policy functions from service delivery and operational functions, and acknowledges that while it is the responsibility of government to fund public good activities, such as the management of protected areas, these should be purchased from the most efficient provider, whether private or public.

Corporatization and privatization

These approaches may be used to improve financial management and to deliver services more efficiently. Corporatization is often required to provide services to meet explicitly identified community service obligations, and has advantages in more efficient service delivery, increased customer focus, user pays concepts that can expose the real cost of services, and identification of the full cost of inputs, which allows a more rational use of resources. There may be problems in balancing autonomy and commercial responsibilities with community and environmental obligations and with broader objectives of government. In Kosciuszko National Park, Australia, a major government hydroelectric scheme organization (the Snowy Mountains Hydroelectric Authority) was corporatized to form the Snowy Corporation, and as part of the negotiations, funds were transferred to the New South Wales Department of Environment and Conservation for catchment management and catchment rehabilitation. The funds were sourced from water and hydroelectricity revenue (Manson and Enders, 2004). Privatization involves the total or partial transfer of public assets, goods or services to the private sector. While the profit objective may seem inconsistent with protected area management, some commercial operators of private protected areas not only achieve profits, but achieve solid results in threatened species recovery. Private game reserves adjoining Kruger National Park in South Africa (such as Sabi Sabi Game Reserve) operate commercially and provide ecotourism services, but act as protected areas contributing to the conservation of the greater ecosystem for fauna outside of the park (Eagles and McCool, 2002).

Leading

Leadership in protected area management at the global and regional level may be seen through the work of organizations such as the United Nations Educational, Scientific and Cultural Organization (UNESCO), the United Nations Environment Programme (UNEP), the World Conservation Monitoring Centre (WCMC), IUCN and the Secretariat for the Convention on Biological Diversity (CBD). NGOs such as Conservation International (CI), The Nature Conservancy and the World Wide Fund for Nature (WWF) play critical global leadership roles (see Chapter 3, p73).

In the context of individual protected area organizations, leading takes on a much more specific focus, influencing others' work behaviour towards achieving organizational goals. In the process of leading, effective managers become catalysts in encouraging innovation, motivating staff to perform at higher levels. Most protected area organizations are made up of people who are committed to the ideals of conservation and who are prepared to work long hours in support of this commitment. Staff or volunteers who are supported by positive leaders can harness extraordinary energy to achieve conservation goals. Conversely, a lack of leadership can result in the development of less productive behaviour. Managers must also take care not to take unreasonable advantage of staff and volunteer commitment and dedication.

Good leaders are an indispensable ingredient when it comes to effective protected area management regardless of the circumstances and cultural differences around the world. Good leaders:

• always set a good example and don't ask their people to do anything that they wouldn't do themselves;
• keep people informed about and involved with what is going on, what the goals are, detailed plans to reach the goals, and the standards they will be measured by;
• delegate responsibility and authority, don't try to do everything themselves, encourage independent action and do not continually look over a person's shoulder;
• keep people challenged by giving them important and worthwhile work;
• listen attentively and courteously so that people know that what they have to say is important, and that it will be given due consideration;
• are consistent so that they are dependable, don't change their minds too often or hastily, and act the same way in the same situation;

- give recognition when recognition is due, making sure that staff get credit for a job well done and receive public praise, but never a public reprimand; and
- make decisions that need to be made.

Chief executive officers and senior staff

The roles of CEOs and executive teams of protected area agencies are pivotal if conservation outcomes are to be achieved. At this level, leadership takes on additional strategic dimensions, requiring the ability to anticipate, envision, maintain flexibility, and empower others to create strategic change as necessary (Ireland and Hitt, 1999). Strategic leadership is required to successfully use the management process at the whole-of-agency level. Successful strategic leadership is exemplified by several key actions:

- *Determine strategic direction* of the protected area agency, including developing a long-term vision of the organization's strategic intent (Falbe et al, 1995).
- *Capitalize on core competencies* by utilizing a protected area agency's functional skills, such as 'response speed' (an ability to act quickly when facing environmental pressures) or 'user knowledge base' (the familiarity of the users of a protected area with the area's attractions and facilities). Core competencies cannot be capitalized upon effectively without developing the capabilities of human capital.
- *Develop human capital* by expanding the knowledge and skills of an agency's entire workforce (Sandberg, 2000). Effective strategic leaders view human capital as a resource to be maximized, rather than as a cost to be minimized.
- *Sustain an effective organizational culture* by maintaining the complex set of ideologies, symbols and core values shared throughout a protected area organization that influences the way in which it operates. Shaping an agency's culture is a central task of effective strategic leadership.
- *Promote ethical practices* through setting specific goals to describe the agency's ethical standards, such as using a code of conduct and rewarding ethical behaviours (Trevino et al,

1999).
- Develop and use *effective organizational controls* (Kirsch, 1996) through which strategic leaders provide adaptive organizational direction.
- Adhere to the principles of *good governance* (see Chapter 5).
- Ensure leadership functions are *sustained* in the face of staff changes or other perturbations by having in place succession and contingency plans.

As leaders, top-level managers or motivators are an important organizational resource that is required for a protected area agency to develop and take advantage of opportunities. Top management teams are the key managers in the organization who are responsible for formulating and implementing the agency's strategy for their protected area. Team characteristics have been shown to affect the strategy of organizations. For example, a top management team with varied functional backgrounds, experiences and education is more likely to formulate an effective strategy. Additionally, heterogeneous top management teams have been shown to positively affect performance such as innovation and strategic change in organizations.

The selection process for a CEO is critical. Because management functions are universal (see p146), managerial skills can also be regarded as transferable from organization to organization (Koontz and O'Donnell, 1955). There are instances of this principle working for protected area agencies. In such cases, CEOs have used prior managerial experience gained in another context to provide effective leadership for protected areas management. However, it should also be recognized that people who have been successful leaders elsewhere will not automatically be effective in a protected area organization. A willingness and capacity to rapidly gain an understanding of protected area management imperatives as well as access to sufficient content knowledge to underpin sound decision-making, are also required. CEOs who have both general managerial skills and operational experience with protected areas may therefore be particularly effective leaders. Such individuals will be well-placed to respond appropriately in times of crisis, when inadequate decisions could lead to the extention of species or

IUCN management study group, Tarako National Park Visitor Centre, Taiwan

Source: Graeme L. Worboys

destribution of heritage. The large number of professional protected area management organizations around the world provides a pool of suitable candidates.

Executive leadership for protected areas ultimately involves decision-making about natural ecosystem processes, biodiversity and cultural conservation. Wise executive decision-making ensures that organizational systems and budgetary management, staff competencies and capacities, management performance evaluation, and other essential systems are in place, supporting priority conservation outcomes. To this end, the following four understandings relate to effective protected area leadership:

1   All protected area managers need to have a basic understanding of the four functions of management and how the management process works.
2   Professional, experienced and competent leadership and organizational loyalty are vital for achieving conservation outcomes.
3   Chief executives and senior staff require a broad set of perspectives and executive competencies necessary for effective functioning at a senior level. While such staff may, in some instances, be recruited from other fields, often a person with professional protected area

experience may be best equipped to lead protected area organizations and secure conservation outcomes for the long term.
4   Protected area corporate knowledge and professional competencies gained by individuals over many years of field-based and policy-based protected area management are important assets for protected area organizations.

Decision-making

Decisions made by managers are critical to achieving conservation outcomes. Long-term conservation outcomes are dependent upon competent decisions at every level of management. Protected area managers are constantly being asked to make judgements on how to best allocate their resources or which management intervention strategies to employ in order to achieve the greatest long-term conservation benefit. This balancing act can be assisted by adopting a decision-making process as illustrated in Figure 6.5.

Managers should recognize that, no matter how astute they are or how much experience they have, their ability to acquire and utilize information is nevertheless limited. In almost all decision situations, information is incomplete, whether because there is insufficient time to gather all of

Figure 6.5 The decision-making process

the available data, or because it is too costly, or because it simply does not exist. Different managers may well perceive situations, alternatives, consequences and weightings quite differently. As well, personal biases, motivational factors and issues associated with group decision-making may also create difficulties. Groups can either have a negative influence, as in increasing goal conflict, or can improve rationality through enhancing the quantity and quality of decision alternatives.

Scanning the external 'environment' is a critical part of decision-making, and managers are repeatedly required to consider internal and external environments. In particular, managers need to be aware of at least six critical decision-making considerations: environmental/ecological; economic; social and cultural; political; legal; and managerial. All of these considerations are informed, even driven by, frequently conflicting values (see Chapter 4).

Environmental/ecological considerations

Life on the planet is dependent upon the retention of natural systems and processes. The primary purpose for the reservation of protected areas is to conserve ecological processes and values (including natural and cultural heritage). Management decisions need to be made in the context of this primary purpose. The objectives of most protected areas will not be achieved without active management intervention.

Economic considerations

Protected areas play an important part in the community, providing important economic benefits (see Chapter 4, p105). From an economic perspective, efficient and effective protected area

management is critical to the long-term economic well-being of citizens and regions. Protected area management decisions may include economic considerations such as those appraised in benefit-cost analysis (see Chapter 12).

Social and cultural considerations

Most communities care about their environment and many depend upon it for their very survival and have strong cultural associations with it. There is an understandable expectation that protected areas will be well managed. The process of management for conservation includes the whole community. Protected areas are only part of a total conservation effort. Conservation of the world's heritage will fail if it relies on the government-established protected areas alone. Working with the community and recognizing various forms of protected area governance, as well as the other social influences discussed in Chapter 2, are critical. Community needs (social considerations) are important inputs to the management decision-making process. The community needs to be empowered in managing protected areas. They need to value the critical importance and benefits of protected areas, thereby fostering a culture of pride and stewardship.

Political considerations

Executive government can intervene in the process of managing organizations at any time and can change the ground rules for how protected area management goals are to be achieved. They can also change the very goals for protected areas. Politicians, in addition to ideology, are strongly influenced by community attitudes and aspirations in providing leadership at the provincial or national level. Managers need to be sensitive to the political process. In making decisions, they need to be politically astute in relation to their organizational responsibilities. More generally, effective engagement with political decision-makers is a function that managers need to master in order to secure positive outcomes for protected areas.

Legal considerations

Courts and the judicial process can provide direction that either strengthens or is contradictory to the policies and priorities of executive government. When the balance of power in parliament is held by minority non-government independents or minor parties, legislation may not have the policy support of the government. Managers are required to make decisions within this environment. They are also required to make decisions in the context of all relevant legislation.

Managerial considerations

People within organizations, their commitment, their enthusiasm, their corporate knowledge and wisdom, their competence, and their teamwork determine the difference between the efficient and effective conservation of protected areas and the loss of heritage. How organizations are structured, how they operate, their culture, their goals, and how leaders perform all profoundly influence effective and efficient management. Management decisions influence how organizations work. They impact upon people. They need to be made carefully and with great judgement if conservation goals are to be realized.

Working with and motivating staff

The performance of staff has been shown to be a function of ability, motivation and environmental conditions. Whereas natural instincts and life skills are important, an understanding of motivation will ensure that 'natural managers' are even better at their work and will equip them for more senior management roles. The many definitions of motivation encompass three common attributes. Motivation is primarily concerned with:

- what energizes human behaviour;
- what directs or channels such behaviour; and
- how this behaviour is maintained or sustained.

Each of these three components represents an important factor in understanding human behaviour at work. The first component points to energetic forces within individuals that drive them to behave in particular ways and to environmental forces that often trigger these drives. Second, there is the notion of goal orientation on the part of individuals: their behaviour is directed towards something. Third, this way of viewing motivation contains a systems orientation: that is, it considers those forces in individuals and in their surrounding environments that feed back to the individuals either to reinforce the intensity of their drive and the direction of their energy, or to dissuade them from their course of action and redirect their efforts (Porter et al, 2003).

The socio-cultural context for leadership and teamwork needs to be understood by managers. Aycan (2004) provides a useful review of relevant socio-cultural characteristics for low and medium HDI countries, including communication patterns; family, performance, control and authority orientations; power and relationship orientations in leadership; and leadership profiles.

A systems perspective on motivation identifies variables that affect motivation in the workplace:

- *individual characteristics:* the motivations, interests, attitudes and needs of the individual;
- *job characteristics:* attributes inherent in the task;
- *work situation characteristics:* the organization's staff and reward policies, organizational climate, and attitudes and actions of peers and supervisors; and
- *community spirit*, or the ethic of working together as a community, for the collective good of all.

Managers need to understand what prompts people to initiate action, what prompts their choice of action and why they persist in that action over time – that is, managers ideally need to develop an appreciation of motivational theory. Content theories of work motivation assume that factors exist within the individual that energize, direct and sustain behaviour. These approaches to motivation are concerned with the identification of important internal elements and the explanation of how these elements may be prioritized within the individual. In contrast, process theories of motivation attempt to describe how behaviour is energized, directed and sustained. Process theories place heavy emphasis on describing the functioning of an individual's decision system as it relates to behaviour. It is beyond the scope of this chapter to go into detail of such theories – we recommend that the aspiring (or practising!) CEO refers to one of the many management and psychology textbooks that deal with this topic.

Controlling

Controlling is concerned with monitoring the performance of an organization against management benchmarks. Managers need to set performance measures and the criteria for how they will be evaluated. Controls help managers and staff to cope with uncertainty, detect irregularities, identify opportunities, handle complex situations and decentralize authority. Management control can be thought of as the process through which managers ensure that actual activities conform to planned activities. The basic control process involves establishing standards, monitoring performance and comparing performance with those standards, and responding with any necessary corrective actions (see Figure 6.6 and Chapter 24).

Managing for performance

How successful a protected area agency is in achieving its goals and in meeting society's needs depends upon how well the agency's managers do their jobs. Performance can be measured in terms of two concepts: effectiveness and efficiency. As Drucker (1964a, 1964b) puts it, effectiveness means 'doing the right thing', and efficiency means 'doing things right'. Effectiveness is the ability to select appropriate goals, and an effective manager chooses the right things to do. Efficiency is the ability to get things done correctly.

A manager's responsibilities in a protected area agency require performance that is both effective and efficient, and while efficiency is undeniably important, effectiveness is absolutely critical. In undertaking the process of management, managers and staff will employ the optimum balance of planning, organizing, leading and controlling to achieve management goals.

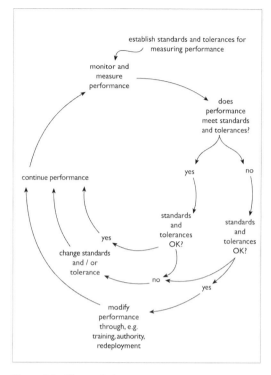

Figure 6.6 The control process

Attributes of a competent protected area manager

Competent managers do the right thing, at the right time and in the right way. Managers can be trained, but they must be willing to learn from experience. Good managers have a number of attributes.

- They are willing to learn from experience.
- They clearly understand the organization's goals.
- They actively pursue excellence and best practice.
- They are sensitive to trends and conditions inside and outside of their organization.
- They have analytical, problem-solving and decision-making skills.
- They possess emotional resilience and can work effectively under pressure.
- They work ethically.

- They understand the impact on others of their use of power.
- They can see the bigger picture.
- They are able to be innovative.

These 'process of management' principles apply equally to all protected area management staff. Even a temporary staff member brought in to do a small job of piecework ought to grasp the aims of the organization, and proceed to plan, organize, control and lead as appropriate for their area and task. This is not to deny that some people in the agency – those commonly referred to as top-level managers – will have wider responsibilities. It might seem that of the four main functions of management (planning, organizing, leading and controlling), the function 'lead' is not appropriate to an officer who has no one 'under' them. Yet, this is to make the mistake of assuming that instruction and knowledge must come down from above. It is often the person on the ground who leads those 'above' them to a more concrete understanding of what can and should be done. The most effective, dynamic and innovative conservation agency will be one in which each officer is a team player, yet is also his or her own main manager in helping to achieve the organization's mission.

As has been noted, to perform the four functions of management, managers need a mix of technical, human and conceptual skills. The relative importance of these three skills varies with the level of managerial responsibility (see Figure 6.4). The attributes of a competent protected area manager can be described in the context of these three skills. Such competencies are further discussed in 'Capacity for what, capacity for who, and what capacity?' in Chapter 7.

Technical skills

Technical skills involve process, knowledge and proficiency. Protected area staff must have a cross-section of technical skills and practical skills to manage protected areas. Conserving ecosystems and species, preserving heritage buildings, protecting significant heritage sites and making critical decisions during incidents such as bushfires, oil spills, floods, tsunamis, earthquakes and other natural episodic events all need

sound judgement as well as a fundamental understanding of conservation issues. Whether staff are at top, middle or front-line levels, they must also understand the ramifications of decisions being made. There needs to be a continuous process of learning and systems available to achieve this. Staff need to be open minded, perceptive and sensitive to such information.

Human skills

Protected area managers must be able to work and interact effectively with people and draw on the fundamentals of organizing and motivating their staff. Managers are advocates for their agency's policies when interacting with local communities, neighbours, and the various levels and instrumentalities of government. They are partners in local cooperative projects. They must have sound facilitation, negotiation and conflict-resolution skills. They assist in a range of projects that involve volunteers. They work with the central agencies of government or with commercial or business partners in facilitating conservation. Managers in more senior positions are expected to be trusted by staff, to be ethical in their behaviour, and to work to invest in the professional careers of people and their working conditions.

Conceptual skills

These skills involve the formulation of ideas. Protected area managers need to understand abstract relationships, develop ideas and solve problems creatively. Thus, technical skill deals with things, human skill concerns people, and conceptual skill has to do with ideas (Katz, 1974). Protected area managers may be selected in competitive interview processes for their demonstrated ability to understand the contextual relationship of their managerial role, to visualize beneficial futures for the organization, and to proactively pursue opportunities with internal and external partners towards conservation goals. Conceptual skills provide the basis for goal-focused active leadership, for efficiency and effectiveness, and are particularly important for staff in senior positions. Managers who have the combined skills of conceptual insight, hands-on and social skills are highly sought after.

Further reading

Bartol, K., Martin, D., Tein, M. and Mathews, G. (1998) *Management: A Pacific Rim Focus*, McGraw-Hill, Roseville

Bazerman, M. (1998) *Judgement in Managerial Decision Making*, 4th edition, John Wiley and Sons, New York

Robbins, S. P. and Coulter, M. (2005) *Management*, 8th edition, Prentice Hall, Englewood Cliffs

Robbins, S. P., Bergman, R., Stagg, I. and Coulter, M. (2003) *Foundations of Management*, Prentice Hall, Frenches Forest

7

Developing Capacity

John Hough

This chapter provides guidance on the process by which the capacity of individuals, organizations and society, as a whole, to plan and manage protected areas can be increased. The term 'capacity-building' is often used as a synonym for training, or training and institution-building; but the process of developing capacity covers much more in that it is not just about learning from someone else 'out there' who already knows the answer, it is about developing new knowledge and practices as well. In particular, since we do not know all the answers about how to plan and manage protected areas, we need the ability to continually develop new approaches, and the 'we' involves individuals, organizations and society as a whole. A key implication of this is to recognize that as well as being able to achieve the objectives of protected areas and protected area systems, individuals, organizations and, indeed, society as a whole must also have the capacity to set objectives – because who else 'out there' is setting protected area objectives if it is not those involved in protected areas themselves:

> Capacity requires establishing effective processes for decision-making and action, carried out by appropriate actors (individual or collective), organized in effective structures for accountability, who understand what they have to do, who have the skill, motivation and material support to perform effectively, who are supported in this by rules, norms and values that are acknowledged and upheld by all actors involved (including those not active but able to influence). Capacity is a property of a 'goal-seeking system' that can be described in terms of its processes, structures, and actors, the roles they play, and the rules and norms that their behaviours reflect (UNDP, 1988).

One way to think about this is to imagine a protected area manager faced with a particular problem. His or her ability to address this problem will depend not only upon their skills and training, but also upon the resources and equipment at their disposal. Since these are generally provided by the organization for which the protected area manager is working, we can see that the capacity of the individual is intimately linked to, and interacts with, the capacity of the organization of which they are a part. However, we must then go on to ask what determines the capacity of the organization? How did the organization get there? Who supplied it with resources? Answering this question will probably lead us into a historical web of interacting forces, complex processes, chance events and certainly motivated individuals. However, it will also show us that, in the end, the existence of protected areas and protected area institutions and organizations is a result of societal choice. Society, or some part of it, chose to establish protected areas. Hence, if we are to improve the ability of protected areas to conserve, we need to think not only about how to improve the skills of protected area employees and the ability of their organizations, but also about how to improve the capacity of the societal context in which they operate. A simple example of this is management of invasive species – for example, goats on the Galapagos Islands. The most efficient solution might be to 'hunt and shoot them' but if public opinion reacts against this, then the option is closed and another solution must be found:

> *Capacity development is about creating conditions that allow and support the right people to take up the right roles in effective decision–action processes. It is both a means of goal realization and an end in itself (Joy, 1999).*

Developing capacity is about facilitating and encouraging a process of transformation or change by which individuals, organizations and societies develop their abilities, both individually and collectively, to perform functions, solve problems, and set and achieve their own goals. Developing capacity for protected areas is then about improving our ability to do everything associated with protected areas – plan, manage, establish, monitor, communicate, deploy staff efficiently and so on – and by 'our' we mean not only individuals and organizations, but also society as a whole.

This chapter describes the levels at which protected area capacity needs to be developed, outlines the components of a capacity development framework and assessing capacity needs, and examines implementing programmes designed to secure the desired change. It should be noted that this approach applies equally to government, whether national or local, community, NGO, or private protected areas.

Capacity levels

When capacity is examined at the individual, organizational and societal levels, a number of elements of capacity emerge.

Individuals

While it is easy for us to accept that protected area managers need specific training in order to work in a specific setting, or in a specific job, the ability to do this job effectively does not just depend upon their own skills, it also depends upon their personality, their motivation, their access to equipment, information, and a variety of other elements. Hence, building skills or training is only

Working group at the World Conservation Learning Network Mesoamerican meeting, Guadalajara, Mexico

Source: Cecilia Nizzola-Tabja

a part of the process of enhancing the capacity of individuals. If we are really to develop capacity, we must look at the context within which the individual works.

Organizations

While some aspects of the context within which protected area people work are beyond the ability of the protected area manager to influence, others are not. In particular, the institutional setting is critical. A poorly managed organization may assign people to jobs for which those individuals do not possess the necessary skills or aptitude. In addition to not knowing how to do the job, they might not have the information, equipment or financial resources they need to carry out the jobs assigned. In contrast, a well-managed organization will assign staff appropriately, have the requisite resources, structures and processes, and be able to motivate staff to carry out their work well.

An assumption is often made that the provision of all of the above conditions depends simply upon the presence or absence of a skilled manager. However, the manager is generally in exactly the same situation as any other employee: his or her effectiveness depends not just upon individual skills and motivation, but also upon the institutional context within which he or she must operate. Hence, in order to develop the capacity to manage protected areas, we must look beyond individual skills to the ability of the organization as a whole to achieve its purpose of protected area management. It is from this understanding that the notion of institution-building originated, and the term capacity-building is often taken to mean a combination of both training and institution-building.

At this point, it is important to draw a distinction between the terms 'organization' and 'institution'. An organization is an entity of some kind with its own structures and procedures. In addition, over time most organizations develop a particular culture that includes shared values and unwritten and informal ways of thinking and doing things. The organizational culture may also manifest itself externally as an 'attitude' or set of values. An institution is broader than an organization in that it includes the context in which an organization operates – the protected area laws, policies, regulations and procedures (both formal and informal) that govern it. In most capacity development work and thinking, the institution is treated as part of the broader societal context or system, and is very different from the discrete entity of an organization.

Systems, institutions and society

The ability of a protected area organization to do its job depends heavily upon its human resources, and hence the importance of training and good management. However, even good managers with all the skills and resources they require will be unable to operate effectively if it is not clear what they are supposed to be doing. An ongoing study in Southern Africa, for example, has concluded that the majority of protected areas do not have clear objectives. The objectives of protected area organizations are rarely set by the managers of those organizations; they are set by boards or higher levels of government. Furthermore, the protected area organizations have to operate in the context of other organizations, such as forest agencies and agriculture departments, or ministries of transport who wish to drive a road through the middle of a protected area. They also have to operate in particular legal and regulatory frameworks. These, in turn, are an outcome of the overall policy environment, both at local, subnational and international levels, and these all interact with each other. In turn, the policy envi-

ronment is set primarily by the overall societal context, again operating at local, national and global levels. Hence, when we examine how to improve the capacity of protected area organizations, we have to look, too, at the societal context of these organizations. Good managers, while not controlling their own environment, must manage this environment as much as they manage those things that they do have control over.

Capacity for what, capacity for who, and what capacity?

The first step in a capacity development programme is to assess what capacity is to be developed for – capacity for 'what'? For protected areas we can assume that the 'what' in general terms is about how to improve protected area planning and management. However, while there are various checklists of the specific 'whats' that are needed, these should only be regarded as providing useful guiding frameworks and should be adjusted specifically for every particular situation. A good example of a checklist of some of the 'whats' required for protected areas is that established by the Convention on Biological Diversity Working Group on Protected Areas (see Table 7.1).

The various 'whats' that are needed for protected area capacity are not necessarily all required at the same scale. While the emphasis tends to be on those required for both individual sites and for national systems of protected areas, some are also required at global levels; others at regional levels, provincial levels and local levels; and in the case of protected areas managed by communities or the private sector, also at these levels.

Having established 'capacity for what', the next question is 'capacity for who'. While the importance of addressing capacity development in the context of society as a whole was identified above, the key actors who are going to drive the changes in society, organizations and individuals outside protected area systems are those individuals currently directly involved in protected areas. These include the following:

*   political leaders, decision-makers and high-level policy-makers;

Table 7.1 Steps and related types of activities required in establishing and managing protected areas

Steps	Types of activities
Identification	Identification of large-scale conservation targets (species, habitats, biomes, ecosystems requiring protection as per Annex 1 of the Convention on Biological Diversity – CBD)
	Identification of landscape/seascape mosaic
	Protected area design
	Assessment of biological values of protected areas
	Assessment of other values of and threats to potential or existing protected areas
	Ecosystem assessments
Designation	Completion of legal establishment of protected areas
	Negotiation and agreement with stakeholders about protected areas, buffer zones and participatory approaches
	Agreement on management objectives of protected areas (according to IUCN category)
Management	Development of management plans and annual work plans
	Development of business plans
	Implementation of capacity-building for staff
	Management interventions to maintain biodiversity and ecological integrity (e.g. by establishing ecological networks or ecological corridors)
	Management interventions to maintain other values, including cultural values through involvement of indigenous and local communities
	Sustainable management options in IUCN Category V and VI protected areas and buffer zones
	Restoration initiatives as needed to increase value of protected areas
	Outreach to the public
	Management of uses (such as recreational, scientific and other uses) in protected areas
Monitoring and evaluation	Monitoring and evaluation of protected areas
	Adaptive management (see 'Approaches to planning' in Chapter 11) of protected areas as necessary

Source: Convention on Biological Diversity Working Group on Protected Areas (2005)

- protected area system managers;
- heads of individual protected areas and middle managers;
- advisory and management committee members;
- species, habitat and resource managers;
- scientists and researchers;
- field technicians concerned with wildlife, fire management and so on;
- law enforcement staff;
- community, religious and indigenous managers and planners;
- private managers and planners;
- training specialists;
- education and awareness specialists;
- community development and outreach staff;
- park interpreters, visitor liaison and guides;
- communications and information specialists;

- national and local policy planners, analysts and advocates;
- global policy planners, analysts and advocates;
- business managers and financing specialists;
- administrative staff working in personnel, finance and support; and
- facilities and infrastructure staff working on roads, maintenance and so on (adapted from Appleton et al, 2003).

The third question in this progression, after knowing the 'what' and the 'who', is the question of 'what capacity?' At an individual level, this is essentially the specific skills and competencies required to perform particular jobs or professions within the protected areas system. Different professionals within the system will require different levels of skill in each of the competencies. The Association of South-East Asian Nations (ASEAN) Regional Centre for Biodiversity Conservation, for example, through an extensive process of analysis with the six ASEAN countries, developed the following list of protected area competencies:

- advocacy and leadership;
- business development;
- collaborative management and participatory approaches;
- communications, information and outreach;
- community development;
- conservation biology;
- data gathering, inventory and research;
- enforcement and compliance;
- environmental education;
- facilities and infrastructure – planning and management;
- field craft;
- fire management;
- geographic information systems (GIS) and mapping;
- institutional structures and arrangements;
- interpretation for visitors and guiding;
- legislation and regulation;
- management – personnel, administration and finance;
- management – resources (wildlife, fisheries, rangelands and water);
- management – organizational (team, time and change);

- management – strategy and planning;
- marketing;
- negotiation, consensus-building and conflict resolution;
- planning and zoning;
- policy analysis and development;
- system planning;
- training; and
- visitor and tourism planning and management (adapted from Appleton et al, 2003).

Similarly, the International Ranger Federation has put forward what it considers to be a set of 'universal essential competencies' for professional rangers:

- Apply basic ecology and conservation principles and processes to monitor changes and manage conservation actions.
- Connect audiences to the importance of protected areas through interpretation, education and information services.
- Build relationships with all relevant communities and other stakeholders.
- Manage and maintain technology and infrastructure.
- Care for oneself and others in emergency situations.
- Write effective reports and manage an office or a project, and be financially responsible.
- Communicate well with team members and maintain strong working relationships (Smith, 2003).

Looking beyond the individual to the level of organizations, institutions and society, as a whole, the United Nations Development Programme (UNDP) has put forward a framework that includes five essential areas of capacity:

1 *Capacity to conceptualize and formulate policies, legislations, strategies and programmes.* This category includes analysing broader societal conditions that may affect needs and performance in a given protected area or system developing a vision; long-term strategizing; and setting of objectives. It also includes conceptualizing broader sectoral and cross-sectoral policy, as well as legislative and

Rangers, Lake Turkana National Park, Kenya

Source: IUCN Photo Library © Jim Thorsell

regulatory frameworks, including synergies between them. It further contains prioritization, planning and formulation of programmes and projects.

2   *Capacity to implement policies, legislations, strategies and programmes.* This category includes process management capacities that are essential to implementing any type of policy, legislation, strategy and programme. It also includes execution aspects of programmes and projects – that is, protected area system and site management. It includes mobilizing and managing human, material and financial resources, as well as selection of technologies and procurement of equipment.

3   *Capacity to engage and build consensus among all stakeholders.* This category includes issues such as mobilization and motivation of stakeholders; creation of partnerships; awareness-raising and developing an environment in which government, civil society and the private sector can work together; stakeholder identification and involvement; managing large group processes and discussions, including mediation of divergent interests; and the establishment of

partnerships and other collaborative mechanisms.

4   *Capacity to mobilize information and knowledge.* This category pertains to the mobilization, access and use of information and knowledge. It includes issues such as effectively gathering, analysing and synthesizing information; identifying problems and potential solutions; as well as consulting experts and peers. It further covers specific technical skills that are related specifically to the requirements of protected areas, including the capacity to carry out scientific and technical assessments.

5   *Capacity to monitor, evaluate, report and learn.* This category pertains to the monitoring of progress; measuring of results; codification of lessons; learning and feedback; and ensuring accountability. It also covers aspects such as reporting. It naturally links back to policy dialogue, planning and improved management of implementation.

It should be clear by this point that there is no universal framework that specifies what capacities are required for protected areas. Capacity requirements and capacity development needs must be determined on a specific case-by-case basis and will depend upon a large number of external and internal influences, such as neighbouring communities and interested and affected parties around the protected area, leadership, skills within the protected area, and political support.

Assessing capacity needs

As noted above, the first steps in capacity development are to determine 'capacity for what' and 'capacity for who' – including individuals, organizations and the societal context – and then 'what capacity?' Capacity development effort should then be concentrated where it will make the most difference. Determining this requires that a 'capacity needs assessment' be conducted.

The scope of a capacity needs assessment depends upon the responsibility of the particular protected area manager. While all managers will have to address capacity needs associated with their own organization, the individuals working within it and the societal context around it, these might vary from those of an entire national protected area system, through provincial and local subunits, to individual protected areas. However, while the scope might vary, the same analytic tools for assessing capacity needs can generally be used, whatever the scope.

The importance of self-assessment

As with all plans and strategies, 'ownership' is critical if the resulting plans are to be implemented. This is particularly true in capacity development where self-identification, ownership and commitment are critical to engendering change. The notion of having an outside 'specialist' come in to study the situation and generate a report is therefore of little value. Who participates in the assessment will significantly influence the outcome of the assessment. It is easy to see how law enforcement rangers might argue that their primary capacity development needs are stronger regulations, while the interpretive staff might argue that the main emphasis should be on training all staff in persuasion techniques. It is therefore those whose capacities are to grow who must undertake the assessment. The role of outsiders in this process is one of facilitation, not one of conducting a study.

Tools for assessing capacity needs

A wide array of tools exists for assessing capacity needs, many of them being quite widely used standard social science techniques. Most experienced facilitators will be able to provide guidance in choosing and adapting the right set of tools. Tools are needed both for guiding the analysis, and to structure the overall process and guide participation. Some of the common tools used, and the capacity levels where they might be used, are listed in Table 7.2. An example of an assessment process that used several of these tools is given in Case Study 7.1.

Critical diagnostic questions

As our understanding of the holistic nature of capacity development has evolved, a key set of diagnostic concerns has emerged. These are listed below, together with some specific notes applicable to protected areas.

Assessing capacity constraints at the individual level

Capacity development at the individual level refers to the process of changing awareness and attitudes, expanding knowledge and developing skills. Guiding questions are as follows:

- *Job requirements and skill levels*. Are jobs correctly defined; are the required skills available?
- *Training/retraining*. Are the appropriate training plans and activities taking place?
- *Career progression*. Are individuals able to advance and develop professionally?
- *Personal/professional networking*. Are individuals exchanging knowledge with peers?
- *Accountability*. Is responsibility delegated effectively and is performance measured? Are individuals held accountable?
- *Access to information and resources*. Can individuals access needed information and resources?
- *Morale, motivation and security*. Are individuals motivated to do their best?
- *Attitudes and integrity*. Are these appropriate and strong?
- *Teamwork and interrelationships*. Do individuals interact effectively and form functional teams?

Table 7.2 Tools for assessing capacity needs and related capacity levels

Tools	Societal levels	Organizational levels	Individual levels
Brainstorming	X	X	
Case study analysis	X	X	X
Concept mapping	X	X	
Consensus-building discussions	X	X	
Delphi process	X		
Direct observation	X		
Document reviews	X	X	X
Expert panels	X	X	
Focus groups	X		
Force field analysis	X	X	
Gap analysis	X	X	X
Informant interviews	X	X	X
Job analysis	X	X	
Logical framework analysis	X	X	
Nominal group techniques	X	X	X
Organizational audits	X		
Participatory appraisals	X	X	
Prioritization matrix	X	X	X
Problem tree/root cause analysis	X	X	
Questionnaires and surveys	X	X	
Site visits	X	X	
Stakeholder analysis	X	X	
Staff audits	X		
SWOT (strengths, weaknesses, opportunities and threats) analysis (see Chapter 11, p302)	X	X	
Systems analysis	X	X	
Terms of reference	X	X	
Testing	X	X	X
Work plans	X	X	
Workshops/working groups	X	X	

Case Study **7.1**

A capacity assessment for protected areas in Namibia

The Namibian Ministry of Environment and Tourism (MET) undertook a comprehensive capacity assessment and review of protected areas during 2004 to 2005. The work built on an earlier partial study from 2003 to 2004 that examined broader capacity issues for biodiversity management as a whole, but only in certain parts of the country. The methodology used key informants, site visits, direct observation, document review, case study analysis, informant interviews with a wide variety of stakeholders both inside and outside the MET, focus groups, and workshops. A team of four analysts facilitated the whole process. Elements examined included the policy, legal and regulatory frameworks, institutional structures and management accountability, and the organizational structure and competency of the MET, including the various divisions and subdivisions responsible for protected areas, wildlife management, science, and administration and support services. It also examined staffing structures; roles; responsibilities; competencies; deployment; administrative processes; accountability; and decision-making capabilities; as well as financial management and human resource management. At individual levels, it examined skills, experience, learning, training and career opportunities, and accountability and performance.

Key recommendations from the assessment included a reorganization of institutions and their responsibilities, comprising significant decentralization; changed staffing structures; and the operationalization of a performance management framework and specific training plan.

The potential value of such actions is illustrated by the case of Mount Kitanglad Natural Park in the Philippines, where management was strengthened by devolving decision-making from central to local levels, and by providing experiential training on issues including leadership, accounting, value formation, lobbying, negotiating and legal issues (Mirasol, 2003).

Source: adapted from Booth et al (2005)

- *Workloads.* Are these reasonable? Do individuals have a reasonable balance between work and other parts of their life?

Assessing capacity constraints at the organizational level

Capacity development at the organizational level focuses on the structure, function and performance of specific organizations (within government, NGOs/civil society and the private sector), as well as the ability of these organizations to adapt to change. This includes looking at sectors and sectoral organizations (such as tourism and tourism organizations). Possible questions are as follows:

- *Mission/mandate.* Does the organization have clearly defined missions and a mandate?
- *Performance and accountability.* Is success clearly defined, being monitored and being evaluated, and are the responsible parties held accountable?
- *Structure and management.* Is the institution effectively structured and managed, focusing on core competencies, strategy and culture?

- *Management processes.* Do organizational processes, such as strategic planning, operations, quality management, performance monitoring and evaluation, work effectively?
- *Human resources.* Are human resources adequate, sufficiently skilled, motivated and appropriately deployed?
- *Financial resources.* Are financial resources managed efficiently and allocated appropriately to enable effective operations?
- *Information resources.* Is the information required to support available operations and is it effectively distributed and managed?
- *Infrastructure.* Are material requirements, such as buildings, offices, vehicles and computers, allocated appropriately and managed effectively?

Assessing capacity constraints at the societal or systemic level

Capacity development at the systemic level emphasizes the overall societal framework in which individuals and organizations interact with each other and their external environment. Guiding questions are as follows:

- *Policy framework.* Is the overall policy environment conducive to achieving results?
- *Legal and regulatory framework.* Is appropriate legislation in place and are laws enforced effectively?
- *Management accountability framework.* Are organizational responsibilities clearly and logically defined and well coordinated? Are the responsible protected area organizations held publicly accountable?
- *Economic framework.* Do markets and the private sector function effectively and efficiently vis-à-vis protected area resources and values?
- *Systems-level resources.* Are the required human, financial and information resources available? These may be found in government, the private sector, NGOs and civil society.
- *Processes and relationships.* Do organizations and processes, whether in government, the private sector, NGOs or civil society, interact and work effectively together (that is, are the institutions efficient)?

Inter-linkages and bottlenecks

We have already seen that capacity development must occur at various levels, from the individual to society as a whole, and it is critical to stress again that these levels are all interconnected. Simply developing the skills of a protected area manager will have no effect on the management of a protected area if the societal context prevents the application of these skills, or as a result of poor organizational management the protected area manager is deployed to the wrong job. Hence, it is critical that, in addition to assessing capacity at each of the three levels, analysis and diagnosis looks across levels to identify the key capacity bottlenecks that must be addressed. It is generally by focusing effort here that the most progress in improving overall protected areas capacity can be achieved.

Time frames

Capacity is relevant in both the short term (the ability to address an immediate problem) and in the long term (enabling protected areas to not only keep up with, but ideally to get ahead of, the issues and challenges they will be facing in the future). A good example is the ability of protected area systems, particularly in the low Human Development Index (HDI) countries, to address the current financial challenges as donor aid switches out of conservation, where it has been for the last 15 years or so, to other priorities. Many are now scrambling to develop this capacity, instead of having already put it in place ahead of this predictable change. A capacity needs assessment must consider, and differentiate between, varying time scales.

Developing capacities

Once a capacity needs assessment has been completed, connections have been established, bottlenecks identified, priorities set, trade-offs made and decisions finalized, the results should be articulated in the form of a strategy and action plan, complete with responsibilities, costings, timelines and performance measures. It is also critical that feedback loops are established so that there is ongoing learning and adaptation during implementation.

At present, most of the protected area literature on capacity focuses on training rather than the broader processes of capacity development at organizational and societal levels. However, much has been written on this process in other fields, and since this is largely the same whatever the focus, this section draws primarily from other areas to provide guidance on the process of developing capacity.

As we have seen earlier, capacity development is much more than just training or institution-building: it involves an ongoing process of change or transformation that aims to induce various actors to adopt new responsibilities, skills, behaviours, approaches, values and policies. The process of actively facilitating capacity development involves actively managing change. This can be overlooked in the design and implementation of interventions that focus on discrete activities such as training workshops or technology-transfer activities. While important, the latter should always be seen in the context of a broader ongoing change management process.

Training involves the transfer of skills and behaviours to particular targets. 'Vertical' transfer occurs when specialists or more senior persons within an organization provide training. Another form of vertical capacity development is the process of mentoring, where a knowledgeable and experienced individual guides another less knowledgeable or skilled individual. Behaviours and skills can also be transferred through horizontal exchange, where one individual or group learns from a peer. A key advantage of peer exchange is that learning occurs in both directions; as such, there is greater potential for new ideas to emerge. Horizontal capacity development is more likely to be informal and loosely structured, compared with the typical formality and discipline associated with vertical transfer. A capacity development strategy should include both vertical and horizontal approaches.

Capacity development is normally driven by an identified need to do something better – that is, more efficiently or more effectively. This 'something' might be, for example, fire management or interpretation for visitors. Where better methods of doing something are already known, it is a fairly straightforward matter to organize training or, at organizational levels, a task force to look into and adapt, for example, an existing fire management system to the local situation. This is so-called 'incremental' capacity development. It starts from an existing situation and makes it incrementally better through small and progressive changes.

However, such an incremental approach can also have significant limitations. Most notably, it tends to preclude broader-scale thinking about more radical change that, while perhaps disruptive in the short term, can result in tremendous gains in efficiency and effectiveness. This is known as 'transformational capacity development'. Instead of asking the question 'how can we do what we are doing better?', it asks the question 'how could we get this done?' Rather than focusing on training, organizational strengthening and improving policies, laws and regulations, transformational capacity development focuses on learning, on new institutional arrangements, and on visioning and scenario development. As such, it has the potential to identify radically new ways of doing things, rather than simply doing existing things better. Again, a capacity development strategy, or change management process, should include both approaches.

Many capacity development processes focus on either the creation of new capacity, or enhancing existing capacities; however, there is often latent capacity within a system and this should not be overlooked. Redeploying staff is the most obvious form of mobilizing latent capacity; but there are often many other ways. One view of capacity development is simply articulated as 'doing more with less' – or at least with the same!

Tools and methods for developing capacity

Changes in capacity depend upon changes in knowledge, attitudes and practices or behaviours. Much work has been done on how to induce change among individuals, organizations and society, and a wide variety of tools and methods for changing these is available. Like all tools and methods, each has its own advantages and disadvantages and works differently in different situations. As always, it is important to pick the right tools for the right jobs, and in almost all cases a combination of tools should be used rather than relying on a single approach.

Individual levels

The ways in which a wide range of protected area training approaches can be applied at the individual level are summarized in Table 7.3. Several of these approaches are considered in more detail below.

Formal education and professional training

This is the most prevalent approach to developing the capacity of individuals and is what most people immediately think of when capacity development is discussed. While effective for transferring specific knowledge and behaviours, it is not necessarily effective at problem-solving, or at developing new thinking and approaches. Since there is inevitably also a significant time lag between new practices being developed and making their way into formal training programmes, the content of much training is several years behind cutting-edge thinking. Formal training is therefore most useful for basic and well-established knowledge and practice.

For managers, scientists, educators and administrative staff, there are well-established

Table 7.3 Suggested individual in-service training plan

Training method	Training approach/category	When	Where	Who conducts or initiates training
Orientation: 1 organizational level		First week (two days)	Headquarters	Personnel and administration department (PAD)
2 park level	On-the-job training – instruction (formal)	(three days)	Protected area	PAD
3 job level		Second week (one day)	Department	Department head/ranger
4 learner level		(four days)	Work site	Supervisor
Study tour (of protected area)	On-the-job training – observation	Third week (five days)	Entire protected area	Supervisor and/or colleagues
Coaching	On-the-job training – instruction (formal)	Fourth week (five days) then ongoing	Work site	Supervisor
Manager shadowing	On-the-job training – observation	Fifth week (five days) then ongoing	Work site	Supervisor
Colleagues	On-the-job training – instruction (informal)	Sixth week (five days) then ongoing	Work site	Colleagues
Meetings	On-the-job training – instruction (informal)	Biweekly Monthly	Work site Department	Supervisor Department head/ranger
Mentoring	On-the-job training – instruction (informal)	Monthly exchange	Protected area	Mentor

Reading:
  1 organizational and departmental policies and plans
  2 work-related and educational
	On-the-job training – self-taught	First month
		
		Ongoing
			Work site, home, protected area	Employee

Experience	On-the-job training – performance related	Ongoing	Work site	Employee
Trial and error	On-the-job training – performance related	Ongoing	Work site	Employee
Informal discussion	On-the-job training – instruction (informal)	Ongoing	Work site	Colleagues
Videos	On-the-job training – self-taught	Ongoing	Work site, home, protected area	Employee
Outside organization colleagues	On-the-job training – instruction (informal)	Case by case	Work site or protected area	Non-work colleagues

Table 7.3 Continued

Training method	Training approach/category	When	Where	Who conducts or initiates training
Lectures	On-the-job training – instruction (formal)	Case by case	Protected area	Outside expert/NGOs
Outside experts and researchers	On-the-job training – instruction (formal)	Case by case	Protected area	Outside expert
Technical assistance	On-the-job training – instruction (formal)	Case by case	Work site	Technical adviser
Filling in for a supervisor	On-the-job training – performance related	Case by case	Work site	Employee
Guided delegation	On-the-job training – instruction (informal)	For special tasks only	Work site	Supervisor
Computer tutorials	On-the-job training – self-taught	For special tasks only	Work site	Employee
Attachment	On-the-job training – instruction (informal)	Once a year	Work site	Supervisor
Workshop or seminar	In-service training (off site)	During first two years and every two years thereafter	Work site or off site	Department and/or PAD
Job rotation	On-the-job training – performance related	Every three years	New protected area or work site (or department, if applicable)	Department and/or PAD
Study tour	On-the-job training – observation	During third year of work and every three years thereafter	New protected area in country or in outside country	Department and/or PAD
Short course	In-service training (off site)	After two years of work if already received formal training, and every two years thereafter	Training institution off site in country or outside country	PAD
Certificate, Diploma, BSc, MSc	Formal training (off site)	After two or three years of work	In country or outside country	PAD

professional training courses leading to formal qualifications in their subject of specialization. However, these are generally not protected area specific. Protected area specific training is generally only available for mid- to lower-level staff, particularly field rangers, although there are a few formal professional training programmes now beginning to emerge for protected area managers (see Case Study 7.2). One of the consequences of this is that senior-level protected area managers tend to be either rangers who have moved up through the ranks, or professionals who have moved laterally into protected areas from other closely related professional fields. In consequence, a key training need in protected areas are short courses to enable both junior and senior rangers, as well as specialized professionals from outside protected areas, to both move up to higher levels and to extend their range of skills into subjects such as strategic planning, financial and personnel management, public relations, conservation biology, and the like. In practice, there are many such courses available, ranging from short specialized courses of a few days, to year-long master's degrees; however, since most staff in mid career cannot take a year off for such training, the majority of professional courses tend to be between two and four weeks in duration. Case Study 7.2 provides an example of the range of protected area training available in South Africa.

Many of the formal training institutions also offer short courses ranging from a few days to a few weeks, as do other organizations, such as some of the conservation NGOs, private tourism operators and projects funded by external donors. Such courses are pitched at a variety of levels, from village guides to senior managers. Mid-level and lower-level courses generally tend to emphasize practical hands-on skills rather than academic or theoretical approaches. They also, particularly at higher levels, often draw in or go out to practising specialists in the field, rather than relying simply on their own staff. Senior protected area managers can also advance their knowledge through partic-ipating in international-level training, such as the one-month International Seminar on Protected Areas Management offered by a consortium, including the US Forest Service International Program and the universities of Montana, Idaho and Colorado State.

Short courses and in-service training

Short courses can be very effective for conveying new knowledge and practices in specialist areas; however, attitudinal change can be more difficult to achieve in short time frames. Many organizations offer short courses in a wide range of subjects relevant to protected areas; similarly, protected area professionals can find a wide range of short courses in topics in other fields, such as business administration, planning, marketing and the like. Short course topics might cover many of those listed in the earlier section on 'Capacity for what, capacity for who, and what capacity?'.

While short courses are obviously important, a common mistake is to imagine that they are some kind of 'magic bullet' – something that will solve all of the problems by 'teaching' individuals how to do particular things. However, as explained above, what individuals do depends upon much more than their knowledge or a prac-tised behaviour. Issues such as their attitudes and motivation, and the availability of resources and information, all play important roles in determining individual capacity, even before the constraints of the organizational and societal contexts come

Case Study **7.2**

Protected area training available in South Africa

Formal training opportunities in South Africa range from a 14-month master's degree in conservation biology at the University of Cape Town, to courses lasting a few hours on specialist subjects for junior protected area personnel with limited education offered in the field by private managers. In between, there is a full range of different possibilities, including year-long diploma and certificate courses at the Southern African Wildlife College, which are intended to prepare mid- and junior-level protected area managers. More general two- and three-year certificate-level training is also available through regional agriculture and natural resource colleges that prepare rangers and field technicians. Critical differences between the kinds of formal training available for protected area professionals include the background level of education and experience of the trainee; the scope of the training – from all aspects of protected areas to very specialized subjects; and realistic expectations regarding the kind and levels of jobs that the trainees are likely to move on to as a result of the training.

into play. This is particularly true where a short course is designed around the message the proponent wants to get across, rather than being designed in the context and from the perspective of the learner. Hence, it is important to recognize that even with 'retraining' of individuals, it is not necessarily easy for them to apply these new skills if the institutional culture of the organization is not changing as well.

Apprenticeships, internships, mentoring and coaching

Pairing experienced individuals with junior individuals can be a very effective way of developing the capacity of both parties. The younger person often brings recent ideas from formal education, and an enthusiastic willingness to ask new questions and look at things in new ways. The older person obviously brings experience, perspective and balance. Successful pairings require openness on the part of both, as well as a formal recognition by management of the additional responsibilities being placed on both.

Exchanges

Short-term staff exchanges can provide an effective way of transferring knowledge and practices between both individuals and organizations, provided the exchange is designed with organizational learning in mind and appropriate internal reporting and briefing/debriefing and consultation are put in place. If not, while useful to the individuals being exchanged, the costs to the organizations in lost productivity and coaching can be high.

Study visits

Formal study visits between different protected areas have some similarities with staff exchanges, except that the focus is more on organizational learning and exchange rather than on individual learning and exchange. The key to effective study visits is that all parties undertake sufficient preparation. Often, advanced visits are required by a facilitator from one or both protected areas involved in order to design the exchange and ensure that all substantive and logistical arrangements are in place.

Meetings and workshops

There are an increasing number of substantive international and regional meetings on protected area topics. These can be political in nature (as are those associated with international conventions, such as conventions on biodiversity, wetlands, migratory species and world heritage) or much more technically focused (as are those of professional societies, such as conservation biology, wildlife and wilderness). Most of the latter, and those organized by the IUCN, such as the World Conservation Congress and the World Parks Congress (see Box 2.2 in Chapter 2), are specifically focused on technical exchange and can be important for individuals to acquire specific new knowledge. They are also of use in developing personal professional networks. Their main drawback is their cost in accommodation, travel and time.

Publications, professional societies and networking

There is an ever-increasing amount of published material on all aspects of protected area planning and management in many languages. Professional societies such as the International Ranger Federation are emerging, and there are numerous websites, list servers and networks dedicated to protected area-related issues on the internet. However, while there can be information overload for some protected areas staff, many of those in remote areas are often in the opposite position – essentially, being starved of information. There are also language barriers that can segment knowledge. So, while there is much information available, it does not necessarily mean that it is being seen, read or adopted.

Constraints to learning at individual levels

Given the wide range of training and learning opportunities that now exist, the extent to which these will lead to changes in knowledge and attitudes will depend to a great extent upon two interdependent factors: the financial and time resources available; and the extent to which learning and adoption of new practices is encouraged by the protected area organizations of which individuals are a part. Generally, the emphasis of most people concerned about training is on the former; however, the latter, which is often ignored, is perhaps equally or more important, particularly given the wide availability of information.

Organizational levels

Developing the capacity of organizations is considerably more complex than developing the capacity of individuals; but significant amounts of work have been done on 'institution-building', so it is a process that is reasonably well understood, even if it is difficult to achieve. Organizational change normally emerges from a combination of external forces and internal reflection, although sometimes it is solely the result of one or the other. But if it is to succeed, it will always require a certain amount of internal reflection. The three key elements in organizational change are its structure, its culture and its procedures. Additionally, capacity can be enhanced by increasing the human, material, financial and informational resources available to the organization, although this only works if there are concomitant changes in structure, culture and procedures.

A key element in developing the capacity of an organization is its own self-assessment, and this in itself can result in significant changes. However, getting an organization to the point of undertaking this assessment is not always easy. Most people resist change because it brings uncertainty, and also because it implies changes in responsibilities, power and influence. Even if decreed by senior management, changes are not fully internalized until they are owned by all of the stakeholders – in this case, the staff of the organization. Key steps in starting organizational capacity development are:

- raising awareness of the possibilities of increased capacity – doing things better, more effectively and more efficiently;
- providing the data and evidence to support this;
- asking provocative questions;
- analysing the stakeholders – identifying champions who will help to drive the process within the organization and the resistors (the people who will most strongly oppose change);

- stimulating the champions, building alliances between those interested in change and devising strategies to overcome (and manage conflicts with) the resistors;
- identifying the 'spaces' for change;
- ensuring ownership of the change process by all of the key stakeholders;
- allocating resources to the change process;
- developing a shared vision;
- maintaining flexibility and a long-term commitment to seeing the changes through;
- putting in place incentives and disincentives; and
- institutionalizing the changes with new structures and procedures, and working to develop a new culture (Pasteur, 2001).

Societal levels

The institutional and societal constraints on individual- and organizational-level change have already been pointed out; and yet it is these that have often been neglected in capacity development initiatives in the past. The challenges have many similarities to those of the organization, except that because the histories, cultures, values, economic issues and power relationships are much greater, resistance to change can be considerable. As with organizational change, it is essential that there are champions – in this case, probably a protected area organization as a whole. As with organizations, the protected area agency will be the one raising awareness: asking provocative questions, identifying and stimulating the champions, and so on. Knowing the stakeholders and their interests, is of course, equally important. Currently, there are three common entry points for a protected area organization seeking changes at an institutional and societal level in order to improve protected area management: treating the government as an organization; awareness and education; and lobbying and high-level policy change.

Treating the government as an organization

This is particularly applicable where the protected area organization is a line agency inside a government. In this case, the strategy pursued is essentially similar to that described under organizational capacity development, except that the actors are organizations rather than individuals. The same capacity assessment process can be applied as at the organizational level, except it is within the structure of agencies, the procedures and rules governing them (policies, laws, regulations and the procedures between them), their interactions, reporting and resource allocations where change will be sought. For protected area organizations that are not line agencies, such as parastatal organizations, private or community protected areas, the approach will contain elements of this approach, but will probably be more similar to the other two below.

Awareness and education

Most protected area organizations have significant communication capacities; but normally these are targeted at protected area visitors, particularly schoolchildren. Targeting them rather differently can be very effective in bringing about societal change more broadly (see Case Study 7.3). However, identifying the key targets can be challenging. Awareness and education are key tools for shifting attitudes and behaviours of society as a whole in ways that can improve protected area management – or, more particularly, can eliminate bottlenecks to such improvement.

Lobbying and high-level policy change

Particularly where power is concentrated (and when the key bottlenecks to enhancing the capacity of protected areas lie within these power structures), high-level lobbying and negotiation are generally required to effect change. In this case, identifying allies outside a responsible government protected area agency may be critical to pursuing effective action. Wheat (1999) provides a detailed account of the lobbying and negotiation process required to establish the Death Valley National Park in the US. An example of a high-level change process that built governance capacity in the Philippines protected area system is given in Case Study 7.4.

It is worth noting that one of the key tools for societal-level change – economic leverage – is not really available to protected area organizations since, in general, they are highly dependent upon, rather than suppliers of, financial resources. Currently, exceptions occur where a particular protected area is a key part of the local economy. This seems to be particularly true of a number of small island tropical countries where coral reefs are recognized as the basis of tourism-based economies; in such cases, protected areas can use economic levers to effect changes to eliminate societal-level constraints to their effectiveness.

Education centre, Guardaparque, Bariloche, Argentina

Source: IUCN Photo Library © Jim Thorsell

Case Study **7.3**

Using awareness and education to develop social capacity: An example from Australia

Parks Victoria is a parastatal agency with responsibility for delivering park management in the Australian state of Victoria. Parks Victoria discovered the value of developing societal capacity through an effort to encourage people to visit parks and play a role in their care. The first step was to identify a 'message' that was perceived by the public as conveying the qualities and attributes of custodianship, environmental protection and a contribution to civil society. This resulted in the coining of the expression 'Healthy Parks, Healthy People' – implying that environmental health and community health were deeply intertwined. The second step was an eight-week radio and print promotion of activities celebrating active outdoor recreation. This was coupled with the development of a number of partnerships with the health sector, which resulted in posters and brochures being distributed to doctors' offices throughout the state, and even a congratulations card being provided to the mother of each new baby. This was followed by a variety of events, such as the World's Greatest Pram Stroll. A second partnership was with a national television station that developed a series of short programmes featuring an actual park ranger. This became so popular that it was placed during peak viewing times. Throughout, the message was maintained: 'Healthy Parks, Healthy People'. Resulting from this were three different awards for marketing and innovation! An additional step taken was active engagement in a variety of collaborative social and volunteer programmes that developed skills and delivered services which benefited both parks and communities. Consequently, there has been public recognition of Parks Victoria as a socially responsible organization and the development of a collective community consciousness. Parks Victoria recognizes this as 'social capital' – but it is also an example of the successful development of societal capacity that now enables Parks Victoria to move ahead with further protected areas agendas.

Source: adapted from Senior and Townsend (2005)

Case Study **7.4**

Building governance capacity for protected areas in the Philippines

In order to establish effective governance of protected areas in the Philippines, the National Protected Area Programme (NIPAP) adopted the following process:

- A senate committee on natural resources and ecology first admitted that there was a problem with managing the system. This provided the impetus to launch organizational reforms, including the legal establishment of local management boards for each individual park.
- These boards met with much scepticism and there was little progress until, five years later, NIPAP recognized that the boards had to be linked to community interests.
- NIPAP undertook internal training of its staff, and then launched a process of dialogue and workshops on protected areas for local community leaders, using local languages and dialects.
- As a result, local leaders became involved and local governments started to provide direct financial support.

This case study reflects a change process initiated by a leader on the senate committee, top-down driven institutional change followed by bottom-up outreach, and a communication and training process, which, in turn, led to the improved effectiveness of the protected area system.

Source: adapted from Manila (2003)

Holistic approaches

In almost all cases, it is necessary to approach capacity development from an integrated perspective – the individual, organizational, institutional and societal levels (see Case Study 7.5). This is challenging; but as we have seen, addressing one without the others is unlikely to succeed. Furthermore, addressing them simultaneously is unlikely to be feasible. As described earlier on p170, identifying the key capacity bottlenecks, addressing them and then moving on systematically to the next ones will become a continual process of self-assessment, learning, change and improvement.

Developing capacity for protected areas requires us to focus holistically on the entire protected area system. It goes beyond transferring existing skills, lessons and knowledge from individuals to individuals, and even protected area institutions to protected area institutions, but seeks more broadly to continually enhance our ability to imagine new protected areas and protected area systems, set goals for these and then achieve them. According to the experts on protected area capacity who gathered at the World Parks Congress in Durban in 2003, this requires five key elements (Carabias, 2004):

1   supportive policy and legal frameworks;
2   strong organizations and institutions;
3   skilled and able professionals;
4   adequate and sustainable financial resources; and
5   awareness and support.

Progress and standards

As with any activity, it is important to measure progress in capacity development. This includes monitoring progress, measuring results, learning and codifying lessons, ensuring feedback and adaptive management, and ensuring accountability. This requires that the use of indicators and (as with other performance evaluation) needs to be SMART: specific, measurable, appropriate, realistic and time bound.

Since capacity is not abstract but is directly linked to the setting and achievement of goals for something in particular – 'capacity for what?' – changes in capacity will be reflected in changes in the ability to do 'what'. For example, we might measure an increase in the number of infractions recorded by staff trained in monitoring protected area boundaries compared to the number of infractions recorded by untrained staff. It is important to note, however, that measuring the

Case Study 7.5

Developing a capacity development strategy

In 1997, the IUCN Commission on Education and Communication assisted five countries in Central Europe to develop a capacity development programme to help protected area managers prepare for accession to the European Union (EU). The first step involved roundtable meetings in each of the five countries, and this was followed by a workshop for decision-makers from ministries and agencies in all five countries to assist them in understanding the change implications of accession. As a result, all five countries sent four participants to a ten-day training session on problem-solving where participants discovered the importance of identifying the real problem, rather than focusing on preconceived solutions. The training session generated a set of guiding questions that included issues of perceptions, stakeholders, motivation and the like. Additional questions included asking 'How can we bring about changes in the wider system to sustain the positive effect of our actions?' and 'In what ways could our efforts cause reaction in the wider system and weaken our results?' Together, a four-part strategy was devised which would:

1   establish a network of change agents in and between the five countries;
2   develop a critical mass of 'early adopters' around the change agents;
3   have the participants themselves discover the individual, institutional and societal barriers to change; and
4   successfully overcome some of these barriers.

Source: adapted from Hesselink et al (2003)

number of staff trained in monitoring protected area boundaries would tell us nothing about whether capacity had increased, only something about the level of effort put into developing capacity.

Hence, in order to measure progress in developing capacity for protected areas effectively, there must first be a set of 'whats' or standards with respect to what protected areas must be able to do. This is very similar to the approach detailed in Chapter 24, which covers the broader issues of individual and societal capacities. As discussed earlier in 'Capacity for what, capacity for who, and what capacity?', a number of approaches to defining the 'whats' of protected areas have been made, and a number of organizations are beginning to develop capacity development scorecards. A sample of a scorecard currently being tested by UNDP for measuring change in the capacity of national protected area systems is given in Table 7.4.

Establishing a global set of 'whats' or standards for protected areas is likely to be quite difficult given the wide range of protected areas that exist and their different objectives, management categories and management authorities – from central government through provincial and local governments, to private and community areas. Each system might have its own particular set of 'whats' and indicator scorecards associated with it. Nonetheless, the ASEAN countries have shown that despite their differences, they have been able to establish a basic set of competence standards for protected areas staff. Similarly, the International Ranger Federation has defined a basic set of ranger competencies (see p166). It is likely that in the near future we will see the emergence of standards associated with these competencies, followed by a system of professional certification maintained by professional associations, for a number of different kinds of protected area professionals.

Sustaining capacity: Becoming a learning organization

Capacity development is a process of self-enhancement, a continuous cycle of learning and review. While at individual levels new skills can be learned and applied, unless they continue to be used they will be lost. Sustaining capacity at the individual level is dependent not only upon new skills being learned, but also on an organizational environment that deploys and redeploys individuals effectively in the context of the evolving nature of the problems and issues being addressed. Similarly, organizations or entities must continually adjust their operations if capacity to deal with current issues is to be sustained. At a systemic level, public perceptions, policies, and organizational mandates, alignments and responsibilities must also be continually reshaped, adjusted and redrawn in response to the changing situation.

Hence, sustaining capacity or capacity retention is a matter of establishing learning systems – an environment conducive to ongoing learning, review and change at all levels: individual, organizational and systemic. A successful capacity development process will be largely self-sustaining. The sustainability of capacity development is about maintaining change and adaptability at all levels. The very notion of having to make capacity development 'stick' implies an unsuccessful approach to capacity development. The UNDP (1998) offers some suggestions for sustaining capacity across all levels:

1   Systemic levels:
    • strategic management:
        • strengthening and sustaining participatory processes;
        • decentralization and devolution to the lowest appropriate levels;
        • delegation and empowerment to those responsible;
        • maintaining flexible and responsive legislative and regulatory environments;
        • strengthening and maintaining transparency and accountability at all levels;
        • ensuring meaningful access to information;
    • good governance:
        • effective linkages between executive and legislative branches of government;
        • effective executive decision-making and decision support;
        • implementing integrated results-oriented budgeting and financial management systems;

- strengthening communication processes between public, private and civil
  sectors;
- involving the private sector, NGOs
  and civil society partners and partnerships in service delivery;
  - teamwork and coordination:
    - foster teamwork;
    - adopt best practices;
    - ensure appropriate incentives and
      disincentives;
    - participatory management;
    - maximize networking;
    - encourage individual mobility within
      the system.
2   Entity/organizational levels:
    - involve employees in decision-making;
    - offer meaningful work;
    - enable workers to take responsibility for
      their work;
    - use self-managing teams rather than
      depending upon authority;
    - reduce the layers of hierarchy;
    - encourage individual identity and
      expertise;
    - give employees responsibility for their
      own development;
    - invest in human resources;
    - establish an atmosphere of mutual respect
      and trust;
    - cultivate existing strengths;
    - expect continuous learning;
    - balance home and work demands;
    - reward superior performance;
    - minimize group size;
    - encourage diversity;
    - encourage entrepreneurialism;
    - encourage risk-taking;
    - ensure a workplace open to constructive
      criticism.
3   Individual levels:
    - enable continuous education and training;
    - establish incentives and security;
    - link responsibility, performance and
      accountability;
    - develop leadership and management
      abilities;
    - pursue cooperative teamwork environ-
      ments;

- maximize access to information.

As the pace of global change increases, our ability
to continually adapt, learn and apply this learning
will be under continual pressure. The aim of
taking a broad view of capacity development is to
get ahead. The only way we will stay ahead is by
becoming learning organizations – by ongoing
capacity development becoming 'business as usual'
for us as individuals, organizations and societies
concerned about protected areas.

Further reading

Appleton, M. R., Texon, G. I. and Urarte, M.T. (2003)
*Competence Standards for Protected Area Jobs in South
East Asia*, ASEAN Regional Centre for
Biodiversity Conservation, Los Banos

Booth, V., Martin, R. and Wilson, E. (2005)
*Strengthening the System of National Protected Areas
Project, Namibia: Capacity Assessment for Parks
Management in Conservation at Individual,
Institutional and Systemic Levels*, Environment and
Development Group, Oxford

Carabias, J., de la Maza, J. and Cadena, J. R. (eds)
(2003) *Capacity Needs to Manage Protected Areas:
Africa*, The Nature Conservancy, Arlington

Carabias, J., de la Maza, J. and Gonzales, J. R. (2004)
'Building capacity to manage protected areas in an
era of global change', in Barber, C. V., Miller, K.
and Boness, M. (eds) *Securing Protected Areas in the
Face of Global Change: Issues and Strategies*, IUCN,
Gland and Cambridge

Carabias, J. and Rao, K. (eds) (2003) *Capacity Needs to
Manage Protected Areas: Asia*, The Nature
Conservancy, Arlington

Pasteur, K. (2001) *Changing Organizations for
Sustainable Livelihoods: A Map to Guide Change –
Lessons for Change in Policy and Organizations, No 1*,
Institute for Development Studies, Brighton

UNDP (United Nations Development Programme)
(1988) *Capacity Assessment and Development in a
Systems and Strategic Management Context*,
Technical Advisory Paper no 3, Management
Development and Governance Division, Bureau
for Development Policy, New York, www.magnet.
undp.org/docs/cap/main.htm

UNDP–GEF (Global Environment Facility) (2003)
*Capacity Development Indicators: A UNDP–GEF
Resource Kit*, UNDP, New York

Table 7.4 Scorecard for assessing protected area capacity

Strategic area of support	Capacity level	Outcome	Outcome indicators (scorecard)			
			Worst state (score 0)	Marginal state (score 1)	Satisfactory state (score 2)	Best state (score 3)
1 Capacity to conceptualize and formulate policies, legislations, strategies and programmes	Systemic	The protected area agenda is being championed effectively/driven forward	There is essentially no protected area agenda	There are some individuals or organizations actively pursuing a protected area agenda, but they have little effect or influence	There are a number of protected area champions who drive the protected area agenda, but more is needed	There are an adequate number of able 'champions' and 'leaders' driving forwards a protected area agenda effectively
1 Capacity to conceptualize and formulate policies, legislations, strategies and programmes	Systemic	There is a strong and clear legal mandate for the establishment and management of protected areas	There is no legal framework for protected areas	There is a partial legal framework for protected areas, but it has many inadequacies	There is a reasonable legal framework for protected areas, but it has a few weaknesses and gaps	There is a strong and clear legal mandate for the establishment and management of protected areas
1 Capacity to conceptualize and formulate policies, legislations, strategies and programmes	Organizational	There is an organization responsible for protected areas able to strategize and plan	Protected area organizations have no plans or strategies	Protected area organizations do have strategies and plans, but these are old and no longer up to date or were prepared in a top-down fashion	Protected area organizations have some sort of mechanism to update their strategies and plans, but this is irregular or is done in a largely top-down fashion without proper consultation	Protected area organizations have relevant, participatorially prepared and regularly updated strategies and plans
2 Capacity to implement policies, legislation, strategies and programmes	Systemic	There are adequate skills for protected area planning and management	There is a general lack of planning and management skills	Some skills exist but in largely insufficient quantities to guarantee effective planning and management	Necessary skills for effective protected area management and planning do exist but are stretched and not easily available	Adequate quantities of the full range of skills necessary for effective protected area planning and management are easily available

Table 7.4 Continued

Strategic area of support	Capacity level	Outcome	Outcome indicators (scorecard)			
			Worst state (score 0)	Marginal state (score 1)	Satisfactory state (score 2)	Best state (score 3)
2 Capacity to implement policies, legislation, strategies and programmes	Systemic	There are protected area systems	No or very few protected areas exist and they cover only a small portion of the habitats and ecosystems	Protected area system is patchy both in number and geographical coverage and has many gaps in terms of being representative	Protected area system is covering a reasonably representative sample of the major habitats and ecosystems, but still presents some gaps and not all elements are of viable size	The protected areas include viable representative examples of all the major habitats and ecosystems of appropriate geographical scale
2 Capacity to implement policies, legislation, strategies and programmes	Systemic	There is a fully transparent oversight authority for the protected area organizations	There is no oversight at all of protected area organizations	There is some oversight, but only indirectly and in an un-transparent manner	There is a reasonable oversight mechanism in place, providing for regular review, but it lacks transparency (e.g. is not independent or is internalized)	There is a fully transparent oversight authority for the protected area organizations
2 Capacity to implement policies, legislation, strategies and programmes	Organizational	Protected area organizations are effectively led	Protected area organizations have a total lack of leadership	Protected area organizations exist, but leadership is weak and provides little guidance	Some protected area organizations have reasonably strong leadership, but there is still need for improvement	Protected area organizations are led effectively
2 Capacity to implement policies, legislation, strategies and programmes	Organizational	Protected areas have regularly updated, participatorially prepared and comprehensive management plans	Protected areas have no management plans	Some protected areas have up-to-date management plans, but they are typically not comprehensive and were not participatorially prepared	Most protected areas have management plans, though some are old, not participatorially prepared or are less than comprehensive	Every protected area has a regularly updated, participatorially prepared and comprehensive management plan

Table 7.4 Continued

Strategic area of support	Capacity level	Outcome	Outcome indicators (scorecard)			
			Worst state (score 0)	Marginal state (score 1)	Satisfactory state (score 2)	Best state (score 3)
2 Capacity to implement policies, legislation, strategies and programmes	Organizational	Human resources are well qualified and motivated	Human resources are poorly qualified and unmotivated	Human resources qualification is spotty, with some well qualified, but many only poorly and in general unmotivated	Human resources, in general, are reasonably qualified, but many lack motivation, or those that are motivated are not sufficiently qualified	Human resources are well qualified and motivated
2 Capacity to implement policies, legislation, strategies and programmes	Organizational	Management plans are implemented in a timely manner, achieving their objectives effectively	There is very little implementation of management plans	Management plans are poorly implemented and their objectives are rarely met	Management plans are usually implemented in a timely manner, although delays typically occur and some objectives are not met	Management plans are implemented in a timely manner, achieving their objectives effectively
2 Capacity to implement policies, legislation, strategies and programmes	Organizational	Protected area organizations are able to adequately mobilize sufficient quantity of funding, and human and material resources to implement their mandate effectively	Protected area organizations typically are severely under-funded and have no capacity to mobilize sufficient resources	Protected area organizations have some funding and are able to mobilize some human and material resources, but not enough to implement their mandate effectively	Protected area organizations have reasonable capacity to mobilize funding or other resources, but not always in sufficient quantities for fully effective implementation of their mandate	Protected area organizations are able to adequately mobilize sufficient quantity of funding, and human and material resources to implement their mandate effectively

Table 7.4 Continued

Strategic area of support	Capacity level	Outcome	Outcome indicators (scorecard)				
			Worst state (score 0)	Marginal state (score 1)	Satisfactory state (score 2)	Best state (score 3)
2 Capacity to implement policies, legislation, strategies and programmes	Organizational	Protected area organizations are managed effectively, efficiently deploying their human, financial and other resources to the best effect	While the protected area organization exists, it has no management	Organizational management is largely ineffective and does not deploy the resources at its disposal efficiently	The organization is reasonably managed, but not always in a fully effective manner and at times does not deploy its resources in the most efficient way	The protected area organization is effectively managed, efficiently deploying its human, financial and other resources to the best effect
2 Capacity to implement policies, legislation, strategies and programmes	Organizational	Protected area organizations are highly transparent, fully audited and publicly accountable	Protected area organizations are totally un-transparent, not being held accountable and not audited	Protected area organizations are not transparent, but are occasionally audited without being held publicly accountable	Protected area organizations are regularly audited and there is a fair degree of public accountability, but the system is not fully transparent	The protected area organizations are highly transparent, fully audited and publicly accountable
2 Capacity to implement policies, legislation, strategies and programmes	Organizational	There are legally designated protected area organizations with the authority to carry out their mandate	There is no lead organization or agency with a clear mandate or responsibility for protected areas	There are one or more organizations or agencies dealing with protected areas, but roles and responsibilities are unclear and there are gaps and overlaps in the arrangements	There are one or more organizations or agencies dealing with protected areas and the responsibilities of each are fairly clearly defined, but there are still some gaps and overlaps	Protected area organizations have clear legal and organizational mandates and the necessary authority to carry this out
2 Capacity to implement policies, legislation, strategies and programmes	Societal	Protected areas are protected effectively	No enforcement of regulations is taking place	Some enforcement of regulations, but this is largely ineffective and external threats remain active	Protected area regulations are regularly enforced but are not fully effective, and external threats are reduced but not eliminated	Protected area regulations are enforced highly effectively and all external threats are negated

Table 7.4 Continued

Strategic area of support	Capacity level	Outcome	Outcome indicators (scorecard)			
			Worst state (score 0)	Marginal state (score 1)	Satisfactory state (score 2)	Best state (score 3)
2 Capacity to implement policies, legislation, strategies and programmes	Individual	Individuals are able to advance and develop professionally	No career tracks are developed and no training opportunities are provided	Career tracks are weak and training possibilities are few and not managed transparently	Clear career tracks are developed and training is available; human resources management, however, has an inadequate performance measurement system	Individuals are able to advance and develop professionally
2 Capacity to implement policies, legislation, strategies and programmes	Individual	Individuals are appropriately skilled for their jobs	Skills of individuals do not match job requirements	Individuals have some or poor skills for their jobs	Individuals are reasonably skilled but could further improve for optimum match with job requirement	Individuals are appropriately skilled for their jobs
2 Capacity to implement policies, legislation, strategies and programmes	Individual	Individuals are highly motivated	No motivation at all	Motivation uneven: some are motivated, but most are not	Many individuals are motivated, but not all	Individuals are highly motivated
2 Capacity to implement policies, legislation, strategies and programmes	Individual	There are appropriate systems of training, mentoring and learning in place to maintain a continuous flow of new staff	No mechanisms exist	Some mechanisms exist, but unable to develop enough and unable to provide the full range of skills needed	Mechanisms generally exist to develop skilled professionals, but either not enough of them or unable to cover the full range of skills required	There are mechanisms for developing adequate numbers of the full range of highly skilled protected area professionals
3 Capacity to engage and build consensus among all stakeholders	Systemic	Protected areas have the political commitment they require	There is no political will at all, or worse, the prevailing political will runs counter to the interests of protected areas	Some political will exists, but is not strong enough to make a difference	Reasonable political will exists, but is not always strong enough to fully support protected areas	There are very high levels of political will to support protected areas

Table 7.4 Continued

Strategic area of support	Capacity level	Outcome	Outcome indicators (scorecard)			
			Worst state (score 0)	Marginal state (score 1)	Satisfactory state (score 2)	Best state (score 3)
3 Capacity to engage and build consensus among all stakeholders	Systemic	Protected areas have the public support they require	The public has little interest in protected areas and there is no significant lobby for protected areas	There is limited support for protected areas	There is general public support for protected areas and there are various lobby groups, such as environmental NGOs, strongly pushing them	There is tremendous public support in the country for protected areas
3 Capacity to engage and build consensus among all stakeholders	Organizational	Protected area organizations are mission oriented	Organizational mission not defined	Organizational mission poorly defined and generally not known and internalized at all levels	Organizational mission well defined and internalized but not fully embraced	Organizational missions are fully internalized and embraced
3 Capacity to engage and build consensus among all stakeholders	Organizational	Protected area organizations can establish the partnerships needed to achieve their objectives	Protected area organizations operate in isolation	Some partnerships in place, but significant gaps and existing partnerships achieve little	Many partnerships in place with a wide range of agencies, NGOs, etc., but there are some gaps, and partnerships are not always effective and do not always enable efficient achievement of objectives	Protected area organizations establish effective partnerships with other agencies and organizations, including provincial and local governments, NGOs and the private sector, to enable achievement of objectives in an efficient and effective manner
3 Capacity to engage and build consensus among all stakeholders	Individual	Individuals carry appropriate values, integrity and attitudes	Individuals carry negative attitude	Some individuals have notion of appropriate attitudes and display integrity, but most don't	Many individuals carry appropriate values and integrity, but not all	Individuals carry appropriate values, integrity and attitudes

Table 7.4 Continued

Strategic area of support	Capacity level	Outcome	Outcome indicators (scorecard)			
			Worst state (score 0)	Marginal state (score 1)	Satisfactory state (score 2)	Best state (score 3)
4 Capacity to mobilize information and knowledge	Systemic	Protected area institutions have the information they need to develop and monitor strategies and action plans for the management of the protected area system	Information is virtually lacking	Some information exists, but is of poor quality, is of limited usefulness or is very difficult to access	Much information is easily available and mostly of good quality, but there remain some gaps in quality, coverage and availability	Protected area institutions have the information they need to develop and monitor strategies and action plans for managing protected area system
4 Capacity to mobilize information and knowledge	Organizational	Protected area organizations have the information needed to do their work	Information is virtually lacking	Some information exists, but is of poor quality and of limited usefulness and difficult to access	Much information is readily available, mostly of good quality, but there remain some gaps both in quality and quantity	Adequate quantities of high-quality up-to-date information for protected area planning, management and monitoring are widely and easily available
4 Capacity to mobilize information and knowledge	Individual	Individuals working with protected areas work together effectively as a team	Individuals work in isolation and don't interact	Individuals interact in limited way and sometimes in teams, but this is rarely effective and functional	Individuals interact regularly and form teams, but this is not always fully effective or functional	Individuals interact effectively and form functional teams
5 Capacity to monitor, evaluate, report and learn	Systemic	Protected area policy is continually reviewed and updated	There is no policy or it is old and not reviewed regularly	Policy is only reviewed at irregular intervals	Policy is reviewed regularly but not annually	National protected areas policy is reviewed annually
5 Capacity to monitor, evaluate, report and learn	Systemic	Society monitors the state of protected areas	There is no dialogue at all	There is some dialogue going on, but not in the wider public, and restricted to specialized circles	There is a reasonably open public dialogue going on but certain issues remain taboo	There is an open and transparent public dialogue about the state of the protected areas

Table 7.4 Continued

Strategic area of support	Capacity level	Outcome	Outcome indicators (scorecard)			
			Worst state (score 0)	Marginal state (score 1)	Satisfactory state (score 2)	Best state (score 3)
5 Capacity to monitor, evaluate, report and learn	Organizational	Organizations are highly adaptive, responding effectively and immediately to change	Organizations resist change	Organizations do change, but only very slowly	Organizations tend to adapt in response to change but not always very effectively or with some delay	Organizations are highly adaptive, responding effectively and immediately to change
5 Capacity to monitor, evaluate, report and learn	Organizational	Organizations have effective internal mechanisms for monitoring, evaluation, reporting and learning	There are no mechanisms for monitoring, evaluation, reporting or learning	There are some mechanisms for monitoring, evaluation, reporting and learning, but they are limited and weak	Reasonable mechanisms for monitoring, evaluation, reporting and learning are in place but are not as strong or comprehensive as they could be	Organizations have effective internal mechanisms for monitoring, evaluation, reporting and learning
5 Capacity to monitor, evaluate, report and learn	Individual	Individuals are adaptive and continue to learn	There is no measurement of performance or adaptive feedback	Performance is irregularly and poorly measured and there is little use of feedback	There is significant measurement of performance and some feedback, but this is not as thorough or comprehensive as it might be	Performance is measured effectively and adaptive feedback is utilized

Source: adapted from UNDP-GEF (2003)

Part II

Principles and Practice

8

Establishing Protected Areas

Mohamed I. Bakarr and Michael Lockwood

The current global network of protected areas is not yet sufficient to protect the full range of species on Earth (see Chapter 1, p12). As a consequence, the establishment of new protected areas is recognized as a key component of international conservation efforts. The Convention on Biological Diversity (CBD), for example, specifically highlights the need to develop guidelines for the selection and management of protected area systems. Protected areas can be established by governments under legislation, by local and indigenous communities, NGOs and private landowners (see Chapter 5). Until recently, the process of identifying target areas and declaring them for protection has been largely driven by political, social and economic interests. As a result, the overall representation of biodiversity conservation is inadequate in many protected area systems around the world (Brooks et al, 2004).

In this chapter, we consider the principles and processes that guide protected area identification and selection to maximize representation of biological and geophysical diversity. The results from such processes indicate what needs to be protected to secure those values (see Chapter 4) that depend upon the conservation of plants, animals and ecosystems.

We first introduce the need for a comprehensive global system of protected areas, particularly in relation to the gaps in the current system. System-wide principles for identifying and establishing national protected area networks in terrestrial and marine environments are considered. We then outline processes for identifying land for reservation as protected areas, including formal scientific reserve selection methods, and the integration of ethical, socio-economic and cultural selection criteria in the context of wider land-use and marine planning processes. We conclude the chapter with a summary of the principles that should guide reserve selection in the future.

The need for comprehensive global systems

The current distribution of protected areas around the world is briefly summarized in 'Extent of the world's protected areas' in Chapter 3 and in Appendix 5. Considerable progress has been made with the establishment of protected areas over the last three decades. The global network of protected areas now covers over 12 per cent of the planet's land surface. For 9 out of 14 major terrestrial biomes (see Chapter 1, p28), this surpasses the 10 per cent target proposed a decade earlier, at the IVth IUCN World Parks Congress in Caracas. We refer here primarily to government-designated areas: the information base on other forms of protected areas, including community conserved areas (CCAs) and private protected areas (other than those already included in official protected area networks) is not adequate to provide a picture of their distribution, extent and representativeness.

National and international conservation planning commonly uses targets based on percentage areas. However, Rodrigues et al (2004a) questioned the scientific basis and conservation value of such 'percentage area' targets. They showed that the percentage already protected in a given country or biome is a very poor indicator of additional conservation needs. While such targets can be very useful political tools, they do not take sufficient account of the fact that biodiversity is not evenly distributed across the planet. The regions with greatest need for expansion of the global protected area network are not necessarily those with a lower percentage of their area protected;

rather, they typically are those with higher levels of endemism. The results demonstrate that if the conservation goal is species representation, then the expansion of the global network of protected areas must account for biodiversity patterns, rather than rely primarily on general percentage-based targets. A more multidimensional specification of global reserve network was developed at the Vth IUCN World Parks Congress (see Box 8.1).

There is a need for a science-based approach to assessing gaps in coverage and defining targets for the establishment of protected areas. Such

---

Box 8.1 Targets for a global protected area network

The action plan developed in 2003 as part of the Vth IUCN World Parks Congress urged governments, NGOs and local communities to maximize representation and persistence of biodiversity in comprehensive protected area networks in all ecoregions by 2012, focusing especially on threatened and under-protected ecosystems and those species that qualify as globally threatened with extinction under the IUCN criteria. The following specific targets and strategies were identified in the action plan.

All globally threatened species are effectively conserved *in situ* with the following immediate targets:

- all critically endangered and endangered species globally confined to single sites are effectively conserved *in situ* by 2006;
- all other globally critically endangered and endangered species are effectively conserved *in situ* by 2008;
- all other globally threatened species are effectively conserved *in situ* by 2010; and
- sites that support internationally important populations of congregatory and/or restricted-range species are adequately conserved by 2010.

Viable representations of every terrestrial, freshwater and marine ecosystem need to be conserved effectively within protected areas, with the following immediate targets:

- a common global framework for classifying and assessing the status of ecosystems established by 2006;
- quantitative targets for each ecosystem type identified by 2008;
- viable representations of every threatened or under-protected ecosystem conserved by 2010; and
- changes in biodiversity and key ecological processes affecting biodiversity in and around protected areas to be identified and managed.

Systematic conservation planning tools that use information on species, habitats and ecological processes to identify gaps in the existing system should be applied to assist in selecting new protected areas at the national level.

Regional landscape and seascape planning should consider locally generated maps, and incorporate zoning and management planning processes to assist in designing and enhancing comprehensive protected area networks that conserve wide-ranging and migratory species and sustain ecosystem services.

Protected area systems need to be established by 2006, which adequately cover all large intact ecosystems that hold globally significant assemblages of species and/or provide ecosystem services and processes.

The coverage of protected areas in freshwater ecosystems needs to be increased as proposed by the Convention on Biological Diversity (CBD) to establish and maintain a comprehensive, adequate and representative system of protected inland water ecosystems using integrated catchment/watershed/river basin management by 2012.

A representative network of marine protected areas should be established by 2012.

Source: adapted from IUCN (2003a)

approaches are possible for two reasons. First, knowledge of species distribution ranges across ecosystems and biomes has increased tremendously over the last several decades, and efforts are under way to synthesize these data and make them publicly available. Second, the World Database on Protected Areas (WDPA) has established a framework for integrating spatial data to map the extent of protected area coverage at all levels, from national to regional and global. The combination of species range maps and protected area coverage now makes it possible to systematically identify gaps and improve targeting of new areas for protection (Brooks et al, 2004; Rodrigues et al, 2004a). This will be crucial to achieving comprehensive coverage of protected areas beyond the current level.

Gap analysis is a conservation planning approach based on assessing the comprehensiveness of existing protected area networks and identifying gaps in coverage. A widely used gap methodology developed by the US Geological Survey National Gap Analysis Program has four basic steps:

1   Create a map of land use/land cover that maps vegetation at the level of natural assemblages of plant species.
2   Map predicted distributions of vertebrate species.
3   Classify the study area according to type of land (protected areas and other land-use categories).
4   Analyse the representation of vertebrate species and vegetation alliances in protected areas (Rodrigues et al, 2003).

Assessment of the highest priority areas for establishing new protected areas requires consideration of irreplaceability and threat. Irreplaceability measures the extent to which species representation is reduced if a site is not protected. Threat can be calculated as the number of threatened species present at a site, giving higher weighting to those with higher extinction risk (Rodrigues et al, 2003).

Rodrigues et al (2003, 2004b) combined five global datasets on the distribution of species and protected areas to identify gaps in the global

protected area network in terms of representing species diversity. This project overlaid species distribution maps onto protected area maps using geographic information systems (GIS) to assess how well each species is represented in protected areas. The analysis did not cover aquatic biodiversity.

The global gap analysis demonstrated that the global protected area network is still far from complete. In interpreting the results, it should be noted that the analysis does not take account of CCAs and private protected areas where these are not yet part of the officially recognized protected area systems. Overall, 1424 species (12 per cent of all species analysed) were identified as not being located within any protected area. Amphibians are the most poorly represented group. Threatened and restricted-range species are those of most conservation concern. Overall, 20 per cent of all threatened species analysed were identified as 'gap species'. Of course, it must also be recognized that presence within a protected area is insufficient to ensure the long-term persistence of many species, particularly those with demanding habitat or area requirements, and does not consider threats such as global climate change (Rodrigues et al, 2004b).

The global distribution of sites requiring urgent protection is summarized in Figure 8.1. Areas identified as urgent are mainly concentrated in tropical forests and on islands. Most unprotected sites highlighted in Figure 8.1 lie in the tropics (80 per cent by area and 87 per cent of the number of urgent unprotected sites), whereas 39 per cent of the planet's land area is in tropical regions. Current protected areas are mainly outside the tropics (53 per cent by area and 74 per cent of sites). Islands (defined as those being smaller than Australia and Greenland, meaning that New Guinea, Madagascar and Borneo are the largest) comprise 5.2 per cent of the total global land area, yet 27.6 per cent of unprotected urgent sites are on islands. Islands support 45 per cent of all species analysed, including 57 per cent of threatened birds, 49 per cent of all mammals and 39 per cent of all amphibians. They also display very high levels of endemism: over 50 per cent of island species do not occur on continental areas. Thus, islands are of critical importance for vertebrate species conservation, and there is an urgent

Ascending Peak, Mount Huangshan, China

Source: IUCN Photo Library © Jim Thorsell

need to expand the representation of islands in the global protected area network (Rodrigues et al, 2003, 2004b).

Unfortunately, tropical and island countries tend to be those that can least afford the costs of establishing and managing protected areas. These costs may outweigh the local benefits because a large proportion of the benefits relate to existence and bequest values (see Chapter 4) that are realized at a global scale. It is crucial therefore that a significant proportion of the costs of establishing protected areas in urgent regions must be met by the global community, as represented by multilateral and bilateral institutions, foundations, and private corporations and individuals (Rodrigues et al, 2003, 2004b). Such sources of protected area finance and the mechanisms that can be used to raise the necessary funds are considered in 'Financing protected areas' in Chapter 12. It must also be recognized that other hurdles to be overcome include empowerment of communities, capacity development and clarification of tenurial and governance arrangements.

Proportionally, Asia is a higher priority for establishing new protected areas, while the need for strengthening the existing network is mainly emphasized in Africa and South America (Rodrigues et al, 2003, 2004b). South-East Asia has the densest concentrations of areas requiring urgent new investment, especially in Vietnamese, Philippine and Indonesian islands. Northern Thailand and the southern Malay Peninsula are also high priorities for mammals. The regions highlighted in Figure 8.1 include many widely recognized centres of endemism, such as Yunnan Province and the mountains surrounding the Sichuan basin in southern China, the Western Ghats of India, Sri Lanka, the islands of South-East Asia and Melanesia, the Pacific islands, Madagascar, the Cameroon highlands, Mesoamerica, the tropical Andes, the Caribbean, and the Atlantic Forest of South America (Rodrigues et al, 2003, 2004b). Note that these findings apply only to mammals, amphibians and globally threatened birds, which were the only taxonomic groups for which the authors were able to obtain global map coverage in digital format.

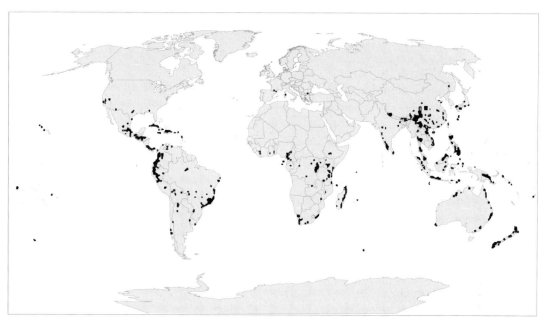

Figure 8.1 Global distribution of unprotected sites of high urgency for the coverage of mammals, amphibians and threatened birds

Source: Rodrigues et al (2004b, p67)

The dominant biomes of the planet in terms of area are deserts and xeric shrublands (19 per cent); tropical and subtropical moist broadleaf forests (14 per cent); and tropical and subtropical grasslands, savannas and shrublands (13 per cent). The current network of protected areas represents each biome in similar proportions, with temperate coniferous forests and tropical and subtropical moist broadleaf forests being the two biomes with a higher percentage of their area protected (24.5 per cent and 15.6 per cent, respectively), and lakes and temperate grasslands, savannas and shrublands being the biomes proportionally less represented (2.4 per cent and 4.2 per cent, respectively). Urgent unprotected sites are heavily dominated by tropical and subtropical moist broadleaf forests (67.9 per cent), with tropical and subtropical coniferous forests also appearing as disproportionately much more important than their actual area suggests. Non-tropical biomes correspond to less than 17 per cent of the total area recommended as a priority for the expansion of the current network of protected areas.

There is considerable overlap between the results of the Rodrigues et al (2003) analysis and

Mountain gorilla (*Gorilla gorilla*), Volcano National Park, Rwanda

Source: IUCN Photo Library © Jim Thorsell

Conservation International's (CI's) 25 global biodiversity hotspots (see Chapter 1, p37). However, there are important exceptions to this overall correspondence. Concentrations of unprotected urgent sites that are not biodiversity hotspots include the Albertine Rift, the Kenyan Highlands and the Ethiopian Highlands in Africa; south-east China and Taiwan in Asia; and the

Queensland wet tropics and Papua New Guinea in Australasia.

Similarly, nearly all protected and unprotected urgent sites highlighted in the global gap analysis are included in the Global 200 (see Chapter 1, p34). However, many of the Global 200 ecoregions hold no urgent sites. This is because the global gap analysis does not target ecoregions of low endemism (such as boreal forests) or low threat (such as many deserts), whereas the Global 200 selects the most representative ecoregion within each habitat type (Rodrigues et al, 2003).

It is important to note that the Rodrigues et al (2003) analysis was necessarily done at a very 'coarse' scale – urgent priority areas need to be assessed at a finer scale to enable more specific identification of crucial sites for expansion of the protected area network. Identifying a comprehensive protected area network requires that assessments be conducted in all regions and nations, and for all governance types. Given the increasing threats to biodiversity, such expansion should be made strategically by focusing on those regions that would contribute most to the global system and prioritizing, within those, the regions where the urgency for conservation action is greatest (Rodrigues et al, 2004b). To assist this effort, there is a need to:

- improve the structure and content quality of the WDPA, especially with respect to accurate boundary information and comprehensive identification of protected areas by IUCN category, especially CCAs (see Chapter 21); and
- undertake regular habitat and species gap analyses at national, regional and global levels (Chape et al, 2005).

We believe that it is also important to eventually extend analyses beyond the adequacy of biological representation to include values based on geo-heritage, as well other characteristics of land and sea (cultural, aesthetic, recreational, economic and spiritual). It is only in this way that the full potential of protected areas to deliver the full range of values and benefits identified in Chapter 4 can be realized.

National and bioregional reserve systems

Many governments have independently developed approaches for establishing and managing new protected areas (see Case Study 8.1). The approaches have tended to draw on criteria and guidelines developed by the IUCN, particularly with regard to categories for designation of protected areas. The guidelines developed by Davey (1998) give a detailed list of considerations and tasks for national-level planning:

- developing a national rationale and mandate for a protected area system;
- identifying the goals and performance criteria for the national system;
- establishing a protocol for community and stakeholder (including rights-holder) participation in plan development and implementation;
- defining the relationships between various categories of protected area;
- defining the relationships between protected areas and other land-use and tenure categories;
- assessing the current system of protected areas, including the distribution across IUCN categories and governance types;
- assessing 'gaps' in the system in terms of its potential to achieve the goals and meet the performance criteria;
- identifying candidate areas to fill these gaps, taking into account:
  - habitat requirements of rare or other species and their minimum viable population sizes;
  - connectivity between units (corridors) to permit wildlife migration;
  - perimeter–area relationships;
  - natural system linkages and boundaries;
  - traditional use, occupancy and sustainability;
  - cost of achieving protected area status; and
  - determining the most appropriate mechanisms for protection, including IUCN category and governance.

Davey (1998) also argued that systems of protected areas should strive to meet the following five criteria:

1 *Representativeness, comprehensiveness and balance.* The highest-quality examples of the full range of environment types within a country need to be incorporated within the protected area system. Protected areas should provide a balanced sampling of the environment types they represent. This applies to biodiversity (at genetic, species and habitat levels), as well as other features, such as landform types, and to cultural landscapes.

2 *Adequacy.* This criterion refers to the integrity and effective management of the protected areas. An adequate system will strive to ensure that the features and associated values of protected areas persist over time. This requires taking into account factors such as the shape, size and connectivity of protected areas at a landscape scale. Replication of sites with similar characteristics may be needed to provide a buffer against local catastrophes.

3 *Coherence and complementarity.* Proposed sites for inclusion in the system should possess particular values that complement existing protected areas, so that reservation brings benefits at least in proportion to the costs.

4 *Consistency.* Management actions should address objectives, which are themselves consistent with the appropriate IUCN category (see Chapter 3, p82).

5 *Cost effectiveness, efficiency and equity.* This criterion emphasizes the need to consider the magnitude and distribution of the costs as well as the benefits of protected area establishment. Protected areas should not be established such that the rights of local and indigenous communities are violated. Efficiency in selection involves identifying the minimum number and area of protected areas needed to achieve system objectives.

To apply these criteria, it will often be helpful to employ a systematic conservation planning tool, such as those described in the following section on 'Systematic reserve selection methods'. It is also important to recognize, however, that the need to undertake systematic identification of an overall reserve network must be balanced with the possible need to act swiftly to reserve critical areas.

Important areas can be designated in advance of a systems plan.

The process for developing and implementing a national systems plan for protected areas should also meet the principles for good governance described in Chapter 5, p134.

Marine reserve systems

The need for a systematic and representative approach to establishing protected areas in marine environments was first articulated at the International Conference on Marine Parks and Protected Areas, convened by the IUCN in Tokyo in 1975 (Kenchington, 1996). In 1990 the 17th General Assembly of the IUCN adopted a primary goal of reserving and conserving marine environments. Resolution 17.38 was as follows:

> *To provide for the protection, restoration, wise use, understanding and enjoyment of the marine heritage of the world in perpetuity through the creation of a global representative system of marine protected areas and through the management, in accordance with the principles of the World Conservation Strategy, of human activities that use or affect the marine environment.*

Over the few years, moves towards the attainment of this goal included:

• the publication and wide distribution of guidelines that describe the approaches that have been successful in establishing and managing marine protected areas in various social and ecological situations (Kelleher and Kenchington, 1992);

• division of the world's coastal seas into 18 major biogeographical regions, the recruitment of working group leaders for these regions and one for the high seas, and the establishment of regional working groups consisting of scientists and managers, government and non-governmental people;

• establishment of working groups in the countries of each region; and

• establishment and empowerment of networks of professionals and activists concerned with marine protected areas to collaborate with the working groups.

Case Study 8.1

National system planning for terrestrial environments, Australia

Managers of protected areas in Australia realized that they needed urgently to acquire not just any natural lands that were available, but representative samples of the different habitat types, and especially of rare and threatened ones. Unfortunately, there was an inevitable bias in the types of land available. The easiest land to acquire for reserves is public land that is unsuitable for agriculture or forestry. There was also political pressure from lobby groups to conserve the 'tall green end of the spectrum of ecosystems' (Thackway and Cresswell, 1995a). This meant that some types of habitat were over-represented in reserves, while others were left unprotected.

Managers began to investigate and actively counter this bias in their own areas; but the job really needed to be done at the national level. The will to cooperate was there; but there was a need to standardize the data and to reconcile the different categories that managers in different regions were using to classify and count types of habitat. The result was the Interim Biogeographic Regionalization for Australia (IBRA) (Thackway and Cresswell, 1995b).

The original IBRA recognized 80 biogeographic regions for Australia's land mass. The biogeographic regions vary in size from 2372 square kilometres (Furneaux Island in Bass Strait) to 423,751 square kilometres (Great Victoria Desert). The larger IBRA regions are mostly in flatter arid or semi-arid areas, whereas its regions are smaller near the coast where rainfall and elevation fluctuate more widely. Even so, each IBRA region is a broad category and contains many smaller habitats.

Thus, even when a high proportion of a given IBRA region is protected in reserves, many of its internal environments may not be. It turned out that some types of region suffer more than others from such 'internal bias' in the way that their smaller habitats are represented. Only in western Tasmania and small areas in Victoria and South Australia (less than 1 per cent of Australia's land mass) are there regions whose whole range of internal environments or ecosystems were represented, without bias, in reserves. The situation was worst in arid and semi-arid lands (Thackway and Cresswell, 1995b).

In 2000, IBRA Version 5 was developed, with 85 bioregions delineated based on the major environmental influences on flora and fauna distribution. Regional- and continental-scale data on climate, geomorphology, landform, lithology, flora and fauna were interpreted to develop the bioregional boundaries.

The National Reserve System (NRS) for Australia is using IBRA as its planning framework to develop a comprehensive, adequate and representative reserve system for Australia's bioregions. It was established in 1992 as a collaborative programme between the national government, states and territories. State and territory conservation agencies have the primary responsibility for selecting and managing new protected areas.

The NRS seeks to addresses the gaps in the existing reserve network at a national scale for terrestrial ecosystems (other than forest and marine ecosystems that are considered under separate processes). Gaps in the representation of ecosystems are identified on a regional basis using IBRA. Consideration is also given to rare or threatened species and ecosystems, as well as species with specialized habitat requirements, wide-ranging or migratory species, and species vulnerable to threatening processes (NRMMC, 2004). A strategic approach has been developed to identifying the requirements of an NRS, based on a number of criteria and principles, including the following:

- *Comprehensiveness.* The NRS aims to include the full range of regional ecosystems within each IBRA region.
- *Adequacy.* The NRS aims to provide reservation of each ecosystem to the level necessary to produce ecological viability and integrity.
- *Representativeness.* Areas selected for inclusion in the NRS should reflect the variability of the ecosystems that they represent.
- *Threat.* Priority should be given to ecosystems where there is a high risk of loss (irreplaceability).
- *Precautionary principle.* The absence of scientific certainty is not a reason to postpone measures to establish protected areas that contribute to a comprehensive, adequate and representative protected area system.
- *Landscape context.* Biodiversity conservation outcomes should be, as far as possible, optimized through the application of scientifically established protected area design principles.
- *Highly protected areas.* The NRS aims to have some highly protected areas (IUCN Categories I and II) located in each IBRA region.
- *Public land.* Priority should be given, in the first instance, to meeting the above criteria from public land, with private land targeted to fill any gaps that remain.
- *Least-cost approach.* Selection should consider long-term and short-term environmental, economic, social and equity implications so that an optimal protected area network is established with minimal economic and social cost.

- *Consultation*. Consultation should be undertaken with community and interest groups to address social, economic and cultural issues.
- *Indigenous involvement*. The biodiversity conservation interests of Australia's indigenous peoples should be recognized and incorporated within decision-making (NRMMC, 2004).

Gaps in the current protected areas network have been identified based on:

- percentage area of reservation within each IBRA (see Figure 8.2);
- level of bias between regions in terms of comprehensiveness (nil, low, moderate, high, no reserves); and
- level of threat to biodiversity within each IBRA according to degree of modification, existing land uses, species extinctions, and abundance of introduced species.

Based on these data, each IBRA has been given a priority classification with regard to its priority for the inclusion of land within the NRS (see Figure 8.3).

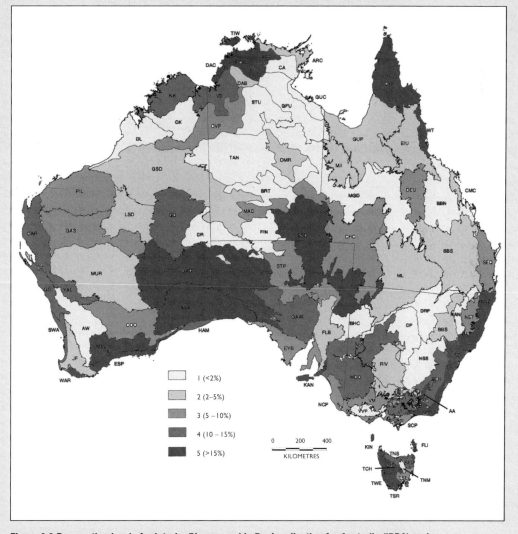

Figure 8.2 Reservation levels for Interim Biogeographic Regionalization for Australia (IBRA) regions

Source: NRMMC (2004, p14)

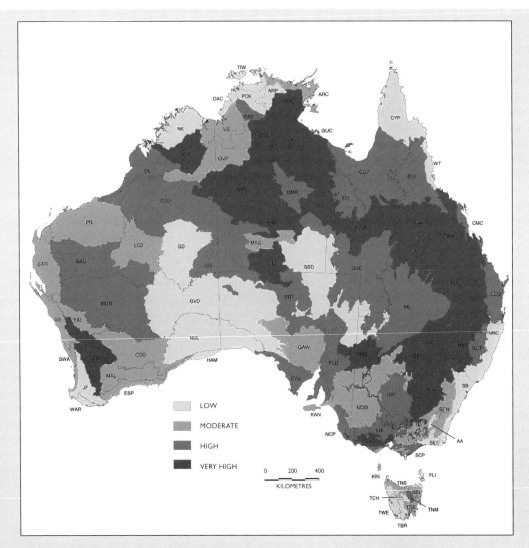

Figure 8.3 Reservation priorities for IBRA regions

Note: Both levels and priorities change over time. Note also that most bioregions, including those with 'low priority', contain particular regional ecosystems that are poorly conserved.

Source: NRMMC (2004, p14)

In 1995 the IUCN, the World Bank and the Great Barrier Reef Marine Park Authority published *A Global Representative System of Marine Protected Areas* (Kelleher et al, 1995). This four-volume report listed the existing marine protected areas in each country. It identified the highest priorities for establishing new marine protected areas or for converting paper parks into effective marine protected areas. It proposed a series of actions necessary to achieve the primary conservation goal, a goal not confined only to marine protected areas. Progress since then has been highly variable. Marine protection has increased at approximately 3 to 5 per cent per year, and at the current rate will not meet the target set at the Vth IUCN World Parks Congress to protect 20 to 30 per cent of marine habitats by 2012 (Wood et al, 2005). Particular challenges associated with establishing a marine protected area network include:

- limited knowledge of marine environments and the effects of human activities on them;
- difficulty of resolving complex jurisdictional issues that may involve international, national, regional and local claimants;
- difficulties in setting clearly identifiable boundaries;
- the differences in scale of the marine systems and processes; and
- a relative lack of community understanding regarding marine protected area values (WCPA, 2006).

Some countries, such as Canada, have produced well-crafted marine protected area systems plans (see Case Study 8.2), but effective plan implementation remains an ongoing challenge. Canada's difficulties arose because it did not integrate socio-economic factors effectively in its process for assessing and making decisions. Others countries, such as in South-East Asia and the Baltic, are moving with determination and commitment to involve local communities. They are establishing marine protected area systems that bring ecological and economic benefits.

As with terrestrial protected areas, principles for establishing networks of highly protected marine areas include representativeness, replication and viability. The high mobility of most marine organisms means that connectivity between marine protected areas is critical. Larvae of species may travel long distances, and juveniles and adults regularly migrate between habitat areas. There is also strong connectivity between marine and terrestrial environments, particularly in relation to movement of water, nutrients, sediment and organisms such as sea birds that use both environments (Vierros, 2004). The effectiveness of the protection afforded to marine organisms within an marine protected area will depend upon the size of the area protected; the activities that are restricted and allowed within the marine protected area boundaries; and activities that occur outside the marine protected area but threaten life within it.

The Convention on Biological Diversity Ad Hoc Technical Expert Group (AHTEG) on marine and coastal protected areas suggested that marine protected area network design should be considered in an ecosystem context, taking into account each national or regional area, including the exclusive economic zones and the high seas. The network should provide for a range of levels of protection, comprising:

- a representative network of highly protected areas or zones where extractive uses are prevented and other significant human pressures are minimized;
- a complementary network of areas that supports the biodiversity objectives of the highly protected areas, where specific perceived threats are managed in a sustainable manner for the purposes of biodiversity conservation and sustainable use; and
- sustainable management practices over the wider coastal and marine environment (Vierros, 2004).

In their work in the northern Gulf of Mexico, Beck and Odaya (2001) specified the following steps in identifying priority sites for conservation with a particular bioregion:

- *Definition of the units to be analysed.* These units may be, for example, species, habitats or some other appropriate biophysical classification of the marine environment. Marine biodiversity can be identified at the scale of major oceanic ecosystems as influenced by large-scale processes, such as currents and upwellings, as well as coastal and oceanic physiography and topography (Day et al, 2003a). Biodiversity also occurs at intermediate and finer scales (communities, habitats and specific sites). Ideally, all of these scales must be taken into account in systems design. Biodiversity can be classified at the genetic, species and ecosystem levels. The protection of genetic variation for a species or for a population is important for maintaining their long-term viability. A species approach to conservation planning provides the ability to focus on restricted or threatened species. An ecosystem-based

Case Study 8.2

Canada's federal marine protected areas strategy

Canada has the world's longest coastline, stretching over 243,000km along three oceans (Atlantic, Pacific and Arctic), as well as the second largest exclusive economic zone (EEZ). The drive for a federal marine protected areas strategy arose from the need for a cooperative and collaborative approach to developing a network of marine protected areas in Canada as a means of helping to address the declining health of oceans. The Oceans Act 1997 provided Fisheries and Oceans Canada with a leading and coordinating role. The intent of the strategy is to clarify the roles and responsibilities of federal departments and agencies with marine protected area mandates (Fisheries and Oceans Canada, Environment Canada and the Parks Canada Agency), and to describe how federal marine protected area programmes can collectively be used to create a cohesive and complementary network of marine protected areas.

The strategic framework is specified in terms of a goal and related objectives and activities.

Goal

The goal comprises the establishment of a network of marine protected areas, established and managed within an integrated oceans management framework, that contributes to the health of Canada's oceans and marine environments.

Objective 1

The first objective is to establish a more systematic approach to marine protected area planning and establishment.

Activities include the following:

- Establish or formalize mechanisms for interdepartmental cooperation.
- Collaboratively develop and use science-based guidelines and decision tools to identify and select new marine protected areas by:
  - identifying and mapping ecologically significant sites and candidate representative areas within integrated management planning areas and other strategic planning initiatives;
  - selecting appropriate tools for conservation;
  - identifying priorities for advancing the marine protected areas network; and
  - developing shared criteria and guidelines and seeking opportunities for achieving multiple conservation objectives.
- Work together to enhance intergovernmental, aboriginal and stakeholder engagement in marine protected area planning and establishment:
  - use integrated management planning as the prime vehicle for marine protected area site identification, including involvement of provinces and territories; aboriginal groups, management committees and boards; other stakeholders and interested parties; and
  - develop mechanisms or procedures for collaboration with other jurisdictions.

Objective 2

The second objective involves enhancing collaboration for managing and monitoring of marine protected areas.
Activities include the following:

- Develop site-specific collaborative models, including the:
  - development of management plans that link marine protected area objectives and other conservation objectives (such as species at risk, fisheries, biodiversity and unique ecosystems);
  - exploration of options for working with aboriginal peoples on marine protected area issues;
  - development of a science and traditional ecological knowledge programme; and
  - development of common public education and awareness programmes.
- Conclude collaborative management arrangements on individual marine protected areas, including with aboriginal groups.
- Work together to identify targets and indicators (ecological, socio-economic and government) to evaluate the effectiveness of marine protected areas and the network.
- Conduct joint or complementary enforcement activities, where possible.

Objective 3

Objective 3 is to increase the awareness, understanding and participation of Canadians in the marine protected areas network.

Activities include the following:

- Establish a marine protected area research programme (natural and social science considerations).
- Launch an internet-based geo-referenced marine protected area mapping system.
- Develop common marine protected area communications and public outreach tools to increase awareness of marine issues and enhance Canadian marine literacy.
- Develop widely accepted definitions of key legislative and policy concepts common to all federal marine protected area programmes (that is, ecological sustainable use, ecosystem-based management and the precautionary approach).

Objective 4

The fourth objective is to link Canada's network of marine protected areas to continental and global networks.

Activities include the following:

- Establish a regional marine protected area action plan with the US and Mexico as part of the Security and Prosperity Partnership to consider:
    - ecological protected area network considerations for species and habitat on each coast; and
    - working arrangements and priorities with the relevant international bodies.
- Provide Canadian leadership and experience to the international community on tools, techniques and approaches to achieving existing global marine protected area commitments and additional marine protected area requirements:
    - within the Convention on Biological Diversity (CBD);
    - with the Arctic Council and its working groups (in the context of the Arctic Marine Strategic Plan);
    - within the context of the World Summit on Sustainable Development (WSSD) commitment to complete a representative network by 2012; and
    - for conservation and protection of the high seas.

These objectives and activities are a shared responsibility of Fisheries and Oceans Canada, Environment Canada and the Parks Canada Agency. To ensure that progress on the protected area network continues, the above mentioned federal departments and agencies will move forward in establishing areas that have previously been identified as candidate sites. In addition, the strategy outlines how collective planning efforts will be undertaken to identify a suite of sites that may be added to the network in the future.

Source: adapted from Government of Canada (2005)

approach to conservation aims to protect a range of habitats, their species and ecological processes within a particular geographic area. However, as with terrestrial environments, there is no generally accepted ecosystem classification and available data on ecosystem distribution are often poor. Consequently, a 'surrogate' is often used to represent changes in biodiversity. The most commonly used surrogates are habitats in marine environments and vegetation communities in terrestrial situations (Smart et al, 2000).

- *Collection of data on the ecology and distribution of these units.* Sampling across, for example, habitat units is undertaken to document distribution of environmental types, species and the relationships between them. For example, planning conservation zoning in the Great Barrier Reef Marine Park involved assessing biological and physical information across 30 reef and 40 non-reef bioregions (Day et al, 2003a).

- *Determination of conservation goals for the amount of each unit that must be protected.* A conservation goal is the amount of habitat or bioregion that must be preserved to protect the full range of diversity. According to Vierros (2004), most recent studies indicate that at least 20 to 30 per cent of each habitat type should be included in highly protected areas in order to secure fisheries benefits from the marine protected area network. While there is less agreement about appropriate goals for biodiversity, Vierros (2004) argues that the 20 to 30 per cent figure might provide a good starting point within the context of adaptive management, provided that it is applied as part of an overall framework as recommended by the AHTEG. In the Great Barrier Reef, a zoning plan has identified no-take areas covering approximately 30 per cent of the marine park (Day et al, 2003a). Sala et al (2002) found that a network protecting 40 per cent of rocky reef habitat in the Gulf of California can satisfy many conservation goals.

- *Identification of a set of sites that meets these goals.* Selection algorithms have been developed that choose sites using rarity and irreplaceability as guiding principles (see the next section on 'Systematic reserve selection methods'). However, the process of identifying marine protected area sites must also take into account socio-economic and cultural criteria, so that formal selection methods are best used in the context of a wider planning process (see p212).

Systematic reserve selection methods

Although a number of countries have designed and implemented protected area system plans, global- (Rodrigues et al, 2003), regional- (Cowling and Pressey, 2003) and sub-national-scale (Margules and Pressey, 2000) studies have confirmed that protected area establishment frequently does not correlate with biodiversity conservation priorities. The largest deficiency is in protection of marine environments (Chape et al, 2005).

The current protected area systems reflect spatial patterns that derive from historical, economic, cultural, political and environmental factors. One outcome of these factors is a certain bias towards some types of landscapes and ecosystems rather than others. In 1918, the US was a leader in the field of protected areas. During that year, the US secretary of the interior, Franklin Lane, instructed the National Park Service director, Stephen Mather, to select national parks on the basis of their having 'scenery of supreme and distinctive quality so extraordinary or unique as to be of national interest and importance'. Scenery was the main selection criterion. Similarly, the first national park in Australia, Royal National Park, was designated in 1879 originally for recreation and public enjoyment. Selecting protected areas on the basis of grand scenery or wilderness quality often results in the targeting of areas remote from intensive uses. Securing the reservation of such areas is typically easier than protecting those economically productive landscapes that support important representations of particular biophysical features (such as endangered species or communities (Margules and Pressey, 2000).

In areas suitable for agriculture, forestry, fishing or human settlement, profitable uses of land or sea have often out-competed conservation. Conservation steps have often been taken only after concerns have arisen over the effects of development (Pouliquen-Young, 1997). Many large parks are in areas of low productivity, which are difficult to access and less suitable for other uses. As a result, many species occurring in productive land or seascapes and those with development potential are not protected even though disturbance, transformation to intensive uses and fragmentation continue (Margules and Pressey, 2000). On the other hand, conservation efforts by indigenous peoples and local communities (see Chapters 20 and 21) within such landscapes and seascapes have largely been ignored by governments and are not yet included in national protected area systems.

Most government-designated protected areas have been established primarily through political processes – that is, government agencies and/or interest groups have supported the reservation of an area, and this support has ultimately been manifested in declaration of the area under appropriate legislation. The political approach to selecting protected areas is often *ad hoc* or opportunistic, is heavily influenced by threat and availability, and is primarily determined by economic and cultural factors (Margules, 1989; Pressey et al, 1994a). While many important natural areas have been protected in this manner, regional conservation of biodiversity and consideration of other significant conservation values are

Iguaçu National Park, Brazil

Source: IUCN Photo Library © Jim Thorsell

• data driven, using features such as species, vegetation types, reserve size or connectivity, and selection units that are divisions of the landscape which are to be evaluated;
• objective led, based on a set of criteria that have quantitative targets for each feature;
• efficient in that they attempt to achieve the goals at a minimum cost in terms of other potential land uses;
• transparent in that reasons behind selection of each reserve are explicit; and
• flexible because features and targets can be varied to explore how changing these parameters influences the configuration and extent of the selected reserve network (Pressey, 1998).

Systematic approaches can:

• encourage planners to be explicit about what they are trying to achieve;
• provide a picture of conservation values in a regional context that can alert planners to the importance of areas they had not previously considered;
• show clearly the implications of using particular data sets and particular goals;
• illustrate the effects of making some areas mandatory for conservation and excluding others from contention;
• allow rapid investigation of alternative policy scenarios; and
• allow transparent, structured and negotiated planning between interest groups, including local communities with strong interests in the outcomes (Pressey, 1998).

not guaranteed. As we have seen in the first section on 'The need for comprehensive global systems', the distribution of protected areas across the various biomes is very uneven, with good representation in some areas and very poor representation in others.

Formal selection procedures, when used as a component of participatory processes, can allow for more informed land-use decisions based on key biological and social criteria. A procedure for the selection of protected areas should be explicit, systematic and straightforward, and should consider the extent to which the options for reservation are lost if a particular site is not preserved, while also recognizing the values of efficiency and flexibility (Pressey et al, 1994b). Systematic approaches to protected area selection are characterized as being:

A number of systematic conservation planning and formal reserve selection procedures have been developed (Kirkpatrick, 1983; Pressey et al, 1993; Margules and Pressey, 2000). More recently, Eken et al (2004) have proposed a framework and criteria for identifying key biodiversity areas (KBAs) as cornerstones for achieving comprehensive protected area coverage (see Case Study 8.3).

The extent to which protected areas are able to conserve biodiversity is determined by how well a protected area network represents the full range of biodiversity and how well the manage-

Case Study 8.3

Key biodiversity areas

The concept of key biodiversity areas (KBAs) emerged from the quantitative criteria-driven approach used by BirdLife International to characterize important bird areas for conservation (Osieck and Mörzer Bruyns, 1981). The KBA approach advocates using universal standards through the application of quantitative criteria for selecting sites of global conservation significance (Eken et al, 2004). Because of the emphasis on site-scale selection, KBAs complement other conservation planning approaches, such as ecoregional planning, that focus on landscape scales.

The KBA selection process is based on the presence of species for which site-scale conservation is appropriate, and the criteria used for selection draw primarily upon two major considerations in systematic conservation planning: vulnerability and irreplaceability (Margules and Pressey, 2000). With respect to vulnerability, the criterion is sites with globally threatened species as determined by the IUCN *Red List*. For irreplaceability, there are three separate criteria: sites with a significant proportion of 'restricted range species'; sites with 'congregatory species'; and sites with 'biome-restricted assemblages'. Eken et al (2004) provide a detailed description of these criteria, and the IUCN World Commission on Protected Areas (WCPA) is currently preparing a guideline for the application of KBAs in developing comprehensive protected area systems.

ment of these areas ensures the long-term survival of this biodiversity by maintaining natural processes and viable populations and excluding threats. This requires attention to the location of protected areas in relation to species distributions and other physical and biological patterns, such as plant communities, as well as wider design considerations, such as the size, connectivity and replication of reserves. A systematic planning approach is useful in identifying reserve networks that meet such criteria (Margules and Pressey, 2000). The six main stages in a typical systematic conservation planning methodology are:

1   Compile data on the biodiversity of the planning region, particularly data on the biodiversity features (such as species or land systems) that will be used as surrogates for biodiversity.
2   Identify conservation goals for the planning region, setting explicit representation criteria and targets for the biodiversity features that are to be analysed.
3   Review existing conservation areas, measuring the extent to which the representation targets have been achieved.
4   Select new protected areas as potential additions to the existing network.
5   Identify the types of reserves to be created,

assess their practicality and feasibility, and set time frames and priorities to establish the enlarged network.
6   Set conservation objectives for each protected area in order to retain the biodiversity features for which the area is important, implementing management actions to achieve these objectives and monitoring key indicators (Margules and Pressey, 2000).

While scientists and technical experts in spatial analysis may play a central role, such a process can be led or facilitated by governments, NGOs, communities, or as managed as a partnership between affected actors.

In the first stage, units are often identified as elements of the landscape that are assigned values and form the pool of land areas from which a protected area network is constructed. A unit can be any spatially defined area such as a watershed, environmental domain (the classification of an area according to climatic, terrain and substrate attributes) or grid square. Units should be small enough to build a reserve with precision, but not so large that a vast number of units are required.

In the second stage, conservation goals (such as representativeness and persistence of biodiversity) are developed into specific, preferably quantitative, targets. These targets allow clear identification of the contribution of existing protected areas to the overall goals (stage 3) and provide the means for measuring the conservation value of different areas during the area selection process in stage 4. A useful criterion will reflect a significant aspect of reserve selection.

Criteria can be divided into four categories: biophysical, social, planning and reserve design. Biophysical criteria include factors such as rarity of species, representativeness of ecosystems, diversity of habitat and naturalness. Social criteria include threat of human interference, community appeal, aesthetics, education value, and recreation and tourism. Planning criteria include adherence to watershed principles, bioregional boundaries, natural boundaries, fire control and availability of the land. Reserve design criteria are concerned with the spatial placement and characteristics of protected area networks and individual units, including their size, boundaries, shape, connectivity and geographic relationship to other units. The use of these criteria reflects the importance of considering the relationship of individual units to a network as a whole. Reserve design criteria are also often employed to combat the problems associated with ecosystem fragmentation or isolation. The way in which a reserve is designed can influence the protection of conservation values and the effectiveness of management. For example, reserve design criteria recommended as part of the forest reserve selection process in Australia included the following:

- Boundaries should be set in a landscape context with strong ecological integrity, such as watersheds.
- Large reserved areas are preferable to small reserved areas.
- Boundary–area ratios should be minimized and linear reserves should be avoided where possible except for riverine systems.
- Reserve design should aim to minimize the impact of threatening processes, particularly from adjoining areas.
- Reserves should be linked through a variety of mechanisms, wherever practicable, across the landscape (Commonwealth of Australia, 1998).

Salm et al (2000) identified a menu of criteria for selecting marine and coastal protected areas that, as well as ecological criteria, included social criteria (social acceptance, public health, recreation, culture, aesthetics, conflicts of interest, safety, accessibility, research and education, and public awareness), economic criteria (importance for commercial species, importance to fisheries, tourism), and pragmatic criteria (urgency, size, degree of threat, opportunism, availability and restorability).

Targets are then specified for each criterion. Targets concern the number of units required to satisfy a given selection criterion. For example, the criterion rarity could have the target 'where possible, each rare species must be found in at least two units'.

Once the criteria to be used have been selected and each unit is measured according to each criterion, the resulting data must be analysed to determine which units perform the best, and so should be included in the reserve network. Several systematic procedures incorporating biological selection criteria have been developed (for example, Kirkpatrick, 1983; Margules et al, 1988; Bedward et al, 1992; Pressey et al, 1994a).

A simple way of testing the units against the criteria is to combine several criteria into a single index and to select the sites that score most highly according to this index. However, often there is no obvious way of weighting and combining criteria. This approach is also inefficient because there is no way to minimize the number of sites required to satisfy each criterion. A better, but more complicated, approach is to use an iterative algorithm. An algorithm is a rule or series of rules that is applied to each unit to determine whether it should be part of the reserve system. Algorithms can efficiently select a reserve system. However, algorithms that incorporate several scientific, social and management criteria can become very complex.

Stage 4 typically makes use of iterative selection algorithms to select areas that efficiently complement existing protected area networks (Margules and Pressey, 2000). Examples of such algorithms are Conservation-Plan (C-Plan) (see Case Studies 8.4 and 8.5), MARXAN, which was developed and tested at the Great Barrier Reef Marine Park, and SITES, developed by The Nature Conservancy.

Case Study 8.4

Using C-Plan to support conservation planning decisions, Australia

Tom Barrett, New South Wales Department of Conservation and Environment, Parks and Wildlife Division, Australia

Conservation-Plan (C-Plan) (Pressey and Logan, 1995) is an example of a reserve selection programme that has been used for conservation assessment in New South Wales (NSW) to support conservation planning decisions. C-Plan was primarily developed for use in the New South Wales Comprehensive Regional Assessment component of the National Forests Policy. In this process, interest groups (conservationists, timber industry and indigenous peoples) negotiate with the aim of designing a reserve network that protects the natural and cultural features on public land while maintaining a viable timber industry.

The algorithm used in C-Plan is designed to achieve a set of conservation goals for as many features as possible in the minimum area (NSW NPWS, 1999). Included in C-Plan is the concept of irreplaceability. Irreplaceability measures how essential the site is based on how much of a feature is contained in other sites and how many times a given site is essential, in combination with other sites, to meet a target (Ferrier et al, 2000). C-Plan was used, for example, in a conservation assessment of the Cobar Peneplain Biogeographic Region in central western NSW. The Cobar Peneplain is a semi-arid area of approximately 73,500 square kilometres (9 per cent of NSW), bounded by the Darling and Bogan rivers. The project involved the use of C-Plan to assess the relative conservation values of land across the region, as well as investigation into ways of incorporating traditional aboriginal ecological knowledge within conservation assessments (Smart et al, 2000).

Used with a geographic information system (GIS), C-Plan:

- maps the options for achieving conservation goals in a region;
- allows users to decide which sites (areas of land or water) should be placed under some form of conservation management;
- accepts and displays these decisions; and then
- lays out the new pattern of options that result.

C-Plan looks at regional biodiversity using the 'irreplaceability' measure. Highly irreplaceable sites are most important for achieving the goal. Sites with a low irreplaceability measure are relatively unimportant for achieving the goal, although some of them must be allocated to conservation management if the regional goal is to be achieved. C-Plan also facilitates the use of resource, cultural and social data and allows the user to design decision rules to select areas based on these data. C-Plan allows decision-makers to identify areas for conservation that will have the least impact upon industries that depend upon forest resources.

After the new protected area has been established (stage 5), the last stage is best done in the context of a management planning project (see Chapter 11, p302).

As has already been noted, advantages of scientific selection methods include their explicit recognition of why each unit was recommended for the reserve network; consistency of assessment – the same method can be used to recommend reserve networks in different regions; ability to ensure that different types of environments, such as deserts and woodlands, as well as the more popular rainforests and mountain areas, are adequately represented in the reserve system; and ability to minimize the area required to adequately satisfy a given set of selection criteria.

Planning processes for protected area establishment

As noted earlier, many protected areas have been established on an *ad hoc* basis rather than using a formal planning framework. While this still occurs, new protected areas are increasingly established through planning processes. Such processes may include a scientifically based selection procedure, such as those described in the previous section, as well as many other elements that provide for community involvement, effective decision-making and implementation. Such processes may be initiated and driven by government agencies, NGOs, and indigenous or local communities. The evolution of land-use planning

Case Study **8.5**

Using C-Plan to support conservation planning decisions, Guyana

In 1994, the Guyana government requested the assistance of the Global Environment Facility (GEF) to help establish a national protected area system. A systematic, country-wide approach was taken to identify areas supporting biodiversity of global and national significance.

Conservation-Plan (C-Plan) was first used to map the irreplaceability of sites across Guyana on a 16 square-kilometre grid. A conservation target was set at 15 per cent representation for each species. This target was chosen for demonstration purposes only. Irreplaceability value was calculated for each of the 941 grid cells. The areas with the highest irreplaceability corresponded closely to previously recognized key ecosystems.

To assess which of these areas require most urgent consideration for protection, the vulnerability of areas with high irreplaceability for biodiversity conservation was also assessed. In this work, a vulnerability index was calculated as the proximity of a grid cell to an existing forestry concession. Other threatening processes can also be included as further analyses are developed.

The vulnerability index map and the irreplaceability value map were overlaid to produce a map of areas with both high vulnerability to logging and high irreplaceability (see Figure 8.4). Most of these areas are in the central, tall evergreen non-flooded forest located in the middle of the state forest; but some highly irreplaceable and slightly vulnerable areas also occur around Kaieteur Falls, the Pakarima and the Kanuku mountains.

Using irreplaceability and vulnerability to map priority conservation areas in Guyana allows for a whole system plan to be proposed, but also modified over time. New and arising issues such as future mineral exploration need to be factored in as part of the vulnerability index. Similarly, patterns of irreplaceability may change as new data become available. The advantage of this approach to system planning is its transparency and flexibility in the light of the complicated and changing land uses in Guyana as the country grapples with sustainable economic development.

Source: adapted from Richardson and Funk (1999)

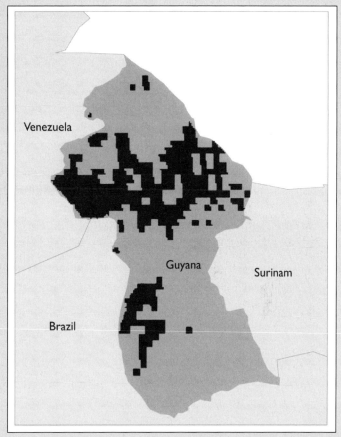

Figure 8.4 Map of Guyana showing areas of high irreplaceability and high vulnerability

Source: Richardson and Funk (1999, p14)

processes in the Cape Floristic Region of South Africa is summarized in Case Study 8.6. An overview of the types of decision-making processes for protected area designation is given in Table 8.1.

Table 8.1 Types of decision-making processes in protected area designation efforts

Type of decision process	Stakeholder role	Governance	Example circumstances
Government initiated; top down	Non-governmental stakeholders are consulted and may have input into decision	Government agency in control (legislation)	Government has a democratic mandate to establish new protected areas
			Local or indigenous communities not significantly affected
Government initiated; participatory	All stakeholders work to achieve a consensus or widely supported decision	Decision-making power shared among stakeholders Decision implemented either by: • government (legislation) • two or more parties in partnership (joint agreement, contract)	Government has a mandate to establish new protected areas Local or indigenous communities significantly affected
Private or NGO initiated	Supporters (government, local community, indigenous people) may be called upon to give assistance and/or approval	Private landowner or NGO in control (private tenure) Government takes responsibility	Landowner or NGO has ownership rights Land or sea is under government jurisdiction Individuals perceive a need to provide leadership and advocacy (see Case Study 8.7)
Indigenous or local community initiated	Supporters (government, NGO) may be called upon to give assistance	Community in control (common property tenure, customary law, traditional use rights)	Community has or assumes ownership and management rights, conferred by law and/or custom

Franklin-Gordon Wild Rivers National Park, Tasmania, Australia was established following conservation protests against a proposed hydroelectricity development

Source: IUCN Photo Library © Jim Thorsell

Case Study 8.6

Protected area planning processes in the Cape Floristic Region, South Africa

Trevor Sandwith, chair, IUCN/ World Commission on Protected Areas (WCPA) Task Force on Transboundary Protected Areas

The history of conservation planning in the Cape Floristic Region in South Africa typifies the evolution of an approach and the coming together of the two main schools of thought that have traditionally emphasized the representation of biodiversity pattern (ensuring that species, populations and ecosystems are included in the protected area system) and biodiversity process (ensuring that ecosystem and evolutionary processes continue to operate at the regional landscape scale despite the threats). Driver et al (2003) identified how conservation planning in the Cape Floristic Region has progressed through a number of approaches:

- *ad hoc and opportunistic approaches*, where protected areas were established in areas where there was least competition with other land uses;
- *scoring approaches*, which attempted to set priorities to address obvious gaps in the set of protected areas;
- *planning for representation*, which used the first reserve selection methodologies to systematically identify a representative system of protected areas based on region-wide databases of species' distributions and the setting of representation targets;
- *planning for persistence*, which by identifying key threats and ecosystem processes in the region determines spatial targets for the continued operation of key ecological and evolutionary processes, such as pollination, migration, herbivory and disturbance factors; and
- *planning for implementation*, which takes into account the social, economic, political, legal and institutional environment as the basis for developing the means to achieve the conservation targets within the desired time frame.

In South Africa, a number of complementary large-scale conservation planning exercises generated key lessons that also have relevance for similar exercises elsewhere in the world. These lessons, as identified by Cowling and Pressey (2003) and Driver et al (2003), are as follows:

- *Plan with implementation in mind.* Policy, legal, institutional and socio-economic requirements for implementation should inform the choices that must be made in conservation planning. This contrasts with many conservation planning exercises, where conservation targets are derived, following which the means to secure effective implementation are worked out. At the outset, it is important to identify who needs the plan and what it is likely to achieve, and then to involve key informants from the outset. It is necessary to ensure that the outputs of planning can be readily taken up, especially by the decision-making process, where most adverse decisions for biodiversity are likely to be made in a piecemeal fashion.
- *Engage local-level stakeholders in committed conservation action.* Key groups can be identified to proactively address key components of the conservation plan, thereby engendering early gains and a rapid build-up of confidence in the emerging plan. In particular, local municipalities are a priority stakeholder group because of their significant influence on local decision-making. It makes sense to include representatives from key constituencies in the planning phase and to engage future implementers in analysing and mobilizing implementation throughout.
- *Coordinate planning frameworks for all types of biodiversity.* It is necessary from the outset to determine a planning framework that is common to all components of biodiversity, including terrestrial, freshwater and marine, and to coordinate the inputs from these different components.
- *Ensure that information is presented at the appropriate scale.* It is necessary to ensure that the appropriate level of detail for decision-making in priority sub-areas of the planning domain is captured from the outset. If decisions are made at the level of individual properties, then property boundaries should be used.
- *Ensure that biodiversity is mainstreamed into sectoral decision-making.* This can be achieved through the elaboration of agreements and mechanisms applied by key sectors based on the new conservation priorities. Priority elements are cross-sectoral agreements, the embedding of spatial targets in land-use plans, and the application of a range of incentives using economic approaches to influence business and industry to adopt and apply biodiversity-friendly practices.
- *Use the conservation planning process to build capacity.* Opportunities should be taken to link scientists and other technical experts with practitioners in relevant fields, and to bring in people from non-conservation careers to rub shoulders with and help influence the language and methods for implementation.
- *Use expert knowledge as well as systematic data analysis.* This can ensure that the conservation planning process is not biased by poor datasets. In this approach, it is necessary to devise ways of integrating expert and systematic processes.

Processes for identifying and establishing new protected areas are undertaken by governments, often as a result of pressure from pro-conservation advocates. A brief account of the establishment of government managed protected areas in Brazil is given in Case Study 8.8. As discussed in Chapter 5, protected area establishment by governments has had a history of causing severe disadvantage to indigenous and local communities. Modern processes must not perpetrate such injustices. Adoption of good governance principles (see Chapter 5, p134), involvement of all stakeholders and recognition of prior rights are crucial.

In the context of marine protected area establishment, Bernstein et al (2004) and Kessler (2003) reviewed six case studies from the US and identi-fied the following lessons that emerged from these case experiences (a summary of one of the cases is given in Case Study 8.9):

- Different processes may contain many of the same elements but lead to a variety of conclusions, depending upon how history and political environment influence the process. Early planning efforts must include a thorough assessment of past history and its potential effects on stakeholder perceptions and the goals to which they will agree, as well as on their willingness to participate and the ground rules they will accept.
- Process managers must have a grasp of the underlying authority for a designation process,

Case Study 8.7

Proposal of Cerro Verde Area as the first marine protected area in Uruguay

Jessica Castro-Prieto and María J. Andrade-Nuñez, CID/Karumbe and Facultad de Ciencias de la Universitad, República Oriental del Uruguay

We conducted a baseline survey of ecological and anthropological data to characterize a marine coastal area of Uruguay and to assess the need for establishing a protected area. Our long-term goal was the designation of this area as the first marine protected area in Uruguay. In September 2003 we started to collect and review existing data, and interviewed biologists and key stakeholders, including fishers, craftspeople, teachers, tourist guides, local government officers and landowners. We then conducted fieldtrips to characterize the area based on physical, biological and anthropological variables, as well as to identify and highlight its primary ecological and cultural values. We also identified and classified land uses and natural resource-related activities, and, where possible, quantified their environmental impacts.

The proposed marine protected area, Cerro Verde, covers over 510 square kilometres of a marine coastal ecosystem, which includes 140 square kilometres of terrestrial and 375 square kilometres of marine environment. The area encompasses a wide variety of ecosystems, such as rocky shores; sand beach arcs; sand dunes; native woody and sandy vegetation; wetlands; islands; and the coastal oceanic shelf. The area represents the greatest richness, diversity, density and biomass of benthic intertidal invertebrate species of sandy beaches in Uruguay. Marine mammal species such as dolphins (*Tursiops truncatus* and *Pontoporia bianvillei*) and sea lions (*Otaria flavense* and *Arctocephalus australis*) can be observed year round. Sea bird species, both resident and migratory from Nearctic and Neotropic zones, utilize these habitats. Migratory species such as whales and sea turtles arrive in the area during the spring season. The prairies, wetlands and forests within the study area constitute important habitats for more than 45 bird species and 26 mammal species. Other important features include marine fossil-bearing deposits; the nation's foremost national historic monument, La Fortaleza de Santa Teresa; archaeological sites; vestiges of shipwrecks; coastal villages; and frontier cities. While resident population density is low, a high volume of tourists visits the area in the summer, attracted by the sandy beaches, low levels of urban development and the rustic character of local buildings, as well as by the wide variety of stores, duty-free products and local crafts.

Cerro Verde is currently being evaluated by the government agency (Dirección Nacional de Medio Ambiente, División Areas Naturales Protegidas) to be incorporated within the National System of Protected Areas.

as well as the ability to explain it to participants.

- Constructive stakeholder involvement in planning is vital to achieving conservation goals, both in establishing sites and in ensuring their effective long-term stewardship. Managers should design and manage processes with an understanding of stakeholder motivation and an expectation that stakeholder goals will differ, and be prepared to handle disagreements and conflict.
- Scientists should not work separately from other stakeholders, even on seemingly non-controversial issues. Scientists should be selected to ensure that their skills match the areas of expertise defined by the objectives of the process, and their role should be made clear to stakeholders.

- Managers must have a vision of the process steps from beginning to end, not just the stakeholder participation stage.
- Processes should incorporate appropriate flexibility and adaptability.
- Planners and managers should treat politics as the natural expression of human and interest group dynamics that reflect stakeholders' genuine interests and perceptions. They are part of the policy process and need to be recognized, accommodated and planned for. Such interest group dynamics often lead to conflict, which should be seen as a natural part of such complex processes.
- Leadership is needed at the political level that initiates and supports the process, at the upper levels of involved agencies that ensure consistent commitment and follow through on

decisions, at the process level where facilitation, negotiation and conflict management skills are crucial, and at the interest group level, where perceived stature, relationships with constituents, and the effective framing, control and communication of a core message are important.

- Value-laden conflicts can and should be addressed through the use of skilled, experienced facilitators.
- Maps have many applications, from identifying gaps to analysing the implications of proposed boundaries. Process planners should consider three important aspects to maps – the process by which they are made, the information they contain, and how, when and by whom they are used.
- Top-level managers must ensure that key programme staff are formally assigned to manage the process from start to finish, and that they have the experience, stature and core skills needed to understand and influence its evolution, and to successfully flag and negotiate emerging issues with the programme leadership.
- Protected area establishment processes take considerable time to complete and, as a result,

require careful planning and realistic time frames.

Management principles

1 Viable representations of every terrestrial, freshwater and marine ecosystem type need to be conserved effectively within protected areas.
2 Systems of protected areas should strive to meet the following criteria: representativeness, comprehensiveness and balance; adequacy; coherence and complementarity; consistency; cost effectiveness; and efficiency and equity.
3 Vulnerability to prevailing threatening processes should influence the priorities for protection.
4 Any use of 'percentage area' targets should take into account their limitations, particularly the fact that they can be poor indicators of additional conservation needs.
5 Each region should contain representative and adequate areas of IUCN Category I, II, III and IV reserves.
6 National reserve systems should recognize and incorporate IUCN Categories I to VI in order to create a landscape-scale matrix of protected areas with varying uses and emphases.

Case Study 8.8

Government processes used to establish Brazilian protected areas

An early attempt to systematically identify a reserve network for Brazil was the Rada na Amazônia (RADAM) project that ran from 1975 to 1983. Survey work identified geology, geomorphology, hydrology, soil and vegetation distribution across the country. This study recommended that 35.2 million hectares of strictly protected areas be established in the Amazon basin, as well as a further 71.5 million hectares of what would now be called IUCN Category V or VI protected areas. The Pico da Neblina, Pacáas Novos, Jaú and Serra do Divisor national parks, and the Rio Trombetas, Lagoi Piratuba and Guaporé biological reserves were created as a result of the project. However, the recommendations were biased towards areas that had no other competing use. Formal reserve network planning then lost momentum until the emergence of three initiatives in the mid to late 1990s.

Biological corridors were used to increase connectivity across landscapes and between existing protected areas. For example, the 2.35 million hectare Amanã Sate Sustainable Development Reserve connects the Jaú National Park to the Mamirauá State Sustainable Development Reserve, thereby contributing to an east–west corridor of contiguous protected areas through the central Amazon. A series of workshops in 1999 and 2000 identified 900 areas that warranted reserve status, and by 2002, 57 of these covering 5,607,146ha had been declared. The Ministry for the Environment's Protected Area Programme for Amazonia used representation of 23 Amazonian ecoregions as the basis for identifying an extra 500,000 square kilometres to be brought under national government protection.

Source: adapted from Rylands and Brandon (2005)

Case Study 8.9

Establishing the Tortugas Ecological Reserve, US

The Tortugas Ecological Reserve in the US was established through a process that was the culmination of a ten-year planning effort. A central component of the design process was the Tortugas 2000 programme (see Figure 8.5).

The Dry Tortugas (the Tortugas) are a cluster of remote islands located in the Gulf of Mexico approximately 113km west of Key West, Florida. The area features biologically diverse marine habitats, including coral reefs and banks, seagrass meadows and rookery islands; the islands have attracted visitors for many years. The Tortugas are popular with recreational divers and have supported diverse commercial and recreational fishing activities.

The area is, in part, protected in the 259 square kilometre Dry Tortugas National Park, established in 1992, and is also at the western edge of the 9800 square kilometre Florida Keys National Marine Sanctuary (FKNMS) created by the US Congress in 1990 and managed under a co-operative agreement between the State of Florida and the National Oceanic and Atmospheric Administration. During the development of the FKNMS management plan, the Tortugas were proposed for an ecological reserve. This proved to be highly controversial, and a seven-year effort to garner support proved unsuccessful. In 1998, a collaborative process to further pursue the proposal was initiated by the FKNMS managers and National Park Service, and became known as Tortugas 2000. The following examples indicate some of the lessons that emerged from an analysis of the Tortugas 2000 process.

project scoping (1998)
⇩
determine goals and objectives for ecological reserve
⇩
ecological forum
⇩
socio-economic forum
⇩
scoping meetings (1998)
⇩
develop and weight criteria
⇩
develop alternatives (1999)
⇩
draft alternative boundaries
⇩
selection of preferred alternative
⇩
develop Draft Supplemental Environmental Impact Statement (1999)
⇩
working group recommendation to Sanctuary Advisory Council on draft boundaries and preferred alternative
⇩
Sanctuary Advisory Council recommendation to NOAA on preferred alternative
⇩
publish Draft Supplemental Environmental Impact Statement (2000)
⇩
public hearings (2000)
⇩
receive and summarize public comment
⇩
revise preferred alternative based on public comment
⇩
publish Final Supplemental Environmental Impact Statement (2000)
⇩
final plan approved (2001)
⇩
implementation begins (2001)

Figure 8.5 Summary of the Tortugas 2000 Reserve establishment process

Source: Kessler (2003, p96)

Don't repeat the past – learn from it. Tortugas 2000 was shaped by relationships and stakeholder perceptions grounded in earlier failed efforts to establish significant ecological reserves in the area. There was time to analyse the mistakes that occurred during the initial development of the marine zoning network and to reflect upon earlier public comments. The already formed relationships, when combined with shared mandates among various government agencies, broad stakeholder participation and a skilled facilitator, set the stage for a relatively rapid series of decisions that led to a robust, widely supported outcome. Significantly, the original reserves concept was completely withdrawn, providing stakeholders with a virtual blank slate from which to work. This created significant good will as interest groups now felt empowered by their defeat of the initial efforts, more in control of their destiny, and more confident of their ability to create a reserve derived from stakeholder prerogatives.

Inclusive stakeholder process breeds success. Organizers recognized that it was important to establish a working group that was as broadly representative as possible. For example, a diversity of fishing interests was identified and represented (commercial, hand-line lobster, Cuban–American, charter, spear and recreational), ensuring that more nuanced perspectives were fully heard and incorporated within the development of proposals. The absence of some of these groups from the initial effort to designate reserves was reported to hamper that process.

Stakeholder representatives must have authority and be accountable. To ensure that reliable decisions were made, it was also important that each working group member had authority to actively represent his or her stakeholder group. As such, members were identified and acknowledged as leaders to those they intended to represent and were held accountable for their commitments. Each member was asked if he or she could speak for a constituency, and efforts were made throughout the process to ensure that members were interacting and receiving feedback from those whom they represented.

Professional facilitators can be very important to the success of the process. The facilitator was viewed as a 'neutral party' by all stakeholders, particularly those on the working group. The facilitator was instrumental in helping participants to identify core interests that underlay their stated positions. He also quickly designed and implemented an effective consensus-building process, ensuring that all members were engaged and involved and that decisions were credible and robust. Because he was clearly not identified with any agency history or position, he was able to provide the kind of neutrality (in terms of both process and outcome) that government representatives typically cannot.

Both traditional science and fishermen's knowledge were equally important. Everyone agreed that the preparation and presentation of numerous types of technical information were integral to the working group's ability to make sound recommendations. The information included oceanic, biological, socio-economic and fisheries information presented by scientists and stakeholders. While the majority of scientific information was provided during two special forum presentations, scientists sat next to fishermen, conservationists and managers throughout the process. The resulting ability of scientists and stakeholders to continuously interact and provide immediate feedback on issues raised around the table helped to build the sense that scientists were there to assist the process. The informational forums allowed community members and other stakeholders to share their knowledge and experience with the working group, managers and scientists. The fact that anecdotal stakeholder knowledge was used directly and given equal weight was crucial to subsequent discussions and consensus-building. Fishers reported feeling more involved, compared to other processes, and that their 'unscientific' but no less valuable knowledge was respected.

Geographic information systems (GIS) as a tool is valuable; but manual map-making is more appropriate in some cases. GIS was used very interactively during working group sessions and was uniformly praised. The ability to quickly and graphically portray new information empowered the working group to make decisions. An extensive database was compiled and information was quickly processed for presentation. In particular, for the first time data showed use patterns in addition to biological information. This allowed the working group to better identify what needed to be protected, and balance those protections with fishery uses. When it came to recording individual preferences for potential boundaries, however, the old-fashioned approach proved better than GIS. A manual method using an acetate overlay on top of the grid cell was employed, and resulted in participants working together over paper charts, sharing stories and perspectives and, according to one observer, avoiding the negative effect that GIS can have on people's ability to have a direct sense of ownership over the map-building process. Each working group member drew out preferred boundary configurations, and the overlays were shared with the group via overheads or provided to staff to use in GIS products. This more intimate, hands-on and interactive technique for recording boundaries proved successful.

Public input was innovative and was solicited throughout the process. Several participants pointed to the interaction between working group members and other stakeholders as essential to the consensus-building process. During working group meetings, members were able to confer directly with members of their stakeholder group to solicit immediate input when necessary. During break-out sessions, the public was invited to sit as a 'second tier' around the working group members, or members could go elsewhere to caucus. Whatever the case, the opportunity for a free and rapid flow of information between members and observers allowed for a full range of perspectives to be incorporated within the discussion. The National Park Service had a simultaneous management planning process under way for the Tortugas National Park, which paralleled the Tortugas 2000 effort. It was important to managers that the simultaneous efforts not confuse the public; thus, they were coordinated as much as possible. This included holding public hearings jointly in which, after initial presentations, the room was divided by topic and individuals could present comments in one of several ways: they could talk into a microphone; write out comments; dictate their comments to staff; or write them up on newsprint on the wall. Comments could be given anonymously, the public could ask questions, and the entire process was relatively informal and non-threatening to those unaccustomed to or uncomfortable with more structured and formal approaches. While some fisheries representatives did not like the rather unorthodox process because they were used to speaking at a podium, the majority felt that it was more inclusive and far less intimidating.

Don't start drawing lines prematurely. Many of the users (particularly fishers) wanted to know where managers thought the ecological reserve boundaries should be. They were familiar with other management processes where several options were presented and debated, rather than created with their input. To their credit, the sanctuary managers remained silent, empowering and, ultimately, compelling stakeholders to do the work of determining the reserve parameters. Managers would not even offer ballpark estimates of the size or location that should be protected, or what the regulations should contain – in public or private. This approach may not work in other cases where trust is not established and where stakeholders may not be as familiar with the geographic area or relevant resources. Here, managers benefited from lessons learned from their earlier efforts, and understood that speculating on the potential boundaries would taint the process and put stakeholders on the defensive, trying to protect what they may have considered their turf or territory. The majority of stakeholders saw the wisdom in this particular part of the process, while a handful had some misgivings, thinking that it protracted the overall efforts. Whatever the perspective, participants unanimously agreed that their input had real meaning and that there was no hidden agenda or predetermined outcome on the part of the managers. Interestingly, the resulting ecological reserve was much larger than any of the managers individually anticipated.

The Tortugas Ecological Reserve was implemented in July 2001. Tortugas North remains open to non-extractive diving and snorkelling, with visitors required to obtain a simple no-cost phone-in permit to ensure that all vessels have access to mooring buoys, to ease enforcement and to assist in monitoring visitor impacts. Regulations prohibit all taking of marine life, restrict vessel discharges to cooling water and engine exhaust, prohibit anchoring, and prohibit the use of mooring buoys by vessels more than 30.5m in combined length. Tortugas South prohibits all taking of marine life and restricts vessel discharges. Regulations also prohibit diving to protect potentially sensitive spawning aggregations from disruption, and require vessels to be in continuous transit through the area with fishing gear stowed. Researchers and educators holding a sanctuary permit may utilize this region.

Almost everyone involved agreed that the Tortugas 2000 process represents how a successful consensus-building process can work when a skilled facilitator is paired with motivated participants in an environment of trust and is empowered by a clear mandate. Building upon efforts leading up to the process and the decision among sanctuary managers to not attempt to predetermine or shape the outcome, participants were free to be proactive and creative rather than reactive and defensive. Success in the Tortugas may also be attributed, in part, to the fact that most participants had some first-hand experience with no-take reserves and thus, perhaps, feared the concept less than in other regions. Moreover, trust was established and more positional bargaining avoided with agreements such as the one between fishers, who agreed not to 'whack and hack' proposals, and conservationists, who agreed not to 'pad and add'. As a result of a successful collaborative process, the building of trust among diverse stakeholders and demonstrably positive ecological measures, even those who initially opposed reserves are now some of their biggest supporters.

Source: adapted from Kessler (2003) and Bernstein et al (2004)

7 National reserve systems should recognize the range of governance mechanisms outlined in Chapter 5, provided an acceptable level of reservation security is afforded.

8 Reserve networks should be designed to take into account the location of protected areas relative to each other and to other land uses, including issues of ecologically optimal boundaries and connectivity.

9 Systematic conservation planning tools that use information on species, habitats and ecological processes to identify gaps in the existing system should be applied to assist in the selection of new protected areas at national and sub-national (bioregional) levels.

10 Reserve selection needs to be based on both traditional knowledge and modern science.

11 Decisions to establish protected areas should be initiated by, or involve participation of,

those with an interest and those affected by any potential reservation.

12 The interests and concerns of indigenous peoples and local communities should be recognized and incorporated within reserve selection decisions.

13 Constructive stakeholder involvement in planning is vital to achieving conservation goals, both in establishing sites and in ensuring their effective long-term stewardship.

14 Those seeking to establish protected areas need to be prepared for a long and drawn-out process; as a result, this requires careful planning and realistic time frames.

Further reading

Brooks, T. M., Bakarr, M. I., Boucher, T., Da Fonseca, G. A. B., Hilton-Taylor, C., Hoekstra, J. M., Moritz, T., Olivier, S., Parrish, J., Pressey, R. L.,

Rodrigues, A. S. L., Sechrest, W., Stattersfield, A., Strahm, W. and Stuart, S. N. (2004) 'Coverage provided by the global protected-area system: Is it enough?', Bioscience, vol 54, pp1081–1091

Chape, S., Harrison, J., Spalding, M. and Lysenko, I. (2005) 'Measuring the extent and effectiveness of protected areas as an indicator for meeting global biodiversity targets', *Philosophical Transactions of the Royal Society B*, vol 360, pp443–455

Davey, A.G. (1998) *National System Planning for Protected Areas*, World Commission on Protected Areas Best Practice Protected Area Guidelines Series no 1, IUCN, Gland and Cambridge

Margules, C. R. and Pressey, R. L. (2000) 'Systematic conservation planning', *Nature*, vol 405, pp243–253

Rodrigues, A. S. L., Andelman, S. J., Bakarr, M. I., Boitani, L., Brooks, T. M., Cowling, R. M., Fishpool, L. D. C., da Fonseca, G. A. B., Gaston, K. J., Hoffmann, M., Long, J. S., Marquet, P. A., Pilgrim, J. D., Pressey, R. L., Schipper, J., Sechrest, W., Stuart, S. N., Underhill, L. G., Waller, R. W., Watts, M. E. J. and Yan, X. (2003) *Global Gap Analysis: Towards a Representative Network of Protected Areas*, Advances in Applied Biodiversity Science 5, Conservation International, Washington, DC

Salm, R.V., Clark, J. R. and Siirilam, E. (2000) *Marine and Coastal Protected Areas: A Guide for Planners and Managers*, 3rd edition, IUCN, Washington, DC

9

Threats to Protected Areas

Graeme L. Worboys, Colin Winkler and Michael Lockwood

The main purpose of protected areas is to conserve biological and geological diversity and cultural heritage. This is achieved by permanent conservation reservation and by active and effective management. However, protected areas are assailed by a multitude of threats and their values can easily be lost. The creation of protected areas without accompanying management is not an option if we are to conserve the values for which they have been reserved. This chapter describes the nature and characteristics of threats to protected areas and provides responses to how such threats may be managed.

Over the past 50 years, humans have changed ecosystems on Earth to meet growing demands for food, freshwater, timber, fibre and fuel, and this has occurred more rapidly and extensively than in any other comparable time in human history. This has had its consequences, and the IUCN *2004 IUCN Red List* recognized 15,589 species threatened with extinction (Baillie et al, 2004). Current extinction rates in mammals and birds are 100 to 200 times higher than the estimated average rate of extinction of species through geological time (SCBD, 2001). All mammals and birds have been assessed for extinction risk, and 24 per cent of mammal species and 12 per cent of bird species were considered globally threatened in 2000 (SCBD, 2001). In 2005, the findings of 1360 experts from 95 countries working with the Millennium Ecosystem Assessment Board advised that human activities were causing environmental damage on a massive scale. They confirmed the underlying threats posed by humans to the environment, and reinforced a common sense view that the capacity of the Earth to absorb human-induced change was finite. Three specific findings of the Millennium Ecosystem Assessment Board (2005) were:

- Fifteen out of 24 global ecosystem services examined were being degraded or used unsustainably, including freshwater, capture fisheries, air and water purification, and the regulation of regional and local climate, natural hazards and pests.
- Changes made in ecosystems are increasing the likelihood of non-linear changes in ecosystems (including accelerating, abrupt and potentially irreversible changes) that have important consequences for human well-being, including disease emergence, abrupt alterations in water quality, the creation of 'dead' zones in coastal waters, the collapse of fisheries, and shifts in regional climate.
- The harmful effects of the degradation of ecosystem services are being borne disproportionately by the poor, are contributing to the growing inequities and disparities across groups of people, and are sometimes the principal factor causing poverty and social conflict.

A convergence of environmental degradation, resource scarcity and social issues is forecast to be influential during the first 50 years of the 21st century, and will test both the social order and the capacity of nations and societies to adapt (Mason, 2003). Governments and protected area managers will need to prepare for, and be adept in, handling potential multiple threats that may arise from such a convergence of events. In this chapter, we briefly consider underlying causes, but provide more detail for direct and indirect threats faced by protected area managers and strategies that can be used to address them. In order to provide a coherent framework for undertaking these tasks, we first present a classification of protected area threats.

Classification of threats

In order to understand and describe threats to protected areas, it is useful to have a classification framework that lists potential threats and shows how they relate to each other and to protected areas. Such a framework can also:

- help practitioners to work out what threats may occur at their sites;
- enable practitioners to search a database of conservation projects and find projects facing similar threats, and to learn how these projects have dealt with these threats; and
- enable tallies of the frequency of threats across projects at various organizational scales (Margoluis and Salafsky, 2001).

Useful frameworks, classifications and information on key threats to protected areas have been researched by WRI et al (1992); IUCN (1999); Carey et al (2000); Margoluis and Salafsky (2001); Rogers and Bueno (2001); Stolton and Dudley (2003); Barber et al (2004); Choudhury et al (2004); WWF (2004); and Millennium Ecosystem Assessment Board (2005). However, none of the classifications entirely suit the purposes of this book. We have therefore drawn on these sources and our own experience to develop a simple classification for threats, shown in Figure 9.1 and Table 9.1. This classification system identifies underlying causes of threats. These underlying causes provide the conditions that generate and drive direct and indirect threats to terrestrial and marine protected areas. Indirect threats arise from outside protected areas, but impact upon values within them. Direct threats are those that arise

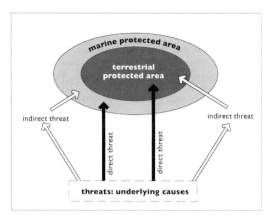

Figure 9.1 Three classes of protected area threats: Underlying causes, indirect threats and direct threats

within protected area boundaries. Thus, direct and indirect threats are simply distinguished by their spatial characteristics. Examples of threats in each of these three broad categories are provided in Table 9.1.

Threats often involve complex chains of cause and effect. For example, a direct threat to a protected area may be encroachment by small farmers. This encroachment may be driven by an indirect cause – the rapid privatization and concentration of agricultural land in adjacent areas. The underlying cause of this situation, in turn, may be subsidies or other changes in government policy aimed at boosting export agriculture to help pay off international debts (Barber et al, 2004). In addition, Carey et al (2000) noted that if a protected area is under threat from one particular factor, there is a strong probability that it is also under threat from others. Troubles seldom come in isolation, particularly where there is a lack of capacity, strained relations with local communities or a more general breakdown in the rule of law.

Managing threats: Underlying causes

The global issues discussed in Chapter 2 (population growth; material aspirations; inadequate legal and political systems; inadequate economic

Table 9.1 Protected area threats: Examples of underlying causes, indirect threats and direct threats

Threat class	Type	Potential consequences that can threaten protected areas	Related sections in this book
Underlying cause	Human population growth	Unsustainable natural resource consumption	'Socio-cultural context' in Chapter 2
	Material aspirations, especially in high Human Development Index (HDI) countries	Unsustainable natural resource consumption	'Economic context' in Chapter 2
	Inadequate legal and political systems	Policies that fail to secure environmental protection	'Economic context' and 'Political context' in Chapter 2
		Lack of political commitment	
		Corruption leading to failures in governance, enforcement and management	
	Inadequate economic systems	Failure to fully account for environmental costs and benefits of decisions	'Economic context' in Chapter 2; 'Financing protected areas' in Chapter 12; 'Public sector support' in Chapter 25
		Poverty, leading to indirect threats	
		Subsidies for environmentally damaging activities	
		Under-resourced conservation management	
		Inequity of ownership, management and benefit flow	'Socio-cultural context' and 'Economic context' in Chapter 2
	Dysfunctional social, cultural or political relations	War and civil conflict impairing capacity to manage	'Political context' in Chapter 2; 'Managing incidents arising from armed conflict' in Chapter 18
	Community attitudes and values	Community attitude and values are at variance to the objectives for conservation	'Economic context' and 'Political context' in Chapter 2
	Knowledge and education deficiencies	Impaired capacity to identify solutions to environmental problems	Chapter 4; Chapter 7; 'General public support' in Chapter 25
		Lack of awareness of protected area benefits	
Indirect threat	Climate change	Changes to habitat and species distribution and abundance, and an increase in extinctions	'Managing indirect threats' in this chapter
		Changes to the physical environment (stream-flow regimes, flood patterns, rainfall, ice distribution, fire frequency and severity, and storm frequency and severity)	
		Inundation of low-lying areas through rising sea levels	
		Thermal impacts to corals and coral bleaching	

Table 9.1 Continued

Threat class	Type	Potential consequences that can threaten protected areas	Related sections in this book
Indirect threat	Inappropriate land- and sea-use decisions	Land-use change, habitat destruction and fragmentation arising from development, agriculture, resource extraction, and human settlement	'Managing indirect threats' in this chapter; 'Importance of linkages' in Chapter 22
		Tourism developments and increasing visitor-use pressure	'Global tourism and environmental performance' in Chapter 19
	Poverty	Lack of options to adopt sustainable practices	'Socio-cultural context' in chapter 2
	Off-site pollution	Polluted water (marine or terrestrial) affecting protected areas	'Managing indirect threats' in this chapter
		Air pollutants damaging biodiversity and scenic values	
	Off-site impoundment of rivers, diversion of water and drawdown of groundwater	Unsustainable water use impacting upon ecosystems	'Managing indirect threats' in this chapter
	Off-site natural events (tsunami, fire, earthquake, volcanicity, avalanche and glacier break-up)	Damage to natural ecosystems, infrastructure and human life	'Managing indirect threats' in this chapter; 'Managing incidents arising from natural phenomena' in Chapter 18
Direct threat	Illegal activities	Poaching of wildlife, hunting, fishing, arson, logging and mining	'Managing direct threats' in this chapter; 'Managing wildlife incidents' in Chapter 18
	War and civil conflict	Damage to natural ecosystems, cultural heritage, infrastructure and human life	'Political context' in Chapter 2; 'Managing direct threats' in this chapter; 'Managing incidents arising from armed conflict' in Chapter 18
	Poor management	Damaging management policies and actions	'Managing indirect threats' in this Chapter; Chapters 6, 7, 13, and 15
		Incompetently executed actions	
	Insufficient management resources	Failure to act, or inadequate management response to threats	'Financing protected areas' in Chapter 12; Chapters 7 and 15
	Introduced animals, including pest animals	Damage to natural ecosystems	'Managing direct threats' in this chapter
	Introduced plants, including weeds	Damage to natural ecosystems	'Managing direct threats' in this chapter; 'Managing weeds and introduced pathogens' in Chapter 16

Table 9.1 Continued

Threat class	Type	Potential consequences that can threaten protected areas	Related sections in this book
Direct threat	Fire	Damage to natural ecosystems, cultural heritage, infrastructure, property and human life	'Managing fire' in Chapter 16; 'Managing fire incidents' in Chapter 18
	On-site pollution	Damage to natural ecosystems, recreation and tourism values	'Managing direct threats' in this chapter
	On-site impacts of chemicals	Damage to natural ecosystems and human health	'Managing direct threats' in this chapter
	On-site impoundment of rivers, diversion of water and drawdown of groundwater	Damage to natural ecosystems	'Sustainability practices for managers' in Chapter 14
	Livestock grazing	Damage to natural ecosystems, recreation and tourism values	'Sustainable use of resources' in Chapter 14
	Urban expansion	Impacts upon habitats and natural ecosystems	Arising from poor land-use decisions – see 'Managing indirect threats' in this chapter
	Unsustainable plant and animal resource extraction	Damage to natural ecosystems, recreation and tourism values	'Sustainability practices for managers' in Chapter 14
	Mineral resource extraction	Damage to natural ecosystems, cultural heritage, recreation and tourism values	'Managing direct threats' in this chapter
	On-site infrastructure and tourism development	Damage to natural ecosystems and cultural heritage	'Managing direct threats' in this chapter; 'Planning systems and tools' in Chapter 19
	Unsustainable visitor use	Damage to natural ecosystems, social and cultural heritage	'Managing direct threats' in this chapter; 'Planning systems and tools' in Chapter 19
	On-site natural events (tsunami, fire, earthquake, volcanicity, avalanche and glacier break-up)	Damage to natural ecosystems, infrastructure and human life	'Managing incidents arising from natural phenomena' in Chapter 18

systems; and dysfunctional social, cultural or political relations) demand national and international leadership. These underlying causes also have major implications for life on Earth. Never before have so many of the life-support systems of Earth been threatened by so many individuals of a single species in such a short period of time. In order to help stop the decline in the Earth's biodiversity, and to maintain a habitable planet for the long term, the Millennium Ecosystem Assessment Board (2005) has brought forward many possible options for managing ecosystems sustainably, from which we highlight four that have particular relevance for protected areas:

1 Change the economic background to decision-making by:
- making sure that the value of all ecosystem services, not just those bought and sold in the market, are taken into account when making decisions (see Chapter 12, p348);
- removing subsidies to agriculture, fisheries and energy that cause harm to people and their environment;
- introducing payments to landowners in return for managing their lands in ways that protect ecosystem services (such as water quality and carbon storage) that are of value to society (see Chapter 12, p328); and
- establishing market mechanisms to reduce nutrient releases and carbon emissions in the most cost-effective way.

2 Improve policy, planning and management by:
- integrating decision-making between different departments and sectors, as well as international institutions, to ensure that policies are focused on the protection of ecosystems;
- including sound management of ecosystem services in all regional planning decisions and in the poverty reduction strategies being prepared by many low Human Development Index countries;
- empowering marginalized groups to influence decisions affecting ecosystem services, and to recognize in law local communities' ownership of natural resources; and
- using all relevant forms of knowledge and information about ecosystems in decision-making, including the knowledge of local and indigenous groups.

3 Influence individual behaviour by:
- providing public education on why and how to reduce consumption of threatened ecosystem services;
- establishing reliable certification systems to give people the choice to buy sustainably harvested products; and
- giving people access to information about ecosystems and decisions affecting their services.

4 Develop and use environment-friendly technology by:
- investing in agricultural science and technology aimed at increasing food production with minimal harmful trade-offs;
- restoring degraded ecosystems; and
- promoting technologies to increase energy efficiency and reduce greenhouse gas emissions.

Managing threats: Planning and procedures

Most protected area organizations have plans and procedures that are designed (among other things) to identify and minimize potential threats and the effects of threats. Important among these are management plans, risk management plans, impact assessment and monitoring, and evaluation procedures.

Sound judgement in using such approaches to address threats is based on professional training and experience, as well as on effective consultation and research. For major threats of an irreversible nature, the precautionary principle should be adopted, such that a lack of full scientific certainty is not used as a reason for postponing cost-effective measures to prevent environmental degradation. Organizations must be willing to take action in advance of full, formal scientific proof. People proposing change should be required to demonstrate that the change will not have a negative effect on the environment.

Management plans, zoning and use limits

Management planning (see Chapter 11) for individual protected areas typically employs a range of subordinate planning tools, models and techniques that help minimize threats.

Management zones

Zoning schemes provide a spatial differentiation of a protected area based on the different objectives of management. Zones can ensure appropriate location of intensive uses; help prevent or minimize the fragmentation of large natural areas within protected areas; provide a spatial limit to development within protected areas; and help to provide special additional

Case Study 9.1

Managing threats to marine habitat, Parc National de Port-Cros, France

Sylvain Dromzee, garde moniteur, Parc National de Port-Cros

Parc National de Port-Cros, located in the Mediterranean Sea, incorporates the islands of Port-Cros, Bagaud and Gabinière (totalling 705ha), as well as the surrounding marine areas (1288ha). An important feature of the park's marine environment is habitat associated with the underwater grass *Posidonia oceanica*, which is a source of food and provides shelter, spawning grounds and nurseries for many species of marine flora, gastropods, shellfish, sea urchins and finfish. *Posidonia oceanica* meadows are found in relatively stable environments, and are important in a number of key geomorphological and ecological processes, such as nutrient recycling and sediment stability (Francour et al, 1999). The ecosystem, regarded as the most significant in the Mediterranean, faces a number of threats.

Over the past 20 years, the toxic algae *Caulerpa taxifolia* and *Caulerpa racemosa* have rapidly colonized the Mediterranean between Spain and Italy. These species form dense blankets that smother the *Posidonia oceanica* meadows. A programme organized by the scientific staff of the Port-Cros National Park, with the assistance of the Total Corporate Foundation, local associations and diving clubs, involves:

- systematic monitoring of the main boat-mooring zones, where there is the greatest risks of the seaweed proliferating;
- eradication by divers using copper-based treatment on the larger patches; and
- eradication by divers manually cutting away the substrate around the weed, putting a whole bundle of weed material in a net, and taking it to the surface to be destroyed.

Anchoring of boats breaks or uproots shoots of *Posidonia oceanica* to such an extent that the habitat is eventually degraded. Anchoring is now excluded from certain zones in the park where the habitat is particularly vulnerable (see Figure 9.2). At popular diving locations, anchor buoys have been installed so that damage to the sea floor and marine biota is minimized. Different mooring systems are used for rock, sand and seagrass environments. Guidelines are also given to boating users about minimum impact methods of anchoring.

The zoning scheme also places various other restrictions on boating, diving and fishing (see Figure 9.2). Shore-based fishing is not permitted anywhere in the park, and boat-based fishing is restricted to certain areas, and then only using the method of trolling from a moving boat. Jet skis and marine scooters are not permitted.

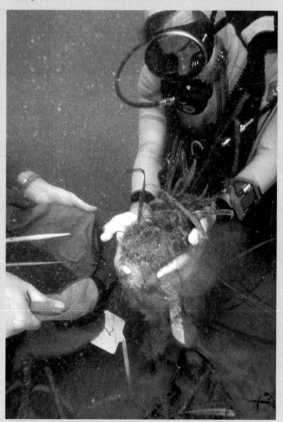

Eradication of toxic algae, *Caulerpa* spp., Parc National de Port-Cros, France

Source: Photoceans

Another potential threat to the marine environment is the 40,000 dives that are undertaken each year within the park. Sites such as those around the Îlot de la Gabinière face considerable pressure both from the divers themselves and their support boats. The number of divers in a particular location is limited to 40 at any one time. Divers enter into an agreement with Parc National de Port-Cros, which commits them, among other things, to refrain from touching the marine substrate or biota; to refrain from feeding marine fauna; to make

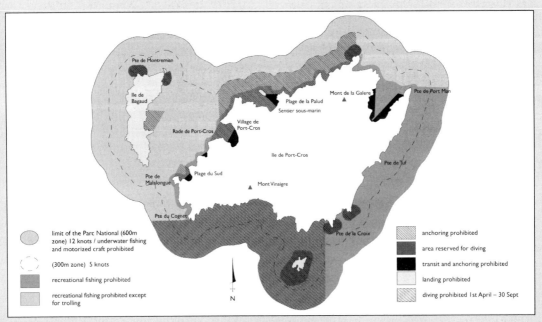

Figure 9.2 Marine zoning regulations, Parc National de Port-Cros, France

limited use of lights; to report the presence of *Caulerpa*, any threats to marine life such as abandoned netting, or any changes in the relative abundance of marine species; and to participate in an annual evaluation of the agreement. The emphasis is on education and encouraging compliance, rather than enforcement, although sanctions are available if necessary. The system, developed with the cooperation and participation of both commercial dive tourism operators and private divers, has proven to be highly successful in ensuring the sustainability of the activity.

Efforts have also been made through brochures, websites and interpretative trails to inform users of the park's marine values. For example, in association with the Total Corporate Foundation, an underwater discovery trail has been established that includes information panels to help divers better appreciate Port-Cros marine biodiversity and the need to actively manage threats.

protective measures for select areas. Zoning schemes (and the objectives of management that underpin each zone) help to convey a consistent message of threat management to the succession of managers who will be accountable for an individual protected area over many years. Consistency of management over the long term is critical for protected areas. Case Study 9.1 indicates how zoning and a number of other management actions are being used to counter threats to marine biodiversity at Parc National de Port-Cros in the Mediterranean.

Managing visitor use using the Recreation Opportunity Spectrum (ROS)

The Recreation Opportunity Spectrum (ROS) is one of a number of recreation planning frameworks (see Chapter 19, p506) that can enhance a zoning scheme. ROS can help to minimize threats by identifying the type and nature of acceptable developments for each ROS category, and by identifying the cross-section of ROS categories that will be managed for a particular protected area. This provides management with a framework for a destination and a basis for eliminating the

Public-Use Coordinator Badiah Badiah works with park staff to develop Recreation Opportunity Spectrum (ROS) zones for Ujung Kulon National Park, Indonesia

Source: IUCN Photo Library © Wiwien Tribuwani Wiyonoputri

inappropriate incremental development or 'hardening' of a site.

Sustainable-use limits

Use limits define a management organization's estimate of the constraints that should apply, for example, to visitor numbers for a given destination, or the number of cattle that may be sustainably grazed in a IUCN Category V protected area. Limits are normally established as part of a consultation process with local protected area managers, researchers, community groups and users. The limit can be formally recognized in a plan of management. Visitor-use limits, for example, can define maximum visitor numbers for a destination or a specific ROS category. Visitor-use demand exceeding such limits threatens the heritage values of destinations.

Environmental impact assessment

In many jurisdictions, there are legislative provisions relating to the prevention or mitigation of threatening processes. Planning legislation generally requires some type of assessment of the impacts of a proposed project on the environment. For protected areas, agencies often have their own internal procedures, as well as being required to meet such formal statutory processes. Environmental impact assessment (EIA) is the appraisal of the likely effects of a proposed policy, programme or project on the environment; alternatives to the proposal; and measures to be adopted to protect the environment. Typical steps in an EIA process are:

- screening the projects that require an EIA and focusing on the significant issues;
- considering alternative proposals and describing proposed actions;
- describing the environmental baseline condition;
- identifying and predicting key impacts;
- evaluating the significance of impacts; and
- assessing the potential of mitigation measures.

These steps are typically written up in an environmental impact statement (EIS). Figure 9.3 illustrates the sequence of steps in the EIA process, emphasizing its cyclical nature.

Protected area managers should check that these generic steps are taken in any EIA process. Approval procedures for developments within protected areas need to be very clear and will normally involve legal advice. Direct responsibility that all procedures have been followed generally rests with the officer who signs the approval. In granting approvals, the credibility of an entire organization is at stake since all aspects of a development approval process can be subject to scrutiny through the courts. Procedures and accountabilities need to be very clear. Wood (2003) recommended that the following questions be used to assist in the design and assessment of an EIA process.

- Is the EIA system based on clear and specific legal provisions?

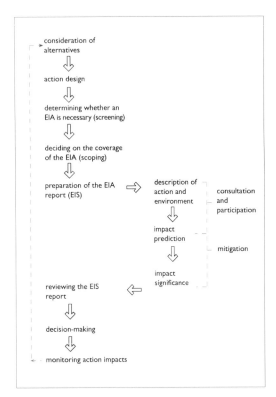

Figure 9.3 An environmental impact assessment (EIA) process

Source: Wood (2003)

- Must the relevant environmental impacts of all significant actions be assessed?
- Must evidence of the consideration, by the proponent, of the environmental impacts of reasonable alternative actions be demonstrated in the EIA process?
- Must screening of actions for environmental significance take place?
- Must scoping of the environmental impacts of actions take place and do specific guidelines have to be produced?
- Must EIA reports meet prescribed content requirements and do checks exist to prevent the release of inadequate EIA reports?
- Must EIA reports be publicly reviewed and does the proponent have to respond to the points raised?
- Must the findings of the EIA report and the review be a central determinant of the decision on the action?

- Must monitoring of action impacts be undertaken and is it linked to the earlier stages of the EIA process?
- Must the mitigation of action impacts be considered at the various stages of the EIA process?
- Must consultation and participation take place prior to, and following, EIA report publication?
- Must the EIA system be monitored and, if necessary, amended to incorporate feedback from experience?
- Are the discernible environmental benefits of the EIA system believed to outweigh its financial costs and time requirements?
- Does the EIA system apply to significant programmes, plans and policies, as well as to projects?

The EIS is the core of EIA. The functions of an EIS are to assist the decision-maker by providing relevant information about the negative and positive impacts of a proposal, and to inform the public to allow them to play an effective part in the decision-making process. An EIS (or an equivalent) is frequently a legal requirement where developments are likely to have a significant impact. An EIS integrates environmental considerations within decision-making processes concerning both private and public sector developments and activities.

Even if an EIS is not required, some protected area management agencies prepare a less detailed 'review of environmental factors' (REF) to assess the potential impacts of a proposed activity. An REF is similar in nature to an EIS, but much less detailed and may well go under different names in different agencies. A review of environmental factors can include many items, and often they are in the form of a checklist, as follows:

- Introduction:
  - location, proponent and name of protected area;
  - the need for the activity.
- The activity:
  - objectives of the activity and justification;
  - description of the activity;
  - associated developments.

- Alternative proposals:
  - description of alternative locations and other ways of achieving the activity.
- The existing environment (description and significance):
  - climate;
  - geology/geomorphology;
  - soils;
  - plants (species/communities);
  - animals (species/habitats);
  - water catchment;
  - indigenous sites/significance to local indigenous peoples;
  - historic sites;
  - recreation;
  - landscape;
  - existing use.
- Environmental impacts:
  - impacts on the natural environment;
  - climate/greenhouse effects;
  - geology/geomorphology;
  - soils (nutrients/erosion);
  - plants (species/communities);
  - animals (species/habitats);
  - water catchment (quality/drainage);
  - exotic species;
  - fire;
  - impacts on the cultural environment;
  - known indigenous sites;
  - significance to local indigenous people;
  - known historic sites;
  - likely impact on unrecorded sites;
  - impacts on the social environment;
  - traffic/roads;
  - noise;
  - neighbours/local residents;
  - safety;
  - lighting and energy use;
  - education;
  - recreation.
- Assessment of alternative proposals.
- Proposed environmental safeguards.
- Consequences of not carrying out the development.
- Conclusions and recommendations.

Risk and incident management systems

Threats to a protected area can be minimized by constantly evaluating threats and their significance or their potential. Often this is completed as part of the planning process for a protected area. Anticipating threats can mean that systems are in place to deal with them, and that other organizations are well briefed on what response approach needs to be undertaken within a protected area (see Table 9.2). Many organizations conduct formal risk management reviews to assess risk from a range of potential threats.

Table 9.2 Some examples of anticipating and preparing for threats

Potential threats	Minimizing the threat
People incidents: Emergency evacuation of injured or sick people	*Minimizing vehicle impacts.* The emergency response procedures for dealing with people incidents have already been agreed to between police, medical and other emergency teams. This minimizes, for example, the potential damage caused by four-wheel drive access to remote areas during an emergency.
Pollution: Oil spill	*Rapid incident response.* The agreed procedures for the safe and environmentally acceptable handling of oil spills within a protected area have been developed. Materials and equipment needed for dealing with oil spills are kept in stock and are deployed immediately when advice of any oil spill is received.
Fire: Forest fire burning into a protected area	*Clear fire-response procedures and accountabilities.* Cooperative fire arrangements have been entered into by authorities and these define fire control accountabilities and agreed special procedures for managing fires in protected areas.
Weeds: Responding to occurrences of new weeds	*Rapid weed-control treatment.* Prior research into potential new weed species has been completed and has established the potential threat of a new weed sighting, as well as the treatment required. The treatment response is rapidly organized and implemented along with any follow-up needs.

Planning for potential threats in cooperation with other organizations is critical, as are the skills needed to deal with such threats. This was demonstrated by an oil spill on the 23 March 1989 when the *Exxon Valdez* ran aground on Bligh Reef, Prince William Sound, Alaska, spilling 36,000 tonnes of crude oil (see Case Study 9.2).

Monitoring and evaluation procedures

Good systems are needed to inventory and establish a baseline for threats (such as weeds or frequent fire events) and to track the effectiveness of management responses (see Table 9.3). The capacity of an organization to respond to threats in a flexible, considered and adaptive manner can help to minimize their impact. A structured approach that is based on fixed internal procedures or, even worse, a non-response may exacerbate threats. Effectiveness reporting provides a direct input into refined planning and adaptive management responses (see Chapter 24).

Trends in threats need to be monitored and evaluated. Managers need to be alert to whether a protected area is subject to a diminishing threat or a worsening threat. The identification of trends in condition from an established baseline can trigger an adaptive response by management. Carey et al (2000) recommend an assessment approach that uses six condition scenarios for established protected areas:

1 *Stable*. This condition is often seen in large protected areas remote from human habitation, or in areas that attract priority funding and have high political status.
2 *Recovering*. This is generally associated with smaller protected areas, where protection can rapidly result in partial recovery, or protection in badly degraded areas.

Case Study 9.2

Response to the *Exxon Valdez* oil spill

The immediate response to the grounding of the *Exxon Valdez* on Bligh Reef, Prince William Sound, Alaska, left much to be desired. This was largely because equipment and overall capabilities to deal with an oil spill were deficient. The only real chance to contain the oil spill came immediately after the accident, when oil floated in calm water. The commissioner of the Alaska Department of Environmental Conservation stated that the industry's response during the first critical 72 hours of the spill was ineffective. He found that this was, in part, because of Alyeska Pipeline Service's (the owner and operator of the Trans-Alaska Pipeline) ten-year efforts to suppress any contingency plan. To decrease operating costs, the staffing and training of spill-response crews had been progressively de-emphasized over time, and equipment was not always in repair and/or available at short notice to deal with an emergency. The inquiries into the oil spill found:

* There was a 14-hour delay in locating ship fenders so that a second tanker could come alongside the *Exxon Valdez* to lighten the un-spilt crude oil cargo – the fenders were eventually found under 4m of snow.
* The boom-deployment barge that carried the off-shore containment and cleanup equipment had been unloaded after being damaged and was out of action. It also took 14 hours before the barge was ready for action.
* There was only one person who could operate a forklift and a crane that was available, so at first, this operator had to run between the equipment in order to deploy containment gear.
* To save costs, Alyeska's 12-person task-dedicated spill-response team had been disbanded in 1982, and their responsibilities assigned to others with their own work loads.

Most of Exxon's cleanup procedures involved the use of chemical dispersants; but it took almost three days to secure US Coast Guard approval to apply the chemicals and for Exxon to move the equipment in place for spraying. The coast guard admitted that it had not realized the immensity of the problem, and even though it was considered to be experienced in oil spill disasters, it did not use its authority to either lead or guide the cleanup crews.

Sources: adapted from Adler (1989); Church (1989); Yagoda (1990); and Mitchell (1999)

Table 9.3 Threats and the use of performance management systems

Management system	Performance reporting
Baseline condition mapping	*Baseline value.* Accurate mapping of a threat (such as weeds) providing a spatial extent of the weed at a particular point in time can be used to measure change in condition in the future.
Works completed	*Treatment mapping.* Mapping areas of weeds treated or locations where pest animals have been treated provides a basis for determining the benefits of treatments in the long term.
Monitoring	*Change in condition.* Measuring changes from baseline over time could identify the success of work programmes completed or identify new adaptive responses that are required. Such performance reporting could provide improved estimates of the amount of resources needed to deal with threats.

3 *Declining.* This is where protected status does not halt a decline in quality. It is often associated with protected areas in heavily populated areas and can result from lack of capacity or 'paper park syndrome', or extreme pressure from illegal commercial operations.

4 *Decline then recovery.* This is when, for example, local inhabitants feel disenfranchised and abandon traditional sustainable practices, but then gradually accept the protected area idea and, perhaps, alternative livelihoods such as ecotourism.

5 *Stability then sudden crisis.* An apparently secure protected area can face a sudden decline due to an unexpected influx of population, an invasive species, new industrial activity or other event.

6 *Recovery then decline.* An improvement in threat abatement outcomes may be short term, only to be followed by a regression back to a previously degraded state.

Using this system, the condition status of precincts within a protected area could be established and used as the baseline from which the effectiveness of management inputs is measured. Identifying trends can assist with organizational resource-allocation decisions and the potential need for external support (Carey et al, 2000).

Managing indirect threats

Many of the most fundamental threats to protected areas come from outside and cannot always be tackled directly by management:

The major threats to conservation in most countries lie outside the protected area system. Unless the linkages between protected areas management and external factors are identified and addressed, fundamental conservation issues are difficult to resolve (Davey, 1998, p10).

Such threats range from changes to the hydrology of a watershed, to national or global issues such as water and air pollution and pollution-related climate change. They also include the impacts of invasive species. Management of such problems relies on what are often distant political decisions. As the reality of issues such as climate change become increasingly accepted, protected area managers are recognizing that they must consider potential indirect impacts in the design and management of protected areas. This section considers the management of indirect threats, including climate change; inappropriate land-use decisions; poverty and the encroachment of human settlements; off-site pollution; off-site use of water; and off-site natural events.

Climate change

Levels of greenhouse gases such as carbon dioxide and methane are rising unnaturally in the atmosphere as a result of emissions from burning fossil fuels. This increased air pollution is having a significant impact on global climates by raising average temperatures and by increasing the frequency and severity of extreme events, such as droughts and storms. The world is entering a period of warmer, less predictable climate. The Intergovernmental Panel on Climate Change

(IPCC) climate change report (IPCC, 2001) was put together by 1000 experts from 120 countries. The report concluded that global average temperatures would rise between 1.4° and 5.8° Celsius by 2100. This will lead to important shifts in climates for regions. Some scientists consider the forecast to be conservative. Changes have already happened, with a 0.7°C increase in temperature since the 1800s (Howden, 2003; Glick, 2004). Some ramifications of global warming (Lowe, 2005) include:

- sea-level rise;
- glacier melt and the loss of perennial freshwater sources;
- flooding of low-lying areas;
- increased drying for some areas;
- increased rainfall for some areas;
- decreased duration of snow cover;
- changes to annual average stream and river flow regimes;
- increased severe storm events;
- increased fire frequency; and
- changes to habitats and species distribution and abundance.

These changes have major implications for protected areas. Marine flooding of lowlands will cause loss of native plant and animal species on islands, mangroves, coastal marshes, mudflats and dune systems. The disruption to human settlements and natural resource extraction will intensify pressures on coastal and island protected areas. Biomes in protected areas will change. For example, high-altitude species on mountains will be lost and potentially displaced by lower-altitude species or weeds (Price and Neville, 2004). Breeding cycles and migration patterns of species will be disrupted. The spatial distribution of many plants and animals will change. Others may be threatened, either because there is nowhere for them to go, or because of environmental changes such as altered fire frequencies or stream-flow regimes. Some habitats are likely to be particularly at threat:

- Many low islands are likely to be inundated as sea-level rises.
- Low-lying coastal areas and especially estuarine, mudflats, sand dune areas and marshes will be affected by marine incursions.
- Mangrove areas are at risk of inundation and salt imbalance due to rising seas.
- High-altitude communities, including montane forests or mountaintop tundra, will continue to experience the loss of species and migration of vegetation from lower altitudes.
- Polar regions will continue to undergo changes from ice melt and warmer temperatures, threatening individual species and the overall ecology.
- Coral reef systems will suffer increased bleaching effects due to increased sea temperatures.
- Cloud forests are at risk from possible drying or changed weather patterns.
- Fire-prone communities will be especially vulnerable, including tropical moist forests where increased drought is likely to result in increased fire risks.
- Relic communities – ecosystems that have survived previous climatic changes in isolated pockets – may be susceptible with more severe climate change.
- Changes in reproduction and migration rates in areas experiencing severe climate change will cause problems for more sensitive, slower-growing and slower-moving species, favouring fast-growing, short-lived weed and invasive species.
- Transition of whole communities will encourage an existing trend towards the replacement of old communities, such as old-growth forests, with younger communities (Carey et al, 2000; Price and Neville, 2004; Flannery, 2005; Tompkins et al, 2005).

These changes have particular implications for protected areas, which are, by their nature, fixed in space but affected by changes over time. Changing weather conditions may force the species within a protected area away from the protected zone; indeed, in some cases the whole ecology of the area may alter in fundamental ways. In situations where the protected area is surrounded by land that has undergone major modification, or by a barrier preventing further development, there may be no space for migration, leading to net losses of biodiversity. Case Study 9.3 highlights a protected area affected by changes in climate.

International efforts to address climate change are coordinated through the United Nations Framework Convention on Climate Change (UNFCCC). This is an international environmental treaty produced at the United Nations Conference on Environment and Development (UNCED), informally known as the Earth Summit, held in Rio de Janeiro in 1992. The treaty aims at reducing emissions of greenhouse gas, pursuant to its supporters' belief in the global warming hypothesis. The treaty as originally framed set no mandatory limits on greenhouse gas emissions for individual nations and contained no enforcement provisions; it is therefore considered legally non-binding. Instead, the treaty included provisions for updates (termed protocols) that would set mandatory emission limits. The principal update is the Kyoto Protocol, which has become much better known than the UNFCCC itself.

Protected area managers can directly and indirectly respond to the influences of climate change, both as individual managers and at a strategic organizational level. Changes can be expected to be evident during the course of a protected area professional's career. Managers can prepare for and mitigate the effects of climate change on protected area values in a number of ways (Noss, 2001; Hannah et al, 2002; Pickering et al, 2004; Price and Neville, 2004; Lowe, 2005; Tompkins et al, 2005; Welch, 2005):

Provide leadership in reducing greenhouse gas emissions. Protected area organizations need to exhibit leadership by minimizing the greenhouse gases that they generate. This includes direct and indirect energy use. This is best approached as a whole-of-organizational response to the issue of global warming. An internal campaign of staff awareness and major changes to purchasing and design policies could be key elements. Opportunities for reducing greenhouse gas emissions include:

- changing the vehicle transport fleet to fuel-efficient vehicles;
- technology permitting, utilizing alternative, low-pollution energy sources;
- encouraging personal action plans for employees, including greater use of public transport;

Case Study 9.3

Climate change impacts on Monteverde Cloud Forest Reserve, Costa Rica

The Monteverde Cloud Forest Reserve is located high on the ridge above the coastal plain near Santa Elena, Costa Rica. It comprises six forest types, and it is located in a much larger forest area of about 60,000ha. Climate change is posing a very real threat to the biological diversity of these forests. A major weakness of all cloud forest reserves in Central America is a failure to include habitats on lower slopes, particularly on the Pacific slope, that are ecologically linked to the higher montane environments. Such areas of dry or humid forest are distinct habitats; but they are also critical to many cloud forest species that have seasonal altitudinal migrations in and out of the cloud forest itself.

Pounds et al (1999) observed that 20 of 50 species of frogs and toads in a 30 square-kilometre study area, including the endemic golden toad (*Bufo periglenes*), disappeared following synchronous population crashes in 1987. The results of the study indicate that the crashes probably belong to a series of demographic changes, which also altered communities of birds, reptiles and amphibians in the area, and are linked to recent increases in sea surface temperatures. The biological and climatic patterns suggest that atmospheric warming raised the average altitude at the base of the orographic cloud bank (which forms as moist air rises up the mountain slope and then cools, condenses and forms clouds). The climate changes at Monteverde are associated with patterns of dry-season mist frequency, which is negatively correlated with sea surface temperatures in the equatorial Pacific and which has declined dramatically since the mid 1970s.

Source: Carey et al (2000)

- using natural heating, natural cooling and energy efficiency in the design of structures and the supporting facilities;
- using alternative energy sources such as solar and wind power;
- purchasing policies that help to achieve energy efficiency following life-cycle assessment of products prior to purchase;
- reducing generation of waste through purchasing policies, reuse and recycling;
- reducing the use of water and energy; and
- taking emissions into account in the design and implementation of management activities such as fuel-reduction burning.

Undertake strategic protected area systems design. 'A good network of large protected areas at the core of biosphere reserves may be wild nature's best climate change shock absorber' (Welch, 2005, p90). Protected area systems-level planning is needed (see Chapter 8, p200). Shifts in biomes at a regional scale need to be understood and factored into the establishment of a protected area system. The changing nature of flora and fauna at an individual protected area level needs to be anticipated, as does the capacity of the system as a whole to conserve a representative sample of a nation's fauna and flora. There will be changes, and the future characteristics of protected areas and their contribution to biodiversity conservation need to be recognized in designing protected area systems. A number of key actions have been suggested:

- Undertake regional-level climate change modelling and biome shift forecasting.
- Identify biomes that are at risk.
- Assess the boundaries of protected areas and determine if they can be adjusted to better cater for anticipated shifts.
- Select and reserve new protected areas that can assist in maintaining biodiversity based on forecast changes.
- Maximize opportunities for the regional biodiversity conservation and landscape connectivity and avoid fragmentation.
- Protect climate refugia at all scales.

Adopt adaptive management planning. Climate change may introduce drier conditions, more frequent fires, new environments for weeds and pest animals, new patterns of visitor use, and other changes. Such forecast changes to biomes need to be accounted for in plans of management (see Chapter 11). Managers may also need to plan specifically for:

- a purpose for protected areas that is more focused on natural processes and biodiversity, rather than specific biomes or species;
- a purpose for protected areas that is more tolerant of biotic changes resulting from natural and anthropogenic changes;
- more focused research on ecosystem changes;
- drier conditions in some areas, with consequences such as changes to the availability of traditional grazing lands;
- a higher fire frequency, with hotter and more volatile fire weather conditions;
- more frequent storm events, which may introduce more lightning-caused fires;
- warmer conditions that may increase the potential for the spread of existing and new weed species;
- warmer conditions that may reduce the length of snow seasons and increase the threat of construction of ski developments at higher altitudes; and
- the predicted loss of species and actions needed to record and preserve genetic information.

Use protected areas as benchmarks of change. Global warming research and monitoring within protected areas can be used as an indicator for local communities of the nature and extent of climate change. Specifically, these could include:

- providing a baseline condition from which change can be measured;
- providing indicators of climate change for a protected area and its natural region, as well as the protocols for measurement, and providing regular and consistent reporting of ecological impacts, including reporting for local communities, authorities and governments; and
- undertaking long-term monitoring to seek causality between climate and biodiversity

responses at several levels of biological organization.

Minimize direct threats. Climate change may provide conditions that aid the more rapid spread of direct threats, such as weeds or pest animals. Attention to these threats within protected areas, and across whole land and seascapes regardless of tenure, reduces the potential for a more rapid spread of such threats under changed climatic conditions.

Adopt responsive and flexible management. Implementing science-based adaptive management will be an important skill for managers of the future. Adaptive management (see Chapter 11, p293) will need to be understood and implemented effectively. Reactive decision-making is likely to be a threat for protected areas. For example, responsive strategic management may require managers to:

- introduce new measures to stabilize watersheds that are affected by higher fire frequencies and more severe temperature regimes;
- translocate animal species from lower altitudes to higher altitudes as biome shifts occur and where natural connectivity opportunities are unavailable; and
- introduce new approaches for managing visitors given changes in the nature of biomes.

Invest in research. Understanding the nature of changes to protected areas is critical for adaptive management. Managers should be at the forefront of introducing ways in which researchers from different scientific organizations can be helped to conduct applied research in protected areas. Major changes in the condition of protected areas need to be tracked.

Manage commercial agreements. Managers need to ensure when entering into legal and commercial agreements for sites that the ramifications of climate change are anticipated and are built into the agreement, including the need for managers to implement adaptive management. Low-lying areas in coastal zones may be inundated. Long-term leases that require a supply of recreation services based on snow or ice may need to be very carefully written. Such changes need to be forecast as part of an agreement.

Manage cooperative agreements. Cooperative agreements between organizations may change. The inability for watersheds to supply historic water volumes in new, hotter, drier climates and the higher fire frequency, for example, may result in changes to the nature of cooperative water supply agreements between a protected area authority and water supply organizations.

Manage for a potential increase in storm events. Higher land and sea temperatures are likely to increase the frequency and severity of storms. Managers who may be affected by such changes can respond by:

- upgrading building codes and design standards for structures in protected areas;
- planning and achieving setbacks for structures from the coastline or areas vulnerable to flooding;
- instigating park closure and evacuation procedures for campers and hikers and other visitors for forecast storm events; and
- training staff to deal with such incidents (see Chapter 7).

Poor land- and sea-use planning decisions

The context of a protected area in a landscape or seascape is critical. A protected area is least threatened when it is surrounded and buffered by natural and semi-natural lands and has connectivity with other natural lands. Poor planning and land- and sea-use allocation decisions have the potential to impact upon protected areas by changing its landscape setting. Landscapes may be affected by settlements, intensive agriculture being established and from mining adjacent to protected areas. In addition, a failure to deliver clear and effective governance and tenure arrangements can also cause threats.

Agriculture is a significant threat to biodiversity and natural ecosystems in terrestrial habitats, and agricultural pollution can affect many protected area freshwater and coastal marine ecosystems. Large agricultural operations near protected areas can disturb the watershed and increase soil erosion (Carey et al, 2000). Major changes in habitat are among the most important factors impacting upon protected areas and often result from human settlement and agricultural conversion. In many of the world's protected areas, human communities form an integral part of the ecosystem (see Chapters 5 and 21); however, human settlements can also act detrimentally on protected areas through:

- expansion of the impact of settlements through illegal activities, such as hunting, or because of increases in agreed activities;
- additional settlement due to land shortages in surrounding areas or because the land offers particular benefits;
- short-term incursions for particular purposes, such as livestock grazing; and
- temporary settlements due to political problems or environmental disaster, such as refugees following war or natural disasters (Carey et al, 2000).

Political, environmental or economic changes can create abrupt but long-term changes in settlement patterns. Some protected areas play a key role in providing a home for indigenous peoples otherwise displaced by land-use activities such as logging or agriculture. This can lead to an increased density of human population, perhaps above the carrying capacity for traditional subsistence activities (Carey et al, 2000).

Ill-defined or disputed protected area boundaries and ill-defined status of lands and waters as protected areas can lead to conflicts over land or water management and ownership. Ill-defined governance often leads to unsustainable resource use. In some jurisdictions, land- and sea-use legislation, including protected area legislation and regulations, are inadequate to provide for wise land-use management. Clarity and leadership must be provided to achieve sustainable use. Where there is legal confusion or inadequate legislation, steps need to be taken to address these fundamental issues.

Protected areas are most viable when they are interconnected with each other and with natural areas under other uses and tenures. They are most vulnerable when they are islands of natural habitats in a land or seascape that has been altered and fragmented. Disturbance at the boundaries and within watersheds directly threatens the integrity of protected areas. For marine areas, disturbance to surrounding marine environments may cause impacts to the protected area. Alteration to natural or semi-natural lands and waters adjacent to protected areas can limit home territories of species and the viability of populations. A protected area is less vulnerable to threats when it is large, roughly circular and still retains its natural interconnections with other unfragmented natural lands. If regional land-use planning and cooperative partnerships can accommodate such opportunities, then this is a major advantage for protected area management in reducing threats to species conservation.

There are a number of regional land-use planning tools that may be used to minimize fragmentation and to maximize the viability of protected areas. The opportunities extend from continental-scale initiatives to very local opportunities for connectivity conservation (Chapter 22). Managers who positively engage with the conservation and management of surrounding natural lands are actively contributing to the long-term survival of species within the protected area. There are a number of ways in which these contributions may be made and include formal responses to planning processes, responses to calls for expert assistance and participation in cooperative projects. Involvement in land-use management outside of protected areas needs to respect prior rights, landownership and cultural ties to land.

Partnerships between private landowners and government organizations can sometimes produce outstanding initiatives that reduce threats to protected areas. Groups of landowners may enter into a cooperative agreement that sees the natural heritage values of their properties retained to serve as a conservation corridor between nearby protected lands. One example of this is the partnership between the Sabi Sabi Game Reserve (which focuses on wildlife ecotourism) and Kruger National Park in South Africa, which are interconnected and enable the free flow of animals across national park and freehold lands (Eagles et al, 2002). Another example on a smaller scale is the Yurangalo Voluntary Conservation Agreement, which was negotiated with a number of property owners on the south coast of New South Wales in Australia. It creates a natural link between the South-East Forest National Park and the Bournda National Park. This is a natural interconnection between protected areas on the coast and those inland at altitudes of about 1000m. It may help to conserve species during biome shift changes induced by global warming.

Protected area managers can provide assistance by way of natural and cultural heritage advice on matters such as rehabilitation of disturbed areas, establishment and management of habitat corridors and recognition of cultural landscape values. Engagement can also include a wide range of projects that are linked to local community groups working to improve the environment, such as the propagation and provision of native plant seed stock, cooperative weed and pest animal control programmes and so on. Assistance may be designed to provide local employment and to help reduce poverty.

Poverty

Poverty among the poorest proportion of the world's population leads to increased pressure on protected areas to supply land and resources. Recent trends indicate a widening gap between rich and poor in many countries. A substantial proportion of the world's population remains in absolute poverty (see Chapter 2, p51).

Overcoming poverty is not only an important human rights issue, it is also necessary for the long-term security of protected areas. Poverty limits people's choices and can prevent the adoption of sustainable resource-use practices:

> *As human well-being declines, the options available to people that allow them to regulate their use of natural resources decline as well. This, in turn, increases pressure on ecosystem services and can create a downward spiral of increasing poverty and further degradation of ecosystem services (Millennium Ecosystem Assessment Board, 2005 p98).*

Elephant calves in privately owned Sabi Sand Game Reserve can move freely between the reserve and Kruger National Park

Source: IUCN Photo Library © Alicia Held

People desperate to survive, and those desperately trying to achieve a minimum acceptable standard of living, may have little option but to exploit natural areas for food, fuel and shelter. These problems may be exacerbated by a lack of education, poor infrastructure and social conflict (Carey et al, 2000). A report from the Asian Development Bank (1990) concluded:

> *Poverty as such cannot be said to cause environmental degradation; however, often the two are associated with each other… As change occurs it leaves behind winners and losers; typically, the losers have few choices available and are forced to adopt short-term survival strategies under which longer-term resource management considerations appear to be an unaffordable luxury.*

Protected area managers need to work with communities and assist, where possible, in dealing with poverty. There may be a range of strategies, from local employment opportunities, sustainable harvesting of some protected area resources, facilitating economic activities such as ecotourism, and other approaches. Some of these are described in Table 9.4.

Off-site pollution

Pollution of protected areas may be subtle and long term, or it may be a consequence of short and sharp events, such as an unplanned incident (see Case Study 9.4). Pollution is a threat to protected areas and the life forms that they protect. Some pollutants are particularly dangerous. Persistent organochlorine pesticides occur in high concentrations in the body fat of marine mammals found great distances from the source of such pollution. Some corals are extremely sensitive to herbicides, while other pesticides, such as chlordane, have caused declines in sensitive invertebrates. Bioaccumulation of pesticides in predators has been responsible for population declines through eggshell thinning and reproductive failure (Carey et al, 2000). Protected area managers, in responding to such issues, are best focused on mitigating impacts, creating awareness of the nature of the problems and providing leadership to influence corrective changes (see Table 9.5).

Off-site water use

Impacts occur from various forms of water diversion. This includes dam construction, drainage and irrigation. Freshwater protected areas are particularly vulnerable because they are susceptible to events in distant parts of the watershed, as well as to the construction of large hydroelectric power schemes, water diversion and changes to water quality. Protected areas with watersheds outside of the reserve boundaries potentially

Table 9.4 Poverty: Potential management responses

Type of instrument	Potential management response
Poverty reduction strategy	Develop a planning document in conjunction with a protected area management plan. Avoid conservation actions that cause or increase impoverishment. Empower local communities through active participation.
Policy instruments	Review policies that may work against sustainability or could be adopted to encourage sustainability.
Economic instruments	Create jobs and incomes for the local area. Work with business to achieve sustainable development involving protected areas. Manage for ecotourism.
Management instruments	Engage in disaster mitigation (floods, droughts, pollution). Protect watersheds. Ensure that there is a rapid response capacity for any pollution event.
Sustainable use management	Identify the limits of natural systems and their carrying capacity. Evaluate the change in condition of natural systems from a predetermined baseline.

Source: IUCN (2005b)

Table 9.5 Pollution: Potential management responses

Pollution type	Potential pollution events	Potential management response
Liquid waste pollution	Background pollution and contamination of streams, rivers, groundwater, water ways and aquatic environments, such as a contaminated river flowing through a protected area	Take steps to ensure that the quality of water flowing from the protected area is higher than the water received.
		Ensure a whole-of-government and community-based partnership response to prevent the pollution.
		Ensure a whole-of-government and community-based partnership response to clean up the pollution.
	Incidents such as liquid pollutant spills that enter a protected area (e.g. an oil tanker spill or chemical truck spill)	Ensure that the management agency has the capacity and the resources to deal with the incident either on or off the protected area.
		Have cooperative arrangements in place to deal with the incident, and ensure that the cleanup does not impact upon the protected area.
Solid waste pollution	A domestic waste tip created on the boundary of a protected area	Negotiate with land-use authorities and neighbours for the removal of the solid waste.
	Dumping of solid waste materials adjacent to a protected area (such as a mine dump)	
Atmospheric pollution	Dust, acid rain, toxic gaseous pollutants and global warming gases	Ensure a whole-of-government and industry partnership response to stop the pollution.
		Ensure a whole-of-government and industry partnership response to clean up the pollution.
Radiation pollution	Radiation fallout due to a nuclear accident	Ensure a whole-of-government response to prevent potential accidents.
		Ensure a whole-of-government response to clean up the pollution.

suffer disruption to their natural flow regimes. This can lead to the demise of natural stream-flow regimes, the non-natural drying of wetlands and other impacts. Some management responses to such impacts are given in Table 9.6.

The ecosystems of the Everglades National Park in the US, for example, are threatened by changed water regimes. Over the past 100 years, flood control and water supply measures have substantially altered the Everglades wetland ecosystem. Too much water now enters the park during the winter dry season, too little water at other times of the year, with both leading to a decrease in wildlife numbers. Canals and highways interrupt overland flow of water. Much of the water entering the park has flowed through urban agricultural areas and contains elevated nutrient levels that have the potential to induce a variety of changes. For example, increased soil phosphorus content has changed periphyton communities (a complex matrix of algae and microbes that serves as an important food source for invertebrates and

Case Study **9.4**

Pollution threats to Doñana National Park, Spain

Doñana National Park is found on the southern Atlantic coast of Spain and is one of the largest and best-known wetlands in Europe. It is an important breeding colony for many bird species and a wintering site for waterfowl (attracting up to 700,000 birds). It represents the last tract of relatively undisturbed marsh in the Guadalquivir Delta, and protects one of the few mobile dune systems on the Iberian Peninsula.

Agricultural practices and mining activities threaten the park's water quality and wildlife. In 1986, an estimated 30,000 birds died in and around the park – poisoned from the uncontrolled use of pesticides in growing rice, cotton and strawberries. In 1998, the park was further threatened by toxic mine waste. The wetlands and wildlife are also seriously threatened by modification of the hydraulic regime from drainage and demand for water from irrigation schemes. In the long term, Doñana is in danger of drying up. Problems such as these led to the inclusion, in 1990, of Doñana National Park in the *Montreux Record* of Ramsar sites requiring priority attention because of the potential for change in their ecological character.

Source: Carey et al (2000)

Doñana National Park, Spain, threatened by agriculture and mining

Source: IUCN Photo Library © Jim Thorsell

some fish) and caused loss of native sawgrass communities (United States Fish and Wildlife Service, 1999). The Comprehensive Everglades Restoration Plan (CERP), approved in the *Water Resources Development Act 2000*, provides a framework and guide to restore, protect and preserve the water resources of central and southern Florida, including the Everglades. Among other things, the plan is designed to improve the quality, quantity, timing, and distribution of flows into the park. CERP involves works that will take more than 30 years to construct and cost an estimated US$7.8

Table 9.6 Off-site water use: Potential management responses

Water use	Threat	Potential management response
Stream or river impoundment	Change to the natural flow regimes within a protected area, including flood cycles	Negotiate a minimum flow regime for the protected area.
		Negotiate a potential artificial cycle of floodwaters to help maintain natural systems.
	Flooding of parts or all of a protected area	Negotiate mitigation strategies and a capacity to record and transfer movable heritage resources.
Pumping or withdrawal of surface water	Incremental withdrawal of water from streams, rivers and freshwater bodies for agriculture and drinking water	Achieve a whole-of-government and community response to water allocations, which ensures a minimum downstream flow for protected areas.
Pumping or withdrawal of subsurface water	Lowering of the water table and subsurface water flows due to over-exploitation	Achieve a whole-of-government and community response to water allocations, which ensures minimum subsurface water for protected areas.

Bushfire in a remote part of Deua National Park, New South Wales, Australia

Source: Graeme L. Worboys

billion. Part of the plan is to remove more than 385km of canals and levees within the Everglades to re-establish the natural sheet flow of water. It is hoped that this will enable the return of the large nesting rookeries of wading birds to the park as well as the recovery of several endangered species such as the wood stork (*Mycteria americana*) and Everglade snail kite (*Rostrhamus sociabilis plumbeus*) (US Army Corps of Engineers, 2006).

Off-site natural events

Natural phenomena may directly or indirectly threaten the integrity of protected areas and the objectives for which they were established. They also threaten human life, property and infrastructure. Emergency responses to such threats may also cause impacts to a protected area. Co-operative contingency plans are necessary to deal with such potential events and the consequent operational threats (see Chapter 18). Natural threats to protected areas that originate outside of their boundaries include:

- lightning-caused fires burning into a protected area;
- tectonic activity – volcanism, faulting and tsunami;

- storm events – wind damage and flooding; and
- mass wasting – cliff collapse, landslide, slump and avalanche.

Fires are natural phenomena. Used as an agent of change or as a management tool, fires may cause changes to habitats and impacts to species, or they may help to sustain species. Natural fire regimes need to be managed (see Chapter 16, p435).

Managing direct threats

Direct threats of widespread relevance to protected areas are identified in Table 9.1. In this section, we will consider the management of such direct threats in more detail.

Illegal activities

Illegal activities threaten protected area values throughout the world. Such activities include poaching, hunting, fishing, mining, clearing, logging, taking of other plant and fungi products, and unlawful vehicle use. International surveys completed by the World Wide Fund for Nature (WWF) (WWF, 2004) and Worboys (2006) confirmed the prevalence of threats as major issues for protected area managers in many parts of the world. Law enforcement is a critical part of

Dead rhinoceros, Pilansberg National Park, South Africa

Source: IUCN Photo Library © Jim Thorsell

protected area management. To be effective, law enforcement needs to include:

- regular risk management assessments for law enforcement operations;
- adequate staff training and equipment support, including weapons training, communications systems, vehicle use and navigation systems;
- regular and effective law enforcement operations on the ground, including monitoring and surveillance of special species at sensitive times;
- evaluating the effectiveness of law enforcement through baseline fauna and flora surveys and ongoing monitoring to assess any change in condition;
- overseeing management information support systems that underpin the evaluations;
- regularly involving the media to generate pro-conservation publicity;
- regularly liaising with other government organizations and, potentially, the military; and
- effectively dealing with any potential for corruption.

Hunting, fishing and poaching. The problem of poaching exists in many countries. Poaching of high-value species is an organized criminal activity in some parts of the world, and management staff are not infrequently injured or killed in the line of duty when trying to counter them. Hunting takes place throughout the world, including in Africa for elephant ivory and rhinoceros horn, and in Asia for tiger (*Panthera tigris*), snow leopard *(Panthera unicia)*, rhinoceros and bears (Carey et al, 2000) for traditional medicinal products. In Australia, illegal sport hunting for feral deer and wild pigs occurs. In the US, all large game species are at least occasionally poached from protected areas. There is a range of potential management responses to hunting, fishing and poaching, depending upon the circumstances (see Table 9.7).

Fuelwood collection and timber harvesting. Fuelwood collection is a fundamental part of life for large numbers of people on Earth, and while it may be sustainable, it can also be destructive. Timber harvesting is usually very destructive to habitats and wildlife, and illegal logging of forests is a growing problem that threatens many protected areas. In 1997, almost 80 per cent of timber harvested in the Amazon was being taken illegally, often from protected areas and indigenous reserves. Illegal logging also damaged Atlantic forest reserves in Brazil (Gamini, 1998). The IUCN and WWF have identified evidence of illegal logging and trade in over 70 countries, and some 65 per cent of WWF's Global 200 forest ecoregions (see Chapter 1, p34) are threatened by illegal logging (Carey et al, 2000). Some management responses are described in Table 9.8. Attempts to address such problems in a remote area of tropical rainforest are described in Case Study 9.5.

Mining, mineral, petroleum and related resource extraction. Many protected areas contain locally or commercially valuable deposits of minerals, oil, natural gas, stone, sand, soil, salt, gemstones and fossils. Illegal extraction of such resources from protected areas is widespread. Mining and mining exploration in any form is typically destructive to protected areas (see Case Study 9.6). The IUCN's official position statement on mining is that:

> … *mining is incompatible with IUCN Categories I to IV protected areas and should therefore be prohibited by law or other effective means. For Categories V and VI, minimal and local extraction is acceptable only when this is compatible with the objectives of the protected area and then only after the assessment of environmental impacts and subject to strict operating and use conditions (IUCN, 2000c).*

Resource shortages place new pressures on protected areas. The combination of increased demand and geo-finite reserves of the world's oil reserves has expert forecasters predicting major shortfalls in oil by the mid 2020s (Foran and Poldy, 2002a; Mason, 2003; Appenzeller, 2004; Roberts, 2004). Fuel prices for aviation kerosene, diesel and petrol (gasoline) and other petroleum products will become much higher, and alternative energy sources such as natural gas, hydrogen, wind power and solar power will become more important. Higher prices will drive activities such as exploration, the extraction of marginal oil

Table 9.7 Management response for hunting, fishing and poaching

Illegal activity	Aspects of the activity	Potential management response
Hunting, fishing and poaching for food	Meat, fish and other food taken for local use	Licensed sustainable subsistence hunting for some protected areas.
	Traditional bushmeat hunting	
		Discussions and negotiations with parties.
	At times of conflict, bushmeat is used for food	
		Law enforcement.
Hunting and fishing for financial return	Bushmeat trade	Law enforcement.
	Fish for sale	Implementation of international agreements, such as the Convention on International Trade in Endangered Species of Wild Flora and Fauna (CITES), which ban or control the sale of animal products.
	Hunting for furs, skins, tusks (ivory), antlers and body parts	
	Hunting for animal body parts for medicinal use	Transboundary agreements and joint law enforcement actions.
		Consultation, if possible, with parties involved in conflict.
	Hunting for the pet trade	Partnerships with customs agents, the police and other government authorities to monitor and check incoming and outgoing wildlife.
		Monitoring nests of endangered bird species to reduce the stealing of eggs, hatchlings and young fledglings.
Hunting and fishing for sport	Trophy hunting	Law enforcement.
Hunting and fishing for cultural reasons	Social customs	Law enforcement.
		Potential agreements with communities.
Hunting and fishing for protection	Human life, livestock and crop protection	Cooperative agreements with communities for dealing with animals that pose threats.
		Fencing of reserves.
Hunting and fishing for research	Animal research and zoo collections	Cooperative agreements with research institutions and zoos.

Sources: Carey et al (2000); Baillie et al (2004); Barber et al (2004); and IUCN (2005b)

deposits and the demand to exploit areas that are environmentally sensitive. Many protected areas may be threatened from oil exploration and extraction activities in the future, and action will be needed to safeguard many areas. As the world's population continues to grow, other shortages in basic commodities, such as water, limestone, timber, gravel and other raw materials, may emerge and may see protected areas placed under the threat of development.

Table 9.8 Management responses for fuelwood collection and timber harvesting

Activity	Potential management response
Illegal extraction of fuelwood for domestic use	Negotiate with users.
	Determine sustainable extraction levels and methods, followed by licensing of the activity.
	Active management may be required to help people who require fuel in refugee camps or urban settlements.
	Monitor impacts.
Fuelwood used for commercially motivated illegal trade	Determine whether sustainable extraction is appropriate and, if so, at what levels and by what methods.
	Sustainable use may be licensed under conditions that ensure that local communities benefit.
	Ensure law enforcement.
Illegal logging	Ensure law enforcement.
	Secure government support for the integrity of protected area regulations.
	Seek international support.

Sources: Carey et al (2000); Baillie et al (2004); Barber et al (2004); and IUCN (2005b)

Illegal mining needs to be controlled and managed to the limit of a country's legal system and law enforcement capacity. Any potential for pollution of protected areas as a result of mining needs to be eliminated. Some management responses are described in Table 9.9.

Clearance of Ituri forest for garden, Okapi Fauna Reserve, Democratic Republic of the Congo

Source: IUCN Photo Library © Jim Thorsell

Case Study 9.5

Addressing illegal activities in and around the Tumucumaque Mountains National Park, Brazil

Marcelo Segalerba, Amazon Conservation Team

The Tumucumaque Mountains National Park, located in the north-western portion of the Brazilian state of Amapá, is the world's largest tropical rainforest protected area. The park, created in 2002, spans 3.867 million hectares and contains one of the most diverse arrays of fauna and flora in the world. Another 5 million hectares of equally species-rich forest surround the national park. These are the territories of five indigenous peoples: the Apalai, Wayana, Kaxuyana, Tiriyó and Txikiyana.

A set of diverse actors is now undertaking the task of protecting the area. The Amazon Conservation Team is an international institution acting in collaboration with the region's indigenous communities on both the Surinamese and Brazilian sides of the border. The government organizations responsible for the Brazilian side are the Instituto Brasileiro do Meio Ambiente e dos Recursos Naturais Renováveis, currently in charge of the Tumucumaque Mountains National Park, and the Fundação Nacional do Indio. Indigenous associations include the Associação dos Povos Indígenas do Tumucumaque and the Associação dos Povos Indígenas Tiriyó-Kaxuyana-Txiquixana. Interactions among these organizations are progressively improving the living conditions of the area's indigenous communities and enabling the implementation of conservation projects in this remote territory.

Surveys by the indigenous peoples and by government agencies have located numerous illegal mining and illegal logging operations, as well as other uncontrolled extractive activities in the Tumucumaque region. Other illegal activities include non-regulated commerce with indigenous communities; extraction of forest products such as Brazil nuts; intrusions and settling in the area; and illegal airstrips. In addition, disease dispersion caused by contact with outsiders, water and soil pollution, and waste accumulation in communities are also problems.

In collaboration with the Amazon Conservation Team and Fundação Nacional do Indio, the indigenous communities of the Tumucumaque developed cultural and land-use maps of the indigenous territory. The maps represent the resources and cultural sites that indigenous communities consider the most important in their territory. Based on this work, indigenous representatives, together with Amazon Conservation Team staff, developed a risk map of the area, identifying the bio-cultural values most under threat. This project is still in progress. The risk map records information such as cultural sites with natural resources in need of protection (sites for hunting, fishing or fruit collection), dangerous sites (such as those associated with illegal animal trade or disease) and important sites for transport and communication (such as entrances to the park or airstrips). The cultural and risk maps are the basis for management plans that will guide indigenous rangers in Tumucumaque.

In 2005, the Amazon Conservation Team commenced a three-year project to train 20 indigenous rangers annually for the protection and management of their territories. The goal of this project is to protect the area from external threats, to protect the cultural and natural values in the region, and to increase the capacity of indigenous communities to work with outside actors in the management of their territories. In addition to training indigenous rangers, the Amazon Conservation Team is also developing the capacity of indigenous leaders so that they will be able to take on responsibility for coordinating indigenous ranger groups. These programmes provide a foundation for an effective response to illegal activities in Tumucumaque indigenous territories.

War and civil conflict

Armed conflict can have significant impacts on protected areas and may also initiate refugee movements that can exacerbate impacts. Protected area staff are threatened with injury or death. Guerrillas and soldiers may kill wildlife for food or for sale. Logging may be used as a way of financing war efforts either directly or by allowing commercial loggers to take timber from protected areas in exchange for money and weapons. Armed conflicts also tend to decrease legal control, precipitating conditions for widespread poaching of fauna and flora for food and as a source of finance. Conflict also gives rise to refugees who source water, food and fuelwood from protected areas. Protected areas may also suffer through the loss of infrastructure, withdrawal of donor funding and loss of tourist revenue, and even the total withdrawal of management structures. Environmental destruction may itself be an instrument of war, as in the use of defoliating herbicides, the deliberate arson in forests and setting fire to oil or gas installations that may pollute protected areas. A list of potential management responses for dealing with armed conflict in protected areas, adapted from Shambaugh et al (2001), is given in Table 9.10.

The International Gorilla Conservation Programme (IGCP) provides an example of this type of work. The IGCP is a coalition of three international conservation organizations and was formed in 1991 to increase their effectiveness in their common objective of mountain gorilla (*Gorilla gorilla*, subspecies *beringei*) conservation. The Virunga Range, home of the mountain gorilla, straddles the borders of Uganda, Rwanda and the Democratic Republic of Congo. The region experienced conflict and instability that had badly affected conservation since the 1990s. The IGCP has responded effectively to crises, maintaining conservation activities while making a significant economic contribution to sustainable livelihoods (Plumptre et al, 2001, cited in Shambaugh et al, 2001). Following the wars and refugee crises, forest cutting and land degradation occurred, and the IGCP instigated a programme of ranger-based monitoring of the mountain gorillas as a basis of directing limited funding resources (Shambaugh et al, 2001).

Poor management

Incompetent protected area management is a threat to protected areas. Poorly considered, poorly researched and poorly planned and executed works by management organizations can lead to negative outcomes. Responses to incidents and emergencies can also cause serious impacts and may also compound existing threats. Protected area organizations need to establish standards, policies and systems for management. Staff need to be disciplined and to have suitable training and skills.

Protected area legislation or regulations often provide a mandate for managers to address threats and to enforce corrective or preventative action. In addition, there is a range of management systems and policies that are employed to help minimize the chances of threats to protected areas. Some practical examples of such policies are given in Table 9.11.

Introduced animals and plants

With globalization and the rapid movement of people around the world there has been an increase in introduced alien species (McNeely, 2001). Invasive plants and animals can displace endemic species and often pose a serious threat to the survival of rare or vulnerable biota.

Introduced animals can be controlled by poisoning, shooting, trapping or mustering; by exclusion from areas; by biological control; or by

Case Study 9.6

Okapi Faunal Reserve, Democratic Republic of the Congo

The Okapi Faunal Reserve occupies some 20 per cent of the Ituri Forest in the Haut-Zaire region in the north-east of the Democratic Republic of the Congo. The Democratic Republic of the Congo is included in the top 25 countries in the world that possess the most species and endemism. The faunal reserve is of great ecological importance. The forest is a Pleistocene refuge, providing exceptional species richness with 15 per cent endemicity, one of the highest in the world.

The nearby area of Kivu is one of the Democratic Republic of the Congo's most densely populated regions, and over the last decade people have been migrating from Kivu into the Ituri Forest in search of new land for cultivation. The forest ecosystem is further threatened by gold mining, commercial logging, poaching, commercial hunting and elephant poaching for ivory (IUCN, 1994). At the 1999 meeting of the World Heritage Committee, the threats to protected areas in the Congo were widely recognized. Park staff still operated despite poor equipment, lack of pay and the threat of armed forces and poachers.

Source: Carey et al (2000)

Table 9.9 Management response for mining and other extraction activities

Activity	Potential management response
Fossil, mineral and gemstone collecting	Develop an education programme to help prevent collecting.
	Ensure law enforcement to prevent collecting.
Prospecting for gold, precious metals and gemstones	Develop and deliver education programme to help prevent prospecting.
	Secure local community support to help prevent the extraction.
	Increase emphasis on law enforcement.
	Secure government support to prevent prospecting.
	Prosecute cases through the courts.
	Providing alternative livelihood options for artesianal prospectors.
Mineral and petroleum exploration or extraction in IUCN Category I–IV areas	Promote landscape planning and strategic environmental assessments to avoid mining concessions in protected areas.
	Ensure law enforcement to prevent exploration and extraction.
	Establish legislative gazettal of protected areas to the centre of the Earth to prevent subsurface mining.
	Secure government and international support to prevent exploration and extraction.
	Provide alternative livelihood options for artesianal miners.
Mineral and petroleum exploration or extraction in IUCN Category V–VI areas	Promote landscape planning and strategic environmental assessments to avoid mining concessions in protected areas.
	Allow limited exploration or extraction subject to an approved environmental impact statement (EIS) and community support.
	Negotiate licence arrangements which ensure that protected area values are not compromised.
	Where possible, negotiate licence arrangements that yield economic benefits to the protected area management agency and the local community.
	Require a security bond.
	Ensure that rehabilitation funds are set aside for repairing damage after exploration and mining works are completed.
	Provide alternative livelihood options for artesianal miners.

Sources: Carey et al (2000); Baillie et al (2004); Barber et al (2004); and IUCN (2005b)

changing the habitat. The key to control is understanding the biology and the nature of the damage of introduced animals. Controls may, for example, be most effective when populations are stressed or at their lowest levels. The control of introduced animals is a science and needs to be researched carefully. Priorities must first be determined. For example, in some settings, small mammals are particularly vulnerable to non-native predators (such as foxes and cats in Australia), and many jurisdictions have aggressive programmes for reducing these predator species. The work undertaken in Western Australia (see Case Study 9.7), and the eradication of feral animals from New Zealand islands (see Case Study 9.8) are excellent examples of pest animal control. A number of

Table 9.10 Management responses to armed conflict

Management goal	Potential management actions
Invest in local community needs	Identify local community needs.
	Demonstrate a commitment to the welfare of the community.
	Assist the community.
Strengthen capacity to maintain a presence	Strengthen the capacity of staff and field offices.
	Increase autonomy and self-reliance of staff and NGOs.
	Maintain neutrality and impartiality.
	Maintain safety of staff.
Gather strategic information	Assess threats and opportunities.
	Assess capacity to respond.
Undertake contingency planning	Undertake pre-conflict planning to identify strategic responses to potential conflict situations.
	Identify during-conflict capability and strategies.
	Have procedures in place to undertake post-conflict planning and implementation.
Collaborate with other organizations	Establish communication and work with organizations such as the military, governments, international aid agencies, the United Nations (UN) and local communities to help prevent, minimize the effects of and aid recovery from conflict.
	Focus efforts on improving communication, developing goodwill and identifying common goals.
	Make information available on the importance of protected area values and benefits.
Secure ongoing funding	Keep donors informed.
	Seek alternative emergency funding.
	Repackage environment programme language to suit an environment of conflict.
Post-war reconstruction	Rehabilitate infrastructure.
	Assist democratic governance.
	Assist policy and legislation development.
	Provide information.
	Assist capacity-building.

Source: Shambaugh et al (2001)

practical management considerations are provided in Table 9.12.

Introduced plants are a serious threat to protected area values. If they develop self-sustaining populations in natural or semi-natural ecosystems, become dominant or disruptive to native floras (an agent of change) and threaten native biological diversity, they are recognized by the IUCN (2000a) as an invasive alien species. Island floras, in particular, are susceptible to such plants (Marinelli, 2004). Some management responses to dealing with introduced plants are described in Table 9.13.

Table 9.11 Operational systems and policies aimed at reducing threats

Management system or policy example	Threat targeted
Locate visitor-use developments outside of the protected area	*Tourism development and natural areas* Encourage the development of visitor facilities (such as accommodation and restaurants) in towns and villages outside of protected areas and provide simple destination facilities within a protected area. This helps ensure that the natural integrity of the destination is retained.
Create 'hardened' visitor access routes	*Impacts of large numbers of visitors at key destinations* For high-use visitor areas of a suitable Recreation Opportunity Spectrum (ROS) category, the provision of hardened walking routes (gravel, paved, bitumen or elevated walkways) can help to keep visitors on designated walking routes and prevent soil erosion impacts.
Limit visitor numbers	*Excessive use of very sensitive destinations* Provide a planned limit for visitor-use numbers (annual) and limit the number of visitors during sensitive times, such as very wet conditions or during a species breeding season. The control of visitor numbers and frequency of use through tickets and guided walks and other techniques can be used.
Use clean earth moving equipment	*Introducing pathogens into pristine natural areas* The introduction of non-natural soil-borne pathogens and weeds into a protected area is a major threat. Machinery to be used in protected areas may need to be cleaned of all soil and sterilized.
Rehabilitate immediately following works	*Soil erosion* Earthworks are commonly undertaken within protected areas. A policy of immediately completing rehabilitation works following earthworks helps to eliminate any potential for soil erosion.
Use sterile plants or local native species for rehabilitation	*Preventing the introduction of weed species* Soil conservation works often use quick-growing species such as grasses to immediately pioneer plant growth for disturbed sites. Sterile (single-season) grass species are often used in conjunction with suitable local native species seed stock for rehabilitation. This helps to reduce the risk of weeds.

Fire

While fire is a natural phenomenon, it can also be a threat to natural environments. For some environments such as rainforest, many native species are poorly adapted to fire and can be killed. Habitats adapted to fire can be affected by changed fire frequencies. Fires that are too frequent can develop a fire climax community and affect soil cover and catchment values. Fires that are unnaturally infrequent can cause an ageing of plant communities and compositional changes. Managers must have a clear understanding of the ecological condition that they are managing for in dealing with fire. Unplanned (non-natural) and illegal fire events (arson) can be a threat to natural habitats, wildlife, cultural heritage and human property and life. Some management responses to such fire threats are described in Table 9.14.

On-site pollution

Pollution may be as simple as waste left lying about or soap used in a pristine creek by bushwalkers, or it may be as severe as tanker-polluters dumping toxic waste in a national park. Land, air and water pollution are all problems. Countermeasures include:

Table 9.12 Management responses to a threat of introduced animals

Management goal	Focus for the response	Potential management actions
Prevent introductions	A whole-of-government approach	Stringent quarantine measures at the borders of countries and islands.
		National prohibition policies for some animal species.
		International conventions restricting trade in animal species.
	Individual protected area approach	Protected area policies preventing the introduction of non-native animal species.
Plan responses for potential introductions	Individual protected area vulnerability to introduced animal species	Research of animal species that may be introduced.
		Analysis of the management response required.
Prevent the spread of existing introduced animals	Minimizing the spread of introduced species	Containment (if possible) and treatment of introduced animal species.
		Priority provided to those introduced animal species with the greatest potential for impact.
Control introduced animal species	Use of a range of humane control techniques	Control techniques include: • herding and removal • live trapping • tranquilizing and removing • targeted poisoning • shooting.
Undertake performance evaluation	Monitoring of introduced animal populations	Completion of a baseline evaluation for the introduced animals pre-treatment.
		Completion of change in condition (from baseline) evaluations following management treatments.

- codes of practice for visitors to protected areas;
- environmental management systems that systematically establish standards for operation and management of waste disposal systems relative to approved standards;
- efficient systems for dealing with wastewater and solid waste (including earthworms or other methods for aerobic decomposition of human waste);
- sewerage works that use advanced aeration treatments and/or chemicals to remove contaminants such as phosphates and nitrates;
- natural wetland filters to reduce nutrients flowing into streams from sewerage plants;
- stockpiles of chemicals and other aids to clean up oil pollution (on land or sea);
- improved policing to reduce illegal dumping of refuse and toxic wastes; and
- constant evaluation of environmental management performance against baseline standards established from environmental best practice standards for protected areas.

Table 9.13 Management responses to the threat of introduced plants

Management goal	Focus for the response	Potential management actions
Prevent introductions	A whole-of-government approach for preventing introductions	Stringent quarantine measures at the borders of countries.
		National prohibition policies for some commercial nursery species.
	Individual protected area approach for preventing introductions	Protected area policies preventing the planting of introduced species.
		Use of local native plant species for rehabilitation.
		Cleaning and sterilization of earth-moving equipment.
		Use of clean seed-free fill, gravel and other introduced materials.
Plan responses for potential introductions	Individual protected area vulnerability to introduced species	Research of plant species that may be introduced.
		Analysis of management response required.
Prevent the spread of existing introduced plants	Minimizing disturbance to soils	Rapid rehabilitation of any disturbed soil areas.
		Use of local native plant species for rehabilitation.
	Minimizing the spread of introduced species	Containment and treatment of introduced plant species.
		Priority for those introduced plant species with the greatest potential for spreading.
	Minimizing the influence of vectors	Management of the movement of vehicles and people may be required to minimize the spread of introduced plants.
Control introduced plant species	Use of a range of techniques to control introduced plants	A range of techniques, guided by careful scientific research, may be used, including the: • application of fire • use of shading control from native species • intensive hand weeding by volunteers (see Case Study 9.1) • use of carefully researched and selected pathogens • use of insect predators • use of chemicals (see Case Study 9.1).
Undertake performance evaluation	Monitoring of area of introduced plants	Completion of a baseline evaluation for the introduced plants pre-treatment.
		Completion of change in condition (from baseline) evaluations following management treatments.

Table 9.14 Management responses to the threat of unplanned (non-natural) and illegal fires

Management goal	Focus for the response	Potential management actions
Prevent non-planned fire	A whole-of-government approach for preventing unplanned fires	Seasonal burning-off bans as summer approaches.
		Total fire bans during extreme (very hot and windy) fire weather days.
		Prevention of arson through cooperative surveillance with police and other organizations.
	Individual protected area approach for preventing unplanned fires	Seasonal fire bans based on a scientific indicator, such as a dryness index.
		Twelve-month 'fuel stove only' policies for hiking areas.
Manage fire events (see also Chapter 18)	Planned response to fire events	Multi-organization and cooperative fire operations.
		Use of pre-planning and incident-control procedures.

On-site use of chemicals

Chemicals either used within or introduced to protected areas by management include fertilizers; herbicides; pesticides; limestone (concrete); trace elements (such as zinc from galvanizing and arsenic from treated pine); salt; explosives; and petroleum-based fuels and products (such as bitumen). Managing these chemicals requires great care. Considerations include:

- pH impacts to natural streams from concreting;
- salt impacts to waterways from road de-icing;
- trace element impacts to plants through leaching from galvanizing (such as trace zinc toxicity to plants);
- secondary and residual impacts of the use of pesticides and herbicides;
- toxic impacts of petroleum products caused during spills or use in outboard motors in natural waterways; and
- impacts from nitrates and other chemicals associated with explosives used for road or other forms of construction.

On-site water use

Uncontaminated natural water is critical for wildlife and habitats. Any impact to natural water flow or availability will threaten protected area values. Water may be used for management facili-

ties administration and work offices, and for fire management support purposes. There may also be some facilities for wildlife. Tourism facilities within protected areas also consume water. Some considerations to ensure that the use of water by management does not threaten the values of protected areas include:

- Use natural supplies only, and limit extraction based on natural flow regimes of streams (or the recharge of aquifers) and the needs of other downstream users, including wildlife.
- Ensure that consumption limits take into account dry and wet cycles.
- Ensure that discharge water is at the same standard (or better) than the water originally extracted.

Infrastructure development

Roads, railways, canals, power lines, pipelines, telecommunication towers and other infrastructure are all developments that can impact upon protected areas. Roads into protected areas can encourage damage through increased visitor use or by potentially increasing illegal use and settlement, or as conduits for pests and diseases. A similar range of issues relates to other transport systems, including railways and canals. Shipping lanes and the activity of private boats can have impacts on marine and freshwater protected areas.

Case Study 9.7

Western Shield

Jim Sharp, Department of Conservation and Land Management, Western Australia

Endangered native animals such as the bilby (*Macrotis lagotis*), numbat (*Myrmecobius fasciatus*) and western quoll (*Dasyurus geoffroii*) are making a comeback in Western Australia due to the groundbreaking wildlife recovery programme Western Shield. Launched in 1996, Western Shield is working to bring at least 13 native fauna species back from the brink of extinction by controlling introduced predators: the fox and cat. The main weapon in the fight against the fox and cat is use of the naturally occurring poison 1080, found in native plants called gastrolobiums, or 'poison peas'. While Western Australia's native animals have evolved with these plants and have a high tolerance to the poison, introduced animals do not. Western Shield makes use of this natural advantage. In the south-west forests, scientific research and monitoring has shown that where baiting has reduced fox numbers, there has been a dramatic increase in native animal numbers.

Western Shield involves aerial and hand-baiting on almost 3.5 million hectares of department-managed land. Baiting operations take place four times a year throughout the state from as far north as Karratha to Esperance in the south. Smaller nature reserves are baited more frequently. Around 770,000 1080 baits are dropped from a twin engine *Beechcraft Baron* during each baiting operation – that is, more than 3 million baits each year. The plane flies 55,000km during each baiting operation. Monitoring is showing that animals once on the brink of extinction in Western Australia are returning and breeding in their natural habitats as a result of fox baiting. Since Western Shield began in 1996, the department has also carried out translocations of animal species. These include the western quoll; dibbler (*Parantechinus apicalis*); numbat; bilby; southern brown bandicoot (*Isodon obesulus*); western barred bandicoot (*Parameles bougainville*); brush-tailed bettong (*Bettongia penicillata*); rufous hare-wallaby (*Lagorchestes hirsutus*); Tammar wallaby (*Macropus eugenii*); Shark Bay mouse (*Pseudomys praeconis*); noisy scrub-bird (*Atrichornis clamorosus*); western bristlebird (*Dasyornis brachypterus longirostris*); malleefowl (*Leipoa ocellata*); and western swamp turtle (*Pseudemydura umbrina*). Baiting has been so effective that translocations of between 20 and 40 animals result in the successful establishment of new populations. Western Australia is one of the few areas in the world where three mammals – the Tammar wallaby, the southern brown bandicoot and the brush-tailed bettong – have been taken off the endangered fauna list because of scientific management action The small hopping marsupial, the brush-tailed bettong, has been relocated to more than 30 places. Ten years ago there were just three surviving populations. Long-term success is happening at the Dryandra Woodland, the Tutanning Nature Reserve, the Boyagin Nature Reserve and the south-west forest areas.

An important element of the programme's success is the cooperation and support of local communities, and many private landowners and land conservation district committees have helped with fox baiting by laying baits on their own land where it is next to conservation reserves and state forest.

Power transmission lines also constitute potential threats, heightened when associated with maintenance access roads. In managing for infrastructure development, a number of considerations are important (see Table 9.15).

When infrastructure developments are approved in protected areas, there are ways of reducing damage. Attention to detail is critical. Details such as the parking of construction equipment, the on-site storage of materials, the access to the construction site, the temporary erosion-control measures, even pH controls for construction discharge waters are important. Techniques for limiting their impacts include:

- effective liaison with the construction company and their contractors and any subcontractors;
- providing background environmental information and guidelines to the developers, both verbally and in writing;
- setting a substantial bond that can be used to repair any environmental damage;
- constantly monitoring the development;
- having an approved development design that includes a waste treatment system (preferably a completely internalized one) for minimizing such effects as stream pollution from sediments, from grease and oil waste, or from the runoff of acid or alkaline waters;

Case Study 9.8

Eradication planning for invasive alien animal species on New Zealand islands

Pam Cromarty and Ian McFadden, New Zealand Department of Conservation

New Zealand's Department of Conservation is a world leader in the field of invasive alien animal species eradication on islands, particularly rodent eradication. Eradication efforts have focused on Tuhua/Mayor Island (1277ha in extent); Raoul and Macauley islands (2938ha and 306ha, respectively); and Campbell Island (11,216ha).

The difference between eradication and control is that control operations manage the impact of invasive alien animal species and are not concerned with removing the 'last animal', while eradication permanently removes the impacts of invasive alien animal species by eliminating the entire population. A number of issues must be dealt with in planning an eradication operation. Failure to consider any one of these can result in an unsatisfactory outcome. Planning for an eradication operation involves research, contingency measures, incorporation of best available techniques, and the flexibility to cope with unexpected difficulties.

One challenge facing the Department of Conservation as eradication operations become more complex is to ensure that effective communication and knowledge transfer take place within the organization. It is vital that the lessons learned from each operation are recognized and disseminated. The Department of Conservation has a commitment to learn from all eradication attempts, to reduce the risk of failed operations and to build the capacity to attempt more complex projects. The approach adopted when planning invasive alien animal species-eradication programmes on islands has several key components:

- a strategic approach considering all eradication programmes;
- team-building, including consideration of team dynamics;
- skills development for project teams;
- peer review to evaluate readiness prior to an operation taking place; and
- review and debriefings throughout the operation.

The next major challenge is improving the planning and implementation of island quarantine and contingency. Further research needs to be conducted into the long-term effects of eradication, defining long-term restoration goals for islands and island groups, and the improvement of eradication techniques for detecting and managing invasive alien animal species at low numbers.

- cordoning off of the development site to delimit the area within which disturbance is permitted;
- starting rehabilitation while the development is still under way;
- offering bonus payments for good environmental results;
- having a proviso in the contract that allows managers to halt work for environmental reasons; and
- contingency plans that deal with potential accidents, such as explosions or fire.

Management principles

1. Protected area managers need to intervene so that the impacts of human-caused threatening processes are reduced.
2. Threats to protected areas are inevitable. They

need to be anticipated with pre-planned responses, appropriately trained personnel and readily available logistic support. This planning should take into account the probability that threatening processes will increase over time, especially in response to changing population and use patterns.

3. Dealing with threats may require long-term activity. Interventions need to recognize the long-term budget commitments and stable organizational environment that are necessary to achieve successful conservation outcomes.

4. Threats can arise as a tyranny of small development decisions over time and can change the nature of values of protected areas. This means that tools such as monitoring and condition reporting are critical for helping to maintain conservation standards.

Table 9.15 Management responses to the threat of developments within protected areas

Management goal	Focus for the response	Potential management actions
Manage development to prevent or minimize reduction in protected area values	Use the legislative basis and purpose of protected areas to exclude inappropriate development	Ensure that there are no weak links in the legal basis and framework of protected areas, including:
	Adopt a whole-of-government approach	• legislative support for conservation and protection • clarity of the purpose of protected areas • a management plan with clear best practice conservation objectives supported by the community • zoning to exclude inappropriate developments from specified areas, with associated clear conservation objectives for each zone.
	Use established formal and legal processes for development approval	Ensure that the community is fully informed of the development proposal. Implement fully transparent environmental impact assessment processes.
Manage approved developments	Performance bonds	Prior to formal approvals, secure substantial replenishable financial performance bonds for non-compliance.
	Accountability for compliance	Prior to final approval, accountability for environmental performance is conveyed on all operatives for the development organization (including subcontractors), based on an approved development plan and environmental impact statement (EIS).
	Monitoring of compliance	Final approval for the developments depends upon resources provided to fund agency staff and resources needed for the monitoring of environmental compliance.
	Designated areas	Final approval defines designated areas that are required to be used for development construction.
	Stop work	The power of stop work is vested in the officer in charge of the protected area, and may be invoked for contraventions of the approved development.
	Infringements	Any contraventions to the governance basis for the protected area may invoke infringement proceedings and penalties.
	Rehabilitation	The development is not officially completed until the rehabilitation work has been finished and approved by the protected area manager.

5   Be aware of shifting environmental baselines –
    there may be intergenerational changes in
    how people perceive the state of their natural
    environment. This can mask the true extent of
    environmental change.

6   Immediate, decisive intervention to deal with
    some threats may save significant future costs.

7   Threatening processes will be diminished
    where protected areas are managed as part of a
    community effort to achieve conservation
    outcomes at a landscape scale.

8   Effective environmental planning processes are
    necessary to combat threats to protected areas.

9   Effective community education will help to
    reduce threats to protected areas.

10 Regulations coupled with adequate policing
    may be required to deal effectively with some
    threats.

11 Managing threats to protected areas typically
    involves identifying all human-caused threats
    that require intervention; assessing the poten-
    tial severity of each threat in terms of their
    impact on protected area values; determining
    the priority of threats in terms of manageabil-
    ity and cost effectiveness of management
    actions; developing strategies and actions to
    address the threats and to ameliorate/reduce
    the level of impacts; and being alert to unin-
    tended consequences.

Further reading

Baillie, J. E. M., Hilton-Taylor, C. and Stuart, S. N.
(eds) (2004) *2004 IUCN Red List of Threatened
Species: A Global Species Assessment*, IUCN, Gland
and Cambridge

Barber, C.V., Miller, K. R. and Boness, M. (eds) (2004)
*Securing Protected Areas in the Face of Global Change:
Issues and Strategies*, IUCN, Gland and Cambridge

Brandon, K., Redford, K. H. and Sanderson, S. E. (eds)
(1998) *Parks in Peril: People, Politics and Protected
Areas*, The Nature Conservancy and Island Press,
Washington, DC

Carey, C., Dudley, N. and Stolton, S. (2000)
*Squandering Paradise? The Importance and
Vulnerability of the World's Protected Areas*, WWF,
Gland

Flannery, T. (2005). *The Weather Makers: The History
and Future of Climate Change*, The Text Publishing
Company, Melbourne

IUCN (2000) *Guidelines for the Prevention of Biodiversity
Loss Caused by Alien Invasive Species*, IUCN, Gland
and Cambridge

McNeely, J. A. (2001) *The Great Reshuffling: Human
Dimensions of Invasive Alien Species*, IUCN, Gland
and Cambridge

10

Obtaining, Managing and Communicating Information

Terry De Lacy, Juliet Chapman, Michelle Whitmore and Graeme L. Worboys

Quality data and information are essential to inform sound management decisions for protected areas. It is not possible to know everything or to predict the consequences of all decisions. Nevertheless, access to, and use of, the most relevant, recent and cutting-edge information is a first step.

The terms data and information are often used interchangeably, but they are distinct. There is a hierarchy of 'knowingness' (see Figure 10.1) that moves from the 'real world' to data that represents aspects of the real world, to information (data integrated and organized) and to knowledge (understanding derived from analysis and interpretation of information). The ideal at the top of the hierarchy is wisdom achieved through intelligent use of knowledge. Managers should be familiar with the different types of data, the differ-

ent ways in which it may be accessed or organized, and the different places where it may be collected and stored (from the heads of old-timers or skilled trades people to books and databases).

Having information and managing it is only the first part of the process. Another important aspect is how best to communicate that information to stakeholders and the broader community. A communication strategy is fundamental to protected area management from the planning stages, through implementation and evaluation. A wide array of people needs to be involved, from staff members, government agencies, scientists, business operators, visitors, local communities and so on. In this chapter we explore the processes of collecting data, facilitating and managing research, establishing and using information systems, disseminating information and communicating with stakeholders.

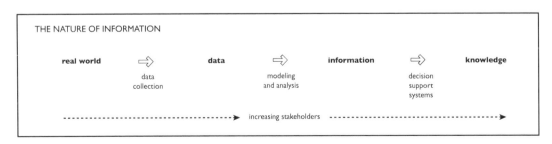

Figure 10.1 The nature of information

Source: adapted from Heywood (1995, p614)

Scope of information needs

There is a range of information required for managing protected areas, from detailed geo-diversity and biodiversity information, to visitation figures and financial records. International agreements that encompass protected areas, such as the Convention on Biological Diversity (CBD), the Convention on International Trade in Endangered Species of Wild Flora and Fauna (CITES), Chapter 15 of Agenda 21, the World Heritage Convention and the Global Biodiversity Strategy all encourage increased use of information relating to biodiversity and its supporting environment.

Since the range of relevant information is extensive, protected area managers must distinguish from the outset between information that is necessary, information that is desirable and information that can be disregarded. The IUCN category to which a protected area belongs (see Chapter 3, p83) has a bearing on the information requirements. Table 10.1 indicates the shifting emphasis of information requirements across the six IUCN protected area categories.

Information types

Geodiversity inventory

Abiotic features such as mountains, canyons, lakes, waterfalls and rock formations are spectacular features of the landscape that draw visitors to a protected area. The structure and processes of abiotic features shape the aesthetic, cultural and biotic elements of a protected area. Inventory and assessment of the abiotic elements and the overall structure of the landscape are essential in protected area management. As a minimum requirement, the landscape features should be mapped.

Biodiversity inventory

It is vital to have in-depth information about the ecosystems and species within a protected area in order to conserve them. For some species, there may be extensive amounts of data, and storing and analysing this data may be the greatest challenge. For other species, there may be very little known, and primary research will need to be conducted, either by the management organization or by a

Volunteer Venturer scout assisting penguin research, Montague Island Nature Reserve, New South Wales, Australia

Source: Graeme L. Worboys

consultant. Data may include species composition, diversity, distribution, habitat and vulnerability, or it may be time-series data, tracking the effects of factors such as climate change.

Cultural inventory

Since protected areas are also designated on cultural values, it is important to establish and maintain data on cultural artefacts, sites, beliefs, practices and rituals. Maintaining maps indicating sites of significance assists in planning activities and developing infrastructure, and can ensure that these sites are not inappropriately intruded upon. Detailed descriptions of these sites should be annotated and maintained. Information can then be provided to front-line managers to assist with management and providing interpretation for visitor groups. Cultural information often has special significance for the local population, as well as being of interest to visitors.

Table 10.1 Management information needs relating to IUCN protected area categories

IUCN category	Primary management objectives	Information type	Examples of information required
Ia Strict protection	Scientific research Preservation of species and genetic diversity	Geodiversity Biodiversity Boundaries Laws Regulations (for research) Finances Threats Traditional knowledge	Site map Species inventories Population size and distribution Habitat condition Rare and endangered species Ecosystem types Landforms, topography, watersheds, soil types and natural features Cultural/social significance Research projects Infrastructure costs
Ib Strict protection	Wilderness protection Maintenance of environmental services	Ia + Environmental services	Biodiversity inventory International agreements relating to the area Risk assessment
II Ecosystem conservation and recreation	Preservation of species and genetic diversity Maintenance of environmental services Tourism and recreation	Ib + Environmental condition Visitation Infrastructure and facilities Social and demographic characteristics	Potential threats Visitor numbers and activities Infrastructure and facility inventory Financial details: income, expenditure and balance sheet
III Conservation of natural features	Preservation of species and genetic diversity Protection of specific natural/cultural features Tourism and recreation	II + Cultural heritage History	Cultural heritage inventory Location and extent of sites of significance
IV Conservation through active management	Preservation of species and genetic diversity Maintenance of environmental services	Ib + Land-use history Social and demographic characteristics	Threats, type, location and extent Cost–benefit analysis

Table 10.1 Continued

IUCN category	Primary management objectives	Information type	Examples of information required
V Landscape/seascape conservation and recreation	Protection of specific natural/cultural features Tourism and recreation Maintenance of cultural/traditional attributes	III + Traditional knowledge	List of cultural/traditional attributes Social and land-use history Oral history
VI Sustainable use of natural ecosystems	Sustainable use of resources from natural ecosystems Preservation of species and genetic diversity Maintenance of environmental services	Ib + Sustainable use criteria	Types of use and users Extent of use Methods of extraction Community statistics – e.g. economics, employment and demography

Traditional knowledge

Traditional knowledge includes inventories of local biological resources, such as animal, bird, insect, local plant and tree species; knowledge about the seasonal cycles of the plants and animals; and indicators of changes in seasons, weather patterns, animal and invertebrate behaviour, and flowering, fruiting and seeding. This frequently comprises knowledge that is integral to the survival of a local community or indigenous people, as well as knowledge that is often useful to scientists and protected area managers.

Environmental condition

The condition of the land, including its stability, chance of erosion and likelihood of rock fall or landslides is surveyed as part of the environmental condition of a site. This may be a result of natural processes or generated through human intervention. Threats to the integrity of the natural system, such as degree of pest and weed invasion, need to be documented and managed. Fire fuel load, water quality and quantity, watershed condition, and the health of the wildlife population and

vegetation are all considerations relating to the overall condition of the protected area and potentially have considerable management implications. New developments within or adjacent to protected areas will have an environmental impact that will need to be assessed. Ongoing monitoring of the impacts will be required.

Infrastructure and facilities

Protected areas often contain a diverse array of structures and equipment. Some of these relate to visitor use – walking tracks, visitor centres, camping areas, signage and car parks; or for marine areas, jetties, pontoons, marker buoys, and so on. Other incidental infrastructure, such as transmission lines and water storage, needs to be considered by management. Infrastructure is often required to support management activities and may include staff accommodation, power supply, transport systems and telecommunications facilities. In terrestrial areas there is usually an access network of roads and tracks. Some reserves contain resident populations or visitor accommodation that will need to be documented.

Uses by indigenous peoples, local communities and others

Depending upon their IUCN category, protected areas can be subject to a range of domestic consumption, livelihood and commercial uses. Examples include scientific research, access to genetic resources, honey production, fishing, water use and harvesting of non-timber forest products (NTFPs) such as rattan. Information is needed to ensure the effective and appropriate management of such uses.

Visitor use

It is important to monitor the level of visitor use at protected areas. Visitation figures are necessary to estimate environmental impacts and carrying capacity, to make decisions about infrastructure investments, to calculate the regional economic benefit of parks and to monitor visitor satisfaction. Many protected areas are valuable tourist attractions and visitor monitoring programmes need to be implemented. The impacts of visitors at sensitive sites should also be measured and monitored.

Community inventory

Understanding the local community and its economic, cultural, demographic, employment and social structure is crucial. Much of the data may be available from government (national, regional or local) statistics. Some information can only be obtained by surveys (written, interviews, focus groups, etc.). Human uses – such as business and residential development, hunting, fishing, cutting wood, clearing areas for agriculture and recreation – need to be considered. In the case of community conserved areas (CCAs) (see Chapter 21) and other protected areas in which indigenous and local communities reside, the community's own understanding of history, biodiversity conservation and sustainable resource utilization is critical.

Social and land-use history

Being informed about the human or social history of the area is invaluable to protected area managers. In combination with the environmental history and the current situation, this information can provide a complete picture of what has occurred in the area. For example, the variety of land uses may help to explain the composition of the landscape. Like cultural resources, social history can be used to provide interpretation for visitors.

Financial management

All management requires effective and transparent financial administration. Consequently, a financial accounting system must be put in place with adequate collection, recording, analysis and presentation of financial data – for example, income, expenditure, inventories, payrolls, reconciliations, assets, balance sheets, profit-and-loss reports and so on.

Data and information collection methods

Ideally, protected area managers will have scientists and/or other knowledgeable individuals working within the organization to undertake research where there are gaps; monitoring will be carried out by dedicated staff members; and research institutions will be keen to contribute to the body of knowledge in order to solve management issues. In reality, protected area managers need to find the resources to source information, to generate new information and to monitor the systems that they are managing. Managers rarely have the resources for collecting large amounts of data; but they have ways of facilitating such work. Around the world, this ranges from protected areas that are well supported and resourced by national and local government to other areas that have minimal infrastructure, are operating 'on a shoestring' and rely on support from international agencies or conservation NGOs. In most CCAs, there are no formal research structures or units, although some or many may have collaborations with institutions or agencies providing such research inputs.

The following five issues need to be considered in data and information collection:

1   Data and information collection must be strategic. The following questions should be asked:
    •   What information is the most critical to the organization's goals?
    •   What data must be collected to supply this information?

Monitoring at Cocha Cashu Biological Station, Manu National Park, Peru

Source: IUCN Photo Library © Jim Thorsell

- Who will collect and analyse the data, and who will be the end-users?
- What is the best and most efficient way of collecting this data?
- How should the data be presented?

2   Decisions need to be made about the means of collecting data and information – for example, in-house, contracting out or a combination of both.

3   Systems need to be put in place to manage data and information and to ensure that they are compatible for use of a range of needs.

4   Data analysis needs to be coordinated to supply the information required.

5   The target audience will be the determining factor in deciding what methods are suitable for information dissemination.

The Rapid Assessment and Prioritization of Protected Areas Management (RAPPAM) method was developed and field-tested by the World Wide Fund for Nature (WWF) International. This tool assesses the management effectiveness of protected area systems at a multiple protected area level. It collects and compares information on the sites within a system (Ervin, 2003a). Evaluation consists of a review of available information and a workshop-based assessment using the *Rapid Assessment Questionnaire*, analysing findings and making recommendations. The process involves park staff, local communities, scientists and NGOs. The results allow comparisons to be made across sites with the intention of:

- identifying relative strengths and weaknesses;
- analysing threats and pressures;
- identifying areas of high ecological and social importance and vulnerability;
- indicating the urgency and conservation priority for individual protected areas; and
- helping to improve management effectiveness at the site and system level.

Case Study 10.1 provides an example of the use of RAPPAM in China.

Case Study 10.1

Implementing the Rapid Assessment and Prioritization of Protected Areas Management methodology in the Upper Yangtze Ecoregion, China

To support the systematic conservation planning project, the World Wide Fund for Nature (WWF)-China Programme Office has adopted the Rapid Assessment and Prioritization of Protected Areas Management (RAPPAM) methodology to assess the management effectiveness of existing protected areas in the forests of the Upper Yangtze Ecoregion. The Upper Yangtze Ecoregion occupies the south-western portion of China. The forests in the area are extremely rich in biodiversity and several international nature conservation organizations have identified the area as having high value for biodiversity conservation. Eighty-eight protected areas, across three sub-regions, were selected for assessment.

The review of existing data utilized the master plans and resource inventories from many of the protected areas, as well as the ecoregion's conservation plan and a national forest protected area systematic plan. These plans provided information on biodiversity conservation and social economic factors. Information included vegetation and infrastructure details, management level and management outputs for most of the protected areas. Other data sources included a workshop for biodiversity conservation, national wildlife surveys and published documents.

Data collection included the use of questionnaires addressing personnel, investment, monitoring, research and other critical management activities. The answers provided baseline data for most of the questions in the *Rapid Assessment Questionnaire*. Protected area managers completed assessment questionnaires during training workshops. A three-day RAPPAM workshop was also held, during which each aspect of the *Rapid Assessment Questionnaire* was discussed. The data obtained through the workshops and feedback from managers was used to identify key threats and management weaknesses.

The ecoregion is surrounded by local communities who traditionally depend upon the resources within or around the protected areas. As such, the major pressures and threats identified for the ecoregion were logging; animal poaching; collection of non-timber forest products (NTFPs); grazing; tourism; agriculture; and mining. The main management weaknesses were lack of funding; low staff capability; and insufficient facilities and infrastructure.

Analyses of the data provided an evaluation of management effectiveness across all of the protected areas in the three sub-regions in categories of planning, inputs and processes. In order to improve management effectiveness and biodiversity conservation, conservation priorities for protected area management need to be set. Priorities can be established using three criteria: biological importance, degree of pressures and threats, and management effectiveness.

Recommendations that emerged from this evaluation covered the topics of financial sustainability; protected area management; threat prevention, mitigation and monitoring; and policies related to protected areas.

Source: adapted from Diqiang et al (2003)

Sourcing existing information

When collecting information about a protected area, it is logical to start with work that has already been done. Finding existing information can be time consuming, especially if there is no central location where such material is kept.

Reference data and information are typically held at a local level, but could also be retrieved from other organizations. This may include accessing information from bibliographies, web searches, manuals, databases, oral histories of local people, visitor surveys, censuses, media articles, maps and photographs. Reference material, such as plant and animal collections, audio and video collections, field reports, books, journals and conference proceedings, could also be useful. Large amounts of heritage, social and economic data may be obtained from nominations for protected area status. Case Study 10.2 discusses the range of information that is included in a nomination for World Heritage status. As information is collected and collated, the information gaps become obvious and the research that needs to be undertaken becomes clear.

Case Study 10.2

IUCN technical evaluation for World Heritage nomination

As part of the nomination for World Heritage status a technical evaluation is undertaken by the IUCN. Such evaluations are approximately ten pages long and provide an excellent starting point for further information-gathering. The technical evaluation includes a list of documents; reports and journal articles relating to the area; a summary of natural values; information about the management and planning framework; threats to the integrity of the area; cultural heritage considerations; the criteria for which the area is nominated; and an explanation of the reasons why the nomination fits those criteria.

The Tropical Rainforest Heritage of Sumatra technical evaluation informs us that the biodiversity of the forests of Sumatra is considered exceptional. The forests contain 10,000 plant species, including 17 endemic genera. Animal diversity is also impressive, with more than 200 mammal species, including the Sumatran orang-utan (*Pongo abelii*), and 580 bird species, including 21 endemic species. The nomination has a total core area of 2,595,125ha. It comprises three national parks: Gunung Leuser National Park, Kerinci Seblat National Park and Bukit Barisan Selatan National Park. It includes the highest mountain in Sumatra, which is an active volcano. Most of the nominated parks are mountainous, with only small lowland areas, and are therefore characteristic of the Bukit Barisan Mountain Range.

Source: adapted from IUCN (2004)

Another crucial source of information is the oral knowledge of local people (indigenous peoples, local communities, local government staff and NGOs). Methodologies for systematically collecting such knowledge are available that enable access to this knowledge while ensuring that the rights and interests of the local people are protected. In particular, issues of obtaining prior consent from the holders of such oral knowledge, and informing them of the purpose of the collection, are important.

Generating new information

If there is not already information available, baseline surveys should be undertaken to assess the status of the protected area and surrounding environs. Primary data collection methods include conducting geological, vegetation, wildlife, visitor or community surveys, and undertaking experiments, case studies and interviews.

Research is a critical means of collecting and analysing data in order to provide information to advise management. Research identifies and assesses the presence, significance, functioning and interdependence of natural, cultural, social, and economic resources and ecosystems. It reveals our rich cultural heritage and shows the antiquity and diversity of indigenous cultures. It helps to make

plans to recover endangered species, manage fires, manage visitors, understand communities and improve operational systems. Managers need to constantly interact with researchers and facilitate their vital work.

Managers can actively attract research to their area by liaising with research institutions and potential researchers. An area can gain a reputation as being a good place for students and others to do research. Managers may be able to provide technical or logistical assistance. Matters such as reliable access, communications, emergency support and accommodation are all important for researchers. In this way, managers can greatly increase a researcher's chance of completing a project. Researchers can then focus more on their own work, to the benefit of both.

It can be beneficial to all parties involved if protected area agencies form partnerships with research institutions. Case Study 10.3 gives an example of this for government-designated protected areas and Case Study 10.4 provides an example for a CCA. Managers may pay consultants, or team up with universities or other research organizations. Volunteer and community groups can also provide research support and the private sector may sponsor research programmes.

Case Study 10.3

Transboundary Protected Area Research Initiative, Africa

The Transboundary Protected Area Research Initiative is a collaboration between the Carnegie Mellon University Center for Integrated Study of the Human Dimension of Global Change, the University of Witwatersrand School for the Environment and the IUCN. Close relations and partnerships exist with other Southern African, European and North American universities and non-governmental agencies.

The initiative conducts integrated assessments in transboundary protected areas (TBPAs) in Southern Africa. Its objective is to determine the nature of the social and natural transformations brought about by TBPAs. The initiative will provide an independent research service to contribute critical and constructive input to policy and decision-making.

The first research phase began in 2003 using the Great Limpopo Transfrontier Park (GLTP) – a joint initiative between Mozambique, South Africa and Zimbabwe – and the wider Great Limpopo Conservation Area (GLCA) as a pilot study. The initiative will conduct research on the following themes:

- ecoregional planning framework and linkages between planning processed across scales and boundaries;
- historical vulnerabilities and adaptation of local people to climate variability, resource limitations and political ecologies;
- social and economic framework of the GLCA, with an emphasis on landownership and land reform;
- tourism development and community-based tourism initiatives launched in the GLTP area over the last decade, with special emphasis on community–public–private partnerships; and
- the decision-making process and governance.

Source: adapted from Center for Integrated Study of the Human Dimensions of Global Change (2004)

Case Study 10.4

Study circles in Mendha-Lekha, India

Ashish Kothari, co-chair, IUCN Theme on Indigenous/Local Communities, Equity and Protected Areas

Mendha-Lekha is a small *adivasi* (tribal) village in the heart of India. It has for the last couple of decades practised a form of self-rule involving taking decisions on most matters related to the village through the village assembly, which consists of all adult women and men. This includes the conservation and sustainable use of about 1800ha of forest.

In order to help with its decision-making, Mendha-Lekha's inhabitants are part of a series of *abhyas gats*, or study circles. These are informal gatherings of people, meeting as and when desired for discussions on any issue. Outsiders are also called in for specific sessions, when the villagers feel the need for external expertise. Conversely, outside researchers and interventionists can also request such circles to be formulated on specific topics.

This institution has provided villagers with critical inputs in taking informed decisions at the village assembly meetings. Specific study circles during the last few years include the use of forest produce, non-violent honey extraction, land/forest encroachments and the impact of forest fires. Some of these have led to modifications in traditional practices in order to make them more sustainable.

Other participatory research and studies carried out in Mendha-Lekha include surveys on bird diversity in the conserved ecosystems (in collaboration with the NGO forum Pakshi Mitra Mandal, or Friends of Birds); impact assessments of the collection of forest produce, such as *Madhuca indica*, *Buchnania lanzan*, *Diospyros melanoxlon* and *Embilica officinalis* (in collaboration with the NGO Vrukshamitra); and an assessment of the dynamics of community-led conservation of forests (in collaboration with the NGO Kalpavriksh).

The study groups have given the villagers the power of information and the ability to assert their rights, and have also improved their conservation performance.

Monitoring

Effective conservation requires data about changes occurring in the ecosystem. Overall management requires data about changes occurring in social, economic and cultural systems, as well as the environmental system being managed. This requires collecting, storing and presenting information on various environmental indicators.

The most important parts of implementing a monitoring programme are to establish the indicators that should be measured and to determine the process of monitoring, including who will be involved. Choosing what indicators will depend upon the site, its environment and management objectives, its use and the resources available to collect data. For example, monitoring visitor impact on a camping site might use indicators such as the:

- number of visitors to the site;
- concentration of E coli in the stream next to the camping area;
- compaction index of soil at the site; and
- a crowding index obtained from visitor surveys.

Regular benchmarking of monitored indicators is required. This will reveal if the site is deteriorating and, hence, requires remedial management action. As indicated, monitoring involves comparing current data with benchmark data. This can include:

- maintaining fixed-photographic points;
- maintaining scientific transects for such variables as vegetation histories;
- fauna censuses (against benchmarks), especially as part of recovery programmes for endangered species;
- measuring environmental impacts at visitor sites;
- counting visitors and their activities;
- assessing the numbers of pest animals;
- measuring the effect of culling programmes on native fauna; and
- collecting socio-economic data in local communities and so on.

Within a protected area there may be many different monitoring programmes to be managed over the year in order to assess the state of the protected area. For example, species recovery plans are monitored to determine whether they are reaching their targets effectively. This forms the basis for adaptive management, where procedures that are not producing the desired outcomes can be amended and more innovative techniques applied. Case Study 10.5 illustrates the benefit of systematic monitoring.

Case Study 10.5

Monitoring programmes: The Mingan thistle, Canada

Mingan Archipelago National Park consists of a series of limestone islands and granite islets and reefs in north-east Canada. Parks Canada runs a number of monitoring programmes in the area, one of which is an inventory of the Mingan thistle (*Cirsium scariosum*).

The Mingan thistle is threatened in each of the provinces in which it grows. Ninety-nine per cent of the known population exists within the Mingan Archipelago National Park. Monitoring of the species has been carried out since 1995, with annual counts and measures being taken. The location of plants is mapped and the numbers in each colony are recorded. Such data provide an indication of the growth and decline of colonies, and are used to predict long-term survival chances for the species. The plants are divided into nine colonies and the variation in plant numbers across these colonies is largely influenced by weather conditions.

During 2001, it was found that no colony had the requisite number of plants (270) to ensure long-term survival. As a result, a recovery programme was implemented to increase the population in vulnerable colonies. Nets were placed over the plants in flower in order to catch the seeds. The seeds were then planted using a protective metal grid to prevent predation from birds and mammals. Results have shown that use of the metal grid improves seed germination fourfold. Parks Canada will continue to monitor the Mingan thistle and implement the necessary measures to ensure its survival.

Source: adapted from Parks Canada (2004a)

Storage, retrieval and analysis

Good data analysis can assist managers to do first what needs doing first – from senior management down to operational level. Strategic-level management is likely to require data analyses that show:

- the actual cost of conserving individual heritage sites, species, habitats and ecosystems;
- the likely economic benefits to the community of conserving ecological systems and processes;
- the relative costs and benefits to local people and non-local stakeholders;
- the success of heritage conservation programmes in reaching their targets;
- how such programmes have performed, by national and international benchmarks, and how well they have fulfilled national and international agreements; and
- the long-term trends of conservation management.

Tactical management requires data analyses that show:

- conservation priorities at a bioregional level, including data that is required for conservation programmes and the effectiveness and cost effectiveness of regional programmes;
- the status of the environment;
- whether conservation and other management targets are being met;
- how well particular programmes are working; and
- staffing details.

Operational management needs data analyses that show the:

- conservation priorities for the local area;
- effectiveness of local conservation programmes;
- case for various land-use options for all sites in the area;
- effectiveness of recovery programmes for endangered species; and
- success of visitor infrastructure investments and so on.

Data analysis requires access to the stored data. Appropriate data storage is as important as accurate data. Huge amounts of environmental data are collected during day-to-day activities within protected areas. For example, operational staff members collect data on the conditions at specific sites (such as ambient temperature and rainfall), record incidents (for example, accidents involving visitors) and list maintenance requirements. Most of the data are unstructured raw data that need a considerable amount of processing before the data can be used for decision-support purposes.

The true value of this data depends upon how it is stored for later retrieval and analysis. Documents on individual heritage resources may not mean much by themselves. One needs to be able to collate, compare and analyse them in order to see overall patterns and draw conclusions.

In protected areas with considerable resources there are often large quantities of data to deal with, and the challenge is how to process and present the data effectively. In protected areas where there is little or no access to global information networks and limited resources available for the systematic collection of local data, the challenge is how to gather, store and manage the basic data essential to the site. One way forward for both types of challenge is to develop partnerships. Many such partnerships already exist at different levels. This will be discussed further in the section on 'Supporting institutions and partnerships'.

While useful, it is not necessary to have the latest computer technology to collect and manage data and information. Well-organized data and information on paper in the form of maps, card files, field notes and ledger books are all important in information management. Preparing the intellectual framework in which the original data will be collected and organized is more important than employing the most modern tools. Large gaps in information due to lack of resources or new protected area status could be discouraging. However, developing a phased approach to information management can assist in overcoming this difficulty. Early phases focus on meeting short-term goals, while keeping long-term goals in view. This allows a new institution to use staff, budgets and tools that are readily available and to

Table 10.2 Types of information systems

Type of system	System purposes
Transaction processing systems	Process data about transactions for classification, calculation, sorting, summarizing and storage
Management information systems	Provide information for decision support where information requirements are regular and can be identified in advance
Decision-support systems	Assist managers with unique (non-recurring) strategic decisions that are relatively unstructured
Executive-support systems	Assist top-level executives in acquiring and using information needed to run the organization – brief them on day-to-day activities and provide information to identify emerging problems
Work group-support systems	Assist and support managers, staff and employees in carrying out day-to-day activities – combine computer processing, data communications, electronic message transmission and image processing
Expert-support systems	Use computer programmes to store facts and files to mimic the decisions of a human expert

Source: adapted from Senn (1990, p13)

move to more advanced approaches when the organization is more established. The key is to design projects that can be transferred readily between management tools (Heywood, 1995).

Information management systems

As much as 80 per cent of the typical executive's day is dedicated to information – receiving, communicating and using it in a wide variety of tasks. Because information is the basis for virtually all activities performed in an organization, systems must be developed to produce and manage it. The objective of such systems is to ensure that reliable and accurate information is available when it is needed and that it is presented in a useable form (Senn, 1990, p8).

The 21st century is, in many ways, defined by the widespread application of information management systems. When developing information management systems, it is important to consider who will be the users of the information; how to make the information easily accessible; what information is required; how to manage it; and how to control the use of terminology (Orna and Pettitt, 1998). Once this is confirmed, the information needs to be documented and a policy for information management developed. Senn (1990) described six different types of information system, each of which is aimed at processing data

to either capture details of transactions, enable people to make decisions or communicate information between people and locations. These six information systems are presented in Table 10.2.

The Tasmanian Parks and Wildlife Service in Australia has developed an integrated information management system that fulfils all the functions described in Table 10.2, and also provides information maps and photographs to a public website (see Case Study 10.6).

It should also be noted that indigenous peoples and local communities have their own sophisticated methods of information management and transmission, including oral methods. These are not necessarily well understood, and even less well used, by formal-sector researchers and managers, but are important tools that communities themselves use in natural resource conservation and management.

There is a myriad of options in terms of electronically storing and retrieving data. State-of-the-art computer technology enables data to be analysed and stored in ways that are user friendly and accessible to managers at all levels. For example, satellite data can be transformed into digital images and geographic information system (GIS) layers that can provide visuals of the terrain, vegetation and water courses, and be used as a basis for further research. GIS is a powerful storage, analysis and presentation tool. In Nepal,

Case Study **10.6**

Tasmanian Parks and Wildlife Service Information Management System, Australia

Steve Sallans, Tasmanian Parks and Wildlife Service, Australia

How does a strategic manager know what is happening on the ground? How can a programme manager work out if the effort going into a programme is efficiently achieving its required outcomes? And, given the tight time frames in which budgets are compiled and the vast range of responsibilities our budgets have to cover, on what basis do project bids get approved? These were some of the important questions exercising my mind as a regional manager in Tasmania's Parks and Wildlife Service (PWS). The answer to these questions lay in the analysis of relevant information about all aspects of the management of the PWS's responsibilities; however, the problem was how to find and access that information, and then how to make sense of it.

The Tasmanian PWS compiles and stores a great deal of information; however, the different information types were being husbanded away in separate and unrelated repositories. The finance system, for example, had its own databases, esoteric rules and power users; visitor statistics was over in its corner, with its own unrelated database; the wildlife branch, and particularly heritage information, was being jealously guarded in its specialist vaults; and each district was out in the field, happily designing their own information systems.

This was not too much of a problem for individual data managers working with their own data; but there was no way for strategic decision-makers to see the big picture. Analysing the relationships between the different disciplines was extremely difficult; you simply could not get an overview that would allow a truly strategic approach to management. We required a meta-system that would pull all of the information together, make clear relationships between the different fields, and finally make the data useful for strategic decision-making.

In 2000, I had the opportunity to do something about this problem. I had been given the task of setting up a new asset management system and successfully argued that the accomplishment of such a system relied, first, on the integration of all the datasets being managed by the park service. Without that context, truly strategic asset management decisions could not be made. This led to creating a vision:

The vision is for one to be able to conduct simple, graphical desktop audits, in real time, of the performance of the PWS in its attempts at achieving optimum productivity from its assets and other inputs in meeting its required outcomes.

We envisaged an intranet portal, a one-stop shop to access all of our data and be able to undertake spatial analysis of it. It needed to be accessible to users at all levels without requiring intimate knowledge of function keys and endless cryptic menus. It needed to be 'point and click' so that even senior managers could feel comfortable with undertaking analysis and 'what ifs' on the fly.

From this vision developed the concept of the PWS Information Management System (PIMS). A data model was constructed to demonstrate the required relationships between the various datasets and how they would function under the intranet portal (see Figure 10.2). A key information link, or database field, common to all of the datasets in the system was required to make the system work. This is essential so that data can be correlated, relationships recognized and analysed, and conclusions drawn. To meet our vision for a point-and-click graphic-based system, the data also required a common spatial element so that they could be analysed spatially and so that graphic reports could generated. We were seeking, for the first time, to achieve 'hard-wired' links between planning; asset management; the finance system; visitor safety and occupational health and safety polices; visitor statistics; and various science projects; among many others. This had never been attempted before.

Coincidentally, the asset management team was in the process of developing a 'levels-of-service' system to provide context for the asset management system and visitor risk management (see Case Study 19.5 in Chapter 19). Essentially, this system classified all of the land under our management (that is, our visitor sites) for the purpose of defining the use of the site and the standard of service and facilities that would be provided on the site. Since all of the datasets can be referred back to the land, this classification became the common data field for every piece of information in the system.

Using the internet portal, a 'visitor site' could be interrogated to discover what plans relate to it; what assets belong to it and what their purpose is in relation to those plans; what work is being planned or being undertaken, if this work is in accordance with the required standards; what threatened species are on the site; and so on. Since the financial system is also keyed to the site, one can thus begin to construct true 'bang-for-bucks' equations. On a broader scale, Recreation Opportunity Spectrum (ROS) analysis can assist strategic decision-making by having the system generate maps of the spread of the different classes of sites, their densities and the costs

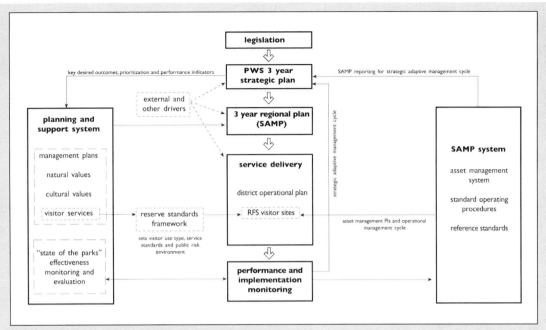

Figure 10.2 Strategic asset management system components

Note: RSF = Reserve Standards Framework; PI = Performance Indicator; SAMP = Strategic Asset Management and Planning.

associated with bringing them up to standard. All in all, this comprised the very tools needed by a resource manager to begin to plan in a realistic and strategic way.

To succeed, however, several roadblocks had to be cleared. First, the data owners had to be convinced of the worth of the project, and the information technology (IT) section had to be brought into the project with the right attitude. It is often at this first stage that many individuals with a similar vision strike trouble. Data owners have often invested heavily in their projects and have no desire to adjust data structures, even marginally, to facilitate integration. IT branches can feel that their territory has been stepped on and can prove to be, at best, not particularly cooperative and, at worst, downright obstructive.

Our approach was to construct a working model and then build a business case around the benefits that the model could demonstrate. My first priority, therefore, was to put together a team with the abilities to do just this. The first team member was a person with strong MapInfo – a desktop geographic information system (GIS) package – development skills to build the spatial aspects and, using MapInfo's internet-enabling product MapExtreme, to demonstrate how the final product would look and feel over the intranet. These products are simple enough for reasonable IT-competent lower-level staff to work with without having to involve the main IT branch. A MapExtreme application, MapLink, had already been implemented over the intranet to produce active maps from the departmental GIS system. The field staff's familiarity and confidence in this system brought immediate credibility for the proposed broader PIMS system.

The second team member had strong skills in technology and database design and was able to put up the model system on our own server, thus avoiding the IT branch issues during the demonstration phase. The third team member worked up the theory that related the various datasets. This important work, the Reserves Standards Framework, a 'levels-of-service' system, provided the land classification system that enabled all of the different datasets to be commonly related (see Case Study 19.5).

Once a working model was live on the net, it became the key to successfully promoting and selling the business case for the project, and to convincing the individual data owners of the enormous benefits to be gained by buying in. With a clear product in mind, the IT branch had no problems in realizing exactly what we wanted and became enthused about being involved. It is often the case that clients go to the IT people expecting them to solve their problems – for instance, 'We need an asset management system.' In fact, the IT people only know about IT, not about asset management (that's our job) – they need a really clear specification of what is required of them, and if the client doesn't know what they want, then IT can't provide it. In fact, this issue often leads to endless frustration for all sides, resulting in very poor relationships. The take-home message is: know precisely what you want before you get the IT technologists involved.

The growing understanding of our operations that this enhanced information management is beginning to provide, and the system's ability to produce thematic mapping reports, has already enhanced our capacity to communicate management issues to stakeholders in a manner that is rapidly building and enhancing their confidence in our professionalism. Budget arguments can now carry vastly more weight when backed up by solid information aligned to whole-of-government objectives.

Now, with the ability to monitor the service's performance from the desktop, the resource managers will have to learn to use the system in order to inform and enhance their decision-making performance and thus move from the crisis management end of the spectrum towards true strategic managers. The development and introduction of the PWS Information Management System is progressively moving the Tasmanian PWS from an essentially reactive organization to an organization that can formulate strategic plans based on effective analysis of complex real time information.

where negotiating the terrain is difficult and time consuming, remote sensing was used to provide important preliminary information to protected area managers (see Case Study 10.7).

Supporting institutions and partnerships

The rapid expansion of protected areas globally has created a demand for data, information and knowledge relating to all aspects of managing protected areas. This has led to international, national, regional, local and trans-sectoral partnerships and consortia providing resources and expertise to fund and carry out research, develop information management systems, develop capacity, and assist with the development and implementation of management plans.

International organizations such as the United Nations Environment Programme (UNEP), the United Nations Educational, Scientific and Cultural Organization (UNESCO), the IUCN, the World Wide Fund for Nature (WWF) and Conservation International (CI) provide funding and services to assist in the management of protected areas. These organizations work closely with other NGOs, governments, the private sector and community groups to progress the conservation effort around the world. One important initiative has been UNEP's World Conservation Monitoring Centre (WCMC) (see Box 10.1).

There are many examples where national environmental information systems are available on the internet for public use. One example is the Inter-American Biodiversity Information Network (IABIN), set up to promote compatible means of collection, communication and exchange of information relevant to decision-making.

Traditional and community knowledge

In many parts of the world, government-designated protected areas are places that people have occupied and used for thousands of years. In such cases, it is important to work with communities in and around the protected area and to incorporate indigenous knowledge within planning and park management. Working in partnership with local communities is essential to successful protected area management. Equally, there are thousands of CCAs (see Chapter 21) where communities continue to use, or have revised the use of, traditional and community knowledge.

The Netherlands Organization for International Cooperation in Higher Education/Indigenous Knowledge (NUFFIC/IK unit) and UNESCO's Management of Social Transformations Programme (MOST) have jointly established a database and publication on best practices on indigenous knowledge. These organizations provide the following definition for indigenous knowledge:

Case Study **10.7**

Remote sensing in protected area management, Nepal

The Makalu Barun National Park and Conservation Area of east Nepal was established in 1992. It encompasses a wide diversity of habitats and bioclimatic regions. The park and its surrounding conservation buffer zone cover over 2230 square kilometres with habitats ranging from tropical monsoonal rainforests to alpine meadows. The area also contains some of the highest mountain peaks in the world.

The management of such an area requires detailed physiographic, geomorphic and ecological information. However, as for many parks in developing countries, reliable information is often lacking due to physical remoteness, lack of funds and personnel for research, and/or political considerations. In remote mountainous areas, such as the eastern Himalaya, even basic geographic data may be unreliable or even unavailable.

Landscape analysis based on satellite remote sensing is known to provide an efficient, cost-effective way to gain up-to-date landscape-level information. The effectiveness of this method in complex mountainous terrain was assessed using the Makalu Barun National Park and Conservation Area as an example. Remote sensing images of the study area encompass the extreme of possible altitudinal change and local topographic relief.

Six field trips between 1992 and 1997 surveyed forest ecology and established approximately 500 ground-control points. Geographic information system (GIS) datasets for the study were obtained from the International Centre for Mountain Research and Development (ICIMOD) database (see Figure 10.3).

The results from the project were not as accurate as typically expected from using this remote sensing method. The difficulties encountered with the process included the level of cloud cover, deep shadow and getting accurate ground-control points. However, given the lack of other reliable data, it was considered a suitable technique for assessing remote mountainous protected areas. This methodology provides a basis for building an accurate GIS land management database, from which intermediate map products could be produced for rapid ecological assessments, preliminary surveys or as the basis for detailed field mapping.

Source: adapted from Zomer et al (1999)

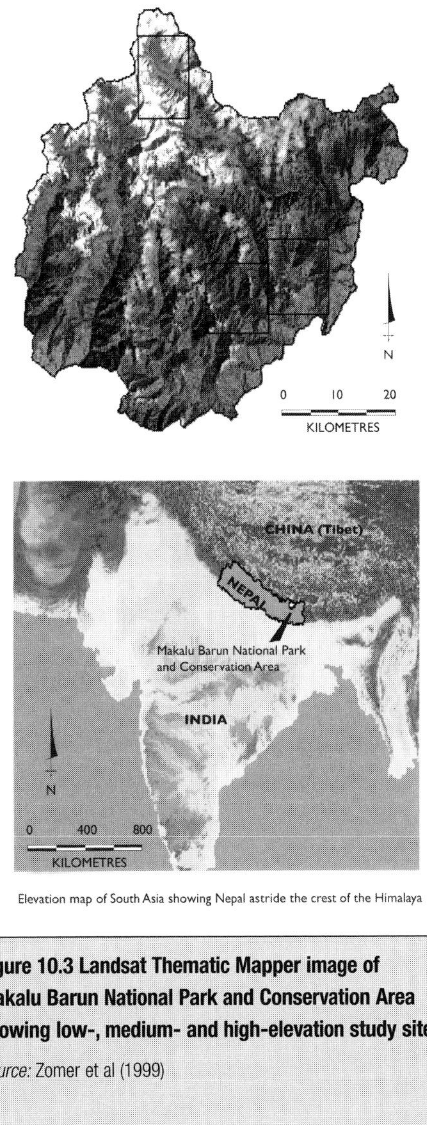

Elevation map of South Asia showing Nepal astride the crest of the Himalaya

Figure 10.3 Landsat Thematic Mapper image of Makalu Barun National Park and Conservation Area showing low-, medium- and high-elevation study sites

Source: Zomer et al (1999)

Indigenous knowledge, also referred to as 'traditional' or 'local' knowledge, is embedded in the community and is unique to a given culture, location or society. The term refers to the large body of knowledge and skills ... that has been developed outside the formal educational system and that enables communities to survive (de Guchteneire et al, 1999).

The database collates case histories to provide guidelines for policy-making and planning. The aim is to encourage researchers and policy-makers

---

Box 10.1 World Conservation Monitoring Centre (WCMC)

Originating in 1979, the World Conservation Monitoring Centre (WCMC) developed from an IUCN initiative to monitor endangered species worldwide. Based in Cambridge, England, it became an independent non-profit UK foundation in 1988 supported by a partnership between the IUCN, the World Wide Fund for Nature (WWF) and United Nations Environment Programme (UNEP).

In 2000, an agreement was made that the WCMC should be responsible to UNEP. As UNEP–WCMC, it has become UNEP's resource centre for assessment, information and policy implementation on biodiversity conservation and sustainable management. The IUCN and WWF remain important collaborators with UNEP and the WCMC.

UNEP–WCMC undertakes a range of work including:

- providing high-quality cost-effective services, in collaboration and partnership with networks, organizations and agencies that have similar goals,
- gathering and assessing a range of data and information to present a global overview of conservation, adhering as much as possible to a principle of free exchange of data, and placing data in the public domain;
- running a website that includes project and species information, databases, maps, publications, contact lists and links to other websites relating to biodiversity conservation;
- undertaking programmes on individual species, forests, mountains, protected areas, marine and freshwater habitats, habitats affected by climate change, and the relationship between trade and the environment;
- working with other organizations to harmonize datasets across the world in order to make it easier to fulfil the reporting requirements for projects relating to international agreements;
- working towards a network of biodiversity centres of excellence in low Human Development Index countries to forward the biodiversity objectives adopted at the World Summit on Sustainable Development;
- providing tools and training for biodiversity assessment and monitoring;
- assisting with the creation of the Global Dive Log, a database into which snorkellers and scuba divers enter observations, such as key indicator species and human-induced pressures; and
- managing, along with the IUCN World Commission on Protected Areas (WCPA) and the World Database on Protected Areas Consortium, the World Database on Protected Areas that provides information on protected areas from 185 countries through access to a geographic information system (GIS) database and a series of Excel spreadsheets.

Source: adapted from UNEP–WCMC (2003)

---

to incorporate indigenous knowledge within their projects and to consider it in all activities affecting local communities. The database will enable a wide range of audiences to learn from the experiences in other projects where indigenous knowledge has been used (de Guchteneire et al, 1999). Examples of where indigenous knowledge has been used to develop cost-effective and sustainable survival strategies are considered best practice. These may include indigenous land-use systems that encourage labour-sharing arrangements or using indigenous knowledge to increase the fuel-efficiency of local stoves instead of replacing them.

In areas where baseline data is not available, it is possible that community knowledge may provide information from which broad-spectrum baseline data may be determined. Community workshops could be conducted when first commencing a project in order to obtain a natural and cultural history of the area and to learn from the intrinsic experiences of the locals.

The importance of protecting intellectual property owned by traditional and indigenous communities has been recognized, and increasing efforts are being made to extend current legal instruments to cover communities (Hansen and Van Fleet, 2003; Borrini-Feyerabend et al, 2004b). It is in the interests of traditional and indigenous communities to have their intellectual property protected, acknowledged and rewarded appropriately. Claiming intellectual property rights for a community under current laws is complex but not impossible. National legislation is often in place and varies between countries. Intellectual property is also codified at an international level through a series of legally binding treaties, including the International Covenant on Economic, Social and Cultural Rights, the CBD, the International Labour Organization Convention No 169 and the Draft Declaration on Indigenous Rights (Hansen and Van Fleet, 2003). It is important that benefits gained from indigenous and traditional knowledge in protected areas are owned by the community, and that protected area staff acknowledge the source of interpretive material and biodiversity knowledge used in management plans and reports.

Communication

Communicating the benefits and values of protected areas and their relationship to the wider economic, social and political community has become essential for protected area agencies. The recommendations with regard to communication and education that emerged from the Vth IUCN

World Parks Congress are detailed in Box 10.2.

Managers have much work to do to build a good reputation, reduce conflict and to demonstrate that protected areas provide benefits to people beyond their boundaries. Reputation is the social capital of the protected area manager (IUCN–CEC, 2003). The one-way approach to protected area management where communities are told, rather than consulted, and excluded from land that was previously theirs or was open for their use has created suspicion and ill will towards protected areas in many regions.

A model of communication is emerging that breaks down barriers and generates cooperation and commitment by communities towards protected areas. This participatory approach requires more commitment, in terms of time and effort, from both protected area managers and stakeholders; but it is proving to be beneficial for all parties. Case Study 10.8 describes a community consultation process that resulted in the community taking ownership and jointly managing the protected area.

Box 10.2 World Parks Congress Recommendation 5.32

The participants in the Stream on Building Broader Support for Protected Areas at the Vth IUCN World Congress in Durban, South Africa (8–17 September 2003):

Recommend that all relevant parties work towards a common agenda for communication for protected areas, from a local to global level.

Further recommend that all relevant parties:

- Incorporate communication into the management and establishment of all protected areas from the beginning.
- Integrate a multilevel communication strategy into all protected area management plans and practices.
- Ensure that adequate funding for communication is included in budgets.
- Develop the capacity and skills for effective internal and external use of strategic communication.
- Support protected area agencies to develop the capacity to deal with developments in a resilient and flexible manner.
- Include professional communicators as part of the management team.
- Strengthen communication networks.
- Improve relations with other sectors to create channels for placing protected area issues on their agendas.
- Develop a participatory approach with stakeholders to encourage their collaboration in protected area management.
- Support communication and media professionals to better understand the benefits of protected areas.
- Recognize that communication must be research based, monitored for effectiveness, evaluated for impact and linked to protected area objectives.
- Use communication tools to promote the sustainable use of biodiversity.

Source: IUCN (2005b)

Working with stakeholders

In order to work with other organizations or with the community towards common goals one needs a range of techniques, from conflict resolution to group decision-making. Community participation work requires many skills, which improve with experience. At the heart of the process are human interactions – individuals and groups working together with understanding, integrity and commitment. The community, by being involved in the management process, comes to better understand protected area issues and their complexities (see Case Study 10.9).

Communication planning

Managers and staff need to be prepared for the activities they must undertake when working with the community. Staff need to be briefed about the relevant people and equipped with the skills for the job. In order to facilitate this, communication plans should be developed by all protected area managers. Case Study 10.10 provides one example of a communication plan.

Understanding communities and stakeholders

In order to solve conservation problems, we must first ask: 'What is their cause?' To work with people on solutions we need to know more about the community in question: its structure, its power relationships, its micro-economy, how it communicates and so on. Some of these considerations are relatively new to conservation agencies, which have traditionally focused on biogeographical studies. Social sciences, on the other hand, have amassed a large body of knowledge since the 1960s, which is very relevant (Machlis, 1992). These include ethnography and community assessment; psychology of attitudes and behaviour; communication and education; social impact assessment; organizational sociology; media studies; and conflict resolution. Some social science methods that can be applied to protected area management are introduced here.

Social and cultural impact assessment. Social and cultural impact assessment (SIA) is a means of assessing and predicting the probable effects of a development project or a policy change on individuals and communities. Issues include:

Case Study 10.8

Community participation, Apo Island Marine Protected Area, the Philippines

In 1976 a research team from Silliman University in the Philippines decided that it wanted to create a marine sanctuary off Apo Island. The team members knew that in order to do so they needed the support of the 700 residents on the island, most of who relied on fishing for their livelihood. Initial presentations explaining the benefits of a marine protected area were met with scepticism. The locals believed that a reduction in fishable area would mean a reduction in catch.

Over the next four years support for the idea increased. In 1982, the majority of the community gave their support for a two-year trial. A no-take zone was set aside. This area contained approximately 10 per cent of the coral reef, which was also considered an important fish breeding ground. The deal was that if fish catch increased after two years, the community would agree to continue the no-take zone.

After the two-year trial, fish catches were up 85 per cent. The spill-over of mature marine species from the sanctuary to the fishable waters was increasing. The community and the university team jointly devised a management plan. The main goal was to protect the fishery by maintaining the no-take zone. Community members managed the area from 1985 to 1994, with assistance from the Silliman University and the municipal government (particularly for law enforcement).

In 1994, the Apo Island Marine Protected Area became part of the integrated protected area initiative of the national government, and management shifted accordingly. However, a strong community management focus is maintained. The community sees the benefits of the marine protected area as being a sustained fish catch, pride in the community and minimized illegal fishing practices.

Source: adapted from Loimann (2003)

Case Study **10.9**

Kuronian Spit National Park, Russia

The Kuronian Spit National Park, which spans the border between Russia and Lithuania, was inscribed onto the *World Heritage List* in 2000. It was listed under cultural criteria, but also plays a significant role in bird migration. The sandy peninsula was created through natural processes and human activity. The terrain consists of some of the highest sand dunes in Europe. Damage to forest cover 250 years ago caused the sand dunes to become active, burying roads, villages and forest. Restoration is possible by reforestation and covering the dunes with plants.

There are three villages within the active dune area with a small permanent population. During the summer season the population more than doubles when the number of tourists visiting the area is taken into account. To control the impact of visitors, numbers are limited. Informing the visitors and residents about the fragility of the dune system was essential. To do this a series of pedestrian trails, a museum and an information centre were established.

Local people, particularly the unemployed, have been trained as guides and to organize a range of youth and visitor activities. Both visitors and residents have been involved in projects to restore the dunes. Through their involvement in the environmental volunteer programmes, residents and visitors have developed a deeper understanding of the interrelationship between people and nature and the need for protection.

Source: adapted from Elcome and Baines (1999)

Case Study **10.10**

Communication plan: Southern region of New South Wales, Australia

The New South Wales (NSW) Parks and Wildlife Division (previously the National Parks and Wildlife Service) needed to address a number of problems in the southern part of NSW during the late 1980s and early 1990s. These issues included:

- poor information services for visitors;
- limited responses to neighbours, stakeholders and the local community about what was happening within protected areas;
- inability to deal with a range of negative media articles; and
- few 'good news' stories.

The resulting community relations/communications plan (reviewed and updated annually) produced the following actions:

- a five-year investment in high-quality visitor information displays at important destinations throughout the region;
- a complete upgrading of all visitor information brochures;
- a complete upgrading of the agency's high-quality protected area destination marketing posters;
- employment of a professional media officer;
- training for all senior staff and media contact staff in media interview techniques;
- developing a database of neighbours;
- producing a newsletter for neighbours;
- systematic release of positive press articles;
- targeting areas of 'anti-park opinion' with regular talkback radio features about 'what was happening';
- developing cooperative visitor information projects (such as visitor touring maps) with local tourism organizations;
- providing immediate responses to negative press stories, including deploying spokespersons to major events that have the chance of becoming negative;
- proactive engagement of the media in positive conservation stories;
- familiarization tours (by bus) for prominent locals and the media; and
- open days, openings and other media launches.

The outcome was very positive for the NSW Parks and Wildlife Division and the community.

- physical and psychological health;
- material well-being and welfare;
- traditions, lifestyles and institutions; and
- interpersonal relationships (Furze et al, 1996).

Surveys and questionnaires. Agencies often use surveys and questionnaires to understand visitor activity, attitudes, preferences, characteristics and so on. Methods are derived from the long history of survey research in the social sciences, as well as from modern market research techniques. The basic steps in developing a survey are as follows:

1   *Identify the information required.*
2   *Sampling.* Specify the number of people to be contacted (sample size) and the process for selecting them (for example, random selection from a population stratified into groups).
3   *Choose the type of survey.* Surveys can be conducted on a group or on a one-to-one basis. They can be done in person, by mail or over the phone. They can involve in-depth interviews or responses to multiple-choice questions. They can be administered by the researcher or self-administered by the respondent.
4   *Design the survey instrument.* The instrument itself can be in the form of a booklet for a mail survey, or a script for a telephone or personal interview. Visual material such as maps and photographs may be required. Questions can be open ended and qualitative ('How...?'), or closed ended and quantitative ('How many...?'). Focus groups of stakeholders are often used to help refine the survey instrument and to make sure that respondents will answer the questions in the terms intended.
5   *Pre-test.* Pre-tests are trial runs of the survey, using a small group of respondents. Even after extensive use of focus groups, surveys can contain errors or problems that can be sorted out at this stage. It is important to ensure that the 'delivery' and administration procedures will be efficient and effective.
6   *Data analysis and interpretation.* Analysis and interpretation of quantitative data typically requires the use of statistical techniques. Statistical packages also exist for the analysis of qualitative responses, and these usually involve

identifying key phrases or detecting underlying meanings and themes.

Rapid rural appraisal. Rapid rural appraisal is a technique used to gain a quick, yet effective, understanding of the social, economic and political processes in any community. Typically, a team of two or three researchers spends a week in a community, gathering a range of different data, including:

- secondary data review – a review of published and unpublished data;
- direct observation – personal visits and observations aided by an observational checklist;
- key indicators – shortcuts to insights about community social conditions and change;
- semi-structured interviews – interviews that follow a set of points that permit probing and allow the interviewer to follow up on unexpected responses, without the requirement that all of the checklist points must be covered in any one interview; and
- key informants – identifying those best able to give information on particular topics or to give special points of view.

Rapid rural appraisal is becoming much more widespread with the increasing demand for protected area managers to work with their local community.

Community assessment. Community assessment can be a valuable tool for improving the focus and effectiveness of interaction and communication with the local community. Such an assessment looks at several issues:

- *Community history.* What historic events and experiences may affect their perceptions of the protected area and of conservation?
- *Social and political climate and the dynamics of decision-making.* Begin by identifying formal and informal community leaders. These are the people who act as spokespersons or to whom others look for advice. Consider the relationships among community members and groups – are they all included in the political process and how do they interact? Do not neglect more formal channels of

communication, such as committees and other organizational networks.

- *Channels of communication and preferred forms of interaction.* This involves examining and ranking the available media or channels of communication: local newspapers, radio, leaflet drops, public meetings and so on (Forrest and Mays, 1997).

Good communication

Communication involves putting forward a particular concept. This can be difficult if the parties involved have opposing ideals or are not familiar with the terminology. For example, there is no value in using scientific terms in a forum where most people find these terms incomprehensible. Being able to phrase your message so that the audience understands is a valuable skill. Communication is a two-way process in which listening is at least as important as speaking. Learning to listen is the first step to effective communication.

Listen first

Listening is a significant part of communication and is crucial to understanding the perspective from which the other side is approaching an issue. Listening to learn what others know, think, believe and do provides a background from which to frame your speaking. It allows you access into their world. Whether speaking to one person or a group of a thousand, creating a relationship with them makes a huge difference to the way in which your message is heard. Being genuinely interested in their experiences is the most effective way of creating that relationship.

Identify stakeholders

Managers often consult the public when making decisions with a wide impact. To ensure that the process is efficient and fair, they must carefully consider who should be involved: is it some local matter relevant to park neighbours who share a risk from fire, or is it a conservation matter of national concern? The people who are to be consulted are often referred to as 'stakeholders'.

Stakeholders are those people affected by the protected area or who have an interest in participating. They include people living in and around the protected area, businesses such as tourism operators, service providers, all levels of government and NGOs. Some stakeholders are also rights holders in that they have particular historic or legal property or resource rights, and/or assert claims based on human rights. A baseline of stakeholders' attitudes, knowledge and practices should be established at the outset. Developing a participatory approach with stakeholders empowers them to collaborate in protective area management. Substantive and secondary target groups need to be identified, such as media professionals or celebrities. These are people who create an enabling environment or opinion leaders who promote the objectives of protected area management.

Stakeholders may approach the agency voluntarily; but managers should attempt as comprehensive an outreach programme as possible. This may include contacting major groups, placing notices in the mass media or on-line, mail-outs to local people, and visiting neighbours and local institutions. Sometimes a core set of stakeholders may already exist in the form of a regional joint committee that has been formed on a previous occasion.

Design for specific audiences

A common agenda for protected areas, at an international, regional and national level, is needed to establish priorities. The content needs to be consistent; but the context has to be tailored to suit the audience. In order to change attitudes, one needs to shift the perception of the listener on three levels: brain (intellectual understanding), heart (emotional affinity) and instinct or gut level (where the new attitude becomes 'right' and motivates action). The communication medium needs to be appropriate to the target audience. Find out to which medium the audience attaches the most respect and use it. Use means of delivery that are appropriate, credible and enjoyable to that audience. Table 10.3 provides a list of possible communication methods to be used for different audiences.

Interpersonal communication

Interpersonal (face-to-face) communication is known to be the most effective form of communication (IUCN-CEC, 2003). This is because it provides direct dialogue and the opportunity to

Table 10.3 Communicating with local communities

Method	Approach
Face to face	Informal contact involving listening and talking to people, especially locals, is simply the best way to communicate about a local area and its protected area. This could happen informally at the local market, in the town or village, in a protected area or during social functions. Getting to know and listening to as many neighbours and occupants of a protected area as possible is an advantage. Joining and participating in local community groups is also an advantage.
	Formal meetings on a range of protected area–local community-related issues provide multiple opportunities to listen and to discuss all aspects of management. The results of the discussions usually need to be made available to a wider audience, and a newsletter, a web-based report or an article in a local newspaper are methods that can be used.
Telephoning	While not as personal, contact by telephone still provides a human touch to communication and is a very useful way of discussing issues that need to be dealt with rapidly. It can be used to provide briefings to key local people on events affecting the protected area, or to listen and learn about new events affecting local communities.
Meeting with leaders of the community	Constant face-to-face formal and informal meetings with leaders representing different parts of the community are critical. They provide opportunities to listen and obtain feedback about the protected area and its management.
Meeting with local experts and user groups	Advisory group meetings, whether formal or *ad hoc* for a particular issue, provide excellent feedback about local issues and an opportunity for local experts to provide input to protected area management. This is also another mechanism for communicating about what is happening in a protected area.
Meeting with marginalized groups and individuals	Women, landless people or other marginalized sections of a community/society may not speak in the midst of mixed groups where more powerful sections are also present. It is useful to have separate sessions with such people.
Meeting with leaders of other organizations	Other government or private organizations may have accountabilities within a protected area. They may deal with incidents (such as an army or a police force), they may build roads, respond to fires, install and service utilities, provide accommodation and recreation services, or make planning decisions. These operations within a protected area can impose threats. Working with these organizations and their leaders can help to prevent impacts.
Meeting with local politicians	Regular briefing meetings with local politicians provide an opportunity to ensure that they are up to date with what is happening in the protected area. In addition, they can be a means by which local issues of concern are identified and discussed.
Official events	Publicity associated with official openings, events, the launch of new products or other reasons provides an official platform for politicians and guarantees media coverage. This media exposure profiles positive happenings within a protected area.
Newsletter	Low-cost, short, regular and reliable newsletters circulating to local communities can be a very useful tool for advising locals of the very latest happenings within a protected area.
Temporary signs	People are always interested in what works are being carried out within protected areas. It is easy to provide a temporary sign explaining what projects are being undertaken, why they are happening, when they are expected to be completed and other information. Handwritten signs on weather-proof plasticized paper mounted on a temporary stake is all that is needed; but temporary typed signs are just as easy. It does not need to be elaborate to be effective.

Table 10.3 Continued

Method	Approach
Print media: newspapers	Local newspapers are always looking for good stories. Press releases provided regularly by managers about events and good stories within a protected area ensure that information is transferred to many locals. Regular news columns are even better if they can be maintained.
Print media: magazines	Feature articles within prominent magazines may be achieved by special invitations and exclusive access to 'newsworthy stories' or by other means. They can be a valuable way of achieving a positive profile for protected areas at a regional or national level.
Brochures and maps	Brochures and maps about protected areas cover a range of topics and may be generated as an official response to a controversial issue. They are also produced to help visitors achieve access to protected areas. Practical, helpful tourist brochures provide a real service to local businesses and the tourism industry.
Posters	Special posters of superb natural phenomena within protected areas can provide compelling and memorable images, and may become the 'unofficial' symbols of a particular protected area. Appropriately framed, they can become gifts for local organizations or for important events.
Electronic media: radio	Regular radio interviews are a useful means of getting the message across to local communities. Often, a standard time slot is achieved for feedback and stories about protected areas. Radio as a medium also provides an immediate opportunity to respond to controversial 'misinformation' about issues.
Electronic media: television	Television news interviews can be positive and can also be associated with controversial issues. They provide an opportunity for the views of a protected area manager to be widely known. Special media skills are usually needed and some protected area organizations employ specially trained staff for such roles.
Electronic media: videos, DVDs and CDs	Some protected area managers have collaboratively generated short films about the special values of a protected area. These films are typically launched on television. They are then made available on video, DVD or CD formats and can be sold commercially. The footage can also be used for tourism promotion films to assist local communities.
Computers: emails	Emails can be a powerful way of responding immediately to issues if local communities have access to computers. They are, however, an impersonal approach and are no substitute for face-to-face contact.
Computers: websites	Websites that are constantly updated can be a powerful tool for protected area managers. They play a critical role in incidents (such as fires), when immediate updates can keep local communities informed of what is happening.
Public communication campaigns	Public communication campaigns may be needed to deal with important issues where major changes are proposed. Typically, they are planned and designed to ensure that the community is well informed about the proposed change, the reasons for change, the benefits resulting and any negative aspects. Usually, such campaigns are underpinned by an expert report and may be supported by briefing notes, media presentations, advertisements and public meetings.
Public hearings	Open-forum meetings that are announced well in advance and that are organized where most convenient for local people are needed to bring in the voices of otherwise left-out groups. Such forums also provide people with an opportunity to question each other, to question official agencies and to gain further information relevant to them.
Cultural and social events	Cultural or social occasions can be a powerful means of eliciting participation, and of exchanging information and experiences in a non-threatening, non-formal manner. These could include festivals, rallies, art performances and so on, organized in a manner that links to conservation and related issues.

Table 10.3 Continued

Method	Approach
Familiarization and briefing meetings	Annual (or frequent) familiarization tours may be conducted by protected area staff. Typically, they target local tourism information officers, media representatives, policy advisers to politicians and other key people. The tours usually include an expert guide and travel to key destinations in protected areas. Background information about protected areas, their benefits and how they are managed are provided.
Workshops, conferences, seminars and presentations	Workshops, conferences, presentations and seminars may be conducted regularly about protected areas. They may involve visiting or local experts and may deal with details of the history, social importance, culture, natural heritage and management of protected areas. Involvement of locals in such events helps to convey the importance of protected areas.
Education centres	Many protected areas provide the support of education centres for visiting school groups. These centres may be very simple, such as a shelter or an outdoor classroom with rudimentary seating. They may also be more complex, such as visitor centres.

address concerns, allows for new ideas to emerge, and can generate agreement and ownership. It is a slow process because it only reaches a small number of people at one time. However, regular face-to-face communication with key people may be more beneficial to meeting your management objectives than public meetings or events to reach the masses.

Communication is a process

Communication is an ongoing process, not a product. For as long as people are involved in managing aspects of the protected area, a communication strategy will be necessary. It is essential that a communication budget is developed for all programmes and agencies. Monitoring and evaluation indicators should be built into the communication process from the start so that communication impact can be assessed (IUCN–CEC, 2003).

Working with print and electronic media

Staff can establish an effective working relationship with local media people, and can assist by providing ideas for stories and by helping them to meet tight media deadlines. They can also provide supporting factual information, photos and other aids and props. One tip in working with the media is that there is never a situation where comments can safely be made 'off the record' and

the camera is 'always rolling' – never assume that filming has stopped at the end of the formal questions. The strongest advice we can offer is to receive professional training before dealing with the media. Adversarial interviews are common and staff need to be adequately prepared. The following tips have been adapted from Kennedy (1999) and Dawson and Cohen (1999).

The interview:

- It is your interview.
- Pick the right location, preferably outside.
- Dress sensibly. Look professional. Create the image that suits the message and the audience.
- Prepare 'A' points (points that you will make at any possible opportunity during the interview).
- Prepare 'B' points (points that you may need to respond to if the journalist raises them, but not otherwise).
- Prepare 'C' points (points that you need to be aware of, but will not respond to or only very briefly).
- Do a practice run.
- 'Add value' to everything you say.
- Turn all negatives into positives.
- Beware of making admissions that may be used out of context.
- Say 'no' nicely – sometimes it is not possible to answer a question.

Simple low-cost information sign, Minnamurra Rainforest, Budderoo National Park, New South Wales, Australia

Source: Graeme L. Worboys

- Never repeat a negative phrase used by the interviewer.
- Refocus questions by choosing key words from the question.
- Steer the interview your way – be concise; do not use jargon.
- Control the interview by returning to your 'A' points.
- Silence the interjecting interviewer.
- Summarize the 'A' points.

Fact sheets. These information sheets can be handed out at an interview along with a press release. They make it easier for the interviewer. Commonly, for adversarial interviews, they address the key issues and provide statistics and other evidence supporting your agency's position. These sheets often take the sting out of what may otherwise be a threatening news story and can even change the direction of an interview. For interviews where the agency is taking the initiative, fact sheets are essential allies.

Media releases. These are usually brief. They should carry that day's date and be on official letterhead, with a catchy headline. The lead para-

Aboriginal rangers briefing visitors, Lake Mungo National Park, New South Wales, Australia

Source: Graeme L. Worboys

graph encapsulates the newsworthy issue. The media release should cover the basic questions of who, what, when, where, how and why. The release should include quotes and factual information, be simple and be interesting. It should list a person and a phone number to contact for further information. Note that journalists are trained to ignore media releases with the previous day's date and also that a release may be ignored if it arrives too late in the day.

Recognizing items of interest to the media. Too often very interesting stories are not told because staff have seen them as un-newsworthy or 'more of the same' in the daily routine. Journalists might have a different view. They see news value in stories that are linked to:

- proximity – 'the fire was 3km from town …';
- prominence – 'the minister said today …';
- timeliness – 'reports just to hand reveal …';
- impact – 'over 70 whales have stranded …';
- extremes – the longest, the biggest, the shortest, the oldest; and
- conflict – 'the premier today attacked the agency over …'.

Education

We continue to learn throughout our lifetime. Education is not only about institutions, it includes any activity in which learning takes place. It occurs in formal and informal settings. In the communication process, learning occurs whenever you are listening. Whenever you are required to think or question what you take for granted, education is occurring. Environmental education is teaching about, and for the benefit of, the environment. Principles for environmental education are outlined in Box 10.3.

Raising awareness

Environmental education begins by raising awareness. It is about establishing and confirming the personal relevance of environmental issues. Useful guides for teaching environmental protection include:

- respect for and appreciation of the interdependence of all natural biotic and abiotic forms;

- recognition of the resilience, fragility and beauty of the natural environment;
- recognition that the Earth has finite resources upon which we depend;
- understanding of the direct dependence of many indigenous peoples and local communities on natural ecosystems and biodiversity; and
- acknowledgement that human ingenuity and creativity has a role in ensuring human and non-human survival, and in identifying appropriate strategies for sustainability.

Educating to alter values challenges current practices and beliefs and has a controversial aspect. One approach is to have people focus on their personal use of resources and to understand the consequences of their actions. Presenting different ways of managing resources is also important. Increasing the importance and value of individual responsibility and action can cause people to change their behaviour.

Developing knowledge and skills

Acquiring relevant knowledge and skills is considered the basis of conventional education. The knowledge and skills required to participate in environmental education are wide ranging and not confined to a particular discipline. In order to gain a rounded understanding of environmental concerns, it is necessary to integrate disciplines such as biophysical sciences, social science, politics, law, economics, governance, communication and education. Protected area managers are well placed to improve understanding of local and global biodiversity, threats to the natural and cultural heritage, the importance and benefits of conservation and protected areas, and individual roles and responsibilities for conservation.

Altering attitudes does not automatically lead to action consistent with the change of attitude. There has to be a personal incentive or disincentive to change behaviour. In the past, protected area managers have used the 'fines and fences' model to control behaviour. There is now a shift to have people take on responsibility and ownership of the protected area and to contribute to its management. Training local people as educators provides employment opportunities and rein-

---

Box 10.3 Environmental education principles

The 1977 Tbilisi Conference in Georgia, the USSR, was the world's first intergovernmental conference on environmental education. Convened by the United Nations Education, Scientific and Cultural Organization (UNESCO) and the United Nations Environment Programme (UNEP), the conference was attended by 265 delegates and 65 representatives and observers. It followed soon after the launch of UNEP and is recognized as having spearheaded clarification on the nature of environmental education.

The conference resulted in a declaration about the importance of environmental education at all levels and for all age groups. The following guiding principles for environmental education were endorsed. Environmental education should:

- consider the environment in its natural, built, technological and social capacity;
- be a lifelong educational process that continues at all levels of education;
- be interdisciplinary in its approach;
- examine major environmental issues to give students an insight into other geographical areas;
- promote the value and necessity for cooperation at a local and international level to solve environmental problems;
- consider environmental aspects in development and growth;
- enable learners to plan their own learning experiences; and
- relate environmental sensitivity, especially to the learners' own community at a young age.

Source: adapted from EEAW (2004)

---

forces the values of the protected area in the local communities (see Case Study 10.11).

Disseminating information

There are various methods of disseminating information to staff, interest groups and government officials, as well as to the general community. Information can be distributed to the community via traditional means, such as story telling and singing; holding public meetings; distributing newsletters; fliers sent in the mail; posting information on a notice board or website; through fact sheets; and so on. The internet provides a fast and effective way of disseminating up-to-date information to the wider community. Fact sheets may take on a number of roles, instructing visitors about developments in a protected area, providing guidelines on behaviour within the area, or informing visitors about the local wildlife or natural features. On-site fact sheets may complement interpretation facilities, including visitor centres, signage and guides. Information can be visual as well as textual and, hence, can include physical displays or images. Protected area managers might make use of the media – print,

radio or television – in order to communicate information to the general public, particularly if there are risk warnings regarding protected areas or if specific events are planned.

Management organizations often have specific reporting requirements such as annual reports, project or programme reconciliations, and state of the environment or state of the park reports. These reports are an effective way of informing the general public and partner organizations about the environmental, cultural and financial achievements of the protected area, and provide a way of checking accountability. An accumulation of internal organization reports on topics such as the status of financial and staffing records, the effectiveness of management programmes, visitation levels, the conservation status of species, and performance against other benchmarking criteria may go towards compiling an annual report.

Visitor centres are effective places to present information about the area, to raise awareness about natural and cultural heritage, and to educate people about the values and benefits of the park, as well as their responsibilities as visitors.

Case Study 10.11

Environmental education in Kruger National Park, South Africa

My Acre of Africa is a unique conservation and environmental education initiative conceived in 2001 and led by Nelson Mandela as patron in chief. Their mission is to:

Enhance the long-term sustainability of Southern Africa's wildlife and wild lands ... by raising money to create a significant endowment fund that will supplement seriously depleted conservation budgets – and also, by educating our children about the importance of their natural heritage.

The Kids in Kruger project is part of the education programme. It brings school children from grades four to seven, from ten communities around the local region, to Kruger National Park on educational day trips. The trips integrate history, culture, tourism and the environment. The visits provide the children with access to the national park and educate them about the importance and relevance of this asset to their own lives.

The vision of My Acre of Africa is to inspire people to protect the natural environment and to nurture a generation of individuals who understand the importance of environmental sustainability. Central to this is ensuring that local communities become active stakeholders in, and beneficiaries of, the activities taking place in national parks. The Kids in Kruger project has been carefully structured to ensure that the maximum number of economic opportunities is provided to entrepreneurs from local communities. The project manager is from a local community. Guides and rangers are appointed from the local communities. The shirts supplied to each child are manufactured locally. Meals provided on the day trips are sourced locally.

As at the end of 2003, 1000 children from six schools have participated in Kids in Kruger. It is hoped that ambassadors selected from these schools will start eco-clubs at their schools, and initiate environmental understanding and appreciation programmes within their communities.

Source: adapted from My Acre of Africa (2004)

Management principles

1   Effective stewardship requires the best available information on all aspects of protected areas and their surrounding environments, including natural heritage, cultural heritage, economic and social aspects, indigenous and local community traditions and resource uses, and visitor values, attitudes and behaviour. It is also critical to understand the limitations of such data.

2   Access to and the ability to use the most relevant, recent and cutting-edge information, including scientific, traditional and community knowledge, is essential to achieve management objectives.

3   A systematic approach to collecting, organizing, storing, accessing and analysing data is fundamental to delivering useful information. Recent advances, such as GIS and electronic databases, are important tools.

4   Research is a core function of protected area

management and should be facilitated by protected area organizations. Research priorities should be clearly documented. Research partnerships should be developed with universities, science organizations and other research providers.

5   Monitoring (including the appropriate selection of indicators and participation of local people) provides critical information for evaluating progress, understanding the consequences of management actions and establishing the basis for adaptive management.

6   Processes should be in place to ensure that information is easily accessible to all interested parties. It needs to be recognized that those accessing the data have different levels of skill and access; hence, the information needs to be provided in different formats and often in different languages.

7   Agencies should ensure that staff have the capability to access, understand, interpret and

apply information, made available from research, monitoring and other sources.

8 Effective protected area management can only occur with the support of the community. Human values will always drive management goals.

9 The needs and desires of people must be considered from the outset and throughout the management process.

10 Agencies, in working with the community to achieve conservation outcomes, must understand the community and be part of it.

11 To communicate effectively, agencies need to understand the community's perceptions, needs, attitudes, values and behaviour.

Further reading

Hamu D., Auchincloss, E. and Goldstein W. (eds) (2004) *Communicating Protected Areas. Commission on Education and Communication*, IUCN, Gland and Cambridge

Reynold, J. H. (ed) (1998) *WCMC Handbooks on Biodiversity Information Management*, Volumes 1–7, Commonwealth Secretariat, London

Websites

World conservation monitoring centre: www.unep-wcmc.org/

World database on protected areas: sea.unep-wcmc.org/wdpa

PALNet Protected areas learning network: www.parksnet.org

IUCN Commission on Education and Communication: www.iucn.org/themes/cec

WWF education: www.panda.org/news_facts/education/index.cfm

11

Management Planning

Michael Lockwood

Planning is something most of us do in one form or another every day. It is also a specialized skill practised by corporate managers, town planners and natural resource managers. In essence, planning is concerned with the future, particularly with future courses of action. Planning is a process for determining 'what should be' (usually defined by a series of objectives) and for selecting actions that can help to achieve these objectives. Other definitions of planning include:

> *Planning is intervention with an intention to alter the existing course of events (Campbell and Fainstein, 2003).*

> *Planning is the generic activity of purposeful anticipation of, and provision for, the future (Selman, 2000).*

Planning can occur at various geographic scales. *Land-use planning* is the process of deciding in a broad sense which areas of land and sea will be used for what purpose, including which areas will be designated as protected areas (see Chapter 8). This may be undertaken at a national, provincial or more limited scale. *Area management planning* is concerned with how to manage these areas once their land-use designation has been determined. A management plan for a national park is an example of an area management plan.

Site planning deals with design details associated with, for example, the development of a visitor facility. A protected area management plan might recommend the establishment of a camping area of a certain standard in a particular location to provide for a specified number of people. A separate and subsidiary site plan will specify the location and design of access, barriers, campsites, toilets and so on within the camping area. *Operational plans* or works programmes then detail the disposition of staff and resources at particular times to carry out specific activities. *Functional planning* focuses on a particular issue – for example, fire management or conserving a significant species. *Organizational planning* is concerned with the purpose, structure and procedures of a management agency. Within an organization responsible for managing natural areas there may be several levels and types of policy and planning documents. A typical hierarchical relationship between such plans and policy instruments is shown in Figure 11.1. If an organization is working well, all of these plans and policies should be coordinated and integrated. For example, the objectives of a plan for an individual protected area should relate to, and be consistent with, a plan at a higher level, such as a regional, tactical or corporate plan. A corporate plan identifies an organization's collective goals, objectives, policies and activities, and provides a context and guidelines for area management and functional plans.

There are many other types of planning and related activities associated with establishing and managing protected areas. Examples include *impact assessment, economic planning, financial planning, business planning* (see Chapter 12), *species recovery planning* (see Chapter 16) and *incident planning* (see Chapter 18). It is important that

Figure 11.1 An illustrative planning hierarchy

Source: adapted from ANZECC (2000)

management plans are well integrated with such plans. The information systems approach described in Case Study 10.6 in Chapter 10 provides a model for how this might be done.

This chapter concentrates on area management planning, with a particular emphasis on government-designated protected areas. For example, the approaches described in the following section on 'Approaches to planning' largely pertain to formal government-designated protected areas and may not be as relevant to community conserved areas (CCAs), where planning is not so structured, but is a part of day-to-day economic and social life. Many indigenous and some local communities have their own planning systems, often based on cultural and ethical criteria, as well as priorities related to agriculture, forestry, fisheries and other resource-use regimes. This chapter does not directly address these systems.

There are several reasons why one needs to plan for the management of protected areas. In general, planning can help to conserve a resource while providing for its appropriate use. More specific reasons for embarking on a planning project include:

- meeting global responsibilities under such agreements as the Convention on Biological Diversity (CBD);

- meeting statutory obligations – in some countries legislation requires management plans to be prepared for reserved areas;
- directing management towards achieving the goals established in legislation or elsewhere;
- enabling adaptive management – that is, providing a framework so that managers can take advantage of new knowledge and respond to altered circumstances;
- refining broad goals into specific, achievable objectives;
- facilitating the making of sound decisions;
- facilitating the resolution of conflicts over resource management;
- aiding communication between different levels within a hierarchical organization – for example, between top-level staff and front-line staff such as rangers who are often responsible for on-ground implementation of actions;
- providing continuity of management despite staff changes;
- making explicit decisions and the means by which they were arrived at – important components of management that might otherwise remain hidden;
- giving all relevant groups and persons, including indigenous peoples and local communities, government agencies and other interested parties, an opportunity to take part in decisions; and
- providing for public accountability.

In my view, these reasons justify managers placing a high priority on achieving high-quality planning. This chapter describes the different ways in which a planner might approach his or her task, the process that might develop from the chosen approach, and an account of a typical area planning project. It concludes by identifying principles for high-quality planning.

Approaches to planning

Before looking at the specifics of land-use and management planning, it is important to consider how one might, in theory, approach a planning problem. Most planning practitioners disregard theory: 'There has always been a gap between what academics think planners should do, and what planners actually do' (Sorensen and Auster, 1999).

Why, then, should we study planning theory? Although in their day-to-day work many planners rely on professional experience, this cumulative professional knowledge can be understood as assimilated theory. Even without conscious adoption, theory is latent in planning practice, and is implicitly used to guide and establish frameworks for this practice. Theory allows us to see the assumptions and value judgements that underpin planning practice. Good theorizing can motivate, define, contextualize, drive forward and inform practice (Campbell and Fainstein, 2003). Theory also provides a means for practitioners to understand planning processes in a way that is outside experience, intuition or common sense.

Historically, professional planning has been dominated by planners working in urban contexts. Much of the theory and practice of planning has been, and continues to be, heavily influenced by this heritage. Since the 1970s, planning has also emerged as an important activity for non-urban land and sea uses, such as protected areas, landscape-scale regions such as watersheds, and natural resources such as forests, fisheries and water. In contrast with urban planning, these more 'natural' and 'rural' areas of planning practice initially were heavily influenced by the biophysical problems they sought to address, principally protection of biodiversity and prevention of resource depletion. Planners working to address such issues were typically trained in the natural and physical sciences, and so they tended to adopt planning practices and processes that were consistent with their systematic scientific understandings.

Early environmental planning focused on natural systems and the protection of natural values, working in a 'top-down' fashion. Top-down planning is initiated and conducted by planners or a small group of 'experts', such that there is little or no opportunity for staff at other levels of the organization, or for other stakeholders, to exert an influence on its outcomes. In contrast, 'bottom-up' planning includes extensive stakeholder and non-planning staff involvement in planning processes. It is now recognized that planners need to take a more 'bottom-up' approach that considers:

- integration of social, cultural, economic and natural concerns;
- development of social and cultural values, as well as maintenance of natural values;
- sharing or devolution of decision-making power;
- interdependence of conservation and development; and
- managing ecosystems in a human context (Maltby, 1997; Mercer, 2000; Selman, 2000).

Over the last 40 years or so, protected area management planning in countries such as Australia and Canada has gone through several phases. Plans during the 1970s and early 1980s tended to be dominated by extensive inventories of natural and cultural resources. They were developed with little community participation, and the data collection effort tended to be at the expense of strategic considerations and substantive management decisions. In the mid 1980s until the early 1990s, plans were more focused on specific management objectives and actions, often framed by a zoning scheme. Community participation also became an important component of planning processes. While these plans provided more management guidance than the earlier plans, they often quickly became out of date and were generally written with little regard to available management resources. They tended to be 'wish lists' rather than realistic management prescriptions. Such rigidity and implementation difficulties meant that they often suffered from the 'sitting on the shelf' syndrome and consequently did little to guide day-to-day management.

As a reaction against these failings, and under the influence of wider trends such as the increasing popularity of strategic planning derived from business management, plans from the mid 1990s were typically much leaner documents. They articulated a strategic direction, but often did not detail specific outcomes or management decisions. Such plans were politically expedient in that in the absence of any performance measures, agencies could not be held to account. Their lack of specificity meant that they also provided little guidance for day-to-day management. Of course, specific decisions were still needed – these tended to be made in within-agency operational planning processes that took place out of the public gaze.

We are now entering an era where plans are attempting to address these various limitations. State-of-the-art planning now seeks to produce relatively short strategic documents that nonetheless contain a realistic set of objectives to enable performance evaluation, as well as actions that, in the immediate future, are considered the best options to meet the objectives. Ideally, the plans are also flexible enough to allow modification of actions on the basis of experience and new information, as well as some adjustment of objectives and performance measures – that is, they facilitate adaptive management. In addition, the planning process itself is now required to be much more participatory – in particular, involving indigenous peoples and local communities living in and around the protected areas.

Area management planning inevitably involves many stakeholders, often with widely diverging values and opinions. This raises a number of questions that planners need to address when designing their planning project:

- How should people be organized to facilitate the planning process?
- Who should have the power to make decisions?
- What knowledge and information should be used?
- What planning methods or procedures should be used?
- Who should decide what the planning objectives should be?
- What criteria should be used to select the best courses of action?

The answers to these will largely depend upon the approach adopted by the people initiating the planning activity, as well as the governance arrangements that apply to the protected area (see Chapter 5). Other influences on the approaches that are adopted include agency traditions, the prevailing mode of public policy development, institutional structures, and the intellectual traditions most influencing those people directing the planning process. This section considers four ways of approaching a planning project: rational

comprehensive, strategic, adaptive and participatory planning. In general, planning processes can be described in terms of mixtures of these approaches.

Rational comprehensive planning

So called 'rational comprehensive planning' is a top-down approach that attempts an objective and exhaustive inventory of current conditions, analyses these conditions, develops possible solutions to issues based on these descriptions and analysis, and selects a preferred solution according to a set of measurable criteria (Briassoulis, 1989). For example, as part of a management planning project for a wetland protected area threatened by altered flow regimes, the following process might be adopted under a rational comprehensive approach:

- Identify the relationship between current flow regimes and species requirements.
- Determine the water requirements for each species.
- Model the outcomes of various management options for meeting these requirements.
- Select the option that is predicted to generate the best outcome.

This simplified example illustrates some of the key characteristics of rational comprehensive planning. It is a scientific and technically demanding approach, in which experts assume a key role. It relies on high-quality data, and often makes use of mathematical models.

Such formality and rigour are both a strength and a weakness. On the strength side, rational comprehensive planning should produce decisions that can be clearly explained and justified. Debate about the decisions tends to focus on technical issues such as the reliability of the data used or the validity of the models used to process the data. The often inefficient processes of public decision-making can be avoided, and political bias minimized. However, the weaknesses of the rational comprehensive approach are that it is inflexible and is disposed to ignoring social and political factors. The rational comprehensive approach to planning tends to give rise to a static planning process, in which a particular set of objectives is established and a number of decisions made that will apply for some specified period of time. Uncertainty and risk are difficult to accommodate. The role of other stakeholders in the decision-making process tends to be minimal. The recommendations from a rational comprehensive process may therefore not reflect community values or aspirations, and may ignore political and institutional limitations.

Strategic planning

David (2001) described strategic management as the art and science of formulating, implementing and evaluating decisions that enable an organization to achieve its objectives. Strategic planning has been used to describe a number of different planning styles. However, there are some common elements that constitute the core of strategic planning processes:

1   Develop a vision and mission. A vision statement answers the question: 'What do we want to become?' A mission statement is an enduring expression of purpose that addresses the question: 'What is our purpose?'
2   Identify an organization's external opportunities and threats, and determine internal strengths and weaknesses. SWOT (strengths, weaknesses, opportunities and threats) analysis is a traditional technique used by planners as part of a strategic planning exercise. Depending upon the scope of the planning and the budget, such an analysis may be undertaken by consultants or as an in-house planning exercise. For the purposes of a SWOT analysis:
    •   A strength is an internal aspect that can improve an organization's competitive situation.
    •   A weakness is an internal aspect where the organization is potentially vulnerable to a competitor's strategic moves.
    •   An opportunity is an environmental condition that can significantly improve an organization's situation relative to that of competitors.
    •   A threat is an environmental condition that can significantly undermine an organization's competitive situation (Bartol et al, 1998).

Characteristics of a SWOT analysis include an assessment of an organization's environment and the factors that influence the ability of an organization to achieve its goals. Strategies are needed to take advantage of external opportunities and to avoid or reduce the impact of external threats. The process of researching and assimilating information on opportunities and threats is sometimes called environmental scanning or industry analysis. Internal strengths and weaknesses are an organization's controllable activities.

3   Establish objectives. Objectives are specific results that an organization seeks to achieve. They are essential for success because they state direction, aid evaluation, reveal priorities and provide a basis for effective planning, organizing, motivating and controlling activities. Objectives should be challenging, measurable, consistent, reasonable, clear and prioritized.
4   Generate alternative strategies and choose particular strategies to pursue. Strategies are the means by which long-term objectives will be achieved.

Benefits of taking a strategic approach to planning are that it:
•   identifies, prioritizes and exploits opportunities;
•   develops a shared vision;
•   provides a framework for coordination and control of actions;
•   minimizes effects of adverse conditions;
•   allows decisions to better support objectives;
•   provides a framework for internal communication;
•   integrates individual efforts within a total effort;
•   encourages forward thinking;
•   gives work a degree of discipline and formality;
•   empowers staff – involving, learning, educating, supporting, owning and enabling;
•   reduces resistance to change; and
•   enhances problem-prevention capabilities (Kaufman and Jacobs, 1996; Koteen, 1997; David, 2001; Hunger and Wheelan, 2001).

Adaptive planning

Adaptive planning treats management as an itera-tive process of review and revision, not as a series of fixed prescriptions to be implemented (as in the rational comprehensive approach). Management interventions are seen as a series of successive and continuous adaptations to variable conditions. The approach emphasizes flexibility, requires willing-ness to learn through experience, and may require sacrificing present or short-term gains for longer-term objectives (Briassoulis, 1989). The emphasis is on learning how the system works through management interventions that are both issue oriented and experimental (Dovers and Mobbs, 1997).

Some adaptive planning places considerable emphasis on the use of predictive models to guide actions. Where outcomes are not as expected, the models are modified to improve their predictive power. In this respect, adaptive planning has some similarities with the rational comprehensive approach. The essential difference is that adaptive planning is flexible and responsive to changing circumstances, whereas rational comprehensive planning tends to be rigid and prescriptive. Adaptive planning recognizes that there is often considerable uncertainty about the outcomes of any particular action. This uncertainty is built into plans, so that information about the actual results of actions is used to inform and, where necessary, modify management practices.

Adaptive planning can be understood as an essential component of an adaptive management process (see Figure 11.2). Adaptive management in its earlier forms concentrated on ecological modelling that aimed to put possible management interventions in terms of scientific hypotheses, capable of being tested. It was an attempt to combine the methods of scientific research with the practicalities and realities of management. More recently, the approach has been expanded to integrate social and institutional aspects with the ecological and managerial dimensions (Dovers, 1998). The main features of this expanded notion of adaptive planning are:

- recognition of the contribution that the natu-ral and social sciences can make to dealing with management problems;

- recognition of uncertainty, complexity and long time scales;
- acknowledgement that management interven-tions are essentially experimental, and while directed towards improving environmental and human conditions, also allow for testing and improving understanding and capabilities along the way; and
- design and maintenance of sophisticated mechanisms (institutions and processes) to allow feedback and communication between theory, policy and practice, and across different situations (Dovers, 1998).

It is a process of learning by experience. This means that mistakes may, and probably will, be made. It is not possible to predict accurately the precise outcome of any course of action – there are always too many variables involved and the interactions between the variables are too complex. A planner can develop models to help forecast and predict the future; but these predic-tions will only be as good as the information on which they are based and the model that processes this information. This means that planning will inevitably involve uncertainty. In this sense, a plan is not a blueprint. While one might reasonably expect a house constructed on the basis of a blue-print plan to be accurately represented by that plan, the same cannot be said for plans addressing the future of protected areas.

There is always the risk that a predicted result will not occur and that the consequences of a recommended action will not be those desired. A planner needs to recognize this fact, and include an awareness of uncertainty and risk into the planning process. This is particularly important for irreversible decisions. However, the difficulty of making decisions, especially when they are irre-versible in nature, should not be used as an excuse to avoid making a decision altogether. 'Non-deci-sions' also have consequences.

Effective stakeholder participation in the adaptive approach demands an ongoing and long-term involvement. Such extensive and open-ended commitment places considerable demands on all stakeholders – demands that may be impossible to meet. It is probable that the only stakeholders to maintain engagement with an adaptive process would be those with the most to gain (or lose). Stakeholders such as urban residents in regional centres and city-based environmental groups often find it difficult to make a meaningful contribution to such processes. Any approach that disadvantages certain stakeholders will pose problems of legitimacy and credibility for the outcomes.

Conventional plans tend to be inflexible and have limited ability to adapt to changing circumstances and a developing knowledge base. Although review processes are usually built into such processes, the opportunity for making major new management decisions is limited to specified review periods, usually held at three- to five-year intervals. This means that many of these management plans are perceived to become quickly out of date and tend to be ignored. Here, an adaptive process has an advantage. If the planning team has an ongoing responsibility for management planning, then the contact with the implementation staff will also, of necessity, be ongoing.

Participatory planning

The participatory and adaptive approaches are emerging as particularly influential components of modern natural resource planning and management (Dovers, 1997). Demands for greater community participation reflect concerns about the legitimacy and efficacy of modern systems of representative government. Perceptions of community participation vary, largely in terms of the extent to which the community exercises decision-making power, with notions of participation ranging from the provision of information through to local control of decision-making (Arnstein, 1969).

There are ethical and pragmatic reasons for involving the public in decision-making. Public participation is believed to legitimize planning outcomes; reduce citizen alienation; avoid conflict; give meaning to legislation; build support for agency programmes; tap into local knowledge; provide feedback on programme outcomes; contribute to community education; and enhance democratic processes by increasing government accountability (Creighton, 1981; Daneke, 1983; Lyden et al, 1990).

Considerable debate exists about two contrasting forms of government. The 'representative' form is where citizens provide legitimacy to a smaller set of representatives to take key decisions: this is necessarily more centralized. The 'participatory' form is where citizens are themselves involved in key decisions, implying a degree of decentralization.

The participatory approach has its philosophical and political roots in liberal–democratic notions of equality of persons and rights of the individual. If the principle of equality of persons is accepted, then the objectives and outcomes of protected area planning should reflect a synthesis of the interests of stakeholders and not relate to the interests of a single individual or subgroup of individuals. Stakeholder participation is a mechanism for improving the efficacy of representative democracy. Indeed, increased stakeholder involvement in decisions reflects a shift from a purely representative model of democracy to a participative democracy in which there is an expectation among citizens that they will not just be represented by elected officials, but actively and continually engage with the processes of policy development and implementation (Daneke, 1983).

If stakeholders are adequately represented in decision-making, and if decision-making processes are adopted that allow stakeholders to cooperate in an honest and open exchange of views, stakeholders can develop empathy for the positions of others, and it is possible for agreed positions to be reached that are accepted as fair to all parties (Kaplan and Kaplan, 1989; Landre and Knuth, 1993). Ostrom (1990) believed this 'social capital' would allow stakeholders to develop cooperative mechanisms to resolve common pool resource dilemmas as alternatives to reliance on market forces or a central authority.

So, involvement of a wide range of groups and individuals throughout the planning process has the following advantages:

- provides the planner with access to a range of information and advice that might otherwise be difficult to obtain;
- enables early identification of major issues and an ongoing check of any further issues that arise;

- generates more creative solutions to problems;
- reduces implementation failure;
- increases plan acceptance;
- manages competing interests and mediating conflict;
- enhances public ownership and commitment to solutions;
- supports the rights of citizens to be involved in decisions that affect them;
- increases government accountability; and
- articulates and represents the diversity of interests and values involved in a decision (Pimbert and Pretty, 1997; Curtis and Lockwood, 1998; Tuler and Webler, 1999; Wondolleck and Yaffee, 2000; Barham, 2001).

Disadvantages include:

- the time-consuming nature of a genuine public participation programme;
- the potentially high financial cost;
- the difficulty of obtaining constructive debate when interest groups have entrenched and opposing views; and
- the difficulty of accommodating conflicting interests under circumstances when only one view can prevail.

From approach to process

Planning is often connected with the word 'process'. This means that planning is not simply an event or an outcome. Planning is best seen as an interrelated sequence of stages. These stages are linked in a dynamic fashion – the interactions between them may occur in one or more directions and change over time. In addition, while there may be a clearly defined starting point to the process, it is often difficult to define an end point. Indeed, many planning practitioners emphasize the ongoing nature of planning, with the need to regularly review the success and relevance of both a particular plan and even the planning process itself.

The approach or mixture of approaches adopted by a planner will determine the particular stages undertaken in the planning process, as well as the relative importance given to each stage. Most of the approaches would only very rarely be found in their pure form in an actual planning project. More commonly, a project is made up of a combination of approaches. This section briefly describes how a management planning project might implement the adaptive approach, and introduces a mixed approach to preparing a protected area management plan.

Adaptive planning process

As noted above, adaptive planning treats management as an iterative process of review and revision. The approach requires willingness to learn through experience, with an emphasis on learning how the system works through management interventions that are both issue oriented and experimental. Adaptive management processes systematically test options and assumptions in order to learn and thereby improve outcomes. It is best applied to complex systems that are constantly and unpredictably changing, where full information is not available, and for which immediate action is required (Salafsky et al, 2001). One model for an adaptive management process is given in Figure 11.2 and two practical examples are given in Case studies 11.1 and 11.2.

Figure 11.2 shows that planning is the initiating phase in adaptive management, during which objectives are established and actions chosen to address these objectives. The actions are then carried out in the 'doing' phase. Results from the actions are subsequently evaluated and management effectiveness is determined in relation to the objectives. Learning that has occurred through the cycle is incorporated within the next and subsequent cycles so that, over time, management performance can be improved.

A mixed planning process

An outline of a planning process that incorporates rational, adaptive and participatory elements is given in Figure 11.3.

Note that the extent that each of the components indicated in Figure 11.3 are addressed will vary according to the significance and complexity of issues and the capacity of the governing organization to undertake planning. In this regard, it is useful to identify four broad levels of planning engagement: holistic, focused, constrained and nominal (see Table 11.1).

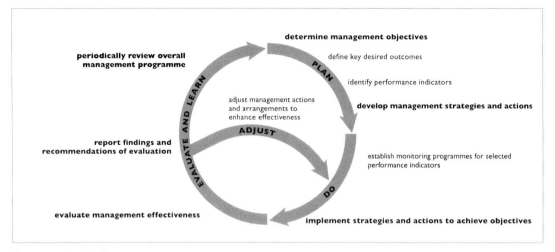

Figure 11.2 An adaptive management process

Source: Tasmania Parks and Wildlife Service (2004)

Case Study 11.1

Adaptive management in Canadian protected areas

The wolves of Algonquin Provincial Park are the largest protected population of the eastern wolf (*Canis lycaon*) in central Ontario, Canada. Algonquin Provincial Park is estimated to support a population of 150 to 175 individuals in 35 packs, from a total species population of approximately 2000 individuals.

During the early 1960s, studies showed that approximately 300 individuals used the park. Public education sessions regarding wolves were held in the park over summer, including the Public Wolf Howl, where rangers would imitate howls and the assembled visitors (up to 2500 people) would wait to see if the real wolves responded. During the late 1970s and early 1980s, the success rate at the Public Wolf Howl was low. Concerns were then raised about the long-term viability of the wolf population, so further studies were undertaken.

Several factors were found to have affected the population of wolves in Algonquin Provincial Park. Changes in habitat have altered the overall numbers and seasonal distribution of prey. More significantly, trapping and hunting of wolves when they leave the park in winter to find food were shown to be a major cause of wolf mortality, and overall mortality was higher than recruitment. A scientific study estimated that in order to ensure sustainability of the population, human-caused mortality needed to be reduced by about 10 to 15 per cent of the population.

An active adaptive management approach was proposed that involved a large-scale experiment manipulating hunting and trapping in different zones around Algonquin Provincial Park over a six-year period, including monitoring of wolves and prey inside and outside the park. This was rejected as being too costly and time consuming. An alternative passive adaptive management approach was adopted that involved regulatory changes designed for 'best bet' conservation action and a commitment to monitoring the long-term trends in both prey and wolves to track the effectiveness of these actions.

A moratorium on hunting and trapping wolves and coyotes, as well as chasing wolves with dogs in and around the park, was implemented in 2001. During the moratorium, the monitoring programme showed that the ban around Algonquin Park improved wolf survival. In May 2004, the moratorium was made permanent and became law.

Source: adapted from Algonquin Wolf Advisory Group (2000) and Ottawa Valley Chapter of the Canadian Parks and Wilderness Society (2004)

Case Study 11.2

Recreational use in Kluane National Park and Reserve, Canada

Management in the Alsek River area of Kluane National Park and Reserve in the Yukon, Canada – an area of 21,980 square kilometres – seeks to provide maximum protection to grizzly bears (*Ursus arctos*) and their habitat, as well as providing opportunities for visitors to experience solitude, natural quiet and self-reliance. Research has shown that seasonal movement of grizzly bears to lower elevations coincided with the main season for river users, and that rafters were camping at sites adjacent to bear movement corridors, near rub trees and within or adjacent to prime bear foods. Based on these findings, researchers supported a commercial operator's suggestion to schedule rafting departures every second day. This reduced crowding at the departure point and lowered the potential for displacement of grizzly bears from their preferred habitats. Rafters are now also required to camp at designated campsites with a lower risk for bear encounters and displacement. Using input from affected users, the new measures were phased in over three years. These changes in visitor use have enhanced grizzly bear protection, public safety and wilderness experiences.

Source: Parks Canada (2004b)

Grizzly bear in the Canadian Rockies

Source: IUCN Photo Library © Jim Thorsell

Figure 11.3 Outline of a rational, adaptive and participatory planning process

A *holistic plan* might take several years to develop until the initial implementation phase and might require a number of planning staff, as well as the contributions of many other professionals and stakeholders. Detailed attention would be given to each of the steps outlined in Figure 11.3.

A *focused plan* might also take a considerable time to develop until the initial implementation phase, but would require less involvement from professional planning staff, other professionals and stakeholders. Attention would be focused on particular steps from Figure 11.3, typically identifying the highest priority issues, setting objectives and related actions for these, implementing this limited range of actions, and evaluating the outcomes.

A *constrained plan* would further contract the scope and detail of the planning project, concentrating, perhaps, on one or two key issues, together with associated actions and their implementation. Planning staff support might involve short-term advice or training.

Table 11.1 Levels of management planning projects

		Significance and complexity of issues		
		High	Medium	Low
Capacity to undertake planning	Well developed	Holistic	Focused	Constrained
	Moderate	Focused	Focused	Constrained
	Minimal	Constrained	Constrained	Nominal

A *nominal plan* would contain the bare minium to guide management. It might, perhaps, be prepared by one person based on their local knowledge, and involve a few simple goals and related actions.

Preparing protected area management plans

Once land-use planning decisions have been made regarding the tenure and broad purpose of a particular area, decisions still need to be made about how the area will be managed. This is the function of an area management plan. Typically, writing a plan involves the compilation and consolidation of material arising from numerous planning process stages into a coherent document. There are several potentially important questions to consider in this regard:

- Who is involved in preparing the plan?
- What should be the time frame for the plan?
- Who is the audience for the plan (and what should be the writing and presentation style)?
- How much, if any, background 'resource inventory' information should be included? Should it be located at the beginning of the plan, at the end or integrated within particular sections?
- Should the process used to develop the plan be explained in the plan itself?
- Should methods used to make the decisions articulated in the plan be described?
- Should involvement of all stakeholders who helped to establish the plan content be described and if so, how?
- Will the plan be written at a broad strategic level, or will it include specific actions?

- Will specific actions be given for each goal/objective, and will time frames and responsibilities be attached to these actions? Some further commentary on this point is provided below.
- What, if any, spatial representations of planning decisions will be required (for example, zoning maps)?

The topics considered in a management plan will vary according to the category of protected area and the particular values that it protects. A list of commonly encountered topics and their general relationship with IUCN protected area categories is given in Table 11.2. Note that the correspondence between topic and protected area category is only indicative – there will be particular instances where the emphasis indicated in the table may not apply. Typical plan contents are further illustrated in Case studies 11.3 and 11.4, which give the tables of contents for a Category V protected area in the UK and a Category II protected area in New Zealand. Both plans deal with core biodiversity and cultural heritage conservation issues. Note the emphasis on economic and social topics in the Dartmoor plan, and on recreation management in the Mount Cook plan. The ongoing nature of planning processes is illustrated with respect to Kosciuszko National Park in Australia in Table 11.3, Figure 11.4, and the latest process of plan revision (Case Study 11.5).

I do not believe that it is useful to prescribe a 'cookbook' approach to preparing plans. However, there are some steps that will be common to most planning processes. When reading the description of such steps as detailed below,

Case Study 11.3

Contents of the Dartmoor National Park Management Plan, UK

Part 1 Introduction

Part 2 A Vision for Dartmoor National Park

Part 3 Conservation and Enhancement of the Natural Beauty, Wildlife and Cultural Heritage of Dartmoor

    3.1 Moorland landscapes

    3.2 Farmed landscapes

    3.3 Woodlands and trees

    3.4 Wetlands and rivers

    3.5 Wildlife and geological conservation

    3.6 Historic built environment

    3.7 Archaeological and historical heritage

    3.8 Customs and traditions

Part 4 Promotion of Opportunities for the Understanding and Enjoyment of the Special Qualities of Dartmoor

    4.1 Information services

    4.2 Interpretation and communications

    4.3 Education services

    4.4 Visitor management

    4.5 Tourism

    4.6 Traffic and transport

Part 5 Economic and Social and Well-Being of Local Communities

    5.1 Housing

    5.2 Employment and economic activity

    5.3 Community services and facilities

Part 6 Planning and Development

    6.1 Development planning and development control

    6.2 Major development

Part 7 Cross-related Themes

    7.1 Agenda 21

    7.2 Military activity

Part 8 Implementation

    8.1 Corporate management and administration

    8.2 Ranger and volunteer services

    8.3 Conservation works service

    8.4 Financial resources

    8.5 Human resources

    8.6 Partners

Part 9 Monitoring and Review

    9.1 State of the National Park monitoring, reporting and review

    9.2 Research strategy

Appendix The State of the National Park

Indicators and targets relating to the state of the Dartmoor environment

Source: Dartmoor National Park Authority (2001)

Case Study 11.4

Contents of the Aoraki/Mount Cook National Park Management Plan, New Zealand

Preface
How to Use This Plan

1 Introduction
    1.1 Management planning
    1.2 Legislative context
        1.2.1 The National Parks Act 1980
            1.2.1.1 National Park Bylaws 1981
        1.2.2 The General Policy for National Parks 1983
        1.2.3 The Conservation Act 1987
            1.2.3.1 The Canterbury Conservation Management Strategy
        1.2.4 The Resource Management Act 1991
        1.2.5 Te Rünanga o Ngäi Tahu Act 1996
        1.2.6 Deed of Settlement between the Crown and Ngäi Tahu and the Ngäi Tahu Claims Settlement Act 1998
            1.2.6.1 Aoraki/Mount Cook and Töpuni
            1.2.6.2 Deed of Recognition
            1.2.6.3 Protocols
            1.2.6.4 Taonga species
            1.2.6.5 Name changes
        1.2.7 Non-statutory planning
        1.2.8 Other statutory bodies with administrative responsibilities
    1.3 Background
        1.3.1 Introduction
        1.3.2 Ngäi Tahu values relating to Aoraki/Mount Cook National Park
            1.3.2.1 Aoraki/Mount Cook Töpuni
        1.3.3 The park – physical character and location
            1.3.3.1 Landform, geology, soils and climate
            1.3.3.2 Vegetation, flora and fauna
        1.3.4 Park heritage
            1.3.4.1 Establishment of Aoraki/Mount Cook National Park
            1.3.4.2 South-west New Zealand (Te Wähipounamu) World Heritage Area
        1.3.5 Recreational and tourism values
            1.3.5.1 ROS and visitor management settings
            1.3.5.2 Visitor groups
        1.3.6 The park within the region
        1.3.7 Further information
2 Management Issues and Objectives
    2.1 Management issues
        2.1.1 Preservation and use
        2.1.2 Aircraft use
        2.1.3 Aoraki/Mount Cook Village
        2.1.4 Huts
        2.1.5 Introduced plants
        2.1.6 Park boundary changes

Source: Department of Conservation (2004)

Aoraki/Mount Cook National Park, New Zealand

Source: IUCN Photo Library © Jim Thorsell

Table 11.2 Management planning topics and IUCN protected area categories

| Topic | IUCN category (see Box 3.3) | | | | | |
	I	II	III	IV	V	VI
Biodiversity conservation	✔	✔	✔	✔	✔	✔
Geodiversity conservation	✔	✔	✔	✓	✓	✓
Cultural heritage conservation	⊗	✔	✔	✔	✔	✓
Visitor-use management	⊗	✔	✔	✓	✔	✓
Water and soil conservation	✓	✓	✓	✓	✓	✓
Management of threats	✔	✔	✔	✔	✔	✔
Management of resource extraction	⊗	(✔)	⊗	✓	✔	✔
Management of human habitation	⊗	(✔)	(✔)	✓	✔	✓
Research and education	✔	✔	✔	✔	✔	✔

Notes: ✔ Typically of high management priority.

✓ Typically of moderate management priority.

(✔) May be of moderate management priority in some areas, while not relevant for others.

⊗ Typically not relevant to the category.

keep in mind that the IUCN category; the governance authority; the prevailing social, cultural, political and economic context; the type of issues to be addressed; and the particular mix of approaches guiding the planning process will all influence exactly how these steps are carried out, their relative importance and their relationship to each other – that is how they fit into the overall planning process.

The following descriptions of the components indicated in Figure 11.3 are given in the context of a holistic planning project. Compromises and omissions must be made in relation to these components for focused and constrained planning projects.

Establish participatory mechanisms and structures

The type and degree of public participation adopted in a planning project will depend upon the governance arrangements and the approach taken by the planner and management agency. Stakeholders may come together in a formal setting, such as an advisory committee meeting, or

a planner may receive an informal deputation or phone call from an interested and sometimes irate individual. In many planning projects, the planner is in the position of being a facilitator or leader of a group of people. For example, the planner might be the convenor of a departmental steering committee set up to direct the planning project, as well as an advisory committee made up of representatives of key interest groups.

Groups and individuals who might be included in a participation programme can be drawn from within the department itself, from other government departments and agencies, and from the general public. Some of the participation methods used in protected area planning, and linkages with level of participation, best practice guidelines and performance measures are summarized in Table 11.4.

Collect relevant data

High-quality information is an important basis for many aspects of protected area management (see Chapter 10), and area management planning is no exception. Incorrect, insufficient or inadequate

Table 11.3 Kosciuszko National Park planning, 1965–2004

Year	Action taken	Notes
1965	Kosciuszko State Park plan	First plan for the park prepared for the state park trust – not formally adopted
1974	Kosciuszko National Park management plan	First plan for the new national park, prepared in the head office, Sydney
1979	Decision to upgrade and amend the plan	Planning team assembled and budget provided
1980	Community information brochure released	Marketing leaflet advising the public that the plan was to be amended
	Key issues identified and the need to obtain additional community input recognized	Issue statements circulated on fire management, resorts, summit area and huts
	Extensive consultation taken, both within the New South Wales National Parks and Wildlife Service (NPWS) and among stakeholders	Leaflet outlining how people can get involved in the process, media interviews, articles and meetings – submissions received on key issues
1981	Draft plan published	Leaflet encouraging comment and advising where the draft plan can be obtained
1982	Final plan published	
1984	Plan amended to deal with construction of the ski tube	Amendments linked to an environment impact statement (EIS)
1987	Supplementary plan published	Objectives and actions related to the Cooleman Plain karst area
1988	Plan amended; ski resorts	Proposed expansion of ski resorts to the Ramshead Range and Twin Valleys not approved
1994	Plan amended; ski resorts	
1999	Plan amended; ski resorts	Expansion of Perisher Valley bed limits following a commission of enquiry
2001	Commencement of a major plan revision	See Case Study 11.5
2004	Draft plan of management placed on public exhibition	See Case Study 11.5

resource data can severely hamper the effectiveness and quality of a management plan. However, complete knowledge of a resource is, of course, unobtainable. Collecting and compiling information takes time and costs money, and both of these factors usually place stringent limits on the data collection effort. It is therefore particularly important to concentrate on collecting relevant data. Planning is not about collecting information for its own sake. Comprehensive statistics on visitor

activities may be essential for an area with a significant recreation component, while another area may require only general impressionistic information on visitor activities.

After pursuing all potential sources of information, a planner may find that a key area has not been covered adequately. For example, the distribution and requirements of endangered plant species recorded in the planning area may not be known. In this case, the planner has two options.

Case Study 11.5

A new plan of management for Kosciuszko National Park

Penny Spoelder, New South Wales Department of Environment and Conservation, Australia

Kosciuszko National Park, which encompasses 690,425ha, is the largest national park in New South Wales (NSW) and one of the largest conservation reserves in Australia. It is one link in a chain of protected areas that stretches along the spine of the Australian Alps for a distance of some 340km.

The park attracts over 1 million visitors per year who enjoy alpine and cross-country skiing, sight-seeing, rock climbing, ice climbing, horse riding, bushwalking, fishing, camping, caving and canoeing. The park contains glacial landforms and possesses an exceptional diversity of alpine plant communities and species that provide habitats for a number of rare and unusual animal species. Elsewhere, the park contains significant karst systems, deep river valleys and frost hollows, as well as vegetation communities ranging from snow gum woodlands and sub-alpine grasslands, to extensive eucalypt forests, pockets of cool temperate rainforest and stands of native cypress pines. The snow-fed rivers of the mountains provide some of Australia's most important water catchments. The park contains major commercial interests in the form of alpine resorts and the Snowy Mountains Hydroelectric Scheme, which contribute significantly to state and regional economies. The park is also rich with evidence of, or associations with, aboriginal culture and the phases of historic land uses, scientific endeavour, and recreation and conservation efforts of many generations. The park's cultural heritage values reside as much in intangible values as they do in physical form. Places within the park have been the scenes of innumerable human experiences. Some of these have survived as legends or anecdotes; others are remembered within place names, songs, literature, art, customs, symbolism or spiritual observance.

In February 2001, the NSW government announced that the *Kosciuszko National Park Plan of Management* would be reviewed. The review commenced in January 2002, involving wide public consultation. A team of people were employed with expertise in protected area management from all over Australia to prepare the new plan. At the outset, they agreed that the new plan would provide a management framework for the National Parks and Wildlife Service (NPWS) and the community for the next 10 to 20 years, protecting the park's values for future generations. As a first step, a number of plans of management prepared for reserves throughout Australia and overseas were reviewed, and park planning specialists were consulted for advice on what they believed to be the strengths and weaknesses of each plan. Other key documents, such as the *ANZECC* [Australian and New Zealand Environment Conservation Council] *Best Practice in Protected Area Management Planning* (Tasmania Parks and Wildlife Service, 2000) and the National Parks and Wildlife Service Plan of Management Manual (NSW NPWS, 2001) were also used as reference documents for the development of the project plan.

Snow gum (*Eucalyptus pauciflora*), Kosciusko National Park, New South Wales, Australia

Source: Graeme L. Worboys

A process was designed that centred around encouraging the involvement of the general public, as well as park users, neighbours, scientists, interest groups, individuals and local communities, in the review of the plan of management. The process was developed following detailed consultation with these groups. This resulted in some modifications to the original design, but ensured that there was general agreement that the planning process would be acceptable to all and involve the relevant interests. The process represented a shift from consulting the public to asking them to share the responsibility for making decisions about their park. This approach was considered the cornerstone to help build public understanding, ensure sound decision-making and increase the probability that the plan would be supported by them. The following consultation mechanisms were established and, to date, have proven to be a successful way of involving relevant groups in plan-making:

- establishment of an independent scientific committee (ISC) made up of recognized scientists and management experts in various disciplines;
- establishment of an independently facilitated and chaired community forum consisting of representatives from various interest groups to discuss and recommend strategies that address the key threats identified by the ISC;
- establishment of an Aboriginal working group representing Aboriginal communities and families who have connections to country that is now known as Kosciuszko National Park.

An inter-agency government working group and a staff working group were also established to assist with the plan review. A representative from each of these four groups attended the meetings of the other groups as a way of ensuring strong communication links between them.

The ISC found that, while many values were in good and stable condition, various pressures could lead to degradation of significant values if not adequately managed. Such pressures include the expansion of development, the imposition of inappropriate fire regimes, the increase in summer visitation, possible climate change, and introduced plants and animals. The ISC prepared an interim report on its findings for community input. Interested organizations and individuals were invited to provide comments, thoughts and suggestions to the ISC. The submissions were then reviewed and incorporated as appropriate within the final ISC report.

A series of workshops was held in local communities in and around the park, as well as in Sydney and Canberra. Media releases, brochures, radio announcements and advertisements in local and national press were also used to inform the public that the review process had commenced. A free call number was established for enquiries and the agency website was also used as a key source of information about the process with links to other relevant sites. The strong cultural connection that some of the communities held with the park was very apparent. The communities also identified key issues that needed addressing in the new plan. They included, among others, the protection of natural and cultural values, the control of weeds and pest animals, sustainable use and access, ski resorts and fire management.

Following the workshops, the community forum was established and met 14 times over two years to work through the issues raised by the community at the workshops. Meetings were generally held over two days and involved a combination of general discussion; field visits to specific parts of the park; presentations from NPWS staff, stakeholders and specialists; and small-group work where specific questions and issues were worked through in more detail. The community forum developed a series of principles to assist them in the development of strategies associated with the management of the park. The principles related to the protection of Kosciuszko's natural values; recognition and celebration of cultural heritage values; respect for aboriginal culture; interpretation, education and awareness; maintaining the economic importance of the park; the need for partnerships and participation by all involved in using and managing the park; and the need for ongoing strategic research and monitoring.

The forum also tackled some difficult issues, such as the management of:

- Kosciuszko's huts, particularly following the loss of 17 huts from bush fires in January 2003;
- increasing visitation at the summit area;
- alpine resorts with growing development pressures and possible implications of climate change;
- recreation activities, such as horse riding and mountain bike riding; and
- control of weeds and pest animals.

The community forum prepared a summary of these principles and its thoughts on the key issues. Interested organizations and individuals were invited to provide comments, thoughts and suggestions to the forum. The submissions were then reviewed and considered by the community forum at its subsequent meetings.

The Aboriginal working group advised NPWS that the new plan should, among other things:

- recognize, acknowledge and celebrate Aboriginal people's connections to their country, now known as Kosciuszko National Park;
- strengthen participation by Aboriginal people in looking after the country by working in partnership with the NPWS;
- recognize the importance of recording history and knowledge, and sharing this with people;
- include opportunities for young people in managing the park through employment, education and training;
- rename places in the park with Aboriginal names.

The group agreed that the section of the new plan relating to the management of Aboriginal cultural heritage should be primarily written by them.

The advice received from the community forum, Aboriginal working group, the ISC, other government agencies and NPWS staff has been invaluable in the development of the new plan of management for Kosciuszko National Park. Greater recognition has been given to the cultural values of the park; community involvement in park management; greater emphasis on environmental stewardship by all agencies and organizations operating in the park; simple zoning schemes; and management strategies identified that ensure sustainable use. The new plan acknowledges the importance of the park's cultural and social values, and the need to protect these values from key threats, such as inappropriate fire regimes, climate change, introduced plants and animals, inappropriate development and unmanaged increases in visitation. The strategies in the plan are commensurate with Kosciuszko's status of one of the great national parks of the world.

Table 11.4 Good practices in government-designated protected area planning participation

Level of participation: Agency/community	Best/good practices	Participation techniques	Performance indicators
Inform/comply The agency informs the community (e.g. no dogs allowed in park). The community is required to comply with agency requirement	• Be proactive • Apply a bottom-up approach • Research the ways in which people get their information • Ensure that people are aware of their reasons for decisions • Establish a feedback loop to enable the community the opportunity to have their say	• Public meetings • Presentations • Internet and mass media • Communication plans • Press releases • Standard operating procedures • Signs • Education campaigns • Printed brochures and newsletters	• Level of participation in agency education programmes • Number of requests for information • Number of informed people (survey results) • Number of infringement notices issued • Number of complaints • Number of ministerials • Number of internet hits
Consult/cooperate The agency seeks input into decision-making process (e.g. in developing a plan of management for a park, the community is encouraged to provide input into the planning process) The community agrees to support decisions and becomes involved in programmes and activities (e.g. Friends of the Park group agrees to undertake planting programme in accordance with agency requirements)	• Consultation takes time and resources – successful outcomes may be undermined where these are insufficient • Be clear about the basis for involvement • Value people's contributions • Promote the inclusion of a diverse range of people and interest groups • Use language that is inclusive of the community	• Workshops • Stakeholder meetings • Surveys • Plans of management • Letters to stakeholders • Advertisements in the media • Public displays • Internet	• Quality of submissions • Number of issues raised • Number of stakeholders reached • Diversity of stakeholder input • Level of customer/client satisfaction (measured through surveys/customer feedback) • Number of staff trained in consultation techniques (e.g. facilitation and conflict resolution)

Table 11.4 Continued

Level of participation: Agency/community	Best/good practices	Participation techniques	Performance indicators
	• Ensure that the community is fully aware of issues and what they are asked to do • Acknowledge stakeholder/community input/cooperation • Be very clear if there is no opportunity for people to have a say in the programme		• Number of volunteer days and quality of conservation outcomes • Number of volunteer hours • Number of people attending community education programmes
Collaborate/participate The agency invites community to share in decision-making process (e.g. nomination of new marine and terrestrial parks by the community) The community has a formal role in decision-making process	• Maintain integrity/honesty • Be open to new ideas • Respect cultural diversity • Identify areas of common interest • Don't make commitments that can't be kept • Provide opportunities for real involvement • Be clear about the powers and functions of advisory groups	• Advisory councils • Task forces • Stakeholder feedback • Conservation partnerships with the community, landholders and industry	• Level and type of participation • Level of integration of regional planning decisions with agency management decisions • Number of resolutions • Number of people nominating for advisory consultative groups • Support for decisions
Partner/participate The agency and community (stakeholders) share responsibility for decision-making (e.g. Aboriginal-owned land leased to government for management as national park)	• Maintain dialogue – ensure that all issues are open to discussion • Provide legislative framework for participation • Ensure ongoing management of participation • Set clear outcomes/outputs	• Joint management • Statutory boards of management	• Number of partnership agreements • Quality of relationships • Number of jointly managed protected areas
Handover/self-directed action The agency hands over control and decision-making to the community. The agency may facilitate management by the community through the provision of resources and expertise. The community/stakeholder has autonomy in decision-making and may seek agency management input (e.g. landowner wishes to contribute important privately owned land to national reserve system)	• Establish mutual benefits, trust and support • Establish a transparent process • Support projects that have good conservation outcomes	• Where government agencies sit on community boards • Provide advice and other resources that result in conservation outcomes • Indigenous protected areas • Voluntary conservation agreements • Review mechanisms	• Number of private conservation reserves and quality of conservation outcomes • Number of conservation agreements and quality of conservation outcomes • Number and quality of covenants • Area of private land added to the reserve system

Source: Parks and Wildlife Commission of the Northern Territory (2002, pp16–18)

The required information can be gathered in the course of the planning project so that it is available to assist management decisions contained in the plan, or the plan can simply specify an action in relation to the collection of this information.

The first option is by far superior because it will enable a management decision to be made regarding (in this case) the endangered species, which can then be integrated within the planning process. This means that there can be public input and discussion of the issue, the options for managing the species, and decisions regarding the preferred management actions. However, time and money may preclude selection of this option and the planner may simply have to include a recommendation in the plan regarding future research on the species.

In some cases, it may be appropriate to publish the resource data collected as a separate document – a resource inventory. This can be particularly valuable in two respects. First, if there has been very little published information available on the planning area it gives interested parties access to relevant information early in the planning process. This can considerably improve the quality and utility of input received from people and groups outside the planning team. Second, it can help the planner to avoid cluttering up the management plan with a large volume of background information. An excess of such information can distract the reader from the plan itself and make the document too long and unwieldy. The information needs described in Chapter 10 (p263) give an indication of what is required to support a planning project.

Identify and analyse the issues

The process of compiling a resource inventory should provide a good basis for identifying and analysing problems and issues associated with the planning area. The public participation component of the planning process is also used to identify issues. Issues may involve conflicts between:

- various uses and conservation of natural values – for example, between cattle grazing and conservation of a significant species, or building of a major visitor access route and preservation of scenic quality;

- one resource component and another – for example, between an introduced species and a native one;
- various uses and the resource upon which they depend – for example, the quality of a bush camping experience can be diminished by problems of vegetation depletion, rubbish, disposal of toilet wastes and so on that are the result of camping; and
- one use and another – for example, fisherfolk and water-sport users; forest-dwelling peoples and wildlife tourists; bushwalkers and trail bike riders; or water-skiers and swimmers.

Classifying issues according to this framework can assist the planner in understanding the nature and context of the issue. This can be the first step in identifying the underlying cause of the issue or problem. In addition, tackling a problem involving two resource components is likely to require a very different approach in comparison to one involving two conflicting uses.

Another product of analysing problems and issues could be a list of all possible topics for which management objectives and related actions may be required. Typically, the subject matter of objectives and actions covers flora and fauna conservation, various aspects of visitor management, management for other authorized uses and regulation of use to minimize impacts.

Establish goals and objectives

Planners have used a confusing array of terminology when dealing with means and ends. Words such as 'goal', 'aim', 'objective', 'strategy', 'policy', 'action', 'indicator' and so on tend to be used ambiguously and, in some cases, interchangeably. This makes it rather confusing for a professional not involved in the plan preparation, the staff who have to implement the plan, and the general public who wish to interpret and understand a planning document. A common usage and understanding of these terms is desirable. To this end, this chapter suggests that the following definitions for key planning terms be adopted and applied consistently in management plans.

A *goal* is a general statement of ends. It is not necessarily achievable in the planning period, but indicates the broad ends to which management aspires. Examples of goals that might appear in a protected area management plan are to:

- conserve native plants and animals;
- secure a culturally important site or a site of critical livelihood importance;
- provide a range of recreation opportunities; and
- control pest plants and animals.

Goals, because of their very general nature, are by themselves insufficient for directing management. However, it is still important to specify these broad statements of direction in a management plan. They can indicate which goals established in legislation or by the government and the managing agency are particularly relevant for the planning area. A statement of goals is important for establishing the links between broader national, state or regional planning considerations and a particular management plan. They can also provide a level of detail not included in a broad strategic vision (see Case Study 11.6).

An *objective* is a statement of realistic, measurable and specific ends to be achieved within a specified period of time. Objectives are required for effective evaluation of a plan since if it is unclear what a plan intends to achieve, it is not possible to determine its success or failure. Without objectives, a manager cannot know when a particular action achieved the desired result (and therefore move on to achieving other objectives). Nor can the manager discover if a particular action is, in fact, not achieving the desired result, and whether another action should be tried instead. Ideally, an objective should be:

- specific;
- clearly stated;
- measurable;
- realistic; and
- where appropriate, time limited.

The objectives given in Case Study 11.6 generally satisfy these ideals. However, in many cases it may not be possible to formulate an objective that satisfies all of these points. In particular, there is often insufficient information to craft a measurable objective. Nonetheless, in the 'objectives' contained in many plans are what I would call

goals, and these could be considerably improved, particularly through greater specificity and measurability.

Strategies are general statements of means – that is, they provide a broad indication of how a goal or objective will be achieved. *Actions* are specific statements of means that ideally include enough detail to enable their unambiguous implementation by field staff.

Performance indicators are scales that are used to assess the degree to which a desired outcome has been achieved. *Standards* specify the required level of a performance indicator in order for an objective to be met. Generally, there is a hierarchy from vision, goal and objective through to performance indicator and standard, as shown in the example in Figure 11.4.

An example of a goal, and related performance indicators and actions, is given in Case Study 11.7. An example of a plan that uses 'strategies', 'actions', 'key deliverables', 'key indicators' and 'target indicators' is given in Case Study 11.8.

Develop options (actions) for achieving objectives

Once goals and specific objectives have been established for each management issue, a planner must explore the possible options for achieving these objectives. Some options will be evident to the planning team from their own professional experience and knowledge of the planning area. Others may be generated through stakeholder and agency staff participation in the planning process. A useful way of getting all of these ideas down on paper is to hold a 'brainstorming' session.

In a brainstorm session the planning team considers each objective in turn and lists all ideas that come to mind, no matter how apparently impractical or crazy. This helps to prevent premature narrowing of the range of options being considered. Narrowing options too early in the planning process can stifle lateral thinking and make it more difficult for novel and creative solutions to emerge.

Sometimes the range of options and their possible implications are such that the planning team may decide to prepare and publish a separate issues and options paper, as was done in the Kosciuszko planning process (see Table 11.3).

Case Study **11.6**

Example goals and objectives from Dry Tortugas National Park, US

National Park Service goal

Natural and cultural resources and associated values are protected, restored and maintained in good condition and managed within their broader ecosystem and cultural context.

Park-specific goal

All natural resources and associated values are protected, restored and maintained in near pristine condition.

National Park Service objective:

- By 30 September 2005, exotic vegetation on 6.3 per cent of targeted area of park land (67,786ha of 1,075,140ha) is contained.

Park-specific objective: • By 30 September 2005, 16ha of disturbed parkland is restored.

In 1999, 100 per cent of *Casuarina* trees (a native of Australia) standing in the northern half of Loggerhead Key (about 6ha) were cut and/or treated with herbicide. This action completed the treatment of *Casuarina* for the entire 16ha island, a project that began almost ten years ago. Approximately 30 per cent of the island requires further work (re-treatment and prescribed burns) before it can be considered restored.

National Park Service objective:

- By 30 September 2005, 19 per cent of the 1999 identified park populations (84 of 442) of federally listed threatened and endangered species with critical habitat on park lands or requiring National Park Service recovery actions have an improved status, and an additional 18.1 per cent (80 of 442) have stable populations.

Park-specific objective: • By 30 September 2005, breeding populations of loggerhead (*Caretta caretta*) and green sea turtles (*Chelonia mydas*) increase.

Florida International University researchers and park staff monitor populations of loggerhead and green sea turtles in the park. The total crawl count in 1999 was 5 per cent lower than the five-year average, and the number of false crawls about 10 per cent less than the five-year average. These numbers are within the natural variability of the long-term ranges. Results of future monitoring will report to this objective.

Park-specific goal

All submerged and land-based cultural resources have been identified, documented, protected and/or stabilized.

National Park Service objective:

- By 30 September 2005, 50 per cent (12,113 of 24,225 structures) of the historic structures on the 1999 List of Classified Structures are in good condition.

Park-specific objective: • By 30 September 2005, three structures listed on the 1999 List of Classified Structures are in good condition.

Fort Jefferson's masonry has severely deteriorated because of the harsh marine environment. In some areas, large sections of the outer brick wall have fallen into the moat. Stabilization projects are under way to improve the condition of classified structures, where feasible. Examples include replacement of the slate roof on the engineer's quarters; repairs to the harbour light; preservation work on the sally port and its granite arch; repairs to cistern structures; and stabilization of the fort's exterior walls. All effort to improve the condition of classified structures is to be reported to this objective.

National Park Service goal

Visitors safely enjoy and are satisfied with availability, accessibility, diversity and quality of park facilities, services and appropriate recreational opportunities.

Park-specific goal

Available park facilities, infrastructure and services are sufficient to support operational needs, park staff and visitors; appropriate recreational opportunities are safe and adequate for visitors and employees.

National Park Service objective:

• By 30 September 2005, 95 per cent of park visitors are satisfied with appropriate park facilities, services and recreational opportunities.

Park-specific objective: • By 30 September 2005, 95 per cent of park visitors are satisfied with appropriate park facilities, services and recreational opportunities.

All efforts directed towards the preservation, protection, restoration, operation and maintenance of the park's resources, facilities and visitor services are to be reported in this objective. A visitor survey was conducted in Dry Tortugas National Park during the 1999 fiscal year. The survey results indicated that 87 per cent of park visitors were satisfied with appropriate facilities, services and recreational opportunities.

Source: adapted from NPS (2000b) to match the terminology used in this chapter and the metric units used in this book

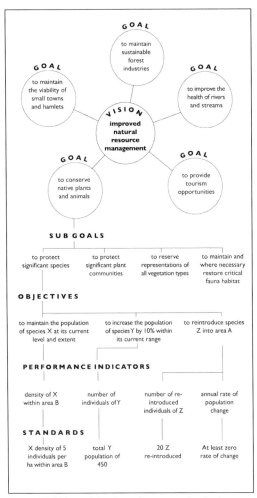

Figure 11.4 From vision to performance standard

These papers can be particularly valuable in a major planning project that involves a number of major and complex issues and is of considerable political significance. An issues and options paper can facilitate extensive formal and informal public involvement in establishing and evaluating management options. It can also help to avoid major conflicts by bringing potentially contentious options into the open early in the process, and allowing plenty of opportunity for their ramifications to be debated.

Select actions

Once the range of possible options for achieving each objective has been established, some basis is required for selecting the best option or combination of options. There is a wide range of methods that could be used to test the options:

• professional judgement;
• dialogue involving planners and stakeholders through informal discussion or formal proceedings, such as enquiries or conferences; and
• systematic application of procedures such as benefit–cost analysis (BCA) (see Chapter 12), multi-criteria analysis, impact assessment or voting.

In much protected area planning, evaluation of options is done implicitly. That is, the planner,

Case Study 11.7

Example goal, performance indicators and actions, Sapo National Park, Liberia

Goal

To ensure that stakeholders have knowledge of and practise actions that conform to the conservation goals and objectives of Sapo National Park (SNP) in Liberia.

Performance indicators

There is no hunting, farming, logging, mining, settlement and fishing within SNP.

Commercial hunting is reduced outside of SNP by a measurable and significant amount (to be monitored under another component of the plan).

At least 50 per cent of the local inhabitants around the SNP are involved in environmental conservation practices.

The private sector (loggers, fishermen, miners, hunters and farmers) conform to conservation practices in the vicinity of the park.

Liberian government officials and agencies are aware and supportive of the goals and objectives of the SNP.

Sinoe River, Sapo National Park, Liberia

Source: IUCN Photo Library © Jim Thorsell

Actions

Install 15 billboards and 36 signposts indicating regulations through symbols and script around SNP and at checkpoints along the Greenville–Zwedru Highway.

Identify priority messages for the stakeholders listed in the results section of the plan.

Translate messages through drama; visual aids such as slides, films and video screenings; electronic media such as radio and television; printed media; sports (football leagues); nature clubs; T-shirts; and school curricula as they relate to conservation. Messages must be delivered in both English and local vernacular languages.

Introduce all SNP staff and local village volunteers to basic community outreach and relations principles.

Train one or more specialized environmental education officers at SNP in environmental awareness and education techniques.

Establish local community action groups in support of conservation around the park.

Meet with the private sector, government officials, including other government agencies than the Forestry Development Authority (the management agency for the park), and local chiefs to solicit their cooperation and support.

Source: Suter (2001a, 2001b)

Case Study 11.8

Actions and indicators, Kgalagadi Transfrontier Park Strategic Management Plan, South Africa

In May 2000, the presidents of Botswana and South Africa created a historical precedent by signing an official treaty that formally established the Kgalagadi Transfrontier Park (KTP). The 38,000 square kilometre park situated in the southern Kalahari, a vast semi-desert area that extends from southern Botswana into the Northern Cape. The management plan for the area specifies a number of strategies, actions and indicators. Those for exotic plants and animals are given in Table 11.5.

Table 11.5 Example strategies, actions and indicators from the Kgalagadi Transfrontier Park Strategic Management Plan

Strategies	Actions	Priority	Key deliverables	Key indicators	Target for indicator
Control the spread and impacts of exotic plants, and control the impacts of non-invasive exotic plants and animals.	Actively maintain the clearing of the priority invasive plant species in the park – mesquite (*Prosopis* sp.) and Mexican poppy (*Argemone subfusiformi*) – notably in the river courses of the Auob and Nossob.	High	Procedures for the introduction and keeping of domestic animals and birds	Extent of areas invaded by declared invasive plant species	No priority invasive plant species present in park
	Monitor and control the spread of alien plants planted within the park tourist camps and staff facilities.	Low	Procedures for control of alien species (plants and animals)		Reduction in area of habitats invaded by invasive plant species
	Opportunistically plant and nurture appropriate indigenous trees within existing and new rest camps, and phase out the current exotic species once they reach the end of their lifespan.	Moderate		Extent of exotic tree species in the day/overnight visitor sites	No new exotic species planted or spread
	Maintain research into the impacts of feral cats on the hybridization of the African wild cats.	High			
	Maintain and update procedures on the introduction and keeping of domestic animals and birds in the park.	Moderate		Domestic species kept by staff without incident and within regulations	No problems with domestic pets

Source: South African National Parks (2004)

planning team or stakeholder committee discusses and assesses the options using their professional judgement. In these assessments the criteria against which the options are being judged are often unstated, and the reasoning behind the testing process is not articulated. The disadvantage of this process is that people who are not directly involved will not have an appreciation of the reasons or justification for the superiority of some actions over others. The decision-making process remains hidden.

One way of making explicit the testing and evaluation steps is to develop a formal assessment procedure. This enables the planner to communicate to interested parties the process by which preferred options were selected and permits justification of these selections. The decision-making process thus becomes more transparent.

Most formal evaluation systems require that the decision-makers identify criteria that can be used to judge the worth of different options. Multi-criteria analysis (MCA), for example, is a widely used approach to assisting decision-making when a range of options needs to be assessed according to several criteria – a common occurrence in protected area planning. MCA is a general term used to describe a number of procedures that organize information relevant to the decision-making process. The basic element common to all MCA is an effects table that indicates the performance of each management option in relation to a set of selected criteria. MCA can be used to choose one or more superior alternatives, generate a complete or partial ranking of alternatives, or analyse the acceptability of each alternative (Lahdelma et al, 2000). At its most basic, no attempt is made to formally aggregate across the different criteria to determine the best option. In this case, MCA serves simply as a means of organizing and presenting the value of implications of each alternative. The decision-maker(s) can use the MCA effects table as a means of assisting choice and clarifying the nature of the options; but some professional judgement must be explicitly applied to select a preferred alternative. This method has been used, for example, in comparing road access options for a nature reserve (Cape Woolamai Steering Committee, 1989).

If the analyst wants to compare options more formally, they can be scaled against a qualitative index. This scaling typically proceeds by determining the performance of each alternative against each criterion using some common measure, multiplying this performance score by a weighting that reflects the relative importance of the criterion, and aggregating across criteria to produce an overall score for the option. This method has been used, for example, in assessing zoning options for marine reserves (Villa et al, 2002) and incorporating connectivity into conservation planning (Fuller et al, 2006).

Integrate actions within a cohesive plan

Most planning processes have as a major outcome the production of a written management plan. Example plan structures were given in Case Studies 11.3 and 11.4. A plan typically incorporates elements such as:

* a description of values and resources;
* identification of issues;
* goals;
* management tools such as a zoning scheme;
* objectives and performance measures; and
* actions for which priorities may be established.

I have discussed these elements earlier, with the exception of zoning. Zoning is a technique that involves spatially organizing a planning area to facilitate the achievement of management goals and/or objectives. Zoning can direct management towards achieving specific objectives in certain sub-areas of the overall planning area. It can also provide the basis for partitioning the planning area in order to separate incompatible uses and to exclude inappropriate uses from certain areas. Zoning can concentrate use into small areas to facilitate control of service provision and restrict the spatial extent of environmental effects. On the other hand, it can also be used to disperse use where impacts may be unacceptably concentrated so that important values are being threatened (Eagles et al, 2002).

Ideally, a zoning scheme should be developed from a wide range of spatial resource information, including:

- land capability factors, such as slope, soil type and hydrology;
- a general description of vegetation communities;
- sites of botanical and zoological significance;
- sites of cultural and historical significance;
- landscape values;
- recreation activities and opportunities;
- current land uses;
- timber and non-timber forest resources (for a forest management plan); and
- management decisions regarding land use.

Spatially representing some of these resource factors can be done with the aid of other planning tools. For example, the Recreation Opportunity Spectrum (ROS) (see Chapter 19, p506) can be used to define recreational opportunities. By combining all of this information, a planner should be able to develop a zoning scheme that takes into account both these resource factors and the goals and objectives for the planning area. Some protected area management agencies have standardized zoning templates or guidelines that can be applied to individual protected areas within a jurisdiction. For example, Parks Canada applies a framework involving five zones differentiated according to purpose, boundary criteria, management resources and public opportunities (see Table 11.6). An example of a zoning scheme from Þingvellir National Park in Iceland is given in Case Study 11.9.

To be useful, zoning must reflect real and significant differences in management emphasis. In some plans, there is very little difference between the various zones, and it seems the planners have either been unable to make some hard decisions – for example, to exclude certain uses from 'preservation' zones – or they have simply used zoning because it is standard practice, without considering whether it really contributes to the particular planning problem at hand.

Descriptions of values and resources, issues, zoning, goals, objectives and actions need to be integrated within a written document, which may be a published draft plan (under a conventional approach) or a 'loose-leaf' document that is continually modified according to a formal process (under an adaptive approach). In an adaptive approach, there is also the additional challenge of incorporating the proposed actions within an experimental design that enables their effectiveness to be tested against the relevant objectives. Other content and structural issues that often confront the writers of management plans include whether to present resource information, and, if so, how much should be provided and where it should be located.

Implement the plan

As noted earlier in 'Approaches to planning', effective implementation is a problem that has long plagued the planning process. It is important that in the effort of developing and compiling a management plan, linkages to the implementation phase are not neglected. Processes must be in place to develop detailed budgets and works programmes based on actions specified in the management plan. Such supporting documents indicate the allocation of time, staff and money required to accomplish each task. Works programmes detail who will be carrying out what tasks on what day.

Review effectiveness of actions in achieving objectives

Monitoring the consequences of actions recommended in a management plan enables a planner to determine whether the actions are, in fact, achieving the objectives set out in the plan (see Chapter 24). Once the actions have been completed and the corresponding action achieved, management can proceed to deal with a new objective. If the action is not making adequate progress towards achieving the related objective, then a new action or series of actions may need to be developed.

Management agencies often have a stated intention to review plans every five years. Such a review enables a plan to be updated to take into account changing circumstances or the availability of new information. It also provides an opportunity for a major review of the objectives and the success of the actions in achieving them. However, if an adaptive approach is adopted, the process of monitoring and revision can be a continuous one. There is not necessarily a 'draft' or 'final' plan at all. There is simply an ongoing

Table 11.6 Parks Canada zoning system

Zone class	Zone purpose	Boundary criteria	Management framework	
			Resources	Public opportunity
I Special preservation	Specific areas of features that deserve special preservation because they contain or support unique, rare or endangered features, or the best examples of these features	The natural extent and buffer requirements of designated features	Strict resource preservation	Usually no internal access Only strictly controlled non-motorized access
II Wilderness	Extensive areas that are good representations of each of the natural history themes of the park and that will be maintained in a wilderness state	The natural extent and buffer requirements of natural history themes and environments in areas of 2000ha and greater	Oriented to preserve the natural environmental setting	Internal access by non-motorized means Dispersed activities providing experiences consistent with resource preservation Primitive camping areas Primitive roofed accommodation, including emergency shelters
III Natural environment	Areas that are maintained as natural environments and that can sustain a minimum of low-density outdoor recreation activities with a minimum of related facilities	The extent of natural environments providing outdoor recreation opportunities and required buffer areas	Oriented to preserve the natural environmental setting	Internal access by non-motorized and limited motorized means, including in the north; authorized air charter access to rivers/lakes; usually dispersed activities, with more concentrated activities associated with motorized access Rustic, small-scale permanent fixed-roof accommodation for visitor and operational use Camping facilities at the semi-primitive level
IV Recreation	Limited areas that can accommodate a broad range of education, outdoor recreation opportunities and related facilities in ways that respect the natural landscape and that are safe and convenient	The extent of outdoor facilities and their area of immediate impact	Oriented to minimize the impact of activities and facilities on the natural landscape	Outdoor opportunities in natural landscapes or supported by facility development and landscape alteration Camping facilities of the basic serviced category Small and decentralized accommodation facilities

Table 11.6 Continued

Zone class	Zone purpose	Boundary criteria	Management framework	
			Resources	Public opportunity
V Park services	Towns and visitor centres in certain existing national parks that contain a concentration of visitor services and support facilities, as well as park administration offices	The extent of services and facilities and their immediate area of impact	Oriented to emphasize the national park setting and values in the location, design and operation of visitor-support services and park administration functions	Internal access by non-motorized and motorized means Centralized visitor support services and park administration activities Facility-based opportunities Major camping areas adjacent to, or within, a town or visitor centre

Source: Eagles et al (2002)

working plan that is adapted and modified as objectives are achieved, problems are identified with existing objectives and/or actions, or some external change (such as a major natural event) forces reconsideration of the entire plan.

Overview of good planning practice

Most protected area planning has been undertaken using some mix of participative, rational comprehensive and adaptive approaches. This mix has generally reflected the imperatives of dealing with the issues at hand and the nature of the organizations responsible for planning and policy development. The move towards adaptive management is, in part, recognition of problems with a purely rational, comprehensive style of planning. Inadequacies of current natural resource management plans as identified by Fallding (2000) include:

*   plans that are either too long and scientific or too short and general;
*   plans that have unrealistic expectations;
*   objectives that do not have effective implementation mechanisms; and
*   the absence of an adaptive framework.

Other failures or shortcomings include a lack of 'buy-in' from key stakeholders, especially due to non-participatory process, and mismatch between objectives and the human, technical and financial resources provided or available.

The range of protected area issues and environments, together with uncertainty surrounding the effectiveness of the various approaches, mean that there is no 'perfect' mix of approaches or a 'perfect' process arising from such a mix. There are, however, several elements that need to be incorporated within the selection of planning approaches and the development of an effective process. In general, this chapter recommends that planning processes be based on the adaptive and participatory approaches. The requirements necessary to support an intelligent mix of the adaptive and participatory approaches are considerable:

*   sophisticated and accessible systems of research, monitoring and communication;
*   availability of sound, adequate and appropriately accessible information;
*   integration across disciplines and professions;
*   commitment to persistence and accountability;

Case Study **11.9**

Zoning of Þingvellir National Park, Iceland

Þingvellir National Park in Iceland is divided into three zones that reflect differing use, conservation criteria and cultural significance. In this case study, each zone is described, and the current situation, limits of acceptable change and policy for each are briefly explained. The zoning of the national park is shown in Figure 11.5.

Zone S1: Þingvellir lava field and other leisure areas

The Þingvellir lava field covers the majority of the area of the national park; the lava is covered with low-growing vegetation and dwarf birch. In several places, coniferous trees have been planted. Within the lava field, the abandoned farmsteads of Hrauntún and Skógarkot form hubs for a network of footpaths, which are ancient routes and thus constitute heritage sites in their own right.

Limits of acceptable change

The overall appearance of the zone should not change to any noticeable degree, and traffic will be managed in such a way that random encroachment does not have an impact on the land. There will be no further spread of coniferous woods.

Figure 11.5 Zoning map for of Þingvellir National Park

Source: Þingvellir Commission, 2004

Policy for this zone

There will be no important human-made structure in the zone other than paths that harmonize well with the environment for those who wish to walk in the lava field and enjoy the environment, or to visit the abandoned farmsteads. Skógarkot shall be made accessible to visitors with limited mobility by means of a path that is suitable for wheelchairs. Coniferous woods will be thinned and confined so that the natural vegetation of the area is allowed to thrive. Heritage sites will be maintained and information on them provided for passers-by.

Mid Atlantic Rift, Þingvellir National Park, Iceland

Source: IUCN Photo Library © Jim Thorsell

Zone S2: Leirar

In this zone a service centre for visitors is now located, along with staff facilities, the national park administrative offices and a campsite. The zone is not deemed to be particularly sensitive, and there is some scope for extension of the current services.

Limits of acceptable change

The entire zone may be developed, but in a style and appearance that harmonizes as far as possible with the surroundings. Emphasis is on durable, low-maintenance building materials that retain a good appearance in spite of use and weathering.

Policy for this zone

At Leirar, development will not exceed what is necessary in order to serve a rising number of visitors in keeping with other services in the area. Staff facilities and administrative offices will remain there. Buildings are to be low-rise structures north of the road.

Zone S3: Lakeshore

The lakeshore is a strip of land by the lake, about 50m across, contiguous with the parliamentary site at the west. Along the shore, there is considerable wear and tear, and visible impact on vegetation.

Limits of acceptable change

Along the shore the interplay of lake, lava and vegetation will be protected, without any structures other than those necessary in order to provide sufficient access for anglers and others seeking outdoor activity. The overall appearance of the zone will not be altered, and traffic will be managed in such a way that random encroachment does not have an impact on the land.

Policy for this zone

Good car parks and easy access to the lakeshore from the road will be provided. Anglers will be directed to specified areas (angling sectors) where the surface will be altered to some extent in order to tolerate the pressure. Many important heritage sites are also located in this zone. At Vatnskot, instruction will be provided on the heritage sites and the utilization of the lake, and there will be access from there to the lakeshore for those with limited mobility. Special attention must be paid to Vellankatla, where the water flowing from beneath the lava field is visible, leading to the possibility of instruction on the groundwater system of the national park.

Source: adapted from Þingvellir Commission (2004)

- having 'spare capacity' in natural and human systems so that managers can honestly adapt and make adjustments;
- democratized, open and accessible processes, with participation structured in order to be clear and to persist over time;
- political, stakeholder and community will to engage in difficult long-term processes; and
- persistent yet flexible institutional arrangements to allow fulfilment of all the other requirements (Dovers and Mobbs, 1997; Dovers, 1998).

In addition, successful planning processes have or develop:

- clear articulation of the process;
- links to larger-scale strategies, providing a strategic focus;
- a clear understanding of the issues;
- explicit measurable objectives;
- decisions that are justified and transparent;
- explicit linkages between objectives and actions;
- actions that allow for consistent interpretation and application;
- explicit links between actions, available resources and budgets;
- explicit lines of responsibility regarding implementation and evaluation; and
- availability of suitably trained staff to guide the process and implement the plan.

The IUCN guide to good practice in planning is provided in Thomas and Middleton (2003), extracts from which are given in Box 11.1.

Box 11.1 IUCN guidelines for management planning

The IUCN *Guidelines for Management Planning of Protected Areas* (Thomas and Middleton, 2003) give detailed procedures for preparing management plans. Overall, the guidelines encourage managers to allow time to prepare simple, flexible and dynamic plans that have involved all stakeholders in the preparation. Plans should contain a vision, a set of management objectives, an analysis of the threats and opportunities, and prescriptions or actions to achieve the objectives that are time-specific, realistic, achievable, within budget and resourced. An evaluation and monitoring process should be built in and the plan reviewed within a specified time frame. At least a year should be given to the process or longer if complex issues are involved.

All people affected by management of the protected area should be involved as early as possible in the planning process. Two audiences are identified: external stakeholders, including local people, visitors and so on; and internal staff who are to implement the plan. It is recognized that, increasingly, NGOs or local communities are preparing and implementing management plans.

There is increasing demand by communities to be consulted and involved in management, particularly where communities rely on the natural resources contained within and around a protected area for their livelihood. Sometimes protected area managers need to provide appropriate incentives for communities to participate. Communities may need assistance to understand the processes involved in planning, management and providing information so that they are fully informed and able to articulate their concerns and ideas.

A plan must have flexibility to ensure that management can adapt according to changing circumstances. A simple plan is considered easier and more cost effective to develop. The plan should be focused on management, the vision, the management objectives and actions to implement the objectives. Plans containing too much information or description about the site can lose their impact and clarity.

Management plans must also take into consideration the broader context within which the protected area fits. Regional concerns, links to requirements of national systems or other plans, and policies and legislation need to be considered and integrated within the plan. Consideration has to be given to ensuring the capacity of staff and community to undertake the planning process. Commitment has to be gained from all of those involved in implementing the plan that they will apply it according to the plan.

Many protected areas share national or provincial boundaries. There needs to be consistency built into the management of protected areas over such boundaries. Coordinated planning is essential and can ensure that partners develop an appreciation of the biophysical, political, social and economic contexts of their neighbours. The IUCN promotes closer cooperation between neighbouring administrations in such situations. Ideally, management plans should be prepared jointly.

Problems encountered in planning and implementation include people not being sufficiently trained, not enough funding to support the process, an unsupportive local community and poor communication with stakeholders. The plan itself can also lead to problems in the implementation phase, particularly when there are unrealistic expectations, lack of clarity in objectives and actions, and poorly defined responsibilities.

A 13-step process is described that provides the requirements for successful preparation and implementation of management plans:

1   appointment of planning team, scoping of the task and defining the process to be used;
2   data gathering and issues identification;
3   evaluation of data;
4   identification of constraints, opportunities and threats;
5   development of a management vision and objectives;
6   development of options for achieving the vision and objectives, including zoning;
7   preparation of a draft management plan;
8   public consultation on the draft;
9   assessment of submissions, revision of draft plan and production of a 'final' plan;
10 approval or endorsement of the plan;

Box 11.1 Continued

11　implementation of the actions in the plan;

12　monitoring and evaluation of the outcomes; and

13　review and, where necessary, revision of the plan.

Each step has accompanying guidelines and suggestions. Feedback is considered fundamental to the process. It allows a planner to correct future action in light of past experience. The feedback loop could be thought of as the 'quality cycle', where the monitoring and review of the plan ensures that all parts are realistic, appropriate, efficient, economic and effective. It is desirable that this is a continuous process, which would ensure flexible, adaptive management of the protected area.

Source: adapted from Thomas and Middleton (2003)

Management principles

There is no single best way to undertake a planning project. This means that, in our view, it is not very useful to offer rigid prescriptions on how to conduct planning. Nonetheless, some principles of high-quality management planning may be suggested:

1　The scope and level of detail of the planning project should take account of the importance of the issues to be addressed and the planning capacity available to the governing organization or individual.

2　The priorities established in a plan should be consistent with the intent of the protected area's IUCN category.

3　Planners should clearly identify the purpose, scope, resources and staff available for the planning project.

4　Planners should consciously adopt planning approaches and processes that are:
- respectful of the laws, customs and values of the society concerned;
- participatory at a level that matches the interests and concerns of stakeholders;
- participatory in the identification of issues;
- cognisant of the multi-value, multicultural context of protected area management;
- rational and participatory in the collection and identification of information to inform management, and the integration of scientific understandings with input from stakeholders;
- rational in the application of formal procedures to assess any changes in land-use or

major investment issues;
- rational and participatory in the assessment of action options and in the selection of preferred actions.
- adaptive in the implementation, assessment, refinement and modifications of objectives and actions.

5　Effective linkages should be established across planning levels such that:
- strategic planning occurs at the organizational and regional levels, including specification of goals and guidelines;
- specific planning occurs at the local level, including development of measurable and realistic objectives that are framed in the context of strategic goals and have clear performance indicators;
- explicit linkages are present between objectives and actions and outcomes; and
- actions are consistent with broader strategies, and at a level of detail that allows for consistent interpretation and application.

6　Effective implementation of actions arises from:
- availability of suitably trained staff to guide the planning process and implement the plan;
- links between actions, available resources, the budget process and performance evaluation;
- definitions of roles and lines of responsibility in the managing agency regarding implementation of particular actions; and
- works programmes that are linked with the plan, contain dates for completion of

actions and are fed back into the performance evaluation.

The implementation phase of a planning process should not be seen as a separate task – while implementation itself may be organized through a works plan, the management plan should have explicit links to such lower-level plans, including resourcing, reporting and accountability and review procedures.

7 Formal evaluation of success is an important part of a successful planning process and involves:

- lines of responsibility in the managing agency regarding evaluating performance against objectives;
- mechanisms for ensuring participation of key stakeholders and ensuring transparency of the process;
- mechanisms for formal recognition (and removal from the plan) of objectives that have been met and completed;
- mechanisms for addressing objectives and/or actions that have not been met, including, where appropriate, their modification; and
- clear guidelines for reviewing plans, objectives and actions, including participants, responsibilities and periodicity of revisions.

8 Management plans need to:

- be accessible and easy to read, including availability in local languages;
- be concise yet comprehensive;
- identify and focus on the significant values and issues;
- offer clear direction for future management that incorporates both a long-term vision and measurable statements of what is to be achieved (objectives);
- indicate how the objectives will be met; and
- identify how performance of management under the plan will be assessed, and how the plan itself will be reviewed.

Further reading

Briassoulis, H. (1989) 'Theoretical orientations in environmental planning: An inquiry into alternative approaches', *Environmental Management*, vol 13, pp381–392

Eagles, P. F. J., McCool, S. F. and Haynes, C. D. A. (2002) *Sustainable Tourism in Protected Areas: Guidelines for Planning and Management*, IUCN, Gland and Cambridge

Fallding, M. (2000) 'What makes a good natural resource management plan?', *Ecological Management and Restoration*, vol 1, no 3, pp185–193

Salafsky, N. R., Margoluis, R. and Redford, K. (2001) *Adaptive Management: A Tool for Conservation Practitioners*, Biodiversity Support Program, WWF, Washington, DC

Tasmania Parks and Wildlife Service (2000) *Best Practice in Protected Area Management Planning*, ANZECC Working Group on National Parks and Protected Areas Management Benchmarking and Best Practice Programme, ANZECC, Canberra

Thomas, L. and Middleton, J. (2003) *Guidelines for Management Planning of Protected Areas*, IUCN, Gland and Cambridge

12

Finance and Economics

Michael Lockwood and Carlos E. Quintela

If protected areas are to conserve biodiversity and promote economic development, they must be adequately funded. However, during the past decade there has been little growth in the resources available in many countries. At the same time, there has been a rapid growth in the number and extent of protected areas, the pressures upon them and the demands of management. Moreover, many countries with the highest levels of biodiversity find particular difficulty in securing the necessary funds because of the imperative of poverty alleviation.

In this chapter, we first consider the costs of protected area establishment and management, and the consequent problem of financing protected areas. We outline the main features and steps of business planning, an important tool to assist managers with the task of identifying and securing financial resources. We then discuss the contributions that environmental economics can make to protected area management, including measuring the economic value of protected areas; identifying appropriate pricing policies for visitor services and other uses of protected areas; assessing the economic benefits arising from recreation use, investment of public funds or from creating new protected areas; and documenting the contribution that protected areas make to regional economies.

Note that finance is concerned with the processes and institutions involved with securing and managing funds. Economics is concerned with the allocation of scarce resources, encompassing the analysis and operation of markets (including supply of, and demand for, goods and services); pricing policy; determination of economic welfare; and assessment of both market and non-market economic values (costs and benefits).

Financing protected areas

Financial sustainability for protected areas has been defined by Emerton et al (2006) as the ability to secure sufficient, stable and long-term financial resources, and to allocate them in a timely manner and in an appropriate form, to cover the full costs of protected areas and to ensure that they are managed effectively and efficiently with respect to conservation and other objectives. Ensuring the viability of protected areas is an exercise in effective risk management. These risks come in many forms, intensity and periods in the life of a given protected area. The Vth IUCN World Parks Congress in 2003 identified financial sustainability as a priority concern. As indicated in the seventh recommendation of the World Parks Congress, government policies and other institutional obstacles that, intentionally and unintentionally, restrict the flow of funding to protected areas include:

- insufficient priority allocated to the conservation of nature and associated cultural values against other competing budget programmes;
- revenues from tourist income and environmental services provided by protected areas

Back country helicopter operations, Yosemite National Park, US

Source: Graeme L. Worboys

not being earmarked for protected area management;

- inappropriate management structures that fail to channel funding to protected area management;
- lack of mechanisms to encourage donor organizations to participate in supporting protected areas; and
- limited use of business planning at both a protected area systems level, as well as for specific protected areas.

The financial risk associated with protected areas is expressed in two direct and clearly identifiable ways. First, funding baselines are often below the minimum required to ensure that protected areas serve their function as one of the most important tools for the protection of the world's biodiversity, as well as generating benefits – financial and otherwise – to local communities. Second, the often sharp and unpredictable fluctuations in

funding, primarily in low Human Development Index (HDI) countries, prevent, in a very significant way, these protected areas and the protected area systems from consolidating themselves as operating units. The short-term funding cycle of many donor organizations tends to exacerbate this problem even further.

Assessing the costs

Financial resources often constrain effective management of protected areas and fall well short of needs. Global expenditure on protected areas in the year 2000 was estimated to be approximately US$6.5 billon per year (Balmford, 2003). However, this spending falls well short of that needed to meet management objectives, address the opportunity costs imposed upon local communities, and secure the necessary expansion of the global protected area network identified in Chapter 8. Balmford et al (2003) used a number of different methods in combination to calculate the costs of establishing and running a global reserve system that covers 15 per cent of the land and 30 per cent of the sea. The resulting estimate, US$30 billion per year is nearly five times the expenditure in the year 2000. Spergel (2001) estimated that protected areas in low HDI countries on average receive less than 30 per cent of the funds necessary for basic conservation management, and most of this is sourced from development assistance by multilateral and bilateral agencies and from private donations channelled by national and international NGOs.

Although the numbers may change from assessment to assessment, the reality of the situation is that the world is falling behind in its financial obligation to support the conservation of biodiversity in protected areas. The gap is due to a number of factors, including a failure to keep pace with the rapid increase in the number and extent of protected areas (see Figure 2.1); widespread institutional changes in the public sector leading to protected area management authorities being integrated within broader environmental ministries, with a consequent dilution of specific protected area funds; and widespread economic liberalization, deregulation and decentralization that has resulted in tighter public expenditure (Emerton et al, 2006). The gap is largest, and getting larger still, in tropical countries where most of the planet's biodiversity is found and where the economic problems are most difficult.

Securing adequate funds is a necessary but not sufficient condition for financial sustainability and effective protected area management. It is also necessary to:

- develop cost-efficient systems for management and administration of funds;
- incorporate financial considerations within planning and management processes;
- provide incentives and opportunities for managers to generate and retain funds;
- strengthen institutional capacity to use financial and business planning tools; and
- establish more supportive economic policy and market conditions (Emerton et al, 2006).

In practical terms, however, just increasing the amount of funding rapidly, without acting on developing modern management tools and training local area managers and system administrators to use them effectively, would not achieve the expected results in the field. On the other hand, the limited local capacity cannot be used as an excuse by wealthier nations to delay their contributions. The situation is so urgent that firm action is required on both fronts.

Sources of finance

In order to meet the full costs of managing protected areas, we must radically change our approach to securing the necessary funds. First, we must destroy the false dichotomy between conservation and development. Government mismanagement and failed economic policies hide behind this fallacy. Investment in protected areas can and should be considered an investment for improving the quality of life of the people who live in and around them. Second, we must find ways to increase the efficiency of managing protected areas. We must make the most of the funds available by adopting cutting-edge business planning and management approaches. Finally, we must diversify the available funding to both increase the financial base and to dampen the funding oscillations. A stable funding base typically includes:

- government funding;
- private sector funding as payment of access to, and use of, the protected area;
- local communities' in-kind contributions;
- grants from NGOs and development agencies;
- debt-for-nature swaps;
- endowments, sinking funds and/or trusts; and
- business enterprises that have the potential for generating more or less stable income flows, employment and other benefits for the key stakeholders.

Significant efforts are being made by many conservation finance specialists to open up options for expanded revenue generation for protected areas. Establishing a sustainable and secure financial base for protected areas generally requires a diversified funding strategy that provides a buffer against the failure or reduction in any one source. It also facilitates funding growth by establishing the policy mechanisms and institutional structures necessary to establish new partnerships. Important sources of protected area financing include governments, multilateral and bilateral development agencies, international financial institutions, the private sector, NGOs and individual donors (together with protected areas users, who are covered in the section on 'Pricing services and facilities').

Government funding

Most protected areas are managed by government agencies and (especially in high HDI countries) have a heavy reliance on government funds derived from taxation revenue. Funding to government protected area management agencies is typically provided through annual appropriations from national and sub-national treasuries. These appropriations are usually divided into recurrent and capital expenditure components. Recurrent expenditures are ongoing commitments to staff salaries and the like. Capital expenditures concern investments in specific projects, including new or modified equipment and facilities.

Where possible, governments need to continue to fund protected areas because of the public good benefits that they provide, as well as meeting the wider obligation to maintain the intrinsic and non-use values of natural areas (see Chapter 4) and to protect the natural assets that belong to the people they serve. The private sector, when they use a protected area to generate profits, should be expected to cover their proportional share of the management costs.

Consider the situation shown in Figure 12.1. The demand for private goods (such as commercial recreation tours) from protected areas is shown by the lower demand curve. A market in protected areas would produce an efficient level of supply of these goods from Q_1 protected areas at price P_1. However, the total demand for protected areas (private + public good components) is given by the upper demand curve. The combined demand for private and public values for protected areas is much greater than the private demand alone. The efficient level of supply based on this total demand is Q_2. Thus, a market will undersupply protected areas by an amount equal to $Q_2 - Q_1$.

This provides a rationale for government funding. The private goods associated with protected areas can be bought and sold through markets; but the public good values must be funded by a government subsidy equal to the amount $P_2 - P_1$. From an economic perspective, undersupply of public goods constitutes a failure to maximize social economic welfare.

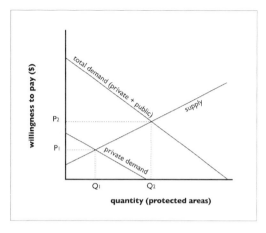

Figure 12.1 Undersupply of public goods

International protected area finance

All multilateral development agencies (such as the World Bank and the United Nations (UN) through its executing organizations) and regional development banks (such as the Inter-American Development Bank, the Asian Development Bank, the African Development Bank, the European Bank for Reconstruction and Development and the Andean Development Corporation) have among their stated objectives the implementation of sound environmental management practices and social safeguards in the projects that they fund. When these projects are near or affect protected areas, they tend to include funding for direct mitigation measures; in some cases, they also make funding available to address the indirect effects of their projects. The Global Environment Facility (GEF) is a unique type of multilateral environmental finance agency that has among its top priorities funding biodiversity conservation and sustainable use, and has been an important source of funding for protected areas around the world (see Chapter 3, p73). Many high HDI countries have their own bilateral aid agencies that, in addition to more general development activities, also support environmental initiatives, including protected areas. Notable among them is the French Global Environment Facility that has been established specifically to support an agenda similar to that of the GEF.

Private sector funding

Many opportunities exist for protected area management agencies to develop constructive partnerships with the private sector. A growing number of business sectors are seeing opportunities in partnership with protected areas and with the communities who surround them. For example, there is a wide range of tourism options that could be exploited through partnerships between the protected area managers and potential investors. Payment for potable water has the potential to become an important source of revenue for protected areas. In this case, the partner may be municipalities, private companies where water services have been privatized, or the agricultural sectors if the water is used for irrigation. The energy sector is another important business partner. Many protected areas are an important source of water to move the turbines of hydroelectric plants, thus contributing to the power generation sub-sector. There is also revenue-generating potential from the scientific value of specific protected areas, where researchers may pay an access fee as a contribution to the management of the reserve, in addition to the cost of their food and lodging. The pricing scheme for each of these types of activities would obviously differ, as is described in the section on 'Pricing services and facilities' in this chapter.

Another important service that protected areas may be able to provide, particularly if there are associated restoration activities, is carbon sequestration. Under the Kyoto Protocol and other international agreements that govern the efforts of governments to curb greenhouse gas emissions, there are provisions for the production and sale of greenhouse gas reduction certificates. These certificates are issued when an enterprise (a protected area included) can demonstrate that it has been able to reduce or mitigate the emission of greenhouse gases (as measured in tonnes of carbon dioxide equivalent) by increasing the efficiency in the use of energy, substituting fuels (as in replacing fossil fuels for hydropower) or increasing the sequestration of carbon in plants, as in reforestation.

Non-governmental organizations

A wide range of international conservation organizations, among them the World Wide Fund for Nature (WWF), Conservation International (CI), The Nature Conservancy, the IUCN, the Wildlife Conservation Society, Flora and Fauna International and Birdlife International, offer some funding, but mostly opportunities for technical assistance and partnerships in the development and implementation of innovative ideas for managing protected areas. Frequently, their support to government agencies is channelled through local partner NGOs. With respect to the specific issue of financial sustainability, the Conservation Finance Alliance is particularly important since it brings together a diverse membership for the purpose of developing and implementing innovative sustainable finance solutions, as well as providing financial training and capacity-building.

Foundations and individual donors

Private donors are a major source of support for protected area management. In low HDI countries, these sources, which include individual donors, foundations and corporations, are particularly important. However, there has been a tendency for support to be directed more towards specific projects with limited time horizons, rather than long-term investment in ongoing management requirements (James et al, 1999).

Fiscal incentives in the form of tax exemptions for donations supporting conservation (and other allowed charitable activities) are important to encourage the development of private philanthropy. In the US, for instance, legislation of this sort has resulted in the growth of a wide range of foundations created by wealthy individuals and corporations for the purpose of funding a range of charitable initiatives. It has also encouraged individuals to give personal gifts for their preferred causes. Their contributions have not only supported the management of public and private protected areas in the US, they have also helped US-based conservation organizations to support their conservation efforts overseas in low HDI countries.

Tax exemptions, although a very powerful tool, are just one of the factors that induce individuals and companies, either directly or through institutional channels, to contribute to conservation. There is a growing trend in corporations to contribute to conservation and charitable causes, in general, as a way of sharing the responsibility for improving the quality of life of the communities with whom they do business. The drive to be a respected corporate citizen is also a powerful force that cannot be dismissed.

Many low HDI countries have a relatively small philanthropic community. In these cases, partnership with NGOs from wealthier countries can be a mechanism to attract funding from individuals, foundations and corporations. These partnerships can take many forms and the specific nature of the transfer of funds can be regulated by tax legislation in the donor country. Nevertheless, these types of partnerships are very common and

have produced significant accomplishments for the conservation of biodiversity and the effective management of protected areas.

Finance mechanisms

Mechanisms for financing protected area establishment and management include environmental taxes and levies, trust and endowment funds, debt-for-nature swaps and ecosystem service markets. Just as a diversity of funding sources can be important for financial capacity, so using a range of methods can contribute to the financial sustainability of a protected area system. In Brazil, for example, government funding of protected areas is supplemented by an environmental compensation mechanism, a National Environmental Fund and internationally funded area-specific programmes (see Case Study 12.1).

Environmental taxes and levies

Governments can impose taxes to generate revenues and/or to discourage activities that are detrimental to the environment. Most countries require an act of their legislature to create new

Case Study 12.1

Protected area funding in Brazil

Over the last ten years, investment in Brazil's protected areas has grown significantly as a result of increased government allocations, in combination with sources such as the National Environmental Fund and the Amazon Region Protected Areas (ARPA) programme.

The National Environmental Fund, created from international loans and agreements and supplemented by fines imposed for environmental crimes, assists in the implementation of Brazilian environmental policy. Since it was set up, the fund has supported more than 900 projects, including integrated management of protected areas.

Brazilian law requires that development projects that may have significant environmental impacts must be licensed by an appropriate federal or state environmental agency. In July 2000, an additional condition of licensing was enacted that required developers to financially support the establishment or management of IUCN Category I to IV protected areas. IUCN Categories V and VI can also benefit whenever they are directly affected by a development project. At least 0.5 per cent of the total project cost must be allocated for such purposes. By 2003, US$130 million had been allocated to protected areas through this mechanism.

Beginning in 1998, the Brazilian government assumed, as a result of a cooperation process with the World Bank and the World Wide Fund for Nature (WWF), a commitment to protect an area equivalent to 10 per cent of Amazon forests in IUCN Category I, II and VI protected areas under the ARPA programme. More than half of the resources of ARPA will be used to establish an endowment fund to be managed by Brazil's Biodiversity Fund (Funbio). In the first phase of ARPA (2002 to 2006), US$81.5 million has been sourced from the Brazilian government (US$18.1 million), the Global Environment Facility (US$30 million), WWF (US$16.5 million) and Kreditanstalt für Wiedereaubau (US$14.4 million), and US$2.5million from other partners. With these resources, approximately 9 million hectares of Category I and II and 9 million hectares of Category VI protected areas will be established. One of the first results of ARPA was the creation of the Tumucumaque Mountains National Park, the largest tropical forest national park on the planet, with 3.9 million hectares.

Source: adapted from Ferraz (2003)

taxes; however, there are certain types of fees that may be put in place without requiring legislative action. For instance, a tourism fee, collected at the airport, has been adopted by Belize to fund its Protected Area Conservation Trust. During the late 1990s, Costa Rica established a fuel tax to support carbon sequestration and forestry projects, a measure that greatly contributed to placing Costa Rica among the leaders in the development of environmental markets. Taxes can be applied to a wide range of transactions, from surcharges for hotel rooms to the purchase of equipment and or the payment for services. However, as appealing as taxes can be to expand the funding contribution of governments for protected areas, they must be carefully considered since they may become an unreasonable burden to those interested in using and supporting protected areas and conservation, in general.

Conservation funds

Most, if not all, protected areas or protected area systems have as one of their sustainable finance objectives the establishment of a fund that, through the investment of its capital, could generate stable and predictable income flows. There are several options that could be considered depending upon the source and the needs of particular protected areas. Two that have been used effectively by many organizations that support protected areas are the sinking fund and the endowment fund. A *sinking fund* is a specific amount of money, the capital, which is invested, typically in a variety of financial instruments. All the income and dividends earned from the investment, in addition to the capital, are then expended on relevant projects. As with the sinking fund, in an *endowment* the capital is invested in a variety of financial instruments; but only the income and dividends are spent for project support. This ensures that the principal of the fund remains untouched and ideally would increase to retain its real value against inflation.

It may be worth clarifying that the term *trust fund* tends to be used interchangeably with 'endowment'; but they are not the same. A trust fund is a contract in which a grantor assigns management and oversight responsibilities of a set of assets to a trustee on behalf of a beneficiary.

These assets could be an endowment fund, a sinking fund or any other financial mechanism, which the trustee must manage on behalf of the beneficiary. The trust adds legal protection against any pressure for the proceeds of the fund to be directed to priorities other than the ones for which the fund was established.

Among the most successful environmental funds that use the whole array of options are Brazil's biodiversity fund (Funbio), Peru's protected areas fund (see Case Study 12. 3) and the Bhutan's Trust Fund (BTF) (see Case Study 12.2). The latter was established by the Bhutan government as a national trust fund with the help of international donors to support conservation activities, including protected area management.

Debt-for-nature swaps

Debt-for-nature swaps are transactions in which a country or financial institution that is owed money by another country foregoes repayment of some or all of this debt in exchange for the debtor country investing an amount equivalent to a portion of the principal and/or interest in nature conservation. The amount of this conservation investment is known as the counter-value and is some fraction of the original debt, often less than 50 per cent.

Many debt swaps have been done since the 1990s. These swaps involve transferring debt from one government to another (official debt) or from private financial institutions to governments (commercial debts). Peru, for example, has conducted a number of such swaps (see Case Study 12.3). These transactions support specific projects and/or are managed by a well-respected environmental fund. During recent years, a new type of debt swap for the poorest countries is being put in place under the Highly Indebted Poor Country (HIPC) programme. Its aim is primarily poverty alleviation; but since poverty and environmental degradation are inextricably linked in most high biodiversity countries, efforts are being made to include environmental components in HIPC debt-relief projects.

Payments for ecosystem service provision

Protected areas provide a range of ecosystem services (see Chapter 4) that benefit people outside their boundaries, such as potable and irrigation

Case Study 12.2

Bhutan Trust Fund

Tobgay S. Namgyal, director, Bhutan Trust Fund for Environmental Conservation

More than one quarter of Bhutan is protected through ecologically representative national protected areas, including four national parks, four wildlife sanctuaries, one strict nature reserve and a network of biological corridors linking all parks (see Figure 12.2). However, until the early 1990s, Bhutan had few means of financing its environmental commitments. As a low Human Development Index (HDI) country with less than 1 million people, of whom 80 per cent are engaged in subsistence agriculture, social and economic development consumed the national budget. Even with per capita gross domestic product (GDP) at US$755, relatively high in the sub-continent, almost all development activities depend upon external assistance (Royal Government of Bhutan, 2003). Therefore, the initiative during the late 1980s to mobilize and sustain substantive funding for conservation was a practical and far-sighted vision by conservationists, donors and the political leadership of Bhutan.

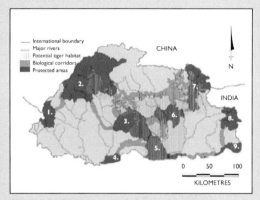

Figure 12.2 Bhutan protected area network

Source: Namgyal (2003)

The Bhutan Trust Fund (BTF) was created to reduce the social 'debt' of financing conservation by sustaining essential conservation programmes, thereby allowing the national treasury to focus on direct poverty reduction. The BTF was established in January 1991, with US$1 million from the World Wide Fund for Nature (WWF) and technical assistance from the United Nations Development Programme (UNDP). Following the Rio Earth Summit in 1992, the fund received US$10 million from the Global Environment Facility (GEF), the latter's second-ever grant and the first to an environmental fund. By 1996, Bhutan mobilized a matching US$10 million from several European countries. Project management strongly contributed to the fund's growth, with GEF grant disbursements tied to fulfilment of major policy and operational progress benchmarks. Guided by Bhutan's strong political will and dedicated donors, the project concluded satisfactorily two years ahead of schedule.

In mid 1996, when the high transactions costs incurred to meet the United Nations' (UN's) financial regulations compromised the fund's sustainability, the original mechanism was dissolved and the current institution was legally incorporated under Royal Charter in Bhutan. Its assets (then US$21 million) were immediately invested in the global capital markets through US-based professional fund managers. The fund is exempted from federal income taxes.

One of the biggest constraints to effective conservation is the absence of local capacity. In the financial year of 1998 to 1999, almost US$4 million was awarded to recruit and train new staff in six priority parks, central regulatory agencies (including the National Environment Commission, the parks' parent agency, and the Ministry of Agriculture), and Bhutan's only environmental NGO, the Royal Society for Protection of Nature. BTF financing enabled the mobilization of 142 conservation professionals, from park guards to atmospheric scientists and graduate ecologists. The collective impact on Bhutan's scientific and management capability for conservation is tremendous, with the conservation sector one of the least dependent upon external technical expertise. On the ground, too, the increased institutional capability for conservation achieved with BTF support complements the goals of other donor-financed interventions. If necessary, BTF can sustain the core costs of Bhutan's parks that amount to about US$1.5 million per annum (Namgyal, 2001).

Manas River, Bhutan

Source: IUCN Photo Library © Jim Thorsell

Case Study 12.3

Debt-for-nature swaps in Peru

Alberto Paniagua V., executive director, Peruvian Trust Fund for National Parks and Protected Areas

From the 1990s, bilateral debt-for-nature swaps were negotiated by several debtor Latin American countries, including Argentina, Brazil, Costa Rica, Ecuador, El Salvador, Guatemala, Honduras, Jamaica, Panama, Peru, the Dominican Republic, Trinidad and Tobago, and Bolivia. The main creditor countries were Germany, Belgium, Canada, the US, Finland, France, Holland, Norway, the UK, Sweden and Switzerland.

By 2003, Peru, for example, had reduced about 70 per cent of its debt with Germany, Canada, the US, Finland, Holland and Switzerland. With the corresponding swaps, it had created local funds for environmental programmes worth US$57 million. The Peruvian Trust Fund for National Parks and Protected Areas (PROFONANPE) was actively involved in bringing about these transactions.

PROFONANPE is Peru's first private environmental fund and the only one to focus on conserving biodiversity in protected areas. It has been designed so that it can capture, manage and channel local and international funds. The fund was a result of negotiations by the Government of Peru, a team of local NGOs devoted to environmental conservation and the Global Environment Facility (GEF). The GEF gave PROFONANPE a seed contribution of US$5.2 million to create an endowment fund, the interest from which would be used to pay the organization's basic operating expenses. Thanks to this arrangement, in eight years PROFONANPE has grown its seed capital about 15-fold to create an overall fund worth US$83.8 million in 2003.

PROFONANPE has negotiated several debt-swap transactions with Germany, Canada, Finland and the US. As a result of the amount of resources involved (US$34.6 million) and the number of operations (eight are under way), this scheme has provided PROFONANPE with the largest portion of its financial portfolio's resources (41.3 per cent). Six of the debt swaps are sinking funds and another two are endowments. PROFONANPE has also established a mixed scheme where the whole of the principal of a sinking fund is disbursed to projects, while the annual accrued interest goes to a separate account that creates an endowment fund once the project comes to an end. Each fund is managed by Peruvian private financial organizations, with investment guidelines set down with the donors.

At present, debt-swap arrangements allow PROFONANPE to fund biodiversity conservation and sustainable development programmes in 18 protected areas with about 11.8 million hectares, or approximately 72 per cent of the Peruvian protected area network. Programmes and projects under way in these areas are carried out by government and private organizations through agreements signed with PROFONANPE.

As countries like Peru near the end of their bilateral foreign debt rescheduling processes, the chance of entering new swap options will become more restricted. Nevertheless, this stage will leave as an undeniable legacy a new breed of institutions, like PROFONANPE, which, building on other and new financing schemes, will continue to contribute to the country's protected areas.

water, water for hydroelectric power, carbon sequestration and retention. For example, the quality of many cities' and companies' water supply is, in part, due to the watershed protection afforded by protected areas some distance from these cities. About one third of the world's largest cities obtain a significant portion of their drinking water directly from protected areas (Dudley and Stolton, 2003). Undisturbed watersheds provide higher-quality water that has less sediment and pollutants. Such services are often taken for granted, in part because the beneficiaries are generally not required to pay for them; however, if they were no longer provided, communities,

companies and, indeed, whole economies would suffer and even collapse completely. Payments for environmental service provision help to ensure a continuity of supply by generating funds to enable proper protection and management of the land and waters from which these benefits derive. In the water supply example, downstream users can be asked to pay for the services they receive from protected watersheds upstream, as has occurred, for example, in Costa Rica (Case Study 12.4).

Georgieva et al (2003) noted that effective development of ecosystem service markets requires that the proponent:

- clearly identifies the services being provided (is able to specify the particular services that are derived from particular areas);
- analyses the demand for services, including who requires them and in what quantities and locations;
- creates supporting institutional structures that enable collection of payments and effective reinvestment in maintaining the supply of services;
- monitors management effectiveness to enable demonstration of service supply characteristics and to identify any potential delivery problems;

- employs flexible mechanisms so that changing demand-and-supply conditions and new knowledge about how ecosystems generate services can be accommodated;
- ensures wide opportunity to participate, considering the needs of poor and marginalized groups in design and implementation; and
- makes a strong business case to potential buyers that this approach is preferable to alternatives such as using technology to treat water to the required standard, or suffering the damage resulting from the loss of services.

Case Study 12.4

Charging for ecosystem services

Costa Rica has instituted a scheme that creates opportunities for private sector firms to pay for environmental service provision. Examples of firms involved in this scheme are given in Table 12.1.

Table 12.1 Examples of companies involved in Costa Rica's payments for environmental service scheme

Company	Watershed	Area protected (ha)	Payment (US$/ha/year)
Energía Global (hydroelectric company)	Río Volcán	2493	10
	Río San Fernando	1818	10
Platanar SA (hydroelectric company)	Río Platanar	1400	10
La Manguera SA (hydroelectric company)	La Esperanza	3000	10
Florida Ice and Farm (drink bottlers)	Río Segundo	1000	42

Source: adapted from Georgieva et al (2003, p3)

The hydroelectric company Inversiones La Manguera Sociedad Anonima (INMAN) signed a contract with the Monteverde Conservation League (MCL) to pay for ecological services provided by the protected area managed by MCL. The Bosque Eterno de los Niños (Children's Eternal Rainforest) is a 22,000ha private reserve managed by MCL. Approximately 3000ha of the protected forest is part of a watershed that is used by INMAN for generating electric power. Recognizing the benefits that they receive from protection of this watershed, INMAN entered into an agreement with MCL to pay for the protection of the ecological services provided by Bosque Eterno de los Niños. The contract recognizes services such as stabilization of land, soil protection, humidity and nutrient retention, water protection and protection of species biodiversity. INMAN pays MCL:

US$10 per hectare (a negotiated price) × Y (a factor that accounts for the amount of energy generated and sold by the hydroelectric plant) × 3000 (for the hectares in the watershed).

The money from this tax is used directly to pay for reserve protection programmes (IUCN, 1998).

Business planning

Business plans are used to guide business development activities. They are being more widely adopted by conservation agencies. Business plans must be developed in the context of a wider management plan that has clearly defined goals and objectives (see Chapter 11). This ensures that generating revenue is a means towards the end of more effective management and does not become an end in itself (IUCN, 2000b). A typical business plan contains the following sections:

- an executive summary that outlines the mission and objectives of the business;
- a summary that provides an overview of the business, including an assessment of resources, location and facilities, ownership structures and so on;
- identification of the goods and services that will be provided and the business's comparative advantage in providing these;
- a market analysis that describes market segments, needs, competitors, trends and growth, and then uses this to develop a market strategy that outlines which customers will be targeted and why;
- a marketing strategy that identifies strategic alliances and explains how the business will position and promote itself, and price and distribute its goods and services, together with a sales strategy with forecasts;
- an indication of the organizational structure, staff and decision-making structures needed to implement the business plan; and
- a financial plan that specifies:
  - key financial indicators that will be used to track performance and the amount of financing required to accomplish the goals;
  - viable funding sources to meet these needs; and
  - a projected cash flow and balance sheet (IUCN, 2000b).

Importantly, these documents are brief, to the point and constantly reviewed. One would expect the board to assess the performance of the venture on an annual basis. As well, there would be at least monthly assessments of business performance throughout the year. Usually this would be undertaken by an executive committee.

As indicated in the list of typical business plan contents, a key component is a financial plan. The financial plan determines the amount and timing of funding required to achieve management objectives, and identifies income sources to meet these needs. Financial planning differs from budgeting (see Chapter 13) in that it is more focused on forecasting required funding, as well as the best potential sources to meet short-, medium- and long-term needs. A summary of the Iwokrama International Centre business plan is given in Case Study 12.5.

Pricing services and facilities

Resource managers are under increasing pressure to adopt user-pays approaches and, where possible, to recover the costs of providing recreation and other services. Managers should be able to justify their pricing of recreation goods and services so that decisions are neither arbitrary nor inequitable (Loomis and Walsh, 1997). The extent of user-pays approaches in protected areas around the world varies greatly. However, in general, revenue falls far short of the real cost of servicing tourism and maintaining the recreation values of protected areas. Most protected area agencies have insufficient funds to adequately carry out both natural resource management and visitor infrastructure management simultaneously. Some agencies charge a fixed fee for all protected areas, some charge for only certain protected areas, and some have fees for particular uses or value-added services, including:

- admission to a particular attraction (such as an historic building);
- use of a specific site or opportunity (for example, many agencies charge camping fees at developed sites);
- instruction and education;
- a licence or permit to undertake an activity (such as commercial film-making);
- a licence or permit to offer a commercial service to visitors (such as accommodation or restaurant); and
- direct purchase of goods, such as maps, books and so on.

Case Study 12.5

Iwokrama International Centre business plan, Guyana

The Iwokrama International Centre in Guyana began operations in 1998. The centre is a body corporate, created by the Guyana parliament with management rights for the 370,000ha Iwokrama Forest in central Guyana. A business plan was developed to present the Iwokrama Centre to prospective business partners and donors and to guide Iwokrama activities for the three-year period of 2004 to 2006. The plan focused on obtaining financing of US$1.05 million for 2005 to 2006 to match projected earned revenues of US$1.155 million and estimated committed and contributed revenues of US$719,000.

The plan is designed to move the centre substantially towards financial self-sufficiency in 2007. It was the culmination of an institutional restructuring that led to a reduction of annual operating costs from US$2.5 million to US$1.5 million and to much greater cost effectiveness and efficiency through better institutional management systems. The business plan is a key instrument for enabling Iwokrama to achieve its mission:

To promote the conservation and the sustainable and equitable use of tropical rainforests in a manner that will lead to lasting ecological, economic and social benefits to the people of Guyana and to the world, in general, by undertaking research, training and the development and dissemination of technologies.

The business planning objectives for Iwokrama for 2005 and 2006 are to:

- reduce Overseas Development Agency (ODA) support from 70 per cent to 35 per cent of revenue;
- convert net earned revenues from a US$300,000 loss in 2004 to a US$60,000 gain in 2006;
- raise US$5 million for an endowment fund to provide an annual revenue in perpetuity;
- triple the number of tourists to over 1500 by 2006; and
- ensure the continued conservation of the Iwokrama Forest through partnerships with local communities and enhanced enforcement capacities.

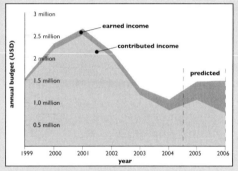

Figure 12.3 Actual and predicted income for the Iwokrama Centre, 1999–2006

Source: Iwokrama International Centre (2004)

Iwokrama's approach is based on developing cross-sectoral partnerships between private sector companies, local communities and the public sector that generate sustainable returns from the assets of the forest. The plan also recognizes a number of risks and associated alleviating actions. For example, the potential for business failures in timber, tourism, training or merchandising are alleviated by thorough market analyses and target monitoring for business revenues.

The major task facing Iwokrama during the plan period is to complete a radical transformation of the way in which it is financed. The organization has been heavily reliant on the patronage of a number of key donors, and while it continues to seek grant funding and assistance from donor agencies, the plan aims to diversify income sources by creating an endowment fund and generating sources of income from its own activities. Actual and predicted income is shown in Figure 12.3.

Under the plan, Iwokrama will concentrate its efforts on the development of business partnerships across four different industry sectors: timber, tourism, merchandising and value adding, and training services. Specific activities identified in the plan include:

- opening five new tourism cabins;
- creating the endowment fund and raising an initial round of US$2 million;
- building human resource capacity for protected area management (15 rangers, 15 guides and 15 managers);
- constructing a new Kurupukari Visitor Centre;
- publishing a ten-year master plan, portfolio and investment prospectus; and
- establishing online purchasing for centre merchandise.

Source: adapted from Iwokrama International Centre (2004)

Justification for user pays

Demand for the benefits afforded by protected areas is likely to continue to rise, particularly with respect to recreation demand (see Chapter 19). This growth is promoted by, among other things, population growth, resource demand, enhanced information availability about the attractions of protected areas, improved access, and transport connections, together with a growing consumer preference for 'quality-of-life experiences', including outdoor recreation. Increased users and visitor numbers will impose additional costs on protected area management agencies. Environmental damage and, therefore, the need to expend resources on rehabilitation, will increase. Services and facilities (car parks, walking tracks, toilets, visitor centres and so on) will require upgrading and expansion. Costs may also be imposed on visitors in high-use areas as congestion diminishes the quality of recreational experiences.

These increased costs make the problem of who should pay for them particularly pressing. Conservation of natural and cultural resources is rightly regarded as a community service obligation for government agencies, and a user-pays system is not applicable to secure the continued supply of these values (QPWS, 2000). However, the costs of providing appropriate infrastructure, facilities and services, repairing environmental damage, and limiting congestion are generated by 'private' consumption of protected area values. The beneficiary and polluter-pays principles suggest that these costs should not be borne by taxpayers, but by users who either gain benefits from the infrastructure, facilities, and services (beneficiaries pay), or who impose environmental or congestion costs on others (polluter pays).

Non-users effectively subsidize users when fees are not charged. Subsidies may be justified to enable low-income earners to visit natural areas. However, at sites primarily visited by high-income earners, the poor may be worse off since they subsidize the free entry of rich visitors through their taxes. A related issue arises when sites have a significant number of foreign visitors who are wealthier than the local taxpayers. This is particularly an issue when visitors from high HDI countries visit low HDI countries (Lindberg, 1998).

Recreation activities are not the only uses that impose environmental costs. Some protected areas are subject to honey production, fishing, cattle grazing and other extractive uses. Again, the beneficiary and polluter-pays principles have application here. However, while local communities often benefit from such activities, they frequently also have to forego potential benefits from alternative uses, such as timber production or mining, and local support can be crucial in achieving successful management outcomes. Such equity and strategic considerations may make it inappropriate to impose additional costs on locals.

Supply costs

Supply costs that may need to be considered in relation to a user-pays pricing policy include:

- capital costs to acquire land and to develop access roads and facilities;
- environmental resource protection and rehabilitation costs;
- agency operation maintenance and replacement costs;
- administrative overhead costs;
- congestion costs for users; and
- opportunity costs of foregone resource development (Loomis and Walsh, 1997).

Measuring expenditure on facilities that are for the sole benefit of visitors is relatively straightforward. However, for many costs it may be difficult to separate out recreation expenditure from other management costs. How much, if any, of the costs associated with running the management agency should be allocated to recreation? How does one separate out the staff costs associated with biodiversity conservation from those associated with recreation? The latter question may be further complicated if some of the biodiversity conservation activities are associated with mitigating the effects of visitor use. The exact proportion of total management cost spent on recreation-related services and facilities is often unclear (Beal and Harrison, 1997). In the end, some judgement must be made based on a reasonable assessment of factors, such as approximate staff time spent on conservation versus recreation-related activities.

Setting a price

The level of charges in a user-pays system should be determined by a clear set of objectives. An agency's choice of revenue objectives can vary according to the type of value and the beneficiary. Objectives for developing a user-fees policy may include:

- equitable allocation of costs;
- cost recovery;
- economic efficiency through identification of a 'market rate';
- maximizing appropriation of consumer willingness to pay (WTP);
- generation of revenue in excess of costs so that other activities, such as biodiversity conservation, can be financed;
- improving facilities and management;
- generating foreign exchange and/or tax revenues from tourist purchases; and/or
- demand management – that is, using fees to limit or redistribute the number of visitors in

order to reduce environmental damage, congestion or user conflicts (Lindberg, 1998; QPWS, 2000).

A brief explanation of some of these objectives and the economic terms related to them is given in Box 12.1.

Some potential relationships between the type of facility, service or value being provided by a protected area, an associated revenue objective and other factors that may justify modification of this objective are summarized in Table 12.2.

For walking tracks, camping areas and the like, revenue objectives are usually limited to partial or full cost recovery. As indicated in Box 12.1, this generally will not constitute the same level of charges as would arise from an objective of economic efficiency. Setting rates below cost recovery can be justified on the basis of the external benefits created by recreation, such as improved health, that reduce costs for other publicly funded welfare programmes. On the

Table 12.2 Revenue objectives for facilities, services and values

Facility, service or value	Potential revenue objective	Mitigating considerations
Infrastructure use – e.g. access roads, visitor centre, car parks, walking tracks or campsites	Cost recovery	Equity, competitive neutrality, demand management, transaction costs, external benefits
Entry to special attractions – e.g. historic buildings or caves	Cost recovery	Equity, competitive neutrality, demand-management transaction costs and external benefits
Commercial products – e.g. on-site accommodation, books, maps or food	Market rate	External benefits
Extractable resources – e.g. honey, fodder, other plant products or fish	Market rate; scarcity rent	Local beneficiaries
Ecosystem services – e.g. clean water or carbon sequestration	Market rate; scarcity rent	Local beneficiaries feasibility and transaction costs
Rental items – e.g. recreation equipment	Market rate	External benefits
Non-extractive occupancies – e.g. power, water and communications infrastructure	Market rate; scarcity rent	Public service and fairness
Non-commercial non-recreation uses – e.g. scientific research	Cost recovery	Value for informing management
Other commercial non-extractive uses – e.g. filming	Market rate	Education or promotion value

Box 12.1 Supply, demand and recreation pricing

A well-functioning market will 'automatically' result in a situation in which supply equals demand. Economists use graphs to show how supply and demand change with the price of a good. In Figure 12.4, at price P_1 the demand for visits is Q_1. However, assuming the management agency can capture visitors' willingness to pay (WTP), they can still cover costs even if more people visit the area. At Q_2 visits, however, WTP is less than the costs of providing this number of visits, so that at this level of visitation the manager would suffer an economic loss. In a perfect market, what tends to happen is that an equilibrium is approached between supply and demand so that Q_3 visits made are produced at price P_3.

This level of visitation is efficient because it maximizes the benefits to both the 'producer' (the protected area agency) and the consumers (visitors). To have one less visit would mean that the agency would miss some potential revenue. To have one more would mean that the agency would make a loss on this additional visit.

With regard to the objectives for a user-pays policy, an agency could, first, set fees per unit at the average cost. This approach would ensure full recovery of costs. At present, most agencies set fees below the level required for full cost recovery.

Second, an agency could set fees at the 'market price' – that is at P_3. This may result in an economically efficient outcome in that benefits would be maximized. However, in general, the shape and disposition of the supply-and-demand curves may be such that an efficient price may not cover the average total costs faced by an agency. Effective competition among private suppliers tends to drive user fees to minimum cost levels; but protected area agencies often do not operate in such a competitive environment and may have a different cost structure. Charging a price equal to the average total cost will ensure that an agency does not make a loss; but this may not maximize benefits (Loomis and Walsh, 1997).

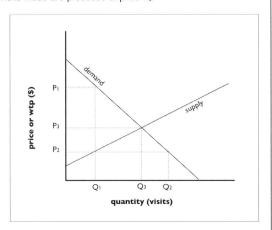

Figure 12.4 Supply, demand and market efficiency

Third, an agency could attempt to capture a larger proportion of users' WTP. They may be in a position to do this because they control a unique resource, for which they are the sole provider. In perfect competitive markets, a surplus accrues to the consumer. However, where a supplier has exclusive control over a particular resource, such as access to a protected area, they can potentially charge a higher fee (a 'scarcity rent') so that the provider appropriates some of the benefit that would otherwise go to the consumer.

The differential between what visitors are willing to pay and what they actually pay is the consumer surplus. In Southern and Eastern Africa, for example, international visitors to protected areas enjoy large consumers' surplus due to disparities between their WTP and the relative low prices (Krug et al, 2002; Turpie et al, 2004). To maximize revenues, as much as possible of this consumer surplus should be captured by the management agency. However, raising prices will also tend to reduce demand and make other destinations relatively more attractive. Elasticity of demand is a measure of the extent to which an increase in price will reduce demand. High elasticities suggest that a price increase will cause a significant drop in demand and, consequently, reduce the number of 'paying customers'. For a protected area with so-called 'inelastic' demand, a price increase will have little impact on visitor numbers. A further complication is that foreign visitor demand is typically inelastic compared with domestic demand, suggesting that a multi-tiered pricing structure is required (see Case Study 12.7).

other hand, fees could be set above cost-recovery level if there is a desire to use price as a mechanism for reducing or redistributing demand. The equity implications of charges should also be considered, with concessions available to low-income earners.

Activities and infrastructure in protected areas such as resorts, shops and commercial tours are usually licensed and a fee is often charged. The magnitude of such fees should ensure that, at minimum, the full costs associated with the activity are recovered and advantage taken of any commercial opportunities. Commercial products, rental equipment and other commercial services should generally be priced at a market rate. However, if such goods and services have associated external benefits, such as educational or safety value, consideration can be given to charging less than a market price.

Many protected areas include residences that could be utilized to generate a financial return. However, in some cases, it may be more appropriate for an agency to encourage provision of services outside a protected area. Such a strategy can minimize environmental costs, pass on the risk to the private sector, and allow the agency to concentrate on the core business of managing biodiversity, cultural heritage and recreation. For example, the US National Park Service has established a collaborative relationship with Delaware North Companies, whom they contract to provide guest services. This concession arrangement has enabled investment in a capital improvement fund, a US$12 million environmental clean-up programme and investment by Delaware North of US$40 million in renovating and upgrading park facilities (Southey, 2004).

Most protected area agencies provide some basic visitor facilities at destinations, but rely on regional towns to provide services such as accommodation, food and fuel. Some agencies do provide accommodation within protected areas, and manage these facilities themselves; but most lease such facilities for a fee. However, as noted above, they also incur costs, and there is a need to carefully evaluate the real costs of providing and managing such developments.

Many protected areas include power transmission lines or other utilities such as gas pipelines. In

some cases, protected area agencies may fund the access roads required to service these facilities. These costs should be recovered. It may also be appropriate to license such utilities and to charge a licence fee.

As we saw in Case Study 12.4, it is possible for a protected area provider to generate revenue through pricing of ecosystem service values. For many protected areas, provision of ecosystem services, such as water supply, is assured because of the mandated management regime applied by the protected area agency. Another authority or company has no need to enter into a contract with the protected area manager because they know that they will continue to obtain the ecosystem services for free. However, it is possible to envisage circumstances where environmental degradation that occurred prior to establishing a protected area may still be compromising potential ecosystem service values. In this case, it may be possible for the management agency to recover some or all of the rehabilitation costs from an organization that will gain ecosystem service benefits from such rehabilitation. It may even be possible to negotiate a market rate or resource rental for the enhanced availability of the valued service.

For resource extractive activities such as sustainable gathering of plant or animal products (Chapter 14), an appropriate objective could be total cost recovery, if not a market rate. However, in many low HDI countries, the need for local communities to make subsistence use of resources mitigates against such pricing policies. The decision regarding which approaches to adopt will be influenced by obligations to assist regional economic development, equity considerations, political acceptability and the need to build good relationships with local communities.

Collection arrangements

Managers can collect fees directly from users, or they can sell collection rights to another individual or organization, who seeks to recoup their costs and generate profit by charging visitors for the value-added services that they provide within the protected area. Managers who collect fees directly from users may have more control over the users and the activities that they undertake. However, they are also then responsible for providing the services on which the fees are based, which can detract attention away from core business, such as biodiversity protection. On the other hand, establishing commercial tourist concessions through licences or contracts with a private operator can generate revenue to protect biodiversity values against the pressures such uses create (see Case Study 12.6). If this option is pursued, it is crucial that contracts have clear and enforceable performance and reporting requirements so that the manager retains control over the nature, timing and intensity of the licensed activities.

Case Study 12.6

Commercial tourism concessions in South Africa

Peter Fearnhead, head of commercial development, South African National Parks

South African National Parks (SANParks) receives an annual appropriation from the South African government, as well as having the right to retain all revenues generated in national parks and to spend these funds on executing its mandate, as determined by a board of trustees.

Late last century, SANParks grew into one of the three largest players in the tourism industry in South Africa, and the largest in ecotourism or nature-based tourism, with in excess of 5200 beds and a further 1000 campsites. Having many of the best natural areas under its management and control, SANParks had a significant influence on the development of the entire industry. However, in 1999 SANParks reviewed its commercial operations and found inefficient delivery of tourism products, often mediocre service standards and poorly rationalized pricing structures.

This led SANParks to develop a Commercialization as a Conservation Strategy, which aimed to generate additional revenue in order to better conserve South Africa's protected areas; provide a foundation and regulatory framework for tourism; and transfer management of commercial operations to private sector operators. A key component of the strategy has been to let concessions in areas such as Kruger National Park for the provision of tourism services.

In most cases, the concessionaire is granted exclusive commercial use rights to a defined area of land, typically between 5000ha and 15,000ha in extent within a protected area, in return for payment of concession fees. At the end of the contract term, all facilities revert to SANParks. The concession contract gives rights of occupation and commercial use of the land, together with a set of obligations on the part of the concessionaire regarding financial terms, environmental management, social objectives, empowerment and other factors. Infringement of any of these requirements carries specified penalties, underpinned by performance bonds, and the sanction of contract termination, with the assets reverting to SANParks. All aspects of biodiversity management continue to be performed by SANParks.

Although the primary objective of the concession process was to generate more revenue for the organization, the processes were designed to encourage partnerships that exhibited the correct mix of financial strength, requisite experience and strong empowerment credentials. The focus of empowerment was on promoting and providing business opportunities for historically disadvantaged entrepreneurs – in particular, those from local communities living adjacent to national parks. This was especially necessary because South Africa's history has been such that the majority have been excluded as users and beneficiaries of the protected area system. In order to encourage a constituency for conservation and support for national parks among the majority of South African citizens, their empowerment is vital. The SANParks concession process placed an emphasis on effective grassroots empowerment at the community level by providing profitable opportunities for community-based businesses and individuals.

As of late 2003, 11 concessions had been awarded to private operators, 7 of which are in Kruger National Park, 2 in Addo Elephant National Park and 2 in Cape Peninsula National Park. In addition, an agreement has been entered into for a private company to manage the one hotel that SANParks has in its portfolio – the Brandwag Hotel in the Golden Gate Highlands National Park.

The results have been beyond expectations. SANParks can depend upon, with a high degree of certainty, the guaranteed minimum stream of income over the concession period, equivalent to 65 per cent of the projected fees. Starting with the guaranteed income, the net present value (see Box 12.3) at a 5 per cent discount rate is 253 million rand, in constant 2003 rand for the 20-year period. The undiscounted, un-inflated equivalent of this amount is 436 million rand. The actual total amount forecast to be paid to SANParks (undiscounted) over the 20-year period is 677 million rand. This represents a major contribution to the future finances of the organization.

Similarly, from a tax perspective, it is estimated that, at maturity, tax receipts will be in excess of 60 million rand per annum, which exceeds the annual operational budget that SANParks receives from the government.

In general, the empowerment results achieved by the bidding process were also good. Three of the successful bidders were black-controlled consortia, and all of the other bidders have significant percentages of black shareholding, with some specifically focused on communities adjacent to the protected area in question. This is considered to be an excellent result in a tourism sub-sector in which black representation in ownership has hitherto been virtually non-existent. In total, the new game lodges are projected to create 683 new permanent jobs, excluding employment created during the construction phase. In terms of the detailed schemes for affirmative action, according to agreed timetables, the concessionaires have undertaken that a minimum of 79 per cent of their employees will be recruited from historically disadvantaged communities, most of which will be those living adjacent to national parks. Concessionaires have also undertaken to outsource minimum guaranteed rand amounts of contracts with local historically disadvantaged business people for the supply of various services. The total of these commitments is 7.8 million rand per annum by the third year (in 2003 terms).

SANParks has had to develop a small, but strong contract management function, which is critical to the continued success of the approach. Any number of issues, from shareholder disputes to environmental breaches, have arisen that needed to be managed carefully, and being able to do so has maintained the integrity of the overall process. In resolving issues and monitoring compliance, SANParks has attempted to be fair minded but firm in its approach and flexible when necessary. On several occasions, SANParks has ordered concessionaires to correct deficiencies, such as the removal of a radio tower, moving board walks and upgrading roads; in other cases, it has fined concessionaires for misconduct. Interestingly, the concessionaires complain regularly that SANParks does not adhere to the same level of environmental standards as applicable to themselves. This was anticipated, and rather than relaxing these standards, SANParks will, over time, have to comply with its own regulations.

The process has greatly expanded the range and extent of sustainable economic activity generated by the national parks without sacrificing their biodiversity objectives. The private ecotourism sector has accepted higher environmental standards and has proposed imaginative schemes, with real benefits to local communities and employees. Initial external fears that the government would remove its subsidy as a result of the generation of additional revenue have proven to be of little substance; in fact, the converse has happened. The process has vastly improved the image of SANParks in the eyes of the South African government, which is seeing that national parks are being put to sensible and sustainable use for the economic development of the country. Correspondingly the South African government has increased its annual financial commitment to SANParks specifically for the creation of new protected areas and the expansion of existing protected areas. Finally, the process has been a two-way street and, in time, SANParks will be forced to meet the same high standards that apply to concessionaires, which can only be to the overall benefit of conservation.

Source: based on Fearnhead (2003)

Note that the beneficiary-pays principle suggests that user charges should not be employed to cross-subsidize biodiversity conservation. While it is consistent with this principle to charge to repair damage arising from use, and to protect environments from such impacts, the wider non-use benefits of biodiversity protection (see Chapter 4) are enjoyed by many non-visitors from around the world. Theoretically, this wider protected area community should pay for general biodiversity management. However, in practice, extracting payments from such a widely dispersed population can be difficult, if not impossible. In high HDI countries, often the best solution is to fund biodiversity conservation from tax revenue. In low HDI countries, this can be more problematic, and

such countries often rely heavily on support provided by international NGOs and institutions such as the GEF.

The cost of collecting user fees is an important factor in establishing a pricing policy. Costs associated with the implementation and administration of a user-pays system are called transaction costs. There is no point in charging user fees if the transaction costs are such that they substantially offset the revenue collected. For a protected area with many entrances, the transaction costs associated with establishing numerous fee collection stations would be high. For a protected area with low annual use, the revenue generated would be low. In both cases, transaction costs are likely to be a high proportion of total costs. Full recovery of these costs is difficult to justify, relative to the value of the damage being caused and/or the services being provided. Of course, transaction costs are also dependent upon the collection method employed, and with changing technology, opportunities may arise to significantly reduce transaction costs.

Typical methods of collection include ticketing in advance, tollbooths, roving staff and honesty boxes. Collection of fees can be done on site. This has the advantage of making a direct connection between the payment and the service provided, and can also facilitate informing visitors about particular activities or regulations. However, such methods are costly in terms of staff salaries and may not be practical for sites with multiple entry points. Alternatives include an honour system with drop boxes for payment, or a system where visitors can purchase a pass to visit any protected areas within a specified period of time. Spot checks may be necessary to give such a system

credibility. Advantages and disadvantages of various revenue collection mechanisms are summarized in Table 12.3.

If demand management is the objective, peak load pricing can be used to control visitor numbers or to redistribute them over different time periods. Peak load pricing refers to the practice of charging different prices over time for the same service. The cost of having excess capacity during off-peak periods can be covered by increasing the amount charged to peak users. Charging higher fees for prime camping sites can help to spread use more evenly. Higher peak-period prices can also be used to perform a rationing function. Variable charges can be used to cover two cost components associated with peak-use periods: increased operating costs of providing services to a large number of visitors; and capital costs of providing adequate facilities to meet peak demand (such as sufficient car park capacity).

Table 12.3 Comparison of revenue collection methods

Fee collection method	Advantages	Disadvantages/constraints
Payment through the post	Administrative convenience; information can be sent	Delay for clients
Credit card payment over the phone or internet	Speed; administrative convenience	Credit card security, staffing telephones or maintaining an automated system
Over the counter payment at protected area offices	Face-to-face staff contact, client briefing and high compliance	Costs of offices and staff; security of cash transactions
Roving rangers	Staff contact and compliance	Auditing problems; security; time consuming; staff costs
Protected area entry stations	Staff contact	Costs of construction and staffing; security
Self-registration stations	Cheap to operate (e.g. in South Australia, 5–10 per cent of revenue raised)	Compliance and enforcement; less staff contact; vandalism
Fixed-location automatic payment machines	Computerized records, low labour costs, and security	As for self-registration stations, plus costs of installation and power supply
Third-party outlets (shops, etc.)	Externalized labour costs and security risks; involvement of local community	Revenue shared with the provider; there may be no knowledge of protected areas at the point of sale

Source: adapted from QPWS (2000)

Another common practice is price discrimination – that is, charging different prices for the same goods or services where the price differences are not proportional to differences in costs. There are a number of reasons why price discrimination may be used. For equity reasons, certain individuals may be charged low prices, or given goods or services free of charge. Such equity-based price discrimination may apply to the very old or very young, local residents or low-income earners. In general, local communities and indigenous peoples should not be charged for access and legitimate subsistence use. Different prices may also be charged to the same person for consuming large amounts of the same good – as in daily versus weekly rates for ski-lift tickets (Loomis and Walsh, 1997).

An important factor to consider is that users are more likely to accept the legitimacy of fees if revenue is retained in the local area, and if an explicit connection is made with improvements to services and facilities (see Case Study 12.7). Care must be taken, however, that facility improvements and the potential increase in visitation that will arise are consistent with strategic objectives for the protected area (QPWS, 2000).

Case Study 12.7 also demonstrates that communication with affected businesses can also be crucial to successful implementation of a user-pays system. Initial industry opposition to increased fees for people undertaking commercial tours to the Great Barrier Reef (see Case Study 12.8) may have arisen, in part, from the fact that the introduction of the new fee did not allow operators to incorporate price changes within pre-sold package tours. A common industry recommendation is for 18 months' notice to be given of price changes. It must be noted, however, that many other industries do not enjoy similar forewarning of cost changes. Implicit in industry opposition to fees is that taxpayers should subsidize their businesses. In practice, who actually receives the subsidy depends upon how much the business can pass cost savings on to clients (Lindberg, 1998). No or low fees at public sites may also disadvantage private providers who must compete with cheaper public alternatives.

Clearly, establishing a recreation pricing policy is a complex task. It is not surprising, therefore, that many agencies are having difficulty grappling with these complexities. Good practice guidelines recommended by the Queensland Parks and Wildlife Service (QPWS, 2000) include the following:

- There must be clear definition of revenue-raising objectives for different types of charges.
- Fees should be set to reflect the level of service, the revenue objectives, estimated public WTP and comparative charges in the marketplace.
- Charges should be presented as a fee for

Case Study 12.7

Recreation pricing in Bunaken National Park, Indonesia

Bunaken National Park is a 89,000ha marine protected area in Indonesia. In 1999, a new national policy of decentralization allowing user fees to be retained locally gave the incentive to the park managers to develop a two-tiered user-pays system. The system was designed with the participation of the tourism industry; the introduction of fees was widely publicized and well understood prior to commencement; and revenue and expenditure figures are available to interested stakeholders. Initially, fees were set at US$7.50 for international users and US$2 for Indonesian visitors. Although visitors' willingness to pay (WTP) was thought to be higher, initially charges were designed to facilitate acceptance of the user-pays approach. In 2001, the first year of operation, receipts were US$42,000, with the 34 per cent of foreign visitors contributing 95 per cent of the revenue. Half of the revenue was used to increase patrol efforts and thereby reduce illegal fishing and damage to coral reefs; 10 per cent was used for a communication programme with local villagers; 20 per cent went to the four levels of government with authority over the park; and the remainder was set aside for the following year. In 2002, entrance fees were doubled, resulting in revenue of US$110,000 from 25,697 visitors.

Source: adapted from Erdmann et al (2003)

services provided, not a fee for entry or access rights.

- Agencies should have the ability to adjust fees, at least to the level of inflection, and the public should be informed to expect these small rises at regular intervals.
- Discounts should be available for children and concession cardholders.
- Accounting procedures should enable estimation of cost effectiveness or profitability of user-pays enterprises.
- Good relationships with, and controls over, all types of commercial operators should be established.
- All conditions of permits, leases and other agreements should be adequate and enforceable.
- New or increased fees for commercial operators should be advised 12 to 18 months in advance.
- Full revenue retention should be achieved by the management agency, with retention of at least a proportion of funds within the local area.
- Disbursement of funds should be in keeping with management objectives.
- The user-pays system should also be used to collect data to assist management, such as visitor numbers and preferences.
- Core management objectives should not be overridden by commercial interests.
- Where necessary, a decline in revenue in the interests of environmental protection should be accepted.
- High-compliance levels should be achieved through workable infrastructure, regular compliance checks and good public support.

Demonstrating economic benefit

As noted in Chapter 4, protected areas make significant contributions to local and national economies. Building political and community support for protected area establishment and management, including adequate financing, requires better communication of these economic benefits. Managers are often in the position of having to justify continued investment in protected areas, to argue for additional funds to

undertake new projects, or to demonstrate the benefits arising from protected areas as a counter to competing or hostile uses and interests. An economic perspective on the issue of who loses and who gains from protected area establishment is given in Box 12.2.

Furthermore, if resources are not individually owned or are un-priced, they tend not to be recognized like other assets, and there is no economic incentive to protect them. Consequently, they tend to be overused or abused, resulting in environmental damage both at regional and global scales. Environmental economists see a partial solution to environmental problems in ensuring that the environment is properly valued to reflect the relative scarcity of protected area benefits.

Measuring economic benefit and cost is fundamental. Credible and reliable estimates of economic value are needed to support the case for investing funds into protected area establishment and management, as well as taking proper account of those who might be disadvantaged from such activities. This section considers several valuation methods and then shows how the results can be used in a benefit–cost analysis (BCA).

Value measurement

Economic values are expressed through the exchange of one thing for another. Such exchange often occurs through the buying and selling of goods in markets, typically involving giving something of value (money) in exchange for a desired good or service. More generally, the exchange value of a good is measured by the amount that an individual is willing to pay for it, or willing to take in compensation for giving it up. Such WTP or willingness to accept compensation are not restricted to market contexts and can also apply to non-market goods, such as biodiversity protection. Biodiversity value also has a non-economic (non-tradable) aspect – some biodiversity is essential to support human life and no amount of another good can compensate for its loss (this value aspect has no price). Many people also consider that the intrinsic value of nature (see Chapter 4) cannot be traded off. Thus, protected area values such as biodiversity are complex, having both economic and non-economic

Case Study 12.8

Great Barrier Reef Marine Park, Australia, environmental management charge

Commercial tourism operators in the Great Barrier Reef Marine Park in Australia are required to pay an environmental management charge (EMC). Most commercial operations in the marine park are subject to the charge, including tourist operations, aquaculture activities, vessel chartering, vending operations, discharge of sewage and resorts. Users who require a permit are required to pay permit application assessment fees (including the costs of environmental impact assessments (EIAs)). The growth in revenue over the period of 1993 to 2003 is shown in Figure 12.5, and the relative importance of the EMC compared with other income sources is depicted in Figure 12.6.

Commercial operations exempt from the charge are private navigational aids, commercial fishing operations, and direct transfer operations from one part of Queensland to another. Commercial fishing does not attract a charge because one is already levied by Queensland fish management organizations. Transfer trips between islands, or islands and the mainland, are exempt on the basis that such passengers are transiting the marine park, not taking part in tourist excursions.

For most tourist operations, the fee is Aus$4.50 per day for each tourist carried. There are some discounts available. All charges are indexed annually to the Consumer Price Index. The total income from the charge during the 2002 to 2003 financial year was Aus$6.7 million, approximately 20 per cent of the budget of the Great Barrier Reef Marine Park Authority. It was originally proposed to introduce the charge on a formula basis. This was not supported by tourist operators since many believed that the actual numbers of visitors undertaking a tourist programme are a more accurate measure of an operator's use of the park. This system has been adopted and involves the addition of new logbooks in which data on park use is recorded. Aggregate data relating to trends in park use provide valuable information on trends and possible problems emerging with increased human activity.

Great Barrier Reef Marine Park, Australia

Source: IUCN Photo Library © Jim Thorsell

A range of activities that may adversely affect the environment within the park requires a permit. Applicants are required to pay a permit application assessment fee (PAAF) prior to the assessment of any application for a permit. The fees range from Aus$510 for a small tourist programme or a vessel mooring to Aus$3660 for a tourist programme carrying more than 150 passengers. Where significant impact assessment is required, higher fees can be levied, up to Aus$79,120 when an environmental impact statement (EIS) is required. A tourism facility such as a new tourist pontoon is usually charged a PAAF of Aus$29,300. Generally, these fees are set at cost recovery or below.

Source: adapted from QPWS (2000) and Skeat and Skeat (2003)

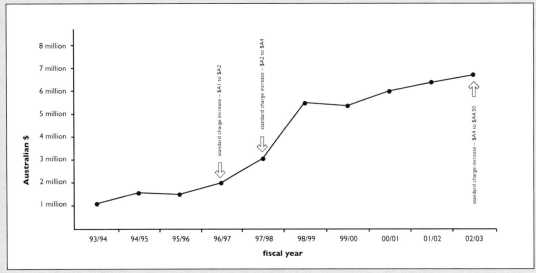

Figure 12.5 Environmental management charge (EMC) revenue in Australian dollars from 1993 to 2003

Source: Skeat and Skeat (2003)

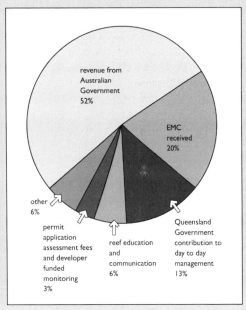

Figure 12.6 Great Barrier Reef Marine Park, Australia, revenue sources for 2002 to 2003

Source: Skeat and Skeat (2003)

Box 12.2 A generalized economic view of the benefits and costs of protection

Establishment of protected areas is typically of benefit to some people and imposes costs on others. To simplify this illustration, imagine that protecting the area in question provides only existence benefits (see 'Value language and classification' in Chapter 4) while imposing costs that prohibit one or more extractive activities undertaken by local people (for example, hunting wildlife and grazing cattle). Of course, any protected area will have a much more complex array of values to be considered (see Chapter 4); but the overall logic of the following simplified analysis would still hold.

The current benefits that local people enjoy from the area are shown by the segments X and Y in Figure 12.7. A decision to protect the area and prohibit hunting, for example, would cause local people to be economically worse off by an amount equal to the size of segment X. The size of the lost surpluses X and Y relative to other sources of economic well-being also give an indication of the level of incentive that people have to ignore or not cooperate with reservation.

The economic benefits that strict reservation would generate for those people who hold existence values for the area are shown in Figure 12.8 by the segments E (hunting prohibition) and F (grazing prohibition). A decision to protect the area and prohibit hunting would cause these people to be economically better off by an amount equal to the size of segment E.

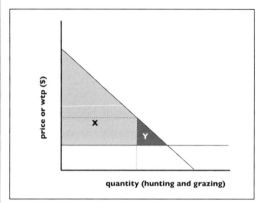

Figure 12.7 Costs of reservation to local people

Source: Adapted from Bagnoli and Rastogi, 2003

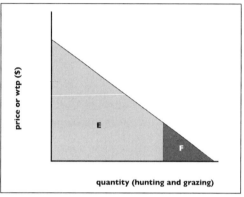

Figure 12.8 Benefits of reservation to local people

Source: Adapted from Bagnoli and Rastogi, 2003

For the limited reservation option to be warranted on economic grounds, $E > X$; and for strict reservation to be economically justified, $E + F > X + Y$. Let us assume that the second condition holds, and that strict reservation yields the best net economic gain. *Distributional issues* then arise relating to whose rights should be recognized. Society as a whole would benefit from reservation; but if local people's rights to hunting and grazing are accepted, then they are at least entitled to compensation for the amounts of X and Y. Alternatively, while they have been using the resources, if local people are not considered to have rights over them, compensation may not be warranted.

Compensation can be in the form of direct payment or through provision of alternative opportunities for income generation or reciprocal agreements for the development of social infrastructure such as schools, medical facilities and water supply (Bergin, 2001; Lovett, 2001). Bruner et al (2001) found that for 93 protected areas across 22 tropical countries, compensation to local communities was strongly correlated with preventing land clearing within protected area boundaries and good condition of the protected area relative to surrounding areas. Community conservation areas (CCAs) (see Chapter 21) are another way in which distributional and supply questions can be addressed simultaneously.

Let us take the argument one step further. People standing to gain existence benefits from reservation reside either in the country in which the area is located (domestic benefit $E_d + F_d = B_d$) or in other countries (international benefit $E_i + F_i = B_i$), where $B_d + B_i = E + F$. Since governments can redistribute resources within their national jurisdictions, when $B_d > X + Y$, it is good economic policy within the country to conserve the region and vice versa. Furthermore, when $B_d < X + Y$, but $B_d + B_i > X + Y$, economic welfare will be improved if an international mechanism can be used to ensure that local people are

---

Box 12.2 Continued

compensated. Those who gain should, in principle, be sufficiently advantaged in order to compensate those who lose and still be better off, accounting for both domestic and international beneficiaries.

Furthermore, consider a world where both supply of protected area values and the demand for them are spread evenly across the planet. Global equity and economic efficiency would require each country to supply their per capita share of global demand. This would involve each country establishing a protected area network sufficient to meet the demands of both domestic and foreign populations without the need for any transfer of money between countries. However, we know that the world is, in fact, highly heterogeneous, with differing levels of endowment and income. Without considerable sacrifice and/or coercion, the right supply of protected areas and their services will not be provided unless additional steps are taken to reconcile the winners and losers. For example, since leisure is a 'luxury good' (demand increases disproportionately with income), income will strongly influence a country's degree of preference for protected areas. In addition, some protected areas may have particular value for local cultures, but not be as highly valued by people from other places. Such considerations affect the relative contributions that should be made by individual nations and the global community. Knowledge of the protected area costs and benefits is a first step in addressing the international distributive aspects of their establishment and management.

Source: adapted and developed from a similar analysis in Bagnoli and Rastogi (2003)

---

aspects. It is the job of economists to measure the economic aspect. Policy-makers then need to include such economic data alongside the non-economic values when making decisions about the establishment and management of protected areas.

Economists use two classes of techniques to measure economic values – revealed preference and stated preference methods. Conventional revealed preference approaches have relied on measurements based on behavioural expressions of value. People reveal the value that they place on a good or service through transactions they make in a market. A technique that uses market prices to estimate the economic implications of a decision is 'change in productivity' analysis. For some goods, such as recreation undertaken in protected areas, direct markets may not exist; but visitors still reveal their value though their willingness to spend time and money in order to gain access to a site. Such revealed preferences for recreation can be measured using indirect market methods based on travel cost.

Recently, economists have also developed methods based on what people say, for example, about their willingness to pay for nature conservation, rather than what they reveal through their behaviour. Such stated preference methods are particularly important with respect to natural areas because many of the potential benefits provided by such areas are not revealed in markets and cannot be recovered through indirect market techniques. At present, the most significant stated preference technique is contingent valuation. Another stated preference technique that has been used to measure protected area values is choice modelling (see, for example, Mathews et al, 2001).

Change in productivity analysis

The economic value of a change in the quantity, quality or availability of a market good or service can be measured using the market price for that good or service. For example, the economic cost of stopping the harvesting of timber products following the reservation of an area as a protected area is equal to the market value of this timber. Such computations can also include the value of lost income when people are put out of work as a result of the productivity change. Another example of the application of this technique is in estimating the economic value generated by the creation of a new tourism opportunity in a protected area.

Travel cost method

The major factor in the production of visitor

services in protected areas is that individuals must transport themselves to the recreation site to consume the service, rather than have the commodity transported to them. Time and transportation services are scarce resources that are central to the individual's decision on whether to use the resource (and to what extent). The recreation consumer relates the time and money costs associated with various outdoor activities to their own resources before making the decision about what activities to undertake and where to pursue them. These features of the visitor experience can be analysed to determine the value of a recreation site.

The travel cost method (TCM) is an indirect market technique that is used for estimating the economic value of recreation. The method uses travel costs to measure how much people are willing to pay to come to an area. The method presumes that, as with other economic transactions, people will make repeated trips to a site until the marginal value of the last trip is worth just what they have paid to get there. Assumptions also need to be made regarding the estimated cost of travel, the unit of observation (individual or group), and how costs are allocated when people visit more than one site.

The method has been used to evaluate recreation in a wide range of settings, including protected areas – for example:

- visitation to Dorrigo and Gibraltar Range National Parks, New South Wales, Australia (Bennett, 1995);
- recreation use of Prince Albert National Park, Saskatchewan, Canada (Loewen and Kulshreshtha, 1995);
- ecotourism value of Monteverde Cloud Forest Reserve, Costa Rica (Menkhaus and Lober, 1996)
- users' benefits from access to Dartmoor National Park, England (Liston-Heyes and Heyes, 1999);
- use value of the Mount Buffalo National Park, Victoria, Australia (Herath and Kennedy, 2004); and
- gorilla tracking in Bwindi Impenetrable National Park, Uganda (Andersson et al, 2005).

Contingent valuation

Contingent valuation is a survey technique that, in its simplest form, asks people how much they are willing to pay for some change in the provision of an amenity, usually a non-market good. The WTP valuations are determined in the context of a hypothetical market that is constructed in the survey. Participants are asked for their WTP contingent upon the existence of the hypothetical market as described in the survey instrument (Wilks, 1990). This hypothetical market typically comprises:

- a description of the amenity;
- the change in its provision; and
- the means (payment vehicle) by which the participant can purchase a particular allocation of the amenity.

Thousands of contingent valuation surveys have been conducted on a wide range of goods, including recreation, wetlands, lake preservation, deer hunting, wildlife preservation, the aesthetic and health benefits of air and water quality, and wilderness. Examples include:

- national park reservation of national estate forests in East Gippsland, Australia (Lockwood et al, 1993);
- recreational economic value of wildlife viewing at Lake Nakuru National Park, Kenya (Navrud and Mungatana, 1994);
- welfare losses from land-use restrictions associated with a newly established national park in Madagascar (Shyamsundar and Kramer, 1996);
- protecting biodiversity and habitat in Siberut National Park and Ruteng Nature Recreation Park, Indonesia (Kramer et al, 1997);
- WTP for the maintenance and preservation of Borivli National Park, India (Hadker et al, 1997);
- lost passive-use benefits associated with damage to Israel's Carmel National Park (Shechter et al, 1998);
- improvements in infrastructure and services at Poas National Park and Miguel Antonio National Park, Costa Rica (Shultz et al, 1998);

- tourists' WTP for visits to Seychelles marine national parks (Mathieu et al, 2000);
- tourists' WTP for maintenance and conservation of the Khangchendzonga National Park, India (Maharana et al, 2000); and
- use and preservation values of natural and cultural resources in five Korean national parks (Lee and Han, 2002).

There has been considerable controversy in the literature concerning the ability of contingent valuation surveys to provide valid measures of environmental economic values. The arguments both for and against contingent valuation are complex and, at times, very technical – they are not detailed here. Suffice to say that efforts to further test and refine the method are continuing.

Input–output analysis

Economic valuation techniques such as TCM and contingent valuation are directed towards estimating the impacts that a particular protected area or policy proposal has on economic welfare. Another approach is to assess the contribution that a protected area makes to an economy. This can be done at a local, provincial or national scale. Economic activity associated with protected area management and tourism expenditure is a significant component of employment and economic activity in some areas. A technique used to perform such an assessment is called input–output (I–O) analysis. I–O analysis measures how an allocation of resources would affect regional income, expenditures and employment.

Expenditure by protected area tourists, for example, generates additional direct and indirect income. Protected area tourism adds value to economies from products and services provided directly to tourists, such as accommodation, restaurants, transportation, crafts and so on. Value added is the net value of the goods and services produced, taking into account the cost of inputs to the production process, such as raw materials and labour, as well as capital depreciation. There is also indirect income from the demand generated in the rest of the economy by the tourism industry. In order to provide services to tourists, accommodation providers must purchase goods and services such as food, clothing, fuel and telecommunication. Industries producing these goods and services must, in turn, employ workers and purchase inputs. People employed in supplying these goods and services earn wages that are used to purchase other goods, and so on, so that there is a flow-on effect that indirectly contributes additional value to an economy. The ratio of the direct impact to the total (direct plus indirect) contribution is called a 'multiplier' (Turpie et al, 2004).

The Australian state government agency, New South Wales National Parks and Wildlife Service (NPWS), has used I–O analysis to evaluate the direct and indirect effects on regional economies of agency and tourist expenditure on areas such as Montague Island Nature Reserve, Fitzroy Falls Visitor Centre and Warrumbungle National Park. For example, the annual contribution of Warrumbungle National Park to the Coonabarabran regional economy was estimated to be Aus\$2.08 million per year of 'value-added' activity, with Aus\$1.37 million of this spent on wages and salaries – the equivalent of 66 full-time jobs (Conner and Gilligan, 2003). Another example of an input–output result was presented in Case Study 4.2 in Chapter 4.

Benefit–cost analysis

BCA is the standard economic technique used to assess the economic benefits and costs of public decisions, including those affecting protected areas. BCAs have been conducted, for example, on issues such as the proposed construction of the Gordon-below-Franklin dam in what is now a world heritage national park in Tasmania, Australia (Saddler et al, 1980); various development options for 'Donau-Auen' National Park in Austria (Kosz, 1996); dredging of the Benji Dam in Zimbabwe's Gonarezhou National Park (Tafangenyasha, 1997); and establishment or exploitation of the Ream National Park in Cambodia (De Lopez, 2003).

If a project is to be judged worthwhile according to BCA, the aggregated benefits to society must exceed the aggregated costs. For example, Figure 12.9 compares the (simplified) costs and benefits of two alternative land uses – clearing a forest area for grazing pasture, and reserving the forest as a protected area. Forest

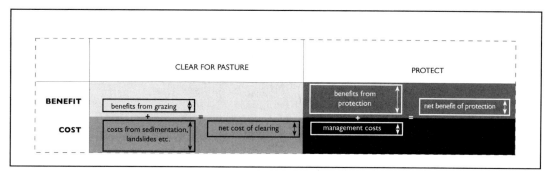

Figure 12.9 Illustration of the net benefits of protecting forested watersheds

Source: adapted from Georgieva et al (2003)

parks protect water catchments, preventing sedimentation, soil erosion and landslides that, among other things, degrade water quality and adversely impact upon communities and industries reliant on clean water for domestic use, irrigation, industrial processes, fishing and recreation. Forest clearing also results in a net increase in carbon emissions to the atmosphere, exacerbating the greenhouse effect and global warming. In the case illustrated in Figure 12.9, the loss of these services would not be outweighed by the benefits arising from land clearing, so reservation is the economically superior option.

BCA is concerned with public benefits and costs. Public costs may include impacts on recreation values (measured using the TCM) or impacts on the non-use values of a natural area (measured using contingent valuation). Some of the basic elements of a BCA are described in Box 12.3.

An economist conducting a financial analysis of a private investment for a company will use many of the same principles as BCA, but will only consider benefits and costs that directly impact upon the company. Furthermore, company managers may be more interested in what the analysis says about the return on their investment, rather than using a measure such as Net Present Value (NPV), which is commonly employed in the assessment of public policy. A private company will also consider such matters as the impact of an investment on their share price, their strategic position in the marketplace and taxation implications.

Balmford et al (2002) calculated that an effective terrestrial and marine reserve system would cost around US$45 billion per year and provide benefits worth between US$4400 billion and US$5200 billion, depending upon the level of resource use permitted within protected areas. This is a cost–benefit ratio of about 100:1. Turpie et al (2004) estimated that the costs of Namibia's protected area system of about 160 million Namibian dollars are far outweighed by benefits of between 940 million and 1900 million Namibian dollars. A summary of the on-site economic benefits of Ream National Park in Cambodia, together with a BCA of conserving mangroves in the park, are given in Case Study 12.9.

While protected areas afford large economic benefits, the often significant opportunity costs on local communities should also be recognized. For example, the value of foregone resource use due to the creation of Khao Yai National Park in Thailand was estimated at 27 million baht per year (about US$675,000). This is about nine times the cost of managing this park (Emerton et al, 2006). In such cases, in the interests of equity, some of the net benefits from establishing a protected area should be used to compensate local people for lost or reduced access to resources.

Management principles

The following principles summarize the key messages from this chapter and also incorporate key points from the recommendations and actions adopted by the Vth IUCN World Parks Congress.

Box 12.3 Steps in a benefit–cost analysis (BCA)

The basic steps in a benefit–cost analysis (BCA) are:

1   Identify the alternative proposals to be examined and the 'lifetime' of each proposal – for example, the productive life-time of a visitor centre might be 20 years.
2   Identify the values associated with each proposal that can be measured in economic terms.
3   Identify each of these values as either a benefit or a cost.
4   Quantify these benefits and costs in dollar terms, using a suitable economic valuation methodology.
5   Assess the project according to a decision rule. Two commonly used decision rules are the benefit–cost ratio (a project has a positive net social benefit if benefits/costs > 1) and the Net Present Value (NPV) (an activity is economically bene-ficial if NPV > 0).

The NPV for a proposal is calculated by adding up the net benefits over the lifetimes of the proposal. If the NPV is positive, then benefits outweigh costs and the project makes economic sense. If the NPV is negative, then from an economic point of view the project should not proceed. The higher the NPV, the more economically valuable the project is. NPV is given by the following formula:

$$NPV = \sum_{t=1}^{t=n} \frac{B_t - C_t}{(1 + r)^t}$$

where:

- t is a particular year of the project, which ranges from 1 at the start of the project to the lifetime of the project at n years;
- $\displaystyle\sum_{t=1}^{t=n}$ means 'the sum of, over the years between and including year 1 and year n';
- B_t are the benefits in year t;
- C_t are the costs in year t;
- r is the discount rate – e.g. for a discount rate of 10 per cent, $r = 0.1$.

The formula therefore means that NPV is given by the discounted value of benefits minus costs, added up for each of the years during the life of the project. To calculate NPV, we must work out the net value for each time period, apply the discount rate and then add up the results for all time periods.

Accounting for time

The idea of using a discount rate requires a brief explanation. A complicating factor in BCA is the temporal nature of both costs and benefits. Comparing the benefit stream with the cost stream over time requires that all present and future values be put into a common frame of reference called present value (PV). The determination of PV is done through the use of a discount rate.

Using a discount rate, the value of a dollar in five years' time is considered to be less than the value of a dollar today. To see this, consider your own attitude to having $100 in your hand today and $100 in your hand at the end of the year – which would you prefer? If you prefer the money today, then the value of the money in a year's time must be less than it is today. The discount rate r is a measure of how much the value of money decreases over time: the longer the time, the less the value. To be precise, the net value for each year is divided by a factor of $(1 + r)^t$ where t is the time period. Note that we are not talking about inflation here – the value decreases even in the absence of inflation.

Case Study 12.9

Economic value of Ream National Park, Cambodia

Ream National Park in Cambodia is an important economic resource for 30,000 local people. Up to 84 per cent of households depend upon park resources for their basic subsistence and income. Products from terrestrial areas include firewood, timber, wild plants for food, medicines and handicrafts. In addition, about 500 fishing boats operating in or near the park harvest about 30 species of marine fishes, crustaceans and shellfish, along with 8 species of freshwater fish. These activities yield a net value of US$1.24 million per year, an average of US$233 for every household in and beside the park. This is in an area where the median family income is US$316 per year.

A benefit–cost analysis demonstrated the high value of mangrove conservation in the park. It was estimated that clearing the mangroves would reduce local income by US$620,000 a year. Other economic losses included in the analysis were damage to houses, infrastructure, farmland, employment and markets, and loss of ecosystem service values, including carbon sequestration benefits. Taking these indirect economic benefits into account, the total annual economic value of conserving Ream's mangroves was estimated to be US$900,000 a year. This was far more than a one-time gain of clear-cutting the mangroves and converting them to prawn farms.

Source: adapted from ICEM (2003a)

1 Protected areas deserve significant financial support owing to the substantial benefits that they provide. Securing the necessary finance necessary for effective protected area establishment and management will require managers to:
   - compile information for the development of a credible estimate of funding needs for protected areas;
   - improve financial administration and effectiveness to ensure that funding is allocated and spent in a way that supports conservation goals;
   - communicate the results of investments in protected areas more effectively to the global and national communities;
   - develop and implement sustainable financing plans;
   - increase, diversify and stabilize the financial flows to protected areas through the implementation of diverse portfolios of financing mechanisms and cost-effective management approaches, including user and service charges, trust funds, private philanthropy, private sector partnerships, debt relief and significant government investment;
   - enhance the opportunities for public–private–community partnerships in protected area management and funding;
   - foster partnerships with potential donors that develop a shared vision for conservation outcomes;
   - adopt business planning, marketing and related techniques appropriate to the management of protected areas;
   - use private sector expertise to manage financial assets;
   - ensure that there is proper valuation of the goods and services provided by protected areas so that decisions about economic development are made with the full understanding of the costs and benefits involved;
   - ensure that where specific private sector activities affect biodiversity, natural or cultural heritage adversely, the responsible parties should meet the costs of avoiding, minimizing, mitigating, restoring or compensating for damage caused, including through support for protected areas;
   - ensure that protected areas, and the surrounding local communities and indigenous peoples, as primary beneficiaries are granted access to the benefits from the increasing number of opportunities to gain remuneration from protected areas; and
   - encourage governments at all levels to increase the financial flows to protected

areas by reducing and redirecting funding currently allocated to subsidies for fishing, agriculture and other sectors that contribute to environmental degradation and biodiversity loss.

2   Protected area assets have significant economic values, a portion of which can be captured through user-pays approaches, including recreation and other user charges, as well as concessions combined with firm contract management. Economic principles can be used to help develop fair and efficient pricing polices for visitor services and other protected area uses.

3   Protected area advocates must work to reduce the perverse subsidies, policy and institutional failures that prevent integration of protected areas within the mainstream of development strategies.

4   Managers need to encourage collection of economic data related to protected area values in order to better inform decision-making and enable better communication of protected area benefits to communities, governments and donors. Assessment of the costs and benefits of protected area management and investment strategies should take full account of the relevant market and non-market economic values. Well-executed analyses of economic benefits can convince governments, communities and the private sector of the importance of investing in protected areas.

5   Economic understanding can help an agency to justify investments and make decisions that maximize net benefits. Information about the economic benefits of protected areas can be used in planning decisions about protected area management and investment strategies.

6   By securing revenue return to local managers and allowing managers to retain the greater proportion of those funds for works (on sites where the revenue was collected), local managers are empowered and have the incentive to collect revenue. They also have the ability to demonstrate directly to visitors the benefits of the revenue collection.

7   Some aspects of protected area management are likely to benefit from being run like a business. Protected area managers need to adopt business and financial management techniques to secure the funds necessary to achieve management objectives. Business planning, in particular, is an important tool for achieving sustainable financing of protected areas.

8   Protected area managers need to be aware of the different economic impacts of protected area management and expenditure on different groups. Attention should be paid to the distributional consequences of protected area establishment and management, including impacts on local communities and indigenous peoples. Managers should seek to ensure that local communities and indigenous peoples who bear costs associated with protected area establishment and management are recognized and adequately compensated.

9   While it is important to adopt imaginative financing strategies, protected area planners and managers should also weigh up the pros and cons of different funding options against their core management objectives.

Further reading

Conservation Finance Initiative (2004) *Conservation Finance Guide*, www.guide.conservationfinance.org

Emerton, L., Bishop, J. and Thomas, L. (2006) *Sustainable Financing of Protected Areas: A Global Review of Challenges and Options*, IUCN, Gland and Cambridge

IUCN (1998) *Economic Values of Protected Areas: Guidelines for Protected Area Managers*, IUCN, Gland and Cambridge

Loomis, J. B. and Walsh, R. G. (1997) *Recreation Economic Decisions: Comparing Benefits and Costs*, 2nd edition, Venture, State College

QPWS (Queensland Parks and Wildlife Service) (2000) *User-Pays Revenue: Benchmarking and Best Practice Program*, ANZECC, Canberra

Quintella, C. E., Thomas, L. and Robin, S. (eds) (2004) *Proceedings of the Workshop Stream 'Building a Secure Financial Future: Finance and Resources', Vth World Parks Congress*, IUCN, Gland and Cambridge

13

Managing Staff, Finances and Assets

Graeme L. Worboys and Colin Winkler

Managing staff, finances and assets lies at the heart of a protected area organization's capacity to operate. People are needed to achieve an organization's primary mission. Staff (and contractors) must be hired and paid. They need a base from which to operate. Hence, offices and workshops must be purchased, constructed or leased. People need to be mobile and to have access to equipment and materials. This may require the use, hire or purchase of transport, vehicles, heavy construction plant and other equipment. Staff also need a supportive operating framework, which ranges from employment contracts to workplace safety rules and skills training. Financial budgets need to be secured and managed. Bills have to be paid. Staff should be treated fairly. Workplaces need to be safe. Systems need to be in place to evaluate and monitor the staff's performance so that professional standards remain high. Numerous routine administrative tasks and systems are required to support the conservation of a protected area. Organizations must operate fairly and equitably relative to their staff, and need to be accountable. Well-designed administration systems help to manage these needs. In this chapter we give an applied perspective on such basic systems.

Texts that provide more in-depth treatments that may be of interest to some protected area managers include Mitchell (2002), who provides a comprehensive, fully integrated statement of administration and management strategies, processes and cultures that must be considered and implemented by organizations striving to excel; and Finkler (2001), whose book is intended for managers who must obtain and use financial information, and accordingly provides the foundation of managerial accounting. Additional guidance on ethical decision-making can be found in McNett and Søndergaard (2004).

Human resource management

Human resource (HR) management needs to be distinguished from management as discussed in Chapter 6. Both are concerned with people; however, management as outlined in Chapter 6 is essentially a 'line' issue (directly focused on attaining an organization's key goals), whereas HR management is basically a 'staff' matter (that is, concerned with supporting the line management process and indirectly linked with the organization's goals). How people are supported will vary between organizations and also will vary between nations with their different cultural, linguistic and socio-economic circumstances.

A process for human resource management

The steps taken by an organization to provide the right people in the right positions at the right times is known as the HR management process. It is about being organized in securing staff and ensuring that administrative systems support them and their work. This is critical if a protected area management organization is to achieve its goals. Nine steps are recognized:

1   HR planning;
2   recruitment;
3   selection;
4   induction;
5   training and development;
6   performance management;
7   compensation (payment or reward for services);
8   movements (promotions, demotions or lateral movement within an organization); and
9   employee welfare and services (Stoner et al, 2004).

The relationships between these steps are indicated in Figure 13.1.

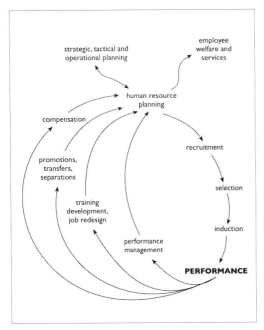

Figure 13.1 The human resource management process

Source: Stoner et al (2004)

Human resource planning

An organization usually plans for the people resources that it will need to accomplish its goals. HR planning is designed to ensure that the people needs of an organization are met constantly and appropriately. Typically, an analysis of internal factors, such as the implications of strategic plans for current and anticipated needs, and external factors, such as the labour market and emerging technology, is conducted. Once this has been completed, managers can compare future staffing needs against the existing human resource situation. This will help to determine what recruitment, induction, training and development, and other internal people-support procedures will be required. The internal and external environments of an organization constantly change, which means that managers must monitor these environments to keep their HR plans up to date.

Sometimes there is very little HR planning, and organizations tend to be reactive rather than proactive. Long-range planning is not seriously considered, to the detriment of achieving protected area conservation goals. This happens because the planning departments of organizations often lack personnel with expertise in statistics, forecasting, organization development and strategic HR management. So, if any planning is done at all, it is usually confined to setting general and departmental goals and rarely includes carefully developed strategic plans. Often HR issues are not integrated within organizational strategies (Debrah, 2002). The internal environment of a protected area organization, as well as its external environment, will broadly define the limits within which an HR plan will operate. Within these limits, a manager can compare staffing needs with the existing staffing profile to determine recruitment and training requirements.

Recruitment

Recruitment is the process of seeking and employing candidates to fill staff positions. It is also used to hire people on contract to complete short-term positions. Recruitment is typically achieved through avenues such as newspapers and other media advertisements, the internet, employment agencies, head-hunting firms and word of mouth. The recruitment process is supported by descriptions of the position to be filled and the advertisement.

Position descriptions. Every position in an organization should have a position description listing the tasks, duties and responsibilities that the position entails. Typically, it will include a position title, reporting arrangements, a summary of the position's primary responsibilities and a list of core duties.

Rangers, Manas Wildlife Sanctuary, India

Source: IUCN Photo Library © Jim Thorsell

Position specifications (competency standards). Position specifications define the background, experience, knowledge, skills and other personal characteristics that an individual needs to perform effectively and efficiently in a particular position. Organizations may require a certain minimum operating standard for specified positions. Competency standards specify the theoretical and practical knowledge and skill required in the workplace. Salary bonuses are often linked to enhanced competencies and may involve evaluating a number of relevant skills. Competency standards provide a way of comparing qualifications and skills for staff of the same name (such as 'ranger') between different jurisdictions. This matters when staff move or are exchanged between agencies. Performance management systems link competency agreements, performance agreements and performance evaluation.

Job advertisements. These are the brief written statements used to advise potential applicants that a position is vacant and that candidates are being sought for filling the position. Typically, they include a position title and reference number, a brief description of the principal duties, and a contact name and phone number for further information. They will also have a closing date for applications. Advertisements are typically posted on websites and placed in newspapers and specialized magazines. Advertisements need to be carefully written. These should not unfairly exclude or advantage certain groups, yet should be clear about the qualities needed for a position. Potential applicants should know the skills and background sought. In addition, a clear statement of the information required for an application needs to be stated. If not, the organization will be disadvantaged since unnecessary time will be absorbed in dealing with applications received from unqualified people. Staff responsible for responding to calls from applicants will need to be thoroughly briefed on the nature of the advertised position.

Selection

Selection is the process of choosing a new staff member from (usually) a number of potential candidates. An interview panel is usually appointed early in the process, and great care is taken to ensure that the panel's composition reflects cultural, social and expertise considerations that support a fair interview process. The advertisement is placed, and candidates complete an application and usually submit this along with a brief résumé. Depending upon the number of suitable candidates, the panel may be required to reject some applicants with the correct qualifications. A shortlist of applicants is usually completed using very clear and agreed criteria. The selection typically involves a face-to-face meeting between the panel and candidates, where each candidate responds to a number of set questions. The interview process may also involve interview tests and usually includes background investigations and confirmation of qualifications cited. The selection process is essentially mutual decision-making, with management deciding if an applicant can be appointed (and is the best candidate), and the applicant deciding if he or she wishes to work for the organization. Depending upon demand and supply, the process could be rather one sided. An indicative selection process is presented in Figure 13.2. The use and order of steps may well vary depending upon the nature of the position in question.

Recruitment and selection are by no means rigid procedures, and not only vary considerably between countries, but also between organizations within the same country. National culture and governing institutions have significant effects on the ways in which people are recruited and selected.

Sometimes, rather than using systematic procedures for recruitment and selection, such as advertising jobs in newspapers, reviewing applications, holding interviews and testing applicants, the process of recruitment and selection can be a bureaucratic and administrative formality. There are cases where vacancies are filled before they are advertised. It is also a practice to hire new employees without necessarily having vacancies. In some areas it may be difficult to get employ-

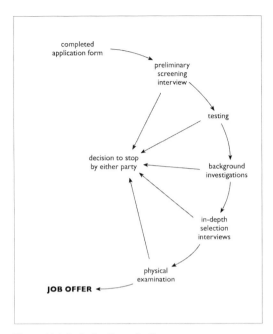

Figure 13.2 An indicative selection process

Source: French (2006)

ment without having contacts with people within an organization. Friendship and kinship can take precedence over qualifications and abilities, as managers feel obliged to support their relatives and friends. Reciprocity occurs from new employees given that they agree with those who hired them (Branine, 2002). Given that the task of achieving protected area management outcomes requires the best people for the jobs at hand, such practices may not be in the best interests of achieving long-term conservation outcomes.

Temporary staff. Temporary staff provide assistance to full-time employees during seasonal peak-load periods, such as a fire season or during holiday periods. They may be selected by an interview panel or, if only required for short periods, may be directly appointed by a manager. Temporary staff may also be employed as a consequence of grants or from revenue earned within protected areas. They are not contract staff and are typically employed under temporary staff provisions of employment awards. Managers need to take care to spell out and record the terms and conditions of employment for such staff.

Contract staff. In some protected areas, certain work is undertaken by contract staff, such as track maintenance or conducting an expert survey on a cultural heritage site. People are usually contracted for short periods to do specific tasks and generally are paid for actual work completed. Management of contractors includes preparing an order or contract, which may be standard legal documents that are supplemented with specific task descriptions and performance measures. Managers need to ensure that the terms of reference are as clear as possible, including specification of the standards that contractors are required to adopt while working in protected areas. There may be provision for progress payments to be made on the basis of reaching specified targets, with a final payment made upon successful completion of the project. Issues such as who owns intellectual property (for reports and research work) and mechanisms for terminating the contract should be specified in the contract.

Induction of staff

Induction is designed to help successful candidates commence work at their new workplace. It assists people in fitting in smoothly within an organization in terms of personal relationships, job responsibilities and organizational policies. The importance of the induction process is often underestimated by managers. When staff are new, they are highly receptive to new ideas and ways of doing things. They tend to closely observe their new environment and appraise the strengths and weaknesses of the organization and its managers. Managers need to ensure that at this time new staff get the attention, skills and training they need. Often, mentors are assigned to assist with the induction process.

The induction programme may comprise a formal course or consist of a more casual process facilitated by an experienced staff member. An induction manual should be provided that describes the organization's structure and mission, as well as:

* strategic priorities;
* code of conduct;
* personnel policies and systems covering such areas as work and family, leave, staff accommo-

dation, uniforms and smoking in the workplace;
* competency required (for a given position);
* training and skill development opportunities;
* customer service policies and protocols;
* how and where to access important corporate information; and
* how to use internal information systems (such as an intranet).

As part of an induction programme, managers may set up a familiarization scheme of protected areas and the key destinations for their new staff. This is important for field staff. Staff may also be trained, prior to a fire season, winter season or a busy tourist season, with the handling of plant and equipment that is used for dealing with such operations and for resolving potential incidents.

Training and development

Staff training is aimed at improving staff knowledge, skills and attitudes in relation to an immediate task or work requirement, and staff development has a longer-term investment context, such as equipping selected staff with the skills needed for higher positions within an organization. Training and development is aimed at increasing the ability of individuals and groups to contribute to organizational effectiveness.

For long-term success, an organization needs to invest in the training and development of its staff. Training needs to be directed towards those competencies that an organization's corporate mission requires. The first step is to determine the current competencies of the staff, to identify any gaps and to design a training scheme to bridge these. Then, resources must be planned to underpin the training. Training needs should be constantly monitored.

Staff need to have basic protected area management competencies; if possible, they need to be up to date with advances in legislation, project management techniques, accounting systems, computer software and other organizational skill needs. Training helps to create an internal culture focused on constant improvement. It can also help to maintain a corporate culture by providing background and information about the history and identity of an organization. Training is commonly undertaken at all levels within an organization. It can be formal and informal. Practical operational training is typically 'on the job' and is conducted at a local level. If there are risks or hazards involved, such as using a firearm, a chainsaw or operating a four-wheel drive, all such training must be completed in accordance with best practice standards for safety and with qualified instructors. More formal training courses are usually administered through an organization's human resources section. A protected area organization may also arrange formal accreditation for its training with a college or university. Other types of training may be contracted to universities or colleges. Many organizations foster an environment of continuous learning, and explicitly encourage and recognize their staff's vocational training. Staff may also benefit from time-release schemes that allow them to be seconded to other organizations or to undertake specialist study or project work. Developing capacity for protected area management is addressed in more detail in Chapter 7.

Larger protected area organizations need to be continuously developing the skills of individual staff in order to achieve conservation outcomes and to meet corporate responsibilities. They will always need to have replacement staff with sufficient skills and experience to achieve smooth succession capacities as staff retire or leave an organization. This approach is relevant to front-line, middle-level and top-level staff. An organization needs to be actively grooming people for appointments at higher levels. All key positions (not only senior appointments) should be subject to a succession plan. Relevant academic qualifications are an advantage for staff, but this may not always be possible. The optimum is where operational staff possess practical skills, combined with suitable academic qualifications. Tertiary-level qualifications, for example, can provide ranger staff with basic knowledge and skills in protected area management. These qualifications are an essential grounding; but they need to be augmented by on-the-job training, professional experience and continuous professional development.

Performance management

Performance management compares an individual's job performance against agreed-upon goals, and provides systematic and comprehensive feedback to the employee. It may also provide an opportunity for 'feed-forward' concerning an employee's plans, and may form the basis for changes in salary, job redesign and job movement. Performance management is an important task for any manager; yet it is one that many managers freely admit they often have difficulty in handling adequately. It is not always easy even to appraise a subordinate's performance accurately, and it is even more difficult to convey that assessment to the subordinate in a constructive and painless manner.

Performance management and development systems are important ways of measuring and improving the contributions that staff members make. These systems can also empower staff to plan their own careers by giving them confidence that they and their supervisors are using the same standards to judge their performance. Such systems link training and development with the requirements of the job and the mission of the organization. Typically, such systems work in three stages.

1   A work plan is developed between a supervisor and an employee. It is clearly linked to the organization's strategic plan.
2   From this work plan and the personal needs of the employee, a personal plan (a 'staff development plan') is developed so that the employee will gain the necessary skills.
3   Progress is reviewed at regular and agreed intervals. At least once a year there is a major review and a report is prepared.

In some countries, culture strongly influences how performance management may be conducted. It is difficult for managers in many countries to accept a Western concept of performance management, with its emphasis on setting specific goals and objectives or giving face-to-face feedback, as well as the newer practices of peer and subordinate evaluations. These practices are at variance with some traditional values. In some cultures, one cannot be critical of a person in his or her presence; consequently, giving negative or critical feedback and, in fact, any face-to-face appraisal is difficult for managers (it may be considered an attempt to ruin someone else's career). There is very little discrimination between good and poor performance, and because of the lack of objectivity, appraisal information is unreliable. This makes pay-for-performance systems more difficult to implement in such countries (Ovadje and Ankomah, 2002).

Payments and benefits (compensation)

Compensation is concerned about pay and other benefits provided to employees and contractors for services provided. It includes ensuring that internal relativities between employees are equitable, and that external competitiveness of pay and benefits is maintained. The salaries or wages for staff (other than contractors) may be set by agreements, by negotiated legal agreements such as industrial awards, or by workplace enterprise agreements. Typically, these agreements specify matters such as normal payments, overtime payments, annual leave and work hours. They define how people are expected to operate in the workplace, and their entitlements and payments. Managers may be directly involved in the negotiation of such agreements. In applying agreements, managers need to pay attention to the detail of staff rosters. During an incident, for example, managers will need to carefully roster their staff for shifts, otherwise double-pay rates may apply for any extended hours worked. Safety issues also come into play, with workers needing regular periods of sleep during extended incidents. Most managers have a fixed budget for salaries, and this needs to be planned for an annual cycle of staffing needs.

Employee welfare and services

Protected area organizations need to ensure that their staff work in a safe and healthy environment. Employee welfare may include considerations for safety in the workplace; health support, such as immunization assistance and sick-leave provisions; a suitable working environment and conditions; assistance programmes, such as housing support, especially for appointments to remote locations;

potentially some financial assistance (such as transfer costs); superannuation schemes; the administration of staff leave entitlements; and counselling services. Some of these matters are discussed in more detail here because of their importance.

Safety and health in the workplace. Managers need to be eternally vigilant about personnel safety. They must ensure that workplaces meet at least accepted benchmarked standards for occupational health and safety. Chemicals or fuel must be stored at a safe distance from workers, and in a prescribed manner. Welding and many other engineering tasks need special and safe workplace environments. Office workers need ergonomically suitable furniture and an office layout that is safe. An office should permit rapid evacuation in the event of a fire. Fire evacuation plans and training drills need to have been completed. There should be a trained first-aid officer (and a comprehensive first-aid kit) in each workplace. Other arrangements may include a sick room. The safety of visitors to protected areas is also a prime concern.

Staff housing. Staff housing may be provided on protected areas that are very remote or where staff need to be present to provide special security. More commonly today, staff live in nearby towns. On-site housing may be rented at the market rate or it may be subsidized, especially where the *quid pro quo* is that staff are nearby and thus potentially on call for serious incidents. Managers will need to ensure that such housing is adequate and in good repair. Much of the rental income may be required for maintaining and occasionally upgrading or replacing the housing. Sometimes staff living in protected areas, but near major metropolitan areas, need special security. This could be arranged with local police or managed through contract security services.

Staff rosters. Managing a protected area may require having a suitable cross-section of staff (and skills) on duty or at least on call at all times. For this reason, carefully planned staff rosters will be required. Rosters should be prepared some two to four weeks in advance and, if possible, longer so that staff can plan their personal lives. Operational needs will require additional staff on duty during peak holiday periods or during periods of high potential for incidents (such as summer bushfires or winter storms). There are also periods when wildlife management may need extra attention or protection. Staff may have special needs for leave such as sick leave, maternity leave and study leave. It is especially important to maintain staff rosters during incidents. In the chaotic 'order' that is brought about by incident-control systems, it is very easy to lose track of how long someone has been on duty. Attention to detail and persever-ance with incident administration systems is essential for effective management. The situation of dangerously overtired staff remaining on duty must be avoided.

Employee assistance programmes. For staff that have personal problems, either in the workplace or at home, some organizations provide confidential personal counselling services. Often, this is extended to the immediate family as well. Apart from being a responsible action, the cost is justified by the fact that staff with unresolved troubles are unlikely to work well. Employee assistance programmes that offer counselling services can help with marriage and family problems, alcohol and other drug problems, emotional stress, legal prob-lems, interpersonal conflicts, financial problems, and work-related difficulties. These services are confi-dential and are normally provided by independent consultants whom staff are invited to contact free of charge. This has the advantage of avoiding managers becoming involved in complex personal issues, as might happen if they felt solely responsi-ble for the welfare of troubled staff members. The disadvantage is that the manager should be aware of some of these problems (such as interpersonal conflicts and other work-related difficulties), as these are likely to impinge upon an employee's performance. There may also be safety issues involved. Striking the right balance between the two approaches is difficult, but needs to be pursued.

A principled organization

Most organizations responsible for managing protected areas have a clear statement of what they stand for. This is usually set out in a corpo-rate plan, and is a group of values and principles that the organization considers important. These principles and values set the scene for how an organization will deal with its staff members, its customers and its external stakeholders, and how

it will go about the business of conservation. This is an important aspect of the administration of protected areas. A principled organization states what it stands for and how it will respect and support its staff.

An organization's values are reflected in the vision and mission statements that drive an organi-zation's strategy. Strategy and ethics are linked via the idea of purpose. Assumptions about an organi-zation's underlying purpose are essentially ethical and are likely to be influenced by culture. To leave these assumptions unstated may result in significant misunderstandings. To be effective, values have to be particularly evident at the operational levels in the thoughts and actions of those who implement strat-egy. Discussions within the protected area organization and with stakeholders, particularly if they are from different cultures, are important in order to build understanding of the others' and the protected area manager's own implicit, culturally influenced ethical assumptions. Such discussions can be a source of strength (McNett and Søndergaard, 2004). For instance in Australia, the 2000–2003 *New South Wales National Parks and Wildlife Service Corporate Plan* provided statements of value for conservation, respect for Aboriginal culture and heritage, social cohesion, active community involvement, fairness and equity, professionalism and ethical conduct. The corporate plan then goes on to describe how these values will be addressed (NSW NPWS, 2004).

Organizations may also prepare a service char-ter or a guarantee of service, which sets out the standards that the public and customers can expect from them. It may invite feedback, as well as giving background on the organization's history, structure, mission and values.

A principled organization states how it will respect and support its staff. In addition, basic guidelines for behavioural standards expected of managers and staff are often prepared.

A code of conduct establishes how employees are expected to behave. It provides guidance to help people to work together comfortably and with mutual respect, despite individual differences of background, personality or style. Usually, the code aims to assist employees when they are faced with ethical issues that may arise during the performance of their duties. It typically deals with

Rwenzori Mountains National Park headquarters, Uganda

Source: IUCN Photo Library © Jim Thorsell

subjects such as professional behaviour; conflicts of interest; gifts, gratuities and hospitality; personal use of organizational resources; giving and accepting direction; dress; dealings with the public; public comment; confidentiality; other employment; and notification of dishonest or unethical behaviour. Such codes of conduct may form part of a broader guarantee of service.

Managers are at the forefront of their workplace. They are continually being judged on the way in which they tackle their daily tasks. They are expected to show honesty, integrity, fairness and balanced judgement. A manager's behaviour and standards will set an example for how the workplace operates. They should be guided, especially in times of stress, by the organization's code of conduct and by its internal policies on ethical management.

Financial management

The management of finances is a critical part of a protected area manager's job. It ensures that important conservation works are achieved effectively and efficiently through funding for staff, support infrastructure, equipment and materials. Managing finances is essentially concerned with controlling money, measuring actual revenue and expenses, comparing these to budget plans, and taking any necessary corrective actions to bring the two into line. Financial sustainability of an organization managing a protected area is an obvious pre-condition for its effective operation.

Many techniques are used to control the sources and uses of funds in organizations managing protected areas; but budgets are the chief means of achieving monetary control. They outline financial goals and are used as measuring and corrective devices at virtually every level of management. A budget is a written, quantified statement of the planned use of money. It includes the source(s) of finances and proposed use. Transparency in preparing budgets and statements of accounts is essential, especially when managing a protected area under the direction of a management board or equivalent. The financial management of organizations is normally audited on a 12-monthly basis.

The budget process

Three key areas of a budget process are the way in which budgets are drawn up and approved; the role played by specialist budget staff and budget committees; and the way in which budgets are managed.

Developing and approving a budget

The budgeting process generally starts with top-level management timetabling the overall process and seeking budget forecasts in the context of strategic objectives that have been set. Depending upon the nature of a protected area's governance, this is completed in the context of whole-of-government processes; the requirements of a company board; the requirements of a management committee; or the requirements of a community committee. Budget proposals are typically generated by front-line and middle-level managers in a clear context of organizational priorities. Some top-level management staff may require certain tasks to be completed and these are normally built into such budget proposals. The final budgets allocated are typically approved by top-level management, or the board, or committees of management, or the community committee, as appropriate.

Budgeting seldom occurs without some drama within organizations. There are always competing priorities for the insufficient funds available. Project champions will jostle for advantage. Competition for the available resources is normal, even though people are working in a collegiate manner to achieve the same vision. It is clear that at each stage in the development of a budget, organizational, social and political priorities can influence the way in which funds are divided. There may also be regional issues. When finally allocating scarce funds for a given action, managers will need to have taken into account all such considerations, including issues such as the safety and health of staff and the general public, the value and condition of assets, and the critical needs of environmental conservation.

An organizational budget will contain separate summary statements of individual budget proposals from functional and/or geographic divisions within an organization. At another level of detail, full budget statements underpin those divisional budget requests. Divisional budgets may be made up of budgets for routine maintenance; routine administration; specialized training; capital improvement works; plant and equipment purchases; event management; investments to prepare for incidents; and other works or actions required by the organization. Such detailed budgets are documented and typically include the following elements:

- *Budget plans.* For a project, task or action, there will be a clear plan, with a series of objectives or milestones and a programme of work over time. Some managers will use a Gantt chart (a chart that typically displays tasks, task duration and accountabilities for tasks in two dimensions) or basic computer programmes such as Microsoft Excel or Microsoft Project to help manage the progress of work. Forecast expenditure is determined for the project milestones, and actual expenditure performance is measured against these during the life of the project. For routine maintenance and administration budgets, budget performance milestones are typically forecast based on previous experience for seasonal and workload demands, and are monitored.
- *Fund source.* The source of funds for the project is clearly identified. This may be sourced from funds that are provided for the annual operating costs and capital funds. Capital funds are typically provided for the purchase equipment, buildings or other fixed assets, and also fund new works. Grant funds may provide both operating and capital-type funds. Often, many grant applications require the organization to provide a percentage of the funds for the project or at least in-kind funding.
- *Estimating the cost of employees.* Managers will need to ask how many personnel are required, and of what types and skills. Will the work be done in house or by contract? When and for how long are specific tradespeople required? Will there need to be double shifts or a continuous 24-hour operation to finish on

time? Some tasks may need to be undertaken outside office hours to minimize disruption to normal business, and this may cost more. Innovative managers may use a special project to train their staff by assigning them the special project task and by putting on temporary staff to replace them. Additional management costs (on-costs) should usually be budgeted for.

- *Estimating costs of services.* There is a costing of project support services. This may include specialist advice and technical designs, such as architectural, engineering, quantity surveyor, geotechnical and other specialist reports.
- *Material costs.* There is a costing of materials. For large projects, quantity surveyors may need to supply these estimates on contract. For smaller projects, estimates will be needed for local materials secured from sustainable sources.
- *Logistic support costs.* There is a cost estimate for logistic support arrangements. This covers all temporary equipment, from offices at a construction site to the hire of vehicles to transport additional staff and the hire of supplementary plant, such as generators and compressors. It may include the cost of aircraft use or the hire of animals to transport equipment to remote locations.
- *Project consumables.* There is a costing for basic items such as electricity, water, waste disposal, office supplies, postage, telephones and other consumables.

Budget specialists

Developing detailed budgets (based on corporate priorities) is the responsibility of front-line managers. Typically, however, they receive support and technical assistance from budget specialists. Some large organizations may have specialized budget departments. Such departments report to a senior manager (typically a top-level manager) and prepare an organizational master budget plan; provide budget assistance to front-line managers; provide budget performance reporting information; and help to design and maintain budget systems and their documentation. There may also be a budget committee comprising senior managers from most functional areas of an organ-

ization with the responsibility of reviewing individual budgets and referring the integrated budget to an organization's governing body. Such a committee may have the additional responsibility of reviewing the monitoring reports.

Budget management

Typically, budgets are for a 12-month period. A reasonable degree of stability should be built into budgets. They should not be revised at managerial whim, but only when forecasts are overtaken by actual events. On the other hand, budgets should not be excessively rigid, although, as a general principle, revisions should be confined to instances where necessary deviations are of such a magnitude as to render the original budget unrealistic. Budgets should be reviewed at set intervals through comparisons of actual performance with budgeted performance. Periodic progress reports from subordinate managers should be audited by those responsible for budget control (including a budget committee, if appointed), with the responsible managers being required to explain significant deviations. Budget management can be severely affected by unplanned events, although it is possible to anticipate this 'incident down-time' and to programme the year to make sure that tasks, wherever possible, are managed around such potential events.

An annual financial audit is generally obligatory, and others may also be taken from time to time. Typically, an internal audit occurs at a local cost-centre office that manages the budget of a given area or section. Audit checks look for compliance between actual and planned or budgeted expenditure. They also examine documents such as invoices and authorizations to check that proper processes have been followed. Internal audits may extend beyond finances to include checks on salary payments, the use of vehicles or equipment, and time sheets. They are a mechanism to help guarantee that funds have been properly spent against the items prescribed in the budget. Annual reports are usually prepared and cover all aspects of management, especially the responsible management of finances. They should contain a breakdown of how the various parts of the budget have been spent. To help develop an annual report, local managers may need to submit a balanced financial report for their areas, as well as a statement of their achievements.

Budget management in some low and medium Human Development Index (HDI) countries may need special management considerations. They may have weak systems development and ability, system inefficiencies and corruption. Weak systems ability means that such countries are unable to utilize human, financial, physical and informational resources efficiently. Corruption may be widespread, and it is widely believed that bribery is necessary in order to get anything done (Rahman and Thai, 1991; Gould, 1991). Managers must be equipped to deal with and, as far as possible, prevent such abuses.

Preventing fraud and corruption

Protected area organizations are not immune from fraud and corruption. Examples of corrupt conduct could include:

- outright theft;
- unauthorized use of an organization's vehicles or other equipment;
- misuse of official or inside information for personal gain;
- illicit use for private gain of official powers, or of computers or records;
- sale or disposal of assets or services at less-than-fair value;
- arranging payment for goods or services that were either overpriced or not received;
- falsifying records or computer programmes in order to commit or conceal fraud;
- appointing a friend or relative to a position for which there are better qualified applicants; and

- providing or receiving a bribe to facilitate a contract.

Administrative areas most at risk from fraud include HR management; information systems; tenders and contracts; licensing and regulation; financial systems and procedures; and arrangements for the use of equipment. Managers normally prepare a plan to guard against fraud and corruption. Such guidelines must be firm. Audits and tip-offs can help to bring fraud to light; but managers should themselves be alert to irregularities. When serious fraud is detected or suspected, criminal investigations and charges, or at least internal disciplinary actions, may follow. Upon suspicion of corrupt behaviour, managers may need to move swiftly to impound all documents and other evidence that investigators would require. Managers have a responsibility to maintain an organizational culture of propriety. The World Bank works with countries in their anti-corruption efforts and also has a number of mechanisms in place to prevent corruption and fraud in bank-financed projects. The World Bank's Department of Institutional Integrity has a 24-hour fraud and corruption hotline.

Reporting requirements to external organizations

The institutions that fund various protected areas or projects (see Chapter 12, p328) have their own requirements insofar as proposals and progress of works are concerned. Case Study 13.1 identifies some of the World Bank's administration requirements for work relevant to protected areas. Other bodies, such as the World Wide Fund for Nature (WWF) and The Nature Conservancy, have their own reporting requirements.

Case Study 13.1

World Bank reporting requirements

The World Bank is one of the United Nations' (UN's) specialized agencies. The bank's environmental strategy sets out three goals for its programmes and projects: to improve the quality of life; to improve the quality of growth; and to protect the quality of the regional and global commons. The World Bank is the world's largest financier of biodiversity conservation and assists in improving the management capacity of protected areas, building the capacity of communities to manage biodiversity resources, and working with governments to design and implement policies that support effective management at local, national and regional levels.

The financial management requirements for World Bank-supported projects are covered in various manuals, guidelines, handbooks and memoranda. Accounting information submitted to the bank, for example, must adhere to accounting standards acceptable to the bank, such as the International Accounting Standards (IAS). These are published annually by the International Accounting Standards Committee and are widely adopted by the accounting profession. The IAS in current use that may be of particular relevance to World Bank projects managed by protected area managers include:

- IAS 1, 'Presentation of financial statements';
- IAS 2, 'Inventories';
- IAS 7, 'Cash flow statements';
- IAS 8, 'Net profit or loss for the period';
- IAS 11, 'Construction contracts';
- IAS 16, 'Property, plant and equipment';
- IAS 18, 'Revenue';
- IAS 19, 'Employee benefits';
- IAS 20, 'Accounting for government grants';
- IAS 26, 'Accounting and reporting by retirement benefit plans'; and
- IAS 27, 'Consolidated financial statements'.

The World Bank imposes a number of requirements on approved projects:

- *Project financial reporting.* A World Bank project normally requires that, within six months of the end of each fiscal year, a borrower and project-linked bodies provide the bank with annual audited financial statements of the project that are acceptable to the bank.
- *Auditing.* The World Bank requires the borrower and project-linked bodies to have the required financial statements audited in accordance with standards acceptable to the bank and by an independent auditor acceptable to the bank.
- *Operational manual.* The World Bank requires that a project is managed in a prescribed manner. An operational manual is provided and is complemented by various guidelines, such as the World Bank's *Financial Accounting, Reporting and Auditing Handbook* (World Bank, 1995). This handbook provides information on accounting system design, the linkage of financial information to key indicators of project objectives and financial reporting, and audits. It includes material on:
  - project appraisal;
  - project implementation;
  - financial reporting;
  - audit compliance; and
  - a country-based review of financial accountability.
- Annexes to the handbook provide additional details, including:
  - accounting standards;
  - use of financial information to monitor physical project implementation;
  - the elements of financial statements;
  - samples of financial statements; and
  - international auditing standards.
- *Chart of accounts.* World Bank projects have a minimum requirement that expenditure is presented by disbursement categories and by project components. In designing a chart of accounts for a particular project, a protected area manager should consider:
  - the need for comparisons;
  - the need for consolidations of project figures into government accounts;
  - the need for comparison of actual with budgeted project figures; and
  - the reporting requirements of the government and the World Bank.

Sources: adapted from World Bank (1995, 1997, 1998, 2005a, 2005b)

Asset management

Assets are items of value that an organization owns or controls. Assets include constructed items such as roads, sewer lines, bridges, buildings, trails and various cultural heritage structures, as well as tools, vehicles and intellectual property. Most organizations have a range of assets to manage, and generally this is inventoried. Asset management systems allow managers to predict when assets will need to be refurbished or replaced ('maintenance cycles'). They can allow for these expenses in their annual budget and can also keep track of the total value of assets, which is important in 'accrual accounting'. Asset management should be part of an integrated management system. This system should include data management and information technology (IT) support systems; integrated organizational management programmes for development projects; annual maintenance programmes; performance review and assessment; and financial management. The Tasmanian Parks and Wildlife Service (PWS) developed an integrated planning, asset, risk, financial and visitor service system that provides a useful model for protected area management agencies worldwide. Elements of this system are described in Case studies 10.6 in Chapter 10 and 19.5 in Chapter 19.

Asset management measures include benchmarks that, in turn, serve to define 'best practice'. Benchmarks establish an organization's reference objectives, with benchmarking a systematic process for measuring best practice and comparing the results to corporate performance in order to identify opportunities for improvement and superior performance. Benchmarking enables managers to compare their organization's performance with that of similar organizations and to seek improvements. The benchmarking and improvement process (see Figure 13.3) has four essential elements:

1 selecting a comprehensive set of parameters for comparison;
2 selecting reliable internal and external sites or measures for comparison;
3 based on performance, comparing the organization's performance with the 'best-of-the-best' measures; and
4 identifying areas of greatest opportunity for improvement.

Which areas of management are selected for benchmarking depends largely upon the characteristics of the organization concerned and its environment, but may include areas such as leadership, planning and scheduling, preventive and condition-based maintenance, contract maintenance, and fuel costs. Benchmarks will vary between organization types and over time – Table 13.1 provides some specimen benchmarks.

There are some established standards and codes, such as:

- design standards and codes for engineering, construction and equipment;
- corporate designs and standards for such things as letterheads, signs, park furniture and uniforms;
- landscape design codes and rehabilitation manuals;

Table 13.1 Specimen best practice benchmarks

Category	Benchmark
Annual maintenance cost/replacement asset value of the equipment	< 3%
Planned maintenance/total maintenance	> 85%
Training for at least 90% of workers (hours per year)	> 80 hours per year
Spending on worker training (percentage of payroll)	~ 4%
Safety performance: recordable injuries per 200,000 labour hours	< 2

Source: Bahrami (2002)

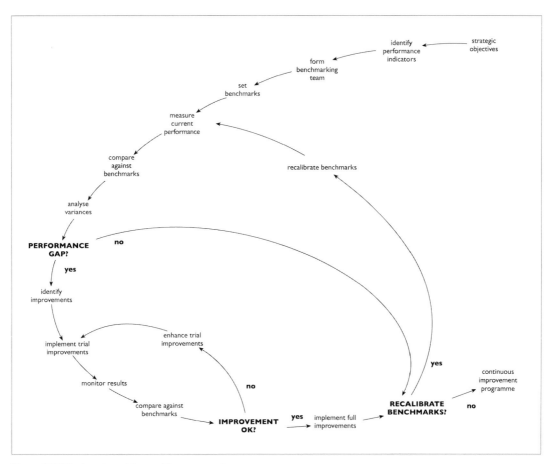

Figure 13.3 The benchmarking and improvement process

Source: Mitchell (2002)

- occupational health and safety codes and manuals, including dangerous goods and chemical safety; and
- contract management manuals, and leasing and licensing manuals.

Such standards help to ensure the safety and health of visitors and staff, as well as protect the environment.

Assets also include intellectual property, a key aspect of which concerns the genetic resources of protected areas. Legislation may need to be upgraded and management processes developed to deal with such rights. Case Study 13.2 provides an example of the sorts of issues that may be experienced with regard to intellectual property and patenting.

Management principles

1   Administration is at the heart of a protected area organization's capacity to operate effectively. Organizations need to strive for continuous improvement in their administration structures and systems.
2   Capacity and skills development of staff are an essential component of the HR management systems.
3   People make the difference when it comes to achieving conservation outcomes. Effective administration of recruitment, induction and other staff-related processes is essential. People need to be managed fairly, equitably and have a clear sense of purpose. They should understand their role, delegations, authority and

Case Study 13.2

Access to genetic resources in Australia's protected areas: Intellectual property and patenting issues

Charles Lawson, Catherine Pickering and Susan Downing, Griffith University, Australia

The National Strategy for the Conservation of Australia's Biological Diversity recognized that Australian genetic resources were valuable and that the social and economic benefits should accrue to Australia (Objective 2.8). Implementing this objective is no easy task given Australia's federal system that requires regulation at the Commonwealth, state and territory tiers of government. To date, a comprehensive access scheme covering all protected areas in Australia remains unfulfilled. Furthermore, some key issues about the preferred approach to regulating access to genetic resources in protected areas have the potential to undermine the likely economic and other benefits from access to these valuable resources.

In dealing with genetic resources in all areas, including protected areas, Australia law-makers have adopted a broad meaning for this term so that, in effect, it includes all manner of living organisms and their parts and components. This includes whole organisms, parts of organisms, organs, fluids, information macromolecules (such as DNA and polypeptides) and biochemicals, and any other living materials or derivatives of those materials sourced within the Australia land area and its recognized ocean boundaries.

Any access scheme to protected areas in Australia must be consistent with Australia's commitments to international agreements, such as the United Nations Convention on Biological Diversity (CBD), the United Nations Convention on the Law of the Sea and the World Trade Organization's Agreement on Trade Related Aspects of Intellectual Property Rights (TRIPS).

In Australia, proposed Commonwealth regulations under the *Environment Protection and Biodiversity Conservation Act 1999* (EPBC Act) are consistent with the preferred approach under the CBD for contracts with access between the resource holder and the bio-prospector. Some protected areas are within the scope of this legislation where they are 'Commonwealth areas' for the purposes of the EPBC Act. The EPBC Act empowers the making of regulations for the equitable sharing of the benefits arising from the use of biological resources; the facilitation of access to such resources; the right to deny access to such resources; and the granting of access to such resources and the terms and conditions of such access. The concept of access adopted by the proposed regulation deals with the collection of samples from individual organisms and then the determination of their genetic, biochemical and other attributes, together with their potential uses. This will include the taking of native species for conservation, commercial uses or industrial applications, such as collecting living material, analysing and sampling stored material, and exporting material for purposes such as conservation, research and potential commercial product development. The EPBC Act scheme proposes access permits and a model contract that may then be negotiated between the resource holder and the bio-prospector.

These regulations are based on the hope that the contracting parties will negotiate an adequate level of benefit-sharing and access to the technology in order to exploit and conserve the genetic resources. The weaknesses in this approach are the burdens of responsibility on those negotiating the individual contracts to properly value the resources accessed and to ensure the transfer of adequate benefits and technology. This will continue to be a difficult area for protected area management where there is some expectation that access to genetic resources will deliver real and tangible financial and conservation benefits.

Some state governments are also developing access schemes consistent with the Commonwealth's contract model and the requirements of the CBD. Private landowners are being encouraged to adopt the same or similar arrangements as the Commonwealth and states. Again, however, negotiating contracts that equitably share benefits and access technology are likely to be a significant hurdle for managers expecting financial and conservation benefits from access to the resources under their management.

Patenting genetic resources

In Australia, the *Patents Act 1990* grants various exclusive rights for any inventions that satisfy the threshold criteria of being new, not obvious, useful and described in a way that can be followed by others. This includes inventions involving whole organisms and parts or components of organisms such as organs, organelles, biological molecules, and the workings of these parts and components. The consequence of using language to define the scope of a patent is the potential for broad claims. As a result of this, broadly claimed patents can be enforced against later inventors across a broad range of products, processes and uses.

The exact limits of patenting are difficult to predict in detail, as the language of the claims determines the scope of the patent, and these depend in large part upon the circumstances in which the patent claims are made and then processed by the Patent Office. The imperative for those drafting the patent claims is to seek to claim the 'invention' as broadly as possible and to deliver to the inventor the widest possible scope of 'exclusive rights'. Furthermore, the ingenuity of those drafting patent claims to use language to make broad claims should not be dismissed lightly – the breadth and inclusiveness of language are considerable.

Our concern of the proposed scheme relates to the undermining effects of the internationally agreed minimum standards intellectual property requirements imposed by TRIPs, implemented in Australia under the *Patents Act 1990*. This is significant, as patents are considered to be one of the main mechanisms of benefit-sharing and valuing genetic resources. Such patents provide the prospect of a royalty stream from the commercialization of accessed genetic resources. The exclusive rights allow the patent holder to commercialize the invention without competition, in this way capturing economic and other benefits as the reward for investing in the development of new and useful inventions. In our view, the problems may only be resolved through genetic resource holders carefully negotiating access contracts that deal in detail, and with some sophistication, with ways of sharing benefits and accessing appropriate technology. We also consider that there is a role for governments in ensuring adequate technology transfer since the CBD (which includes the access schemes proposed by the United Nations Convention on the Law of the Sea and the United Nations Food and Agriculture Organization's International Treaty for Plant Genetic Resources for Food and Agriculture) is concerned with delivering national benefits. These national benefits include outcomes that may not necessarily be in the immediate interests of individuals. For example, access to a new technology might benefit all Australians (through increased economic activity in Australia and employment), whereas an individual resource holder might consider a minor royalty adequate.

    opportunities to improve.

4 Acting ethically is a fundamental part of good administration.

5 Managing finances wisely is a crucial part of any protected area manager's job. Financial management must be consistent with statutory requirements and audit processes.

6 To achieve organizational goals, procedures must have sound budget, financial monitoring and performance systems, and an overall annual business plan.

7 Standards should be set for administration systems and regular monitoring should be carried out. To conserve continuous improve-

Rangers, Lake Turkana National Park, Kenya

Source: IUCN Photo Library © Jim Thorsell

ment in performance, the systems should be benchmarked.

8   Protected area organizations should have administrative systems that are accountable, transparent, auditable, well documented, and founded on written and public policies.

9   Protected area organizations should adopt environmental best practice and ecologically sustainable technologies in their use of power, water, paper and other resources.

10 Administration system, policies and procedures should directly support a protected area organization's conservation objectives.

Further reading

Budhwar, P. S. and Debrah, Y. A. (eds) (2002) *Human Resource Management in Developing Countries*, Routledge, London

Dessler, G. (2004) *A Framework for Human Resource Management*, Prentice-Hall, Englewood Cliffs

Farazmand, A. (ed.) (1991) *Handbook of Comparative and Development Administration*, Marcel Dekker, New York

Finkler, S. A. (2001) *Financial Management for Public, Health, and Not-for-Profit Organizations*, Prentice-Hall, Englewood Cliffs

Harzing, A. and van Ruysseveldt, J. (eds) (2004) *International Human Resource Management*, Sage, London

Mitchell, J. S. (ed) (2002) *Physical Asset Management Handbook*, 3rd edition, Clarion Technical Publishers, Houston

Stoner, J. A .F., Freeman, R. E. and Gilbert, D. R. (2004) *Management*, Prentice-Hall, Englewood Cliffs

14

Sustainability Practice and Sustainable Use

Juliet Chapman, Terry De Lacy and Michelle Whitmore

Protected areas play a large part in a sustainable world by maintaining and enhancing a wide range of values and benefits (see Chapter 4). They should also provide models for best practice conservation. Protected area management itself must therefore implement best sustainability practice. The processes and activities of protected area management consume energy and natural resources and produce wastes. Roads and buildings are constructed; light and energy for heat or cooling are used to make offices functional; human wastes must be disposed of; and so on. Managers have a responsibility to adopt sound environmental management practices and behave in a manner consistent with wider sustainability principles.

At the World Summit on Sustainable Development in 2002, most national governments recommitted to preparing national sustainable development strategies. Protected area managers need to adopt practices consistent with such instruments. For example, Parks Canada's role in relation to Canada's sustainable development strategy includes contributing to the overall sustainable development of the country through the establishment of a protected area network, as well as managing its daily operations according to the guidelines set out in *Greening Government* (Government of Canada, 2002). This is a government-wide initiative to provide a coordinated approach to sustainable development, which recommends best practice in seven priority areas of operations: procurement; waste management; energy efficiency; water conservation and wastewater management; vehicle fleet management; human resources management; and land-use management. Targets and performance indicators are collaboratively developed and each department is required to participate (Government of Canada, 2000).

In some types of protected areas, particularly those designated as IUCN Category V or VI (see Chapter 3, p82), resource extractive uses may be consistent with the area's management objectives. Such uses must be sustainable: economically, environmentally and socially. Sustainable practice and resource use is an attempt to integrate conservation, social fabric and livelihood needs, as well as financial security. This requires strong governance systems; sound planning and adaptive management; multidisciplinary information; development of capacity; scientific, social and economic research; monitoring and evaluation; long-term commitment by all stakeholders to common goals; use of the precautionary principle where sufficient information is not available; patience; and a willingness to cooperate.

In this chapter two aspects of protected area management are addressed – implementing sustainable practices within management organizations, and sustainable management of extractive uses. Sustainable tourism management is addressed in Chapter 19.

Sustainability and protected area organizations

Protected area operations provide many opportunities for developing and adopting sustainable practices. Key areas for managers to consider are use of energy, materials and water, and production of waste. As well as paying attention to aspects of product use and design in relation to such specific topics, management systems are also needed so that managers can develop an integrated organization-wide approach to sustainability.

Energy

Common sources of energy around the world include plant fibre, oil, coal, gas, water, sun, wind and uranium. Some are renewable energy sources that may have few associated waste products; others are non-renewable and may be a significant source of pollution. Electricity for use in homes and offices in high Human Development Index (HDI) countries and urban areas of other countries is typically generated from non-renewable sources such as coal or natural gas, or from nuclear power with its associated safety and waste-storage problems. The cost of connection to an electricity grid to provide power to remote areas may be prohibitive, so such places often rely on diesel generators and operate on limited energy supplies. There are energy and emission costs associated with the transport of diesel, as well as the direct emission of greenhouse gases from the burning of fossil fuels.

Expert forecasters have predicted major shortfalls in oil by the mid 2020s due to a combination of increased demand and geo-finite reserves of the world's oil reserves (Foran and Poldy, 2002b; Mason, 2003; Appenzeller, 2004; Roberts, 2004). Prices for aviation kerosene, diesel and petrol (gasoline) and other petroleum products will become much higher, and alternative energy sources such as nuclear, natural gas, hydrogen, wind power and solar will become more important. Higher prices will drive activities such as exploration, the extraction of marginal oil deposits and a demand to exploit areas that are environmentally sensitive. A demand-driven search for oil would be a threat to environmentally sensitive areas such as Alaska's Arctic National Wildlife Refuge.

In response to such concerns, some protected area managers are adopting measures for energy conservation and are gradually introducing renewable energy systems within their operations. Although, at present, renewable resources only provide a small fraction of global energy production, wind and solar power are the fastest-growing energy sources in the world (Sawin, 2003). Micro-hydro schemes, photovoltaics, wind turbines and biomass are all potential energy sources that can be used to generate sufficient energy to power equipment, facilities and dwellings.

Photovoltaic cells convert sunlight to electricity. They can be used in most climates, although obviously they are most effective in places that receive high levels of sunlight. The cells are expensive to install; but over the longer term these costs can be offset by reduced running and maintenance costs. The capital cost of photovoltaic cells is also decreasing, further enhancing their competitiveness. Small self-contained photovoltaic battery systems are widely used for warning lights, electric fencing and communication links because they are often the cheapest option for such applications. Larger systems can be used as the primary energy source for protected area operations (see Case Study 14.1). Photovoltaics have a further advantage of being able to be sited so that they are relatively unobtrusive.

Wind turbines at exposed sites may be more economic than solar cells. Electricity generation using such turbines is highly dependent upon the strength of wind, with a doubling of wind speed typically producing an eightfold increase in generation output. Average annual wind speeds of 20 kilometres per hour (6 metres per second) or more are considered suitable for wind turbines. Effective siting of turbines requires the availability of data on average wind speeds over an extended period. The disadvantages for wind turbines in protected areas are their visual impact and their potential impacts on birds.

Micro-hydro installations need strong and constant stream flow, as well as a height differential sufficient to run a turbine. Where stream flow is less reliable, a back-up battery array may be required. When electricity is not needed for lighting, it can be diverted to other uses to keep a steady load on the turbine. These systems are ideal

Case Study 14.1

Sustainable energy generation in the Channel Islands National Park, US

Channel Islands National Park is off the coast of southern California. The park consists of Anacapa, Santa Barbara, Santa Cruz, San Miguel and Santa Rosa islands and the surrounding waters extending out 1.6km. The total area is 1009 square kilometres. The relative isolation has created challenges for managing the national park since operating in remote locations makes the logistics of providing facilities and energy for park operations both costly and difficult. One of the operational goals is to eliminate, wherever possible, any reliance on non-renewable energy, and as new facilities are constructed, greening technology will be incorporated whenever possible. Currently, there are 72 renewable energy applications in operation in the park. These range in size from single module solar installations, which power remote communications, weather stations and provide lighting/ventilation for pit toilets, to a large-scale hybrid wind/photovoltaic system on Santa Rosa Island. Projects also include use of bio-diesel to operate a research boat and to make Anacapa and Santa Barbara Islands petroleum free.

One of these energy systems is composed of:

- two 10 kilowatt (kW) wind turbines and a 12.6kW photovoltaic array;
- one 30kW inverter to control battery charging and provide continuous 208/120 AC electricity;
- a system controller to regulate power generation and activate backup generators as needed; and
- a 300kW capacity battery bank.

This system replaces a 35kW diesel generator. These sources enable the displacement of 163,800 litres of diesel fuel each year, thereby preventing annual emission of:

- 385,200kg of carbon dioxide;
- 9315kg of nitrogen oxides;
- 356kg of particulates;
- 225kg of sulphur dioxide; and
- 6390kg of carbon monoxide.

Source: adapted from NPS (2000a) and Chemical Engineers Resource Page (2004)

in remote areas, particularly in mountainous or hill country (see Case Study 14.2).

Biomass combustion is a common form of energy used for heating and cooking. Wood-burning appliances have improved dramatically in efficiency and emissions during recent years. Wood is far cheaper than fossil fuels, particularly in remote and rural areas, even when the extra labour of cutting wood and refuelling appliances is taken into account. On the other hand, managers need to take into account the greenhouse gas emissions produced by burning such fuels, as well as the environmental effects associated with their collection. Changes to landscapes and habitats can occur from the production and harvesting of biomass. A significant shift to biomass use could result in major conversions of natural habitat to biomass (or displaced agricul-

tural) production and to unsustainable harvests of biomass from natural or managed systems.

Energy conservation is also an important factor in the purchase and use of equipment. Simple and effective measures include using low-wattage energy-efficient light globes; making sure the appliances purchased are energy efficient; turning off power points in the office so that equipment is not left on standby; making every car trip count; using water saving shower roses in residences so that not as much hot water is used; insulating buildings so that they are cool in summer and warm in winter; and designing and siting buildings in order to make the most of the natural light and heat or cooling that are available.

Protected area agencies may also reduce energy consumption through practices such as:

Case Study 14.2

Micro-hydro systems in Sabah, Malaysia

Construction of the micro-hydro system in Terian, a village in Sabah, Malaysia, was carried out by two local NGOs – Sahabat Alam Malaysia and Sabah-based Partners of Community Organizations (PACOS). PACOS installed the micro-hydro system in Kampung Terian, 25km from Penampang, Sabah. Like other remote villages, the community living along the boundary of the Crocker Range National Park has relied on diesel-powered generators.

Diesel supply had to be replenished once a week. Villagers carried the fuel on their backs in an arduous trek through hilly terrain. The burden also meant that they could not transport other household items or groceries. However, the 180 villagers can harness clean energy with the completion of the 5 kilowatt (kW) micro-hydro system.

The community has already worked with PACOS to develop a medicinal garden, an ecotourism project and watershed management plans. The renewable energy system brings electricity to the primary school, pre-school, community centre, church and communal rice mill, along with individual homes. After the water passes through the micro-hydro system, it can be channelled to irrigate rice fields in an efficient and environmentally sustainable way. In this way, the energy system will have multiple effects, from improving livelihood, to preserving the watershed, to bringing the community together.

The Kampung Terian project also includes the installation of solar home systems for five families who live in the national park. Another village in the protected area, Kampung Longkogungan, is tapping solar energy to power its Communication Technology Centre in a primary school to bring the internet to the forest community.

Source: adapted from Chiew (2005)

- vehicle fleet purchasing or leasing policies, which achieve energy-use reduction targets;
- human resource (HR) management policies, which achieve energy conservation through transport services, improved office and workplace environments, and workplace training and induction programmes; and
- operational systems, which utilize low energy options for achieving outcomes.

Materials

Any work we do uses materials and energy and creates waste. Knowing the flow of materials in and out of a protected area and the circulation of materials internally is central to sustainability management. The relative environmental impact of materials is also vital, and whether they are sourced internally (raw materials inside the protected area) or externally (raw and processed materials outside the protected area) are also key factors in the sustainable use of materials.

Construction of roads, walking tracks, buildings and so on in protected areas consumes a wide range of materials. Where possible, preference should be given to using materials that are sourced locally, thereby reducing transport costs and contributing to local economic development. Preference should also be given to materials that are long lasting and have minimal associated environmental impact. Second-hand building materials or products made from wastes such as plastics, paper and scrap wood may be preferable to using virgin materials. If virgin materials are to be used, there may be an opportunity to source them from producers that use environmental best practice. Opportunities to employ sustainability principles also arise when structures are upgraded or are subject to routine maintenance.

Administrative centres typically use a wide range of materials and equipment, including furniture, electronic equipment and stationery. Often office equipment and supplies may be part of an organization's policy on sustainable practice, so protected areas under the auspices of a national or state government department may have sustainability standards to meet. For example, the state of North Carolina in the US has established Executive Order 156: State Government Environmental Sustainability, Reduction of Solid Waste, and Procurement of Environmentally Preferable Products. This orders each state agency to manage its operations within specific environmental

Recycling bins, South-East Forests National Park, New South Wales, Australia

Source: Graeme L. Worboys

parameters. All electronic office equipment, including computers, monitors, printers, scanners, photocopy machines and facsimile machines must be compliant with the US Environment Protection Authority Energy Star programme. State agencies are directed to purchase and use recycled paper for all letterhead stationery, reports, memoranda and other documents when feasible and practicable. All new and re-manufactured photocopy machines and laser printers purchased are required to have the ability to use xerographic paper having at least 50 per cent recycled content, 30 per cent of which should be post-consumer content. Office paper waste should be reduced by avoiding unnecessary printing and copying. All documents are to be printed on both sides of the paper. Electronic communication, such as email, voicemail and the internet, is to be used for routine announcements, memoranda, documents, reports, manuals and publications. Recycling facilities are to be available for aluminium, glass, plastic beverage containers and reusable products favoured over disposable items where economically viable (State of North Carolina, 1999). Such measures can be adapted to any administrative centre where management objectives require sustainable practices. Indeed, protected area managers should be providing leadership by exceeding minimum regulatory requirements where possible.

Water

Potable freshwater is one of the world's scarcest natural resources. Yet we waste huge volumes and pollute even more by mixing our waste with otherwise freshwater supplies in rivers and underground aquifers. Freshwater is also critical in ecosystem processes as a vital element in the life of all biota. It has been estimated that half of all accessible surface runoff has been commandeered for human use, reducing the natural flows available to ecosystems (environmental flows) by half (Yencken and Williamson, 2001). In protected areas, water is used for domestic purposes such as washing, cooking and drinking; washing down equipment; fire fighting; and irrigation. Sustainability issues concern the source of water supply, the level of water use, environmental flows and the disposal of wastewater. Strategies to deal with these issues include water conservation measures and education; ensuring sustainable water off-take from natural waterways; and reducing, treating and reusing wastewater.

Water for a protected area can be taken from a reticulated supply, collected in rainwater tanks, dams or reservoirs, or extracted from natural water bodies within the protected area. Typically, in a natural system 80 per cent of rainfall is held in the vegetation and soil and 20 per cent runs off the surface into the nearest basin (such as a stream, river or wetland). Over time, excess water travels through the subsurface, providing water for plants, soil biota and recharging underground aquifers. When we take water out of the natural cycle there is some environmental impact. The extent of that impact needs to be kept to a minimum.

When constructing camps, shelters, housing,

car parks, roads and tracks, it is important to keep the area of non-porous surface to a minimum so that the maximum amount of water possible follows its natural cycle in the environment. Where there are non-porous surfaces that increase surface runoff, it is beneficial to provide drainage lines that are vegetated so that particulate matter picked up by rainwater on roads and car parks does not become a pollutant in the main waterway and the rate of flow is also slowed.

It is valuable to determine the current human-related water use in a protected area. Unless water is a scarce resource that is already closely monitored, it is likely that considerable water efficiencies could be implemented. Water conservation can be achieved by, for example, using reduced water-flow shower heads and taps; limiting showers through coin-operated or press-button systems that deliver water for a set time period; providing composting or dry toilet systems; and signage on rainwater tanks requesting users take only limited amounts of water. Ensuring that hoses or taps are not left dripping or leaking also saves significant amounts of water. It is also worth considering replacing old appliances, such as washing machines and dishwashers, with current models as they can be both water and energy efficient. The initial capital outlay could be recouped by savings in energy and water costs. Wastewater is integral to water management, and a cradle-to-grave approach should be adopted for water management.

With visitor increases, demand for water will increase, prompting a need for monitoring and management. The provision of water to campgrounds and to visitors is a decision that needs to be made according to benefit–cost analysis, environmental impact assessment (EIA) and a variety of other considerations regarding visitor convenience and priorities for the protected area in question. For example, protected areas in arid environments where freshwater is scarce may not provide water in the protected area for campers and day visitors. Case Study 14.3 covers a situation where water is scarce, but where park priorities focus on providing education camps and ways of supplying extra water may need to be found.

Waste

Solid, liquid, gaseous and energy waste is generated by every operation undertaken in the protected area. Wastewater is a by-product of water use and is integral to water management. Wastewater should be dealt with on site. Reducing water use means less wastewater to deal with. Typically, wastewater is generated through sanitation and washing (of people, dishes, clothes, animals and equipment, including vehicles). Water waste from these kinds of activities can have a range of pollutants, including particulate matter, oil or grease, chemical residues, nutrients, and detergents or soaps. The risk of the pollutants leaching into the surrounding environment must be considered in managing the wastewater disposal. Hazardous wastes must be contained appropriately and disposed of in accordance with best practice.

There are many alternatives for on-site treatment, such as using composting toilets or other water-free toilets, and using septic tanks followed by drainage pipes into leach areas where soil micro-organisms complete waste treatment. Effluent may also be released to polishing ponds or evaporation ponds as a final form of treatment. Activated sludge systems or micro-filtration systems are required for larger volumes of effluent.

Systems for grey water (all wastewater from a domestic facility except that from toilets) reuse are becoming more prevalent. Examples include wetland systems, sand or gravel filters. The aim of these systems is to clean the water through physical and biological processes so that it can be reused in some way, usually as irrigation or for toilet systems. Black water or toilet waste can be disposed of through septic systems or sewage treatment plants.

Protected area operations also generate a significant amount of solid waste that must be properly managed to avoid environmental damage and loss of amenity. Waste comes from all infrastructure building and maintenance, office operations and visitor services. Wherever products are introduced onto the site, waste is bound to occur. *Reduce, reuse and recycle* is a useful catchphrase that has been employed in waste management education campaigns. Recycling

Case Study **14.3**

Sustainable water use in Biscayne National Park Florida, US

In Biscayne National Park in the US, a study of water use and projected water use was carried out as part of an assessment of a proposed new education camp at Adams Key. The camp would require an increase in potable water of over 8000 litres per day. A study evaluated the current water usage, including plumbing and other on-site uses, on Adam's Key, as well as the potential to have a reverse osmosis (RO) system adapted to an existing cistern (tank), the potential for water to be pumped from a saltwater well and treated via RO, and the possibility of increasing the storage capacity of the rainwater collection system.

Using current water management practices, the site would need an RO system capable of delivering between 8200 and 10,000 litres per day. It was recommended that the design of the camp include efficiency measures and rainwater collection to allow for a smaller RO system. Greater water efficiency could be achieved by retrofitting bathroom taps (with current flows of approximately 9 litres per minute) with aerators that have flows of 4.5 litres per minute. Washing machines in the homes were estimated to use between 160 and 180 litres per load. A number of washing machines on the market were known to use about half the water per load. The dishwashers at the residences use approximately 40 litres per load. It is recommended that they be replaced with models that use 25 litres per load or less.

It is estimated that the measures would have a cost of approximately US$4500 for the efficiency measures and US$1500 for the extra storage capacity. Table 14.1 describes the current water usage from the water-using equipment and the expected usage after water conservation measures have been implemented.

Table 14.1 Current and prospective annual potable water usage, both residences

	Current usage (litres)	Proposed efficiency measures	Proposed annual usage (litres)	Estimated savings (litres)	Estimated installed cost of efficient appliances (US$)
Bathroom sinks	25,480	Tap aerators	12,740	12,740	10
Washing machines	143,330	Install high-efficiency washing machines	59,880	83,450	3600
Dishwashers	33,120	Install high-efficiency dishwashers	20,380	12,740	800
Leaks	12,740	Fix all leaks at hose bibs (US$40); add shut off nozzles at hose bibs (US$50)	0	12,740	90
Other appliances	260,800	No change	260,800	0	–
Annual total	475,470		353,810	121,670	4500
Total monthly usage	39,620		29,480	10,140	

Source: US Department of Energy (2004)

Source: adapted from US Department of Energy (2004) and NPS (2005)

Solar toilets, Sorak Mountain National Park, Korea

Source: IUCN Photo Library © Jim Thorsell

results in significant savings in greenhouse gas emissions, atmospheric pollution, water use and solid waste. Simple changes to work practices, such as recycling or reusing paper, can make a significant difference.

In many protected areas where there are designated accommodation areas, such as standing camps or camping areas or resorts, there are usually facilities for waste disposal. In some cases where it is appropriate, there may be the opportunity to separate garbage into recyclables, food waste and rubbish. Food waste often attracts wild animals to waste disposal areas. Most protected areas have waste receptacles designed to keep animals out. It may be necessary to educate visitors about correct use of recycling and waste receptacles. In more remote situations where strict protection applies, hikers may be required to carry out all their solid waste, including toilet waste.

Vehicle emissions, emissions from diesel generators and smoke from appliances using fire are the most likely sources of gaseous emissions in protected areas. There may also be methane from waste dumps, where these are unavoidable in the protected area. Levels of emissions can be minimized by using fuel-efficient vehicles and appliances, ensuring that they are well serviced and used effectively.

Environmental management systems

Environmental management systems (EMS) provide a framework for managing environmental responsibilities by achieving specified environmental goals, as well as managing environmental risks and liabilities. EMS are based on standards that specify a process of continuously improving environmental performance and complying with legislation. There are a number of international standards that can be used to guide the implementation of EMS. ISO 14001 is one such standard that provides a structure for the development of environmental performance control and auditing for all types of businesses and organizations.

Some organizations have developed their own EMS that can significantly reduce threats to protected areas. For example, an EMS developed for Parks Victoria in Australia has four major interconnected components:

1   directions and priorities involving analysis of the matters that need management attention, as well as assessment of natural assets and the threats to them;
2   programme development that evaluates ways of avoiding, sharing, minimizing or accepting risks;
3   programme delivery that involves setting targets and methods for risk reduction, and estimating the likely level of risk after action is taken, as well as the likely condition of the assets; and
4   information and evaluation that assesses the results of the works (Parks Victoria, 1998).

These components can be located within a more general model for an EMS (see Figure 14.1 and Table 14.2).

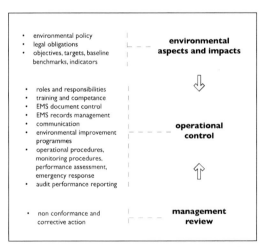

Figure 14.1 Environmental management system (EMS) for the State of Victoria, Australia

Source: State of Victoria (2004)

Performance assessment and monitoring

One process in sustainability performance assessment involves assessing the products and services to be used for an operation, including a life-cycle assessment. Life-cycle assessment can assist identification of the most sustainable option for alternative materials and processes – for example, a decision between wood and steel as building components. Life-cycle assessment is:

> … a method for assessing the biophysical and health impacts and resource consumption of a product over its entire life cycle (from raw materials to final disposal) and identifying opportunities for reducing those impacts (Higgins and Thompson, 2002, p293).

As indicated by Trusty (2003), assessing the merits of standard building materials, such as wood, plastic, concrete or steel, can be complex because consideration must be given to each of the composite materials and processes used in manufacturing. A comparative example might be deciding whether to purchase porcelain cups or disposable cups. On the one hand, porcelain cups utilize considerable energy and resources during manufacturing. They need to be transported from the factory to the warehouse and out to individual stores, and because they are quite heavy, this would involve considerable fuel consumption. Once purchased, they require washing after each use, consuming water and the use of potentially nutrient-rich detergents. Using an estimate per cup of coffee, the resources consumed could be calculated. Alternatively, a disposable paper cup requires energy and resources for manufacturing; but it is much lighter than a porcelain cup and would not use as much fuel during transportation. Nevertheless, these cups are designed to be disposed of, contributing to waste production and pollution of the atmosphere. This simple example demonstrates that a life-cycle assessment can be quite complex, and even give results that differ from normal expectations.

Performance monitoring can be achieved through establishing sustainability indicators and performance benchmarking (De Lacy et al, 2002). Monitoring should be conducted on a systematic basis and across strategic aspects of an operation in order to determine the success of previous actions and where and how new improvements can be made. Monitoring will be guided by an organization's information systems (see Chapter 10) and its evaluation strategy (see Chapter 24).

Table 14.2 Explanation of the key components of Victoria's environmental management system (EMS)

Component	Comments
Environmental policy	A statement of the organization's intentions and principles for environmental performance
Environmental aspects and impacts	Identification of aspects of the organization that will have an impact on the environment and their relative significance
Legal obligations	An organization needs to know its environmental legal obligations and comply with them or work towards compliance
Objectives, targets, benchmarks and indicators	Baseline data from which to measure improvement, stasis or decline
	Benchmarks are standards against which to measure performance
	Objectives and targets are short-term, specific, measurable, achievable and realistic time-bound aims
	Indicators can be observed to show the presence or state of a condition or trend
Environmental improvement programmes	A schedule of actions to achieve the improvement objectives and targets set by the organization
Roles and responsibilities	Definition of roles, responsibilities, authorities and competencies required for each role need to be formally defined
Training and competence	Everyone must be competent in their role to fulfil their responsibilities within the EMS
	Formal identification of training needs is required, as well as carrying out training, testing competences, after training and generating auditable records
Communication	Communication between those in environmental management roles, other staff and external actors involved, as well as interested parties, is crucial in the EMS and also encourages participation and raises awareness
Operational control	Operational controls (containment measures, work procedures and training) should reduce the risk of environmental impacts and non-compliance with legal obligations
Monitoring	Sound environmental management requires monitoring, measurement and recording of operations that have environmental impact
Emergency response	Identifies potential incidents and emergency situations and addresses prevention or mitigation of any environmental impacts associated with them
Document control	Documents such as instructions and procedures should be controlled to ensure that current authorized documents are being used and are available to all of those who need them
Records	Records are essential in auditing, demonstrating compliance and due diligence, and help to avoid duplication of effort in projects; they are also critical for reporting
Audits	Audits are used, for example, to measure the extent to which the EMS is operating properly or meeting its legal obligations
Non-conformance corrective action	A formal process is required for capturing non-conformances, devising corrective action and ensuring that they are implemented
Management review	Senior management must periodically review the EMS to ensure its continuing suitability adequacy and effectiveness

Source: State of Victoria (2004)

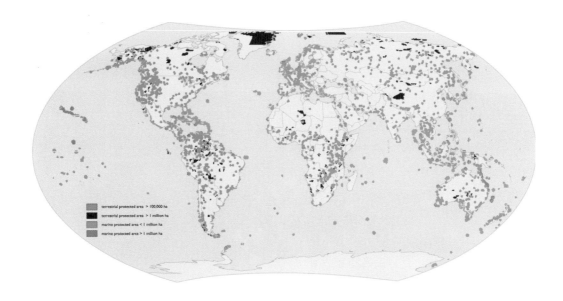

Figure 3.2 Extent of the world's protected areas

Source: based on data from UNEP–WCMC

Travertine pools, Huangshan Mountain World Heritage Area, China

Source: IUCN Photo Library © Jim Thorsell

Saguro National Monument, Arizona, US

Source: IUCN Photo Library © Jim Thorsell

Sundarban Biosphere Reserve, India

Source: IUCN Photo Library © Jim Thorsell

Camels in Aïr and Ténéré Natural Reserves, Niger

Source: IUCN Photo Library © Jim Thorsell

Great Barrier Reef Marine Park, Australia

Source: IUCN Photo Library © Jim Thorsell

Arrayan (*Luma apiculata*) trees, Los Arrayanes National Park, Argentina

Source: IUCN Photo Library © Jim Thorsell

Pyrénées Occidentales National Park, France

Source: IUCN Photo Library © Jim Thorsell

Manu National Park, Peru

Source: IUCN Photo Library © Jim Thorsell

Butterfly, Kinabalu National Park, Malaysia

Source: IUCN Photo Library © Jim Thorsell

Lago del Toro and peaks, Torres del Paine National Park, Chile

Source: IUCN Photo Library © Jim Thorsell

Cyclamen (*Cyclamen purpurascens*), Triglavski Narodni Park, Slovenia

Source: IUCN Photo Library ©
Jim Thorsell

Orchid (*Oncidium* sp.), Central Volcanic Cordillera Conservation Area, Costa Rica

Source: IUCN Photo Library ©
IUCN/Enriqué Lahmann

Lake Turkana National Park, Kenya

Source: IUCN Photo Library ©
Jim Thorsell

Lesser flamingo (*Phoeniconaias minor*), Lake Bogoria, Ramsar Wetlands, Kenya

Source: IUCN Photo Library © Jim Thorsell

Waterfalls, Iguazú National Park, Argentina

Source: IUCN Photo Library © Jim Thorsell

Muleteers in Simien National Park, Ethiopia

Source: IUCN Photo Library © Jim Thorsell

Cloud forest, Rwenzori Mountains National Park, Uganda

Source: IUCN Photo Library © Jim Thorsell

In Australia, the Sustainable Tourism Cooperative Research Centre has developed EMS software that facilitates performance reporting. The system uses a series of earthcheck indicators (see Table 14.3) with relevant baseline data from which to compare the performance of individual operations. These indicators provide a basis to monitor, benchmark and enhance environmental, social and economic performance. Baseline data is founded on accepted minimum performance standards, and these are utilized to set the bench-mark. Baseline performance figures will vary depending upon location, climatic conditions and socio-economic context. If the average per capita performance for a number of environmental management considerations is used as a baseline performance measure, then this can be a starting point for comparative quantitative environmental performance (see Table 14.4). Establishing baseline performance levels becomes a policy decision by organizations. Operators are expected to meet or exceed baseline standards and to consistently improve upon these over time. Green Globe 21 (see Case Study 14.4) is a certification scheme for the travel and tourism industry for improving sustainability performance, utilizing earthcheck benchmarking baseline performance levels and indicators.

Performance reporting

The triple bottom line refers to accounting for environmental, social and economic factors, each of which is to be addressed when assessing an organization's performance. Environmental reports are used by organizations to demonstrate their triple bottom line credentials. Such reports typically utilize indicators and enable reporting on appropriateness, efficiency and effectiveness of programme delivery (Moore et al, 2003). It is important for managers, stakeholders, government and the community to have reliable information on an organization's environmental, social and

Table 14.3 Indicators and measures utilized in analysing accommodation providers' performance compared to baseline levels

Environmental and social performance areas	Benchmarking (earthcheck) indicators and measures
Policy and planning	Sustainability policy: policy in place
Energy management	Energy consumption: energy consumed/guest night or area under roof
Freshwater resources	Potable water consumption: water consumed/guest night or area under roof
Wastewater management	Cleaning chemicals used: biodegradables used/total chemicals used
Waste minimization	Solid waste production: volume of waste landfilled/guest night or area under roof
Ecosystem conservation	Resource conservation: eco-label products purchased/products purchased
Social and cultural impact	Social commitment: employees living within 20km/total employees
Optional indicators	Value of products purchased locally: funds donated to species conservation

Source: De Lacy et al (2002)

Table 14.4 Average per capita performance for environmental management parameters

Country	Energy use (mega joules per person per day)	Carbon dioxide emissions (kg per person per day)	Water withdrawals (litres per person per day)	Solid waste (kg per person per day)	Solid waste (cubic metres per person per day)
Australia	629	47	2299	1.9	0.00291
Canada	910	38	4447	1.3	0.00207
China	104	8	1203	1.5	0.00231
UK	443	24	438	1.3	0.00202
US	926	54	4595	2	0.00303

Source: Green Globe Asia Pacific (2003)

economic performance through 'triple bottom line' reporting. De Lacy et al (2002) describe the contents of triple bottom line reporting as including measures to minimize resource, water and energy consumption; the volume and toxicity of wastes generated; extent of damage to plant and animal species and habitat; and conservation measures such as land offsets and contributions to environmental groups, projects and research.

Protected area managers have a responsibility to work with the local community and stakeholders and to regularly inform them of progress that

Case Study 14.4

Green Globe 21 and earthcheck benchmarking indicators

Green Globe 21, a global environmental benchmarking and certification programme for the travel and tourism industry, assists tourism enterprises and communities with monitoring, improving and reporting on their environmental management performance (De Lacy et al, 2002). It is a commercial company and was launched by the World Travel and Tourism Council in 1994 and based on the principles of *Agenda 21* (WTTC, 1997). The Sustainable Tourism Cooperative Research Centre (CRC) developed the benchmarking system earthcheck, utilized by Green Globe 21. All operators applying for benchmarked status by supplying environmental management performance data are assessed against baseline performance standards.

There are four types of Green Globe 21 registration and, currently, there are certification standards developed for companies, destinations, design and construct infrastructure, and ecotourism, with one being developed for tourism precincts. In order to be benchmarked, operators must address the requirements of the relevant Green Globe 21 Standard, as well as annually measure and submit information with regard to a number of benchmarking key performance indicators (KPIs). To achieve certified status, operators have to complete the benchmarking process; following approval at this stage, they are submitted to an independent audit to assess and ensure compliance.

Detailed infrastructure design can also positively contribute to achieving sustainability objectives. As well as delivering improved environmental performance, it can lower construction costs, enhance aesthetics and lower long-term maintenance costs. Earthcheck has developed a Design and Construct Standard and benchmarking indicators to ensure that effective design is implemented at the initial phase of construction, maximizing the environmental and economic benefits. Benchmarking performance criteria for design and construction include positioning (orientation on the north–south axis and impact on the ground); energy efficiency and conservation (use of solar panels, insulation and ventilation); building materials and processes (items with low volatile emissions, recycled materials, sourcing from local suppliers and reduction of on-site waste); and protection of air, earth and water (water recycling, evaporation of wastewater, construction processes and local employment) (Hyde and Law, 2001).

is made in meeting environmental, social and economic performance targets. Triple bottom line reporting can be utilized in state of the parks reports. Information on environmental performance assessment, monitoring, improvement of energy and water consumption and waste production, and social commitments need to be included in these reports. Publicly reporting this information provides an example to other organizations and informs the community of the benefits of adopting sustainable practices.

Sustainable resource use, primarily in Category V and VI protected areas

Around the world people in low HDI countries have subsistence livelihoods that rely heavily on the products available from natural environments (see Case Study 14.5). In order to conserve biodiversity, protect ecosystem integrity and ensure a long-term secure future for dependent communities, it is essential that use of these products is sustainable. This is a complex undertaking. It is estimated that up to 25,000 wild plant products alone are used by people in the tropics (Heywood, 1999). Managers need to know what wild products are utilized by local communities, how they are harvested and what quantities are extracted. They need to monitor whether the use is sustainable or not. Each product has its own biological characteristics, and is part of a population, community and ecosystem. In many cases, there may be little science known about the plant, animal, fungus or invertebrate in question.

There is no one-size-fits-all answer. The combination of factors that enhances sustainable

Case Study 14.5

Sustainable use of protected areas in Cambodia

Cambodia established a network of 23 protected areas, set up on the king's initiative in 1993 and managed by the Cambodian Ministry of the Environment. Since then, several other areas have been added, including the Cardamom Mountains World Heritage Area and Tonle Sap Biosphere Reserve, which are managed by the Ministry of Agriculture Forestry and Fisheries. Protected areas now cover more than 20 per cent of the country, with plans to increase it to 25 per cent in the near future.

Cambodia is a low Human Development Index (HDI) country with an estimated 35.9 per cent of the population classified as poor. Rural households, especially those for whom agriculture is the primary source of income, account for almost 90 per cent of the poor. Eighty-five per cent of the population are rural dwellers who depend upon agriculture, fisheries and forest products for their subsistence. Harvesting wood and non-wood products is a critical part of subsistence livelihoods. In general, the more isolated communities close to protected areas are the poorest and most dependent upon common forest and aquatic resources.

Poverty alleviation is the underlying theme of national development strategies, and protected areas will increasingly be measured on their performance in supporting local communities in sustainable livelihoods and forms of sector development that bring local benefits.

The 2002 *National Biodiversity Strategy and Action Plan* bases its strategies on the notion that protected areas will be engines of development. The strategy provides a framework for action at all levels, with the aim of enhancing the country's ability to ensure the productivity, diversity and integrity of its natural systems. It is suggested this will result in the ability, as a nation, to reduce poverty and improve the quality of life of all Cambodians. The strategy promotes the conservation of biodiversity and the sustainable use of resources. Challenges include:

* clarifying the contributions that protected areas do and can make to poverty alleviation;
* providing infrastructure to support remote communities in and around protected areas;
* engaging communities in collaborative protected area management in a timely manner; and
* providing alternative sustainable livelihoods to the large percentage of the population currently relying on subsistence agriculture in order to satisfy the rapidly modernizing material aspirations of the local community.

Source: adapted from ICEM (2003b)

resource use in one protected area is unlikely to be identical to the factors that influence another located in a different country or socio-economic environment. While there may be some commonalities that can be extrapolated between species, countries and environmental conditions, this cannot be taken for granted, so that good research and ongoing monitoring are required.

The challenge to establish sustainable use of wild products requires an international approach. The IUCN Sustainable Use Specialist Group Technical Advisory Committee was established with members from different areas of expertise (sociology, economics, ecology, agro-ecology, wildlife management and statistics) to distinguish factors that influence or affect the probability of a use being sustainable. The committee has developed an Analytic Framework for Assessing Factors that Influence Sustainability of Uses of Wild Living Natural Resources (IUCN-SUSG, 2001). The framework is based on four suites of factors:

1   usable living natural resources;
2   user population;
3   institutional, political and cultural conditions in which use occurs; and
4   economic conditions under which use takes place.

The probability of a use being sustainable is affected by the interaction of these factors, as well as wider influences such as poverty, foreign debt, powerful commercial- or political-vested interests, national and international market forces, and natural disasters, which may interact with the factors included in the model and change the conditions of sustainable use. Sustainability is considered a dynamic process towards which we strive. To this end there must be indicators and a continuous evaluation and monitoring of all key factors. Adaptive management is required so that adjustments can be made in response to changing circumstances and knowledge.

The IUCN framework document influenced the development of the *Addis Ababa Principles and Guidelines for Sustainable Use of Biodiversity* (CBD, 2004a). The Addis Ababa document is a framework to assist all users of biodiversity to manage their use so that biodiversity and ecosystems do not decline over the long term, thereby also avoiding an associated decline in cultural and socio-economic conditions. It includes a set of principles, operational guidelines and instruments for their implementation. The principles apply to both consumptive and non-consumptive use of components of biodiversity. They consider policy, law and regulation, biodiversity management, socio-economic conditions, and information research and education. Application of the principles and guidelines is set within the context of an ecosystem approach. The 14 principles are as follows:

1   Supportive policies laws and institutions should be in place at all levels of governance and there should be effective linkages between these levels.
2   Recognizing the need for a governing framework consistent with international and national laws, local uses of biodiversity components should be sufficiently empowered and supported by rights to be responsible and accountable for use of the resources concerned.
3   International and national policies, laws and regulations that distort markets which contribute to habitat degradation or otherwise generate perverse incentives that undermine conservation and sustainable use of biodiversity should be identified and removed or mitigated.
4   Adaptive management should be practised, based on:
    •   science, and traditional and local knowledge;
    •   iterative, timely and transparent feedback derived from monitoring the use, environmental and socio-economic impacts, and the status of the resource being used; and
    •   adjusting management based on timely feedback from the monitoring procedures.
5   Sustainable use management goals and practices should avoid or minimize adverse impacts on ecosystem services, structure and functions as well as other components of ecosystems.
6   Interdisciplinary research into all aspects of the use and conservation of biological diversity should be promoted and supported.

7 The spatial and temporal scale of management should be compatible with the ecological and socio-economic scales of the use and its impact.

8 There should be arrangements for international cooperation where multinational decision-making and coordination are needed.

9 An interdisciplinary participatory approach should be applied at the appropriate levels of management and governance related to the use.

10 International and national policies should take into account:
   • current and potential values derived from the use of biological diversity;
   • intrinsic and other non-economic values of biological diversity; and
   • market forces affecting the values and use.

11 Use of biodiversity components should seek to minimize waste and adverse environmental impacts, and optimize benefits from uses.

12 The needs of indigenous and local communities who live with and are affected by the use and conservation of biological diversity, along with their contributions to its conservation and sustainable use, should be reflected in the equitable distributions of the benefits from the use of those resources.

13 The costs of managing and conserving biological diversity should be internalized within the area of management and reflected in the distribution of the benefits from the use.

14 Education and public awareness programmes on conservation and sustainable use should be implemented, and more effective methods of communications should be developed between and among stakeholders and managers (CBD, 2004a).

Local and indigenous communities generally have considerable knowledge about the species they use, especially where they have been using the product for many generations. In many such cases where the external pressures are not too great and traditional life is intact, use of the product is likely to be sustainable. This knowledge is critical in managing community conserved areas (CCAs) (see Chapter 20) and many co-managed protected areas (see Chapter 21), and can be invaluable for conservation scientists.

Traditional livelihoods are being increasingly modified by external factors. There are a multitude of pressures on people using wild forest, grassland, wetland and coastal resources, including rapid economic development, rapidly changing landscapes, population growth, migration and so on. Much of the responsibility for managing the protection of the world's biodiversity hotspots rests on the shoulders of low HDI countries that are also working to improve economic performance and alleviate poverty, which includes aspirations for greater material and energy consumption.

Some products that have traditionally been used by local communities have been commercialized in regional or global markets, offering cash returns to communities. This has occurred with wild animal products, plants for herbal medicines, cosmetics, pharmaceuticals and marine products. Economic pressures arising from commercialization can place considerable pressure on traditional community and government regulatory structures. Two examples illustrate the problem.

In Nepal, plants for Ayurvedic medicine are in high demand for markets in India. Clearing houses are set up on the border and agents contract local people to collect and deliver the plants. They are paid by weight and there is no concern by agents about where the plants are harvested. Illegal harvesting in protected areas is common (Battharai et al, 2003).

In Cambodia, an internationally owned company set up a rattan processing factory on the border of Ream National Park. Local villagers were encouraged to harvest rattan and were paid by the stem. The only source of rattan was in the national park. The rattan supply was quickly exhausted and the company closed its operations, leaving Ream National Park and the local community worse off (ICEM, 2003b).

Protected area managers need to find ways of working with local communities and indigenous people to protect biodiversity and ecosystem processes, and, at a minimum, to do no harm to human livelihoods (Borrini-Feyerabend et al, 2004b). This may require compromise on both sides, and it may take years before agreements are reached and fully implemented.

The IUCN category of each protected area is an important guide for management decisions about sustainable resource use. Since Category I permits no extraction of resources, it is important that people living nearby are fully cognisant of the restrictions. Provision for compensation for any loss of resource use needs to be put in place. Where this has not happened, much time, effort and resources go into patrolling and preventing illegal activity (Chhetri et al, 2004). In Categories II to VI, biodiversity conservation is also paramount, along with conservation of cultural heritage. In some countries and provinces, some extraction of renewable resources on a sustainable basis may be provided for in a management plan, primarily for Category V and VI protected areas; but again such uses must be consistent with the overriding purpose of all protected areas, as expressed in the IUCN definition: that of biodiversity conservation. This will generally necessitate controls to limit extraction levels, manage environmental impacts and, where necessary, appropriate rehabilitation. In all cases, it is important to work out if there is a sustainable rate and level of extraction that does not compromise biodiversity objectives. Users need to be involved in the process of determining these rates and in establishing control mechanisms.

In the rest of this section, we illustrate some approaches to sustainable resource extraction within protected areas using examples of subsistence agriculture, livestock grazing, harvesting of wild plant products (fruit, reeds, seeds and medicinal plants), hunting of animals for meat, and fishing in marine environments. We also briefly consider the emerging issue of bio-prospecting.

Subsistence agriculture

Subsistence agriculture describes a situation where people are harvesting and producing enough resources to meet their own personal needs. Crop–livestock systems are frequently supplemented by resources from natural ecosystems. Nearby forests and wetlands are used for a number of purposes, including leaf litter, pest control products, medicines, food, fodder and fuel.

Shifting 'slash-and-burn' cultivation, or swid-den, is widely practised as a form of subsistence farming across the world, particularly in parts of Asia, Africa, the Pacific Islands and Central and South America. A small patch is cleared from the forest and is subsequently burned and cropped for a few cycles before being abandoned due to weed invasion and fertility decline. The site is left fallow for a number of years while other patches are cleared and cultivated elsewhere. Re-growth of forest vegetation during this period leads to a restoration of the soil's fertility, and the farmer eventually returns to the site for reuse as a cropping area. The site is also used as it regenerates since particular species are useful at various times. Shifting cultivation incorporates a range of highly adaptable and site-specific systems that have developed in response to particular environmental and socio-cultural conditions. Crops grown include food, medicinal plants, spices and plants for crafts (Heywood, 1999). Typically, under low population densities, and when practised by traditional swiddeners, shifting cultivation has minimal long-term impact on a tropical forest (Shriar, 1999). This system is sustainable in areas of low population density and when the period during which the land lies fallow is at least six to eight years. As population or migration increases, the fallow period shortens, decreasing crop yields; meanwhile, the required weeding labour, which is mostly done by women, increases (Pehu, 2003).

In some protected areas where people have been practising subsistence agriculture, zoning is a tool that has been used to define areas where agriculture is permitted. In American Samoa National Park, for example, the National Park Service has leased the land and marine environment in the park for 50 years from several villages, who wanted to protect the forest. The park service manages the land and reefs within the park; but the villagers reserve the right to traditional use, which includes subsistence agriculture. Under the park lease provisions, native American Samoans can continue to carry out subsistence activities with traditional tools and methods on currently active and managed lands leased to the park, while clearing and cultivation are prohibited in primary and mature secondary forest. Subsistence agriculture typically includes maintaining small plots of land for the cultivation of traditional Polynesian crops such as bananas, taro, breadfruit and coconuts. Managed lands are defined as areas that were farmed or left fallow within the last 15 years (Graves, 2004).

Livestock grazing

Livestock grazing in protected areas is often considered a threat to biodiversity. Livestock production in high HDI countries has been associated with overgrazing, erosion, water pollution and biodiversity loss. Nonetheless, some livestock grazing can be essential in maintaining certain highly diverse grasslands, and the removal of people and livestock has led to decreases in biodiversity (Infield, 2003). Where cultures are based around herding livestock, the systems they have established over hundreds or thousands of years have shaped the landscape, and their use of the land has become integral to maintaining biodiversity (Farvar, 2003; Borrini-Feyerabend et al, 2004a). Grazing livestock in protected areas is very much a case-by-case decision. In Africa and West Asia, nomadic pastoralists grazed cattle on a sustainable basis for centuries. In Europe, much of the biodiversity in protected areas has co-developed with traditional agricultural practices. In Australia, livestock grazing causes significant damage to native vegetation, soils and waterways and has recently been prohibited in the Victorian Alpine National Park. In some cases, pressures to increase agricultural production have led to overgrazing in some protected areas, and measures have had to be introduced by managers to minimize the damage (see Case Study 14.6). In many CCAs, communities voluntarily regulate grazing to ensure that negative impacts are not felt by the ecosystem or wildlife. This includes a temporary or seasonal stoppage of all grazing activity, allowing degraded landscapes to regenerate.

Harvesting wild animal and plant products

Protected forests, wetlands grasslands and marine environments are the source of a wide range of non-timber products. Forests, in particular, provide important non-timber products. Non-timber forest products (NTFPs) are defined as all biological material other than industrial round wood and resulting products that are harvested

Wood collection, Kibale National Park, Uganda

Source: IUCN Photo Library © Jim Thorsell

from within and on the edges of natural, manipulated or disturbed forests (Chamberlain et al, 2004). NTFPs constitute a large proportion of the 'informal economy' and are often used by rural communities to supplement their nutritional needs during times of shortage or poor harvests. Table 14.5 provides a number of examples.

Plant biodiversity hotspots often occur in low HDI countries in the tropics, where pressure to increase economic and human development is high. Well-managed NTFP harvesting can assist the local economy. Negotiating with communities to stop practices that are damaging the protected area may be needed in the case of government-managed protected areas. In the case of CCAs, such negotiations are usually carried out internally by community members. Other ways of dealing with subsistence resource use in protected areas is to limit the resource extraction to certain areas, to allow only specific people to collect the

Case Study **14.6**

Sustainable grazing in Retezat National Park, Romania

Retezat National Park, located in the west of Romania, is the country's oldest national park. It protects a unique corner of the Carpathian Mountains, a rich assemblage of vegetation and viable populations of various large mammals. In 1979 the park was designated as a biosphere reserve under the United Nations Educational, Scientific and Cultural Organization's (UNESCO's) Man and the Biosphere programme.

Traditional grazing is still practised by local people in the park. More than 20 per cent of the alpine areas are pastures owned and used by local villages as grazing areas for livestock. The villagers' rights to these pastures date back to a governmental agreement of 1922. Over the years, control over the grazing in this area has diminished and the area has been overgrazed. This was demonstrated to have altered the natural diversity and richness of the alpine pastures to the extent that overgrazing had become one of the main threats within the park.

Nevertheless, the aim was to maintain traditional grazing activity on the park's alpine pastures, but within its ecological capacity. The challenge for the Park Management Authority has been to encourage local people to work towards sustainable use of the mountains' natural resources, and to reduce the damaging levels of grazing. The current park administration, established in 1999, organized meetings with local communities and authorities to raise awareness of the purpose of the national park, the effects of overgrazing, and to gain local input for park planning.

A small grants programme was developed within the framework of the Romanian Biodiversity Conservation Management Project to encourage projects that decrease grazing pressure on the alpine pastures, while promoting sustainable grazing and other activities on lands around the villages. A grants committee was established, which includes representatives from all of the communities with ownership rights or another stake in the park. Training is provided to local people to enhance their capacities for project writing and fundraising activities.

In 2001, grazing contracts were negotiated for the use of alpine pastures inside the central zone of the national park. Local authorities have assisted in developing protocols and joint programmes that establish rules for grazing activities and protect the grazing rights of local animal owners. As a result, the level of grazing activities in the alpine meadows was successfully reduced in 2002 and 2003.

The Park Management Authority has recognized the importance of working with local stakeholders to retain local knowledge and to develop support for conservation. Participatory activities are needed to successfully manage a park where landownership and land-use rights are so complex. Through working with the national park, local stakeholders are securing opportunities to continue traditional activities in the area. In addition to this, support from the national park, in the form of training and small project grants, is leading to new opportunities and helping local people to gain confidence in developing their own initiatives.

Source: adapted from Wieting (2004)

resource, to establish quotas based on a sustainable yield, and to establish plantings of coveted species outside the protected area.

In Kibale National Park in Uganda, the community and park management developed agreements to limit extraction of resources. The protected area is surrounded by 27 parishes where approximately 120,000 people live. The boundary communities extract more than 20 products from the park to meet some of their subsistence, commercial, cultural and medicinal needs. Prohibition was the first management strategy attempted; but it was found that law enforcement was becoming very time consuming and expen-

sive for park managers. With the aid of the Kibale Semuliki Conservation and Development Project, collaborative resource management agreements were negotiated with local boundary communities, which set limits on who could harvest in the park and what products could be taken. Initially, it took two years to identify, negotiate and sign the first agreements, then six months, on average, for the following agreements. The success of the collaborative agreements was greater where assistance was given to develop alternatives to harvesting park resources. Community–park relations improved, a significant drop in illegal activity was noted and community members became

Table 14.5 Examples of non-timber forest product (NTFP) uses around the world

Place	Users	Number of species	Purpose
Peruvian Amazon	Iquitos people	57 wild fruit species	Sale at local markets
Colombia	Maraca Indians	51 bird species	Domestic consumption
Bolivia	Siriono Indians	23 mammal, 33 bird and 9 reptile species	Domestic consumption
Michigan, US	Rural community	138	Non-market use
Indonesia	Various	1260 plant species	Medicinal use
India	275 forest dwellers, farmers and pastoralists	At least 10,000 plant and animal species (mostly plants)	Medicinal use, energy, housing and wild foods
Sarawak, Malaysia	Hunters	26 mammal, 12 bird and 5 reptile species	Domestic consumption and market use
South Africa	Various	500	Medicinal use
Central African Republic	Hunters	33 mammal, 7 reptile and 3 bird species	Domestic consumption and market use
Germany	Various	1543	Medicinal use

Sources: based on Chamberlain et al (2004); TPCG and Kalpavriksh (2005)

involved in reporting illegal activity (Chhetri et al, 2004).

Often, traditional and indigenous communities have customary law that limits the extraction of resources. In the case of Shirakami World Heritage Area in Japan, strict practices were maintained by a few '*matagi*' (hunters), based on a traditional ethic of reciprocity with the mountains, which was also subsequently adopted by members of the local community and conservationist s who joined in to lobby for protection for Shirakami and who continue to visit the area to assist with rehabilitation activities (see Case Study 14.7). In many of the CCAs around the world, traditional restrictions have been revived after having been eroded for a period, often along with new restrictions born out of the necessity of responding to changed circumstances. In the Indian village of Mendha-Lekha, for instance, the community has fought to restrict the previously unsustainable bamboo extraction by a paper mill, and has regulated its own use of timber and other forest produce in its bid to conserve the forest (see Case Study 21.4).

Protected area managers with responsibilities for areas where harvesting plants or grazing livestock over a long period has taken place need to determine if the use has beneficial, detrimental or neutral implications for achieving management objectives. It is also necessary to determine at what level the activity is sustainable and to establish limits. For example, harvesting grass from a wetland area may be beneficial to bird habitat; but increasing or decreasing the harvest or changing the way in which it is carried out may make the activity detrimental. Ongoing monitoring of environmental and social conditions to assess the impact of such activities is required. A number of CCAs across the world are beginning to use monitoring methods to judge the sustainability of their resource uses, ranging from traditional 'rule-of-thumb' indicators to complex scientific ones. Where external expertise is used to study impacts, research should include participatory methods

Case Study 14.7

Traditional use in Shirakami-sanchi World Heritage Area, Japan

Kumi Kato, School of Language and Comparative Culture, University of Queensland, Australia

Shirakami-sanchi (hereafter, Shirakami) in the north-west of Honshu in Japan is a mountain range of approximately 130,000ha that includes seven peaks above 1000m. In 1993, approximately 13 per cent of the range was inscribed on the *World Heritage List* as a natural property. The nominated area of 16,971ha is divided into 60 per cent core and 40 per cent buffer zone, and encompasses parts of two prefectures, Aomori and Akita, whose names in characters – green forests and autumn rice fields – represent the two local landscape types. With the nomination, Shirakami has come to be known for its beech (*Fagus crenata*) forest, known as 'buna' in Japanese. The buna forests in Shirakami are one of the largest intact forest systems in Japan.

The main livelihoods of people living around the World Heritage Area consist of rice farming and apple growing, and traditionally they also engaged in river fishing, harvesting edible wild plants (*sansai*) and fungi, small-scale logging for firewood, charcoal burning, and collecting leaves and weeds for fertilizer and cattle feed. These widely practised traditional uses are referred to as *Yamazumi* (mountain inhabitation). *Matagi* (traditional hunters) also hunted bear and other animals. This sustainable and strictly regulated hunting has now been banned, which *matagi* consider to upset the balance of the mountains.

Traditional activities in Shirakami are based on strict rules. It was a *matagi* tradition that hunters enter the mountain as a group of eight, and work required cooperation and equal share of all harvests. Unwritten but strict regulations applied to all traditional practices regarding the use of tools (hand or knife), location, species and harvesting seasons. If harvest took place in one area, then that area was off limits for two years. The amount taken was to ensure future harvest and respect for the mountain. One *matagi* said that they would know exactly where and when, for example, rare fungi are ready for harvest and would never disturb the mountain unnecessarily. These secrets were not passed on to anyone. It took any *matagi* at least four years to learn all of these practices, as well as related rituals, languages and taboos.

A *matagi* explained that they say 'be blessed' rather than 'take'. He said: 'If the Mountain god allows us to be blessed with harvest, we gratefully receive; but if not, we are not meant to have any.' A similar sense of respect, awe and affinity towards Shirakami was expressed by community members, who 'feel so grateful for this place because it is always there' and 'simply want to return the blessing we receive from the land'.

The community's sense was that their existence and actions would not damage nature. They said that 'the mountain needs us' and they knew how to reciprocate the favour and blessing by showing deep appreciation, making the best use of what is allowed according to self-regulation, and also in a form of restoration and conservation work (collecting beech seed, planting seedlings, thinning saplings and weeding). Volunteers and 'commuting' community members also became part of the restoration and conservation work. Such reciprocity and sense of connection was what they sought in their involvement with Shirakami and the community. A founder of a nature school says that he 'used to take food (plants) from the mountains, and so now I want to return by planting trees, caring for the mountains and running educational programmes'.

involving the people undertaking the harvesting (Case Study 14.8).

Harvesters, once they have been involved in a survey and have witnessed the results for themselves, may willingly take on monitoring over time if they can see that it will help to ensure the long-term survival of the resource. Conservation education is a key factor in any sustainable resource use and is one of the greatest contributions that protected area managers can make (see Chapter 10).

Medicinal plants

It has been estimated that for 80 per cent of the world's population, wild plants are a major source of medicine (Bowles et al, 2001). In most instances, this resource use has been sustainable over long periods of time, often regulated by customary law. However, increasingly, people are becoming involved in commercial ventures that are driven by market demand with contracts outside the traditional structures.

The Himalayan region, for example, is a major

source of medicinal plants integral to Ayurvedic and other traditional medicine systems. There is a strong demand for such plants, especially in India. The alternative health industry in Europe, North America, Australia and New Zealand uses a wide variety of herbal medicines, and has adopted many of the practices of Ayurvedic, Buddhist and Chinese traditional medicines so that it has become a fast-growing multi-billion dollar industry. In 2004, the global herbal medicine industry was valued at more than US$60 billion annually. Harvesting wild medicinal plants has thus become an organized commercial venture in many places, where agents employ local people to undertake the work (Battharai et al, 2003).

Protected areas often contain valuable resources of medicinal plants. In many cases where wild harvest occurs, it is through the local knowledge of the harvester that the plant is found, particularly as resources become scarcer and demand increases. Knowledge about plant properties is also often embedded in the local culture. From the point of view of sustainability, two principles are threatened – social equity and biodiversity conservation; illegal harvesting in protected areas is high in some areas as populations of plants outside the protected area become exhausted (McClelland, 2004).

Hunting, wildlife trade and fishing

Many protected areas contain important wildlife species that are sought either directly for food or as marketable merchandise for their meat, skin, tusks and medicinal qualities, or as live pets or zoo specimens. Wild game has long been important for many rural communities, and some protected

Case Study 14.8

Researching sustainable harvest levels of a bromeliad species, Los Tuxtlas Biosphere Reserve, Mexico

Aechmea magdalenae, a typical non-timber forest product (NTFP) species, is a clonal understorey bromeliad harvested from the buffer zone of the Los Tuxtlas Biosphere Reserve in the state of Veracruz, Mexico. The strong, silky fibre extracted from its leaves is used to embroider expensive leather articles in an art known as *el piteado*. The ramets (above-ground stems) are also harvested for use in forest cultivation programmes. Although non-governmental and governmental agencies have been promoting the harvest of *A. magdelanae* as a strategy to encourage local harvesters to conserve the standing forest, the elevated economic value of *A. magdalenae*'s fibre has also resulted in high harvesting pressure on wild populations. The species, collected by local harvesters throughout south-east Mexico and Guatemala, is reported to have disappeared from several regions due to over-harvesting.

At least three things are necessary to protect NTFP species from over-harvest and for NTFP extraction in buffer zones to contribute to forest conservation:

* identification of optimal harvest regimes;
* accurate estimation of maximum harvest limits; and
* implementation of those limits among local harvesters.

The first and third tasks require the participation and cooperation of local harvesting communities. The accurate estimation of maximum harvest limits poses more technical problems. First, it necessitates a sound description of the effects of environmental variation on maximum sustainable harvest rates. Second, the methods used to estimate maximum sustainable harvest must be validated.

The results of a study conducted on harvested populations of *A. magdelanae* showed maximum sustainable harvest to be greater than previous studies that attempted to estimate maximum rates of harvest for NTFPs by simulation methods.

Participatory research on establishing harvest limits for NTFP extracted from buffer zones may help to ensure the conservation of over-harvested NTFP and the integrity of the reserves. Participatory research involves the cooperation of local harvesters in a simultaneous research and education process. It can be a critical component of conservation efforts because when NTFP species are over-harvested in buffer-zone forests, harvesters often meet their economic needs by illegally harvesting them in the reserve.

Source: adapted from Ticktin et al (2002)

Collecting medicinal plants, Chiang Mai, Thailand

Source: IUCN Photo Library © Jim Thorsell

areas may allow limited subsistence hunting. Where traditional bushmeat hunting is undertaken at a sustainable level, it can be compatible with protection. Bushmeat is a term commonly used to describe meat gained from hunting wild animals, mostly in forest environments where domestic livestock is not common. It is an important subsistence and commercial business in Africa and, to a lesser extent, in South America and Asia.

However, there are problems associated with the activity that pose a significant threat to protected areas. Until recently, bushmeat hunting was generally a subsistence activity. Now it has become a commercial venture and 90 per cent of bushmeat is sold, rather than kept for family consumption. Hunters sell the animals to women, who process and sell the meat in 'chop bars' and restaurants in urban areas. Weak governance structures at the local level and poor industrial practice make regulation and management of the trade difficult. As the trade is largely illegal, working out

the level of wildlife being taken and the species mix involved is also problematic (Brown, 2003).

In Africa, rare and already endangered species are threatened by the illegal expansion of the bushmeat trade, including chimpanzees, elephants and gorillas. Poaching is widespread and many protected areas are targeted because they are known to contain the resources that poachers seek (CITES, 2001).

Global markets for wildlife raise another set of issues. Market forces can create value for wildlife and drive the establishment of private or community conservation reserves. For example, the commercially operated Campbell Private Game Reserve in South Africa provides hunting experiences resembling those of the Bushmen of the Kalahari, and management of the activity takes into account the carrying capacity for individual game species (Campbell Private Game Reserve, 2004). On the other hand, the market can cause over-exploitation of populations through poach-

Uru boat-building with tortora reeds, Lake Titicaca, Bolivia

Source: IUCN Photo Library © Jim Thorsell

ing and illegal trade. In Cuc Phuong National Park, Viet Nam, hunting has reduced populations of large mammals, and conflicts with local human populations hamper effective management. During 1996 to 1997, police detected 1270 cases of illegal trade involving 69,000 animals. Endangered species are often openly on sale (Compton, 1998; McNeely, 1998). The slipper orchid (*Paphiopedilium rothschildianum*) and the pitcher plant (*Nepenthes raja*), both from the Mount Kinabulu National Park in Malaysia, have become the objects of theft and trade, while stealing of butterflies and other insects occurs in Khao Yai National Park in Thailand. Many aquatic environments within protected areas face problems of over-fishing caused by incursion from neighbouring communities or by the illegal presence of larger-scale operations.

There have been successes at regulating hunting to a sustainable level. This has mainly occurred through agreements and by making wildlife management the responsibility of local communities (see Case Study 14.9). In many of the relatively new CCAs, a mix of traditional restrictions and new ones may be adopted (see Chapter 21). In the state of Nagaland in India, for example, several dozen villages have declared a seasonal prohibition on hunting, and/or designated forest areas where hunting is totally prohibited (Kothari and Pathak, 2005).

Sustainable use of marine resources

Extraction from marine ecosystems occurs for both subsistence and commercial use. Harvest includes edible resources such as finfish, shellfish, marine mammals and seaweeds; resources for construction such as mangrove poles, coral blocks, sand and lime; ornamental uses such as shells, pearls and coral; scientific uses, which includes a wide array of species; and industrial uses such as giant clams and species yielding pharmaceuticals, and for mariculture such as mussels and oysters.

Fish catch, Sundarbans, India

Source: IUCN Photo Library © Jim Thorsell

Many millions of people inhabiting the coasts of the world have small cash incomes and subsist on local resources. Some communities have customary practices that ensure sustainable management; but often they need assistance to monitor their activities in a way that demonstrates sustainable harvest (Salm et al, 2000). The biodiversity of coasts is readily accessible to users. Rock pools accessible at low tide contain molluscs, bivalves, crustaceans, octopus and sea cucumber that can often be gathered by hand. Seaweed is also available in this way. In subtropical and tropical areas, mangroves are another highly productive system where crabs and other invertebrate species can be gathered and fish can be caught. Mangroves themselves are used as building material for housing and boats and for fuel. Coral reefs provide fish, invertebrates and building materials. Beaches are places where turtle eggs (in the tropics), bird eggs and birds can be found, and off the beach, sandy bottom bays are home to various fish species that are caught in nets or on lines.

Marine mammals such as seals, whales and dolphins are also traditional foods of indigenous people in arctic and temperate zones, as well as the tropics. As with use of terrestrial resources, indigenous and traditional societies had regulations in place through customary law to protect against overuse of resources. For example, in Korea, diving is traditionally done by women. To ensure sustainability they agreed not to use scuba equipment when it became available so that all they could take was what they could gather by holding their breath and diving in the traditional way. They typically dive for four to six hours a day about ten days per month, when conditions are right. The best divers can hold their breath for almost two minutes and dive to a depth of around 15m. They collect octopus, abalone, sea urchins, sea slugs sea cucumber and seaweed, and have been selling their produce since the 1970s (Onishi, 2005; Pfeiffer, 2005).

In some places, self-regulated systems are still operating effectively; but more often, changes in land use and tenure have disrupted practices that have been in place for millennia. Case Study

Case Study 14.9

Meat harvesting and distribution, Namibia

Christopher Vaughan, Department for International and Rural Development University of Reading, UK

In Namibia's communal land areas, managing wildlife is primarily concerned with managing social relations, as well as managing biological resources and the law. In order to support the local management of wildlife and other natural resources, the Namibian government has implemented progressive policy, which allows for the establishment of new community wildlife and natural resource management (NRM) institutions, called conservancies. A conservancy is the name given by the Namibian government to legally recognized institutions established to manage new rights over wildlife. It is an IUCN Category VI protected area. A conservancy consists of a group of commercial farms or areas of communal land on which neighbouring landowners or members have pooled resources for the purpose of conserving and using wildlife sustainably. Members practise normal farming activities and operations in combination with wildlife use on a sustainable basis. Understanding social relations is a critical aspect of understanding the processes involved in achieving community wildlife management objectives since community conservation is not simply about technical choices or changes in laws or formal organizations, but is also a part of wider processes of social change and about attempts to redistribute social and political power.

The implementation of legal community wildlife utilization (such as game meat hunting and distribution) provides direct livelihood benefits and is an incentive for collective management. Wildlife hunting for community use can provide immediate tangible benefits that give local communities the incentive to engage in conservation wildlife management practices. It also ameliorates some of the suffering associated with human wildlife conflict. It has lead to a change in perception by local communities as to who is responsible for wildlife management. No longer do communities feel that the distant state is responsible, but increasingly they are able to see the link between their own community conservancy management and the wildlife that surrounds them. The most commonly hunted species are springbok (*Antidorcas marsupialis*) and oryx (*Oryx gazella*). Members of the conservancy staff use high-powered rifles to cull animals and record numbers of off-take. Meat is divided up by conservancy staff and either delivered to houses or dropped at collection points. In other cases, meat from joint venture trophy hunting is butchered and delivered to communities. Hunted wild meat can also be requested for special social occasions, such as a chiefs' meeting or independence day celebrations. In some instances, conservancies are exploring opportunities to harvest large numbers of springbok and to butcher them for sale to external markets. In all cases, conservancies must record numbers of off-take and inform the Ministry of Environment and Tourism of their plans. Conservancies are limited to a few species that are classified as huntable game, while others remain specially protected and permission must be sought through a special quota and permit system from the ministry. Of critical importance is the availability of wildlife in relation to the human population; fortunately, in Namibia's north-west there is a relatively low human population and high wildlife population. However, in Caprivi, where it is the reverse, some larger species, such as Cape buffalo (*Syncerus caffer*), African elephant (*Loxodonta africana*) and hippopotamus (*Hippopotamus amphibius*), are offered to communities for meat consumption as a result of problem animal control or trophy hunting, or, on rare occasions, are slaughtered for ceremonial purposes. One of the main problems in the process other than a lack of adequate resources is maintaining clear and transparent means of communication and equity in the distribution process. If this is not handled in a transparent and equitable manner, it can lead to community conflict and resentment.

Official conservancy harvesting and meat distribution is limited to conservancies with higher ratios of available wildlife than human populations. However, the extent to which meat distribution contributes to livelihood security and changes behaviour is currently limited, although the timing of hunts and the species hunted are deemed appropriate and desirable by local people. Creating a direct link between managing and benefiting from wildlife is important. Even in areas where meat distribution takes place, some people continue to hunt illegally for the pot. Illegal wildlife use continues to play a critical role in people's livelihoods and is governed by complex local social arrangements. Recent research by the Wildlife in Livelihoods Diversification project indicates that approximately one quarter of households use wildlife and that it is important to livelihoods, particularly for poorer households. Wildlife use, even if 'illegal', allows the least secure households to meet food requirements and to reserve resources, such as livestock or crops, for future use. Community members report a wide variety of wildlife species utilization; yet this local indigenous knowledge and diversity of use is not celebrated or a focus of programme support activities. It is unlikely that illegal wildlife will ever be totally stopped. Community 'own-use' hunting and meat distribution is the beginning of the process to provide immediate tangible benefits to local communities and can act as an important incentive for communities to begin to feel ownership and benefit from their wildlife in a legal and sustainable way.

14.10 describes the breakdown in traditional use after the declaration of a nature reserve, followed by restoration of sustainable practices under a negotiated agreement between protected area managers and traditional users.

Marine protected areas are taking a leading role in developing sustainable use of marine resources where customary law has ceased to be effective due to external pressures or where pressure from population increase has caused overuse of resources. In Tanzania, marine protected area agreements were reached that sea cucumber would only be harvested from rock pools and not by diving. In Monterrico, a multiple-use area on the Pacific Coast of Guatemala, managers let fishermen take 80 per cent of turtle eggs from every turtle nest that fishermen find. They say that most eggs would not be successful anyway. The fishermen have to give the protected area the remaining 20 per cent, which are cared for very well. The little turtles are freed in front of tourists and all reach the sea (Gambarotta, pers comm, 2005).

Often, community struggles to maintain or revive sustainable use have been embedded in, or led to, wider political struggles for control. This is illustrated by the case of the Tagbanwa people of the Philippines, who inhabit a limestone island for which they have established stringent use regulations (Ferrari and De Vera, 2003a). The forest resources are to be used for domestic purposes only. All of the freshwater lakes but one are sacred. Entry to those lakes is strictly forbidden except for religious and cultural purposes. The only lake accessible for tourism is Lake Kayangan, which has regulations concerning the number of people allowed in, waste disposal, resource use and so on. Until recently, the Tagbanwas' territorial rights were not legally recognized, leading to encroachment by migrant fishers, tourism operators, politicians seeking land deals and government agencies. This caused several problems, chief among which was the impoverishment of the marine resources, essential for the local livelihood. During the mid 1980s, however, the islanders organized themselves into the Tagbanwas Foundation of Coron Island and started lobbying to regain management control over their natural resources. First, they applied for a Community Forest Stewardship Agreement, which was granted in

1990 over the 7748ha of Coron Island and a neighbouring island, Delian, but not over the marine areas. The Tagbanwa continued their struggle and, in 1998, managed to get a Certificate of Ancestral Domain Claim for 22,284ha of land and marine waters. In 2001, after having produced a high-quality map and an *Ancestral Land Management Plan*, they managed to obtain a Certificate of Ancestral Domain Title, which grants collective right to land (Ferrari and De Vera, 2003a).

Unlike terrestrial areas where agricultural systems provide commercial food production, the vast majority of commercial fisheries rely on wild fish. Naturally productive ecosystems such as coral reefs and estuaries provide continued fish production if they are conserved appropriately. It is widely recognized that fisheries need to be managed in a sustainable way. Case Study 14.11 illustrates the often rocky path to agreement and sustainable use of resources.

The following factors have been found to affect sustainability of resource use and management within marine protected areas:

- The local community should be directly involved in the establishment and management of the marine protected areas.
- Different user groups must have a strong commitment to sustainable resource use for the long term.
- An institutional framework needs to be established that incorporates all relevant stakeholders and includes a decision-making process that takes their interests into account.
- A stable political and economic base is needed that includes a strong commitment by government to manage marine resources in the context of marine protected areas.
- A comprehensive management plan, based on an adaptive approach (see Chapter 11), is needed for the marine protected area, which ensures that resource use will take place in a sustainable manner and user conflicts will be minimized (Senaratna, 2002).

Strong national policies and legislation covering marine protected areas are also needed, as well as resources to ensure their enforcement (Senaratna, 2002).

Case Study **14.10**

Mussel harvesting in Mapelane Reserve, South Africa

Mapelane Nature Reserve is part of the Greater St Lucia Wetland Park in Kwazulu-Natal Province in South Africa. It is a traditional mussel harvesting site for the Sokhulu people. They know that when the *Msintsi* tree is flowering, the mussels are ready for harvest. Mussel shell middens on this part of the coast date back 2000 years, indicating that this resource has been harvested here for at least that long. A system of rotational harvesting was used allowing each mussel bed a few years to recover between uses. Mussels were harvested by young women and were considered good food, especially for children.

Commercial forestry started in the region during the 1930s, and the right of the Sokhulu people to harvest mussels was challenged by foresters, loggers and recreational campers. The conflict escalated when the area was declared a nature reserve in 1984, and its rich habitat and biodiversity was added to the World Heritage site of the Greater St Lucia Wetland Park. At this time, Mabelane Reserve came under the authority of Ezemvelo Kwazulu-Natal Wildlife. However, the Sokhulu people still claimed the area to be their territory.

Mussel harvesting was now an illegal activity, carried out at night. The manner of harvesting changed from careful selective collection to fast wholesale removal of mussels, which significantly damaged the mussel beds. The efforts of park personnel to protect the shoreline were actually contributing to significant damage to the coastal resources, and also perpetuated tension and violence between park officials and the Sokhulu community.

With the assistance of a researcher from the University of Cape Town, the officer in charge of Mapelane Reserve convinced higher officials to try a different approach. A research project to establish a sustainable level of harvesting was undertaken, along with finding ways of resolving conflict and negotiating an agreement between park staff and the harvesters. An agreement to co-manage the mussel harvest was made. Sokhulu Buhhlebemvelo Joint Mussel Management Committee was established, comprising park staff, harvesters, researchers from the University of Cape Town and a few professional staff, including a community liaison officer whose role was to translate and keep open communication between the parties.

The joint committee controlled most aspects of the mussel harvest. It identified subsistence collectors, issued harvest permits, specified harvest methods, and set the schedule and location of the harvest, as well as the quantity of mussels per harvester. Monitors were hired to record and oversee the collection process. Processes were put in place to ensure fair representation on the joint committee and full participation by all members.

The Sokhulu community and Kwazulu-Natal park authorities have recently signed a contractual agreement setting out the roles and responsibilities of the co-management partners and confirming their commitment to work together. Harvesters are typically female and poor: factors that limit their influence in most other decision-making arenas. They have become empowered and gained skills in being part of the joint committee, which is now seeking employment opportunities for members of the Sokhulu community.

Sources: adapted from UNDP, UNEP and the World Bank (2003)

Bio-prospecting

Bio-prospecting is the search for components of biological diversity that may be of value for commercial development. Since protected areas are a major reservoir of genetic and biological resources, they come under pressure from bio-prospecting. The potential benefits from bio-prospecting have been hailed as one important reason to conserve biodiversity. Many as-yet undescribed species may yield considerable benefits to humanity – benefits that will be foregone if we do not conserve and sustainably use current biodiversity. Large multinational pharmaceutical companies are involved as the process requires large capital inputs, and returns may be 10 to 20 years into the future. Despite the initial capital input and the long time frame, finding a plant with properties that are developed into a widely used drug is worth billions. Pharmaceuticals are worth around US$300 billion per annum. Of the top 150 prescriptive drugs in the US, 118 were derived from living organisms: 74 per cent plants, 18 per cent fungi and 5 per cent from vertebrate species (Hall, 2003). The agrochemical industry is also interested in the benefits of bio-prospecting and spends hundreds of millions of dollars on developing new products such as pesticides and

Case Study **14.11**

Soufriere Marine Management Area, St Lucia

The Soufriere Marine Management Area is a multiple-use area including no-take marine reserves, fishing priority zones and other use zones. Prior to its establishment in 1994, there were numerous ongoing conflicts between users. The area was home to 150 fishers with 78 boats, and fishing was a traditional source of income. They fished off the beach using seine nets, off the reef with gill nets and in the reef with fish traps. There were 4500 dives per month on the reef, mainly from tourists – most staying at one of the three major hotels. Other visitors came for half-day visits from other hotels on the island or from cruise ships. Yachters cruising the West Indies also visited Soufriere. Visiting divers cut holes in fish traps to release reef fish; yachtsmen anchored in sandy bays, interfering with local fishing for coastal pelagic fish; and access to the beach and sea had been restricted by the development of tourist facilities. The reef fish populations were under threat from illegal spear fishing and pot fishing, and anchors from yachts and diving boats were damaging the structure of the reef (Salm et al, 2000).

After several unsuccessful attempts to resolve conflicts, a new process was started in 1992 by the Department of Fisheries and the Caribbean Natural Resources Institute. Interest groups were assisted by professionals in a negotiation, conflict resolution and participatory planning process. Development cooperation funding from the US and French governments assisted implementation. Mapping of all uses of the coastal area was undertaken, and a final map was developed showing coastal resources, uses and areas of conflict or concern. A preliminary agreement was reached covering 11km of coastline and was a zoning agreement with specific rules for each zone.

The implementation process began successfully; but after two to three years it broke down as procedures were bypassed and agreements were reached between users without informing the full user group or the management organization. The process lost credibility and regulations were ignored. However, it was agreed by all stakeholders involved that there were fundamental problems that needed solving. An institutional review was held, which uncovered that stakeholders were not aligned on the mission and objectives of the Soufriere Marine Management Area – they had only reached a consensus on the zoning. Other shortcomings were that the original agreement was not binding and there was not an adequate legal basis for operation. A new management regime was developed based on a clear agreed mission, transparent management structure and strong legal basis (Salm et al, 2000; Renard, 2001).

In 2005, Soufriere Marine Management Area celebrated its tenth anniversary. Commercial fish biomass in the marine reserve has shown a fourfold increase, and a threefold increase in the fishing zone, and the area is financially self-sufficient, thanks to diving and yacht mooring fees. Institutional capacity has increased in all stakeholder groups and tourism is bringing benefits to the local community. The area is also used for scientific study. Challenges continue to arise; but there is a commitment from the stakeholders, and the legal and management structures to deal with them are working at this point in time (Gell and Roberts, 2003).

herbicides. For both these industries, around 37 per cent of the research and development budget goes into the search and discovery of new compounds. Other industries engaged in bio-prospecting include health food and beauty product companies (MED, 2002).

Bio-prospecting can be like looking for a needle in a haystack. The odds of finding a plant useful for medicine by random screening are estimated to be 1:10,000 to 1:50,000; but it has been found that with the aid of traditional knowledge of indigenous and local communities, the odds are shortened dramatically (McClelland, 2004). In current circumstances where traditional healers have been involved, it has been estimated that returns to those who have assisted in preservation, research and discovery efforts are 0.0001 per cent of the overall profits (Bowles et al, 2001).

There are conventions and treaties that are attempting to address the inequities inherent in this arrangement and to protect the intellectual property rights of indigenous people and local communities. The one most relevant here is the Convention on Biological Diversity (CBD). Key obligations relating to bio-prospecting concern principles of state sovereignty, conservation and sustainable use, access to genetic resources, sharing benefits equitably, and the protection of indigenous knowledge. In 2002, the Sixth Convention of the Parties to the Convention on Biological Diversity produced the Bonn Guidelines to guide the benefit-sharing arrangements between countries. Benefits to be considered are both monetary and non-monetary, including access fees, royalties, licence fees, research funding, institutional capacity-building, collaborative and cooperative research, technology transfers, and scientific information.

Management principles

1   Protected area managers must ensure that they put in place best practice EMS that address sustainability considerations regarding the legal use of resources.
2   Sustainability provides a strategic direction and framework in which protected area managers should work.
3   Participation of all stakeholders in sustainable resource-use decisions is essential.
4   Both scientific and traditional and local knowledge and practices need to be considered in establishing sustainable use of biodiversity.

5   Education for sustainability is a key factor in building a sustainable future. Protected areas can be an important demonstration for sustainable practices.

Further reading

Borrini Feyerabend G. and Buchan D. (eds) (1997) *Beyond Fences: Seeking Social Sustainability in Conservation, Volumes 1 and 2*, IUCN, Gland and Cambridge

Tilbury, D. and Wortman, D. (2004) *Engaging People in Sustainability*, IUCN Commission on Education and Communication. IUCN, Gland and Cambridge

Websites

Analytic Framework for Assessing Factors that Influence Sustainability of Uses of Wild Living Natural Resources: www.iucn.org/themes/ssc/susg/anafra.html

IUCN Sustainable use specialist group URL: www.iucn.org/themes/ssc/susg/

Convention on Biological Diversity Addis Ababa principles and guidelines: www.biodiv.org/programmes/socio-eco/use/addis.asp

15

Operations Management

Graeme L. Worboys and Colin Winkler

A feral animal thrashing in its capture cage, the repetitive thump of a weed spray unit, the clang of picks and shovels on a mountain walking track, and dust rising from road access maintenance works are all sights and sounds from protected area management operations. Protected areas need active and effective management to retain the values for which they were reserved. Threatening processes such as weed and feral animal invasions are undermining the conservation integrity of many protected areas, and these threats must be dealt with. Intervention management is often required to conserve biodiversity on reserves through actions such as disturbance simulation, translocation of species and species population management. Nature can no longer take care of its own for many reserves in fragmented landscapes:

> ... across the globe, human actions have directly and indirectly undercut the self-sustaining and naturally regenerative capacity of many ecological systems ... conservation management, while critically important, is only a set of tools and approaches whose usefulness and appropriateness are measured by the extent [to which] they contribute to long-term conservation of natural patterns and processes ... management that is logically linked to long-term solutions, to stewardship of the environment can provide the critical intervention needed to conserve biodiversity (Meffe and Carroll, 1997, pp350–351).

Law enforcement may be needed to deal with human pressures such as unsustainable harvesting, poaching and vandalism. Poverty contributes to these problems, and civil disorder and war can directly impact upon protected areas. Protected area operations management is at the forefront of addressing such issues. Operations are essential activities and tasks that underpin the conservation management of protected areas. Managed correctly, operations help in achieving conservation outcomes. They are the major difference between so-called 'paper parks' (legally reserved areas with no active management) and parks that are managed effectively and contribute to conservation outcomes.

Operations management is defined as the management of the productive processes that convert inputs into goods and services (Slack et al, 2001). It is considered to be part of the 'controlling' function of management (see Chapter 6) because much of the emphasis is on regulating the productive processes that are critical to reaching organizational goals (Bartol et al, 1998). Protected area management operations are those inputs, processes and systems that directly contribute to achieving conservation outcomes. There are many and varied operational activities that are undertaken in protected areas.

Operational management must be conducted professionally, effectively and always in the context of the status of land or sea as a protected area. Otherwise, it can become a threatening process in itself. There have been some instances of 'cowboys' at work in managing parks. Lazy research, poor planning, poor execution of works and damaging operations should never happen. Protected areas are fast becoming the last natural lands and seas of Earth and their special status demands respect and caution.

There is an extraordinary wide scope of protected area management operations. This book describes many of these throughout its chapters on protected area management practice. This chapter focuses on generic operations planning and management, and the principles and practices described here apply wholly or in part to most operations. It has been designed to directly assist effective and responsible operations management. We describe important operational planning considerations; discuss the types of planning approvals that may be needed; encourage the development of effective operational policies and procedures; and offer a range of practical considerations that may assist with the implementation of operations. Monitoring and reporting of operations are also discussed.

Planning for operations

Operations management is guided by a plan. Usually, this document is for a 12-month to 3-year period and is directly linked to an organization's strategic plan, the plan of management for a protected area or areas, the annual budgeting process, and the management effectiveness evaluation system. The operations plan should indicate the priority operations for a protected area organization for a defined geographic area. Operations are typically action events. They are not the place to establish 'policy or procedures on the run' – instead, policies and procedures need to be in place. There is a clear role for organizational field management policies that are developed and made available publicly. However, operations management also needs an adaptive capability so that effective responses can be mounted to changes in circumstances. For some operations, this adaptive response may have to be very rapid.

Procedural statements for operations are also essential. Safety is one of the principal drivers for the development of procedural statements. The training courses that accompany them are just as important. Successful implementation of an operational plan will also be influenced by an institution's structure and its governance systems and procedures. Typically, the operations plan will deal with many essential, but individual, protected area operations. Each individual operation will have its own specific plan and will have been influenced by a range of critical planning considerations. Some considerations are exemplified in the Australian setting by Operation Bounceback (see Case Study 15.1).

Operational planning guidance. In some countries, there are 'natural heritage charters' or some form of convention or other standards that provide clear guidance for protected area management operations. Where these exist, they should be essential background research reading and inputs for all protected area management operations managers.

Purpose of an operation. The purpose of an operation needs to be clear and identified as a strategic priority. In the case of weed and pest animal operations, the purpose is protected area threat abatement, with the most strategically important introduced species to be targeted first. A rationale for the threat response and the commitment of resources will normally have been identified.

Operational context knowledge. An operation needs to be well researched. If it is an introduced species control programme, then the biology of weeds or pest animals needs to be known and control techniques must be designed to match these characteristics. If it is a fire management operation, such as prescription burning, then fire behaviour characteristics for the treatment area need to be known, as should the prevailing conditions that best suit the nature of the fire behaviour and fuel reduction sought. If it is the provision of a hardened walking track surface, then research into suitable material types needs to have been completed. Too often, this background research has either not been done or has been poorly completed. This is a major mistake, and has led to the wasting of precious dollars available for conservation operations. Even worse, it may compound the problems that originated the conservation action response. Operations managers need to obtain the best information possible in designing an operation. This may mean involving researchers, technical experts and local

Case Study 15.1

Operation Bounceback, South Australia, Australia

Damien Pierce, Department for Environment and Heritage, South Australia

Declaring a patch of land a conservation reserve doesn't guarantee you any conservation outcomes, and if you stood in the Flinders Ranges National Park and Gammon Ranges National Park pre-Bounceback, you'd have encountered the usual suspects. Big numbers of feral goats (*Capra hircus*), more than enough euros (*Macropus robustus*) and rabbit (*Oryctolagus cuniculus*) infestation approaching 150 warrens per square kilometre in some areas all contributed to excessive total grazing pressure. Operation Bounceback has developed from an initial feral goat control effort during the early 1990s, to an evolving programme looking at long-term ecological recovery with the following broad aims:

- Link efforts to conserve and enhance biodiversity across the Northern Flinders region.
- Restore the natural ecological processes, with particular focus on core areas of the Flinders Ranges National Park and Gammon Ranges National Park.
- Remove major threats to biodiversity and ecological integrity in the region.
- Develop and demonstrate a best practice model of integrated ecological management.

There are four key components to Bounceback operations:

1 *Monitoring and research.* Monitoring is conducted for system response and threatening processes. The majority of our monitoring is long term, based on indicators of response, such as vegetation condition, indicators of habitat quality or the status of populations, such as the viability of yellow-footed rock-wallaby (*Petrogale xanthropus*) colonies. We also monitor the threats or pests themselves, such as rabbit, European red fox (*Vulpes vulpes*) or goat populations, to gain quicker feedback.

2 *Removal of threats.* Our threat abatement activities aren't necessarily radical, innovative or spectacular. They are based on good science and delivered as an integrated package. The basics address total grazing pressure, introduced predation and pest plants. The activities include:
   - fox control (ground and aerial baiting with dried-meat 1080 baits);
   - feral goat control (ground and aerial mustering and culling);
   - rabbit control (warren destruction with a bulldozer and explosives for follow-up);
   - feral cat control (culling and trapping in targeted areas);
   - kangaroo management (targeted areas where over abundant); and
   - weed control of, for example, wheel cactus (*Opuntia robusta*) and prickly pear (*Opuntia* spp.).

3 *Active and direct recovery.* Active recovery is activity that doesn't knock out the bad, but directly promotes the good. With revegetation, we are re-introducing plants or a seed source through direct seeding. Obviously, this is linked heavily with our threat abatement activities to allow any recruitment to survive. It can also include re-introduction of a fauna species, and Bounceback will continue to investigate this option.

4 *District involvement/community partnerships.* The northern Flinders Ranges contains many stakeholders with differing land uses, primarily pastoral production, conservation and tourism. Many Bounceback activities are found off-reserve with the support of land-holders. Strong partnerships have been formed with members of the community and various volunteer groups.

Is it working? The short answer is yes. We are seeing signs of recovery in the form of habitat and fauna recovery and vegetation recruitment, and we have arrested the decline of some key species. A major focus of ours is the yellow-footed rock-wallaby, and with the help of Bounceback, populations have increased throughout much of the region.

community experts. It may involve commissioning special reports that will aid the design of an operation.

Previous operations knowledge. Repeating opera-

tional mistakes of the past (or 'reinventing the wheel') is a common problem for protected area management, and a lot of time and money can be wasted because of this. The history of an operation

Track closure sign, Whakawerawera Thermal Area, Rotorua, New Zealand

Source: Graeme L. Worboys

needs to be researched and understood. Assuming that operations have been adequately planned and documented, this information should be available. Unwritten history and local knowledge can assist with gaps in knowledge. Interviewing, recording and involving previous managers, researchers, practitioners, local experts, user groups and stakeholders in providing background information and insights are very valuable tools.

Local knowledge. Involving the local community and local experts in the operation is a wise investment. This may be more than initial consultation and briefing about the operation. It may involve the employment of local advisers to provide input to the detailed planning and implementation. It may also involve the employment of locals to undertake works.

Environmental impact assessment (EIA). Assessing the environmental impact of an operation is important and may be a legal requirement. Chapter 9 on managing threats covers EIAs; in the case of simple operations, EIAs may be brief but,

nevertheless, need to be consistent with any standard internal procedures that may apply. For repetitive or maintenance operations, an EIA may only be needed initially. Social considerations, especially the views and attitudes of the local community, form an important part of such planning.

Environmental management system (EMS). Operational systems such as an EMS (see 'Sustainability practices for managers' in Chapter 14) may provide a formal systems framework for managers managing for operations. This may be recognized in an EIA. One well-known system, ISO 14001, the international standard for EMS, defines an EMS as 'the part of the overall management system which includes organizational structure, planning, activities, responsibilities, procedures, processes and resources for developing, implementing, achieving, reviewing and maintaining the environmental policy' (Thompson, 2002). The ISO 14001 framework may not be suitable for all operations; but it may influence how individual operation plans are developed. Planning, training, procedures, systems and monitoring are important aspects of an EMS. Monitoring and performance evaluation are critical parts of the 'plan–do–monitor–revise–act' continuous improvement cycle that an EMS promotes.

Planning approvals. Before an operation proceeds, there may be a range of approvals required by law by policies within the protected area organization, and by local community requirements and procedures. Some examples are shown in Table 15.1. In their operational timetable, managers need to take into account the lead times that are inherent in gaining planning approvals and build into their operations schedule sufficient 'slack' to cover any delays.

Sustainability assessment. Protected area management consumes non-renewable resources and causes environmental impacts in its pursuit of conservation outcomes. A holistic approach to environmental management of protected areas is both responsible and desirable. Protected area organizations of the future will adopt sustainability

assessment standards for operations. This is most likely to include benchmarking systems that help direct management to ensure best practice environmental performance.

Administrative systems that support operations should track actual environmental operational performance against predetermined 'best practice' standards. This information may also be required for future triple bottom line reporting requirements or strategic environmental performance targets set by protected area organizations. Sustainability approvals for protected area operations may be required for:

- the sustainable design of new structures and built facilities for protected areas;
- operations in which considerable non-renewable fossil fuels will be used and where substantial greenhouse gases will be generated;
- operations that will consume large volumes of water; and
- operations that will generate solid and liquid waste.

Table 15.1 Examples of operational planning approvals

Protected area operation	Example of approval required
Major construction or development	Satisfactory environmental impact assessment (EIA)
Large building construction	Management plan
	EIA or equivalent
	Building approval
Visitor access improvements	Management plan
Visitor facilities	Management plan
Maintenance operations	Operations plan
	EIA
Fire operations	Fire plan
	EIA
Pest animal operations	Pest animal plan
	EIA

Budget approval. A budget is needed to undertake an operation. Securing budget approval through institutional systems takes time and human energy, and this time factor and workload need to be planned for. Sometimes the budget is approved out of synchrony with planning processes and money is available, but the design is unfinished or the EIA needs to be completed. This is where pragmatism can readily replace responsible planning systems. A philosophy of 'the money is here, lets get on with the job' can place enormous pressure on operations managers to proceed despite unfinished or rushed planning. Operations managers need to have the discipline to correctly follow procedures. Operational planning must be satisfactorily completed before an operation commences.

Operations schedule. Time and event planning is a critical part of operations management. Given that all operational approvals have been achieved, an operation now needs to be organized so that it is implemented efficiently. Scheduling techniques are necessary to ensure that managers can be sure that they are moving. Some operations use a Gantt chart to help achieve this. Gantt charts are used to monitor progress by identifying the range of actions for an operation and the sequencing of those actions (Hitt et al, 2005). A key element of any effective operation is the sequence and timing of the specific steps that the operation requires. The Gantt chart shows when actions are to be started and how long they are expected to last. It shows which actions are first, second or last in the operation, and whether a preceding action must be completed before a subsequent one can be started, or whether there is some anticipated overlap in the timing of specific actions. As well as the planned sequence and timing, the actual progress of the operation can be charted. This allows protected area managers to better assess their progress against the plan and potentially make adjustments where necessary. There are sophisticated computer programmes that will help in devising complex operational plans; however, manually drawn Gantt charts (or their relatives) are generally quite sufficient.

Staff competency and capacity. Staff need to be competent to manage an operation, and there should be sufficient staff to meet the forecast work loads and the number of shifts needed (capacity). Specialist operational skills may be required for certain operations, and such skills need to be recognized in job descriptions, interviews and statements of accountability. On-the-job induction for new workers and site-specific protected area sensitivity training for operations are critical for achieving effective and efficient operations.

Operation logistics planning

Operations planning requires, among other things, consideration of a number of important logistical matters.

Transport. Access to and from a workplace will be required. Protected areas may require work in remote locations that could involve the transport of people and equipment on yaks, llamas, donkeys, horses (or other animals), bicycles, motor cycles, four-wheel-drive vehicles, aircraft, canoes and boats.

Accommodation. In certain circumstances, it may be cost effective or more practical for operations staff to be accommodated at the actual operations site during a working week. Through local arrangements or workplace agreements of mutual benefit to employer and staff, longer day shifts and shorter working weeks are sometimes negotiated for working at remote and difficult-to-access sites. Accommodation at the work site that meets workplace standards; sanitation; catering; communications; entertainment; first aid; safety; and emergency evacuation are some logistical considerations that will need to be addressed.

Equipment. Operations staff will need to be equipped with the correct personal safety equipment. They will require gloves, masks, and eye and other protective gear for dealing with poisons; they will need ear protection gear for noisy machinery; and they will need hard hats, gloves, boots and safety glasses for construction sites, as well as other safety equipment. All of the correct safety gear should be in place prior to the start of an operation. Communications equipment and a working communications system will be essential for safety and logistics.

Evacuation. An emergency evacuation plan should be prepared for any potential medical or other emergency that could occur at an operations site. Such a plan would have endorsement

Manufacturing workshop for information display panels, Dorrigo, New South Wales, Australia

Source: Graeme L. Worboys

Heavy machinery for remote area trail work, Kosciuszko National Park, New South Wales, Australia

Source: Graeme L. Worboys

from local medical and emergency authorities. Rehearsing 'mock emergencies' with the multiple authorities involved in such operations is recommended.

Shelter. Poor weather, poor visibility, extreme winds, extreme temperatures, fires and heavy rain and snow may be encountered during operations in protected areas. The provision of suitable on-site shelter facilities is an important planning consideration.

Environmental impacts. There are many potential operational environmental impacts that need to be managed. Many relate to the quality of supervision, training and leadership. Training of operational staff and leadership, including setting the required standards and demonstrating the required procedures on site, is a critical part of an operation. Training and supervision are especially important if the work is delegated to non-protected area contractual staff with a non-environmental management background. The following questions provide indicative guidance for operational managers:

- How will the environmental guidelines for the operation be supervised and monitored?
- How will solid, liquid and gaseous waste impacts generated by operations be minimized?
- What measures will be used by the operation to minimize fossil fuel use?
- What types of fossil fuels or other energy sources will be used?
- What amount of greenhouse gases will be generated?
- Will there be impacts from dust and noise, and how will these be dealt with?
- Is there any potential for operational impacts to streams and water bodies, and how will these be dealt with (for example, pH impacts from concreting and petroleum impacts from refuelling spills)?
- How will the application of herbicide and pesticide chemicals be kept from affecting streams, water bodies, karst systems and other non-target effects?
- Will there be impacts on local communities living in or adjacent to the protected area?

Road grading, Ben Boyd National Park, New South Wales, Australia

Source: Graeme L. Worboys

- How will noise impacts be minimized for wildlife, for staff and for visitors?
- Has all equipment been cleaned and sterilized effectively? This includes transport, heavy plant and earth-moving equipment. Soil transfer (with potential soil pathogens) and seed transfer on equipment comprise a major potential problem.
- How will the actual disturbance area of an operation be minimized?

Safety considerations. Safety is paramount, both for operational staff and for those who may be affected by an operation. Operational safety planning questions that may need to be considered by the operations manager include the following:

- Do key operational personnel have the necessary qualifications and experience to undertake the proposed operations?
- Is the correct operational equipment available, and has it been maintained so that it can be used safely and effectively?
- Are there any hazards on site that need to be considered (such as unsafe trees, unstable geological features or dangerous animals)?
- Are there hazards associated with an operation that need to be managed (such as helicopter operations, use of explosives, use of welding equipment and use of cutting and grinding equipment)?
- Are any weapons to be used for animal culling or tranquilizing?
- How is public safety to be managed during operations? What public information will be provided?
- Is there a chance that an operation will cause an incident (such as a fire or a pollution event)? What precautionary action is required to deal with this?

Marine operations. Marine operations involve another dimension of planning and implementation complexity. All of the general principles discussed above need to be considered, along with the following additional matters:

- What marine operations specialist qualifications are required (such as boat operations licence, swimming and diving qualifications)?
- What actual time is available to conduct work given tidal variation, currents, weather cycles and the presence or absence of ocean animals that may cause harm to workers?
- What special considerations are needed for noise impacts (underwater acoustic impacts) and the use of explosives, chemicals and materials (saltwater corrosion)?
- Is there any potential conflict between the operation and commercial or other fishing interests?
- Is there any potential conflict between the operation and marine species (such as migratory whales or birds)?
- What special arrangements are needed to deal with major natural incidents, such as storm events, impacts from ice, tsunamis and underwater volcanic eruptions?
- What special arrangements are needed to deal with threats from humans, such as shipping incidents, oil pollution events, conflict and acts of piracy?

Risk management

Risk is a measure of the possibility of some particular harm being realized upon a protected area. Risk management, while accepting that accidents can and do happen, focuses on manipulating circumstances in order to increase the odds in favour of non-harmful outcomes. Ultimately, by accepting and acting on any level of risk, we gamble with the well-being of the protected area and/or the safety of field staff. Risk can be quantified as a function of two interlocking parameters: likelihood (the probability or frequency of an occurrence) and consequence (the outcome or impact of that occurrence). Risk management planning is often closely linked with EMS. A risk profile may be developed for an organization after completing a risk management evaluation process. The risk management process typically involves the following steps:

- *Establish the risk review context.* Set objectives and goals of the risk review process; establish a structured approach, including an overall review plan with roles, responsibilities and deliverables; establish a communications strategy/plan for the process; set criteria against which the risk will be evaluated; and document the entire process, thereby leaving an audit trail.

- *Identify risks.* Define all potential areas of risk, their source and their impact, including people/processes affected; use a team workshop approach involving 'what if' scenarios in order to identify potential risks and consequences.
- *Analyse risks.* Build a risk profile (register); determine existing controls and analyse risks in the context of these controls. Prepare a risk matrix to both rate and prioritize all identified risks, where Risk = function of (Likelihood + Consequence).
- *Evaluate risks.* Evaluate risks against management's risk acceptance criteria (political, financial, legal, environmental and social). From this assessment, each risk is either accepted or rejected, and prioritized mitigation plans can be established.
- *Treat risks.* Review each unacceptably high risk and identify potential treatment options (avoidance, reduction, transfer and retention) per risk. Prepare risk mitigation plans for each risk and implement prioritized action plans (actions, responsibility and resources, timing and priority). Review, report and follow up action plans regularly.
- *Monitor and review.* Monitor all steps in the risk management process and continuously review and improve the process, drawing upon stakeholder feedback and results of action plans.
- *Communicate and consult.* Continually communicate and consult with both internal and external stakeholders as appropriate at each stage of the risk management process.

Design and materials

Sustainability and environmental impact considerations should provide guidance in selecting and purchasing materials, and in designing structures and facilities. Immediate cost may be important; but planning considerations should take into account both short-term and long-term factors (see Case Study 15.2). Key lessons from this case study include:

- the value of using local recycled materials suitable for the environment in which they were to be used;
- the use of local knowledge (traditional techniques) of how to lay the walking track pavers in difficult terrain; and
- the use of high-cost but very efficient transport (helicopters) and making them cost effective by thorough preparation and minimizing operational time.

Environmental considerations. An operations manager must pay attention to detail when materials are being purchased. Has the purchasing officer been briefed on the appropriate detailed material specifications derived from the environmental impact statement (EIS)? Some materials contain chemicals that are toxic to the environment. Zinc in galvanizing, and copper and arsenic (and/or other chemicals) in treated timber may be toxic to native plants and aquatic organisms. Chemicals used to protect hulls in marine environments may adversely affect marine protected areas. These are just some examples of materials that will need to be used with care.

Sustainability considerations. Recycled timber and building materials, plantation timbers, weed-free gravel from environmentally approved sources, and materials that have been assessed for their life-cycle suitability (Thompson, 2002) are all examples of sustainability-influenced purchasing. Preferential suppliers for these goods and services would be local people with environmental credentials. Operations managers will need to monitor material purchases to ensure that sustainability requirements are implemented.

Maintenance considerations. Many protected area operations are very costly. They may be remote, require intensive human involvement and may necessitate costly transport. High capital cost structures and facilities with low long-term maintenance costs may be compelling material choices for many sites. Consideration of long-term repetitive maintenance costs should always form part of the initial costing and decision-making about the type of materials to be used. Maintenance operations can also threaten protected area values if they are not undertaken with sustainability in mind.

Light-transmitting steel-mesh elevated walkway, alpine area, Kosciuszko National Park, New South Wales, Australia

Source: Graeme L. Worboys

Contingency management

Problems (other than incidents – see Chapter 18) do arise in the management of any operation. Some problems can be anticipated and dealt with to help minimize any chance of them occurring. Other problems are unavoidable, but can be anticipated and prepared for. The following contingency considerations need to be built into operations management:

- *Preventing accidents.* A well-organized staff roster offering suitable rest periods; staff using safety equipment; and equipment that is well maintained, with qualified and competent people using the equipment can all help to minimize accidents.
- *Dealing with accidents.* A trained first-aid officer on site; access to a well-equipped first-aid kit; and radio communications and emergency evacuation capacity can minimize the impact of any accidents that do happen.
- *Avoiding material shortages.* Shortfalls in materials can jeopardize operations. Material stockpiling well in advance can help to ensure a smooth operation.
- *Avoiding loss of staff.* Staff working on or supervising an operation may be transferred (for a short term) to deal with an emergency or incident (such as a fire). This can be a real issue for some protected areas. One way of minimizing impacts to a project is to contract

Case Study 15.2

Track restoration and maintenance on the Pennine Way, Dun Hill, UK

The Pennine Way is Britain's oldest and most famous national trail. It starts in the Peak District at Edale and crosses the high moorland of the Peak National Park *en route* to Scotland, 440km away. The route is wild and remote, passing through blanket peat bogs that are wet for most of the year. The peat bog vegetation is unique to the southern Pennines; however, the wet and boggy nature of the moors makes them vulnerable to erosion, not only from the natural processes of wind, rain and frost, but also from the trampling effects of walkers.

The National Park Ranger Service and volunteers carried out routine maintenance work; nevertheless, the ranger service was not coping with the enormous pressures put on this increasingly popular path. The Pennine Way Management Project was set up to investigate solutions to these problems and to work on practical restoration, maintenance and sustainable management. The aim of the project was to provide a durable route that enables people to enjoy the walk without worsening the damage to the moors. The path work uses stone-flag paving and stone-pitching, ensuring that the work blends well into the environment. Once a firm path surface has been provided, work can begin to restore the surrounding trampled and dead vegetation. Year-round use of the national trail, coupled with popular day-walker use, means that the path is used by around 15,000 people a year.

The problem

A combination of pressure from walkers on the fragile vegetation and the nature of the peaty soils had led, over the years, to severe vegetation and soil loss. The problem was further compounded by overgrazing by sheep and a legacy of acid rain damaging the already fragile vegetation. As a result, an area of up to 26ha of moorland was damaged by trampling.

Solutions

The Pennine Way Management Project perfected techniques for creating sustainable footpath surfaces in keeping with the surrounding wild landscape. The technique employed depends upon the nature of the problem; but the objectives have consistently been to ensure that:

- natural surfaces are sustained, where possible;
- all surfacing solutions must use *in situ* materials if available or, if not, materials similar to those locally; and
- traditional techniques are used, where possible.

On stretches of path with heavy use on fairly level, deep peat, the natural surface is usually unsustainable. The traditional technique of creating a durable path on soft, level ground in the Pennines is known as the 'causey'. This method of laying sandstone flags directly onto the subsoil has been used for hundreds of years. The project has copied this traditional technique by using local materials, but employing modern methods, such as using helicopters and mechanical barrows.

Materials

The ideal material for a causey path is recycled mill-floor flagstones recovered from the floors of demolished factories. The flagstones are readily available, are relatively cheap and assimilate well into the moor.

Logistics

The eroded section of path is 3km from the nearest road, with the only access being on foot across wet peaty moors. The 312 tonnes of stone was delivered to the road head at Crowden on 24-tonne trucks and moved to the helicopter airlift site by fork-lift and dump truck. Over the winter, the stone was sorted, weighed and banded on site, ready for the summer airlift.

Laying the path

The job of laying the stones to produce a footpath rested with the five-person Pennine Way Maintenance Team. With four years' experience, they had perfected techniques of carefully positioning stones of up to 0.5 tonnes each, keeping them level and without 'trip points'. The chosen line for the path closely followed the eroded line, thus minimizing disturbance of intact vegetation and preserving the legal and 'desire' line on the ground. The gentle curves in the path break up the visual impact for the walker. Altogether, the team spent 294 working days on Dun Hill laying the flags and carrying out revegetation work. This involved walking 3km to the site nearly every morning for five months, in weather conditions varying from the dry heat of the summer to snow and fog in winter.

The finished path

What had been a muddy and unpleasant slog up to the plateau of Black Hill is now an improved path for nearly 2km, at a cost of about UK£76 per metre. The path surface uses local stone laid in a traditional style, but using the most modern of techniques. The restoration work involved the Pennine Way Team working in the most remote part of the south Pennines in varyingly difficult weather conditions for almost a full year; but the result is a durable path that will provide pleasant walking in wild surroundings without detracting from that wilderness. The re-vegetation work on the surrounding damaged ground, helped by the relief from the impact of walkers' boots, will enable the recovery of 26ha of protected moorland.

Source: adapted from Peak District National Park Authority (2001)

specialist teams to undertake the work. Such teams would not usually be deployed to an emergency.

Operation debrief

At the end of a major operation, there is typically a debriefing on all aspects of the management. A typical debriefing would include:

- an appraisal of the task completed to assess whether it met the objectives established;
- its total cost, including the number of staff who worked on it;
- the cost effectiveness of the operation;
- the strengths and weaknesses of the management;
- feedback from staff about what improvements are necessary for the next project; and
- positive feedback for staff about their achievement.

Such an operations debriefing should be recorded and made available for future operations managers. The full management evaluation for operations is described in Chapter 24.

Communication and liaison

People are often interested in operations in protected areas, whether for professional, personal or neighbourly reasons. At times, for operational logistic reasons, it is essential for people to know exactly what is happening. A range of consultative arrangements can be put in place depending upon the nature of the operation. It is basic courtesy (and good publicity) to advise neighbours, the local community and stakeholders of operations. It is also essential for cooperative ventures or for operations that involve potential public hazard, such as prescription burning, pest animal or weed control, and wildlife relocations. At the site of an operation, a simple temporary sign is all that is needed. A cheap plastic-coated (weather-proof) sheet of thick paper with the nature, purpose and timing of an operation described and securely attached to a temporary display stake works well. People are frequently interested in what is happening, and it is so easy to inform them. Other useful methods include:

- press releases and other media announcements;
- a newsletter for neighbours and the community that describes the nature and the purpose of the operation;
- a website describing operations for a protected area that are under way; and
- formal liaison meetings with local communities, users, authorities, unions, contractors and staff.

Senior protected area operations managers are typically highly qualified, trained and experienced individuals, and have the responsibility to complete planned operational actions. They have been charged by the community (through their organization) as relatively short-term custodians of protected area systems, individual protected areas or smaller areas of operational responsibility. Operations managers need to be clear that their custodian role is essential but successional, with a responsibility to ensure that the best information is available for decisions, that investments of essential new research are made, and that the operation is adaptive as new and better information comes to light. This is a managerial and inclusive approach that needs to engage communities, stakeholders and experienced professionals in an exchange of information.

Operations implementation

Leadership is required during the implementation of any operation. Key considerations include the personal safety, needs and circumstances of the operations team; project timetable and scheduling of events; media management; budget management; reporting requirements; political awareness; and local community needs. Effective rosters will ensure that staff who are needed for long-term tasks are adequately and regularly rested. The operations manager would also have a relieving officer. 'Burn out' of operations managers through lack of rest leave or unwillingness to delegate responsibilities is unnecessary and constitutes bad organizational management. It also potentially threatens an operation. Reporting on the progress of operations is both routine and important. Finance reports ensure that expenditures match estimates and that the project is on target

Getting supplies, Montague Island Nature Reserve, New South Wales, Australia

Source: Graeme L. Worboys

financially. Operational progress reports track progress of an operation against the planned project milestones and outcomes. Sustainability reporting provides environmental management performance information. Staff reporting ensures that payments, leave entitlements and roster arrangements are all current. Such reporting also enables an operation to remain efficient and effective. There is also a need to adequately document an operation upon completion for the record.

Management principles

1   Effective protected area management operations are an essential and integral part of the conservation of natural and cultural heritage. Protected areas require active, effective and continuous management if the purposes for which they were reserved are to be retained.

2   Operational standards, best practice systems, staff competencies, operational procedures, on-site leadership and operations team discipline are integral and essential parts of effective protected area operational management. Leadership during an operation is vital to counter the constant threat of operational impact through accidents, lack of discipline or poor planning and implementation techniques. Effective pre-planning should anticipate impacts and accidents and ensure an on-site capacity to deal with contingencies.

3   The safety and welfare of operations staff are the primary concerns of operations managers.

4   Operational management leadership, inclusiveness and attention to operational detail are essential parts of successful operational management. All aspects of the operation – initial design, location, the manner in which it is to be conducted, the materials to be used and the types of expertise to be employed – are equally critical. Pre-planning for an operation must be high quality.

5   Research, operational performance monitoring and adaptive management are essential parts of successful operational management.

6   The use of local knowledge and involvement of the local community in operations are a fundamental part of an operation.

7   The provision of adequate and timely public information about operations is an essential part of operational management.

Further reading

There is very little information available on this subject, in general, and nothing widely available on the specifics of protected area operations. Two sources that do provide some measure of relevant information are as follows.

Margoluis, R. and Salafsky, N. (1998) *Measures of Success: Designing, Managing and Monitoring Conservation and Development Projects*, Island Press, Washington, DC

Schroeder, R. G. (1993) *Operations Management: Decision Making in the Operations Function*, McGraw–Hill International, New York

16

Natural Heritage Management

Jamie Kirkpatrick and Kevin Kiernan

The process of natural area management commences with a vision, progresses through planning and allocating resources, and culminates in a range of outcomes (Hockings et al, 2000). Management to conserve natural heritage involves assessing the significant qualities of an area, and ensuring the survival or restoration of these qualities, ideally in a self-sustaining condition rather than one that requires continual intervention. Achieving this end typically requires protection of functioning natural systems, rather than merely localized features and sites (ACIUCN, 2002).

The concept of 'natural' is a difficult one, given that *Homo sapiens* is one of millions of species that have evolved on planet Earth and depends upon the rest of the biosphere for survival. It is useful to distinguish between the human species and the rest of nature when discussing protected area management, although it may still be difficult to discriminate between the natural and the artificial, since people have often affected the nature of the atmosphere, the geosphere, the hydrosphere and the biosphere.

With organisms apart from *Homo sapiens*, the distinction is usually made between those organisms that we have helped to evolve and those that have evolved without our direct intentional intervention. The truly natural are those that have totally escaped our influence, such as species associated with submarine volcanic vents on mid-oceanic ridges. Such ecosystems are seldom the subject of protected area management, making it necessary to draw a line somewhere across the continuum between the natural and the anthropogenic. This line, for our purposes, approximates the edge of cultivated land, although we also recognize that some IUCN Category V and VI protected areas include cultivation.

The components of what we call 'nature' exist irrespective of human culture; but 'heritage' is a cultural construct – the 'things we want to keep'. Political processes determine what is accorded 'official' natural heritage status, a situation that inevitably disenfranchises some. It is the management of this 'official' heritage upon which we focus here, though it is appropriate that managers remain cognisant of other views and accommodate them, where possible, within the context of their consciences and formal duty statements. Formal instruments for protection exist at global to local scales. At the international level, there are World Heritage criteria (see Chapter 3), to which many nations subscribe. At other political divisions, such as the national level, there are differing interpretations of outstanding heritage.

In this chapter, we discuss general principles and approaches for managing natural heritage, and then address specific aspects of natural heritage management: water, geodiversity, fire, weeds, plant pathogens, animals, the impacts of people, and restoration and rehabilitation. In all cases, the specifics of protected area management for natural values will be highly contingent upon the nature of the protected area and the environment and society in which it is embedded. Thus, the chapter emphasizes ways of thinking about, and ways of conducting, natural heritage management.

Principles of, and approaches to, natural heritage management

The typical protected area has very few management staff. These managers often have a major role in the facilitation of tourism-related activities, and, consequently, relatively little time to maintain the natural values that attract at least some of the tourists and are usually the reason for the existence of the reserve. Some protected area managers also have to manage commercial or traditional use of resources within their parks. All of these human activities can affect the natural elements and processes in protected areas. In the context of these activities and other influences on natural ecosystems, any potential management intervention, or non-intervention, is likely to have benefits for some elements of nature, but may harm others. For example, the removal of domestic sheep from chalk grasslands in England favours trees and the native animals that use them, but is disastrous for many native herbs and the animals that feed off them.

Little time, conflicting goals, what to do? This section suggests some principles of, and approaches to, natural heritage management in the context of limited resources. The first step is to determine priorities for action. The next step is to be as efficient as possible in achieving these priorities.

Manage for those values most dependent upon particular protected areas

The manager needs to determine those natural elements and processes that their protected area is most important in protecting. The question that needs to be asked of your protected area is:

Are there any species, communities, landforms, geological features or processes that depend upon protected areas and are unrepresented, poorly represented or unprotected in other protected areas?

If the manager has, for example, the only viable population of dwarf hippopotamus in the world in his or her reserve, but nothing else of any great significance, they should avoid constructing parking areas or visitor centres in areas that the species depends upon and should resolve any management conflicts in favour of the species. If their reserve also has the best example in the world of a particular type of rainforest, which is encroaching on hippopotamus habitat, the test of irreversibility needs to be applied. Holding back the best example of a common rainforest type is not going to destroy it – but losing a few more individuals of the dwarf hippopotamus might nudge them towards extinction, which is irreversible.

Understand your natural systems

In conjunction with heritage charters and management guidelines, a grounding in the biological sciences and geosciences is useful in helping protected area managers to understand what conservation management needs to be done in a reserve. However, reserves and their ecosystems are all different to the degree that a management recommendation developed in one place in one type of ecosystem might prove counterproductive in another place in the same or another ecosystem. Managers need to learn from their predecessors, scientists and locals, and then learn for themselves. The world is full of appalling conservation outcomes resulting from well-intentioned decisions by people unaware of the limitations of their expertise and the costs of this deficiency. Do not become one of them – seek advice even if you think you know it all or believe that the value closest to your heart, or in which you have trained, is inevitably the most important, or the only one, likely to be affected by an action.

Some managers consider scientific research in their areas to be detached from practical management issues. However, a cooperative scientist can provide invaluable insights into how ecosystems work and can be encouraged to collect data that you want for management purposes. Natural scientists tend to return regularly to their research sites, making them valuable repositories of all sorts of histories apart from the data they collect for their projects. Older people whose families have had a long history of exploiting, living in or recreating in your protected area can be invaluable

Lunnan stone forest, China

Source: IUCN Photo Library © Jim Thorsell

sources of information on how ecosystems work. Indigenous people with orally transmitted cultures can give particularly good insights to long-term processes, rare events and previous management regimes.

Before you have finished talking with all of these people, you may have been moved on to your next posting, leaving behind written briefings for your successors on what you have learned and done. All of this knowledge-seeking induces efficiency in conservation management because it helps to discriminate between things that *really* need to be done to protect important values, and actions that are either a waste of time or potentially destructive.

Do not obsess about naturalness

It is impossible to manage a protected area back to its 'pristine' landscape, and misguided attempts to duplicate older ways of management may, in fact, lead away from the 'purity' that is sought. For example, while attempted returns to indigenous-style fire regimes may serve the interests of biological diversity and may reverse trends towards ecosystem degradation (Marsden-Smedley and Kirkpatrick, 2000), the question inevitably remains: are the results 'natural'? Case Study 16.1 briefly examines some of the evidence for major vegetation transformation due to human activity, including the issue of fire-induced environmental change in Madagascar.

Think about processes

Conservation management should be based not just on localized phenomena, but on functioning natural systems. There are many reserves that present managers with insuperable obstacles because this reality has not been recognized – for example, cave reserves that protect the cave entrance but not the source of the water that forms the cave stream or seeps through its roof to form the speleothems, such as stalactites and stalagmites, which may have been the very reason that the cave was protected.

Case Study 16.1

Human impacts on fire and large-scale vegetation changes

Humans have used fire for over 1 million years, setting in motion a great wave of environmental transformation that continues today. In Africa, evergreen forests shrank and grasslands and savanna expanded. In North America, fire set by the first human settlers expanded the prairies and ate into woodlands and forests. In Australia, the vegetation of the continent was transformed first by Aboriginal firestick farming, and then by the burning practices of European settlers.

Most aspects of a fire regime can be modified to a greater or lesser degree by human intervention. Prescribed burns are nearly always constricted by the risk of damage to people and property, and can produce very different effects from the wildfires under which natural vegetation patterns evolved.

Large-scale human impacts on fire and vegetation have been claimed in many parts of the world; however, the evidence is circumstantial and controversial. The problem is that climate has changed over the long period of human settlement, and it is difficult to separate the respective effects of human occupation and climate.

Where human settlement has been relatively recent, vegetation change is less likely to be confounded by climate change. Madagascar, the world's fourth largest island, was first settled by humans only some 2000 years ago, and through a lethal combination of shifting agriculture and burning, vast areas were thought to have been transformed into grasslands and wooded grasslands. While there has been undeniable human modification of the island's vegetation, the importance of humans and fire in transforming Madagascar's great central plateau from forests to grassland is more controversial, with pollen and charcoal studies from a lake in central Madagascar indicating that open grassy vegetation and fire existed in the area for thousands of years prior to human settlement. Accordingly, it is difficult to attribute Madagascar's current vegetation to the human use of fire. Much the same problem occurs in other large-scale examples of supposed fire-driven vegetation change.

Source: adapted from Bond and van Wilgen (1996)

Deficiencies related to reserve boundary design may be beyond the control of the manager; but managers should never fail to identify the extent of the natural systems over which they have even partial jurisdiction and to ensure that they are managed in order to safeguard the values that depend upon them. For example, roadside drains and toilets should not be sited where seepage can enter underground karst drainage systems and their associated caves.

In a few cases, it may be possible to safeguard a feature with less consideration of the surrounding environment; for example, a geological exposure that exhibits an important fossil assemblage is likely to be essentially fossil itself, a relict of processes that no longer operate. The objectives of geo-conservation are not simply to safeguard geological features, landforms and soils, but also the natural processes by which these things come into being.

Floods, landslides, earthquakes, volcanic eruptions, wildfires, tornados and the like are perceived as disasters when the aspirations of humans place them in the path of these largely natural processes. However, the occurrence of such a major event in a natural area does not imply that it is an unprecedented disaster, however dramatic its short-term effects. Meteorological records or data on river discharge for remote protected areas are likely to be very short if they exist at all, and even a record over 200 years may not be sufficient to illustrate the magnitude of a flood with a recurrence interval of 100 years. Many high magnitude natural events have a still longer recurrence interval. It is important that managers incorporate sufficient time depth in their thinking – one of the many situations in which fostering good relations with scientists can be of immense benefit. It may not only change your attitude to 'disasters', but may better inform any attempts at environmental manipulation that you are considering.

The one exception to this long-term perspective on putative disasters arises when park managers are charged with protecting a critical natural heritage asset in a spatially constrained area that represents the last scraps of a former habitat

Karst, Gunung Mulu, Malaysia

Source: IUCN Photo Library © Jim Thorsell

and in which recovery of a species from localized damage is no longer possible. But in most cases, natural hazards in populated areas are, when they occur in protected areas, best regarded as part of the ongoing natural environmental systems.

Thinking about processes is efficient because one process intervention may be more effective than a thousand restoration or protection activities related to individual elements of natural diversity. In a similar vein, until you have learned as much as is available on the ecosystems of your protected area, hasten slowly.

Be cautious in changing management regimes

Many protected areas have been managed in the same way for decades, up to millennia. You know that the species, features and ecosystems of the reserve have survived this treatment. You do not usually know the potential impacts of altered management regimes. If you suspect that the current management regimes are leading to a progressive loss of the more important values of your protected area, experiment with limited change in a process of adaptive management, rather than imposing change on the whole system – otherwise you might end up with an unnatural disaster, like those intense and extensive wildfires induced by the fire suppression policies associated with Smoky the Bear in the US. Of course, there may be desperately needed management changes in natural areas that require no more than a few seconds' thought before implementation, such as preventing the dumping of rubbish in sink holes.

Observe the 'canaries'

Caves are the major features of many protected areas. In northern Thailand and many other places, colonies of bats sleep out the day clinging to their roofs. Their profuse droppings react with the floor of the caves, drawing oxygen from the air. Candles, rather than the canaries of miners, are used by guides to indicate this danger to the lives of tourists. Looking for such 'canaries' is efficient because no manager can afford to monitor everything, and early diagnosis gives the best prospect of a cheap cure. The protected area manager is well advised to seek canary or candle surrogates that can be used to indicate imminent danger to the important values of their protected area.

Caves again provide a good example. These typically contain a wide variety of resources that may include important palaeoenvironmental archives in the form of sediments, accumulations of fossil bones, archaeological relicts, attractive speleothems, rare minerals, unusual hydrological and microclimatic characteristics, and ecosystems comprising biota adapted to existence in a stable low-energy environment of permanent darkness. In some cases, access to caves has been limited in recognition of the particular sensitivity of natural cave microbiota (a phenomenon that has generally been annihilated by the inevitable contamination caused as soon as humans enter). Moreover, safeguarding this most-at-risk value simultaneously allows the other values for which the site is important to also be protected.

Undertake efficient inventories and monitoring

A knowledge of the distributions of the key environmental assets of any protected area is a fundamental requirement for effective management. It is axiomatic that such inventories should be as objective as possible, unsullied by policy considerations – inventories should not be distorted by second guessing political intentions. The development of policy and practical measures to further the protection, or destruction, of the inventoried assets should be a distinct and separate process. Regionalization (based on the idea that an assemblage of different areas can be sufficiently unified by enough common characteristics as to outweigh the factors that allow distinction between them) can be useful where the area is large, poorly known and there are insufficient resources for a detailed inventory. More detailed inventories can be developed using genetic classifications or measures of objective physical and biological characteristics. Generalized surveys of broad areas can be employed to identify important phenomena, although they may be unintentionally skewed by the inventory compiler if that person's expertise is limited to only one or a few attributes.

Maps, in whatever form, are valuable tools for recording the locations of natural assets, including vegetation types, rare or threatened species and geomorphologic and geologic features; artefacts, such as roads, tracks, huts and visitor centres; management activities, such as weeding, planned burning and restoration; monitoring sites; unplanned disturbance events, such as wildfire and land slips; and permitted activities, such as zones in which hunting is an allowable activity. These layers of information can be used as a planning tool. For example, the location of a new walking track can be planned to avoid rare or threatened species habitat and boggy ground, as indicated by particular vegetation types (Kirkpatrick, 1990).

Aerial photographs and similar imagery, coupled with sophisticated computer software, are valuable aids in mapping and monitoring natural phenomena. Monitoring can be difficult to implement effectively, although it is essential if decline in the condition of park assets is to be identified sufficiently early for appropriate remedial action to be taken. Many management plans include a provision for monitoring; but frequently neither an appropriate monitoring strategy has been formulated, nor resources committed to this end.

More detailed (and time-consuming) monitoring should be restricted to what is necessary to determine changes in population or those elements of biodiversity and geodiversity for which the protected area is most important and which are thought to be subject to some threat. For such monitoring, adopt the cheapest and quickest option that gets the outcome you need. In the cases of plant species and vegetation, permanent photo points can be extremely efficient and effective. Photo-monitoring in caves is feasible, but is more difficult than it sounds due to the vagaries of consistently reproducing comparable artificial lighting conditions. It is a waste of time, and unnecessarily distressing to the animals, if you have an expensive trapping programme for a rare vertebrate when you can design a way to get an approximate idea of the trend in their numbers by counting scats, diggings or scratchings in permanent plots or transects (see Table 16.1).

Nevertheless, sound design is necessary for monitoring, so consult your scientific contacts. This may be particularly important in terms of fitting the sampling protocol to the phenomenon – sampling undertaken at a consistent time or date each week may miss the key events you most need to identify, such as pulses of water contamination related to rainfall and runoff events.

It is particularly important to monitor the impact of your own intervention in natural systems, such as those related to infrastructure development. There must be commitment to responding appropriately and rapidly if there is evident harm outside the parameters set in management plans.

Managing water

Water is a fundamental resource for sustaining natural environmental processes, scenery, ecosystems and people in protected areas. Management needs to be based on an understanding of natural drainage systems, including groundwater, streams, rivers and lakes. The fundamental principle of

Table 16.1 Fauna inventory: Some field survey techniques used

Fauna field survey technique	Notes
Direct identification – observation and listening	Skilled observers are invaluable for enhancing information about wildlife. Bird, frog and some mammal species have distinguishing calls or sounds from which they can be identified. Standard fauna inventory forms have been produced by many organizations to facilitate the recording of observations.
Observation – fauna tracks and diggings	While often difficult to discern, signs of fauna, such as footprints and scratchings, are an invaluable aid to fauna observers and researchers.
Collection and analysis of fauna scats	Predator scats can be valuable for rapid inventory of native fauna populations. Researchers have found that the scats from such animals are deposited close to the food source. After *carefully* collecting the scat (given the chance of contracting a disease such as hydatids), it can be dried and analysed for hair and bone content. Scats from native animals themselves are important inventory diagnostics.
Collection and analysis of bird pellets	Some birds regurgitate bone, feather, fur and other fragments of their meals that they are not able to digest. Owl pellets, for example, contain a wealth of small mammal bones in stratified deposits at some cave sites. They have provided valuable contemporary and historical records of small mammal populations used as prey by the birds.
Fauna signs in their habitat	Animal runways in heath and native grasslands, burrows, nesting hollows, incisions in trees that mark nesting sites, claw marks on trees, and litter and damage to trees and shrubs from animal feeding are all signs that indicate the presence of fauna.
Trapping and collection of insects	Water traps, flight interception traps, light traps and bait traps are methods used for collecting insects.
Spotlighting	Many species are only active during the night. The use of a portable light will reflect the retina colour of animals' eyes. The colour, shape and size will help in identifying species.
Call playback	Many animals have distinctive calls, and when these are recorded and played back through a loud speaker, species can be prompted to respond.
Use of pit-traps	This is a technique used by zoologists to capture small mammals, reptiles and invertebrates. Use is made of a barrier and a small container that is sunk into the ground. Animals are directed to the container by the barrier and are captured in the pit as they try to pass through the 'opening' in the barrier.
Reptile searches	This technique is usually undertaken for a small area and during the middle of the day. Favoured habitats for these species (under logs and rocks, in leaf litter, in hollows and so on) are searched.
Use of hair tubes	A hair tube is a length of plastic pipe (about 90mm in diameter for small species) that has a bait sealed at one end and double-sided sticky tape on the side of the pipe. When feeding, the small mammal leaves some hair on the tape, which is subsequently analysed to determine the species.
Use of small mammal traps	Collapsible aluminium traps (Elliot traps), which capture their specimens live using a bait, pressure pad and spring rear-door trap, are a common tool of scientists undertaking fauna inventories. Typically, specimens are captured, identified, weighed, measured and released on site. Larger live traps (cage traps) are used for the capture of larger specimens.
Use of nets, including harp nets and 'fish' nets	Harp nets (vertical filaments of nylon organized to form a barrier to bats) are generally placed on bat flight paths. They are designed to minimize their detection from bat sonar signals and to minimize any impact on the bats. Nets are commonly used for the capture of birds.

Table 16.1 Continued

Fauna field survey technique	Notes
Use of specialized traps	Large traps are often used for the capture of bigger animals, such as salt-water crocodile (*Crocodylus porosus*) of northern Australia. This technique is used when a 'problem' animal needs to be relocated.
Aerial monitoring	Aerial methods of monitoring fauna and their environment offer distinct advantages when dealing with remote areas or areas that are otherwise inaccessible, such as major waterways or other water bodies to count waterfowl and eagles. Even relatively small fauna may be indirectly monitored in this way – for example, beaver dams. Analysis of aerial surveys may be facilitated using computer programmes.
Global positioning systems (GPS) and geographic information systems (GIS)	GPS and GIS permit efficient and accurate collection of spatial data, while combining and comparing time-sequential maps and satellite imagery for estimating, for example, global change and environmental degradation. GIS are also ideal for comparing flora or fauna species diversity with variables in their habitats in order to help manage conservation areas. Conversely, habitats can be identified with overlay analysis, producing maps of where field teams might locate rare or endangered species of plants and animals (see Case Study 16.2).

Source: adapted from Worboys et al (2005)

Monitoring bats using a harp net, Central Eastern Rainforest Reserve, Australia

Source: IUCN Photo Library © Jim Thorsell

water management is that strategies need to be catchment based, rather than attempting to manage on the basis of individual parts of the system in isolation.

Managers should also recognize the possibility that components of drainage systems that appear to be inactive (such as normally dry channels in arroyos, alluvial fans or in karst) are there for a reason – that discharge is likely to occur through them during low-frequency high-magnitude events, and that failing to manage them appropriately may ultimately incur harmful erosion, ecological damage, damage to infrastructure or risk to human life. Managers must try to maintain the magnitude, timing and rate of natural processes in as near to natural condition as possible; this is of particular significance in water management, where the critical issues are the maintenance of discharge, flow regimes and water quality. Where any of these elements is compromised in a manner that is beyond the control of the manager, she or he is faced with the challenge of trying to cope or adapt.

Dams can change the flow regime, sediment load, temperature and oxygen status of stream systems. Construction of a dam may flood natural or cultural assets, as in the case of the Hetch

Case Study 16.2

Determining panda populations using global positioning systems (GPS) and geographic information systems (GIS), China

The State Forestry Administration in China has revealed that increased national efforts at protecting wildlife such as the giant panda (*Ailuropoda melanoleuca*) have seen dramatic increases in the population of this endangered species, including more than 500 new pandas born within the past 16 years.

The inventory began in 1999 and was carried out in the endangered bear's major habitats, including the western provinces of Sichuan, Shaanxi and Gansu. It was the third ever conducted in China, with earlier counts carried out during the 1970s and 1980s. The latest inventory found that the number of giant panda in the wild has increased from 1100 in 1988 to more than 1590 in 2003.

Global positioning systems (GPS) and geographic information systems (GIS), along with specially designed computer software, were used to annotate the exact spots where wild pandas or their footprints, droppings and bamboo stem fragments or other traces were found, thereby improving the accuracy of the inventory. The increase of the panda population is attributed to the improvement of their habitat and successful research in artificial insemination and conception. The inventory of the giant panda has been complemented by a national survey of major wild fauna and flora and wetland resources from the mid 1990s.

Source: adapted from Zhuo Rongsheng (2004)

Hetchy dam in Yosemite National Park, which inundated a valley as significant as the more famous Yosemite Valley. Wave action may erode slopes that are not naturally adjusted to that form of disturbance, and soil moisture changes related to periodic draw-down of the reservoir may cause landslides. Dams act as settling ponds that may limit the through-flow of natural sediments and nutrients, as has occurred below the Glen Canyon dam on the Colorado River, with harmful consequences for the Grand Canyon, such as sandy shorelines being washed away and native fish species disappearing. Channels downstream of dams can progressively become filled with sediment once regular flushing by high flows is halted; as a result, during a major flood event there may be insufficient channel capacity to accommodate the water that spills onto the surrounding landscape, causing flooding. Change in downstream water quality, including oxygen status and temperature, can have ecological repercussions.

Protection of water quality is essential. The fact that many natural waters have suffered contamination highlights the importance of those pristine waters that remain; but many managers are faced with the need either to repair previous degradation or prevent matters from becoming worse. An important principle is to focus initial efforts to improve water management on more

upstream sites and *then* extend them downstream, reducing the potential for efforts to be sabotaged by continued 'bleeding' from higher in the watershed.

Groundwater is particularly important in some protected areas. In some arid and semi-arid environments, the groundwater has accumulated during times when climatic conditions were very different than now. In coastal and island settings, a freshwater lens may be perched on denser, more saline groundwater, and overexploitation of the freshwater may lead to unexpected salinization of bores. Water-bearing rocks (aquifers) may be generally porous and permeable, permitting only slow flow, or they may be fractured and fissured, permitting faster flow. The most rapid flow occurs in conduit aquifers, such as those formed in karst areas or volcanic landscapes in which subsurface lava tubes are present. There is often a dangerous assumption that groundwater is inherently pure; but groundwater in conduit aquifers has limited exposure to any of the natural self-purification processes (sunlight, biological processes and ionic exchange with surrounding materials), posing severe dangers for humans and for groundwater-dependent ecosystems.

Difficulties arise in karst terrain because directions of groundwater drainage are typically governed by geological structures, rather than by surface topography, meaning that topographic maps will provide little guidance. Streams often flow underground from one valley into another. Because karst landscapes can be like a giant underground sponge in which there are many interconnected spaces, water may flow in one direction when conditions are relatively dry, but spill in various other directions as conditions become wetter and there is more water in the 'sponge'. Hence, contaminant transmission by groundwater or unexpected floods bursting from the ground in apparently unlikely places can pose hazards for ecosystems and humans alike. There is no 'quick fix' available – responsible management of karst areas requires careful water tracing experiments to enable an adequate understanding of the groundwater systems.

Managing geodiversity

Physical features, such as the landforms that surround us, sustain and enrich our lives in much the same way as do the plants and animals with which we share the planet. They are equally deserving of careful stewardship as valid parts of the cosmos significant in their own right, for their underpinning of functioning natural environmental systems, including ecosystems, and for the instrumental opportunities they offer humans. Gray (2004, p8) defines geodiversity as:

> ... *the natural range (diversity) of geological (rocks, minerals, fossils), geomorphological (land form, processes) and soil features. It includes their assemblages, relationships, properties, interpretations and systems.*

The management of geodiversity involves safeguarding important geological sites, landforms and soils, as well as sites of natural geo-processes. There is a common perception that the prefix 'geo' implies phenomena made of rock that are therefore likely to be inherently robust and require little consideration. However, this misconception is soon obvious to the manager who has to confront:

• theft of important fossils;

Ha Long Bay, Viet Nam

Source: IUCN Photo Library © Jim Thorsell

- destabilization of sand dunes;
- vandalism or accidental damage to fragile speleothems in a karst cave; or
- serious soil erosion problems.

Many landforms are relics of environmental conditions over millennia. Breeding geological sites or landforms in zoos or botanical gardens is not an option when geodiversity is lost.

Just as there are different species of plants and animals, so too are there many different types of waterfall, sand dune and other landform categories. There are also different types of landform assemblages, much as there are communities of plants and animals, and there are composite landform communities, such as those that occur where glacial processes are superimposed on limestone. Like biotic species, some landform types are common and some are rare, some are robust and some are fragile – hence, a variety of management actions may be required.

Some sites of geo-conservation significance are very fragile, while many others are relatively robust, and still others are seemingly indestructible. Accordingly, it is unnecessary that all significant geo-conservation sites be protected; however, it is useful to have an indication of just how robust or fragile a specific site is. This may be built into a landform classification system such as the one outlined in Box 16.1, which distinguishes between sites on the grounds of their vulnerability, based on the intensities and patterns of disturbances entailed in particular land-use practices. Disturbing a site may not *necessarily* degrade its geo-conservation values – it is the vulnerability of those values that is important.

Box 16.1 Vulnerability of geo-conservation values

1   Values are vulnerable to inadvertent damage simply as a result of diffuse, free-ranging human pedestrian passage, even with care. Examples include fragile surfaces that may be crushed underfoot, such as calcified plant remains, or gypsum hairs in some karst caves that can be broken by human breath.

2   Values are vulnerable to the effects of more focused human pedestrian access, even without deliberate disturbance. Examples include risk of damage by entrenchment through the advent of pedestrian tracks; coastal dune disturbance; drainage changes associated with tracks leading to erosion by runoff; risk of damage as a result of changes caused by changes to fire regime; and defacement of speleothems simply by touching their surface.

3   Values are vulnerable to damage by scientific hobby collecting or sampling, or by deliberate vandalism or theft. Examples include exploitation of some fossil and mineral sites and karst caves.

4   Values are vulnerable to damage by remote processes. Examples include hydrological or water-quality changes associated with the clearing or disturbance of watersheds; fracture/vibration due to blasting in adjacent areas (potentially causing such damage as breakage of stalactites in caves); and sites susceptible to damage if subsurface seepage water routes change due to the creation of new fractures.

5   Values are vulnerable to damage by higher intensity, shallow linear impacts, depending upon their precise position. Examples include vehicular tracks, minor road construction and the excavation of ditches or trenches.

6   Values are vulnerable to higher intensity but shallow generalized disturbance on site. Examples include clear-felling of forests and replanting, but without stump removal or major earthworks and associated drainage changes.

7   Values are vulnerable to deliberate linear or generalized shallow excavation. Examples include minor building projects, simple road construction or shallow borrow pits.

8   Values are vulnerable to major removal of geo-materials, or large-scale excavation or construction. Examples include quarries and sites of large dam construction.

9   Values are vulnerable only to very large-scale contour change. Examples include mega-quarries.

10   Special cases include erosion caused by sea-level rise resulting from humanly induced greenhouse warming, and sites where the value is rendered inaccessible through inundation beneath an artificial reservoir, although the physical characteristics of the site may remain intact.

Source: Kiernan (1997)

Landforms are the product of interactions between geological substrates, geomorphological processes and time. Diversity is not everything – many of the most cherished landforms are, in fact, examples of relatively common phenomena. The World Heritage-listed Skojcan Caves in Slovenia are viewed as outstanding, even though they are but one example of a phenomenon – limestone caves – of which there are hundreds of thousands around the world. While Earth's geo-environments encompass a diverse range *at a global scale*, at a local scale there may be monotonous repetition, as within the outstanding dune fields of some large deserts. The lack of diversity at a local scale does not diminish the conservation value of such a place on a broader canvas. The fact that there are many waterfalls in the world, further-more, does not diminish the beauty and local significance of a local cascade that is dear to the heart of a small community.

Managing geo-heritage

Geo-heritage management, whatever the spatial scale of significance and whatever the extent of the area, requires respecting the phenomena involved; minimizing intervention in the func-tioning of the healthy natural systems that sustain it; the application of knowledge and experience derived from a wide range of specialists, including, but by no means limited to, scientists; and that cognisance be taken of all aspects of the natural significance of a place, including its possible cultural heritage significance. Geo-heritage may be regarded as being worth conserving for three main reasons:

1   From the perspective of intrinsic values (see Chapter 4), physical features do not require human approval or certification to be a valid part of the cosmos, but simply deserve respect in their own right.
2   Protection of geo-heritage is important in order to safeguard natural process values, recognizing the interdependence of all things and the impossibility of achieving other conservation outcomes unless hydrological, geomorphic and life-support systems are respected.
3   Physical features such as landforms have

myriad instrumental uses to humankind as objects of spiritual, aesthetic, recreational, scientific, educational, economic or other significance to humankind, including the provision of environmental system services such as clean air and water.

In assessing geo-heritage significance, there is a need to recognize:

*   why the site is significant;
*   to whom it is significant;
*   the scale of its significance;
*   whether that significance is likely to be temporary or permanent; and
*   the adequacy of the information base or expertise upon which the evaluation is founded.

It is essential that a clear distinction is maintained between the values for which a geo-heritage site is considered important and the instrumental uses to which it may be put. Tourism may be a poten-tial use of a particularly scenic site or one that contains an endearing animal species; but as noted above, the site also has value in its own right. Failure to recognize and act upon this distinction can erode the fundamental asset. Beware of the content-free manager, politician or developer who tries to tell you that a resort deep inside a park is appropriate because the tourism potential of the area is one of its conservation values. A limestone cave and its contents represent a conser-vation value for which protective management is required; development of that cave for commer-cial tourism represents a use value.

Geological sites

Significant geological sites may include outcrops of particular rock types, sites where fossils occur, exposures that reveal the nature of subsurface structures and a variety of other phenomena. 'Type sites' that provide the earliest or best exam-ple of particular phenomena provide important reference sites against which evidence found else-where can be compared in order to advance geological knowledge of broader regions. Such sites can be lost during some construction activi-ties, such as bulldozing embankments to establish

Artificial cast of fossils at Ediacara, South Australia

Source: Kevin Kiernan

roads. An adequate inventory of geological assets and prior examination of proposed development sites by appropriate specialists is desirable. Theft of gemstones or fossils may be a problem. Geological sites are vulnerable to unscrupulous people harvesting fossils for a thriving collectors' market. Such issues can be particularly acute where no manager is present on site to provide advice or protection, or where the establishment of protective structures is impossible for practical or other environmental reasons. There may be nothing to prevent the clients of an 'eco' tourism enterprise later returning independently to an unsecured sensitive site with a group of their equally inexperienced friends. For example, at Ediacara, South Australia, all that remains is an artificial cast of the fossils that once made the site important.

Landforms

For many traditional societies, respect for the natural environment stems from a spiritual connection to particular physical features. Some of the earliest formal reserves were created to safeguard physical scenery imparted by the juxtaposition of landforms, largely irrespective of the biological values that have tended to dominate the language of conservation management over recent decades. Hence, the first reservation of land in what is now Banff National Park in Canada was in order to protect a small limestone cave that contained a warm spring.

Geomorphology is defined by the contours of the land; any artificial change to those contours, at whatever scale, by definition represents damage to the natural geomorphology. The question that arises is whether the landform is significant and the extent of the damage. A feature made of solid rock is more robust than one formed of unconsolidated fine sediment, such as a sand dune, that may blow away if de-vegetated. Fire-induced spalling (flaking) may remove weathering features such as surface solution sculpture (karren) on limestone, and smoke can discolour speleothems in karst caves due to airflow underground as the cave atmosphere continually equilibrates with changes in air pressure or temperature in the outside environment.

Cave management

In addition to the importance of karst caves as landforms in their own right, they often also contain other natural values related to geology, mineralogy, hydrology or climatology. They may be warehouses of palaeoenvironmental information, housing ecosystems in which organisms are physiologically adapted to a life of constant darkness and limited nutrient input, existing in such low numbers that the loss of even a few individuals may be sufficient to cause genetic drift or even extinction. Caves may contain bones of extinct animals, fossil pollen or chemical isotopes, and cultural legacies such as archaeological sites.

Karst caves illustrate many broader natural area management issues in microcosm, but on a particularly sensitive palate. Cave management needs to be founded on an understanding of the stream and seepage water catchments that sustain both speleothems and ecosystems, and maintaining the exchange of water and air between surface and subsurface environments in as natural a condition as possible. Particular care needs to be taken in utilizing any chemicals, control of feral animals and development of infrastructure both above and below ground. The closure of natural infiltration routes through the construction of sealed roads and car parks in close proximity to caves is to be avoided, although in the wider catchment sealing traffic areas may sometimes be preferable to allowing an unsealed surface to contribute sediment into the karst system. Composting toilets or removal of wastes is preferable to septic systems sited where seepage can enter karst systems to the detriment of physical features and sensitive cave ecosystems.

Concepts such as carrying capacity may be of little use because features such as broken stalactites do not grow back relatively rapidly like vegetation, but instead form over geological rather than human time scales. Below ground, there may be a need for rationing of use and well-trained guides to minimize potential damage by inexperienced visitors. Routes may need to be delineated through sensitive areas and promoted as a means of centralizing damage. Even if visitors do not break stalactites, permanent disfiguration may result from people merely touching speleothems because dirt and body oils can become sealed beneath the next layer of clear calcite that forms. Infrastructure facilitating visitor access or asset protection underground should be constructed to allow easy removal with minimum impact, using a material that will not cause problems, such as corrosive or toxic runoff from some metal fixtures, or the unnatural food resource provided by rotting wooden structures. Visitor safety is a particular concern given the massive damage that can be inflicted trying to rescue an injured visitor from a cave – vegetation cut away to allow movement of a patient on a stretcher may grow back relatively quickly, but stalactites broken during a similar process may take millennia to reform. Inappropriate lighting may cause the build-up of damaging algae, dirt carried underground on clothing and footwear will accumulate and its removal will pose challenges, and the cave climate

may be modified. Carbon dioxide levels may sometimes pose dangers for visitors, and accumulated exposure of staff to radioactive radon gas in caves may be an issue.

The management response must include managing recreational cavers, tourists, scientists *and* the managers themselves. Thousands of years of history have commonly lain protected in caves through the coming and going of ice ages and the rise and fall of different human cultures. Its potential removal to nourish a few pages of a 21st-century scientific journal that may be ashes or compost within a few decades warrants utterly scrupulous evaluation. Managers changing light globes in off-track sections of tourist caves or repeatedly visiting sensitive sites to monitor impacts will generate their own impacts.

Soils

It is appropriate that examples of different soil types and catenas (soil groupings that are typically found in certain topographical conditions) are given protective management as important elements of geodiversity. But soils are also essential to the functioning of most natural systems in protected areas, from plant communities to the herbivores that graze upon them and the karst cave systems that may be dissolved from the rock beneath them by water that has become acidified while percolating through soil.

Soils may be damaged by direct impacts, such as quarrying or infrastructure development. They may become subject to unnatural erosion resulting from disturbance to vegetation that allows running water or wind to remove soil particles. Soils may be compacted or their profiles inverted due to the passage of inappropriate vehicles, with long-lasting damage particularly evident in permafrost environments when traffic is allowed on the seasonally thawed uppermost horizons during summer. Soils may be polluted or contaminated due to direct application of chemicals or atmospheric fallout of industrial pollutants or vehicle emissions. Soil nutrients are volatilized during fires and can be removed with the highly erodible ash fraction that remains. Hence, management of these pressures is fundamental and may require regulation of activities, strategies to maintain ground cover and construction to

Table 16.2 Examples of soil management actions

Management goal	Possible management actions
To control soil erosion	Regulate activities that can cause soil erosion, including overuse of visitor destinations, illegal four-wheel-drive activities and excessive use of horses.
	Manage for a minimum suitable natural ground cover.
	Take steps to control soil erosion, where necessary, including re-vegetation of disturbed areas and 'roll-over' drains for management access tracks.
To minimize the impacts of introduced soil pathogens	Clean earth-moving plant and equipment prior to entry into protected areas.
	Use, if necessary, pathogen treatment solutions for plant and equipment prior to their use in protected areas.
	Provide boot-cleaning stations for hikers at trailheads to reduce the artificial spread of soil pathogens such as cinnamon fungus – this method is used in protected areas in South-Western Australia (Barrett and Gillen, 1997).
To minimize the impacts of soil compaction	Confine plant and equipment to defined routes.
	Use alternative transport techniques, such as helicopters, to eliminate the use of vehicles in areas prone to soil disturbance.
	Use elevated walkways for areas of intensive visitor use to prevent soil disturbance.
To minimize the impacts of trace elements	Many trace elements such as zinc are highly toxic to plants and animals when leached into soils – galvanized and similar products must be used with care and knowledge.
To minimize the impacts of introduced seeds	Use clean earth-moving equipment in natural areas.
	Use only clean (weed-seed free) soil, gravel or hay mulch.

Source: adapted from Worboys et al (2005)

address problems in areas subject to damage. The latter can involve improvements to drainage or construction of elevated walkways. Materials used for construction may need to be chosen with care to reduce the risks of toxic effects, such as those associated with some products that contain zinc. Treatment of equipment to reduce the risks of transferring soil pathogens is an important consideration. Some of the major soil management actions are summarized in Table 16.2.

Managing fire

Determining what is appropriately regarded as a natural fire regime can be difficult (see Case Study 16.1). In 'natural' landscapes, fires tend towards particular regimes (patterns of frequency, intensity and seasonality), controlled largely by rates of fuel accumulation since the last fire, and temporal patterns in both fuel moistness and natural ignition incidences. These regimes vary from the almost total absence of fire, as in most areas covered with evergreen rainforest, to annual burning, as in many grasslands. The most worrying fire regimes for managers are ones of intermediate frequency. If fires occur annually or biannually, as they do in savannas in the wet/dry tropics, they are regarded as much a part of the normal environment as the wet and lightning seasons. If there is little evidence of fire anywhere, as in the rainforests of the Peruvian Yungas, managers do not perceive fire as a major concern. However, if fires tend to occur at intervals of decades, they are perceived as highly destructive events, often invoking in managers a desire to reduce the hazard.

The controls on the incidence and severity of fire in natural ecosystems are well understood.

Fire requires fuel. This is potentially any dead organic material smaller in diameter than the little finger of a medium-sized human being. Once the dead material ignites, green material of the same size range may also burn. However, vegetation that is all green is unlikely to burn because of its high moisture content. Similarly, dead organic material needs to be relatively dry before it will support flames. Thus, past and present weather conditions are critical in determining whether a fire will ignite and carry at any one time. If the soil is moist at its surface, dead fuel on the ground is also likely to be moist.

Given that the weather is uncontrollable, fuel moistness is also uncontrollable. However, managers can control fuel levels by planned burning. Alternatively, managers may decide that the best way to prevent extensive and severe unplanned fires is to prevent those ignitions that can be prevented, and to suppress the ones that cannot be prevented as soon as possible after ignition. Neither of these approaches has been widely successful in preventing the severe and extensive unplanned fires that can occur in extreme weather conditions.

When applied in close proximity, fuel reduction has proven to be successful in protecting fire-susceptible assets in extreme fire weather conditions, but only if the assets themselves are not in a highly flammable state. Broad acre hazard-reduction burning may create relatively safe places from which to back-burn, and may prevent crown fires; but, except for a very short time after the planned burn, it cannot prevent the spread of fire in extreme weather conditions. Some recent modelling studies indicate that huge areas would have to be hazard-reduction burned each year even to have any effect on the average size of all unplanned fires.

On top of its ineffectuality in preventing the spread of the severest of fires, broad acre hazard-reduction burning may also prevent a transition from highly flammable vegetation to less flammable vegetation. For example, in New Zealand, introduced gorse (*Ulex europaeus*) forms highly flammable thickets that act as a nurse crop for some native rainforest trees. If the fire hazard presented by gorse is kept temporarily low by burning, the gorse survives, but the rainforest

species do not. If the vegetation is left unburned, the rainforest trees eventually shade out the gorse, and the understorey becomes largely bare, with rapidly decaying litter that is usually too moist to support fire.

Fire suppression is a difficult option. In many parts of the world there is a culture of fire lighting that may take a generation to change. It is impossible to rapidly change the culture of pathological fire lighters, who tend to light fires in the severest of conditions. Lightning storms tend to light many fires at once, stretching suppression resources. In severe weather conditions, fires must be accessed extremely quickly, as they rapidly become unstoppable by all but weather change. In less severe weather conditions, successful suppression means that vegetation remains unburned that could have been burned, thereby increasing fuel loads and, thus, the potential severity of a future fire. The general outcome of suppression strategies has been a reduction in the frequency of fire, but an increase in fire severity and fire size, creating the very problem that they were designed to avoid. A second negative outcome, wherever managers have access to heavy machinery when fighting fires, has been the creation of mazes of bulldozer-cut tracks. These are destructive of nature in themselves, a major cause of sedimentation of streams and caves, and they improve access for exotic plants, animals and pathogens to previously undisturbed ecosystems.

Given the above, we conclude that, except directly around specific assets, both fuel-reduction burning and fire suppression are likely to be counterproductive strategies in protected area management. However, there are a large number of examples of inappropriate fire regimes within protected areas leading to the gradual decline to extinction of vegetation types and species of conservation significance, and fire is one of the tools available to repel the invasion of some exotic organisms.

Why, if fire regimes are as natural as rain, do we require burning of parts of protected areas for conservation purposes? Most of the terrestrial natural vegetation of the Earth has not only been ignited by natural causes, such as lightning, but also by people, who have thereby influenced biotic patterns over most of the 10,000 years of present climatic conditions. A lack of traditional burning would not be so much of a problem for nature conservation if natural vegetation still covered most of the planet. After all, almost all of the species on the planet are likely to have been present before human beings evolved. However, protected areas increasingly tend to be islands of natural vegetation in seas of cultural vegetation. Your reserve may be smaller than the pre-agricultural size of individual fires, and less likely to burn at this size than as a part of an unbroken expanse of natural vegetation; yet, fire is still needed for ecosystem survival and functioning, and unburned areas within your reserve are necessary as sources of disseminules (reproductive plant parts, such as seeds or spores, that facilitate dispersal) of the species that recolonize burns through wind dispersal.

There are few protected areas in the world that have not been changed by the biotic diaspora associated with the European invasions and the development of modern trade networks. Exotic organisms have both caused the extinction of native organisms and become components of the naturalized biota. The presence of exotic organisms in a protected area and the absence of native organisms previously present can both require variations from the natural, or pre-industrial, fire regimes. For example, the sweet pittosporum (*Pittosporum undulatum*) is an Australian rainforest tree that has invaded many other parts of the temperate and tropical world. As an individual, it is easily killed by fire; but if left unburned, it will form a closed community resistant to the ingress of flames.

All forms of planning for nature conservation management require clear objectives. In fire management these should relate to asset protection and the maintenance of conservation-significant environmental diversity.

Assets can be elements of geodiversity, biodiversity or cultural heritage of conservation significance that could be severely damaged, or destroyed, by a single fire, or too frequent fire, or they may be artefacts such as park infrastructure. It should not be assumed that protective action is needed for all natural phenomena. In most cases, the fire-susceptible natural phenomena survive in protected areas because they are protected by their locations (such as in deep rocky gorges) or by their inherent qualities (such as non-flammable foliage and very low ground-fuel levels).

The situations in which protective action is needed to maintain natural phenomena are generally those in which the probabilities of ignition and spread have been increased by improved vehicle access, or an increased use of fire for land management upwind of the reserve, or a decreased use of fire in upwind vegetation, leading to high fuel accumulations. In some cases, disturbances by introduced animals, such as cattle, may make forest edges more flammable than they otherwise would have been. In other cases, invasive introduced plants may be more flammable and have greater biomass than the native species.

Protective actions for assets do not necessarily have to be the establishment of a low fuel zone around its margin. In the examples given above, restrictions on land use upwind of the reserve, the removal of cattle, and herbicide application to the exotic plant could provide protection. Of course, each of these alternatives has their own hazards, which need to be assessed. If low fuel zones are to be established, they do not need to be wide. They also do not need to be bare or involve the removal of all trees. Mowing beneath trees, or in open vegetation, is an effective option to create a low fuel zone in many areas. Wet season burning can eliminate highly flammable annual grasses from the ground layer in monsoon forests and woodlands, providing adequate protection for built assets.

Planned burning for the purpose of maintaining elements of nature requires an understanding of the fire responses of these elements. In planning ecological burns, it should be understood that planned burns are unlikely to eliminate unplanned burns, so a planned fire regime needs to be a response to an inadequate number or type of unplanned fires. It is very difficult for planned burns to simulate some fire regimes, such as the fires that regenerate Californian redwood (*Sequoia sempervirens*) forests, because the intensity of the planned fire would have to be such that escape and damage would almost be guaranteed. We have to leave regeneration burns in such situations to chance. Planned fires in less demanding vegetation tend to be low intensity and patchy, although the patterning of ignition can be used to create local hotspots, if needed. Managers also tend to demand relatively secure boundaries. Ideally, these should be recently burned areas of the same vegetation type, streams and other water bodies, or the boundary of the burned vegetation type with other less flammable vegetation types.

If a particular vegetation type needs to be 'planned burned' in order to maintain a favoured species or community, it is important that not all the vegetation type in any particular protected area is burned at once as the nature of post-fire vegetation succession is known to be affected by the particular climatic conditions that prevail after any fire, as well as the distance of the burned area from sources of wind-dispersed obligate-seeder species. Many plants, fungi, invertebrates and vertebrates are dependent upon particular successional stages after fire. Unless all stages are present in a reserve, there is a danger of losing some of these species.

There are general rules for safe and effective planned burning. Burning should only occur when fuel dryness and wind conditions are (and are likely to continue to be) in the appropriate window for the vegetation type at its present fuel load, and only after a test fire. Burning is ideally conducted in late afternoon so that increased relative humidity at night can help to prevent escapes. The fire needs to be ignited into the wind and/or downhill to mitigate the chances of it leaping the leeward boundary. However, the specifics of prescriptions for safe fire lighting vary enormously between vegetation types and environments. Laws related to fire vary enormously between jurisdictions. Managers need to obtain or develop the appropriate specific prescriptions for their land and follow their local laws and regulations.

Managing weeds and introduced pathogens

Weeds are plants that we do not want, commonly because they are perceived to be a threat to native species. They may also impinge on the character of landforms, as in the case of marram grass (*Ammophila arenaria*), which usually fosters a dune morphology quite different from that which results from sand trapping by native grasses in places where it has been introduced. In protected areas, most weeds are species that have recently invaded from other continents, or other regions on the home continent, usually through the agency of our species. In some protected areas, such as many of those in continental alpine areas, there are few or no weeds, and weed management is not a major issue. In others, such as those on remote oceanic islands, weeds can be a major management issue.

Most weeds are ruderals (short-lived plants that colonize disturbed areas). However, a subset of weed species can establish in undisturbed native vegetation. Another subset can establish in response to natural disturbances and be far from short lived. The weeds that most threaten nature conservation values are those that have adaptations for long-distance dispersal, usually by wind, birds or water, and also fall in one of the latter two subsets.

Newly introduced weeds have a period of grace within which they are relatively free of damage from herbivores and diseases. In most cases, local animals and diseases, or other introductions, eventually make use of them. By this time the weed may be widespread and abundant. In some cases, the weed may even have become an important resource for some native animals. This needs to be taken into account in any weed management planning.

Prevention is better than cure

Quarantine measures are never going to be effective at a national level while trade and tourism are regarded as more important than nature conservation and primary industry. Accidental introductions are unavoidable in this situation. Quarantine should be able to prevent most deliberate introductions. However, plants present particular difficulties in import screening of ornamentals and crops – it has proven impossible to reliably predict which species might be dangerous invaders. The best tactic seems to be extreme caution.

Within any particular protected area, quarantine can be effective for many weed species. The disseminules of a large proportion of weed species

Removing weeds, Gir National Park, India

Source: IUCN Photo Library © Jim Thorsell

can be spread in building and road materials, and in mud and dirt adhering to machinery and vehicles. This is a strong argument for minimizing road and building construction within protected areas, cleaning vehicles and machinery before entry, and sterilizing construction and road materials. It is dangerous to bring in pot plants, even if grown from local seed or cuttings, in case this becomes the source of an infestation. Protected area managers need to consider if concessionaires and leaseholders should be allowed to plant ornamentals in their ski villages and around their 'ecotourism' resorts.

Determining priorities for weed control

Once introduced to a new region, a plant that is going to become invasive necessarily takes some time to attain this state, if only through the shape of its exponential population growth curve. A new weed in your protected area should therefore be subject to precautionary extirpation as the highest priority in your weed management programme.

Weeds that should *not* be removed are those that are important for maintaining populations of some of the most significant species and that present little danger to other significant park assets. These are generally introduced species that have become well integrated within the ecosystem and provide food resources or shelter no longer available from native plants because the relevant native plants have been eliminated.

There seems little point in expending scarce resources to remove weeds that do not threaten the future of any element of biodiversity or geodiversity in your protected area. There are some introduced plants that have been around so long that they occur in low numbers everywhere in suitable habitat dominated by natives and do not appear to suppress native species richness. Many of these species would be impossible to eliminate from even very small areas without destroying the intermixed natives or causing damage to other assets.

The highest priority in weed control, after the new invaders, should be given to species that threaten biodiversity and geodiversity. Among these, weed species that are still in a state of expansion and those that can be most cheaply eliminated should have highest priority; but all should be controlled to the degree necessary to maintain or improve the critical conservation values. There are relatively few such damaging weeds that can be permanently eliminated from large areas. Control, rather than elimination, is usually the aim of action.

Options for weed control

Techniques for dealing with weeds include biological control, herbicide sprays, cutting, slashing, replanting with native species, controlled burns to selectively target weed seedlings, and hand clearing. An effective combination is to remove weeds and then replant with vigorous native species to prevent reinvasion.

Herbicides. Herbicide application is a widely used approach to controlling agricultural weeds and is also employed in protected areas, particularly on species that have clumped or localized distributions. This management option is usually expensive. Where a decision is made to employ herbicides, particular care is required in planning and implementation to minimize damage to non-target species, including aquatic species and soil biota.

Over-planting. Small areas with dense infestations of weeds can be difficult to convert back to native vegetation unless the natives can be used to shade them out or to steal the resources they need for growth. Local soil, seed and cuttings should be used for propagation to avoid the introduction of new weeds and pathogens.

Hand weeding can be highly effective with scattered weeds among predominantly native vegetation. This requires weeds that can be relatively easily killed using hand tools and cheap or voluntary labour. Native litter placed on disturbed ground encourages native regeneration.

Grazing or burning, or grazing and burning, can be used to control some weeds. The combination of burning, followed by grazing, can be more effective than either one of the methods used in isolation.

Mechanical removal may work for some weeds in very limited areas with good access. Steam treatment can be highly effective, but can only take place near roads, as with most mechanical techniques.

Introduction of new organisms for biological control is initially a highly expensive option if the proper controls on introductions are followed, and has a low success rate.

Engage with the community. The source of your weed problem may be the nursery in the nearby settlement that is selling your weed. You may need to talk with the local community to remove weed species from nurseries and gardens.

Weed control should be part of a protected area management plan, with actions taking into consideration the biology of the weed species involved (see Case Study 16.3).

Managing introduced plant pathogens

Plant pathogens are fungi, bacteria, viruses or prions that kill or damage plants. Like weeds, these have transgressed the boundaries or biotic realms and regions – in this case, with largely unconscious human help. Once introduced, they are almost impossible to eliminate as their symptoms usually postdate their presence. Their rate of spread can be slowed through strict quarantine measures; but it is difficult to impose these measures and to get all to conform to them. It seems that some plant species will depend upon cultivation in pathogen-free settings for their future on the planet.

In the hope that local populations of susceptible species will evolve resistant genotypes if the spread of the pathogen is slowed sufficiently, managers should be aware of the symptoms of

Case Study 16.3

Management of two invading woody plants in the Everglades, Florida, US

The Everglades National Park in Florida consists of an extensive complex of wetlands and pine barrens and is closely adjacent to intensively developed areas. Two major woody weeds that have invaded the park are the Brazilian pepper (*Schinus terebinthifolius*) and the Australian paperbark (*Melaleuca quinquenervia*). A first stage in managing the populations of any weed is understanding its ecology and distribution. With Brazilian pepper, it has proven possible to detect dense populations using hyperspectral imagery, but not possible to use such imagery to locate isolated trees (Lass and Prather, 2004). This species has been shown to prefer human-disturbed sites with relatively high phosphorus levels (Li and Norland, 2001). At one such disturbed site within the Everglades National Park, 4000ha of abandoned agricultural land, which had been subjected to break-up of the limestone layer and fertilizer additions, complete soil removal proved necessary to prevent the reinvasion of the species and to enable its replacement with native wetland plants (Dalrymple et al, 2003). The paperbark is a wetland species, pre-adapted to Florida's conditions. It has proven so invasive, totally displacing native plants, that a biological control, *Oxyops vitiosa*, was introduced to chew on developing new season foliage. This it has done, with the surprising outcome of no less foliage, but 36 times less reproduction (Pratt et al, 2005).

various introduced pathogens. For example, the cinnamon fungus (*Phytophthora cinnamomi*) preferentially attacks certain shrub species, but has little effect on sedges or grasses, so can easily be deduced to be present. Diversion of tracks and area closures may slow down the spread of root pathogens, such as the cinnamon fungus, from spot infestations.

Managing animals

The conservation of vertebrate animal species has been the major reason for the establishment of a large proportion of the protected areas of the world. Yet, most of the individual animals and species of animals in protected areas are invertebrates. Invertebrates play a critical role in ecosystem functioning, with the survival of particular invertebrate species often being critical for the survival of plant and vertebrate species, and are important to conserve for themselves as major elements of biodiversity.

While there is some argument over whether predators normally have much of an influence on the populations of their natural prey, there is little doubt that herbivores can have substantial influence on the nature of vegetation, and that introduced predators can cause extinctions of their new prey, as with the extinction of rails (family *Rallidae*) on Pacific Ocean islands with the introduction of the Polynesian rat (*Rattus exulans*). Different animals have different tastes in foodstuffs, creating the possibility of manipulating the ecosystem to favour the most conservation-significant elements of biodiversity and geodiversity by varying the populations of particular animals. To serve this end, translocation, induced reduction of existing populations and induced increase of existing populations are options.

Translocation

The translocation of vertebrate carnivores can be used to reduce populations of species that threaten other species. For example, canines prey on the young of the fox (*Vulpes vulpes*), a species that threatens medium-sized native mammals.

Translocated herbivores can eliminate invasive non-native plants, promote diversity in native vegetation and prevent tree thickening. For example, the loss of elephants from the savanna system is likely to lead to tree thickening, given their role in tree destruction. The introduction of diseases and their vectors can be effective in nature conservation, as with the introduction of a flea to transport *Myxomatosis* between rabbits on sub-Antarctic Macquarie Island.

Animal welfare considerations have induced some research organizations to seek novel diseases to induce sterility in target populations without killing them. This is highly dangerous research that should be discontinued. The animal that is an ecologic and economic disaster in some countries is a precious native in others, and humans have not been particularly effective in stopping diseases transgressing national boundaries.

Translocation is an extreme form of manipulation, to be undertaken only after thorough research and deliberation. Conservation goals will usually be better achieved through management measures that adjust the sizes of populations of species already present in reserves, rather than introducing new ones.

Adjusting animal population downwards

Large vertebrate animals that inhabit open country can be efficiently and specifically culled by shooting either from helicopters or on the ground. The Judas technique is often effective in locating groups of social animals such as goats in country unsuitable for shooting from helicopters. A member of the species is captured and released with a radio transmitter attached. They find a herd, which is subsequently conveniently located and dispatched. Shooting is undertaken by rangers in many protected areas, and in others licensed or authorized shooters may be involved in culling operations (see Case Study 16.4).

Poisoning has the disadvantage that it tends to be less species specific than shooting in its lethal outcomes, with secondary poisoning and biological accumulation being typical problems. However, poisons can kill animals that are impossible to control by shooting. Successful poisoning of an undesirable animal must affect its population more than that of its competitors and prey. This can be achieved by the use of chemicals that induce a higher mortality in the target animal than in others, as is the case with 1080 poison in Western Australia, where the native

Case Study 16.4

Elimination of cats on the sub-Antarctic Marion Island, South Africa

The introduction of cats (*Felis catus*) by human beings has been thought to have caused the extinction of large numbers of species, these extinctions having been concentrated on islands. Feral cat elimination attempts have been successful on at least 48 islands, ranging from Baja California to the tropics, to the sub-Antarctic. The success rate has been greater on small than on large islands. The largest island from which cats have been eliminated is Marion, a 290 square kilometre sub-Antarctic island belonging to the Republic of South Africa. The elimination was the result of a 19-year programme, the first stage of which was research on the impacts of cats and the characteristics of the cat population. This was followed by the development of a management policy and the selection of methods of control. The feline panleucopaenia virus was released in 1977 and its effects were monitored. This proved an insufficient measure by itself, so a second method of control, hunting at night, was trialled, then fully implemented, while its effects and that of the disease continued to be monitored. The combined effects of these two control measures proved insufficient for elimination of the species. In a final assault, trapping and poisoning were used. By 1991, no cats survived on Marion Island.

Sources: adapted from Bester et al (2002) and Nogales et al (2004)

animals are adapted to the active ingredient, which occurs in local plants, while introduced animals are not. Alternatively, the form of presentation or application of the bait can be used to eliminate or minimize mortality in non-target species.

Adjusting animal populations upwards

Managers may wish to increase the populations of particular animal species as part of recovery from endangerment, or to achieve a particular management purpose, such as the control of a weed species. The key to increasing the population of any animal species is the recognition and correction of the factor or factors that limit an increase in numbers. These may operate to limit fecundity, as with DDT-induced thinning of bird shells, or relate to mortality in the juvenile or later stages of life, as with long-line kills of female albatrosses. There may be particular temporal pinch points that control the overall population, such as the amount of food available in a particular season or the number of nest sites available in spring. The population may succumb to diseases at particular population densities or be subject to increased predation once more readily available as a food source in an environment. Population regulation is sometimes complex and its causes are not always easily determinable, as may be seen in the account of

the Gould's petrel (*Pterodroma leucoptera*), an endangered species found nesting on small coastal islands off the Australian state of New South Wales (see Case Study 16.5).

Animals have been threatened by infrastructure within reserves. Vehicles are a major cause of mortality of threatened species, although large windows in visitor centres present their own dangers for birds. Sewerage ponds seem to be more of a resource for water birds and animals than a threat. Poorly designed gates installed to secure sensitive caves have, in some cases, proven disastrous for bat populations through restricting nocturnal flights for feeding and the return of this energy to cave ecosystems as guano – a situation that potentially raises the risks of insect predation for park vegetation or local croplands.

The best option to solve these problems is to withdraw tourist traffic and/or infrastructure to sites outside the protected area. Where this option is not possible, traffic can be slowed within reserves through the use of 'speed humps' and avoiding long straights. Animal overpasses and underpasses can lower mortality but, in most cases, need to be combined with barrier fencing to be effective and are highly expensive.

Many threatened species have their populations limited by predation from other animals, usually, but not always, by introduced species. The solution lies in reducing the numbers of the

Case Study 16.5

Recovery of an endangered species: Gould's petrel

David Priddel, New South Wales Department of Environment and Conservation, Parks and Wildlife Division, Australia

The Gould's petrel is Australia's rarest endemic sea bird. The only place it breeds in the world is on two small islands at the entrance to Port Stephens, New South Wales. The vast majority of the birds nest in rock cavities on the rugged rainforest-covered slopes of Cabbage Tree Island, and a dozen or so pairs nest on nearby Boondelbah Island.

The first comprehensive census of the Gould's petrel was undertaken in 1982. The initial survey revealed some disturbing facts. Fewer than 300 pairs nested, and breeding success was drastically low (less than 20 per cent). Surveys repeated in each of the subsequent two years yielded similar results. It was also found that the population had declined by more than 25 per cent during the past two decades. The causes of the species' demise were poorly understood.

A research project was initiated to identify the causes responsible for reproductive failure. As expected, the rate of nest failure was exceptionally high. More alarmingly, however, was the discovery that nesting adults were dying in relatively large numbers. Many petrels perished after becoming entangled in the sticky fruits of the birdlime tree (*Pisonia umbellifera*). The most prevalent cause of mortality, however, was predation by pied currawongs (*Strepera graculina*) and, occasionally, Australian ravens (*Corvus coronoides*). These predators would kill both chicks and nesting adults to feed their own developing young.

Experimental recovery actions were implemented immediately before the 1993 to 1994 breeding season. Poisoning destroyed birdlime trees within the breeding grounds of the Gould's petrel. Follow-up measures prevented new plants establishing from seed. Shooting reduced pied currawong numbers. Their nests were located and destroyed, along with any eggs and young. Ongoing monitoring of the petrel population revealed an immediate rise in the number of petrels incubating eggs and a marked improvement in breeding success. The culmination of these factors was a fourfold increase in fledgling production. Breeding success now regularly exceeds 55 per cent, and in most years more than 300 young fledge (see Figure 16.1).

Clearly, the threats posed by the birdlime tree, pied currawong and Australian raven were able to be ameliorated by appropriate management intervention. The question remained, however, as to why these unusual threats arose, particularly on an island essentially remote from the influences of people. The answer lay in the changes to the vegetation wrought by rabbits since their introduction to Cabbage Tree Island in 1906.

The Gould's petrel breeds in two deep rainforest-covered gullies on the western slopes of Cabbage Tree Island. Rabbits had destroyed much

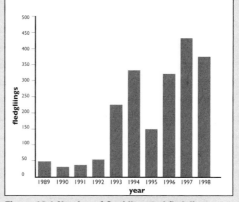

Figure 16.1 Number of Gould's petrel fledglings produced on Cabbage Tree Island, New South Wales, for ten seasons, 1989–1998 (years refer to commencement of breeding season)

of the rainforest understorey. Without adequate concealment, nesting petrels have been exposed to predators. The sparseness of vegetative cover also makes the petrels more vulnerable to entanglement in the fruits of the birdlime tree. An intact understorey captures many of these fruits before they fall to the ground. Fruits caught up in vegetation pose little or no threat to petrels moving about the forest floor.

It was considered that the requirement for long-term control of pied currawongs could be eliminated if rabbits were eradicated and the understorey given the opportunity to re-establish. Rabbits were successfully eradicated. The procedure involved the sequential use of three mortality agents: *Myxomatosis*, rabbit calicivirus and poisoning. Significant changes in the vegetation of Cabbage Tree Island were evident within just weeks of the last rabbit being removed. Before implementing recovery actions, fewer than 50 young fledged each year. During the late 1990s, reproductive output had risen to 300 young per annum. Following this success, an attempt to establish a second viable colony on Boondelbah Island was initiated and 100 nest boxes were established there between 1999 and 2000. Two hundred chicks were transferred and all but five successfully fledged, with some returning to breed. In 2002 to 2003, 12 nest boxes were occupied and five eggs were laid. Surveys in 2001 to 2002 found that, in total, there were 1000 birds breeding with 450 young being produced per annum (NSW NPWS, 2003).

threatening species. This has been highly successful in recovering threatened bird species in New Zealand, where predators have been eliminated from small islands to which the species have been translocated.

A species may be declining because a successional stage in the vegetation is in decline. This is relatively easily reversed if the species depends upon early successional stages, but is less easily reversed if it depends upon old growth. In this case, there may be some chance of increasing the numbers of the species if the resource that it depends upon in old growth can be replaced artificially, as with nest boxes that substitute for nesting hollows.

Managing the impact of people on natural environments

Some people maltreat protected areas or see them as an opportunity to make a living at the expense of their natural values (threats to protected areas from human activities, such as pollution, are considered in Chapter 9). Others can love protected areas to death through:

- defoliation and erosion of camping areas;
- trampling and vehicle impacts;
- polluting with their wastes;
- unconsciously introducing pathogens, weeds and pests;
- disturbing animals through misplaced kindness or accident; or
- accidentally starting fires.

Critical concepts in understanding when and where people need to be managed are resistance and resilience. For example, a vegetation type is highly *resistant* if the act of a large number of people walking on it does not cause its death. The vegetation type is *resilient* if death is caused, but recovery is rapid. Different degrees of resistance and resilience interact to determine how much human pressure of any type can be placed on an ecosystem before it collapses, irreversibly, into another less desirable state. These concepts have been used by managers for many purposes, such as locating tracks, determining the need for toilets at camping areas and assessing the need for access restrictions.

When does a human-induced change become unacceptable? This is a critical question in the management of natural values. The worst type of threshold to set is a proportional one. Proportions are essentially arbitrary, so are easily shifted as a result of political pressure. For example, if a threshold was that the natural vegetation cover be removed from no more than 1 per cent of a protected area, and a new ecotourism resort proposal came up that would take removal to 1.02 per cent, the threshold may be shifted to 1.025 per cent and those who objected would be mocked. The best types of thresholds are 'no' ones that relate to the values for which the protected area is most significant: for example: 'providing tourist facilities should cause no irreversible changes to landforms and soils at the century time scale'.

Options for mitigating trampling damage

There are basically three options to prevent trampling causing irreversible and expanding damage to ecosystems and aesthetic naturalness:

1. reducing the number of tramplers to carrying capacity (politically difficult);
2. restricting tramplers to small hardened lines (can be immensely expensive); and
3. separating tramplers from the natural (can be immensely expensive).

Rationing can take place by privilege, booking, cost or lottery, or some combination. All of these techniques have been used to control access to back country in the US and elsewhere. Alternatively, removing tracks from maps, obscuring track entrances and periodic closures are all potential approaches.

Management costs can be minimized by not bothering too much about easily reversible damage, like that in some boggy areas, where the discomfort might prevent people going further. However, the cheapest option is not necessarily the best in the long term – some of the more expensive forms of track and campsite construction, such as stone steps, not only blend in better with their surroundings than cheaper forms, such as boardwalks and wooden camp platforms, but also last much longer, with lower maintenance costs.

Options for preventing the introduction or spread of new organisms by users of protected areas

Codes of practice are one mechanism that has been used to mitigate the undesirable effects of park users. They can be effective in reducing reversible or gradually incremental damage. However, they are of little use for preventing the unwitting introduction of new organisms because they are never universally adopted among users, and it takes only one introduction to establish a potentially damaging organism in a new place. For hygiene to be effective, it must be compulsory and policed. Vehicles, camping equipment, clothes and boots must be cleaned, requiring easily used cleaning stations outside the protected area, or within the protected area when leaving an infested or infected area. This is very expensive. Prevention of access to those parts of a protected area from which a disease could be spread by people is an alternative. However, to be effective, such quarantining requires a high level of policing or unanimous social support.

Options to reduce disturbance of animals

Recognizing the high likelihood that the feeding of animals within protected areas will result in harm to people, animals or ecosystems, most jurisdictions ban, or highly regulate, this activity. Nonetheless, people are still injured or killed as a result of illegal feeding, prompting the shooting or translocation of the most aggressive individuals of potentially lethal species. Access to areas important for the breeding of animals is often also regulated in order to ensure that people are not there at times of the year when their presence could cause high levels of mortality, or, if present, do not disturb the animals.

Managing the natural aesthetic resource

The natural aesthetic resource incorporates the smell, sound, touch, taste, spirituality and view of natural phenomena and natural landscapes. The beauty of wild landscapes has long been a prime motivation for establishing protected areas. Beauty is, of course, in the eye of the beholder, and beholders are well known to vary in their perceptions. Most early national parks contained a juxtaposition of water and steep land, characteristics still dominant in the wild land art of most contemporary cultures. There also seems to be a high degree of cross-cultural constancy in the perception that a view of water from an open glade, through a partial vegetation screen, is to be desired, as it would have been in East Africa in the early days of our species. However, those who live on plains tend to appreciate their natural beauty as much as those who live in mountains appreciate the splendour of their habitat. We grow into landscapes by living in them and perceive a beauty, that may be unfelt by others, in familiar natural objects and scenes. Conversely, visual contrasts to familiar landscapes may be the major attraction for visitors to natural areas, such as the stunning limestone towers of the Ha Long Bay World Heritage Area in Viet Nam. City dwellers may be drawn to natural areas largely by the visual contrast with their normal habitat.

Management options to maintain or increase the natural aesthetic resource

It is impossible to avoid all negative impacts on the natural aesthetic resource if infrastructure and facilities are built within protected areas. The best option is not to build within them; but if developers are too powerful to resist, it may be possible to persuade them to spend a little extra money on disguise, or, at least, to have disguise as a design criterion. Disguise should relate to all of the senses. The aesthetic experience at the lookout may be visually outstanding; but if music can be heard and cooking food smelled, the feeling of being at one with the beauty of nature may evaporate.

The normal approach to natural aesthetic value management is highly utilitarian – the greatest scenic good for the greatest number. Trees are carefully culled in front of the lookout to leave the ones that hide the atomic power station in the valley below; roads are located to minimize views of scenic disruptions; visitor centres and car parks are built to blend into their surroundings. Quietness and solitude, as important components of the natural aesthetic experience, tend to be ignored, as does the need to preclude artificial light at night. If visitors want the full natural aesthetic experience, they must escape from roads, visitor centres and lookouts to more natural places, more remote from mechanized access and intrusive interpretation. Low standards of aesthetic management may still permit momentary gratification of visitors whose more lasting passions may lie elsewhere, but disappoint, disenfranchise and disillusion those with higher standards who are potentially the most committed and effective advocates for your reserve.

If one adopts the position that the natural aesthetic resource is independent of the number of people who might experience it in any one place, or that it is inversely related to this number, it is possible to quantify its potential loss from any development within or outside a protected area. Viewfields can be analysed. The greater the proportion of the viewfield that is occupied by human disturbance and artefacts, the lesser the natural aesthetic experience. If these variables are measured, then it is easy to calculate their relative losses from alternative development plans, inside or outside protected areas, or, alternatively, to measure the potential gains from road closure and rehabilitation (Kirkpatrick and Haney, 1980).

Managing remoteness

Remoteness of an area from human disturbance is an important consideration in terms of the potential for natural phenomena, such as functioning natural systems, to both persist in an undisturbed condition, and to impart a sense of the wildly primeval environment from which we have come as a species. The concept of wilderness is a Western cultural construct that may sometimes include pre-agricultural humanity as part of the natural landscape, but which excludes the artefacts of agricultural, industrial and post-industrial societies as elements of naturalness. The fact that some people find the concept offensive because they take it, often incorrectly, to imply that they or their ancestors did not use and influence land now designated as wilderness, does not reduce its usefulness in managing naturalness.

A useful indicator of remoteness is the time it takes a walker to reach a given area from the nearest point of mechanized access. However, care is required in the use of such measures. For some people, a mere four hours' walking or canoeing

may be sufficient for them to need to spend the night sleeping among nature, an exciting prospect in protected areas with crocodiles, lions or grizzly bears, and a potentially spiritual experience in less megafauna-blessed areas. Others require greater time distances in order to be motivated to camp in the wild. If assessment is not based on faster, more capable walkers, then those people most committed to wilderness and its protection may find no wilderness in your putative wilderness zone. The absolute distance from human disturbances can also be measured. This relates to the dissipation of unnatural sounds and smells, and to the feeling of remoteness experienced by people, although again people differ in their perception of what constitutes an adequate distance to imply wilderness.

Restoration and rehabilitation

In 'damage control', protected area managers inevitably find themselves involved in efforts to restore the natural environment to something resembling a known past condition by:

* eliminating detrimental processes;
* repairing degradation;
* removing introduced species; or
* re-introducing species that have vanished.

A viable, well-handled restoration exercise can have enormous benefits; but a non-viable or poorly handled attempt can be enormously costly in both economic and environmental terms.

From a geomorphological perspective, the potential to restore a damaged site depends upon the nature of the landforms and the processes that formed them. Little damage may have accrued where the features are formed of solid rock. Hence, the solid rock walls that surround the artificial reservoir in Hetch Hetchy Valley, Yosemite National Park, in the US have not suffered due to wave action, but only merely discoloured by a temporary 'bath-tub ring' caused by the death of lichen growing on the rock, making restoration entirely viable. Conversely, where reservoir or riverbanks are formed from unconsolidated soft sediments, waves may cause significant damage to the structure of the perimeter landforms, and reservoir-level fluctuations may induce damaging landslides on surrounding slopes. However, in both situations landforms that are more than a few metres below the reservoir surface will not be eroded by wave action because the short wavelength of wind waves does not allow them to scour a lake bed at depth.

Construction of an artificial facsimile of a destroyed landform does not constitute restoration, which instead involves working with nature to effect recovery. There is no capacity for a damaged landform to heal itself if it is the product of geomorphological processes that no longer operate at the site due to changed climatic conditions, such as a moraine deposited by a glacier during the Pleistocene in an area that is now entirely deglaciated. Conversely, if the processes originally responsible for formation of the landform are still operating at the site, a degree of self-healing *is* possible. Careful assessment of all elements in the landform community is required. And it is infinitely better, and cheaper, not to allow damage to occur in the first place.

Many ecosystems will restore themselves after damage, providing the underlying environmental conditions have not been changed. In most situations in which conditions have been changed, revegetation, with species suited to the new conditions, will occur without any human intervention. Where damage has initiated positive feedback, as with an eroding track, intervention may be necessary to stabilize the substrate before natural recovery can occur. Some forms of human-induced damage can have highly detrimental effects on aesthetic naturalness. In these cases, restoration may take the form of artificial inputs of fertilizers and direct seeding, or planting, of native species.

Management principles

1 Managers need to determine the natural elements and processes that their protected area is most important in protecting, and give management priority to maintaining these elements and processes.

2 It is impossible to manage a damaged protected area back to its 'pristine' landscape, but it is possible to rehabilitate a site so that it recovers some of its natural values.

3 Management decisions should be based on sound science and knowledge, including local traditional knowledge.

4 In most circumstances, changes in management regimes should be experimental, using adaptive management processes, rather than comprehensive.

5 Managing natural heritage in protected areas must go beyond localized phenomena to include functioning natural systems.

6 Protected area managers should seek indicators that signal imminent danger to the important values of their area, and should follow an adaptive approach consistent with emerging threats and management needs.

7 All management interventions should be:
   - consistent with the strategic plan and conservation objectives;
   - based upon knowledge of the distribution of the area's key environmental assets; and
   - monitored to assess their impact on biodiversity and other protected area objectives.

8 Biodiversity conservation and viability of populations of key species often depend upon factors beyond protected area boundaries; therefore, protected areas should be managed as part of wider regions.

Further reading

Bond, W. J. and van Wilgen, B. W. (1996) *Fire and Plants*, Chapman and Hall, London

Buck, L. E., Geister, C. C., Schelhas, J. and Wollenberg, E. (2001) *Biological Diversity: Balancing Interests through Adaptive Collaborative Management*, CRC Press, London

Gray, M. (2004) *Geodiversity: Valuing and Conserving Abiotic Nature*, Wiley, Chichester

Yaffee, S. L., Phillips, A. F., Frentz, I. C, Hardy, P. W. Maleki, S. W. and Thorpe, B. E. (1996) *Ecosystem Management in the United States*, Island Press, Washington, DC

17

Cultural Heritage Management

Jane Lennon

Conservation of cultural heritage is a social, educational and technical process that depends upon an appropriate understanding of the values contained in the heritage resource – an understanding that develops with the changing values and requirements of society. The modern concept of cultural heritage embraces all the signs that document human activities over time. It relates to the tangible built environment in an ecological context, and requires the reading of layers of evidence present in the environment. It also encompasses the intangible heritage of culture, such as language, dance, music, folk ways and craft skills. Intangible heritage is often associated with particular localities, giving meanings and significance to these places. These cultural links should be conserved.

Since antiquity, special objects and sites have been protected by decrees or customs. Protection of cultural heritage began in Europe after the Renaissance (17th century), and attention was given to monuments and works of art so that cultural heritage was synonymous with museums. In the pre-industrial era, people and their built habitats were more directly dependent upon nature than they are today. Massive destruction caused by wars and major industrial development since the 1950s have made people realize that their environment is a source of cultural identity and is valued for the many attributes creating a sustainable life. After World War II, many European countries enacted laws to preserve historic towns and cities (Feilden and Jokilehto, 1993). The legal and administrative developments in European countries influenced Asian, African and Latin American countries in two directions: systems were developed following European models, as in Japan, and in colonies or colonized countries, heritage protection was conducted by European rulers (Ito, 1995).

Following the foundation of the United Nations Educational, Scientific and Cultural Organization (UNESCO) (see 'Institutions working for protected areas' in Chapter 3) and a suite of other organizations concerned with cultural heritage, such as the International Council on Monuments and Sites (ICOMOS), the International Council of Museums (ICOM) and the International Centre for the Study of the Preservation and Restoration of Cultural Property in Rome (ICCROM), the concept of heritage has evolved across the world. During the 1950s and 1960s, the growing interest in historic areas provided the incentive for new methodologies for their preservation. From the 1970s, concern for the environment and ecology gave rise to policies of environmentally sustainable development. In the 1990s, increasing attention was given to cultural diversity and intangible heritage. Characterization of cultural heritage and its diverse values requires a range of policies for its management and protection, including various international recommendations and conventions promulgated by UNESCO. Recommendations provide guidance for specific types of heritage, such as archaeological sites, historic buildings, museums and movable cultural heritage, whereas conventions are ratified by state parties as legal instruments.

The first convention for cultural heritage was the Convention for the Protection of Cultural Property in the Event of Armed Conflict (The Hague Convention), adopted in 1954 and followed by the Convention on the Means of Prohibiting and Preventing the Illicit Import, Export and Transfer of Ownership of Cultural Property in 1970. Concern resulting from increased threats to natural and cultural heritage worldwide, and the desire to protect internationally significant places and their values, prompted the general conference of UNESCO in 1972 to adopt a special Convention Concerning the Protection of the World Cultural and Natural Heritage (see 'Conventions' in Chapter 3).

Article 1 of the convention defines cultural heritage as:

- *monuments:* architectural works, works of monumental sculpture and painting, elements or structures of an archaeological nature, inscriptions, cave dwellings and combinations of features, which are of outstanding universal value from the point of view of history, art or science;
- *groups of buildings:* groups of separate or connected buildings which, because of their architecture, their homogeneity or their place in the landscape, are of outstanding universal value from the point of view of history, art or science; and
- *sites:* works of man [sic] or the combined works of nature and of man [sic], and areas including archaeological sites which are of outstanding universal value from the historical, aesthetic, ethnological or anthropological points of view.

These definitions have subsequently influenced many countries to protect cultural heritage places in their legislation. Amendments to World Heritage definitions in 1992 included cultural landscapes in the types of places to be conserved, and the 2003 Convention on Intangible Cultural Heritage further expanded the definition of cultural heritage. This is particularly important for

cultures that do not create monuments, but have beliefs associated with landscape features or seasonal rituals that leave no tangible evidence.

To separate cultural heritage from its environment and from natural heritage often seems tidy and convenient for management; but conservation staff should remember that this is somewhat artificial. People shape land, and the land, in turn, shapes people and their culture. Many protected areas in the Americas, Africa and Australasia are predominantly natural environments but include strong cultural links to communities. This is in contrast with English and French national parks, for example, which protect landscapes that include towns and villages. Cultural heritage plays a vital part in defining group identity, and the value put on certain sites or objects (whether by individuals, groups or significant proportions of the community) demands that they be actively conserved. Such significant sites or objects are known generally as 'cultural heritage resources'. These are the physical evidence of past and contemporary cultural activities. They are valuable, often rare and could not be replaced if lost.

This chapter describes some of the ways in which cultural heritage resources are conserved. It is a brief coverage, but it also offers guidance as to where comprehensive reference material may be found. The focus is on cultural heritage that is found within protected areas, and on the practicalities of conserving cultural heritage sites.

Significance of cultural heritage in protected areas

In the ages of Classicism (700 BC to 500 AD) and the Enlightenment (1450 to 1650 AD), scholars tried to find universal values, the idea or ideal, and Greek art was imitated. But with the age of Romanticism (18th century), appreciation of the plurality of cultural values led to critical appraisal of truthfulness and authenticity in historical sources. The values of cultural resources refer to the material, workmanship, design and setting of a site – its physical environment. As an historic resource, it may have been degraded and altered by natural weathering and continued use, as well as modifications, which themselves are part of the accumulated historical character and material properties. These accumulated attributes represent the inherent values of the cultural heritage, illustrating historical testimonies and associated cultural values. The aim of conservation is to protect these qualities and values of the heritage resource, to protect the physical properties and to ensure their integrity for future generations.

The most important policy document circulating internationally is the *International Charter for the Conservation and Restoration of Monuments and Sites*, known as the *Charter of Venice*, which resulted from the deliberations of practitioners about restoration of flood-damaged buildings in Venice in 1964. It has become the fundamental reference for cultural heritage conservation policies. Various nations have used its generic principles while adapting it to suit their particular resources, such as Australia's 1981 *Burra Charter*, the 2004 *China Principles*, *A Preservation Charter for the Historic Towns and Areas of the United States of America* (US/ICOMOS, 1992) or the *Charter for the Preservation of Quebec's Heritage* (ICOMOS, 1982).

Conservation should be based on a clear definition of the heritage resource in relation to its setting as part of a critical process of developing conservation management. A rigorous process encompassing three fundamental stages – understanding significance, developing policy, and management – involves a series of ten steps (see Figure 17.1). This conservation process facilitates a logical flow from evidence to significance, policy development, implementation and management.

Understanding the significance of the heritage resource drives the conservation process. The term 'significance' is used in heritage conservation to mean the degree to which the heritage resource possesses defined values. These values include aesthetic, historic, scientific or research, social or spiritual value for past, present or future generations. They vary for different groups at different periods in their social history. These values can be checked against criteria established for defining significance, as illustrated by Case Study 17.1, which describes three World Heritage cultural landscapes.

Significance is embodied in the heritage resource itself, in its fabric, setting, use, associations, meanings, records, related places and objects, and its tangible and intangible properties. There are many guidelines currently in use for

STAGE 1:
gather and analyse evidence;
describe the heritage values

1. identify the site / place / landscape and its associations
2. identify / contact people or groups with an interest in the place
3. gather and record information about the place sufficient to understand significance (historical, documentary, oral, physical)
4. provide a description of the heritage values as a statement of significance

STAGE 2:
develop policies

5. identify obligations arising from identified and heritage values
6. gather information about other factors affecting the future of the place (owner/manager's needs and resources, external factors, physical condition, constraints)
7. develop policy

STAGE 3:
implement policy and undertake
ongoing management

8. prepare management plan for implementation of policies
9. manage place in accordance with management plan
10. monitor and review

Figure 17.1 Cultural heritage management process

Source: Australia ICOMOS (1999)

determining significance of the heritage resource object or place (see the 'Further reading' section for some of these).

To determine significance first requires understanding the history of the resource. The sequence of its phases forms the historical timeline. This linkage with the developmental sequence becomes the fundamental reference for evaluating heritage. Alois Reigl, an Austrian art historian and conservator, developed the concept of '*kuntswollen*' to describe how an object created at a given time both reflects the artistic trends of its period and contributes to those trends (Reigl, 1996 [1903]). He describes artistic and historical monuments as having:

*   age value – emotional response to its appearance;
*   historical value based on its specific stage in human development;

Case Study **17.1**

World Heritage cultural landscapes

Villa D'Este, Italy

The Villa d'Este at Tivoli in the Roman hills, with its palace and garden, is one of the most remarkable and comprehensive illustrations of Renaissance culture at its most refined. Owing to its innovative design and the creativity and ingenuity of the architectural components in the garden (fountains, ornamental basins, sculptures, etc.), it is a true water garden and a unique example of an Italian 16th-century garden. The Villa d'Este, one of the first *giardini delle meraviglie*, served as a model for, and had a decisive influence on, the development of later gardens in Europe.

Palmeral of Elche, Spain

The Palmeral (palm groves) of Elche represents a remarkable example of the transference of a characteristic landscape from one culture and continent to another, in this case from North Africa to Europe. The palm grove or garden from Al-Andalus is a typical feature of the North African landscape that was brought to Europe during the Islamic occupation of the Iberian Peninsula and has survived to the present day. The ancient irrigation system, which is still functioning, is of special interest.

Champasak cultural landscape, Lao People's Democratic Republic

The Champasak cultural landscape, including the Vat Phou Temple complex, is a remarkably well-preserved planned landscape more than 1000 years old. Vat Phou exhibits a remarkable complex of monuments and other structures over an extensive area between river and mountain, with some outstanding architecture, many containing great works of art, and all expressing intense religious conviction and commitment.

It was shaped to express the Hindu vision of the relationship between nature and humanity, using an axis from mountaintop to riverbank to lay out a geometric pattern of temples, shrines and waterworks extending over some 10km. Two planned cities on the banks of the Mekong River are also part of the site, as well as Phou Kao Mountain. The whole site represents a development ranging from the 5th to 15th centuries, mainly associated with the Khmer Empire.

Sources: UNESCO (2006a, 2006b, 2006c)

- deliberate commemorative value to keep a monument alive in social consciousness; and
- contemporary use value, including practical newness value, as in reconstruction.

Reigl's values are constantly interacting – newness and historical, commemorative and age – and will continue in a state of flux as one generation's contemporary values are added to the previous generation's historical values.

Heritage is also what past generations have preserved and sometimes altered. Hence, 'the valid contribution of all periods to the building of a monument must be respected' (*Venice Charter*, Article 13). The character of a monument changes according to the amount of knowledge and interpretation of today's individual beholders. In considering such interpretations, the concepts of value and authenticity are fundamental:

Conservation of cultural heritage in all its forms and historical periods is rooted in the values attributed to the heritage. Our ability to understand these values depends, in part, on the degree to which information sources about these values may be understood as credible or truthful. Knowledge and understanding of these sources of information, in relation to original and subsequent characteristics of the cultural heritage, and their meaning, is a requisite basis for assessing all aspects of authenticity…

All judgements about values attributed to cultural properties, as well as the credibility of related information sources, may differ from culture to culture, and even within the same culture. It is thus not possible to base judgements of values and authenticity within fixed criteria. On the contrary, the respect due to all cultures requires that heritage properties must be considered and judged within the cultural contexts to which they belong (Nara Document on Authenticity, 1994, Articles 9 and 11).

So, there must be a dual authenticity: documented historic authenticity as shown in the timeline and materials, or physical authenticity, both equally important and complementary. For African sites, it has been argued that 'the spirit of the site took precedence over substance', and using the site as a living site reinforces the authenticity of spiritual values as part of the cultural context (Munjeri, 1998, p17).

Depending upon the type of cultural heritage and its cultural context, sites, places and landscapes meet the conditions of authenticity if their cultural values are truthfully and credibly expressed through a variety of attributes, including:

* form and design;
* materials and substance;
* use and function;
* traditions, techniques and management systems;
* location and setting;
* language and other forms of intangible heritage;
* spirit and feeling; and
* other internal and external factors (UNESCO, 2005j, paragraph 82).

The *Operational Guidelines for the Implementation of the World Heritage Convention* discuss the application of conditions of authenticity and integrity (UNESCO, 2005j, paragraphs 79–95). Attributes such as spirit and feeling are recognized as difficult to apply to conditions of authenticity, 'but nevertheless are important indicators of character and sense of place, for example, in communities maintaining tradition and cultural continuity'.

The heritage resource must maintain its integrity with respect to the elements of authenticity. Authentic materials underlie the design and workmanship in its original setting. Copies and reproductions are not acceptable, except in rare cases based on complete and detailed documentation of the original, as in the case of the World Heritage listed Mostar Bridge, destroyed in the Bosnian–Croatia war.

Until the 1992 amendments to the World Heritage criteria, the 'test of authenticity' was primarily directed towards built architectural and artistic monuments, arguably with a bias towards certain values associated with such monuments in particular cultures – for example, medieval Christian. In contrast to monuments of this type, indigenous cultural places do not represent a built heritage, but rather a process of close interaction between people and their environments over a long time. In many instances, the cultural values are manifestations of the ability of people to respond effectively to the challenges and opportunities presented by their natural environment. The statement in the preamble to the *Venice Charter* that 'the historic monuments of people remain to the present day as living witnesses of their age-old traditions' is applicable to a range of values, whether related to built monuments or landscapes shaped by generations of interaction between people and the natural environment (Sullivan, 1998). Many indigenous people see the presence of cultural sites in the landscape as evidence of their direct and continuing link between the present and the ancient past.

Identifying the cultural values and assessing their significance (see Case Study 17.2) will determine the degree of interest in the place/site/object and its setting, the interpretation of its character and the development of policies to conserve the values through various types of treatments or works.

Cultural sites and landscapes

What is landscape? The word 'land' has it roots in the Middle Ages and possibly earlier in Old Saxon, and denotes a geographical unit, a meadowland, heathland or common land, or units combined to form a larger land unit. 'Scape' is a variant spelling of shape: to modify and create. In its root meaning, landscape is a land shaped by its people, their institutions and customs (Tuan, 2002).

Landscape is both a way of viewing the environment surrounding us and a means of describing the environment in order to include both its natural and cultural aspects. Landscapes may refer to both an environment, usually one shaped by human action, and to a representation (particularly a painting) that signifies the meanings

Case Study **17.2**

Significance assessment, Kurnell Peninsula Headland, Australia

Kurnell Headland in Botany Bay National Park, Australia, is of outstanding heritage value to the nation. It is listed on the *Australian National Heritage List* and was assessed against the following criteria.

Criterion a: the place has outstanding heritage value to the nation because of the place's importance in the course, or pattern, of Australia's natural or cultural history.

The Meeting Place Precinct, Kurnell Peninsula, was the site of first recorded contact between indigenous people and Britain in Eastern Australia, and the dispossession of indigenous people. The discovery of Botany Bay, including Kurnell Peninsula, in April 1770 by Lieutenant James Cook, commander of the *Endeavour*, was a precursor to the colonization of Australia by Britain. The association of Cook's visit with the place is clear and well substantiated, and has been celebrated since 1822.

The Meeting Place Precinct, including Captain Cook's Landing Place, includes memorials and landscape plantings commemorating the events of 1770. Place names such as Inscription Point and Point Solander, the remnant watercourse, the memorials to explorers and indigenous inhabitants, and Cook's maps of the peninsula, in conjunction with Cook's journal, and those of officers and scientists, clearly illustrate the events of 1770. Attributes specifically associated with its indigenous values include the watering point and immediate surrounds, and the physical evidence of Aboriginal occupation in the area broadly encompassed by the watering place and the landing stage.

Criterion b: the place has outstanding heritage value to the nation because of the place's possession of uncommon, rare or endangered aspects of Australia's natural or cultural history.

As the first landfall made by Cook on continental Australia during his successful mapping of the eastern coastline, and the point of first recorded contact between the British and indigenous Australians in Eastern Australia, the place possesses rare aspects of Australia's cultural heritage and is of outstanding heritage value to the nation.

Criterion g: the place has outstanding heritage value to the nation because of the place's strong or special association with a particular community or cultural group for social, cultural or spiritual reasons.

Captain Cook's Landing Place at Kurnell Peninsula is considered by many to be of outstanding heritage value to the nation for its association with the 'the birth of the nation'. The events hold a different meaning for indigenous Australians, marking the commencement of colonization of Australia, and dispossession, underpinned by the doctrine of *terra nullius*. The story of Cook's first landing on the east coast of Australia is nationally important, and Captain Cook's Landing Place has become a symbolic place representing an important national story.

The story of Cook's voyage, including Cook's landing place at Kurnell and first contact between the British and indigenous Australians on the eastern seaboard, has become an integral part of Australian folklore and our collective psyche. There are Captain Cook stories in many parts of Aboriginal Australia, including remote areas such as Central Australia and the Victoria River Downs, Northern Territory. The events have been well documented by many authors, acknowledging the place's important association with indigenous Australians at a national level.

Criterion h: the place has outstanding heritage value to the nation because of the place's special association with the life or works of a person, or group of persons, or importance in Australia's natural or cultural history.

On this, Cook's first of three voyages in the Pacific, Joseph Banks was botanist, assisted by Daniel Solander and the artists Sydney Parkinson, Alexander Buchan and Herman Sporing. The artists were to produce botanical, zoological and ethnographic drawings. Banks and Solander collected 83 specimens, many of which are now the type specimens of species and genera, including *Banksia*. Both Banks and Solander as scientists on Cook's crew are remembered by local geographical place names; Cape Banks and Point Solander have defined the entrance to Botany Bay since 1770.

Attributes clearly associated with the landing are included within the Meeting Place Precinct. Although the location of botanical specimens collected by Banks and Solander was referred to generically as 'Botany Bay', the landing place, as the site of first exposure to the environment, was a key source of botanical specimens and species types. A number of species, including *Angophora costata* woodland on the adjacent headland areas and a native violet at the watering place, named after Banks, occur in close proximity to the landing site.

Source: Department of the Environment and Heritage (2005)

attached to the setting. While landscape painting is a mode of representation that signifies ideas and values about the scene depicted, the construction of monuments, lakes, groves and avenues turns the land itself into a signifier, a process colonizing nature by landscape (Olwig, 1993).

Some civilizations and cultures do not have a word for landscape. The peoples of India, the ancient Greeks and the Australian Aborigines have a specific relation, physical and associative, with their environment; but this relation cannot be described in terms of landscape. The first use of the term 'landscape' as a way of viewing the environment (especially in painting), was in China around the 4th century AD, later in Italy and Flanders in the 15th century.

The definition of the term 'landscape' has evolved and different disciplines have favoured their exclusive definitions – art historians, geographers, anthropologists and archaeologists. Landscape can be:

- the topography of a region;
- terrain that people inhabit and embed with reciprocal meanings;
- a piece of land overseen from a vantage point;
- an object;
- an experience; or
- a representation of something.

It has different meanings for different social groups and is understood and experienced in many different ways. Currently, there are converging approaches to landscape: through an ecological approach focused on complex interactions of natural processes that shape characteristic land areas, and extending its concerns to the ways in which human activities interact with these natural processes; and through a cultural studies approach emphasizing context and processes where meanings shape 'nature' through human cognition and representation in symbols, signs and language (Cosgrove, 2003).

Cultural landscapes

Cultural landscape has been a fundamental concept for geographers since its first use in Germany in the 1890s when the social geographer Friedrich Ratzel defined *Kulturlandschaft* as an area modified by human activity as opposed to the primeval natural landscape. The German school emphasized the material aspects of culture, such as buildings still visible in the landscape, rather than the non-material aspects, such as customs and traditions (Livingstone, 1992). At the same time, the French school of *géographie humaine* enquired into how people, environment and lifestyle determine the face of the countryside (Aitchison, 1995). The French geographer Vidal de la Blanche acknowledged that different regions, *le pays*, have their own characteristics as a result of human influences. The American geographer, Carl Sauer, introduced the term 'cultural landscape' to the English-speaking world:

> The cultural landscape is fashioned out of a natural landscape by a culture group. Culture is the agent, the natural area is the medium; the cultural landscape is the result. Under the influence of a given culture, itself changing through time, the landscape undergoes development, passing through phases and probably reaching the end of its cycle of development. With the introduction of a different, that is, alien culture, a rejuvenation of the landscape sets in, or a new landscape is superimposed on remnants of an older one. The natural landscape is of course of fundamental importance, for it supplies the materials out of which the cultural landscape is formed. The shaping force, however, lies in culture itself (Sauer, 1925, p46).

Sauer's contribution contains many of the ideas that are now the current concern of heritage conservation – interrelationships over time, distinguishable patterns in the landscape of changing activities and layers of evidence. However, it was suggested then that since the cultural elements in the landscape merely constitute a collection of parts of the total landscape, 'unaltered natural landscapes and those uncontrolled by man' might be called 'wild landscapes' in contrast to 'tamed' or 'cultivated' landscapes (Hartshorne, 1939, p348).

Cultural landscapes became a concept for analysing the ties between culture and the environment in two methods of study: examining visual material evidence in the landscape, such as building types and field patterns, and examining cultural perceptions and visual preferences. Landscapes were seen as the repository of history and the storehouse of both collective and private memories:

> The landscape as a whole – that largely manmade tapestry, in which all other artefacts are embedded ... which gives them their sense of place (Lowenthal, 1981, p12).

The ambiguity of the use of the word 'landscape' for vernacular, ordinary, designed or inspirational places, problems of translation between disciplines and uncertainties of exact meaning have been discussed frequently. But the United States National Park Service has provided direction for the cultural landscape movement (Alanen and Melnick, 2000).

In 1981, the US National Park Service recognized cultural landscapes as a specific resource type and in 1984 published *Cultural Landscapes: Rural Historic Districts in the National Parks System* (Melnick et al, 1984) that set out criteria for identifying and defining cultural landscapes. Since then, the US National Park Service has provided intellectual and practical leadership through its register bulletins and publications, and through its own research, interpretation, treatment and management of cultural landscapes within the protected area system. The National Park Service defines the cultural landscape as:

> ... a geographic area, including both cultural and natural resources and the wildlife or domestic animals therein, associated with a historic event, activity or person, or exhibiting other cultural or aesthetic values. (NPS 1994).

Four general types of cultural landscapes, not mutually exclusive, are also their management responsibility: historic sites, historic designed landscapes, historic vernacular landscapes and ethnographic landscapes (see Box 17.1). These categories have been highly influential internationally for land-use planners and protected area managers.

The concept of 'place' linking natural heritage and cultural values was applied in Australia through the Australia ICOMOS *Burra Charter*. This enabled the idea of conserving an extensive place – a landscape with cultural significance resulting from associative values through symbolic meanings given to it. The Australian Heritage Commission, established in 1975, registered modified landscapes such as historic precincts, townships and mining areas. The initial *Register of the National Estate* concentrated on sites, buildings and natural areas. However, the term cultural landscape was not used by the commission until 1980 when the Tasman Peninsula was promoted as a cultural landscape as a means of linking all of the historic convict sites and their surrounding landscapes (Lennon, 2005a).

Box 17.1 US National Park Service cultural landscape categories

1   *Historic site:* a landscape significant for its association with a historic event, activity or person.
2   *Historic designed landscapes:* a landscape that was consciously designed or laid out by a landscape gardener, architect, engineer or horticulturalist according to design principles, or an amateur gardener working in a recognized style or tradition. The landscape may be associated with a significant person, trend or event in landscape architecture, or illustrate an important development in the theory and practice of landscape architecture. Aesthetic values play a significant role in designed landscapes.
3   *Historic vernacular landscape:* a landscape that evolved through use by people whose activities or occupancy shared it. Through social or cultural attitudes of an individual, a family or a community, the landscape reflects the physical, biological and cultural character of everyday lives. Function plays a significant role in vernacular landscapes. This can be a farm complex or a district of historic farmsteads along a river valley – rural historic districts or agricultural landscapes.
4   *Ethnographic landscapes:* a landscape containing a variety of natural and cultural resources that associated people define as heritage resources – contemporary settlements, sacred religious sites, massive geological structures with small plant communities, animals, and subsistence and ceremonial grounds.

Source: NPS (1994)

Cultural landscapes and World Heritage

Although the World Heritage Convention brought together natural and cultural places under one framework in 1972, there was no mechanism for recognizing sites that were the result of the interplay between cultural and natural values – that is, landscapes of outstanding universal value. Many properties inscribed on the *World Heritage List* are, in fact, landscapes and might have been inscribed as cultural landscapes if such nominations had been possible prior to 1992. These include some of the great gardens such as Versailles and the Alhambra, archaeological sites such as Stonehenge and Hadrian's Wall in the UK and the M'Zab Valley in Algeria, or the mixed sites of Mount Athos and Meteora in Greece and Hierapolis-Pamukkale in Turkey. Many natural sites, such as Sagarmatha in Nepal, St Kilda in the UK and the Grand Canyon in the US, have important cultural values that must be accounted for by management.

Cultural heritage protection in Europe was dominated by the ideas of art historians and focused on single monuments. This led to preservation or reconstruction of single, unique objects at some clearly defined phase in their existence, a museum-like approach that excluded dynamic processes and context. Nature protection reflected the goal of protecting threatened species and 'untouched' nature, and natural areas were similarly excluded from their surrounding context, including human activities. The emphasis in nature conservation on nature reserves and species protection saw humans as 'a nuisance', and human influences and modifications signified loss in value (Plachter and Rössler, 1995).

The World Heritage Convention was also criticized for its narrow interpretation of culture and its failure to address the concept of cultural continuity. The Australian World Heritage nominations of Kakadu National Park, the Willandra Lakes Region and the Tasmanian Wilderness National Parks, in accordance with cultural criterion (iii), which includes the notion of a 'civilization which has disappeared' (UNESCO, 1997, paragraph 24), highlighted this deficiency. The significance of Kakadu National Park resided not only in Kakadu's sacred sites, but also in the

way 'the region as Aboriginal land symbolizes Aboriginal control over such important places and the survival of Aboriginal communities as political, social and spiritual entities' (McBryde, 1990, p15). Cultural criterion (iii) did not in any way express this significance of Kakadu or any other cultural landscape in Australia as a place symbolically representative of the continuing survival of Aboriginal culture in Australia.

These concerns were shared globally through the convergence of fieldwork in anthropology, archaeology and heritage management, creating a platform for new perspectives on the concept of cultural landscape. Archaeology shifted from the antiquarian focus on the alienated artefact, towards a concern with social and spatial context in the landscape (Thomas, 1993). Landscape was where adaptive relations between people and the land have been maintained so that today the landscape is processual and transforming. It is also subject to poetic interpretation and a place where values and emotion coincide (Morphy, 1993). The inevitability of this dynamic operating in landscape was also recognized in 1992 by the IUCN in its acceptance of cultural landscapes as a category of protected areas (Lucas, 1992).

Changes to the World Heritage cultural criteria were discussed in the context of recognizing the past and continuing role of hunter–gatherer societies in managing and maintaining the landscape and acknowledging the continuing associative values of landscapes and landscape features to indigenous peoples. It was recognized that the cultural criteria failed to incorporate the idea of cultural continuity from prehistoric times to the present-day existence of living traditional cultures. Accordingly, criterion 24 (a) (iii) was altered in 1992 to read 'a civilization which is living or which has disappeared'. Revisions to the cultural heritage criteria included reference to 'landscape design', 'landscape' and 'land use' in criteria (ii), (iv) and (vi), respectively In addition, reference to 'cultural tradition', 'significant stages(s) of human history' and 'living traditions' were included to recognize the continuing traditions of local indigenous peoples in cultural heritage criteria (iii) and (iv), respectively. The concept of surviving 'living traditions' and cultural continuity were incorporated within the text of criterion (vi) and the associative values referred to in that criterion were expanded to include reference to 'artistic or literary works' (Layton and Titchen, 1995, p23). The following categories of World Heritage cultural landscape are now recognized:

1   The most easily identifiable category is the clearly defined landscape designed and created intentionally by humans. This embraces garden and parkland landscapes constructed for aesthetic reasons that are often (but not always) associated with religious or other monumental buildings and ensembles.

2   The second category is the organically evolved landscape. This results from an initial social, economic, administrative and/or religious imperative, and has developed its present form by association with, and in response to, its natural environment. Such landscapes reflect that process of evolution in their form and component features. They fall into two sub-categories. A relict (or fossil) landscape is one in which an evolutionary process came to an end at some time in the past, either abruptly or over a period. Its significant distinguishing features are, however, still visible in material form. A continuing landscape is one that retains an active social role in contemporary society closely associated with the traditional way of life, and in which the evolutionary process is still in progress. At the same time, it exhibits significant material evidence of its evolution over time.

3   The final category is the associative cultural landscape. The inclusion of such landscapes on the *World Heritage List* is justifiable by virtue of the powerful religious, artistic or cultural associations of the natural element, rather than material cultural evidence, which may be insignificant or even absent (UNESCO, 2005j, Annex 3, paragraph 10).

In 1993, Tongariro National Park in New Zealand became the first property to be inscribed on the *World Heritage List* under the revised criteria describing cultural landscapes. The volcanic mountains at the heart of the park play a fundamental role through oral tradition in defining and confirming the cultural identity of the Ngati Tuwharetoa iwi (Maori) people: the two are indissolubly linked. A basic sense of continuity through *tupuna* (ancestors) is manifested in the form of profound reverence for the mountain peaks. The natural beauty of Tongariro is the spiritual and historical centre of Maori culture.

By way of contrast, the Kalwaria Zebrzydowska (Poland) cultural landscape was inscribed in 1999 on the basis of criteria (ii) and (iv). It is a cultural landscape of great beauty and spiritual quality. Its natural setting, in which a linked series of symbolic places of worship relating to the passion of Christ and the life of the Virgin Mary was laid out at the beginning of the 17th century, has remained virtually unchanged and is today a continuing place of pilgrimage – a living spiritual place. However, it was inscribed primarily as a place of cultural tradition, not as a place of associative spiritual value. It is a prototype of an Eastern European tradition, just as the use of the symbol of *coquille St Jacques* (French for 'cockle [a shellfish] of St James') became a prototype motif in Western European tradition in places of pilgrimage, such as Santiago de Compostela.

In 1995, UNESCO published *Cultural Landscapes of Universal Value – Components of a Global Strategy* (von Droste et al, 1995), which provided examples of cultural landscapes from all regions of the world. It included specific studies on 'the identification and protection of routes, canals, rice cultures and their terraced landscapes, as well as associative cultural landscapes in the Asia-Pacific region'. It was hoped that these would provide baselines for future assessments of cultural landscapes using comparative studies of similar types within a region (Plachter and Rössler, 1995, pp17–18).

The term 'cultural landscape' now embraces a diversity of manifestations of the interaction between humankind and its natural environment:

Cultural landscapes are cultural properties and represent the 'combined works of nature and man'… They are illustrative of the evolution of human society and settlement over time, under the influence of the physical constraints and/or opportunities presented by their natural environment and of successive social, economic and cultural forces, both external and internal (UNESCO, 2005j, paragraph 47).

Cultural landscape can be seen as the repository of collective memory. Since the advent of industrialization and the evolution of a scientifically oriented culture, many people have realized that they have lost their spiritual connection with landscape. Inspirational landscapes may become familiar to people through their depiction in paintings, poetry or song. This is the case with Hallstatt-Dachstein for Austrians, with their love of alpine scenery, and with Mount Huangshan, an archetype of landscape in Chinese painting in the Tang dynasty when countless *shanshui* (mountain and water) paintings celebrated 'the loveliest mountain in China'. The Lake District of England is a good example of landscape associated with poetry.

Associative cultural landscapes may include large or small contiguous or non-contiguous areas and itineraries, routes or other linear landscapes or seascapes — these may be physical entities or mental images embedded in people's spirituality, cultural tradition and practice. Important examples include the sacred mountains of Taishan, Lushan and Mount Emei in China; Aboriginal dreaming tracks in Australia; the spread of Polynesian culture across the Pacific Ocean; the Silk Road from China to the West; and the pilgrimage routes to Jerusalem, Santiago de Compostela and Mecca.

Landscapes and nature conservation

Many cultural landscapes are important for nature conservation and may contain habitats valuable to the conservation of biodiversity. The *Operational Guidelines for the Implementation of the World Heritage Convention* summarize the natural qualities of cultural landscapes:

> *Cultural landscapes often reflect specific techniques of sustainable land use, considering the characteristics and limits of the natural environment they are*

Lake District National Park, UK

Source: IUCN Photo Library © Jim Thorsell

established in, and a specific spiritual relation to nature. Protection of cultural landscapes can contribute to modern techniques of sustainable land use and can maintain or enhance natural values in the landscape. The continued existence of traditional forms of land use supports biological diversity in many regions of the world. The protection of traditional cultural landscapes is therefore helpful in maintaining biological diversity (UNESCO, 2005j, Annex 3, paragraph 9).

Protected landscapes (IUCN Category V, discussed in Chapter 3, p82) are landscapes whose exceptional natural and cultural values have led to measures for their protection. They are natural landscapes that have been transformed by human action, but also places where the natural setting has shaped the way in which people live, their types of settlement and their way of life. These protected landscapes may provide some important lessons on how to achieve sustainable living. They are usually places of outstanding visual quality, rich in biodiversity and cultural value because of the presence of people. Importantly, they represent a practical way of achieving conservation objectives on private working lands.

Category V 'Protected landscapes or seascapes' relate most closely to cultural landscapes of the World Heritage categories. For example, the open low-impact grazing system that has led to the development of a steppe-like ecosystem and the survival of a rich diversity of endemic plant species on Sweden's Southern Öland was one of the reasons for its World Heritage cultural landscape designation (see Case Study 4.3 in Chapter 4).

IUCN (1994) has also identified the following benefits within protected landscapes/seascapes:

- conserving nature and biodiversity;
- buffering more strictly controlled areas;
- conserving human history in structures and land-use patterns;
- maintaining traditional ways of life;
- offering recreation and inspiration;
- providing education and understanding; and
- demonstrating durable systems of use in harmony with nature.

The protected landscape approach has been most used in Europe; but there is evidence of its wider application in the small island states of the Pacific and Caribbean, the mountains of the Andes, the traditional coffee-growing areas of Central America, the landscapes of New England and the rice terraces of the Philippines. Many of these are also cultural landscapes in the World Heritage categories. Case Study 17.3 describes a transborder area that is both a cultural landscape and a national park.

As noted in Chapter 2 (p67), a major paradigm shift has occurred in which protected area management has moved from a focus on 'islands' of protected habitats to embrace the wider landscape, including lived-in, working landscapes. There is a new understanding of the link between nature and culture, where healthy landscapes have been shaped by human interaction and biological diversity often coincides with cultural diversity. The new paradigm promoted by the IUCN for protected landscapes was further reinforced at the 2003 World Parks Congress, where it was recommended that 'all protected area systems recognize and incorporate spiritual values of protected areas and culture-based approaches to conservation' (Recommendation 5.13).

In the following two subsections, Europe is used as an example of how cultural landscapes are treated in a particular region, and forests are used as an example of how cultural landscapes relate to a particular biome.

European landscapes

The European Landscape Convention adopted by member states of the Council of Europe and the World Heritage Committee in Florence in October 2000 is a recent example of high-level cooperation. It is also recognition that landscape is an essential feature of human surroundings, that it contributes to the formation of local cultures and that it is a basic component of the European natural and cultural heritage, contributing to human well-being and consolidation of the European identity.

The convention notes that developments in agriculture, forestry, industrial and mineral production techniques, and in town planning, transport, infrastructure, tourism and recreation practices, including, at a more general level,

Case Study 17.3

Mont Perdu World Heritage Site, France and Spain

The Mont Perdu World Heritage Site of 30,639ha lies within two national parks, contiguous along the national frontier between France and Spain in the central Pyrénées. There are 2000 inhabitants distributed between three villages in France, with 700 inhabitants distributed between five villages in Spain. The Gavarnie area was a significant tourist destination of the European Romantic Movement during the early 19th century, and is now a skiing destination. In the south, around le Parc d'Ordesa y Monte Perdido, considerable rural desertion has occurred and little modernization. The whole landscape is visually dominated by Mont Perdu (3353m) and a range of spectacular mountains.

The two parks are very different environmentally: on steep north-facing slopes, much rain and winter snow has resulted in a ski-tourism industry, and wide areas of upland summer pasture; along south-facing slopes, a dissected and eroded landscape experiences long droughts, resulting in both densely vegetated gorges and sparsely vegetated uplands. The natural characteristics of geology, altitude and climate have resulted in a landscape above 2000m that is free of trees and scrub, studded with broad grassy areas. This pattern occurs on both the drier Spanish side and the wetter French side.

Transhumance (seasonal movement of herds) is the cultural mechanism that links the two areas. Grasslands west of Gavarnie in France provide summer pastures for Aragonese herds from the Broto Valley in Spain; but the practice documented over 700 years predates such national distinctions. It results in short-cropped herbage, which is clearly not 'natural' on the French slopes, linking habitats across the boundary of two national parks and the frontier of two countries. Yet, for the people following this pastoral lifestyle, there is no frontier. Mont Perdu is perceived by the local population as one space without boundaries – a cultural landscape.

At the time of World Heritage inscription, the two national parks had negotiated a charter of cooperation, identifying common objectives and practices. However, there was a lack of understanding by local people of the significance of transhumance as a way of life, and also of the natural and human geography through which it moves. The local Association Mont-Perdu Patrimoine mondiale stated that, in future, it will concentrate on collaborating with those who work the land in order to reconnect land use and landscape in exemplary ways 'to encourage our other partners more concerned with the short term than [with] the historical continuity of these open spaces'.

Such issues are familiar worldwide, wherever countryside management intersects with local landowners and workers. Meanwhile, transhumance continues, supported by both national parks. Their primary management aim is to maintain the conditions for transhumance, not merely as an interesting historical survival, but very much as the basis of the way of life of the communities affected by the inscription of the World Heritage cultural landscape on both sides of the frontier.

Source: adapted from de Bellefon (2000)

changes in the world economy, have the effect of continually transforming landscapes. It also acknowledges that the public expect to play an active part in the development of landscapes and to enjoy high-quality landscapes; and that landscape is a key element of individual and social well-being and that its conservation entails rights and responsibilities for everyone.

The contracting parties to the convention agreed to implement four general measures at national level: recognition of landscapes in law; implementation of landscape protection policies; public participation in landscape planning; and integrating landscape within regional and town planning, and cultural, environmental, agricultural, social and economic policies, as well as any

others with possible direct or indirect impact on the landscape. Terms used in the convention are defined to ensure uniform interpretation: 'landscape', 'landscape policy', 'landscape quality objective', 'landscape protection', 'landscape management' and 'landscape planning' (Déjeant-Pons, 2003).

Some European landscapes are also of World Heritage status, and residents and managers have also sought national park status for such areas as a means of ensuring national government support for conservation.

Conservation planning for European rural landscapes involves examining generic problems; but the solutions have to be specific and practical, while recognizing the cultures and institutions of

Case Study **17.4**

Cinque Terre, Italy

The Ligurian coastal region between Cinque Terre and Portovenere in Italy is a scenic and historic landscape. The form and siting of the five small towns and the shaping of their surrounding landscape, overcoming the disadvantages of a steep and broken terrain, graphically encapsulate the continuous history of human settlement over the past millennium. The site was inscribed on the *World Heritage List* in 1997. The landscape, with its steep terraces rising from the shoreline of the Mediterranean Sea, was seriously damaged by post-World War II external changes that disrupted the traditional system: people emigrated, the land was abandoned, terraces were collapsing due to lack of maintenance, and viticulture on an economic scale broke down so that grapes had to be imported during the 1980s.

Revitalization has come from within the five communities – people concerned about loss of identity formed a cooperative to produce and market the traditional wine of the region, and to redevelop the landscape. This requires complexity in design to preserve the whole: zoning the terraces according to soils and drainage; prescribing building and housing upgrades; new subdivision; connecting tourists with the terraced landscapes through trekking and education; and being able to purchase abandoned terraces so that external funds flow into site restoration.

The 5000 residents asked for national park status to protect their World Heritage-listed landscape. Now, skilled Albanian refugees are moving in to repair the stone terraces, house prices have risen 300 per cent since inscription, and the new threat is tourism – there are 2 million visitors annually, of whom 60 per cent are from overseas. A management plan for Cinque Terre National Park integrates protection and conservation of the landscape and its continuing use for cultivation. Survival of the landscape and its inscribed heritage values is dependent upon its continuing economic viability.

Source: adapted from Lennon (2001)

Terraces above Riomaggiore, Cinque Terre, Italy

Source: Jane Lennon

places (Besio, 2003). Determining limits of acceptable change in these landscapes and managing that process of change is fundamental to their conservation, as illustrated in changing viticulture in, and tourism to, the terraced landscapes of the Italian Cinque Terre (see Case Study 17.4) or Amalfi coast (Lennon, 2001).

In French regional parks, which are similar to English national parks with their stricter planning controls, much restoration and rehabilitation is under way. In the Parc Naturel Régional du Luberon, many villages belong to the 'prettiest villages in France' designation and are thriving tourist attractions. Surrounding working farms may offer restored *gîtes* in old farm buildings; these are popular with hikers crossing the countryside on long-distance paths. Local authorities – and there are 36,000 *mairies* – can protect rural villages through designation of *secteurs sauvegardés*; national incentives then apply through a tax rebate equivalent to the amount spent, which is deducted from the total tax payable.

In summary, there is an increased awareness across Europe of the value of the landscape and, especially, designated cultural landscapes. This is reflected in the huge range of incentives to manage these landscapes and promote their stories and attractions. It is also recognized in the adoption of uniform terminology and planning provisions for landscape conservation.

Cultural landscapes and forests

The forest as a landscape type has been regarded in Western history as a wilderness, a place of darkness and evil spirits (Schama, 1995). However, evidence now shows how pre-Christian era populations manipulated these forests for their own use by fire, and the forested landscape today is a result of these long-term impacts.

It has been shown that the European forest existed only in relatively discrete pockets, confined to upland regions, and that the grazing habits of Holocene large mammals created the landscape patterns which were then sustained and exploited by human occupation (Vera, 2002). This has ramifications for the current landscape conservation policy of preserving remnants of primeval forest by excluding grazing animals, and has led to dense re-growth of Bielowieza Forest, on the Polish–Byelorussian border, in which the bison grazing meadows are kept artificially open by mowing. This ecological management supports the argument that 'nature' is as much an outcome of human discourse as of 'natural' processes (Cosgrove, 2003). Forest landscapes have provided symbols of antiquity and group identification, as shown in Case Study 17.5.

Guidance for protected area managers in relation to actions they can take to conserve cultural landscapes is discussed in the further section on 'Conserving historic sites'.

Conserving indigenous heritage

The heritage of indigenous and minority groups is part of living culture, and its expression is often invisible in the landscape managed by the dominant group, especially in colonized settler societies such as Canada, the US, the Amazon basin, Australia and South Africa. The adoption by the World Heritage Committee of the cultural landscapes categories established a mechanism, in 1992, for recognizing cultural values in natural areas and living cultural values expressed in the landscape (see the earlier section on 'Cultural sites and landscapes' and Case Study 17.6).

There is a growing literature on the cultural and spiritual values of biodiversity (see, for example, Posey, 1999). These cover bio-cultural diversity linking language, knowledge and the environment (Maffi, 2001); conserving the sacred in the landscape, in groves and mountains (Ramakrishnan et al, 1998; Ramakrishnan, 2003); and managing intangible knowledge of indigenous people in the landscape by merging values-based and knowledge-based systems (Andrade, 2000; English and Lee, 2003).

The environment represents a storied landscape resounding with cultural values, and environmental dialogue can be predicated not on the repression of indigenous people and the mystification of wilderness, but on an awareness of nature as contested terrain. This does not excuse 'deforesting the Earth'; but Michael Williams, professor of geography at Oxford University, through his detailed global audit, challenges naive characterizations of 'pristine forests' (Williams, 2003).

There are many examples all over the world of forests and plants conserved for their spiritual

Case Study 17.5

Qadisha Valley, Lebanon

Over centuries, Maronite monks have found the Qadisha Valley a suitable place for the development of eremitic life. Its natural caves, carved into the hillsides – almost inaccessible, scattered, irregular and comfortless – provide the material environment necessary for their life of contemplation and mortification. A specific spiritual relationship developed between this landscape and the needs of hermits. Caves laid out as hermitages or chapels and monasteries – with interiors covered with frescoes, façades added, flights of stairs cut into the rock and hillsides transformed into terraced fields – are techniques specific to the practical use of the Qadisha Valley by these hermits. This is the largest concentration of hillside hermitages going back to the very origins of Christianity.

The ancient text known as the *Epic of Gilgamesh*, found in central Mesopotamia, makes reference to the Qadisha Forest and describes the cedars of Lebanon (*Cedrus libani*) as sacred trees. The forest contains 3000-year-old trees, the last direct witnesses to Biblical times. They are mentioned 103 times in the Bible. These giant trees know the history of humankind and are worthy of international protection. Pilgrims have been coming since the 17th century from all over the world to admire this beautiful forest. The cedar has been adopted as the emblem of the Lebanese national flag.

In 1998, this area on the western flank of Mount Lebanon was nominated as a cultural landscape of outstanding universal value. However, an overall management and conservation plan was required for the monastic sites and monuments of the Qadisha Valley and for the cedar forest. This was done, and the site was inscribed on the *World Heritage List*. One of the major problems today is the implementation of the management plan, including the establishment of a commission to coordinate the activities of the different owners and agencies involved, and the definition of an effective buffer zone.

Source: adapted from Rössler (2001)

values. Ancient trees, such as redwoods in the US, yews in Europe and sacred trees in India, are revered along with 'sacred groves' found in Ghana, Kenya, Venezuela, Nepal, China and India (Barrow and Pathak, 2005). The Dai people in the Xishuangbanna region, Yunnan Province, of south-west China manage holy hills or *nong*, where the gods reside; these forested hills, numbering about 400 between 30,000ha and 40,000ha in extent, form green islands in which all utilization of timber is prohibited (Shengji, 1999). The sacred forest groves of Ghana were also set aside and protected by customary law; these often small areas support sacred, totem or tabooed species, burial grounds and shrines. The 5 square kilometre Nkodurom grove has been preserved for over 300 years by village chiefs who are responsible for maintenance, with a management regime that is governed by taboos, including prohibition on all forms of use, no access except for those performing traditional rites, no access on Thursdays (the day when spirits are resting) and no access for menstruating women. Sacred groves, islands of biodiversity, have survived because of

strong spiritual and cultural attachments to the groves; but erosion of traditional beliefs is threatening their survival (Ntiamoa-Baidu, 1995). This is also the case in the Philippines rice terraces (see Case Study 17.7).

How do we ensure the conservation of indigenous heritage by its own custodians, those who inherited it and have a duty to care for their storied landscapes?

Community conserved areas (CCAs) are one example (see Chapter 21). While these areas might be primarily conserved for providing subsistence living needs or to arrest environmental degradation, they also conserve cultural heritage and biodiversity. They include coastal fishing areas, village forests, sacred ponds and grasslands (Pathak et al, 2003). Other models involve formal joint management arrangements with national park authorities. In 2002, the Alto Fragua-Indiwasi National Park was created on the highly biodiverse piedmont of the Colombian Amazon, the first time that an indigenous community was the principal designer and manager of a protected area recognized by the government of Colombia.

Case Study 17.6

Indigenous values of Uluru–Kata Tjuta National Park, Australia

In 1994, Uluru–Kata Tjuta National Park became the second World Heritage property, after Tongariro, to be listed for its associative cultural values. It had already been listed for its natural values; however, it is an outstanding example of the traditional land use known as hunting and gathering. Relatively few contemporary hunting and gathering cultures now exist throughout the world. The World Heritage values include the continuing cultural landscape of the Anangu Tjukurpa that constitutes the landscape of Uluru–Kata Tjuta National Park and which:

- is an outstanding example of a traditional human type of settlement and land use – namely, hunting and gathering – that dominated the entire Australian continent up to modern times;
- shows the interactions between humans and their environment;
- is, in large part, the outcome of millennia of management using traditional Anangu methods governed by the *Tjukurpa* ('the Law');
- is one of relatively few places in Australia where landscapes are actively managed by Aboriginal communities on a substantial scale, using traditional practices and knowledge that include:
  - particular types of social organization, ceremonies and rituals which form an adaptation to the fragile and unpredictable ecosystems of the arid landscape;
  - detailed systems of ecological knowledge that closely parallel, yet differ from, the Western scientific classification; and
  - management techniques to conserve biodiversity, such as the use of fire and the creation and maintenance of water sources, such as wells and rock holes.

Uluru–Kata Tjuta National Park is directly and tangibly associated with events, living traditions, ideas and beliefs of outstanding universal significance. The World Heritage values include:

- the continuing cultural landscape of Uluru–Kata Tjuta National Park, which is imbued with the values of creative powers of cultural history through the *Tjukurpa* and the phenomenon of sacred sites;
- the associated powerful religious, artistic and cultural qualities of this cultural landscape; and
- the network of ancestral tracks established during the *Tjukurpa*, in which Uluru and Kata Tjuta are meeting points.

The *Tjukurpa* is an outstanding example of an indigenous philosophy. It is founded upon a time when heroic beings, who combined the attributes of humans and animals, camped and travelled across the landscape. As they did, they shaped and created the features of the land. The actions of the heroes established the code of behaviour followed by Anangu today, which regulates all aspects of life, from foraging behaviour and management of the landscape to social relationships and personal identity. It is expressed in verbal narratives through lengthy inma (song cycles and associated ritual), through art and through the landscape itself. For Anangu, the landscape is the narratives, songs and art of the *Tjukurpa*.

Source: adapted from Lennon (2001)

In the Peruvian highlands, six communities of the Quechua people have established el Parque de la Papa to conserve 1200 potato varieties occurring in over 8500ha of communal land, as well as natural ecosystems of the Andes. This is the pilot project for the Ruta Sagrada del Condor-Wiracocha network of protected landscapes based on traditional agriculture across seven countries from Venezuela to Chile, covering the pre-Hispanic Andean region (Sarmiento et al, 2005).

In Australia, the development of Indigenous protected areas conserving biodiversity and culture has proceeded rapidly. Indigenous protected areas covered 2.6 million hectares and indigenous people managed nearly 15 per cent of Australia's land area in 1996 (Lennon et al, 2001, p116). This reflects, in part, the passage of land rights legislation in various states and territories during the 1970s and 1980s, and the 1993 Commonwealth *Native Title Act*, which recognizes that pre-existing rights of Indigenous Peoples to land and waters may have survived the process of

Case Study 17.7

Rice terraces of the Cordilleras, the Philippines

The rice terraces in the Cordillera mountain range in the far north of Luzon Island, the largest island in the Philippine archipelago, are at altitudes varying from 700m to 1500m above sea level. They cover 20,000 square kilometres, or approximately 7 per cent of the land mass of the Philippines, and extend over the five provinces of Kalinga-Apayao, Abra, the Mountain Province, Benguet and Ifugao. The human population is comprised of eight major ethno-linguistic groups, with a density of 100 to 250 inhabitants per square kilometre.

The fragile terraced landscape was the first living (continuing) cultural landscape inscribed on the *World Heritage List* in 1995, and owes its preservation to the strong spiritual values of the Ifugao culture that has been guiding all aspects of daily life for over 1000 years. The spirit world of the tribal mountain culture is deeply rooted to the highland lifestyle and environment, expressed in a wealth of artistic output and in the traditional environmental management system and agricultural practices that remain in place today. The special high-altitude rice is traditionally harvested by women chanting the *hud hud*, a chant proclaimed by the United Nations Educational, Scientific and Cultural Organization (UNESCO) as one of the 19 masterpieces of the Oral Intangible Heritage of Humanity in 2001.

On the national level, maintaining the traditional values, whether spiritual or physical, is under severe threat due to the pressing demands of modernization, the urgent socio-economic needs of the community, and the lack of support from national authorities who are not aware that preservation of the cultural values that reinforce the continuation of the traditional agricultural system must be supported along with the physical conservation of the terraces. Airports, highways and tourism infrastructure are also threatening the endangered site and its community.

Change is difficult to manage in the Philippine Cordilleras. The terraces follow the contours of the highest peaks of the mountain range. The narrow rice fields are built in clusters from stone and mud. Privately owned forests (*muyong*) that play an important part in maintaining the water cycle encircle terrace clusters. A traditionally designed hydraulic system with sluices and canals democratically delivers an unobstructed water supply, starting from the highest terrace and descending to the lowest. Access severely limits the introduction of farm animals or machinery into the terraces, making all agricultural activities and wall maintenance manual work. The irrigation system has suffered extensive earthquake damage that has misaligned the distribution system. Portions of the traditional system constructed of natural materials, which possessed a pliability that allowed the network to adjust to minor Earth movements or heavy rain, have been lost. Natural materials are no longer readily available, and recent experiments in repairing the system with rigid concrete have been a failure.

Visual characteristics of the landscape are disappearing. Clusters of villages with steep pyramidal roofs of thatch were the most striking landscape features. An existing programme assists owners of houses to replace galvanized iron sheets with thatch once again. Technical solutions are being carried out on site in the areas of agriculture, forestry and hydraulics. Joining traditional knowledge with technology, a UNESCO-aided project for geographic information system (GIS) mapping of the site commenced in January 2001 to generate the non-existent baseline data needed for site management planning.

Despite the formation of the Ifugao Terraces Commission and preparation of a master plan for the four terrace clusters that are the nucleus of the World Heritage site, lack of awareness was preventing proper management. National authorities needed to simultaneously preserve the intertwining network of culture, nature, agriculture and environment that are the elements of the site. In 2001, the World Heritage Committee placed the property on the *List of World Heritage in Danger*.

As a result, financial aid of US$1 million was granted from the National Commission for Culture and the Arts for site rehabilitation under the responsibility of the Ifugao provincial government, which has returned responsibility to the community. Cultural revival programmes at schools and transfer of traditional ecological knowledge are occurring, and a revised management plan has been developed.

Source: adapted from Villalón (2005)

European occupation. In 2000, a new category of Indigenous protected areas was established and 13 areas have been declared, covering almost 13.5 million hectares.

Traditional owners and Indigenous custodians must be involved in managing their heritage in protected areas (see Case Study 17.8). They rightly fear misappropriation or theft of their intellectual

Case Study 17.8

Indigenous management of Uluru–Kata Tjuta National Park, Australia

The expansion of values recognized in the World Heritage listing facilitated changing priorities in managing Uluru–Kata Tjuta National Park, Australia, as reflected in the current management plan, which states that acknowledgement of the place as a cultural landscape is fundamental to the success of the joint management arrangement. This plan is the first to recognize the primacy in land management of the cultural practice of the traditional owners, a point highlighted by its bilingual presentation.

The plan details how traditional owners and the Australian government work as partners by combining Anangu natural and cultural management skills with conventional park practices (Uluru–Kata Tjuta Board of Management and Parks Australia, 2000, pp8–9). In the context of *Tjukurpa* (Anangu law), the actions of ancestral animals have important roles in the evolution of the landscape. For example, Aboriginal people learned how to patch burn the country from the *Tjukurpa* of *lungkata*, the Centralian blue-tongued lizard (*Tiliqua multifasciata*). Although modern methods are now used, the practice of lighting small fires close together during the cool season continues to leave a mosaic of burned and unburned areas. This traditional knowledge and practice has been adopted as a major ecological management tool in the park. *Tjukurpa* also teaches about the care of rock holes and other water sources (Calma and Liddle, 2003).

The *2001 Cultural Heritage Action Plan and Cultural Landscape Conservation Plan*, which operates under the *2000 Plan of Management*, provides a more detailed operational guide for implementing cultural site and landscape management programmes. It was compiled through a series of community workshops in the park. This plan provides for the conservation of the cultural values of specific sites, storylines and story places, including sacred sites, birthplaces, rock art, camping places, rock holes and places important in the recent Anangu and Piranpa ('white fella') history of the area.

Equally important, this plan also provides for the conservation of the cultural landscape in which these places exist and from which they are inseparable. It requires both physical conservation actions and attention to the maintenance of cultural heritage values that enliven it. This will be achieved through training of young Anangu, involvement of traditional owners who live outside the park, keeping the stories about places strong, providing privacy for ceremonies, explaining cultural restrictions to visitors, and recording oral history connected to people's early experiences in the park, including the struggle to win back their land. In addition to this park-wide cultural landscape plan, there are plans for specific sites, such as Mutitjulu Kapi (Mutitjulu waterhole), associated rock art sites and the physical features of the *Kuniya* and *Liru* stories, which require actions for managing visitor use, as well as for vegetation, fire, rock art and the restoration of trampled areas and the waterhole.

Tourism to such a spectacular location has also evolved a new approach, where Indigenous People guide tourists around the base of the rock and explain its significance, its ecology and their management role. The park offers access to some sites, including information about their history and significance (available at the cultural centre); but access to other sacred sites is not granted, with some sites restricted to women and some to men. A large proportion of the area of Kata Tjuta is associated with ritual information and activities that must remain the exclusive prerogative of senior men (Calma and Liddle, 2003, p108).

Anangu regard the popular climb up the dangerously steep monolith as inconsistent with their spiritual veneration of the site, as the tourist climbing route follows that of a spiritual Dreaming ancestor. They request tourists not to climb Uluru and hope to educate people through interpretive programmes, but choose to leave the decision of whether or not to climb to the tourists (Calma and Liddle, 2003). The numbers of tourists climbing the rock fell by 40 per cent during the three years to 2000, showing that understanding brings respect.

The evolution and current practice of planning and management at Uluru–Kata Tjuta illustrates how cultural heritage values now underpin land management, and it is an exciting example of traditional owners reclaiming their ways of living in the land, referred to as 'keeping country straight'. It also represents reconciliation between Europeans, whose practices often damaged the land, and the Anangu, whose traditional methods can assist ecological restoration.

Source: adapted from Lennon (2005b)

property rights and violation of sacred sites through tourism or resource extraction pressures (Stevens, 1997b). Indigenous involvement in active conservation of cultural places such as art sites assists in maintaining traditional 'connections to country'. This has also been achieved through employment of local indigenous people in the maintenance of long-established national parks such as Chaco Canyon and Mesa Verde in the US.

Conserving historic sites

Specific historic sites provide small-scale evidence of human interactions in cultural landscapes. These include prehistoric sites such as Stonehenge in England or Lascaux in France, and thousands of minor site features such as dolmens and barrows in wider landscapes. Smaller landscapes may themselves form part of more extensive evolving cultural landscape areas, such as the Minori Valley along the Amalfi coast in Italy or the townscape of Ravello in the same area, or the chapels along pilgrimage routes in the countryside, or in the Hortobagy of Hungary or the Po Delta, where the wetland areas contrast strongly with the dryer plains and different rural structures were erected in response to this. Evidence of land-use activities often remain in lands now reserved as protected areas. Many also continue to be lived-in land-scapes.

Designed landscapes are represented by gardens and grand estates, such as Studley Royal Park in England and Versailles in France; botanic gardens, such as those at Kew, England; or cemeteries. Relict landscapes contain prehistoric and archaeological sites, including those associated with industrial processing, such as Ironbridge in the UK, the birthplace of the modern iron industry. Many protected areas contain evidence of previous resource use, particularly mining and logging – the latter sometimes results in changes to species distribution and forest composition. This is particularly apparent in the American Rocky Mountain parks.

English Heritage is now using the technique of 'characterization', an approach based on field evidence as a means of identifying the important components of a landscape and then defining how these elements should be conserved through zoning. An understanding of ecology; geology; vegetation; water; past management regimes; patterns of past land use; architecture; the use of local materials; archaeological evidence of past occupation; current use patterns; and socio-economic factors is required. It is often a complex, multidisciplinary task. Characterization is a way of defining patterns and drawing together data on different types of uses to assist management. The significance and integrity of heritage features in protected areas largely derive from the relationship between the landscape and the historic elements within that landscape. The larger landscape provides the setting for many features that should be separately described. However, these features only display their full meaning and significance when considered in their broader landscape setting.

For example, historic landscape character types have been defined for Cornwall in the UK as:

- rough ground;
- prehistoric enclosures;
- medieval enclosures;
- post-medieval enclosures (17th to 18th century);
- modern enclosures;
- ancient enclosures;
- plantations and scrubs;
- settlements (pre-20th century);
- settlements (20th century);
- industrial (active);
- industrial (relict);
- communications (roads, airfields, etc.);
- recreation;
- military;
- ornamental;
- reservoirs; and
- natural water bodies (Fairclough, 1999).

Heritage conservation has focused previously on the management of individual structures. But conservation practice has moved from identifying sites as items or 'dot points' on a map, to examining the spatial context and connections of those sites/places. This results in a cultural landscape framework that examines landscape processes, landscape features, land use and the evidence of the relationships between them.

Components in the landscape may be classified as follows (NPS, 1990):

- *Structures:* the physical remains of a deliberately constructed feature associated with human activity, such as a house, garden or water race.

- *Complexes:* a number of features that are related to each other in some way – for example, through use or function, such as structures associated with a farm or military barracks.
- *Sites:* the location of an event, structure, earthwork or complex where no above-ground evidence remains.
- *Features:* component or element of a landscape, including structures, sites or complexes and field boundaries, as well as natural features, such as an avenue of exotic trees or alluvial streamside deposits containing minerals.
- *Linear networks:* long, narrow landscape or landscape components, such as a river, canal/aqueduct or transport route and its associated elements.

Guidelines for managing historic buildings provide much advice on identifying, analysing and repairing construction details (Feilden, 1982). There has been much less written on the management of structures, whether standing or archaeological ruins, within a landscape or protected area context (Conservation Studies Institute, 2005).

Elements and characteristics that relate historic structures to other features in the landscape, and to the broader landscape, must be identified. This includes identifying linkages, such as historic access routes to a structure; understanding the topographic reasons for its siting; considering the importance of sight lines to and from it; and considering structures or features that relate it to other components in the landscape – for instance, by virtue of common usage. There is a need for all interventions in historic structures and archaeological sites to be based on adequate research and a full understanding of the landscape context. On the basis of analysing this information, it may be necessary to restore or reconstruct access and sight lines to a structure in order to reinstate its historical meaning in the landscape context (see Case Study 17.9).

Identifying and documenting threats to historic sites and their landscape setting allows assessment of the vulnerability of the conservation values, and preparation of an appropriate management response for protecting the significant values. Threats to sites, landscapes and their structural features result from both natural processes and human activities and include:

- wind or water damage;
- erosion;
- wildfires;
- undermining of foundations or earthworks by feral animals;
- decay and rot;
- weed invasion;
- road construction and associated works;
- trampling;
- vandalism;
- badly sited and designed buildings;
- destructive management techniques;
- farming practices that destroy heritage values;
- uncontrolled mining and quarrying;
- poorly designed new infrastructure such as pipelines, power lines and so on;
- depopulation and consequent loss of skilled traditional workforce; and
- gentrification of rural areas.

The extraordinary diversity of vernacular architecture in rural heritage ranges from stonewalls and *truli* shelters to timber barns, byres, granaries, thatched cottages, mills and fish traps. Rural heritage is increasingly viewed as an attractive resource for tourism. In Central and Eastern Europe, where traditional peasant farming survived under the socialist regime, a rich and diversified cultural heritage remains: wooden houses and churches, crafts and embroidery, folk and religious festivals, local food processing and culinary skills (Passaris and Sokolska, 2001). There are pressures to modernize these rural heritage structures, as illustrated in Case Study 17.10.

Consideration of the vulnerability of heritage values leads to asking: what are the limits of acceptable change? In other words, what changes can be permitted (new houses, roads or crops) in the protected area landscape without compromising its significant heritage values and integrity? And to what extent should the managing authority intervene to change, restore or rebuild historic elements in the landscape? The answer to the questions is resolved in the context of a management planning process (see also Chapter 11).

Case Study **17.9**

Studley Royal Park, UK

Studley Royal Park in England is one of the most significant 18th-century planned landscapes in Europe centred on a formal water garden. It was created by John and William Aislabie, and incorporates vistas of the ruins of Fountains Abbey, the greatest English Cistercian Abbey. The landscape and structures are protected by national legislation, and in 1986 it was inscribed as a cultural World Heritage site. The National Trust has owned the site since 1983.

The water garden is characterized by its use of the natural landscape of the steep-sided, twisting Skell Valley, which contrasts with the formal canalization of the river itself, artificial ponds and classically inspired garden buildings and ornaments. These buildings and structures, as well as plantings, are essential in retaining its significance. The site is an outstanding example of landscape design. The abbey ruins have major archaeological value. The site also has national and international natural values, as well as being of major significance aesthetically and spiritually, and as a local amenity and tourist attraction.

When acquired by the National Trust, the water gardens were in need of major works. Maintenance of the hard landscape and buildings, and of the plantings, had been neglected. The site continues to be subject to floods and silting of the water channels by the River Skell. Continued decay would have led to the loss of form and significance.

The National Trust embarked upon a major conservation programme to revive the garden's original splendour. Between 1983 and 1987, work was carried out in parallel with field surveys and research led by a small working party composed of consultants and National Trust staff. Their collective knowledge compensated for some lack of historical and archaeological information. Where evidence was available, the objective was to restore John and William Aislabie's landscape. Where there was none, educated and pragmatic choices were made, informed by ongoing surveys. The work programme combined emergency repairs, restoration of the major built features (a banqueting house, statues and temples), extensive work on the water features (dredging, bank reinforcement, ponds and canal revetments, and repairs to the cascades) and to the soft landscape features (hedge pollarding, lawn flattening, planting and tree clearance). Since the major restoration was completed, the National Trust has followed a policy of active maintenance to counteract the pressures of flooding and silting, as well as of natural decay.

Source: adapted from National Trust (2000)

Management planning process

A management plan should detail the significant cultural values and contain a framework for defining the management objectives and priorities; developing management actions; implementing these; and monitoring their impact. All objectives must relate to the statement of significance for the heritage values exhibited in the protected area. By using a values-based management approach, compared to an issues-based management approach, objectives and actions will address the retention of significance. Such objectives and actions focus on the vulnerability of specific heritage values in the context of limits of acceptable change – how much of the 21st century should be permitted to intrude in protected areas before their values are compromised and changed in meaning? The heritage values are derived from the interaction of peoples with nature in a specific place or ecosystem. Can this interaction remain authentic, while using modern techniques?

Decisions about the appropriate techniques to be used in managing cultural heritage in the protected area should be presented as a major component with a protected area management plan, or, if necessary, as a subsidiary plan to an overarching area management plan. Information required for developing such a plan or plan section includes requirements for retaining heritage values; a description of the physical condition of the historic components and their landscape; the external requirements and constraints; community interests; resources and costs; and a list of priorities.

In the context of a planning process the management plan should outline objectives and actions covering the following elements.

Type and degree of physical intervention in the historic fabric to retain significance. Fabric refers to all

Case Study **17.10**

Vlkolínec, Slovakia

This remarkably intact traditional Central European settlement composed of 45 wooden dwelling houses and associated infrastructure, such as barns, is surrounded by narrow strip fields and meadows in a steep mountainous area. There are a few original inhabitants; the settlement is partly used for weekend cottages. It was inscribed on the *World Heritage List* in 1993 under cultural criteria (iv) and (v).

At the time of inscription, property ownership had not generally been transferred to the state, as in other parts of Slovakia; estates and houses were retained mostly in private possession. However, there was a lack of respect for World Heritage values among local people and authorities. Despite the existing master plan, there was no detailed policy on sustainable habitation of the site. It had insufficient infrastructure – only electricity (no water supply system and no sewage) – although this offered energy conservation possibilities.

Some traditional land-use forms had been extinguished by nationalization, and only sheep-breeding survived in Vlkolínec after the socialist era; individual grazing was partly replaced by that organized in co-operative farms. This resulted in no further need for barns, especially hay barns – characteristic elements in the landscape of the surrounding meadows. Traditional skills and use of local materials and techniques were replaced, and woodworking became a general problem.

By 2000, government funding allowed local road reconstruction and the construction of a water supply system. Government programmes that focused on safeguarding the cultural heritage of Vlkolínec were adopted, and there was increased interest in permanent residency (even families with children). The activities of local school teachers focused on environmental education and traditional skills on the basis of Vlkolínec traditions.

Increasing tourism pressure in a very limited area has caused problems, especially the lack of appropriate infrastructure (no public toilets, only a small bar in a museum house and no regular store), which is partly regulated by exclusion of public transport to a more distant parking place. The residents do not accept being part of a 'permanent exhibition' and try to find individual solutions, such as construction of hedges with gates, which did not exist in the centre of settlement before inscription.

Growing pressure to improve the standard and quality of living now focuses on enlarging the internal capacities of the buildings by regular use of under-roof spaces. This involves issues of lighting, either roof windows or dormer windows, both atypical for this site. Present inhabitants, who are weekenders or holiday householders, have no clear idea of future land use.

Source: adapted from Dvoáková (2001)

---

the physical material of the place, including components, fixtures, contents and objects. It also refers to subsurface remains and spaces in the landscape. Procedures for controlling intervention in the physical evidence of the site/landscape should be developed. Intervention may be necessary as part of the ongoing management of traditional uses, for conservation treatment, for interpretation purposes, during adaptation to a compatible use, or as part of a research project to reveal more information about the landscape or a feature within it. Mitigation strategies need to be identified to minimize impacts. When archaeological sites, structures and buildings are involved, appropriate mitigation will nearly always require investigation and recording. There may also be cultural, social or religious reasons for not intervening. Non-intervention might be a requirement to maintain associative values of the landscape.

Case Study 17.11 illustrates that management techniques do not need to be expensive or intrusive. In this case, insertion of new cattle sheds into the landscape is a trade-off to ensure greater protection of the primary resource – archaeological heritage. Protection also requires effective communication when so many players are involved.

Use. The suitability of current uses needs to be assessed, along with likely changes and whether theses are compatible with the retention of the cultural significance of the protected area.

Interpretation. Methods for revealing the significant values of the place to the public should be outlined. This may involve highlighting the fabric to show historic meanings; treating the place in a way that is consistent with its original use; using introduced interpretive material; or employing local people as guides.

Traditional housing, Vlkolínec, Slovakia

Source: Jane Lennon

Constraints on investigation. There may be cultural, social, ethical or religious reasons that prevent or limit investigation of the landscape or access to historic sites by researchers, workers or the public.

Future developments likely to occur. The conservation plan must examine possible future developments and their impact on the heritage values. Developments of any scale should also be assessed through environment impact assessment (EIA) procedures and appropriate mitigation strategies should be developed. The aim is for a flexible conservation plan that can be adapted to changing conditions, while retaining the significance of the heritage values expressed in the landscape.

The physical and social impact of implementing the plan on systems outside the boundary of the protected area should also be considered. For example, will prohibiting developments within this area overload the capacity of neighbouring infrastructure? Will prohibiting new developments within the protected area lead to loss of economic viability for its resident population?

Case Study 17.11

Management of archaeological earthworks, Hadrian's Wall, UK

Hadrian's Wall is the most complex frontier of the Roman Empire, stretching across northern Britain. It consists of linear barriers, forts and other sites, surviving in a wide variety of conditions, rural and urban, partly as visible features, with much buried archaeology. It was inscribed in 1987 as a cultural World Heritage site. Archaeological elements are protected by national legislation and the visual setting is controlled through the local development planning control system. Less than 10 per cent is publicly owned; the remainder is privately owned, principally as farmland. It also has high landscape scenic values, natural aspects of national and international significance, is an important agricultural area, and has high economic values through tourism.

Many upstanding archaeological earthworks are subject to pressure from visitors or farm stock. This pressure can cause significant damage to archaeological deposits. It was necessary to apply techniques for protection and proactive management of earthworks. With partners, English Heritage developed the Proactive Earthwork Management Project.

Existing monitoring by the partners featured a baseline condition survey, produced as part of the project to highlight when and where action is required to prevent deterioration of the archaeological resource. Actions to protect earthworks include one-off interventions, sustained actions and a combination of both. Sustained actions are preferable since these include continuing, low-cost, minimum intervention techniques, such as management agreements to control stock levels or grassland management to reduce the impact of recreation. One-off actions include the repair of erosion scars and the insertion of permanent paths where a grass sward is unsustainable. An important combination approach has been the erection of cattle sheds within the Northumberland National Park to remove the threat of damage by cattle during winter months when the soils are waterlogged.

Source: adapted from Rimmington (2001)

Hadrian's Wall: Walking to Once Brewed from Housteads

Source: F. Leblanc

Management principles

Since conservation involves all of the processes of looking after a site, place or landscape in order to retain its cultural significance, there are common principles arising from the *Venice Charter* and its offspring charters that apply. Given that the primary aim of heritage management is to retain the cultural values in the protected area landscape, all conservation treatments must respect the existing fabric or associations and maintain authenticity in materials, design, workmanship and setting in order to prolong the integrity of the site within the landscape and to allow it to be interpreted. Care should be taken introducing any new elements and adapting to changed circumstances.

What treatments are used depends upon the management objectives and conservation strategies. The objective of a proposed treatment should be defined and a method of achieving this should then be found that enhances and does not degrade the heritage significance. Treatment actions range from cyclical maintenance to varying degrees of

consolidation, restoration, continuing traditional ways of living, or even adaptive reuse. The appropriateness of particular treatments should be carefully evaluated before any works commence.

The appropriateness of treatments will also vary depending upon the type and scale of the protected area. For example, in designed landscapes there may be reconstruction of missing elements, as at Lednice in the Czech Republic; rehabilitation and restoration following damage, as at the Hampton Court Palace gardens in England; and reconstruction via replanting, as at Versailles in France, following the destructive storms of 1998.

Cultural associations must be maintained to keep the associative values alive as detailed in the significance assessment. This requires much effort by elders and area managers to establish education programmes or seasonal activities, intergenerational meetings and festivals to transmit rituals and crafts.

In managing cultural heritage in protected areas, managers must know what cultural values are found in their landscapes and must ensure that their management protects and enhances both the intangible expression of these values and their physical evidence. But values are dynamic and evolve and change. Evaluation of condition and knowledge about the values must be updated; therefore, management strategies must be able to change to protect the values expressed in protected areas.

Protected areas have a range of values that communities recognize as important and want to conserve. Cultural and natural values are the qualities that make a place or landscape important. We tend to separate those qualities into natural and cultural, with the latter including historic and indigenous; but increasingly, managers are finding that the categories overlap to such an extent that these heritage values must be catered for simultaneously.

For conserving cultural heritage values expressed in places – that is, monuments, buildings and structures, ruins, archaeological sites and landscapes – there are key messages:

• The place itself is important.
• Managers must understand the cultural significance of the place.
• Managers must understand the fabric and associations of the place.
• Cultural significance should guide management decisions.
• Managers should do as much as necessary to manage the place, and as little as possible.

These ideas are summarized in the following set of management principles:

1 The objective in managing heritage places is to identify, protect, conserve, present and transmit, to all generations, their heritage values.

2 The management of heritage places should use the best available knowledge, skills and standards for those places, and include ongoing technical and community input to decisions and actions that may have a significant impact on their heritage values.

3 The management of heritage places should respect all values of the place.

4 The management of heritage places should ensure that their use and presentation and interpretation to visitors are consistent with the conservation of their heritage values.

5 The management of heritage places should make timely and appropriate provision for community involvement, especially by people who have a particular interest in, or associations with, the place, and may be affected by the management of the place.

6 Indigenous people are the primary source of information on the value of their heritage, and their active participation in identification, assessment and management is integral to the effective protection of indigenous heritage values.

7 The management of heritage places should provide for regular monitoring, review and reporting on the conservation of heritage values.

Further reading

Clark, K. (2001) *Informed Conservation: Understanding Historic Buildings and Their Landscapes for Conservation*, English Heritage, London

Conservation Studies Institute (2005) *A Handbook for Managers of Cultural Landscapes with Natural Resource Values*, National Park Service, Woodstock, www.nps.gov/csi

de la Torre, M. (ed) (2005) *Heritage Values in Site Management: Four Case Studies*, The Getty Conservation Institute, Los Angeles

Feilden, B. (1982) *Conservation of Historic Buildings*, Butterworth Scientific, London

Marquis-Kyle, P. and Walker, M. (2004) *The Illustrated Burra Charter: Good Practice for Heritage Places*, Australia ICOMOS, Melbourne

Mitchell, N., Brown, J. and Beresford, M. (eds) (2005) *The Protected Landscape Approach: Linking Nature, Culture and Community*, IUCN, Gland and Cambridge

UNESCO (United Nations Educational, Scientific and Cultural Organization) (2005) *Operational Guidelines for the Implementation of the World Heritage Convention, Intergovernmental Committee for the Protection of the World Cultural and Natural Heritage*, WHC02/05, UNESCO, Paris

Website

International Council on Monuments and Sites (ICOMOS): www.icomos.org

18

Incident Management

Graeme L. Worboys and Colin Winkler

For protected areas, an incident can be formally described as 'an event or cluster of events, which may be accidental, intentional or natural in origin, and which requires an emergency or law enforcement response'. Protected areas that are directly influenced by natural events such as fires, volcanic eruptions, earthquakes, tsunami, blizzards, floods and storms. Non-natural events such as road accidents, airplane accidents, oil spills, pollution events and civil conflict also affect protected areas.

Incidents in which protected area managers may be involved may concern wild animal attacks on human life or property, fires, floods, storm damage, search and rescues, whale strandings, pollution, social unrest and civil conflict. Fire incidents include wildfires in natural vegetation, as well as building, chemical and vehicle fires. Wildlife emergencies such as animal impacts on crops, dangerous animal presence and whale strandings can involve managers working in close cooperation with community groups and volunteers. People frequently get lost within protected areas, requiring search and rescue operations to be undertaken. People may create incidents through poaching, cruelty to animals, road kills, and illegal collection of flora and fauna. Protected area managers may also need to consider engineering-based problems, including the failure or collapse of buildings or structures such as roads and bridges.

While incident management responses are well developed and sophisticated in some protected areas systems around the world, in others capacity and resources are limited. Nevertheless, the adoption of even basic incident management procedures and practices will pay dividends in terms of improved responses, ultimately delivering better conservation outcomes.

In this chapter, we provide background information about planning and preparing for incidents, the organizational systems for incident management, and specific responses to some more common incidents that affect protected areas. While we address incidents at a local community conservation area (CCA) level, our emphasis is more on the management systems needed to manage incidents and responses to more common incidents.

Organizations with incident management responsibilities

Managing land and water means that protected area management organizations will sooner or later deal with incidents. The degree and complexity of an incident will usually dictate the nature and extent of involvement. Small incidents may be handled locally by staff. Larger incidents may see many organizations and individuals joining forces to cooperatively manage and resolve an incident. The degree of participation in major incident management operations will depend upon the legal responsibilities that protected area organizations actually have. Through prior research and planning, managers will know the legal rights or powers of each member of any co-operative group or individual involved in an incident, and their likely demands and needs. When an oil spill threatens sea birds, for example, protected area managers will know which authority and which organization has jurisdiction over that particular class or location of oil spill. In some countries, laws give emergency powers to some management bodies during such incidents. It is important to understand this legal context and to have good relations with relevant organizations and their leaders.

If human life and property are at risk, the management authority of a protected area manager will usually be overridden by other authorities with wider emergency powers. Given this potential, it is critical that those authorities are made aware of the special needs of protected areas, such as the need to protect threatened species or culturally significant sites. This will help to limit any unavoidable damage to protected areas caused by ill-informed use of emergency powers. Ideally, the need to protect the environment should be an integral part of the preplanning for an incident; however, where this need has not happened, briefings should be given as early as possible during an incident. For instance, when working with fire authorities, managers may need to negotiate predetermined understandings related to:

- fire-fighting vehicle access;
- use of natural or pre-existing fire-control lines;
- use of bulldozers and hand-tool constructed lines, or natural features such as rivers, water bodies, rock areas or rainforest gullies;
- types of fire-fighting chemicals used; and
- location of sensitive plant or animal communities, or culturally significant sites.

Major incidents can involve a complex mix of government authorities and military forces, as well as volunteer organizations. Incidents can quickly become chaotic. This is particularly the case when different authorities are collaborating, but using different command-and-control systems. There are major advantages in utilizing a common incident management system, such as that described later in 'Incident control systems'.

Managing incident responses

While predicting actual incidents is difficult, a protected area manager for a given geographic region should have a reasonable idea of what sort of incidents are likely to happen, the sort of terrain in which they may occur and in roughly what season. Managers will be able to draw upon their own experience and the wisdom of the local community to enable them to anticipate and plan for potential incidents. Such pre-planning and the development of a capacity to respond (which includes suitable and adequate logistic support, good systems and trained staff) are critical. Such preparedness and expertise may help to prevent serious damage to life, property and the natural environment. Managing for incidents includes:

- analysis – identification of potential incidents for a protected area;
- research – assessment of incident management protocols and systems at all levels of the protected area organization and government;
- understanding the jurisdictional responsibilities of different agencies involved in incident management and inter-agency pre-planning requirements;
- policy formulation for protected areas – development of organizational responses to incidents;
- incident plans – including incident response systems, heritage protection needs, incident operational techniques and equipment;
- organization of logistics – such as plant, equipment and communication training and staff preparation;
- incident response management;
- staff management – potential trauma counselling;
- rehabilitation – potential repair of disturbed areas; and
- debriefing – post incident assessment.

Managers of protected areas may need to act in the interests of people living in adjacent areas, even if there is no immediate risk to lives or property. In developing an organized response to incidents, a range of questions should be asked:

- Does a particular event require incident response action? Does it threaten life, property or a protected area?
- What incidents are likely to occur for a protected area?
- What action is needed to deal with the incident? How is this action to be delivered? How do the control-and-command systems work?
- Who needs to be consulted or involved? Who are the stakeholders?
- For this kind of incident, what plans or systems are already in place at various levels of the protected area agency or government?
- What organizations should carry out these plans, and what legal and other powers do they have? What is the correct role of the protected area manager?
- How can damage be reduced, both during and after the incident?
- What safety measures are needed?
- What skills must staff have to deal with the incident?
- What legal and bureaucratic conditions must the manager comply with during the incident?
- What legal, social, political, economic and environmental issues will have to be addressed after the incident?

Management systems for dealing with major incidents

While many protected area authorities, regional fire authorities and comparable organizations are able to manage small- to medium-sized incidents quite successfully in their own right, experience has shown that some incidents rapidly develop to exceed the response capacity of a single organization. There is often a need for multiple organizations to be involved. When managing such a large incident and working with multiple organizations, there is a major advantage in utilizing a common incident management system. Such a system exists and is generically known as an incident control system (ICS).

For example, the National Interagency Incident Management Systems (NIIMS) (or variant) has been adopted by various American states and counties, by the US Coast Guard, by the Panama Canal Authority and by some Caribbean countries for their emergency operations centres. It is used by private organizations in dealing with oil-well blow-out control. NIIMS also forms the framework for managing emergencies in other countries, including New Zealand, where it is known as the Coordinated Incident Management System, and Australia, where it is known as the Australasian Inter-service Incident Management System. Apart from their utility in managing emergencies within such countries, this system has proven its worth in cooperative incident management where cross-border cooperative management has been required. The NIIMS system is described later in detail in 'Incident control systems' because of its utility for managing protected area incidents in a variety of situations.

Incident management skills and training

When media news programmes show an incident, they rarely depict the work of incident managers, finding more interest in the dramas being played out by crews in the field, such as fighting fires or carrying out a helicopter rescue. However, without the work of the people behind the scenes – the incident managers and planners – the work of the crews can be wasted. The battle against an incident is more likely to be decided by those back at base who plan the strategy.

The greatest resource that managers have is the collective knowledge and skills of their staff. Teamwork, itself a skill, and leadership are needed. Training is a fundamental part of preparing for an incident, and managers need to ensure that their staff are trained in the cross-section of skills necessary to deal with the spectrum of events. Some of the roles, and the corresponding skills, needed by an incident response team managing a fire, for example, are listed in Table 18.1.

Occupational health and safety

The safety of all staff involved in an incident is the overriding priority in incident management. Staff who are undertaking the demands of incident management need to be physically and psychologically fit, and able to undertake the work; systems must also be in place to manage this requirement (see Chapter 13). A manager must be conservative in the deployment of staff to an incident no matter

Table 18.1 Skills required for a fire incident

Skill	Incident controller*	Planner*	Operations personnel*
Leadership	✓	✓	✓
Decision-making	✓	✓	✓
Negotiation	✓	✓	✓
Teamwork	✓	✓	✓
Media management	✓	✓	
People management	✓	✓	✓
Counselling	✓		✓
Mentoring	✓	✓	✓
Time management	✓	✓	✓
Computing		✓	
Weather data analysis	✓	✓	
Multivariate analysis		✓	
Incident behaviour forecasting	✓	✓	
Air photo interpretation	✓	✓	✓
Advanced mapping	✓	✓	✓
Back-burning	✓	✓	✓
Mopping up	✓	✓	✓
Incident control system operation	✓	✓	✓
Chainsaw operation			✓
Four-wheel-drive vehicle driving (basic)	✓	✓	✓
Four-wheel-drive vehicle driving (advanced)			✓
Remote area fire fighting			✓
Heavy vehicle driving			✓
Tanker operation			✓
Motor cycle riding			✓
Motor vehicle maintenance			✓
Pump maintenance			✓
Bulldozer supervision		✓	✓
Bulldozer operation			✓
Tractor operation			✓
Helicopter safety	✓	✓	✓
Helicopter winching			✓
First aid	✓	✓	✓
Advanced first aid			✓
Radio procedures	✓	✓	✓
Fire fuel assessment	✓	✓	✓

Note: * Key incident control team positions – see this chapter's section on 'Incident control systems'.

Source: NSW NPWS (1997a)

how skilled or experienced they are. This is even more critical when inexperienced staff or volunteers are involved. For all personnel, it must be made clear that risk-taking and bravado are unacceptable and may imperil others.

Fighting wildfires in or adjacent to protected areas is a very hazardous operation. Recognizing that safety in fire-fighting situations is not only an ethical imperative, but that it also makes 'dollars and sense', the International Labour Organization (ILO) included fire fighting within the *Safety and Health in Forestry Work ILO Code of Practice*. This code was not intended to be legally binding or to supersede the legislation of any country, but was designed to provide guidance to ILO constituents in their endeavour to improve the safety and health of all those working in forests. The code is based on international experience, and is intended to be relevant and practicable in most countries. From a fire-fighting standpoint, the code (drawn up in 1997 by 30 experts representing the views of governments, employers and workers) aims to protect fire fighters from hazards and to prevent or reduce the incidence of occupational illness or injury.

An efficient system for rotating crews is also needed. Exhausted, overtired or hungry people are more likely to make mistakes that risk lives and threaten incident operations. Managers need to consider how they will keep track of personnel once they are in the field. The appropriate length of shift time varies: fire crews may work 12 hours at a time. However, people working with stranded whales in cold water may need to warm up on land after only 20 minutes, otherwise hypothermia may occur. When an incident goes on for weeks, it becomes important to rest people and not keep rotating them back onto duty.

Managers have a range of safety obligations. They need to keep an eye on the reliability and maintenance condition of equipment. In most countries, there are strict rules for air safety, such as pilots only working a fixed number of hours per day, with enforced rest days. Managers must insist on a roster system for pilots, and may need to arrange for aircraft to be exchanged, or rested for service, at regular intervals. This is especially important during long and intense incident response campaigns.

Incident administration

A manager may need to set up forward control centres for incidents, such as the case of fire. It is crucial to put these in the right places and to think ahead. What happens, for example, if a fire changes direction? Setting up a forward control centre at the height of an incident is a skill honed by experience. Such centres need to work efficiently from the moment they are set up. Trial and error is unacceptable; the layout and structure of such bases must be carefully planned. A common but serious mistake is to mix crews that are resting with the bustle of crews departing for the incident. Helicopter pads should be set up near the camp, but away from resting personnel. Resting crews need real rest. Food must be adequate, and site cooking and ablution facilities free of health risks: staying healthy in the field is itself a safety issue. Always plan to be ready to treat and evacuate sick or injured personnel. Do not lose sight of the budget. Aircraft are not cheap to hire or use. Managers will need to make sure that all flights are justified and cost effective, and that the right type of aircraft is being used. Managing the budget as the incident proceeds is a fundamental responsibility.

Community consultation during incidents

Managers need to keep the community informed about serious incidents. Early on during an incident, they should provide background fact sheets to politicians and the media, and continue to provide regular bulletins. Major incidents may require press conferences, the handling of which requires training and specialist support. Smaller incidents may require regular press releases and media interviews, or briefings with individuals. The incident control system prescribes regular briefings for stakeholders, neighbours, local politicians and the media.

Maintaining routines during an incident

Incidents may completely occupy the limelight for a given time; yet, managers need to manage the normal routine as well. Visitor facilities must be maintained, accounts and wages paid, and government commitments and deadlines need to be kept. Part of planning for an incident involves planning to keep up with day-to-day routine management.

Post-incident management

Rehabilitation. Any incident will impact upon protected area values to some degree. Consideration should always be given to rehabilitation work and recovery action. Any damage caused during an incident should therefore be rehabilitated immediately after the incident, with the cost of this work being a cost against the incident. Some damage can, however, take many years to repair and may require persistent rehabilitation work.

Debriefing. Incident debriefs are a critical part of managing the total incident operation. Inevitably, most incidents are characterized by confusion and conflicting stories about what has happened. Debriefs provide a valuable insight into a whole operation, and how operations can be improved for the next event. Staff stress counselling may be required immediately following some incidents, and professional assistance should be obtained for this type of service.

Legal issues. Incidents can lead to loss of life or property. Formal inquiries, such as coronial inquests, are called in some countries immediately after the event, and managers may be summoned to give evidence. They will be expected to tell the inquiry exact dates and times, the reasons why certain decisions were made or not made, and who made the decisions and why. This means keeping an accurate account of events during the incident. Like police officers, managers must be trained to record and recall all the legally relevant aspects of an incident. Typically, incidents are recorded in an operational 'log', although protected area managers are wise to keep a personal log of time and of events in which they were involved. For inquests, inquiries, insurance inquiries, and other legal inquiries or actions that can follow an incident, well-organized and accurate information about the incident will be required. Some staff may be subpoenaed and may need some coaching on legal protocols and seek guidance on their behaviour as witnesses. It can be an unsettling experience to be cross-examined in an adversarial coronial or court atmosphere. After a major incident and before going into the witness box, managers should seek legal advice to confirm that they have collected full, accurate and relevant information, as well as ensuring that they have been briefed on court proceedings and questioning. They are advised to have legal representation, if possible.

Economic impacts of incidents. Managers need to bear in mind that incidents that lead to closure of a protected area may result in serious losses for licensed commercial operators and nearby towns that rely on tourism. Where fault is determined through a legal process, it may lead to compensation payouts. The insurance premiums for protected areas can be influenced by the nature, frequency, and cost of incidents.

Incident control systems

ICSs derived from the NIIMS provide standard procedures that allow different organizations to 'speak with one language' and arrange themselves under a single command. Based on a structure of delegation, an ICS can be used for any incident or emergency, large or small, where various activities or organizations must be coordinated. An ICS sets out a framework for the effective management of incidents that:

- is adaptable and scaleable to any type or size of incident;
- is suitable for use regardless of jurisdictions or agencies involved;
- employs a common organization structure;
- utilizes common command structures and consolidated action planning; and
- utilizes common terminology.

An ICS has a specific set of operating requirements. It must have:

- a balance of agency jurisdiction versus agency involvement, including considerations for single jurisdiction and single agency involvement, single jurisdiction with multi-agency involvement, and multi-jurisdiction with multi-agency involvement;
- an organizational structure that must be able to be adapted to any incident to which the relevant agencies would be expected to respond;

- an organizational structure that must be applicable and acceptable to all users no matter where they are situated;
- an organizational system that must be able to expand in a logical manner from an initial situation into a major incident;
- basic common elements in organization, terminology and procedures that allow for the maximum application and use of already developed qualifications and standards;
- the least possible disruption to existing systems when implemented; and
- low operational maintenance costs (NIIMS, 2002).

An ICS has several components that function interactively. In order that diverse users can work effectively towards a common goal, they need to share a terminology in relation to the various resources that are needed to manage incidents and the facilities that are an integral part of the hierarchy of authority. These include key words such as command post, incident base and staging areas, and organizational functions, including the set of distinguishing position titles that are needed at the various organizational levels (see Table 18.2).

A system of integrated communications should follow this structure with, for example, radio networks organized to include a command network involving incident command members; a tactical network coordinating across different agencies; a support network linking with operational staff; and a specialized network providing ground-to-air communications. A unified command structure may be necessary because many incidents involve multi-jurisdictional situations, and the responsibility and authority of individual agencies is normally legally confined to one jurisdiction. Unifying command means that all relevant agencies contribute to determining overall objectives in handling the incident. They are involved in choosing strategies, tactical planning, the development of action plans, the integration of tactical operations and making optimal use of all resources.

Linked with the unified command structure are ideas of assigning incident facilities in a hierarchical pattern, such as command post, incident base, camps, staging areas and helipads. Managing the incident according to objectives is also fundamental. The approach includes the following:

- establishing overarching objectives;
- developing and issuing assignments, plans, procedures and protocols;
- establishing specific, measurable objectives for various incident management functional activities, and directing efforts to attain them; and
- documenting results to measure performance and facilitate corrective action.

The unified command concept includes using a manageable span of control. In an ICS, as a general rule, the span of control for any individual with emergency management responsibility should

Table 18.2 Organizational levels for an incident and related position titles

Organizational level	Position title
Incident command	Incident commander
Command staff	Officer
Section	Section chief
Branch	Branch director (an optional level)
Division/group/sector	Division/group/sector supervisor
Unit	Unit leader

Source: AIIMS (1992)

range from 3 to 7 groups or individuals, with 5 seen as an optimum maximum. The number depends upon the kind of incident, the nature of the tasks involved, hazard and safety factors, and the distances involved. During the initial response to an incident the incident controller may operate alone; but if an incident grows, the incident controller will need to delegate functions, while retaining overall control. Shift work will be critical for lengthy incidents. The incident controller is responsible for:

- assessing the severity and implications of the incident;
- preparing an initial departmental action plan in consultation with the main agency affected and any regional emergency team to deal with the incident, and preparing updates during the course of the incident;
- coordinating the activities of environmental agencies at various levels of government;
- conducting legal and technical investigations of the incident;
- meeting regularly with section chiefs of the incident management system;
- maintaining records of all meetings, decisions and other incident documentation;
- regularly briefing the media and providing news releases;
- coordinating cost recovery and compensation for environmental damages if required; and
- monitoring and evaluating the overall performance of the incident response team.

As an incident escalates, an ICS team may be divided into three sections: planning, operations and logistics. An example of an ICS structure for a large incident is shown in Figure 18.1. The degree of sophistication of the incident response relates to the size and complexity of the incident, and the three sections are scaled up or scaled down accordingly. The incident controller has overall responsibility for managing the incident, and must prepare the objectives for action and approve the incident action plan.

Planning

The planning section is responsible for the collection, evaluation and dissemination of tactical

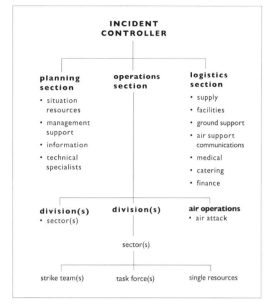

Figure 18.1 The incident control team

Source: AIIMS (1992)

information about the incident. It is responsible for developing the incident action plan, a most critical document. The section maintains information on the current and forecast situation, and on the status of resources assigned to the incident (such as maintaining registers that list where resources and equipment are, and how they are being used). The section has four primary units and may also have various technical specialists to assist in evaluating the situation and forecasting requirements for additional personnel and equipment. These include:

1   situation unit:
    - weather service;
    - situation information processing;
    - mapping;
    - incident prediction;
    - technical specialists and analysis;
2   resources unit:
    - where resources are deployed and what they are doing;
3   management unit:
    - administration support;
    - communication services; and

4   information services:

- accurate information about the nature of the event (AIIMS, 1992).

Operations

The operations section is responsible to the incident controller for managing all tactical operations at the incident site that are directed towards reducing the immediate hazard, saving lives and property, establishing situation control, and restoring normal operations. Depending upon the circumstances, agencies that might be part of the operations section include fire, law enforcement, public health, public works and emergency services. The way in which operations will be organized and managed will depend upon the type of incident, the agencies involved, and the objectives and strategies that have been determined. Typically, an operations section has divisional commanders for functions such as air operations and particular sectors.

Logistics

The logistics section assists in developing the initial action plan and is crucial to its successful implementation. When it is mobilized, the logistics section is responsible for meeting all support needs for an incident by providing facilities, services and materials to the operations staff. These responsibilities will include ordering resources via appropriate procurement authorities, as well as providing facilities, transportation, supplies, equipment maintenance and fuel, food service, communications and medical services. Logistics typically has eight functions to manage:

1   supply;
2   facilities;
3   ground support;
4   air support;
5   communications;
6   medical;
7   catering; and
8   finance (AIIMS, 1992).

Logistics may be responsible for:

- assessing initial incident reports and identifying solutions to anticipated logistical problems;

- contributing to the initial departmental action plan and its regular updating;
- liaising with other responding agencies to coordinate shared logistics requirements;
- ensuring that all facilities are quickly adapted to emergency mode and are maintained as such for the duration of the incident;
- ensuring appropriate accommodation and catering;
- coordinating air, water and ground transportation needs in consultation with other agencies;
- requesting logistical assistance from local communities;
- facilitating the procurement of needed supplies and services;
- ensuring that communications equipment is deployed, operational and maintained to meet emergency response needs; and
- coordinating the systematic compilation of costs associated with personnel time, service contracts and other incident-related expenses (AIIMS, 1992).

Shift change

The ICS system relies on a 24-hour response to an incident, with a shift change on a frequency suitable for the incident. Major fire operations typically have a shift change every 12 hours, while marine mammal strandings with in-water operations may have a much more frequent cycle. The shift change represents the complete transfer of accountability to new teams. It is a major operational exercise that requires great coordination. It is an area of incident management that can become very messy, very quickly. Typically, the shift change is organized to occur in daylight and during non-crises times during an incident. The shift change order is as follows (AIIMS, 1992):

- The incident controller shift change occurs during the first part of the operations shift change and after briefing the incoming incident controller.
- The next to change over is the operations section. Outgoing operations staff will have been briefed on the plan for the next 12 hours, and they, in turn, brief their incoming replacements.

- The planning section changes after the operational shift change.
- Logistics will change with the operations personnel, but some (who manage the shift change) will change over during the middle of the operational cycle.

Adaptability of the ICS system

The ICS system is particularly adaptable: in a large incident, each section might employ scores of people; in a small incident managed by only two people, the second one might be told: 'You'll be in charge both of planning and logistics.' In either case, the same range of duties applies. An incident action plan is developed by the incident management team for the particular incident, and is reviewed and approved by the incident controller. It contains objectives and strategies with specific time frames. The incident command system is ideal for 'multi-agency' incidents. While some people have criticized the amount of paperwork involved, the system has proven to be successful in dealing with incidents ranging from fires and hailstorms, through to outbreaks of livestock disease.

Managing fire incidents

Fire is one of the more common types of incident managed in many fire-prone countries. Fires may be natural (caused by lightning) or due to accident or arson. Because of the danger to life and property, they need to be responded to. Planned fires have the same potential and must be managed very carefully. Large-area prescription burns for management, cultural and ecological purposes may be undertaken. So, too, are smaller prescription burns carried out to protect property or for ecological management. Typically, such planned burns are managed using ICSs.

Woodland fire, Nokolo-Koba National Park, Senegal

Source: IUCN Photo Library © Jim Thorsell

Ranger back-burning, Muogomarra Nature Reserve, New South Wales, Australia

Source: Graeme L. Worboys

Fire season preparation

Planning for fires is a routine task for many protected area managers. They will generally work in conjunction with local fire brigades. This planning is conducted at a number of levels. There is a fire management plan for an entire protected area that documents the strategic objectives for fire management in the context of its ecosystems and its surroundings. There is a fire operational plan that provides all logistic details (contacts, policies and procedures). This is updated every 12 months. The timing of fire preparation activities may vary from season to season, influenced by climatic and fuel conditions. The response to a particular fire is described by an incident action plan. Being ready for a fire season involves making sure that staff have knowledge, skills, attitudes and physical fitness appropriate to the demands that may be placed upon them. Other tasks include ensuring that:

- there are cooperative arrangements amongst agencies;
- fire plans are up to date;
- computer software for simulating fire behaviour is operational;
- heritage data is accessible;
- staff rosters are clearly established;
- a programme of prescription burning has been completed;
- a fire-trail maintenance programme has been completed;
- radio communication systems are working;
- fire observation towers are serviceable and accessible;
- plant and equipment are serviceable;
- supplies of fuel, incendiaries and retardants are available;
- contracts for aviation support have been arranged; and
- contracts for major plant (such as bulldozers) have been organized.

During the fire season

Several methods are used by managers for the early detection of wildfires, including the staffing of fire towers at vantage points during the summer season. The towers report local weather, as well as any fires they sight. Surveillance flights, particularly during afternoons of thunderstorm activity, provide very early warnings for new fires. Mid-morning surveillance flights the day after thunderstorms are also used to detect fires caused by lightning that have smouldered through the rain or the night-time humidity, and have been reactivated by the morning's heat. Frequently, however, local residents and visitors may raise the alarm for fires. Immediate attack on a fire as soon as it is detected is the best control strategy. Crews may be able to directly attack the fire and suppress it while it is small. In many remote areas, this is one of the few options that managers have in controlling fires. Remote areas often consist of rugged terrain that is unsuitable for the bulldozers and large tankers used to control fires in other areas. Instead, small remote fires are often directly attacked by specialist fire fighters using dry fire-fighting techniques and may be supported by water-bombing aircraft. In some countries, experiencing very wide-scale fires for the first time, new systems for dealing with fire management have had to be introduced (see Case Study 18.1).

Techniques for rapid response to a wildfire sighting include the following options:

- Water-bombing can be carried out using aircraft and environmentally acceptable fire retardants. A second observation aircraft may be used to direct the water-bomber to the target. Often water-bombers provide a holding strategy until on-ground crews arrive at the scene.
- The fire can be directly attacked by tankers and crews. Small tankers are useful to reach fires that are inaccessible to larger tankers.
- Earth-moving equipment can be used to block or encircle the fire with a control line.
- Helicopter-based fire crews can attack more remote fires. Typically, the first crew member is winched down or rappels (controlled descent, utilizing ropes and abseiling techniques) from

a helicopter to cut a helipad clearing in the forest. Direct attack on the fire can then begin. Evacuation can also occur, if necessary. Following this, the same helicopter may begin to drop water on the fire using a water bucket serviced by nearby water sources. In volatile conditions, water bucketing helps to keep the fire fighters safer by reducing the fire's behaviour. It may not put out the fire; but it can dampen it enough for fire crews to safely attack its flank.

Fire-response tactics will depend upon the terrain and the type of fire. When open fields or road systems near a town allow vehicles to move almost at will, direct attack by large tanker units is often very successful. This is especially so if water is available and if control lines (which may be existing roads) are easily set up. For more remote fires, dry fire-fighting techniques are mainly used.

Dry fire-fighting techniques are the most common approach to control fire in protected areas. Combustion requires three things: fuel, oxygen and heat. No fuel means no fire. Bare-earth ('mineral-earth') fire breaks basically mean no fuel. These fire breaks can be made by bulldozers, tractors, graders or by crews using hand tools. They should usually surround the fire or link to natural fire barriers such as dams, lakes, rivers or rock barriers. This linkage forms a control line. On rare occasions, 'wetlines', or water-soaked barriers, may be used for an urgent back-burn. Typically, mineral-earth control lines are put in place well before the fire arrives, and small fires termed 'back-burns', are then set to burn back towards them from the fire-ward side. This creates a much wider 'blackened' area with little or no fuel. The matters that managers should consider in dry fire fighting include:

- a drought index rating – a measure of the relative dryness of the forest and other fuels and, therefore, their potential flammability;
- a fire danger rating index – an index that combines a range of parameters and provides an evaluation of rate of spread or suppression difficulty for specific combinations of fuel, fuel moisture content and wind speed;

Case Study 18.1

Response to the 1997/1998 East Kalimantan fires, Indonesia

Human-caused burning in combination with El Niño-influenced dry conditions resulted in 5.2 million hectares of forests burning in East Kalimantan, Indonesia, in 1997 and 1998. Large-scale land clearance was the dominant reason for the fires, with fires also being lit for agriculture and transmigration reasons. The fires caused major economic losses for Indonesia, and because of smoke/haze pollution, caused tensions with many of its East Asian neighbours. Many local East Kalimantan communities were also affected by the fires and their consequences.

The Indonesian government responded to what has been described as a disaster. It provided new fire management legislation in 1999 and 2001, instigated institutional development to assist all stakeholders in land and fire management, and established forest fire brigades. It focused on new policies (prevention, suppression and impact mitigation), including law enforcement, early warning and fire detection capability, and a capacity for fire suppression and post-fire rehabilitation. It also focused on empowering the local community to deal with land and forest management and fire management, including the establishment of village fire brigades. Education campaigns were also conducted and fire prevention was emphasized (Sukotjo, 2004).

The IUCN and the World Wide Fund for Nature (WWF) (supported by the US Forest Service) were also involved. They instigated a project called Project Fire Fight South-East Asia (Hoffman et al, 2003). This work focused on prevention and targeted three themes: community-based fire management; legal and institutional frameworks for forest and land fires; and the economics of fire and fire use. The IUCN and WWF identified as solutions the increased involvement of the private sector, stronger incentives for rural communities to manage local fires, and education to improve understanding of the fire problem and to correct any misconceptions. They recognized four key fire management elements:

1   analysis of the fire problem;
2   preparedness to respond to fires;
3   response (suppression) to the fires; and
4   recovery (rehabilitation of ecosystems and repair of built assets) (Hoffman et al, 2003).

They found that government agencies, in cooperation with the private sector, should create and support conditions and opportunities for community-based fire management. These include capacity-building, materials, information (such as fire weather conditions and maps) and secure land rights.

CARE (a humanitarian aid agency) was also involved in East Kalimantan. It found that, in 2001, most of the affected communities were still trying to recover from the disasters. It developed a humanitarian approach to forest fire management based on community development, in combination with a disaster response. CARE's activities included six clusters of activities:

1   participatory action and learning;
2   training in disaster management;
3   building a local emergency response capacity;
4   improving land-use mapping;
5   organizing stakeholder planning workshops; and
6   establishing stakeholder forums on disaster management at a subdistrict level (Kieft and Nur, 2002).

From an original position of being fatalistic about the fires, local communities were motivated by the project to undertake a number of initiatives, including:

- planting commercially valuable bananas as a fire break in conjunction with rubber cultivation;
- making land accessible by leasing, thereby reducing the need to burn the forest to achieve new land;
- growing crops with low biomass (such as onions) around villages as fire breaks;
- organizing forest fire brigades; and
- establishing paddy fields on burned peat swamps (Kieft and Nur, 2002).

Sources: adapted from Kieft and Nur (2002), Hoffman et al (2003) and Sukotjo (2004)

- the rate of spread of the fire for existing and forecast conditions;
- the amount and kinds of fuel present near the proposed control line;
- how long it will take to construct the control line (by whatever mechanism);
- how wide the control line needs to be in these conditions before one can safely back-burn from it;
- safety aspects, such as escape routes for personnel;
- the use of expert navigators (using air photos) to help place the control lines, particularly where heavy plant is employed;
- environmental and heritage assets at risk;
- the possible use of natural fire barriers, such as scree slopes, cliffs and streams (remember that fires sometimes cross these barriers, even with low fuel loads);
- the risk that fire can burn underground and, in very dry conditions, beneath a control line by burning stumps and roots;
- the risk from any soils with enough peat or organic matter that will burn underground;
- the need for support systems, such as helicopter water-bombing using small portable reservoirs (buoy walls) set up on ridge tops nearby;
- the use of very small portable pumps (in backpacks) for use along creeks and river systems to provide backup when back-burning, or when putting out fire in the numerous logjams or tangles of vegetation along creek beds;
- the use of satellite-based navigation, such as global positioning systems (GPS), to map and place control lines precisely;
- the use of aerial thermal imaging to help locate hotspots when thick smoke is obscuring the fire;
- the use of laptop computers to carry data-rich maps of the area into the field and to help decision-making, especially if infrared images and other field data can be promptly downloaded;
- the use of automatic weather stations (temporarily installed) to give precise data on local weather and weather changes to be linked to a fire's behaviour;
- the use of portable phone systems that can be set up at remote fire-control centres to augment satellite technology; and
- the use of portable two-way radio transmitter/receiver stations that can keep all teams reliably in touch during the operation.

Fire incident controllers need the best fire intelligence information possible. Their planning team needs to be constantly providing critical information to service the incident strategic decision-making process. Incident control planners require a range of competencies to achieve this. Skills such as local terrain and heritage knowledge; air photo interpretation; meteorological interpretation; and fire behaviour expertise, such as rate of spread calculations (for variable terrain and variable forest/grassland fuel types) are essential. More advanced skills, such as knowledge of computer-based geographic information systems (GIS), infrared mapping of active fire fronts, use of satellite technology, use of computer fire-perimeter forecasting programmes, and the ability to predict fire behaviour for back-burns and optimal burn times using computers, are major assets. Fire planners may anticipate a range of questions from incident controllers:

- What is the fire rate of spread for the next 12-hour and 24-hour period?
- Where will the fire perimeter be in 12 hours and 24 hours?
- What is the three-day prognosis for rates of spread of the fire?
- Where will the estimated fire perimeter be located in three days?
- For the fire terrain type, how long will it take to construct fire control lines using hand tools and/or bulldozers?
- Where are the optimum locations for those control lines (for time, heritage protection considerations and safety considerations)?
- Is there sufficient time to construct the control lines ahead of the approaching fire front?
- What are the optimum weather conditions (for safety and controllability) for a back-burn from the control line?
- When are those optimum conditions going to occur during the window of fire weather available?

- How much time will there be to put in place the back-burn before the next major weather system?
- Is it possible to put in place the fire-fighter resources for the back-burn in time?
- Where are the safety routes for fire fighters for a remote location?
- How long will it take to evacuate all fire fighters from a remote location by helicopters?

There will be many more questions. Too often, however, fire-control strategies are put in place with inadequate homework. Repeatedly, the wildfire overruns proposed control lines through poor analysis and planning. Too often, damaging bulldozer lines are left half finished. As a consequence, the fire expands to a much larger set of control perimeters. The role of the fire planner is critical in incident control decision-making processes. Fire planners need to be able to

complete this task adequately under extreme time and event deadlines.

Managing wildlife incidents

There is a range of wildlife incidents that must be dealt with, many of them distressing to both animals and the people involved. Incidents range from wildlife threatening human life and property, illegal hunting of native animals, and acts of cruelty, to dealing with animals that are injured in road or marine accidents. Managers may be required to deal with wild animals that are damaging crops, may need to disentangle fishing lines from seals and other marine fauna, or may need to relocate wild animals to more natural environments. A frequent marine wildlife incident is the stranding of marine mammals, particularly whales. The account of a whale stranding given in Case Study 18.2 provides an insight into some of the practical details of managing such an incident.

Case Study 18.2

A whale rescue at Seal Rocks, New South Wales, Australia

Rosemary Black, Charles Sturt University, Australia, former ranger with New South Wales National Parks and Wildlife Service, Australia

The New South Wales National Parks and Wildlife Service (NPWS) was responsible for coordinating and managing a stranding of 50 false killer whales (*Pseudorca crassidens*) at Seal Rocks, a location to the north of Sydney, Australia. A marine mammal stranding of any scale calls for excellent organizational and planning skills. It also demands good cooperation between all of the individuals and organizations involved. At Seal Rocks, it was estimated that 30 different organizations were involved. The district office at nearby Raymond Terrace served as the headquarters for the incident team. The incident control system (ICS) team coordinated and procured the required equipment and answered all of the media and public enquiries. The incident attracted national and international media and public interest. On day one, telephone enquiries jammed the four lines of the office, with an estimated one call every 30 seconds. NPWS regional and head office media officers coordinated the massive interest and produced regular media releases. Such incidents have a huge potential to promote a positive image for conservation agencies and to raise public awareness of marine mammals.

At the scene of the whale stranding there were two sector leaders located at each of the beaches. They were responsible for coordinating the personnel and equipment, as well as implementing the incident controller's decisions for managing the whales. This type of operation requires coordinating large numbers of people and ensuring that their needs are met. In addition to over 100 NPWS staff, there were about 800 volunteers and over 50 army personnel who required portable toilets, food and equipment, such as wet suits. The St John's Ambulance was on site to assist with medical problems that included hypothermia and dehydration, and the Salvation Army supplied meals and hot drinks. Marine mammal experts were brought in from Taronga Zoo, Seaworld and ORRCA (a volunteer organization caring for whales, dolphins, seals and dugongs in Australian waters) to assist with expert advice to the NPWS staff. Any incident comes at a financial cost. With the Seal Rocks rescue, it was estimated to be Aus\$85,000. There have been few whale strandings in Australia of this scale in which whales were successfully returned to the ocean. Every time this happens, we learn a little bit more about coordinating these types of incidents and marine mammal management. To be ready for such incidents, all coastal areas should develop a marine mammal rescue action plan.

Threats to life and property

Wildlife can threaten human life and property. Large animals can be particularly threatening to humans. Elephants, for example, are one of the most formidable instigators of human–wildlife conflict in Asia and Africa, causing hundreds of deaths and financial losses to crops and property. In the floodplain of Waza Logone (Waza National Park and Biosphere Reserve), Cameroon, large elephant herds are known to destroy crops and kill humans in their migrations (Madden, 2004). Retaliation does occur, and often little is done by governments to provide an alternative. Despite this, there is often a high level of tolerance for coexistence, and elephants may be venerated by some local communities (Madden, 2004). Large fences that contain wildlife, is one tool for dealing with this issue. In Uganda, trenches have been dug by local communities to prevent the elephants of Kibale National Park from destroying their crops (Blomley and Namara, 2003).

In Bwindi Impenetrable National Park, Uganda, problem animals include bush pigs, baboons, elephants and mountain gorillas. Bush pigs and baboons have been declared vermin; while elephants and gorillas – because of their high conservation value – are more difficult to manage (Roberts, 2003). Control measures that have been attempted (within the reality of financial constraints) include:

- scare shooting;
- noise making;
- planting thorn hedges; and
- constructing boundary trenches (Roberts, 2003).

Crop raiding by gorillas may be minimized by using local community volunteers who guard crops at the boundary of the park. The volunteers are supported by the International Gorilla Conservation Programme, which supplies field equipment. Non-palatable crops such as tea or pasture are encouraged on cultivated land near the boundary of the park (Roberts, 2003).

Gorilla guards, Volcano National Park, Rwanda

Source: IUCN Photo Library © Jim Thorsell

Anti-poaching post, Masai Mara National Reserve, Kenya

Source: IUCN Photo Library © Jim Thorsell

Poaching

Poaching of animals in protected areas is a major issue (see Chapter 9). Such activity may develop into a major conflict incident when it is associated with the illegal trafficking of endangered species or products (such as ivory), or the exploitation of protected species. The International Rangers Federation identified that between 1998 and 2003, 31 rangers were killed and a further 32 injured following physical attacks. Rangers have been killed in Bolivia, Colombia, Portugal and South Africa. Attackers have ranged from off-road quad bikers and fishermen to bands of poachers, hunters and rebels. During 2002, at Murchison Falls National Park in Uganda, rebel soldiers killed seven rangers (Gamborotta, 2003). Protected area managers may need to develop specialist skills, including an ability to deal with an armed conflict, or to access such capacity by establishing cooperative partnerships with police or military forces.

Marine pollution events and wildlife

In marine pollution events, protected area managers will generally deploy crews to retrieve affected wildlife, establish treatment facilities, and contact veterinarians and wildlife volunteer groups for assistance. Where large numbers of animals are affected, zoos and NGOs such as the Royal Society for the Prevention of Cruelty to Animals, the American Society for the Prevention of Cruelty to Animals or other comparable organizations may need to be consulted. An example of an incident response to an oil spill in Australia is provided in Case Study 18.3.

Managing incidents arising from natural phenomena

Natural events are a normal part of a dynamic planet Earth; but some of these may be severe, causing incidents that impact upon humans, other species or property. These may need an incident response from protected area managers.

Case Study 18.3

Wildlife response to the *Iron Baron* oil spill in July 1995, Australia

Irynej Skira, formerly of Tasmania Parks and Wildlife Service, Australia

On 10 July 1995 at 7.30 pm, on a dark and squally night, there was a distress call from the captain of the Broken Hill Proprietary-chartered bulk ore carrier *Iron Baron*. He reported that it had run aground on Hebe Reef at the entrance to the Tamar River in northern Tasmania. The ship quickly began to leak some of its 543 tonnes of heavy oil used for fuel and 54 tonnes of diesel. The *State Oil Pollution Plan* was immediately put into action. Federal and industry officers were notified. They made all resources available to assist in cleaning up the oil spill, in salvaging the fuel oil and other cargo, and in treating wildlife that had become covered in oil. Resources were also used in preventing further spread of oil and protecting the shoreline.

From a wildlife perspective, the greatest concern was for nearby colonies of little penguin (*Eudyptula minor*). The *Iron Baron* incident was the first oil spill in Australian waters where large numbers of birds were covered in oil. Despite the relatively small amount of oil, the impact on wildlife was extensive. Prevailing winds and currents in the region are predominantly westerly. Over the following month, oiled penguins were recovered up to 20km west and 120km east of Hebe Reef. Little penguin made up 98 per cent of the six species of birds and mammals that were taken for treatment or discovered dead due to oiling. Other birds affected included 34 black-faced shags (*Leucocarbo fuscescens*), six Australian pelicans (*Pelecanus conspicillatus*), two black swans (*Cygnus atratus*), one little pied cormorant (*Phalacrocorax melanoleucos*) and two water rats (both dead on arrival). Seals and albatrosses were visibly affected by oil, but could not be captured for treatment. The rehabilitation programme commenced on 11 July and was completed on 29 August, some 50 days later. The Low Head colony was home to about 1500 little penguins. As the oil slick spread to the Furneaux Group, larger penguin colonies were affected. Of the penguins brought in for treatment, 682 were from Low Head, 1119 from Ninth Island and the remainder from 13 other localities (Holdsworth and Bryant, 1995). In total, 2063 penguins were treated, of which 1959 were released and 104 died. Only 20 penguins died at Low Head; the remainder were either dead on arrival or euthanized by veterinarians. A very efficient capture and rehabilitation programme was organized and became the most prominent public feature of the oil spill response. The initial assistance of Sydney Taronga Zoo was invaluable. Zoo staff set up the Parks and Wildlife Service's (PWS's) oiled sea-bird response, using the oiled wildlife treatment equipment provided by the oil industry. Approximately 50 specialists from around Australia became involved. Some 200 volunteers assisted in night searches for oiled penguins, as well as washing and rehabilitation. An estimated 90 per cent of staff from the nature conservation branch and 70 per cent of PWS rangers and land management staff were directly involved in animal care or incident control at some stage.

Following the incident, a long-term environmental impact study was commissioned to evaluate the effectiveness of the remediation activities. The collaborative study involved Broken Hill Proprietary and relevant government agencies. Public interest groups were consulted throughout. The study report, finalized in 1999, reported favourably on the scope and nature of remediation efforts, and stated that the results clearly indicated that the affected environments either recovered or were well established on a course of recovery after two years.

Extreme weather

Types of violent weather that affect parts of the globe include storm events that go by various names (cyclones, hurricanes, typhoons and tornadoes), extreme rainfall, freak storms with strong winds and hail, blizzards, prolonged cloud and fog, and dust storms. These become 'incidents' mainly when they affect people. It is usually a matter, after the incident, of repairing damage to installations and facilities in the protected area or giving assistance to neighbours in need. Managers may also be responsible for part of a community response –
for instance, in clearing or rebuilding roads outside their management areas.

Extreme winds. Storms events do not respect the boundaries of protected areas. Since the main issue is the risk to residents and visitors in the region, managers will usually work closely with community emergency services. A prime concern is the safety of staff members, and especially of those dealing with the incident. The risk from falling trees can be greater some time after a major storm event, requiring a precautionary approach to visitor safety and access.

Floodwaters, Kosciuszko National Park, New South Wales, Australia

Source: Graeme L. Worboys

Extreme rain. Extreme rainfall can occur anywhere around the globe, but especially in high-rainfall or cyclone-prone zones. Flooding may be confined to low-lying areas; but dangerous landslips and slower mass movement of waterlogged soils can occur anywhere. Flooded rivers may trap hikers in remote areas, or else tempt them into dangerous crossings that can lead to injury or death. Canoeists and white-water rafters may also be trapped. Helicopters provide an ideal means of rescue in such cases if they are available; but they have limitations. Flood weather often means driving rain with fog and mist. Clouds can descend to ground level. In such situations, helicopters usually cannot be used when they are most needed, or else must be used with great caution. Cold, wet weather brings the threat of hypothermia, especially to injured people. When soils are saturated, four-wheel-drive vehicles can do great damage to tracks in sensitive areas. As well, the media, volunteers, politicians and other observers often demand access to the incident. Managers may need to plan adroitly to fill empty places in the vehicles and thus limit the number of vehicles used and the damage done. Media helicopters in misty, foggy conditions can add to confusion and be hazardous to other aircraft. Afterwards, damage done to tracks must be fixed, equipment repaired and the site cleared of any discarded equipment.

Cave systems. Water inside cave systems can rise very quickly during heavy rain and be life threatening for cavers. Many limestone cave systems have small catchments. A storm in the watershed can flood underground streams. These can cut off passages upon which cavers rely or flood whole caves. Rescuing cavers is a job for specialists, and is often a race against time to avoid rising waters and the onset of hypothermia. Contingency plans should emphasize both quick response and the need to minimize damage to the caves during the rescue.

Snow. Snowstorms and blizzards may cause incidents in many countries. They can involve protected area managers in several kinds of incidents. Hikers and skiers can misjudge the severity of an oncoming blizzard or become disorientated in 'whiteout' conditions. Managers may need to ensure that snow safety information is provided to visitors. Search and rescues can be regular winter events, and rangers are usually involved in at least a supporting role. Avalanches are frequent in the steep and high snowfields of some continents and can cause incidents. The alpine parks and resorts in protected areas are vulnerable in other ways. Deep cold and heavy snow can close roads and bring down power lines. Cold can also disrupt services such as water supplies and sewerage systems. Service pumps can break down, and water pipes can freeze or burst. Heavy snow loads can severely damage trees and buildings. Branches that break and fall increase the fuel load for summer fires and may require an upgraded fire plan.

Geological incidents

Geological incidents such as earthquakes, mass movement and cliff collapse occur in protected areas.

Earthquakes. Earthquakes of a moderate to severe scale occur irregularly throughout the world. They are commonly associated with movements along faults and other features of the Earth's crust. Earthquakes of a magnitude of 6 or more can cause damage if they are shallow and close to populated areas. The tsunami that occurred in the Indian Ocean on 26 December 2004 was caused by a massive disturbance along the northern part of a 1200km fault line off the northern tip of Sumatra. Energy released by the movement sent massive waves from the earthquake epicentre. At their maximum, the waves towered 25m to 30m in height. Around 200,000 people in 11 countries lost their lives and 1.5 million were left homeless, with impacts to protected areas in a number of countries. It was the second most powerful quake on record, at a magnitude of 9.3. Many coastal protected areas, including limestone reef systems, were affected. Natural mangrove systems helped to protect other parts of the coast.

Mass movement. The influence of gravity causes loose material to move down slope. The movement can seem slow and subtle from day to day, but may be large over months or years

(Montgomery, 1997). It can also be sudden, swift and devastating, as in a landslide or cliff collapse. The steeper the slope, the more likely it is to slip. Since many protected areas have very steep and broken terrain, the potential for such geological incidents is high. Loose substrates, such as unconsolidated rocks and gravel, clay-rich soils and soil–rock mixes, also invite mass movement. So, too, do unstable strata structures, such as fault planes or joint planes, and steeply dipping structures parallel to the slope. Heavy rain, flooding, earthquakes or human interference can all trigger mass movement. Most of these natural events occur without warning, such as landslides (see Case Study 18.4).

Dangerous terrain and sensitive areas. Steep terrain is also a hazard when dealing with incidents such as fires. Bulldozers are often used to prepare control lines for fires; but in doing so they can encounter small cliffs, unstable block fields of boulders, scree slopes, steep inclines and patches of limestone that may be hollow. Bulldozers are best deployed in protected areas with an interpreter/navigator who uses a set of aerial photos and/or maps to aid navigation. This officer navigates around potentially dangerous or unstable terrain, as well as any sensitive natural or cultural sites. It is their responsibility to know the location of important heritage sites and to protect them from impact. Unstable scree slopes can also be very dangerous when a number of staff are deployed in the same place.

Memorial honouring Virunga National Park guards killed on duty, Democratic Republic of the Congo

Source: IUCN Photo Library © Jim Thorsell

Case Study 18.4

Nepalese protected areas, floods and landslides

Nepal's national parks and wildlife reserves are under a constant threat of natural disasters, such as floods and landslides during the 100 days of rainy season where more than 80 per cent of the total annual rainfall (about 1500mm) falls in Nepal. Rain washes out geologically unstable soil in the hills and causes floods in the plains. Almost all of Nepal's major rivers either originate in the national parks or pass through them. Soldiers stationed to protect a conservation site have been swept away by landslides. A sudden landslide killed 20 security personnel at a check post in the village of Ramche who were positioned to protect Langtang National Park. Floods and landslides cause damage to the habitats of endangered animals, as well as to infrastructure. Indian rhinos (*Rhinoceros unicornis*) have been killed by floods; an Indian elephant (*Elephas maximus indicus*) breeding centre has been inundated.

The Nepalese Department of National Parks and Wildlife Conservation has built embankments along rivers; but they have proved insufficient to prevent the floods from entering into park areas. Chitwan, which occupies 932 square kilometres in the subtropical lowlands in Terai, is home to around 600 endangered rhinos and about 80 Royal Bengal tigers (*Panthera tigris*). The World Wide Fund for Nature (WWF) has provided support in emergency situations to rescue endangered species trapped by floods.

Source: adapted from Poudel (2003)

Where terrain may be unstable, managers must plan cautiously for the safety of visitors. A geotechnical report may be required before any proposed structures (including buildings, lookouts, walking tracks and bridges) are built. Once they are constructed, an appropriately qualified engineer should confirm that they are safe to use. Managers should check often, and not hesitate to close sites or tracks that may have become unstable.

Managing incidents arising from armed conflict

Armed conflict regrettably occurs in or near protected areas in many countries:

> *Armed conflicts add complexity and present new challenges, difficulties and risks for conservation. Often, there is little that the conservation sector and its collaborators can do to avoid adverse environmental impacts: the forces that cause them are much larger than any efforts that conservation staff can undertake to prevent them. Sometimes, though, there are actions that can be taken to reduce these impacts, even if they cannot be avoided entirely. Actions at the right time and in the right place can collectively make a significant difference in conserving natural resources and biodiversity, and, ultimately, in promoting sustainable livelihoods and maintaining long-term stability in an area once conflict ends (Shambaugh et al, 2001).*

Protected area managers can take a number of actions at different levels in situations of armed conflict. These are adaptive approaches to management and include internal organizational arrangements as well as on-ground responses. Some of these are described in Table 18.3. In some circumstances, protected area organizations may be able to work with NGOs and other international organizations to help protect parks.

Management principles

1   Sooner or later, incidents will occur.
2   Preparedness is essential. Managers can and should plan in advance, using the 'principles of precaution'.
3   Human life and property take precedence over the environment during an incident.
4   The safety of staff is paramount. Undisciplined or risky behaviour is not acceptable.
5   Staff may need extra job-related support during and after an incident.
6   Proven and widely recognized management systems are the best way to protect an area during an incident. It helps if both staff and stakeholders are skilled in the use of standard incident management systems, such as the NIIMS/ICS.
7   Having efficient plans, appropriately skilled staff and suitable plant, equipment and stores

Table 18.3 Actions that may be taken during situations of armed conflict

Potential action	Notes
In response to conflict, increase flexibility of management	Conservation organizations need to be flexible in a situation of armed conflict
	They need to stay calm and ensure that staff are safe, adapt to new circumstances quickly, adjust and intensify planning, and strengthen the capacity of local staff and field offices
Emphasize livelihood linkages, while staying focused on long-term goals	The first priority is to save lives
	Improved collaboration between environment, relief and development sectors can help to avoid harmful impacts
	Flexibility: use of natural resources may be required to support basic survival needs for a period
	Link community needs during conflict and incorporate these within conservation activities
	Demonstrate a commitment to the local community and build trust
Strengthen capacity to maintain a presence during and especially immediately after conflict	Staff need to be aware of all emergency plans
	Staff need the right to dissent and leave if they wish
	Staff need to be well trained to work under high stress and in potentially dangerous situations
	Additional incentives and motivation may be required for personnel to perform during a period of civil unrest
	Increase the autonomy of local staff and NGOs
	Maintain neutrality and impartiality
	Actively build trust with different actors in the conflict
Use reliable, up-to-date information to assess the situation	Collect relevant information
	Assess threats and opportunities
	Assess organizational capacity to respond
Ensure good planning	Develop contingency plans before, during and after conflict
	Prepare staff security guidelines
	Determine the basis for pulling out of an area
Collaborate with all groups involved	Improve communication
	Develop good will and trust

Source: Shambaugh et al (2001)

accessible allows for prompt action that can minimize the impacts of incidents.

8   Full and timely data on heritage assets, and on other matters, is crucial. A calm analysis of data, even in the heat of an incident, allows decisions to be made that preserve life and property and limit the impact on the environment.

9   Anticipate official post-incident enquiries and collect appropriate information during the incident.

10 Staff will respond, and perform better, if given real roles and scope and recognition for their skills.

11 Mutual trust and respect is critical when working with other organizations if effective

incident management is to be achieved. Such trust is usually achieved through constant professional and respectful interaction over a long period.

12 Working extensively and professionally with the community is a critical investment for cooperative management. Direct contact with senior local officials and local members of parliament or government, and constant briefing about the progress of incident events are critical.

13 During incidents, expect the unexpected; anticipate the inevitable.

Further reading

AIIMS (Australian Inter-service Incident Management System) (1992) *Incident Control System: The Operating System of Australian Inter-service Incident Management System*, Australian Association of Rural Fire Authorities, Melbourne

NIIMS (National Interagency Incident Management Systems) (2002) *Operational System Description: National Interagency Incident Management System*, www1.va.gov/emshg/apps/kml/docs/NIIMS_ICS_OperationalSysDesc.pdf

Shambaugh, J., Ogelthorpe, J., Ham, R. and Tognetti, S. (2001) *The Trampled Grass: Mitigating the Impacts of Armed Conflict on the Environment*, Biodiversity Support Program, Washington, DC

US Department of Homeland Security (2004) *National Incident Management System*, US Department of Homeland Security, Washington, DC

19

Tourism and Recreation

Terry De Lacy and Michelle Whitmore

Protected areas attract millions of visitors each year. This will increase as the world becomes more crowded and beautiful natural areas become rarer and more sought after. Tourism can have benefits for protected areas. The areas can be used to educate people about conservation. The economic value of tourism from protected areas can benefit local communities and act as leverage for political support. But, of course, large numbers of visitors affect the environments of protected areas and the communities who depend upon them. Protected area managers are required to balance the demands for a quality visitor experience with the need to protect the environment. Managers of protected areas need to be aware of the trends in tourism and their implications for management (Eagles, 2004).

In this chapter we provide a global context for tourism and protected areas and discuss management issues. Case Study 19.1 outlines many of the issues related to tourism and protected areas discussed at the Vth IUCN World Parks Congress in South Africa. These issues are further developed throughout the chapter. We also address the characteristics of the tourism industry, visitor management models, institutional systems for tourism management and local community involvement.

Global tourism and environmental performance

Growth in global tourism has been one of the great phenomena of the late 20th and early 21st centuries. In 2003, international tourism expenditure was valued at US$523 billion, and there were approximately 691 million international visitor

Case Study 19.1

Tourism and protected areas at the Vth IUCN World Parks Congress, Durban, South Africa

Robyn Bushell, University of Western Sydney, Australia

Visitation to protected areas is growing significantly worldwide and is therefore a major focus for protected area management. The theme of the Vth IUCN World Parks Congress in 2003, *Benefits Beyond Boundaries*, epitomized some of the critical issues facing protected areas globally and the importance of visitors and visitor management.

Tourism and recreational visitors can provide considerable economic benefits to protected areas and the communities adjacent to or within them. High-quality visitor experiences and effective environmental education contribute to increased understanding and commitment to the protection and conservation of biodiversity.

However, if poorly planned and managed, tourism can contribute to the deterioration of cultural landscapes, threaten biodiversity, contribute to pollution and degradation of ecosystems, displace agricultural land and open spaces, diminish water and energy resources, and drive poverty deeper into local communities. Christ et al (2003) show how tourism development can have a profound impact on biodiversity conservation with a strong correlation between biodiversity hotspots and popular nature-based tourism locations.

Therefore, in order for tourism in and around protected areas to be a tool for conservation, careful and strategic implementation of policy, together with proactive and effective management of tourism, is essential. This requires considerable capacity-building of protected area staff and communities. It also requires a much better level of understanding of protected area visitation patterns, numbers and trends; of visitor motivation and satisfaction; and guidance in issues such as the most effective policies on licensing, concessions and permits (Skeat and Skeat, 2004).

Partnerships with traditional owners are an important mechanism of protected area management to ensure support for indigenous communities.

Protected areas worldwide require more sophisticated understanding of effective conservation education and interpretation strategies (Staiff et al, 2002).

In order to deal with these issues the World Commission on Protected Areas (WCPA) has had a Taskforce on Tourism and Protected Areas since 1997. Tourism-related issues also involve the activities of other IUCN commissions: the Commission on Environmental, Economic and Social Policy and the Commission on Education and Communication, all concerned with tourism as a form of sustainable use of biodiversity.

At the provincial and country level, and within IUCN national committees, there are several programmes relating to tourism. For example, IUCN South Africa founded the Fair Trade for Tourism Initiative, which certifies sustainable accommodations facilities. Member organizations and affiliates of IUCN with tourism and conservation programmes include the United Nations Educational, Scientific and Cultural Organization (UNESCO), the United Nations Environment Programme (UNEP), The Nature Conservancy, Conservation International (CI), the World Wide Fund for Nature (WWF) and Birdlife International. The relationship between tourism and protected areas is highlighted in World Parks Congress Recommendation 5.12.1, which states that the tourism sector, including appropriate institutions, associations and operators, works together with protected area managers and communities to ensure that tourism associated with protected areas, in both developed and developing countries:

- respects the primacy of the role of conservation for protected areas;
- makes tangible and equitable financial contributions to conservation and to protected area management;
- ensures that tourism contributes to local economic development and poverty reduction through:
  - support to local small- and medium-sized enterprises;
  - employment of local people;
  - purchasing of local goods and services; and
  - fair and equitable partnerships with local communities;
- uses relevant approaches that encourage appropriate behaviour by visitors (such as environmental education, interpretation and marketing);
- uses ecologically and culturally appropriate technologies, infrastructure, facilities and materials in and/or near protected areas;
- monitors, reports and mitigates negative impacts and enhances the positive effects of tourism;
- communicates the benefits of protected areas and the imperative for conservation; and
- promotes the use of guidelines, codes of practice and certification programmes.

arrivals worldwide (WTO, 2004a). The World Travel and Tourism Council (WTTC) forecast that the number of international arrivals will increase to nearly 1.6 billion by 2020 (WTTC, 2004). However, the high cost and reduced availability of aviation fuel may influence this forecast. Many of the countries expecting significant growth in travel and tourism demand are also those in which key Global 200 ecoregions (see Chapter 1, p34) are located (Font et al, 2004).

While protected areas in high Human Development Index (HDI) countries may currently receive a greater number of visitors than low HDI countries, the trend is for significant growth in visitation to protected areas in low and medium HDI countries, mainly as a result of international tourism. Low HDI nations currently have a limited capacity to fund management of visitation to protected areas, and will need to be strategic in the way that they source funding from tourism.

The tourism industry and protected areas can potentially enjoy a mutually beneficial relationship. Tourism can provide an economic justification for the establishment of protected areas, as well as opportunities for local people to reduce their dependence upon resource extraction. It can build a supportive constituency that promotes biodiversity conservation, and it can provide an impetus for private conservation efforts (Christ et al, 2003). However, the health of this relationship depends upon the compatibility of their respective needs and recognition by the industry of all the values afforded by protected areas.

Tourism definitions

Common terms used to describe various aspects of tourism, are defined as follows.

Tourism is travel away from home for business, recreation or pleasure, and the activities that go with this. The World Tourism Organization (WTO) definition recognizes the trip to be more than 50km, and for the stay to be overnight but less than 12 months. The term also covers industries and services that aim to satisfy the needs of tourists. The tourism system includes businesses linked to the point of origin, transit and the destination.

Visitor use is defined as any use of protected areas by visitors. These include official visitors, volunteers, contractors, protected area workers and educational groups, as well as tourists and local recreationists.

Recreation is activity voluntarily undertaken, primarily for pleasure and satisfaction, during leisure time (Pigram and Jenkins, 1999). *Recreation settings* are areas that allow a given activity, such as sightseeing, picnicking, camping, rock climbing or canoeing. They are sometimes referred to as destinations.

Nature-based tourism involves travel to unspoiled locations in order to experience and enjoy nature. It usually involves moderate and safe forms of exercise, such as hiking, cycling and camping. *Wildlife tourism* typically involves travel to observe animals in their natural habitats. *Adventure tourism* is nature-based tourism with a kick: it requires physical skill and endurance (rope climbing, deep-sea diving or kayaking) and involves a degree of risk-taking, often in little-charted terrain. *Car camping* is usually conducted in family groups to locations with enough facilities to make the experience in nature more comfortable (Eagles, 1995). Nature, wildlife, adventure and car camping tourism are defined solely by the recreational activities of the tourist.

Ecotourism is defined by its benefits both to conservation and to people in the host country. Coined by Herbert Ceballos Lascurain in 1983, the term *ecotourism* implies a genuine attempt to respect nature and to manage for the future. Sirakaya et al (1999) produced a definition of ecotourism following consultation with ecotourism operators in the US. Their definition considers that ecotourism involves non-consumptive and educational visits to low-use sites of high natural, cultural or historical quality. The expected results from ecotourism include low impact on the host environment; increasing contributions to environmental protection and conservation; funds to protect ecological and socio-cultural assets; improved understanding; interaction between visitors and local communities; and employment opportunities and spending contribution to the local economy. Tourism activities in protected areas:

- may be run on a commercial basis by a protected area organization, with profits being returned to the protected area, or may be run by a private operator, with some profits returned to the protected area;
- may be certified by an independent accreditation body and employ environmentally qualified staff;
- should provide high-quality environmental education for visitors; and
- should have associated investments of time and resources to help minimize impacts and make a positive contribution to achieving conservation outcomes.

Wildlife safari in Ngorongoro Crater, Tanzania

Source: Michelle Whitmore

There is a much greater awareness among operators of the need to conduct 'sustainable' tourism, as indicated by the adoption of environmental accreditation programmes such as Green Globe. Certification is being introduced as protected area agencies seek higher standards of operation in protected areas, and some concerned and committed companies provide leadership in environmental management (see Case Study 19.2).

Tourism and the environment

Modern transport systems, especially aircraft, have delivered visitors quickly and efficiently to visitor destinations around the world. Tourism is important to the economies of many nations and brings many benefits to local communities. The tourism industry uses materials, water and energy, contributes to greenhouse gas emissions and produces solid wastes. Transport is a major component of the tourism system and is one of the greatest producers of greenhouse gases.

Tourism's consumption of resources at a global scale is considerable:

> *International and national tourists use 80 per cent of Japan's yearly primary energy supply (5000 million kWh per year), produce the same amount of solid waste as France (35 million tonnes per year), and consume three times the amount of freshwater contained in Lake Superior, between Canada and the US, in a year (10 million cubic metres) (Christ et al, 2003).*

Despite the efforts of a few outstanding companies, the tourism industry has been slow to achieve substantive environmental performance improvements (Worboys and De Lacy, 2003). If tourism in protected areas is to be managed sustainably, then the emission of greenhouse gases, as well as the consumption of energy and water and the production of wastes, must be reduced (see Chapter 14). The susceptibility of the tourism industry to climate-induced redistribution or

Case Study **19.2**

Binna Burra Mountain Lodge, Lamington National Park, Australia

Linus Bagley, manager, Binna Burra Mountain Lodge

Binna Burra Mountain Lodge, founded in 1933, is located just inside the World Heritage-listed Lamington National Park in south-east Queensland, Australia. Much of the property displays natural rainforest regrowth and revegetated areas, while developed sections support the lodge and a campsite.

The original prospectus of the company, dated 10 March 1933, clearly expressed the company's early intentions with respect to environmental protection. Romeo Watkins Lahey, one of the company's founders, was a great influence in establishing sound environmental principles at the company's inception:

> The company is being formed with the objects set out in the Memorandum of Association and, in particular, to provide tourist facilities and accommodation in beauty spots throughout the State of Queensland and, as far as possible, to assist in preserving such in their natural state for future generations in accordance with the ideals of the National Parks Association of Queensland.

During recent years, Binna Burra Mountain Lodge has adopted a more formalized approach to all aspects of its environmental management. An environmental management plan and a land management plan have been developed to underpin all aspects of the company's operation. Key environmental indicators have been identified and benchmarked through the Green Globe process (see Case Study 14.4). In 1996, the company received advanced accreditation certification through Ecotourism Australia's National Eco-Certification Programme.

Binna Burra was one of the initial applicants to the Queensland government's Cleaner Production Partnership programme. This programme, delivered through the Queensland government Environmental Protection Agency's Sustainable Industries Division, assists industry to identify areas where environmental performance can be improved and operating costs reduced. The company invested over Aus$40,000 to implement the recommendations of an eco-efficiency assessment. As a result, annual savings of almost Aus$17,000 were achieved. This included savings in diesel fuel (Aus$6500 per annum); water heating (Aus$2700 per annum); ultraviolet water treatment chemical savings (Aus$800 per annum); and sewage-treatment plant chemical savings (Aus$950 per annum). The initiatives achieved electricity savings of 234 megawatt hours (MWh) and greenhouse gas reductions of 189 tonnes carbon dioxide equivalent per year.

Through the Green Globe programme, the company's environmental performance is monitored and benchmarked. The major areas of attention include:

- landscaping and land management;
- water and wastewater;
- solid waste;
- cleaning materials;
- energy efficiency;
- air and noise pollution;
- contribution to the local community;
- interaction with wildlife;
- biodiversity conservation;
- safety and emergency procedures; and
- staff environmental education.

Environmental interpretation is fundamental to the operation. Binna Burra Mountain Lodge attracts visitors who wish to interact with the natural environment and, in doing so, develop their knowledge, awareness, appreciation and enjoyment. Interpretation of the natural history and cultural heritage of Lamington National Park is provided by suitably qualified guides. Staff at Binna Burra are dedicated to following best practice methods with regard to environmental conservation, education and quality of service.

The company's management recognize the importance of working closely with the protected area managers and local rangers. Regular meetings to discuss track maintenance, health and safety, fire control, monitoring outcomes and visitor activity in the park facilitate a good cooperative working relationship that results in beneficial outcomes for the environmental sustainability of the park.

extinction of wildlife populations and changing visitor management challenges, particularly due to natural disasters, is a reality that must be confronted (Higham and Hall, 2005). There could be a complete change in peak tourism regions as travellers seek more comfortable climates. Preston–Whyte and Watson (2005, p140) provide one perspective on how climate change may affect key tourism attractions in Africa:

> … *the melting of the Mount Kilimanjaro ice cap; the desiccation of the Okavango, Chobe, Zambezi, Kafue and St Lucia hydrological systems; rising temperature in the trout-rich waters of the Drakensberg Mountain foothills; and the disappearance of the spring annuals in the Succulent Karoo. However, in general, a warmer and drier climatic scenario should enhance the promotion of popular images of the 'African bush' experience, given that the expansion of the eutrophic savannas favours flat-topped thorn trees, large ungulate herds and the 'Big Five'.*

There are numerous conventions, charters and guidelines that can assist protected area managers in dealing with the tourism industry, local communities and visitors. These include:

- Convention on Biological Diversity (CBD) Guidelines on Biodiversity and Tourism Development;
- International Council on Monuments and Sites (ICOMOS) International Cultural Tourism Charter: Managing Tourism at Places of Heritage Significance;
- Quebec Declaration on Ecotourism;
- IUCN World Commission on Protected Areas (WCPA) Sustainable Tourism in Protected Areas: Guidelines for Planning and Management;
- Convention Concerning the Protection of World Cultural and Natural Heritage; and
- United Nations World Tourism Organization (WTO) Global Code of Ethics for Tourism.

The WTO *Global Code of Ethics* calls for tourism to work closely with the local community to ensure a sustainable future for natural and cultural resources, as well as for tourism (WTO, 2004b).

Rangers, wetland protected area, Taipei, Taiwan

Source: Graeme L. Worboys

The WTO has contributed to a variety of international declarations on tourism and the environment. In conjunction with the WCPA and the United Nations Environment Programme (UNEP), for example, the WTO developed guidelines for the practical management of tourism to protected areas. It sponsored the first international conference on climate change and tourism, and supported the subsequent *Djerba Declaration on Tourism and Climate Change*, which encouraged the tourism industry to use more energy-efficient and cleaner technologies, and urged governments to support all relevant intergovernmental and multilateral agreements that would promote sustainable tourism, especially the Kyoto Protocol.

At the conclusion of the Third Global Travel and Tourism Summit held in May 2003, more than 500 of the world's most influential businesses and political leaders called on the WTTC to create a new vision and strategy for travel and tourism. The resulting strategic document, *Blueprint for New Tourism*, was launched by the WTTC on 7 October 2003. The blueprint sets as a key goal balancing economics with environment, people and cultures; and indicated that 'new tourism' looks beyond short-term considerations to focus on benefits for local communities and the environment, as well as for travellers.

Similarly, key messages from Conservation International (CI) and its UNEP partner reinforce the importance of global sustainable tourism:

> *Over the past three decades, major losses of virtually every kind of natural habitat have occurred... Many of the ecosystems in decline are the very basis for tourism development... Tourism will require careful planning in the future to avoid having further negative impacts on biodiversity... At the same time, an increasing number of examples have shown that tourism ... can have a positive impact on biodiversity conservation (Christ et al, 2003).*

The United Nations Educational, Scientific and Cultural Organization (UNESCO) has several initiatives to promote tourism that responsibly uses natural and cultural assets as outlined by UNESCO (2005l):

> *Joint activities with the Institute of Responsible Tourism aim to promote sustainable development and protection of natural and cultural heritage in the tourism industry.*
>
> *A cooperative arrangement [exists] with UNEP and WTO in the Tourism Operators' Initiative for Sustainable Tourism Development, which aims to develop and implement tools for sustainable tourism development.*
>
> *The World Heritage Centre monitors the effects of tourism on the inscribed values of world heritage areas.*
>
> *Several NGOs affiliated with UNESCO, such as the International Scientific Council for Island Development (INSULA) and the International Council for Science's (ICSU's) Scientific Committee on Problems of the Environment (SCOPE), have also carried out projects on the impacts of tourism.*

Various tourism organizations are committed to achieving sustainable tourism through self-regulation of the industry and by promulgating the principles and practices of *Agenda 21*. Many operators are gaining certification in environmental, social and economic sustainability. Membership of such schemes implies best practice. Certification can provide tour companies with a marketing advantage, as consumers are influenced by the presence or absence of environmental codes and many are concerned about environmental impacts.

The Asia-Pacific Economic Cooperation (APEC) and the Australian Sustainable Tourism Cooperative Research Centre (STCRC) launched a programme for delivering sustainable tourism based on cooperation and quantified environmental performance targets (De Lacy et al, 2002). The STCRC has been responsible for important research into sustainable tourism throughout the Asia-Pacific region. Private hotel chains, ecotourism organizations, magazines devoted to green outcomes and environmental certification schemes such as Green Globe have all helped. The Rainforest Alliance, a New York-based NGO, has provided leadership for the introduction of a Global Sustainable Tourism Stewardship Council. The council aims to provide a minimum standard for tourism environmental certification schemes and an accreditation process. Despite these initiatives, the extent of on-ground improvement in environmental performance has been disappointing. More effort is needed to implement the principles enunciated in documents such as those cited above.

The tourism industry

The search for an experience with nature is a growing phenomenon in the tourism industry. Newsome et al (2002) suggest that tourism to natural areas has increased from 2 per cent of all tourism during the late 1980s to approximately 20 per cent of all leisure travel. There is no doubting the capacity of protected areas to attract visitors to a destination, and most often these destinations are in rural or provincial areas that may otherwise not receive significant tourist numbers. A recent study by Tourism and Transport Forum (TTF) Australia and STCRC (2004) estimated that Australian national parks receive approximately 80 million visitors per year and they are fundamental to provincial tourism success. Protected areas in Thailand were reported as receiving more than 15.4 million visits in 1996 (Pipithvanichtham, 2005). Protected areas such as Yellowstone, the Grand Canyon and Yosemite in the US have attracted millions of visitors every year for decades. A global estimate of tourism to protected areas is difficult to obtain because there are no consistent protocols for collecting and analysing data on visitation.

Characteristics of visitors

Adventure holidays and opportunities to learn about and experience local cultures are in demand. Visitors are increasingly discerning and environmentally aware, and are likely to avoid locations that are known to be congested or have environmental problems. All visitor markets expect the protected area destinations that they visit to be well managed. They expect a quality experience and are becoming more demanding with regard to facilities and activities. It is not always possible or appropriate to meet all of these demands. Protected area managers need to decide which activities best fit with the character and purpose of the protected area and to create a balance between visitor use and environmental management issues.

Identifying the characteristics of specific visitor groups allows managers to control the visitor experience and to target programmes and services to visitor interests. There are various tourist 'typologies' or 'segments' that have been identified. Typically, each location allocates their own segments that suit their distinct visitor groups; but this makes it difficult for comparisons between sites (Hvenegaard, 2002). Palacio and McCool (1997) propose a segmentation of the nature-based tourism market using a benefit approach:

> Nature-escapists *appreciate and are interested in learning about nature. They are also motivated by the desire to escape from the pressures of everyday life.*
>
> Ecotourists *are strongly motivated by the desire to learn about nature, interested in physical fitness and adventure, want to escape their home surroundings, and are interested in associating with others.*
>
> Comfortable naturalists *are interested in nature and escape, but want to do it in comfort.*
>
> Passive players *have low motivation with respect to their interest in nature, desire for escape, adventure and social activity (Palacio and McCool, 1997, pp239–240).*

Being aware of this segmentation can assist with the design of education and marketing campaigns. Directing advertising at suitable mediums will help in attracting the desired target market – for example, those that support conservation and are interested in learning about the environment (Eagles et al, 2001). While the majority of visitors to many protected areas may be domestic visitors, understanding international visitor use is also important for many protected areas, especially in countries with large nature or wildlife tourism visitation. Keeping abreast of tourism industry research on international visitors assists the planning process to meet visitor demand, where possible. Close proximity to major metropolitan centres or the international status of a protected area as a World Heritage site will result in a larger number of international visitors.

Wildlife tourism

Wildlife often attracts people to protected areas, and wildlife tourism is a growing industry. Like other types of tourism, wildlife tourism can contribute to conservation through *in situ* and *ex situ* management and research (Higginbottom et al, 2002), or threaten the very resource on which it relies. Areas with substantial concentrations of wildlife, particularly larger mammals, tend to provide the greater tourist attractions.

To effectively manage wildlife tourism, the impacts of the activities on all species within the protected area need to be assessed since different species have different tolerance levels.

Understanding the long-term impacts of tourism on wildlife behaviour, stress, reproduction and health is a time- and resource-intensive process. Adaptive management (see Chapter 11) is a key platform for the sustainable management of wildlife tourism given its uncertainty and complexity (Newsome et al, 2005).

Sustainable tourism

Management responses to achieving sustainable tourism in protected areas vary between 'direct' and 'indirect'. Direct responses regulate behaviour by implementing permits, zoning and restricting activities. Indirect approaches include applying visitor fees, interpretation and site 'hardening'. Site hardening is often considered the simple solution. Hardening a site means changing boggy tracks to boardwalks, replacing pit toilets with composting toilets, and so on. This cannot be used as a general solution because the very type of site that many visitors wish to see and experience in protected areas (natural destinations) becomes increasingly scarce. As soon as there are infrastructure improvements, the nature of the recreation setting changes. Therefore, in order to provide a range of recreation settings and visitor facilities, natural sites may need to be actively managed so that use is sustainable without 'hardening'. If many visits are causing damage, then action can be taken to change the way in which visitors use the site, as well as when they use it and how many use it. The advantage of this approach is that it preserves a diversity of destinations by protecting those most vulnerable to change, particularly sites that are currently undeveloped.

Management techniques that can be used to help achieve sustainable visitor use include:

- completing a survey of natural and cultural

Tourist on a guided mokoro safari in the Okavango Delta, Botswana

Source: Michelle Whitmore

heritage values and identifying sites of significance;

- determining the recreation setting for a destination and estimating how many visitors a site can handle;
- determining whether infrastructure or facilities are appropriate for a destination, and, if so, their layout and how they are to be blended harmoniously with the site;
- visitor management practices such as limits; permits; tour operator concessions and lease agreements; dispersal of visitors; concentration of visitors; rules on the length of stay; segregating different recreational activities; seasonal limits; zoning; and limits on the size of party;
- environmental education and interpretation;
- codes of practice;
- facilitating environmental certification schemes for tourism operators;

- using renewable energy sources (such as wind and solar power) (see Chapter 14); and
- designing for recycling facilities, if appropriate, but also encouraging visitors to take home their waste.

There are typically few sites in protected areas that cannot be visited; but there are many that can only accept a few visits a year by a few people, and then in conjunction with expert guides. There are numerous other sites where larger numbers of visitors are sustainable and can be actively promoted. Zoning is a planning tool commonly used to manage visitor use by spatially dividing a protected area according to key management objectives (see, for example, Table 11.6). Zones can allocate where development is allowed, as well as identify areas that will be strictly protected. Other mechanisms include quota systems that allow only a certain number of visitors per year.

Bhutan has a largely intact natural environment. The Bhutanese government recognizes the benefits that tourism can provide (such as foreign exchange and employment), and is utilizing a precautionary approach to minimize the negative influences and increase the economic benefits of tourism. Limitations are posed on the number of people who can enter the country by setting a high fixed price for tours. Pricing is an effective way of regulating numbers for maximum yield (that is, maximum economic return for minimum impact). This high-yield management approach limits social problems often associated with major tourist destinations (Brunet et al, 2001).

Developing specific tourism management plans is a strategy for highly visited areas: these plans should integrate with the overall protected area management plan and align with the tourism plan for the region. In Sweden, the recent designation of Fulufjället National Park (FNP) was coordinated with tourism marketing and promotion for the surrounding region and the country (see Case Study 19.3). Collaboration between protected area managers and all tourism stakeholders is imperative. Involving tourism operators in management decisions and maintaining communication channels can assist in developing a trusting relationship. Case Study 19.4 outlines

the importance of communication between protected area managers and tourism operators.

Key destinations

The majority of visitors to protected areas focus on only a few well-known attractions. Detailed planning of such key destinations is critical. Careful selection of the location for key destinations can potentially spread the economic benefits of tourism. Key destinations have the potential to achieve iconic status, along with their host protected area, and thereby assist provincial economies. Tourism marketing campaigns generally focus on these iconic sites. In such places, attention to design detail is critical. For example, walks may be designed for brief-, medium- and long-stay visitors. Visitation limits can be built into the design of key destinations in order to protect sites and to improve the quality of the visitor experience. The integrity of the site must be at the forefront of design considerations. In addition, key destinations can concentrate visitors and keep them away from highly sensitive areas when visitation is likely to significantly degrade fragile ecosystems.

Visitor management models

Planning, active management of sites, monitoring and rapid response to unsustainable actions should be the four basic elements of effective visitor management. There are a number of management models designed to guide this process. The more widely recognized models are described below.

Recreation Opportunity Spectrum (ROS)

The ROS was developed by the US Forest Service (Clarke and Stanley, 1979). It is a planning tool for managing natural areas for recreation and aims to distinguish a range of recreational settings, from remote natural wilderness through to urban and 'developed' settings, in order to offer visitors a range of high-quality outdoor recreation opportunities. This range of settings has been described as a recreation opportunity spectrum. Nature-based tourism experiences range from a short stopover at a scenic lookout, to a guided walk and talk by a ranger, to high-risk adventure activities, or to extended camping tours through remote country lacking in any visitor facilities. Some

Case Study **19.3**

Incorporating the social with the ecological in Fulufjället National Park, Sweden

Peter Fredman, European Tourism Research Institute, Sweden

In Sweden, national park legislation has recently changed so that the focus is no longer just ecological, but also social. As a result, in designating the recent Fulufjället National Park (FNP), it was important to assess the social needs of the park, as well as the ecological. Key issues were Recreation Opportunity Spectrum (ROS) zoning, a tourism development project, an in-depth visitor survey and an 'inside-out' designation process.

Fulufjället was designated as a national park because it provides habitat to the four predators in the area – brown bear (*Ursus arctus*), wolverine (*Gulo gulo*), wolf (*Canis lupis*) and lynx (*Lynx lynx*) – and it is the only mountain area in Sweden unaffected by the Sami people grazing reindeer. Hence, the area features a unique flora of lichens and mosses not found elsewhere in the Swedish mountain region. Prior to its establishment as a national park, Fulufjället was a regularly visited nature reserve, and so the park was important to local people for recreation. The core visitor attraction is Sweden's highest waterfall, Njupeskär. Other popular activities include trekking, hunting, fishing and ice climbing.

The park was not established in isolation. Extensive community consultation occurred in the years leading up to its designation as a national park. This ensured that the public were aware of the changes that would occur. The focus was on the opportunities that would be created around the park (Wallsten, 2003). In the year before and the year after designation, extensive visitor surveys were conducted to guide the park management plan and further development. These surveys also monitored changes in visitor characteristics, activities and impacts (Fredman, 2004; Fredman et al, 2005).

In designating FNP, complementary infrastructure was developed. This included a visitor centre, new trails and new signage clearly indicating the new park zoning. The park was zoned using ROS. See p506 and Tables 19.1–19.3 for an explanation of this method. Four zones were allocated, ranging from wilderness to more developed zones. Zones 1 to 3 make up the majority of the park and offer opportunities for a tranquil experience of nature. The smallest zone, zone 4, is a high-use zone around the waterfall.

The region directly surrounding the protected area is referred to as the 'gateway' community. Many of the tourism businesses providing services for visitors to Fulufjället are located here. In tandem with the national park designation process, a tourism development project was implemented by Swedish authorities with European Union (EU) funding. The park managers now work closely with these tourism operators to market the park. This includes the recently established Protected Area Network of Parks (PAN) Accommodation. The park is jointly promoted as one of the key attractions in the region and in the country. As a result, FNP is increasingly becoming a major revenue generator for the region. According to the visitor surveys, park visitation increased by 40 per cent following designation.

activities, such as wilderness walking, require a much greater area of natural land than those that rely on built infrastructure or intensive interaction. The ROS categorizes areas by their physical factors, such as the naturalness of the area and the presence or absence of roads and visitor facilities; by social factors, such as the number of other users; and by managerial factors, such as the presence of barriers and signs (NSW NPWS, 1997b).

The ROS has been adopted, but not always fully used, by many protected area agencies. An example of a ROS classification system developed for use in the Australian state of New South Wales (NSW) is shown in Table 19.1. This table also gives the different category labels used in the

states of Victoria and Queensland. Indicative activities associated with the five ROS classes are given in Table 19.2. The associated visitor expectations within each of these classes are shown in Table 19.3. Further development of this approach is demonstrated in Case Study 19.5.

Limits of acceptable change

Limits of acceptable change (LAC) (Stankey et al, 1985) is based on the premise that human use does cause damage. It sets managers the task of defining (through objectives of management and performance criteria) how they want their destinations to be managed. This approach is quite different from monitoring visitor use to

Case Study **19.4**

Collaboration between protected area managers and tour operators, Kimberley Region, Western Australia

Aggie Wegner, Murdoch University, Western Australia

It is a political and economic reality that protected areas in Australia serve the dual purpose of nature conservation and recreation and tourism provision. Protected areas are tourism assets, and tour companies regularly access protected areas, often in remote locations. There is considerable potential for conflict between the objectives of tour operators and protected area managers. It is, therefore, imperative that protected area managers and tourism operators learn to work collaboratively. This case study focuses on the importance of effective communication between protected area managers, in this case, the Western Australia (WA) Department of Conservation and Land Management (CALM), and tour operators in the Kimberley region of WA.

Interviews conducted with protected area managers and tour operators provided evidence that, while they share many of their core values and objectives, they do not necessarily assign the same meanings to the words they use to communicate with one another. For example, protected area managers often see communication as the simple task of providing information on daily operations, while operators seek communication to build relationships and for product enhancement.

Tour operators appreciate it when a ranger joins the tour group for an informal discussion, even if this is during the process of collecting fees. The direct contact of rangers with passengers is perceived to add to the passengers' experience and improves the tour product. Personal contact, in the field, between rangers and tour groups provides enhanced interpretation of environmental, social and cultural factors in protected areas. It ensures that the agency's message on conservation and protection is communicated as they intended, while reducing potential misinformation from tour guides. It can also provide tour operators and their passengers with a greater awareness of conservation issues and the importance of sustainable management.

determine if impacts are occurring. The LAC approach sets limits, which can be measured, to the human-induced changes that will be permitted, and identifies the remedies that managers should provide. The LAC system, whose focus is on wilderness areas, employs nine steps (Stankey et al, 1985):

1 Identify area concerns and issues.
2 Define and describe opportunity classes.
3 Select indicators of resource and social conditions.
4 Inventory resource and social conditions.
5 Specify standards for resource and social indicators.

Boardwalk, Point Pelée National Park, Canada

Source: Graeme L. Worboys

Table 19.1 Recreation Opportunity Spectrum (ROS) as utilized by the New South Wales National Parks and Wildlife Service (NPWS)

New South Wales ROS category	Class 1	Class 2	Class 3	Class 4	Class 5
Equivalent Victorian ROS category (Department of Conservation and Environment, undated)	Remote	Semi-remote	Roaded natural	Semi-developed	Developed
Similar Queensland ROS category	Remote	Semi-remote, non-motorized	Semi-remote, motorized	Natural	Divided into two classes – intensive and urban
General description	Essentially unmodified environment of large size	Predominantly unmodified environment of moderate to large size	Predominantly natural environment; generally small development areas	Modified environment in a natural setting – compact development area	Substantially modified environment; natural backdrop
Access	No roads or management tracks – few or no formed walking tracks	No roads – management tracks and formed walking tracks may be present	Dirt roads – management tracks and walking tracks may be present	Two-wheel-drive roads (dirt and sealed); good walking tracks	Sealed roads; walking tracks with sealed surfaces, steps and so on
Modifications and facilities	Modifications generally unnoticeable – no facilities; no structures unless essential for resource protection and made with local materials	Some modifications in isolated locations – basic facilities may be provided to protect the resource (such as pit toilets and BBQs)	Some modifications, but generally small scale and scattered; facilities primarily to protect the resource and public safety; no powered facilities	Substantial modifications noticeable – facilities may be relatively substantial and provided for visitor convenience (such as amenity blocks), and caravans may be present at times	Substantial modifications that dominate the immediate landscape – many facilities (often including roofed accommodation) designed for large numbers and for visitor convenience
Social interaction	Small number of brief contacts (e.g. less than five per day); high probability of isolation from others; few if any other groups present at campsites	Some contact with others (e.g. up to 20 groups); but generally small groups – no more than six groups present at campsites	Moderate contact with others; likely to have other groups present at campsites; families with young children may be present	Large number of contacts likely; variety of groups, protracted contact and sharing of facilities common – may have up to 50 sites	Large numbers of people and contacts: groups of all kinds and ages; little likelihood of peace and quiet
Visitor regulation	No on-site regulation – off-site control through information and permits may apply	Some subtle on-site regulation, such as directional signs and formed tracks	Controls noticeable but harmonized (such as information boards and parking bays)	On-site regulation clearly apparent (such as signs, fences and barriers), but should blend with natural backdrop	Numerous and obvious signs of regulation – rangers likely to be present

Source: NSW NPWS (1997b)

Table 19.2 Indicative tourism and recreation activities undertaken for recreation opportunity classes

Activity	Class 1	Class 2	Class 3	Class 4	Class 5
Alpine skiing					✓
Snow boarding					✓
Cross-country skiing	✓	✓	✓	✓	✓
Ice climbing	✓	✓	✓	✓	✓
Picnicking (facility based)			✓	✓	✓
Camping (no facilities)	✓				
Camping (facility based)		✓	✓	✓	✓
Scenic driving			✓	✓	✓
Four-wheel driving and registered trail-bike riding on road			(✓)	(✓)	
Nature study or cultural awareness	✓	✓	✓	✓	✓
Horse riding		(✓)	(✓)	(✓)	
Canoeing/kayaking/white-water rafting	(✓)	(✓)	✓	✓	✓
Boating (motorized)		(✓)	✓	✓	✓
Sailing/sail boarding		✓	✓	✓	✓
Adventure activities	(✓)	(✓)	(✓)	(✓)	
Fishing	✓	✓	✓	✓	✓
Non-powered flight: hang-gliding, hot air ballooning and paragliding		(✓)	(✓)	(✓)	(✓)
Powered flight: low altitude			(✓)	(✓)	(✓)
Cycling (on existing roads and trails)		(✓)	(✓)	✓	✓
Bushwalking (on formed tracks; not overnight)	(✓)	✓	✓	✓	✓
Bushwalking (remote areas or long-distance trails)	✓	✓	✓		✓
Orienteering/rogaining		(✓)	(✓)		
Cross-country running			(✓)	(✓)	
Caving	(✓)	(✓)	(✓)	(✓)	(✓)
Organized mountain biking				(✓)	(✓)

Notes:

✓ Activity permitted.

(✓) Activity may be permitted subject to certain conditions, such as designated sites only.

Source: adapted from NSW NPWS (2002)

6   Identify alternative opportunity class allocations.
7   Identify management actions for each alternative.
8   Evaluate options and select an alternative.
9   Implement actions and monitor conditions.

It is a relatively costly and complex process; but adaptations are possible. The greatest strength of LAC is determining when 'enough' change has occurred. The two weaknesses of LAC have been selecting standards and gaining stakeholder support (Newsome et al, 2002).

Visitor impact management

Visitor impact management (VIM) was developed by Graefe et al (1990). The model recognizes that managing visitor use is complex, and that impacts are influenced by factors other than use levels. VIM identified five major sets of considerations critical to understanding the nature of recreational impacts that should be incorporated within any programme which models such impacts:

1   interrelationships between types of impact;
2   use–impact relationships;
3   varying tolerances of impact;

Table 19.3 Visitor expectations of services relative to the nature of visitor destination settings based on the Recreation Opportunity Spectrum (ROS)

ROS category (see Table 19.1)	Class 1	Class 2	Class 3	Class 4	Class 5
Ranger patrol and monitoring	*	*	*	*	*
Natural setting; no modifications	*				
Large expanses of natural scenery	*				
Natural settings; very basic modifications		*	*		
Natural settings; basic modifications with basic road access			*	*	
Fire management trails		*	*	*	*
Walking tracks, basically maintained		*	*	*	*
Walking tracks developed to a higher standard				*	*
Pit toilet facilities		*	*	*	*
Composting toilets		*	*	*	*
Septic toilets				*	*
Showers				*	*
BBQ sites		*	*	*	*
Parking areas			*	*	*
Formalized camping facilities (basic)			*	*	*
Formalized camping facilities, including furniture				*	*
Visitor information signs (basic)			*	*	**
Visitor information signs and display panels			*	*	*
Information maps	*	*	*	*	*
Brochures	*	*	*	*	*
Booking systems (walking in some areas)	*	*	*	*	*
Booking systems (camping in some areas)	*	*	*	*	*
Clean facilities	*	*	*	*	
Sites or areas managed sustainably	*	*	*	*	*
Facilities and services maintained in a safe, hygienic condition	*	*	*	*	
Vandalism repaired rapidly and basic maintenance achieved for facilities and access	*	*	*	*	

Source: NSW NPWS (1997b)

4   activity-specific influences; and
5   site-specific influences.

The VIM process uses eight steps:

1   reviewing data;
2   reviewing objectives of management;
3   selecting key indicators of impact;
4   selecting standards for these key impact indicators;
5   comparing existing conditions;
6   identifying probable causes of impact;
7   identifying management strategies; and
8   implementing the strategies.

VIM relies on reviewing existing literature and applying the knowledge gained to manage visitor impacts. A weakness is that it does not allow for dealing with potential future impacts.

Visitor experience and resource protection

Visitor experience and resource protection (VERP) is an indicator-based approach. It can be used in wilderness and non-wilderness settings. The result is a series of management zones based on quality resources and visitor experiences (Brown et al, 2006).

Visitor Activity Management Programme

Visitor Activity Management Programme (VAMP) assesses the appropriateness of visitor activities at a site and matches these with suitable facilities and services (Payne and Nilsen, 2002). It makes use of marketing techniques.

Tourism Optimization Management Model

Tourism Optimization Management Model (TOMM) was initially developed for monitoring tourism on Kangaroo Island, South Australia. It

has three major parts – context description, monitoring programme and implementation (Newsome et al, 2002). It has broad application and involves a diversity of stakeholders, but requires the availability of detailed information.

A comparison between these various frameworks is given in Table 19.4. If there are not sufficient resources, staff or finances to conduct one of the more complex visitor management models, an adapted planning framework could be instigated. Such a framework could place greater

Table 19.4 Comparison of visitor management frameworks

Visitor management framework	Developed	Applied	Related to carrying capacity	Scope	Scale	Stakeholder involvement	Information on impacts
Recreation Opportunity Spectrum (ROS)	US Forest Service	US, Australia, Sweden and New Zealand	Yes, social carrying capacity	Social	Landscape	Not specific	No
Visitor Activity Management Programme (VAMP)	Parks Canada	Canada	No	Design and social	Landscape and site	Not specific	No
Visitor impact management (VIM)	US National Parks and Conservation Association	US, Australia, Canada, Argentina, Mexico and The Netherlands	Yes	Social and ecological	Site specific, but can be used at landscape level	Not specific	Yes
Limits of acceptable change (LAC)	US Forest Service	US and Australia	Yes, through its connection to ROS	Social and ecological	Site specific, but can be used at landscape level	Yes	Partially
Visitor experience and resource protection (VERP)	US National Parks Service	US and Australia	Yes	Social and ecological	Landscape and site	Yes	Partially
Tourism Optimization Management Model (TOMM)	Manidis Roberts Consulting, Australia	Australia and Canada	Yes, through its association with LAC	Social and ecological	Landscape	Yes	Yes

Sources: adapted from Newsome et al (2002) and Payne and Nilsen (2002)

emphasis on the abilities of 'on-the-ground' staff to establish planning limits. This response is primarily applicable at the site scale, and should generally be instigated where the more tested approaches are not applicable. Reference sites can be used to evaluate the planning limits established, and these limits can be reviewed through a community consultation process. Regular monitoring against management objectives can determine whether a strategic response is required.

Visitor service and support

Visitors require good service and support. They directly benefit from good planning and the initiative taken by managers early in the establishment of a new protected area. There are several non-invasive ways in which staff can help people to have a high-quality experience when they visit protected areas:

- Information about destinations should be made readily available in a clear, corporately consistent and concise form, whether in brochures, videos, press releases, articles or the internet.
- Roads to sites should be safe, well-maintained examples of whatever category they are claimed to be (bitumen road, gravel road or four-wheel-drive track).
- Tourism operators who transport people to destinations should be using the journey as an opportunity to inform people about protected area management. Protected area staff could provide information kits and brief videos, to be shown by coaches en route to destinations. Formal training could also be provided for tour leaders.
- Destinations should be thoughtfully designed or sensitively adapted for the recreation intended. Different sites for a given recreation should offer a range of facilities, from minimal to sophisticated, and visitors should be given reliable information as to what they can expect at a site.
- Design of facilities should be in keeping with the character of the recreation settings in which they are located. Variation in the level of visitor facilities (from no infrastructure to urban-style facilities) should be planned based on the desired mix of recreation settings.
- For destinations with no facilities, considerable effort may be needed to ensure minimal evidence of human use. Special arrangements may be required to deal with waste.
- Information provided to visitors prior to their arrival at a destination should ensure that their expectations of the facilities and services available match those present.
- This variety of sites and facilities should mean that licensed commercial tour operators can select and offer a range of recreation settings. Visitors who prefer more natural settings will have that choice. This type of experience may be increasingly desired and is already an important niche market.

Walkers, Ben Boyd National Park, New South Wales, Australia

Source: Graeme L. Worboys

Case Study 19.5

Reserves Standards Framework: A levels-of-service approach, Tasmania, Australia

Mark Poll, Tasmania Parks and Wildlife Service, Australia

One of the ongoing challenges for Tasmania's Parks and Wildlife Service (PWS) is ensuring that services are provided where they are needed and at a standard appropriate to visitors' requirements. In addition to this, consideration needs to be given to the diversity of services (recreation opportunities) provided nearby, within the regions and across the state. Equally important, service provision and its maintenance must be both environmentally and economically sustainable. All protected area managers face these challenges, as well concerns about risk management.

The Reserves Standards Framework (RSF) (Poll, 2003) was developed as a strategic planning and management tool to address risk management from a public policy perspective. Recognition of the aforementioned challenges and a review of related initiatives by the Department of Conservation in New Zealand (Visitor Asset Management System), Parks Canada (Visitor Risk Management) and Parks Victoria in Australia (Levels of Service) reinforced the need to consider risk management as an integral part of the broader management context. As such, characteristics of those initiatives are reflected in the RSF and can be seen in the integration of the following elements:

- visitor management;
- risk management;
- asset management; and
- finance management and resource allocation.

Visitor management strives to provide quality recreation experiences and to ameliorate the impacts of visitors on natural and cultural values. In order to achieve this, it is necessary to understand the types of people who visit the protected areas. Of particular interest are visitors' expectations, the types of experiences and activities sought, and the levels of risk that are commensurate with those experiences. Such insights allow managers to target service provision in order to match the characteristics of the visitors. By communicating the levels of service provided across the protected areas, visitors are better able to self-select recreation opportunities that match their needs (Shelby and Heberlein, 1986).

Risk management involves limiting or removing the likelihood of incidents and accidents. Foresight is essential to successful risk management because a proactive approach is more effective in reducing the probability of accidents, incidents and their consequences than after-the-fact reactions.

Asset management. Adherence to construction, maintenance and environmental standards and codes of practice is fundamental to the ongoing integrity of natural, cultural and built assets for which the PWS is responsible. Standards, such as those developed by Standards Australia and Standards New Zealand (2004), and those prescribed by legislation, government agreements and policy, set the benchmark for management.

Finance management and resource allocation. Effective asset management requires the strategic allocation of finite funding and resources to provide and maintain appropriate levels of service and the value of the assets managed by the agency, whether they are built, natural and/or cultural. This is essential in ensuring the safety and well-being of visitors who use the facilities, the long-term integrity of the assets and the quality of the recreation opportunities provided.

Finding a common thread to link these four elements was critical to the success of the RSF. The early realization that these four elements share a common spatial characteristic was fundamental to its development. The *visitor site* provides the link, as it is the on-ground location where visitors recreate, risks are managed, assets are provided and resources are spent. From a technical viewpoint, the RSF is underpinned by a spatial (geographic information system, or GIS) database that links often discrete management functions and information sources (see Case Study 10.6).

Visitor sites are classified according to their predominant visitor group. Visitor sites may be defined along a spectrum from 'day use comfort' sites at one end, through to 'bushcamping remote/natural' sites at the other (see Table 19.5). 'Day use comfort' sites cater to visitors whose stay is usually brief and undertaken *en route* to another destination. Such visits often incorporate a drink/meal break, a stretch of the legs or a short walk viewing natural features accompanied by interpretive signs/information. These sites also provide the opportunity for day-long visits that are restricted to the site and are often associated with a family or group outing. Visitors to such sites can enjoy low-risk experiences associated with high-standard facilities. In contrast, 'bushcamping remote/natural' sites provide visitors with the opportunity to stay for one or several nights in areas where few, if any, facilities are provided. Visitors to these sites must be capable of coping with potentially high-risk levels associated with remote natural environments.

Table 19.5 Reserves Standards Framework (RSF) site classification and the associated acceptable level of risk

RSF classification	Acceptable risk level
Day use comfort	Low risk
Day use get away	
Easy access campers	
Bushcamping backcountry	
Bushcamping remote	
Natural	High risk

Once the predominant visitor group has been identified, the boundaries of the visitor sites are defined and mapped. The boundary between visitor sites is the point at which there is a change in the predominant visitor group or the number of visitors.

Various levels of service can be provided for each RSF site category (see Figure 19.1). To determine the *descriptive* level of service at a visitor site, an inventory of existing services is undertaken, recording the location, type and condition of services. This information is stored within the Parks and Wildlife Service Information Management System (PIMS) (see Case Study 10.6). Comparisons are then made between the existing service level at the site and the model service levels to determine the site's *descriptive* classification. The model service levels are detailed in a set of tables that outlines the type, level and standard of service to be provided at visitor sites of different classifications. Such details include specific standards for walking tracks, amenities, roads, information and signage that are to be provided and maintained for each visitor site category and its level of service. All visitor sites managed by the PWS are thus classified, mapped and recorded on the PIMS. An example of a RSF mapping is given in Figure 19.2.

So, how does this information help in addressing the challenges outlined earlier? From a *visitor management* perspective, communication of the existing level of service at a site is a critical step that facilitates visitors' site selection. Visitors can make more informed choices with respect to recreation venues that are

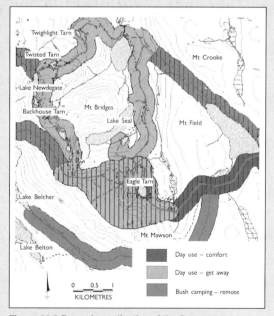

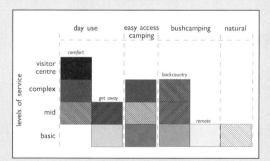

Figure 19.1 Reserves Standards Framework (RSF) visitor site classification matrix

Figure 19.2 Example application of the Reserves Standards Framework from Mt Field National Park

aligned with the type of experience they desire and their skill level. In this way, both the quality of visitors' experiences and their safety are enhanced.

In terms of *risk management*, identification of the predominant visitor group provides the contextual foundation for determining the acceptable level of risk for the site (see Table 19.5). The level of risk can then be communicated in a uniform fashion in accordance with the PWS's Public Risk Management Policy (Sallans, 2003). This policy builds on the foundation of the National Safety Council of Australia's methodology for risk calculation and is consistent with the 2004 Australian and New Zealand Standard for Risk Management AS/NZS 4360.

An understanding of the levels of service, and a register of the assets supplied at each visitor site, provides the basis for the development of site-based maintenance and inspection schedules. Completion of scheduled works (including statutory maintenance, and mandatory condition and safety monitoring) are then logged via the asset management module of the PIMS, automatically confirming that the scheduled service requirement has been met. As works are programmed and their completion recorded, it is possible to track performance and the cost of management at the visitor-site level. Such data can then inform future fund allocation and, when aggregated to a region or agency level, can be used to support budget bids.

From a planning perspective, examination of the existing (descriptive) levels of service, using the thematic mapping and analysis capabilities of the PIMS, provides the foundation for strategic decision-making, such as that encompassed by the Recreation Opportunity Spectrum (ROS). Specifically, the insights provided by such analyses can and should inform decisions with respect to determining the desired (aspirational) levels of service. In doing so, several important questions are considered:

- Is the current level of service (and use) at a visitor site consistent with the management of the natural and/or cultural values?
- Does the existing level of service at a visitor site match the needs of the predominant visitor group?
- Does the existing level of service at a visitor site fit with the spectrum of recreational opportunities that the PWS wants to provide within the protected area, across the region and across the state?
- How does the existing service offered, at a site, region or state-wide level, relate to other government and non-government initiatives?
- How does the existing range of recreation opportunities fit with the present and likely future resource capacities of the PWS?

In addition to the above questions, the existing and likely future levels of visitation are taken into account when determining aspirational service levels. Such decisions are influenced by the importance of sites for recreational and educational experiences, their potential to enrich/foster visitors' appreciation and understanding of Tasmania's natural and cultural values, and/or to increase visitors' understanding of the need for the protection of those values.

As a result, a site's *aspirational* level of service may prescribe:

- the maintenance of existing levels of service;
- a change to the level of service within a visitor site category;
- a shift in management from service provision for one visitor site category and level of service to another;
- closure of the site due to over-servicing, lack of resources, unacceptable level of risk to visitors, and natural and/or cultural values; or
- development of a new site with a specified level of service due to under-servicing or re-siting of existing services to mitigate environmental impacts – for example, rerouting a walking track to inhibit the spread of *Phytophthora cinnamomi*, a soil-borne organism that causes root rot.

Once the aspirational levels of service have been identified, the on-ground managers are provided with clearly defined guidelines with respect to the standard of service provision they are to provide and to the acceptable level of risk. Incidence of under- or over-servicing, due to a lack of defined standards of service provision, is then highlighted and minimized.

In cases where services at a visitor site meet the aspirational standards, resources can be directed to visitor sites where aspirational levels of service are yet to be met. Where a gap exists between the existing and the aspirational levels of service, analyses can be undertaken to determine the cost involved in meeting the desired standard of service provision, and bids for funding can be made.

In conclusion, it can be seen that the development of the RSF enhances the strategic management capabilities of the PWS. Specifically, the RSF provides the foundation for critical analysis and informed decision-making with respect to meeting the challenges of providing a spectrum of quality recreation opportunities that are safe and environmentally and economically sustainable.

Managers need to keep in mind the inventory of protected area assets and facilities, as well as those available in surrounding areas. Case Study 19.5 describes the asset management system used by the Tasmanian Parks and Wildlife Service (PWS) in Australia. As well as addressing provision of quality visitor services and risk management, these systems draw together other aspects of visitor management considered in this chapter: data requirements, market segmentation, ROS and recreation planning.

Visitor monitoring

Tourism and recreation are dynamic, as are the seasonal patterns of visitor use. A change in either can bring peak loads of visitors that exceed the capacity of destinations. Managers should constantly analyse the relationship between the supply (capacity of destinations or sites) and the demand (of visitors who seek or would prefer a given setting). With knowledge of any patterns, they will be in a better position to manage for sustainability.

There is a general lack of quality time-series data for visitation to protected areas. In addition, the number of protected areas monitoring impacts from visitation is low. Visitor statistics would assist in deciding on the most appropriate management approach. Monitoring can provide information on visitor numbers, characteristics, activities, preferences, expectations and motivations, to name a few. Data on visitor numbers is important for budget and resource allocation; reports on sanitation; fire suppression; requirements for facilities and staff; visitor services; interpretation and education material; planning; marketing; assessing the economic value of visitation and environmental impacts; and public liability (Hornback and Eagles, 1999). Monitoring and reporting on visitor impacts and management is one way in which protected area managers can provide justification for changing or maintaining visitor opportunities.

Techniques for obtaining visitation figures can range from direct measurements with automatic counters (such as heat and impact recognition, and vehicle counters) to indirect measurements using mathematical equations (for example, esti-

mates of visitor numbers from regional tourism surveys). Depending upon the site and requirements for visitor data, there is a range of options available. These include automatic sensors and detectors, secondary recordings, visitor registers, ticket sales, observations, counter rotation and partial counts. These techniques are often used in combination.

Visitor perspectives on management approaches and perceptions of social and environmental resource conditions can be ascertained through surveys There is a multitude of survey techniques, from self-response questionnaires to interviews. This information can help to direct visitor management and resource allocation for visitor services. Table 19.6 provides a summary of visitor monitoring techniques.

Interpretation of protected area values

> Interpretation communicates what is special about protected areas and, by creating a greater understanding, makes them better appreciated. It helps visitors have more positive and meaningful experiences. It is also important to long-term conservation. Interpretation is an educational activity which aims to reveal meanings and relationships through the use of original objects, by first hand experience and by illustrative media, rather than simply to communicate factual information (Tilden, 1982, p8).

Interpretation has long been at the heart of managing protected areas. Interpretation needs to translate scientific information into a format that non-scientists can understand and find interest in (Ham, 1992). The style of interpretation has changed over the last century in accordance with varying demands. Protected areas have been likened to open-air museums, providing instructive information. Staiff et al (2002) describe what they call the 'new museology'. Visitors no longer accept that there is one 'correct' interpretation of an object. Rather, it may have multiple meanings implied through ecological, indigenous, aesthetic, historical and recreational perspectives.

Table 19.6 Summary of visitor monitoring techniques

Visitor monitoring technique	Advantages	Disadvantages	Application
Counting visitors – includes automated counters, entrance records (e.g. ticket sales), manual counts, visitor books, tour records and aerial photos	Provides simple measure of extent of use of natural area; automated counters are one of the most reliable ways of estimating numbers	Most methods provide estimates only; automated counters are expensive to purchase and some may have significant margins of error	Traffic counters can be employed on most roads used by vehicles; aerial photos are useful for marine areas and difficult-to-access locations, such as beach dunes
Questionnaires and personal interviews – includes site-based, main and/or telephone data collection	Questionnaires provide comprehensive information on visitors, their activities and expectations; they are widely used, making results comparable with those obtained elsewhere	Can be expensive to design, administer and analyse	Best used where detailed information on visitors and their visit characteristics, preferences and expectations are required for planning and impact management
Observing visitors – used to count numbers and observe behaviour	Useful for counting numbers when other means are not available; observing behaviour can be correlated with other techniques, especially self-reporting by visitors	Counts of numbers are approximate only; observing behaviour is expensive and training of observers is essential	Best used where information on numbers and behaviour is unavailable via other means
Focus groups and other interactive techniques – users brought together to provide data, often on more than one occasion	Efficient means of accessing a range of ideas at one time (focus group) or seeking determination and agreement over time on indicators and standards (task force)	Extremely time consuming to organize and administer; data may be difficult to analyse if consensus is not reached	Using task forces only warranted for large, complex natural areas with multiple stakeholders

Source: Newsome et al (2002, p286)

Role of interpretation and interpreters

Interpretation can educate the community, elucidate management objectives, and give visitors an enjoyable and profound experience. Interpretation is one of the major ways in which staff interact with visitors. The best interpretive experiences are long remembered. Effective interpretation can have an impact on visitor behaviour and attitudes. The effect of different styles of interpretation on visitor behaviour in Lamington National Park, Queensland, is described in Case Study 19.6.

There are four roles for interpretation: promotion, enjoyment, management and conservation (Beaumont, 1999).

A protected area management agency can promote public understanding of its goals and objectives, as well as disseminate information about the managed area and advertise recreational programmes. While there are marketing aspects to this role, integrity is required to avoid propaganda that can undermine community relations. Marketing for a protected area can help managers match demand with supply (taking into account visitor use limits) and assist with conservation by promoting appropriate visitor behaviour. Promotion and marketing should be guided by the goals and objectives of the protected area and portray appropriate use and values. Promotional efforts can develop an identity and image for the

Walkers, Peak District National Park, UK

Source: IUCN Photo Library © Jim Thorsell

site through logos or slogans. A clear outline for promotional strategies can be attained through discussions between protected area organizations and tourism operators (Wearing and Nelson, 2004).

Visitor enjoyment is a major objective of interpretation and is especially important in ecotourism. Interpretation helps to develop a keener awareness, appreciation and understanding of the area visited and enriches the visitor's experience. It helps to orientate visitors, allowing them to find preferred recreation opportunities and to do so safely and with enjoyment.

Effective communication of management needs can persuade visitors to treat sites respectfully, without need for regulation and enforcement. It can be used to subtly direct most visitors' attention towards less fragile sites, promote suitable behaviours and reduce visitor impacts. Use of the internet can be highly effective in disseminating management information. A significant proportion of travellers utilize the internet to gain information on their destination. Maintaining an up-to-date internet site enables protected area managers to provide information to a large audience instantaneously. Information

Case Study **19.6**

Using interpretation to manage recreation in Lamington National Park, Australia

Carolyn Littlefair, Griffith University, Australia

Protected area managers often prefer to use interpretation as a management technique because it is perceived to be the most cost-effective method; it is a light-handed approach and allows visitors the freedom of choice; and it enhances visitor experiences and satisfaction. However, the ability of interpretation to bring about a reduction in the environmental impacts of visitors to natural areas has rarely been quantified. I conducted a research project to assess how well environmental interpretation works as a management tool – specifically, to determine the extent to which interpretation reduced the environmental impacts of visitors on guided walks in national parks.

The research was conducted in Lamington National Park, in the south-east of Queensland, Australia, with the assistance of Binna Burra Mountain Lodge. Five different interpretive programmes were created and used. The programmes were a combination of environmental interpretation, role modelling by the guide of appropriate behaviour, and verbal appeals from the guide for visitors to modify their behaviour. Three common and experimentally convenient environmental impacts were measured: shortcutting of corners, picking up litter already on the track and the noise level of the group. Between 2000 and 2002, 41 walks were studied. The impacts of each group were measured and statistical analysis was undertaken on all results.

Results from the measurements of shortcutting found that the interpretive programme, which consisted of a combination of environmental interpretation, role modelling and verbal appeals, was always the most effective in reducing shortcutting. Results of the picking up litter measurements found that verbal appeals from the guide was the only factor that influenced whether litter was picked up. Analysis of the noise results found that no interpretive programme significantly reduced the noise level of visitors.

This study reveals that it is possible for interpretation to reduce some environmental impacts of visitors. Environmental interpretation alone did nothing to modify the behaviour of visitors or reduce impacts. It is important that interpretative programmes expressly address an impact or behaviour in order to have any chance of reducing it. When the required behaviour is unfamiliar or uncertain to the visitor, role modelling of the correct behaviour by the guide was essential for visitors to behave that way themselves.

on track closures or recreation activities can be easily downloaded from an internet site without the cost to the managers of printing and distribution. As protected areas become increasingly popular as international tourist destinations, it will be important to provide multilingual information, and this is most easily provided on-line.

With respect to conservation, interpretation of protected area values can:

- instil interest in, and support for, conservation activities;
- encourage donations of time and money to conservation;
- explain the rationale for management decisions that favour conservation over visitor convenience – for example, why at some sites it is appropriate to not provide any facilities or infrastructure; and
- provide educational information that may have wider benefits for conservation.

Good interpretation will always use a mix of methods and media. However, the appropriate mix will depend upon the audience. Visitor surveys and other social science methods described earlier can be used to classify an audience. As well, some agencies now attempt to divide an audience into 'market segments' in order to identify its different requirements. Skilled presenters can adapt or personalize their presentations accordingly.

Plain language is especially important when dealing with visitors. Inappropriate jargon can easily alienate the general public or cause misunderstandings. Hence, staff members needs to be able to adapt their language to their hearers. Staff can vary their register, both in speech and writing (including public signage). Register is a term for the tone and style that makes speech or writing suitable for a given audience. Different registers may be required for writing, conversation and formal speech. Note that the two elements that most readers find off-putting are long sentences and long abstract words. When preparing publications, staff may seek advice on the appropriate register; but they will need their own sense of register when they meet with or give talks to the public. Engaging people by writing or speaking in a lively way can enthuse the public (or a team of one's co-workers) and activate their emotions.

Guides lead many of the interpretive activities (tours, talks, group activities and so on). To meet the broad goals of interpretation, a guide needs to take on many roles. Recently, standards and measures for interpretation have been formalized – for example, the EcoGuide Certification Programme developed by Ecotourism Australia specifically for nature and ecotourism guides. A number of aspects of the guide's role have been formally defined, including:

- a leader and organizer of group activities;
- an educator communicating messages and skills to the group;
- a public relations representative for their organization and its goals;
- a host for visitors, attending to their needs, desires and safety;
- a motivator for the group to act in environmentally sensitive ways;
- an entertainer providing fun and comradeship; and
- a conduit through which the experiences (both conscious and subliminal) of the site are facilitated (Pond, 1993).

Interpretation methods and media can be broadly classified as:

- personal – attending services such as information centres, conducted activities, talks, live interpretations and cultural demonstrations; or
- non-personal or 'static' interpretation – printed materials, signs, exhibits, self-guided walks, pre-recorded tour commentaries on cassettes or videos, virtual tours, and other electronic media.

Using new technology, a variety of different interpretation techniques can be implemented. Case Study 19.7 provides two examples of interpretation for remote wildlife communities. In all cases, information should be arranged around a theme since it makes it more interesting and is more likely to be remembered. A summary of a number of interpretation techniques and their strengths and weaknesses is presented in Table 19.7.

Local community involvement in tourism

Tourism can both provide opportunities for and impose burdens on local communities. Protected areas are often located in sub-national regional locations where employment options may be limited. Evidence of employment and financial benefits reaching the community, and legitimate participation in tourism and wildlife management, can help generate support for protected areas and tourism. Wherever possible, local staff and products should be used and promoted. A holistic approach to tourism and protected area management, which addresses local poverty, rural settings, education, local values and culture, and legal and tenure systems, as well as the issues of equity and empowerment, will have a greater chance of achieving effective community participation (Burns, 2004). Without clear land tenure agreements, for example, it will be unclear who has the rights to benefit from, or manage, tourism. The Community-based Natural Resource Management (CBNRM) programme instigated in Namibia has addressed many of these issues (see Case Study 19.8). An evolving association between tourism in the South Luangwa National Park (SLNP) in eastern Zambia and communities in the surrounding Lupande Game Management Area is discussed in Case Study 19.9.

Tourism is increasingly being utilized as a tool for poverty alleviation (see Case Study 19.10), gender equity and introducing sustainable development principles. International aid organizations have recently begun providing funding for tourism development. The Cambodian government, for example, is taking advantage of these funds to promote natural and cultural sites in provincial areas, providing opportunities for people in these areas.

Table 19.7 Strengths and weaknesses of some interpretive techniques

Technique	Application	Strengths	Weaknesses
Publications and websites	Pre-trip information Supports on-site information Provide updates on conditions	Cost-effective method of reaching a wide audience Portable information	Communication is passive Expensive if subject to frequent updates Limited internet access globally
Visitor centres	Information on macro- and micro-management scales Face-to-face contact Often located at the entrance gates to protected areas	Recognizable information points A wide range of audiovisual techniques	Expensive to establish Need to cater for different audiences Can be overwhelming and crowded
Brochures	Available through visitor centres Support self-guided trails	Portable information In-depth information Low cost Not intrusive on landscape	Require a certain level of reading skills One-way communication
Self-guided trails and signage	Provide a focus for the attention of visitors Opportunity to provide messages throughout a site Provide information and direction	Visitors can explore at their own pace Visitors read only what they are interested in Relatively low cost Suitable for remote areas	Subject to vandalism Interpretive story not flexible Generally not suitable for children Can be obtrusive on the natural environment
Guided touring	Wide application in all environments	Messages can be very powerful and effective Can be adapted to client needs Can be spontaneous and up to date Interpreter can facilitate active involvement	Requires well-trained and effective interpreters Audience attention is needed to be successful May only be available for a small portion of visitors

Sources: adapted from Beaumont (1999) and Newsome et al (2002)

Management principles

1   It is important that visitor use is managed sustainably as part of the overall protected area management framework.
2   The sustainable management of tourism requires the development of partnerships between protected area managers, the tourism industry and the local community.
3   Effective management requires the evaluation of visitor impacts. High-quality environmental and cultural conditions need to be maintained

Case Study **19.7**

Providing interpretation on remote wildlife communities

Interactive computer programmes and remote technology have been used to provide interpretation on remote wildlife communities (Moscardo et al, 2004). Interactive programmes allow visitors to self-direct their information search and work at their own pace. Remote technology, such as cameras and microphones, allows visitors to observe wildlife at a distance. This is particularly useful for presenting wildlife that is typically elusive or to show behaviour that is often not seen. It also reduces the negative effects on wildlife.

Cameras and microphones can be placed in hides, burrows or nests by wildlife experts and the information relayed to visitor centres. In this manner, large numbers of visitors can observe wildlife without major disturbance. This can be of benefit for sites that are difficult to access or have limits on the number of visitors allowed entry due to the sites' sensitivity.

This technique has been used at Taiaroa Head on the South Island of New Zealand for viewing northern royal albatross (*Diomedea epomophora sanfordi*) (Moscardo et al, 2004). Located in the visitor centre, a live broadcast of the birds is relayed from cameras hidden within the nesting site. The broadcast is combined with a range of static and audiovisual displays, guide presentations and tours to provide visitors with a holistic experience.

The Scottish Seabird Centre utilizes multimedia and interactive technology to provide interpretation on nearby bird colonies. This is in addition to the standard themed displays, videos, boat tours and volunteer staff. A multimedia show focuses on gannets and a viewing deck with telescopes allows visitors to observe the gannet colony on Bass Rock and puffins on the nearby island of Fidra. A live feed from cameras situated on the islands allows visitors to observe the birds in their normal behaviour. The live screenings are interactive in that the visitors can remotely zoom, pan and rotate the cameras to scan the islands for birds, and focus in on nests and chicks during the breeding season (Newsome et al, 2002).

Ecotourists learn about medicinal herbs from a local expert in Tatras National Park, Slovakia

Source: Robin Rigg

Case Study **19.8**

Tourism and community-based natural resource management, Namibia

Christopher Vaughan, Department for International and Rural Development, University of Reading, UK

Tourism activities within Namibia's communal land areas historically benefited private-sector lodge owners, tour operators and tourists, often to the exclusion and detriment of local resident communities. With the development of the national Namibian Community-based Natural Resource Management (CBNRM) programme and implementation of new community projects and activities, this is changing. Increasingly, local communities are developing their own community campsites and negotiating beneficial joint venture agreements for training, employment and revenue with private-sector tourism investors. Tourists are increasingly aware of the complex socio-ecological nature of the environment within which they are visiting and relationships are being built between local communities, tourists and tour operators.

In this early stage in the CBNRM programme's development, tourism benefits the livelihoods of a limited number of people by delivering income, employment, capacity-building and career path development. This is substantially more than under the pre-independence apartheid era, and there are now firm foundations to expand the scope and scale of benefits to local residents. Recent research by the Wildlife in Livelihoods Diversification project (WILD) indicates that only 3.6 per cent of the work force in Namibia's Kunene region, and less than 1 per cent of survey respondents in Caprivi region, listed CBNRM and tourism-related employment as their main occupations. In Caprivi, incomes from tourism employment, which amount to 6000 Namibian dollars (US$909) per annum, are slightly less than the average of household incomes from livestock, cropping and natural resource sales. This means that incomes from tourism, while providing new livelihood diversification opportunities, do not currently provide more than existing livelihood strategies. However, those who gain tourism-related employment are able to generate a stable income and support larger social networks.

Communities traditionally had few rights to control unregulated tourism and to negotiate benefits from existing concessions. With increased localized control, the ability to negotiate and lobby, and a new favourable policy and service provider environment, this is changing. However, tourism development can also bring site-specific costs in terms of restricting access to resources resulting from changes in land use – for example, restricting grazing mobility seasonally and geographically. Community-based tourism enterprises have, in some instances, failed where local governance and service provider support has been lacking. The CBNRM programme has provided a foundation for communities to develop new tourism enterprises and seek joint ventures with the private sector. While bringing new opportunities, it has also brought costs and, in several cases, has resulted in increased community conflict.

It is still early days for the programme; but a number of opportunities exist for tourism to further provide sustainable livelihoods and conservation efforts. The government could adopt, develop and operate a pro-poor tourism policy. This should focus on tourism developments that have positive impacts, contributing directly to poverty reduction, enhanced livelihood security and social empowerment. Good local governance should be encouraged to deal with tourism enterprises and to address conflict. Conservancies need support to develop inclusive stakeholder integrated land-use planning processes that mitigate site-specific livelihood costs. This should be in conjunction with rights provision to communities to further develop tourism-related activities.

to ensure the economic benefits brought by tourism.

4   Management should facilitate rewarding, safe and enjoyable experiences for visitors, without compromising conservation objectives.

5   Planning tools such as ROS are essential to manage visitor opportunities effectively. Protected area managers, in cooperation with other land managers, should facilitate at a regional scale the provision of an appropriate range of recreation opportunities.

6   Regular communication of current and qual-

ity information should be provided to the public. Visitors will be more supportive of protected area management if they are aware of the real cost of maintaining visitor sites and if revenue from tourism is reinvested in providing these services.

7   Ham (1992), Newsome et al (2002), Griffin and Vacaflores (2004) and Moscardo et al (2004) have suggested a number of principles for interpretation of protected area values:

• Interpretation is neither teaching, nor 'instruction' in the academic sense. It seeks

Case Study 19.9

Communities and protected area tourism, Zambia

Allison Rossetto, James Cook University, Australia

The relationship between tourism in protected areas and adjacent communities is dynamic and negotiated. This case study explores the value of the national park as a community resource, both directly and indirectly, due to the presence of the tourist sector.

South Luangwa National Park (SLNP) in eastern Zambia is considered one of the greatest wildlife sanctuaries of the world (Zambia National Tourist Board, 2005). The conservation and tourism potential of the SLNP was recognized as early as the 1950s (Norman Carr Safaris, 2003); but the park, in its current form, was created during the 1970s. The SLNP is located in Mambwe District in eastern Zambia. It is bordered by four game management areas.

The existence of the SLNP and the demand for photographic and hunting safaris present considerable opportunities for the surrounding community to leverage benefits. While the community receives no direct financial return from the SLNP, it is paid a proportion of revenues raised by hunting concessions relating to the Lupande Game Management Area. Funds are distributed among democratically elected organizations and are used for a mix of community projects and household dividends. Possibly of more value to the community is the tourism sector associated with the SLNP. Already, the park attracts more than 12,000 international visitors annually (Phiri and Butler, 1998) and tourism is the major employer in the local area, employing in excess of 500 people during the peak season (June to October) (Dalal-Clayton and Child, 2003). The tourism sector is a key provider of support for social and infrastructure projects, such as the construction of wells, schools and teachers' houses, and support for education in the form of scholarships and bursaries, usually with funds sourced directly for this purpose from tourists.

A recent study conducted in the area exploring tourism as a means of poverty alleviation found that while considerable links exist between the tourism sector and the surrounding community, many more had yet to be exploited. In 1998, 80 per cent of the population in the Eastern Province lived in poverty, with 66 per cent in extreme poverty (Ministry of Finance and National Planning, 2002). The study attributed the community's failure to capitalize on the tourism sector's presence to a multiplicity of factors, including a limited understanding of the tourism system and its integration with other economic activities (Sofield et al, 2004); a lack of decision-making power in relation to tourism; a lack of cooperation and communication within the community in relation to tourism and between the community and the tourism sector; and limited skills in relation to the sector.

The study concluded with more than 20 recommendations relating to new or improved means for the community to harness the benefits of tourism to the SLNP. These strategies were devised to address the factors identified as inhibiting beneficial links. Recommendations ranged from broad measures, such as public education and awareness campaigns, and to improving coordination and cooperation within the community for direct involvement in the tourism industry. For example, the study noted:

- the potential to establish community managed co-operatives for the sale of fresh produce to safari lodges;
- the opportunity to develop cultural experiences that have potential socio-economic benefits for community members who provide the products and services to the tourist sector; and
- the potential to establish a community managed lodge or game farm where profits are returned to the community in the same manner as current hunting concessions.

While the strategies recommended are tailored to the SLNP context, they demonstrate the potential benefits that can be harnessed from appropriate linkages between rural communities and tourism based on protected areas. The socio-economic benefits of capitalizing on tourism are significant. These can only be achieved by addressing the barriers to participation that are present.

to foster self-discovered insights.

- Interpretation must be enjoyable for visitors. Entertainment is not the main goal in using interpretation; but it is one of its essential qualities. Participation activities can be effective.

- Interpretation must be relevant for visitors. Understanding visitor characteristics, needs and motivations helps to direct the provision of information.
- Interpretation should provide varied experiences, using different mediums to

Case Study 19.10

Economic benefits for the Tibetan community at Jiuzhaigou Biosphere Reserve, China

Fung Mei Sarah Li, Murdoch University, Western Australia

Jiuzhaigou Biosphere Reserve in Sichuan Province, China, is a great example of how tourism can contribute to poverty alleviation. The reserve gained World Heritage status in 1992 due to its outstanding biodiversity and landforms. Its high alpine environment provides habitat for a number of endangered species, including the giant panda (*Ailuropoda melanoleuca*). There were originally nine Tibetan villages inside the reserve boundaries ('Jiuzhaigou' means valley of nine stockaded villages); but currently only six remain. There is a residential population in the reserve of approximately 1000 people. The communities were subsistence herders and farmers until these activities were prohibited in the reserve in 1994. Revenue from tourism has virtually eliminated poverty from the Tibetan communities living inside the reserve.

Tourism became an approved activity in the reserve in 1984. Visitor numbers have increased from 340,000 in 1998 to 1.35 million in 2004. Tourism provides employment and income generation for the rural communities. There are approximately 200 permanent and 200 casual staff employed by the management authority in the reserve – most of these are Tibetans (the ethnic minority). Income generation includes park entrance fees; homestays and the accommodation sector; and transport and catering, restaurant and souvenir entrepreneurship. This has resulted in a substantial increase in local incomes. The annual revenue generated through entrance tickets was US$19.8 million in 2003. As a result, the tax paid by Jiuzhaigou Biosphere Reserve to the prefecture government was US$4 million.

A number of Tibetan communities have invested in small hotels and cultural centres along the main road to the reserve as an alternative to homestays. As the numbers of tourists to the reserve have grown, so has the size of the community on the main road to the reserve. The township of Jiuzhaigou has grown from approximately 150 people in 1984 to 10,000 in 2004.

The reserve management and the local communities established a co-operative to purchase a fleet of 'green' buses. In 1999 the green buses, which run on natural gas, replaced diesel- and petrol-fuelled vehicles. The company started with 112 buses, and by 2004 there were 352 buses of various sizes. Initially, each bus had a local Tibetan driver and a Tibetan guide; but as bus numbers increased additional personnel had to be employed. The bus company was very successful, both environmentally and economically. In 2001, each of the 1000 members of the Tibetan community achieved a per capita income of US$11,000 from bus fares. In 2002, the Prefecture government took over control of the bus company in order to access its earnings for wider prefecture development, for which the villagers were offered compensation.

Another joint venture between the communities and reserve management was the establishment of a catering complex in 2004. This included a 5000-seat restaurant complex and 200 souvenir outlets – one for each family.

Although there have been many changes in the level of community involvement in tourism activities in Jiuzhaigou Biosphere Reserve, the outcome has been positive. Most of the literature recommends that pro-poor tourism should be small scale. In the case of Jiuzhaigou, it is the large-scale managed visitation that has provided the Tibetan community with the economic capacity to underwrite various developments.

encourage the use of all five senses.
- Interpretation must be well organized with a logical structure so that visitors can easily follow it.
- Interpretation should have a theme, not simply a topic. Themes provide a framework that helps people to retain information.
- Interpretation can be most effective when it is dealt with as part of an overall management plan.

8 Well-managed tourism in protected areas offers opportunities for poverty alleviation and consequent community support for conservation.

Further reading

Christ, C., Hillel, O., Matus, S. and Sweeting, J. (2003) *Tourism and Biodiversity: Mapping Tourism's Global Footprint*, UNEP and Conservation International, Washington, DC

Eagles, P. F. J. and McCool, S. F. (2002) *Tourism in National Parks and Protected areas Areas: Planning and Management*, CABI, New York

Eagles, P .F .J., McCool, S. F. and Haynes, C. D. A. (2002) *Sustainable Tourism in Protected Areas: Guidelines for Planning and Management*, IUCN, Gland and Cambridge

Ham, S. H. (1992) *Environmental Interpretation: A Practical Guide for People with Big Ideas and Small Budgets*, North American Press, Golden

20

Collaboratively Managed Protected Areas

Ashish Kothari

Collaborative management of natural resources, broadly speaking, involves management by two or more partners. It is a rapidly spreading and evolving approach, increasingly favoured by governments and civil society for being, under many circumstances, more robust than single agency management approaches. Applied to protected areas, it normally means the partnership of government agencies with other sections of society, most often indigenous peoples or local communities, but also frequently NGOs or the private sector.

For the purposes of this book, collaboratively managed protected areas (CMPAs) are defined as:

> ... *officially designated protected areas where decision-making power is shared between state agencies and other partners, including indigenous peoples and local communities, and/or NGOs and individuals or private sector institutions.*

In this book, the terms collaborative management, co-management, joint management and multi-stakeholder management are used synonymously.

A wide range of CMPA arrangements are evident around the world due to widely varying interpretations of what co-management actually means. These range from one partner being dominant and involving other partners only in occasional consultations or for benefit-sharing, to all partners being equally represented in decision-making and implementation. Usually, but not necessarily, co-management includes multiple

partners being involved in making or negotiating plans for the protected areas, taking on conservation responsibilities, sharing benefits and costs, and participating in relevant institutional structures.

This chapter considers these various manifestations of CMPAs, how they can be most effective, and some of the challenges involved in achieving this. Although CMPAs include arrangements between state agencies and NGOs or the private sector, this chapter focuses mainly (though not exclusively) on arrangements between state agencies and indigenous peoples or local communities. In compiling the chapter, I have borrowed heavily from Borrini-Feyerabend (2003b) and Borrini-Feyerabend et al (2004b).

Common features of co-managed protected areas

The sheer diversity of CMPAs makes it difficult to distinguish features that are common to all of them, other than the fact of their being multiple partnership arrangements. But the following characteristics can be said to be fairly universal amongst CMPAs.

CMPAs are based on some clearly identified interests that all the partners share, or at least recognize and respect. Different partners may benefit differently and differentially from the CMPA arrangement; but these are felt in some way to be complementary.

CMPAs involve clearly laid out institutional structures and rules of partnership in which all partners have a role to play. These structures and rules may be initiated by one partner and accepted by others, or they may be evolved jointly.

CMPAs are situations of social engagement, encounter and experimentation. Many protected area co-management settings are relatively new, and even those that have had several decades of experimentation may still be exploring options. As such, they are an interesting arena for learning and change, provided that flexibility and adaptability are maintained by the partners.

CMPAs capitalize on multiplicity and diversity. Co-management is not only multiparty; it is also multilevel and multidisciplinary. Different social actors possess different capacities and comparative advantages in management, and the CMPA arrangement stresses and builds upon their complementary roles. Different social actors, however, may also possess contrasting interests and concerns, which in a successful CMPA setting would be resolved through the partnership arrangement and the recognition of the greater mutual benefit of collaborating.

CMPAs are based upon a negotiated, joint decision-making approach and some degree of power-sharing and fair distribution of benefits among all institutional actors. While the type and extent of power-sharing and benefit distribution vary from situation to situation, all entitled actors receive some benefits from their involvement. This may help to empower the least powerful stakeholders, redressing power imbalances in society and fostering social justice – though by no means is this a universal phenomenon.

CMPAs are more a 'process' than a stable and definitive end point or 'product'. Co-management is a process requiring ongoing review and improvement, rather than the strict application of a set of rules. Its most important result is not a management plan but a management partnership, capable of responding to varying circumstances and needs. Successful co-management agreements and organizations themselves have a healthy tendency to evolve.

It is important to recognize that in CMPA arrangements involving indigenous peoples and local communities, such communities are both stakeholders and rights-holders by virtue of their cultural ties with and direct livelihood dependency upon the local environment. In particular, such people should be recognized as having important historical rights of association with a territory.

There are many routes to creating a co-managed protected area. In many countries in the world, co-management is enshrined in the legislation that establishes and regulates protected areas. Management boards are prescribed to have a certain composition, reserving representation to the social actors considered by the legislators to be the bearers of the most relevant entitlements and concerns. A large number of European protected areas are of this kind (see Case Studies 20.1 and 20.2).

In most countries, official protected areas have conventionally been managed by a national or regional agency, but are brought under CMPA arrangements due to protests, pressures and conflicts with other concerned parties (particularly local communities). In some cases, the contribution of communities is invited only in the form of consultation, or through a benefit-sharing arrangement (see Case Study 20.3). In others, they are included in the management organization and given the power of influencing decisions as a minority voice (see Case Study 20.4). In still others, they are included in an organization with technical and/or decision-making capacity that requires deliberation by consensus.

Whenever a pluralist management body exists, a distinction needs to be made between decision-making bodies acting by voting, and those acting by consensus. In the first case, the critical factor is obviously the number of voting members assigned to each management partner, and the alliances likely to be created among them. In the second case, the arrangements can be much more sophisticated (see Case Study 20.5). While voting involves fairly straightforward procedures and results, consensus procedures allow the integration of incentives towards social arrangements that are both equitable and sustainable.

In many countries, territories under the occupation or management of indigenous peoples or local communities, including community conserved areas (CCAs) (see Chapter 21), are brought under the protected area network either at the insistance of the communities or through government initiative. The same could happen with private lands. This may result in a co-management

Case Study 20.1

French regional nature parks

Federation des Parcs Naturels Regionaux

For over 35 years, France has been experimenting with a policy of conservation and sustainable development carried out by local stakeholders. Elected people, NGOs, inhabitants and private industries together define a project that meets the stakes of a rural area recognized for its rich but threatened cultural and natural heritage, and with a fragile socio-economical base. After a validation process, the government classifies the area as a regional nature park (RNP). Such parks vary greatly in size and type, and are found in mountains, the plains, on the coast, in forests and on wetlands. Their size varies from 25,000ha (Haute Vallée de Chevreuse) to 300,000ha (Guyane), averaging about 150,000ha in extent. This corresponds to the territory of about 80 villages.

Each RNP is managed by an organization of the elected people of the local communities (regions, departments and villages), which associates local stakeholders in their decision-making. A multidisciplinary technical team runs it and its financial means are essentially provided by public funds. By 2004, there were 44 RNPs representing:

- 3689 towns and villages;
- 7 million hectares, or 12 per cent of the land;
- 68 counties;
- 23 regions; and
- 3 million inhabitants.

The missions of each RNP are as follows.

- Protecting heritage: to manage its rural area harmoniously, to maintain the biological diversity of its environment, and to preserve and improve its resources and its most remarkable or fragile sites.
- Implementing economic and social development: to promote economic development based on the environmental heritage, which can guarantee a quality of life for its inhabitants by supporting local economy and improving the land and the natural and human resources.
- Participating in the spatial planning of its area: to provide inputs to towns and villages regarding landscape planning.
- Involving and informing the public: to facilitate public contact with nature, promoting the understanding and awareness of environmental problems, and the discovery of local culture through activities and equipment that respect nature and the countryside.
- Carrying out experiments: to try and perfect experimental procedures and methods.

Each RNP is based on a charter, drawn up for the region. Its signatories are committed for ten years. The charter sets the objectives of the RNP and the measures that will set these in action. It helps to guarantee the coherence and coordination of actions carried out within the Park by the various local authorities. After ten years, a revision procedure for the charter leads to the redefinition of a new ten-year project and, if necessary, the renewal of its classification.

The limits of an RNP are negotiated between all its partners; but the defined area corresponds to those of the local counties, which voluntarily adhere to the park's charter. These limits are therefore not fixed with respect to administrative boundaries and they may overlap several counties or regions.

RNPs are networked within France, and their federation is actively involved in European and other international cooperation. Linked to over 30 countries, the RNP federation aims to share the experiences of sustainable development and good governance.

arrangement (see Case Studies 20.6 and 20.7). Among the most interesting co-management governance models are the 'mixed models', which strongly combine local/traditional and Western/'modern' policies and practices (see Chapter 5).

Lands and resources can be set aisde voluntarily by indigenous and local communities under special management regulations and practices through either customary or legally established procedures that have received official recognition by government agencies and are thus integrated

Case Study 20.2

North York Moors National Park, UK

Andy Wilson, North York Moors National Park, UK

The North York Moors National Park is situated on the east coast of England. It has a wide diversity of landscapes and habitats, including sea cliffs, traditional villages, ancient woodland and farmed dales. At its centre is a large block of moorland vegetation. The area is extremely rich in archaeological remains from the Mesolithic and the Bronze Age, to the industrial archaeology of the alum, ironstone and jet mining. The area around Whitby has a great seafaring and ecclesiastical history, which along with the rich farming traditions of the area, has left its imprint on the landscape we see today.

The moorland area is noted for its key bird species – golden plover (*Pluvialis apricaria*), curlew (*Numenius arquata*) and merlin (*Falco columbarius*) – and for its habitat. The park contains the largest contiguous block of heather-dominated heathland in England, and for these reasons the area is protected under European designations.

Stakeholders

The area has a complex system of management. Much of the area is privately owned and large areas of moorland are managed for grouse shooting. There are 25,000 residents, approximately 8 million visitors per year, various regional and national agencies, and two tiers of local authorities. All of these have a stake in the park and all require consultation on the issues and factors affecting its management.

Management and responsibility

The National Park Authority exists to conserve the area and promote understanding and enjoyment of its special qualities; however, this broad remit is tempered by its relatively limited statutory powers. The main area of direct control is the organization's position as a strategic and local planning authority.

The National Park Authority works hard to engage with landowners, national and government agencies, and individuals in order to bring these groups together to find common ground and initiatives that will benefit the area.

The authority is made up of members appointed by a government minister, representatives from local communities and nominations from local authorities. The authority also draws in representatives from specialist interest groups to aid its decisions. In addition, the authority itself is a member of a number of wider discussion groups and decision-making bodies that bring a variety of influences to bear.

Accountability

Because of the complex structures and the nature of the stakeholders, ensuring accountability is not always easy. In order to achieve this, communication with all of the groups and stakeholders is an essential tool, and one that requires a great deal of time and commitment but has proved to be effective and essential. The authority's performance and financial affairs are independently audited and subject to public scrutiny.

Strengths and weaknesses

The authority's key strength is in its culture. It concentrates on developing trust and relationships between its diverse range of stakeholders, customers and partner agencies in order to achieve consensus and joint working, which results in more positive outcomes than the authority or the individual constituents could accomplish solely.

Communication can always be improved. Although the authority uses a range of media, benefit could be achieved from more resources being made available in this area.

within national protected areas systems. These areas tend to have similar characteristics to other official protected areas in terms of size, ecological condition and management objectives; but they are strongly informed by the customary traditions and practices (see Case Studies 20.6 and 20.7).

Some lands and resources traditionally belonging to indigenous or local communities

Case Study 20.3

Opening protected areas to people in Central Africa

Across Central Africa, there are examples where conservation NGOs and governments have agreed to allow local people limited and regulated access to protected areas in order to satisfy at least part of their subsistence requirements. This development is extremely significant because it provides an avenue to increasing formal roles for local people in the management of parks, currently very scant. It provides much-needed fora for dialogue between park managers and local communities, upon whose shoulders the long-term sustainability of these protected areas depends. In Lobeke, Cameroon, local communities negotiated limited access to the park resources (despite this being legally forbidden). Similar access is being negotiated in many countries across Central Africa, including allowing special community access to grazing lands and fishing areas (Waza Logone, Cameroon); providing formalized access to forest resources within a park to clearly specified user groups and for collection of agreed products (Bwindi, Uganda); instituting special forest reserves, where local people can hunt or fish (Dzangha-Sangha, Central African Republic); and permitting indigenous people to remain within the reserve itself (Mbuti in the Okapi Reserve, Democratic Republic of Congo).

Bwindi Impenetrable Forest National Park, Uganda

Source: IUCN Photo Library © Jim Thorsell

The next step is for local and indigenous communities to secure the right to become actively involved in management. This would open up a space for more equitable dialogue between conservation agencies and local and indigenous communities. Decentralization of government authority and responsibility is an essential component of change if the protected area managers are to develop long-term local agreements with communities; unfortunately, current attitudes and national laws in many countries prevent this from happening.

A logical extension of the 'opening up' process is the restitution of lands and/or natural resources to communities from whom these were forcibly taken away in the past. In some countries, this has been accompanied by arrangements in which communities to whom land/resources have been restored, agree to manage them or let them be managed for conservation (see Case Study 20.7).

Source: adapted from Nelson and Gami (2003)

Case Study 20.4

Cooperative management with Aboriginal people in Canada's national parks

Jim Johnston, Parks Canada, Canada

Parks Canada has increasingly found common ground with Aboriginal peoples on the establishment and cooperative management of national parks. This approach offers a way of working together to conserve natural areas that are vital to sustaining traditional ways of life, while simultaneously contributing to the achievement of national conservation goals. Creation of new national parks through a consensus-based approach and cooperative management is in keeping with the new paradigm for protected areas (see 'Protected areas and "the new paradigm"' in Chapter 2) and the goals and programmes of work of the United Nations Convention on Biological Diversity (CBD) (see Appendix 4).

Parks Canada is the oldest government-protected area organization in the world. In 1998, it was given a new governance structure as an agency of the Canadian government through the *Parks Canada Agency Act*. It reports to parliament through the minister of the environment and has responsibility for national parks, marine conservation areas and national historic sites.

Formal cooperative management arrangements between Parks Canada and Aboriginal people date back to the 1970s. The first such arrangement was at Wood Buffalo National Park, established in 1922 and one of the first in the world to permit traditional use of a protected area by indigenous and local communities. By the 1970s, due to the growth of the number of people eligible to obtain a permit, wildlife resources were being depleted. Hunters and trappers and park officials worked cooperatively to solve the problem by creating a hunters' and trappers' association. It sets limits on the number of harvesting permits as a means of conserving wildlife and ensuring sustainability of traditional harvesting activities.

A more formal framework for cooperative park management evolved through the process to settle land claims of Aboriginal groups. In negotiating comprehensive land claim agreements, starting during the 1970s, it became apparent that this process could involve the creation of national parks that could be beneficial to the Aboriginal claimant group in whose traditional territory the proposed park was situated. Set aside for conservation and to encourage understanding and enjoyment by all Canadians, these parks also could provide a protected area where Aboriginal people could continue their traditional harvesting activities. Such activities are of economic, cultural and nutritional importance. New national parks could also provide economic benefits to Aboriginal communities through employment as park staff or providing ecotourism services. The land claims process also provides an opportunity to negotiate the formal structure for cooperative management.

To date, Parks Canada has entered into successful agreements with Aboriginal groups and communities to cooperatively manage 13 national parks that protect over 180,000 square kilometres of land in all ecoregions of the country. Under these agreements, parks officials or others with expertise in protected area management, together with representatives of local Aboriginal communities, participate as members of a cooperative management board. These boards provide advice to the minister responsible for national parks on numerous issues. For example, the management board for Ukkusiksalik National Park advises on harvesting and use of park wildlife to support traditional lifestyles, cultural resource management, and recruitment and hiring of park staff. It also gives guidance on implementing economic measures provided by government that benefit local communities through employment, enhanced tourism and capacity-building. The board also plays a critical role in preparing the management plan.

The cooperative management boards operate within the parameters of the *Canada National Parks Act*, which assigns final decision-making authority to the minister responsible for national parks. However, in the 30 years that the cooperative style of management has been used, there has been no occasion where the minister has rejected or altered a board's management advice. This is a testament to the ability of Parks Canada and Aboriginal peoples to work together to achieve significant shared objectives.

have been incorporated within official protected areas without specific agreements with these communities. In such situations, communities requiring restoration of traditional land and resource rights over all or part of an official protected area can be assisted by a variety of processes. Co-management boards and specially formulated regulations are two useful approaches (see Case Study 20.8).

Case Study 20.5

Consensus in a co-management board, Galapagos Marine Reserve, Ecuador

Located approximately 1000km from the Ecuadorian mainland, the volcanic Galapagos Islands contain remarkable terrestrial and marine ecosystems, and became, some years ago, the focus of complex and violent multi-stakeholder conflicts. The rapid economic and demographic change, the presence of unregulated industrial fishing, the appearance of high-value fisheries for Asian markets, the state-imposed policy and regulations, and the general non-compliance with the management plan of the marine reserve were all factors fuelling these conflicts. In 1998, in response to national and international concern about the threats facing them, Ecuador passed innovative legislation through a special law that, among other measures, introduced the control of migration within the country, created one of the largest marine reserves in the world (about 130,000 square kilometres in extent), prohibited industrial fishing, and established institutions for participatory management of the marine reserve. The creation of the Galapagos Marine Reserve was the fruit of an exhaustive local participatory planning process, which took two years (74 meetings of a multi-stakeholder planning group called Grupo Núcleo, 2 fisheries summit meetings and 3 community workshops) and produced a consensus management plan. The implementation of this plan, through a legally based participatory management regime, has been in progress now for more than three years.

The Galapagos co-management institution essentially consists of a three-party arrangement uniting a local participatory management board (PMB), an inter-institutional management authority (IMA) and the Galapagos National Park (GNP). The PMB is made up of the primary local stakeholders, while the IMA comprises representatives of ministers and local stakeholders. In the PMB, the members present specific management proposals (concerning, for example, fisheries or tourism), which are analysed, negotiated and eventually agreed upon by consensus. The consensus-based proposals are channelled for approval to the IMA and then to the GNP, for implementation and control. Proposals that have reached a consensus in the PMB carry an important weight at the IMA level. However, if no consensus is reached in the PMB, the different stakeholder positions are submitted to the IMA, where the decision is left in the hands of a majority of mainland ministerial officials. Statistics are compelling. Nearly 100 per cent of consensus-based PMB proposals (which, incidentally, managed to secure excellent conservation results) are approved without modification in the IMA. Obviously, the consensus-based co-management setting creates a very strong incentive for local stakeholders to develop and agree on viable proposals in the PMB.

Source: adapted from Heylings and Bravo (2001)

Types of co-managed protected areas

Various elements of CMPAs can be used to distinguish between and understand their characteristics:

- *Kinds of partners*. Is the partnership between government and communities, or NGO and communities, or private party and communities, or some other permutation and combination?
- *Origin of the CMPA*. Was the move towards collaborative management initiated by the state or by the other partner(s)? What was the motivation for such a move? What process was carried at the initial stages?
- *Relative roles of partners*. Among the various partners, who are the owners or rights-holders of the land/resources being conserved? Who is involved in decision-making and implementation? Who are the key participants?
- *Length of time the CMPA arrangement has been in place*. Is the CMPA an historically well-established one or is it relatively recent? Has it had the time to adjust its governance structure and procedures to the context at stake?
- *Extent of engagement of various partners in the CMPA*. Is there unequal involvement of various partners in decision-making, implementation and other aspects of the CMPA arrangement, or is the involvement more or less equal? Are all partners equally serious and committed to the arrangement, and do they have equal powers and capacities?
- *Flexibility and adaptability of the arrangement*. Is the institutional setting rigidly prescribed by legislation – for instance, regarding who should be the members of the management board – or is it left with room for local

Case Study 20.6

Co-management of a cultural landscape, Arizona, US

Stephanie Tuxill, Quebec–Labrador Foundation (QLF), Atlantic Center for the Environment, US

At the centre of the Navajo (Diné) homeland in the Colorado Plateau of the south-west US is Canyon de Chelly. In 1931, the US National Park Service and the Navajo Nation agreed to designate this area as a national monument. Together they manage the canyon's natural and cultural resources across approximately 33,929ha and support the Navajo community, which continues to live within the monument's borders. While this relationship has not always been smooth, during recent decades the National Park Service has embraced more inclusive, participatory approaches to managing its nationwide system of protected areas, and Canyon de Chelly National Monument aims to be a model for other federally protected tribal sites in the US.

The exact arrival time of the Navajos in Canyon de Chelly is unclear; but landforms such as Spider Rock have a deep cultural and spiritual significance for the tribe, and Navajo families raise sheep and harvest peaches and maize in agricultural traditions dating back 300 years or more in this region. The sandstone cliffs, riparian zones and upland regions of the canyon also display an impressive array of archaeological resources from earlier cultures, including cliff dwellings, pit houses, artefacts, petroglyphs and pictographs. This evidence indicates that there has been 5000 years of human occupation in the canyon and its tributaries, including a series of well-established ancestral Pueblo settlements between the 3rd and 14th centuries, and subsequent use of the area by Hopis, Navajo and other tribes.

Following years of skirmishes and wars with US soldiers, a 1868 treaty enabled the Navajo to retain control of Canyon de Chelly as part of a reservation known as Navajo tribal trust lands. By the early 1900s, however, archaeologists, government officials and tribal members desired better protection of the canyon's archaeological resources, which were threatened by looting, vandalism and destruction by natural forces such as erosion.

There was initial resistance from the Navajo to a national monument designation; but the National Park Service overcame this by reassuring the tribe that the lands would remain in tribal trust, and that Navajo rights would be protected and respected. For example, subsistence activities such as hunting and sheep grazing are permitted, which at the time was unusual for lands within the protected area system. The monument regulations require visitors to gain permission before taking photographs of people, and to hire an authorized Navajo guide in order to camp or travel beyond designated trails, visitor centres and campgrounds.

Tourism at Canyon de Chelly has grown steadily over the years, from 400 visitors in 1931 to 167,000 in 1964, and to more than 881,000 in 2004. Besides visitor management, watershed restoration has emerged as a top priority for the monument due to the impact upon natural and cultural resources and the residents who depend upon the canyon for their livelihood. These Navajo communities have experienced a general decline in the productivity of the renowned historic peach orchards and other agricultural crops due to erosion, water shortages and invasive species, such as tamarisk (originally planted for erosion control).

Today, the National Park Service affirms the importance of Canyon de Chelly's administrative partnership and management activities that support both the living and historic cultural landscape. The current mission of Canyon de Chelly National Monument is to 'work in partnership with the Navajo people and other Indian tribes to protect and interpret Canyon de Chelly as a landscape of historical, sacred and national significance, as well as enhancing the cultural and social aspirations of the Navajo people'. In 2003, the monument staff consulted partners and stakeholders and held open community meetings to gain input on creating a general management plan.

Case Study 20.7

Kaa-Iya del Gran Chaco National Park, Bolivia

Oscar Castillo and Andrew Noss, Wildlife Conservation Society, Bolivia

The Kaa-Iya del Gran Chaco National Park (KINP) covers 3,440,000ha, making it the largest protected area in Bolivia. It contains the largest area of dry tropical forest under full protected area status anywhere in the world. It is also the first national park in Latin America established as a result of the initiative of a Native American people, and the only one where a Native American organization shares primary administrative responsibilities with the national government. The KINP was created in 1995 by presidential decree, and the

Capitanía de Alto y Bajo Isoso (CABI) indigenous organization signed a ten-year agreement with the Ministry of Sustainable Development and Planning in 1996 to co-administer the KINP with the national park service, Servicio Nacional de Areas Protegidas (SERNAP).

Capitanía de Alto y Bajo Isoso's territorial and spatial strategy

CABI represents 10,000 Isoseño-Guaraní people living in 25 communities along the Parapetí River in the Bolivian Chaco. CABI's territorial strategy has two complementary components that are integrated within a long-term vision of environmental management and sustainable development: the creation of the KINP and the provision of communal title to the Isoseño people of the 1.9 million hectare Isoso Tierra Comunitaria de Origen (TCO) adjoining the KINP to the west.

The management plan for the KINP, developed by CABI with support from Wildlife Conservation Society (WCS), was approved by the national government in 2000, while the management plan for the Isoso TCO is being developed by the same two partners, using the same environmental and socio-economic zoning criteria so that the two areas, totalling 5.3 million hectares, are managed in a consistent and complementary manner.

Governance and management

For the Sustainable Development Ministry and SERNAP to partner with an indigenous organization, rather than a conservation body, leads towards new levels of active community participation in protected area management. Through the co-administration agreement, both parties must jointly agree on annual work plans and budgets, and on the selection of the KINP director. CABI recruits park guards, ensuring considerable influence over personnel and creating strong links between the Isoseño community and the park's daily operations, while SERNAP ensures technical oversight by giving the guards government contracts. CABI provides the administrative back-up to the KINP's operations through a shared office in Santa Cruz.

The principal demonstrated strength of the co-administration experience, between 1996 and 2005, is that CABI is an effective independent partner, bringing to the table three key factors: personal and institutional stability, direct budgetary contributions and new partners. In comparison to responsible government authorities' variability and rotation – five Ministerio de Desarrollo Sostenible y Planificación (MDSP) ministers, five directors of SERNAP and three park directors since 1995 – CABI leaders and its organizational and institutional principles have not changed and bring a long-term perspective and cultural and institutional memory to park administration.

Steps towards financial sustainability

CABI has also generated important financial support for the KINP through agreements with private companies, including the gas pipeline consortia operating the Bolivia–Brazil pipeline, which support park guard activities, but also established a trust fund with annual returns dedicated to environmental education, training and other complementary park programmes. A similar agreement with the Inter-American Development Bank (IDB)-funded *Environmental and Social Management Plan*, tied to Santa Cruz–Puerto Suárez highway corridor, will supplement resources for the management of the KINP.

CABI efficiently administered a total budget of US$1.3 million, including over US$500,000 in CABI co-financing, representing 41 per cent of the KINP budget during the seven fiscal years of 1998 to 2004. In 1999, SERNAP faced a severe financial crisis, and CABI, in effect, saved the KINP by contributing 70 per cent of the budget. These figures do not include resources from WCS and the US Agency for International Development (USAID) to develop the KINP management plan and initiate wildlife research and environmental education activities in and around the KINP, as well as to strengthen the administration of the KINP.

Steps towards strategic partnerships

Finally, in addition to the obligatory compensation package negotiated in the context of the Bolivia–Brazil gas pipeline and highway, CABI has established a long-term cooperative relationship with the owners and operators of the Bolivia–Brazil gas pipeline, Gas Transboliviano SA (GTB), creating the Kaa-Iya Foundation (KIF) in 2002, with directors from both CABI and GTB. The KIF's mission is to promote conservation and sustainable development with long-term financing mechanisms in and around the KINP, integrating additional competent public, private and social actors. This new partnership has generated additional funds from WCS and GTB for wildlife research, environmental education and ecotourism initiatives, and for promoting bi-national coordination with Paraguay. Initial resources are being utilized to leverage new donor support and to attract additional partners.

Case Study 20.8

The Makuleke story, South Africa

Christo Fabricius, Rhodes University, South Africa

In 1967, the Makuleke people were forced to move from the Pafuri area, one of the most productive and richest regions of South Africa's famous Kruger National Park. These days, 20,000ha of Kruger's Pafuri area are called the Makuleke region, with the Makuleke as the legal managers of this land. This was made possible through a simple piece of legislation, promulgated on the eve of South Africa's democracy: the *Restitution of Land Rights Act of 1994*.

The Makuleke land claim created waves through South Africa's conservation community. At that time, conservationists were not used to dealing with local communities and their grievances, and were far from prepared for a land claim on one of the icons of conservation. Doom prophets predicted 'the end of Kruger', and the Makuleke and Kruger conservationists soon found themselves at opposite ends of the table, negotiating for their own best positions.

A drawn-out process of negotiations and 'give-and-take' politics, facilitated by intermediaries such as NGOs, resulted in an historical agreement in 1999. It committed South African National Parks (SANParks) and the Makuleke to joint management of the Makuleke region of Kruger National Park for the next 25 years. A joint management board (JMB) was formed, giving SANParks the responsibility for law enforcement and the Makuleke the right to commercial and cultural rights. Both parties agreed to abide by a conservation master plan.

The Makuleke had already begun organizing themselves by forming a legal communal property association and a land trust, training community members in management skills and expanding their social networks. Their vision was to develop tourism lodges in partnership with the private sector in their sector of Kruger. This was easier said than done: the first years were not 'plain sailing'. Investors were slow to respond to calls for development proposals because of the remoteness of the Makuleke region, the perceptions of risk and the uncertainties about the exact roles of SANParks and the Makuleke. There was also an element of disrespect for the Makuleke on the side of authorities. Complaints arose that the JMB was constantly overruled by park management, and that its authority was not recognized. Says Livingstone Maluleke, one of the community leaders: 'This created a situation in the JMB where we were treated as a nuisance, rather than respected for not moving back onto our land.'

Fortunately, the stakeholders, donors and facilitators persisted in their reconciliation and capacity development efforts. Today, almost ten years after the initial agreement, many of these problems appear to have become manageable. The authority of the JMB is becoming recognized, and the private sector has begun showing an interest. A luxury private-operated game lodge has been opened under lease agreement with the Makuleke and a second acclaimed international Safari operator recently signed a long-term (45-year) cooperative agreement with the Makuleke. More than 200 jobs have been secured through this arrangement. Makuleke field rangers are being employed by the joint venture partner. This private partner will shortly develop two luxury game lodges in the Pafuri area.

What are the key lessons from the Makuleke case? First, collaborative management requires an enormous investment in capacity development on all sides. Second, patience and trust-building is essential and requires skilled and dedicated intermediaries. Third, the capacity for joint management lies in functional social networks working together at different levels. Fourth, the relationship between local communities and conservationists must be productive. Benefits must be generated and each stakeholder must understand what they are gaining from the process. Fifth, there needs to be recognized governance structures at several levels. Separate organizational structures are needed to generate and maintain agreements, enforce rules, manage revenue, act as legal entities and manage day-to-day operations. Sixth, there is a need for 'champions'; but their powers must be balanced by spreading responsibilities evenly and rotating powerful positions.

More than ten years after it started, the Makuleke story is still in its infancy. New developments and changes take place almost monthly, and new actors enter and depart regularly. The Makuleke story shows that joint management has many ups and downs and, like the end of the rainbow, has no magical end point.

adjustment and experimentation, responding to the specific characteristics of the context? Is there adaptive management?

- *Fairness of process.* Is the CMPA supported by NGOs or other agencies capable of facilitating the process, especially on behalf of those who might have less power or influence? Is anyone in charge of guaranteeing fairness, transparency and adequate sharing in the evolution of the partnership?
- *Distribution of costs and benefits of the process.* Are the costs (financial, time, human and material) and benefits (revenues, resource uses, ecosystem benefits and so on) clearly distributed among the partners? Is there relative equity in this distribution? Does the CMPA have the ability to sustain recurrent costs for social communication, negotiated decision-making, collective operations and monitoring?
- *Ecological and social performance.* Is the CMPA effective in meeting its conservation objectives? Is it effective in meeting the needs and interests of its partners, including livelihood and other benefits to communities?

These characteristics, in various combinations, can help to distinguish between 'strong' and 'weak' CMPAs. The former would be where the arrangement has been sustained for a substantial period of time, partners have clear and equitable roles, costs and benefits are equitably distributed, locally appropriate adaptations are possible, the arrangement is transparent and fair, and both conservation and social/economic goals are being effectively met. The latter would be where one or more of these features are absent, the weakest being where all are absent. However, it is important to understand the full context of the CMPA initiative before coming to such conclusions. A CMPA that appears 'weak' at a point in time may simply be at an initial stage of development or going through a temporary low period.

A regional review commissioned by the IUCN Theme on Indigenous and Local Communities, Equity and Protected Areas (TILCEPA) in South-East Asia, for instance, analysed a series of cases and identified CMPAs with varying weaknesses (Ferrari, 2003). In Malaysia, Viet Nam, Laos and Cambodia, protected area agencies have only recently begun to accept that concerned communities need to be involved in managing protected areas, but only of their non-core parts or their buffer zones and peripheries. The same is happening in some countries in West Africa, such as Burkina Faso, Niger and Bénin (Borrini-Feyerabend, pers comm, 2005). This management participation is not codified in law, but is left to the good disposition of individual managers.

There are also often situations where there is a strong policy statement on CMPA, but weak implementation. An example of relatively weak CMPAs is the Philippines, where each protected area is expected by law to be run by a management board composed of government officers, NGOs and community representatives. Unfortunately, this has not yet been functioning effectively due to various limitations – from lack of documents in local languages and resources for meetings and workshops, to the fact that the local people are too shy to voice their concerns in the presence of the board chairperson, who is a government officer. For the time being, the decision-making power still remains firmly in the government's hands.

In Australia, relatively strong co-management arrangements for protected areas have been developed over the last 20 years, following the passing of legislation that recognized Aboriginal rights to land and natural resources. In 1981, Gurig National Park became the first jointly managed national park in Australia (see Case Study 20.9), and since then further co-management arrangements have been developed for other parks in various states and territories, according to several different models (see Table 20.1). Joint management represents a trade-off between the rights and interests of traditional owners and the rights and interests of government conservation agencies and the wider Australian community. In the most sophisticated arrangements, the trade-off involves the transfer of ownership of the national park to Aboriginal people in exchange for continuity into the foreseeable future of national park status over the land and shared responsibility for park management.

A key element in these arrangements is that

the transfer of ownership back to Aboriginal people is conditional on their support (through leases or other legal mechanisms) for the continuation of the national park. In other words, the land occupied by a park is simultaneously returned to Aboriginal ownership and leased back to a government conservation agency under a co-management board and with the agreement of an arbitration process in case of disputes. In the early cases, such as Gurig National Park in Australia, however, the land was not leased at all. The more recent form of protected area established voluntarily on existing Aboriginal-owned land presents a challenge to all co-management models since it is more advanced in terms of self-determination of the Aboriginal owners and in terms of self-management practices.

Case Study 20.9

Garig Gunak Barlu National Park, Australia

Dermot Smyth, James Cook University, Australia

In the Iwaidja language, *Garig Gunak Barlu* means 'the land and the deep blue sea'. Garig Gunak Barlu National Park comprises the Cobourg Peninsula and surrounding coastal waters, approximately 200km east of Darwin in Australia's Northern Territory. These areas were formerly established as separate terrestrial and marine protected areas (Gurig National Park and Cobourg Marine Park).

Garig Gunak Barlu National Park includes sandy beaches, dunes, coastal grasslands, mangroves, rainforest patches, swamps, lagoons, coral reefs, seagrass meadows and abundant marine life. The protected area includes populations of dugong and marine turtles: loggerheads (*Caretta caretta*); hawksbill (*Eretmochelys imbricata*); Pacific Ridley (*Lepidochelys olivacae*); leatherback (*Dermochelys coriacea*); and flatbacks (*Natator depressus*).

For thousands of years, the Cobourg Peninsula and its surrounding sea formed the traditional lands of four Aboriginal clans. In 1924, the peninsula became North Australia's first flora and fauna reserve. During the 1950s, all of the remaining Aboriginal traditional owners were removed to a government settlement on nearby Croker Island. In 1981, the establishment of Gurig National Park was agreed to by the Northern Territory government and the Aboriginal traditional owners in order to resolve a pending land claim under the *Aboriginal Land Rights Act* of the Northern Territory. Rather than proceed with the claim, the traditional owners consented to the establishment of the national park in return to regaining title to their traditional lands. The key features of the joint management of Garig Gunak Barlu National Park are:

- declaration of the park under its own legislation – the *Cobourg Peninsula Land and Sanctuary Act 1981* (NT);
- vesting of the land in a land trust on behalf of the traditional owners;
- establishment of a board of management comprising eight members, of whom four are traditional owners and four are representatives of the Northern Territory government (the board is chaired by one of the traditional owner members, who also has a casting vote);
- payment of an annual fee by the government to traditional owners for use of their land as a national park (the fee was set at Aus$20,000 in 1981 and increased annually by a percentage equal to the percentage increase in the average male wage in Darwin);
- responsibility for day-to-day management rests with the Conservation Commission of the Northern Territory (now the Parks and Wildlife Commission); and
- recognition of the rights of traditional owners to use and occupy the park.

The *Cobourg Peninsula Land and Sanctuary Act 1981* sets out the respective functions of the board and the commission. In summary, the functions of the board are to:

- prepare the management plans;
- protect and enforce the rights of the traditional owner group to use and occupy the park;
- determine, in accordance with the plan of management, the rights of access to parts of the sanctuary of persons who are not members of the traditional owner group;

- ensure adequate protection of sites in the park of spiritual or other significance in Aboriginal tradition;
- make by-laws with respect to the management of the park; and
- carry out other functions as imposed on the board by the plan of management.

The functions of the commission are to act on behalf of and subject to the direction of board in preparing the management plans and controlling and managing the park. The act also states that where differences of opinion arise between the board and the commission with respect to the preparations of plans of management or the control and management of the park, the matter will be resolved by a resolution of the board. The plan contains many practical details relating to the exercise of the rights and interests of traditional owners on the park, including:

- the location of Aboriginal residential areas;
- the recognition of traditional hunting and fishing; and
- a commitment to train and employ Aboriginal people as rangers and in other capacities in the park (subject to budgetary constraints).

In 1996, the act was amended to extend the powers of the board to include supervision of the management of the adjacent Cobourg Marine Park, which includes customary marine clan estates of the traditional owners. In summary, the joint management arrangements for Garig Gunak Barlu National Park provide Aboriginal people with secure tenure over their traditional lands, as well as nominal control over policy and planning matters via their voting majority on the board. The Northern Territory government, through its representation on the board and through the operations of the Parks and Wildlife Commission, maintains a strong role in determining the management of the park. It is significant that these arrangements do not require traditional owners to lease their lands back to the government.

In Latin America, experimentation with co-responsibility in protected area management between the civil society and the state has been gaining significant strength and recognition during the last decade (see Case Study 20.7). One of the TILCEPA regional reviews identified 79 specific experiences in Central America, with an important variety of management types taking

Table 20.1 Four co-management models from Australia

Garig Gunak Barlu National Park model	'Uluru' model	Queensland model	Witjira National Park model
Aboriginal ownership	Aboriginal ownership	Aboriginal ownership	Ownership of land remains with the government
Equal representation of traditional owners and government representatives on board of management	Aboriginal majority on board of management	No guarantee of Aboriginal majority on board of management	Aboriginal majority on board of management
No lease-back to government agency	Lease-back to government agency for long period	Lease-back to government agency in perpetuity	Lease of the national park to traditional owners
Annual fee to traditional owners	Annual fee to traditional owners, community council or board	No annual fee paid	
Example: Garig Gunak Barlu National Park	Examples: Uluṟu–Kata Tjuṯa, Kakadu, Nitmiluk, Booderee and Mutawintji National Parks	Example: none finalized	Example: Witjira National Park

Source: adapted from Smyth (2001)

advantage of the relative state of flux and openness of the relevant legislations and policies (Solis et al, 2003). Similarly, experiences in the Andean region are offering several inspiring examples.

If Australia, the Philippines, Canada and Bolivia are already positively accepting and recognizing the value of co-management experiences, many other countries are currently still at an 'experimental' stage. Among those are Argentina, Panama, the Democratic Republic of Congo and India (see Case Studies 20.10 and 20.11).

Continuing challenges

Co-managed protected areas are not without their fair share of problems and challenges.

Denial of cultural identity and rights of communities. In many countries, indigenous peoples and local communities are still struggling to establish their distinct identities, and their rights to customarily held territories, resources and knowledge. This is especially true with regard to protected areas, where fear of ecological damage or of losing

Case Study 20.10

Mapuche indigenous people in the Lanin National Park, Argentina

Bruno Carpinetti, Administración de Parques Nacionales, Argentina, and Gonzalo Oviedo, IUCN, Switzerland

At the time of the establishment of the Lanin National Park in Argentina in 1937, the Mapuche people living in the area were excluded from any meaningful input into how, where, when or why a natural protected area would be created on their traditional territory. This policy of exclusion has had significant negative social and economic impacts on Mapuche communities, and their lack of control over decisions taken in their traditional territory was the most critical issue for them throughout the 20th century.

The Mapuche people, organized in the Neuquen Mapuche Confederation (Confederación Mapuche Neuquina), have been struggling for some time for the recuperation of land and resource rights in the Neuquen Province. In particular, they cared for a place within the Lanin National Park where they traditionally placed sacred values and where a powerful symbol, the Rewe (a wood and stone monument representing a traditional tree of values, or cosmic tree), had been built in ancient times for ritual purposes. The Rewe fulfilled a totemic function for the Mapuche – it was a representation of their clans and a symbol of cultural unity, belonging and identity.

The communities proposed the creation of a protected indigenous territory in their lands, once legally recognized, and took the Rewe as a symbol not only of sacredness, but also of biodiversity protection. Negotiations had been unsuccessful for a long time until a more sensitive protected area administration took office in 2000. This opened up a process that led, finally, to an agreement on a number of principles and procedures. In May 2000, a co-management committee was established in the area, with the participation of the Mapuche communities and the National Park Service.

Since the creation of the management committee, three broad principles have guided the building of this new partnership between the Mapuche people and the National Parks Service:

- the recognition of community rights of ownership of their traditional lands;
- the need to build up formal and informal structures that facilitate community participation in park management; and
- the operation of effective mechanisms for sharing the benefits of park management with the communities.

The co-management committee comprises half national government and half Mapuche appointees. It has two members appointed by the Neuquen Mapuche Confederation; two members elected by the seven Mapuche communities living within the Lanin National Park; one member appointed by the National Parks Administration Board of Directors; the director of protected areas conservation; the park manager; and one member appointed by the National Institute for Indigenous Affairs. The committee deals with all matters regarding indigenous land claims, forest management, carrying capacities for cattle grazing and all aspects of communal land management within the national park.

The concerned parties on the co-management committee have already agreed that the process should be based upon the recognition of the rights of the communities over their 'territory' (not simply their lands), that the area will be co-managed, and that the links between conservation of biological diversity and conservation of cultural diversity are inextricable – a principle illustrated in the respect for the Rewe as the central philosophical element of the Mapuche culture and community life.

Case Study 20.11

A tiger reserve and a Himalayan park: Towards participatory management

Ashish Kothari, co-chair, IUCN Theme on Indigenous/Local Communities, Equity and Protected Areas, with inputs from Pramod Krishnan, deputy field director, Periyar Tiger Reserve, and Sanjeeva Pandey, director, Great Himalayan National Park, India

A remarkable transformation is taking place in the relationship between government officials managing the Periyar Tiger Reserve in southern India and the villagers inside or adjacent to the reserve. Over the last six to seven years, a once conflicting relationship has turned into one of cooperation, trust and mutual support. Since the late 1990s, reserve officials have worked with villagers to rid them of their economic indebtedness, to obtain better prices for their agricultural products, to introduce new activities linked to wildlife tourism that are generating direct income to the villagers, and even to help solve social problems, such as the trafficking of women. Over 100,000 person days of employment have been created, and annually the community-managed ecotourism is bringing in 6 million rupees (approximately US$150,000) for 500 families.

In turn, villagers have taken up patrolling of the reserve, reporting poaching and wood theft, managing a part of the large tourist inflow, and helping with more effective management. Institutional structures that partly build on traditional skills and systems have been created to manage these initiatives. Several dozen people earlier identified as poachers have now taken to these or other activities, and although some of them actually earn less than they used to when they were poaching, they prefer the new situation since it comes with greater security and dignity. Most remarkably, about 100 women from several settlements have taken to voluntary patrolling of the reserve, stating simply that they are doing this 'for their children's future'. Increasingly, reserve officials are talking of bringing the villagers into the entire planning process. They openly say that 'sharing power with people has actually increased our power' since it has helped them to deal more effectively with violators and vested interests. People's involvement in conservation is also saving the government about 10 million rupees annually.

Consultative meeting at Periyar Tiger Reserve, India

Source: Ashish Kothari

This transformation has taken place under a Global Environment Facility (GEF)-funded eco-development project; but what is clear is that the credit must go to an extremely creative set of officials who went well beyond the initial concepts of the project. They approached local communities with humility, with a clear message of wanting to find mutually acceptable solutions, and with few prescriptions set in stone. But this has also raised the serious question: how sustainable are initiatives like this? In 2004, as the GEF-funded project was coming to an end, the effort was faced with the question: will the work be sustained if this set of officials is transferred out or if fund-flow stops? Some of the villages have created robust enough institutions and fund mechanisms to enable continuity; but others have still not been able to do this.

In yet another creative solution, the wildlife officials convinced the state government to set up a Periyar Foundation in 2004, a public trust with autonomy. This foundation, comprised of senior government officials, village representatives, scientists and NGOs, is free to generate financial resources from any source. It has started by levying tourists an 'eco-development fee'. A number of social welfare and conservation research activities have already been initiated under the foundation.

A similar initiative is unfolding in the Great Himalayan National Park (GHNP), one of India's most important mountain protected areas, home to the endangered western tragopan (*Tragopan melanocephalus*) and many other species. This area, too, was a hotbed of conflicts between park officials and villagers who entered the area for grazing, collection of medicinal plants, hunting and other pursuits. A top-down approach had not yielded much result. By the late 1990s, the process of settlement of rights, under India's *Wild Life (Protection) Act*, had taken away many of the customary rights of access that these villagers enjoyed, a process that was heavily criticized by NGOs and activists. A new park director then took it upon himself to win over the trust of women in the villages, helping them to set up some small-scale enterprises through the creation of Women's Savings and Credit Groups (WSCGs). Each woman member is encouraged to save 1 rupee a day, which by now has become a substantial sum of 700,000 rupees in about 95 WSCGs. Through these savings, the women have so far conducted business worth 3 million rupees, including vermi-composting, apricot oil production, hemp products, ecotourism, street theatre and wage labour. The park management has opened two shops to market the produce of the WSCGs, and provided training in various skills. The WSCGs are now being federated into a Village Forest Development Society at the *Panchayat* (village council) level, and have set up an NGO called Society for Advancement of Hill and Rural Areas (SAHARA). Villagers have been helping in patrolling and monitoring, inside and on the periphery of the park. In December 2003, many of the *Panchayats* came together and formed a group called Jujurana Jive (Long Live Western Tragopan), in which three men and three women from each *Panchayat* have been identified to take an active role in wildlife protection. The group is quite upbeat and says that it will not only keep an eye on villagers and poachers, but also on the activities of the park staff!

With concerns regarding sustainability similar to the Periyar case in mind, GHNP's director has set into motion the creation of a Biodiversity Conservation Society (BiodCS). This society comprises government officials, independent experts and some local community representatives. It has the power to keep the park's tourism revenues and to raise funds in other ways. It regularly interacts with local people through SAHARA and other local institutions, channelling employment and income-generation opportunities, such as medicinal plant cultivation and sale. By early 2005, however, the biggest worry was that BiodCS had not yet been given full institutional status by the state government or a corpus fund promised by the government.

Neither of the above cases can be called full joint or collaborative management, especially since tenurial rights are not all secure yet and equitable decision-making processes are not fully established. However, the move towards such a system seems to be set. Appropriate changes will be needed in India's wildlife legislation to enable this process to fulfil its potential; but meanwhile a group of innovative and bold officials has shown that participatory conservation can be initiated if only the requisite willingness and creativity are present.

control has led formal conservation agencies to resist any move towards participatory conservation.

Inadequate or absent policies/laws. Many, if not most, countries still do not have participatory protected area management as part of their conservation policies and laws. Informal arrangements towards co-management, such as at some protected areas in India (see Case Study 20.11) find it hard to stabilize, upscale or spread in the absence of supportive legal regimes. In many countries where some arrangements towards co-management are built into policy and law, these remain weak and inadequate, especially with regard to sharing decision-making powers.

Application of rigid, universally applied prescriptions. Too often, CMPA arrangements are not flexible enough to allow the local situations and partnerships to express themselves. Many national legislations assign a fixed composition to a protected area management board (for instance, a fixed number of seats for national government representatives, regional or local government representatives, NGOs, expert institutions and communities) without the possibility of adjusting the setting to local reality. Many also prescribe standard management regimes to ecologically and culturally diverse settings, or constrain adaptation by universally specifying the kind of ownership and rights regimes that are allowed.

Local and national inequities in power. The CMPA arrangement may, through design or by default, provide unequal powers and benefits to some partners vis-à-vis others. For instance, some laws give full privilege to elected administrators (and, thus, to party politics, often only weakly related to the local situation). The co-management structures can quickly be filled by individuals whose allegiance is more towards a national political party than a sincere concern for the protected area at stake, making a mockery of the pluralist decision-making structure. In Europe, as elsewhere, politicians are extremely sensitive to the powerful lobby in favour of recreational/tourist or even industrially exploitative use of protected areas, or to the wishes of constituencies in urban areas. These interests can become dominant and displace local rights, needs and aspirations.

Inadequate, short-term or see-saw government commitment. A frequent problem in CMPA arrangements occurs when dynamic officials, who have made the critical difference between success and failure, are transferred before the arrangement has been fully established. Governments can also fail to maintain adequate financial, technical or legal support for reasons extraneous to the arrangement (see Case Study 20.12).

Inadequate capacity. Many countries have policies, laws and programmes for CMPA in place, but do not have adequate capacity to effectively implement them. This lack of capacity may be among one or more of all partners, and may relate to financial, technical, human or other resources necessary to make CMPA work.

Continuing threats from external sources. Several CMPA arrangements have been undermined, or continue to be threatened, by external forces. Most common among these are unsustainable or destructive 'development' processes and projects, such as extractive industries, tourism, power projects, infrastructure facilities, demands from the national and international markets, and so on. Cultural and economic changes in local systems, brought about under influence from outside forces, can also be serious threats to CMPA arrangements.

Although CMPA policies and programmes are spreading across the world, in some regions they remain the exception rather than the rule. In Africa as a whole, it is estimated that only 1 per cent of forest estates comes under community-based or joint state–community management (Alden-Wily, 2002), despite the remarkable recent evolution of land tenure norms. Paradoxically, the weakness of state institutions is often responsible for the scarcity of effective co-management experiences. Weak institutions tend to 'grab' power via highly centralized laws and are plagued by the lack of accountability over the allocation and regulation of state-sanctioned extraction rights. In India, a strongly entrenched forest management bureaucracy, backed by a small but powerful conservation lobby, has resisted changing from conventional top-down to participatory approaches, even though such changes have been signalled in some policy-level documents, such as the 2002 *National Wildlife Action Plan* (Kothari, 2004).

The way forward for collaboratively managed protected areas

The TILCEPA-sponsored studies of CCAs and CMPAs in different world regions (Ferrari, 2003) came to recognize that the engagement, recognition and effectiveness of community involvement in conservation are highly context dependent. In Europe the key struggle is to deepen the engagement – from pluralist management structures based on delegation to party officials, to participatory management structures based on direct involvement and fair political 'weight' for the social actors most directly concerned. In Central America, the most urgent challenge is to develop

Case Study 20.12

Developing collaborative management in the Retezat National Park, Romania

Erica Stanciu, Scientific Council, Retezat National Park, Romania

The Retezat National Park in Romania covers an area of about 38,000ha in the southern range of the Carpathian Mountains. It is a representative site for this European mountain range, which was declared one of the World Wide Fund for Nature's (WWF's) Global 200 ecoregions.

Forests cover 52 per cent of the area and are well preserved, with more than 30 per cent of these old growth and at least 50 per cent natural forests. The alpine area (48 per cent) is covered by dwarf pine (*Pinus mugo*), Cembra pine (*Pinus cembra*) (28 per cent) and alpine meadows (14 per cent), with the remainder consisting of stone edges and peaks, and slopes covered with scree and stones. The beautiful blue patches of the more than 80 glacial lakes and the numerous springs that take their clean water from this magnificent place make this remote mountain a very special part of the Carpathians and a unique experience for those who have the chance to visit.

The Retezat National Park Administration (RNPA) was established in November 1999 as a subunit of the National Forest Administration, a para-statal organization that administers state forests in Romania. At the very beginning of its activity, in March 2000, the RNPA brought together major stakeholders and initiated the establishment of two new management bodies: the Scientific Council and the Consultative Council.

The Retezat National Park can be considered an example of how to start a process that can eventually lead to a co-managed protected area. Formal decision-making authority, responsibility and accountability rests mainly with one agency, the RNPA (ultimately, the National Forest Administration); but Law 462/2001 requires that management activities are discussed and consensus on main decisions obtained through consulting with stakeholders represented on the Consultative Council. Major conservation decisions are also influenced by an independent body, the Scientific Council.

In 2001, the first meetings with key stakeholders in the framework of the newly established Consultative Council laid the basis for a long-term dialogue with the RNPA. Since then, biannual meetings have been organized where communities have had the opportunity to learn about the initiatives of the park administrators and bring their input to the development of key documents: the park regulations and the Retezat National Park Management Plan. After two years of data-gathering, workshops and working group meetings, with representatives of local communities involved in the whole process, the first management plan of a national park in Romania was approved by the Ministry of the Environment.

A similar process, initiated at two other large protected areas, the Piatra Craiului National Park and the Vanatori Neamt Forest Park, helped to develop a *Management Planning Manual for Protected Areas*. The manual strongly emphasizes the significance of participatory management and gives important information on how to conduct the participatory process. This manual and the experience of the Retezat National Park are being used to develop the management plans for the 14 other national and nature parks in Romania.

However, if the long-term benefits of co-management are to be realized, there is a need for key stakeholders and, particularly, local communities to continue their active involvement in implementing the management plan at Retezat National Park. The experience of four years of park management shows that lack of understanding and commitment to biodiversity conservation among most of the stakeholders, particularly when this occurs within the local communities, can undermine the process of developing participative management and, thus, park management effectiveness. Only a motivated and very active team, and a competent and efficient park management body, one that brings in constantly innovative ideas and processes to improve cooperation with local communities, will be able to further develop the collaborative management system in Retezat National Park. Lack of financial and human resources can hinder the process of developing sound cooperation between the park administration and local communities, and the process that should eventually lead to co-management practices.

Based on the example of Retezat National Park and the two other 'sister parks' (Piatra Craiului National Park and Vanatori Neamt Forest Park), supported during the last five years by Global Environment Facility (GEF) funding, 15 new park management bodies were established in 2004 as a first important step in transforming paper parks into real national and nature parks. But this excellent development is not being accompanied by adequate government support for protected area management. Even in Retezat National Park, as GEF funding is running out, the park administration faces severe financial constraints that affect its entire activity – but, most of all, its relationship with local communities.

new legislation and policy, based on the lessons learned in a variety of pilot field operations. In the Caribbean, the vigorous emergence of interest on the co-management of coastal and marine protected areas still needs to be backed by substantial funding and political will. In Spanish-speaking South America, exciting innovations have brought about new protected area models that, at the same time, foster conservation and secure the land and resource rights of indigenous peoples.

In South–East Asia, community involvement in conservation is both a matter of socio-cultural livelihood and reappropriation of natural resources from the state and the powerful economic forces that covet and seek to control them. In the Horn of Africa, the plight of pastoral communities is the most evident and urgent issue as 'ethnic conservation' practices are being obliterated. In Australia, various models of CMPA are leading towards an effective engagement of Aboriginal peoples. In South Asia, several community conservation models are being tried,

from weak CMPA arrangements, such as bureaucracy-led consultations and benefit-sharing arrangements (but no formal power-sharing) in India, to stronger arrangements, including joint management structures in Nepal and Pakistan (Kothari, 2005). In their context of dense population settings, human–wildlife conflicts are quite prominent in the debates surrounding these initiatives.

In Central Africa, protected area co-management approaches with communities are relatively rare, a primary obstacle being weak state institutions, highly centralized laws and lack of accountability in natural resource management. In Southern Africa, key lessons have been developed during the last couple of decades, pointing to the need for communities to achieve tangible and secure benefits from the sound management of their natural resources, which, in turn, depends upon collective proprietorship and devolution of relevant management authority and responsibility. In Brazil, the emphasis seems to be on realizing the potential of many management opportunities,

Machilu village, Karakoram National Park, Pakistan

Source: IUCN Photo Library © Jim Thorsell

and revitalizing, on the one hand, the economic benefits of sustainable management, but also, on the other, a spiritual and emotional 're-enchantment' with nature.

Besides the distinctive experiences and needs just mentioned, the analysis of the above case studies highlights a number of elements of broad global validity. First is the recognition that much knowledge, skills, resources and institutions with great potential for conservation still exist in civil society, in general, particularly among indigenous and local communities throughout the world (Banuri and Najam, 2002). Despite the inherited troubles and negative historical circumstances mentioned at the beginning of this chapter, the potential for engaging civil society in conservation is still enormous.

At the heart of initiatives across the world, such as the ones highlighted in this chapter, is the recognition that 'conservation' is changing in a fundamental way. It is responding to the interests and concerns of a variety of social actors, including relevant indigenous and local communities. For this, conservation can no longer be pursued as a lone value, independent or superior to all other concerns, or be controlled by small groups of professional experts. Rather, it must be pursued by society as a whole, along with and through other important social goals, such as livelihoods, cultural diversity, community-based appropriate development and social equity.

In the 1990s the above statement would have been bold and potentially subversive. Not today. Fundamental changes are visibly taking place, carried along by many other changes in society, described in Chapter 2. Most countries of the world still have a long distance to travel on the path towards CMPA; but at the international level, clear direction has been set for this in the Convention on Biological Diversity Protected Area Programme of Work (see Appendix 4) and in other key documents of the global conservation community, such as the outputs of the vth IUCN World Parks Congress (see Appendix 3). Precisely because so much is happening, however, there is a danger of a backlash, especially from some conventional conservation agencies that become reactive. This would be a mistake. Engaging indigenous and local communities in conserva-

tion can be a powerful means of coping with the global changes sweeping our planet. It may require a sharing of power not favoured by many of the agencies currently in charge; but, on the eve of socio-economic and environmental change of great proportions, conservation can no longer afford to consume its precious resources in fighting its best and most promising allies.

Management principles

1   Most government-managed protected areas have been long inhabited by humans or have been used by humans even when non-resident. Tens of millions of people depend substantially upon the resources found within protected areas for their survival, livelihood, health and well-being. These people have also influenced the landscape and seascape. Most 'wildernesses' are influenced, to varying degrees, by indigenous peoples and local communities. Such people also have customary and, at times, statutorily recognized rights and claims to lands, waters and resources within protected areas. Collaboratively managed protected areas are a key mechanism for giving recognition to these facts.

2   Conservation that attempts to keep communities out of the decision-making process, and/or out of the sharing of benefits, is unlikely to be sustainable for long. Community support is needed to achieve long-term conservation objectives. There is no substitute for engaging with people. Indeed, public communication and collaboration can significantly enhance conservation objectives and outcomes.

3   In order to work successfully with local communities, protected area managers must recognize that human relationships and trust are crucial, and that much can be achieved by approaching decisions on the basis of mutual benefit.

4   Effective collaboration among partners to manage protected areas requires facilitative legal and policy regimes; attitudinal changes in all partners; trust-building and increase in capacities to handle processes of collaboration; institutional structures and rules to govern the partnerships; clarity in the relative rights and

responsibilities and functions of each partner; and the ability to adapt.

5   CMPAs face a number of challenges, including denial of cultural identity and rights of communities; inadequate or absent policies and laws in many countries; application of rigid, universally applied prescriptions without flexibility to deal with site-specific situations; local and national inequities in power that make for unequal decision-making and benefit-sharing; inadequate, short-term or see-saw government commitment; inadequate capacity among various partners; and continuing threats from external sources, including development processes and projects. Protected area managers should contribute to processes and actions that seek to address these challenges.

6   Protected area managers need to work to secure governmental recognition and support for CMPAs, including policy and legislative measures, as well as supporting civil society and community mobilization.

Further reading

Borrini-Feyerabend, G., De Sherbinin, A., Diaw, C., Oviedo, G. and Pansky, D. (eds) (2003) *Policy Matters*, vol 12 (joint CEESP–WCPA special issue on community empowerment for conservation)

Borrini-Feyerabend, G., Pimbert, M., Farvar, M. T., Kothari, A. and Renard, Y. (2004a) *Sharing Power: Learning-by-Doing in Co-management of Natural Resources throughout the World*, IIED and IUCN/CEESP/CMWG, Tehran

Borrini-Feyerabend, G., Kothari, A. and Oviedo, G. (2004b) *Indigenous and Local Communities and Protected Areas: Towards Equity and Enhanced Conservation*, WCPA Best Practice Series 11, IUCN WCPA, Gland and Cambridge

Brown, J., Kothari, A. and Menon, M. (eds) (2002) *Parks*, vol 12, no 2 (Special issue on local communities and protected areas)

Jaireth, H. and Smyth, D. (eds) (2003) *Innovative Governance: Indigenous Peoples, Local Communities and Protected Areas*, Ane Books, New Delhi

Websites

IUCN Commission on Environmental, Economic and Social Policy (CEESP)/World Commission on Protected Areas (WCPA) Theme on Indigenous and Local Communities, Equity and Protected Areas (TILCEPA), www.tilcepa.org

IUCN Commission on Environmental, Economic and Social Policy (CEESP), www.iucn.org/themes/ceesp/index.html

21

Community Conserved Areas

Ashish Kothari

Possibly the most exciting conservation development of the 21st century is the global recognition of community conserved areas (CCAs). The conservation of sites and species by indigenous peoples and local communities is age old; but the fact that these are equivalent in many ways to conventional government-managed 'protected areas' has not been recognized until recently. It is only with the struggles waged by communities for recognition of their initiatives and rights, along with the work of some international organizations and the exploration of new conservation models by some countries, that CCAs have burst into the global scene during the first few years of this century. In particular, the two events that marked this recognition were the Vth IUCN World Parks Congress in 2003 and the Seventh Conference of Parties to the Convention on Biological Diversity (CBD) in 2004. A definition of CCAs that emerged from the congress was:

> … *natural and modified ecosystems with significant biodiversity, ecological and related cultural values, voluntarily conserved by indigenous and local communities through customary laws or other effective means.*

This definition, as well as many of the concepts regarding CCAs described in this chapter, is still evolving, given that in formal conservation circles the idea and acceptance of CCAs are very recent. The term 'communities' is used here as a convenient short form for indigenous peoples and local communities. Community conservation efforts are of diverse kinds, but all contain three essential characteristics:

1 One or more communities closely relate to the ecosystems and/or species because of cultural, livelihood, economic or other ties.
2 Community management decisions and efforts lead to the conservation of habitats, species, ecological benefits and associated cultural values, although the conscious objective of management may not be conservation *per se* and could be related to livelihoods, water security or cultural values.
3 Communities are the major players in decision-making and implementing actions related to ecosystem management, implying that some form of community authority exists and is capable of enforcing regulations.

This chapter describes the range and extent of CCAs, discusses how they can be categorized as protected areas, indicates the range of benefits that they provide, and provides examples of the wide variety of socio-cultural and political contexts in which they occur. I have borrowed heavily from Pathak et al (2004) and Borrini-Feyerabend (2003b).

Range and significance of community conserved areas

There is a diverse array of CCAs across the world. Spread across low, medium and high Human Development Index (HDI) countries, they include:

- indigenous peoples' territories managed for sustainable use, cultural values or, in more recent times, explicit conservation objectives;
- territories (terrestrial or marine) over which mobile or nomadic communities have traditionally roamed, managing the resources through customary regulations and practices;
- sacred spaces, ranging from tiny forest groves and wetlands to entire landscapes and seascapes, often (but not necessarily) left completely or largely inviolate;
- resource catchment areas, from which communities make their essential livelihoods or from which key ecosystem benefits are derived, managed such that these benefits are sustained over time;
- nesting or roosting sites, or other critical habitats of wild animals, conserved for ethical or other reasons explicitly oriented towards protecting these animals; and
- landscapes with mosaics of natural and agricultural ecosystems, containing considerable cultural and biodiversity value, and managed by farming communities or mixed rural–urban communities.

Although they may occasionally contain private lands, CCAs are mostly found on common or collectively held property, or on government lands that the community considers as part of its commons.

There is no clear idea of the extent of area that CCAs cover across the world. Some scholars estimate that about 420 million hectares of forests (11 per cent of the world's total) are under community ownership or administration (Molnar et al, 2004), and that this could double in the near future due to spreading policies of decentralization (White et al, 2004). This includes over 22 per cent of forests in low HDI and some medium HDI countries. Of this, about 370 million hectares are under some level of conservation management by communities (Molnar et al, 2004). Add to this other ecosystems (wetlands, marine areas, grasslands, deserts and so on) that would be under CCAs, and the sheer magnitude of this conservation effort becomes impressive.

The following characteristics of CCAs can assist in their analysis and classification:

- *Size of the area being protected.* This ranges from less than 1ha, such as several sacred sites in South Asia and West Africa, to entire mountains, lakes or landscapes, such as Titicaca Lake in Peru/Bolivia.
- *Biodiversity being conserved.* The range of biodiversity protected by CCAs ranges from a single species, such as the demoiselle crane (*Anthropoides virgo*) in the village of Kheechan, western India, to particular habitats containing many species, to mosaics of different ecosystems.
- *Motivations for conservation.* These range from purely ethical values or a concern for threatened wild animals, to the security of ecological benefits being derived, to economic and financial benefits from the site.
- *Origins and history.* The CCA could be initiated by the community itself or by an outside agency, and the subsequent process of establishment could be led from within or by external actors who continue to play a role.
- *Type of management institution.* The entire relevant community could be involved through a general council, as in the case of Mendha-Lekha village in India (see Case Study 21.4). There could be sections of the community responsible for management, as in most of the other CCAs described in this chapter. The institution could be comprised entirely of community members, as in case of the Comarca Ngöbe–Buglé in Panama (considered in Case Study 21.10), or may contain representatives of outside agencies, as at the Alto Fragua–Indiwasi National Park in Colombia (see Case Study 21.8).
- *Type of community rules and regulations being enforced.* Governance can be based on written or unwritten rules; traditional customary or new regulations; enforcement through social sanctions; financial penalties; or other means.
- *Type of social and economic benefits.* The conserving community can derive specific benefits, which could be related to the motivations for initiating the CCA, as well as unanticipated or side benefits (see Table 21.1).
- *Nature of ecological benefits.* CCAs can support intrinsic values and non-use benefits, as well as providing ecosystem services (see Table 21.1).

- *Legal or tenurial relationship of the community to the CCA.* The community may own the site and its resources, as in the indigenous protected areas described in this chapter; have non-ownership control, such as legal rights to utilize resources; have only *de facto* control with no legal backing, as in the case of many Indian CCAs listed in Table 21.1; or have a combination of these arrangements over different aspects of the CCA.
- *Length of time that the initiative has been sustained.* The CCA may be 'age old', with no clear community memory of its establishment, as in the case of many sacred sites; have a long recorded history, as with the 1000-year-old accounts of the Italian Regole d'Ampezzo (considered in Case Study 21.9); or may be very recently established.

The above characteristics, in various combinations, can help to distinguish between 'strong' and 'weak' CCAs. For instance, a regional review of South–East Asia commissioned by the IUCN's Theme on Indigenous and Local Communities, Equity and Protected Areas (TILCEPA) analyses a series of cases from weak (an externally originated, community-based initiative in Burma, which secured only temporary tenure rights through a 25-year lease) to strong (an internally originated ancestral domain in the Philippines, fully backed by local practice and culture, strongly supported by NGOs, and with the community entitled to ownership rights because of relevant national legislation). However, one has to be careful before categorizing CCAs in this way. A CCA that appears 'weak' may simply be at an initial stage of development or going through a temporary low period.

Are CCAs protected areas?

Given the international recognition that CCAs have obtained since the World Parks Congress of September 2003 (as exemplified in Appendices 3 and 4), governments and conservation organizations will increasingly be faced with the question: are all CCAs to be considered protected areas? This question was the subject of discussion at the World Parks Congress, and has been considered and extensively discussed within fora such as TILCEPA and the Theme on Governance, Equity

and Rights of the IUCN's Commission on Environmental, Economic and Social Policy (CEESP) (see, for example, Kothari et al, 2003). As noted in 'Types of protected areas' in Chapter 3, the IUCN definition of a protected areas is:

> *… an area of land and/or sea especially dedicated to the protection and maintenance of biological diversity, and of natural and associated cultural resources, and managed through legal or other effective means. (IUCN, 1994, p7)*

As noted in 'Conventions' in Chapter 3, the CBD uses the following definition: 'a geographically defined area which is designated or regulated and managed to achieve specific conservation objectives'.

Key elements of protected areas according to these definitions are:

- geographical limits or boundaries;
- predominantly aimed at achieving conservation benefits, but not excluding other related benefits;
- designation and management by legal or other effective means;
- existence of a body of governing rules; and
- a clearly identified organization or individual with governance authority.

The examples presented in this chapter and in sources such as Kothari et al (2003) suggest that many or most CCAs have all of these elements. The IUCN protected area category system is being updated to include a governance dimension, as indicated in Table 5.1. This has made it possible to include non-official conservation areas, such as CCAs, in national protected area systems. This dimension is also to be added to the World Database on Protected Areas (WDPA) (see Box 10.1 in Chapter 10), which will make it possible to list CCAs in the database. Following on from the governance typology for protected areas described in Chapter 5, Table 21.1 shows how CCA types can be allocated to each of the six IUCN protected area categories.

Key motivations

National governments often establish and manage protected areas with the primary objectives of

Table 21.1 Community conserved areas (CCAs) as protected areas in the IUCN category system

IUCN category (see Chapter 3, p82)	Community conserved area (CCA) type	Site examples
Categories Ia and Ib Strict Nature Reserve and Wilderness Areas	Sacred/forbidden or otherwise 'no-use' groves, lakes, springs, mountains, islands and so on with prohibition on uses, except in very particular occasions, such as a once-a-year ceremony, once-a-year collective hunting or fishing strictly regulated by the community A special case here may be the territories of un-contacted peoples (such as in the Amazons) The main reasons for the communities to protect the area may be cultural or religious, rather than aesthetic, scientific or intrinsic values	Coron Island, Palawan, the Philippines (sacred beaches, marine areas and lakes) Hundreds of sacred forests and wetlands in India Mandailing Province, Sumatra, Indonesia (forbidden river stretches) Life Reserve of Awa People, Ecuador Intangible zones of Cuyabeno–Imuya and Tagaeri–Taromenane, Ecuador Indigenous reserves, Peru Forole sacred mountain of northern Kenya
Category II National Park	Watershed forests above villages, community declared wildlife sanctuaries (at times also for ecotourism use)	Tinangol, Sabah, Malaysia (forest catchment) Safety forests, Mizoram, India Isidoro–Secure National Park, Bolivia Cuvu Tikina, Fiji Islands Alto Fragua–Indiwasi National Park, Colombia
Category III Natural Monument	Natural monuments (caves, waterfalls, cliffs and rocks) that are protected by communities for religious, cultural or other reasons	Limestone caves, Kanger Ghati National Park and elsewhere, India Mapu Lahual network of indigenous protected areas (coastal range temperate rainforests), Chile Sites of ancestor graves, Madagascar
Category IV Habitat/Species Management Area	Heronries and other village tanks, turtle nesting sites, community managed wildlife corridors and riparian vegetation areas	Kokkare Bellur, India (heronry) Pulmarí Protected Indigenous Territory, Argentina (proposed)
Category V Protected Landscape/Seascape	Traditional grounds of pastoral communities/ mobile peoples, including rangelands, water points and forest patches; sacred and cultural landscapes and seascapes, and collectively managed river basins Such natural and cultural ecosystems have multiple land/water uses integrated with each other and are given a context by the overall sacred/cultural/productive nature of the ecosystem; they include areas with high agricultural biodiversity	Palian river basin, Trang Province, Thailand (rainforest, coast and mangroves) Thateng district, Sekong Province, Laos (agriculture and forestry mosaic) Coron Island, the Philippines Indigenous reserves, Peru Potato Park, Peru Migration territory of the Kuhi nomadic tribe (Iran), including the Chartang–Kushkizar community protected wetland

Table 21.1 Continued

IUCN category (see 'Types of protected areas' in Chapter 3)	Community conserved area (CCA) type	Site examples
		Borana territory, Oromo region, Ethiopia (pastoral territory, with protected savannah, forest and volcanic areas of Categories Ib and III)
		Ekuri Initiative, Nigeria
		Community conservancies, Namibia
		Island of Eigg, United Kingdom
Category VI Managed Resource Protected Area	Resource reserves (forests, grasslands, waterways, coastal and marine stretches, including wildlife habitats) under restricted use and communal rules that ensure sustainable harvesting through time	Jardhargaon, Mendha-Lekha, Arvari, Dangejheri and hundreds of others, India
		Pathoumphone district, Champassak Province, Laos
		Pred Nai, Thailand
		Amarakaeri Communal Reserve, Peru
		Takietà forest, Niger
		Kinna, Kenya (bordering Meru National Park)
		Community forests in the Val di Fiemme, Italy

Source: adapted from Kothari et al (2003)

biodiversity conservation – a concept understood as having a positive impact for the provision of goods and services to human communities, but which may impose some separation between humans and nature. Biodiversity is perceived as having intrinsic value (see Chapter 4), independent from consideration of other human and social interests and concerns.

Indigenous and local communities, on the other hand, are motivated by a diversity of interests and concerns, while establishing their own conserved areas, or entering into a partnership to manage protected areas established by other social actors or the state. These may include one or more of the following motivations.

A concern for the protection of wildlife. This may especially relate to wildlife that is considered to be special in some way. The village wetlands of Kokkare Bellur in southern India harbour the globally threatened spotbilled pelican (*Pelecanus philippensis*). Wintering or breeding grounds of migratory species are protected in areas such as

Kheechan in western India, which has a large population of demoiselle cranes (*Grus virgo*). Habitats of threatened species are protected in areas such as Khonoma in north-eastern India, which supports a large population of the threatened Blyth's tragopan (*Tragopan blythii*) (Pathak et al, 2006).

To secure a sustainable provision of resources related to livelihoods. Most CCAs are likely to have this as a main or one of the main motivating factors, especially when communities are faced with serious depletion of such resources (see Case Study 21.1).

To maintain crucial ecosystem functions from which communities benefit. Ecosystem functions that are critical in supporting human welfare include soil stabilization and the maintenance of hydrological cycles (see Chapter 4). In the north-eastern Indian state of Mizoram, for instance, villagers have protected forested water catchments designated by the government as 'safety forests' (Singh, 1996), and in the US, communities protect or acquire

Case Study 21.1

Cuvu Conservation Initiative, Fiji

Floyd Robinson, Partners in Community Development, Fiji

Coastal resource-owning communities in Fiji have taken proactive steps to conserve their depleting inshore fisheries resources. These communities have customary rights of usage of resources, which legally belong to the state. Coastal fisheries have been depleted for a number of reasons, including over-fishing, use of enhanced and destructive methods, land-based sources of pollution, lack of awareness and complacency. In Cuvu district, Nadroga, Fiji, seven villages have worked with a local NGO, provincial authorities, ministries relating to natural resources, and a private resort to improve their skills and management of coral reefs.

The NGO Partners in Community Development (PCD) Fiji implemented two community-based conservation projects in 1999 that had different funding sources, but shared similar fundamental principles. The Wai Bulabula project aimed to support conservation of coral reefs by managing land-based sources of pollution. On the other hand, the coral gardens project focused on developing workable models to enhance community capacity to conserve coral reefs. These projects were coordinated through a Cuvu district environmental committee, comprising community leaders, PCD Fiji, government ministries and the Shangri La's Fijian Resort.

Through a series of participatory learning and action workshops conducted in 1999, communities considered their state of environment, identified concerns and underlying reasons, and developed management plans. Specific activities that arose out of the management plans included the establishment of no-fishing zones, replanting of mangroves, training of fish wardens and replanting of coconut seedlings along the coastline.

A fundamental principle of the Cuvu project was the integrated approach, which aimed to work through existing traditional structures and systems with the goal of sustainability. The district environmental committee, while coordinating project activities, played a key role in updating both the high chief and provincial authorities. Seaweed workshops also ensured training opportunities for the women and youth of the district.

A feature of the project was the involvement of the private sector, Shangri La's Fijian Resort, which provided logistical and financial support for the projects. An artificial wetland system was built at the resort to biologically reduce nutrient loading of wastewater through the use of plants.

The Cuvu conservation project was one of the initial marine community-based conservation projects in Fiji, from which numerous lessons have been learned. Through their initiative, communities of Cuvu have demonstrated how they can work, together with the private sector, resorts, NGOs and government ministries, to conserve coastal marine resources.

forests for the same purpose (see Case Study 21.2).

To sustain religious, identity or cultural needs. Honouring the memories of ancestors or the deities, guarding burial sites and ritual places from external interference, and securing aesthetic values are common motivations behind establishing CCAs. Thousands of sacred sites across the world have been motivated by cultural values; many indigenous protected areas continue to have strong cultural motivations (Bernbaum, 1999; Chambers, 1999; Laird, 1999; Posey, 1999). Several community forests in the US are secured for aesthetic enjoyment (see Case Study 21.2).

To secure collective or community land tenure. Communities often seek to obtain legal recogni-tion of their customary rights, and to gain assur-ance from governments that the land will be protected and not subjected to a variety of forms of exploitation. In a climate of tenure insecurity, lack of confidence in state institutions and poli-cies, and after a long history of abuse of indigenous and community rights, people are searching for all possible instruments to secure long-term access to natural resources. In certain situations they have discovered that a protected area regime can offer them such a security, apart from attracting funding, support, visibility, politi-cal empowerment and livelihood options. Examples include indigenous protected areas in Australia (see Case Study 21.7) and the Ekuri Initiative in Nigeria (see Case Study 21.3).

Case Study 21.2

Community forests in the US: Good neighbours of protected areas

Martha West Lyman, Quebec–Labrador Foundation (QLF), Atlantic Center for the Environment, US

The economy and culture of the northern New England region of the US is rooted in forests. The region hosts the flagship forests of the country's national forest system, as well as numerous other protected areas, including wildlife refuges, state forests and parks, and privately conserved land. Ownership and management of forest land by towns is not a new idea here, but rather an old one with new relevance since it relates to conserving land adjacent to existing protected areas, as well as linking protected areas.

The town of Conway, New Hampshire, owns over 650ha of forest, including one large chunk of 367ha known as the Common Lands. These lands date back to colonial times when they were made available for use by townspeople who were, 'through economic misfortune, in need of firewood'. During the 1930s, Gorham, New Hampshire, acquired over 2000ha of land from a paper company to protect the town's water supply. While the land is still managed in keeping with this principal priority, the Gorham Town Forest now serves as an outdoor classroom and produces revenues from timber harvests that support community activities. In 2000, the town of Randolph, New Hampshire (population 320), acquired about 4100ha of land to manage growth, to preserve the forest-based economy of the town, and to provide a vital corridor and link between the two sections of the White Mountain National Forest. And in 2005, the town of Errol, New Hampshire (population 303), acquired about 2100ha of privately owned forest that it recognized as an important community asset. This forest is a critical part of a growing corridor of public and private conservation land between the White Mountain National Forest, Nash Stream Forest, and Lake Umbagog National Wildlife Refuge.

Access and rights to natural resources are two of the principle tenets of sustainable development. Community-based natural resource management also shows that if the values of natural resources can be availed of by the landholder (in this case, the community), then there is a strong likelihood that the resources will be conserved and will result in improved management, expanded participation, improved governance and increased benefits (Child and Lyman, 2005).

Randolph community forest project, New Hampshire, US

Source: Martha West Lyman

These concepts are increasingly important in this region, where the globalization of the forest products industry has resulted in large absentee landowners selling vast areas of land. This, coupled with development pressures, has combined to cause fragmentation of the forests. While there have been impressive conservation initiatives to secure the land, virtually all of the ownership still remains in the hands of absentee landowners, such as timber investors, state and federal agencies or state or national non-profits. Although communities gain some benefits from improved stewardship and a forest base that is still available for recreation, the decision-making power and economic returns from the land continue to flow out of the region. As mechanization in the forest industry reduces employment in both the woods and the mills, even wage income is sharply reduced.

According to this scenario, increasing local equity in forest land, the region's core asset, is a positive step in the direction of supporting local self-determination, resource protection and economic growth, while preserving and enhancing local traditions.

In 2003, the Quebec–Labrador Foundation (QLF), Atlantic Center for the Environment, conducted a study of the economic, environmental and social contributions of town ownership of forest land (Bisson and Lyman, 2003). The findings of the study include the following:

- Forests either pay their way or produce revenue for towns, and in all cases impose no net costs on towns.
- Forests provide a mix of monetary and non-monetary benefits, including timber revenues, non-forest product revenues, water supply and quality, recreation, wildlife habitat and open space.
- Forests provide support for other community priorities, including social services, education, building community capacity and social capital.

QLF is currently working with other communities and organizations in the region to determine the potential for community ownership and management of forest land as a component of a regional conservation and community development strategy.

To provide security. Communities may establish CCAs to obtain a physical assurance for their own security, as well as the security of their properties and settlements. This may be associated with an expectation of invasion by enemies or harsh ecological conditions, such as droughts or floods. Examples include the Kaya forests of Kenya and the humid elevated forests in Ethiopia.

To obtain financial benefits. CCAs can enable communities to access new markets for their products or the experiences available on their lands or seas. For example, protected area status makes it more likely that communities will be able to attract ecotourism business.

Benefits of CCAs

CCAs are critical from an ecological and social perspective in many ways:

- They help to conserve critical ecosystems and threatened species.
- They maintain essential ecosystem functions, including water security and gene pools.
- They sustain the cultural and economic survival of tens of millions of people, especially communities directly dependent upon

natural resources for survival and livelihoods.

- They provide corridors and linkages for animal and gene movement, including often between two or more officially protected areas.
- They help to synergize the links between agricultural biodiversity and wildlife, providing larger land/waterscape level integration.
- They offer crucial lessons for participatory governance, useful even in government managed protected areas, lessons already employed in several countries to resolve conflicts between protected areas and local people.
- They offer lessons in integrating customary and statutory laws, and formal and non-formal institutions, for more effective conservation.
- They are often built on sophisticated ecological knowledge systems, elements of which have wider positive use.
- They are frequently part of community resistance to destructive development, an attempt to save territories and habitats from mining, dams, logging, tourism, over-fishing and so on.
- They can help to create a greater sense of community identity and cohesiveness. This has

Case Study 21.3

Ekuri community requests for a community conserved area, Nigeria

Chief Edwin Ogar, Ekuri community, Nigeria

The Ekuri community in Nigeria is made up of Old Ekuri and New Ekuri, two villages 6km apart located on the edge of Cross River National Park in its buffer zone. This park is found in the Cross River State of Nigeria, on the border with Cameroon. The community belongs to a small indigenous group called Nkukorli with a unique tradition, culture and language, who occupy only five villages. The Ekuri community jointly possesses 33,600ha of pristine tropical forest on their communal land – probably the largest communally controlled forest remaining in Nigeria. They are predominantly forest gatherers and farmers.

Until 1990, members of both villages had a four-hour walk to the nearest trafficable road. This meant that all the products harvested from the forest and farms were head carried to the road and then sold to 'middlemen' for ridiculously low prices. Both villages badly wanted a road because they realized that with a proper road, they could take larger quantities of these products directly to markets in nearby cities and sell them for much better prices than those obtained at the roadside. The community was being approached on a regular basis by logging companies, trying to make agreements with each village separately in order to divide them, dangling the prospect of a road in exchange of logging rights.

However, these overtures were not appealing to the Ekuri people, who instead resolved, in 1992, to manage their forest by themselves. This they did by forming and establishing the Ekuri Initiative, a community NGO charged with the responsibilities for the conservation and sustainable management of the Ekuri community forest, with the purpose of community development and poverty reduction.

Many factors motivated the Ekuri people to take this decision, chief among them being to:

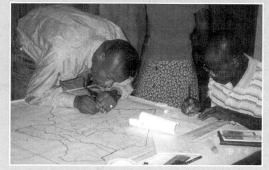

Ekuri Initiative: Land-use mapping for a community forest

Source: Alix Flavelle

- protect and safeguard the inheritance of ancestors;
- protect their cultural-, spiritual- and economic-based livelihoods;
- ensure the protection of watersheds for free flow of freshwater for their uses and for other communities downriver;
- generate incomes from their rich forest for community development and poverty reduction;
- ensure the protection of diversity of species and long-term survival of their forest; and
- avail of the negative lessons learned/drawn from other communities whose forests are unsustainably managed.

Since 1992, the Ekuri community (with a population of 6000), through the Ekuri Initiative, have been engaged in a community forestry project to sustainably harvest timber, vegetables, rattans and other products from their community forest. Proceeds have enabled them to implement laudable and concrete community development and poverty reduction programmes. With support from other agencies, they have conducted a boundary survey to demarcate 33,600ha, taken up two 50ha inventory plots and prepared a detailed five-year plan, including a preliminary land-use plan. The initiative is a recipient of the prestigious United Nations 2004 Equator Award for its outstanding efforts and commitments to reducing poverty through conservation and sustainable use of biodiversity.

However, in spite of the tremendous successes of the initiative, the state government has approved an illegal forest concession in Ekuri community forest against the wishes of the Ekuri people. Outside of urban areas where most land is owned individually, all of the remaining land of Nigeria is owned by the state. Although communities administer local lands and function very much like their owners, they do not have legal ownership rights. This has led to exploitation, denials of the customary rights of communities and outright expropriations. Against this backdrop and current threats to the Ekuri community forest, the Ekuri people have requested the IUCN Theme on Indigenous and Local Communities, Equity and Protected Areas (TILCEPA) to assist them in acquiring the status of a community conserved area (CCA). TILCEPA has been helpful in collaborating with the Ekuri people to ensure the realization of a CCA for the Ekuri community forest for its protection and integration within the international regime of protected areas.

been part of the very characteristics that ensured the survival of many communities through history and today may lead to other social benefits, such as community organization and action for improved education, health and sanitation. CCAs may even lead towards a more just and egalitarian society – for instance, through joint initiatives among different local classes and castes, the empowerment of women, or the enhanced transparency and accountability in governance of all sorts of community affairs (see Case Study 21.4).

- They conserve biodiversity at relatively low financial cost. Costs of maintenance of CCAs are often largely covered as a part of normal livelihood or the cultural activities of communities through existing systems and structures. These costs are low compared to those official state-managed protected areas. Costs in human labour can, however, be significant.

Case Study 21.4

Transparency: More than an empty word in Mendha-Lekha, India

Mendha-Lekha village in India exhibits a high level of transparency in the management of its community conserved area (CCA) and other affairs. Located in the central Indian tribal belt, the Gond residents of this village have been part of the wider 'tribal self-rule' movement, aimed at ensuring that all key decisions relevant to the settlement are taken locally. During the 1970s, these communities were faced with displacement by a government-sponsored hydroelectric project. Strong opposition to this project stopped it and helped to spur the local population to organize around the management of their forests. Subsequently, the village also stopped a paper mill from over-exploiting bamboo, and started imposing restrictions on its own residents regarding the use of forest resources. A forest patch of 1800ha is under Mendha-Lekha's protection, and neighbouring villages are being inspired to bring several hundred hectares more under conservation.

During the early 1980s, the village established an institution called the Gram Sabha (the village assembly), comprising all adults. All decisions are discussed threadbare in the Gram Sabha until everyone is satisfied and a consensus emerges. Often these discussions are preceded by deliberations in a study circle, attended by anyone from the village, as well as outside agencies who are interested in the particular issue. Accounts are managed by multiple institutions and are regularly made available to the Gram Sabha. Even government officials who come to implement schemes in the village are made to present all details to the Gram Sabha and are forced to make modifications that the villagers want.

Mendha-Lekha's community conserved forests, India

Source: Ashish Kothari

In many of these and other ways, CCAs are eminently suited to helping meet the United Nations Millennium Development Goals (MDGs), especially those related to eradicating poverty and ensuring environmental sustainability. Indeed, they provide an essential link or bridge between these goals, which is otherwise weakly developed in most country policies and programmes (Pathak et al, 2006). Table 21.2 provides a glimpse of the kinds of ecological and socio-economic benefits of CCAs and community-based conservation. The examples in this table are from South Asia, but can be extrapolated to CCAs in other parts of the world.

Table 21.2 Ecological and socio-economic benefits of community-based conservation in South Asia

Type of initiative	Ecological benefits	Socio-economic benefits	Illustrative examples
Traditional protection of sacred sites	Protection, often total, of forests, grasslands and village water tanks	Cultural sustenance; protection of community identity	Several thousand in India and Bangladesh, usually small in extent
Traditional protection of sacred species	Protection of key species	Cultural sustenance, aesthetic enjoyment, marginal livelihood and economic benefits	Blue bull (*nilgai*) (*Boselaphus tragocamelus*), Rhesus macaque (*Macaca mulatta*) and fig (*Ficus* spp.) all over India; blackbuck (*Antelope cervicapra*) and other species in the Bishnoi community area, Rajasthan, India; fig (*Ficus* spp.), mahua (*Madhuca indica*), khejri (*Prosopis cineraria*) and other trees in many countries
Traditional sustainable use practices for habitats	Conservation of habitats, such as village water tanks, pastures and forests, and wildlife species resident in them, as well as corridors or gene movement between official protected areas	Sustenance of traditional means of survival and livelihoods; in some cases, sustenance of financial revenues	Kokkare Bellur heronry, India; *bugiyals* (pastures) and *Van Panchayats* (village forest council-managed areas) in the Indian Himalaya; several marine sites with traditionally regulated fisheries in India and elsewhere
Traditional sustainable use practices for species	Conservation of wildlife species, along with or independent of their habitats	Sustenance of traditional livelihoods and cultural practices	Trees such as mahua, harvested with great restraint in many parts of tribal India; hunting restraints for several species
Recent initiatives to revive degraded habitats and to sustainably use them	Regeneration of forests, grasslands and other ecosystems, and of species dependent upon them	Revival of traditional livelihoods; sustenance of survival resources; generation of new livelihoods, including financial revenues and employment; political and social empowerment, including, in many cases, greater equity (gender, class, caste and so on)	Several million hectares of forest lands in India (joint forest management or community initiated) and several hundred thousand hectares in Nepal and Bhutan

Table 21.2 Continued

Type of initiative	Ecological benefits	Socio-economic benefits	Illustrative examples
Recent initiatives to conserve and/or sustainably use relatively intact ecosystems	Conservation of important ecosystems and their resident species; reduction in threats to them	Generation of new livelihoods, including financial revenues and employment; revival of old or generation of new cultural practices and identity; political and social empowerment, including, in many cases, greater equity (gender, class, caste and so on)	Mendha-Lekha, India; Annapurna Conservation Area, Nepal; Muthurajawela Marsh and Lagoon, Sri Lanka; eco-development at Periyar Tiger Reserve, India; community wildlife and forest reserves in Nagaland, India
Recent initiatives at sustainable (consumptive and non-consumptive) use of species	Revival of threatened populations of wildlife, such as ibex (*Capra ibex*), and reduction in overexploitation (e.g. of plant and aquatic species)	Generation of new livelihoods including financial revenues and employment	Hushey, Pakistan; Rekawa, Sri Lanka; Biligiri Rangaswamy Temple Sanctuary, India; Baghmara, Nepal
Resistance to destructive commercial forces	Reduction or elimination of factors threatening ecosystems and species	Protection of survival and livelihood base; protection of political and social identity	Protection of Indian coastline and marine areas by traditional fisherfolk from destructive fishing and aquaculture; several movements against big development projects in several countries; movement against mining in Sariska Tiger Reserve, India

Source: adapted and updated from Kothari et al (2000)

Harvesting barley, Annapurna Conservation Area, Nepal

Source: IUCN Photo Library © Jim Thorsell

Baghmara Community Forest, Nepal

Source: IUCN Photo Library © Jim Thorsell

While most CCAs are motivated by social, economic or cultural needs and values, an emphasis on community benefits does not at all imply that biodiversity conservation is undervalued. It just means setting biodiversity into a perspective of human well-being and peaceful development. The case of the Alto Fragua–Indiwasi National Park in Colombia (see Case Study 21.8) is an excellent example of this. A community-promoted refuge provides both biodiversity protection and a secure livelihood to people in a context of armed violence, drug trafficking and the many social problems that affect the surrounding areas. In another case, in the Ecuadorian Andes, the indigenous communities have established use restrictions and management regulations in areas adjacent to the San Pablo Lake in order to prevent the further deterioration of the lake's environment – a genuine conservation objective, and yet fully related to community livelihoods (Oviedo, 2002).

Importantly, community initiatives have often integrated the conservation of both wild and domesticated species, and tend to look at them as part of a continuum from predominantly wild to semi-wild and semi-domesticated, to predominantly domesticated. Indeed, their perception indicates that the conventional divide between 'wild' and 'domesticated' biodiversity is not as sharp as is often made out. Several traditional practices of optimizing this range of biodiversity (such as home gardens in southern India and Sri Lanka) continue to exist, and new ones are being tried out by many communities. In some Indian villages in the Himalayan belt, the farmers involved in forest conservation are also the ones reviving a range of agro-biodiverse practices (such as trials of several hundred traditional varieties of rice, beans and other crops), and they make explicit connections between the two (TPCG and Kalpavriksh, 2005). In the Peruvian Andes, the Quechua indigenous peoples have established a

Potato Park as a bio-cultural heritage site where a mosaic of agricultural and natural ecosystems are conserved, along with the revival of potato diversity in its place of origin (Pathak et al, 2004; Alejandro Argumedo, pers comm, 2005).

Legal and policy context

CCAs have a diversity of legal and policy features. Many are based on customary law and traditional practice, with no statutory backing in national law, and often existing as a struggle in the face of adverse national law. Others are based on national or local government policies and laws that provide general autonomy or authority to indigenous peoples or local communities over their territories and resources, with no specific conservation-related law applied to the CCA. Some, though less numerous, are based on national or local government policies and laws that specifically enable the designation of the CCA as a conservation area.

In the first category, CCAs are entirely based on customary rules and agreements, with no intervention of government agencies or relation to official policies, and at times even imply a degree of confidentiality regarding exact location, boundaries, resources and so on. In most countries, CCAs are 'informal' in the sense of being officially unrecognized. Their contribution to a country's conservation system goes unnoticed and unsupported. Worse still, some official protected areas have been established on the very territories where CCAs were already in place, disrupting the traditional management system.

In the second category, CCAs survive because there is a general policy or legal backing to the territorial or resource rights of the concerned communities. Most common among these are some areas managed by indigenous peoples in Bolivia, Columbia, Canada, Australia, India, the Philippines and other countries where the territorial identity and boundaries of such peoples are established in law. In many of these cases, the boundaries of the CCAs themselves may not be officially demarcated (although they may be clear to the communities concerned), and such CCAs are not explicitly recognized in the official conservation or protected area system of the country (see Case Studies 21.5 and 21.6).

In the third category are CCAs that are offi-cially recognized as conservation entities by the relevant government. In this case, there are two possible consequences. First, the recognition does not substantially reduce the autonomy and decision-making power of the local communities. Here, the community gets legal authority to enforce its decisions (for instance, notification under a wildlife legislation as a protected area can offer a CCA protection against destructive industrial processes). Examples of full state recognition of CCAs include the indigenous protected areas of Australia (see Case Study 21.7), a number of CCAs in South America (see Case Study 21.8), community conservancies in Namibia, and several protected environments dedicated to the sustainable management of valuable natural resources, such as the alpine forests and pastures of the Valle d'Ampezzo and the Magnifica Cumnita della Val di Fiemme in Italy (see Case Study 21.9). In all of these cases, a system of conservation has been voluntarily established by the owner communities and recognized with legal backing by the relevant states. Indeed, the indigenous protected areas of Australia, the Alto Fragua–Indiwasi National Park and the Comarca Ngöbe–Buglé are fully integrated within the respective national protected area systems. The Italian case, which is much older, offers an example of a CCA where communities managed to develop agreements with dominant powers over hundreds of years – from the Republic of Venice at the time of Marco Polo, to the Austro–Hungarian Empire, to the Italian national state. In the case of Madagascar, the government is, at the time of writing, considering legal options for the recognition of CCAs as part of its protected area system (see Case Study 21.6).

Second, the recognition is based on the sharing of authority and responsibility with governmental agencies, which substantially alters the governance situation and transforms the CCA into a co-managed protected area, examples of which are given in Chapter 20.

Similar cases involve lands traditionally belonging to indigenous or rural communities that, in the past, had been incorporated within official protected areas and now, through a variety of processes, have been 'restituted'. The communities now own and manage them, possibly as a CCA corresponding partially or totally to the

Case Study 21.5

Community conservation in Nagaland State, India

Neema Pathak, Kalpavriksh, India

Nagaland State of India, bordering Burma, is occupied by 16 tribal communities, each culturally and geographically distinct from the other. Unlike other parts of India, nearly 90 per cent of the land is under community ownership and 85 per cent is still under forest cover. Originally hunter–gatherers, these communities have developed an intricate land-use system, with land distributed between shifting cultivation (communal ownership of land), settled agriculture (private landownership) and forest reserves (could be family, clan or community owned) to meet food, fruit, fuel, timber and other requirements. Wild meat is an integral part of tribal culture here. Most families own guns and go hunting nearly every day. Easy availability of guns (because of a few decades of political insurgency in the state) and non-implementation of wildlife protection laws have led to unsustainable hunting. Increasing population and heavy dependence upon timber and forest produce for livelihood have also affected forest quality.

During the late 1980s and early 1990s, the effects of these activities began to manifest themselves in the drying-up of water resources, declining availability of wild foods and declining populations of wild animals. In 1988, the Khonoma Village Council in Kohima district declared 20 square kilometres of forest and grassland as the Khonoma Nature Conservation and Tragopan Sanctuary. Rules were formulated to strictly ban hunting (not only here, but over the whole of Khonoma's 135 square kilometre territory) in order to stop all resource uses in the sanctuary area and to allow only a few ecologically benign uses in the buffer area. A trust was set up for management. A proposal is currently under discussion to extend the sanctuary area to the adjoining forest. The villagers are also trying to persuade neighbouring villages to take up similar measures, which, if successful would conserve 200 square kilometres of unique habitat, with several endemic and threatened species.

In the same district, the village council of Sendenui resolved to set aside an area of about 1000ha after some discussions initiated by the village youth concerning the decline in wild animal populations. The village has issued its own wildlife protection act, with rules and regulations for managing the sanctuary. In neighbouring Phek district, several villages have taken up conservation measures. In 1983, the Luzaphuhu village student's union resolved to conserve a 5 square kilometre patch of forest land above the village as a watershed. In 1990, they declared another 2.5 square kilometres as a wildlife reserve, with hunting strictly prohibited. Similarly, Kikruma village is regenerating and protecting 70ha. Several villages centred around Runguzu are protecting an entire range, with perhaps several thousand hectares of forest, and six villages led by Chizami are reviving traditional protection of a few hundred hectares. Along many roads in the state, notices have been put up by village youth associations warning that the area is under strict protection.

Khonoma youth at the Khonoma Nature Conservation and Tragopan Sanctuary, India

Source: Ashish Kothari

Different villages have varying ways of dealing with violations, a simple fine being the most common. Some are more sophisticated, with a higher fine for more endangered species.

There is no specific conservation law backing these initiatives. What is helping, however, is the 1978 Nagaland Village and Area Council Act, under which settlements have considerable powers over land use in their territories. Sendenui's wildlife protection act, for instance, derives its formal basis from this general act.

Case Study 21.6

Community-based management initiatives in Madagascar

Joanna Durbin, Durrell Wildlife Conservation Trust, Madagascar

There has been dramatic environmental change in Madagascar since the arrival of humans 2000 years ago, with significant loss of forests, changes in hydrology, sedimentation of lakes and rivers, and loss of Madagascar's unusual endemic species.

Despite the apparent spiral of degradation, there are many examples of local initiatives where those relying on valued natural resources have developed institutions and rules to maintain resources. For example, at the Manambolomaty Lakes, a closed season is respected to allow fish stocks to recover during the spawning season under the orders of a traditional leader known as the *tompon-drano*, or lord of the water. In the south-east of the country it is *fady*, or taboo, to cut down the hovao tree (*Dilobeia thouarsii*) in the rainforest because the nuts provide a valued source of cooking oil. In the south-west, the Bara people protect Zombitse and Vohibasia forests as a pasture area and to hide cattle from cattle thieves.

Many natural areas with cultural and spiritual importance for the Malagasy people are protected through traditional management. Angavo is one of the many sacred forests in the south of Madagascar where spiny forest covering around 3000ha is protected from deforestation, fire and any wood extraction. Many forests throughout Madagascar are protected by local customs because they contain tombs or ritual sites, although the areas protected are usually small, typically up to 100ha. In the west of Madagascar, there are sacred lakes where nets, boats or other uses are prohibited. A council of elders, often in collaboration with a traditional leader, such as the head of a local royal family (*mpanjaka*), reinforces the rules (*dina*) and decides on any sanctions (*vonodina*) after these have been agreed at a meeting of the community (*fokonolona*). Unfortunately, there are also many examples where societal changes and outside pressures have undermined traditional practices.

Recent government policies have explicitly aimed to reinforce community management of natural resources through the 1996 GELOSE law (Gestion Localisée Securisée, or Secure Local Management law). This enables communities to sign a contract with the state to manage specific natural resources on their lands. The *cahier de charge* defines management objectives, rules and quotas. As of January 2005, almost 500 contracts had been signed covering around 500,000ha. These contracts legalize traditional forms of management that rely upon the notions of *fokonolona*, *dina* and *vonodina*, and are of great significance in a country where government agencies are generally under-funded, de-motivated and corrupt.

Madagascar is currently poised to further recognize the contribution made by community conservation. Following the president's statement at the World Parks Congress in Durban in 2003 that Madagascar would triple its protected areas to cover 6 million hectares, or 10 per cent of the country, there is a strong move towards developing a more flexible approach to protected area management. The new conservation sites are being planned with different levels of co-management, often incorporating GELOSE contracts as a management unit within the area. A number of CCAs are under evaluation for inclusion in the new protected area system, and legislation is being developed to recognize traditional management as a contribution to the nation's protected areas.

entire official protected area. In these cases, recognition of communities' traditional land and resource rights and management attributions is done through official means, including the establishment of co-management agreements and joint management institutions. Again, the extent of autonomous decision-making power determines whether such a situation can be considered a CCA or a co-managed protected area.

The existence and status of CCAs are strongly dependent upon the particular local, national and regional context. In the Horn of Africa, for instance, conservation initiatives conceived, wanted and implemented by local communities through their own exclusive means are at the heart of traditional cultures throughout the country. These initiatives are culture based and culture specific, and tend to relate in complex ways to the ethnic identity of a community, including its governance systems, norms, symbolic constructions and rituals (Bassi, 2003). Unfortunately, these practices have not been recognized and supported by state governments. On the contrary, the active policies of subsequent dominant political powers and developers have often undermined the relevant indigenous resource management systems

Case Study 21.7

Indigenous protected areas, Australia

Dermot Smyth, James Cook University, Australia

In Australia, a very strong form of community conserved area (CCA), known as an indigenous protected area (IPA), was officially recognized by the federal government in 1998. An IPA is an area of land and/or water that traditional indigenous owners have voluntarily declared to be a protected area as defined by the IUCN, and to which they have made a public commitment to manage for the conservation of its biodiversity and associated cultural values. In exchange for this declaration, the Australian government, through the Indigenous Protected Area Programme of the Department of Environment and Heritage, provides financial support and technical assistance to develop and implement a management plan for the declared area. Once declared, IPAs are formally recognized as part of the National Reserve System (NRS), which has the goal of establishing a comprehensive, adequate and representative system of protected areas, encompassing all bioregions of Australia (see Case Study 8.1).

The first IPA was formally proclaimed in August 1998 over an Aboriginal-owned property called Nantawarrina in the northern Flinders Ranges of South Australia. There are now about 20 declared IPAs throughout the country, comprising approximately 20 per cent of the total terrestrial protected area (TPA) estate in Australia.

Although part of the NRS, IPAs remain under indigenous ownership and control, with the level of government participation in management determined by the indigenous owners. IPAs can be established as formal conservation agreements under state or territory legislation, or independently of government legislation (as provided by the IUCN definition). Indigenous people use a variety of legal mechanisms to control activities on their IPAs, including local government by-laws, privacy laws and traditional indigenous laws.

The declarations of IPAs represent the first occasions in Australia in which indigenous people have voluntarily accepted protected area status over their land and water. Because the process is voluntary, indigenous people can choose the level of government involvement, the level of visitor access (if any) and the extent of development to meet their needs. IPAs are attractive to some indigenous groups because they bring management resources without the loss of autonomy usually associated with joint management of protected areas. IPAs also provide public recognition of the natural and cultural values of land and water, and of the capacity of indigenous peoples to protect and nurture those values. IPAs are attractive to government conservation agencies because they effectively add to the nation's conservation estate without the need to acquire the land, and without the cost of establishing all of the infrastructure, staffing, housing and so on of a national park.

that allowed the people to survive for centuries in difficult and fragile environments because of the existence of CCAs.

Contrasting with the experience of the Horn of Africa is that of CCAs and collaboratively managed protected areas (CMPAs) in South America. These are making a significant contribution to biodiversity conservation and are actually prompting national governments to set more of national lands under a conservation regime. It is estimated that about 84 per cent of national parks in South America overlap with community lands, and in many of these areas communities are regaining legal land and management rights (Amend and Amend, 1995). In addition, several countries (Brazil, Bolivia, Colombia and Panama) have legal provisions recognizing the indigenous

peoples' direct right to manage their land (see Case Study 21.10). Soon, a vast proportion of existing protected areas of the region may be community managed, totally or partially.

Many CCAs stretch our understanding of the concept of 'area' since the territories under protection do not have clear borders, being associated with forces of undetermined nature or place, or with changing seasons and climatic phenomena. This is particularly true with reference to mobile communities (on land or at sea), who generally relate to very broad territories and resources that are profoundly affected by varying climatic conditions (see Case Study 21.11). In general, however, this is true for all ethnic groups, as ethnic conservation does not tend to work through a univocal association between one

Case Study 21.8

Alto Fragua–Indiwasi National Park, Colombia

Gonzalo Oviedo, IUCN senior adviser for social policy, Ecuador, based on information provided by Ignacio Giraldo from the Amazon Conservation Team

The Alto Fragua–Indiwasi National Park of Colombia was established in February 2002 as a result of agreements between the Colombian government and the Association of Indigenous Ingano Councils Tandachiridu Inganokuna. It is a landmark in the evolution of the protected areas model in Latin America as the first national park of Colombia to be created on the ancestral lands of an indigenous people at their request, and on the basis of their own culture (Zuluaga and Giraldo, 2002).

The park covers 68,000ha in the southern department of Caquetá, and is named after the headwaters of the Fragua River and the Ingano term *Indiwasi* (House of the Sun). Located on the piedmont of the Colombian Amazon, the park is within a region considered to be one of the top 'biodiversity hotspots' of the world (Colombia Environment Ministry, 2002).

The Ingano, with a population of approximately 35,000, are descendents of various ancient ethnic groups, unified through the Inga language and culture, belonging to the Quechua linguistic family (Zuluaga et al, 2003).

Following the declaration of the area, the Special Administrative Unit for the National Parks System of Colombia (UAESPNC) and the Tandachiridu Inganokuna Association signed a memorandum of understanding for the management of the park. A board composed of four representatives from each of the two parties was created (putting this case into the category of co-managed protected area, as discussed in Chapter 20, but retained here because of its predominantly community-based origin), and the following commitments were established:

- UAESPNC will facilitate the adaptation of national regulations for the administration of national parks to the conditions of the area so that local needs are met, while still complying with national obligations under the protected area system;
- the board will undertake at least one annual assessment of progress; and
- the document produced by the Ingano communities, *Our Thinking – Alpa Ñucanchipataita Karadu*, will serve as the basis of the park's management.

The main challenge that the Ingano and the area administration face is the adoption of a management regime based on a bio-cultural approach. A key objective is monitoring the colonization process in the areas surrounding the park. A research project undertaken jointly by the Tandachiridu Inganokuna Association, the Colombia National University, using geographic information system (GIS)-based analysis, and UAESPNC indicated that land below 400m was the most affected by colonization. The limits and zonation of the park were updated based on these results, aided by scientific inventories by the Von Humboldt Institute. An assessment of management effectiveness identified a number of weak areas: lack of sufficient qualified personnel, funding and coordination with local authorities.

One of the strategies proposed by the Tandachiridu Inganokuna Association to overcome these problems is the establishment of a network of Indiwasikama families – 'families that guard the House of the Sun'. Indigenous families have been located in critical areas of the park borders, and have been given plots for practising traditional horticulture integrated with forest management. Apart from serving their own subsistence purposes, the plots are pilot sites for a demonstration of sustainable management techniques, which are to be disseminated to colonizers' families in the vicinity of the park. Besides, the families will continue practising their traditional rituals and ceremonies in these areas in order to maintain an active cultural setting.

Creating a protected area of this magnitude as an indigenous-owned area, moving towards a co-management regime, and using an intercultural or bio-cultural approach is feasible, but not easy. Neither the unilateral methods that formal protected areas have had in the past, nor an isolationist approach that leaves the indigenous peoples alone would deal with all of the challenges. Partnership between the indigenous organizations, the government-protected area agency and a NGO bringing technical expertise and advocacy capacity (the Amazon Conservation Team) allows for the combination of different skills, roles and responsibilities. Devolving the authority and management capacity to the indigenous communities is not enough; without broader partnerships, the effectiveness of their role could be compromised.

This experience shows the importance of integrating traditional knowledge and formal science. The landscape dimension of management is also highlighted, mainly due to the socio-ecological and cultural interactions with the broader area. The application of the management effectiveness assessment tools has also brought some important lessons, including the need for integration of cultural variables in the assessment process and ways of strengthening critical areas of management. The establishment of the proposed network of Indiwasikama families is a creative response to these issues.

Case Study 21.9

Italian traditional institutions

Long-established traditions of community forestry and pasture management in the north of Italy date from the Middle Ages, and some can be traced to well before the Roman conquest. In some places, such as the Fiemme Valley, community control over forests was maintained thanks to the armed struggles of local residents in the mid 19th century, when the nascent Italian state was attempting to incorporate all forests within the national *demanio*. Such struggles took place all over Italy; but only in the north were they so serious and prolonged as to convince the government to carve out special exceptions in the national law.

An example of community forestry that still exists today thanks to such legal exception is the Magnifica Comunità di Fiemme. In the Magnifica Comunità, the forest-managing institutions are strong, maintain a spirit of mutual assistance and solidarity, and provide an important cultural basis for the use of the forest resources. Legally, the forest is owned by 'all people of the Fiemme Valley' who comprise the '*vicini*' of 11 townships (a *vicino* is a person who has been living in the valley for 20 years at least, or who is a descendant of a *vicino*). Community forests are inalienable, indivisible and collectively owned and managed. Traditionally, wood was distributed according to the citizen's need to build a house (once in a lifetime) and for maintenance work and heating (once a year). Today, the financial income from the sale of timber is used to support community needs.

Another example is the Regole d'Ampezzo of the Ampezzo Valley (where the famous Cortina resort is located), which has a recorded history of approximately 1000 years. The Regole manage the common property resources initially made available by the extensive work of the early Regolieri (extensive pasture creation and maintenance out of the original woods). To date, the Regolieri comprise only the descendants of the early founders of the community and their sons, who remain residents in the valley, a more stringent requirement than in the case of the Magnifica Comunità di Fiemme. They hold the property under inalienable and indivisible title. Their general assembly takes management decisions after extensive discussion and by a 'qualified majority', a procedure more akin to consensus than voting. The decisions and rules (which, incidentally, is the meaning of the word '*regole*') are carefully crafted to use the resources sustainably and in non-destructive ways. Unlike in the Fiemme Valley, no dividends are shared among the Regolieri, and all of the income from the natural resources (for example, from tourism and timber sales) is reinvested in their management.

About 15 years ago, the Regole finally received major recognition as the sole and full legal managers of the Parco Naturale delle Dolomiti d'Ampezzo. Thus, this regional protected area is established on the land and the resources that the local community has conserved throughout the centuries. From an economic point of view, the Regole are today less directly reliant on the natural resources that they manage, although the unique tourism and real estate value of their valley depends upon the magnificent landscape that they have maintained. It is notable that they have obtained a tax-free status from the Italian government, and secured major project funds and subsidies from the European Union (EU), the Italian state and the Veneto regional government.

Sources: adapted from Merlo et al (1989), Jeanrenaud (2001) and Lorenzi (pers comm, 2005)

ethnic group and a defined territory. Different ethnic groups may also have unclear or competing claims over the same territory; but despite this, their conservation areas may remain effectively managed (see Case Study 21.12).

Limitations and problems

Despite their impressive spread and efficacy, CCAs are not necessarily a solution to all conservation problems. They often suffer from serious limitations and face a host of problems.

CCAs have suffered through the undermining of traditional institutions by colonial or central-ized political systems. In many countries, governments have taken over most of the functions and powers that communities used to traditionally enjoy. Even well-intentioned government policies to support conservation involve taking over functions and powers, or establishing uniform and parallel institutional bodies based on representative politics, rather than facilitating and improving upon an existing system. In many parts of Asia, for example, there is a strong tradition of local management of small irrigation reservoirs that also support large populations of birds and other animals. In many cases, these reservoirs – together

Case Study 21.10

Comarca Ngöbe–Buglé, Panama

Vivienne Solís Rivera, Cooperativa Autogestionaria de Servicios Profesionales para la Solidaridad Social RL (CoopeSoliDar RL), Costa Rica

The constitution of the Republic of Panama recognizes the territorial rights of indigenous people. In 1997, through Law Number 10, the Comarca Ngöbe–Buglé was created. This region is located in the Provinces of Veraguas, Chiriquí and Bocas del Toro. The Ngöbe–Buglé are the most numerous indigenous community of the country, with a population of 180,000 people and a territory of 277,762ha. Conservation activities have been supported by the Worldwide Fund for Nature (WWF) with the informed consent of the Comarca Ngöbe–Buglé and financial support from the Manfred Hermsen Stiftung.

This territory is considered collective property of the Comarca ('indigenous region'), with property use and rights enjoyed only under the observance of the Ngöbe–Buglé law and collective practices. Governance and administration are in the hands of the local traditional authorities. The maximum authority is the General Congress of the Comarca, which is an organization that arises from the local congresses.

Panama is one of the few countries in the region that has recognized and accepted the creation of Comarcas within the national legislation as territory that rightfully belongs to the indigenous people. National law not only protects the natural resources of their lands, but also the cultural resources that are patrimony of the indigenous communities.

Within this territory, important examples of biological and cultural wealth that are strongly related to each other are found. Among them is Playa de Chiriquí, located in the area of the Ñö Kribo. This beach is an important nesting site of the critically endangered hawksbill turtle (*Eretmochelys imbricata*) in the Caribbean. The decrease of the presence of this turtle on this specific beach and along its area of distribution is attributed to hunting, especially to supply the international commerce of the hawksbill shell. Nesting decreased by 98 per cent during the 1950s. Currently, about 3000 to 5000 leatherback turtle (*Dermochelys coriacea*) nests are found on this same beach each year, placing Playa Chiriquí as the second in importance regarding this species in the Caribbean and the first in Central America. A hawksbill turtle conservation and recuperation project, in its first two-year phase, seeks to conserve and revive turtle populations, while improving the quality of life of their guardians. Participatory monitoring of the turtle population was initiated by the Caribbean Conservation Corporation in 2003. This project intertwines conservation, research and management functions, and strengthens community organizations. This is complementary to the work of other associates in the region, such as Panamá's National Environmental Agency (ANAM) and Centro de Estudios y Accion Social Panameno (CEASPA), with an emphasis on the sustainable use of terrestrial and marine resources.

Playa Chiriquí is part of the Damani–Island Escudo de Veraguas Wetlands Reserve, an area of approximately 9700ha. This is a protected territory proposed by the Ngöbe–Buglé people themselves and is declared a wetland of international importance under the Ramsar Convention. It includes valuable tropical humid and mangrove forests.

In all, the natural resources of the Playa Chiriquí region represent an important asset for the development of the Ngöbe, Río Caña, Río Diablo y Río Chiriquí communities, who inhabit various ends of the beach. These populations currently live under extreme poverty, illness and lack of access to land, electricity or potable water. Río Caña and the Laguna de Damani include a section of lakes and lagoons that represent a wetland ecosystem of great value, not only because it is the nesting site of the green (*Chelonya mydas*), leatherback and hawksbill turtles, but also because of the presence of other endangered species, such as the manatee (*Trichechus manatus*) and the harpy eagle (*Harpia harpyja*).

This area contains the necessary characteristics to be acknowledged as a community conserved area (CCA); but more analysis is required before it is recognized within the national system of protected areas of Panamá, El Sistema Nacional de Áreas Protegidas de Panamá (SINAP), and the General Ngöbe–Buglé Congress, which could be a way of fortifying its management by the community.

---

with sacred forests or landscapes – have been included into protected areas, breaking down the intricate community management systems and generating resentment by the surrounding populations (Pandey, 2000). Bassi (2003) records the conflicts created when the Awash National Park in Ethiopia caused displacement and reduced territorial access among the Karrayu (Oromo)

Case Study 21.11

Community-conserved landscape of the Oromo–Borana, Ethiopia

Marco Bassi, Bologna University, Italy

The whole ethnic territory of the Borana, in Ethiopia, can be considered as a community (ethnic) or indigenous conserved area. The territory has been managed for centuries according to specific rules that ensured the sustainable use of renewable natural resources. Some specific provisions embedded in culture ensured biodiversity conservation *per se*, and the sound management of natural resources was promoted through norms of inclusion/exclusion designed for pastoral activity and known as *seera marraa bisanii* – 'the law of grass and water'. The Borana 'law of grass' shares the basic principles of most East African pastoral groups. It differentiates between dry season pastures (with permanent water points) and wet season pastures (with good grass, but only accessible during rains), imposing the maximization of use of wet season pasture whenever possible (during rains) in order to minimize pressure on the most intensely utilized rangelands served by permanent water points. The 'law of water' is, instead, peculiar to the Borana and their environment, characterized by the presence of numerous well complexes (the nine *tulaa* wells are the most famous among them). This law is extremely well articulated, regulating in various ways the social and economic investment necessary to develop traditional wells and water points, access and maintenance. Through the normal cycle of well excavation and collapse, over-exploited dry season areas are abandoned and new ones are developed.

The juniper forests found in Borana lands have a special role, which is common to many East African forests used by pastoralists. Being too humid, they are not suitable for permanent pastoral settlement. Some open patches, however, contain excellent pasture, and the forest also provides permanent springs. For centuries, such forests have never been permanently inhabited, but were reserved as excellent dry season pasture. They had a crucial function as a last refuge for grazing in case of drought and as a reserve for medical and ritual plants, and had an overall symbolic and ecological meaning. They were not subject to special management provisions besides the very strict prohibition to start fires inside them, but were an integral and essential part of the survival system of the Borana.

The environmentally sound management of natural resources in Borana land has ensured the conservation of a unique biodiversity patrimony right until the 1970s, despite the establishment of some small towns close to the main forests at the beginning of the 20th century.

The Acacia–Coommiphora open woodlands and bushlands of the area support 43 species of mammals, including the endemic Swayne's hartebeest (*Alcelaphus buselaphus swaynei*), and 283 species of birds, including the endemic Abyssinian bush crow (*Zavattariornis stresemanni*) and the white-tailed swallow (*Hirundo megaensis*). It is possible that the Abyssinian bush crow, found only in the land of the Borana, is actually dependent upon a pastoralism-modified ecology. A recent roadside count by Borghesio and Giannetti (2005) indicates a population decline by 80 per cent from 1989.

Dry evergreen forests and patches of forests with *Juniper procera* are also important because they occur in low rainfall habitat (below 1000mm). The endemic Prince Ruspoli's turaco (*Tauraco ruspolii*) is only found in Manquubsaa (Nagelle) and Areero juniper forests. The larger three Juniper forests found in Boranaland, Manquubsaa (Nagelle), Arero and Yabello have been classified as national forest priority areas.

Since the 1970s, the Borana environment has been facing major changes in land-use patterns. The socialist government limited movement within the ethnic territory and promoted agriculture. After the change of government, the United Nations High Commission for Refugees facilitated the resettlement of people in Boranaland who were not actually from the area. More land resources were lost by the Borana in the process of economical liberalization and globalization. Large ranches were acquired by international investors, and extensive portions of land around the towns, located in their critical dry season pastures, were assigned to town dwellers and to non-Borana immigrants for smallholding cultivation. All of this has severely disrupted the regulatory system of the Borana.

Sources: adapted from Tache (2000) and Bassi (2002)

---

pastoral people, who had protected the landscape's important biodiversity for centuries.

Local communities are not homogenous, and their initiatives are often affected by inequities and social injustices. Conservation or resource-exploitation decisions may be taken by the powerful (the men, the landowners, the upper caste people); but the brunt of these decisions may

Case Study 21.12

Forole Sacred Mountain and the Gabbra mobile pastoralists, Kenya

Chachu Ganya, Pastoralist Integrated Support Programme, Kenya

The Gabbra pastoralists in Kenya use mobility to cope with ecological variability in a very arid environment. Their mode of range use follows spatial and temporal patterns of resource distribution. The grazing zones of the Gabbra's five phratries' (*gossa*) mobile ritual centres are separated. Each phratry's mobile ritual centre, with 50 to 100 households, has a fixed grazing zone, and its movement is restricted to avoid environmental degradation.

Culture is an important element that determines the management and conservation of the bio-cultural landscape of the Gabbra. The Gabbra holy symbol sites include unique landscapes, special hills such as the Forole Sacred Mountain, a single grove of trees or even some unique tree species, among others. In the Gabbra territories of northern Kenya and southern Ethiopia, there are over 100 such sacred sites/symbols. These ritual sites are protected and preserved by each Gabbra phratry, and the access is limited to only ceremonial occasions. In order to minimize environmental degradation, only a few animals are brought by the Gabbra during the ceremonies to these sacred sites.

Forole is an important cultural site of one of the Gabbra phratry. The Galbo tradition (the Galbo are one of the five groups of the Gabbra) demands very strict environmental conservation measures for such sacred areas. It is, by tradition, forbidden to hunt, and no plants or parts of plants may be removed from the holy sites; even a fibrous twig used as a toothbrush has to be thrown away before one leaves the area. No herding sticks or traditional twigs are cut there. These restrictions are instituted in order to ensure the survival of the flora and fauna of this geographically small but culturally highly valued site. In the absence of such environmental protection and wise management, cultural sites such as the Forole Mountain would long have been degraded of its unique flora and fauna. In addition, to the Gabbra camel nomads, Forole is also a grazing area of the Borana, who are cattle-rearing pastoralists. The two communities share the same language, but have a distinct leadership and some different ritual and cultural practices.

The Gabbra and the Borana utilize the Forole grazing reserves as the wet season grazing zone due to lack of permanent water sources around the Forole area. During recent years, the two resource-sharing communities have had strained relationships and even armed conflicts. The increasing conflicts are triggered by competition for the pastoral resources and by politically related pressures from both communities, which largely advocate for rivalry and dominance rather than harmonious utilization of the available resources. However, even during such conflicts, the Boranas fully respect the sacredness of the Gabbra ritual sites, such as the Forole Mountain, and the inherent restrictions, directly ensuring conservation of these unique sites.

be felt by the powerless (the women, the artisans, the head-loaders, the pastoralists – all highly dependent upon the closest village resources).

Conflict with neighbouring communities or inter-village inequities in access to land and resources tend to undermine CCA initiatives. In the Himalayan state of Uttaranchal in India, communities have often conserved forests effectively under the system of *Van Panchayats* (village forest councils). But the distribution of forest land among various villages may be highly skewed, with some villages having miniscule and unsustainable portions, or a few hectares, while others have massive territories of thousands of hectares that are impossible to manage (FES, 2003).

Traditional management and belief systems

have also been eroded in many places due to breakdown in community spirit and institutions caused by the monetization of the economy, 'development' projects and the growing dominance of party politics in public life. Market forces, sudden inflows of capital and cultural change undermine traditional leadership. Sectoral interests have, in several cases, found collaborators from within the community who are willing to violate community regulations in order to make quick profits, and over whom the community may not be able to exercise control. Party politics often takes a serious toll on traditional systems of justice and conflict resolution, and creates unhealthy competition and factionalism within the community. In India, several hundred sacred sites have been wiped out due to such forces; sacred sites in other countries also face such challenges.

Batoufan in western Cameroon is an area controlled by around 100 independent chiefdoms that possess and guard a series of sacred forests through various community-based and secret societies. Many of these forests are of high biodiversity value, and different types of forest possess different cultural and spiritual status for the communities concerned. Access to these sacred forests is strictly controlled by community institutions; but community members can enter either to collect key medicines needed by sacred healers or through limited annual access, when all community members can go into the forests to harvest a wide range of products. Key dilemmas faced by this community-based conservation model include the diversification of cultural norms due to immigration, which tends to dilute the authority of the customary system, and the conflicting rules between national forest and conservation laws, on the one hand, and customary protection measures and spiritual practices, on the other (Nelson and Gami, 2003).

Newer generations are often not interested in carrying on conservation-oriented traditions, influenced by 'modern' education that devalues such traditions, or finding them irrelevant in the face of severe livelihood problems.

Many CCAs are on lands that the community does not have ownership to or control over, making the maintenance of CCAs difficult, especially in the face of outside pressures. A majority of CCAs in India, for instance, are on lands owned by the state and managed by specific government departments (forest, irrigation and revenue). In other words, although *de facto* management is by the community, land-use authority remains vested in the government, which often assigns the areas for mining, urban growth, industry, land redistribution or other non-conservation uses (Pathak et al, 2006).

National or local government policies and development processes often threaten CCAs, even where the community has legal ownership or control, and especially where it does not have clear legal title to the land. This is particularly true of the large territories of mobile or nomadic populations, or of shifting cultivators, portions of which are laid claim to by governments or other communities (see Case Study 21.12).

Human and livestock population increases have, in several places, shrunk the total available resource base and led to over-exploitation that the community is unable to curb on its own.

Communities sometimes find it difficult to sustain the current costs of managing CCAs, such as investment in time and labour; funds for the salaries of village guards; conflict situations with neighbours or migrating communities; opportunity costs related to the inability to access or utilize certain land or resources; crop depredation; property loss; and loss of lives as a result of increased wildlife populations. Different communities are able to withstand or compensate those costs to varying degrees, with shifting impacts on the viability of the CCAs.

Previously sustainable levels of resource use may now be causing over-exploitation as a number of extraneous circumstances may have led to the decline in extent or abundance of these resources. This is the situation, for instance, with traditional hunting of wild animals, where the populations of these species have declined due to various factors emanating from within and outside the community.

Many communities who rely on agriculture as their main livelihood activity assert claims to wide sections of forest around their settlement areas, but do not (or cannot) exercise any formal institutional defence against outsiders who come to hunt, log or mine.

While these and other problems should not be underestimated, it is also important to recognize that none of them are insurmountable. The experiences of a number of CCAs highlighted in this chapter, and many others, demonstrate that there is both resilience and adaptability among communities. These experiences also demonstrate that support from outside agencies can often be critical in tackling such problems or, in general, in helping to sustain CCAs. It is in this connection that governments and NGOs need to urgently heed the recommendations emanating from the World Parks Congress (see Appendix 3) and the CBD (see Appendix 4). This is particularly important in terms of extending recognition, legal backing, technical and financial support, or other kinds of aid (as deemed appropriate by the communities themselves) to peoples and communities who are struggling to maintain and spread CCA initiatives.

Management principles

The way forward depends upon the following measures by protected area managers, governments, NGOs and expert institutions (all with the full and meaningful involvement of the concerned communities):

1   CCAs that are within the broad framework of areas defined in this chapter, or which an individual country's legal or customary systems recognize as CCAs, should be recorded as part of the national protected area systems, and their governing communities recognized as protected area managers.
2   CCAs often need legal backing, as felt appropriate by the concerned communities, which allows the flexibility to accommodate local contexts and concerns.
3   Systems of rights and responsibilities, building on traditional or customary arrangements, where appropriate, need to be established or strengthened.
4   CCAs need support in other ways, as felt appropriate by the concerned communities, such as social recognition, economic and financial support, support to address internal and external threats, conflict resolution mechanisms, and institutional and networking support.
5   Concerned communities need help to resist destructive developmental or commercial pressures, including by foregoing short-term commercial gains from the CCA resources.
6   There is an urgent need to help tackle equity (including gender) issues, within communities and among communities, as well as between communities, on the one hand, and government agencies and other non-local actors, on the other.
7   There is a need to support participatory monitoring and evaluation of CCA initiatives by providing appropriate resources and capacity-building for communities.

8   Protected area managers and advocates need to help build the capacity of relevant communities, in terms of resource management, assessment, evaluation of external impacts and technical capacities in conservation and income generation.
9   CCA representatives need to be involved in larger protected area and conservation systems, such as at landscape and seascape levels, and with national and sub-national conservation bodies.
10 CCAs need to be integrated within international regimes, such as the *United Nations List of Protected Areas*, the Global Database on Protected Areas, the World Conservation Monitoring Centre (WCMC) protected area database and the IUCN protected area category system.
11 Protected area managers and advocates need to generate international support for CCAs from relevant international programmes, treaties and donors, including the Ramsar Convention, World Heritage designation, the CBD and so on.
12 Protected area managers, advocates and CCA organizations need to support the exchange of ideas, information and personnel relating to CCAs, particularly exchange of community members themselves.

Further reading

Borrini-Feyerabend, G., De Sherbinin, A., Diaw, C., Oviedo, G. and Pansky, D. (eds) (2003) *Policy Matters*, vol 12 (joint CEESP–WCPA special issue on community empowerment for conservation)

Borrini-Feyerabend, G., Kothari, A. and Oviedo, G. (2004) *Indigenous and Local Communities and Protected Areas: Towards Equity and Enhanced Conservation*, WCPA Best Practice Series 11, IUCN WCPA, Gland and Cambridge

Brown, J., Kothari, A. and Menon, M. (eds) (2002) *Parks*, vol 12, no 2 (Special issue on local communities and protected areas)

Pathak, N., Bhatt, S., Balasinorwala, T., Kothari, A. and Borrini-Feyerabend, G. (2004) *Community Conserved Areas: A Bold Frontier for Conservation*, TILCEPA/IUCN, CENESTA, CMWG and WAMIP, Tehran

Websites

IUCN Commission on Environmental, Economic and Social Policy (CEESP)/World Commission on Protected Areas (WCPA) Theme on Indigenous and Local Communities, Equity and Protected Areas (TILCEPA), www.tilcepa.org and www.iucn.org/themes/ceesp/wkg-grp/TILCEPA/community.htm

IUCN Commission on Environmental, Economic and Social Policy (CEESP), www.iucn.org/themes/ceesp/index.html

22

Linking the Landscape

Trevor Sandwith and Michael Lockwood

Achieving a comprehensive and effective protected area system requires the targeted and strategic establishment of protected areas (see Chapter 8). In addition to their biodiversity conservation objectives, protected areas provide a range of other values to society, including social, economic, spiritual and cultural values, which extend far beyond protected area boundaries. Protected areas are, in turn, affected by land-use activities and impacts in the surrounding areas, as well as by global change. These include agriculture, fisheries and settlements that fragment landscapes and impact upon ecosystem processes, as well as the pervasive threats of climate change and the impact of invasive alien species (see Chapter 9).

No system of protected areas can achieve its potential if protected areas become isolated fragments surrounded by incompatible land uses. There are numerous definitions of, and approaches to identifying spatial scales for, connectivity conservation planning and management. In this chapter we are primarily concerned with regions and landscapes, which have been defined by Forman (1995, p13) as follows:

> A region is a broad geographical area with [a] common microclimate and sphere of human activity and interest. This concept links the physical environment of microclimate, major soil groups and biomes with the human dimensions of politics, social structure, culture and consciousness... A landscape, in contrast, is a mosaic where the mix of local ecosystems or land uses is repeated in a similar form over a kilometres-wide area. Familiar examples are forested, suburban, cultivated and dry landscapes. Whereas portions of a region ecologically are quite dissimilar, a landscape manifests an ecological unity throughout its area. Within a landscape several attributes tend to be similar and repeated across the whole area, including geologic land forms, soil types, vegetation types, local faunas, natural disturbance regimes, land uses and human aggregation patterns. Thus, a repeated cluster of spatial elements characterizes a landscape.

Protected areas must be established and managed as components of regional- and landscape-scale conservation strategies. The biological rationale is that whereas the protected area estate has performed relatively well in securing representative samples of biodiversity pattern (distribution of species, communities and ecosystems), it remains inadequate to conserve the ecosystem processes that will secure persistence either of the protected areas or of biodiversity in the wider landscape and region. Multiple-agency, regional-level and landscape-level approaches can contribute to the resolution of this problem. Establishing conservation linkages at such scales is necessary to mitigate negative impacts and to achieve conservation and rural sustainability objectives. Equally important is that people from all walks of life value protected areas and biodiversity throughout a region and landscape, and are involved in their protection and management.

Landscapes arise from the interaction of people with their environment over time (Phillips, 2002), and conservation itself can be regarded as an expression of human values and goals in relation to the landscape, governed by and through the institutions of society. In many parts of the world, there has been a breakdown of this holistic approach, and there is therefore a need to learn how to work across fragmented jurisdictional distinctions, such as those between public, communal and private land; national park and state forest; or one local government area and another. The goal must be to achieve connectivity conservation, to establish networks of protected areas and to manage these cooperatively in the context of sustainable management of the whole matrix of land uses. Attention should also be paid to establishing a robust and appropriate mix of protected areas across all IUCN categories (see 'Types of protected areas' in Chapter 3) within each region or landscape.

In many developing countries, sustainable natural resource management is the primary source of livelihoods, and protected areas can and should be managed in such a way that they serve human development, poverty alleviation and livelihood needs without compromising the value and integrity of the resource base. In effect, this approach requires that regional and landscape management must integrate social, cultural, economic and institutional concerns with biodiversity outcomes and values, and that the relevant institutions cooperate to achieve this.

Within this landscape and organizational matrix, the specific function of protected area management is undertaken by a wide range of people and organizations. There is an enormous range of alternative management traditions and arrangements, including state, community and private sector models and various combinations of these. In many situations, governmental or parastatal organizations manage protected areas. On the other hand, there is an extensive tradition of community conserved areas (CCAs) for protected area management, and there is a growing realization of the need to reinstate community involvement in protected area management where it has lagged or has been displaced (Borrini-Feyerabend et al, 2004b). In particular regional-and landscape-scale management demands a coordinated effort from national, state and local government; NGOs; community-based organizations; communities; and private land managers. It is a challenge to formulate cooperative management systems that function effectively for conservation at this scale; but a wide range of 'experiments' are in progress worldwide.

It is clear from the Convention on Biological Diversity Protected Area Programme of Work (see Appendix 4) that protected area systems and networks are a key strategy for conservation. Parties to the convention have an imperative to mobilize these at the national scale, and to collaborate with neighbouring countries to achieve the goals at the scale of regional networks. Delegates at the 2003 IUCN World Parks Congress in South Africa, which had as its central theme 'Benefits beyond boundaries', were also concerned with how integrated landscape management can support protected areas, and recommended that governments, NGOs and communities:

- adopt design principles for protected areas that emphasize linkages to surrounding ecosystems and ensure that the surrounding landscapes are managed for biodiversity conservation;
- recognize the need to restore ecological processes in degraded areas, both within protected areas and in their surrounding landscapes, to ensure the ecological integrity of protected areas;
- recognize that the presence and needs of human populations, consistent with biodiversity conservation within and in the vicinity of protected areas, should be reflected in the overall design and management of protected areas and the surrounding landscapes; and
- recognize the importance of participatory processes that link a diverse array of stakeholders in stewardship of the landscape linkages.

This chapter outlines the major features of connectivity conservation management at a landscape scale. We begin by summarizing those characteristics of ecosystems that require us to establish linkages and manage towards an integrated landscape approach to biodiversity conservation. We then examine biodiversity conservation at a regional scale, recent developments in the development of transboundary conservation areas, and efforts to establish continental-scale protected area systems.

Importance of linkages

Protected area linkages can be established at local, regional, trans-jurisdictional, national, international and continental scales. Although there is not unanimous support among conservationists, establishing and maintaining linkages, whether biophysical, social, economic or institutional, is backed up by an extensive body of evidence. Some of this is briefly described below to illustrate the importance of establishing and maintaining regional and landscape connectivity.

Biophysical linkages

Many ecosystems are fragmented, with relatively undisturbed areas located within an extensive matrix of moderately and severely disturbed environments. Human activities such as urban, agricultural and industrial development have isolated populations of native plants and animals into islands surrounded by environments that are often hostile to them:

> Animal species vary greatly in their level of habitat specialization and their tolerance to habitat disturbance and change. These attributes are important influences on how they perceive a particular landscape and the level of connectivity that it affords. Such species are tolerant of human land use and are able to live in, and freely move through, a patchwork of degraded natural habitats… In contrast, there are many organisms that are sensitive to habitat change and degradation… For these species, survival and maintenance of connectivity in disturbed landscapes depends on the provision of suitable habitat (Bennett, 2003, p49).

Fragmentation of natural habitat occurs when a large expanse of habitat is transformed into a number of smaller patches that are isolated from each other (Wilcove et al, 1986). When the landscape surrounding the fragments is inhospitable to species of the original habitat, and when dispersal is low, remnant patches can be considered 'habitat islands', and local communities will be 'isolates'.

Fragmentation can lead to the extinction of species. The principal issue here is that local extinctions, which will inevitably occur from time to time due to chance factors, are no longer reversible. Additional reasons may be that:

- the remaining fragments are smaller than the minimum home range or territories needed by a species;
- the fragments lack the diversity of habitats some species need;
- predators and pests may build up and invade from the cleared land between the fragmented habitats;
- species that tend to utilize the margins or edges of natural habitats will be unduly favoured;
- the fragments may be too small to sustain balanced ecological relationships, such as predator–prey, parasite–host and plant–pollinator associations; and
- small populations contain less genetic variation, are more sensitive to chance variations over time, and may be wiped out by maladaptive genetic drift or by natural catastrophes (Soulé, 1986; Wilcove et al, 1986).

In some regions, only a small fraction of the original vegetation is located within protected areas. For example, the Cape Floristic Region of South Africa is considered to be one of the world's 25 most threatened biodiversity hotspots (Myers et al, 2000). The region is characterized by high endemism and highly localized distributions, and is under serious threat as a result of the conversion of natural habitat to permanent agriculture and to rangelands for cattle, sheep and ostriches; inappropriate fire management; rapid and insensitive infrastructure development, such as dams; over-exploitation of water resources, marine resources and wild flowers; and infestation by alien species of terrestrial, freshwater and marine habitats. Some important terrestrial habitats have been reduced by over 90 per cent and less than 5 per cent of land in the lowlands enjoys any conservation status (Sandwith et al, 2004). These severely depleted systems are the most urgent focus for a landscape approach to conservation management. Even where relatively large areas of natural environment remain, a landscape approach can add to the protection of native species, as well as addressing land degradation problems.

With the fragmentation of a habitat, the size of populations of particular species may be reduced considerably, whereas other species are able to colonize the area once it has become fragmented. For example, Temple (1991) distinguished three types of bird populations that differ in their sensitivity to habitat fragmentation:

1   area-sensitive birds, which have large spatial requirements that cannot be met in fragments of their habitat below a critical minimum size;
2   isolation-sensitive birds, which have difficulty dispersing between isolated fragments of their habitat; and
3   edge-sensitive birds, which originated in extensive and contiguous ecosystems that featured few ecological edges, where different systems abut each other (such as forest and farmland).

One of the most damaging landscape-level effects of fragmentation is the loss of a keystone species – that is, a species that provides a key link between a number of species, such as a pollinator, seed disperser or important prey species. The introduction of non-indigenous species may also have a major effect on small remnants. The reduced interior-to-edge ratio that accompanies fragmentation results in increased pressure from predators, competitors, parasites and disease. Edge effects can penetrate far into a habitat. In a severely fragmented landscape, virtually all of the remaining habitat may be so close to edges that almost no interior habitat remains. Edge-sensitive species are particularly vulnerable to population decline.

A patchy landscape can be characterized by the size and type of patches (their internal quality), as well as how those patches are arranged in space and time (that is, the connectivity of the ecosystem). An understanding of ecosystem connectivity across the landscape can inform effective biodiversity management at a landscape scale. Connectivity concerns how patches of relatively undisturbed environment are connected spatially, temporally, genetically and ecologically.

Links between patches can be made through physical connections, such as corridors of native vegetation, or through dynamic processes, such as dispersal mechanisms (for example, a tree growing within a forest can transmit and receive pollen from any other tree that lies within the range of bees or other pollinating insects – pollination provides a connection among the trees).

Conservation linkages attempt to build and connect areas of natural habitat, thereby reducing fragmentation and the extent of environments 'hostile' to native plants and animals. There is considerable evidence that linkages can enhance the viability of populations (Bennett, 2003), and corridors may help to mitigate the impacts of climate change along rainfall and temperature gradients. Landscape linkages can involve:

•   linear strips of suitable vegetation or habitat that provide a pathway or corridor between two or more larger areas of habitat;
•   a series of 'stepping stones' that enables movement of native biota between two or more larger areas of habitat; and
•   a habitat mosaic in which boundaries between suitable and hostile environments are not clearly defined, but which occur as gradients so that species can make some use of a range of habitats (Bennett, 2003).

The loss of connectivity of patches in a landscape occurs in three phases: *connected* (most of the landscape is connected, with only a few isolated patches); *critical* (a single large section may be connected, but the remainder of the landscape remains as isolated patches); and *disconnected* (the landscape is broken into many isolated sites and becomes fragmented). When spatial connectivity is critical, the dynamics of systems are inherently unpredictable, and changes in landscape connectivity can result in rapid fragmentation of habitats. Landscape management should aim to provide for and, where necessary, recreate as much connectivity as possible between patches of natural vegetation. Disconnected landscapes need to be modified so that they move through the critical phase and, where possible, return to a connected state. Modifications typically involve reinstating connections through the establishment of corridors and consolidation of patches so that their edge area is minimized.

Although there is still much to learn, the message from landscape ecology seems to be to:

- retain large, minimally disturbed areas that contain stable source populations;
- reconstruct and restore ecosystems where there are no remaining large areas of intact environment to provide a stable source population;
- build upon isolated remnants as the core of a restoration effort;
- retain and protect small habitat remnants;
- establish and maintain connections among the large, minimally disturbed areas, the restored areas and the remnants; and
- retain and regenerate isolated trees, or other elements, which can be of some value for certain fauna when restoration is not possible.

Institutional linkages

Of equal importance is our ability to institutionalize and manage regional- and landscape-level conservation programmes. Managing protected areas demands organization at a number of scales. First, at the protected area level, effective management includes identifying the reasons for establishing the protected area; maintaining or putting in place a management system, including a statement of objectives, the implementation options for management, and the means to ensure adaptive management of the protected area in relation to its objectives and purpose; and maintaining relationships with stakeholder groups.

Strong institutions are essential if national systems of protected areas are to be effective in conserving biodiversity. There are a number of models for protected area and nature conservation management agencies that are being applied around the world, but no readily available analysis of the effectiveness of the range of organizational designs. Most common is the establishment of separate agencies for protected area management and for wildlife management in the areas outside of protected areas. Less common are organizations that have nature conservation as their primary responsibility across the whole of a region or landscape, including protected areas. The latter

approach is regarded as highly effective in achieving conservation goals that require an integrated approach.

Several recommendations from the Vth IUCN World Parks Congress (see also Appendix 3) emphasized the governance and institutional arrangements for regional- and landscape-level conservation, including:

- the potential for transboundary conservation initiatives to conserve biodiversity and cultural resources at a landscape level, to foster peaceful cooperation among communities and societies across international boundaries, and to engender regional economic growth and integration (Recommendations 11 and 15);
- the need to recognize the legitimacy and importance of a range of governance types (see Chapter 5) in order to promote connectivity at the landscape and seascape level (Recommendation 17);
- the need to embed the marine protected area network within wider integrated coastal and marine management frameworks and to ensure linkages among marine coastal and terrestrial protected areas (TPAs) to address potential threats beyond protected area boundaries (Recommendation 22); and
- the need to support the establishment and implementation of integrated river basin management in which networks of protected areas and regimes of protection are a key development strategy (Recommendation 31).

These recommendations demand that attention be placed on institutional design, in that there is a requirement to mainstream biodiversity considerations into the policies, plans and programmes of other economic sectors, such as agriculture, fisheries or forestry, and industrial and commercial sectors of the economy. The means must be found to ensure cooperation among different levels of government, across government sectors and with civil society. In some cases, purpose-built authorities have been established with new and extraordinary powers, such as the Great Barrier Reef Authority in Australia. In other cases, memoranda of understanding have been entered into, defining cooperative governance arrangements to achieve agreed strategies and goals – for example, the memorandum of understanding that governs the Cape Action for People and the Environment (C.A.P.E.) programme in South Africa (Sandwith et al, 2004).

Regional- and landscape-scale conservation also encompasses situations where the unit of conservation interest spans jurisdictions, and even international boundaries. Where this is the case, transboundary conservation arrangements among adjacent countries must be facilitated, and cooperative governance that takes into account the administrative regimes of different countries has to be accommodated. The larger the initiative, the more layers and complexity there will be in the organizational design, so that the most complex transboundary conservation initiatives will contain all of the afore-going layers of organization, right down to the local community institutions far from the central powers of nation states and regional governments. Regional- and landscape-level conservation programmes, by definition, have a range of objectives and a range of implementation arrangements, and protected areas and protected area management agencies become just one of a suite of essential organizational actors that must interact to achieve these aims.

National protected area systems

National systems of protected areas include the full range of protected areas of all categories and governance types in a region or country (see Chapter 8, p200). National plans for protected areas must encompass the full range of protected area categories, and must be developed in the context of national conservation planning that includes areas that are important for conservation, but which might never be contained within protected areas, or that support ecosystem processes that maintain the functioning of protected areas and natural ecosystems. Approaches and methods for conservation planning have been considerably enhanced in the recent past, supported by the availability of data at the landscape scale, derived from Landsat Thematic Mapper imagery, digital terrain modelling and the modelling of biodiversity distributions in space and time, and by the avail-

ability of computer hardware and software capable of handling complex reserve selection algorithms.

At a national level, protected area systems plans will set the agenda for regional and local implementation. But, as has been discussed earlier, there is a need for integration with other development processes. More generally, the biodiversity targets represented in national systems plans must be reflected in national frameworks, sectoral policies and plans, particularly in statutory land-use plans that provide spatial linkages for biodiversity and processes for trading off biodiversity objectives against other developmental objectives. The real challenge is to ensure that protected area systems do not unnecessarily compete with, but – as far as possible – complement other developmental processes, and that sustainable protected area development is itself viewed as a valid and valuable land-use choice. This is the challenge of 'mainstreaming' biodiversity and protected areas into social and economic development in such a way that the net impact on sustainable development is positive.

Although it might be difficult to provide a precise definition of this process, situations where mainstreaming of biodiversity has occurred can be characterized by:

- the incorporation of biodiversity and sustainable use considerations within policies concerning economic development;
- the simultaneous achievement of gains in biodiversity and gains in an economic sector (the 'win–win' scenario), as well as careful consideration of environment–development trade-offs;
- sectoral activity being recognized as based on, or dependent upon, the sustainable use of biodiversity; and
- situations where sectoral activities result in overall gains for biodiversity, exceeding biodiversity losses (Pierce et al, 2002).

Mainstreaming is, however, not necessarily a matter of intent or design that can be simply put in place as a policy measure. It may arise with a gradual and growing understanding of the dependence of a sector on biodiversity, or it may occur suddenly, when sectoral and biodiversity partners are presented with a shared need, and are opportunistic in their actions. More importantly, for mainstreaming to achieve lasting impact, it must occur at a very local level and become a part of ordinary peoples' lives. Mainstreaming outcomes are most likely to occur when protected areas and biodiversity are embedded in regional- and landscape-scale approaches to conservation and development. The rationale and likelihood of achieving this is further developed in the next section.

Conservation at a bioregional scale

Many issues confronting conservation managers occur at scales that do not match the familiar national, state and local tiers of government. Many environmental problems are best addressed at the scale of the region, ecosystem or watershed, cutting across other jurisdictions and involving other actors, such as local communities, private landowners, trusts and corporate structures. This has meant that public institutions alone have not been well placed to mount effective responses to these issues. Chapter 5 considered various modes of governance that can be used to establish protected areas. This broadening of governance possibilities beyond traditional government-managed protected areas is being manifest in an emerging emphasis on working at other levels, such as local community or regional scales, and involving a much broader range of stakeholders in the process. Regions have become the focus of environmental governance, particularly through integrated watershed and natural resource management approaches.

Potential advantages of regional-scale conservation planning include the:

- capacity to engage stakeholders;
- opportunity to build on activity at the property and local levels;
- capacity to integrate social, economic and environmental dimensions; and
- appropriateness of this scale for negotiating trade-offs, determining priorities and investment sharing (Meadowcroft, 1997; Read and Bessen, 2003).

Two terms are commonly applied to these regional approaches to conservation: bioregional conservation programmes and ecoregional conservation programmes.

Bioregional and ecoregional approaches

Bioregional approaches to conservation are not new, and the concept of defining political and/or jurisdictional boundaries based on biophysical elements has been explored and debated over centuries (Fall, 2005). Miller (cited in Fall, 2005) reviewed the origins of the 'bioregion' concept and concluded that bioregions could be defined not only by the biological resources in a particular area, but also by the cultural, societal, institutional and political elements represented there. More recently, the application of the ecosystem approach, guided by the Convention on Biological Diversity (CBD), has resulted in the development of bioregional conservation programmes in several parts of the world.

Ecoregional conservation programmes, on the other hand, are more strictly based on science-based criteria, drawing on the enhanced technologies for systematic conservation planning to define ecoregions, primarily determined by their biodiversity characteristics. The World Wide Fund for Nature (WWF) defines an ecoregion as:

> *A large area of land or water that contains a geographically distinct assemblage of natural communities that:*
> - *share a large majority of their species and ecological dynamics;*
> - *share similar environmental conditions; and*
> - *interact ecologically in ways that are critical for their long-term persistence (Dinerstein et al, 2000, p241).*

Examples of these ecoregional programmes are the Global 200 ecoregions identified by the WWF (see Chapter 1, p34) and the biodiversity hotspots recognized by Conservation International (CI) (see Chapter 1, p37).

Taking an ecoregional approach to conservation offers a number of opportunities. It enables scientists to set targets for representation of biodiversity for the ecoregion as a whole, and offers opportunities to develop strategies that address threats to biodiversity in a holistic, integrated and systematic manner. It also enables a meaningful engagement with the social and economic forces driving biodiversity loss at a range of scales, including regional and global. According to WWF (1998, p1):

> … *the approach is providing practitioners with innovative ideas, methods, tools and approaches that can drive and support the conservation of species, spaces and processes within clear spatial boundaries, while recognizing and responding to the aspirations, needs and motivations of people and their governments.*

Furthermore, it permits the development of enabling frameworks of coordinated policy, laws and institutions to protect biodiversity. Ecoregional planning offers opportunities for an engagement with major stakeholders across political and administrative boundaries by developing a consensus on goals and strategic objectives and in creating a coordinated programme of action. It can also enable a commitment to powerful partnerships and the potential to mobilize significant resources to achieve its goals and strategic objectives. A further advantage of action at the regional scale derives from the increased potential for raising public awareness of the economic and social consequences of biodiversity loss.

Ongoing analysis of the world's most species rich and threatened areas has identified 34 hotspots, each holding at least 1500 endemic plant species and having lost at least 70 per cent of its original habitat extent (CI, 2005a). Collectively, these hotspots contain approximately 80 per cent of the world's species and at least 150,000 or 50 per cent of the world's endemic species. CI has, especially through the Critical Ecosystem Partnership Fund, supported investments in the richest and most threatened biodiversity 'hotspots' and wilderness areas worldwide, and 14 programmes are currently being implemented. A biodiversity corridor approach is taken where conservation effort is focused on linking major sites for maintaining biodiversity and regional- or landscape-scale ecological processes across wide geographic areas. The main function of the corridors is to connect important areas for biodiversity conservation through a network of sustainable land uses, thereby increasing mobility and genetic exchange among individual plants and animals (CEPF, 2006). From an institutional point of view, the purpose of the conservation corridors is to stimulate new levels of civil society empowerment and participation in practical and political processes as a way of underpinning and multiplying the effect of government and corporate responses to conservation.

The combined application of these bioregional, ecoregional and corridor hotspots programmes, together with a range of other similar initiatives around the world, represents a significant investment in conservation that extends beyond the boundaries of protected areas. In the Cape Floristic Region (CFR) of South Africa, where one of the world's six floral kingdoms is contained entirely within the borders of a single country, four of WWF's ecoregions and CI's Cape Floristic Province hotspot coincide. The region is regarded as one of the world's most important biodiversity hotspots owing to its extraordinary species richness and to the high levels of threat to its persistence. A major conservation and development programme, supported by the WWF, the Critical Ecosystem Partnership Fund and the Global Environment Facility (GEF), is attempting not only to arrest biodiversity loss, but to ensure that the benefits of biodiversity conservation are felt throughout the sub-regional economy (see Case Study 22.1).

Protected areas, ecoregions and ecological networks

Natural resource management at the landscape scale provides a context for the development of protected area systems within production landscapes, and fulfils the need for linkages between protected areas and surrounding areas. No ecoregional approach would be complete without the key role of protected areas and their specific contribution to a conservation-based economy. In particular, though controversial in some contexts, the direct and indirect use of some categories of protected areas for sustainable harvesting or nature-based tourism is widespread, with a key challenge to define the types and limits of such use so that protected area values are maintained while benefits flow to the people of the region.

As noted in Chapter 3 (p82), protected landscapes (IUCN Category V) support the sustainable use of natural resources across landscapes that have been significantly shaped by people. Many more areas, particularly in the developing world, have the potential to be recognized as protected landscapes (Phillips, 2002). Managed resource areas (IUCN Category VI) offer the opportunity to incorporate a mosaic of uses, while still having as their primary objective the conservation of biodiversity.

Activities outside protected areas also need to be managed to foster the vitality of local communities, while maintaining the long-term health and viability of watersheds and ecosystems. Protected area managers can provide expertise and technical support, and, in turn, can benefit from local knowledge and experience. Protected areas can therefore be regarded as catalytic for the development of ecoregions, and are the anchors and role models around which sustainable natural resource management can be built.

Case Study 22.1

Cape Action for People and the Environment (C.A.P.E.), South Africa

Amanda Younge, development consultant, South Africa

The Cape Action for People and the Environment (C.A.P.E.) programme is an important example of ecoregion-based conservation, integrating terrestrial, aquatic, institutional and socio-economic concerns within a coherent conservation strategy and implementation programme. C.A.P.E. was able to gain the support of key stakeholders, create commitment to implementation by executing agencies, and demonstrate significant levels of financial support from local agencies, as well as from the international donor community. It established clear targets for conserving a representative sample of biodiversity patterns and ecological processes, and developed mechanisms to enable effective monitoring and review of achievements. The C.A.P.E. process has raised a number of questions regarding this approach to conservation, and continues to provide useful opportunities to evaluate the effectiveness of the ecoregional approach in addressing biodiversity pressures.

The Cape Floristic Region (CFR) is only 90,000 square kilometres in extent. The CFR and adjoining marine areas have spectacularly high levels of plant and animal biodiversity (over 1400 threatened plant species), three marine provinces, important Ramsar wetland sites and many sites of scenic beauty. At least 70 per cent of its 9600 plant species are found nowhere else on Earth. Due to significant levels of threat to the biodiversity of the CFR, South Africa was granted US$1 million by the Global Environment Facility (GEF) in 1998 for the development of a strategy and action plan to conserve the terrestrial, marine and freshwater ecosystems of the CFR.

Key issues identified included the spread of invasive alien species on both land and in the water; poor fire management; poor and uncoordinated watershed management, with loss of water availability, erosion and siltation; inappropriate agricultural practices, leading to excessive water use, invasions of alien vegetation and nutrient/toxic chemical pollution; and poor land-use planning controls, inadequate to address intensive development pressures for both formal and informal land uses. Underlying drivers of these threats were identified as including a failure to value the environmental services provided by intact ecosystems; an inability to recognize the socio-economic opportunities linked to conserving the biome, notably for alien species removal, flower harvesting and nature-based tourism-related activities; lack of general public awareness of the potential for economic gain and social opportunity arising from conservation; poverty and inequity of access to opportunities; and fragmented, uncoordinated and inappropriate laws, poor intergovernmental communication, lack of reliable funding for long-term contracts, and contradictions in property rights law over the status of privately owned resources.

The terrestrial component of the C.A.P.E. project was based on the systematic conservation planning approach, and pioneered its application at the ecoregional scale. In revisions of the conservation planning component, it has also been possible to completely integrate freshwater and marine components, as well as threats and connectivity considerations.

A key objective of the C.A.P.E. strategy process was to generate a sense of ownership and commitment from implementing agencies (primarily government bodies). C.A.P.E. focused on building partnerships between implementing agencies, NGOs, research institutions and the private sector, and on creating legitimacy for the process and its outcomes through an inclusive, participatory planning process.

The strategic planning process identified actions supporting both conservation and sustainable use. In addition, a range of cross-cutting supportive and enabling actions was identified, focusing on institutional strengthening and governance. Each of these programmatic themes comprises a number of strategic components, addressing the key issues identified in the situation assessment (see Table 22.1).

Table 22.1 Elements of the Cape Action for People and the Environment (C.A.P.E.) strategy

Programme themes	Strategic components
Conserving biodiversity in priority areas	Strengthening conservation within and beyond protected areas
	Supporting bioregional planning and biosphere reserve development
Using resources sustainably	Ensuring that watershed management embraces a concern for biodiversity
	Improving the sustainability of harvesting
	Promoting sustainable nature-based tourism
Strengthening institutions and governance	Strengthening institutions
	Enhancing cooperative governance
	Promoting community involvement

Source: CEPF (2004)

The themes and strategic components complement and reinforce one another in order to ensure effective conservation both inside and outside protected areas. Conservation stewardship, sustainable use practices and sustainable nature-based tourism also support effective protected areas. Conserving the fragments of rare habitat in commercial farming districts requires land-use planning to be based on sound biological information and meaningful off-reserve conservation strategies, again supported by conservation stewardship on farms. It also calls for appropriate laws and policies, creating incentives for the right kinds of investment and practice. Sustainable marine harvesting requires effective marine protected areas for restocking. Being able to show positive impacts on watershed management increases incentives to remove alien vegetation because water supply is an important issue in this relatively dry region.

Source: adapted from Younge (2002)

Another generic term that is widely used is that of ecological networks. The Convention on Biological Diversity Protected Area Programme of Work (see Appendix 4) includes a goal to apply the ecosystem approach through ecological networks. Bennett and Wit (2001, p16) reviewed the origins and scope of ecological networks, and as a working definition described them as:

A coherent system of nature and/or semi-natural landscape elements that is configured and managed with the objective of maintaining or restoring ecological functions as a means to conserve biodiversity, while also providing appropriate opportunities for the sustainable use of natural resources.

Bioregional and ecoregional conservation programmes, as well as conservation corridors, are forms of ecological networks, although their socio-economic linkages have been emphasized more strongly than the definition given above would indicate. Bennett and Wit's (2001) review reveals that there are many other expressions of ecological networks, at both smaller and larger scales. At smaller scales are networks within municipalities, such as metropolitan open-space systems. At much larger scales are mountain conservation corridors, migratory flyways or supra-continental programmes such as the Western Hemisphere Shorebird Network.

At the heart of many connectivity conservation initiatives are a number of models of landscape management. From a biodiversity point of view, the most widespread is that of biosphere reserves, which are centred on core zones surrounded by transition and buffer zones that introduce a gradient of land uses that ultimately form part of the surrounding production landscape.

Biosphere reserves

Over the past three decades, the United Nations Educational, Scientific and Cultural Organization's (UNESCO's) Man and the Biosphere programme has promoted a people-centred approach to conservation through the establishment of biosphere reserves. The biosphere reserve concept, introduced in Chapter 3, is one approach to management at a landscape scale. Biosphere reserves aim to preserve genetic resources, species, ecosystems and landscapes; foster sustainable economic and human development; and act as a demonstration of what can be done in relation to local, national and global issues of conservation and sustainable development. Each biosphere reserve should contain three elements: one or more *core areas* devoted to long-term conservation of nature; a clearly identified *buffer zone* in which activities compatible with the conservation objectives may occur; and an outer *transition area* that is devoted to the promotion and practice of sustainable development (Cresswell and Thomas, 1997), and may contain a variety of agricultural activities, settlements or other activities. The strength of biosphere reserves is the emphasis in their management objectives on integrating human and natural systems. In particular, the biosphere reserve model is not so much about the space that is contained within its boundaries, but about the institutions of collaborative management which the model demands are put in place to ensure that the objectives can be met across a range of jurisdictions. Case Study 22.2 describes the management approach taken for the Fitzgerald River Biosphere Reserve, which includes the Fitzgerald River National Park (FRNP) as a core area.

Transboundary protected areas

Although transboundary natural resource management is generally regarded as a relatively recent phenomenon, there are numerous examples of longstanding cooperative resource management arrangements in river basins, lakes, marine areas and mountains throughout the world, involving local communities and other authorities (Singh, 1999). Whereas many of these arrangements are concerned with regulating competitive resource use and therefore supporting peaceful cooperation among communities, there is often also an underlying conservation purpose. In 1999, the Biodiversity Support Programme defined transboundary natural resource management as 'any process of cooperation across boundaries that facilitates or improves the management of natural resources (to the benefit of all parties in the area concerned)' (Griffin et al, 1999). Transboundary natural resource management has found support and practical application for conservation and wilderness preservation purposes.

During the past 50 to 80 years, possibly as a result of increasing global demand for natural resources, but also because of increased international attention to sovereign rights and obligations of states (Singh, 1999), there has been an increase in the number and complexity of formalized transboundary natural resource management arrangements and agreements between countries. This has been particularly true with respect to key shared resources, such as water and fisheries, but has also emerged where protected areas are adjacent across an international boundary. There is also a growing literature that reflects on the objectives and practice of transboundary natural resource management and transboundary conservation (see, for example, van der Linde et al, 2001).

Worldwide, there is an impressive array of transboundary conservation initiatives being implemented on virtually all continents and countries. The development of these since the declaration of the Waterton–Glacier International Peace Park in 1932 is reviewed in Sandwith et al (2001). An historical overview and further examples are provided in Mittermeier et al (2005). Today, there are at least 188 examples of transboundary conservation areas spanning the borders of more than 122 countries (Besançon and Savy, 2005). In effect, there has been experimentation on a grand scale, with transboundary conservation practice reflecting a range of methods of implementation, expression and achievement of all or

Case Study 22.2

Stepping outside: A landscape approach to nature conservation, Australia

John Watson, Western Australia Department of Conservation and Land Management

Fitzgerald River National Park (FRNP) in Western Australia is relatively large (about 330,000ha in extent) and is considered to be mostly in 'pristine' condition – a true benchmark in a world network of protected areas (Watson and Sanders, 1997). Because it has a large central wilderness zone (about 70,000ha), is located on a remote section of Australia's coastline and has low visitor levels in most of its areas, it should therefore surely be able to 'look after itself'. Wrong!

The FRNP may be more secure than many smaller areas; but it is not immune to internal or external influences that, over time, will lead to a deterioration of its true 'representativeness' and its nature conservation value. In December 1989, three lightning strikes 40km apart on a day of extreme fire weather resulted in a wildfire of some 149,000ha – almost 50 per cent of the park by area – and most of this burned within eight hours!

Lesson 1: even large protected areas can be significantly affected by natural 'catastrophic' events that may be quite normal and, indeed, beneficial in a pristine landscape, but which have severe ramifications in what is now an 'island' reserve in a 'sea' of cleared agricultural land.

The FRNP is mainly composed of a low plateau and a series of river basins with significant upper catchments outside the park in the cleared farmlands. Changes in groundwater and surface hydrology have resulted in rising water tables, increased salinity, more rapid surface runoff and greater silt levels in waterways, all of which then impact upon the downstream FRNP, particularly its riparian systems, inlets and estuaries, and adjacent marine values.

Lesson 2: undesirable impacts can occur even on large protected areas through inward drainage processes and can reach right into central core areas. Protected areas with predominantly outward drainage, such as mountains, are clearly less vulnerable in this context (although they do have their own suite of other threatening processes).

The FRNP has not escaped the alien invasive fox (*Vulpes vulpes*) that is believed to have had a major impact on Western Australia's native fauna species. Whereas baiting programmes (using the naturally occurring 1080, sodium mono-fluoroacetate, poison) have been outstandingly successful in combating this predator, foxes continue to move in from outside reserve boundaries.

Lesson 3: you may be able to control feral animals within your protected area; but there is typically a further population waiting to move in again from outside and to replace them when the opportunity arises.

For all of the above reasons – and many other examples that could have been used – it is clear that we must take a *landscape* approach to protected area management and must 'network' outwards, both physically and socially.

Physical networks and linkages

Over the past 22 years since its designation as a world biosphere reserve, the Fitzgerald Biosphere Reserve has evolved from the original gazetted 'core' area of 278,000ha to a 'model' biosphere reserve of some 1.3 million hectares, including a 'buffer and corridor zone' around the national park core and a 'zone of cooperation' that incorporates the farming areas and towns beyond the buffer zone.

Conservation managers are now working together with the local community at three levels within the 1.3 million hectare 'Fitzgerald biosphere' landscape to address physical linkages and networks:

1   In addition to the buffer zone around the outside of the national park, major corridor linkages of uncleared vegetation, sometimes up to 10km wide, are recognized. These extend in both directions along the coast from the national park core area, and inland along several river foreshore reserves and through a broad linkage via the Pallinup River area and Ravensthorpe Range (see Figure 22.1). These buffer and major corridor linkages are mainly public land – essentially, existing or proposed protected areas, whether formally part of the conservation estate or shire reserves with other primary purposes.
2   During 1996, Environment Australia (the national government conservation agency) provided funding to produce an integrated vegetation management plan for the zone of cooperation. This was completed in March 1997 and identified important remnant vegetation patches, poorly conserved vegetation types and rare vegetation communities (Robinson, 1997). A review of all catchments was carried out and priority actions were identified. Salinity prediction maps and vegetation change maps, produced by the Commonwealth Scientific and Industrial Research Organisation (CSIRO), were used to help identify suitable areas where corridors

could be re-established to provide interconnected east–west and north–south linkages between large remnant patches of vegetation. These strategic plantings have now been fine-tuned to include prescriptions for species selection and placement.

3   Within the framework described in points 1 and 2, individual farmers and local catchment groups are continuing to develop re-vegetation and cropping strategies to further combat rising groundwater salinity, and to provide more localized vegetation corridors and protection of on-farm remnant vegetation.

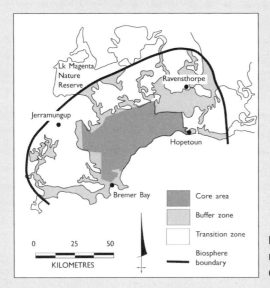

Figure 22.1 Fitzgerald Biosphere Reserve showing national park core area and surrounding buffer-corridor zone

Social networks and linkages

It is often said that the most important resource in an organization is its people; the same is true for protected areas. In the social context, protected areas must look outward and encompass ownership and support from the broader landscape around them. The biosphere reserve model provides an identifiable framework to achieve this – the challenges are to increase community awareness of protected area values, to extend that awareness to the expanded physical networks and linkages discussed earlier, and to encourage pride and support for working and living together in the total biosphere landscape.

There are various ways in which this can be achieved – for example, through 'friends groups' and public involvement in planning. Two examples are:

1   Around 1994, as part of a major biological study of the buffer/corridor zone and zone of cooperation around the FRNP (Sanders, 1996), a schools monitoring programme was established. Every school within the biosphere reserve was provided with basic equipment and, with the assistance of staff, was encouraged to set up ongoing monitoring of 'their bit of bush' – typically, an area of remnant vegetation relatively close to the school. The methods used included direct observation, fauna trapping and vegetation/plant identification in transects and quadrats. The studies were incorporated within the school curriculum. This programme provided a valuable educational opportunity for the students. It also provided useful data and further consolidated community support for the biosphere reserve. Approximately 25 per cent of the entire community population assisted or visited at least one of the sites – imagine extrapolating that proportion to a 'hands-on' conservation project in a city! The project ran over a three-year period and has continued in those schools with appropriately skilled teachers.

2   The Malleefowl Preservation Group is a voluntary organization based around the west of the Fitzgerald Biosphere Reserve. Two of the group's main study sites, where the threatened malleefowl (*Leipoa ocellata*) still survives, are located in the zone of cooperation in the Cocanarup Nature Reserve and the Peniup Reserve. The group produced a community action plan for malleefowl in its area, and has been successful in promoting the bird as a 'flagship' species. This has provided a focus for on-farm conservation of wildlife habitats. Since the malleefowl lives throughout the Fitzgerald Biosphere Reserve, this local community action has made a significant contribution towards nature conservation at the landscape level.

Bringing it all together

Clearly, cooperation is required between people at all levels to ensure a landscape-scale approach to nature conservation and protected areas – local residents, school children and teachers, agency personnel, and funding bodies at the local, state, national and even international level. At the physical/social interface, an even broader landscape approach is currently being used – namely, the expanded implementation of these principles from the 1.3 million hectare biosphere reserve to the whole of the South Coast Region. The 'flagship' for this is not a species, but our landscape-scale corridor concept. This is a vision of an unbroken network of wide corridors along the coast from Esperance to Albany and inland to other major protected areas – some 500km long and 100km or so inland – with the Fitzgerald Biosphere Reserve as the central 'hub' (see Figure 22.2). Hopefully, this initiative will galvanize broad community awareness in our entire region and benefit not only the Fitzgerald Biosphere Reserve, but all of the other 150 or so protected areas within the region.

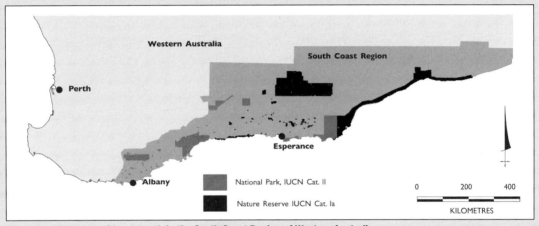

Figure 22.2 Macro-corridor network in the South Coast Region of Western Australia

some of the goals given above. This has led to difficulty in defining precisely what is meant by transboundary conservation, and how best it should be undertaken. In the light of increasing support for transboundary conservation initiatives by national states, international conservation organizations and bilateral and multilateral donors, some work has been done to review practice, to propose organizing frameworks and to provide advice for implementation.

A proposed typology of transboundary conservation practice

An expert group was convened at a workshop arranged by the IUCN–World Commission on Protected Areas (WCPA) Task Force on Transboundary Protected Areas in May 2004 to develop a proposed typology for transboundary conservation initiatives. The product of the group's work is summarized in this section as an input into an ongoing discussion regarding the need for standardization of terms. Although not in itself of concern, the growing number of terms and definitions can mitigate against the development of a broad-based understanding of the nature of transboundary conservation and can hinder communication and any comparative analysis of best practice and lessons learned.

The term 'transboundary conservation and development initiatives' is proposed to represent the broad scope of partnerships ranging from very local-level initiatives with narrowly circumscribed objectives, to large-scale global initiatives involving many nations and wide-ranging goals. Within this context, a variety of experiences of transboundary conservation have emerged. These include situations where:

Waterton–Glacier International Peace Park, US and Canada

Source: IUCN Photo Library © Jim Thorsell

- two protected areas adjoin one another across a jurisdictional boundary;
- a matrix of land uses occur in the transboundary area, and where protected areas might be a component of the matrix in either or both countries;
- areas have been specifically set aside to commemorate or draw attention to peace and/or cooperation, in addition to conservation goals; and
- there are linked or disparate areas involving two or more countries in which a biological migratory process occurs.

In general, international transboundary conservation and development initiatives will include:

- areas that straddle at least one international boundary;
- a biodiversity conservation goal that can only be met through international collaboration in addition to national action;

- transboundary social and economic development goals, in addition to local and national goals;
- protected areas, conforming to one or more of the IUCN protected area categories (IUCN, 1994), but also areas that are not protected areas; and
- a willingness and means for ongoing collaboration and cooperation.

The initiatives may include:

- processes of natural resource management that extend across an international boundary;
- communities who have kinship or resource-use links across an international boundary;
- efforts to broker or maintain peace during and after armed conflict; and
- processes to maintain peaceful cooperation.

The analysis of objectives and contexts has suggested a typology, which is proposed as an organizing framework for transboundary conservation and development initiatives. Four main types are described below, drawing on case studies and perspectives from the literature: transboundary protected areas; transboundary conservation and development areas; parks for peace; and transboundary migratory corridors.

Transboundary protected areas

Protected areas that adjoin across an international boundary and that involve cooperative management have provided the most easily defined of transboundary conservation initiatives. Examples of these are the La Amistad International Park between Costa Rica and Panama; the Kgalagadi Transfrontier Park between Botswana and South Africa; the Neusiedler See/Seewinkel–Fertö Hansag Transfrontier Park between Austria and Hungary; and a transboundary initiative between Uzbekistan, Kazakhstan and Kyrgystan (see Case Study 22.3). Sandwith et al (2001, p3) defined transboundary protected areas as follows:

> *A transboundary protected area is an area of land and/or sea that straddles one or more borders between states, sub-national units such as provinces and regions, autonomous areas, and/or areas beyond the limit of national sovereignty or jurisdiction, whose constituent parts are especially dedicated to the protection and maintenance of biological diversity, and of natural and associated cultural resources, and [are] managed cooperatively through legal or other effective means.*

Transboundary conservation and development areas

There are extensive examples of transboundary conservation initiatives where protected areas may be, although are not necessarily, a feature of the region and landscape, but where conservation and sustainable development goals have been asserted within a framework of cooperative management. Examples of transboundary conservation initiatives in this category include the Maloti–Drakensberg Transfrontier Conservation and Development Area (Lesotho–South Africa); the cooperation between the Palatinate Forest Nature Park–Northern Vosges Regional Natural Park (Germany–France);

and Sungai Kayan Nature Reserve and the proposed Pulong Tau National Park (Indonesia–Malaysia). Transboundary conservation areas can be defined as follows:

> *Transboundary conservation (and development) areas are areas of land and/or sea that straddle one or more borders between states, sub-national units such as provinces and regions, [and] autonomous areas and/or areas beyond the limit of national sovereignty or jurisdiction, whose constituent parts form a matrix that contributes to the protection and maintenance of biological diversity, and of natural and associated cultural resources, as well as the promotion of social and economic development, and which are managed cooperatively through legal or other effective means (Transboundary Protected Areas Taskforce, 2005).*

Parks for peace

Some transboundary conservation initiatives have the explicit objective of securing or maintaining peace during and after armed conflict, or of commemorating a discordant past. The term 'peace park' has been used to describe these situations; but this term is rather loosely applied to all sorts of situations, including memorials in city parks, battlefields and the like. To ensure a more consistent application of terms to situations where both conservation and peaceful cooperation are goals, Sandwith et al (2001, p3) defined parks for peace as follows:

> *Parks for peace are transboundary protected areas that are formally dedicated to the protection and maintenance of biological diversity, and of natural and associated cultural resources, and to the promotion of peace and cooperation.*

Examples of such parks include the Si-a-Paz project (Costa Rica–Nicaragua) and a similar initiative between Equador and Peru along a portion of their common border. The Waterton–Glacier International Peace Park (Canada–US) symbolizes the peace and collaboration that exists between these two countries.

Transboundary migratory corridors

The final group of transboundary conservation initiatives includes situations where the habitat

Case Study 22.3

Transboundary conservation in Central Asia

A transboundary initiative between Uzbekistan, Kazakhstan and Kyrgystan is currently under way in the West Tien Shan Mountains of Central Asia. There are currently four protected areas that could be considered as a potential transboundary conservation area. Discussions are in progress on an interstate agreement for a West Tien Shan transboundary conservation area that would improve coverage of representative habitats and promote connectedness. The four protected areas are as follows:

1   Aksu–Djabagly Reserve, Kazakhstan (IUCN Category Ia; 8575ha) (juniper forests, steppe and meadows);
2   Sary Chelek Reserve, Kyrgyz Republic (IUCN Category Ia; 2390ha) (juniper forests with walnut, spruce and fir apple);
3   Besh Aral, Kyrgyz Republic (IUCN Category Ia; 6329ha) (juniper forests, steppe and meadows); and
4   Chatkal Reserve, Uzbekistan (IUCN Category Ia; 3570ha) (juniper and tugai forests, steppe and meadows).

Support is being provided to the four protected areas through a mix of investments in capacity-building (including training, transport, communications and infrastructure), community awareness and education, and research and monitoring.

In addition to national-level activities, the initiative supports strong regional cooperation, including development of framework laws on protected areas and an interstate agreement for a West Tien Shan transboundary conservation area. The three countries are collaborating in joint planning efforts to designate wildlife corridors and appropriate land uses to maintain the protected areas in a linked protected area network, as well as joint training, research and monitoring of key wildlife species, especially those predators and ungulates known to require large home ranges in these mountain habitats.

The initiative is promoting regional cooperation in managing the West Tien Shan to strengthen protected area and corridor management, natural resource management and incentives for local communities. Good progress has been made through collaborative approaches to adopting new technical and social standards for protected area management, improvements to biodiversity laws and regulations, establishment of a transboundary protected area network, and organization of ecotourism in the West Tien Shan. A bioregional plan for conservation in the greater West Tien Shan ecosystem will integrate activities within the protected areas, their buffer zones and corridors that connect them. The plan is being developed using an integrated geographic information system (GIS) platform for the three countries.

Importance to biodiversity

Situated at a biological crossroads, the West Tien Shan in Central Asia, the westernmost range of the great Himalaya chain, is species rich, with some 3000 recorded species of flora and fauna. The region covers a range of climatic conditions, from subtropical to tundra and glaciers, and from semi-arid steppe to snow-covered peaks. The mountains harbour unique stands of walnut (*Juglans regia*) forest, wild ancestors of cultivated fruit-bearing species such as apple, pear, pistachio and almond, as well as medicinal plants and endemic flowers and species of tulip and crocus. Rare and threatened animals include the snow leopard (*Uncia uncia*), the Argali sheep (*Ovis ammon*) and the Himalayan griffon vulture (*Gyps himalayensis*).

Importance to regional economic growth and integration

The main economic activity in the ecoregion is agriculture, and mostly in the livestock sub-sector. More than half of the population lives in poverty, and the situation is worsening due to problems associated with the transition from centrally planned to market economies. During the Soviet era, a highly intensive regional (now international) system of livestock and pasture management was in use, which managed the seasonal movements of millions of sheep and goats between the mountain summer and winter lowland pastures. After independence in 1991, livestock numbers dropped sharply as a result of the suspension of price controls and subsidized feed imports, and the collapse of intra-Soviet Union trade arrangements. Despite the decline in livestock numbers, the problem of overgrazing persisted, but at a different level. There is over-utilization of the more accessible pastures, while those furthest from settlements are under-grazed. A large part of the pasture resource is in poor condition, with low productivity, topsoil erosion and occasional mudflows in highly degraded areas. The project is now preparing a bioregional plan that takes a holistic approach to economic development and nature conservation.

Importance in promoting a culture of peace and cooperation

Cooperation among the countries has been historically strong, even before the Soviet period, and the project has helped to strengthen this in approaches to managing the greater West Tien Shan ecosystem. Nonetheless, the transborder region is characterized by inter-mingled national boundaries (a legacy of the Soviet era), with attendant border disputes, and conflicts over managing water flows for agriculture and energy production. The project has been successful in promoting good will among the countries on nature conservation and led to the preparation of a bioregional plan for the greater West Tien Shan Ecosystem. This plan, when completed, will be integrated with other high-level instruments of regional cooperation.

Main partners

Support for the project is strong in government agencies, and local communities and NGOs have been closely involved in the process – although the desire for a peace park came first from local communities and there are also a number of indigenous communities in the area. Substantial financial support has come from the Global Environment Facility (GEF) (US$10.15 million). Other important international partners have been:

- the European Union (EU)/Tacis, which has provided technical support in improving legal frameworks (also assisted by the United Nations Food and Agriculture Organization, or FAO) and in drafting an interstate agreement, as well as support to tourism development and other rural livelihoods;
- the Swiss Agency for Development and Cooperation, which has provided assistance in training on community-based tourism development and alternative livelihoods and energy; and
- the Dutch government, which assisted with conservation and the use of medicinal plants.

The four protected areas are managed at the national level; but the project has fostered adoption of compatible management standards. The project is being implemented under the guidance of the Transnational Steering Committee.

Conclusion

The project's main challenge has been in introducing modern methods in conservation biology collaboratively among the three countries. While regional projects are generally more complex to implement than national ones, this project demonstrates the value of a single regional approach to transboundary ecosystem management – particularly, building cooperation among the three countries.

Source: adapted from Brylski (2005)

needs of species require the persistence of areas in several countries – for example, all elements of a migratory route. These migration routes could involve two or more adjacent countries (for instance, for the seasonal movement of elephants), or might constitute the feeding, resting or breeding areas of a migratory species, such as birds, sea turtles or whales, wherever these occur. Transboundary migratory corridors can be defined as follows:

> *Transboundary migratory corridors are areas of land and/or sea in two or more countries, which are not necessarily contiguous, but are required to sustain a biological migratory pathway, and where cooperative management has been secured through legal or other effective means (Transboundary Protected Areas Taskforce, 2005).*

Examples of such transboundary initiatives include the Palearctic Flyway (Siberia to Senegal), the European Green Belt and the Meso-American Biological Corridor.

It should be noted that these four types are not mutually exclusive, and may not be inclusive of all situations prevailing worldwide. The proposed definitions and designations are descriptive and are not intended to replace or become official designations at this stage. Furthermore, in addition to these types, there are two other official designations of transboundary conservation initiatives, which can be superimposed on any combination of the above four types:

1   A transboundary World Heritage site is where protected areas on either side of an interna-

tional boundary fall collectively into the designation of the area as a World Heritage site. These initiatives are likely to be a small subset of transboundary protected areas.

2   A transboundary biosphere reserve is where areas on either side of an international boundary fall within a biosphere reserve. Transboundary conservation and development areas (as defined above) conform most closely to the concept of a biosphere reserve, provided they meet UNESCO's designation criteria (UNESCO, 2000).

Key elements of a transboundary conservation initiative

Practical guidance for establishing transboundary conservation areas is provided by Sandwith et al (2001) and by van der Linde et al (2001). One of the main difficulties that practitioners face is distinguishing what is really needed when it comes to the transboundary aspects of these initiatives. Many discussions are dominated by reference to all of the other important considerations that would be applied to any protected area initiative, resulting in a lack of focus. Yet, transboundary conservation has some unique characteristics that require attention. In this section, only the major transboundary issues will be highlighted.

Perhaps the most important question that proponents of transboundary initiatives should ask is whether it is necessary to 'go transboundary' to achieve their goals. This is related to the identification of the underlying objectives of the initiative. For example, if there is a conservation goal, it must be assessed whether or not this will require a transboundary intervention. In the case of a migratory species that moves seasonally across the international boundary, this need could be asserted if there are differences in protection status and management regimes on either side of the border, requiring harmonization of policies and management programmes. In other situations, such as where a tropical forest spans the boundary, it may be desirable, but not essential, that a transboundary cooperation or management intervention be established. Van der Linde et al (2001) recommend that multi-step scoping studies are undertaken.

Undertaking the scoping of transboundary issues at site level

Step 1. An initial scoping of the important natural resource issues is conducted by the relevant government department, nature conservation agency, NGO or district council. At the end of this step, it should be possible to list likely transboundary issues for attention. If none have been identified, it may not be necessary to continue any further.

Step 2. Stakeholders are identified, followed by exploratory meetings to discuss the issues identified in step 1 with key actors and to broaden the initial scoping beyond the natural resource issues. Any new transboundary issues should be listed.

Step 3. A further, more detailed, scoping is undertaken where the identified likely transboundary issues are explored to determine whether they are significant or not. The purpose of this step is to make a clear distinction among those activities that require a transboundary approach, those where a simple exchange of information would suffice, and those that should, instead, be implemented at a national level.

This initial scoping helps to determine, first, whether there are any substantive issues for attention and, second, helps to initiate stakeholder involvement in the earliest stages. In many existing examples, a clear message emerges that stakeholders should be involved from the outset. The transboundary situation, involving complex levels of involvement in adjacent countries, as well as the potential for the issues to be wide ranging, can make this an expensive and difficult exercise. Following the scoping study, and provided that important transboundary issues have been identified, there is a need to pursue a more rigorous analysis of the issues.

An example of a situation requiring such scoping is in Central Asia, where the conservation of the Argali sheep (*Ovis ammon*) may depend upon the cooperation of three adjacent countries (see Case Study 22.3). Scoping would assist in determining the current status of the population, whether it is a meta-population (that is, the populations in each country are subpopulations of a formerly more wide-ranging population) and whether there is any movement among the three countries. This might result in the flagging of these issues as aspects to consider in whether or not a cooperative transboundary programme might be necessary to achieve conservation goals for the species. In addition, scoping would assist in identifying the key stakeholders involved in this issue, including researchers, managers, and local and national government administrators.

Undertaking the analysis of transboundary characteristics at site level

Van der Linde et al (2001) recommend that a more extensive analysis should follow scoping. Since biodiversity conservation is likely to be the most relevant objective of the exercise, it is useful to probe the biodiversity issues in more depth and to determine what relationship, if any, there is with other objectives, including social, economic, political and institutional issues. A procedure is suggested whereby a matrix is drawn up that will allow an iterative probing of the issues. The basic steps of analysis, when applied to biodiversity considerations, include:

- identifying a biodiversity or natural resource management objective or target;
- determining whether there is a transboundary relationship that affects the achievement of the objective or target; and
- analysing the threats and opportunities for achieving the natural resource management objective or targets.

Using Case Study 22.3 as an example, it would clearly be necessary to examine the prevailing status of the Argali sheep in each country, and to determine what the desired objective for the conservation of this species should be. It would then be necessary to examine whether there is movement across the borders and to determine the nature and scale of this movement, and whether there are any impediments to movement, such as physical barriers or management regimes. In addition, options for improved management would have to be discussed, and legal and institutional requirements for harmonized management regimes identified. It would be important to establish whether the *status quo* or proposed management regimes would differentially affect social or economic situations in the adjacent

countries. Most importantly, it would assist in determining whether or not there are national or transboundary options for management.

If such an analysis is performed, goal by goal and issue by issue across the matrix of biodiversity, social, economic, political and institutional dimensions, a picture will gradually emerge regarding the nature of the issues and whether they are amenable to transboundary solutions. Furthermore, this analysis must be conducted from the point of view of each country involved in the initiative in order to determine whether there are unrelated, conflicting or aligned issues. Together with this understanding, an analysis of the costs and benefits of alternative options should inform decision-makers. Clearly, the option to go transboundary will be strengthened where there is a mutual interest among the countries involved, and where multiple objectives are aligned, rather than conflicting. If there is misalignment, such as where one country's abstraction of water affects a conservation priority of another country downstream, there might be a strong rationale and even a need to 'go transboundary'; but it will be readily appreciated that the cost and complexity of doing so will be much greater.

Van der Linde et al (2001) conclude by pointing out the key lessons that should be taken into account. Transboundary conservation programmes:

- can be effective, under the right conditions;
- are not a universal panacea;
- are dependent upon effective natural resource management in the countries concerned and cannot be a substitute for this;
- have no blueprint, and every situation needs to be carefully assessed;
- are popular; but their effectiveness has not currently been unequivocally demonstrated with any rigour;
- should be assessed for feasibility prior to implementation, and should evolve and develop adaptively in practice;
- should be conducted at the most local level possible and should focus on the key issues only;
- should be built on trust and partnership, both depending upon good communication;

- should involve the full range of stakeholders, all of whom need to be involved in appropriate ways, and within a sound governance arrangement;
- should result in a net gain taking into account all benefits and costs;
- require additional investments of money and time;
- depend upon political will and commitment from all involved countries;
- are subject to sovereignty and security conditions;
- should work with existing institutions and include capacity-building elements; and
- often depend upon key individuals as champions and drivers.

Best practice guidance

It is readily apparent that the implementation of transboundary conservation programmes is likely to be even more complex and demanding than the already difficult task of establishing and managing protected areas effectively. Management issues may be especially difficult to address at the scale of transboundary programmes, where there is the additional requirement of seeking cooperation among very different sets of authorities working with different policies and laws. Many transboundary conservation programmes are initiated at a diplomatic level among neighbouring states, and may even be cited as solutions to existing conflicts and contribute to peace-making programmes. However, protected area managers are likely to be given responsibility for developing the implementation programme at the site level. Where there are already good relations between the managers of adjacent sites, the outlook is promising for cooperation at that level; but it is always going to be a challenging, albeit engaging, task.

With this in mind, the IUCN, through the WCPA, drew upon experiences worldwide and distilled a set of guidelines for protected area managers that address nine main areas (Sandwith et al, 2001):

1 identifying and promoting common values;
2 involving and benefiting local people;
3 obtaining and maintaining the support of decision-makers;
4 promoting coordinated and cooperative activities;
5 achieving coordinated planning and protected area development;
6 developing cooperative agreements;
7 working towards funding sustainability;
8 monitoring and assessing progress; and
9 dealing with tension or armed conflict.

Many of these will resonate with protected area managers as being common issues that are relevant to any protected area situation, especially when applied in a regional or landscape scale. This, in fact, poses a challenge for transboundary conservation programmes since protected area managers and stakeholders find it difficult to determine those issues that have a specific transboundary element. For example, it is self-evident that transboundary protected areas must involve and benefit local people. But what does this mean in a transboundary situation? A transboundary programme may well involve many other aspects, such as communities who were previously divided by the imposition of an international border or who have been displaced by armed conflict. Furthermore, there may be trading ties or local resource harvesting agreements among communities who share a transboundary river or lake system. There is a need for the transboundary conservation manager to discriminate between which issues are, indeed, transboundary and to relate these to the results of the scoping and analysis process described earlier.

General principles for dealing with the nine areas of guidance listed above are provided in other chapters. Some of the key transboundary issues that should be considered under each heading are given below.

Identifying and promoting common values

- Focus on those issues that unite, rather than those that divide.
- Undertake parallel and compatible actions and share experiences.
- Identify a common vision based on a shared priority, such as endangered species.
- Collaborate in communication and tourism marketing.
- Host joint meetings and field days.

Involving and benefiting local people

- Engage with local stakeholders in each country from an early stage, and especially identify transboundary relationships where these exist.
- Identify issues that either unite or divide communities across the border, including shared heritage, cultural values and languages, and promote activities for reconciliation, sharing or better understanding.
- Determine land tenure rights and obligations, and identify transboundary conflicts or disputes.
- Identify ways of using the transboundary conservation programme to address local needs, with particular emphasis on ensuring equity and parity on both sides of the border.

Obtaining and maintaining the support of decision-makers

- Determine the status of any transboundary bilateral agreements or frameworks among the countries concerned, and promote harmonization of applicable policies and laws.
- Inform and seek official endorsement of the transboundary conservation initiative in each country, especially among the security community in each country (including the military, police and district or municipal authorities), and keep them informed.
- Communicate the benefits of transboundary conservation, as well as the need for careful and gradual development of these initiatives.
- Involve neutral third-party NGOs that can assist in brokering or facilitating dialogue and exchange among the parties.

Promoting coordinated and cooperative activities

- Undertake joint activities for awareness-raising and capacity development among professionals in each country involved, with a specific focus on promoting compatible language and technical skills.
- Share expertise, both within neighbouring sites and between transboundary conservation areas, and promote exchanges, study tours and knowledge networking.
- Work towards compatible communications infrastructure, including radio and electronic communications.
- Standardize monitoring programmes, collaborate in research, share results, and develop a joint bibliography of publications and reports.
- Collaborate in contingency planning for emergencies and develop joint security, fire management or rescue plans.
- Develop compatible strategies for the control of alien invasive species, and plan and implement joint restoration strategies for species that span the boundary.
- Plan and develop joint trail systems that link the different components of the transboundary conservation area, and institute joint conservation education programmes.

Achieving coordinated planning and protected area development

- Convene a transboundary planning team and coordinate planning activities in each participating country, to result in a joint planning and development framework.
- Formulate a zoning plan that takes into account the opportunities and constraints presented by the juxtaposition of conservation areas in each country.
- Formulate joint or compatible management plans, either for the whole area or for key management issues that are common to all parties.
- Develop compatible environmental impact assessment (EIA) procedures and protocols for notification of potential transboundary impacts.
- Work towards jointly developed and marketed tourism products and opportunities.

Developing cooperative agreements

- Promote cooperation and develop informal agreements on specific issues that will benefit all parties, and demonstrate to national and sub-national stakeholders that cooperation is constructive.
- Obtain information on existing agreements between the countries concerned: these may form the basis of extended or new agreements for natural resource management (NRM) in the transboundary conservation area.

- Identify specific issues that require formal agreements; consider the appropriate form of agreement and the process required to put an agreement in place.
- Consider the need for sub-national cooperative agreements between tiers of government in each country and with local community structures prior to entering into transboundary agreements.

Working towards funding sustainability

- Identify at an early stage the likely costs for each party involved in a transboundary conservation programme, as well as the efficiencies that can be achieved through joint or complementary programmes.
- Identify opportunities for joint revenue-generating activities – for example, a transboundary trail – and consider the establishment of a transboundary financial mechanism, such as a trust or not-for-profit entity.
- Initiate joint fund-raising programmes through the cooperative development of funding proposals and common approaches to donors.
- Consider innovative funding mechanisms, where appropriate, such as payments for environmental services, especially where there are transboundary implications – for example, as with water supplies.

Monitoring and assessing progress

- Monitor the level of cooperation on the whole transboundary programme or on specific activities as the relationship progresses through the continuum of non-cooperation, communication, consultation, collaboration, coordination and, ultimately, full cooperation.
- Evaluate the transboundary programme on the basis of its success in obtaining additional resources, achieving coordinated ecosystem management, averting threats, promoting enhanced nature-based tourism, increasing management effectiveness, involving communities at all levels, promoting peaceful coexistence, sustaining joint meetings, and maintaining free and open communications among the parties.

Dealing with tension or armed conflict

- Use the opportunity to collaborate on transboundary conservation to reduce longstanding disputes regarding boundaries or resource use in the transboundary region. For example, the Cordillera del Condor area was established in 1998 to symbolize and implement the peace treaty adopted by Ecuador and Peru (see Case Study 22.4).

Case Study 22.4

Transboundary conservation for peace in the Cordillera del Condor, Ecuador and Peru

The Cordillera del Condor initiative between Ecuador and Peru currently includes two international adjoining small protected areas, linked to a much larger 'reserved zone' in Peru. The areas are:

- El Condor Park, Ecuador (2540ha);
- Zone of Ecological Protection, Peru (5440ha); and
- Santiago–Comaina Reserved Zone, Peru (initially 863,280ha, expanded to 1,642,570ha in 2000).

It is therefore a transboundary protected area, but the aim is to develop a far larger El Condor–Kutukú Conservation Corridor along the entire border area, including the Llangantales National Park (IUCN Category II; 219,707ha), the Chimborazo Fauna Reserve (IUCN Category VI; 655,781ha), El Cajas National Park (IUCN Category V; 28,808ha) and Podocarpus National Park (IUCN Category II; 146,280ha) in Ecuador, and the Santiago–Comaina Reserved Zone (1,642,567ha), the Tabaconas–Namballe National Sanctuary (IUCN Category III; 29,500ha) and Cutervo National Park (IUCN Category II; 2500ha) in Peru. Additional areas in the Kutukú and El Condor mountains in Ecuador could also be linked. It is hoped to extend the initiative to incorporate other ecosystems shared by the two countries – namely, mangroves and dry forest on the Pacific coast and lowland rainforests in the Amazon region, as well as paramos and coastal and marine ecosystems.

Importance to biodiversity

The area contains dense cloud forests, with an exceptionally rich biodiversity, including several endemic species. The remoteness and, particularly from the Peruvian side, inaccessibility means that species under threat in other areas of the Amazon are still plentiful here. Endangered species found in the region include a local subspecies of the long-haired spider monkey (*Ateles belzebuth belzebuth*), the spot-winged parrotlet (*Touit stictoptera*), the white-chested swift (*Cypseloides lemosi*) and the golden-plumed conure (*Leptosittaca branickii*). Bird species such as the Traylor's forest falcon (*Micrastur buckleyi*) are not only endangered, but also endemic.

Importance to regional economic growth and integration

The region currently suffers from poor infrastructure and poverty. The transboundary conservation initiative is built around a ten-year *Bi-national Development Plan*, which aims to carry out activities and projects that will allow greater regional economic integration, thus speeding up its productive and social development and addressing poverty alleviation. The *Bi-national Development Plan* provides a political umbrella for the design and implementation of basic infrastructure and social development projects, along with protection and sustainable use of natural resources. The plan is estimated to cost US$3 billion, to be met by the two governments, the international donor community and private enterprise. In addition, the environmental benefits of the region are recognized. Cloud forests are particularly important in maintaining hydrological cycles, and this role was highlighted in research that helped to develop conservation plans for the region.

Importance in promoting a culture of peace and cooperation

The mountainous Cordillera del Condor region between Peru and Ecuador has been an area in dispute for decades. The concept of using a peace park to help reduce conflict and build cooperation has been discussed since the 1980s, and was the first driver for the initiative. Interest in conservation and a strong desire for peace among local inhabitants led to the signing of a Presidential Act in October 1998, where both countries reached an agreement that ended hostilities and opened new avenues for bilateral cooperation on conservation issues. The peace process has been consolidated by both the establishment and management of protected areas and the promotion of sustainable development projects for local communities.

Main partners

The governments of Ecuador and Peru have been closely involved in the process of creating a transboundary protected area, although the desire for a peace park came first from local communities. There are also a number of indigenous communities in the area. The International Tropical Timber Organization provided technical and financial support for a scoping study to assess the feasibility of different conservation strategies and to consolidate the network of transboundary protected areas present in the region. It then funded twin projects, one on each side of the border, worth a total of US$1.4 million, to identify potential land-use zones (including the Santiago–Comaina Reserved Zone) through the use of land-use maps, biological inventories, participatory rapid assessments, and monitoring and evaluation programmes, to consolidate land tenure, and to create a local protected area co-management framework and management plan for the operation of the protected areas. These two projects are now under way. Further support for the initiative has come from the United Nations Foundation and the John D. and Catherine T. MacArthur Foundation.

Organization

The individual reserves are run by national protected area agencies, but there is a bi-national steering committee to oversee the initiative and those parts of the *Bi-national Development Plan* that are being conducted jointly. The individual countries have committed to certain time-limited actions, including (for Ecuador) agreeing on a model of regional environmental management, strengthening participatory mechanisms and fostering sustainable economic alternatives; and (for Peru) agreeing on a subsystem of protected areas through a rapid participatory assessment programme and working on sustainable development projects with local indigenous communities.

Conclusion

The area still remains tense, and much work will be needed to build a lasting peace. There are also many pressures, both on the environment and on local communities, and an inevitable tension between the needs of development and poverty alleviation, on the one hand, and the needs of conservation, on the other. Although local communities have lobbied for a peace park for some years, the momentum increased once funding was available to carry out research and to draw up comprehensive proposals. The fact that the area contains important biodiversity was a key factor that has helped to leverage additional support for impoverished human communities living in the area.

Source: adapted from Ponce and Ghersi (2003)

- Promote the awareness and use of the Draft Code on Transboundary Protected Areas in Times of Peace and Armed Conflict (Sandwith et al, 2001).
- Provide timely and accurate information to authorities in both countries regarding the adverse impacts of security activities on the transboundary conservation area.
- In times of peace, develop mechanisms that can provide for strictly neutral liaison during times of armed conflict or other emergency situations.
- Contribute to the mobilization of appropriate responses to emergency situations, especially regarding humanitarian assistance, and ensure that decisions regarding refugees are undertaken in accordance with the United Nations High Commission on Refugees (UNHCR) guidelines for prevention of environmental impacts related to refugee operations (UNHCR, 1996).

Continental-scale linkages

Internationally, there are important attempts to achieve continental-scale connectivity conservation. Hamilton (1997) described a vision for the protection of entire mountain ranges, including initiatives in the Americas, Yellowstone to Yukon (see Case Study 22.5), and the Himalayas. The Greenbelt Initiative in Europe straddles the former iron curtain and serves, through transboundary cooperation, to reunite the divided countries of Eastern and South-Eastern Europe. Embedded within this broad conservation belt are many existing and potential transboundary protected areas, as well as other transboundary conservation areas (Schneider-Jacoby, 2004). In Australia, WildCountry is a continental-scale conservation initiative involving several NGOs, governmental organizations and community organizations, including the Wilderness Society and the Australian Bush Heritage Fund. There are currently WildCountry projects in Western Australia, South Australia, Cape York and Northern Australia. Proposals have also been put forward for a continental-scale conservation corridor along the Great Escarpment of Eastern Australia and the Australian Alps (Pulsford et al, 2003).

Another form of transcontinental, and even intercontinental, transboundary programme is that represented by the fourth 'type' – namely, transboundary migratory corridor. In this type, relatively disjunct components that are needed to sustain a biological process are linked through international agreements. An example of this is the Agreement on the Conservation of African–Eurasian Migratory Waterbirds (see Case Study 22.6).

Management principles

1   Establishing conservation connectivity in the landscape is vital for achieving nature conservation goals, as well as for the health and sustainability of rural communities.
2   Protected areas are only one of a number of land-use types within a region, but an essential component of any bioregional conservation programme. Integrated planning and management across regions, landscapes, political boundaries and land tenures is essential for achieving natural resource management goals, including biodiversity conservation and ensuring that people are involved and benefit.
3   Protected areas should be integrated within their regional and landscape contexts to ensure that there is connectivity of all biodiversity components of biodiversity, as well as ecosystem processes.
4   Protected area agencies are part of the social and economic fabric of regions, and must develop partnerships with other agencies and individuals to further both conservation and regional development outcomes.
5   Protected area managers should engage with adjacent land managers and communities to ensure that activities outside protected areas are compatible with protected area objectives, while fostering opportunities for sustainable livelihoods involving local communities and maintaining the long-term health and viability of catchments and ecosystems.
6   Transboundary protected areas, while not a panacea, are an important mechanism for helping to achieve biodiversity and community development goals, as well as peaceful cooperation among governments and communities. They should be assessed for

Case Study 22.5

Yellowstone to Yukon Conservation Initiative, North America

Rob Buffler, executive director, Yellowstone to Yukon Conservation Initiative, US

The Yellowstone to Yukon Conservation Initiative (Y2Y) is a joint Canadian–US initiative encompassing a partnership of more than 250 organizations collectively representing more than a million voices for conservation working together to restore and maintain the unique natural heritage of the Yellowstone to Yukon region and the quality of life it offers. Y2Y acts as guide and connector throughout the vast region.

As a guide, we both commission scientific research and rely on the work of others to better understand the entire region's landscapes and wildlife. In organizing and sharing this knowledge we provide an overall context that not only identifies the conservation priorities for the whole region, but also brings together different organizations to help them work more collaboratively and effectively.

As a connector, we link innovative conservation strategies to key individuals, ground-breaking science and the necessary funding sources. By facilitating the exchange of ideas and research as well as attracting international attention and funding we have been able to assist other conservation organizations to achieve more than they could on their own. Connections are integral to the scientific rationale driving Y2Y's conservation efforts. Moreover no lasting conservation will happen without making connections between the many diverse peoples, organizations, businesses and communities that are part of the landscape.

The Y2Y ecoregion is part of the western mountain system of North America. From Cokeville in west-central Wyoming, Y2Y stretches north-west for 3200km to the Peel River in the northern Yukon, only 60km south of the Arctic Circle. The region ranges from 200km to 800km wide, corresponding with ecological boundaries along the eastern montane foothills and the western inland coastal watersheds (see Figure 22.3). Within this region, we are working to define and designate a network of connecting movement corridors and transition areas. The existing protected areas will help to anchor the network.

The Y2Y has identified 17 critical cores and corridors that are crucial to the survival of key wildlife species throughout the region (see Figure 22.4). Maintaining these habitats and the key lands connecting them will allow the Rocky Mountains to continue supporting all of the natural and human communities that depend upon them. These 17 areas cover much of the Y2Y region and provide a framework for the core areas and the linkages necessary to keep the entire Y2Y ecosystem intact.

Because of the urgent threats facing them and the ability of Y2Y to have an impact, four of these areas have been targeted for priority attention. They were chosen because they were either:

- core protected areas embedded in a landscape needing more holistic management;

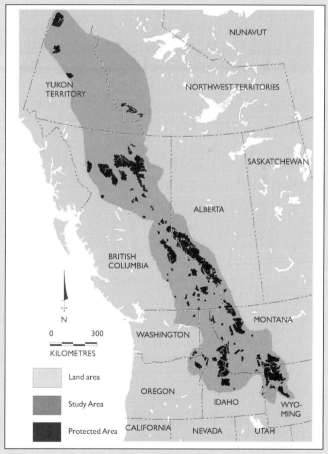

Figure 22.3 Yellowstone to Yukon Conservation Initiative ecoregion

Source: Based on maps from the Yellowstone to Yukon Conservation Initiative

- unprotected source areas needing protection as core areas;
- linkages important to maintaining connectivity between core areas; or
- linkages that have been severed and require restoration.

We are now beginning the process of identifying the organizations and campaigns that will ensure the conservation of these critical cores and corridors.

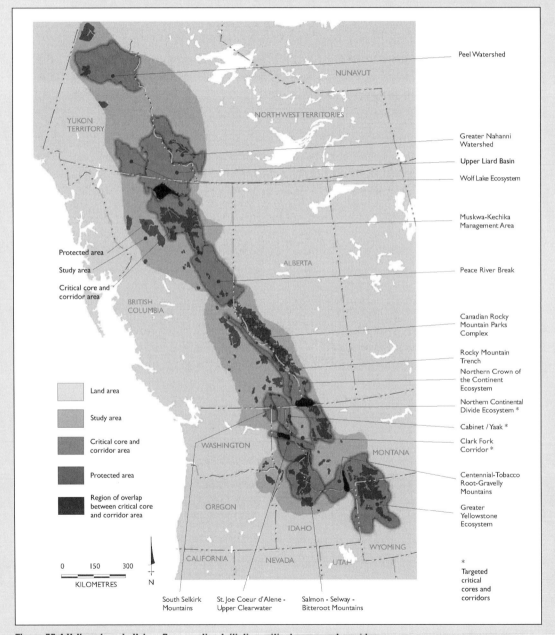

Figure 22.4 Yellowstone to Yukon Conservation Initiative critical cores and corridors

Source: Based on maps from the Yellowstone to Yukon Conservation Initiative

Case Study 22.6

Agreement on the Conservation of African–Eurasian Migratory Waterbirds

Margaret Sandwith, Percy FitzPatrick Institute of Ornithology, University of Cape Town, South Africa

The extent of the African–Eurasian transboundary migratory corridor network includes 117 countries connecting Canada, Europe, Asia, the Middle East and Africa. The agreement coordinates conservation action of the range states for the protection of the migratory pathway of waterbirds, particularly the protection of wetlands utilized by the waterbirds during migration. Two hundred and thirty-five species have been identified that depend upon the availability of these wetlands during their annual migration cycle.

A proposal for an Agreement for Western Palearctic Anatidae made during the 1988 Bonn Convention ultimately led to the formulation of an Agreement on the Conservation of African–Eurasian Migratory Waterbirds. The agreement emerged in its present form in 1993 when the African component was given more weight. The agreement was adopted in The Hague in 1995 and came into force in 1999 with its ratification by seven states from Africa and seven from Eurasia.

An African–Eurasian Flyway Global Environment Facility (GEF)-funded project was approved in 2003 and is under the joint management of Wetlands International and BirdLife International, involving local and national stakeholders. Matching funding was provided by the Ministerie van Landbouw, Naturbeheer en Visserij in The Netherlands, the United Nations Environment Programme (UNEP) and the Convention on the Conservation of Migratory Species of Animals.

The purpose of the project is 'to develop the transboundary strategic measures necessary to conserve the network of critical wetland areas upon which migratory waterbirds depend throughout the African–Eurasian flyway'. An action plan (2003–2005) details the requirements for conservation actions, such as species and habitat conservation, management of human activities, research and monitoring, education and information, and implementation.

feasibility prior to implementation, be designed to evolve and develop adaptively, be built on trust and partnership, and focus on addressing a small number of key issues.

7 The biosphere reserve model should be considered an effective institutional instrument for integrated decision-making involving protected areas across jurisdictions within bioregions, and including transboundary situations.

8 Protected area managers should engage with other institutions to promote more effective coordination and avoid overlapping or competing jurisdictions and mandates. Protected area agencies should lobby for, and create opportunities for, improved coordination among government, community and private sector agencies at all levels to facilitate integrated funding, planning, implementation and monitoring for landscape-scale conservation.

9 Protected area agencies should assist with building capacity among other sectoral agencies to enable them to contribute more effectively to biodiversity conservation goals.

10 Maintaining and enhancing nature conservation values on private land can be achieved through a mix of policy instruments, including regulations, economic incentives, partnerships, management agreements and conservation purchases.

11 Protected area managers should base implementation programmes on sound and defensible conservation planning, and on an analysis of the potential efficacy of proposed management programmes, followed by effective measurement of outcomes.

Further reading

Bennett, A. F. (2003) *Linkages in the Landscape: The Role of Corridors and Connectivity in Wildlife Conservation*, 2nd edition, IUCN, Gland and Cambridge

Golder, B. (2004) *Ecoregion Action Programmes: A Guide for Practitioners*, WWF, Washington, DC

Mittermeier, R., Mittermeier, C. G., Kormos, C., Sandwith, T. and Besançon, C. (eds) (2005) *Transboundary Conservation: A New Vision for Protected Areas*, CEMEX/Conservation International, Washington, DC

Sandwith, T., Shine, C., Hamilton, L. and Sheppard, D.

(2001) *Trans-boundary Protected Areas for Peace and Cooperation*, Best Practice Protected Area Guidelines Series no 7, IUCN, Gland and Cambridge

Website

Building the Global System – Transboundary Protected Areas: www.iucn.org/themes/wcpa/theme/parks/parks

23

Marine Protected Areas

Jon Day

Globally, the protection of marine areas has been a comparatively recent initiative compared to the use of protected areas for terrestrial conservation and resource management. The long-held belief that marine resources are infinite has now proven to be a myth; while living marine resources may be renewable, there are finite limits to exploitation. Over-fishing that led to the social and economic collapse of communities dependent upon the Grand Banks fisheries in the north-west Atlantic is a striking example of the far-reaching consequences of poorly managed marine resources and untimely responses to warning signs.

Unfortunately, commercial fisheries are not the only activities that have impacts upon our marine environments. The combined effects of over-fishing, by-catch, habitat degradation and food-web changes have had significant impacts, resulting in formerly abundant species now being rare. Many coastal ecosystems have been or are being polluted and physically degraded. Invasive species and diseases are proliferating, and the impacts of climate change on marine ecosystems are increasingly documented. The following points put into perspective the importance of mounting an effective response to these threats and protecting marine environments.

Oceans cover 70 per cent of the Earth's surface and contain 97 per cent of the Earth's water. They drive climate and weather, regulate temperature, generate much of the oxygen in the atmosphere, absorb much of the carbon dioxide, and replenish freshwater to both land and sea through the formation of clouds. Oceans comprise more than 90 per cent of the planet's biologically useful habitat and contain most of the life on Earth, including nearly all of the major groups of animals, plants and microbes. This watery living system is absolutely critical to how our world works. Oceans supply food, provide leisure opportunities and generate billions of dollars for national economies.

In recent decades, considerable efforts have been directed worldwide to establishing marine protected areas (MPAs). However, the most optimistic estimates indicate that less than 1 per cent of the world's oceans are currently in MPAs (Jones, 2006; see also Chapter 3, p97). There has been a growing understanding that far more needs to be done to adequately manage our use of coasts, seas and oceans in order to ensure environmental and economic sustainability. There is an emerging realization that effective marine protection requires us to identify and protect representative examples of marine habitats, rather than trying to protect specific threatened species, or special or scenic areas (Day and Roff, 2000; see also Chapter 8, p200). To be effective in protecting marine biodiversity, this approach needs to be applied in offshore waters and the open sea, as well as in near-shore and coastal areas.

In setting up the spatial framework for marine protection, we then seek to manage the human values, behaviours and uses that affect marine environments. Everything done towards establishing and managing MPAs is directed towards maintaining 'good' behaviours or changing 'bad' behaviours. Of course, this raises the issues of who decides which behaviours are acceptable, and with what legitimacy and how unacceptable behaviours may be be modified. Such matters of governance are dealt with in Chapter 5, and the range of approaches outlined there sets a context for addressing them in marine environments.

Aspects of MPA establishment and management are introduced in several other chapters throughout this book, including values (Chapter 4), governance (Chapter 5) and establishing protected areas (Chapter 8). This chapter builds on this material and examines various types of coastal and marine environments, and the interrelationships between them; discusses the differences between managing marine versus terrestrial ecosystems; considers what is meant by an MPA; indicates why a network of MPAs is far more effective than a single MPA; explains how MPAs fit in with other approaches to marine conservation; considers the key aspects of MPA governance; describes the main MPA management tools; and raises some key emerging issues for MPAs.

A limited number of case studies have been provided in this chapter, with a bias towards Australia and the Great Barrier Reef Marine Park (GBRMP). However, there are many good examples of case studies of MPAs worldwide. Readers are therefore encouraged to refer to those texts and websites listed in the section on 'Further reading', most of which contain examples of various MPA case studies of many different types and sizes in both low and high Human Development Index (HDI) countries.

Characteristics of coastal and marine areas

Effective conservation of the marine environment demands consideration of:

- watersheds that affect the oceans mainly via rivers and non-point sources of pollution;
- coastal lands where human activity is concentrated and any use directly affects adjacent waters;
- coastal waters (such as estuaries, lagoons and shallow inshore waters) where the effects of land-based activities are dominant;

- offshore waters that are mainly out to the edge of national jurisdictions (200 nautical miles offshore); and
- high seas that are marine environments beyond the limit of national jurisdictions.

Although the natural processes in these five areas are highly interrelated, it is difficult to integrate management regimes across them because:

- marine resources are not evenly spread across them, with 90 per cent of the marine fish catch either coming from coastal waters or dependent upon them during larval stages, though coastal and offshore waters occupy only 10 per cent of the Earth's oceans (FAO, 1991);
- of the variable nature of tenure and ownership, with:
  - private property tending to predominate in inland areas;
  - a mix of public and private property on coastal lands;
  - public property issues dominant in coastal and offshore waters; and
- the focus of government institutions generally differs in each of these key areas, and these often compete with each other for dominance on behalf of their constituent industry.

Problems arise when marine and coastal resources, such as fish and coral reefs, are regarded as 'common property resources' with 'open' or 'free' access to virtually all users. Free access often leads to excessive use, pollution and habitat degradation. These generalizations, of course, vary from country to country according to cultural conceptions of private, public and common property. Increasingly, in the Pacific and South-East Asia, coastal lands, islands and waters are being locally managed or community-controlled by traditional institutions, such as village-level councils of elders (Tawake et al, 2005). The re-allocation of property rights (legal or non-legal) from one user to another, either by direct (such as licences and permits) or indirect means (such as allowing the growth of one use over another), is a major factor in the degradation of marine resources, particularly in low and medium HDI countries.

Differences between terrestrial and marine ecosystems

The similarities and differences between marine and terrestrial ecosystems also need to be understood in order for marine conservation to be successful and to highlight the difficulties of attempting to protect marine biological diversity in ways that are developed for terrestrial systems. Marine ecosystems are inherently complex, interconnected and physically influenced across a range of spatial–temporal scales. Unlike terrestrial ecosystems, their fundamental attributes – their biological characteristics and species – are not directly visible to us (Day and Roff, 2000).

At a very broad conceptual level, marine and terrestrial systems do have some similarities:

- both are composed of interacting physical and biological components;
- both are complex patchworks of differing environments that are occupied by different communities and species; and

- both marine and terrestrial species show a gradient in diversity with latitude – that is, species diversity generally increases with decreasing latitude (Day and Roff, 2000).

However, there are many more differences than similarities between marine and terrestrial ecosystems. These differences can be found in such variables as space and time scales of physical processes; mobile versus sessile lifestyles; size, growth rate and trophic position relations; and the fundamental physical properties of water itself (Carr et al, 2003).

Problems can arise if it is assumed that knowledge gained from terrestrial ecosystems will transfer directly to marine contexts. As Rice (1985) warned, marine ecosystems are not simply wet, salty terrestrial ones! The principles of marine conservation, and the way in which marine ecosystems need to be addressed, are very different from the ones derived from experience on land. Marine ecosystems are:

Sian Ka'an World Heritage Area, Mexico

Source: IUCN Photo Library © Jim Thorsell

Tarutao National Park, Thailand

Source: IUCN Photo Library © Jim Thorsell

- highly dynamic, subject to natural changes (often rapid);
- three dimensional (much more than terrestrial ecosystems);
- highly interconnected, with such concepts of 'connectivity' (see Case Study 23.1) and 'downstream' issues needing to be considered in all dimensions, due to the fluid nature of water;
- poorly known;
- not easily delineated, managed, viewed or monitored; and
- complex in terms of ownership and differing sectoral views.

Management of marine areas or marine species is complex, but may require some knowledge of terrestrial, as well as marine, environments. Consider, for example, the green turtle (*Chelonia mydas*). In the Great Barrier Reef World Heritage Area in Australia, green turtles lay their eggs on the mainland or islands outside the Great Barrier Reef Marine Park. Once they hatch (and if they survive), they then move into near-shore marine areas in the park, feeding on seaweed and seagrasses. They then migrate thousands of kilometres in open sea to other countries, where they may be hunted and caught. Those females that survive then return to the same stretch of beach back in Australia to nest. This means that effective conservation of this species alone needs to consider local, provincial, national and international jurisdictions. One of the world's largest MPAs is still not large enough to encompass the full life cycle of the green turtle.

Definitions and types of marine protected areas

The term 'marine protected area' (frequently shortened to MPA) has arisen out of a historic array of meanings that formed as protected areas were declared in coastal and marine areas around the world, each with its own label and implications (Salm et al, 2000). The diverse array of MPA goals, and their order of priority, varies enormously from place to place – so much so that one could almost say that every MPA is unique, having been tailored to meet the specific circumstances of the place where it is established (Agardy, 1997).

MPAs are variously defined as purely in-water designations, as coastal management units that include terrestrial and marine areas, or as any kind of marine managed area (Agardy, 1997). Put most simply, an MPA is any marine area afforded some kind of special protection, usually to benefit marine values such as conservation and/or fisheries. The oldest legally established MPA that still exists in the world was recognized by *MPA News* as Royal National Park in the state of New South Wales, in South-Eastern Australia. When the park was designated in 1879, its regulations included bans on dredging and the removal of sand, rocks and vegetation. Soon after, prohibitions on the use of explosives, net fishing and the commercial exploitation of oysters were added (Brown, 2001).

The IUCN First World Conference on National Parks, held in Seattle in 1962 (see Box 2.2 in Chapter 2), was probably the first time the need for protection of coastal and marine areas was internationally recognized and agreed. By 1995, there were at least 1306 sub-tidal MPAs worldwide, with a median size of 1584ha (Kelleher et al, 1995). In the last decade, there has been a rapid and accelerating progress in MPA establishment, with virtually every coastal country having implemented some form of MPA. The United Nations Environment Programme (UNEP)–World Conservation Monitoring Centre (WCMC) assessment of protected areas in 2005 identified 4526 MPAs (this includes terrestrial protected areas, TPAs, with a marine component). These cover over 1.6 million square kilometres, or less than 1 per cent of the world's oceans (Wells and Day, 2004). More detail on the distribution and extent of MPAs is given in Appendices 5 and 6.

The widely adopted IUCN definition of a protected area (see Chapter 3) explicitly covers land or seas. However, following resolutions to IUCN's General Assembly in 1988, the IUCN developed a more specific, but compatible, definition of an MPA:

> *Any area of intertidal or sub-tidal terrain, together with its overlying water and associated flora, fauna, historical and cultural features, which has been reserved by law or other effective means to protect part or all of the enclosed environment (Kelleher and Kenchington, 1992, p13).*

Some users have found certain difficulties in applying this definition; for example, Nijkamp and Peet (1994) suggest:

- the definition refers primarily to terrain rather than to marine waters, which seems to emphasize the value of the seabed rather than the value of the overlying water or associated flora and fauna;
- the reference to fauna and flora is too restrictive since it might exclude such marine features as ocean vents, upwelling areas and so on; and
- an area that is reserved by law is not necessarily protected by law.

Nijkamp and Peet (1994) therefore suggested a modified definition of an MPA as:

> *Any area of sea or ocean – where appropriate, in combination with contiguous intertidal areas – together with associated natural and cultural features in the water column within, or on top of the seabed, for which measures have been taken for the purpose of protecting part or all of the enclosed environment.*

Other definitions have also been developed. The Convention on Biological Diversity (CBD) defined a marine and coastal protected area as:

> *… any defined area within or adjacent to the marine environment, together with its overlying waters and associated flora, fauna, and historical and cultural features, which has been reserved by legislation or other effective means, including custom, with the effect that its marine and/or coastal biodiversity enjoys a higher level of protection than its surroundings (CBD, 2004b, p135).*

In the US, MPAs have been defined as:

> ... *any area of the marine environment that has been reserved by federal, state, territorial, tribal or local laws or regulations to provide lasting protection for part or all of the natural or cultural resources therein (US Presidential Executive Order 13158, 26 May 2000).*

None of these definitions explicitly recognize that the air above the water surface should also be part of an MPA. The air supports much of the bird life that can play an important role in the marine environment, and can be subject to human uses that are detrimental to marine systems and species, such as aircraft use, noise and air-borne pollution, as well as hovercraft, helicopters and so on.

It is also important to note that, as with TPAs, a huge variety of marine and coastal terms have been used to label different types of MPA. Inevitably, the same term or title may mean different things in different countries. For example, the terms 'national park' and 'marine park' are some of the most commonly used, but differ significantly in how they are applied around the world. The term 'sanctuary', as used in the US context, is a multiple-use MPA that is designated under the jurisdiction of the US National Oceanic and Atmospheric Administration's (NOAA) National Marine Sanctuary Program (such as in the Florida Keys National Marine Sanctuary). However 'sanctuary' takes on a different meaning elsewhere in the world – in the UK, the term has been used, on occasion, to refer to strictly protected marine reserves in which extractive use is prohibited (Jones, 2006). MPAs can be applied to all six IUCN categories (see 'Types of protected areas' in Chapter 3), and may range from highly protected, no-take areas, intended for scientific research (Category IA), to multiple-use areas, created to foster the sustainable use of natural ecosystems and resources (Category VI).

This multitude of labels, definitions and terminologies has the potential to confuse many users through misunderstanding and uncertainty. The confusion is all the more reason for emphasizing an international system of protected area categorization that does not depend upon terms or titles (Wells and Day, 2004). This book uses MPA as a broad generic or 'umbrella' term, reflecting the accepted IUCN definition. In addition, this chapter refers to 'no-take' and 'multiple-use' MPAs.

A *no-take MPA* (sometimes referred to as a marine reserve, or refugia) is a special type of MPA or a zone within a multiple-use MPA, where any removal of marine species and modification or extraction of marine resources are prohibited (by such means as fishing, trawling, harvesting, dredging, mining or drilling), and other human disturbance is restricted. No-take areas have become an important tool for both marine biodiversity protection and fisheries management (Roberts and Hawkins, 2000; Palumbi, 2003; Jones, 2006). They may comprise a whole MPA or be a core zone within a multiple-use MPA.

A *'multiple-use' MPA* is a particular type of MPA in which the use and removal of resources may be permitted in some areas, though not all, but where such use is controlled to ensure that long-term conservation goals are not compromised. Multiple-use MPAs generally have a spectrum of zones within them, with some zones allowing greater use and removal of resources than other zones. No-take zones are commonly designated as one of the zones.

One of the best known MPAs in the world is the multiple-use GBRMP, covering 344,400 square kilometres. Because of the iconic status of the Great Barrier Reef, many people think the entire area is a marine sanctuary or a marine national park, and therefore protected equally throughout. While the entire area is protected by law, many do not understand that the GBRMP is a multiple-use area, in which a wide range of activities and uses is allowed, including extractive industries, while still protecting one of the world's most diverse ecosystems. The comprehensive, multiple-use zoning system provides high levels of protection for specific areas, while allowing a variety of other uses, including shipping, dredging, aquaculture, tourism, boating, diving, commercial fishing and recreational fishing, to continue in certain zones.

As a result of a zoning review between 1999 and 2003, the proportion of the GBRMP protected by no-take zones (locally known as 'green zones') (see Table 23.1) increased from less than 5 per cent to more than 33 per cent of the MPA, and now 'representative' examples of each of the 70 broad habitat types across the entire park are protected in 'green zones' (GBRMPA, 2004). Anyone can enter a 'green zone', and activities such as boating, swimming, sailing and snorkelling are allowed; however, all extractive activities, such as fishing or collecting, are not allowed.

Table 23.1 Activities matrix for zones in the Great Barrier Reef Marine Park, Australia

ACTIVITIES GUIDE (see *Zoning Plan* for details)	General Use Zone	Habitat Protection Zone	Conservation Park Zone	Buffer Zone	Scientific Research Zone	Marine National Park Zone	Preservation Zone
Aquaculture	Permit	Permit	Permit [1]	✗	✗	✗	✗
Bait netting	✓	✓	✓	✗	✗	✗	✗
Boating, diving, photography	✓	✓	✓	✓	✓ [2]	✓	✗
Crabbing	✓	✓	✓ [3]	✗	✗	✗	✗
Harvest fishing for aquarium fish, coral and beachworm	Permit	Permit	Permit [1]	✗	✗	✗	✗
Harvest fishing for sea cucumber, trochus, tropical rock lobster	Permit	Permit	✗	✗	✗	✗	✗
Limited collecting	✓ [4]	✓ [4]	✓ [4]	✗	✗	✗	✗
Limited impact research	✓	✓	✓	✓ [5]	✓	✓ [5]	Permit
Limited spearfishing (snorkel only)	✓	✓	✓ [1]	✗	✗	✗	✗
Line fishing	✓ [6]	✓ [6]	✓ [7]	✗	✗	✗	✗
Netting (other than bait netting)	✓	✓	✗	✗	✗	✗	✗
Research (other than limited impact)	Permit	Permit	Permit	Permit	Permit	Permit	Permit
Shipping (other than in a designated shipping area)	✓	Permit	Permit	Permit	Permit	Permit	Permit
Tourism program	Permit	Permit	Permit	Permit	Permit	Permit	✗
Traditional use of marine resources	✓ [8]	✓ [8]	✓ [8]	✓ [8]	✓ [8]	✓ [8]	✗ [8]
Trawling	✓	✗	✗	✗	✗	✗	✗
Trolling	✓ [6]	✓ [6]	✓ [6]	✓ [6,9]	✗	✗	✗

PLEASE NOTE: This guide provides an introduction to Zoning in the Great Barrier Reef Marine Park.

1. Restrictions apply to aquaculture, spearfishing and harvest fishing for aquarium fish and coral in the Conservation Park Zone. Refer to the Regulations for details.
2. Except for One Tree Island and AIMS which are closed to public access.
3. Limited to 4 catch devices (eg. crab pots and dillies) per person.
4. By hand or hand-held implement and generally no more than 5 of a species. Refer to the Regulations for details.
5. Other than limited impact research (extractive) which requires a permit.
6. Maximum of 3 lines/rods per person with a combined total of 6 hooks.
7. Limited to 1 line/rod per person and 1 hook per line.
8. Activities that are not 'as of right' in the zone, or that involve the take of protected species, require either a permit or a Traditional Use of Marine Resources Agreement.
9. Pelagic species only.

Detailed information is contained in the Zoning Plan available from the Great Barrier Reef Marine Park Authority.

A. Permits are required for most other activities not listed above.
B. All Commonwealth owned islands in the Great Barrier Reef Marine Park are zoned "Commonwealth Islands Zone". Refer to the Zoning Plan for details about use and entry of Commonwealth islands.
C. Special Management Areas may provide additional restrictions at some locations.
D. The Zoning Plan does not affect the operation of s.211 the *Native Title Act 1993*.

ACCESS TO ALL ZONES IS PERMITTED IN AN EMERGENCY.

Source: Great Barrier Reef Marine Park Authority, www.gbrmpa.gov.au

Marine protected area networks

The benefits of MPAs are greatly increased if they are linked together into ecologically coherent networks. Such an MPA network would comprise an organized collection of individual MPAs, connected in some way by ecological or other processes, or operating cooperatively and synergistically to fulfil ecological aims more effectively and comprehensively than the individual MPAs could alone. Wherever possible, such a network should comprehensively represent the region's spectrum of marine life characteristics, rather than just a subset of habitats or species of special interest; in this way, networks provide significant improvements in the management of the wider seas and oceans.

A number of global and regional agreements that governments have signed reflect a political commitment to establishing networks of MPAs. This relatively recent focus on MPA networks is in recognition of the fact that such a carefully organized approach will fulfil ecological, social and economic aims that a single MPA site alone could not fulfil (Roberts et al, 2001b), assuming that it is not possible to have a single large MPA that protects all critical habitats across a range of locations. Broad-area integrated management utilizing a network that has been developed and managed successfully is generally far more effective than a series of small highly protected areas surrounded by 'a sea' of unmanaged activities because:

- ecologically, a network can recognize temporal/spatial scales at which ecological systems operate and help to ensure functioning ecosystems;
- socially, a network helps to resolve and manage conflicts in the use of natural resources and ensures that all reasonable uses can occur in various areas with minimal conflict; and
- practically, a network can facilitate more effective use of resources, rather than each small, isolated highly protected area having to maintain its own set of duplicate resources for management (Pressey and McNeill, 1996).

A network of MPAs can therefore represent better value for money and effort than that expended on individual, isolated MPAs. When investigating possible networks, it is useful to also consider various types of marine linkages and oceanographic connections, such as:

- species-specific localities (such as known spawning aggregation sites; nesting or feeding areas);
- geographic connections (such as upwellings that influence food-web dynamics and productivity);
- sink-source patterns (such as transport by currents and circulation patterns);
- seasonal migratory patterns (such as locations that are used by certain species during migration); these areas may be geographically constrained, such as straits or estuaries, and are often geographically distant and ecologically different – for example, the humpback whale (*Megaptera novaeangliae*) spends the summer feeding in the nutrient-rich waters of Antarctica and breeds in the winters in the warmer waters of the tropical Pacific – a vast oceanic migration;
- coastal linkages (such as haul-out areas for seals or known nesting beaches for turtles); and
- cross-shelf connectivity (see Case Study 23.1).

Networks can provide greater opportunities to deliver social and economic goals, alongside benefits for wildlife and ecosystems.

There are several challenges, however, in establishing effective national and regional networks of MPAs and the related efforts required to coordinate actions at these scales. These challenges include broadening current efforts directed at individual MPAs to establish effective networks, and translating policy concepts and existing scientific principles about network design into practical actions that benefit the marine environment. Actions will be required at many levels and in many different ways; but governments, as well as national and regional bodies, have an important role in helping to develop the necessary capacity.

The best available scientific data estimates a minimum of 20 to 40 per cent of marine

Komodo Island National Park, Indonesia

Source: IUCN Photo Library © Jim Thorsell

environments need to be in MPA networks to protect biodiversity and manage resources. However, it is also important to recognize that such percentage targets can be problematic (see Chapter 8) and they may create a false sense of security that marine conservation issues are being adequately dealt with once they are achieved. A real problem can arise if the remaining 60 to 80 per cent becomes degraded, over-fished or unmanaged so that, in time, even the 20 to 40 per cent that is 'protected' becomes unviable because of the intrusion of these external effects.

Given that it is unlikely that the resources or capacity will exist to fully implement a complete MPA network in a single step, a staggered approach to implementation may be needed after the overall design and goals of the network have been agreed. This will involve selecting initial sites and developing a subsequent growth strategy for implementing the full network. It may help to focus initially on developing a few well-managed

MPAs that benefit local areas and communities. Success of these areas can then be used as demonstrations during visits to educate key policy-makers about the value of MPAs and the proposed network. In choosing initial sites, it may also be prudent to create a foundation of representation across the system by selecting a set of sites that represents subunits of the larger biogeographic area. Additional selection criteria for the initial sites may include social and institutional aspects, such as supportive local communities and partners, as well as ecological factors, such as high likelihood of success to deliver benefits rapidly. Further details on approaches to reserve selection are given in Chapter 8.

Role and benefits of marine protected areas

The values and benefits associated with protected areas, both terrestrial and marine, were outlined in Chapter 4. MPAs sustain local economies, support

Case Study 23.1

Cross-shelf connectivity, Great Barrier Reef, Australia

The red emperor (*Lutjanus sebae*) belongs to the family of tropical snappers and sea perches, and is well known as a popular eating fish in Australia's Great Barrier Reef. At different stages of its life cycle, red emperors look different and are dependent upon various habitat types. For example, its tiny larval and juvenile stages utilize inshore estuarine environments as nursery habitats; but as they grow and migrate offshore, they show dramatic changes in life form and colour, and utilize other habitats, such as the inshore seagrass beds, the reefal isolates and the deep water algal 'lawns'.

Figure 23.1 was produced as a poster by the Australian Coral Reef Society and proved useful when engaging with the public during the re-zoning process in the Great Barrier Reef, particularly to explain:

- the dependence of the red emperor upon different habitats during varying stages of its life cycle (and there are many fish and other marine species that similarly use different habitats);
- the importance of protecting examples of all the different habitats that fish and other species depend upon (not just the more spectacular coral reef areas); and
- the concept and importance of ecosystem connectivity.

Many fishers previously thought the red emperor was only a coral reef fish, and were unaware of the different roles of the various habitat types for the different life stages of this species. The poster also helped fishers and other users to understand the high level of interconnectivity between marine habitats.

Figure 23.1 Habitats utilized during the life cycle of the red emperor (based on a concept developed by Russell Kelley and illustrated by Gavin Ryan, © R Kelley/G Ryan)

Source: Cappo and Kelley (2001)

tourism and recreation experiences, and provide opportunities for research and education. Two other benefits are highlighted in this section: maintaining marine biodiversity and enhancing fish stocks.

Maintaining biodiversity

MPAs can play an important role in maintaining marine biodiversity (that is, all life forms – species, communities and populations – in the oceans). The biodiversity of the marine realm is continually being discovered and described. There are estimates of millions of species that have not been catalogued, and new species are being discovered every year.

Many marine plants and animals, and their young, swim or drift at will. Many other marine species, however, migrate and use different habitats at different stages in their life cycle (see Case Study 23.1). Marine ecosystem can therefore be considered as a chain with many links – break any of the links and it may have implications for entire suites of species. The act of setting aside some areas that contain different types of plants, animals and habitats means that we are protecting the immense range of biodiversity that makes these areas special (and in some areas, sustains the livelihoods of entire communities).

In many countries, rare or threatened species have specific legislative protection (for example, all six species of marine turtle are protected by national legislation, as well as international agreements in Australia, the US and various other countries); but it is also important to protect their habitats. Seagrass beds, in particular, because of their importance as feeding grounds, need special consideration (see Case Study 9.1 in Chapter 9). Previously unknown seagrass meadows have recently been discovered in north-eastern Australia in deeper waters many kilometres offshore.

Other important roles in which MPAs may engage to help maintain biodiversity include:

- protecting key ecological functions and processes, such as upwellings, which are the 'engines' of many marine areas;
- acting as a source of seedbank locations for the production of eggs and larvae of commercial and recreational species, which may then

move from MPAs to 'seed' adjacent marine areas;
- assisting species that depend upon different habitats at certain stages of their life cycle (see Case Study 23.1); and
- providing 'insurance' to mitigate the effects of accidental impacts, or unfavourable or changed environmental conditions.

It must be stressed that MPAs alone will not save biological diversity in the oceans and should be accompanied by other marine management measures, discussed in the further section on 'Relationship of marine protected areas with other marine management approaches'. MPAs can be effective in conserving certain types of habitats and biological communities, particularly if they have been chosen by using a science-based framework. For example, coral reefs are particularly well suited to MPA status because they are physically defined areas harbouring a characteristic diversity of species (Thorne-Miller and Catena, 1991). Other benthic communities may also receive adequate protection from an MPA; but pelagic and high seas communities are less amenable to such protection. Similarly, if MPAs are likely to be significantly influenced by impacts originating outside of the MPA (such as pollution from mainland runoff), then the MPA status may have only partial benefit.

Some might argue that rotational or seasonal closures, as sometimes used in fisheries management, are sufficient tools for protecting some fish species. However, such temporal closures, or other tools such as size limits, are not appropriate for a significant range of other non-fish species. The establishment and effective management of appropriately zoned representative networks of MPAs is the most effective way to protect the full range of plants and animals in the marine environment, not just fish.

In particular, a system of no-take MPAs or zones can maintain or restore ecosystem structure, function and integrity by (Sobel and Dalgren, 2004):

- protecting physical habitat structure from fishing gear impacts and other anthropogenic and incidental impacts;

- protecting biodiversity in terms of:
  - preventing loss of vulnerable species;
  - restoring population size and age structure;
  - restoring community composition;
  - protecting the genetic structure of populations;
- protecting ecological processes from the effects of exploitation by:
  - maintaining the abundance of keystone species;
  - preventing second-order and 'cascading' ecosystems effects;
  - preventing threshold effects;
  - maintaining food-web and trophic structure;
  - ensuring system resilience to stress;
- maintaining high-quality feeding areas; and
- promoting a holistic approach to ecosystem management.

Enhancing fish stocks

MPAs can protect important fish breeding and nursery areas, such as seagrass beds, mangrove communities and reefs. In no-take MPAs, eggs, larvae and young fish can develop unhindered. Once fish stocks have increased, surplus adult fish, as well as their offspring, can then move into adjoining areas, effectively creating a spill-over effect that helps to replenish fish stocks in areas where fishing is allowed. Improved fishery yields can enhance commercial, recreational and indigenous fishing in adjacent areas. The effect of no-take areas on fisheries has been likened to a retirement savings plan, with the accumulated interest on natural capital paying valuable and sustainable dividends in the long term.

Spatial closures have long been recognized by fisheries managers and responsible fishers as a tool to protect critical habitats and important stages of fish life cycles. Spatial closures can assist by protecting spawning aggregations, lowering overall fishing mortality rates, minimizing by-catch interactions and protecting essential fish habitat.

The size, abundance and fecundity of fish are greater in no-take zones and other types of fisheries closures. In a study of some 89 marine reserves, Halpern (2003) found that the biomass inside no-take areas was, on average, nearly three times higher than in unprotected areas, while the organism size and diversity was 20 to 30 per cent greater. There are also other flow-on benefits for many species in areas outside a no-take area – for example, spill-over of adults and juvenile fishes, as well as larval recruitment (Russ and Acala, 1996; Ward et al, 2001). It is not surprising, therefore, that many fishers choose to 'fish the line', fishing just outside the boundary of no-take areas.

Other important roles of MPAs for enhancing fish stocks include preventing over-fishing by providing refugia for an intensely harvested species, and assisting in the re-establishment of linkages between functional groups that have been depleted or suppressed by exploitation, thus, locally at least, helping to re-establish their ecological integrity. In general, a system of no-take MPAs or zones can improve fisheries by (Sobel and Dalgren, 2004):

- increasing the abundance of over-fished stocks;
- reducing fishing for vulnerable species;
- reducing by-catch and incidental fishing mortality;
- simplifying enforcement and compliance;
- reducing conflicts between users; and
- enhancing species reproduction through:
  - increasing spawning stock biomass;
  - increasing spawner density;
  - providing undisturbed spawning sites;
  - increasing spawning potential and stock fecundity; and
  - providing the export of eggs and larvae.

Relationship of marine protected areas with other marine management approaches

MPAs can provide a key contribution to long-term viability and maintenance of marine ecosystems provided that the MPA (or, preferably, the network of MPAs) has been designed using a representative basis (see, for example, Day et al, 2000) and provided that the MPAs are adequate in size and connectivity. However, MPAs should be regarded as only part of the jigsaw to achieve marine conservation (Allison et al, 1998); without a broader integrated strategy, any MPA or network of MPAs lacks a fundamental context. In fact, MPAs can only be as 'healthy' as the surrounding marine waters because of the nature of the fluid environment and biological interdependency of neighbouring communities. If there are options, the choice should be for large sustainable-use management areas (and as broad a representation of marine ecosystems as possible), as well as a range of zone types or a network of MPAs, in preference to isolated highly protected enclaves surrounded by a sea of unmanaged activities.

While MPAs often provide specific area protection for valuable features or defined areas, the traditional approach to MPAs usually means that the surrounding and connecting seas, as well as upstream land areas, remain subject to resource extraction, harvesting and management by other resource agencies, or, in some cases, subject to no management at all. Thorne-Miller and Catena (1991) suggest that as well as MPAs, the requirements for the effective protection of marine biodiversity include:

- regulation of land-based and maritime sources of pollution;
- integrated coastal zone management; and
- direct regulation of harvesting marine resources.

Regulation of land-based and maritime sources of pollution

Marine pollution is the single greatest ubiquitous threat to marine species and marine ecosystems, particularly with respect to long-term damage. Reducing pollution from both land and sea sources is critical to conserving marine and coastal ecosystems. Aside from a single catastrophic event, the greatest source of marine pollution is land-based human activity. Often mainland environmental problems become reflected downstream in marine problems.

While storm-water runoff and erosion are natural environmental processes, human activities that increase these natural processes or add pollutants can have major impacts on marine environments, including increased soil erosion resulting in suspended sediments, often with nutrients attached, being conveyed to the sea. Different types of pollutants in the marine environment can produce a range of impacts and can enter the marine environment in a variety of ways.

Sedimentation can smother inshore habitats, decrease water clarity, reduce photosynthesis or increase scouring. This may be the result of inappropriate sea dumping or poorly managed land-based activities including logging, agriculture or coastal or industrial development (for instance, port or road construction).

Excess nutrients (especially nitrogen and phosphorus) resulting from inadequate treatment of human waste (for example, sewage) or animal waste (for instance, animal feedlots or aquaculture), or from excess fertilizers, are likely to lead to elevated algal growth, changes to aquatic community structure and increased fish kills.

Toxic substances or pathogens (including oils or other hydrocarbons, toxic substances, heavy metals, hazardous material and bacteria) cause cumulative impacts in the tissue of fish and shellfish. A US National Academy of Science study estimated that the oil running off US streets and driveways and ultimately flowing into the ocean was equivalent to an *Exxon Valdez* spill (49.5 million litres) every eight months (NRC, 2002). No country in the world has the capacity to adequately combat a major oil spill, and actions to minimize the likelihood of spills are important, rather than just preparing for their clean up. Despite action by the International Maritime Organization (IMO – the United Nations (UN) agency responsible for improving ship safety and security, and preventing marine pollution from ships), such spills are still likely, so adequate preparation is still a priority.

Other impacts may arise from the discharge of ballast water (often with the major problems of invasive species) or from marine debris, including waste.

The natural occurrence of some pollutants (such as nitrates, phosphates and some hydrocarbons, including oil) confounds the issue. Some are distributed in the marine environment as part of the background of natural bio-geochemical cycles, such as volcanic activity, or splits and breaks in the Earth's crust.

Another distinctive and significant feature of the distribution of contaminants in the marine environment is their localization at the water–atmosphere and water–bottom sediment boundaries. In most instances, their concentrations are massively higher in the surface micro-layer of water and in the upper layer of bottom sediments (Patin, 1999).

Water quality issues can be exacerbated where the loss of wetlands or other coastal habitats has reduced nature's ability to filter nutrients or other pollutants before they reach an MPA. Hence, watersheds are important areas for management, with implications for downstream areas.

While land-based pollution is one of the major causes of coral reef loss and degradation in many areas worldwide, ship-sourced pollution in some areas can have major impacts on an MPA. For example, it is estimated that a 3000-passenger cruise ship can in one week generate about 955,000 litres of sewage, 4.5 million litres of grey water (shower, sink and dishwashing water), 168,000 litres of oily bilge water, more than 8 tonnes of solid waste, ballast water containing potential invasive species, and toxic wastes from dry-cleaning and photo-processing (Pew Oceans Commission, 2003). The 2006 ratification of the IMO 'Convention on the Prevention of Marine Pollution by Dumping of Wastes and Other Matter' will help to address these issues.

Integrated coastal zone management

It is estimated that half of the global population resides within 60km of the coastline. Further increases of populations and economic activities in coastal areas mean that there is competition for coastal and marine resources. Multiple demands by society for outputs and services from a coastal area usually exceed the capacity to meet all of the demands.

As with the definition of MPA, there are many differing views on what the 'coastal zone' actually comprises. The preferred approach is a fully integrated programme of both coastal and marine management. The most effective way to determine the mix of outputs is integrated coastal zone management (ICZM), encompassing all five key parts, including the watershed and oceanic and marine aspects outlined earlier in 'Characteristics

of coastal and marine areas', within the broader context of 'the coastal zone'.

As it is not always possible to set aside totally protected MPAs, especially in near-shore and coastal areas, ICZM is becoming increasingly accepted as an effective means of dealing with such complex issues and areas. This approach recognizes the interrelationship of the coastal zone to the marine environment and abandons the segregated 'sector' management, where particular activities are regulated without taking into account other activities affecting the same resources.

Worldwide, wetlands are being transformed into agricultural lands or by coastal development. Tourism will not flourish if the area loses its attraction to visitors; fish stocks can be negatively affected, particularly by upstream impacts. Without proper management, industry and energy facilities can degrade the environment for many other activities. Similarly, excavation, mining (such as sand and aggregate extraction), the building of ports and marinas, and the construction of coastal defences and activities linked to urban expansion can cause alterations of coral reefs, shorelands, beachfronts and the seafloor. Although such activities may be environmentally detrimental, they are driven by economic factors that people support (subsistence resource use, growth, jobs, leisure opportunities and so on). The problem is to find a way to make an activity acceptable, or finding an alternative activity that provides equivalent economic and social benefits. There is, therefore, a need to bring sectoral activities together to achieve a commonly acceptable coastal management framework.

Direct regulation of harvesting marine resources

The harvesting of fisheries resources is an important use of the marine environment and often occurs within, or adjacent to, MPAs. For example, four of the seven marine zone types within the GBRMP in Australia allow some form of fishing, with various restrictions on gear types (see Table 23.1). Fishing and MPAs are therefore not incompatible, provided the fishing is done sustainably. As previously outlined, MPAs can also play a role in enhancing fish stocks.

In most areas of the world (whether inside an MPA or not), 'fishing ain't what it used to be'. There are fewer fish, the average size is smaller, some species are less common and there is increased competition between sectors. It is estimated that some 70 to 80 per cent of the world's fisheries are fully exploited, over-exploited or depleted. The effective regulation of fisheries and other harvesting activities in the oceans is becoming increasingly essential.

Regulations need to be more than just catch limits on target species. Regulations for non-target species (known as 'by-catch') are also required for other fish, marine mammals, turtles and a range of other marine species. By-catch is an enormous issue, with estimates that fishermen discard about 25 per cent of what they catch. Global estimates of by-catch and discards range from 17.9 million to 39.5 million tonnes each year, either because it is not economically worth retaining or because of regulatory restrictions on retention (Alverson et al, 1994). By-catch and discard levels can be reduced by modifying fishing gear or techniques to increase selectivity, improving the targeting of single species, and/or establishing no-take zones in areas that have high levels of by-catch.

Unsustainable fishing directly affects the abundance of marine fish populations, as well as the age of maturity, size structure, sex ratio and genetic makeup. When combined with habitat degradation, by-catch and incidental mortality, fishing can contribute to altered ecosystem structure and function; as commercially valuable populations decline, people begin fishing down the food web, which has resulted in a decline of the mean trophic level of the world's fish catch (Pauly et al, 1998)

In addition, a range of other fishery management techniques need to be applied (such as species quotas, gear restrictions and regulations of times, areas and numbers of licences). Ongoing and effective communications with stakeholders associated with fisheries in or adjacent to an MPA (including commercial, recreational and indigenous fishers, conservation groups, other community groups and government agencies) are fundamental, and may be done in various ways.

Through collaboration with fisheries manage-ment agencies and stakeholders, MPA managers need to:

* minimize ecological impact through the restriction, cessation or mandatory adoption of new technologies of those fishing activities that can be judged (using the best available information) to be significantly damaging marine ecosystems;
* establish ecologically sustainable fishing practices; and
* ensure that adequate monitoring and assessment are undertaken to determine the impacts of fishing activities and the status of harvested stocks, non-target species and the ecosystems upon which they depend.

Examples include:

* management options to minimize impacts upon the inter-reefal and lagoonal benthos areas adjacent to areas fished by commercial trawlers;
* mesh-net fishery restrictions; and
* harvest quotas for some species.

Many commercial fisheries in developed countries have specialist advisory committees, and whenever possible MPA managers should work with them to ensure that fisheries management plans for any fisheries in or adjacent to an MPA have clear objectives of sustainability.

Some sites, such as fish spawning aggregation areas or migratory routes are critically important, and the species concerned are vulnerable at specific and predictable times of the year. Over-exploitation can quickly occur, compromising reproduction and decimating fish populations. The Society for the Conservation of Reef Fish Aggregations estimates that 15 per cent of the world's spawning aggregations are already gone, with a further 60 per cent in decline due to over-exploitation. However, for the rest of the year, these areas may not need any greater management than the surrounding areas. For this reason, the European Union (EU) has allowed for the establishment of conservation 'boxes' within which seasonal, full-time, temporary or permanent controls are placed on fishing methods and/or access. For example, the Irish Sea Cod Box is designed to conserve cod stocks by restricting fishing activities during the spawning period.

Many of the ecological, political and economic problems associated with fishing are considered by many to be due primarily to commercial fishing or foreign fishers. However, recreational fishing has increased markedly during the past 20 years, rivalling commercial fisheries for landings in many major fish stocks. If we are to sustain viable populations and ecosystems, then recreational fishing also requires effective regulations (Coleman et al, 2004).

In a number of countries, including some in South-East Asia and the Pacific, commercial operators from elsewhere have been permitted to access fish stocks using sophisticated technology, providing relatively short-term benefits for only a privileged few, and compounding the pressures for local communities. Unsustainable fishing, mariculture, and the issue of abandoned/lost fishing gear, including 'ghost nets', are also considered in 'Marine issues and their implications for marine protected areas as key emerging issues for marine protected areas management.

A fully integrated approach for marine conservation

A fully integrated approach, comprising MPAs and the three aspects as outlined above, is really the logical and sustainable mechanism to achieve effective marine conservation, as well as long-term social and economic sustainability for those communities and industries dependent on the marine environment. To be effective, integration must include the following dimensions:

- intergovernmental – all jurisdictions and the various levels of government (national, provincial and local) that have a role in ICZM;
- inter-sectoral – across different user groups (minimize segregated sector management);
- intergenerational:
  - activities undertaken today will have implications for future generations;
  - tracking environmental change over the long term must take into account 'shifting environmental baselines' (successive generations comparing changes against already altered baselines);
- interdisciplinary – ecological, social, economic

and cultural; and
- across the land–water interface (clearly, integration across this land–water boundary is essential and must minimize habitat destruction) (Knecht and Archer, 1993).

Marine protected area governance

Most institutional arrangements for marine governance have arisen over many years, with separate agencies operating within certain limits 'carved out in the past and zealously guarded ever since' (Holmes, 1976). Such arrangements have often been devised to meet the demands of the time, and then progressively modified, rather than effectively addressing the emerging needs for developing viable MPA networks or to fulfil long-term sustainability objectives. In most marine governance arrangements, the main problems can be attributed, at least partially, to the fragmentation that occurs. For example, in the US, at least 20 federal agencies implement over 140 federal ocean-related statutes. In addition, some 35 coastal states and territories have authority to make rules about the oceans (Crowder et al, 2006).

A monolithic system for marine governance at the national level is not considered to be the ideal model. A single federal authority is likely to be overburdened by its own bureaucracy, be unable to respond to important provincial and local concerns and variations (Eichbaum, 2002), and will not of itself give voice to the needs and rights of local communities and indigenous peoples. On the other hand:

> … *a decentralized system with decision-making authority left entirely up to local entities would be hard pressed to identify and properly respond to national interests, work under common standards or manage issues that extend beyond local regions. Reconciling these issues requires a hybrid system that contains both an overarching coordinating and priority-setting structure, as well as implementing mechanisms for decentralized planning and action (Eichbaum, 2002, p4).*

These conclusions are broadly consistent with those offered in Chapters 2 and 5. A marine governance system based on a federalist model (which is well developed for land-based resource management) that distributes authority between different levels of government (federal, state and, perhaps, even local) seems the most appropriate if the situation will allow it. The top level within such a model ensures that broad national objectives are met while being responsive to, and building the capacity of, regional and local parties to ensure that they can properly address unique issues and circumstances. As well as the principles developed in Chapter 5, good MPA governance practices should consider:

- a 'nested governance' structure operating simultaneously at multiple scales and levels, integrating local aspirations, national strategies and international obligations;
- an integrated and holistic approach, taking account of all the components of the marine ecosystem and the pressures upon it;
- appropriate mechanisms for the vertical integration among different levels of government, and horizontal integration among agencies with different mandates, as well as involving the roles and responsibilities of local communities, indigenous peoples and regional groups; and
- the use of reinforcing and complementary instruments (see Case Study 23.2) or international obligations (such as World Heritage or Ramsar obligations) to ensure matching appropriateness of the conservation management goals.

Nevertheless, best practices in MPA management are those that adequately fit the circumstances of the place, including environmental and ecological circumstances, the cultural and socio-political context, and the economic and logistic feasibility of undertaking management. Given that these circumstances vary so widely, no single approach to MPA management can be universally advocated, nor should one be applied (Gubbay, 1995).

Most MPAs in the world have either a legal or customary basis for their declaration. Governments are ultimately responsible for managing the marine environment within their jurisdictional limits, and apply their own policies and laws to establish and manage MPAs. However, in some countries, NGOs have taken on management responsibility for some MPAs (such as in Belize), while in others, community conserved areas (CCAs) (see Case Study 21.1 in Chapter 21) and collaboratively managed MPAs (see Case Study 20.5 in Chapter 20 and Case Study 23.3) have been established. Community conserved MPAs are increasingly being referred to as locally managed marine areas.

The success or failure of an MPA often depends upon its boundaries, especially how well recognized they are by users (see Case Study 23.4). When there is a legislative basis, MPAs are generally managed within a broad institutional structure, comprising some form of legal framework, policy and processes established by government, together with various marine-related agencies and stakeholders.

In most coastal countries, there is a wide range of national and provincial/state statutes and agencies relating to the protection and use of marine environments and resources, including protected area and fisheries legislation, wildlife legislation and shipping legislation. MPAs may therefore be administered at the national, regional or local level by one or more separate agencies, institutions, NGOs or communities, whose primary mandate may be either one, or more, of conservation, tourism, fisheries and cultural protection. Sometimes the responsible agency may also be the national protected area agency and have TPAs as its primary mandate, so difficulties arise if the differences outlined earlier in 'Characteristics of coastal and marine areas' are not recognized.

The unfortunate reality is that most countries have a plethora of single-purpose and uncoordinated marine-related legislation, along with a variety of agencies with marine responsibilities, and are also signatories to conventions with marine implications. The problems arise because of the competing mandates, overlaps, gaps and inefficiencies resulting from this poorly integrated array.

Consequently, for most MPAs, legislation and regulations are narrowly focused, and often do not consider the broader spectrum of overlapping issues and conflicts. Considering the suite of international, national and other legal frameworks will assist in the development of more coherent and integrated national ocean and MPA policies.

Case Study 23.2

Effective coordination and linkages across sectors and jurisdictions, Great Barrier Reef Marine Park, Australia

The Great Barrier Reef Marine Park (GBRMP) is one of the world's largest marine protected areas (MPAs), covering 344,400 square kilometres (an area bigger than the UK, Holland and Switzerland combined; or if measured against the west coast of the US, it would stretch virtually from the Canadian border to the Mexican border). The entire GBRMP is a multiple-use park, with eight different zone types designated in specific areas to separate conflicting uses (seven marine zones and one Commonwealth island zone). The zoning, which is a cornerstone of the GBRMP management approach, underwent a major review from 1999 to 2003, and a new zoning plan became law on 1 July 2004 (Table 23.1). Zoning is only one of a range of management 'tools' used in the GBRMP; others include permits, education, management plans and site plans. Collectively, these tools are used to regulate access and to control and mitigate impacts associated with the human use of the GBRMP (Day, 2002b).

The number of staff within the federal managing agency (the Great Barrier Reef Marine Park Authority or GBRMPA), that is directly responsible for the GBRMP, comprises less than 200 people, so how do they manage such a huge and complex area effectively? The primary way is through effective coordination and linkages across sectors and jurisdictions. This includes:

- coordinating day-to-day management activities (such as field patrols, enforcement, aerial surveillance and intelligence-gathering) by a range of state agencies (such as the Queensland Parks and Wildlife Service, the Queensland Boating and Fisheries Patrol and the Queensland Water Police), in conjunction with various federal agencies such as Coastwatch, the Customs National Marine Unit and the Australian Maritime Safety Authority;
- all day-to-day management activities coordinating by a special unit within the GBRMPA, which also works closely with each agency and the Federal Department of Public Prosecutions, providing an effective surveillance and enforcement capability and maximizing the resources of, and cooperation between, numerous agencies;
- complementary legislation for adjacent marine park areas under Queensland (state) jurisdiction (hence, a user does not need to know the boundary between state and federal waters as the rules in all waters are virtually identical);
- encouraging regular users, such as tourism operators, to assist in managing the GBRMP through a number of cooperative measures (for example, compliance with best practice approaches, monitoring programmes such as Bleachwatch, crown of thorns starfish watch (COTSWATCH), and 'Eye on the Reef', and training and accreditation);
- effective community engagement through a range of local marine advisory committees, expert advisory committees and other participatory processes encouraging and understanding stewardship; and
- encouraging sectors such as agriculture, aquaculture and local government to assist management through industry codes of practice and involvement in regional planning.

Sources: adapted from Day (2002b) and the GBRMPA website, www.gbrmpa.gov.au

International law and marine protected areas

Most maritime countries are signatories to conventions with marine implications and need to operate within the context of these international agreements and obligations. Nijkamp and Peet (1994) suggest various reasons why MPAs are strongly influenced by international law.

International law sets limits to the competence of coastal states to regulate activities at sea that may threaten particular areas (such as navigation, fisheries, and exploration and exploitation of offshore oil and gas). In 1994, the United Nations Convention on the Law of the Sea (UNCLOS) came into force. UNCLOS provides an international basis upon which to pursue the establishment of MPAs and the conservation of marine resources beyond the 12 nautical mile territorial seas. The convention establishes a comprehensive framework for regulating the oceans, including:

- the extension of sovereign rights over marine resources, such as fish, within national 200 nautical mile exclusive economic zones (EEZs);

Case Study 23.3

Community participation to raise capacity and achieve benefits from marine protected areas, Tanzania

In the urban areas of Tanzania, rapid population growth, combined with poor management of the coastal area, has led to the rapid and extreme degradation of coral reefs, shoreline change and deforestation. The large urban demand for resources from the coast also exerts pressure on the natural environment along the entire coast. For example, the urban demand for timber (poles for construction and charcoal for fuel), ornamental shells, coral for lime, lobster, crabs, octopus and all types of fish products is a driving force of growing resource exploitation in rural areas.

Concern with growing and cumulative threats to coastal and marine resources and degradation of the coastal environment led to the establishment of the Marine Parks and Reserves Unit (MPRU) in 1994 under the Ministry of Natural Resources and Tourism. MPRU has the mandate to establish marine protected areas (MPAs) of the Tanzania mainland in order to ensure their sustainable conservation. After the establishment of the MPRU, Mafia Island Marine Park was gazetted in 1996. The Mnazi Bay–Ruvuma Estuary Marine Park was gazetted in 2000. There are also fishery management areas in the Tanga Region, managed collaboratively by local government and local communities. These were developed with the support of the Tanga Coastal Zone Conservation and Development Programme (TCZCDP), with technical assistance from the IUCN and funding from the government of Ireland.

TCZCDP was established in 1994 to promote the sustainable use of coastal resources in three districts – Pangani, Muheza and Tanga municipality – and to address critical coastal issues. When the programme started, low fish catches, destructive fishing practices (including dynamite fishing) and illegal mangrove cutting were the major threats. Through a participatory approach, six collaborative management areas have been delineated. Each collaborative management area has a collaborative management area plan (CMAP), which is jointly implemented by the communities and the district council. The plans include reef closures, enforcement and monitoring. A reef team, comprised of villagers and district staff, monitors the impact of the reef closures. The information collected is fed back into the management process and is used by the villagers to review and revise the plans. Since the TCZCDP started, dynamite fishing has declined significantly and coastal marine resources have recovered, much of this due to the CMAPs, demonstrating that management of coastal resources and development activities can be undertaken effectively at the local level. Some key lessons learned from the TCZCDP are:

- collaborative fisheries management, with the inclusion of enforced no-take zones, can stabilize or improve the densities of commercial reef fish on both open and closed reefs, with higher densities in the closed reefs;
- involving communities in the environmental monitoring programme provides them with first-hand information of the impacts of their management interventions; and
- participatory establishment of closed reefs in Tanga encourages compliance and reduces the costs and needs for an extensive enforcement system.

Source: adapted from Belfiore et al (2004)

- access and navigation;
- obligations to adopt measures to manage and conserve natural resources;
- a duty to cooperate regionally and globally with regard to environmental protection and research related to this protection;
- a duty to minimize marine pollution, including land-based pollution;
- restrictions on marine dumping by ships;
- regulation of seabed mining and the exploitation of non-living resources; and
- the settlement of disputes (UNEP, 2002).

International law offers instruments to regulate activities at sea for which coastal states have no exclusive jurisdiction (particularly fisheries and shipping). The IMO is recognized as the only international body responsible for establishing and recommending measures at an international level concerning ships' routing. While the primary purpose is to improve the safety of navigation, it has been used to designate particularly sensitive sea areas (PSSAs), such as the Great Barrier Reef, the Galapagos Archipelago and the Baltic Sea.

Case Study 23.4

Addressing marine protected area boundaries and jurisdictional uncertainties, Queensland, Australia

Jon Day, Great Barrier Reef Marine Park Authority (GBRMPA) and Vanessa Coverdale, Queensland Parks and Wildlife Service, Australia

When declaring a marine protected area (MPA) and determining legal boundaries, it is important to consider the normal tidal ranges in the proposed MPA, particularly in any near-shore areas. In general, if an MPA is proposed adjacent to urbanized areas, highly modified mainlands or important ports, the boundaries will often exclude major ports and marinas, and may be declared, for example, a specified distance from the high water mark to reduce social and economic impacts. Alternatively, to improve public understanding of MPA boundaries, tide-related or moving boundaries might not be used, but, instead, coordinates marked on a general map. In this case the legal description for the park might simply be 'the area shown and described on map X'.

In pristine areas and adjacent to low-population areas, MPA planners should try to encompass as much as possible (within legal and political constraints), using either highest astronomical tide or high water marks. Highest astronomical tide generally suits areas with large tidal ranges, whereas high water suits small tidal ranges.

In addition, if an MPA shares a boundary with another protected area (for example, a fish habitat area or a national park), it is prudent to provide an integrated and coordinated approach to all of the protected area boundaries, with high water mark being the most suitable basis for this.

Low water mark is a complex and difficult boundary for legal and administrative purposes; issues include:

- the position of low water is not surveyed or marked in most parts of the coast;
- low water mark constantly moves with erosion and accretion;
- the definition for 'low water' may differ – for example, mean low water differs from lowest astronomical tide;
- the low water mark is usually covered by water, so it is difficult to inform the public of its precise location and it is impractical as a boundary from an enforcement perspective; and
- there are no clear principles for defining low water in rivers, estuaries or narrow bays, so it may be unclear which bays and channels are part of an MPA, and which may be regarded as 'internal waters', often under a different jurisdiction.

Ever since the Great Barrier Reef Marine Park (GBRMP) was declared in 1975, the landward boundary has been low water (Queensland is the only state in Australia where a Commonwealth marine park abuts the coast at low water). To complicate matters, the definition applied by the Commonwealth (mean low water) differs from that used by Queensland (lowest astronomical tide). The GBRMP also excludes:

- tidal lands and tidal waters around most islands within the outer boundaries of the GBRMP (although some islands are Commonwealth islands and, hence, are part of the GBRMP);
- internal waters of the adjoining state of Queensland, and
- a number of small exclusion areas (also state waters) around major ports/urban centres.

In the early days of the GBRMP, zone boundaries were described as a specified distance from a geographical feature, such as a reef edge. This proved extremely difficult to understand and enforce, so the 2004 zoning plan used coordinate-based zone boundaries. Most of these coordinates are shown on the zoning maps and may be identified with global positioning systems (GPS), plotted on a chart or loaded into electronic navigation aids. Inshore boundaries are usually aligned with identified landmarks or other features.

The complexities arising out of different zoning plans for Commonwealth and state (Queensland) waters were largely alleviated when the state determined, in November 2004, to 'mirror' the new zoning for the GBRMP in most of the adjoining state waters. Now there is complementary zoning for virtually all of the state and Commonwealth waters within the entire Great Barrier Reef World Heritage Area (that is, from high water mark to the outer/seaward extent of the GBRMP). Queensland also has a policy position of showing zoning out to 3 nautical miles; however, in areas of overlap or confusion, Commonwealth provisions have normally been applied.

Elsewhere along the Queensland coast, the state of Queensland has been declaring state marine parks over tidal land and tidal waters for many years, and given the complexities outlined above, has applied differing MPA boundaries, depending upon the circumstances.

Isla del Coco National Park, Costa Rica

Source: IUCN Photo Library © Jim Thorsell

Cape Cross Seal Reserve, Namibia

Source: IUCN Photo Library © Jim Thorsell

Internal marine waters

All waters on the landward side of the agreed baseline of the territorial sea are termed 'internal waters'. This baseline may be at low water mark or may be many nautical miles offshore. Within internal waters, a coastal state is free to impose any requirements it sees fit, including implications for foreign vessels. Various legal concepts can be applied to determine internal waters including:

- geographical bays surrounded by the territory of the coastal state and intimately connected with it;
- straight baselines, provided that there is a coastal fringe of islands or a deeply indented coastline; the lines do not depart to any appreciable extent from the general direction of the coast; and the waters enclosed have a close linkage to the land; and
- historic waters over which the coastal state can prove an exclusive exercise of state authority, long usage or passage of time.

Territorial seas, exclusive economic zones and the continental shelf

Territorial seas are 12 nautical mile strips around the coast, measured from the agreed maritime zone baseline. Territorial seas are, however, still subject to the rules of international law that enable the 'innocent passage' of foreign ships. As noted, the EEZ extends 200 nautical miles from the agreed maritime baseline. Within the EEZ, Article 56 of UNCLOS grants coastal states:

> … *sovereign rights for the purpose of exploring and exploiting, conserving and managing the natural resources, whether living or non-living, of the waters superjacent to the sea bed and of the sea bed and its subsoil.*

The coastal state (country) is also granted jurisdiction over the protection and preservation of the marine environment, although this has to be exercised with due regard to the rights and duties of other coastal states. If the continental shelf of a coastal state extends beyond the 200 nautical mile EEZ, the coastal state may still retain 'sovereign rights' in the seabed for the purpose of exploring and exploiting its natural resources.

The 'high seas'

While most maritime countries have now extended their jurisdiction seaward out to 200 nautical miles (the EEZ), about 50 to 60 per cent of the world's oceans are still outside these national jurisdictions. These 'high seas' have no comprehensive policy or management framework, and include some of the least explored and rarely studied areas on earth, yet are used extensively for fishing and other forms of marine use.

High seas biodiversity conservation and high seas MPAs have been the subject of discussion in various international arenas during recent years (for example, at the 2002 World Summit on Sustainable Development; the Vth IUCN World Parks Congress in 2003; the United Nations Informal Consultative Process on Oceans and the Law of the Sea 2004; and the International Marine Protected Areas Congress 2005). It is now widely recognized that the oceans and deep seabed beyond national jurisdictions should be managed according to an ecosystem-based approach that considers all uses and impacts. This framework should be complemented by special efforts to control human activities that may impact upon the productivity and biodiversity of important and vulnerable areas, such as seamounts, hydrothermal vents and deep water corals, and to protect spawning grounds and nurseries for juvenile species (Gjerde, 2003).

Coastal states can agree to establish an arrangement to cooperatively manage a specific area through regulating their own national and flag vessels, as well as through mutual enforcement procedures. Tools such as codes of conduct, environmental impact assessments (EIAs) and strategic environmental assessments can aid integrated and precautionary management for the area. However, there are significant obstacles impeding the declaration of high seas MPAs. There is a lack of political will among countries reluctant to restrain their activities for the purposes of biodiversity conservation on the high seas. This stems, in part, from a poor understanding and valuing of biodiversity and ecosystem services, which leads to prioritizing short-term use over long-term sustainability. There are also difficulties with securing the cooperation of nations that provide havens for illegal, unreported and unregulated fishing.

Territorial and jurisdictional uncertainties

The need to clarify provincial and national jurisdictions, as well as departmental responsibilities, is becoming increasingly important as MPA proposals progress and multiple-use conflicts increase (Case Study 23.4). In many countries, the general rule is that a province, territory or state extends to the low water mark; but in some jurisdictions there are legal precedents or common law exceptions to this. For example, the waters in coastal bays and inlets that are deeper than they are wide (the 'half circle' rule, or 'between the jaws of the land') are usually regarded as part of the provincial/state jurisdiction.

There are also legal precedents ruling that the territorial sea and the continental shelf are outside the boundaries of a province or state, and national governments usually have exclusive jurisdiction over them. However, in Canada, for example, some offshore petroleum legislation indicates that the seabeds in these areas are vested in the province. Such jurisdictional dilemmas have been resolved by functional agreements between the federal and provincial governments. Nevertheless, these are political, rather than legal, solutions to the problems of offshore jurisdiction.

There are many different indigenous peoples who have agreed settlements or land/sea claims over marine waters (such as the Nunavut Settlement Area in Canada and the Croker Island Seas Native Title Settlement in northern Australia). Where agreements have been reached, there may be clear provisions over how marine areas may be managed. Elsewhere there may be uncertainties that need to be clarified with the relevant indigenous peoples well before any MPA proposals are initiated.

Marine management tools

MPA managers rarely manage natural systems or specific marine species *per se*; what they generally do is manage the human impacts associated with those resources. As noted in Chapters 6 and 11, management is usually considered to be a continuous, interactive, adaptive and participatory process, comprising a set of related tasks, all of which must be carried out to achieve a desired set of goals and objectives. It is important that these goals and objectives are clearly established and widely known.

Adaptive management (see Chapter 11) is a key aspect of the effective management of any MPA, and this is particularly challenging due to:

* the interconnectedness of different habitats of the marine environment and the interdependency upon neighbouring biological communities;
* the impacts from adjacent land or sea areas that may threaten the integrity of even the best managed MPA;
* the three-dimensional aspects of what needs to be managed (few MPAs are well known, easily viewed or easily 'delineated' for management purposes);
* the problems that most parts of the marine environment are not easily viewed or understood (hence 'out-of-sight, out-of-mind'); and
* ownership issues (for most marine areas worldwide, open-access resources are poorly or insufficiently regulated).

When used in the context of an adaptive management and planning approach, the following management tools, together with EIAs (see Chapter 9, p228), have particular utility for MPA managers.

Zoning

Zoning for protected areas, in general, was introduced in Chapter 11 (p301). Spatial allocation is an accepted practice in many marine areas around the world. In addition to MPAs, spatial allocations are made under national or provincial legislation for a diverse range of sectoral activities, services and purposes. Although such allocations tend to have meaning only for one sector, MPA managers must take them into account when formulating plans and undertaking management activities within MPAs.

Existing spatial allocation in marine areas may include:

* fisheries management, conservation and licensing zones, and open and closed areas/seasons, including areas closed for

human health reasons (such as shellfish harvesting closures);

- oil and gas management zones, including exploration licence blocks, environmental assessment areas and safety zones around infrastructure;
- ocean dumping and disposal zones, including sea dumping areas and charted locations of munitions;
- marine transportation management and monitoring zones, including vessel traffic zones and separation schemes, commonly used vessel transit lanes, port/harbour authority anchorage areas, ballast water exchange zones and so on;
- aquaculture lease areas, including facilities or grow-out areas for aquaculture;
- military training areas, including inshore and offshore exercise and test areas, and surveillance and patrol areas;
- scientific research and monitoring zones, including fisheries survey and sampling areas; and
- utility zones, such as submarine cable protection zones.

Uncoordinated spatial approaches can lead to conflicts between different types of ocean uses and contribute directly to ecosystem impacts. For example, the areas delineated for fisheries management purposes are rarely mindful of those delineated for conservation purposes (although often they both may be administered by different parts of the same overall agency). As well, simply adopting various existing spatial arrangements or developing new, unconnected management zones will not address many existing issues or constitute effective ocean planning.

Within MPAs, a well-planned and effective zoning can provide an integrated approach and can address many of these issues. Most zoning plans involve the application of between two to eight zones, which may range from general-use zones (the least restrictive, providing for all reasonable uses), through to preservation zones (no entry with the exception of permitted scientific research that cannot be undertaken elsewhere).

Table 23.1 shows an activities guide for the current zoning plan for the GBRMP (GBRMPA, 2004). This multiple-use zoning system governs a wide range of activities, providing high levels of protection for specific areas, while allowing a variety of uses, including fishing, to continue in other zones (Day, 2002a). This zoning plan is a statutory (legal) document that sets out clearly what can be done in each zone. Each zone also has specific zoning provisions that list:

- activities allowed 'as of right' (such as recreational activities that do not involve the taking of plants, animals or marine products); and
- activities that require a permit (such as tourist programmes and certain types of research).

There is also a provision that allows a permit to be issued for 'any other purpose' if the proposed activity is consistent with the objective of the zone. If an activity is not listed 'as of right' or as requiring a permit, it is prohibited. Such an integrated and comprehensive approach, when combined with other management tools outlined in this chapter, can address the interactions and trade-offs between human activities, and can also start to consider cumulative impacts.

Permits and licensing

Permits or licences, used in conjunction with a planning framework and other management tools, can:

- reduce impacts on high-use and sensitive areas;
- separate potentially conflicting activities;
- encourage responsible behaviour in MPA users;
- require, or assist in, the collection of data for planning of MPAs; and
- assist in monitoring activities that may become damaging to the MPAs.

The types of activities that may require a permit in an MPA include:

- most commercial activities, including tourist operations;
- installation and operation of structures, such as jetties, marinas, pontoons and aquaculture facilities;

- any works, such as repairs to structures, dredging and dumping of spoil, and placement and operation of moorings;
- anchoring or mooring for an extended period;
- waste discharge from a fixed structure; and
- certain types of research.

Certain activities should trigger the requirement for an EIA to be undertaken. Examples include proposals to construct pontoons, jetties, pipelines and marinas, as well as dredging operations. Similarly, activities that are outside an MPA, but which might still impact upon the waters or marine resources within it, may be subject to an EIA process.

Enforcement and surveillance

Effective compliance and enforcement includes some of the more important components of any overall marine management approach. Without them, an MPA will not achieve its objectives and, in time, its regulations will neither be accepted nor complied with by users or locals. Enforcement and compliance, however, should not be considered as the only management approach or only as a tool of last resort.

Enforcement and compliance can be very expensive because of the costs of resources, including trained personnel and access to appropriate vessels, aircraft or specialist equipment. However, when combined with effective public education and enlisting the assistance of key stakeholder groups, the result can be an effective strategy to encourage compliance with MPA management principles. A comprehensive education and enforcement strategy should be designed to facilitate compliance through easy-to-understand products, such as clear MPA boundaries and definitions of activities that are easy to understand, comply with and enforce.

Visitors, local communities and regular users, such as tourist operators and fishers, can also be vital to the effective surveillance and enforcement of regulations. When designing surveillance and compliance programmes, some of the factors that need to be considered include:

- the benefits of increased cooperation/coordination between various agencies and stakeholders;

- greater use of intelligence-gathering and analysis to facilitate strategic and tactical planning of operations; and
- the value of achieving and publicizing the successful prosecution of offenders.

The complexity and level of surveillance equipment will depend upon the logistics, costs and practical requirements of a particular MPA. For example, in large offshore areas, greater use of new technologies may need to be considered, including remote surveillance, global positioning systems (GPS), satellite transponders on fishing vessels (vessel monitoring systems), high-resolution photography and even night vision equipment. Other technologies, such as forensic chemical analysis, are also increasingly being used to provide evidence in prosecutions.

As outlined in Case Study 23.2, in the GBRMP in Australia, various federal and state agencies work closely together to greatly increase surveillance and enforcement capabilities in the MPA. For example, in addition to federal marine park managers, state agencies such as the Queensland Boating and Fisheries Patrol undertake specialist surface surveillance and aerial fisheries patrols, targeting offshore areas, as well as inshore areas closed to trawling and netting. Similarly, the federal agency Coastwatch (part of the Australian Customs Service) assists with aerial surveillance and enforcement, making over 600 flights (both day and night patrols) per year for a variety of government departments. Most of this information is readily available to the MPA managers. In addition, Coastwatch can act as forward air support for surface vessels or can readily investigate incident reports such as oil spills.

Research and monitoring

Research and monitoring can help MPA managers to diagnose problems, prioritize and implement solutions, evaluate the results of management actions and forecast future conditions. Having the best available information for decision-making is essential to effective scientifically based management of any MPA.

Monitoring is a fundamental management tool to document environmental impacts, both natural and anthropogenic, and to assess the effectiveness of management actions. Monitoring management performance is an important task in order to know that what we are doing is both efficient and effective (Hatziolas and Staub, 2004). However few MPAs around the world are evaluating their management success effectively. A big challenge for MPA managers, therefore, is to implement sound evaluative management systems as the norm, rather than as the exception (Day et al, 2003b).

MPA managers rarely have time or the resources to also conduct much research or monitoring (Day, 2002b). However, managers need to work as closely as possible with the scientists who conduct research and monitoring, and should define the key management issues for which scientific information or advice is needed. Managers should also be involved in identifying research priorities. Given the difficulties of obtaining resources, it is essential that any research and monitoring be prioritized to address the items that most need management responses. Scientists should also be encouraged to:

- ensure that decision-making is supported by the best available information;
- provide accurate and timely scientific information and advice for MPA management, including reporting on the state of the MPA;
- provide information systems and services that meet the needs and priorities of the managers;
- increase understanding of the natural variability of the marine ecosystems and their response to natural or anthropogenic disturbances; and
- where possible, achieve efficiency gains through the strategic and effective application of information technology.

MPA managers may need to 'think outside the square' and consider supporting research and monitoring occurring outside their MPA. So much of the integrity of an MPA depends upon what goes on beyond the boundaries that some external monitoring may be required or accessed to provide a wider context.

Education

Education and communication for protected areas generally are considered in Chapter 10 (p279) and Chapter 19 (p517). Rarely does the one message or the type of media used suffice for a diverse range of stakeholders using an MPA, so it may need to be targeted for a particular target audience. Salm et al (2000) provide an evaluation in a marine context of a range of education and outreach techniques. Thompson et al (2004) outline many of the barriers to communication for a major planning programme and suggest ways of addressing them.

MPAs with education facilities can play an important role in tourism through providing training, support and information for local people involved in the tourist industry. The centres themselves often provide an attraction for tourist visitors seeking local knowledge of the area. MPAs also have a role in educating people about the culture, history and heritage of the areas that they protect, including local community uses and practices, historic features, customary tenure boundaries, and ceremonial or sacred sites. There are often links to prehistoric use and legends, and traditional practices of use that are important in understanding present values and future options. Educating visitors about sites of historic significance helps to illustrate the relationship between people and marine environments.

Marine issues and their implications for marine protected areas

Application of the tools described in the previous section will be particularly challenging in relation to a number of current and emerging threats to the integrity of MPAs.

Climate change

The threat to protected areas posed by climate change is described in Chapter 9 (p235). Of all the emerging issues facing MPAs and marine environments worldwide, climate change is one of the most challenging. Despite a continuing strong 'denial lobby', climate change is now regarded as a real, serious and long-term threat to our marine ecosystems, with hundreds of peer-reviewed articles leading to widespread consensus within the scientific community.

Among the more significant changes to marine environments expected due to climate change are warming sea-surface temperatures, leading to shifts in circulation patterns; increased ocean acidity; increasing sea levels; and changed rainfall patterns. Of greatest concern is the rate of such changes, with many predicted to have severe negative consequences for marine ecosystems, for MPAs and for the regional communities and industries that depend upon marine environments.

Marine ecosystems are among the most vulnerable to climate change, and many are already showing signs of impacts that can be attributed to shifts in environmental conditions that are consistent with climate change predictions. Most of these impacts also have consequences for species distributions and marine ecosystems. For example, the warming of the California Current in recent decades has been linked to declines in populations of zooplankton and sooty shearwaters (*Puffinus griseus*), and shifts towards a predominance of warm-water species in the fish communities inhabiting kelp forests off the southern California coast.

There is widespread consensus among coral reef scientists that reefs worldwide are at risk of substantial changes due to climate change. Mass mortalities due to coral bleaching have been reported with increasing frequency from around the world in the last two decades. Some sites, such as the Seychelles and Maldives in the Indian Ocean, lost 50 to 90 per cent of their corals during the worldwide bleaching event of 1998. A summary of the worldwide impacts of coral bleaching can be found in the *Status of Coral Reefs of the World* series of reports edited by Wilkinson (for example, Wilkinson, 2002, 2004). Large-scale coral bleaching events, driven by unusually warm sea temperatures, have now had an impact upon every major coral reef system on the planet. Coral reef scientists are concerned that coral bleaching is likely to become more frequent and more severe, even under optimistic climate scenarios produced by the Intergovernmental Panel on Climate Change (IPCC).

Management activities, especially in MPAs, have a critical role to play in influencing how serious these consequences are (see Chapter 9, p235); but, ultimately, the rate and extent of changes to the global climate system will determine the long-term fate of susceptible marine ecosystems.

MPAs can provide a buffer against the effects of climate change and an aid to the natural resilience of marine ecosystems.

Tourism and recreation

In the marine and coastal environment, some areas and habitats, such as islands, coral reef areas and so on, are particularly sensitive to the impacts of non-sustainable tourism. Tourism in MPAs can therefore definitely be considered a 'double-edged sword', and the environment of many coastal areas and islands has been adversely affected by tourism.

As noted elsewhere in this book, tourism has the potential to contribute socio-economic benefits; but, at the same time, its fast and sometimes uncontrolled growth can be the major cause of degradation of the marine environment, as well as loss of local identity and traditional cultures. Tourism's relationship with the environment is highly complex, with the obvious ecological risks of ecosystem and habitat depletion/destruction due to the pressure of growing tourism.

Tourism activities require assessments of their environmental impacts and carrying capacities. Within MPAs with limited budgets and staff, increasing tourism can stretch scarce resources. While tourism's benefits can contribute to awareness and protection, it can be difficult to strike a balance between economic gain and unacceptable impacts.

Unless managed, rapidly expanding tourism activities may contribute to a self-destructive cycle, eventually leading to a lack of quality and diversification, and possibly unsustainable environmental impacts. A progressive trend towards over-crowding and a uniformity of tourists and tourism opportunities can have implications for continuing to attract tourists. Tourism operators may therefore be forced to lower prices to attract tourists, compromising quality and establishing a self-destructive cycle to the point where tourism may eventually end.

Much, therefore, depends upon the type of tourism planning and management, and of societal adaptation. When tourism activities achieve widely accepted levels of environmental impact, and result in positive ongoing interactions with local communities, they may be considered sustainable.

MPAs can be an important component for the recreation for many millions of people worldwide. For those fortunate enough to have recreational opportunities, the marine environment can play a significant role in their enjoyment, health and well-being (whether holidaying at the beach, fishing, boating, sailing, swimming, surfing or diving). For many, fundamental motivations include the experience of being in the natural environment; taking time out from the pressures of modern life; bonding between family members; passing on family traditions and skills; and so on.

There are also significant commercial and economic dimensions to the recreational values associated with the marine environment, including:

* recreational fishing supplies (rods, lines, bait, etc.);
* boat design, construction and associated activities (sail-making, outboard retailing/repairs; jet skis, etc.);
* development, construction and operation of marinas;
* magazines for fishing, yachting and power-boats;
* diving equipment and accessories, and diver training; and
* guided fishing trips, game-fishing trips and so on.

It would appear that there are changing trends in water-based recreation, many of which are consistent with MPA values. For example, in some countries, tag-and-release fishing is becoming more prevalent, along with the trend from spear-fishing to underwater photography and the use of less-polluting motors.

Unsustainable fishing

With the increasing national and global demand for fish resources, increasing populations with more leisure time, and an appreciation of resource use by indigenous fishers, it is important to develop a strategic approach to managing all types of fishing (commercial, recreational and indigenous fisheries) in order to achieve ecological sustainability. Any type of fishing at unsustainable

levels can affect target species, non-target species and their habitats, particularly if there are synergistic impacts, and consequently there is potential for producing ecological effects in both the fished areas and the marine environment as a whole (see the earlier section on 'Role and benefits of marine protected areas').

More 'traditional' fisheries management tools, such as bag and size limits, may help to protect the sustainability of a fishery, but do not fully address the impact of extractive activities on the ecosystem or on a huge range of other non-target species. Targeting particular species of a particular size that play a particular role in the ecosystem and taking them out of the system will alter that system – even if the take is sustainable. Management plans for all recreational and commercial fisheries (including all types of netting, crabbing, line fishing and trawling) are important to the sustainability of the fish stocks; but these more 'traditional' fisheries management approaches do not specifically address habitats or ecological processes.

The issue of abandoned/lost fishing gear is increasingly becoming a worldwide concern, with oceanic circulation patterns causing large accumulations of such gear and exacerbating the problem in some areas. For example, abandoned fishing nets can contribute to 'ghost-fishing' or the entanglement of threatened species.

Pest plants, animals and diseases

Invasive or introduced marine species may enter MPAs by a variety of vectors, including ballast water discharged by commercial shipping, bio-fouling on hulls and inside internal seawater pipes of commercial and recreational vessels, aquaculture operations (accidentally and intentionally) and aquarium imports, as well as marine debris and ocean currents.

Such invasive or introduced species crowd out native species, alter habitats and impose economic burdens on coastal communities. The rate of marine introductions has risen exponentially over the past 200 years and shows no signs of levelling off (Carlton, 2001). For example, Carlton (2001) estimates that in the past decade, some 1 million non-native salmon have escaped from fish farms and established themselves in streams in the US

Pacific north-west. In Australia, a national action plan has been developed; but only time will tell whether such actions are effective.

Dredging and mineral and sand extraction

Dredging is often required to keep harbours and channels open for shipping purposes and may occur in an MPA. Dredging can have major impacts, especially changing the hydrographical conditions within an MPA or in areas adjacent to the MPA. Dredging may also damage habitats and kill marine species unless appropriate controls are imposed. The extent of the effects depends upon a wide range of factors, including the location of the dredged area and the disposal area, the method and rate of extraction, and the type of machinery, as well as the nature of the surface of the sea bottom, the sediments, the coastal processes and the sensitivity of habitats and species.

Potential effects due to dredging or reclamation include alteration of the hydrographical conditions, thereby affecting the strength of currents, water exchange and/or sediment transport. Possible effects include coastal erosion due to alteration of wave and current patterns, particularly if dredging or reclamation is undertaken in shallow waters. Impacts on coastal protection can be extensive, either by interference with the supply of sand and gravel to adjacent beaches, or by reducing offshore wave protection and thereby changing the wave energy and/or direction reaching the coast.

Marine sand and gravel, as well as the minerals of interest found on or in the seabed, are non-renewable resources. Accordingly, pressure may come about to allow their extraction in MPAs. When there are extensive supplies of some types of marine sands, there seems to be more limited resources of gravel suitable to meet demands according to specifications and for beach nourishment. The quantities of sand and gravel currently being exploited are very large. For example, in the north-east Atlantic alone, the extraction of sand and gravel was estimated as an average of 40 million cubic metres per annum during the 1990s.

Oil and gas extraction

Offshore oil and gas operations have increased dramatically within the last two decades and are expanding to include shallow coastal and deep slope waters. Some activities associated with oil and gas operations, including surveys, drilling and production activities, may, if adjacent to MPAs, impact upon the environment in various ways, including:

- the risk of accidental oil spills and long-term consequences of chronic contamination;
- the behaviour and toxicities of oil and gas hydrocarbons, as well as related chemicals and wastes (especially the eco-toxicological characteristics of drilling fluids and their components, spent drilling mud, well cuttings, produced waters, oil spill-control agents and so on);
- transportation issues (such as undersea pipelines and shipping);
- fisheries implications;
- the potential ongoing environmental impacts associated with the exposure of marine organisms to low-level operational waste discharges; and
- decommissioning and abandonment of offshore installations.

Shipping and related issues

Most countries with MPAs also rely heavily upon shipping for coastal and international trade. Ships use specific shipping routes and ports or harbours, and these often occur adjacent to or within MPAs. Ports and harbours may be situated close to, or in direct contact with, important marine and coastal ecosystems, such as estuarine waters, mud flats and wetlands. Ports generally require large areas of land and coastal waters, particularly for storage areas (such as container and oil terminals) and warehouses. Ports and harbours are also places where various industrial activities are performed, either by port authorities or industries located within or in areas close to port areas, such as oil terminals and refineries. Thus, the effects of ports and harbours may not only be in terms of the coastal environment, but the economic and social well-being of local communities dependent upon coastal resources.

Environmental impacts can occur during the construction or expansion of a port or harbour, as well as during subsequent daily operations. Unless precautionary and preventive actions are taken during the construction and operational phases, water pollution can be caused by dredging, shipping or related activities, leading to both short-term and long-term negative impacts for adjacent areas.

Many ships still use bunker fuels with a high sulphur content, which may result in deterioration of air quality within the port area, as well as adjacent areas. Ship-generated waste (oils from cargos and engines, hazardous chemicals, solid waste and sewage) must be handled and treated in an appropriate manner; but few ports have adequate disposal facilities.

Mariculture

Mariculture is considered by many to be sustainable, even within an MPA; but its environmental and socio-economic impacts need careful consideration. Mariculture production worldwide is growing at the rate of about 5 to 7 per cent annually (CBD, 2001), increasing from approximately 9 million tonnes in 1990 to more than 23 million tonnes in 1999 (FAO, 2000).

Mariculture can modify, degrade or destroy marine habitat, disrupt trophic systems, deplete natural seedstock, transmit diseases and reduce genetic variability. For example, in some areas coastal mangroves have been converted into shrimp ponds, enclosed or semi-enclosed waters have been affected by nutrient loading (or stripping), and benthic habitats have been affected by bivalve bottom culture practices, as well as by sedimentation.

Expansion of mariculture in coastal areas can lead not only to significant physical alteration of coastal environments, but can also reduce coastal protection and other functions of the ecosystem. Other impacts include depriving local inhabitants and communities of their traditional livelihoods, exclusion from traditional fishing grounds, destruction of fishing grounds and water pollution (from nutrients, antibiotics and anti-foulants). Wild capture fisheries are affected as spawning and nursery grounds are destroyed.

The environmental and socio-economic impacts of mariculture have led to concern about the sustainability of the industry itself. To be sustainable, the industry must ensure that its impacts are kept within environmentally acceptable limits.

Management principles

1   In most MPAs worldwide, there are real challenges in simply maintaining existing levels of management, let alone coping with rapidly escalating levels of use or increasingly complex issues, such as competing uses and values. Finding the right balance between protection and sustainable use is essential, and issues such as cumulative impacts are becoming increasingly important.

2   MPA legislation and new policies alone are not enough to achieve effective marine conservation. The most fundamental change required is a change in values – not only what we value, but how we value it. People must first care *about* the resource, so eventually they will care *for* the resource.

3   'Out of sight, out of mind' – people don't tend to care for what they cannot see; hence, fundamentally changing the attitudes of society and politicians is one of the most challenging aspects of managing MPAs. Widespread popular support is essential if marine conservation efforts are to be successful and sustainable.

4   Marine conservation begins with people, so communication is an integral part of effective management. Communicators must build awareness of the threats and instil a sense of urgency for action to achieve change. This requires coordinated engagement and consultation processes. Local communities and indigenous peoples must be involved in marine resource management. The most successful mechanisms have either been top down through government and communities as co-management, or bottom up through devolution to community-based management.

5   The declaration of MPAs can act like a magnet; people who have not seen these areas want to visit, especially as the diversity increases, and those who have visited, often want to come back. As both groups fulfil their wish in ever increasing numbers, the enthusiasm for a special area can destroy its natural diversity. Consequently, long-term planning and some hard

decisions need to be made and maintained by MPA managers and politicians in order to ensure an MPA's ecological sustainability.

6 No MPA will be 'perfect' when first developed, and an adaptive approach must be adopted that allows boundaries and zones to be fine-tuned. It is important to recognize that the results are a function of management effectiveness and adaptive management.

7 An organizational framework providing for integrated management is required for effective MPA management. If this is absent or deficient, the energies of managers, agencies, governments and users will continue to be dissipated in inter-sectoral conflicts, incompatible activities and inefficient systems. Integration across use sectors, levels of government and the land–sea boundary, and comprehensive application of the best available science (not waiting for perfect information) are all fundamental to effective ocean governance and marine conservation.

8 Ensure that any exploitation is sustainable – if exploitation is to occur within some areas or zones within a MPA, this should only occur where it can be demonstrated that the type and level of activities are sustainable over the long term.

9 Better technology is not always a better way – given adequate opportunities, nature may be better at repairing environmental damage than any engineering solutions, such as building sea walls or replenishing sand. Mangroves have be replanted successfully, whereas seagrass replanting has been largely unsuccessful.

10 Manage the ecosystem, not a single species. Most fisheries management efforts have focused on attempting to manage a single target species, and most of these efforts have failed. The accepted approach is to manage all components and functions of the ecosystem.

11 No-take MPAs really do work, and in many areas around the world the benefits of no-take areas are now evident and increasing.

12 MPAs are best developed as a network. Small and isolated MPAs are less effective if the surrounding areas are unmanaged and overexploited.

13 Apply the precautionary principle. We will never know everything about our marine ecosystems, our impacts upon it and how to manage it sustainably. But we do know enough now to be aware that we should proceed with caution, adaptively managing as we continually learn. For any new activity, the burden of proof should be on the proponent to show how they will minimize any risks to the structure and functioning of marine ecosystems.

14 Ensure that all MPA planning is open, transparent, collaborative and adaptive, using the best available scientific, traditional and local knowledge. Accommodate the economic, social and cultural aspirations of people within the ecological constraints.

Further reading

Belfiore, S., Cicin-Sain, B. and Ehler, C. (eds) (2004) *Incorporating Marine Protected Areas into Integrated Coastal and Ocean Management: Principles and Guidelines*, IUCN, Gland and Cambridge

Day, J. C. and Roff, J. C. (2000) *Planning for Representative Marine Protected Areas: A Framework for Canada's Oceans*, WWF Canada, Toronto

Ecological Applications (2003) 'The science of marine reserves', *Ecological Applications*, vol 13 (supplement), pp3–228

Kelleher, G. and Kenchington, R. A. (1992) *Guidelines for Establishing Marine Protected Areas: A Marine Conservation and Development Report*, IUCN, Gland and Cambridge

Kenchington, R. A. (1990) *Managing Marine Environments*, Taylor and Francis, New York

Salm, R.V., Clark, J. R. and Siirila, E. (2000) *Marine and Coastal Protected Areas: A Guide for Planners and Managers*, 3rd edition, IUCN, Gland and Cambridge

Sobel, J. and Dalgren, C. (2004) *Marine Reserves: A Guide to Science, Design and Use*, Island Press, Washington, DC

Websites

Great Barrier Reef Marine Park Authority, www.gbrmpa.gov.au

International Maritime Organization, www.imo.org/home.asp

IUCN Global Marine Programme, www.iucn.org/themes/marine

Locally-managed Marine Areas, www.lmmanetwork.org

MPA News, www.depts.washington.edu/mpanews

United Nations, Oceans and the Law of the Sea, www.un.org/depts/los/general_assembly/general _assembly_reports.htm

24

Evaluating Management Effectiveness

Marc Hockings, Fiona Leverington and Robyn James

How well are our protected areas being managed? Are they meeting their conservation objectives and protecting their values? Are we able to manage them to cope with increasing threats and pressures, such as exotic pests, agricultural encroachment, climate change, hunting and over-use? How do we measure this and adapt management so that protected areas will be maintained for now and the future?

In 2003 the global protected area community attending the Vth IUCN World Parks Congress celebrated the achievement of the goal that had been set ten years previously to increase the world's protected area estate to at least 10 per cent of the Earth's land surface. It was recognized that coverage of global biodiversity within protected areas was still incomplete and new areas would need to be acquired. It was also recognized that more attention would have to be paid to the management of existing protected areas (IUCN, 2005b). In many cases, we have little idea of whether management of protected areas is working. What little we do know suggests that many protected areas are being seriously degraded. Carey et al (2000) reported that most protected areas face multiple serious threats and that their values have been significantly degraded. Many seem in danger of losing the very values for which they were originally protected.

We clearly need to find out what is happening and then carefully manage areas to cope with escalating threats and pressures. This often involves allocating scarce resources of time, money and expertise. There is a growing awareness that evaluating management effectiveness and applying the results is at the core of good protected area management. This is indicated, for example, by the Convention on Biological Diversity Programme of Work on Protected Areas (see Appendix 4).

In this chapter, we first consider why management effectiveness evaluation is a critical component of sound protected area management. We then describe a system that can be used to provide a coherent structure for effectiveness evaluation and give guidance on how this system can be implemented. The chapter is based on Worboys et al (2005, Chapter 21), adapted to reflect global experiences and discussions on this topic held during the Vth IUCN World Park Congress.

Purposes of management effectiveness evaluation

Management effectiveness evaluation measures the degree to which a protected area is protecting its values and achieving its goals and objectives. The overall aim is to use results to improve protected area management. Evaluation results enable managers to understand the current situation (what is working and what is not), allocate resources efficiently, plan to address potential threats and take advantage of emerging opportunities. Because evaluation involves judging management, some people see it as negative or threatening. However, management effectiveness evaluation should be a positive process, which allows us to correct and learn from our mistakes and build on success. Four broad purposes for evaluation are outlined as follows:

1   *Promoting better protected area management, including a more reflective and adaptive approach.* By comparing evaluations over time, management actions that are working and those that are not should become obvious. Such information is the basis for an adaptive approach to management where management responses to identified problems or needs are treated like experiments (see Chapter 11, p293). Successful approaches are adopted, while management that fails is analysed and the lessons learned used to develop and test modified approaches. Pressures and threats can also be assessed and attention can be directed to those threats likely to have the most significant impact on protected area values.

2   *Guiding resource allocation, priority-setting and project planning.* Evaluation results can also influence resource allocation, priority-setting and project planning. For example, some conservation organizations are now developing models to help set priorities and allocate resources. Evaluation plays a key role in these models, which generally establish minimum standards for different aspects of management and then assess protected areas against these standards. The conservation importance of protected areas, their suitability for particular uses (such as tourism) and their current threats are usually taken into account.

3   *Providing accountability and transparency.* Evaluation can provide reliable information to the public, donors and other stakeholders about how resources are being used and how well an area is being managed. For example, in New South Wales, Australia, the New South Wales Parks and Wildlife Service is developing a system to evaluate and monitor all aspects of park management within the entire park system of over 600 parks. To improve the agency's transparency and accountability, the information is presented publicly in a *State of the Parks* report (Department of Environment and Conservation, 2005).

4   *Increasing community awareness, involvement and support.* Protected areas cannot survive without strong public support. Building this support has become an important objective for park managers. Providing local communities and interested stakeholders with information about how management is being conducted and what is being achieved is an important ingredient in building this support. Evaluation can also provide a way of involving stakeholders in management and ensuring that their views are heard. Chronic resource shortages are a common feature of protected area systems around the world, and public support – sometimes serious public concern – is needed to convince governments to provide better resourcing. Evaluation processes can alert the community to threats and can demonstrate the need for better support for, or resourcing of, protected areas. Results, especially from independent evaluators, can spur public action on park management issues.

Developing evaluation systems

The IVth World Parks Congress in Caracas in 1992 recommended that the IUCN develop a system for monitoring management effectiveness of protected areas. To address this issue, the IUCN convened an international task force within its World Commission on Protected Areas (WCPA). The work of the task force resulted in a publication, *Evaluating Effectiveness: a Framework for Assessing the Management of Protected Areas* (Hockings et al, 2000, 2006), which provides a framework and principles for evaluating management effectiveness. A summary of the framework is outlined in Table 24.1.

The WCPA task force developed a framework rather than a standard global methodology because different situations require different types of assessment. In particular, there are major differences in the time and resources available for assessment in various parts of the world. Issues of scale and differences in the nature of management objectives, threats and impacts, and available resources all affect the choice of evaluation methodology. The framework provides a structure and process for developing an evaluation system, together with a checklist of issues that need to be measured, suggests some useful indicators, and encourages basic standards for assessment and reporting.

The WCPA framework is based on evaluating the cycle of management (see Figure 24.1). This starts with understanding the context of the park, including its values and threats, existing status and pressures, progresses through establishing a vision, planning and allocating of resources and, as a result of management actions, producing results that (hopefully) lead to the desired outcomes. Monitoring and evaluation of these stages of the management cycle provide the links that enable planners and managers to learn from experience (see Table 24.1).

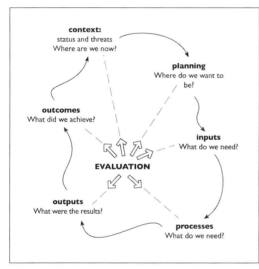

Figure 24.1 Evaluation in the management cycle

Source: Hockings et al (2000, p12)

Ideally, assessments should cover each of the elements in Table 24.1, which are complementary rather than alternative approaches to evaluating management effectiveness. However, assessments are driven by particular needs and resources, and a partial evaluation can still provide very useful information.

The framework provides a structure for designing an evaluation system. Developing a system for monitoring and evaluating management effectiveness using the WCPA framework involves making a number of decisions about the

purpose and scale of the assessment process. Following this process can help in selecting an appropriate methodology from the range of existing systems available, adapting these as necessary to meet particular needs, or developing a methodology to meet local needs and circumstances. A process for establishing an evaluation system is set out in Figure 24.2.

The framework can be used to develop a system for evaluation at any level from a whole protected area system (see Department of Environment and Conservation, 2005) or a portfolio of sites (see Case Study 24.1 for an example of an application to all protected areas supported by the World Wide Fund for Nature (WWF) Forest for Life programme), down to a single protected area or part of it (see Case Study 24.3 for monitoring and assessment programmes under way in the Great Barrier Reef Marine Park (GBRMP), Australia). It can also be used to look at specific issues of management, such as community involvement.

For each of the evaluation framework elements, questions are developed that incorporate measurable indicators of success so that the evaluation meets its objectives. The types of questions for each element are discussed as follows.

Context. This review element looks at the current situation and aims to answer the following questions:

- Why is the area/system important: what are its values on a local, regional and global scale?
- What are the stresses and threats facing the protected area/system?
- What is its broad policy and managerial environment?
- What are the roles and effects of stakeholders on management?

This information helps to put management decisions in context and is also critical for management planning. If the area has a management plan, much of this information may already be compiled. This may be the main assessment used to identify priorities within a protected area network or to decide on the time and resources that can be devoted to a special project.

Table 24.1 Summary of the World Commission on Protected Areas (WCPA) framework

Elements of evaluation	Explanation	Criteria that are assessed	Focus of evaluation
Context	What is the current situation? Assessment of importance, threats and policy environment	Significance Threats Vulnerability National context Partners	Status
Planning	Are the design of the area, planning systems and plans adequate? Assessment of protected area design and planning	Protected area legislation and policy Protected area system design Reserve design Management planning	Appropriateness
Inputs	Are resources for management adequate? Assessment of resources needed to carry out management	Resourcing of agency Resourcing of site	Adequacy
Processes	How is management carried out and does it meet relevant standards? Assessment of the way in which management is conducted	Suitability of management processes	Efficiency and appropriateness
Outputs	What were the results? Assessment of the implementation of management programmes and actions; delivery of products and services	Results of management actions Services and products	Effectiveness
Outcomes	What has been achieved? Assessment of the outcomes and the extent to which they achieved objectives	Impacts: effects of management in relation to objectives	Effectiveness and appropriateness

Source: Hockings et al (2000, p13)

Planning. The planning element of evaluation examines the adequacy of the area's design, planning systems and plans and asks questions such as:

- How adequate is protected area legislation and policy?
- Is the legal status and tenure of the site clear?

- How do site characteristics, such as size and shape, influence management?
- Is the current management planning process adequate and appropriate?

Indicators for evaluation will depend upon the purpose of assessment and its scale. For whole

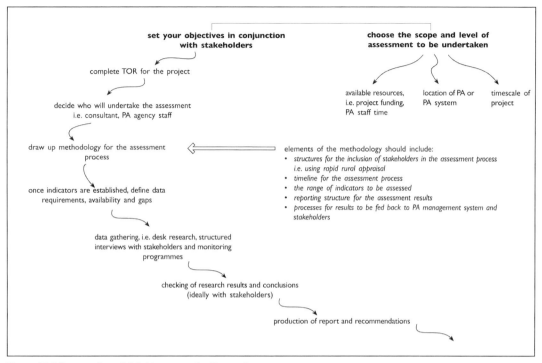

Figure 24.2 Process for establishing an evaluation system

Note: PA = protected area; TOR = terms of reference.

Source: Hockings et al (2000, p26)

protected area systems, ecological representativeness and connectivity will be particularly important (see Chapter 8). Assessment of individual protected areas will focus on the shape, size, location and detailed management objectives and plans.

Inputs. This element considers the adequacy of available resources – staff, funds, equipment and facilities – in relation to the management needs of an area. The evaluation will assess whether:

- the site has the resources needed to meet its management objectives; and
- the resources are being used in the best way.

Processes. Assessment looks at how well management is being carried out. Indicators may include policy development, enforcement, maintenance, community involvement and systems for natural and cultural resource management. Three basic questions are asked:

1. Are the best systems and processes for management being used, given the context and constraints under which managers are operating?
2. Are established policies and procedures being followed?
3. What areas of management need attention in order to improve the capacity of managers to undertake their work (more resources, staff training and so on)?

Outputs. Output monitoring focuses on whether the tasks, such as those set in a management plan or works programme, have been carried out, and the actual consequences that have resulted from such actions (or non-action). The questions are:

- Has the management plan and/or work programme been implemented, and if not, why not?
- What are the results or outputs from the management process?

Case Study 24.1

Evaluating a protected areas project portfolio: The World Bank/World Wide Fund for Nature tracking tool

The World Wide Fund for Nature (WWF) has put in place a system for measuring improvement of protected areas management effectiveness over time. Through this system, it has surveyed management effectiveness in over 300 forest protected areas in 40 countries, using a tracking tool developed with the World Bank and the World Commission on Protected Areas (WCPA). This is the global survey of protected area effectiveness with the widest sampling of countries yet undertaken using a consistent methodology. This case study summarizes key findings.

Status: The good and the bad in management performance

The survey shows patterns of strengths and weaknesses. In general, issues relating to legal establishment, biodiversity condition assessment, boundary demarcation, design and objective setting seem to be satisfactorily addressed, while activities relating to people (both local communities and visitors) are less effective, as are management planning, monitoring and evaluation, budget and education, and awareness. The ten highest scored questions (in descending order) concerned:

1   legal status;
2   biodiversity condition assessment;
3   protected area demarcation;
4   protected area objectives;
5   protected area design;
6   regular work plan;
7   protected area regulations;
8   management of budget;
9   resource management; and
10   research.

The ten lowest scored questions (in descending order) concerned:

1   education and awareness;
2   monitoring and evaluation;
3   current budget;
4   security of budget;
5   fees;
6   management plan;
7   local communities;
8   visitor facilities;
9   indigenous peoples; and
10   commercial tourism.

Staff numbers correlate well with good biodiversity condition and with overall management effectiveness. Adequacy of training is patchy, and many protected areas with low staffing levels also reported that staff faced serious shortfalls in training and capacity-building. There are dramatic differences in average staff numbers in different parts of the world, with Latin America generally having far lower staffing levels.

There is a very good correlation between the success of a protected area in education and awareness-raising and its overall effectiveness, with the highest correlation coefficient out of all those tested. This is highly significant in terms of future interventions because education was one of the issues in which many parks scored lowest.

Analysis suggests that a good monitoring and evaluation system is closely correlated to those protected areas where biodiversity is best being conserved. Unfortunately, few protected areas reported having comprehensive monitoring and evaluation programmes.

One depressingly consistent problem is a failure to manage relations with people. Problems are evident in terms of effectively channelling the input of local communities and indigenous peoples and securing their voice and participation in management decisions. Management of tourists is also problematic, with the provision of visitor facilities and access to commercial tourism scoring lowest of all. In spite of this, respondents identified work with communities among the top critical management activities. This might indicate that the level of awareness of the problem is high and that time and effort are being dedicated to the issue, but that measures taken are more recent and, thus far, are not sufficient to show satisfactory results across the sample surveyed.

Trends

Management effectiveness results were tested against age of protected area, geographical region, IUCN category, and against some international designations (natural World Heritage sites, Man and the Biosphere reserves and the Ramsar Convention sites).

Older protected areas tended to score slightly higher than newer areas, suggesting that given more time and effort, management can be improved. However, it should be noted that there are many exceptions. Analysis also found differences in average total scores between regions.

There is a highly significant relationship between overall score and IUCN category, with the most highly protected categories exhibiting more effective management, although it should be noted that numbers within the sample for IUCN Category III and V protected areas are too low to give a confident picture. However, there were no significant differences in effectiveness among World Heritage, the United Nations Educational, Scientific and Cultural Organization (UNESCO), Man and the Biosphere and Ramsar sites compared to other protected areas.

Threats: What is eroding biodiversity in our forest protected areas?

Protected areas face a series of critical threats. The most severe threats identified within forest protected areas were poaching (identified in one third of protected areas), encroachment and logging (mainly illegal, but also legal logging), with collection of non-timber forest products (NTFPs) also being a common problem. These four were considered to be key threats in more protected areas than all other problems added together. Land conversion for agriculture, ranching and other uses, habitat fragmentation and large infrastructure development projects were threats identified outside the protected areas themselves, which are putting at risk the maintenance of protected areas values.

Critical management activities: Key success factors

Law enforcement and surveillance was by far the most commonly reported key management activity identified, listed by over one third of all sites, followed by working with regional authorities and with local communities, management planning, building institutional and governance capacity and ecotourism.

Enforcement shows one of the strongest relationships to management effectiveness. Enforcement activities carried out by a motivated, competent and empowered corps of rangers are critical, particularly where protected areas face problems of poaching or invasion. However, it should be noted that protected area staff also place a strong emphasis on community issues and sustainable resource use – issues that would not have appeared in most protected area management plans a few years ago.

Biodiversity condition: Success factors for maintaining biodiversity

Biodiversity condition is of primary importance for conservation; therefore, the evaluation results were examined to see how assessment of biodiversity condition correlated with performance in various other aspects of management. The strongest correlation was found with monitoring and evaluation, resource management, staff numbers and legal status.

The initial results of the tracking tool enabled WWF to build a baseline from which to systematically monitor the progress of management effectiveness within the sites where it works. Repeated assessments will take place every two years.

Source: adapted from Dudley et al (2004)

Bringing people together and sharing information from maps, aerial photographs and local on-ground knowledge, Kaziranga National Park, India

Source: Marc Hockings

Outcomes. This element evaluates whether objectives of a protected area have been achieved: principally whether values have been conserved and whether threats to these values are being addressed effectively. Outcome evaluation is most meaningful where concrete objectives for management have been specified either in national legislation, policies or site-specific management plans. The main questions are:

- Has management maintained the values of the site and achieved the other site management objectives?
- Are threats to these values being adequately addressed?

Outcome evaluation is the most important test of management effectiveness. To be accurate, outcome evaluation will often require long-term monitoring of the condition of the biological and cultural resources of the system or site, the socio-economic aspects of use and the impacts of management on local communities. The selection of indicators to be monitored is critical so that resources are not wasted on monitoring features that cannot help to manage the most critical issues (see Box 24.1 and Case Study 24.2 for examples of an approach to selecting indicators to assess ecological integrity). In the absence of quantitative monitoring results, qualitative assessments and expert opinion may still yield useful conclusions.

Applying evaluation methodologies

Several methodologies for evaluating management effectiveness are now being applied in different parts of the world. A number of these,

Box 24.1 Measuring ecological integrity

Parks Canada (2005) defines ecological integrity as:

> *... a state of ecosystem development that is characteristic for its geographic location, has a full range of native species and supporting processes and is viable – that is, is likely to persist.*

Measuring ecological integrity is a critical need for protected areas around the globe. It aims to track the changing status of the biological health of species and ecosystems. It can help to direct our limited resources to the highest priority needs for conservation and is necessary for establishing protected areas and conservation objectives and targets, setting monitoring and reporting activities, and identifying critical research needs. Different components of ecological integrity can be assessed, including elements of biodiversity, ecosystem processes, ecological attributes and threats.

At the World Parks Congress in Durban in 2003, it was highlighted that although ecological integrity is the core element of protected area management, ecological assessment is often under-addressed in conservation strategies and protected area management plans (IUCN, 2005b). Measurement of ecological integrity is, however, becoming a routine part of some organizations' operations. For example, the assessment of ecological integrity has become a legal mandate for Parks Canada. Several case studies from Canada, China, Central America and Australia were presented at the congress. They reported that successful implementation of ecological assessments has led to improved protected area management, especially after being integrated within management planning cycles (IUCN, 2005b).

Often the problem is deciding what to measure. It is important to focus on the critical ecological aspects for the site, otherwise monitoring processes can become too complex and resource hungry and are likely to be abandoned. A number of methods have been developed to address this. For example, The Nature Conservancy (TNC) 5-S Framework (TNC, 2002) focuses on key ecological attributes, status and threats, and the Parks Canada ecological model focuses on identifying key values and key threats to values, as well as maintenance of values. Both systems focus on limiting the data to be measured. Figure 24.3 shows a general process for developing an ecological integrity monitoring framework.

Sound science is essential to measure ecological integrity, and in many cases this will require building science capacity within organizations (IUCN, 2005b). Assessment of ecological integrity also relies on the development of measurable indicators with clear baseline thresholds as future reference points (Parrish et al, 2003).

develop vision and goals
- *agree objectives, stakeholders, terminology, project area, etc.*

select group of ecological attributes of the protected area
- *base these on an understanding of the ecology including agents of change*
- *make an initial choice of measures/indicators to reflect these*
- *compare data needed with existing monitoring processes/data and identify gaps*

carry out a process to identify and validate indicators
- *include thresholds and power to detect change*
- *OPTIONAL: identify responses to a breach of the thresholds*

make final choice of indicators
- *develop a detailed protocol for each indicator*
- *measure indicators to establish a baseline*
- *OPTIONAL: aggregate indicators into overall measures*

develop a data management system   **develop a reporting and communication plan**

Figure 24.3 Developing a monitoring system for ecological integrity

Source: Choudhury et al (2004, p12)

Case Study 24.2

Evaluating a specific protected area: Measuring the ecological integrity of the Serengeti ecosystem

A multi-step process (see Figure 24.4) is currently being developed to monitor the ecological integrity of the Serengeti ecosystem as part of the Enhancing our Heritage project. The monitoring system has been designed to use indicators that capture as much information as possible about different aspects of biodiversity and ecosystem functioning, without costing an unrealistic amount or taking too much time. This approach has been developed from The Nature Conservancy (TNC) Enhanced 5-S Framework.

Eight conservation targets (taken from the site management plan) were chosen to be monitored. They were selected to represent the key elements of biodiversity in the Serengeti ecosystem and to provide an overall indication of the health of the ecosystem. These targets are:

1 the migration;
2 the Mara River;
3 riverine forest;
4 acacia woodland;
5 terminalia (*Combretum molle/Terminalia mollis*) woodland;
6 *kopje* habitat;
7 black rhinos (*Diceros bicornis*); and
8 wild dogs (*Lycaon pictus*).

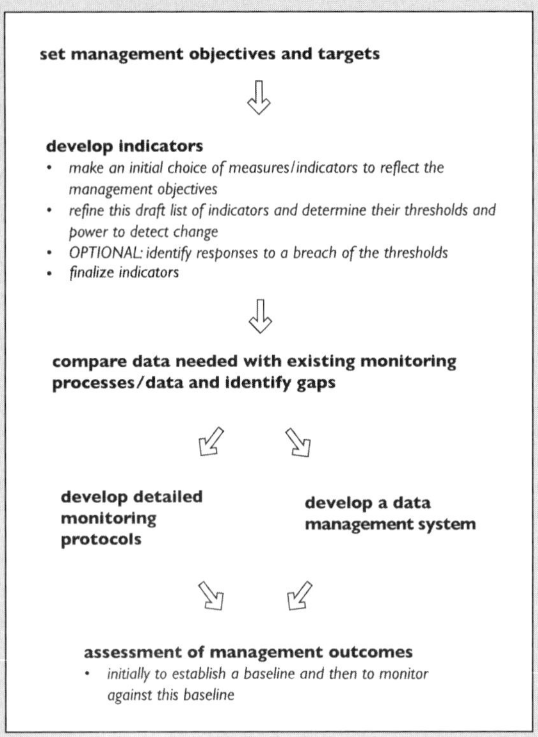

Indicators have been provisionally chosen for monitoring both the key ecological attributes of the targets and the most serious threats facing the targets. For example, for the black rhino (conservation target 7), key ecological attributes or status indicators are suitable habitat, population and productivity. Threats indicators chosen for the black rhino are poaching, unviable population size, in-breeding, human disturbance and availability of secure habitats. The monitoring plan then outlines in detail how and when each indicator will be monitored. For example, the black rhino numbers will be monitored daily by ranger observations in the Rhino Conservation Area. Other conservation targets are subject to less intensive monitoring, such as terminalia woodland, where ground counts of oribi (*Ourebia ourebi*) will be conducted every three years. Examples of the programme for measurement of indicators relating to these two conservation targets are:

- Indicator: increase in poaching mortality;
- Targets: black rhino threat – poaching; and
- Justification for selection: numbers have declined through poaching.

- Indicator: oribi density;
- Targets: terminalia woodland key ecological attributes – herbivores of woodland; and
- Justification for selection: this species is only found in these woodlands.

Source: adapted from Mwangomo et al (2005)

Figure 24.4 Steps taken to develop a monitoring plan for the Serengeti ecosystem

Source: Mwangomo et al (2005)

An ecological monitoring plan has recently been developed and applied at Serengeti National Park, Tanzania

Source: Marc Hockings

including three based on the WCPA framework, are outlined below. Depending upon available time, resources and the objectives of evaluation, processes range from complex to simple and cheap. While most of the developmental work on management effectiveness evaluation was carried out in terrestrial (especially forest) protected areas (TPAs), work in marine protected areas is now accelerating, and additional guidance on relevant indicators and monitoring programmes for marine environments has been prepared (Pomeroy et al, 2004; Day et al, 2003c). Case Study 24.3 provides an example of the application of evaluation in marine protected areas.

World Bank/WWF management effectiveness tracking tool

The World Bank/WWF Alliance for Forest Conservation and Sustainable Use has developed a simple site-level questionnaire-based assessment system for tracking progress in management effectiveness (Stolton et al, 2003). The methodology is designed to provide a relatively quick, easy and

consistent system for reporting progress on management effectiveness in a diverse range of protected areas. It enables protected area managers to identify key trends and issues for protected areas in a region. It is not, however, designed to replace more thorough methods of monitoring and assessment for the purposes of adaptive management. The tracking tool has been applied in over 300 protected areas in 40 countries. Key findings are summarized in Case Study 24.1.

Rapid Assessment and Prioritization of Protected Areas Management (RAPPAM) methodology

WWF International has developed and field tested a tool for assessing the management effectiveness of protected area systems at a national level by collecting and comparing information on all or most of the sites within a country or region (Ervin, 2003b). Evaluation consists of five steps: determining the scope of assessment; reviewing available information; a workshop-based assessment using the *Rapid Assessment Questionnaire*;

Case Study 24.3

Evaluating management effectiveness in the Great Barrier Reef Marine Park, Australia

Jon Day, Great Barrier Reef Marine Park Authority (GBRMPA), Australia

In 2002, over 50 monitoring/assessment programmes were under way in the Great Barrier Reef Marine Park (GBRMP) in Australia across a broad range of physical, biological and socio-economic areas (see examples in Table 24.2). Most programmes were very task specific and were undertaken as 'stand-alone' monitoring or research tasks.

Table 24.2 Examples of specific evaluation assessments undertaken in the Great Barrier Reef Marine Park (GBRMP), Australia

Type of evaluation	Description
Reactive Monitoring Report for Great Barrier Reef World Heritage Area	Annual report (2000–2002) to World Heritage Committee on five priority action areas
Long-term monitoring of key organisms across the Great Barrier Reef	Annual monitoring of status and natural variability of corals, algae and reef fishes from 48 reefs, as well as the crown of thorns starfish (*Acanthaster planci*) from 100 reefs
Environmental effects of prawn trawling in the Great Barrier Reef	Five-year study into the effects of trawling on seabed communities in the far northern section of the Great Barrier Reef
Audit of performance of *East Coast Trawl Management Plan*	Audit of *East Coast Trawl Management Plan* to examine how well trawl fishery is managed against the ecologically sustainable development objectives of Queensland fisheries legislation
Effects of sea dumping on nearby fringing reefs and seagrasses	Reactive monitoring programme with decision thresholds to manage the effects of port dredging and dumping on nearby corals and seagrasses
Cooperative Research Centre project on the effects of line fishing	Ten-year assessment of fish stocks following baseline surveys and manipulations of closure strategies

While some of these programmes can assess the effectiveness of specific management actions, few provide an integrated assessment of the overall state of the entire marine park or enable broad-scale public reporting.

In an attempt to move towards a more holistic marine protected area-wide evaluation, the Great Barrier Reef Marine Park Authority (GBRMPA) has developed key performance indicators derived from the main objectives of the authority's goal. These key performance indicators are not intended to replace any of the more detailed monitoring assessments, but do provide a more 'broad-brush' evaluation in a form useful for public reporting. Simple graphs showing trends with these key performance indicators appear in the agency's annual reports. The key performance indicators also provide a systematic basis against which the agency's budget statement is presented annually to parliament.

Key lessons learned from this approach include the following:

- Clear linkages need to be established between the GBRMPA's goal, the critical issues facing the GBRMP and the key performance indicators.

- Only one broad key performance indicator per desired outcome is necessary for broad public reporting.
- Relatively simple key performance indicators were chosen for one or more of the following reasons:
  - already being monitored – therefore, able to show trends from existing data sets;
  - easily understood by decision-makers; and
  - show either a positive trend (indicating management is working) or indicate clear need for continuing management actions.

Other techniques for management effectiveness have been variously applied within parts of the GBRMP. The World Commission on Protected Areas (WCPA)/IUCN Management Effectiveness Framework has been applied in a rapid dot-point assessment to one key aspect of management in the GBRMP: the recent major re-zoning programme, known as the Representative Areas Programme (RAP), which came into effect in July 2004. The evaluation used a combination of quantitative assessments (for example, overall increase from <5 per cent to >33 per cent in 'no-take' zones) and qualitative assessments (for example, huge increase in public awareness and increased international recognition of the RAP planning process) to summarize the overall effectiveness of this specific management approach.

The World Bank MPA Score Card System approach was applied in 2004 against the specified criteria developed by Staub and Hatziolos (2004). Scores indicating achievements for the GBRMP, overall, against the six management elements are:

- context – score 22/26;
- planning – score 14/14;
- process – score 20/25;
- inputs – score 11/14;
- outputs – score 31/33; and
- outcomes – score 21/27.

The scoring had the real advantage of being very quick, yet useful. The overall final score 119/139 (= 86 per cent) is relatively high by global standards. The rapid assessment was useful in indicating where improvements were desirable, including:

- better integrated research and monitoring relevant to management needs;
- improved mechanisms for controlling unsustainable human activities;
- improved stakeholder awareness;
- increased stakeholder participation in management decision-making; and
- indigenous/traditional people directly participating in management decision-making.

The *State of the Reef* report is a dynamic web-based product that allows the GBRMPA to continuously update information and increase user flexibility and access to information. It is available on the GBRMPA website: www.gbrmpa.gov.au/corp_site/info_services/publications/sotr/index.html.

Some of the challenges regarding evaluating management effectiveness within the GBRMP include:

- problems of 'shifting baselines';
- difficulties of monitoring a dynamic marine ecosystem; and
- maintenance of ecological integrity and natural processes within limits or ranges of variation that are considered 'acceptable' or 'desirable'.

Establishing an effective and appropriate evaluation system has met several challenges. Some monitoring methodologies require destructive sampling/killing of individual species, often at a questionable level of appropriateness in a World Heritage area. New non-destructive sampling practices (such as baited remote underwater videos) have been developed by the Australian Institute of Marine Science, which assist monitoring while minimizing the damaging side effects. There is also a need for complementary monitoring outside of the GBRMP to understand the wider context, as well as more social/economic evaluation and monitoring to enable sound decision-making (the 'triple bottom line' approach to monitoring and reporting).

The GBRMP is not a typical marine protected area because of its enormous size and complexity. Nevertheless, like most marine protected areas, the evaluation of management effectiveness still has a way to go before it becomes totally integrated within the adaptive management cycle.

Identifying threats at a management effectiveness evaluation workshop in Serengeti National Park, Tanzania

Source: Marc Hockings

analysing findings; and making recommendations. The results allow comparisons to be made across sites with the intention of:

- identifying management strengths and weaknesses;
- analysing threats and pressures;
- identifying areas of high ecological and social importance and vulnerability;
- indicating the urgency and conservation priority for individual protected areas; and
- helping to improve management effectiveness at the site and system level.

The process involves park staff, local communities, scientists and NGOs. The methodology has been applied in over 850 protected areas in countries such as China, South Africa, Bhutan, Georgia, Lao and Russia. The objectives of assessment were developed individually for each country. Detailed case studies for each area were then used to improve management in ways such as conservation planning, priority-setting and increasing focus on threatened areas (Ervin, 2003a).

Enhancing our heritage: Monitoring and managing for success in natural world heritage sites

A monitoring and assessment toolkit based on the WCPA framework has been developed to help managers and stakeholders assess current management activities, identify gaps and discuss how problems might be addressed (Hockings et al, 2005). It was developed as part of a United Nations Foundation/IUCN/United Nations Educational, Scientific and Cultural Organization

(UNESCO) project to improve monitoring and evaluation, and management of natural World Heritage sites and is being applied in pilot natural World Heritage sites in South Asia, Latin America and Southern and Eastern Africa. The workbook is designed for use in all natural World Heritage sites and can be adapted for different protected areas.

Indicators and tools for assessing each component of the WCPA framework are presented in a workbook that can be used by managers (with appropriate adaptation to suit site needs) to develop a comprehensive assessment system (Hockings et al, 2005). The assessment tools focus on identifying and monitoring the main values (biodiversity, social, economic and cultural) of the site to ensure that appropriate objectives for these values have been set and that management is achieving these objectives (see Case Study 24.2 for application of ecological monitoring at one of the Enhancing our Heritage sites). Together, they enable a picture of the management effectiveness of the site to be developed. The tools are outlined in Table 24.3, grouped according to the six elements of the WCPA framework.

PROARCA/CAPAS and WWF/CATIE methodologies

Both the WWF/Central American Tropical Agricultural Centre for Research and Education (CATIE) (Cifuentes et al, 2000) and Programa Ambiental Regional para Centroamaerica (PROARCA) Central American Protected Area System (CAPAS) (Courrau, 1999) methodologies for evaluating management of protected areas have been developed and tested over a number of years within Latin America. These methodologies involve scoring systems based on a hierarchy of indicators of different aspects of management performance. For each indicator used, a number of conditions are established – the optimum condition being given the maximum value. Results are presented in the form of a percentage of the maximum obtainable score. This can be calculated as an overall figure for the protected area or as scores for each field of activity, and can be presented in matrix format. The methodologies focus principally on management inputs and process, with some assessment of management outputs and outcomes.

Table 24.3 Evaluation tools for measuring each World Commission on Protected Areas (WCPA) framework element

WCPA framework element	Evaluation tools
Context	Tool 1: Identifying management values and objectives
	Tool 2: Identifying threats
	Tools 3a and 3b: Relationships with stakeholders/partners
	Tool 4: Review of national context
Planning	Tool 5: Assessment of management planning
	Tool 6: Design assessment
Inputs	Tool 7: Assessment of management needs and inputs
Process	Tool 8: Assessment of management processes
Outputs	Tool 9: Assessment of management plan implementation
	Tool 10: Work/site output indicators
Outcomes	Tool 11: Monitoring the outcomes of management

Source: Hockings et al (2005)

5-S Framework for Conservation Project Management

The Nature Conservancy (TNC) has developed a computerized tool to assist park managers and evaluators in assessing the effectiveness of conservation (TNC, 2002). The 5-S Framework is the planning mechanism that TNC uses throughout its portfolio of projects and sites and is based around five main steps:

1 *systems* (identifying a limited set of ecological targets);
2 *stresses* (the elements that impact upon biodiversity);
3 *sources* (the causes of stresses);
4 *strategies* (actions to address the stresses); and
5 *success measures*.

It begins with the identification of key biodiversity and ecological attributes of the area. For these key attributes, indicators are identified that allow the area's biodiversity health to be measured. The status of the indicator is then rated on a four-point scale – poor, fair, good and very good. The rating can then be integrated to rate biodiversity integrity overall.

Measures of success: Designing, managing and monitoring conservation and development projects

A conservation practitioner's guide on how to do project-level adaptive management centres on incorporating research within conservation action (Margoluis and Salafsky, 1998). Specifically, it is the integration of design, management and monitoring to systematically test assumptions in order to adapt and learn. It includes a framework of specific conditions that warrants an adaptive management approach, steps for the process of adaptive management and principles for the practice of adaptive management. Conditions and principles for adaptive management suggest that natural systems are complex in a changing environment, that information will never be complete and that there is always opportunity to learn and improve, especially if a learning environment is created (Margoluis and Salafsky, 2001). The steps for adaptive management are outlined in Figure 11.2 in Chapter 11.

Guidelines for evaluating management effectiveness

Based on experience in management effectiveness evaluation over the past decade, a number of general guidelines have been developed (Leverington and Hockings, 2004). These guidelines began from a discussion held at an international workshop in Australia in February 2003 in preparation for the Workshop on Management Effectiveness Evaluation held at the Vth IUCN World Parks Congress in Durban, and were refined after Durban (see Box 24.2) The guidelines following are grouped according to relevant aspects of evaluation.

Support and participation

Effective evaluation needs a high level of support and commitment from protected area management organizations (especially organization leaders) and important stakeholders. This is essential if evaluation is to be integrated within management so that it becomes an accepted and integral part of doing business.

Box 24.2 Workshop on evaluating management effectiveness, Vth IUCN World Parks Congress, Durban 2003

Many methodologies have been developed for assessing management effectiveness of protected areas since the issue was raised at the IVth IUCN World Parks Congress in 1992. The World Commission on Protected Areas (WCPA) has made an important contribution through the development of a framework that provides a general approach and guidelines for assessing management effectiveness, as well as a system for developing specific assessment methodologies. The aim of this workshop in Durban was to present a comprehensive examination of the status of management effectiveness evaluations, including principles, methods, applications and current issues. The workshop covered four broad themes:

Box 24.2 Continued

- reviewing experience with management effectiveness evaluation over the last ten years and distilling lessons learned;
- the use of indicators and methods for assessing specific aspects of protected area management, such as ecological integrity, engagement with local communities, management of marine protected areas, and various social and economic aspects of protected area management;
- addressing threats through monitoring and evaluation, focusing particularly on the unsustainable harvesting of bush meat, alien invasive species and climate change; and
- discussion of work in progress on the definition of standards and possible certification schemes for protected area management.

Reviewing the experiences and use of different methodologies and indicators

Participants recognized the need for some harmonization of standards and indicators across systems. The WCPA Management Effectiveness Evaluation Framework provides a starting point for this harmonization; but there is still much to be learned about the most relevant, useful and reliable indicators and assessment methods.

It was also strongly recognized that evaluation benefits from long-term commitment and use of a consistent methodology so that data is comparable over time. To be effective, monitoring programmes must become part of core business for a protected area management organization. It is also necessary to commit resources to responses that flow from the assessments.

It was emphasized that there was a need to use good science for management effectiveness evaluations. This is particularly important for assessing ecological integrity. Other requirements are the need to include social and cultural elements, such as traditional ecological knowledge, in the design, implementation and reporting of management effectiveness evaluations.

Threats

The identification and abatement of threats is a key component of the effective management of protected areas. Participants stressed the need to recognize that threats occur at multiple spatial and temporal scales, and occur beyond the boundaries of protected areas. Addressing individual threats is complicated by the compounding and often unanticipated effects of multiple threats operating together. Assessments of management effectiveness are improving our understanding of threats facing protected areas. Other potential threats, such as those arising from genetically modified organisms, have hardly even been identified in the context of protected areas.

Standards and certification of protected area management

Emerging issues of standards and certification were considered, dealing with issues of the certification of protected area category assignment and the development of standards for, and possible certification of, management effectiveness. Support for more work on both concepts was expressed, with encouragement for the WCPA to move forward with the investigation and testing of these approaches in partnership with other relevant institutions.

Outcomes from the congress workshop

Specific work programme proposals were developed and endorsed for future work on management effectiveness evaluation and incorporated within the World Parks Congress Recommendations (Recommendation V.18), the *Durban Action Plan* and the *Message to the Convention on Biological Diversity*. The discussions at the World Parks Congress workshop on evaluating management effectiveness influenced the Convention on Biological Diversity (CBD) Protected Area Programme of Work adopted at the meeting of the Conference of the Parties (COP 7) to the CBD held in Kuala Lumpur in February 2004 (see Appendix 4).

Source: Hockings et al (2004) and IUCN (2005b)

Good communication is essential from the beginning of the evaluation and at all stages throughout. Evaluation always involves a group of people, including, at a minimum, the evaluators and management agency staff, and usually a range of other stakeholders. Building a team with the evaluators and the participants is also important. In most cases, the evaluation process should be regarded as a team effort to obtain positive change, rather than as a potentially threatening and punitive process.

Purpose, objectives and scope

Often, an evaluation process can be designed to fulfil several purposes. Objectives of the evaluation should be clearly defined since these will influence both design and implementation. Expected levels of resourcing and support should also be outlined; finally, an implementation plan should be developed.

The scope and scale of the evaluation need to be established at the outset. The scope of evaluation can be very broad (the evaluation of all aspects of management) or specific (for example, looking at how effective a particular community engagement programme or invasive pest-control initiative has been). The scope should also specify whether this is a one-off evaluation, a time-bound evaluation (for example, over the life of a short-term project) or the establishment of a continuing programme.

The scale can vary from system wide (or even embracing a number of national systems) to a specific protected area or a location. Evaluations of broad scale and scope can provide vital information for management at high levels, such as system wide resource prioritization, advocacy and policy directions.

Localized or issue-specific evaluations are useful for improving management at a practical on-ground level. In practice, an evaluation programme for a large or complex protected area will consist of a number of monitoring and evaluation projects operating at differing scales and with different objectives (see, for example, Case Study 24.3). Integrating these within a coherent programme is frequently a challenge.

Methods

Once the objectives, scope and scale have been clarified, the primary aspects of developing an evaluation methodology are:

- selecting the evaluation team;
- defining the questions or indicators (see Case Study 24.2 for examples of ecological indicators);
- choosing how to obtain information (literature studies, interviews, questionnaires, observations, scientific studies and so on);
- deciding how the information will be analysed and reported; and
- considering how to apply the information to meet the evaluation objectives.

Designing a methodology for evaluation can be a daunting task for managers. However, there has been a great deal of thought put into existing methodologies, and the use or adaptation of these can save considerable resources and allow comparability of results between projects or sites. For example, a guidebook for evaluating marine protected areas has been developed, based on the WCPA framework (IUCN, 2003b).

Adopting a methodology does not mean that all of the indicators, survey methods or reporting proformas of a previous project need to be used. These can be tailored to fit specific requirements. Methodologies can be improved over time, although changes will lessen the comparability of results, so should be carefully considered. The methodology used should be as simple as possible, repeatable and transparent. Limitations to the process, including knowledge gaps, must always be identified. There is a danger that evaluations can oversimplify reality by interpreting indicators to mean more than they really do. In summary, methods should be:

- cost effective – if they are too expensive they will not be adopted;
- replicable – to allow comparability across sites and times;
- simple – very complex tools can alienate field staff and stakeholders;
- statistically valid – they must be able to withstand scrutiny;
- field tested – pilot studies before major projects are essential;

Tourists observing wildlife in Serengeti National Park, Tanzania

Source: Marc Hockings

- documented in manuals or other formats so they can be reviewed;
- credible, honest and non-corrupt – the results need to be shown to be genuine and data gaps must be identified;
- congruent with management and community expectations; and
- rapid – the evaluation process should draw on and review longer-term monitoring, where possible, but should not be overly time consuming.

Analysis and reporting

Results of evaluations can be simply tabulated, compared across time or areas, or analysed more thoroughly to answer complex questions. The general aim is to understand what is happening within a management programme and what is contributing to its success or failure. However, protected area management is complex, making it difficult to attribute causes to results, whether good or bad (for example, is the death of the forest patch due to inappropriate burning regimes, an unknown pathogen, a natural cycle or a combination of all of these factors?). One approach is to examine causal links between the different elements in the management cycle. For example, inadequate staff numbers (input) and poor organization of their work programme (process) may decrease their output and their ability to achieve management objectives (outcomes).

The way in which evaluation findings are reported must suit the intended audiences. Methods of presentation, language and terminology used in collecting and reporting evaluations should be commonly understandable. Methods of communication include reports in hard copy and on the internet, attractive publications to increase public interest, presentations to managers and other stakeholders, media coverage and displays.

Assessment reports should identify the strengths and weaknesses of management and make recommendations.

Applying results

The evaluation process itself is a vital learning experience, which often has impacts upon management. Getting people together to talk about management and to focus on key issues provides a valuable opportunity for increased understanding and the exchange of different viewpoints.

The findings and recommendations of evaluation also need to feed back formally into management systems in order to influence future planning, resource allocations and management actions. Evaluations that are fully integrated within a managing agency's process are more successful in improving long-term management performance.

Management principles

1 Evaluation of management effectiveness is essential for responsive, proactive protected area management.
2 Assessment of each element of protected area management and the links between them will obtain the most comprehensive picture of management effectiveness.
3 Evaluation works best with a clear plan that features a clear purpose, scope and objectives.
4 Existing methodologies can be adapted for new evaluations.
5 Methodologies should be repeatable, as simple and rapid as possible, and relatively cheap.
6 Consistent methodology and long-term commitment enables data to be compared over time.
7 It is essential to use good science for management effectiveness evaluation. This is especially important for ecological integrity that is often the core element of protected area management.
8 Measuring and addressing multiple threats is a key component of effective protected area management.
9 Management effectiveness evaluation must involve appropriate stakeholders – including indigenous and local communities, on-ground park staff, NGOs and experts – in all phases, from design to adoption of recommendations. Evaluations must listen to the needs of local people and staff, and suggest appropriate responses to these needs.
10 Questions and indicators need to be relevant to the objectives of the project and be cost effective. Indicators should have some explanatory power or be able to link with other indicators to explain causes and effects.
11 Evaluation works best where it is considered core business for an organization with a high level of support.
12 Evaluation requires adequate mechanisms, capacity and resources to address the findings and recommendations.
13 Evaluation findings must be reported back. This enables adaptive management – feeding the results of research and monitoring into on-ground management and providing a basis for decision-making.

Further reading

Department of Environment and Conservation (2005) *State of the Parks 2004*, Department of Environment and Conservation, Sydney

Dudley, N., Belokurov, A., Borodin, O., Higgins-Zogib, L., Hockings, M., Lacerda, L. and Stoloton, S. (2004) *Are Protected Areas Working? An Analysis of Forest Protected Areas by WWF*, WWF International, Gland

Hockings, M., Stolton, S., Dudley, N., Courrau, J. and Parrish, J. (2005) *The World Heritage Management Effectiveness Workbook: How to Build Monitoring, Assessment and Reporting Systems to Improve the Management Effectiveness of Natural World Heritage Sites*, revised edition, UNESCO, Paris, and IUCN, Gland and Cambridge, www.enhancingheritage.net/docs_public.asp

Hockings, M., Stolton, S., Leverington, F., Dudley, N. and Courrau, J. (in press) *Evaluating Effectiveness: A Framework for Assessing the Management of Protected Areas* (2nd Edition), IUCN, Gland and Cambridge

Leverington, F. and Hockings, M. (2004) 'Evaluating the effectiveness of protected area management: the challenge of change', in Barber, C. V., Miller, K. R. and Boness, M. (eds) *Securing Protected Areas in the Face of Global Change: Issues and Strategies*, IUCN, Gland and Cambridge

Pomeroy, R. S., Parks, J. E. and Watson, L. M. (2004)

How Is Your MPA Doing? A Guidebook of Natural and Social Indicators for Evaluating Marine Protected Area Management Effectiveness, IUCN WCPA Marine Programme, Gland and Cambridge

Websites

Rapid Assessment and Prioritization of Protected Areas Management (RAPPAM): www.panda.org/about_wwf/what_we_do/forests/our_solutions/protection/tools/rappam/index.cfm

The Nature Conservancy Five-S Framework: www.consci.org/scp

World Bank/World Wide Fund for Nature (WWF) tracking tool: www.panda.org/about_wwf/what_we_do/forests/our_solutions/protection/tools/tracking_tool.cfm

25

Building Support for Protected Areas

Jeffrey A. McNeely, Michael Lockwood and Juliet Chapman

The Convention on Biological Diversity (CBD) has marked a significant shift in the perception of protected areas by governments. It has linked protected areas to larger issues of public concern, such as sustainable development, traditional knowledge, access to genetic resources, national sovereignty, equitable sharing of benefits and intellectual property rights. Protected area managers are now sharing a larger and more important political stage with agricultural scientists, NGOs, anthropologists, ethnobiologists, lawyers, economists, pharmaceutical firms, farmers, foresters, tourism agencies, the oil industry, indigenous peoples, and many others. These competing groups claim resources, powers and privileges through a political decision-making process in which biologists, local communities (including indigenous peoples), the private sector and conservationists have become inextricably embroiled (McNeely and Guruswamy, 1998). The challenge is to find ways for the various stakeholders to work together most effectively in order to achieve the conservation and development objectives of modern society.

Institutions and individuals having a direct, significant and specific stake in a protected area may originate from geographical proximity, historical association, dependence for livelihood, institutional mandate, economic interest, or a variety of other concerns. However, these 'stakeholders' are united in being aware of their own interests in managing the protected area, and in possessing specific capacities or comparative advantages for such management, as well as a willingness to invest specific resources – such as time, money or political authority – for such management (Borrini-Feyerabend, 1997). The different stakeholders generally have different interests, ways of perceiving problems and opportunities about the protected area, and approaches to protected area management.

The list of potential stakeholders in any given protected area or protected area system is a long one. It can include:

- agencies with legal jurisdiction over the protected area, at municipal, provincial or national level;
- individuals, families and households (for example, landowners within or around a protected area, or people living in cities who care about protected areas);
- community-based groups (such as water co-operatives and neighbourhood associations);
- local traditional authorities (such as village councils of elders or traditional chiefs);
- political authorities prescribed by national laws (including elected representatives at village or district levels);
- local governmental service providers (such as health, education, forestry and agriculture extension);
- NGOs dedicated to the environment or development at local, national and international levels;

- businesses and commercial enterprises (local, national or international);
- universities and research organizations;
- national governments; and
- the international community, including other governments and intergovernmental bodies (Borrini-Feyerabend and Brown, 1997).

Building support and understanding is crucial for the sustainability of protected areas and their management. A wider and deeper advocacy from stakeholders is essential for securing legitimacy and credibility, as well as the necessary political and financial support. In this chapter, we consider the ways in which protected area managers can secure and extend such support from key stakeholder groups.

Private commercial-sector support

Private sector activities have profound influences on biodiversity through the use of resources, trading patterns, marketing and a range of cultural influences. Numerous private sector investors are already deeply involved in biodiversity – exploiting, holding or controlling extensive areas of land important for conservation; managing important wildlife habitats; promoting bio-prospecting; carrying out biodiversity-related research; and supporting conservation efforts in the field.

Many industries are becoming much more 'green'; they want to promote a positive corporate image among the public, and a link with conservation can help them do so. Some are even starting to see biodiversity as a focus for profitable investment and therefore can become useful potential partners for protected areas (as well as posing the threat of inappropriate development) (IUCN and WBCSD, 1997). Other motivations for private sector involvement in biodiversity include access to capital (as more and more investors require sound environmental performance, and pension funds favour leaders in a sector), access to markets (for example, organic and certified products) and environmental security (such as protection from flooding or changes in the micro-climate). Understanding the full range of business drivers

becomes particularly important when approaching a company for support – it is essential to suggest to a business how they would benefit.

The trend towards the greening of commerce is most strongly seen in high Human Development Index (HDI) countries; but many low and medium HDI countries are seeking to promote rapid economic expansion, with the consequences that the local business sector will increasingly have the resources to invest in conservation and the emerging consumer class will have the interest, influence and resources to support national conservation efforts (Naisbitt, 1995; ADB, 1997). Building on these trends leads to a focus on identifying incentives for the private sector to play a greater role in providing financial and other forms of support to protected areas, including through active involvement in management.

Already, the International Chamber of Commerce (ICC), the World Business Council for Sustainable Development (WBCSD) and the World Travel and Tourism Council (WTTC) provide business leadership for change towards sustainable development and promote high standards of environmental and resource management in business. Many individual companies are working on innovative approaches to ensure that their activities preserve fragile ecosystems, even when mineral extraction is involved (see Case Study 25.1). This is not to deny that some corporations may not be genuine in their support for conservation, and use sustainability rhetoric to mask a 'business as usual' approach. However, there are clear indications that, although many private commercial interests still fail to integrate environmental responsibility within their operations, at least some are willing and able to contribute more to protected areas, provided that protected area managers and government can provide the policy and management frameworks that will support and encourage their contributions.

Numerous options for private sector involvement in various aspects of protected areas are available. Which ones are adopted will depend upon the interests of the commercial firm, the opportunities available and the policy climate created by government. Options can include:

Case Study 25.1

Mining company support for Bushmanland Conservation Initiative, South Africa

In the Bushmanland region, located on the north-east margin of the Succulent Karoo hotspot, just south of the Orange River and the border between Namibia and South Africa, two initiatives in 2002 turned initial disagreement between mining company Anglo American and conservationists into one of cooperation. The first was the International Council on Mining and Metals Initiative under which Anglo American, as a member, states that it respects legally designated protected areas and will work with others in developing best practice guidance to enhance its contribution to biodiversity conservation, including in and around protected areas. The second was the launch of the Succulent Karoo Ecosystem Programme. These two initiatives were both important in Anglo's understanding of its role not just in minimizing impacts, but also in playing a direct and positive role as a custodian of large tracts of biodiversity-rich land. A new partnership was established between conservation groups, local landowners and the mining company, called the Bushmanland Conservation Initiative.

The Bushmanland region is a priority conservation area identified in the Succulent Karoo Ecosystem Programme. The ancient rocky outcrops known as *inselbergs* that dominate Bushmanland are home to a rich and unique variety of succulent and geophyte plants. In 2002, it had no formal protected area status.

However the Bushmanland Conservation Initiative is working on creating a 60,000ha protected area in the Succulent Karoo biodiversity hotspot, supported by a commitment by Anglo Base Metals for both in-kind donations and future collaboration on conservation. Anglo Base Metals provided co-funding for the first phase of the initiative (18 months) in the form of office space, accommodation for three employees, use of their facilitates and 40,000 South African rand per annum for printing, photocopying and maintenance. The focus is to conserve Bushmanland's biodiversity in this globally unique arid land by establishing protected areas on private land. It is envisaged that the protected areas will be nested within a multi use landscape, including stock farming, mining and ecotourism. The project has focused on new ways of helping local landowners (mining companies, commercial farmers and communal farmers) become stewards of the land and place important areas aside for conservation.

Source: adapted from ICMM (2005) and Botha (pers comm, 2005)

- developing policies that commit to keeping critical wildlife habitats off-limits to certain industrial development activities;
- managing land adjacent to protected areas, such as timber, petroleum or mining concessions, in ways that contribute to the objectives of the protected area;
- providing funding to protected areas, either as a donation or as a means of mitigating the environmental impacts of their activities;
- providing professionally qualified experts in fields such as finance, personnel management, tourism and concession management;
- providing support to forested protected areas targeted at maintaining the carbon-storage capacity of the site;
- paying fees or royalties for prospecting for medicinal plants or other valuable genetic resources;
- providing various kinds of facilities related to tourism in protected areas that pay concession

fees, which can support park management;
- providing logistics support, such as the donation of the use of a helicopter or light airplane for inventory and monitoring; and
- paying for services provided by protected areas, such as protection of a watershed that provides high-quality water to a nearby industry.

While the market system is already providing a range of benefits, it is also leading to over-exploitation in many cases, and considerable challenges face those who are seeking to achieve sustainable use. Thus, expanding the role of the private commercial sector in protected areas carries some risks. These can include at least the following:

- The private commercial sector seeks to maximize profits, so it may tend to focus operations on locations where profits are the highest and seek opportunities to avoid paying rents and other forms of compensation. Because most private firms have no long-term ties to the protected area, their commitment may weaken as time goes by. In addition, market-driven economics fails to capture all of the public interest and intangible values embodied in protected areas.

- Large corporations in the agriculture, forest or fisheries sectors owned by distant shareholders (many of them in foreign countries) and managed out of central offices are unlikely to have great interest in enhancing the biodiversity that exists in a particular setting, or in safeguarding or respecting the rights of indigenous peoples and local communities in the area.
- Even where private sector commitment to conservation is present, it may disadvantage or undermine the rights of indigenous peoples and local communities (as has happened, for example, with some ecotourism ventures and privately managed protected areas).
- In the case of tourism, it may be difficult to control quality of service to the public, while the public assumes the tourism operation is government run. Leasing or granting concession rights may result in political pressures to increase the type and availability of certain services that are inconsistent with the objectives of the protected area.
- Inappropriate commercialization of protected areas is a danger that requires constant vigilance. For example, a private firm established a seaweed farm in Tubbataha Reefs National Marine Park in the Philippines without a permit. It tried to gain support by involving the provincial government in the project and securing the approval of key local government officials. Such developments were clearly contrary to the objectives of the park and its international status as a World Heritage area.
- Many of the problems of protected areas are driven by powerful economic forces that yield high short-term economic profits to selected commercial interests, with society at large paying the very considerable costs. For example, Cesar (1996) found that the total net losses due to threats to coral reefs – poison fishing,

blast fishing, mining, sedimentation and over-fishing – in Indonesia carried net losses to society of 2.3 to 8.2 times greater than the net benefits to commercial interests.
- Public-sector protected area managers must also take care that relationships with the private sector do not afford corporations undue influence over management decisions or quell the potential for critical comment on company performance.

Working with nature can be an economically attractive option for the private sector and could encourage industries to be more willing to consider other investments in protected areas. To give one example, Western Mining Corporation, one of Australia's largest mining companies, has donated Aus\$120,000 to the Department of Conservation and Land Management (CALM) to build a research and management centre on Penguin Island, Western Australia, that will become a regional base for important marine, island and coastal research. CALM and several academic institutions have ongoing research projects based on Penguin Island's plants and animals as part of Shore Water Islands Marine Park (6545ha).

Attracting such private sector investment for protected areas can be facilitated by identifying and prioritizing specific areas as targets for private sector financing, while putting in place safeguards against the above listed risks. Efforts should be made to create biodiversity investment opportunities that will appeal directly to the financial instincts of the various interests within the private sector, ranging from tourism to energy to genetic resources. If suitable incentives can be provided to enterprises to assume a certain degree of financial risk, a wide range of private investments could be secured by protected area managers. Encouraging investment will require an accessible framework for providing information, structuring negotiations and ensuring project security.

Protected areas potentially can provide benefits in the form of genetic resources to the pharmaceutical, biotechnology, agrochemical, seed, horticulture, cosmetic and phyto-medical markets; but these different markets give rise to a wide range of approaches to benefit-sharing.

Creating expensive bureaucratic regulatory systems – for example, to implement the genetic resources provisions of the CBD (Articles 15 and 16) – could act as a disincentive to investment by the industries that have the greatest potential interest in the biological resources held by protected areas. One approach is through the use of intermediaries, including botanic gardens, universities, research institutions, NGOs and even commercial brokers, who will collect, identify and guarantee re-supply of promising materials; acquire government approval for collections; broker benefit-sharing agreements; and ensure that any benefits arising are shared fairly and equitably in the source country. Benefits are likely to be maximized when the governments create incentives for new, varied and equitable partnerships based on the use of biological resources.

The critical factor in enabling the private commercial sector to contribute more effectively to protected areas is for governments to devise policy frameworks appropriate to their country that will allow consistent and realistic goals to be developed and met, with a clear distribution of costs and benefits; for example, tax breaks or other economic incentives for contributions to protected areas could generate greater private sector support. As pointed out by the CBD, each government needs to determine for itself how best to carry out the broad objectives for which protected areas have been established and how it wishes to involve the private sector. But it is clear that such policies must be based on an integrated view of the economy, society and the environment, incorporating good science and assessment of risk, and an appropriate balance of ecological, economic and social objectives.

University and research organization support

Given the increasing demands on protected areas to deliver more benefits to society, partnerships between researchers and protected area managers have become crucial. Research, often carried out by universities and research institutes, provides managers with vital information on the social characteristics of resident and neighbouring communities; the presence or absence of species and their ecological requirements; the geophysical

characteristics of the area; the economic potential of various resources and activities; new interpretations of cultural resource material; trends in ecosystem change; and so forth. On the other hand, researchers are often attracted to protected areas that provide relatively controlled settings for their scientific work, calling on the logistical and political support of protected area managers. Research also often gains in relevancy from the practical discipline imposed upon it by real-life management constraints (Harmon, 1994).

However, in most countries science is not making the contribution to protected area management that is really required. It is difficult to obtain current information about status and trends of habitats and key species within them: information that is essential to protected area management. Furthermore, relatively little research is being done on critical social and economic issues affecting protected areas, including valuation of ecosystem services, impacts of protected areas on rural populations and even such basic parameters as numbers of visitors to protected areas. One of the most important gaps may be the linkage between conservation, sustainable use and development. Inadequate understanding of this very complex area is already impeding the ability to effectively conserve biological diversity and reap its many as yet untapped benefits (Glowka et al, 1994). Another concerns community conserved areas (CCAs) and initiatives, which remain largely undocumented across the world.

For most protected areas systems, most research is carried out by the non-governmental sector, including universities (some of which are government run), research stations, national NGOs and international NGOs. Much of this research is directly relevant to management. Numerous universities have found protected areas to be useful as research sites, and many have made important contributions to protected areas.

International NGOs are also involved in field research. The Wildlife Conservation Society's field division, Wildlife Conservation International (WCI), has the largest field-based research staff of any international conservation organization and its scientists have played direct roles in establishing over 100 protected areas. They have also produced a manual on wildlife field research (Rabinowitz,

1993). WCI is well known for its wildlife surveys that have provided the basis for designing systems of protected areas in Lao PDR and Viet Nam. Its work in China has made important contributions to protected areas designed to conserve the giant panda (*Ailuropoda melanoleuca*) and associated flora and fauna (Schaller et al, 1985; Schaller, 1993). WCI wildlife surveys in Tibet and Xinjiang led directly to the identification of protected areas, including the 4.5 million hectare Arjin Mountains Nature Reserve and the Chang Tang Nature Reserve, at 33 million hectares. Its earlier work in the Himalayas and associated mountain chains identified important areas for wild sheep and goats and their predators, and its work in India set the standard for research on tigers (Schaller, 1967).

The World Wide Fund for Nature (WWF) has provided funds for research on the habitat requirements of pandas, tigers, elephants, rhinos and many others. Birdlife International, with national organizations in many countries, has contributed to protected areas by determining the distribution of species of birds and in identifying 'critical bird areas', which help to identify priorities for protected areas.

The preceding discussion has given a brief indicative overview of research being carried out on biodiversity in protected areas. But, to date, most research is carried out on topics of greatest interest to the researchers themselves, and protected area managers have not taken full advantage of this resource by defining the kinds of research they require. Greater benefits from collaboration between protected area management, universities and research institutions could be promoted through the guidelines given in Box 25.1. Care must be taken to ensure that these guidelines serve as an incentive to research, rather than an obstacle.

One benefit of research in protected areas is that independent researchers often have detailed information on the local situation, tend to be less vulnerable to intimidation by local powers, and tend to have contacts at the central level that can ensure that information reaches those who need it and can put it to effective use (van Schaik and Kramer, 1997).

Research in protected areas is facing some new obstacles. Intellectual property rights issues arising from the CBD have created difficulties for scientists who suddenly find their professional interests or access to genetic resources being addressed through international agreements, rather than conventional scientist-to-scientist exchanges. The basic principle for protected areas should be to provide conditions to encourage research, rather than to discourage it. This need not necessarily imply subsidies to research; but, at the very least, bureaucratic impediments should be avoided, while providing safeguards against misuse of research for commercial purposes.

Increasing pressures on protected areas call for a concerted effort to mobilize additional research in support of protected area management. The extent of research could be significantly increased if greater efforts were made to facilitate collaboration – for example, through accelerating granting of permits and identifying suitable local counterparts, or encouraging indigenous peoples and local communities to take up their own research work with external inputs, where necessary.

For large protected areas with extensive research programmes (such as many biosphere reserves), it will often be useful for a protected area management authority to have on staff a research scientist to oversee research and to ensure that the guidelines indicated above are followed. In some countries, it may be more advisable to engage a university to perform these functions.

Public sector support

Most national governments support the notion of protected areas. Almost all countries have networks of protected areas. However, the level of financial and resource support for protected areas is often low compared to other sectors of the economy:

> In many parts of the world, protected areas are seen as marginal to other areas of policy, such as economic development and agriculture. If protected areas are to have a strong and viable future, this situation must change. Protected areas must be mainstreamed with other policy areas. A key issue is to appropriately identify and communicate the many values and benefits that protected areas offer (Sheppard, 2001, p46).

Box 25.1 Guidelines for managing research partnerships

Protected area management agencies can derive considerable benefits from partnerships with universities and other research institutions and should do everything possible to facilitate all kinds of non-intrusive research in protected areas. Ensuring that these partnerships are effective can be based on the following guidelines:

- Require approval, through a quick and simple process, of all research projects in a protected area before they begin so that the protected area managers know what kinds of research are being done where.
- Proactively define the research that the protected area management agency requires for management purposes and provide incentives to research agencies to carry it out.
- Welcome purely academic research, which can be expected, ultimately, to benefit protected areas. However, research driven by scientific curiosity should be expected to pay its own way and not require the logistics and funding support that might be offered by the protected area agency to relevant applied research.
- Agree on the kinds of support that will be provided to researchers by the protected area agency (for example, transport, housing, laboratory facilities and so on).
- Unless questions of indigenous or local community ownership supervene, require that any specimens collected become part of a museum or herbarium collection that is available to other researchers.
- Ensure that any research carried out is not significantly disruptive of the natural values for which the protected area has been established.
- Ensure that copies of all reports and publications resulting from the research are sent to both the protected area where the research is carried out and to the national protected area agency. Researchers should also make a greater effort to explain their findings in ways that are useful to protected area managers.

Where protected areas are managed by public sector agencies, the organization itself must ensure internal consistency and support. A breakdown within the organization will undermine a united stand for protected areas that can be presented to other government sectors, local government, national governments, international bodies and so on, as well as weaken advocacy for protected areas. The goals and objectives need to be clear and well formulated into plans that everybody can access (see Chapter 11), and lines of communication need to be transparent and open so that rangers on the ground in remote areas are kept informed and are part of strategic-level processes so that strategic managers can easily access operations information necessary for budget committees, grant applications, national and international state-of-protected-areas reporting, and so on. A strong integrated information management system (see Case Study 10.6 in Chapter 10) provides the means to input and access the necessary data and information.

Perhaps more importantly, an integrated information management system also enables a manager to mount evidence-based arguments in support of funding claims to government treasury officials. Drawing on such a system, the argument for increased resources might go something like: 'If you increase our allocation by so much, according to our business plan, this would enable us to meet the objectives set in X park management plan, with resulting benefits Y and Z stakeholders, identified as high priority in our corporate strategic plan.' Similarly, current funding allocations can be defended by pointing out the specific implications of any reduction in terms of services and facilities that would no longer be offered.

A strategic communication plan is a valuable tool for a protected area agency. A team of communicators especially trained to ensure delivery of material in the most appropriate form for the target audience boosts the credibility and professionalism of the organization. Image is also important. Protected area agencies that have spent time devising a logo and standard design for the products they give to other agencies, tourist promoters, the general public and so on have found improved status of protected areas within government and from the general public (see Case Study 25.2).

In inter-agency meetings, there can be significant pressure to undermine conservation values for short-term economic benefit, such as inappropriate tourist development, extractive uses and so on, that may compromise the integrity of the protected area. Public protected area agencies need the power and culture that enables them to stand firm in support of protected area values and related management objectives. Within the government sectors, agencies need to find allies and develop strong working relationships with those people so that they can count on their support.

Protected areas in a state or country are not just about conserving the local environments of that area. They are also about protecting representative ecosystems and biodiversity that contribute to a global network. Government ministers and colleagues need to be reminded that their country's protected area network links to the bigger picture of global biodiversity conservation and international agreements and commitments.

Management support role of NGOs

In organizational and managerial terms, NGOs possess attributes that can complement government initiatives in protected areas. As Lees (1995) has pointed out, NGOs:

> ... *commonly bring qualities of innovation, commitment, flexibility and a history of community-led solution-finding to the complex task of successful management of protected areas. Their skills are an important complement to the role of government, a partnership that needs fostering through mutual respect and resource sharing.*

Because NGOs often have less bureaucratic organizational structures and management processes than governments, they can have the flexibility necessary to adapt to changing conditions. They may be more efficiently operated since they are more closely linked to market processes than governments. NGOs also tend to be more effective in generating meaningful participation from rural people, helping to promote their self-reliance and empowerment.

At the global level, some international NGOs have become extremely important financial conduits and managers, with more resources than

Case Study 25.2

A national identity for Mexican protected areas

The Mexican Commission for Protected Areas (CONANP) found that the absence of a national identity meant that few people knew about or valued natural protected areas and did not recognize which institutions were responsible for them. A strong identity assists with developing a public profile for an organization. As it was, each protected area had produced their own materials to promote themselves, with no specialist communication input. These were of varying quality, often of a poor design and print quality and frequently with long, highly technical content designed more for specialists than the general public.

CONANP created a Directorate of Strategic Communication and Identity to address the problems. As part of a strategic communication plan, a national identity was created that included uniforms, badges for vehicles with the new logo, sign posting and brochures created in a standard design, and a manual that gave clear instructions on how the national identity was to be applied. All of the protected areas and suppliers working with CONANP were obliged to comply with the rules and procedures set out in the manual.

As a result of this and other communication-based initiatives, in the space of two years CONANP became one of the most widely recognized environmental institutions in Mexico. The success of the communications strategy has led to requests from other institutions and businesses to assist with improving their communication efforts. This credibility has enhanced CONANP's capacity to establish effective partnerships with other institutions.

Source: adapted from Lira (2004)

Ceremony to launch Jervis Bay National Park, New South Wales, Australia

Source: Stuart Cohen

some national government departments. This sometimes puts NGOs into an uneasy relationship with government agencies because they have the money, personnel and rapid response capacity for programmes and projects, while national governments have the sovereignty, responsibility and gate-keeping authority, but operate under budget and staff constraints (Murphree, 1994). The challenge here is to find appropriate complementary roles and activities. More generally, NGOs are making an increasing contribution to a plural system of global governance, and environmental NGOs have been particularly prominent as players in international politics (Princen and Finger, 1994, Chapter 2).

NGOs can contribute to protected areas through a variety of mechanisms or roles, including owning and/or managing protected areas (see Case Study 25.3); having a watchdog function to alert the public or carry out advocacy about threats; funding field projects, including through

governments, local communities and other NGOs; supporting and/or carrying out research; facilitating communication and cooperation among stakeholders; and disseminating information, exchanging technical information and networking.

One of the most effective roles for NGOs is tapping the willingness to pay for protected areas by the general public, both domestically and internationally. Conservation finance began with the work of the NGOs that have been raising money and lobbying for conservation actively for at least 100 years. It could be argued that it is largely as a result of the lobbying and advocacy efforts of NGOs over the past several decades that donors and governments have increased their financial support for conservation. NGOs, with their relatively simple organizational structures and considerable experience in obtaining results from limited budgets, are an attractive source of short-term and project-specific funding for protected areas. In addition to donating funds directly, international NGOs can help to organize and capitalize trust funds and debt-for-nature swaps, and can serve as sources of information on various funding mechanisms. NGOs are still in the forefront of innovation in bringing more investors and more financing to the support of conservation (WRI, 1989; Spergel, 1993; Dillenbeck, 1994; Clark and Downes, 1995).

In general, NGO programmes tend to focus on projects, rather than providing long-term sources of operating funds. They are inclined to support activities such as the development of management plans, staff training, research, environmental education and community outreach activities. NGOs generally need to maintain supervision and accounting control over the funds they disburse. Most international NGOs actively seek to closely involve their counterparts in the developing world, as illustrated by the work of The Nature Conservancy (TNC).

NGOs sometimes have the capacity to serve as facilitators of communication and cooperation between governments and local communities, or between the private sector and local communities or governments. This role of facilitator can help to enable a more positive relationship among the stakeholders. The capacity of an NGO to contribute to conflict resolution about protected areas will depend upon the objectives of the NGO, its credibility with local people and the government, and its vision and resources. But in various parts of the world, NGOs have been able to undertake a variety of roles in resolving conflicts, including advocacy, education and facilitation of consensus-building efforts among diverse interests (Lewis, 1996). In a conflict situation, NGOs are often well suited as mediators because they can be perceived as more neutral than protected area managers or other government officials. In other cases, NGOs may negotiate on behalf of certain interest groups, such as local communities or urban conservationists. Partnerships between local communities and NGOs can help to increase their effectiveness in confronting the power of other interests that might operate contrary to the interests of the objectives of the protected area. NGOs play a major role in facilitating and supporting CCAs.

In a time of rapid change, access to information is uneven, and many NGOs have been mobilized to help redress this imbalance. Indeed, many NGOs are best characterized as organizations designed to collect, process and transmit information, especially to influence public opinion or change government behaviour. Many NGOs publish newsletters, issue press releases and publish various kinds of books, field guides and other such products.

NGOs have been major contributors to protected areas in virtually all countries, providing funds and expertise, building public support, promoting action and advocating conservation interests. While NGOs can provide very practical support to protected areas, their contributions are likely to be most useful when a clear understanding has been reached between the NGO and the protected area management authority. NGOs can diversify efforts and approaches to managing protected areas, sometimes using methods very different from those adopted by government agencies. Locally based NGOs can often use their familiarity with local issues and resources to operate effectively where government agencies or national NGOs may have difficulties.

NGOs also have their limitations. It is often difficult to provide oversight of their activities, and they do not have a democratic mandate for their work. Their funding is frequently uncertain, making them dependent upon dynamic donor priorities that can limit their long-term commitment to a project; and they are often dependent upon one or a few charismatic leaders. National NGO leaders are not typically associated socially, economically and culturally with the rural communities whom they seek to empower. Grassroots NGOs do not suffer as much from this problem, but may have difficulties in reaching those in authority. Some government officials view environmental NGOs – particularly those that engage in advocacy work – as foes of economic development and unwelcome monitors of environmental and human rights abuses.

The contributions of NGOs will need to expand to meet growing demands. They particularly need to find ways of working in partnership with many other interest groups, especially the private sector (as sources of funds, influence and

Case Study 25.3

NGOs as private protected area managers

Privately owned and managed protected areas are an important part of national protected area systems in some countries, bringing flexibility to the means by which protected areas may be established.

As an illustration of the range of roles that NGO partners can play in protected area management, consider the following:

- The Nature Conservancy (TNC) owns and manages the largest private protected area system in the world, consisting of more than 47 million hectares of land and 8000km of river, as well as more than 100 marine conservation projects.
- The Programme for Belize (PFB) has been given management responsibility for the 92,614ha Rio Bravo Conservation and Management Area, holding the land in trust for the people of Belize. Originally supported by private donations, PFB hopes to earn sufficient revenue through forest products and tourism to become self-sustaining.
- In Guatemala, the Fundacion Defensores de la Naturaleza was given authority in 1990 by the Guatemalan Congress to manage the operations and administration of the Sierra de las Minas Biosphere Reserve (236,300ha), including the work of the park guards. It is in charge of management decisions, including training, infrastructure and communications, under supervision of the National Council of Protected Areas.
- In Panama, the Asociacion Nacional Para la Conservacion de la Naturaleza has an agreement with Panama's Institute for Natural Renewable Resources to demarcate the boundaries of the Darien Biosphere Reserve (597,000ha), train and equip park personnel, install infrastructure and carry out biological inventories.
- In Bolivia, Fundacion Amigos de la Naturaleza has been granted a ten-year management contract by the National Department for the Conservation of Biodiversity for the Noel Kempff Mercado National Park (927,000ha), with responsibilities for hiring rangers, building infrastructure and helping to reduce poaching.
- In Colombia, the Fundacion Pro-Sierra Nevada de Santa Marta is responsible for managing three areas within the Sierra Nevada de Santa Marta National Park (300,000ha), including land protection and community outreach activities.
- In Ecuador, Fundacion Natura has a formal agreement with the Ministry of Agriculture to participate and collaborate in protected area management, working on staff training and fundraising (including facilitating a debt-for-nature swap valued at US$10 million).
- In Paraguay, Fundacion Moises Bertoni is legally responsible for managing the Mbaracayu Forest Nature Reserve (63,000ha).

expertise), local communities (as those with the most immediate interests being affected) and governments (as those holding sovereignty over land and resources). For example, NGOs could become more effective by strengthening their capacity for working with the private sector through establishing partnerships with private sector actors with a proven track record in tourism, genetic resources and small-scale sustainable enterprise, both national and international.

Local community support

The stakeholders with the most direct dependency upon protected area resources are the local communities. In most parts of the world, rural villagers strongly believe that they have historical rights to the land and resources that governments have declared 'protected' in the national interest

(Dang, 1991; Vandergeest, 1996). In India, for example, at least 3 million people live inside protected areas and several million more live in areas immediately adjacent to protected areas; all have been historically dependent upon the protected areas for various resources, and it would be difficult, if not impossible, to find adequate alternatives for them outside the protected area system (Kothari et al, 1989). For the reason of dependency alone, more inclusive conservation policies are imperative.

As detailed in Chapters 20 and 21, many local communities have long-established protected areas and resource-management practices, including measures such as sacred groves, hunting seasons, taboos and various other ways of asserting community interests above those of the individual. While these measures do not necessarily

African Mountains Association meeting

Source: IUCN Photo Library © Jim Thorsell

address national-level concerns, they have the great advantage of strong local support and can be a significant part of the national protected area system.

The conflict between the ideal of 'undisturbed nature' and the reality of long-term human occupation of the land has led to the wide recognition that conservation cannot succeed unless it is linked to secure tenure over land and resources, involvement in decision-making, and economic opportunities and investments aimed at the rural communities who might otherwise threaten the viability of protected areas through their activities in pursuit of livelihood. For example, the CBD calls for governments to protect and encourage customary use of biological resources that are compatible with conservation or sustainable use (Article 10c); to support local populations to develop and implement remedial action where biodiversity has been reduced (Article 10d); to promote environmentally sound and sustainable

development in areas adjacent to protected areas with a view to furthering protection of these areas (Article 8e); to ensure that an equitable share of benefits from conservation and sustainable use flow back to local communities (Article 8j); and to promote the exchange of traditional and indigenous knowledge (Article 17.2). It is up to each government and to citizens of the country to determine how these objectives are to be implemented at the national level.

In some countries, the message about the value of protected areas has driven land speculation, with land developers buying up rights to use lands bordering protected areas, leading to destabilization of some buffer zone communities as villagers begin to sell their land, often at prices too tempting to reject. At least one danger of this development is that villagers who fail to use their proceeds wisely may face new economic hardships that could force them back into ecosystem encroachment.

Numerous factors can contribute to a

productive partnership between protected areas and local communities. Perhaps most importantly, when they are the primary decision-makers and beneficiaries, local people can reasonably be expected to institute their own conservation measures or support those initiated by government. Numerous examples cited from various parts of the world (UNEP, 1988; Stone, 1991; West and Brechin, 1991; Birckhead et al, 1992; Wells et al, 1992; Kemf, 1993; Western and Wright, 1994; Kothari et al, 1996) support the general point that earning the support of local communities means giving them a real stake in the success of a well-managed protected area.

While community involvement in protected areas or the surrounding buffer zones is widely seen as essential, it is no panacea. First, many of the problems are of fairly recent origin as a result of expanding populations, immigration and levels of consumption; therefore, traditional community-based solutions may not be effective in the new circumstances. Second, some local communities are not noted for their peaceful relations with neighbouring communities; in fact, the history of village boundaries is often one of conflict – so building support networks requiring inter-village cooperation is not easy. And, finally, the fact that local communities are often well adapted to their

local environmental conditions does not automatically mean that they are going to make wise decisions. Deciding how to invest scarce resources in assets that mature over several decades (such as forest trees) or are highly mobile (such as migratory species of waterfowl) is a sophisticated task, and clearly some individuals or communities will be able to organize themselves more effectively and make better decisions than others. Any community faces a challenging set of problems when it tries to govern and manage complex multi-species, multi-product resource systems whose benefits mature at varying rates and are under pressure by competing groups of humans at every step (Ostrom, 1998). The best general approach to this complex of problems appears to be greater commitment from resource management agencies to work with communities, improved community resource management programmes, effective enforcement of agreed regulations, continuing research and monitoring, and long-term commitment by both conservation and development NGOs (Wood et al, 1995).

Denying the traditional tenurial rights of communities means that the traditional rules regulating resource access lose their legitimacy, invariably leading to over-exploitation of resources. This is certainly not to claim that indige-

Banff township, Banff National Park, Canada

Source: Graeme L. Worboys

Cuc Phuong National Park, Viet Nam

Source: IUCN Photo Library © Jim Thorsell

nous people or local communities are always ideal resource managers; but they do depend upon their immediate environment for their livelihood and have many years of experience in determining how resources can be managed to provide sustainable benefits. Any new tenure system imposed from outside – such as a national park – will need to be demonstrably effective and equitable if it is to earn local support.

Unfortunately, establishing protected areas at the initiative of central or provincial government authorities has often alienated at least some local people from the areas which they had traditionally considered 'their territory' and over which they had tenure. In many cases, establishment of protected areas has involved relocating villages, often involuntarily. In almost all cases, local people have been expected to curb traditional uses of the resources contained within the new protected areas. In extreme cases, this has led to violence and bloodshed.

Lacking any significant involvement in the design and management of protected areas and feeling that their traditional tenure rights have been taken without consultation or compensation, local people have seldom supported protected areas and are sceptical of the capacity of governments to manage local resources on their behalf. But following the flush of rapid creation of protected areas over the past few decades, greater attention is now being given to the sustainability and viability of protected areas. It has become widely agreed that conservation is likely to be most effective when it reinforces traditional rights and conservation practices. This, in turn, is leading to many efforts to involve local people more significantly in protected area management, including greater attention to tenure rights (McNeely et al, 1985; Thorsell, 1985; West and Brechin, 1991; Kemf, 1993; Lewis, 1996; Kothari et al, 1997).

Given the great diversity of local communities, a vast spectrum of potential approaches to involving communities in protected area management is available (see Box 25.2). In many cases, it will be a matter of 'learning by doing', building on existing measures such as legal ownership of land, customary tenure rights of local communities, legislative frameworks and so forth. Furthermore, local communities are not the only stakeholders, and finding appropriate ways of involving communities in protected area management often also entails negotiations with other stakeholders, including the private sector, NGOs and research organizations.

Detailed knowledge of the people whose lives are affected by the establishment and management of protected areas is at least as important to protected area managers as information about the plant and animal species to be conserved. The cultural, socio-economic and demographic characteristics of local people, including the age and gender divisions of labour, form the basis for measures to promote the sustainable use of natural resources, alleviate poverty, improve the quality of human life and create support for protected areas.

Involving local communities in protected area management will inevitably face some difficulties (Borrini-Feyerabend, 1997). Some rural communities have little interest in protected areas, and do not want to be involved in management. Other communities may not have the time and resources available to invest in the protected area, even if they have the interest to do so. Some cultures and groups may find the concept of participation to be alien, hesitating to express views and interests that may be different from those of their neighbours. The investment of time and energy required by protected area managers to work with local communities may force them to neglect other duties, such as resource management within the protected area.

Another significant danger of the greater involvement of local communities in protected area management is that various individual and sectional interests are fully capable of turning this good idea to their own ends. The challenge is to be able to sift out these detrimental interests from the local people who genuinely depend for survival upon the natural resources of the protected areas, and empower the latter to be able to live with dignity. This will be an ongoing process as people move in and out of local communities.

It is now widely accepted that local communities have a legitimate right to participate in at least some aspects of protected area management, and to gain recognition of their own conserved sites and conservation practices. Indeed, because of a range of economic factors, the supply of biologically rich protected areas is doomed to be suboptimal without a concerted effort by the world community to make conservation an attractive option to the rural people who have practical jurisdiction over the resources (McNeely and Guruswamy, 1998).

Box 25.2 Policy guidelines for involving local communities in protected area management

- Identify the local communities and other groups and individuals who have a stake in the protected area, and assess the power relationships of the various interest groups to determine patterns of resource use. On the basis of this assessment, enable local residents to derive benefits from the protected area in proportion to their investment in the area and its conservation objectives.
- Build sensitivity towards the inequities within and between communities and make special attempts to empower the underprivileged, including women.
- Ensure that the benefits of the protected area to the local community are equal to or greater than the potential benefits from other uses of the protected area (in other words, develop means of compensating local stakeholders for their opportunity costs). This may require economic incentives provided by other stakeholders with an interest in the area (for example, the tourism industry).
- Specify the functions, powers, rights and responsibilities of local communities in relation to the protected area; acknowledge skills, educational and cultural gaps that might exist, and plan for incremental devolution of responsibilities, along with training.

Box 25.2 Continued

- Where the local people are empowered to protect and utilize resources from protected areas, also raise their awareness of broader environmental issues through the implementation of conservation education programmes.
- Develop institutional structures at local and wider levels to facilitate community participation in various protected area management issues. Provide legislative and policy support to build a strong foundation for such arrangements. Provide firm legal backing. Informal participatory conservation initiatives can be powerful and successful, but often do not last long. Legal backing, through statutory or customary law or both, can be one element in providing such long-term sustenance.
- Develop appropriate attitudes of protected area staff towards local people, replacing the traditional police role with a more cooperative and collaborative role.
- Select the right person to lead the local-level management committee. Many real leaders may not hold any political position; so select the leader through a democratic means, rather than through nomination by the protected area managers.
- Initiate a process of dialogue. Often, genuine and open dialogue among various rights-holders and stakeholders is missing, leading to misunderstandings and lost opportunities to bring their respective strengths together. Such regular dialogue at local, regional and national levels is needed to reduce stereotypes, increase understanding and arrive at mutually acceptable ways forward.
- Encourage ecologically sensitive livelihoods. Clearly, some traditional livelihoods are compatible with conservation objectives, while others may be detrimental: the former need encouragement and support; the latter need alternative approaches. In all cases, the search for secure livelihoods is important to tackle real poverty and to link people's lives with conservation.
- Integrate traditional and scientific knowledge. There is much in traditional practices and knowledge from which modern conservation can learn, and much in modern conservation science from which traditional communities can benefit. A judicious mix of the two, with neither dominating, needs to be attempted.
- Set up accessible and transparent dispute-resolution mechanisms. Disputes among community members, or between communities and others, including official agencies, are commonplace in participatory conservation initiatives. Transparent and accessible mechanisms to resolve such disputes, including through third-party mediation, are a good investment.
- Ensure a public right to information. Secrecy about conservation and development programmes (including budgets) is one major reason for suspicion and misunderstanding. Citizens, particularly local communities, must have full access to all aspects of the conservation initiative and to developmental inputs that have a bearing on it.
- Adapt to site-specific situations. Given the enormous ecological, cultural, economic and political diversity within which protected areas are located, a uniform legal and programmatic approach for an entire country or region is usually counterproductive. Protected area policies and programmes need to be open and sensitive to local conditions. Built-in flexibility should promote creativity, but also contain checks against misuse.
- Since participatory conservation is a relatively new phenomenon in many countries, capacity of several kinds needs to be built: of officials to deal with community issues, of communities to deal with conservation responsibilities and new institutions, and so on.
- Resist destructive development and commercial pressures. Many participatory conservation initiatives have failed due to larger pressures of unsustainable development. Such processes that impinge upon the conservation values of protected areas, or undermine community abilities to conserve and manage, need to be strongly resisted. Given that, in many cases, some parts of government are promoting such destructive processes, this can be difficult, but protected area agencies need to assert their conservation mandate on such matters!
- Treat conservation as a process, not a project. Short-term projects aimed at achieving participatory conservation are often unsuccessful because they try to force an artificial pace or achieve impractical targets. Experience from successful community-based initiatives strongly suggests that a long-term process is important, keeping in mind the varying pace of communities, the need to build sustainable institutional arrangements and so on.

Source: Kothari et al (1997) and Kothari (2004)

As population continues to grow and more economic pressures are put on forests, wetlands, coral reefs and other natural habitats, it is even more important to recognize and implement locally instituted mechanisms to control access to resources, to ensure appropriate participation in decision-making processes and to develop procedures for resolving conflicts. In many cases, the indigenous approaches to these mechanisms are more effective than those imposed from outside.

A key factor is the stability of rural communities, implying that governments need to pay particular attention when contemplating major efforts at relocating people from one part of the countryside to another. Those people who have developed long-term relationships with particular settings, and have developed knowledge on how to manage the resources contained within those ecosystems, are likely to have a very different relationship with the land and its resources than are new immigrants who have no particular linkage to local resources. Given the dynamism of development, communities in and around protected areas often include both indigenous peoples who have a long history in the region and immigrants who have arrived much more recently; the new arrivals frequently are responsible for more destructive land-use practices than the long-term residents. But, of course, new technologies and new markets can be expected to change the behaviour of local villagers irrespective of their traditional conservation practices.

Participatory approaches may be difficult to implement when the conservation need is urgent, human population pressure is high or the various stakeholders are unwilling to negotiate. Assumed links between the development of alternatives and reduced impact on protected areas should be closely monitored because they may not occur, in practice. Management objectives should be clearly defined and participatory activities linked to these.

General public support

The 'general public' is a widely used term that refers to those people who do not necessarily have direct stakeholder interest, expertise or power in relation to, in this context, protected areas. Although such people may lack direct engagement, surveys (see Chapter 2, p42) show

widespread community concern about environmental quality. There is already a considerable level of support for protected areas from the general public. This is evident from the growth of protected areas around the world and the growing number of community-managed and private reserves. A search on the internet for nature conservation and protected areas comes up with over 11 million sites. In some parts of the world, protected areas enjoy a very high degree of public support (see Case Study 25.4). Many people who do not visit parks or live in close proximity to them value their existence and wish to ensure that the current generation pass on a bequest of a well-managed protected area network to future generations. For example, from a sample of 1282 members of the general public from the Australian states of Victoria and New South Wales, over 66 per cent expressed strong positive existence and bequest values for natural areas (Winter et al, 2003).

Managers need to get better at harnessing such support to improve investment in, and commitment to, protected areas. The long-term viability of protected areas requires the 'silent majority' of supporters to become advocates, both personally and politically, for their establishment and sound management. There is also the ongoing work of increasing the level of knowledge in the general community so that people, whether current supporters or opponents of protected areas, can make more informed choices. Of course, managers must also listen to and learn from community concerns and aspirations. A constructive public discourse about the benefits and costs of protected areas and the implications of the new management paradigm (see Chapter 2, p67) can only strengthen and consolidate their position politically, socially, culturally and economically. The support of a critical mass of the world's people is needed to elevate conservation and protected areas to a central position on the world stage.

In many high HDI countries, people donate money and become members of conservation groups acting at international, national, provincial and local scales. People who live in cities, people who have access to information and the big picture, and people who recognize the

Case Study 25.4

General public views on protected areas in Tasmania, Australia

Roy Morgan Research, Melbourne

Protected areas managed by the Parks and Wildlife Service (PWS), a Tasmanian state government agency, cover almost 40 per cent of Tasmania's land area. It is important to the state's future that Tasmanians understand and value their natural heritage and the benefits that it can bring to their community. The PWS commissioned Roy Morgan Research to assist with developing a communications strategy through evaluating levels of awareness and support of protected areas among Tasmanians. Specific areas examined included current levels of national park attendance; awareness of the PWS; the protected area network's natural and cultural value; and the value placed by the community on PWS and the resources and services that it offers.

A total of 506 Tasmanian residents aged 16 years and over were interviewed by telephone. Respondents were randomly selected with quotas applied by gender, age and region, and weighted to ensure that the sample's demographic characteristics represent the total Tasmanian population.

The survey showed that 89 per cent of Tasmanians have visited a Tasmanian national park, 53 per cent in the last 12 months. Other major results included:

- 70 per cent agree that Tasmania has about the right amount of reserve area, while 27 per cent think there is not enough area because some valuable areas are not protected;
- 45 per cent place very high, and 33 per cent place fairly high value on Tasmania's protected areas; and
- 98 per cent think that having the parks and wildlife system in Tasmania is a valuable part of the Tasmanian community.

Results from this survey will assist in establishing key baseline data and setting targets for the PWS communication strategy. The results highlight the opportunity for the communications activities to include awareness programmes for the less prominent parks. Visitation was shown to be a positive way of developing a higher opinion of the PWS.

Cradle Mountain – Lake St Clair National Park, Tasmania, Australia

Source: IUCN Photo Library © Jim Thorsell

importance of protecting the Earth's diversity lobby governments to develop and maintain protected areas and to support international conservation treaties and agreements. While, in the short term, politicians may take notice when large numbers of people rally in support of protected areas, environmentalists are often hard pressed to compete with other public policy issues, such as economic welfare, health and education. Protected area advocates need to become better at demonstrating that the environmental agenda is not necessarily in competition with these other imperatives, but can contribute significantly to them.

As noted in Chapter 2 (p67), many 'paper parks' still exist in the world, and many more that are inadequately resourced and managed. In most countries, protected area agencies struggle to convince their governments to give adequate resources to manage protected areas effectively. So, protected area agencies all over the world have to work hard to create relationships with every aspect of society. International bodies are advocating for protected areas and conservation all over the world, building relationships, alliances and networks so that the message is consistent and united. The IUCN is advocating a common language and framework for protected areas so that the international understandings about protected areas are the same across governments and protected area organizations. Every protected area agency has a role to play in the global advocacy for protected areas. The old slogan 'Think globally act locally' is apt. Actions occur mostly at a local level; but with tools such as the internet, television and film, there is a capacity to influence more widely than ever before. There is also greater capacity for protected area agencies to link with each other and to learn from each other. Organizations such as the International Rangers Federation have the capacity to give rangers all over the world a sense of being part of a much bigger process than managing operations in their own protected area, often in fairly isolated circumstances.

Creating relationships and developing partnerships and alliances is crucial, as is working and relating with people, rather than trying to impose top-down solutions. Managers attempting to build public support may also benefit from:

- having a clear message that is consistent at all levels of an organization;
- utilizing an integrated information system that allows everybody to know what is going on and keeps track of changes;
- developing a communication strategy;
- ensuring that those staff who interact with the public on a day-to-day basis are good communicators;
- being benefits focused and positive (negative messages can be disempowering and do not often inspire people to take creative action);
- celebrating success widely and loudly (cultivating relationships with local and national media, drama groups, musicians and festival organizers, for example, can help here);
- keeping in touch with supporters and letting them know how much they are appreciated (for example, through newsletters or social events);
- recognizing that there is rarely a 'quick fix' (in the Apo Marine Reserve in the Philippines, for example, it took six years of talking with the local villagers before the successful establishment of a no-take zone; see Case Study 10.8 in Chapter 10);
- providing opportunities for people to be involved in protected area operations through volunteer programmes, joint management with local communities and 'Friends of Park' groups (make sure that volunteers know what you are asking them to commit to, and that you expect them to honour the commitment in training, effort and time); and
- being honest and realistic (building trust and a strong relationship depends on delivering what is promised).

If governments and the general public recognize the many economic, social, cultural, ecological, developmental and political values of protected areas; if appropriate institutions are established to manage protected areas in close collaboration with other stakeholders; if sustainable economic benefits are allowed to flow to and from protected areas and to their surrounding communities; and if information from both traditional knowledge and modern science can be mobilized to enable protected areas to adapt to changing conditions, then the protected areas can be the engines for new forms of community identity and development.

Management principles

1   A wider and deeper advocacy from stakeholders is essential to secure legitimacy and credibility for protected area management, as well as the necessary political and financial support.

2   Some private sector actors are willing and able to contribute more to protected areas. Protected area managers and governments need to provide the policy and management frameworks that will support and encourage their contributions. Managers need to encourage private sector involvement in protected areas with respect to providing funding, expertise, facilities and services. Private investors should be provided with appropriate incentives, such as security of tenure, appropriate contractual relations, the removal of perverse economic incentives, correction of market-distorting policies and removal of barriers to entry. Where such conditions are met, private investment in protected areas can increase significantly.

3   Inappropriate commercialization of protected areas is a danger that requires constant vigilance.

4   In most countries, science is not making the required contribution to protected area management. It is crucial that managers establish more effective partnerships with researchers. Care must be taken to ensure that management guidelines serve as an incentive to research, rather than as an obstacle.

5   Public protected area agencies need the power and culture that enables them to stand firm in support of protected area values and related management objectives. Within the government sectors, agencies need to find allies and develop strong working relationships with those people so that they can count on their support.

6   The role of NGOs in protected area management must continue to expand through a variety of mechanisms or roles, including owning or managing land or sea; acting as a watchdog and carrying out advocacy on threats to conservation; funding field projects; carrying out research; facilitating communication and cooperation among stakeholders; disseminating information; and assisting resolution of conflicts and facilitation of consensus-building efforts among diverse interests.

7   The contributions of NGOs will need to expand to meet growing demands. They especially need to find ways of working in partnership with many other interest groups, particulary the private sector, local communities and governments. Public sector protected area managers need to create more effective partnerships with NGOs, thereby establishing complementary roles and activities.

8   The stakeholders with the most direct dependency upon protected area resources are the local communities. For reasons of dependency and social justice, inclusive conservation policies are imperative.

9   Greater commitment is needed from protected area management agencies to work with communities and assist in the creation of improved community resource management programmes, effective enforcement of agreed regulations, continuing research and monitoring, and long-term commitment. In many cases, it will be a matter of 'learning by doing', building on existing measures such as legal ownership of land, customary tenure rights of local communities and legislative frameworks.

10 Detailed knowledge of the people whose lives are affected by the establishment and management of protected areas is at least as important to protected area managers as information about the plant and animal species to be conserved.

11 Participatory approaches may be difficult to implement when the conservation need is urgent, human population pressure is high or the various stakeholders are unwilling to negotiate. Assumed links between development of alternatives and reduced impact on protected areas should be closely monitored because they may not occur, in practice. Management objectives should be clearly defined and participatory activities linked to these.

12 Every protected area agency has a role to play in the global advocacy for protected areas. Creating relationships and developing partnerships and alliances is crucial, as is working and relating with people, rather than trying to impose top-down solutions.

13 Many people who do not visit parks or live in close proximity to them value their existence and good management. Managers need to get better at harnessing such support. The long-term viability of protected areas requires the 'silent majority' of supporters to become advocates, both personally and politically, for their establishment and sound management.

Further reading

Borrini-Feyerabend, G. (ed) (1997) *Beyond Fences: Seeking Social Sustainability in Conservation*, IUCN, Gland and Cambridge

Guruswamy, L. and McNeely, J. A. (eds) (1998) *Protection of Global Diversity: Converging Strategies*, Duke University Press, Durham

McNeely, J. A. (1998) *Mobilizing Broader Support for Asia's Biodiversity: How Civil Society Can Contribute to Protected Area Management*, Asian Development Bank, Manila

Sheppard, D. (2001) 'Twenty-first century strategies for protected areas in East Asia', *George Wright Forum*, vol 18, no 2, pp40–55

Western, D. and Wright, R. M. (eds) (1994) *Natural Connections: Perspectives in Community-based Conservation*, Island Press, Washington, DC

26

Challenges and Opportunities

Michael Lockwood, Graeme L. Worboys and Ashish Kothari

Protected areas are one of the most important land and sea uses on Earth. They are created out of human respect for, and desire to sustain, natural and cultural values. They provide critical elements of a response to the global environmental, social and economic challenges of contemporary societies. They conserve vital biodiversity and represent the variety of the Earth's landscapes and history. They offer one answer to how people can relate to and engage with nature. They provide cultural, spiritual, social, economic and 'quality of life' benefits, and are one of the key mechanisms to sustain life on Earth. Protected areas play a critical role in sustaining the natural resource base that supports the livelihoods of people and the viability of economies and communities. They are sources of knowledge and offer educational experiences from connecting with nature that will become increasingly important as the world becomes more urbanized.

The dramatic growth in number and extent of government-designated protected areas over the last 40 years is an expression of the international consensus that such benefits must be maintained so that they can be passed to future generations, both human and non-human. For this, thanks are due to the people engaged in and supporting their establishment and management, many of whom do so with a commitment and passion that becomes a life's work.

Building on the work of pioneering conserva-tionists, especially those during the 1960s and 1970s, many governments around the world have now established protected area management agencies, staffed by committed and highly skilled professionals. Many of these agencies are now also embracing collaborative management with indigenous peoples and local communities, private landowners or other actors. Longstanding local and indigenous conservation regimes are now recognized in many countries, and in international agreements, as community conserved areas (CCAs). These areas are managed using traditional knowledge and customary law to achieve biodiversity and cultural conservation outcomes, as well as, in many cases, sustaining the livelihoods of local people. There are outstanding examples of nations working together to establish peace parks and transboundary protected areas. Through the work of the IUCN, NGOs and conservation leaders around the world, there is now a compelling global advocacy for the importance of protected areas.

Parallel with a dramatic growth in the number and extent of protected areas over the last 40 years has been a significant shift in the way in which protected areas are conceptualized – so significant a change is this that it has been termed a 'new paradigm' for protected areas. The World Commission on Protected Areas (WCPA) (WCPA, 2006, p2) articulated a vision for protected areas based on this new approach:

> *In this changing world, we need a fresh and inno-vative approach to protected areas and their role in broader conservation and development agendas. This*

approach demands the maintenance and enhancement of our core conservation goals, equitably integrating them with the interests of all affected people. In this way the synergy between conservation, the maintenance of life-support systems and sustainable development is forged. We see protected areas as vital means to achieve this synergy efficiently and cost effectively. We see protected areas as providers of benefits beyond boundaries – beyond their boundaries on a map, beyond the boundaries of nation states, across societies, genders and generations.

The new paradigm provides the context from which we, in this concluding chapter, draw on (and acknowledge our debt to) the WCPA's *Strategic Plan 2005–2012* (WCPA, 2005) to consider some of the key challenges and directions for protected areas over the next decade.

Despite the impressive increase in protected area coverage worldwide, today, more than ever, such areas face serious threats. Climate change, land and seascape fragmentation due to destruction of natural ecosystems and accelerating demand for natural resources threaten protected areas worldwide. With respect to climate change, for example, protected area managers need to prepare for shifts in the location and composition of biomes, loss of species, new development pressures, and increased frequency and severity of flooding, storms, fire and drought, as well as desertification and reduction in snow and ice cover. Given that even our understanding of these phenomena is low, the challenge is acute. Equally, the destruction of ecosystems by unsustainable processes and projects, including large-scale mining, hydropower and irrigation development, infrastructure and energy generation, demands from the national and international markets, and expansion of human settlements, is continuing and, in some places, accelerating.

Addressing such global problems requires enhanced knowledge, as well as its application within land- and seascape-scale planning and management approaches. Protected areas must be established and planned as networks rather than as individual reserves. The most effective protected areas will be those connected with wider land- and sea-use planning and resource management

decision-making systems beyond their boundaries. In recognition of this, the WCPA has initiated a major project responding to climate change which focuses on developing connectivity conservation and adaptive management strategies for mountain biomes. Such projects will contribute to ecosystem-based land and water management in a way that promotes the conservation of nature and culture, as well as sustainable resource use.

Shortages of essential natural resources, such as water, and of important fuels, such as oil and wood, will increase economic and social conflict, make it more difficult for managers to access and afford conventional forms of transportation, exacerbate tensions between government conservation agencies and resource-dependent communities, and constrain aviation-based international tourism. Protected area managers can respond by providing leadership and advocacy in the use of climate and environment friendly alternative energy sources and sustainable resource use. They can learn how to better buffer protected areas and local communities against the global, regional and local 'ups and downs' of volatile industries such as tourism, and address such variability through enhancing their adaptive capability.

Social disorder and conflict pose massive challenges to protected area managers in many parts of the world. Resource shortages, over-consumption by a few and continued growth of the world's human population will also exacerbate the political, religious and social tensions that make the world a dangerous and uncertain place. Reconciling protection of natural and cultural heritage with sustainable use and management of natural resources is therefore particularly pressing. Working with local communities becomes more and more critical. Through transboundary initiatives such as peace parks, protected areas can be an important mechanism for promoting international cooperation and understanding.

Protected area managers must also take account of, and in some cases lead and implement, social and institutional change. Effective responses to changing consumption patterns and human population growth, economic and institutional globalization, democratization and decentralization require the mainstreaming of protected areas and environmental considerations, more generally, into the decisions made by citizens, governments and communities. Building legitimate, widely supported and well-managed protected area networks is a key task for the next decade and beyond. With enhanced communication and education, people from all walks of life, from all nations, ethnic backgrounds and socio-economic conditions, will increasingly recognize and understand the full range of protected area values and benefits – these include what they contribute to them personally, to their community and to the world as a whole. Particular attention should be given to awareness-raising for decision-makers, politicians and their advisers.

It is difficult to secure a high priority for conserving natural heritage in national policy agendas. Pressing matters such as poverty alleviation, economic prosperity, civil security, and health and education services tend to dominate the political landscape, and the benefits that protected areas can provide in each of these fields are not yet sufficiently recognized. Too many businesses and communities consider protected areas as a barrier to their aspirations and activities. Protected area advocates and managers need to become much more adept at explaining the cross-sectoral benefits associated with a comprehensive and well-managed protected area system. One of many approaches required will be enlisting the support of high-profile members of the community to communicate critical messages. Many people living in and around protected areas depend upon them for vital food, medicines, fuel, fodder, clothing and other products. Poverty alleviation, sustainable livelihoods and enhanced productivity of fisheries are but some of the values that need to be better and more forcefully articulated to decision-makers and local communities. It is also crucial to increase the interest and support of people living in urban areas.

Early efforts in this regard are beginning to transform the perception that 'national parks' are a luxury land use that provides benefits to a few, to an understanding that a representative and well-managed global system of protected areas is essential to support life and standards of living for communities across the world. The links between protected areas and the life-support benefits that they provide must be more effectively documented and persuasively communicated.

The world is far from achieving a comprehensive, adequate and representative global system of protected areas. Major gaps remain for freshwater systems, tropical forests and on islands. Marine ecosystems, especially offshore waters and the high seas, are largely unprotected. The number of threatened species continues to rise. Urgent action is required to complete the system. In addressing the deficiencies, attention must be paid to achieving an appropriate mix of reserves across the IUCN categories and across various governance regimes so that the full range of protected area values is secured.

Marine and coastal biodiversity is under increasing stress from intense human pressures, including rapid coastal population growth, urban development, habitat destruction, over-exploitation of commercial and recreational resources, and pollution. At the same time as coastal and marine resources are being degraded and depleted, people around the world are increasingly dependent upon them for food, tourism, shoreline protection and many other ecosystem services. As these pressures intensify, marine protected areas are increasingly recognized as critical to maintain and help restore natural and cultural resources and values.

The World Summit on Sustainable Development, the World Parks Congress and the Convention on Biological Diversity (CBD) have all committed to create more protected areas. Goals from these forums give specific direction to efforts to establish new protected areas over the next decade. Gaps in the coverage of marine protected area system and major biomes need to be more specifically identified using global biodiversity datasets. As knowledge of the specific needs to complete the system grows, efforts to establish new protected areas can become progressively more strategic and targeted. Over the next few years, the WCPA will help to facilitate efforts to:

- develop conservation connectivity and transboundary initiatives in Africa, Asia and South America to link protected areas with each other and with surrounding land uses;
- secure the implementation of an ecologically

representative network of marine protected areas; and

- ensure that 40 per cent of mountain protected areas are linked within collaboratively managed ecosystem networks.

Mountains around the world are relatively well represented in protected areas. This creates an opportunity to achieve connectivity conservation along major mountain ranges such as the Rockies in North America, the Andes in South America, the Himalayas in Asia and the Alps in Europe. Apart from being of value in their own right, mountain protected area networks can facilitate connectivity conservation across other biomes, as well as illustrate the value of regional- and landscape-scale connectivity between reserved areas. Furthermore, mountain ecosystems can allow exploration and demonstration of how such connectivity conservation can address the effects of climate change.

Sound governance is critical for the future of protected areas and is central to ensuring their effective and long-term management. Democratization of societies and decentralization of decision-making authority and management responsibility have widened opportunities for local communities and indigenous people to become involved in protected area governance. In particular, CCAs established and managed by indigenous peoples and local communities have been recognized as essential for conservation in various contexts. As a result, a range of cooperative and community-based governance models has emerged, alongside recognition of the need to retain and enhance a vigorous government policy and management capability. The policy and governance roles of protected area agencies will continue to evolve alongside expanded roles for local communities and indigenous peoples, NGOs and the private sector. Continued governance innovation is essential to address the complexity of achieving conservation outcomes across the wide variety of environmental, socio-economic and cultural settings. Building effective connections between governance actors across scales (local, provincial, national and international) is also crucial for the establishment of coherent and lasting protected area institutions. Irrespective of

which organizations take on or are vested with governance authority, some common principles apply.

Legitimacy and voice. All people should have free expression of views and a voice in decision-making, either directly or through legitimate intermediate institutions that represent their intention. Governance processes should seek to foster trust, constructive dialogue and collective agreement. Rules should be respected because they are accepted and, where possible, 'owned' by stakeholders.

Equity. Governing processes should promote participatory mechanisms for decision-making that encourage the involvement of all. Stakeholders, including those holding or claiming rights over land, sea or resources, must be respected and engaged in the identification and management of protected areas. Such stakeholders include indigenous peoples and local communities, urban constituencies, protected area users, and a wide range of special interest groups. Legal frameworks must be fair and impartially enforced. Establishment of protected areas often imposes considerable short-term opportunity costs onto local communities. While there are also many local benefits, much of the value derived from reservation is enjoyed by non-local people, nationally and internationally, as well as by the non-human life that is protected. National and international support, financial and institutional, is required to ensure that the costs and benefits of establishing and maintaining protected areas are more equitably shared.

Direction. Institutions and individuals should provide effective leadership by fostering and maintaining an inspiring and consistent long-term vision, and should mobilize support for this vision.

Performance. Governance authorities have a responsibility to ensure that there is sufficient and well-coordinated institutional and human capacity to undertake the required processes and actions. Processes and institutions should produce results that are effective and efficient in that they meet needs, while making the best use of resources.

Accountability. Decision-makers must be accountable to citizens and stakeholders, and relevant information must be directly accessible to them.

The capacity to establish and manage protected areas effectively is weak in many countries. The capacity of an institution, organization or individual involves an appropriate mix of willingness, skills, capability and resources. The skills required to establish and manage protected areas are increasingly specialized, diverse and complex. Considerable effort must be devoted in the coming years to upgrade the professional skills of protected area managers worldwide.

Management effectiveness is under pressure, and investment in protected areas continues to decline. These trends must be urgently reversed. Under-investment by governments, as representatives of community interest, means that protected areas are often struggling to meet the objectives set for them. Inadequate human and financial resources mean that many protected areas lack effective management, particularly in low Human Development Index (HDI) countries. Many protected area users, if they pay anything at all, often do not pay an amount that is commensurate with the full cost of their activities. On the other hand, subsidies and other perverse financial settings encourage unsustainable forestry, agriculture and fishing. Such irrational economic policy settings must be reformed. Funding sources must be diversified. Private bequests and donations, debt-for-nature swaps, ecosystem service charges and more economically rational user-pays fee structures are a few examples of the possibilities. At the same time, care must be taken that adoption of more business-like management approaches does not compromise core protected area values, or the cultural and livelihood values of such areas to local people.

Visitors to protected areas are increasing in numbers and demand will continue to grow, generating vital revenue and increasing understanding and awareness of protected areas values. But already this growing tourism is putting enormous strain on protected areas in most parts of the world. As with other uses, care must be taken that tourism and recreation are properly planned and managed to minimize the impacts, achieve sustainable use and secure economic benefits for protected areas and local people.

Various figures are reported for the extent of protected areas worldwide. As of early 2006, the World Database on Protected Areas (WDPA) identified 113,707 protected areas covering 13.2 per cent of the global land surface and about 1 per cent of marine areas. This coverage may actually be much greater, given that CCAs, which number tens of thousands across the world, have not yet been factored into the database or into related gap analyses. Effective protected area management of the current estate is, in part, dependent upon the generation of knowledge and use of biological, cultural, social and economic information. Such knowledge and information needs to be sourced from indigenous people, local communities, scientists, users and stakeholders. Despite significant advances in these areas, protected area managers and policy-makers often make decisions based on inadequate data. For many protected areas around the world, crucial information is lacking, is difficult for managers to access or is in a form that is difficult to use. There are insufficient opportunities for practitioners to learn from others' experiences. Such deficiencies must be urgently rectified.

Considerable progress in documenting and assessing management effectiveness has been made over the last decade. Central to this progress has been the development and application of the WCPA Management Effectiveness Framework. However, in many countries, adoption and implementation of sound monitoring and evaluation systems are lacking. There is often still insufficient knowledge of trends in ecological, environmental, social, cultural and economic factors to support adaptive management and allow informed decisions to be made. When information is generated and used, it is often done so with insufficient regard to the requirements of participatory governance. Greater understanding and recognition of traditional management practices are also required.

Protected areas in the early 21st century face multiple threats. Meeting these will require new standards of protected area management, new paradigms of governance, innovative initiatives and adaptive responses. As one of humanity's most important land and sea uses, protected areas must flourish. This will require acceleration of the already considerable collaborative and cooperative efforts within and among nations, and within and among communities.

Forest of the Cedars of God, Lebanon

Source: IUCN Photo Library © Jim Thorsell

Part III

Appendices

Appendix 1

Chronology of Earth's Evolutionary Development

Graeme L. Worboys

Table A1.1 briefly summarizes the Earth's evolutionary development, in reverse chronological order.

Table A1.1 The Earth's evolutionary development

Geological era/ period/epoch	Million years ago	Atmosphere, climate, major tectonic events, and natural and human phenomena	Flora	Fauna
Holocene Epoch	0–0.01	Sea level reaches its modern level about 6000 years ago	Recovery and establishment of modern vegetation over the last 16,000 years	The sixth mass extinction of species on Earth – impacts by humans
			Extinctions	
		The Australian Great Barrier Reef commences forming about 8000 years ago		
Pleistocene Epoch	0.01–1.6	Many of the world's temperate zones were alternately covered by glaciers and uncovered during the warmer interglacial periods	Cyclic changes from open/dryer vegetation in glacial periods to wetter vegetation in interglacials	
			Repeated glaciation leads to mass extinctions	Repeated glaciation and/or disease and/or hunting by humans leads to extinctions

Table A1.1 Continued

Geological era/period/epoch	Million years ago	Atmosphere, climate, major tectonic events, and natural and human phenomena	Flora	Fauna
		91,000 years ago, earliest *Homo sapiens* fossils (Israel)		
		700,000 years ago, early humans migrated out of Africa across the old world		460,000 years ago, early *Homo* fossils (China)
Tertiary Period	1.6–23.7	Early ancestor of humans in Africa 1.6 million years ago		
Neogene Epochs: Pliocene and Miocene		Africa 2.5 million years ago: tool-making by ancestor of humans	Decline of forests and spread of grasslands	First appearance of hominids
		Cool dryness starts to appear in upper Tertiary		
		Late Miocene cooling – southern ice cap increases about 6 million years ago		Diverse marsupial fauna: frogs at Riversleigh, Australia
Tertiary Period	23.7–66.4		Explosive radiation of flowering plants	Birds: first penguins evolve
Palaeogene Epochs: Oligocene, Eocene and Palaeocene		The Australian continent separates from Antarctica about 45 million years ago and moves northward from high latitudes		Flightless birds
				Modern genera of mammals present
				First whales and rodents appear
				In seas, bony fish abound
			First appearance of grasses	Appearance of first primates
				Rise of mammals
				First placental mammals

Table A1.1 Continued

Geological era/ period/epoch	Million years ago	Atmosphere, climate, major tectonic events, and natural and human phenomena	Flora	Fauna
Cretaceous Period	66.4–144	Rifting in Gondwana between 96 million–132 million years ago	First flowering plants	Appearance of modern birds
		Gondwana fragmenting	Mass extinctions: highest loss in angiosperms, lowest in ferns	The fifth mass extinction on Earth
				Mass extinctions of vertebrates, including dinosaurs
		Chicxulub Mexico meteorite impact event – 170km diameter astrobleme	Last period of fern and gymnosperm dominance	
		Lower Cretaceous marine flooding worldwide about 120 million years ago		
		Cretaceous deposits of the Dorset and east Devon Coast formed	Araucaria: Wollemi Pine, Australia, a living relic of the Cretaceous	Oldest known monotreme, a platypus, in Lightning Ridge Australia
			Major diversification of angiosperms worldwide	
				Pterosaurs
				Dinosaurs
Jurassic Period	144–208	Subtropical	Araucarians and Podocarps	Age of reptiles, including the dinosaurs
		Warm and wet world	Forests of gymnosperms and ferns over most of the Earth	Ancestor of monotremes
		Jurassic deposits of the Dorset and east Devon Coast formed		
		No polar ice		Cicadas
				Multituberculates
				First birds appear

Table A1.1 Continued

Geological era/period/epoch	Million years ago	Atmosphere, climate, major tectonic events, and natural and human phenomena	Flora	Fauna
Triassic Period	208–245	Warm to hot	Gymnosperms dominant: ferns, club mosses and horsetails	Extinctions of marine invertebrates; some land vertebrates lost
		Periods of aridity and seasonal rainfall		Explosive radiation of dinosaurs
		No polar ice		Age of amphibians
		Triassic deposits of the Dorset and east Devon Coast formed		Amphibians: Labyrinthodonts
		Laurasia: Asia and Euroamerica		Reptiles; dinosaurs first appear but are rare
		Gondwana: Africa, Antarctica, Australia, India, Madagascar, New Guinea, New Zealand and South America		First mammals appear in the northern hemisphere
		Single land mass on Earth; super continent Pangeaea splits into Laurasia and Gondwana		Complex arthropods dominant in seas
				First beetles
Permian Period	245–286	Volcanism	Mass extinctions in plants	The fourth mass extinction event on Earth
				The most severe extinction event, marine and terrestrial: 90–95 per cent of marine species disappear
		Warm to hot	Extensive swampy conditions for coal deposition	*Labyrinthodonts* (primitive amphibians)
		Ice cap advances and retreats	*Glossopteris* flora	Appearance of therapsids, mammal-like reptiles
			Decline of non-seed plants	Increase of reptiles and insects
				Decline of amphibians

Table A1.1 Continued

Geological era/period/epoch	Million years ago	Atmosphere, climate, major tectonic events, and natural and human phenomena	Flora	Fauna
Carboniferous Period	286–360	Glaciation	Pro-gymnosperms are replaced in tundra areas	First sharks appear
		Cool	Club mosses and horsetails diminish with the cold	Increase in amphibians
		Warm	Gymnosperms appear	First winged insects
			Widespread forests of giant club moss trees, horsetails and tree ferns provide basis for vast coal deposits	Early reptiles
Devonian Period	360–408	Warm and wet	First extinction crisis in plants	The third mass extinction event on Earth; mass extinctions in marine animals – reef-building organisms were devastated
			Rich flora in swamps	Amphibians diversify into many forms
			First seed plants Development of vascular plants: club mosses and ferns	First land vertebrates appear: amphibians
Silurian Period	408–436	Sufficient ozone in the atmosphere able to screen ultraviolet rays, permitting life outside the seas	First land plants evolve from marine algae	First land invertebrates: land scorpions
		Hot and arid	First vascular plant	Golden age of fishes
Ordovician Period	436–505	Atmosphere unable to support life on land	Algae in the sea	The second mass extinction event on Earth: 1000 families of marine invertebrates perished
		Warm		First vertebrates appear (fish)
				Rich trilobite and shellfish fauna

Table A1.1 Continued

Geological era/ period/epoch	Million years ago	Atmosphere, climate, major tectonic events, and natural and human phenomena	Flora	Fauna
Cambrian Period	505–570	Atmosphere unable to support life on land	Algae in the sea – dominant	The first mass extinction event on Earth caused by rising sea levels
		Hot and dry		Trilobites dominant
		Burgess Shales formed Canadian Rocky Mountain Parks		First vertebrates: jawless fishes; Archaeocyathid (sponges)
				Limestone reefs
				Explosive evolution of marine life
Precambrian Era	570–4500	Living organisms steadily release oxygen to the oceans and atmosphere	Cyanobacteria – living examples of stromatolites in Shark Bay World Heritage Area, Australia	Ediacaran fauna (jellyfish, etc.)
		300 million-year ice age that peaks at 620 million, 770 million and 940 million years ago	3200 million years ago oldest evidence of simple single cells	600 million years ago, oldest multi-cell animal fossils
		Vredefort Dome meteorite impact structure (astrobleme) 2023 million years ago: the world's oldest and largest (360km diameter) known impact (World Heritage area)		
		Life-providing oxygen causes oxidation of ocean minerals and produces 'red beds' 2500 million years ago	Stromatolites are the most common form of life for 3000 million years	1500 million years ago, first complex cells appear in the fossil record
		Ancient atmosphere consists of carbon dioxide, water vapour, methane, ammonia and hydrogen	3500 million years ago, stromatolites appear in Shark Bay Marine Reserve, Australia (World Heritage area)	

Sources: Vandenbeld (1988); White (1990); Vickers-Rich and Rich (1993); White (1994); Long (1998); Mulvaney and Kamminga (1999); Groombridge and Jenkins (2000); Rich and Vickers-Rich (2000); White (2000); Woodford (2000); Groombridge and Jenkins (2002); Allen (2002); Burenhult (2003); White (2003); Earth Impact Data Base (2004)

Stromatolites, Shark Bay Marine Reserve, Western Australia

Source: IUCN Photo Library © Jim Thorsell

Appendix 2

Chronology of Protected Areas

**Michael Lockwood, Graeme L. Worboys and
Ashish Kothari (with contributions from Neville Grove,
Robert Sneddon and Patty Warboys)**

Table A2.1 Chronology of key protected area events

Year	Key event	Source
Through human history	Conservation sites for various reasons, including spiritual and ethical, or for ecological benefits such as water In India, an estimated 10% of land may have been under sacred sites until colonial times; in Nepal, forests were protected for lions or tigers considered to be forest goddesses	Posey (1999); Gokhale et al (1997); HMG/IUCN (1988)
1370 BC	Establishment of a nature reserve in Egypt	Lyster (1985), cited in Harrop (1999)
3rd century BC	Establishment of a sanctuary in Sri Lanka, by King Devanampiyatissa, under Buddhist influence	Nanayakkara (1987)
3rd century BC	Emperor Asoka of India declared sites as protected specially for elephants, and passed an edict for the protection of animals, fish and forests – the earliest recorded instance of a government protecting natural areas and resources	Rangarajan (2001)
684	First Indonesian nature reserve established by order of the King of Srivijaya on the island of Sumatra	McNeely and Schutyser (2003)
1087	William the Conqueror declared the New Forest in England as his royal domain – it later became common heritage, with 259 square kilometres for grazing, timber production and public recreation, administered by the Forestry Commission	Brockman (1959)
12th century AD	Hunting banned by King Kirti Nissanka Malla in a 35km radius around the kingdom of Anuradhapura, Sri Lanka, which is even now considered a protected area	Nanayakkara (1987)
1641	Great Ponds Act, Massachusetts, US, set aside some 36,420 hectares, forever open to the public for 'fishing and fowling'	Brockman (1959)

Table A2.1 Continued

Year	Key event	Source
1810	The English poet William Wordsworth wrote of his vision of the Lake District as 'a sort of national property'	Phillips et al (2003)
1832	Hot Springs Reservation Arkansas, US, were reserved when the US Congress set them aside so that they 'shall not be entered, located or appropriated for any other purpose whatever' – later established as the Hot Springs National Park in 1921	Brockman (1959)
1833	Birth of a national park idea – US explorer and artist George Catlin's writings reflect an emergence of an awareness of the great aesthetic and cultural qualities of 'primitive' America and the need for their preservation; after visiting the native American Indian country of the Upper Missouri, he wrote: *… and what a splendid contemplation, too, when one (who has travelled these realms and can duly appreciate them) imagines them as they might in the future be seen (by some protective policy of government) preserved in their pristine beauty and wildness, in a magnificent park… A nations park, containing man and beast, in all the wild and freshness of their nature's beauty.*	Brockman (1959)
1840	Royal instructions to William Hobson, New Zealand's first governor, to 'reserve land for public use and enjoyment' around the volcanic Mount Egmont	Rata (1975)
1864	George Marsh's influential Man and Nature published on land and water degradation	
1864–1865	Yosemite (California) established by US Congress on 1 July 1864 as the first of a new national-level model of protected areas: *… to commit them [Yosemite Valley and the Mariposa Grove of Big Trees] to the care of the authorities of that state for their constant preservation, that may be exposed to public view, and that they may be used and preserved for the benefit of mankind.*	Brockman (1959); McNeely and Schutyser (2003)
1866	Jenolan Caves Reserve, New South Wales, Australia, declared to protect the values of the caves	Finlayson and Hamilton-Smith (2003)
1872–1883	World's 'first' national park, Yellowstone, formally reserved – the title of national park formally conferred in 1883	Brockman (1959); Sutton and Sutton (1972); McNeely and Schutyser (2003)
1879	Australia's first national park, The National Park in New South Wales near Sydney, was formally declared – later to be renamed The Royal National Park in 1955	Charles (1994); Goldstein (1979)
1882	Mexico's first national park, El Chico National Park, established – the first in Central America	McNeely and Schutyser (2003)
1885	Canada gave protection to 26 square kilometres around hot springs in the Bow Valley of the Rocky Mountains, which was enlarged to 670 square kilometres in 1887 and named Rocky Mountains Park; further enlargements followed, and in 1930 the reserve was renamed Banff National Park	Dearden and Rollins (2002)

Table A2.1 Continued

Year	Key event	Source
1887–1894	Te Heuheu Tukino paramount chief of the Ngati Tuwharetoa tribe and other native chiefs presented tribal lands around Mounts Ruapehu, Ngauruhoe and Tongariro, which were to form the nucleus of Tongariro National Park, established in 1894	Sutton and Sutton (1972); Rata (1975)
1895	The National Trust formed in Great Britain	Charles (1994)
1898	Sabie Game Reserve, South Africa, established to conserve wildlife – later to become Kruger National Park in 1926	Harroy et al (1974)
1906	First Australian national park legislation adopted by the Queensland parliament following a long advocacy by R. M. Collins – provided for the creation of national parks, which could only be alienated by parliament In 1908 Mount Tambourine was the first Queensland national park established under the legislation	Mosley (1968); Goldstein (1979); Mulligan and Hill (2001)
1908	Assam Reserve in Kaziranga established in India – later to become Kaziranga National Park	Harroy et al (1974)
1909	Iguazú National Park, Argentina, initially created (the first in South America) – later formally established in 1934	Harroy et al (1974); McNeely and Schutyser (2003)
1909	Sarek, Stora Sjöfallet, Peljekajse and Abisko National Parks established in Sweden, totalling over 284,900ha	Harroy et al (1974)
1914	Engadine National Park established in Switzerland occupying an area of 16,000ha	Bauer (1962)
1916	United States National Park Service established	Goldstein (1979)
1916	Barguzin and Kedrovaya Pad reserves established in Russia	Harroy et al (1974)
1925	Cambodia's first national park, Angkor Wat, reserved – the first in Asia	McNeely and Schutyser (2003)
1925	Albert National Park, 809,000ha, created in the then Belgian Congo by King Alfred of Belgium – now called Virunga National Park in the Democratic Republic of Congo	Harroy et al (1974)
1931	Japan's National Park Laws established to formally reserve protected areas	Ikenouye (1962)
1932	Waterton–Glacier International Peace Park established, comprising two existing parks: Waterton Lakes National Park in Canada and Glacier National Park in the US	Dearden and Rollins (2002)
1934	Ecuador establishes the Galapagos National Park	Harroy et al (1974)
1936	Establishment of Corbett National Park in India, one of the first parks designated under statutory national law in South Asia	Corbett Park (2006)
1937	Brazil's first national park established – Parcque Nacional de Itatiáia; Venezuela's first park established – Henri Pittier National Park	Strang (1962); Harroy et al (1974)
1945	United Nations Educational, Scientific and Cultural Organization (UNESCO) established	
1948	The International Union for the Conservation of Nature, now the World Conservation Union (IUCN), established as a means of promoting conservation worldwide	McNeely and Schutyser (2003)

Table A2.1 Continued

Year	Key event	Source
1961	The World Wildlife Fund, later to become the World Wide Fund for Nature (WWF), established as an international NGO to mobilize support for conservation	McNeely and Schutyser (2003)
1962	*Silent Spring*, Rachel Carson's influential book, published, which exposed the problems of indiscriminate use of pesticides, especially the impacts of DDT on the food chain	Carson (1962)
1962	Ist IUCN World Conference on National Parks, Seattle, Washington, US – aimed to establish a more effective international understanding of national parks and to encourage further development of national parks worldwide	McNeely and Schutyser (2003)
1963	Establishment of the African College of Wildlife Management at Mweka, Tanzania; by 2000, over 4000 Africans had graduated	McNeely and Schutyser (2003)
1965	International Seminar on National Parks and Equivalent Reserves held by the US National Park Service, Parks Canada and the University of Michigan	McNeely and Schutyser (2003)
1969	At the IUCN General Assembly in Delhi, an agreed definition of a national park was established as 'a relatively large area where one or several ecosystems are not materially altered by human exploitation and occupation'	Phillips et al (2003)
1969–1974	Future of the Great Barrier Reef Symposium conducted by the Australian Conservation Foundation, which provided direct input to state and federal elections Save the Great Barrier Reef Campaign Committee established Two Royal Commissions established; drilling for oil on the reef was prohibited indefinitely (1970) Great Barrier Reef Marine Park (GBRMP) declared (1974) – one of the largest marine parks in the world	Lawrence et al (2002)
1970	UNESCO launches the Man and the Biosphere programme	Batisse (2001)
1970	Bouddi National Park, Australia's first marine national park reserved by protecting 283ha of the seafloor	Charles (1994)
1970	Establishment of the School for Training of Wildlife Specialists, Garoua, Cameroon – well over 3000 people trained	McNeely and Schutyser (2003)
1971	Ramsar Convention on Wetlands of International Importance adopted in Ramsar, Iran; by 2003, 1292 sites covering 109,103,928ha in 137 countries had been designated	Charles (1994); McNeely and Schutyser (2003)
1972	United Nations Conference on the Human Environment, Stockholm, Sweden, held to sound the alarm about the perilous state of the Earth and its resources, with 113 nations attending Concept of sustainable development introduced	UNEP (2002)
1972	United Nations Environment Programme (UNEP) established	UNEP (2002)

Table A2.1 Continued

Year	Key event	Source
1972	IInd IUCN World Conference on National Parks held in Yellowstone, US; key issues addressed included the effects of tourism on protected areas; park planning and management; social, scientific and environmental problems within national parks in wet tropical, arid and mountain regions	Wagner (2003); McNeely and Schutyser (2003)
	Protected area coverage: 1823 sites, 217 million hectares	
1972	UNESCO Man and the Biosphere programme formally endorsed by United Nations Conference on the Human Environment in Stockholm to establish a coordinated world network of biosphere reserves	Batisse (2001)
1972	UNESCO Convention Concerning the Protection of the World Cultural and Natural Heritage adopted; by 2003, 149 natural World Heritage sites and 23 mixed natural and cultural sites had been recognized	UNEP (2002); McNeely and Schutyser (2003)
1972	*The Limits to Growth* (Meadows et al, 1972) published	UNEP (2002)
1972	Landsat satellite launched	UNEP (2002)
1973	Convention on International Trade in Endangered Species of Wild Flora and Fauna (CITES) adopted	UNEP (2002)
1973	Launch of Project Tiger in India, one of the world's most ambitious species recovery and protection programmes	Kothari et al (1989)
1975	First South Pacific Conference on National Parks and Reserves held in New Zealand	Charles (1994)
1977	United Nations Conference on Desertification, Nairobi, Kenya	UNEP (2002)
1977	Training programme for protected area personnel established at Turrialba, Costa Rica – continues until present and has provided trained staff for much of Latin America	McNeely and Schutyser (2003)
1977	Green Belt movement established in Kenya	UNEP (2002)
1977	First World Wilderness Congress held in Johannesburg, South Africa, with 2500 delegates from 27 countries	
1978	IUCN system of categories of protected areas published; sets framework for global assessment of protected area coverage – latest major revision in 1994	McNeely and Schutyser (2003)
1979	First World Climate Conference, Geneva, Switzerland	UNEP (2002)
1979	Convention on the Conservation of Migratory Species of Animals (CMS) adopted	UNEP (2002)
1980	Launch of World Conservation Strategy prepared by IUCN, WWF and UNEP, containing three core objectives: essential ecological processes and life-support systems must be maintained; genetic diversity must be preserved; and any use of species or ecosystems must be sustainable	IUCN, UNEP, WWF (1991)
1981	Protected Areas Data Unit at the World Conservation Monitoring Centre (WCMC) established; provides first global database on protected areas	McNeely and Schutyser (2003)

Table A2.1 Continued

Year	Key event	Source
1981	Gurig National Park becomes the first national park in Australia to be jointly managed by indigenous traditional owners and government	Smyth (2001)
1982	World coverage of protected areas reaches 4 million square kilometres, with protected areas established by 124 countries	Harrison et al (1982)
1982	IIIrd IUCN World Congress on National Parks, Bali, Indonesia, focused on the role of protected areas in sustaining society; the inadequacy of the existing global network of terrestrial protected areas; the need for more marine, coastal and freshwater protected areas; improved ecological managerial quality of existing protected areas; a system of consistent protected area categories to balance conservation and development needs; and links with sustainable development Protected area coverage: 2671 sites, 396 million hectares	Wagner (2003); McNeely and Schutyser (2003)
1982	United Nations Convention on the Law of the Sea (UNCLOS)	UNEP (2002)
1982	United Nations General Assembly adopts the *World Charter for Nature*	UNPE (2002)
1985	Uluru–Kata Tjuta National Park, Australia, returned to aboriginal ownership	Smyth (2001)
1985	International Conference on the Assessment of the Role of Carbon Dioxide and other Greenhouse Gases, Villach, Austria	UNEP (2002)
1987	*Our Common Future* published, a report of a World Commission on Environment and Development Independent Commission chaired by Gro Harlem Bruntland to bring forward a global agenda for achieving sustainable development by 2000 and ways to deal more effectively with environmental concerns – calls for 12% of the land to be given protected area status	WCED (1987); McNeely and Schutyser (2003)
1989	Fall of the Berlin Wall	
1989–1990	Intergovernmental Panel on Climate Change (IPCC) established – warns of impending global warming	UNEP (2002)
1991	Global Environment Facility (GEF) established, providing a major new funding mechanism for protected areas	UNEP (2002); McNeely and Schutyser (2003)
1992	IVth IUCN World Congress on National Parks and Protected Areas, 'Parks for Life', held in Caracas, Venezuela – emphasized the relationship between people and protected areas, the need for identifying sites of importance for biodiversity conservation, and a regional approach to land management, and set a target of protecting at least 10% of each major biome by the year 2000 Protected area coverage: 8641 sites, 7900 million hectares	Wagner (2003); McNeely and Schutyser (2003)
1992	United Nations Conference on Environment and Development (UNCED) held in Rio de Janeiro, Brazil, resulting in an action plan for sustainable development (*Agenda 21*), as well as the Convention on Biological Diversity (CBD)	UNEP (2002)
1992	United Nations Framework Convention on Climate Change	UNEP (2002)
1993	World Wide Web has only 50 pages World Conference on Human Rights, Vienna, Austria	UNEP (2002)

Table A2.1 Continued

Year	Key event	Source
1994	United Nations Convention to Combat Desertification	UNEP (2002)
1997	The UNESCO *World Heritage List* included 500 sites (350 cultural, 100 natural and 50 cultural and natural)	Wagner (2003)
	IUCN Symposium 'Protected areas in the 21st century: From islands to networks' concluded that protected areas face significant challenges, including the need to move from an 'island' to a 'network' view of protected areas; mainstream protected areas into other areas of public policy; manage protected areas for and with local communities; and raise standards through capacity-building	
1997	Kyoto Protocol adopted to limit greenhouse gas emissions	UNEP (2002)
1999	World population reaches 6000 million	UNEP (2002)
1999	Launch of Global Compact on labour standards, human rights and environmental protection	UNEP (2002)
2000	World Wide Web has 50 million pages	UNEP (2002)
	Millennium Summit, New York, US – governments were urged to adopt a new ethic of conservation and stewardship, and, as the first steps, to adopt and ratify the Kyoto Protocol, accommodate 'green accounting' into their national accounts, participate in a Millennium Ecosystem Assessment and prepare the ground for meaningful actions for the Earth Summit +10 in 2002	
2002	World Summit on Sustainable Development, Johannesburg, among other things, calls for loss of biodiversity to be reversed by 2010 and for a system of marine protected areas	McNeely and Schutyser (2003)
2003	Vth IUCN World Congress on National Parks and Protected Areas, 'Benefits Beyond Boundaries', held in Durban, South Africa	
2003–2004	Recognition of community conserved areas (CCAs) as protected areas equivalent to government-managed protected areas at the World Parks Congress (September 2003) and the Seventh Conference of the Parties of the Convention on Biological Diversity (February 2004)	Chapter 21, this volume
2004	Adoption of Programme of Work on Protected Areas at the CBD's Seventh Conference of Parties, held in Kuala Lumpur, Malaysia	Appendix 4, this volume

Sources: as indicated, as well as Worboys et al (2004)

Appendix 3

Vth IUCN World Parks Congress Outputs

Peter Shadie

The IUCN, with leadership and support from its World Commission on Protected Areas (WCPA), stages world parks congresses every ten years for the benefit of the conservation community and the world at large. The congress brings together the largest global assembly of protected area specialists, managers and experts to focus on the state of the planet's protected areas, the challenges they face and the opportunities before them. They act as a catalyst for protected area action and recommend future directions for the world's protected areas. The Vth IUCN World Parks Congress was held in Durban, South Africa, in September 2003.

The theme of the Vth IUCN Congress was identified as 'Benefits beyond Boundaries' and the programme was structured around seven workshop streams, as well as three cross-cutting themes. The workshop streams were:

1 Linkages in the Landscape and Seascape;
2 Building Broader Support for Protected Areas;
3 Governance of Protected Areas: New Ways of Working Together;
4 Developing the Capacity to Manage Protected Area;
5 Evaluating Management Effectiveness;
6 Building a Secure Financial Future; and
7 Building Comprehensive Protected Area Systems.

The three cross-cutting themes were:

1 Communities and Equity;
2 Marine; and
3 World Heritage.

The congress programme and related activities included more than 200 workshops, side meetings, media press conferences, launches and other sessions; more than 50 publications and tools; various policies and partnerships; on-site high-level political commitments to additional protected areas and resources (200,000 square kilometres of new protected areas and pledges of an additional US$35 million); hands-on training through short courses and demonstration centres; and field experiences and an exhibition of the latest in protected areas. Full proceedings of the congress in English, Spanish and French are available in hard copy from www.iucn.org/bookstore and can be downloaded from www.iucn.org/themes/wcpa.

The hosting of the World Parks Congress for the first time in Africa provided an opportunity to focus on the special needs of African protected areas. The World Parks Congress launched the African Protected Areas Initiative and agreed a ten-point agenda for action. All of the congress sessions placed a special focus upon African protected area issues, case studies and approaches.

The Protected Areas Learning Network (PALNet) was also launched as a pilot website at the congress. PALNet is being developed by the IUCN as a knowledge management tool to support managers in dealing with protected area issues in a changing world.

The rest of this appendix summarizes the major outputs from the World Parks Congress.

United Nations List of Protected Areas and the world's protected areas: Status, values and prospects in the 21st century

An important objective of the World Parks Congress was to assess the state of protected areas worldwide. The *United Nations List of Protected Areas*, mandated by the UN, is periodically updated to collect information about the number and extent of the world's protected areas. The 2003 version of the UN list released at the Durban Congress was the 13th report to be produced since 1962. It showed the global protected area estate to have expanded to 102,102 sites covering 18.8 million square kilometres with terrestrial protected areas (TPAs) covering some 11.5 per cent of the Earth's land surface. For further information on the UN list see www.iucn. org/bookstore or www.unep-wcmc.org. The World Parks Congress also generated an accompanying publication, *The World's Protected Areas: Status, Values and Prospects in the 21st Century*, which is currently in press. This document provides a qualitative assessment of the state of the world's protected areas.

The *Durban Accord* and *Durban Action Plan*

The *Durban Accord* was agreed at the close of the World Parks Congress and is a collective statement by the nearly 3000 participants. The accord celebrates the global achievements and sets out a vision for the world's protected areas. At the same time, it voices concern for their future and the urgent need for action in the 21st century. The accord affirms a new paradigm for protected areas, expressed as follows:

> In this changing world, we need a fresh and innovative approach to protected areas and their role in broader conservation and development agendas. This approach demands the maintenance and enhancement of our core conservation goals, equitably integrating them with the interests of all affected people. In this way the synergy between conservation, the maintenance of life-support systems and sustainable development is forged. We see protected areas as vital means to achieve this synergy efficiently and cost effectively. We see protected areas as providers of benefits beyond boundaries – beyond their boundaries on a map, beyond the boundaries of nation states, across societies, genders and generations.

The accord is backed by the *Durban Action Plan*, which suggests a checklist of the activity needed to address the principles of the accord. The action plan is directed towards multiple societal actors and recommends action across ten separate outcomes. Progress against the *Durban Action Plan* will be assessed at the time of the VIth IUCN Congress. For further information, see www.iucn. org/themes/wcpa.

World Parks Congress Recommendations

Thirty-two *World Parks Congress Recommendations*, along with a list of emerging issues, were agreed within the seven workshop streams and three cross-cutting themes (see Table A3.1). The recommendations reflect state-of-the-art thinking on protected areas and represent broad agreement by protected area specialists of the action needed on specific issues. The recommendations have informed policy and strategy at a number of levels and provide a concise set of principles and actions to guide protected area establishment and management. Given that many of the recommendation topics have multiple dimensions and there are areas of overlap, the approximate relationship between them and the chapters in this book is indicated in Table A3.2. The emerging issues (see Table A3.3) are those that workshop participants felt were matters which, in the future, would become globally significant and require a global response. For further information, see www.iucn.org/themes/ wcpa.

Message to the Convention on Biological Diversity

An objective for the World Parks Congress was securing stronger intergovernmental support and action for protected areas as a fundamental contribution to achieving biodiversity conservation and

Table A3.1 World Parks Congress recommendation topics

No.	Recommendation topic
V.1	Strengthening institutional and societal capacities for protected area management in the 21st century
V.2	Strengthening individual and group capacities for protected area management in the 21st century
V.3	Protected areas learning network
V.4	Building comprehensive and effective protected area systems
V.5	Climate change and protected areas
V.6	Strengthening mountain protected areas as a key contribution to sustainable mountain development
V.7	Financial security for protected areas
V.8	Private sector funding of protected areas
V.9	Integrated landscape management to support protected areas
V.10	Policy linkages between relevant international conventions and programmes in integrating protected areas in the wider landscape/seascape
V.11	A global network to support the development of transboundary conservation initiatives
V.12	Tourism as a vehicle for conservation and support of protected areas
V.13	Cultural and spiritual values of protected areas
V.14	Cities and protected areas
V.15	Peace, conflict and protected areas
V.16	Good governance of protected areas
V.17	Recognizing and supporting a diversity of governance types for protected areas
V.18	Management effectiveness evaluation to support protected area management
V.19	IUCN Protected Area Management categories
V.20	Preventing and mitigating human–wildlife conflicts
V.21	The World Heritage Convention
V.22	Building a Global System of Marine and Coastal Protected Area Networks
V.23	Protecting marine biodiversity and ecosystem processes through marine protected areas beyond national jurisdiction
V.24	Indigenous peoples and protected areas
V.25	Co-management of protected areas
V.26	Community conserved areas
V.27	Mobile indigenous peoples and conservation
V.28	Protected areas: mining and energy
V.29	Poverty and protected areas
V.30	Africa's protected areas
V.31	Protected Areas, Freshwater and Integrated River Basin Management Frameworks
V.32	Strategic Agenda for Communication, Education and Public Awareness for Protected Areas

Table A3.2 Relationship between World Parks Congress recommendation topics and book chapters

Chapter	Congress recommendation
3 Global Protected Area Framework	V.10; V.19; V.21
4 Values and Benefits	V.1; V.13; V.14; V.24; V.27; V.29
5 Governance of Protected Areas	V.16; V.17; V.24
7 Developing Capacity	V.1; V.2; V.3
8 Establishing Protected Areas	V.4; V.29; V.31
9 Threats to Protected Areas	V.5; V.20; V.28
10 Obtaining, Managing and Communicating Information	V.3
12 Finance and Economics	V.7; V.8
17 Cultural Heritage Management	V.13
18 Incident Management	V.20
19 Tourism and Recreation	V.12
20 Collaboratively Managed Protected Areas	V.24; V.25; V.27
21 Community Conserved Areas	V.24; V.26; V.27
22 Linking the Landscape	V.6; V.9; V.10; V.11; V.31
23 Marine Protected Areas	V.22; V.23
24 Evaluating Management Effectiveness	V.18
25 Building Support for Protected Areas	V.13; V.14; V.15; V.28; V.29; V.30; V.32

meeting the Millennium Development Goals (MDGs) and World Summit on Sustainable Development targets. The congress was able to play an influential role in leading to the timely adoption of the Convention on Biological Diversity Protected Area Programme of Work in February 2004. The congress plenary sent a message to the convention urging the adoption of a comprehensive, far-sighted and measurable programme of action for protected areas. The timing of the congress was extremely beneficial, leading just five months later to the convention's Seventh Conference of the Parties that placed special emphasis on protected areas. At that time, the 188 parties to the Convention on Biological Diverstiy (CBD) adopted the Protected Area Programme of Work, thereby binding government commitment towards far-reaching action on protected areas (see Appendix 4).

Table A3.3 Emerging issue topics

Number	Emerging issue topic
1	Ecological restoration
2	Building support for protected areas through site-based planning
3	Disease and protected area management
4	Sustainable hunting, fishing and other wildlife issues
5	Private protected areas
6	Collapse from the inside: threats to biodiversity and the ecological integrity of protected areas from unsustainable hunting for subsistence and trade
7	Management of invasive species
8	Gender equity in the management of protected areas
9	Amendment to the IUCN definition of marine protected areas
10	Moratorium on deep-sea trawling
11	HIV/AIDS (acquired immune deficiency syndrome) pandemic and conservation

Appendix 4

Convention on Biological Diversity Programme of Work on Protected Areas

Peter Shadie

Chapter 3 introduced the Convention on Biological Diversity (CBD) and its relevance to protected areas. The principle provisions of the CBD dealing with protected areas are found under Article 8 of the convention. However, almost all other articles of the CBD make reference to protected areas and the contribution that they offer to achieving the overall objectives of the convention. In addition, the Convention on Biological Diversity Conference of the Parties has emphasized the importance of protected areas in the various work programmes adopted under the convention. There are strong references to protected areas within the programmes of work on forest biological diversity, marine and coastal biological diversity, inland water biological diversity and the biological diversity of dry and sub-humid lands.

In February 2004, the Seventh Conference of the Parties (COP 7) adopted a comprehensive Protected Area Programme of Work. This programme details the actions necessary to give effect to those aspects of the CBD dealing with protected areas, principally Article 8, but also others. In essence, the programme commits countries to develop participatory, ecologically representative and effectively managed national and regional systems of protected areas, stretching, where necessary, across national boundaries, integrated with other land uses and contributing to human well-being. The programme imbues a sense of urgency through the adoption of challenging time frames and specific targets.

Although the CBD is not the only global convention dealing with protected areas, it is the core multilateral environmental agreement that addresses issues related to protected areas. While national governments as parties to the CBD bear the responsibility for implementation of the programme, it places special emphasis on the supporting role of partner organizations, such as United Nations (UN) agencies, other conventions, intergovernmental forums, organizations such as the IUCN and international NGOs.

The programme is a complex document with many interlinked and overlapping activities, which can be divided into three general phases (see Table A4.1). The table is not intended as an exhaustive or definitive list of the major outcomes under the programme, nor is it intended as a definitive breakdown of how phases of activity should be carried out. Rather, it is provided as a tool to illustrate the logical sequencing of activities under the programme.

An effective global protected area system is the best hope for conserving viable and representative areas of natural ecosystems, habitats and species, and helps to achieve the 2010 biodiversity target. In adopting the programme, the world community has agreed to work together at the national, regional and international level to meet clearly defined goals and time-bound targets for the world's protected areas.

The programme contains four interlinked and mutually reinforcing elements:

1   direct actions for planning, selecting, establish-

Table A4.1 Phases of the Convention on Biological Diversity Protected Area Programme of Work

Phases	Potential main outcomes of each phase
Phase I (2004–2006)	*'Master plan' for protected areas.* Completing, in effect, a master plan for the system of protected areas (key elements include, for example, plans for filling ecological gaps; securing financial resources; building capacity; promoting governance arrangements; and addressing policy, legislative and institutional barriers).
	Studies and assessments, for input into master plans, covering, for example, socio-economic contributions of protected areas, ecological gaps in protected area systems and types of governance arrangements.
	New protected areas. Establishment of new protected areas where urgent action is required.
Phase II (2007–2008)	*Threats.* Mechanisms in place to address key threats.
	Financial resources. Sufficient financial resources secured.
	Indigenous and local communities. Policies and mechanisms to support indigenous and local community participation and equitable sharing of costs and benefits.
	Standards. Standards adopted for all major aspects of protected areas.
Phase III (2009–2015)	*Effective systems of protected areas.* Comprehensive, ecologically representative and effectively managed systems of protected areas.
	Integration of protected areas within wider landscapes and sectors.

Source: Dudley et al (2005, p7)

ing, strengthening, and managing protected area systems and sites;

2 governance, participation, equity and benefit-sharing;

3 enabling activities; and

4 standards, assessment and monitoring.

In essence, element 1 primarily deals with *what* protected area systems need to conserve and where; elements 2 and 3 cover *how* to implement protected area systems effectively, including issues such as the policy environment, governance, participation, finance and capacity-building; and element 4 covers the steps needed for *assessing and monitoring* the effectiveness of actions taken under elements 1 to 3.

Each programme element has one or more goals (16 in total), which are outcome-oriented statements of purpose. Each goal is accompanied by a more specific target, which in most cases sets a specific date by which the desired outcome is to

be accomplished. Each target is accompanied by a set of suggested Activities of the Parties (92 in total), which represents the consensus recommendations of COP 7 for the 'best practice' actions that countries need to take in order to meet the goals and targets to which they have committed. However, the activities may be treated flexibly since not every country will have the need or capacity to implement every one.

Fourteen of the 16 goal targets noted above contain deadlines of either 2008 or 2010 (for terrestrial areas) and 2012 (for marine areas), with broader integration into wider landscapes and seascapes by 2015. Reaching these targets will require implementing a range of supporting activities, including, for example, the establishment of an enabling policy environment, provision of financial and technical resources, capacity-building, monitoring and evaluation, and ensuring that protected areas are established and managed in an equitable and participatory manner.

The programme reflects fresh thinking on protected areas due to the influence of the immediately preceding Vth IUCN World Parks Congress (see Appendix 3). For example, the inclusion of the major element on governance, participation, equity and benefit-sharing mirrors the vital importance of these considerations to successful protected area management. The programme commits governments to promote the equitable sharing of the costs and benefits of protected areas – particularly for indigenous and local communities – and to enhance and secure the full and effective participation of indigenous and local communities and relevant stakeholders. Similarly, the programme includes the latest professional thinking on evaluating the management effectiveness of protected area systems. Parties agreed that by 2012, all protected areas should be managed effectively:

> … *using participatory and science-based site planning processes that incorporate clear biodiversity objectives, targets, management strategies and monitoring programmes, drawing upon existing methodologies and a long-term management plan with active stakeholder involvement.*

The programme takes into account the ecosystem approach, which is the primary framework for action under the CBD. This emphasizes the relationship of protected areas in the broader land and seascape, the central role they play in delivering ecosystem goods and services, and their consequent value in sustainable development strategies. Parties have therefore committed, by 2015, to:

> … *integrate protected areas within broader land and seascapes and sectors so as to maintain ecological structure and function in such a manner that all protected areas and protected area systems are integrated into the wider land and seascape, and relevant sectors, by applying the ecosystem approach and taking into account ecological connectivity and the concept, where appropriate, of ecological networks.*

The programme places special emphasis on marine conservation, both the pressing need to establish expanded networks of marine protected areas to conserve marine biodiversity, and the need to improve the management of these areas. Explicit measures are included to address the need

for marine protection in areas beyond the limits of national jurisdictions: the high seas.

The programme recognizes the value of adopting the IUCN system of protected area categories to harmonize reporting, compare and contrast national systems, and to provide a measure of progress against the agreed 2010/2012 biodiversity targets.

The programme acknowledges the needs of species and ecosystems to function across national borders by encouraging transboundary cooperation for conservation. Parties have committed, by 2010 (in terrestrial areas) and 2012 (in marine areas), to:

> … *establish and strengthen transboundary protected areas, other forms of collaboration between neighbouring protected areas across national boundaries and regional networks, to enhance the conservation and sustainable use of biological diversity, implementing the ecosystem approach and improving international cooperation.*

The financial resourcing implications of the programme are strongly acknowledged. The programme recognizes and seeks to address the need for sustainable finance and adequate investment in capacity development for protected areas. Parties committed to securing sufficient financial resources by 2008 to implement and manage national systems of protected areas effectively. The Conference of the Parties also signalled the urgency of funding in a number of areas by agreeing to 2006 and 2008 timelines for implementing some crucial activities.

The full Programme of Work on Protected Areas is downloadable from the CBD's website at www.biodiv.org/decisions/?dec=VII/28. Further guidance on the interpretation and implementation of the programme is given in Dudley et al (2005) and downloadable from www.biodiv.org/doc/info-centre.shtml.

Appendix 5

Number and Area of National Protected Areas, by WCPA Region

Compiled from data in WDPA Consortium (2005) by Michael Lockwood and Colin Winkler.

Terrestrial protected areas include inland lakes, rivers and wetlands.

Marine and coastal protected areas include marine protected areas, littoral protected areas and protected areas with both marine and littoral components – these marine protected areas include areas that are fully marine and areas that have only a small percentage of intertidal environment.

National IUCN areas = national protected areas classified as one of the IUCN categories (see Box 3.3).

National other areas = protected areas not yet classified under one of the IUCN categories.

National protected areas = protected areas recognized within a national jurisdiction separately from, but may be overlapping with, World Heritage areas, Ramsar sites or biosphere reserves.

Sites less than 1ha are recorded as having 0ha area.

European national other areas include regional designations, such as those under the Barcelona Convention and Birds Directive – these sometimes overlap, often imperfectly, with other reserve designations, so the data may include some double counting.

Differences between the data here and those in Tables 3.3 and 3.4 are due to Chape et al (2005) using an earlier version of the database, and from our separation of national and international protected areas into two appendices.

Table A5.1 Number and area of national protected areas by World Commission on Protected Areas (WCPA) region

ANTARCTICA

			National IUCN areas						National
	Ia	Ib	II	III	IV	V	VI	Total	other areas
Terrestrial protected areas									
Sites									**Total**
Antarctica	13							13	2
Total	13							13	2
Area (ha)									
Antarctica	49,591							49,591	153,500
Total	49,591							49,591	153,500

Table A5.1 Continued

ANTARCTICA

	Ia	Ib	II	National IUCN areas III	IV	V	VI	Total	National other areas
Marine and coastal protected areas									
Sites									**Total**
Antarctica	42							42	
Total	42							42	
Area (ha)									
Antarctica	250,004							250,004	
Total	250,004							250,004	
REGIONAL TOTAL									
Sites	55							55	2
Area (ha)	299,595							299,595	153,500

AUSTRALIA and NEW ZEALAND

	Ia	Ib	II	National IUCN areas III	IV	V	VI	Total	National other areas
Terrestrial protected areas									
Sites									**Total**
Australia	1937	28	537	664	1503	163	440	5272	3
New Zealand	115	4	12	3217	37	44		3429	424
Total	2052	32	549	3881	1540	207	440	8701	427
Area (ha)									
Australia	19,014,237	3,930,383	25,289,070	362,611	2,286,852	771,449	22,419,787	74,074,389	216,632
New Zealand	22,176	226,256	1,684,315	2,960,219	46,574	1,461,172	6,400,712	156,521	
Total	19,036,413	4,156,639	26,973,385	3,322,830	2,333,426	2,232,621	22,419,787	80,475,101	373,153
Marine and coastal protected areas									
Sites									**Total**
Australia	51	6	130	29	111	8	49	384	
New Zealand	34		3	37	2	1		77	7
Total	85	6	133	66	113	9	49	461	7
Area (ha)									
Australia	1,976,161	33,175	6,128,387	27,446	23,049,813	16,786	37,100,670	68,332,438	
New Zealand	852,584		1,374,547	41,071		2501	746	2,271,449	3523
Total	2,828,745	33,175	7,502,934	68,517	23,052,314	17,532	37,100,670	70,603,887	3523
REGIONAL TOTAL									
Sites	2137	38	682	3947	1653	216	489	9162	434
Area (ha)	21,865,158	4,189,814	34,476,319	3,391,347	25,385,740	2,250,153	59,520,457	151,078,988	376,676

Note: Tokelau (a self-administering territory) has been included within the New Zealand data.

Table A5.1 Continued

BRAZIL

	Ia	Ib	II	III	IV	V	VI	Total	National other areas
Terrestrial protected areas									
Sites									**Total**
Brazil	156		156	4	255	85	66	722	498
Total	156		156	4	255	85	66	722	498
Area (ha)									
Brazil	7,214,670		13,836,242	69,605	499,057	11,324,715	19,770,050	52,714,339	103,398,326
Total	7,214,670		13,836,242	69,605	499,057	11,324,715	19,770,050	52,714,339	103,398,326
Marine and coastal protected areas									
Sites									**Total**
Brazil	24		22	1	4	30	1	82	6
Total	24		22	1	4	30	1	82	6
Area (ha)									
Brazil	605,748		1,786,090	760	7904	2,245,981	98,174	4,744,657	446,183
Total	605,748		1,786,090	760	7904	2,245,981	98,174	4,744,657	446,183
REGIONAL TOTAL									
Sites	180		178	5	259	115	67	804	504
Area (ha)	7,820,418		15,622,332	70,365	506,961	13,570,696	19,868,224	57,458,996	103,844,509

CARIBBEAN

	Ia	Ib	II	III	IV	V	VI	Total	National other areas
Terrestrial protected areas									
Sites									**Total**
Anguilla									3
Antigua and Barbuda			1					1	10
Aruba									3
Bahamas			4		8			12	2
Barbados	1			1	2			4	2
Bermuda		6	7	2	4	1		20	12
Cayman Islands		1	2		1				4
Cuba		1	9	1	12	5	5	33	150
Dominica			2				3	5	4
Dominican Republic	3		11	5	3	6	9	37	22
Grenada							1	1	12
Guadeloupe			1		6	1			8
Haiti			2			6		8	1
Jamaica				1	1		131	133	56
Martinique		1			6	1		8	
Montserrat	1	2	2	1	6	12			
Netherlands Antilles									5

Table A5.1 Continued

CARIBBEAN

	Ia	Ib	II	III	IV	V	VI	Total	National other areas
				National IUCN areas					
Terrestrial protected areas									
Sites									**Total**
Puerto Rico					8		1	9	21
Saint Kitts and Nevis			1					1	6
Sain Lucia	1		1		2		17	21	19
Saint Vincent and the Grenadines					6			6	14
Trinidad and Tobago	2		1	5	7		1	16	77
Turks and Caicos Islands			2	1	4		7	1	
Virgin Islands (British)			1		1			2	1
Virgin Islands (US)									1
Total	7	10	45	19	68	25	174	348	422
Area (ha)									
Anguilla									5
Antigua and Barbuda			–					–	200
Aruba									300
Bahamas			20,555		492			21,047	100
Barbados	–			2	38			40	7171
Bermuda		15	16	5	25	8		69	18
Cayman Islands		240	196		1				437
Cuba	1429		45,866	127	40,837	8074	52,171	148,504	247,812
Dominica			10,322				9542	19,864	345
Dominican Republic	9575		890,900	26,287	118,657	67,500	15,985	1,128,904	381,690
Grenada								618 618	2958
Guadeloupe			17,300		1287	16,200		34,787	
Haiti			5000			2345		7345	9
Jamaica				18	–		91,233	91,251	113,691
Martinique		98			943	62,725			63,766
Montserrat	30		814	6		1	201	1052	
Netherlands Antilles									222
Puerto Rico					2053		11,263	13,316	17,151
Saint Kitts and Nevis			15					15	1400
Saint Lucia		13	–		1500		7899	9412	4
Saint Vincent and the Grenadines				4399				4399	3200
Trinidad and Tobago	4585		8200	66	11,398		–	24,249	1940
Turks and Caicos Islands				576	95	11		682	
Virgin Islands (British)			107		13			120	120
Virgin Islands (US)									59
Total	14,190	1795	999,291	27,087	181,738	156,864	188,912	1,569,877	778,395

Table A5.1 Continued
CARIBBEAN

	Ia	Ib	II	III	IV	V	VI	Total	National other areas
				National IUCN areas					National
Marine and coastal protected areas									
Sites									**Total**
Anguilla									11
Antigua and Barbuda			4		3	3		10	11
Aruba					1			1	1
Bahamas	1		6		19			26	5
Barbados			1		1			2	4
Bermuda		4	57	4	15			80	23
Cayman Islands		2	10		30			42	2
Cuba		1	19		8	1	8	37	43
Dominica			1			1		2	
Dominican Republic			8	3	2	1		14	2
Grenada									20
Guadeloupe					12			12	
Jamaica			1		1	2	6	10	22
Martinique					8			8	
Montserrat				4	1			1	6
Netherlands Antilles	1		5					6	6
Puerto Rico					15			15	18
Saint Kitts and Nevis			1					1	12
Saint Lucia				1	27		3	31	14
Saint Vincent and the Grenadines					19			19	1
Trinidad and Tobago	2				7			9	7
Turks and Caicos Islands			4	2	15	4		25	1
Virgin Islands (British)				4	23			27	16
Virgin Islands (US)		1	1	1	4			7	9
Total	4	8	118	19	211	12	18	390	228
Area (ha)									
Anguilla									–
Antigua and Barbuda			6628		–	–		6628	3550
Aruba					20			20	70
Bahamas	–		121,593		1385			122,978	137,257
Barbados			230		–			230	5020
Bermuda		19	1526	6	13,701			15,252	59
Cayman Islands		1988	1492		20,182			23,662	–
Cuba		4436	1,070,120		267,129	1490	2,027,649	3,370,824	368,382
Dominica			531			–		531	
Dominican Republic			467,810	13,470	374,000	125		855,405	–
Grenada									2335
Guadeloupe					5639				5639
Jamaica			1530		–	187,615	5496	194,641	10,217
Martinique					1700			1700	
Montserrat				8	6		1	15	

Table A5.1 Continued

CARIBBEAN

Marine and coastal protected areas

| | \| National IUCN areas | | | | | | | | National |
Area (ha)	Ia	Ib	II	III	IV	V	VI	Total	other areas
									Total
Netherlands Antilles	55		12,630					12,685	1635
Puerto Rico					17,289			17,289	17,120
Saint Kitts and Nevis		2610						2610	77
Saint Lucia				20	832		134	986	2002
Saint Vincent and the Grenadines					3885			3885	
Trinidad and Tobago	2265				4224			6489	6505
Turks and Caicos Islands		6419	135	61,605	2872	`	71,031	1	
Virgin Islands (British)				365	1608			1973	20,873
Virgin Islands (US)		1000	5308	7695	4258			18,261	–
Total	2320	7443	1,698,427	21,699	777,463	192,102	2,033,280	4,732,734	575,103
REGIONAL TOTAL									
Sites	11	18	163	38	279	37	192	738	650
Area (ha)	16,510	9238	2,697,718	48,786	959,201	348,966	2,222,192	6,302,611	1,353,498

CENTRAL AMERICA

| | \| National IUCN areas | | | | | | | | National |
Terrestrial protected areas	Ia	Ib	II	III	IV	V	VI	Total	other areas
Sites									**Total**
Belize	3		13	2	10		18	46	4
Costa Rica	5		15		36		42	98	100
El Salvador									89
Guatemala			11	33			29	73	9
Honduras	1		14	8	31			54	44
Nicaragua		1	3	2	59		3	68	41
Panama		1	8	2	4	2	2	19	55
Total	10	1	64	47	140	2	94	358	342
Area (ha)									
Belize	45,484		146,848	2484	187,025		395,414	777,255	29,780
Costa Rica	20,478	419,083			19,636		369,305	828,502	399,679
El Salvador									28,309
Guatemala		405,086	188,570			1,927,662	2,521,318		15,845
Honduras	–		396,900	320	131,698			528,918	2,309,064
Nicaragua	295,000		25,327	19,305	437,507		1,247,500	2,024,639	938,889
Panama		24,722	446,195	5404	6107	613	127,520	610,561	1,244,208
Total	360,962	24,722	1,839,439	216,083	781,973	613	4,067,401	7,291,193	4,965,774

Table A5.1 Continued

CENTRAL AMERICA

	Ia	Ib	II	III	IV	V	VI	Total	National other areas
				National IUCN areas					
Marine and coastal protected areas									
Sites									**Total**
Belize			10	1	18	2	1	32	4
Costa Rica	5		10		14		3	32	8
El Salvador			1		1			2	1
Guatemala				1			2	3	1
Honduras			3		14	1		18	18
Nicaragua	1				4			5	2
Panama			7		7			14	11
Total	6		31	2	58	3	6	106	45
Area (ha)									
Belize			19,660	414	174,536	78,162	3300	276,072	7396
Costa Rica	1519		308,253		106,528		82,655	498,955	86,695
El Salvador			3820		2000			5820	602
Guatemala				6265			4043	10,308	38,400
Honduras			78,401		65,490	46,000		189,891	305,670
Nicaragua	50,000				80,400			130,400	69,900
Panama			953,577		50,514			1,004,091	911,782
Total	51,519		1,363,711	6679	479,468	124,162	89,998	2,115,537	1,420,445
REGIONAL TOTAL									
Sites	16	1	95	49	198	5	100	464	387
Area (ha)	412,481	24,722	3,203,150	222,762	1,261,441	124,775	4,157,399	9,406,730	6,386,219

EAST AND SOUTH AFRICA

	Ia	Ib	II	III	IV	V	VI	Total	National other areas
				National IUCN areas					
Terrestrial protected areas									
Sites									**Total**
Botswana			4		8			12	78
Eritrea					3			3	
Ethiopia			13		8		18	39	58
Kenya			33		13		11	57	419
Lesotho					1			1	1
Malawi			5		4			9	209
Mayotte					4		1	5	1
Mozambique			3		2		1	6	30
Namibia			8	3		5	1	17	160
Seychelles			2				6	8	
Somalia					2		7	9	20
South Africa	2	4	37	3	272	5		323	202
Sudan			7		3		16	26	20

Table A5.1 Continued

EAST AND SOUTH AFRICA

	Ia	Ib	II	III	IV	V	VI	Total	National other areas
				National IUCN areas					National

Terrestrial protected areas
Sites

	Ia	Ib	II	III	IV	V	VI	Total	Total
Swaziland					2		3	5	3
Tanzania, United Republic of			14		23		49	86	709
Uganda			7		26	4	17	54	698
Zambia			22	16			39	77	606
Zimbabwe		1	10	2	20	15	20	68	182
Total	2	5	165	24	391	29	189	805	3396

Area (ha)

	Ia	Ib	II	III	IV	V	VI	Total	National other areas
Botswana			4,624,950		5,947,340			10,572,290	17,754,435
Eritrea					500,600			500,600	
Ethiopia			3,035,740		2,481,800		13,092,300	18,609,840	4,071,845
Kenya			3,432,203		53,213		739,260	4,224,676	3,554,418
Lesotho					6805			6805	38,400
Malawi			696,200		362,300			1,058,500	2,150,522
Mayotte					640		1083	1723	–
Mozambique			1,575,000		1,710,000		1,200,000	4,485,000	1,545,358
Namibia			3,188,237	158		55,996	582,750	3,827,141	3,907,351
Seychelles			3720				91	3811	
Somalia					180,200		10,360	190,560	3,300,000
South Africa	4781	123,604	3,733,228	4268	2,519,347	49,414		6,434,642	1,543,955
Sudan			8,473,000		143,000		3,607,000	12,223,000	3,559,000
Swaziland					35,175		24,909	60,084	–
Tanzania, United Republic of			4,099,975		9,686,500		12,445,302	26,231,777	11,696,192
Uganda			766,222		989,610	7598	2,898,543	4,661,973	1,809,909
Zambia			6,358,868	7441			17,325,781	23,692,090	7,533,188
Zimbabwe	950	2,715,660	3086	20,178	362,993	1,595,403	4,698,270	1,054,197	
Total	4781	124,554	42,703,003	14,953	24,636,708	476,001	53,522,782	121,482,782	63,518,770

Marine and coastal protected areas
Sites

	Ia	Ib	II	III	IV	V	VI	Total	Total
Eritrea									1
Kenya			4				7	11	4
Mayotte			1				1	2	
Mozambique			1		4		1	6	4
Namibia			2		1	1		4	
Seychelles	4	1	5				2	12	1
Somalia							1	1	7
South Africa	7		12		13			32	17
Sudan			1					1	4
Tanzania, United Republic of			6		1		5	12	16
Total	11	1	32		19	1	17	81	54

Table A5.1 Continued

EAST AND SOUTH AFRICA

	Ia	Ib	II	III	IV	V	VI	Total	National other areas
Marine and coastal protected areas									
Area (ha)									**Total**
Eritrea									200,000
Kenya			5430				299,739	305,169	199,980
Mayotte			4180				450	4630	
Mozambique			143,000		1,102,000		1,000,000	2,245,000	750,639
Namibia			6,787,019		2288	744,595		7,533,902	
Seychelles	35,086	3	6322				5	41,416	1
Somalia							334,000	334,000	1,290,000
South Africa	41,780	327,755		16,437				385,972	157,462
Sudan			26,000					26,000	262,000
Tanzania, United Republic of			360		30,000		196,923	227,283	2600
Total	76,866	3	7,300,066		1,150,725	744,595	1,831,117	11,103,372	2,862,682
REGIONAL TOTAL									
Sites	13	6	197	24	410	30	206	886	3450
Area (ha)	158,535	124,562	57,303,199	14,953	26,938,196	1,965,193	57,185,050	143,689,688	66,381,452

EAST ASIA

	Ia	Ib	II	III	IV	V	VI	Total	National other areas
Terrestrial protected areas									
Sites									**Total**
China					2	1921	59	1982	3
Hong Kong					17	13		30	52
Japan	5	18	30		20	57		130	639
Korea, DPR			9	12	10			31	
Korea, Republic of					17	16		33	4
Macao									1
Mongolia	3	9	16	22				50	1
Taiwan, Province of China	13		3		8		9	33	
Total	21	27	58	34	74	2007	68	2289	700
Area (ha)									
China					93,400	139,157,839	5,857,134	145,108,373	–
Hong Kong					2485	13,702		16,187	9366
Japan	4957	262,865	370,013		283,004	2,325,145		3,245,984	2,213,123
Korea, DPR			150,143	10,795	155,004			315,942	
Korea, Republic of	36,883	313,182	350,065	3785					
Macao									–
Mongolia	6,212,909	4,001,374	8,837,652	1,939,882				20,991,817	799,360

Table A5.1 Continued

EAST ASIA

	Ia	Ib	II	III	IV	V	VI	Total	National other areas
				National IUCN areas					National

Terrestrial protected areas
Area (ha) — **Total**

	Ia	Ib	II	III	IV	V	VI	Total	National other areas
Taiwan, Province of China	63,801		193,795		21,226		21,739	300,561	
Total	6,281,667	4,264,239	9,551,603	1,950,677	592,002	141,809,868	5,878,873	170,328,929	3,025,634

Marine and coastal protected areas
Sites — **Total**

	Ia	Ib	II	III	IV	V	VI	Total	National other areas
China					33	9		42	
Hong Kong				2	14	16	7		
Japan	16	7	17		35	88		163	39
Korea, Republic of					3	4		7	
Taiwan, Province of China	6		3	7				16	9
Total	22	7	20		47	139	9	244	55

Area (ha)

	Ia	Ib	II	III	IV	V	VI	Total	National other areas
China						1,573,240	54,700	1,627,940	
Hong Kong					44	28,872		28,916	366
Japan	1913	75,704	161,546		2110	760,249	1,001,522	247,928	
Korea, Republic of					13,195	334,122		347,317	
Taiwan, Province of China	665		129,049		3752			133,466	186,545
Total	2578	75,704	290,595		19,101	2,696,483	54,700	3,139,161	434,839

REGIONAL TOTAL	Ia	Ib	II	III	IV	V	VI	Total	National other areas
Sites	43	34	78	34	121	2146	77	2533	755
Area (ha)	6,284,245	4,339,943	9,842,198	1,950,677	611,103	144,506,351	5,933,573	173,468,090	3,460,473

Table A5.1 Continued

EUROPE AND SCANDINAVIA

	National IUCN areas								National other areas
	Ia	Ib	II	III	IV	V	VI	Total	
Terrestrial protected areas									
Sites									**Total**
Albania	4		10	4	20	3	4	45	2
Andorra									2
Austria	3		7	242	530		305	1087	101
Belgium					53	5		58	604
Belize			2		2			4	
Bosnia and Herzegovina		1	1		13	6		21	10
Bulgaria	1	53		605	57			716	37
Croatia	59		4	46	29	44		182	10
Czech Republic	3		2	264	473	26		768	10
Denmark	10	6	5	17	183	64		285	111
Estonia	27	254	197	215	181	101	975	364	
Finland	19	5	31		29		91	175	3291
France			4	23	1119	33		1179	330
Germany, Federal Republic of			8		6185	1024		7217	516
Greece		1	12	46	31	19		109	101
Hungary			5		129	54		188	51
Iceland			3	32	17	18		70	
Ireland			6		69			75	567
Italy	5	7	9	12	196	58		287	609
Latvia	4		24	295	212			535	6
Liechtenstein					9	1		10	
Lithuania	5		4		255	28		292	7
Luxembourg					18	1		19	179
Macedonia	2		3	65	13			83	
Malta	2	45	2	35	3	1		88	6
Monaco									2
Netherlands		5	7	5	45	11	2	75	520
Norway	93		17		21	29		160	1630
Poland	1		14		1382	118		1515	303
Portugal	1	1	1	15	8	12		38	48
Romania	13		14	5	109	8		149	24
Russian Federation									4
Serbia and Montenegro	2	26	6	10	30	27		101	75
Slovakia	607		7	307	189	1		1111	65
Slovenia			1	3				4	1
Spain	14	12		8	115	140		289	453
Svalbard and Jan Mayen Islands	12							12	6
Sweden	618	96	18	306	889	205		2132	2768
Switzerland	1				1937	251		2189	11
UK					351	66	1	418	7436
Total	1506	512	235	2534	14,936	2740	199	22,662	20,260

Table A5.1 Continued

EUROPE AND SCANDINAVIA

	Ia	Ib	II	III	IV	V	VI	Total	National other areas
				National IUCN areas					National
Terrestrial protected areas									
Area (ha)									**Total**
Albania	14,500		19,547	3470	16,003	2497	18,245	74,262	1800
Andorra									3250
Austria	1133		92,216	3732	461,937	1,788,545		2,347,563	4,94,929
Belgium					9462	73,668		83,130	462,596
Belize			500		6052			6552	
Bosnia and Herzegovina		20	20		2974	6572		9586	280
Bulgaria	1463	73,597		243,409	275,023			593,492	523,472
Croatia	25,716		56,762	288	10,727	228,701		322,194	67,944
Czech Republic	10,779		74,820		2184	70,123	1,087,199	1,245,105	193,421
Denmark	11,644	13,810	4635	7429	171,142	37,808		246,468	960,092
Estonia	7901	177,052		120	67,867	96,623	121,441	471,004	423,372
Finland	152,450	107,900	738,460			9251	1,804,478	2,812,539	242,198
France			258,844	1622	298,896	5,500,915		6,060,277	1,452,318
Germany, Federal Republic of			129,111		816,094	9,392,338		10,337,543	1,118,298
Greece		550	78,698	611	126,254	32,914		239,027	763,700
Hungary		224,009			21,152	575,472		820,633	14,149
Iceland			177,000	29,100	75,445	194,228		475,773	
Ireland			61,304		18,373			79,677	1,328,813
Italy	413	220,990	342,345	974	171,646	879,880		1,616,248	4,467,734
Latvia	24,525		217,223	5194	644,919			891,861	151,445
Liechtenstein					161	6247		6408	
Lithuania	20,904		124,900		148,496	360,829		655,129	53,340
Luxembourg					1250	36,000		37,250	92,831
Macedonia	12,730		108,338		61,313 923			183,304	
Malta	1	3694	32	324	203	276	4530	20,359	
Monaco									51
Netherlands		19,857	21,754	14,735	97,287	21,528	226,630	401,791	840,006
Norway	140,454		1,379,440			9918	413,364	1,943,176	12,423
Poland	115		170,656		164,253	2,427,842		2,762,866	6,259,351
Portugal	338	9672	21,100	2657	25,529	485,798		545,094	399,737
Romania	28,921		398,184		249 36,347	12,620		476,321	123,713
Russian Federation									159,058
Serbia and Montenegro	914	2306	142,100	1759	87,790	91,262		326,131	48,953
Slovakia	97,673		243,219	3105	7006	12,284		363,287	871,419
Slovenia			83,807	725				84,532	0
Spain	1390	4329	154,671		1,717,561	2,180,349		4,058,300	3,236,204
Svalbard and Jan Mayen Islands	7779							7779	15,55000
Sweden	88,635	2,585,812	645,602	26,132	68,583	312,086		3,726,850	1,851,106
Switzerland	16,887				300,376	867,943		1,185,206	24,081
UK					137,950	2,616,400	0	2,754,350	5,175,157
Total	667,265	3,219,589	5,969,297	409,132	6,076,973	29,742,188	2,170,794	48,255,238	33,392,600

Table A5.1 Continued

EUROPE AND SCANDINAVIA

	Ia	Ib	II	III	IV	V	VI	Total	National other areas
			National IUCN areas						National other areas
Marine and coastal protected areas									
Sites									**Total**
Albania			1		6			7	
Belgium					2			2	
Bulgaria		1						1	
Croatia	8		3	2	1	4		18	
Denmark	6	3	5	2	28	10		54	
Estonia									3
Finland	1	2	4		6		1	14	3
France			1		75	7		83	
Germany, Federal Republic of			5		14	5		24	
Gibraltar						1		1	
Greece			4	4	3	3		14	1
Iceland	2				4	3		9	
Ireland					12			12	
Italy	1	1	1		31	3		37	6
Latvia			1					1	
Lithuania			1			2		3	
Malta	1	3					1	5	
Monaco					2			2	
Netherlands		1	2	2	4		1	10	9
Norway	9				2	6		17	
Poland			2			2		4	
Portugal	2	1			15	7		25	3
Romania	6		1		1			8	4
Serbia and Montenegro					1	1		2	
Slovenia						41		41	
Spain	1		3		21	13		38	4
Svalbard and Jan Mayen Islands	2		3		1			6	1
Sweden	3	15	2	4	5	58		87	3
UK					66	87		153	72
Total	42	27	39	14	300	253	3	678	109
Area (ha)									
Albania			1250		27,350			28,600	
Belgium					386			386	
Bulgaria		1445						1445	
Croatia	7454		37,950	4	153	204,639		25,0200	
Denmark	34,662	5342	127,752	1061	56,151	8916		233,884	
Estonia									144,870
Finland	4360	17,800	70,764		18,114		2322	113,360	7353
France			2475		49,334	1,114,150		1,165,959	
Germany, Federal Republic of			814,411		11,991	80,660		907,062	

Table A5.1 Continued

EUROPE AND SCANDINAVIA

	Ia	Ib	II	III	IV	V	VI	Total	National other areas
				National IUCN areas					National
Marine and coastal protected areas									
Area (ha)									**Total**
Gibraltar						35		35	
Greece			230,563	15,463	2895	3048		251,969	9267
Iceland	272			2605		502,000		504,877	
Ireland				3008				3008	
Italy	46	284	73,762		160,776	26,755		261,623	146,948
Latvia			26,490					26,490	
Lithuania			26,400			26,950		53,350	
Malta	7	15					1307	1329	
Monaco					51			51	
Netherlands		3759	4855	9400	38,600		23,810	80,424	20,645
Norway	69,240				2540	55,363		127,143	
Poland			29,006			11,862		40,868	
Portugal	3645	20			89,709	140,548		233,922	0
Romania	33,225		580,000		86			613,311	256,700
Serbia and Montenegro					20	12,000		12,020	
Slovenia						65,261		65,261	
Spain	850		65,542		8112	106,890		181,394	3529
Svalbard and Jan Mayen Islands	4,906,519		1,735,711			1140		6,643,370	0
Sweden	1414	14,7564	7450	6423	4748	246,830		414,429	3251
UK					92,776	2,150,841		2,243,617	182,244
Total	5,061,694	176,229	3,834,381	32,351	570,545	4,756,748	27,439	14,457,387	774,807
REGIONAL TOTAL									
Sites	1548	539	274	2548	15,236	2993	202	23,340	20,369
Area (ha)	5,728,959	3,395,818	9,803,678	441,483	6,647,518	34,498,936	2,198,233	62,714,625	34,167,407

Table A5.1 Continued

NORTH AFRICA AND MIDDLE EAST

	Ia	Ib	II	III	IV	V	VI	Total	National other areas
Terrestrial protected areas									
Sites									**Total**
Afghanistan			1		6			7	10
Algeria	4		7		3			14	39
Bahrain					1			1	2
Cyprus			1		3	1		5	7
Egypt	3				5	8	1	17	23
Iran, Islamic Republic of			16	16	35	54		121	10
Iraq					8			8	6
Israel			31	128	6			165	107
Jordan				6	5			11	38
Kuwait				1				1	13
Lebanon			1					1	28
Libyan Arab Jamahiriya			1		4			5	23
Morocco		2			5	2		9	37
Oman					1	1		2	
Qatar			1		1			2	6
Saudi Arabia			5	1	7	54	8	75	47
Syrian Arab Republic									40
Tunisia			4		1			5	55
Turkey	17		17	2	10	11	14	71	442
United Arab Emirates					1	1		2	16
Yemen									24
Total	24	2	54	50	226	143	23	522	973
Area (ha)									
Afghanistan			41,000		177,629			218,629	67,000
Algeria	37,666		11,782,988		43,200			11,863,854	92,537
Bahrain					800			800	–
Cyprus			9117		66,000	840		75,957	17,369
Egypt	313,191				48,140	3,905,126	575,000	4,841,457	1,014,528
Iran, Islamic Republic of			1,619,750		21,008	3,869,719	4,862,817	10,373,294	177,927
Iraq						541		541	620,000
Israel					1889	238,186	9177	249,252	136,946
Jordan					86,100	827,200		913,300	328,503
Kuwait					250			250	32,000
Lebanon			3500					3500	36,328
Libyan Arab Jamahiriya				–	122,000			122,000	70,980
Morocco		3063			230,480	92,000		325,543	378,069
Oman					–	22,000		22,000	
Qatar			–		50			50	–
Saudi Arabia			1,017,800	1,220,000	1,597,125	87,520	77,923,700	81,846,145	10,699,792
Syrian Arab Republic									449,478
Tunisia			27,787		100			27,887	671,735
Turkey	26,202		349,909	274	111,806	104,593	211,528	804,312	2,977,336

Table A5.1 Continued

NORTH AFRICA AND MIDDLE EAST

	Ia	Ib	II	III	IV	V	VI	Total	National other areas
				National IUCN areas					

Terrestrial protected areas
Area (ha) | | | | | | | | | **Total**

	Ia	Ib	II	III	IV	V	VI	Total	National other areas
United Arab Emirates					–	40		40	32,016
Yemen									564
Total	377,059	3063	14,851,851	1,243,171	6,592,126	9,911,313	78,710,228	111,688,811	17,803,108

Marine and coastal protected areas
Sites | | | | | | | | | **Total**

	Ia	Ib	II	III	IV	V	VI	Total	National other areas
Algeria			2		1	1		4	10
Bahrain	1							1	1
Cyprus					3	2		5	11
Egypt	1		3		5	2	6	17	23
Iran, Islamic Republic of					2	6		8	14
Israel			1		16	3		20	16
Jordan					1			1	
Kuwait	1				2	1		4	8
Lebanon					1			1	
Libyan Arab Jamahiriya			3					3	6
Morocco	1				2	1		4	14
Oman			2		2			4	
Qatar			1		1			2	5
Saudi Arabia	1		1			1		3	59
Syrian Arab Republic									2
Tunisia			2					2	10
Turkey			2		10	2		14	10
United Arab Emirates									15
Western Sahara									1
Yemen									35
Total	5		17		46	19	6	93	240
Area (ha)									
Algeria			6920		6000	80,000		92,920	25,130
Bahrain	50							50	5150
Cyprus					2141	134		2275	5709
Egypt	70,000		3,675,650		3,683,500	315,822	180,307	7,925,279	843,455
Iran, Islamic Republic of					410	622,276		622,686	100,080
Israel			3158		42,418	549		46,125	4068
Jordan					4000			4000	
Kuwait	2000				–	25,000		27,000	1850
Lebanon					500			500	
Libyan Arab Jamahiriya			51,000					51,000	47,050
Morocco	6500				7650	33,800		47,950	105,613
Oman			2,928,540		32,300			2,960,840	
Qatar			–		1619			1619	12,234
Saudi Arabia	69,600		200			450,000		519,800	707,800
Syrian Arab Republic									320
Tunisia			17,695					17,695	78,910

Table A5.1 Continued

NORTH AFRICA AND MIDDLE EAST

| | National IUCN areas | | | | | | | | National other areas |
	Ia	Ib	II	III	IV	V	VI	Total	
Marine and coastal protected areas									
Area (ha)									**Total**
Turkey			45,410		372,250	33,950		451,610	189,234
United Arab Emirates									35,120
Western Sahara									1,888,889
Yemen									362,500
Total	148,150		6,728,573		4,152,788	1,561,531	180,307	12,771,349	4,413,112
REGIONAL TOTAL									
Sites	29	2	71	50	272	162	29	615	1213
Area (ha)	525,209	3063	21,580,424	1,243,171	10,744,914	11,472,844	78,890,535	124,460,160	22,216,220

NORTH AMERICA

| | National IUCN areas | | | | | | | | National other areas |
	Ia	Ib	II	III	IV	V	VI	Total	
Terrestrial protected areas									
Sites									**Total**
Canada	684	103	1027	300	534	761	939	4348	1072
Mexico	47		32	6			44	129	19
St Pierre et Miquelon									6
US	58	579	166	257	527	1,230	276	3093	4332
Total	789	682	1225	563	1061	1991	1259	7570	5429
Area (ha)									
Canada	2,231,846	10,134,699	33,269,054	101,566	5,141,710	1,189,735	7,719,743	59,788,353	9,383,427
Mexico	448,540		707,162	16,404			8,687,171	9,859,277	9187
St Pierre et Miquelon									12,666
US	3,569,230	35,817,269	14,925,450	6,314,227	12,313,691	6,721,668	67,026,501	146,688,036	2,339,761
Total	6,249,616	45,951,968	48,901,666	6,432,197	17,455,401	7,911,403	83,433,415	216,335,666	11,745,041
Marine and coastal protected areas									
Sites									**Total**
Canada	40	9	83	13	40	4	30	219	8
Greenland		1	1					2	
Mexico	7		14	1			17	39	
US	8	6	39	18	236	86	7	400	103
Total	55	16	137	32	276	90	54	660	111
Area (ha)									
Canada	87,992	367,123	9,767,851	23,986	12,985,316	1572	176,002	23,409,842	23,790
Greenland		1,050,000	97,200,000					98,250,000	
Mexico	242,239	701,994	664		7,293,918	8,238,815			
US	127,295	158,985	10,478,520	795,407	31,696,334	5,592,930	43,477,437	92,326,908	27,226
Total	457,526	1,576,108	118,148,365	820,057	44,681,650	5,594,502	50,947,357	222,225,565	51,016
REGIONAL TOTAL									
Sites	844	698	1362	595	1337	2081	1313	8230	5540
Area (ha)	6,707,142	47,528,076	167,050,031	7,252,254	62,137,051	13,505,905	134,380,772	438,561,231	11,796,057

Table A5.1 Continued

NORTH EURASIA

	Ia	Ib	II	III	IV	V	VI	Total	National other areas
			National IUCN areas						
Terrestrial protected areas									
Sites									**Total**
Armenia	3		2		23			28	
Azerbaijan	12				20			32	2
Belarus	2		3	340	558			903	1
Georgia	20		4		9			33	7
Kazakhstan	7		4		62			73	27
Kyrgyzstan	6		6	18	55			85	8
Moldova, Republic of	5			22	16	20		63	
Russian Federation	73		35	7883	2379	367	53	10,790	414
Tajikistan	3		2		18			23	8
Turkmenistan	8			2	14			24	17
Ukraine	17		8	3054	2067	19		5165	17
Uzbekistan	8		2	2	12			24	5
Total	164		66	11,321	5233	406	53	17,243	506
Area (ha)									
Armenia	39,285		178,102		81,720			299,107	
Azerbaijan	74,315				319,336			393,651	4400
Belarus	81,023		222,555	18,504	982,253			1,304,335	10,947
Georgia	172,248		71,849		46,179			290,276	1,218,619
Kazakhstan	833,712		838,557		6,069,676			7,741,945	2,172,960
Kyrgyzstan	201,680		91,600	7	315,003			608,290	106,898
Moldova, Republic of	19,378			1184	3485	23,282		47,329	
Russian Federation	16,627,978		8,575,257	2,338,025	61,544,200	1,137,429	8,421,607	98,644,496	33,499,809
Tajikistan	119,325		1,630,000		853,600			2,602,925	793,000
Turkmenistan	819,994			2020	1,061,206			1,883,220	95,000
Ukraine	307,643		492,294	80,804	768,889	287,807		1,937,437	39,724
Uzbekistan	208,354		598,710	3486	1,239,743			2,050,293	96,500
Total	19,504,935		12,698,924	2,444,030	73,285,290	1,448,518	8,421,607	117,803,304	38,037,857
Marine and coastal protected areas									
Sites									**Total**
Azerbaijan	3							3	
Georgia	2							2	
Kazakhstan	1							1	
Russian Federation	18			3	24	1	1	47	12
Ukraine	7			10				17	
Total	31			3	34	1	1	70	12
Area (ha)									
Azerbaijan	117,061							117,061	
Georgia	3730							3730	
Kazakhstan	50,000							50,000	

Table A5.1 Continued

NORTH EURASIA

	Ia	Ib	II	III	IV	V	VI	Total	National other areas
				National IUCN areas					**National other areas**

Marine and coastal protected areas

Area (ha)   **Total**

	Ia	Ib	II	III	IV	V	VI	Total	other areas
Russian Federation	16,089,136			103,910	13,957,124	30,000		30,180,170	2,928,040
Ukraine	138,906				168,626			307,532	
Total	16,398,833			103,910	14,125,750	30,000		30,658,493	2,928,040

REGIONAL TOTAL

	Ia	Ib	II	III	IV	V	VI	Total	other areas
Sites	195	0	66	11,324	5267	407	54	17,313	518
Area (ha)	35,903,768	0	12,698,924	2,547,940	87,411,040	1,478,518	8,421,607	148,461,797	40,965,897

PACIFIC

	Ia	Ib	II	III	IV	V	VI	Total	National other areas
				National IUCN areas					**National other areas**

Terrestrial protected areas

Sites   **Total**

	Ia	Ib	II	III	IV	V	VI	Total	other areas
American Samoa				3				3	3
Cook Islands							1	1	8
Fiji	9							9	48
French Polynesia			2					2	2
Guam							4	4	
Micronesia, Federated States of						1		1	4
New Caledonia	1		4	9	18		1	33	26
Niue					1				
Northern Mariana Islands				1				1	8
Palau			1					1	2
Papua New Guinea			4		1		12	17	49
Samoa			3		1	1		5	16
Solomon Islands			1			2	1	4	2
Tonga			2					2	5
Tuvalu									1
Vanuatu							1	1	28
Wallis and Futuna Islands	1							1	
Total	11		17	13	20	4	20	85	203

Area (ha)

	Ia	Ib	II	III	IV	V	VI	Total	other areas
American Samoa				154				154	266
Cook Islands							155	155	3390
Fiji	15,596							15,596	107,374
French Polynesia			990					990	–
Guam							1185	1185	
Micronesia, Federated States of						5100		5100	40

Table A5.1 Continued

PACIFIC

Terrestrial protected areas
Area (ha)

	Ia	Ib	II	III	IV	V	VI	Total	National other areas
			National IUCN areas						National other areas
New Caledonia	5870		10,257	230	42,848		–	59,205	601,880
Niue									–
Northern Mariana Islands				5				5	2894
Palau			–						–
Papua New Guinea			235,323		740		694,674	930,737	2,692,659
Samoa			5509		150	3		5662	12,086
Solomon Islands			1090			31,300	500	32,890	–
Tonga			6240					6240	20
Tuvalu									–
Vanuatu							3207	3207	11,101
Wallis and Futuna Islands	30							30	
Total	21,496		259,409	389	43,738	36,403	699,721	1,061,156	3,431,710

Marine and coastal protected areas
Sites

	Ia	Ib	II	III	IV	V	VI	Total	Total
American Samoa	1	1	1	1		4	4		
Cook Islands					1			1	7
Fiji	3			1	2	1	9	16	32
French Polynesia			1		9			10	
Guam					6	1	1	8	4
Kiribati	4			6		1	1	12	3
Marshal Islands					3		1	4	4
Micronesia, Federated States of						1		1	30
New Caledonia	1		2	1	20	8	1	33	5
Niue							1	1	3
Northern Mariana Islands	4				4			8	5
Palau			5	1		1	1	8	11
Papua New Guinea			1	1	3		12	17	76
Samoa					4		3	7	8
Solomon Islands							1	1	9
Tonga			1		5	3	2	11	3
Tuvalu								1	1
US minor outlying islands	3		3					6	1
Vanuatu							1	1	25
Wallis and Futuna Islands									1
Total	16		14	11	58	16	35	150	231

Area (ha)

	Ia	Ib	II	III	IV	V	VI	Total	Total
American Samoa	653		4250	142	64			5109	202
Cook Islands					160			160	1502
Fiji	4023			43	498	3500	13,900	21,964	12,576

Table A5.1 Continued

PACIFIC

	Ia	Ib	II	III	IV	V	VI	Total	National other areas
Marine and coastal protected areas									
Area (ha)									**Total**
French Polynesia			–		23,949			23,949	
Guam					6745	779	6135	13,659	–
Kiribati	71			26,731		52,370	1270	80,442	32,113
Marshal Islands					5631		70,100	75,731	10,697
Micronesia, Federated States of						–		–	2482
New Caledonia	17,200		255	120	44,398	21,887	–	83,860	1470
Niue							5400	5400	57
Northern Mariana Islands	1541				292			1833	2190
Palau			20,300	1200		3000	484	24,984	109,852
Papua New Guinea			27	44,240	163		368,348	412,778	599,074
Samoa					11,237		6475	17,712	570
Solomon Islands							8270	8270	1000
Tonga			450		423	1,000,023	3335	1,004,231	300
Tuvalu				3300	3300				
US minor outlying islands	41,199		525,922					567,121	12,995
Vanuatu							3470	3470	1737
Wallis and Futuna Islands									75
Total	64,687		551,204	72,476	93,560	1,081,559	490,487	2,353,973	788,892

REGIONAL TOTAL	Ia	Ib	II	III	IV	V	VI	Total	National other areas
Sites	27	0	31	24	78	20	55	235	434
Area (ha)	86,183	0	810,613	72,865	137,298	1,117,962	1,190,208	3,415,129	4,220,602

SOUTH AMERICA

	Ia	Ib	II	III	IV	V	VI	Total	National other areas
Terrestrial protected areas									
Sites									**Total**
Argentina	36	1	54	8	21	12	156	288	11
Bolivia	1	1	12		5		4	23	10
Chile			17	10	32			59	119
Colombia	3		30	3	2		58	96	313
Ecuador	3	1	8	1		1	9	23	113
French Guiana	3			1	7	8		19	15
Guyana			2		1			3	20
Paraguay			11	3	13	1	3	31	18
Peru			8	4		3	17	32	32
Suriname			2		6			8	7
Uruguay					1	7		8	32
Venezuela			33	31	6	57	49	176	55
Total	46	3	177	61	94	89	296	766	745

Table A5.1 Continued

SOUTH AMERICA

	National IUCN areas								National other areas
	Ia	Ib	II	III	IV	V	VI	Total	
Terrestrial protected areas									
Area (ha)									**Total**
Argentina	718,840	77,020	3,096,969	78,902	1,929,562	10,077	11,432,051	17,343,421	80,000
Bolivia	–	111,411	10,753,928		1,216,345		2,479,907	14,561,591	6,815,590
Chile			1,397,458	15,261	1,237,654			2,650,373	610,266
Colombia	15,365		7,474,309	1,947,640		2053	424,666	9,864,033	26,779,851
Ecuador	170,228	500	2,133,462	3383		400	1,809,429	4,117,402	2,606,878
French Guiana	286,300			17,740	203,550		12,384	519,974	3,102,766
Guyana			126,000		360,000			486,000	234,000
Paraguay			1,519,355	4517	125,731	61,979	124,000	1,835,582	834,829
Peru			3,664,308	309,950		35,392	3,483,652	7,493,302	14,915,699
Suriname			1,608,400		237,400			1,845,800	132,000
Uruguay					8185	21,373		29,558	764,491
Venezuela			12,463,040	5,029,152	147,184	12,483,484	23,432,628	53,555,488	10,485,243
Total	1,190,733	188,931	44,237,229	7,406,545	5,467,664	12,625,089	43,186,333	114,302,524	67,361,613
Marine and coastal protected areas									
Sites									**Total**
Argentina	7		2		10	?	8	20	
Chile			14	3	10			27	
Colombia	2		9		1		1	13	4
Ecuador			2				2	4	
French Guiana	1					2		3	1
Peru				2			1	3	
Suriname					4		3	7	1
Uruguay				2		2		4	
Venezuela			11	3	3		2	19	6
Total	10		38	10	28	6	17	109	12
Area (ha)									
Argentina	19,183		192,000		16,564	10,262	543,809	781,818	
Chile			7,311,902	2410	4,133,624			11,447,936	
Colombia	30,000		777,495		–		3600	811,095	998,460
Ecuador			818,028				13,351,300	14,169,328	
French Guiana	7852					16		7868	2700
Peru				3663			335,000	338,663	
Suriname					52,100		83,320	135,420	–
Uruguay				1650		4782		6432	
Venezuela			843,179	23,346	37,602		1,246,500	2,150,627	175
Total	57,035		9,942,604	31,069	4,239,890	15,060	15,563,529	29,849,187	1,001,335
REGIONAL TOTAL									
Sites	56	3	215	71	122	95	313	875	757
Area (ha)	1,247,768	188,931	54,179,833	7,437,614	9,707,554	12,640,149	58,749,862	144,151,711	68,362,948

Table A5.1 Continued

SOUTH ASIA

	Ia	Ib	II	III	IV	V	VI	Total	National other areas
			National IUCN areas						
Terrestrial protected areas									
Sites									**Total**
Bangladesh					3	4		7	22
Bhutan	1		4		4			9	1
India			83		408		1	492	373
Nepal			9		3		5	17	15
Pakistan			5		66	5	2	78	136
Sri Lanka	28		20		43		91	413	
Total	29		121		527	9	8	694	960
Area (ha)									
Bangladesh					50,946	14,760		65,706	7356
Bhutan	65,000		799,200		376,600			1,240,800	23,569
India			3,561,860		11,729,555		–	15,291,415	7,549,565
Nepal			893,800		97,900		1,206,700	2,198,400	691,300
Pakistan			714,495		2,671,100	122,982	18,137	3,526,714	8,489,531
Sri Lanka	49,499		369,736		218,176			637,411	1,163,700
Total	114,499		6,339,091		15,144,277	137,742	1,224,837	22,960,446	17,925,021
Marine and coastal protected areas									
Sites									**Total**
Bangladesh					4	1		5	2
India	1	1	9		107		2	120	11
Maldives									25
Pakistan			1		4			5	6
Sri Lanka	1		3		15			19	1
Total	2	1	13		130	1	2	149	45
Area (ha)									
Bangladesh					32,426	1729		34,155	11,615
India	133,010	20,000	80,624		235,712		1,138,500	1,607,846	13,500
Maldives									–
Pakistan			167,700		50,501			218,201	2850
Sri Lanka	28,905		86,495		116,719			232,119	–
Total	161,915	20,000	334,819		435,358	1729	1,138,500	2,092,321	27,965
REGIONAL TOTAL									
Sites	31	1	134	0	657	10	10	843	1005
Area (ha)	276,414	20,000	6,673,910	0	15,579,635	139,471	2,363,337	25,052,767	17,952,986

Table A5.1 Continued

SOUTH-EAST ASIA

	Ia	Ib	II	III	IV	V	VI	Total	National other areas
				National IUCN areas					
Terrestrial protected areas									
Sites									**Total**
Brunei Darussalam	21		3			6		30	21
Cambodia			5	1	16	3	3	28	
East Timor			1					1	14
Indonesia	103	3	16	14	26	63	731	956	319
Lao PDR							23	23	18
Malaysia	98		15	1	10	1	2	127	577
Myanmar			1	1	2	2	1	7	55
Philippines			41	2	6	23	54	126	19
Singapore			3	1				4	
Thailand			57	43	37			137	113
Viet Nam			10		50	29		89	86
Total	222	3	152	63	147	127	814	1528	1222
Area (ha)									
Brunei Darussalam	71,233		64,459			1935		137,627	191,127
Cambodia		550,000	10,250	3,093,035	97,000	403,950	4,154,235		
East Timor		800			800	186,800			
Indonesia	815,573	16,850	4,835,423	5270	2,686,711	243,082	15,141,738	23,744,647	22,174,379
Lao PDR				3,508,995	3,508,995	1,030,274			
Malaysia	99,722		797,292	71	467,875	1011	1360	1,367,331	10,688,778
Myanmar			160,671	64,232	29,384	13,478	16,055	283,820	3,785,492
Philippines			451,369	7,797	51,524	116,860	771,516	1,399,066	113,417
Singapore			2891	18				2909	
Thailand			3,411,986	302,402	2,727,545			6,441,933	3,218,834
Viet Nam			265,028		736,009	91,767		1,092,804	361,240
Total	986,528	16,850	10,539,919	390,040	9,792,083	565,133	19,843,614	42,134,167	41,750,341
Marine and coastal protected areas									
Sites									**Total**
Brunei Darussalam	4					1		5	2
Cambodia			2					2	
Indonesia	47	5	21	1	23	19	6	122	148
Malaysia	14		49		4		1	68	114
Myanmar		1						1	8
Philippines		3	11	1	11	21	7	54	7
Singapore					2			2	
Thailand			16	3		1		20	8
Viet Nam			2		12			14	30
Total	65	9	101	5	52	42	14	288	317

Table A5.1 Continued

SOUTH-EAST ASIA

Marine and coastal protected areas
Area (ha)

	Ia	Ib	II	III	IV	V	VI	Total	National other areas
									Total
Brunei Darussalam	1219					2566		3785	14,353
Cambodia			192,250					192,250	
Indonesia	1,119,348	1,526,876	9,184,412	15	925,870	595,353	104,450	13,456,324	4,529,306
Malaysia	10,840		347,306		122,392		20,682	501,220	1,186,815
Myanmar		20,484					20,484		259,699
Philippines		430	472,051	22,202	1,026,104	926,858	126,504	2,574,149	6712
Singapore					140			140	
Thailand			499,622	86,885		13,100		599,607	68,300
Viet Nam			21,200		50,019			71,219	176,248
Total	1,131,407	1,547,790	10,716,841	109,102	2,124,525	1,537,877	251,636	17,419,178	6,241,433

REGIONAL TOTAL	Ia	Ib	II	III	IV	V	VI	Total	National other areas
Sites	287	12	253	68	199	169	828	1816	1539
Area (ha)	2,117,935	1,564,640	21,256,760	499,142	11,916,608	2,103,010	20,095,250	59,553,345	47,991,774

WEST AND CENTRAL AFRICA

Terrestrial protected areas
Sites

	Ia	Ib	II	III	IV	V	VI	Total	National other areas
									Total
Angola			4		5	1		10	7
Benin			2				3	5	57
Burkina Faso			4		9			13	77
Burundi				2	11	2		15	
Cameroon			11		6		1	18	31
Cape Verde									50
Central African Republic	1		4		8		1	14	58
Chad			2		7			9	28
Congo			4		7		3	14	17
Côte d'Ivoire	2		5		1		1	9	313
Democratic Republic of the Congo	2	4	8		2		27	43	47
Djibouti									1
Equatorial Guinea		2	3	2	3			10	
Gabon					1			1	17
Gambia					1			1	66
Ghana	1		6		3		6	16	320
Guinea	1		1				1	3	151
Guinea-Bissau									7
Liberia			1					1	19

Table A5.1 Continued

WEST AND CENTRAL AFRICA

	Ia	Ib	II	III	IV	V	VI	Total	National other areas
				National IUCN areas					
Terrestrial protected areas									
Sites									**Total**
Madagascar	4		16		20		7	47	8
Mali			1	1	11			13	8
Mauritania					4			4	
Mauritius			1		6			7	2
Niger	1		1		4			6	1
Nigeria	8		10		13			31	996
Rwanda			2		3			5	6
Sao Tome and Principe									4
Senegal			2		3		2	7	4
Sierra Leone			4		1		1	6	65
Togo			3		6			9	88
Total	20	6	95	5	135	3	53	317	2448
Area (ha)									
Angola			2,958,000		2,303,000	10,000		5,271,000	7,276,800
Benin			777,500				485,000	1,262,500	1,406,591
Burkina Faso			814,300		2,320,900			3,135,200	2,282,036
Burundi				742	145,500	8500		154,742	
Cameroon			2,502,779		953,083		69,145	3,525,007	1,392,741
Cape Verde									1000
Central African Republic	84,304		3,219,497		4,016,651		343,277	7,663,729	3,690,618
Chad			414,000		11,080,000			11,494,000	1,903,635
Congo			3,566,480		1,326,460		155,000	5,047,940	2,578,431
Côte d'Ivoire	128,000		1,730,000		95,000		62,100	2,015,100	3,437,764
Democratic Republic of the Congo	270,000	1,067,100	9,926,625		604,100		5,432,576	17,300,401	2,340,167
Djibouti									–
Equatorial Guinea		51,500	303,000	39,000	61,500			455,000	
Gabon					80,000			80,000	3,616,286
Gambia			500		500	33,977			
Ghana	38,570		1,058,430		7064		164,506	1,268,570	2,564,354
Guinea	13,000		38,200				119	51,319	1,518,418
Guinea-Bissau									462,646
Liberia			129,230					129,230	1,755,197
Madagascar	208,688		897,343		300,725		335,328	1,742,084	362,037
Mali			350,000	400,000	3,781,989			4,531,989	2,691,462
Mauritania					250,000			250,000	
Mauritius			6574		196			6770	30
Niger	1,280,000		220,000		6,914,100			8,414,100	700,000
Nigeria	50,291		2,805,160		744,869			3,600,320	3,252,183
Rwanda			102,000		98,800			200,800	31,151
Sao Tome and Principe									29,000
Senegal			929,000		1,167,250		60,756	2,157,006	201

Table A5.1 Continued

WEST AND CENTRAL AFRICA

	Ia	Ib	II	III	IV	V	VI	Total	National other areas
				National IUCN areas					National other areas
Terrestrial protected areas									
Area (ha)									**Total**
Sierra Leone			143,587		1200		8573	153,360	288,935
Togo			357,290		71,915			429,205	1,756,464
Total	2,072,853	1,118,600	33,248,995	439,742	36,324,802	18,500	7,116,380	80,339,872	45,372,124
Marine and coastal protected areas									
Sites									**Total**
Angola			2		2			4	
Benin									1
Cameroon			1		1			2	
Cape Verde									13
Comoros			1					1	1
Côte d'Ivoire			3					3	
Democratic Republic of the Congo									2
Djibouti	1						1	2	
Equatorial Guinea					3			3	
Gabon					2			2	3
Gambia			3		2			5	1
Guinea									3
Guinea-Bissau									3
Liberia		1						1	1
Madagascar	1		5				1	7	2
Mauritania	3		2					5	
Mauritius	1		1		16			18	3
Nigeria									1
Senegal			4		3			7	
Sierra Leone									4
Togo									1
Total	6	1	22		29		2	60	39
Area (ha)									
Angola			2,465,000		445,200			2,910,200	
Benin									10,000
Cameroon			260,443		128,360			388,803	
Cape Verde									2915
Comoros			40,400					40,400	5
Côte d'Ivoire			32,500					32,500	
Democratic Republic of the Congo									176,850
Djibouti	–						–	–	
Equatorial Guinea					131,000			131,000	
Gabon					98,000			98,000	394,033
Gambia			18,440		3607			22,047	1000

Table A5.1 Continued

WEST AND CENTRAL AFRICA

	Ia	Ib	II	III	IV	V	VI	Total	National other areas
			National IUCN areas						
Marine and coastal protected areas									
Area (ha)									**Total**
Guinea									4350
Guinea-Bissau									118,354
Liberia		55,400						55,400	145,000
Madagascar	1523		11,391				65,315	78,229	113,000
Mauritania	310,000		1,186,000					1,496,000	
Mauritius	31	–			9004			9035	473
Nigeria									10,000
Senegal			83,450		1775			85,225	
Sierra Leone									111,250
Togo									900
Total	311,554	55,400	4,097,624		816,946		65,315	5,346,839	1,088,130
REGIONAL TOTAL									
Sites	26	7	117	5	164	3	55	377	2487
Area (ha)	2,384,407	1,174,000	37,346,619	439,742	37,141,748	18,500	7,181,695	85,686,711	46,460,254

Source: WDPA Consortium (2005)

Appendix 6

World Heritage Areas, Biosphere Reserves and Ramsar Sites, by WCPA Region

Compiled from data in WDPA Consortium (2005) by Colin Winkler and Michael Lockwood.

Table A6.1 World Heritage areas, biosphere reserves and Ramsar sites, by World Commission on Projected Areas (WCPA) region

AUSTRALIA and NEW ZEALAND

	Biosphere reserves	Ramsar wetlands	World Heritage areas	Total
Terrestrial protected areas				
Sites				
Australia	12	29	7	48
New Zealand		2	1	3
Total	12	31	8	51
Area (ha)				
Australia	4,906,295	2,682,820	1,652,589	9,241,704
New Zealand		16,124	79,596	95,720
Total	4,906,295	2,698,944	1,732,185	9,337,424
Marine and coastal protected areas				
Sites				
Australia		35	10	45
New Zealand		3	2	5
Total				
Area (ha)		38	12	50
Australia		4,689,053	43,076,619	47,765,672
New Zealand		22,744	3,986,792	4,009,536
Total		4,711,797	47,063,411	51,775,208
REGIONAL SUMMARY				
Sites	12	69	20	101
Area (ha)	4,906,295	7,410,741	48,795,596	61,112,632

Table A6.1 Continued

BRAZIL

	Biosphere reserves	Ramsar wetlands	World Heritage areas	Total
Terrestrial protected areas				
Sites				
Brazil	5	5	14	24
Total	5	5	14	24
Area (ha)				
Brazil	125,041,890	3,684,219	6,651,286	135,377,395
Total	125,041,890	3,684,219	6,651,286	135,377,395
Marine and coastal protected areas				
Sites				
Brazil		3	3	6
Total		3	3	6
Area (ha)				
Brazil		2,749,867	1,944,393	4,694,260
Total		2,749,867	1,944,393	4,694,260
REGIONAL SUMMARY				
Sites	5	8	17	30
Area (ha)	125,041,890	6,434,086	8,595,679	140,071,655

CARIBBEAN

	Biosphere reserves	Ramsar wetlands	World Heritage areas	Total
Terrestrial protected areas				
Sites				
Bermuda		5		5
Cuba	1	1	5	7
Dominica			1	1
Dominican Republic	1	1	1	3
Haiti			1	1
Jamaica	1	1		
Saint Kitts and Nevis			1	1
Saint Lucia		2	1	3
Total	2	10	10	22
Area (ha)				
Bermuda		24		24
Cuba	25,000	22,000	–	47,000
Dominica			6857	6857

Table A6.1 Continued

CARIBBEAN

Total Terrestrial protected areas	Biosphere reserves	Ramsar wetlands	World Heritage areas	Total
Terrestrial protected areas				
Area (ha)				
Dominican Republic	476,700	20,000	–	496,700
Haiti			–	–
Jamaica		5700		5700
Saint Kitts And Nevis			–	–
Saint Lucia		85	2909	2994
Total	501,700	47,809	9766	559,275
Marine and coastal protected areas				
Sites				
Aruba		1		1
Bahamas		1		1
Bermuda		2		2
Cayman Islands		1		1
Cuba	5	5	2	12
Guadeloupe	1			1
Netherlands Antilles		5		5
Trinidad And Tobago		1		1
Turks And Caicos Islands		1		1
Total	6	17	2	25
Area (ha)				
Aruba		70		70
Bahamas		32,600		32,600
Bermuda		12		12
Cayman Islands		82		82
Cuba	1,358,708	1,166,411	103,800	2,628,919
Guadeloupe	69,707			69,707
Netherlands Antilles		1940		1940
Trinidad And Tobago		6234		6234
Turks And Caicos Islands		58,617		58,617
Total	1,428,415	1,265,966	103,800	2,798,181
REGIONAL SUMMARY				
Sites	8	27	12	47
Area (ha)	1,930,115	1,313,775	113,566	3,357,456

Table A6.1 Continued

CENTRAL AMERICA

	Biosphere reserves	Ramsar wetlands	World Heritage areas	Total
Terrestrial protected areas				
Sites				
Belize		1		1
Costa Rica	2	5	1	8
El Salvador	1	1	2	
Guatemala	2	2	3	7
Honduras	1	1	1	3
Nicaragua	2	8	1	11
Panama	2	1	2	5
Total	9	19	9	37
Area (ha)				
Belize	6637	6637		
Costa Rica	728,955	294,443	612,600	1,635,998
El Salvador	1571	–	1571	
Guatemala	2,349,566	356,307	57,600	2,763,473
Honduras	800,000	69,711	–	869,711
Nicaragua	3,574,400	405,691	–	3,980,091
Panama	1,514,891	48,919	–	1,563,810
Total	8,967,812	1,183,279	670,200	10,821,291
Marine and coastal protected areas				
Sites				
Belize			1	1
Costa Rica		6	2	8
Guatemala		2	2	
Honduras		4	1	5
Panama		3	2	5
Total		15	6	21
Area (ha)				
Belize		96,300	96,300	
Costa Rica		215,607	241,700	457,307
Guatemala		146,400	146,400	
Honduras		109,969	525,000	634,969
Panama		110,984	804,000	914,984
Total		582,960	1,667,000	2,249,960
REGIONAL SUMMARY				
Sites	9	34	15	58
Area (ha)	8,967,812	1,766,239	2,337,200	13,071,251

Table A6.1 Continued

EAST AND SOUTH AFRICA

	Biosphere reserves	Ramsar wetlands	World Heritage areas	Total
Terrestrial protected areas				
Sites				
Botswana		1	1	2
Ethiopia			7	7
Kenya	4	4	3	11
Malawi	1	1	1	3
Mozambique			1	1
Namibia		2		2
South Africa	4	10	5	19
Sudan	2		1	3
Tanzania, United Republic of	3	3	6	12
Uganda	1	2	3	6
Zambia		2	1	3
Zimbabwe			5	5
Total	15	25	34	74
Area (ha)				
Botswana		6,864,000	–	6,864,000
Ethiopia			22,000	22,000
Kenya	1,463,786	90,969	304,982	1,859,737
Malawi	45,130	224,800	9400	279,330
Mozambique			–	–
Namibia		600,500		600,500
South Africa	3,371,140	283,071	795,813	4,450,024
Sudan	1,250,890		–	1,250,890
Tanzania, United Republic of	5,228,100	4,271,516	6,860,453	16,360,069
Uganda	246,500	37,000	131,692	415,192
Zambia		333,000	3779	336,779
Zimbabwe			679,681	679,681
Total	11,605,546	12,704,856	8,807,800	33,118,202
Marine and coastal protected areas				
Sites				
Kenya	2			2
Namibia		2		2
Seychelles			2	2
South Africa		7	1	8
Total	2	9	3	14
Area (ha)				
Kenya	79,600			79,600
Namibia		29,100		29,100
Seychelles			35,019	35,019
South Africa		215,650	239,566	455,216
Total	79,600	244,750	274,585	598,935
REGIONAL SUMMARY				
Sites	17	34	37	88
Area (ha)	11,685,146	12,949,606	9,082,385	33,717,137

Table A6.1 Continued

EAST ASIA

	Biosphere reserves	Ramsar wetlands	World Heritage areas	Total
Terrestrial protected areas				
Sites				
China	22	18	30	70
Japan	4	7	11	22
Korea, DPR	1		1	2
Korea, Republic of	2	2	7	11
Mongolia	4	11	2	17
Total	33	38	51	122
Area (ha)				
China	4,543,694	2,547,763	2,022,575	9,114,032
Japan	115,796	84,089	28,213	228,098
Korea, DPR	132,000		–	132,000
Korea, Republic of	122,443	960	–	123,403
Mongolia	6,917,000	1,439,530	1,068,693	9,425,223
Total	11,830,933	4,072,342	3,119,481	19,022,756
Marine and coastal protected areas				
Sites				
China	2	3		5
Japan		6	1	7
Total	2	9	1	12
Area (ha)				
China	28,629	90,100		118,729
Japan		15,684	10,747	26,431
Total	28,629	105,784	10,747	145,160
REGIONAL SUMMARY				
Sites	35	47	52	134
Area (ha)	11,859,562	4,178,126	3,130,228	19,167,916

EUROPE AND SCANDINAVIA

	Biosphere reserves	Ramsar wetlands	World Heritage areas	Total
Terrestrial protected areas				
Sites				
Albania		1	1	2
Andorra			1	1
Austria	5	16	8	29
Belgium		3	8	11

Table A6.1 Continued

EUROPE AND SCANDINAVIA

	Biosphere reserves	Ramsar wetlands	World Heritage areas	Total
Terrestrial protected areas				
Sites				
Bosnia and Herzegovinia		1		1
Bulgaria	16	7	9	32
Croatia	1	3	6	10
Czech Republic	6	10	12	28
Denmark		5	3	8
Estonia	1	7	1	9
Finland	1	5	5	11
France	8	12	27	47
Germany, Federal Republic	14	24	30	68
Greece	2	4	15	21
Hungary	5	21	8	34
Iceland		2	1	3
Ireland	2	23	2	27
Italy	7	21	37	65
Latvia	1	6	1	8
Liechtenstein		1		1
Lithuania		5	3	8
Luxembourg		1	1	2
Macedonia		1	1	2
Malta		1	3	4
Netherlands	1	31	7	39
Norway		16	4	20
Poland	9	7	13	29
Portugal	1	5	13	19
Romania	3	2	6	11
Serbia And Montenegro	2	5	4	11
Slovakia	4	12	5	21
Slovenia	1	2	1	4
Spain	26	24	35	85
Svalbard and Jan Mayen Islands		5		5
Sweden	1	41	12	54
Switzerland	2	8	6	16
UK	7	94	21	122
Total	126	432	310	868
Area (ha)				
Albania		13,500	200	13,700
Andorra			4247	4247
Austria	46,837	137,325	0	184,162
Belgium		5085	0	5085
Bosnia And Herzegovinia		7411		7411

Table A6.1 Continued

EUROPE AND SCANDINAVIA

	Biosphere reserves	Ramsar wetlands	World Heritage areas	Total
Terrestrial protected areas				
Area (ha)				
Bulgaria	37,778	13,685	40,660	92,123
Croatia	200,000	68,955	11,500	280,455
Czech Republic	450,525	41,861	0	492,386
Denmark		204,515	0	204,515
Estonia	1,560,000	123,294	0	1,683,294
Finland	350,000	94,528	0	444,528
France	829,568	387,051	11,055	1,227,674
Germany, Federal Republic	1,613,523	125,034	70	1,738,627
Greece	8850	56,111	375	65,336
Hungary	128,884	154,147	0	283,031
Iceland		57,500	0	57,500
Ireland	11,137	33,429	0	44,566
Italy	301,067	16,922	91	318,080
Latvia	474,447	148,363	0	622,810
Liechtenstein		101		101
Lithuania		50,451	0	50,451
Luxembourg		313	0	313
Macedonia		18,920	38,000	56,920
Malta		5	0	5
Netherlands	260,000	254,752	0	514,752
Norway		33,979	0	33,979
Poland	398,007	72,208	10,509	480,724
Portugal	554	1623	15,987	18,164
Romania	662,047	664,586	0	1,326,633
Serbia And Montenegro	236,693	40,837	32,000	309,530
Slovakia	241,298	38,208	0	279,506
Slovenia	0	955	413	1368
Spain	2,036,140	37,191	20,310	209,3641
Svalbard and Jan Mayen Islands		450		450
Sweden	96,500	459,670	940,000	1,496,170
Switzerland	212,059	6593	56,126	274,778
UK	24,515	421,301	0	445,816
Total	10,180,429	3,790,859	1,181,543	1,5152,831
Marine and coastal protected areas				
Sites				
Albania		1		1
Belgium		3		3
Bulgaria		3		3
Croatia		1		1
Denmark		22		22

Table A6.1 Continued

EUROPE AND SCANDINAVIA

	Biosphere reserves	Ramsar wetlands	World Heritage areas	Total
Marine and coastal protected areas				
Sites				
Estonia		4		4
Finland	1	6		7
France		8	1	9
Germany, Federal Republic		8		8
Greece		6	1	7
Iceland		1		1
Ireland		22		22
Italy		25	1	26
Malta		1		1
Monaco		1		1
Netherlands		12		12
Norway		16	1	17
Poland		1		1
Portugal		7		7
Romania			1	1
Spain		25	3	28
Sweden		10	1	11
UK	2	54	4	60
Total	3	237	13	253
Area (ha)				
Albania		20,000		20,000
Belgium		2850		2850
Bulgaria		6621		6621
Croatia		11,500		11,500
Denmark		531,998		531,998
Estonia		95,050		95,050
Finland	420,000	44,218		464,218
France		233,200	12,000	245,200
Germany, Federal Republic		714,993		714,993
Greece		107,390	0	107,390
Iceland		1470		1470
Ireland		33,565		33,565
Italy		40,215	0	40,215
Malta		11		11
Monaco		10		10
Netherlands		562,146		562,146
Norway		81,940	103,710	185,650
Poland		18,247		18,247
Portugal		64,473		64,473
Romania		679,222	679,222	

Table A6.1 Continued

EUROPE AND SCANDINAVIA

	Biosphere reserves	Ramsar wetlands	World Heritage areas	Total
Marine and coastal protected areas				
Area (ha)				
Spain		135,935	63,268	199,203
Sweden		54,830	142,500	197,330
UK	2	326,475	30,521	356,998
Total	420,002	3,087,137	1,031,221	4,538,360
REGIONAL SUMMARY				
Sites	129	669	323	1121
Area (ha)	10,600,431	6,877,996	2,212,764	19,691,191

NORTH AFRICA AND MIDDLE EAST

	Biosphere reserves	Ramsar wetlands	World Heritage areas	Total
Terrestrial protected areas				
Sites				
Afghanistan			2	2
Algeria	4	23	7	34
Cyprus		2	3	5
Egypt	2		6	8
Iran, Islamic Republic of	8	15	6	29
Iraq			2	2
Israel	1	2	3	6
Jordan	1		3	4
Lebanon		4	5	9
Libyan Arab Jamahiriya		2	5	7
Morocco	2	1	8	11
Oman			4	4
Syrian Arab Republic		1	4	5
Tunisia	4	1	7	12
Turkey		5	9	14
Yemen	1		3	4
Total	23	56	77	156
Area (ha)				
Afghanistan			–	–
Algeria	7,349,083	2,744,032	8,000,000	18,093,115
Cyprus		3756	–	3756
Egypt	2,455,800		–	2,455,800
Iran, Islamic Republic of	2,667,675	1,127,577	–	3,795,252
Iraq			–	–

Table A6.1 Continued

NORTH AFRICA AND MIDDLE EAST

	Biosphere reserves	Ramsar wetlands	World Heritage areas	Total
Terrestrial protected areas				
Area (ha)				
Israel	26,600	366	–	26,966
Jordan	30,800		–	30,800
Lebanon		1075	–	1075
Libyan Arab Jamahiriya		311	–	311
Morocco	9,754,151	250	–	9,754,401
Oman			2,750,000	2,750,000
Syrian Arab Republic		10,000	–	10,000
Tunisia	75,602	12,600	–	88,202
Turkey		93,000	9576	102,576
Yemen	2,681,640		–	2,681,640
Total	25,041,351	3,992,967	10,759,576	39,793,894
Marine and coastal protected areas				
Sites				
Algeria		3		3
Bahrain		2		2
Egypt		2		2
Iran, Islamic Republic of	1	7		8
Jordan		1		1
Morocco		3		3
Tunisia			1	1
Turkey		4		4
Total	1	22	1	24
Area (ha)				
Algeria		47,960		47,960
Bahrain		6810		6810
Egypt		105,700		105,700
Iran, Islamic Republic of	85,686	353,570		439,256
Jordan		7372		7372
Morocco		14,100		14,100
Tunisia			12,600	12,600
Turkey		66,300		66,300
Total	85,686	601,812	12,600	700,098
REGIONAL SUMMARY				
Sites	24	78	78	180
Area (ha)	25,127,037	4,594,779	10,772,176	40,493,992

Table A6.1 Continued

NORTH AMERICA

	Biosphere reserves	Ramsar wetlands	World Heritage areas	Total
Terrestrial protected areas				
Sites				
Canada	12	18	10	40
Greenland	1	6	1	8
Mexico	10	18	22	50
US	43	11	15	69
Total	66	53	48	167
Area (ha)				
Canada	4,505,880	5,544,231	7,323,462	17,373,573
Greenland	97,200,000	1,080,120	40,240	98,320,360
Mexico	2,008,759	964,966	104	2,973,829
US	29,491,872	337,580	2,353,845	32,183,297
Total	133,206,511	7,926,897	9,717,651	150,851,059
Marine and coastal protected areas				
Sites				
Canada		10	3	21
Greenland		5		5
Mexico	4	33	2	39
US	4	8	5	17
Total	8	64	10	82
Area (ha)				
Canada		7,507,270	3,340,087	10,847,357
Greenland		262,190		262,190
Mexico	4,874,250	4,136,467	898,950	9,909,667
US	1,843,029	855,150	7,779,772	10,477,951
Total	6,717,279	12,761,077	12,018,809	31,497,165
REGIONAL SUMMARY				
Sites	74	117	58	249
Area (ha)	139,923,790	20,687,974	21,736,460	182,348,224

Table A6.1 Continued

NORTH EURASIA

Total Terrestrial protected areas	Biosphere reserves	Ramsar wetlands	World Heritage areas	Total
Terrestrial protected areas				
Sites				
Armenia		2	3	5
Azerbaijan		2	1	3
Belarus	2	7	2	11
Georgia		1	3	4
Kazakhstan		2	2	4
Kyrgyzstan	2	1		3
Moldova, Republic of Russian		2		2
Federation	31	29	17	77
Tajikistan		5		5
Turkmenistan	1		1	2
Ukraine	5	23	2	30
Uzbekistan	1	1	4	6
Total	42	75	35	152
Area (ha)				
Armenia		492,239	–	492,239
Azerbaijan		99,560	–	99,560
Belarus	305,229	276,307	87,607	669,143
Georgia		513	–	513
Kazakhstan		608,500	–	608,500
Kyrgyzstan	4,335,456	623,600		4,959,056
Moldova, Republic of Russian		79,152		79,152
Federation	25,107,479	9,165,767	7,107,564	41,380,810
Tajikistan		94,600		94,600
Turkmenistan	34,600		–	34,600
Ukraine	286,019	364,376	–	650,395
Uzbekistan	57,360	31,300	–	88,660
Total	30,126,143	11,835,914	7,195,171	49,157,228
Marine and coastal protected areas				
Sites				
Azerbaijan		1		1
Georgia		1		1
Russian Federation		6	3	9
Turkmenistan		1		1
Ukraine	1	10		11
Total	1	19	3	23
Area (ha)				
Azerbaijan		132,500		132,500
Georgia		33,710		33,710
Russian Federation		1,158,000	13,940,015	15,098,015

Table A6.1 Continued

NORTH EURASIA

	Biosphere reserves	Ramsar wetlands	World Heritage areas	Total
Marine and coastal protected areas				
Area (ha)				
Turkmenistan		188,700		188,700
Ukraine	46,403	380,275		426,678
Total	46,403	1,893,185	13,940,015	15,879,603
REGIONAL SUMMARY				
Sites	43	94	38	175
Area (ha)	30,172,546	13,729,099	21,135,186	65,036,831

PACIFIC

	Biosphere reserves	Ramsar wetlands	World Heritage areas	Total
Terrestrial protected areas				
Sites				
Palau		1		1
Papua New Guinea		2		2
Total		3		3
Area (ha)				
Palau		493		493
Papua New Guinea		594,924		594,924
Total		595,417		595,417
Marine and coastal protected areas				
Sites				
French Polynesia	1			1
Solomon Islands			1	1
Total	1		1	2
Area (ha)				
French Polynesia	930			930
Solomon Islands			37,000	37,000
Total	930		37,000	37,930
REGIONAL SUMMARY				
Sites	1	3	1	5
Area (ha)	930	595,417	37,000	633,347

Table A6.1 Continued

SOUTH AMERICA

	Biosphere reserves	Ramsar wetlands	World Heritage areas	Total
Terrestrial protected areas				
Sites				
Argentina	11	11	7	29
Bolivia	3	8	6	17
Chile	7	2	3	12
Colombia	4	2	5	11
Ecuador	2	6	3	11
Paraguay	1	6	1	8
Peru	3	6	10	19
Suriname			2	2
Uruguay	1		1	2
Venezuela	1		3	4
Total	33	41	41	115
Area (ha)				
Argentina	4,176,986	3,310,024	776,200	8,263,210
Bolivia	735,000	6,518,073	1,523,000	8,776,073
Chile	2,479,166	78,318	–	2,557,484
Colombia	3,332,250	47,888	72,000	3,452,138
Ecuador	2,613,215	103,386	271,925	2,988,526
Paraguay	280,000	785,970	–	1,065,970
Peru	3,268,402	4,361,460	2,179,918	9,809,780
Suriname			1,600,000	1,600,000
Uruguay	200,000		–	200,000
Venezuela	8,266,230		3,000,000	11,266,230
Total	25,351,249	15,205,119	9,423,043	49,979,411
Marine and coastal protected areas				
Sites				
Argentina		2	1	3
Chile		6		6
Colombia	1	1		2
Ecuador	1	5	1	7
French Guiana		2		2
Peru		4		4
Suriname		1		1
Uruguay		1		1
Venezuela		5		5
Total	2	27	2	31
Area (ha)				
Argentina		272,565	360,000	632,565
Chile		21,890		21,890

Table A6.1 Continued

SOUTH AMERICA

	Biosphere reserves	Ramsar wetlands	World Heritage areas	Total
Marine and coastal protected areas				
Area (ha)				
Colombia	30,000,000	400,000		30,400,000
Ecuador	14,761,844	55,095	14,266,514	29,083,453
French Guiana		196,000		196,000
Peru		2,415,954		2,415,954
Suriname		12,000		12,000
Uruguay		407,408		407,408
Venezuela		263,636		263,636
Total	44,761,844	4,044,548	14,626,514	63,432,906
REGIONAL SUMMARY				
Sites	35	68	43	146
Area (ha)	70,113,093	19,249,667	24,049,557	113,412,317

SOUTH ASIA

	Biosphere reserves	Ramsar wetlands	World Heritage areas	Total
Terrestrial protected areas				
Sites				
Bangladesh		2	2	4
India	3	12	25	40
Nepal		4	4	8
Pakistan	1	15	6	22
Sri Lanka	2	1	7	10
Total	6	34	44	84
Area (ha)				
Bangladesh		611,200	–	611,200
India	2,565,000	113,257	158,902	2,837,159
Nepal		23,488	208,000	231,488
Pakistan	65,791	1,280,521	–	1,346,312
Sri Lanka	36,687	1397	8864	46,948
Total	2,667,478	2,029,863	375,766	5,073,107
Marine and coastal protected areas				
Sites				
Bangladesh			1	1
India		7	1	8
Pakistan		4		4
Sri Lanka		2		2
Total		13	2	15

Table A6.1 Continued

SOUTH ASIA

	Biosphere reserves	Ramsar wetlands	World Heritage areas	Total
Marine and coastal protected areas				
Area (ha)				
Bangladesh			139,700	139,700
India		535,250	133,010	668,260
Pakistan		63,106		63,106
Sri Lanka		7125		7125
Total		605,481	272,710	878,191
REGIONAL SUMMARY				
Sites	6	47	46	99
Area (ha)	2,667,478	2,635,344	648,476	5,951,298

SOUTH-EAST ASIA

	Biosphere reserves	Ramsar wetlands	World Heritage areas	Total
Terrestrial protected areas				
Sites				
Cambodia	1	3	1	5
Indonesia	3	1	4	8
Lao PDR	2	2		
Malaysia	3	2	5	
Philippines	2	3	5	
Thailand	3	9	4	16
Viet Nam	1	4	5	
Total	8	18	20	46
Area (ha)				
Cambodia	1,481,257	54,600	–	1,535,857
Indonesia	1,068,189	80,000	2,500,000	3,648,189
Lao PDR			–	–
Malaysia		48,098	128,234	176,332
Philippines		29,404	–	29,404
Thailand	54,572	283,100	577,464	915,136
Viet Nam	257,357		–	257,357
Total	2,861,375	495,202	3,205,698	6,562,275
Marine and coastal protected areas				
Sites				
Indonesia	3	1	3	7
Malaysia		1		1
Philippines	2	2	2	6

Table A6.1 Continued

SOUTH-EAST ASIA

	Biosphere reserves	Ramsar wetlands	World Heritage areas	Total
Marine and coastal protected areas				
Sites				
Thailand	1	1		2
Viet Nam	1	1	1	3
Total	7	6	6	19
Area (ha)				
Indonesia	993,410	162,700	2,692,373	3,848,483
Malaysia		647		647
Philippines	1,174,047	39,000	53,402	1,266,449
Thailand	29,936	87,500		117,436
Viet Nam	75,740	12,000	150,000	237,740
Total	2,273,133	301,847	2,895,775	5,470,755
REGIONAL SUMMARY				
Sites	15	24	26	65
Area (ha)	5,134,508	797,049	6,101,473	12,033,030

WEST AND CENTRAL AFRICA

	Biosphere reserves	Ramsar wetlands	World Heritage areas	Total
Terrestrial protected areas				
Sites				
Benin	2	1	1	4
Burkina Faso	2	3		5
Burundi		1		1
Cameroon	3		1	4
Central African Republic	2		1	3
Chad		2		2
Congo	2	1		3
Côte D'Ivoire	2	1	3	6
Democratic Republic of the Congo	3	2	5	10
Djibouti		1		1
Equatorial Guinea		1		1
Gabon	1	1		2
Gambia			1	1
Ghana	1	2	2	5
Guinea	4	6	1	11
Madagascar	2	3	2	7
Mali	1	1	4	6
Mauritania		1	1	2

Table A6.1 Continued

WEST AND CENTRAL AFRICA

	Biosphere reserves	Ramsar wetlands	World Heritage areas	Total
Terrestrial protected areas				
Sites				
Mauritius	1			1
Niger	2	7	2	11
Nigeria	1	1	1	3
Rwanda	1			1
Senegal	3	2	3	8
Sierra Leone		1		1
Togo		2	1	3
Total	33	40	29	102
Area (ha)				
Benin	2,928,313	91,600	–	3,019,913
Burkina Faso	532,000	299,200		831,200
Burundi		1000		1000
Cameroon	876,000		526,000	1,402,000
Central African Republic	1,640,200		1,740,000	3,380,200
Chad		1,843,168		1,843,168
Congo	246,000	438,960		684,960
Côte D'Ivoire	1,770,000	19,400	1,484,250	3,273,650
Democratic Republic of the Congo	282,668	866,000	6,854,625	8,003,293
Djibouti		3000		3000
Equatorial Guinea		33,000		33,000
Gabon	15,000	480,000		495,000
Gambia			–	–
Ghana	7770	8600	–	16,370
Guinea	1,192,670	4,554,050	13,000	5,759,720
Madagascar	353,772	775,595	152,000	1,281,367
Mali	2,500,000	4,119,500	400,000	7,019,500
Mauritania		15,500	–	15,500
Mauritius	3594			3594
Niger	25,128,070	1,476,280	7,956,000	34,560,350
Nigeria	130,600	58,100	–	188,700
Rwanda	12,500			12,500
Senegal	1,093,756	26,000	913,000	2,032,756
Sierra Leone		295,000		295,000
Togo		194,400	50,000	244,400
Total	38,712,913	15,598,353	20,088,875	74,400,141

Table A6.1 Continued

WEST AND CENTRAL AFRICA

	Biosphere reserves	Ramsar wetlands	World Heritage areas	Total
Marine and coastal protected areas				
Sites				
Benin		1		1
Comoros		1		1
Equatorial Guinea		2		2
Gabon		2		2
Gambia		1		1
Ghana		4		4
Guinea		6		6
Guinea-Bissau	1	1		2
Liberia		1		1
Madagascar		1		1
Mauritania		2	1	3
Mauritius		1		1
Senegal		2	1	3
Total	2	24	2	28
Area (ha)				
Benin		47,500		47,500
Comoros		30		30
Equatorial Guinea		103,000		103,000
Gabon		600,000		600,000
Gambia		20,000		20,000
Ghana		169,810		169,810
Guinea		225,011		225,011
Guinea-Bissau	101,230	39,098		140,328
Liberia		76,091		76,091
Madagascar	140,000			140,000
Mauritania		1,215,600	1,200,000	2,415,600
Mauritius		26		26
Senegal	73,720	16,000	89,720	
Total	241,230	2,569,886	1,216,000	4,027,116
REGIONAL SUMMARY				
Sites	35	64	31	130
Area (ha)	38,954,143	18,168,239	21,304,875	78,427,257

Table A6.1 Continued

SUMMARY OF ALL REGIONS

World Commission on Protected Areas (WCPA) Region		Biosphere reserves	Ramsar wetlands	World Heritage areas	Total
Total					
Australia and New Zealand	Sites	12	69	20	101
	Area (ha)	4,906,295	7,410,741	48,795,596	61,112,632
Brazil	Sites	5	8	17	30
	Area (ha)	125,041,890	6,434,086	8,595,679	140,071,655
Caribbean	Sites	8	27	12	47
	Area (ha)	1,930,115	1,313,775	113,566	3,357,456
Central America	Sites	9	34	15	58
	Area (ha)	8,967,812	1,766,239	2,337,200	13,071,251
East and South Africa	Sites	17	34	37	88
	Area (ha)	11,685,146	12,949,606	9,082,385	33,717,137
East Asia	Sites	35	47	52	134
	Area (ha)	11,859,562	4,178,126	3,130,228	19,167,916
North Africa and Middle East	Sites	24	78	78	180
	Area (ha)	25,127,037	4,594,779	10,772,176	40,493,992
North America	Sites	74	117	58	249
	Area (ha)	139,923,790	20,687,974	21,736,460	182,348,224
North Eurasia	Sites	43	94	38	175
	Area (ha)	30,172,546	13,729,099	21,135,186	65,036,831
Pacific	Sites	1	3	1	5
	Area (ha)	930	595,417	37,000	633,347
South America	Sites	35	68	43	146
	Area (ha)	70,113,093	19,249,667	24,049,557	113,412,317
South Asia	Sites	6	47	46	99
	Area (ha)	2,667,478	2,635,344	648,476	5,951,298
South-East Asia	Sites	15	24	26	65
	Area (ha)	5,134,508	797,049	6,101,473	12,033,030
West and Central Africa	Sites	35	64	31	130
	Area (ha)	38,954,143	18,168,239	21,304,875	78,427,257
TOTAL	**Sites**	**319**	**714**	**474**	**1507**
	Area (ha)	**476,484,345**	**114,510,141**	**177,839,857**	**768,834,343**

Notes:

Terrestrial protected areas include inland lakes, rivers and wetlands.

Marine and coastal protected areas include littoral protected areas, and protected areas with both marine and littoral components – these marine and coastal protected areas include areas that are fully marine and areas that have only a small percentage of intertidal environment.

Some World Heritage areas, Ramsar sites and biosphere reserves are overlapping with national protected areas (see Appendix 5).

Source: WDPA Consortium (2005)

References

Abrams, P., Borrini-Feyerabend, G., Gardner, J. and Heylings, P. (2003) *Evaluating Governance: A Handbook to Accompany a Participatory Process for a Protected Area*, Parks Canada and CMWG/TILCEPA, Ottawa

Acha, M. O. (2003) 'Wirikuta: The Wixarika/Huichol sacred natural site in the Chihuahuan Desert, San Luis Potosi, Mexico', in Harmon, D. and Putney, A. (eds) *The Full Value of Parks: From Economics to the Intangible*, Rowman and Littlefield, Lanham

ACIUCN (Australian Committee for the International Union for the Conservation of Nature) (2002) *Australian Natural Heritage Charter*, 2nd edition, ACIUCN and AHC, Canberra

Adam, P. (1994) *Australian Rainforests*, Oxford University Press, Melbourne

ADB (Asian Development Bank) (1990) *Economic Policies for Sustainable Development*, Asian Development Bank, Manila

ADB (1997) *Emerging Asia: Changes and Challenges*, Asian Development Bank, Manila

Adler, J. (1989) 'Alaska after *Exxon*', *Newsweek*, 18 September, pp50–62

Administración de Parques Nacionales (2005) *Monumento Natural Bosques Petrificados*, www.parquesnacionales.gov.ar

Agardy, T. (1997) *Marine Protected Areas and Ocean Conservation*, RE Landes Press, Austin

Agardy, T., Bridgewater, P., Crosby, M. P., Day, J., Dayton, P. K., Kenchington, R., Laffoley, D., McConney, P., Murray, P. A., Parks, J. E. and Peau L. (2003) 'Dangerous targets? Unresolved issues and ideological clashes around marine protected areas', Aquatic Conservation Marine Freshwater Ecosystems, vol 13, pp353–367

AIIMS (Australian Inter-service Incident Management System) (1992) *Incident Control System: The Operating System of Australian Inter-service Incident Management System*, Australian Association of Rural Fire Authorities, Melbourne

Aitchison, J. (1995) 'Cultural landscapes in Europe: A geographical perspective', in von Droste B., Plachter, H. and Rossler, M. (eds) *Cultural Landscapes of Outstanding Universal Value: Components of a Global Strategy*, UNESCO, Paris

Alanen, A. R. and Melnick, R. Z. (2000) *Preserving Cultural Landscapes in America*, John Hopkins University Press, Baltimore

Alcorn, J. B. (1993) 'Indigenous peoples and conservation', *Conservation Biology*, vol 7, no 2, pp424–427

Alcorn, J. B. (2005) 'Dances around the fire: Conservation organizations and community-based resource management', in Brosius, J. P., Zerner, C. and Tsing A. (eds) *Representing Communities: Histories and Politics of Community-based Resource Management*, Altamira Press, Walnut Creek

Alcorn, J. B., Luque, A. and Valenzuela, S. (2005a) 'Global governance and institutional trends affecting protected area management: Challenges and opportunities arising from democratization and globalization', in Pansky, D. (ed) *Governance Stream of the Vth World Parks Congress*, Parks Canada and IUCN/WCPA, Ottawa

Alcorn, J. B., Luque, A. and Weisman, W. (2005b) 'Non-governmental organizations and protected area governance', in Pansky, D. (ed) *Governance Stream of the Vth World Parks Congress*, Parks Canada and IUCN/WCPA, Ottawa

Alden-Wily, E. (2002) 'Participatory forest management in Africa: An overview of progress and issues', Paper submitted for the second international workshop on participatory forestry in Africa, FAO, Rome, www.cbnrm.net/pdf/aldenwily_l_002_cfm.pdf

Alderman, C. (1994) 'The economics and role of privately owned lands used for nature tourism, education, and conservation', in Munasinghe, M. and McNeely, J. (eds) *Protected Area Economics and Policy: Linking Conservation and Sustainable Development*, World Bank, Washington, DC

Algonquin Wolf Advisory Group (2000) *The Wolves of Algonquin Provincial Park: A Report to the Minister of Natural Resources*, Algonquin Wolf Advisory Group, Ontario

Ali, I. (2003) 'Shimshal Nature Trust, Pakistan', Paper presented to the Vth World Parks Congress, Durban

Ali, I. and Butz, D. (2003) 'The Shimshal governance model – A CCA, a sense of cultural identity, a way of life', *Policy Matters*, vol 12, pp111–120

Allen, M. (2002) *Field Guide to the Freshwater Fishes of Australia*, CSIRO Publishing, Melbourne

Allison, G. W., Lubchenco, J. and Carr, M. (1998) 'Marine reserves are necessary but not sufficient for marine conservation', *Ecological Applications*, vol 8, no 1, ppS79–S92

Allmendinger, P. (2002) 'The post–positivist landscape of planning theory', in Allmendinger, P. and Tewdwr-Jones, M. (eds) *Planning Futures: New Directions for Planning Theory*, Routledge, London

Alverson, D. L., Freeburg, M. H., Murawski, S. A. and Pope, J. G. (1994) *A Global Assessment of Fisheries Bycatch and Discards*, FAO Fisheries Technical Paper no 339, FAO, Rome

Amend, S. and Amend, T. (1995) *National Parks Without People? The South American Experience*, IUCN, Quito

Anderson, P. (2003) *The Contribution Made by Private Game Reserves and Landowners to Conservation in South Africa*, Powerpoint presentation to the Vth World Parks Congress, Durban

Anderson, T. L. and James, A. (2001a) 'Introduction: Parks, politics and property rights', in Anderson, T. L. and James, A. (eds) *The Politics and Economics of Park Management*, Rowman and Littlefield, Lanham

Anderson, T. L. and James, A. (eds) (2001b) *The Politics and Economics of Park Management*, Rowman and Littlefield, Lanham

Andersson, P., Croné, S., Stage, J. (2005) 'Potential monopoly rents from international wildlife tourism: An example for Uganda's gorilla tourism', *Eastern Africa Social Science Research Review*, vol 21, no 1, pp1–18

Andrade, G. I. (2000) 'The non-material values of the Machu Picchu World Heritage Site from acknowledgement to action', *Parks*, vol 10, no 2, pp49–62

ANZECC (Australia and New Zealand Environment Conservation Council) (2000) *National Framework for the Management and Monitoring of Australia's Native Vegetation*, Environment Australia, Canberra

Appenzeller, T. (2004) 'The end of cheap oil', *National Geographic*, June 2004

Appleton, M. (2004) Flora and Fauna International/ Cardamom Mountains Wildlife Sanctuaries Project (Cambodia), personal communication

Appleton, M. R, Texon, G. I. and Urarte, M.T. (2003) *Competence Standards for Protected Area Jobs in South East Asia*, ASEAN Regional Centre for Biodiversity Conservation, Los Banos

Archer, M., Hand, S. J. and Godthelp, H. (1994) *Riversleigh: The Story of Animals in Ancient Rainforests of Inland Australia*, Reed, Sydney

Argumedo, A. (2005) Indigenous Peoples' Biodiversity Network, Peru, personal communication

Arnstein, S. (1969) 'A ladder of citizen participation', *Journal of the American Institute of Planners*, vol 4, pp216–224

Asian Development Bank (1990) *Economic Policies for Sustainable Development*, ADB, Manila

Australia ICOMOS (1999) *The Burra Charter: The Australia ICOMOS Charter for Places of Cultural Significance*, Australia ICOMOS Secretariat, Melbourne

Australian Bush Heritage Fund (2005) *Home page*, www1.bushheritage.asn.au

Aycan, Z. (2004) 'Leadership and teamwork in the developing country context', in Lane, H. W., Maznevski, M. L., Mendenhall, M. E. and McNett, J. (eds) *The Blackwell Handbook of Global Management: A Guide to Managing Complexity,* Blackwell Publishing, Oxford

Bagnoli, P. and Rastogi, T. (2003) 'Distributive issues relating to parks: Overview of issues and selected case studies', Paper presented at the Vth IUCN World Parks Congress, Sustainable Finance Stream, Durban

Bahrami, K. (2002) 'Best practice benchmarks', in Mitchell, J. S. (ed) *Physical Asset Management Handbook*, 3rd edition, Clarion, Houston

Baillie, J. E. M., Hilton-Taylor, C. and Stuart, S. N. (eds) (2004) *2004 IUCN Red List of Threatened Species: A Global Species Assessment*, IUCN, Gland and Cambridge

Baird, I. and Dearden, P. (2003) 'Biodiversity conservation and resource tenure regimes – a case study from NE Cambodia', *Environmental Management*, vol 35, no 5, pp541–550

Balmford, A. (2003) 'The global costs and benefits of conserving wild nature', Paper presented at the Vth IUCN World Parks Congress, Sustainable Finance Stream, Durban

Balmford, A., Bruner, A., Cooper, P., Costanza, R., Farber, S., Green, R. E., Jenkins, M., Jefferiss, P., Jessamy, V., Madden, J., Munro, K., Myers, N., Naeem, S., Paavola, J., Rayment, M., Rosendo, S., Roughgarden, J., Trumper, K. and Turner, R. K. (2002) 'Economic reasons for conserving wild nature', *Science*, vol 297, pp950–953

Balmford, A., Gaston, K. J., Blyth, S., James, A. and Kapos, V. (2003) 'Global variation in terrestrial conservation costs, conservation benefits, and unmet conservation needs', *PNAS*, vol 100, no 3, pp1046–1050

Balmford, A., Gravestock, P., Hockley, N., McClean, C. J. and Roberts, C. M. (2004) 'The worldwide costs of marine protected areas', *PNAS*, vol 101, no 26, pp9694–9697

Banuri, T. and Najam, A. (2002) *Civic Entrepreneurship: A Civil Society Perspective on Sustainable Development*, Gandhara Academy Press, Islamabad

Barber, C. V. (2004) 'Designing protected area systems for a changing world', in Barber, C. V., Miller, K. R. and Boness, M. (eds) *Securing Protected Areas in the Face of Global Change: Issues and Strategies*, IUCN, Gland and Cambridge

Barber, C. V., Miller, K. R. and Boness, M. (eds) (2004) *Securing Protected Areas in the Face of Global Change: Issues and Strategies*, IUCN, Gland and Cambridge

Barham, E. (2001) 'Ecological boundaries as community boundaries: The politics of watersheds', *Society and Natural Resources*, vol 14, pp181–191

Barrett, S. and Gillen, K. (1997) 'Mountain protected areas of South Western Australia', *Parks*, vol 7, no 1, pp35–42

Barron, A. E., Bergin, P. and Infield, M. (1997) *Livestock and Wildlife in the Environment – Diversity in Pastoral Ecosystems of East Africa*, African Wildlife Foundation, www.fao.org/WAIRDOCS/LEAD/X6140E/X6140E00.HTM

Barrow, E. and Pathak, N. (2005) 'Conserving "unprotected" protected areas – Communities can and do conserve landscapes of all sorts', in

Mitchell, N., Brown, J. and Beresford, M. (eds) *The Protected Landscape Approach: Linking Nature, Culture and Community*, IUCN, Gland and Cambridge

Bartol, K., Martin, D., Tein, M. and Matthews, G. (1998) *Management: A Pacific Rim Focus*, 2nd edition, McGraw-Hill, Sydney

Bassi, M. (2002) 'The making of unsustainable livelihoods – An on-going tragedy in the Ethiopian drylands', *Policy Matters*, vol 10, no 7–12

Bassi, M. (2003) *Enhancing Equity in the Relationship between Protected Areas and Local Communities in the Context of Global Change: Horn of Africa and Kenya*, www.iucn.org/themes/ceesp/Wkg_grp/TILCEPA/community.htm#A

Batisse, M. (2001) 'World Heritage and Biosphere Reserves: Complementary instruments', *Parks*, vol 11, no 1, pp38–43

Battharai, B., Ojha, H., Ram Banjade, M. and Luintel, H. (2003) *Effect of NTFP Market Expansion on Sustainable Local Livelihoods*, Forest Resource Action Team, Nepal

Bauer, J. G. (1962) 'The Swiss National Park', in Cahalanc, V. H. (ed) *National Parks – A World View*, American Committee for International Wildlife Protection, New York

Bazerman, M. (1998) *Judgement in Managerial Decision Making*, 4th edition, John Wiley and Sons, New York

Beal, D. J. and Harrison, S. R. (1997) *Efficient Pricing of Recreation in National Parks: A Queensland Case Study*, Presented to the AARES Conference, Gold Coast

Beaumont, N. (1999) *Ecotourism: The Contribution of Educational Nature Experiences to Environmental Knowledge, Attitudes, and Behaviours*, PhD thesis, Australian School of Environmental Studies, Griffith University, Brisbane

Beck, M. and Odaya, M. (2001) 'Ecoregional planning in marine environments: Identifying priority sites for conservation in the northern Gulf of Mexico', *Aquatic Conservation: Marine and Freshwater Ecosystems*, vol 11, pp235–242

Bedward, M., Pressey, R. L. and Keith, D. A. (1992) 'A new approach to selecting fully representative protected area networks: Addressing efficiency, reserve design and land suitability with an iterative analysis', *Biological Conservation*, vol 62, pp115–125

Belfiore, S., Cicin-Sain, B. and Ehler, C. (eds) (2004) *Incorporating Marine Protected Areas into Integrated Coastal and Ocean Management: Principles and*

Guidelines, IUCN, Gland and Cambridge

Bell, N. S. (2000) 'On-the-job training for protected area personnel: A crucial but under-acknowledged training approach', Paper presented for the College of African Wildlife Management Conference: African Wildlife Management in the New Millennium, Mweka

Beltrán, J. (ed) (2000) *Indigenous and Traditional Peoples and Protected Areas: Principles, Guidelines and Case Studies*, IUCN, Gland and Cambridge

Bennett, A. F. (2003) *Linkages in the Landscape: The Role of Corridors and Connectivity in Wildlife Conservation*, 2nd edition, IUCN, Gland and Cambridge

Bennett, G. and Wit, P. (2001) *The Development and Application of Ecological Networks: A Review of Proposals, Plans and Programmes*, AID Environment, Amsterdam

Bennett, J. (1995) *The Economic Value of Recreation Use of Gibraltar Range and Dorrigo National Parks*, NSW NPWS, Sydney

Bergin, P. (2001) 'Accommodating new narratives in a conservation bureaucracy', in Hulme, D. and Murphree, M. (eds) *African Wildlife and Livelihoods: The Promise and Performance of Community Conservation*, James Currey, Oxford, pp88–105

Bernbaum, E. (1999) 'Mountains: The heights of biodiversity', in Posey, D. A. (ed) *Cultural and Spiritual Values of Biodiversity*, Intermediate Technology Publications and UNEP, Nairobi

Bernstein, B., Iudicello, S. and Stringer, C. (2004) *Lessons Learned from Recent Marine Protected Area Designations in the United States*, Report to the National Marine Protected Areas Center, National Fisheries Conservation Center, Ojai

Besançon, C. and Savy, C. (2005) 'Global list of internationally adjoining protected areas and other transboundary conservation initiatives', in Mittermeier, R. Mittermeier, C. G., Kormos, C., Sandwith, T. and Besançon, C. (eds) *Transboundary Conservation: A New Vision for Protected Areas*, CEMEX/Conservation International, Washington, DC

Besio, M. (2003) 'Conservation planning: The European case of rural landscapes', in *Cultural Landscapes: The Challenges of Conservation*, World Heritage Papers no 7, UNESCO World Heritage Centre, Paris

Bester, M. N., Bloomer, J. P., van Aarde, R. J., Erasmus, B. H., van Rensburg, P. J. J., Skinner, J. D., Howell, P. G. and Naude, T. W. (2002) 'A review of the successful eradication of feral cats from sub-Antarctic Marion Island, Southern Indian Ocean', *South African Journal of Wildlife Research*, vol 32, no 1, pp65–73

Bigg, T. (2003) *The World Summit on Sustainable Development: Was It Worthwhile?*, www.iied.organization/wssd/wssdreview.pdf

Birckhead, J., De Lacy, T. and Smith, L. (eds) (1992) *Aboriginal Involvement in Parks and Protected Areas*, Australian Institute of Aboriginal and Torres Strait Islander Studies, Canberra

Bird, C. and Sattaur, O. (1991) 'Medicines from the rainforest', *New Scientist*, vol 1782, pp34–39

Biscayne National Park (2005) *Education in the Park*, www.nps.gov/bisc/educate/index.htm

Bishop, K., Dudley, N., Phillips, A. and Stolton, S. (2004) *Speaking a Common Language: The Uses and Performance of the IUCN System of Management Categories for Protected Areas*, Cardiff University, IUCN and UNEP–WCMC, Cardiff, Gland and Cambridge

Bisson, K. and Lyman, M. (2003) *Valuing Forests as Community Assets in the Mount Washington Valley: A Study of the Economic, Environmental, and Social Contributions of Public and Private Forests and Their Potential Role as a Component of a Regional Economic Development Strategy*, Mount Washington Valley Economic Council, Conway

Blomley, T. and Namara, A. (2003) 'Devolving rights or shedding responsibilities? Community conservation in Uganda over the last decade', *Policy Matters*, vol 12, pp283–289

Bond, W. J. and van Wilgen, B. W. (1996) *Fire and Plants*, Chapman and Hall, London

Booth, V., Martin, R. and Wilson, E. (2005) *Strengthening the System of National Protected Areas Project, Namibia: Capacity Assessment for Parks Management in Conservation at Individual, Institutional and Systemic Levels*, Environment and Development Group, Oxford

Borghesio, L. and Giannetti, F. (2005) 'Habitat degradation threatens the survival of the Ethiopian bush crow *Zavattariornis stresemanni*', *Oryx*, vol 39, no 1, pp44–49

Borrini-Feyerabend, G. (ed) (1997) *Beyond Fences: Seeking Social Sustainability in Conservation*, IUCN, Gland and Cambridge

Borrini-Feyerabend, G. (2003a) *Community Conserved Areas (CCAs) and Co-managed Protected Areas (CMPAs) – Towards Equitable and Effective Conservation in the Context of Global Change*, Unpublished report of the IUCN joint CEESP/WCPA Theme on Indigenous and Local Community, Equity and Protected Areas (TILCEPA) for the Ecosystem, Protected Areas and People (EPP) Project

Borrini-Feyerabend, G. (2003b) 'Governance of protected areas: Innovations in the air', *Policy Matters*, vol 12, pp92–101

Borrini-Feyerabend, G. (2004) 'Governance of protected areas, participation and equity', in *Biodiversity Issues for Consideration in the Planning, Establishment and Management of Protected Areas Sites and Networks*, Convention on Biological Diversity Technical Series 15, Secretariat of the Convention on Biological Diversity, Montreal

Borrini-Feyerabend, G., Banuri, T., Farvar, M. T., Miller, K. and Phillips, A. (2002) 'Indigenous and local communities and protected areas: Rethinking the relationship', *Parks*, vol 12, no 2, pp5–15

Borrini-Feyerabend, G. and Brown, M. (1997) 'Social actors and stakeholders', in Borrini-Feyerabend, G. and Buchan, D. (ed) *Beyond Fences: Seeking Social Sustainability in Conservation*, IUCN, Gland and Cambridge

Borrini-Feyerabend, G. and Buchan, D. (eds) (1997) *Beyond Fences: Seeking Social Sustainability in Conservation, Volumes 1 and 2*, IUCN, Gland and Cambridge

Borrini-Feyerabend, G., De Sherbinin, A., Diaw, C., Oviedo, G. and Pansky, D. (eds) (2003) *Policy Matters*, vol 12 (joint CEESP–WCPA special issue on community empowerment for conservation)

Borrini-Feyerabend, G. and Dudley, N. (2005) *Elan Durban … Nouvelles Perspectives Pour les Aires Protégées à Madagascar*, www.equilibrium consultants.com/publications/docs/ElanDurban.pdf

Borrini-Feyerabend, G., Pimbert, M., Farvar, M. T., Kothari, A. and Renard, Y. (2004a) *Sharing Power: Learning by Doing in Co–management of Natural Resources throughout the World*, IIED and IUCN/CEESP, Teheran, www.iucn.org/themes/ceesp/Publications/sharingpower

Borrini-Feyerabend, G., Kothari, A. and Oviedo, G. (2004b) *Indigenous and Local Communities and Protected Areas: Towards Equity and Enhanced Conservation*, WCPA Best Practice Series 11, IUCN WCPA, Gland and Cambridge

Bowles, I., Guérin-McManus, M., Famolare, L., Mittermeier, R. and Rosenfel, A. (2001) *Bioprospecting in Practice: A Case Study of the Suriname*, ICBG Project and Benefits Sharing under the Convention on Biological Diversity, CBD, Montreal

Bramwell, M. (ed) (1973) *Mitchell Beazley Atlas of World Wildlife*, Mitchell Beazley Ltd, The Netherlands

Brandon, K., Redford, K. H. and Sanderson, S. E. (eds) (1998) *Parks in Peril: People, Politics and Protected Areas*, The Nature Conservancy and Island Press, Washington, DC

Branine, M. (2002) 'Human resource management in Algeria', in Budhwar, P. S. and Debrah, Y. A. (eds) *Human Resource Management in Developing Countries*, Routledge, London

Brechin, S. R., Wilshusen, P. R., Fortwangler, C. L. and West, P. C. (2002) 'Beyond the square wheel: Toward a more comprehensive understanding of biodiversity conservation as a social and political process', *Society and Natural Resources*, vol 15, pp41–64

Briassoulis, H. (1989) 'Theoretical orientations in environmental planning: An inquiry into alternative approaches', *Environmental Management*, vol 13, pp381–392

Bridgewater, P. (2002) 'Biosphere reserves: A network for conservation and sustainability', *Parks*, vol 12, no 3, pp15–20

Briggs, D. E. G., Erwin, D. H. and Collier, F. J. (1994) *The Fossils of the Burgess Shale*, Smithsonian Institution Press, Washington, DC

Brockington, D. (2002) *Fortress Conservation: The Preservation of the Mkomazi Game Reserve, Tanzania*, Indiana University Press, Bloomington

Brockman, C. F. (1959) *Recreational Use of Wild Lands*, McGraw Hill, New York

Brooks, T. M., Bakarr, M. I., Boucher, T., Da Fonseca, G. A. B., Hilton-Taylor, C., Hoekstra, J. M., Moritz, T., Olivier, S., Parrish, J., Pressey, R. L., Rodrigues, A. S. L., Sechrest, W., Stattersfield, A., Strahm, W. and Stuart, S. N. (2004) 'Coverage provided by the global protected-area system: Is it enough?', *BioScience*, vol 54, pp1081–1091

Brown, D. (2003) 'Is the best the enemy of the good? Livelihoods perspectives on bushmeat harvesting and trade – some issues and challenges', Paper to the CIFOR–Bonn Conference on Rural Livelihoods, Forests and Biodiversity, www.odi-bushmeat.org/downloads

Brown, G., Koth, B., Kreag, G. and Weber D. (2006) *Managing Australia's Protected Areas: A Review of Visitor Management Models, Frameworks and Processes*, Sustainable Tourism CRC, Gold Coast

Brown, I. (2001) 'Which MPA is the oldest? Reader challenge', *MPA NEWS*, vol 3, no 6, www.depts.washington.edu/mpanews/MPA26.htm#oldest

Brown, J., Kothari, A. and Menon, M. (eds) (2002) *Parks*, vol 12, no 2 (Special issue on local communities and protected areas)

Brown, J. H. and Lomolino, M. V. (1998) *Biogeography*, 2nd edition, Sinauer, Sunderland

Bruner, A. G., Gullison, R. E., Rice, R. E., Da Fonseca, G. A. B. (2001) 'Effectiveness of parks in protecting tropical biodiversity', *Science*, vol 291, pp125–128

Brunet, S., Bauer, J., De Lacy, T. and Tshering, K. (2001) 'Tourism development in Bhutan: Tensions between tradition and modernity', *Journal of Sustainable Tourism*, vol 9, no 3, pp243–263

Brylski, P. (2005) *Central Asia Transboundary Biodiversity Project*, www.tbpa.net/case_07.htm

Buck, L. E., Geister, C. C., Schelhas, J. and Wollenberg, E. (2001) *Biological Diversity: Balancing Interests through Adaptive Collaborative Management*, CRC Press, London

Buckley, R. (2003) 'The practice and politics of tourism and land management', in Buckley, R., Pickering, C. and Weaver, D. B. (eds) *Nature-based Tourism, Environment and Land Management*, CABI Publishing, Wallingford

Budhwar, P. S. and Debrah, Y. A. (eds) (2002) *Human Resource Management in Developing Countries*, Routledge, London

Burbach R. and Flynn P. (1980) *Agribusiness in the Americas*, Monthly Review Press, New York

Burenhult, G. (ed) (2003) *People of the Past – Tithe Illustrated History of Humankind: The Epic Story of Human Origins and Development*, Fog City Press, San Francisco

Burnie, D. (ed) (2004) *Animal*, Dorling Kindersley, London

Burns, G. L. (2004) 'The host community and wildlife tourism', in Higginbottom, K. (ed) *Wildlife Tourism: Impacts, Management and Planning*, Common Ground, Altona

Burroughs, W. J. (1999) *Climate Revealed*, Cambridge University Press, Cambridge

Callicott, J. B. (1986) 'On the intrinsic value of nonhuman species', in Norton, B. G. (ed) *The Preservation of Species: The Value of Biological Diversity*, Princeton University Press, Princeton

Calma, G. and Liddle, L. (2003) 'Uluru–Kata Tjuta National Park: Sustainable management and development', in *Cultural Landscapes: The Challenges of Conservation*, World Heritage Papers no 7, UNESCO World Heritage Centre, Paris

Campbell Private Game Reserve (2004) *Campbell Private Game Reserve*, www.campbell-safari.co.za

Campbell, S. and Fainstein, S. (2003) 'Introduction: The structure and debates of planning theory', in Campbell, S. and Fainstein, S. (eds) *Readings in Planning Theory*, 2nd edition, Blackwell, Oxford

Cape Woolamai Steering Committee (1989) *Cape Woolamai State Faunal Reserve Environment Effects Statement: Visitor Facilities*, CWSC, Cowes

Cappo, M. and Kelley, R. A. (2001) 'Connectivity in the Great Barrier Reef World Heritage Area: An overview of pathways and processes', in Wolanski, E. *Oceanographic Processes of Coral Reefs: Physical and Biological Links in the Great Barrier Reef*, CRC Press, pp161–187

Carabias, J. de la Maza and Cadena, J. R. (eds) (2003) *Capacity Needs to Manage Protected Areas: Africa*, The Nature Conservancy, Arlington

Carabias, J. de la Maza and Gonzales, J. R. (2004) 'Building capacity to manage protected areas in an era of global change', in Barber, C.V., Miller, K. and Boness, M. (eds) *Securing Protected Areas in the Face of Global Change: Issues and Strategies*, IUCN, Gland and Cambridge

Carabias, J. and Rao, K. (eds) (2003) *Capacity Needs to Manage Protected Areas: Asia*, The Nature Conservancy, Arlington

Carey, C., Dudley, N. and Stolton, S. (2000) *Squandering Paradise? The Importance and Vulnerability of the World's Protected Areas*, WWF, Gland

Carlton, J. T. (2001) *Introduced Species in US Coastal Waters: Environmental Impacts and Management Priorities*, Pew Oceans Commission, Arlington

Carr, M. H., Neigel, J. E., Estes, J. A., Andelman, S., Warner, R. R. and Largier, J. L. (2003) 'Comparing marine and terrestrial ecosystems: Implications for the design of coastal marine reserves – The science of marine reserves', *Ecological Applications*, vol 13 (Supplement), pp90–107

Carson, R. (1962) *Silent Spring*, Houghton Mifflin, Boston

CBD (Convention on Biological Diversity) (1992) *Convention on Biological Diversity*, UNEP–CBD, Montreal

CBD (2001) *Jakarta Mandate: Marine and Coastal Biodiversity – Mariculture*, www.biodiv.org/ programmes/areas/marine/mariculture.asp

CBD (2003) *Global Biodiversity Outlook*, Secretariat of the Convention on Biological Diversity, Montreal

CBD (2004a) *Addis Ababa Principles and Guidelines for Sustainable Use of Biodiversity (CBD Guidelines)*, Secretariat of the Convention on Biological Diversity, Montreal

CBD (2004b) *Decisions Adopted by the Conference of the Parties to the Convention on Biological Diversity at Its Seventh Meeting*, UNEP/CBD/COP/7/21. SCBD, Montreal

CBD (2004c) *Annex: Decisions Adopted by the Conference of the Parties to the Convention on Biological Diversity at Its Seventh Meeting (COP 7)*, www.biodiv.org/meetings/cop–07/default.asp

CBD (2005) *Further Development of Tool Kits for the Identification, Designation, Management, Monitoring and Evaluation of National and Regional Systems of Protected areas Areas*, UNEP/CBD/WG-PA/1/4, CBD Secretariat, Montreal

CEESP (Commission on Environmental, Economic and Social Policy) (2003) *Policy Matters*, vol 12 (special issue on Community Empowerment for Conservation for the Vth World Parks Congress), www.iucn.org/themes/ceesp/Publications/newsletter/PM12.pdf

Center for Integrated Study of the Human Dimensions of Global Change (2004) *The Transboundary Protected Areas Research Initiative (TBPARI)*, www.hdgc.epp.cmu.edu/misc/TBPA.htm

Cernea, M. and Schmidt-Soltau, K. (2005) *National Parks and Poverty Risks: Policy Issues in Conservation and Resettlement*, World Development

Cesar, H. (1996) *Economic Analysis of Indonesian Coral Reefs*, World Bank, Washington, DC

Chamberlain, J., Cunningham, A. and Nasi, R. (2004) 'Diversity in forest management non-timber forest products and bush meat', *Renewable Resources Journal*, vol 22, no 2, pp11–19

Chambers, P. (1999) 'Aquatic and marine biodiversity', in Posey, D. A. (ed) *Cultural and Spiritual Values of Biodiversity*, Intermediate Technology Publications and UNEP, Nairobi

Chape, S., Blyth, S., Fish, L., Fox, P. and Spalding, M. (2003a) *2003 United Nations List of Protected Areas*, IUCN and UNEP–WCMC, Gland and Cambridge

Chape, S., Harrison, J., Spalding, M. and Lysenko, I. (2005) 'Measuring the extent and effectiveness of protected areas as an indicator for meeting global biodiversity targets', *Philosophical Transactions of the Royal Society B*, vol 360, pp443–455

Chape, S., Spalding, M. and Sheppard, D. (2003b) *The State of the World's Protected Areas*, Unpublished manuscript, 'Chapter 1: Global overview'

Charles, I. (1994) *Parks, People and Preservation: Recollections of the Establishment and First 25 Years of the NSW National Parks and Wildlife Service*, NSW NPWS, Sydney

Chemical Engineers Resource Page (2004) *A Model of Renewable Energy*, www.cheresources.com/pvwind.shtml

Chhetri, P. B., Barrow, E. G. C. and Muhweezi, A. (eds) (2004) *Securing Protected Area Integrity and Rural People's Livelihoods: Lessons from Twelve Years of the Kibale and Semliki Conservation and Development Project*, IUCN East Africa Regional Office, Nairobi

Chiew, H. (2005) 'Indigenous communities show the way with renewable energy project', *The Star Online Lifestyle*, www.greenempowerment.org/media

Child, B. and Lyman M. (2005) *Natural Resources as Community Assets: Lessons from Two Continents*, Sand County Foundation/Aspen Institute, Madison, www.sandcounty.net/assets

Child, G. (ed) (2004) *Parks in Transition: Biodiversity, Rural Development and the Bottom Line*, Earthscan, London

Choudhury, B. C., Courrau, J., Dudley, N., Dutton, I., Ervin, J., Hockings, M., Margoluis, R., Parrish, J., Paul, S., Salafsky, N., Stolton S. and Woodley, S. (2004) *Workshop Report: Ecological Integrity and Threats Assessment, Enhancing Our Heritage Project*, UQ, UNF and UNESCO, Washington, DC

Christ, C., Hillel, O., Matus, S. and Sweeting, J. (2003) *Tourism and Biodiversity: Mapping Tourism's Global Footprint*, UNEP and Conservation International, Washington, DC

Church, G. J. (1989) 'The big spill: Bred from complacency the *Valdez* fiasco goes from bad to worse to worst possible', *The Times*, 10 April

CI (Conservation International) (2005a) *About Conservation International*, www.conservation.org

CI (2005b) *Biodiversity Hotspots*, www.biodiversityhotspots.org

CI (2005c) *Biodiversity Hotspots*, www.conservation.org/xp/CIWEB/regions/priorityareras/hotspots.xml

CI (2005d) *Conservation Response*, www.biodiversiyhotspots.org/xp/Hotspots/hotspotsScience/conservationresponses

CI (2005e) *Protected Area Coverage in the Hotspots*, www.biodiversiyhotspots.org/xp/Hotspots/hotspotsScience/conservation_responses/protected_areas

CI (2005f) *Endemic Genera*, www.biodiversiyhotspots.org/xp/Hotspots/hotspotsScience/key_findings/endemic_genera.xm

CI (2005g) *Remaining Habitat*, www.biodiversiyhotspots.org/xp/Hotspots/hotspotsScience/key_findings/remaining_habitat.xml

Cifuentes, A. M., Izurieta, V. A. and de Faria, H. H. (2000) *Measuring Protected Area Management*

Effectiveness, WWF Centroamerica, Turrialba

CITES (Convention on International Trade in Endangered Species of Wild Flora and Fauna) (2001) *Summary Report*, Technical Meeting of the CITES Bushmeat Working Group in Central Africa, 5–6 July, Douala, www.cites.org/eng/prog/BWG/0107_wg_report.shtml

Claridge, A. W., Castellano, M. A. and Trappe, J. M. (1996) 'Fungi as a food resource for mammals in Australia', in Mallett, K. and Grgurinovic, C. (eds) *Fungi of Australia Volume 1B: Introduction to Fungi in the Environment*, Australian Biological Resources Study, Canberra

Clark, D. and Downes, D. (1995) *What Price Biodiversity? Economic Incentives and Biodiversity Conservation in the United States*, Centre for International Environmental Law, Washington, DC

Clark, K. (2001) *Informed Conservation: Understanding Historic Buildings and Their Landscapes for Conservation*, English Heritage, London

Clarke, R. N. and Stankey, G. M. (1979) *The Recreation Opportunity Spectrum: A Framework for Planning, Management and Research*, General Technical Report PNW-98, USDA Forest Service, Fort Collins

Coleman, F.C., Figueira, W. F., Ueland, J. S. and Crowder, L. B. (2004) 'The impact of United States recreational fisheries on marine fish populations', *Science*, vol 305, no 5692, pp1958–1960

Columbia Ministerio del Ambiente (2002) 'Nace el Parque Nacional Natural 'Indiwasi' en Colombia', Public communique, Bogata, 25

Commonwealth of Australia (1998) *Comprehensive Regional Assessments and Regional Forest Agreements*, Commonwealth of Australia, Canberra, www.rfa.gov.au

Compton, J. (1998) *Borderline: A Report on Wildlife Trade in Vietnam*, WWF-UK, Godalming, Surrey

Conner, N. and Gilligan, B. (2003) *Socio-economic Benefits of Protected Areas: Concepts and Assessment Techniques as Applied in New South Wales, Australia*, NSW NPWS, Sydney

Conservation Finance Initiative (2004) *Conservation Finance Guide*, www.guide.conservationfinance.org

Conservation Studies Institute (2005) *A Handbook for Managers of Cultural Landscapes with Natural Resource Values*, National Park Service, Woodstock, www.nps.gov/csi

Convention on Biological Diversity Working Group on Protected Areas (2005) *Further Development of Tool Kits for the Identification, Designation,*

Management, Monitoring and Evaluation of National and Regional Systems of Protected Areas, UNEP/CBD/WG-PA/1/4, CBD Secretariat, Montreal

Corbett Park (2006) 'Jim Corbett National Park – A park with history', www.corbettpark.com/jim-corbett-national-park-corbett-park.asp

Cordell, H. K. and Tarrant, M. A. (2002) 'Changing demographics, values and attitudes', *Journal of Forestry*, vol 100, no 7, pp28–33

Cork, S. J. and Shelton, D. (2000) 'The nature and value of Australia's ecosystem services: Framework for sustainable environmental solutions', in *Sustainable Environmental Solutions for Industry and Government*, Proceedings of the Third Queensland Environmental Conference, Institution of Engineers, Australia, and Queensland Chamber of Commerce and Industry, Brisbane

Cosgrove, D. (2003) 'Landscape: Ecology and semiosis', in Palang, H., Fry, G. (eds) *Landscape Interfaces-cultural Heritage in Changing Landscapes*, Kluwer, Dordrecht

Courrau, J. (1999) *Strategy for Monitoring the Management of Protected Areas in Central America*, PROARCA CAPAS Program, The Nature Conservancy, Arlington

Cowling, R. M. and Pressey, R. L. (2003) 'Introduction to systematic conservation planning in the Cape Floristic Region', *Biological Conservation*, vol 112, pp1–13

Creighton, J. L. (1981) 'The use of values: Public participation in the planning process', in Daneke, G. A., Garcia, M. W. and Priscoli, J. D. (eds) *Public Involvement and Social Impact Assessment,* Westview, Boulder

Cresswell, I. D. and Thomas, G. M. (1997) *Terrestrial and Marine Protected Areas in Australia*, Environment Australia, Canberra

Critical Ecosystem Partnership Fund (2004) *Portfolio Review – Cape Floristic Region Biodiversity Hotspot*, CEPF, Washington, DC

Critical Ecosystem Partnership Fund (2006) 'Our strategy', www.cepf.net/xp/cepf/strategy/index.xml

Crowder, L. B., Osherenko, G., Young, O. R., Airamé, S., Norse, E. A., Baron, N., Day, J. C., Douvere, F., Ehler, C. N., Halpern, B. S., Langdon, S. J., McLeod, K. L., Ogden, J. C., Peach, R. E., Rosenberg, A. A. and Wilson, J. A. (2006) 'Resolving mismatches in US ocean governance', *Science*, vol 313, pp617–618

Cumming, D. (2004) 'Performance of parks in a century of change', in Child, B. (ed) *Parks in*

Transition: Biodiversity, Rural Development and the
Bottom Line, Earthscan, London

Curtis, A. and Lockwood, M. (1998) 'Natural
resource policy for rural Australia', in Pratley, J.
and Robertson, A. (eds) *Agriculture and the
Environmental Imperative*, CSIRO, Melbourne

Dalal-Clayton, B. and Child, B. (2003) *Lessons from
Luangwa: The Story of the Luangwa Integrated
Resource Development Project, Zambia*, International
Institute for Environment and Development,
London

Dalrymple, G. H., Doren, R. F., O'Hare, N. K.,
Norland, M. R. and Armentano, T. V. (2003)
'Plant colonisation after complete and partial
removal of disturbed soils for wetland restoration
of former agricultural fields in Everglades
National Park', *Wetlands*, vol 23, no 4,
pp1015–1029

Daneke, A. (1983) 'Public involvement: What, why
and how', in Daneke, G. A., Garcia, M. W. and
Priscoli, J. D. (eds) *Public Involvement and Social
Impact Assessment*, Westview, Boulder

Dang, H. (1991) *Human Conflict in Conservation:
Protected Areas, The Indian Experience*,
Development Alternatives, New Delhi

Danilina, N. (2001) 'The zapovedniks of Russia',
George Wright Forum, vol 18, no 1, pp48–55

Danilina, N. and Boreyko, V. (2003) 'Strictly protected
areas: The Russian system of zapovedniks', in
Harmon, D. and Putney, A. (eds) *The Full Value of
Parks: From Economics to the Intangible,* Rowman
and Littlefield, Lanham

Dartmoor National Park Authority (2001) *Dartmoor
National Park Management Plan*, Dartmoor
National Park Authority, Devon

Davey, A. G. (1998) *National System Planning for
Protected Areas*, World Commission on Protected
Areas Best Practice Protected Area Guidelines
Series no 1, IUCN, Gland and Cambridge

David, F. R. (2001) *Strategic Management: Concepts*, 8th
edition, Prentice Hall, Upper Saddle River

Dawson, A. and Cohen, S. (1999) *Media Training
Manual*, NSW NPWS, Sydney

Dawson, J. and Lucas, R. (2000) *Nature Guide to the
New Zealand Forest*, Random House, Auckland

Day, J. C. (2002a) 'Zoning – Lessons from the Great
Barrier Reef Marine Park', *Ocean and Coastal
Management*, vol 45, pp139–156

Day, J. C. (2002b) 'Marine park management and
monitoring – Lessons for adaptive management
from the Great Barrier Reef', in Bondrup-
Nielsen, S., Munro, N. W. P, Nelson, G., Willison,
J. H. M, Herman, T. B. and Eagles, P. (eds)

Managing Protected Areas in a Changing World,
Proceedings of the 4th International Conference
on Science and Management of Protected Areas,
Waterloo, Canada

Day, J. C., Fernandes, L., Lewis, A., De'ath, G.,
Slegers, S., Barnett, B., Kerrigan, B., Breen, D.,
Innes, J., Oliver, J., Ward, T. J. and Lowe, D. (2000)
*The Representative Areas Program for Protecting
Biodiversity in the Great Barrier Reef World Heritage
Area*, Proceedings of the 9th International Coral
Reef Symposium, Volume 2, Bali

Day, J. C., Fernandes, L., Lewis, A. and Innes, J.
(2003a) 'RAP – An ecosystem level approach to
biodiversity protection planning', Paper presented
at the second meeting of the International
Tropical Marine Ecosystem Symposium, Manila

Day, J. C., Hocking, M. and Jones, G. (2003b)
'Measuring effectiveness in marine protected areas
– Principles and practice', in Beumer, J., Grant, A.
and Smith, D. (eds) *Aquatic Protected Areas – What
Works Best and How Do We Know?*, Proceedings of
World Congress on Aquatic Protected Areas,
Australian Society for Fish Biology, Cairns

Day, J. C., Hockings, M., Jones, M. and Jones, G.
(2003c) 'Measuring effectiveness in marine
protected areas – Principles and practice', in
Proceedings World Aquatic Protected Areas Congress,
Australian Society for Fish Biology, Cairns

Day, J. C. and Roff, J. C. (2000) *Planning for
Representative Marine Protected Areas: A Framework
for Canada's Oceans*, WWF Canada, Toronto

de Bellefon, P. (2000) *Tres Sols – Mont Perdu*, Mont
Perdu World Heritage Association, Gèdre

de Guchteneire, P., Krukkert, I. and von Liebenstein,
G. (1999) *Best Practices on Indigenous Knowledge*,
UNESCO Management of Social
Transformations Programme and Centre for
International Research and Advisory Networks,
www.unesco.org/most/bpikpub.htm#ik

DEG (2005) *Kurnell Peninsula Headland*,
www.deh.gov.au/cgi-bin/ahdb/search.pl

DEH (Department of Environment and Heritage)
(2003a) *Management of Lord Howe Is Marine Park
(Commonwealth Waters)*, www.deh.gov.au/coasts/
mpa/lordhowe/management.html

DEH (2003b) *The Benefits of Marine Protected Areas*,
Commonwealth of Australia, Canberra

DEH (2004) *National List of Extinct, Extinct in the Wild,
Critically Endangered, Endangered, Vulnerable and
Conservation Dependent Species*, www.deh.gov.au

de la Torre, M. (ed) (2005) *Heritage Values in Site
Management: Four Case Studies*, The Getty
Conservation Institute, Los Angeles

De Lacy, T., Battig, M., Moore, S. and Noakes, S. (2002) *Public/Private Partnerships for Sustainable Tourism: Delivering a Sustainability Strategy for Tourism Destinations*, Sustainable Tourism CRC, Gold Coast

De Lopez, T. T. (2003) 'Economics and stakeholders of Ream National Park, Cambodia', *Ecological Economics*, vol 46, no 2, pp269–282

Dean, C. (2005) 'To save its canal, Panama fights for its forests', *New York Times*, 24 May, www.nytimes.com/2005/05/24/science/earth/24pana.html

Dearden, P., Bennett, M. and Johnston, J. (2005) 'Trends in global protected area governance, 1992–2002', *Environmental Management*, vol 36, no 1, pp89–100

Dearden, P., Chettamart, S. and Emphandu, D. (1998) 'Protected areas and property rights in Thailand', *Environmental Conservation*, vol 25, no 3, pp195–197

Dearden, P. and Rollins, R. (2002) *Parks and Protected Areas in Canada: Planning and Management*, 2nd edition, Oxford University Press, Don Mills

Debrah, Y. A. (2002) 'Human resource management in Ghana', in Budhwar, P. S. and Debrah, Y. A. (eds) *Human Resource Management in Developing Countries*, Routledge, London

Déjeant-Pons, M. (2003) 'European landscape convention', in *Cultural Landscapes: The Challenges of Conservation*, World Heritage Papers no 7, UNESCO World Heritage Centre, Paris

Department of Conservation (2004) *Aoraki/Mount Cook National Park Management Plan*, Department of Conservation, Christchurch

Department of Conservation and Environment (n.d.) *An Inventory of Recreation Settings on Major Areas of Public Land in Victoria*, Occasional Paper Series No 4, DCE, Melbourne

Department of Environment and Conservation (2005) *State of the Parks 2004*, Department of Environment and Conservation, Sydney

Department of the Environment and Heritage (2005) 'Australian Heritage Database', www.deh.gov.au/cgi-bin/ahdb/search.pl

Dessler, G. (2004) *A Framework for Human Resource Management*, Prentice Hall, Englewood Cliffs

Dietz, T., Stern, P. and Guagnano, G. (1998) 'Social structure and social psychological bases of environmental concern', *Environment and Behaviour*, vol 30, no 4, pp450–471

Dillenbeck, M. (1994) 'National environmental funds: A new mechanism for conservation finance', *Parks*, vol 4, no 2, pp39–46

Dinerstein, E., Powell, G., Olson, D., Wikramanayake, E., Abell, R., Loucks, C., Underwood, E., Allnutt, T., Wittengel, W., Ricketts, T., Strand, H., O'Connor, S. and Burgess, N., (2000) *A Workbook for Conducting Biological Assessments and Developing Biodiversity Visions for Ecoregion-based Conservation, Part 1: Terrestrial Ecoregions*, WWF-USA, Washington, DC

Diqiang, L., Jianhua, Z., Ke, D., Bo, W. and Chunquan, Z. (2003) *China: Management Effectiveness Assessment of Protected Areas in the Upper Yangtze Ecoregion Using WWF's RAPPAM Methodology*, WWF, Gland

Dolce, J. (ed) (2003) *Extreme Earth*, Harper Collins, London

Dovers, S.R. (1997) 'Sustainability: Demands on policy', *Journal of Public Policy*, vol 16, pp303–318

Dovers, S. R. (1998) *Public Policy and Institutional R&D for Natural Resource Management: Issues and Directions for LWRRDC*, Report to the Land and Water Resources Research and Development Corporation, Centre for Resource and Environmental Studies, ANU, Canberra

Dovers, S. R. and Mobbs, C. D. (1997) 'An alluring prospect? Ecology and the requirements of adaptive management', in Klomp, N. and Lunt, I. (eds) *Frontiers in Ecology: Building the Links*, Elsevier, Oxford

Driver, A., Desmet, P. G., Rouget, M., Cowling, R. M. and Maze, K. E. (2003) *Succulent Karoo Ecosystem Plan Biodiversity Component Technical Report*, Cape Conservation Unit, Botanical Society of South Africa, Cape Town

Drucker, P. F. (1964a) *The Effective Executive*, Harper & Row, New York

Drucker, P. F. (1964b) *Managing for Results*, Harper & Row, New York

Dryzek, J. S. (1997) *The Politics of the Earth*, Oxford University Press, Melbourne

Dryzek, J. S. and Braithwaite, V. (2000) 'On the prospects for democratic deliberation: Values analysis applied to Australian politics', *Political Psychology*, vol 21, pp241–266

Dudley, N., Belokurov, A., Borodin, O., Higgins-Zogib, L., Hockings, M., Lacerda, L. and Stoloton, S. (2004) *Are Protected Areas Working? An Analysis of Forest Protected Areas by WWF*, WWF International, Gland

Dudley, N. and Phillips, A. (2006) *Forests and Protected Areas: Guidance on the Use of the IUCN Protected Area Categories*, IUCN, Gland and Cambridge

Dudley, N. and Stolton, S. (2003) *Running Pure: The Importance of Forest Protected Areas to Drinking*

Water, World Bank/WWF Alliance for Forest Conservation, Washington, DC

Dudley, N., Mulongoy, K. J., Cohen, S., Stolton, S., Barber, C. V. and Gidda, S. B. (2005) *Towards Effective Protected Area Systems: An Action Guide to Implement the Convention on Biological Diversity Programme of Work on Protected Areas*, Secretariat of the Convention on Biological Diversity, Montreal

Dvoáková, V. (2001) 'Vlkolinec, Slovakia', in Lennon, J. (ed) *Management Guidelines for World Heritage Cultural Landscapes*, Unpublished report to the World Heritage Centre, Paris

Eagles, P. F. J. (1995) 'Understanding the market for sustainable tourism', in McCool, S. F. and Watson, A. E. (eds) *Linking Tourism, The Environment and Sustainability*, US Department of Agriculture, Forest Service, Intermountain Research Station, Minneapolis

Eagles, P. F. J. (2002) 'Trends in park tourism: Economics, finance and management', *Journal of Sustainable Tourism*, vol 10, no 2, pp132–153

Eagles, P. F. J. (2003) 'International trends in park tourism: A macro view of park tourism finance', Paper presented at the Vth IUCN World Parks Congress Sustainable Finance Stream, Durban

Eagles, P. F. J. (2004) 'Trends affecting tourism in protected areas', *Working Papers of the Finnish Forest Research Institute 2*, www.metla.fi/julkaisut/workingpapers/2004/mwp0002.htm

Eagles, P. F. J., Bowman, M. E. and Tao, T. C. (2001) *Tourism in Parks and Protected Areas of East Asia*, IUCN, Gland and Cambridge

Eagles, P. F. J. and McCool, S. F. (2002) *Tourism in National Parks and Protected areas Areas: Planning and Management*, CABI, New York

Eagles, P. F. J., McCool, S. F. and Haynes, C. D. A. (2002) *Sustainable Tourism in Protected Areas: Guidelines for Planning and Management*, IUCN, Gland and Cambridge

Earth Impact Database (2004) *Impact Cratering on Earth*, University of New Brunswick, www.unb.ca/pass/ImpactDatabase/essay.html

Ecological Applications (2003) 'The science of marine reserves', *Ecological Applications*, vol 13 (supplement), pp3–228

EEAW (Environmental Education Association of Washington) (2004) *Environmental Education in Washington: Status Report 2004*, www.eeaw.org

Eghenter, C. and Labo, M. (2003) 'The Dayak people and Kayan Mentarang – First co-managed protected area in Indonesia', *Policy Matters*, vol 12, pp248–253

Eichbaum, W. E. (2002) *A Comprehensive Ocean Governance System in the United States*, Testimony by vice president of World Wide Fund for Nature (WWF)-US before the US Commission on Ocean Policy, 24 September, Chicago

Eken, G., Bennun, L., Brooks, T. M., Darwall, W., Foster, M., Knox, D., Langhammer, P., Matiku, P., Radford, E., Salaman, P., Sechrest, W., Smith, M. L., Spector, S. and Tordoff, J. (2004) 'Key biodiversity areas as site conservation targets', *Bioscience*, vol 54, pp1110–1118

Elcome, D. and Baines, J. (1999) *Steps to Success – Working with Residents and Neighbours to Develop and Implement Plans for Protected Areas*, IUCN Commission on Education and Communication, European Committee for EE, Gland

Elphick, J. (1995) *The Atlas of Bird Migration: Tracing the Great Journeys of the World's Birds*, Marshall Edition, London

Emerton, L., Bishop, J. and Thomas, L. (2006) *Sustainable Financing of Protected Areas: A Global Review of Challenges and Options*, IUCN, Gland and Cambridge

English, A. J. and Lee, E. (2003) 'Managing the intangible', in Harmon, D. and Putney, A. D. (eds) *The Full Value of Parks: From the Economic to the Intangible*, Rowman and Littlefield, Lanham

Environment Australia (1999) *Today Shapes Tomorrow: Environmental Education for a Sustainable Future*, Department of Environment and Heritage, Canberra

Erdmann, M., Merrill, P., Arsyad, I. and Mongdong, M. (2003) *Developing a Diversified Portfolio of Sustainable Financing Options for Bunaken National Marine Park*, Presentation at the Vth IUCN World Parks Congress, Durban

Ervin, J. (2003a) 'Protected area assessments in perspective', *Bioscience*, vol 53, no 9, pp819–822

Ervin J. (2003b) *WWF Rapid Assessment and Prioritisation of Protected Areas Management (RAPPAM) Methodology*, WWF, Gland

European Travel Commission (2005) *New Media Review*, www.etcnewmedia.com/review/NMR/h2hchartall.asp

Ewert, A. W., Baker, D. C. and Bissix, G. G. (2004) *Integrated Resource and Environmental Management: The Human Dimension*, CABI, Wallingford

Fairclough, G. J. (ed) (1999) *Historic Landscape Characterisation*, English Heritage, London

Falbe, C. M., Kriger, M. P. and Miesing, P. (1995) 'Structure and meaning of organizational vision', *Academy of Management Journal*, vol 39, pp740–769

Fall, J. (2005) *Drawing the Line: Nature, Hybridity and*

Politics in Transboundary Spaces, Ashgate, Burlington

Fallding, M. (2000) 'What makes a good natural resource management plan?', *Ecological Management and Restoration*, vol 1, no 3, pp185–193

FAO (United Nations Food and Agriculture Organization) (1991) *Environmental and Sustainability in Fisheries, Food and Agriculture of the United Nations*, FAO, Rome

FAO (2000) *Yearbook of Fisheries Statistics: Summary Tables*, FAO, Rome

Farazmand, A. (ed) (1991) *Handbook of Comparative and Development Administration*, Marcel Dekker, New York

Farvar, M. T. (2003) 'Myths, challenges and questions on mobile pastoralism in West Asia', *Policy Matters*, vol 12, pp31–41

Fearnhead, P. (2003) 'Commercial tourism concessions: A means of generating income for South African National Parks', Paper presented at the Vth IUCN World Parks Congress Sustainable Finance Stream, Durban

Feilden, B. (1982) *Conservation of Historic Buildings*, Butterworth Scientific, London

Feilden, B. M. and Jokilehto, J. (1993) *Management Guidelines for World Heritage Cultural Sites*, ICCROM, Rome

Felix, J. (2005) *Governance of Antarctica's Protected Areas: An Evaluation*, Honours thesis, School of Geography and Environmental Studies, University of Tasmania, Hobart

Ferrari, M. F. (2003) *A Regional Review of CCAs and CMPAs in South-East Asia*, Unpublished report of the IUCN joint CEESP/WCPA Theme on Indigenous and Local Community, Equity and Protected Areas (TILCEPA) for the Ecosystem, Protected Areas and People (EPP) project

Ferrari, M. F. and de Vera, D. (2003a) 'Coron Island and rights based conservation in the Philippines', *Policy Matters*, vol 12, pp166–170

Ferrari, M. F. and de Vera, D. (2003b) 'A "participatory" or a "rights-based" approach? Which is best for protected areas and indigenous peoples in the Philippines?', *Policy Matters*, vol 12, pp166–170

Ferraz, C. F. (2003) 'Institutional solutions for the financing of protected areas in Brazil', Paper presented at the Vth IUCN World Parks Congress Sustainable Finance Stream, Durban

Ferrier, S., Pressey, R. L. and Barrett, T. W. (2000) 'A new predictor of the irreplaceability of areas for achieving a conservation goal, its application to

real-world planning and a research agenda for further refinement', *Biological Conservation*, vol 93, pp303–325

FES (Foundation for Ecological Security) (2003) *A Biodiversity Log and Strategy Input Document for the Gori River Basin, Western Himalaya Ecoregion, District Pithoragarh, Uttaranchal*, FES, Uttaranchal

Finkler, S. A. (2001) *Financial Management for Public, Health, and Not-for-Profit Organizations*, Prentice Hall, Englewood Cliffs

Finlayson, B. and Hamilton-Smith, E. (2003) *Beneath the Surface: A Natural History of Australian Caves*, University of New South Wales Press, Sydney

Flannery, T. (2005) *The Weather Makers: The History and Future of Climate Change*, The Text Publishing Company, Melbourne

Flyvberg, B. and Richardson, T. (2002) 'Planning and Foucault: In search of the dark side of planning theory', in Allmendinger, P. and Tewdwr-Jones, M. (eds) *Planning Futures: New Directions for Planning Theory*, Routledge, London

Follett, M. P. (1949) *Freedom and Co-ordination: Lectures in Business Organization*, Management Publications Trust, London

Font, X., Cochrane, J. and Tapper, R. (2004) *Tourism for Protected Area Financing: Understanding Tourism Revenues for Effective Management Plans*, Leeds Metropolitan University, Leeds

Foran, B. and Poldy, F. (2002a) *Dilemmas Distilled: A Summary Guide to the CSIRO Technical Report Future Dilemmas: Options to 2050 for Australia's Population, Technology, Resources and Environment*, Commonwealth of Australia, Canberra, www.cse.csiro.au/futuredilemmas

Foran, B. and Poldy, F. (2002b) 'Between a rock and a hard place: Australia's population options to 2050 and beyond', *People and Place*, vol 11, no 1, pp1–15

Forman, R. T. T. (1995) *Land Mosaics: The Ecology of Landscapes and Regions*, Cambridge University Press, Cambridge

Forrest, C. J. and Mays, R. H. (1997) *The Practical Guide to Environmental Community Relations*, John Wiley and Sons, New York

Francour, P., Ganteaume, A. and Poulain, M. (1999) 'Effects of boat anchoring in *Posidonia oceanica* seagrass beds in the Port-Cros National Park (north-western Mediterranean Sea)', *Aquatic Conservation: Marine and Freshwater Ecosystems*, vol 9, pp391–400

Fredman, P. (2004) 'National park designation: visitor flows and tourism impact', in Sievänen, T., Erkkonen, J., Jokimäki, J., Saarinen, J., Tuulentie,

S. and Virtanen, E. (eds) *Proceedings of the Second International Conference on Monitoring and Management of Visitor Flows in Recreational and Protected Areas*, Finnish Research Institute, Rovaniemi.

Fredman, P., Hörnsten Friberg, L. and Emmelin, L. (2005) *Friluftsliv och Turism i Fulufjället: Före – Efter Nationalparksbildningen*, Naturvårdsverket, Rapport 5467, Dokumentation av de Svenska Nationalparkerna, no 18

Freedman, B. (1995) *Environmental Ecology: The Ecological Effects of Pollution, Disturbance and Other Stresses*, Academic Press, San Diego

French, W. L. (2006) *Human Resource Management*, 6th edition, Houghton Mifflin, Boston

Friedmann, J. (1987) *Planning in the Public Domain: From Knowledge to Action*, Princeton University Press, Princeton

Fuller, T., Munguia, M. Mayfield, M., Sandez-Cordero, V. and Sarker, S. (2006) 'Incorporating connectivity into conservation planning: A multicriteria case study from central Mexico', *Biological Conservation*, in press

Furze, B., De Lacy, T. and Birckhead, J. (1996) *Culture, Conservation and Biodiversity: The Social Dimension of Linking Local Development and Conservation through Protected Areas*, John Wiley and Sons, London

Galal, N., Ormond, R. F. G. and Hassan, O. (2002) 'Effect of a network of no-take reserves in increasing catch per unit effort and stocks of exploited reef fish at Nabq, South Sinai, Egypt', *Marine Freshwater Research*, vol 53, pp199–205

Gambarotta, J. C. (2003) 'Give us better protection urge rangers', *National Parks and Protected Areas Bulletin 10*, August

Gambarotta, J. C. (2005) International Rangers Federation, vice president and ranger, Lagos Di Castello, Uruguay, personal communication

Gamini, B. (1998) 'Mahogany shipment seized by Brazilians', *The Times*, 5 May

Gaus, G. F. (1990) *Value and Justification: The Foundations of Liberal Theory*, Cambridge University Press, New York

GBRMPA (Great Barrier Reef Marine Park Authority) (2004) *Great Barrier Reef Marine Park Authority*, www.gbrmpa.gov.au

GBRMPA (2006) 'Activities guide for the new Great Barrier Reef Marine Park Zoning', www.gbrmpa.gov.au/corp_site/management/zoning/documents/IntroActiveGuide.pdf

Gebhardt, A. and Lindsey, G. (1995) 'Differences in environmental orientation among homeowners',

Journal of Environmental Education, vol 27, no 1, pp4–13

GEF (Global Environment Facility) (2005) *What Is the GEF?*, www.gefweb.org

Gell, F. R. and Roberts, C. M. (2003) *The Fishery Effects of Marine Reserves and Fishery Closures*, WWF-US, Washington, DC

Georgieva, K., Pagiola, S. and Deeks, P. (2003) 'Paying for the environmental services of protected areas: Involving the private sector', Paper presented at the Vth IUCN World Parks Congress Sustainable Finance Stream, Durban

Ghimire, K. B. and Pimbert, M. P. (eds) (1997) *Social Change and Conservation: Environmental Politics and Impacts of National Parks and Protected Areas*, Earthscan, London

Gifford, R. (2003) 'Global climate change', in Attiwell, P. and Wilson, B. (eds) *Ecology: An Australian Perspective,* Oxford University Press, Melbourne

Gjerde, K. M. (2003) *Towards a Strategy for High Seas Marine Protected Areas*, Proceedings of the IUCN, WCPA and WWF Experts Workshop on High Seas Marine Protected Areas, 15–17 January, Malagra, IUCN, Gland and Cambridge

Glick, D. (2004) 'Global climate: The big thaw', *National Geographic*, September, www.magma.nationalgeographic.com/ngm/0409/feature2/fulltext.html

Global Coordinate (2005) *Western Caucasus*, www.redtailcanyon.com/items/13536.aspx

GlobeScan (2004) *Results of First-ever Global Poll on Humanity's Relationship with Nature*, www.globescan.com/news_archives/IUCN_PR.html

Glowka, L., Burhenne-Guilmin, F. and Synge, H. (1994) *A Guide to the Convention on Biological Diversity*, IUCN, Gland and Cambridge

Gokhale, Y., Velankar, R., Subash Chandran, M. D. and Gadgil, M. (1997) *Sacred Woods, Grasslands and Waterbodies as Self-organized Systems of Conservation*, RANWA, Pune

Golder, B. (2004) *Ecoregion Action Programmes: A Guide for Practitioners*, WWF, Washington, DC

Goldstein, W. (ed) (1979) *Australia's 100 Years of National Parks*, NSW NPWS, Sydney

Goldstein, W. (2003) *Communication, Education and Public Awareness for Protected Areas, West Asia and Northern Africa*, Workshop report, IUCN, Gland and Cambridge

Gore, R. (1997) 'The dawn of humans: The first steps', *National Geographic*, vol 191, pp72–99

Gould, D. J. (1991) 'Administrative corruption:

Incidence, causes, and remedial strategies', in Farazmand, A. (ed) *Handbook of Comparative and Development Administration*, Marcel Dekker, New York

Gould, S. J. (1989) *Wonderful Life: The Burgess Shale and the Nature of History*, Norton, New York

Government of Canada (2000) *Sustainable Development in Government Operations: A Coordinated Approach,* www.sdinfo.gc.ca/reports/en/coordinated_approach/index.cfm

Government of Canada (2005) *Canada's Federal Marine Protected Areas Strategy*, Fisheries and Oceans Canada, Ottawa

Government of Nova Scotia (2005) *Protected Areas*, www.gov.ns.ca/enla/pareas/wa_bnlkb.htm

Graefe, A.R., Kuss, F. and Vaske, J. (1990) *Visitor Impact Management, Volume 2: The Planning Framework*, National Parks and Conservation Association, Washington, DC

Graham, J., Amos, B. and Plumptre, T. (2003) 'Governance principles for protected areas in the 21st century', Paper prepared for the Vth World Parks Congress, Durban, South Africa, Institute of Governance, Ottawa, Canada

Graves, A. (2004) *Mapping Subsistence Agriculture in the National Park of American Samoa*, US National Park Service, www.nps.gov/gis/mapbook/tech/30.html

Gray A. (1999) 'Indigenous peoples, their environments and territories', in Posey, D. A (ed) *Cultural and Spiritual Values of Biodiversity,* Intermediate Technology Publications and UNEP, Nairobi

Gray, M. (2004) *Geodiversity: Valuing and Conserving Abiotic Nature*, Wiley, Chichester

Green Globe Asia Pacific (2003) *Performance Level Benchmarks*, www.greenglobe21.com/Documents/General/Performance%20Level%20Benchmarks.xls

Greider, T. and Garkovich, L. (1994) 'Landscapes: The social construction of nature and the environment', *Rural Sociology*, vol 59, no 1, pp1–24

Griffin, J., Cumming, D., Metcalfe, S., t'Sas-Rolfes, M., Singh, J., Chonguiça, E., Rowen, M. and Oglethorpe J. (1999) *Study on the Development of Transboundary Natural Resource Management Areas in Southern Africa*, Biodiversity Support Program, Washington, DC

Griffin, T. and Vacaflores, M. (2004) *A Natural Partnership: Making National Parks a Tourism Priority*, Sustainable Tourism CRC, Gold Coast

Groombridge, B. and Jenkins, M. D. (2000) *Global Biodiversity: Earth's Living Resources in the 21st Century*, World Conservation Press, Cambridge

Groombridge, B. and Jenkins, M. D. (2002) *World Atlas of Biodiversity: Earth's Living Resources in the 21st Century*, University of California Press, Berkeley

Gubbay, S. (ed) (1995) *Marine Protected Areas: Principles and Techniques for Management*, Chapman and Hall, London

Guhrs, T. (2003) Synopsis of *A Thirsty Place*, performed by Tinyeleti Tsa Ditshaba, Vth World Parks Congress, Durban

Guillett, A. (2005) *Legal and Institutional Implications of Systemic Planning and Management of Transboundary Protected Areas: A Comparative Review of Some Case Studies*, Presentation to the Vth IUCN World Parks Congress, Durban

Guruswamy, L. and McNeely, J. A. (eds) (1998) *Protection of Global Diversity: Converging Strategies*, Duke University Press, Durham

Hadker, N., Sharma, S., David, A. and Muraleedharan, T. R. (1997) 'Willingness-to-pay for Borivli National Park: Evidence from a contingent valuation', *Ecological Economics*, vol 21, pp105–122

Hall, K. (2003) 'What is bioprospecting and what are our international commitments?', Background paper for Ministry of Economic Development, Wellington, www.med.govt.nz/ers/nat–res/bioprospecting/general–information/what–is/what–is.pdf

Halpern, B.S. (2003) 'The impact of marine reserves: Do reserves work and does reserve size matter?', *Ecological Applications*, vol 13, no 1 (Supplement), ppS117–137

Ham, S. H. (1992) *Environmental Interpretation: A Practical Guide for People with Big Ideas and Small Budgets*, North American Press, Golden

Hamilton, L. S. (1997) 'Maintaining ecoregions in mountain conservation corridors', *Wild Earth*, vol 7, no 3, pp63–66

Hamilton, L. S. (2000) 'Some guidelines for managing mountain protected areas having spiritual or cultural significance', *Parks*, vol 10, no 2, pp26–29

Hamilton, L. S. (2002) 'Why mountains matter', *World Conservation*, vol 33, no 1, pp4–5

Hamilton, L. S., Worboys, G. L. and Bubb, P. (2003) *State of the World's Protected Areas*, Draft, www.iucn.org/themes/wcpa/wcpa2003/english/outputs/intro.htm

Hamu, D., Auchincloss, E. and Goldstein, W. (eds) (2004) *Communicating Protected Areas*, IUCN, Gland and Cambridge

Hannah, K., Midgley, G. F., Lovejoy, T., Bond, W. J., Bush, M., Lovett, J. C., Scott, D. and Woodward,

F. I. (2002) 'Conservation of biodiversity in a changing climate', *Conservation Biology*, vol 16, no 1, pp264–268

Hansen, S. and VanFleet, J. (2003) *Traditional Knowledge and Intellectual Property: A Handbook on Issues and Options for Traditional Knowledge Holders in Protecting Their Intellectual Property and Maintaining Biological Diversity*, AAAS, Washington, DC

Hanson, D., Dowling, P. J., Hitt, M. A., Ireland, R. D. and Hoskisson, R. E. (2005) *Strategic Management*, Thomson Learning, Melbourne

Hare, A. (ed) (1994) *The World's Natural Habitats*, Duncan Baird, London

Harmon, D. (1994) *Coordinating Research and Management to Enhance Protected Areas*, IVth World Congress on National Parks and Protected Areas, Caracas, Venezuela, IUCN, Gland

Harmon, D. (1996) 'Losing species, losing languages: Connections between biological and linguistic diversity', *Southwest Journal of Linguistics*, vol 14, pp1–33

Harmon, D. and Putney, A. D. (eds) (2003) *The Full Value of Parks: From Economics to the Intangible*, Rowman and Littlefield, Lanham

Harrison, J., Miller, K. and McNeely, J. (1982) 'The world coverage of protected areas: Development goals and environmental needs', *Ambio*, vol 11, no 5, pp238–245

Harrop, S. R. (1999) 'From English moors and meadows to the Amazon rainforest: Land use, biodiversity management and forgotten law', in Walkey, M., Swingland, I. and Russell, S. (eds) *Integrated Protected Area Management*, Kluwer, Dordrecht

Harroy, J.-P., Tassi, F., Pratesi, F. and Humphries, C. (1974) *National Parks of the World*, Orbis, London

Hartshorne, R. (1939) 'The nature of geography', *Annals of Association of American Geographers*, vol XXIX, p348

Harzing, A. and van Ruysseveldt, J. (eds) (2004) *International Human Resource Management*, Sage, London

Hatziolos, M. and Staub, F. (2004) *Score Card to Assess Progress in Achieving Management Effectiveness Goals for Marine Protected Areas*, World Bank, Washington, DC

Healey, P. (1997) *Collaborative Planning: Shaping Places in Fragmented Societies*, Macmillan Press, London

Herath, G. and Kennedy, J. (2004) 'Estimating the economic value of Mount Buffalo National Park with the travel cost and contingent valuation models', *Tourism Economics*, vol 10, no 1, pp63–78

Hess, K. (2001) 'Parks are for people – But which people?', in Anderson, T. L. and James, A. (eds) *The Politics and Economics of Park Management*, Rowman and Littlefield, Lanham

Hesselink, F., Idle, E. and van Boven, G. (2003) 'Beyond training: Protected area institutions as learning organizations – Developing capacity to change towards management in partnership', Paper presented to the Vth World Parks Congress, Durban

Heylings, P. and Bravo, M. (2001) 'Survival of the fittest? Challenges facing the co-management model for the Galapagos Marine Reserve', *CM News*, vol 5, pp10–13

Heywood, V. H. (ed) (1995) *Global Biodiversity Assessment*, Cambridge University Press, Cambridge

Heywood, V. H. (1999) 'Trends in agricultural bio-diversity', in Janick, J. (ed) *Perspectives on New Crops and New Uses*, ASHS Press, Alexandria

Higginbottom, K., Tribe, A. and Booth, R. (2002) 'Contributions of non-consumptive wildlife tourism to conservation', in Buckley, R., Pickering, C. and Weaver, D. B. (eds) *Nature-based Tourism, Environment and Land Management*, CABI Publishing, Wallingford

Higgins, A. and Thompson, D. (2002) 'Life cycle assessment', in Thompson, D. (ed) *Tools for Environmental Management: A Practical Introduction and Guide*, New Society Publishers, Gabriola Island

Higham, J. and Hall, C. M. (2005) 'Making tourism sustainable: The real challenge of climate change?', in Hall, C. M. and Higham, J. (eds) *Tourism, Recreation and Climate Change*, Channel View Publications, Clevedon

Hines, C. (2000) *Localization: A Global Manifesto*, Earthscan, London

Hitt, M. A., Black, J. S. and Porter, L. W. (2005) *Management*, Pearson Prentice Hall, Singapore

HMG/IUCN (1988) *Building on Success: The National Conservation Strategy for Nepal*, His Majesty's Government of Nepal and IUCN, Kathmandu

Hockings, M., Ervin, J. and Vincent, G. (2004) 'Assessing the management of protected areas: The work of the World Parks Congress before and after Durban', *Journal of International Wildlife Law and Policy*, vol 7, no 2, pp31–42

Hockings, M., Stolton, S. and Dudley, N. (2000) *Evaluating Effectiveness: A Framework for Assessing the Management of Protected Areas*, IUCN, Gland and Cambridge

Hockings, M., Stolton, S., Dudley, N., Courrau, J. and

Parrish, J. (2005) *The World Heritage Management Effectiveness Workbook: How to Build Monitoring, Assessment and Reporting Systems to Improve the Management Effectiveness of Natural World Heritage Sites*, revised edition, UNESCO, Paris, and IUCN, Gland and Cambridge, www.enhancingheritage.net/docs_public.asp

Hockings, M., Stolton, S., Leveringham, F., Dudley, N., Courrow, J. (2006) *Evaluating Effectiveness: A Framework for Assessing the Management of Protected Areas*, 2nd edition, IUCN, Gland and Cambridge

Hoffman, A., Moore, P., Simorangkir, D. and House, N. (2003) *Fires in South East Asia – Analysis, Insights and Ideas from Project FireFight South East Asia*, IUCN, Gland and Cambridge and WWF, Gland

Holdsworth, M. and Bryant, S. (1995) 'Rescue and rehabilitation of wildlife from the Iron Baron oil spill in Northern Tasmania', *Tasmanian Naturalist*, vol 117, pp39–43

Holmes, J. (1976) *The Government of Victoria*, University of Queensland Press, St Lucia

Hornback, K. E. and Eagles, P. F. J. (1999) *Guidelines for Public Use Measurement and Reporting at Parks and Protected Areas*, IUCN, Gland and Cambridge

Howden, M. (2003) 'Climate trends and climate change scenarios', in Howden, M., Hughs, L., Dunlop, M., Zethoven, I., Hilbert, D. and Chilcott, C. (eds) *Climate Change Impacts on Biodiversity in Australia*, Commonwealth of Australia, Canberra

The Humane Society of the United States (2005) *Marine Pollution and Habitat Degradation*, www.hsus.org/marine_mammals/what_are_the_issues/marine_pollution_and_habitat_degradation.html>

Hunger, J. D. and Wheelan, T. L. (2001) *Essentials of Strategic Management*, Prentice Hall, Upper Saddle River

Hutton, D. and Connors, L. (1999) *A History of the Australian Environment Movement*, Cambridge University Press, Melbourne

Hvenegaard, G. T. (2002) 'Using tourist typologies for ecotourism research', *Journal of Ecotourism*, vol 1, no 1, pp7–18

Hyde, R. and Law, J. (2001) *Green Globe 21 – Designing Tourism Infrastructure: Steps to Sustainable Design*, Sustainable Tourism CRC, Gold Coast

ICEM (International Centre for Environmental Management) (2003a) *Field Studies in Cambodia, Lao PDR, Thailand and Vietnam: Economic Benefits of Protected Areas*, ICEM, Brisbane

ICEM (2003b) *Lessons Learned in Cambodia, Lao PDR, Thailand and Vietnam: Review of Protected Areas and Development in the Lower Mekong River Region*, ICEM, Brisbane

ICMM (International Council on Mining and Metals) (2005) *The Bushmanland Conservation Initiative*, www.icmm.com/casestudy.php?rcd=20

ICOMOS (International Council on Monuments and Sites) Canada French-Speaking Committee (1982) *Charter for the Preservation of Quebec's Heritage*, ICOMOS Canada French-Speaking Committee, Quebec City

IFAD (International Fund for Agricultural Development) (2001) *Rural Poverty Report 2001: The Challenge of Ending Rural Poverty*, Oxford University Press, Oxford

IISD (International Institute for Sustainable Development) (2003) 'A summary report of the Vth IUCN World Parks Congress', *Sustainable Developments*, vol 89, no 9, pp1–15

Ikenouye, O. (1962) 'National Parks of Japan', in Cahalane, V. H. (ed) *National Parks – A World View*, American Committee for International Wildlife Protection, New York

Infield, M. (2003) 'National Parks as cultural entities', *Policy Matters*, vol 13, pp64–70

INforEEP (2000) *What Is Environmental Education and Why the Need for It?*, www.botany.uwc.ac.za/inforeep/what's_EE2.htm

IPCC (Intergovernmental Panel on Climate Change) (2001) *Climate Change 2001: The Scientific Basis*, Contributions of Working Group 1 to the Third Assessment Report of the Intergovernmental Panel on Climate Change, IPCC, Cambridge

International Wilderness Leadership Foundation (2005) *8th World Wilderness Congress*, www.8wwc.org

Ireland, R. D. and Hitt, M. A. (1999) 'Achieving and maintaining strategic competitiveness in the 21st century: The role of strategic leadership', *Academy of Management Executive*, vol 12, no 1, pp43–57

Ito, N. (1995) '"Authenticity" inherent in cultural heritage in Asia and Japan', in Larsen, K. E (ed) *Proceedings of Nara Conference on Authenticity in Relation to the World Heritage Convention*, UNESCO and Agency for Cultural Affairs, Nara

IUCN (World Conservation Union) (1994) *Guidelines for Protected Area Management Categories*, IUCN, Gland and Cambridge

IUCN (1998) *Economic Values of Protected Areas: Guidelines for Protected Area Managers*, IUCN, Gland and Cambridge

IUCN (1999) *Threats to Forest Protected Areas: A Research Report for the World Bank/WWF Alliance for Forest Conservation and Sustainable Use*, Summary of a survey of 10 countries carried out in association with the World Commission on Protected Areas, IUCN, Gland and Cambridge

IUCN (2000a) *Guidelines for the Prevention of Biodiversity Loss Caused by Alien Invasive Species*, IUCN, Gland and Cambridge

IUCN (2000b) *Financing Protected Areas*, IUCN, Gland and Cambridge

IUCN (2000c) *Vision for Water and Nature: A World Strategy for Conservation and Sustainable Management of Water Resources in the 21st Century – Compilation of all Project Documents*, IUCN, Gland and Cambridge

IUCN (2003a) *The Durban Action Plan*, Vth IUCN World Parks Congress Durban, IUCN WCPA, Gland and Cambridge

IUCN (2003b) *How Is Your MPA Doing? A Guidebook of Natural and Social Indicators for Evaluating Marine Protected Area Management Effectiveness*, IUCN WCPA Marine Programme, Gland

IUCN (2003c) *What is the Vth IUCN World Parks Congress?*, www.iucn.org/themes/wcpa/wpc2003/english/about/intro.htm

IUCN (2004) *World Heritage Nomination – IUCN Technical Evaluation Tropical Rainforest Heritage of Sumatra (Indonesia)*, www.whc.unesco.org/archive/advisory_body_evaluation/1167.pdf

IUCN (2005a) *Welcome to the WCPA*, www.iucn.org/themes/wcpa/

IUCN (2005b) *Benefits Beyond Boundaries: Proceedings of the Vth IUCN World Parks Congress, Durban, South Africa, 8–17 September 2003*, IUCN, Gland and Cambridge

IUCN–CEC (Commission on Education and Communication) (2003) *Voices Beyond Boundaries: Communication for Protected Areas*, www.iucn.org/webfiles/doc/CEC/Public/Electronic/Videos/Voicesfinal2printable.pdf

IUCN–ICMM (International Council on Mining and Metals) (2004) *Integrating Mining and Biodiversity Conservation: Case Studies from Around the World*, IUCN, Gland and Cambridge

IUCN–SUSG (Sustainable Use Specialist Group) Technical Advisory Committee of the Species Survival Commission (2001) *Analytic Framework for Assessing Factors that Influence the Sustainability of Wild Living Natural Resources*, IUCN, Gland and Cambridge

IUCN and WBCSD (World Business Council for Sustainable Development) (1997) *Business and Biodiversity: A Guide for the Private Sector*, IUCN and WBCSD, Gland

IUCN, UNEP, WWF (1991) *Caring for the Earth. A Strategy for Sustainable Living*, Earthscan, London.

Iwokrama International Centre (2004) *Iwokrama International Centre for Rain Forest Conservation and Development Business Plan 2005–2006*, Iwokrama International Centre, Georgetown

Jaireth, H. and Smyth, D. (eds) (2003) *Innovative Governance: Indigenous Peoples, Local Communities and Protected Areas*, Ane Books, New Delhi

James, A., Green, M. and Paine, J. (1999) *A Global Review of Protected Area Budgets and Staff*, World Conservation Monitoring Centre, Cambridge

Jeanreanaud, S. (2001) *Communities and Forest Management in Western Europe: A Regional Profile of the Working Group on Community Involvement in Forest Management*, IUCN, Gland and Cambridge

Jones, B. and Murphree, M. (2001) 'The evolution of policy on community conservation in Namibia and Zimbabwe', in Hulme, D. and Murphree, M. (eds) *African Wildlife and Livelihoods: The Promise and Performance of Community Conservation*, James Currey, Oxford

Jones, P. J. (2006) 'Collective action problems posed by no-take zones', *Marine Policy*, vol 30, pp143–156

Jones, R. and Dunlap, R. (1992) 'The social bases of environmental concern: Have they changed over time?', *Rural Sociology*, vol 57, no 1, pp28–47

Joy, L. (1999) *Capacity Development: An Analysis and Synthesis of its Current Conceptualization and Implications for Practice*, UNDP and UNCF, New York

Kaimowitz, D., Faune, A. and Mendoza, R. (2003) 'Your biosphere is my backyard: The story of Bosawas in Nicaragua', *Policy Matters*, vol 12, pp6–15

Kaiser, F. G., Wolfing, S. and Fuhrer, U. (1999) 'Environmental attitude and ecological behaviour', *Journal of Environmental Psychology*, vol 19, pp1–19

Kant, I. (1956 [1785]) *Groundwork of the Metaphysics of Morals* (translated into English by H. J. Paton), Harper and Row, New York

Kaplan, S. and Kaplan, R. (1989) 'The visual environment: Public participation in design and planning', *Journal of Social Issues*, vol 45, pp59–86

Katz, R. L. (1974) 'Skills of an effective administrator', *Harvard Business Review*, vol 52, no 5, pp90–102

Kaufman, J. L. and Jacobs, H. M. (1996) 'A public planning perspective on strategic planning', in Campbell, S. and Fainstein, S. (eds) *Readings in Planning Theory*, Blackwell, Oxford

Kelleher, G. (1999) *Guidelines for Marine Protected*

Areas, IUCN, Gland and Cambridge

Kelleher, G., Bleakley, C. and Wells, S. (1995) *A Global Representative System of Marine Protected Areas, Volume I–IV*, Great Barrier Reef Authority, World Bank and World Conservation Union, Washington, DC

Kelleher, G., Bleakley, C. and Wells, S. (eds) (2005) *A Global Representative System of Marine Protected Areas*, IUCN, World Bank and Great Barrier Reef Marine Park Authority, Washington, DC

Kelleher, G. and Kenchington, R. A. (1992) *Guidelines for Establishing Marine Protected Areas: A Marine Conservation and Development Report*, IUCN, Gland and Cambridge

Kellert, S. R., Mehta, J. N., Ebbin, S. A. and Lichtenfeld, L. L. (2000) 'Community natural resource management: Promise, rhetoric and reality', *Society and Natural Resources*, vol 13, pp705–715

Kemf, E. (ed) (1993) *Law of the Mother: Protecting Indigenous People in Protected Areas*, Sierra Club, San Francisco

Kenchington, R. A. (1990) *Managing Marine Environments*, Taylor and Francis, New York

Kenchington, R. A. (1996) 'A global representative system of marine protected areas', in Thackway, R. (ed) *Developing Australia's Representative System of Marine Protected Areas*, Proceedings of technical meeting, South Australian Aquatic Sciences Centre, Adelaide, 22–23 April, Department of the Environment, Sport and Territories, Canberra

Kennedy, P. (1999) *Working with Media: Internal Training Notes*, NSW NPWS, Sydney

Kessler, B. L. (2003) *Marine Protected Area (MPA) Process Review: Case Studies of Five MPA Establishment Processes*, NOAA Coastal Services Center, National Marine Protected Areas Center Training and Technical Assistance Institute, Charleston

Kieft, J. and Nur, A. (2002) 'Community-based disaster management: A response to increased risks to disaster with emphasis on forest fires', in Moore, P., Ganz, D., Cheng Tan, L., Enters, T. and Durst, P. B. (eds) *Communities in Flames: Proceedings of an International Conference on Community Involvement in Fire Management*, FAO, Bangkok

Kiernan, K. (1997) 'Landform classification for geoconservation', in *Pattern and Process: Towards a Regional Approach for National Estate Assessment of Geodiversity*, Environment Australia, Canberra

King Mahendra Trust (1994) *Annual Progress Report of the Annapurna Conservation Area Project*, King Mahendra Trust for Nature Conservation, Kathmandu

Kirkpatrick, J. B. (1983) 'An iterative method for establishing priorities for the selection of nature reserves: An example from Tasmania', *Biological Conservation*, vol 25, pp127–134

Kirkpatrick, J. B. (1990) 'A synusia-based mapping system for the conservation and management of natural vegetation', *Biological Conservation*, vol 53, pp93–104

Kirkpatrick, J. B. and Haney, R. A. (1980) 'The quantification of developmental wilderness loss – The case of forestry in Tasmania', *Search*, vol 11, pp331–335

Kirsch, L. J. (1996) 'The management of complex tasks in organizations: Controlling the systems development process', *Organization Science*, vol 7, pp1–21

Knecht, R. W. and Archer, J. (1993) '"Integration" in the US Coastal Zone Management Program', *Ocean and Coastal Management*, vol 21, pp1–3

Knudtson, P. and Suzuki, D. (1992) *Wisdom of the Elders*, Stoddart Publishing, Toronto

Koontz, H. and O'Donnell, C. (1955) *Principles of Management: An Analysis of Managerial Functions*, McGraw-Hill, New York

Kosz, M. (1996) 'Valuing riverside wetlands: The case of the "Donau–Auen" national park', *Ecological Economics*, vol 16, no 2, pp109–127

Koteen, J. (1997) *Strategic Management in Public and Nonprofit Organizations*, 2nd edition, Praeger, Westport

Kothari, A. (2004) 'Protected areas and people: Participatory conservation', in *Biodiversity Issues for Consideration in the Planning, Establishment and Management of Protected Area Sites and Networks*, Convention on Biological Diversity Technical Series no 15, Secretariat of the Convention on Biological Diversity, Montreal

Kothari, A. (2005) 'Community-oriented conservation legislation in South Asia: Halting progress', in Uday, R. S. and Yonzon, P. B. (eds) *People and Protected Areas in South Asia*, IUCN, South Asia and Resources Himalaya Foundation, Kathmandu

Kothari, A., Borrini-Feyerabend, G., Jaireth, H., Oviedo, G., Phillips, A. and Murphree, M. (2003) *Community Conserved Areas and the International Conservation System*, A discussion note relating to the mandate of the WCPA/CEESP Theme Group on Indigenous/Local Communities, Equity and Protected Areas (TILCEPA), www.iucn.org/themes/ceesp/Wkg_grp/

TILCEPA/TILCEPA.htm#cca

Kothari, A., Pande, P., Singh, S. and Variava, D. (1989) *Management of National Parks and Sanctuaries in India: A Status Report*, Environmental Studies Division, Indian Institute of Public Administration, New Delhi

Kothari, A. and Pathak, N. (2005) 'Tragopans and tribals: A Naga transformation', *Sanctuary Asia*, vol 25, no 5, pp60–63

Kothari, A., Pathak, N. and Vania, F. (2000) *Where Communities Care: Community Based Wildlife and Ecosystem Management in South Asia*, Kalpavriksh, Delhi/Pune and IIED, London

Kothari, A., Singh, N. and Suri, S. (eds) (1996) *People and Protected Areas: Towards Participatory Conservation in India*, Sage Publications, New Delhi

Kothari, A., Vania, F., Das, P., Christopher, K. and Jha, S. (eds) (1997) *Building Bridges for Conservation: Towards Joint Management of Protected Areas in India*, Indian Institute of Public Administration, New Delhi

Kramer, R., Pattanayak, S., Sills, E. and Simanjuntak, S. (1997) *The Economics of Siberut and Ruteng Protected Areas*, Final report submitted to the Directorate General of Forest Protection and Nature Conservation, Indonesia, Duke University, Durham

Krug, W. (2001) 'Private supply of protected land in Southern Africa: A review of markets, approaches, barriers and issues', Paper presented at the World Bank/OECD International Workshop on Market Creation for Biodiversity Products and Services, Paris, 25 and 26 January, CSERGE–UCL, London

Krug, W., Suich, H. and Haimbodi, N. (2002) *Park Pricing and Economic Efficiency in Namibia*, DEA research discussion paper no 45, Directorate of Environmental Affairs, Ministry of Environment and Tourism, Windhoek

Lahdelma, R., Salminen, P. and Hokkanen, J. (2000) 'Using multi-criteria methods in environmental planning and management', *Environmental Management*, vol 26, no 6, pp595–605

Laird, S. A. (1999) 'Forests, culture and conservation', in Posey, D. A. (ed) *Cultural and Spiritual Values of Biodiversity*, Intermediate Technology Publications and UNEP, Nairobi

Landre, B. K. and Knuth, B. A. (1993) 'Success of citizen advisory committees in consensus-based water resources planning in the Great Lakes Basin', *Society and Natural Resources*, vol 6, pp229–257

Langholz, J. (2002) 'Privately owned parks', in Terborgh, J. and van Schaik, M. (eds) *Making Parks Work: Strategies for Preserving Tropical Nature*, Island Press, Washington, DC

Langholz, J. and Krug, W. (2005) 'New forms of biodiversity governance: Non-state actors and the private protected area action plan', in Pansky, D. (ed) *Governance Stream of the Vth World Parks Congress*, Parks Canada and IUCN/WCPA, Ottawa

Langholz, J. A. and Lassoie, J. P. (2001) 'Perils and promise of privately owned protected areas', *Bioscience*, vol 51, no 12, pp1079–1086

Lanjouw, A. (2005) *Transboundary Biodiversity Conservation in the Context of Regional Insecurity and Conflict*, Presentation to the Vth IUCN World Parks Congress, Durban

Lass, L. W. and Prather, T. S. (2004) 'Detecting the locations of Brazilian pepper trees in the everglades with a hyperspectral sensor', *Weed Technology*, vol 18, no 2, pp437–442

Lawrence, D., Kenchington, R. and Woodley, S. (2002) *The Great Barrier Reef, Finding the Right Balance*, Melbourne University Press, Melbourne

Layton, R. and Titchen, S. (1995) 'Uluru: An outstanding Australian Aboriginal cultural landscape', in von Droste, B., Plachter, H. and Rossler, M. (eds) *Cultural Landscapes of Outstanding Universal Value: Components of a Global Strategy*, UNESCO, Paris

Leaver, B. (1999) 'Land use allocation in the state of Tasmania, Australia', in *Compendium of Case Studies: Protected Area Management Principles and Practice*, NSW NPWS, Queanbeyan

Lee, C. and Han, S. (2002) 'Estimating the use and preservation values of national parks' tourism resources using a contingent valuation method', *Tourism Management*, vol 23, no 5, pp531–540

Lees, A. (1995) 'Innovative partners: The value of non-governmental organizations in establishing and managing protected areas', in McNeely, J. A. (ed) *Expanding Partnerships in Conservation*, Island Press, Washington, DC

Leiserowitz, A. A., Kates, R. W. and Parris, T. M. (2004) *Sustainability Values, Attitudes and Behaviors: A Review of Multi-national and Global Trends*, CID working paper no 113, Harvard University, Cambridge

Leiserowitz, A. A., Kates, R. W. and Parris, T. M. (2005) 'Do global attitudes and behaviors support sustainable development?', *Environment*, vol 47, no 9, pp22–38

Lennon, J. (2001) *Management Guidelines for World Heritage Cultural Landscapes*, Unpublished report to the World Heritage Centre, Paris

Lennon, J. (2005a) 'Cultural landscapes – A concept for raising forest consciousness', in Calver, M. (ed) *A Forest Consciousness*, Proceedings of the 6th national conference of the Australian Forest History Society Inc, Millpress, Rotterdam

Lennon, J. (2005b) 'The evolution of landscape conservation in Australia: Reflections on the relationships of nature and culture', in Mitchell, N., Brown, J. and Beresford, M. (eds) *The Protected Landscape Approach: Linking Nature, Culture and Community*, IUCN, Gland and Cambridge

Lennon, J., Egloff, B., Davey, A. and Taylor, K. (1999) *Conserving the Cultural Values of Natural Areas: A Discussion Paper*, Jane Lennon and Associates and University of Canberra, Canberra

Lennon, J., Pearson, M., Marshall, D., Sullivan, S., McConvell, P., Nicolls, W. and Johnston, D. (2001) *Natural and Cultural Heritage: Australia State of the Environment Report 2001*, CSIRO, Canberra

Leonard J. (1999) *Capacity Development: An Analysis and Synthesis of Its Current Conceptualization and Implications for Practice*, UNDP/UNICEF, New York

Leopold, A. (1949) *A Sand County Almanac*, Oxford University Press, New York

Leverington, F. and Hockings, M. (2004) 'Evaluating the effectiveness of protected area management: The challenge of change', in Barber, C.V., Miller, K. R. and Boness, M. (eds) *Securing Protected Areas in the Face of Global Change: Issues and Strategies*, IUCN, Gland and Cambridge

Lewis. C. (1996) *Managing Conflicts in Protected Areas*, IUCN, Gland and Cambridge

Li, Y. and Norland, M. (2001) 'The role of soil fertility in invasion of Brazilian pepper (*Schinus terebinthifolius*) in Everglades National Park, Florida', *Soil Science*, vol 166, no 6, pp400–405

Lindberg, K. (1998) 'Economic aspects of ecotourism', in Lindberg, K., Epler-Wood, M. and Engeldrum, D. (eds) *Ecotourism: A Guide for Planners and Managers, Volume 2*, Ecotourism Society, Bennington

Lira, M. S. (2004) 'Strategic communication and visual identity in the National Commission for Natural Protected Areas (CONANP), Mexico', in Hamu, D., Auchincloss, E. and Goldstein, W. (eds) *Communicating Protected Areas*, IUCN, Gland and Cambridge

Liston-Heyes, C. and Heyes, A. (1999) 'Recreational benefits from the Dartmoor National Park', *Journal of Environmental Management*, vol 55, no 2, pp69–80

Livingstone, D. (1992) *The Geographical Tradition*, Blackwell, Oxford

Locke, H. and Dearden, P. (2005) 'Rethinking protected area categories and the new paradigm', *Environmental Conservation*, vol 32, no 1, pp1–10

Lockwood, M. (1999) 'Humans valuing nature', *Environmental Values*, vol 8, pp381–401

Lockwood, M., Loomis, J. and De Lacy, T. (1993) 'A contingent valuation survey and benefit cost analysis of forest preservation in East Gippsland, Australia', *Journal of Environmental Management*, vol 38, pp233–243

Loewen, K. G. and Kulshreshtha, S. N. (1995) *Economic Aspects of Recreation Activity at the Prince Albert National Park*, Prince Albert Model Forest Association, Prince Albert

Loimann, K. (2003) *Community Participation in the Planning and Management of Marine Protected Areas: A Study of Kenya and the Philippines*, Senior thesis, Brown University, Providence

Long, J. (1998) *Dinosaurs of Australia and New Zealand and Other Animals of the Mesozoic era*, UNSW Press, Sydney

Loomis, J. B. and Walsh, R. G. (1997) *Recreation Economic Decisions: Comparing Benefits and Costs*, 2nd edition, Venture, State College

Lorenzi, S. (2005) Secretary of the Regole of Cortina d'Ampezzo, personal communication

Lovett, J. C. (2001) 'Ownership of environmental values and opportunity costs', *Environment and Planning C: Government and Policy*, vol 19, pp681–693

Lowe, I. (2005) *Living in the Hothouse. How Global Warming Effects Australia*, Scribe Publications, Melbourne

Lowenthal, D. (1981) 'Introduction', in Lowenthal, D. and Binney, M. (eds) *Our Past Before Us, Why Do We Save It?* Temple Smith, London

Lucas, P. H. C. (1992) *Guide on Protected Landscapes for Policy-makers and Planners*, IUCN, Gland and Cambridge

Lyden, J. F., Twight, B. W. and Tuchman, E. (1990) 'Citizen participation in long-range planning: The RPA experience', *Natural Resources Journal*, vol 30, pp23–138

Lynch, O. J. and Alcorn, J. B. (1994) 'Tenurial rights and community-based conservation', in Western, D. and Wright, R. M. (eds) *Natural Connections: Perspectives in Community-based Conservation*, Island Press, Washington, DC

Machlis, G. E. (1992) 'The contribution of sociology

to biodiversity research and management',
Biological Conservation, vol 62, pp161–170

Machlis, G. E. and Field, D. R. (eds) (2000a) *National Parks and Rural Development: Practice and Policy in the United States*, Island Press, Washington, DC

Machlis, G. E. and Field, D. R. (2000b) 'Conclusion', in Machlis, G. E. and Field, D. R. (eds) *National Parks and Rural Development: Practice and Policy in the United States*, Island Press, Washington, DC

MacKay, K. T. (2005) *Community Managed Marine Protected Areas in the Pacific Islands: Summary of Case Studies*, www.icriforum.org/itmems/presentations/T3_PacificIslandsKMackay.doc

Mackay, R. (2002) *The Penguin Atlas of Endangered Species*, Penguin Books, New York

MacRae, A. (1995) *Burgess Shale Fossils*, www.geo.ucalgary.ca/~macrae/Burgess_Shale/

Madden, F. (2004) 'Can traditions of tolerance help minimise conflict? An exploration of cultural factors supporting human–wildlife coexistence', *Policy Matters*, vol 13, pp234– 241

Maffi, L. (1999) 'Linguistic diversity', in Posey, D. A. (ed) *Cultural and Spiritual Values of Biodiversity*, Intermediate Technology Publications and UNEP, Nairobi

Maffi, L. (ed) (2001) *On Biocultural Diversity, Linking Language, Knowledge and Environment*, Smithsonian Institution Press, Washington, DC

Maharana, I., Rai, S. C. and Sharma, E. (2000) 'Environmental economics of the Khangchendzonga National Park in the Sikkim Himalaya, India', *GeoJournal*, vol 50, no 4, pp329–337

Mahoney, T. A., Jerde, T. H. and Carroll, S. J. (1965) 'The jobs of management', *Industrial Relations*, vol 4, no 2, pp97–110

Makwaeba, I. M. (2004) 'The use of traditional knowledge in South African National Parks Imbewu Youth Programme: Planting a seed of environmental awareness', in Hamú, D., Auchincloss, E. and Goldstein, W. (eds) *Communicating Protected Areas*, IUCN, Gland and Cambridge

Malhotra, K., Gokhale, Y., Chatterjee, S. and Srivastava S. (2001) *Cultural and Ecological Dimensions of Sacred Groves in India*, Indian National Science Academy, New Delhi

Maller, C., Townsend, M., Brown, P. and St Leger, L. (2002) *Healthy Parks, Healthy People: The Health Benefits of Contact with Nature in a Park Context*, Deakin University and Parks Victoria, Melbourne

Maltby, E. (1997) 'Ecosystem management: The concept and the strategy', *World Conservation*, vol 3, pp3–4

Manins, P., Holper, P., Suppiah, R., Allan, R., Walsh, K., Fraser, P. and Beer, T. (2001) *Atmosphere: Australia State of the Environment 2001*, Commonwealth of Australia, Canberra

Manson, G. and Enders, G. (2004) 'Institutional reforms, water reforms, and hydro-electric operations in protected areas: Some lessons learned from Kosciuszko National Park Australia', in Harmon, D. and Worboys, G. L. (eds) *Managing Mountain Protected Areas: Challenges and Responses for the 21st Century*, Andromeda Editrice, Colledara

Margoluis, R. and Salafsky, N. (1998) *Measures of Success: Designing, Managing and Monitoring Conservation and Development Projects*, Island Press, Washington, DC

Margoluis, R. and Salafsky, N. (2001) *Is Our Project Succeeding? A Guide to Threat Reduction Assessment for Conservation*, Biodiversity Support Program, Washington, DC

Margules, C. (1989) 'Introduction to some Australian developments in conservation evaluation', *Biological Conservation*, vol 50, pp1–11

Margules, C. R., Nicholls, A. and Pressey, R. L. (1988) 'Selecting networks of reserves to maximise biological diversity', *Biological Conservation*, vol 43, pp63–76

Margules, C. R. and Pressey, R. L. (2000) 'Systematic conservation planning', *Nature*, vol 405, pp243–253

Marinelli, J. (ed) (2004) *Plant*, Dorling Kindersley, London

Marquis-Kyle, P. and Walker, M. (2004) *The Illustrated Burra Charter: Good Practice for Heritage Places*, Australia ICOMOS, Melbourne

Marsden-Smedley, J. B. and Kirkpatrick, J. B. (2000) 'Fire management in Tasmania's Wilderness World Heritage Area: Ecosystem restoration using indigenous-style fire regimes', *Ecological Management and Restoration*, vol 1, no 3, pp195–203

Marsh, G. P. (1864) *Man and Nature; or, Physical Geography as Modified by Human Action*, Belknap Press of Harvard University, Cambridge

Marshak, S. (2001) *Earth: Portrait of a Planet*, Norton, New York

Mason, C. (2003) *The 2030 Spike: Countdown to Global Catastrophe*, Earthscan, London

Mathews, L. G., Kask, S., Rotegard, L. and Stewart, S. (2001) 'Using economics to inform national park management decisions: A case study on the Blue Ridge Parkway', in Harmon, D. (ed) *Crossing*

Boundaries in Park Management: Proceedings of the 11th Conference on Research and Resource Management in Parks and on Public Lands, The George Wright Society, Hancock

Mathieu, L., Langford, I. H. and Kenyon, W. (2000) *Valuing Marine Parks in a Developing Country: A Case Study of the Seychelles*, CSERGE working paper GEC 2000-27, University of East Anglia, Norwich

McBryde, I. (1990) 'Those truly outstanding examples. Kakadu in the context of Australia's World Heritage properties – A response', in Domicelj, J. and Domicelj, S.(eds) in collaboration with Raza, M. and Suarez, O. *A Sense of Place? A Conservation in Three Cultures*, AGPS, Canberra

McClelland, L. (2004) 'Bioprospecting: Market-based solutions to biopiracy', *UCLA Journal of Law and Technology*, Notes 8, www.lawtechjournal.com/notes/2004/08_040809_mccelland.php

McGuire, J., Sweis, T. S. and Naroff, J. (1988) 'Effects of top managers' cabinet appointments on shareholders' wealth', *Academy of Management Journal*, March, pp201–212

McLean, J. and Straede, S. (2003) 'Conservation, relocation and the paradigms of park and people management – A case study of Padampur Villages and the Royal Chitwan National Park, Nepal', *Society and Natural Resources*, vol 16, pp509–526

McLoud, P. (2003) 'A day in the life of a ranger', *Ho'opono Mauna Kea Newsletter*, vol 8, Winter, pp1–2

McNeely, J. A. (1998) *Mobilizing Broader Support for Asia's Biodiversity: How Civil Society Can Contribute to Protected Area Management*, Asian Development Bank, Manila

McNeely, J. A. (2001) *The Great Reshuffling: Human Dimensions of Invasive Alien Species*, IUCN, Gland and Cambridge

McNeely, J. A. and Guruswamy, L. (1998) 'Conclusion: How to save the biodiversity of planet Earth', in Guruswamy, L. and McNeely, J. A. (eds) *Protection of Global Diversity: Converging Strategies*, Duke University Press, Durham

McNeely, J. A., Harrison, J. and Dingwall, P. (eds) (1994) *Protecting Nature – Regional Reviews of Protected Areas*, IUCN, Gland and Cambridge

McNeely, J. A., Miller, K. R., Ried, W. V., Mittermeier, R. A. and Werner, T. B. (1990) *Conserving the World's Biological Diversity*, IUCN/WRI/CI/WWF-US/World Bank, Gland and Washington, DC

McNeely, J. A. and Schutyser, F. (2003) *Protected Areas in 2023: Scenarios for an Uncertain Future*, IUCN, Gland and Cambridge

McNeely, J. A., Thorsell, J. W. and Chalise, S. (1985) *People and Protected Areas in the Hindukush Himalaya*, King Mahendra Trust and ICIMOD, Kathmandu

McNett, J. and Søndergaard, M. (2004) 'Making ethical decisions', in Lane, H. W., Maznevski, M. L., Mendenhall, M. E. and McNett, J. (eds) *The Blackwell Handbook of Global Management: A Guide to Managing Complexity*, Blackwell, Oxford

Meadowcroft, J. (1997) 'Planning for sustainable development: Insights from the literatures of political science', *European Journal of Political Research*, vol 31, no 4, pp427–454

Meadows, D. H., Meadows, D. L., Randers, J., Behrens III., W. W. (1972) *Limits to Growth*, Potomac Associates, New York

MED (Ministry of Economic Development) (2002) *Bioprospecting in New Zealand: Discussing the Options*, www.med.govt.nz/ers/nat-res/bioprospecting/review/discussion/index.html

Meffe, G. K. and Carroll, C. R. (eds) (1997) *Principles of Conservation Biology*, 2nd edition, Sinauer Associates, Sunderland

Melnick, R. Z., Sponn, D. and Saxe, E. J. (1984) *Cultural Landscapes: Rural Historic Districts in the National Park System*, United States Department of the Interior, National Park Service, Washington, DC

Menchu, R. (2001) *The Value of Sacred Sites*, www.tierramerica.net/2001/0527/igrandesplumas.shtml

Menezes, Pedro da Cunha e (2005) 'Raising the priority of urban areas in protected area systems in Brazil and beyond', in Trzyna, T. (ed) *The Urban Imperative*, California Institute of Public Affairs, Sacramento

Menkhaus, S. and Lober, D. J. (1996) 'International ecotourism and the valuation of tropical rainforests in Costa Rica', *Journal of Environmental Management*, vol 47, no 1, pp1–10

Menkhorst, P. and Knight, F. (2001) *A Field Guide to the Mammals of Australia*, Oxford University Press, Melbourne

Mercer, D. (2000) *A Question of Balance: Natural Resource Conflict Issues in Australia*, 3rd edition, The Federation Press, Sydney

Merlo, M., Morandini, R., Gabbrielli, A. and Novaco, I. (1989) *Collective Forest Land Tenure and Rural Development in Italy: Selected Case Studies*, FO:MISC/10, FAO, Rome

Millennium Ecosystem Assessment Board (2003) *Ecosystems and Human Well-being: A Framework for Assessment*, Island Press, Washington, DC

Millennium Ecosystem Assessment Board (2005) *Millennium Ecosystem Assessment Synthesis Report*, Island Press, Washington, DC

Ministry of Finance and National Planning (2002) *Zambia Poverty Reduction Strategy Paper 2002–2004*, www.sarpn.org.za/countrypovertypapers/Zambia/prsp_April2002

Ministry of Water, Land and Air Protection (2001) *Economic Benefits of British Columbia's Provincial Parks*, British Columbia Ministry of Water, Land and Air Protection, Vancouver

Mintzberg, H. (1979) *The Structuring of Organizations*, Prentice Hall, Englewood Cliffs

Mitchell, B. A. and Brown, J. L. (1998) 'Stewardship: A working definition', *Environments: A Journal of Interdisciplinary Studies*, vol 26, no 1, pp8–17

Mitchell, J. G. (1999) 'In the wake of the spill: Ten years after *Exxon Valdez*', *National Geographic*, March

Mitchell, J. S. (ed) (2002) *Physical Asset Management Handbook*, 3rd edition, Clarion Technical Publishers, Houston, Texas

Mitchell, N., Brown, J. and Beresford, M. (eds) (2005) *The Protected Landscape Approach: Linking Nature, Culture and Community*, IUCN, Gland

Mittermeier, R., Mittermeier, C. G., Kormos, C., Sandwith, T. and Besançon, C. (eds) (2005) *Transboundary Conservation: A New Vision for Protected Areas*, CEMEX/Conservation International, Washington, DC

Molnar, A., Scherr, S. and Khare, A. (2004) *Who Conserves the World's Forests: Community Driven Strategies to Protect Forests and Respect Rights*, Forest Trends and Ecoagriculture Partners, Washington, DC

Montgomery, C. W. (1997) *Environmental Geology*, 5th edition, McGraw Hill, New York

Moore, S. A., Smith, A. J. and Newsome, D. N. (2003) 'Environmental performance reporting for natural area tourism: Contributions by visitor impact management frameworks and their indicators', *Journal of Sustainable Tourism*, vol 11, no 4, pp348–375

Moote, M. A., McCalaran, M. P. and Chickering, D. K. (1997) 'Research theory on practice: Applying participatory democracy theory to public land planning', *Environment Management*, vol 21, no 6, pp877–889

Morphy, H. (1993) 'Colonialism, history and the construction of place: The politics of landscape in northern Australia', in Bender, B. (ed) *Landscape: Politics and Perspectives*, Berg, Oxford and Providence

Moscardo, G., Woods, B. and Saltzer, R. (2004) 'The role of interpretation in wildlife tourism', in Higginbottom, K. (ed) *Wildlife Tourism: Impacts, Management and Planning*, Common Ground, Altona

Mosely, J. G. (1968) *National Parks and Equivalent Reserves in Australia. Guide to Legislation, Administration, and Areas*, Special Publication No 2, Australian Conservation Foundation, Canberra

Mulligan, M. and Hill, S. (2001) *Ecological Pioneers: A Social History of Australian Ecological Thought and Action*, Cambridge University Press, Cambridge

Mulvaney, J. and Kamminga, J. (1999) *Prehistory of Australia*, Allen and Unwin, Sydney

Munjeri, D. (1998) 'Integrity and or authenticity – an issue of universal values: The case for Africa', in von Droste, B., Rossler, M. and Titchen, S. (eds) *Linking Nature and Culture*, Report of the Global Strategy Natural and Cultural Heritage Expert Meeting, March, Amsterdam, UNESCO, Paris

Murombedzi, J. (2003) 'Pre-colonial and colonial conservation practices in Southern Africa and their legacy today', in Whande, W., Kepe, T. and Murphree, M. (eds) *Local Communities, Equity and Conservation in Southern Africa*, TILCEPA, Africa Resources Trust and PLAAS, Cape Town

Murphree, M. W. (1994) 'The role of institutions in community-based conservation', in Western, D. and Wright, R. M. (eds) *Natural Connections: Perspectives in Community-based Conservation*, Island Press, Washington, DC

Mutebi, J. (2003) 'Co-managed protected areas: From conflict to collaboration – Experience in Bwindi Impenetrable National Park, Uganda', Paper presented to the Vth World Parks Congress, Durban

Mwangomo, E., Stolton, S. and Dudley, N. (2005) *Ecological Integrity: Plans for Monitoring the Serengeti Ecosystem and Threats to the Ecosystem*, Draft report for the Enhancing our Heritage Project, www.enhancingheritage.net/docs_public.asp

My Acre of Africa (2004) *Conservation and Environmental Education Projects*, www.myacreofafrica.com

Myers, N., Mittermeier, R. A., Mittermeier, C. G., da Fonseca, G. A. B. and Kent, J. (2000) 'Biodiversity hotspots conservation priorities', *Nature*, vol 403, pp853–858

Naisbitt, J. (1995) *Megatrends Asia: The Eight Asian*

Megatrends that Are Changing the World, Nicholas Brealey, London

Najder, Z. (1975) *Values and Evaluations*, Clarendon Press, Oxford

Namgyal, T. S. (2001) 'Sustaining conservation finance: Future directions for the Bhutan Trust Fund', *Journal of Bhutan Studies*, vol 3, no 1, pp48–83

Namgyal, T. S. (2003) *Sustaining Conservation Finance in Bhutan: The Experience of the Bhutan Trust Fund*. Paper presented at the Vth IUCN World Parks Congress Sustainable Finance Stream, Durban, South Africa

Nanayakkara, G. L. A. (1987) 'The status of community forestry in Sri Lanka, in Regional community forestry training centre for Asia-Pacific', in Stevens, M. E.(ed) *Report of a Seminar on Regional Community Forestry Training Centre for Asia-Pacific*, RECOFTC, Bangkok

National Trust (2000) 'Studley Royal Park, UK: Restoration and conservation of the formal 18th century water garden', in Lennon, J. (ed) *Management Guidelines for World Heritage Cultural Landscapes,* Report to the World Heritage Centre, Paris

Navrud, S. and Mungatana, E. D. (1994) 'Environmental valuation in developing countries: The recreational value of wildlife viewing', *Ecological Economics*, vol 11, pp135–151

Nelson, J. and Gami, N. (2003) *Enhancing Equity in the Relationship between Protected Areas and Indigenous and Local Communities in Central Africa, in the Context of Global Change*, www.iucn.org/themes/ceesp/Wkg_grp/TILCEPA/community.htm#A

Newsome, D., Dowling, R. and Moore, S. (2005) *Wildlife Tourism*, Channel View Publications, Clevedon

Newsome, D., Moore, S. A. and Dowling, R. K. (2002) *Natural Area Tourism: Ecology, Impacts and Management*, Channel View Publications, Clevedon

NIIMS (National Interagency Incident Management System) (2002) *Operational System Description: National Interagency Incident Management System*, www1.va.gov/emshg/apps/kml/docs/NIIMS_ICS_OperationalSysDesc.pdf

Nijkamp, H. and Peet, G. (1994), cited in Day, J. C. and Roff, J. C. (2000) *Planning for Representative Marine Protected Areas: A Framework for Canada's Oceans*, WWF Canada, Toronto

Nogales, M., Martin, A., Tershey, B. R., Donlan, C. J., Witch, D., Puerta, N., Wood, B. and Alonso, J. (2004) 'A review of feral cat eradication on

islands', *Conservation Biology*, vol 18, no 2, pp310–319

Norman Carr Safaris (2003) *Norman Carr Safaris*, www.normancarrsafaris.com/default.htm

Noss, R. F. (2001) 'Beyond Kyoto: Forest management in a time of rapid climate change', *Conservation Biology*, vol 15, pp578–590

NPS (National Park Service) (1990) *National Register Bulletin No 30: Guidelines for Evaluating and Documenting Rural Historic Landscapes*, National Park Service, Washington, DC

NPS (1994) *Cultural Resource Management Guideline*, NPS-28, National Park Service, Washington, DC

NPS (2000a) *Renewable Energy Applications and Projects at Channel Islands National Park,* www.nps.gov/chis/energy.htm

NPS (2000b) *Dry Tortugas National Park 2001 – 2005 Strategic Plan*, NPS, Homestead

NPS (2005) *Parks and Recreation,* www.nps.gov

NRC (National Research Council) (2002) *Oil in the Sea III: Inputs, Fates and Effects*, National Academy Press, Washington, DC

NRMMC (Natural Resource Management Ministerial Council) (2004) *Directions for the National Reserve System: a partnership approach*, Department of the Environment and Heritage, Canberra

NSW NPWS (New South Wales National Parks and Wildlife Service) (1997a) *Eden District Incident Action Plan*, NSW NPWS, Sydney

NSW NPWS (1997b) *Draft Nature Tourism and Recreation Strategy*, NSW NPWS, Sydney

NSW NPWS (1999) 'C-Plan Conservation Planning Software User Manual for C-Plan (Version 2.2)', Unpublished report by NSW NPWS, Hurstville

NSW NPWS (2001) *Plan of Management Manual 2001*, NSW NPWS, Sydney

NSW NPWS (2002) *Recreation Planning Framework for NSW Parks*, NSW NPWS, Sydney

NSW NPWS (2003) 'NSW saving our threatened native plants and animals: Recovery and threat abatement in action', *2003 Update*, NSW NPWS, Sydney

NSW NPWS (2004) *Corporate Policies and Guidelines*, www.nationalparks.nsw.gov.au

Ntiamoa-Baidu, Y. (1995) *Indigenous vs Introduced Biodiversity Conservation Strategies: The Case of Protected Area Systems in Ghana*, WWF–Biodiversity Support Program, Washington, DC

Ofstad, S. (ed) (1994) *Symposium: Sustainable Consumption*, Ministry of Environment, Oslo

Ogden, P. (2003) 'Protected landscapes: Their role in

promoting the sustainable use of agricultural land' *Parks*, vol 13, no 2, pp3–11

Olson, D. M. and Dinerstein, E. (2002) 'The Global 200: Priority ecoregions for global conservation', *Annals of the Missouri Botanical Gardens*, vol 89, pp199–224

Olson, D. M., Dinerstein, E., Abell, R., Allnutt, T., Carpenter, C., McClenachan, D'Amico, J., Hurley, P., Kassem, K., Strand, H., Taye, M. and Thieme, M. (2000) *The Global 200: A Representation Approach to Conserving the Earth's Distinctive Ecoregions*, Conservation Science Program, WWF-US, Washington, DC

Olson, D. M., Dinerstein, E., Wikramanayake, E. D., Burgess, N. D., Powell, G. V. N., Underwood, E. C., D'Amico, J. A., Itoua, I., Strand, H. F., Morrison, J. C., Loucks, C. J., Allnutt, T. F., Ricketts, T. H., Kura, Y., Lamoreux, J. F., Wettengel, W. W., Hedao, P. and Kassem, K. R. (2001) 'Terrestrial ecoregions of the world: A new map of life on Earth', *Bioscience*, vol 51, no 11, pp933–938

Olwig, K. (1993) 'Sexual cosmology: Nation and nature at the conceptual interstices of nature and culture, or what does landscape really mean?', in Bender, B. (ed) *Landscape: Politics and Perspectives*, Berg, Oxford

Onishi, N. (2005) *An Elderly Vanishing Breed Udo's No Nonsense-free Divers*, www.cdnn.info/news/industry/i050216.html

O'Riorden, T. and O'Riorden, J. (1993) 'On evaluating public examination of controversial projects', in Foster, H. D. (ed) *Advances in Resource Management*, Belhaven Press, London

Orna, E. and Pettitt, C. (1998) *Information Management in Museums*, 2nd edition, Gower, Hampshire

Osieck, E. R. and Mörzer Bruyns, M. F. (1981) *Important Bird Areas in the European Community*, International Council for Bird Preservation, Cambridge

Ostrom, E. (1990) *Governing the Commons: The Evolution of Institutions for Collective Action*, Cambridge University Press, Cambridge

Ostrom, E. (1998) 'The institutional analysis and development approach', in Tusak-Loehman, E. and Kilgour, D. M. (eds) *Designing Institutions for Environmental and Resource Management,* Eward Elgar, Cheltenham

Ottawa Valley Chapter of the Canadian Parks and Wilderness Society (2004) *Environmental Commissioner's Annual Report Comments on Wolves*, www.cpaws-ov.org/algonquinwolves/

Ovadje, F. and Ankomah, A. (2002) 'Human resource management in Nigeria', in Budhwar, P. S. and Debrah, Y. A.(eds) *Human Resource Management in Developing Countries*, Routledge, London

Oviedo, G. (2002) *Lessons Learned in the Establishment and Management of Protected Areas by Indigenous and Local Communities, South America: Enhancing Equity in the Relationship between Protected Areas and Indigenous and Local Communities in the Context of Global Change,* www.iucn.org/themes/ceesp/Publications/TILCEPA/CCA-GOviedo.pdf

Oviedo, G. (2003) *Indigenous Peoples Issues in the IUCN*, IUCN internal discussion note, www.iucn.org

Owen, W. (1993) *Encyclopedia of Animals*, Weldon Owen, Sydney

Palacio, V. and McCool, S. F. (1997) 'Identifying ecotourists in Belize through benefit segmentation: A preliminary analysis', *Journal of Sustainable Tourism*, vol 5, no 3, pp234–243

Palumbi, S. R. (2003) *Marine Reserves: A Tool for Ecosystem Management and Restoration*, Pew Oceans Commission, Washington, DC

Pandey, D. N. (2000) 'Sacred water and sanctified vegetation: Tanks and trees in India', Paper presented at International Association for the Study of Common Property, Bloomington

Pansky, D. (ed) (2005) *Governance Stream of the Vth World Parks Congress*, Parks Canada and IUCN/WCPA, Ottawa

Parks and Wildlife Commission of the Northern Territory (2002) *Public Participation in Protected Area Management Best Practice*, Parks and Wildlife Commission of the Northern Territory, Darwin

Parks and Wildlife Service Tasmania (2004) *A History of the Parks and Wildlife Service*, www.parks.tas.gov.au/manage/about/history.html

Parks Canada (2004a) *Mingan Archipelago National Park Reserve of Canada*, www.pc.gc.ca/pn–np/qc/mingan/natcul/natcul1–6b2_E.asp

Parks Canada (2004b) *Kluane National Park and Reserve of Canada Management Plan*, Parks Canada, Gatineau

Parks Canada (2005) *National Parks of Canada*, www.pc.gc.ca/progs/np–pn/index_E.asp

Parks Victoria (1998) *Directions in Environmental Management*, Parks Victoria, Melbourne

Parrish, J. D., Braun, D. P. and Unnasch, R. S. (2003) 'Are we conserving what we say we are? Measuring ecological integrity within protected areas', *Bioscience*, vol 53, no 9, pp 851–860

Passaris, S. and Sokolska, J. (2001) 'Enhancement of the cultural and natural heritage in Poland',

Naturopa, vol 95, pp28–30

Pasteur, K. (2001) *Changing Organizations for Sustainable Livelihoods: A Map to Guide Change – Lessons for Change in Policy and Organizations, No 1*, Institute for Development Studies, Brighton

Pathak, N., Bhatt, S., Balasinorwala, T., Kothari, A. and Borrini-Feyerabend, G. (2004) *Community Conserved Areas: A Bold Frontier for Conservation*, TILCEPA/IUCN, CENESTA, CMWG and WAMIP, Tehran

Pathak, N., Chowdhury, S. and Bandekar, R. (2006) *Directory of Community Conserved Areas in India*, Kalpavriksh, Pune/Delhi

Pathak, N., Hufeza, T. and Kothari, A. (2003) *Community Conserved Areas: A Bold Frontier for Conservation*, CENESTA, Tehran

Pathak, N., Kothari, A. and Roe, D. (2005) 'Conservation with social justice: The role of community conserved areas in meeting the MDGs', in Satterthwaite, D. and Bigg, T. (eds) *How to Make Poverty History: The Central Role of Local Organizations in Meeting the MDGs*, International Institute for Environment and Development, London

Patin, S. A. (1999) *Environmental Impact of the Offshore Oil and Gas Industry*, EcoMonitor, East Northport

Pauly, D., Christensen, V., Dalsgaard, J., Froese, R. and Torres Jr, F. (1998) 'Fishing down marine food webs', *Science*, vol 279, pp860–863

Payne, R. J. and Nilsen, P. W. (2002) 'Visitor planning and management', in Dearden, P. and Rollins, R. (eds) *Parks and Protected Areas in Canada: Planning and Management*, 2nd edition, Oxford University Press, Don Mills

Peak District National Park Authority (2001) *Pennine Way Management Project Review*, Peak District National Park Authority, Bakewell

Pearce, D. W. and Warford, J. W. (1993) *World Without End: Economics, Environment, and Sustainable Development*, Oxford University Press, Oxford

Pehu, E. (2003) 'Upland agriculture Lao PDR', www.mekonginfo.org/mrc_en/doclib.nsf/0/ AE756EC7F8F7F832C725682C00252034/ $FILE/FULLTEXT.html

Perrow, C. (1986) *Complex Organizations: A Critical Essay*, 3rd edition, Random House, New York

Pew Oceans Commission (2003) *America's Living Oceans: Charting a Course for Sea Change*, Pew Oceans Commission, Arlington

Pfeiffer, C. (2005) *Jeju Women Divers*, www.jejutimes.net/JT/?url=/JT/db/ read.php?idx=455

Phillips, A. (2002) *Management Guidelines for IUCN Category V Protected Areas: Protected Landscapes/ Seascapes*, Best Practice Protected Area Guidelines Series no 9, IUCN WCPA, Gland and Cambridge

Phillips, A. (2003) 'Turning ideas on their head: The new paradigm for protected areas', in Jaireth, H. and Smyth, D. (eds) *Innovative Governance: Indigenous Peoples, Local Communities and Protected Areas*, Ane Books, New Delhi

Phillips, A., Bishop, K., Dudley, N. and Stolton, S. (2003) *Background Paper: An Assessment of the Application of the IUCN System of Categorising Protected Areas*, IUCN, Gland and Cambridge

Phiri, E. and Butler, C. (1998) 'A case study of local community initiatives towards the sustainable use of natural resources: Kakumbi natural resources management business in the Luangwa Integrated Resources Development Project (LIRDP) area in Zambia', Paper presented at the Scandinavian Seminar College: African Perspectives on Policies and Practices Supporting Sustainable Development, 9–11 November, Abidjan, Ivory Coast

Pickering, C. M., Good, R. B. and Green, K. (2004) *Potential Effects of Global Warming on the Biota of the Australian Alps*, Australian Greenhouse Office, Canberra

Pierce, S. M., Cowling, R. M., Sandwith, T. and MacKinnon, K. (2002) *Mainstreaming Biodiversity in Development: Case Studies from South Africa*, World Bank Environment Department, Washington, DC

Pigram, J. J. and Jenkins, J. M. (1999) *Outdoor Recreation Management*, Routledge, London

Pimbert, M. P. (2003) 'Reclaiming diversity and sustainability in community-based conservation', *Policy Matters*, vol 12, pp76–86

Pimbert, M. P. (2004) 'Natural resources, people and participation', in Chambers, R., Kenton, N. and Ashley, H. (eds) *Participatory Learning and Action: Critical Reflections, Future Directions*, IIED and IDS, London

Pimbert, M. P. and Pretty, J. N. (1997) 'Parks, people and professionals: Putting "participation" into protected area management', in Ghimire, K. B. and Pimbert, M. P. (eds) *Social Change and Conservation: Environmental Politics and Impacts of National Parks and Protected Areas*, Earthscan, London

Pipithvanichtham, P. (2005) *Issues and Challenges of Ecotourism in the National Parks of Thailand*, www.recoftc.org/documents/Inter_Reps/

Ecotourism/Piyathip.rtf

Pizzey, G. and Knight, F. (2003) *The Field Guide to the Birds of Australia*, 7th edition, Harper Collins, Sydney

Plachter, H. and Rössler, M. (1995) 'Cultural landscapes: reconnecting culture and nature', in von Droste, B., Plachter, H. and Rössler, M. (eds) *Cultural Landscapes of Universal Value – Components of a Global Strategy*, Gustav Fischer Verlag Jena, UNESCO, New York

Plumptre, T. and Graham, J. (1999) *Governance and Good Governance: International and Aboriginal Perspectives*, Institute on Governance, Ottawa

Poll, M. (2003) *Reserves Standards Framework*, Strategic Asset Management Branch, Parks and Wildlife Service, Hobart

Pomeroy, R., Parkes, J. and Watson, L. (2004) *How Is Your MPA Doing? A Guidebook of Natural and Social Indicators for Evaluating Marine Protected Area Management Effectiveness*, IUCN, Gland and Cambridge

Ponce, C. F. and Ghersi, F. (2003) 'Cordillera del Condor (Peru–Ecuador)', Paper prepared for the Workshop on Transboundary Protected Areas in the Governance Stream of the Vth World Parks Congress, Durban

Pond, K. L. (1993) *The Professional Guide: Dynamics of Tour Guiding*, Van Nostrand, New York

Porter, L. W., Bigley, G. A. and Steers, R. M. (2003) *Motivation and Work Behavior*, McGraw-Hill Irwin, Boston

Posey, D. A. (ed) (1999) *Cultural and Spiritual Values of Biodiversity*, Intermediate Technology Publications and UNEP, Nairobi

Poudel, K. (2003) *Protected Areas Like National Parks Are Under Constant Threat from Natural Disasters like Floods and Landslides*, www.nepalnews.com/contents/englishweekly/spotlight/2003/sep/sep05/national2.htm

Pouliquen-Young, O. (1997) 'Evolution of the system of protected areas in Western Australia', *Environmental Conservation*, vol 24, no 2, pp168–181

Pounds, J., Fogden, M. and Campbell, J. (1999) 'Biological response to climate change on tropical mountain', *Nature*, vol 398, no 6728, pp611–615

Powell, J. M. (1976) *Environmental Management in Australia 1788–1914*, Oxford University Press, Melbourne

Pratt, P. D., Rayamajhi, M. B., Van, T. K., Center, T. D. and Tipping, P. W. (2005) 'Herbivory alters resource allocation and compensation in the invasive tree *Melaleuca quinquenervia*', *Ecological Entomology*, vol 30, no 3, pp316–326

PRB (Population Resource Bureau) (2004) *World Population Data Sheet*, www.prb.org/pdf04/04WorldDataSheet_Eng.pdf

Press, F. and Siever, R. (2000) *Understanding Earth*, W. H. Freeman, New York

Pressey, R. L. (1998) 'Systematic conservation planning for the real world', *Parks*, vol 9, no 1, pp1–6

Pressey, R. L., Bedward, M. and Keith, D. A. (1994a) 'New procedures for reserve selection in New South Wales: Maximising the chances of achieving a representative network', in Forey, P. L., Humphries, C. J. and Vane-Wright, R. L. (eds) *Systematics and Conservation Evaluation*, Oxford University Press, Oxford

Pressey, R. L., Humphries, C. J., Margules, C. R., Vane-Wright, R. L. and Williams, P. H. (1993) 'Beyond opportunism: Key principles for systematic reserve selection', *Trends in Ecology and Evolution*, vol 8, pp124–128

Pressey, R. L., Johnson, I. R. and Wilson, P. D. (1994b) 'Shades of irreplaceability: Towards a measure of the contribution of sites to a reservation goal', *Biodiversity and Conservation*, vol 3, pp242–262

Pressey, R. L. and Logan, V. S. (1995) 'Reserve coverage and requirements in relation to partitioning and generalisation of land classes: Analysis for western New South Wales', *Conservation Biology*, vol 9, no 6, pp1506–1517

Pressey, R. L. and McNeil, S. (1996) 'Some current ideas and applications in the selection of terrestrial protected areas. Are there any lessons for the marine environment?', in Thackway, R. (ed) *Developing Australia's Representative System of Marine Protected Areas*, DEST, Canberra

Preston-Whyte, R. A. and Watson, H. K. (2005) 'Nature tourism and climatic change in Southern Africa', in Hall, C. M. and Higham, J. (eds) *Tourism, Recreation and Climate Change*, Channel View Publications, Clevedon

Price, M. F. and Neville, G. R. (2004) 'Designing strategies to increase the resilience of alpine/montane systems to climate change', in Harmon, D. and Worboys, G. L. (eds) *Managing Mountain Protected Areas: Challenges and Responses for the 21st Century*, Andromeda Editrice, Colledara

Princen, T. and Finger, M. (1994) *Environmental NGOs in World Politics: Linking the Local and the Global*, Routledge, New York

Pulsford, I., Worboys, G. L., Gough, J. and Shepherd, T. (2003) 'A potential new continental scale corridor for Australia', *Mountain Research and Development*, vol 23, no 3, pp291–293

Putney, A. (2003) 'Introduction', in Harmon, D. and Putney, A. (eds) *The Full Value of Parks: From Economics to the Intangible*, Rowman and Littlefield, Lanham

QPWS (Queensland Parks and Wildlife Service) (2000) *User-Pays Revenue: Benchmarking and Best Practice Programme*, ANZECC, Canberra

Queensland Environmental Protection Agency (2005) *Marine Parks*, www.epa.qld.gov.au/ parks_and_forests/marine_parks/

Quinlan, J. F. (1989) *Ground-water Monitoring in Karst Terrains: Recommended Protocols and Implicit Assumptions*, Karst Waters Institute, www.karstwaters.org

Quinlan, J. F. (1990) 'Special problems of ground water monitoring in karst terrains', in Nielsen, D. M. and Johnson, A. I. (eds) *Ground Water and Vadose Zone Monitoring*, ASTM Special Technical Publication 1053, ASTM, Philadelphia

Quintella, C. E., Thomas, L. and Robin, S. (eds) (2004) *Proceedings of the Workshop Stream 'Building a Secure Financial Future: Finance and Resources', Vth World Parks Congress*, IUCN, Gland and Cambridge

Rabinowitz, A. (1993) *Wildlife Field Research and Conservation Training Manual*, The Wildlife Conservation Society, New York

Rahman, S. and Thai, K. V. (1991) 'Context of public budgeting in developing countries', in Farazmand, A. (ed) *Handbook of Comparative and Development Administration*, Marcel Dekker, New York

Rakotoniaina, L. J. and Durbin, J. (2004) 'Culte des ancetres joro et sauvegarde des espèces menacées d'extinction à Madagascar', *Policy Matters*, vol 13, pp248–255

Ramakrishnan, P. S. (2003) 'Conserving the sacred: The protective impulse and the origins of modern protected areas', in Harmon, D. and Putney, A. (eds) *The Full Value of Parks: From the Economic to the Intangible*, Rowman and Littlefield, Lanham

Ramakrishnan, P. S., Saxena, K. G. and Chandrashekhara, U. M. (eds) (1998) *Conserving the Sacred for Biodiversity Management*, UNESCO, Oxford and IBH Publishing, New Delhi

Ramsar Convention Secretariat (2005) *Trilateral Ramsar Platform Set for Morava–Dyje Floodplains*, www.ramsar.org/wn/w.n.trilateral_morava.htm

Rangarajan, M. (2001) *India's Wildlife History*, Ranthambhor Foundation and Permanent Black, New Delhi

Rata, M. (1975) 'Preserving the natural and cultural heritage', *Proceedings of the South Pacific Conference on National Parks and Reserves*, Wellington New Zealand, 24–27 February

Read, V. and Bessen, B. (2003) 'Mechanisms for improved integration of biodiversity conservation', in *Regional NRM Planning Report*, Environment Australia, Canberra

Recher, H. F., Lunney, D. and Dunn, I. (1986) *A Natural Legacy: Ecology in Australia*, 2nd edition, A. S. Wilson, Sydney

Reigl, A. (1996) 'The modern cult of monuments: Its essence and its development', in Stanley Price, N., Kirby Talley Jr, M. and Melucco, A. (eds) *Historical and Philosophical Issues in the Conservation of Cultural Heritage: Readings in Conservation*, The Getty Conservation Institute, Los Angeles

Renard, Y. (2001) *Case of the Soufriere Marine Management Area (SMMA), St Lucia*, CANARI technical report no 1285, www.canari.org/ 285smma.pdf

Rhodes, R. A. W. (1996) 'The new governance: Governing without government', *Political Studies*, vol 44, no 4, pp652–667

Ribot, J. C. (2002) *Democratic Decentralisation of Natural Resources: Institutionalising Popular Participation*, World Resources Institute, Washington, DC

Ribot, J. C. (2003) 'Democratic decentralisation of natural resources: Institutional choice and discretionary power transfers in sub-Saharan Africa', *Public Administration and Development*, vol 23, no 1, pp53–65

Ribot, J. C. (2004) *Waiting for Democracy: The Politics of Choice in Natural Resource Decentralisation*, WRI, Washington, DC

Rice, J. (1985) 'New ecosystems present new challenges', in *Marine Parks and Conservation: Challenge and Promise, Volume 1*, National and Provincial Parks Association of Canada, Ottawa

Rich, T. H. and Vickers-Rich, P. (2000) *Dinosaurs of Darkness*, Allen and Unwin, Sydney

Richardson, K. S. and Funk, V. A. (1999) 'An approach to designing a systematic protected area system in Guyana', *Parks*, vol 9, no 1, pp7–16

Ricketts, T. H., Loucks, C. J. and Dinerstein, E. (1999) *Terrestrial Ecoregions of North America: A Conservation Assessment*, Island Press, Washington, DC

Rimmington, N. (2001) 'Management of

archaeological earthworks, Hadrians Wall World Heritage Site, UK', in Lennon, J. (ed) *Management Guidelines for World Heritage Cultural Landscapes*, Report to the World Heritage Centre, Paris

Robbins, S. P., Bergman, R., Stagg, I. and Coulter, M. (2003) *Foundations of Management*, Prentice Hall, Frenches Forest

Roberts, A. (ed) (2003) *Protected Areas in Uganda: Benefits Beyond Boundaries*, Uganda Wildlife Authority, IUCN, International Gorilla Conservation Programme, Kampala

Roberts, C. M., Bohnsack, J. S., Gell, F., Hawkins, J. P. and Goodridge, R. (2001a) 'Effects of marine reserves on adjacent fisheries', *Science*, vol 294, pp1920–1923

Roberts, C. M., Halpern, B., Palumbi, S. R. and Warner, R. R. (2001b) 'Designing marine reserve networks: Why small, isolated protected areas are not enough', *Conservation Biology in Practice*, vol 2, no 3, pp12–19

Roberts, C. M. and Hawkins, J. P. (2000) *Fully Protected Marine Reserves: A Guide*, WWF Endangered Seas Campaign, Washington, DC, and Environment Department, University of York, York

Roberts, P. (2004) *The End of Oil, the Decline of the Petroleum Economy and the Rise of a New Energy Order*, Bloomsbury, London

Robinson, C. J. (1997) *Integrated Vegetation Management Plan for Fitzgerald River Biosphere Reserve Zone of Co-operation*, CALM, Albany

Rodrigues, A. S. L., Akçakaya, H. R., Andelman, S. J., Bakarr, M. I., Boitani, L., Brooks, T. M., Chanson, J. S., Fishpool, L. D. C., da Fonseca, G. A. B., Gaston, K. J., Hoffmann, M., Marquet, P. A., Pilgrim, J. D., Pressey, R. L., Schipper, J., Sechrest, W., Stuart, S. N., Underhill, L. G., Waller, R. W., Watts, M. E. J. and Yan, X. (2004a) 'Global gap analysis: Priority regions for expanding the global protected-area network', *BioScience*, vol 54, pp1092–1100

Rodrigues, A. S. L., Andelman, S. J., Bakarr, M. I., Boitani, L., Brooks, T. M., Cowling, R. M., Fishpool, L. D. C., da Fonseca, G. A. B., Gaston, K. J., Hoffmann, M., Long, J. S., Marquet, P. A., Pilgrim, J. D., Pressey, R. L., Schipper, J., Sechrest, W., Stuart, S. N., Underhill, L. G., Waller, R. W., Watts, M. E. J. and Yan, X. (2003) *Global Gap Analysis: Towards a Representative Network of Protected Areas*, Advances in Applied Biodiversity Science 5, Conservation International, Washington, DC

Rodrigues, A. S. L., Andelman, S. J., Bakarr, M. I., Boitani, L., Brooks, T. M., Cowling, R. M., Fishpool, L. D. C., da Fonseca, G. A. B., Gaston, K. J., Hoffmann, M., Long, J. S., Marquet, P. A., Pilgrim, J. D., Pressey, R. L., Schipper, J., Sechrest, W., Stuart, S. N., Underhill, L. G., Waller, R. W., Watts, M. E. J. and Yan, X. (2004b) 'Effectiveness of the global protected area network in representing species diversity', *Nature*, vol 428, pp640–643

Rogers, P. M. and Bueno, F. F. D. (2001) 'Protected areas training needs: Lessons from the Philippines', *ASEAN Biodiversity*, vol 1, no 4, pp11–16

Rokeach, M. (1973) *The Nature of Human Values*, Free Press, New York

Rolston, H. (1983) 'Values gone wild', *Inquiry*, vol 26, pp181–207

Rolston, H. (1985) 'Valuing wildlands', *Environmental Ethics*, vol 7, pp23–48

Rolston, H. (2003) 'Life and the nature of life in parks', in Harmon, D. and Putney, A. D. (eds) *The Full Value of Parks: From Economics to the Intangible*, Rowman and Littlefield, Lanham

Rössler, M. (2001) 'Qadisha Valley, Lebanon', in Lennon, J. (ed) *Management Guidelines for World Heritage Cultural Landscapes*, Report to the World Heritage Centre, Paris

Routley, R. and Routley, V. (1979) 'Against the inevitability of human chauvinism', in Goodpaster, K. E. and Sayre, K. M. (eds) *Ethics and Problems of the 21st Century*, University of Notre Dame, Notre Dame

Royal Government of Bhutan (2003) 'Report of annual progress by the government to the National Assembly of Bhutan', Cabinet Secretariat, Thimphu

Russ, G. R. and Alcala, A. C. (1996) 'Marine reserves: rates and patterns of recovery and decline of large predatory fish', *Ecological Applications*, vol 6, no 3, pp947–961

Rylands, A. B. and Brandon, K. (2005) 'Brazilian protected areas', *Conservation Biology*, vol 19, no 3, pp612–618

Saddler, H., Bennett, J., Reynolds, I. and Smith, B. (1980) *Public Choice in Tasmania*, ANU, Canberra

Sala, S., Aburto-Oropeza, O., Paredes, G., Parra, I., Barrera, J. C. and Dayton, P. K. (2002) 'A general model for designing networks of marine reserves', *Science*, vol 298, pp1991–1993

Salafsky, N. R., Margoluis, R. and Redford, K. (2001) *Adaptive Management: A Tool for Conservation Practitioners*, Biodiversity Support Program, WWF, Washington, DC

Salim, E. (1994) 'The challenge of sustainable production and consumption as seen from the South', in Ofstad, S. (ed) *Symposium: Sustainable Consumption*, Ministry of Environment, Oslo

Sallans, S. (2003) *Parks and Wildlife Service Public Risk Management Policy*, Strategic Asset Management Branch, Parks and Wildlife Service, Hobart

Salm, R. V., Clark, J. R. and Siirilam E. (2000) *Marine and Coastal Protected Areas: A Guide for Planners and Managers*, 3rd edition, IUCN, Washington, DC

Sandberg, J. (2000) 'Understanding human competence at work: An interpretative approach', *Academy of Management Journal*, vol 43, pp9–25

Sanders, A. (1996) *Conservation Value of Fitzgerald Biosphere Reserve Bbuffer/Transition Zone Phases I–IV*, CALM, Albany

Sandersen, H. T. and Koester, S. (2000) 'Co-management of tropical coastal zones: The case of the Soufriere Marine Management Area, St. Lucia, West Indies', *Coastal Management*, vol 28, pp87–97

Sandwith, T., Shine, C., Hamilton, L. and Sheppard, D. (2001) *Trans-boundary Protected Areas for Peace and Cooperation*, Best Practice Protected Area Guidelines Series no 7, IUCN, Gland and Cambridge

Sandwith, T., Younge, A., Warner, C., Sekhran, N., Dinu-Wright, A. and Carret, J. (2004) 'Linking mountains to lowlands for biodiversity conservation in the Cape Floristic Region', in Harmon, D. and Worboys, G. (eds) *Managing Mountain Protected Areas: Challenges and Responses for the 21st Century*, Andromeda Editrice, Colledara

Sarmiento, F. O., Rodgriguez, G. and Argumedo, A. (2005) 'Cultural landscapes of the Andes: Indigenous and colono-culture, traditional knowledge and ethno-ecological heritage', in Mitchell, N., Brown, J. and Beresford, M. (eds) *The Protected Landscape Approach: Linking Nature, Culture and Community*, IUCN, Gland and Cambridge

Sauer, C. O. (1925) 'The morphology of landscape', *University of California Publications in Geography*, vol 2, no 2, pp19–53

Sawin, J. (2003) 'Charting a new energy future', in Starke, L. (ed) *State of the World 2003: A Worldwatch Institute Report on Progress Towards a Sustainable Society*, Earthscan, London

Schaller, G. B. (1967) *The Deer and the Tiger: A Study of Wildlife in India*, University of Chicago Press, Chicago

Schaller, G. B. (1977) *Mountain Monarchs*, University of Chicago Press, Chicago

Schaller, G. B. (1993) *The Last Panda*, University of Chicago Press, Chicago

Schaller, G. B. (1997) *Tibet's Hidden Wilderness: Wildlife and Nomads of the Chang Tang Reserve*, Harry Abrams, New York

Schaller, G. B., Hu Jianchu, Pan Wenshi and Shu Jing (1985) *The Giant Pandas of Wolong*, University of Chicago Press, Chicago

Schama, S. (1995) *Landscape and Memory*, Harper Collins, London

Schelhas, J. (2001) 'The USA national parks in international perspective: Have we learned the wrong lesson?', *Environmental Conservation*, vol 28, pp300–304

Schneider-Jacoby, M. (2004) *Conservation without Frontiers – Towards a New Image for the Balkans: A Strategic Plan for the IUCN South–Eastern European Programme*, www.euronatur.org/uploads/media/balkanstrategie_200405.pdf

Schroeder, R. G. (1993) *Operations Management: Decision Making in the Operations Function*, McGraw-Hill International, New York

Schultz, P. W. and Zelezny, L. (1999) 'Values as predictors of environmental attitudes: Evidence for consistency across 14 countries', *Journal of Environmental Psychology*, vol 19, pp255–265

Secretariat of the Convention on Biological Diversity (2001) *Global Biodiversity Outlook*, Secretariat of the Convention on Biological Diversity, Montreal

Selin, S. W., Schuett, M. A. and Carr, D. (2000) 'Modeling stakeholder perceptions of collaborative initiative effectiveness', *Society and Natural Resources*, vol 13, pp735–745

Selman, P. H. (2000) *Environmental Planning: The Conservation and Development of Biophysical Resources*, 2nd edition, Chapman, London

Senaratna, S. (2002) *Sustainable Use – Lessons Learned: Factors Influencing the Sustainability of Multiple Use Marine Protected Areas*, Leaflet, IUCN Sri Lanka country office, www.iucn.org/themes/sustainableuse/docs/ll/leafletsonali.PDF

Senior, J. and Townsend, M. (2005) '"Healthy parks, healthy people" and other social capital initiatives of Parks Victoria, Australia', in Trzyna, T. (ed) *The Urban Imperative*, California Institute of Public Affairs, Sacramento

Senn, J. A. (1990) *Information Systems Management*, 4th edition, Wadsworth, Belmont

Shambaugh, J., Ogelthorpe, J., Ham, R. and Tognetti, S. (2001) *The Trampled Grass: Mitigating the Impacts of Armed Conflict on the Environment*, Biodiversity

Support Program, Washington, DC

Shechter, M., Reiser, B. and Zaitsev, N. (1998) 'Measuring passive use value: Pledges, donations and CV responses in connection with an important natural resource', *Environmental and Resource Economics*, vol 12, no 4, pp457–478

Shelby, B. and Heberlein, T. (1986) *Carrying Capacity in Recreation Settings*, Oregon State University Press, Corvallis

Shengji, P. (1999) 'The holy hills of the Dai', in Posey, D. A. (ed) *Cultural and Spiritual Values of Biodiversity: A Complementary Contribution to the Global Biodiversity Assessment*, UNEP, Nairobi

Sheppard, D. (2001) 'Twenty-first century strategies for protected areas in East Asia', *George Wright Forum*, vol 18, no 2, pp40–55

Shields, R. (1991) *Places on the Margin: Alternative Geographies of Modernity*, Routledge, London

Shindler, B. and Brunson, M. (1999) 'Changing natural resource paradigms in the United States: Finding political reality in academic theory', in Soden, D. and Steel, B. (eds) *Handbook of Global Environmental Policy and Administration*, Marcel Dekker, New York

Shriar, A. (1999) 'Resource conservation and rural neglect: An example from Petén, Guatemala', *Delaware Review of Latin American Studies*, vol 1, no 1, www.udel.edu/LASP/vol1Avrum.html

Shultis, J. (2003) 'Recreational values of protected areas', in Harmon, D. and Putney, A. D. (eds) *The Full Value of Parks: From Economics to the Intangible*, Rowman and Littlefield, Lanham

Shultz, S., Pinazzo, J. and Cifuentes, M. (1998) 'Opportunities and limitations of contingent valuation surveys to determine national park entrance fees: Evidence from Costa Rica', *Environment and Development Economics*, vol 3, pp131–149

Shyamsundar, P. and Kramer, R. A. (1996) 'Tropical forest protection: An empirical analysis of the costs borne by local people', *Journal of Environmental Economics and Management*, vol 31, no 2, pp129–144

Singh, D. (1996) *The Last Frontier: People and Forests in Mizoram*, Tata Energy Research Institute, Delhi

Singh, J. (1999) *Study on the Development of Transboundary Natural Resource Management Areas in Southern Africa: Lessons Learned*, Biodiversity Support Programme, Washington, DC

Sirakaya, E., Sasidharan, V. and Sonmez, S. (1999) 'Redefining ecotourism: The need for a supply-side view', *Journal of Travel Research*, vol 38, pp168–172

Skeat, A. and Skeat, H. (2003) 'Financial issues and tourism systems to make tourism and others contribute to protected areas – The Great Barrier Reef', Paper presented to the Vth World Parks Congress Sustainable Finance Stream, Durban

Skeat, A. and Skeat, H. (2004) 'Systems to make tourism and others contribute to protected areas – The Great Barrier Reef', in Bushell, R. and Eagles, P. F. J. (eds) *Tourism and Protected Areas: Benefits beyond Boundaries, the Vth World Parks Congress 2003*, CABI Publishing, Wallingford

Slack, N., Chambers, S. and Johnston, R. (2001) *Operations Management* (3rd edition), Prentice Hall, London

Smart, J. M., Knight, A. T. and Robinson, M. (2000) *A Conservation Assessment for the Cobar Peneplain Biogeographic Region: Methods and Opportunities*, NSW NPWS, Sydney

Smith, R. (2003) *Universal Essential Competence for Professional Rangers*, Unpublished report, International Ranger Federation

Smyth, D. (2001) 'Joint management of national parks', in Baker, R., Davies, J. and Young, E. (eds) *Working on Country: Contemporary Indigenous Management of Australia's Lands and Coastal Regions*, Oxford University Press, Melbourne

SNH (Scottish Natural Heritage) (1999) *National Parks for Scotland: SNH's Advice to Government*, SNH, Perth

Sobel, J. and Dalgren, C. (2004) *Marine Reserves: A Guide to Science, Design and Use*, Island Press, Washington, DC

Sofield, T., Bauer, J., De Lacy, T., Lipman, G. and Daugherty, S. (2004) *Sustainable Tourism – Eliminating Poverty (ST–EP): An Overview*, Sustainable Tourism CRC, Gold Coast

Solis, V., Cordero, P. M., Cruz, I. A., Borras, M. F., Gonzales, F. M. and Dreja, A. S. (2003) *A Regional Review of CCAs and CMPAs (Focusing on Terrestrial and Non Indigenous PAs) in Central America*, Report of the IUCN joint CEESP/WCPA Theme on Indigenous and Local Communities, Equity and Protected Areas (TILCEPA) for the Ecosystem, Protected Areas and People (EPP) project

Sorensen, T. and Auster, M. (1999) 'Theory and practice in planning: Further apart than ever?', *Australian Planner*, vol 36, no 3, pp146–149

Soulé, M. E. (ed) (1986) *Conservation Biology: The Science of Scarcity and Diversity*, Sinauer, Sunderland

Soulé, M. E. (1995) 'The social siege of nature', in Soulé, M. E. and Lease, G. (eds) *Reinventing Nature? Responses to Postmodern Deconstruction*,

Island Press, Washington, DC

South African National Parks (2004) *Kgalagadi Transfrontier Park: Draft 1 – Strategic Management Plan 2004–2007*, South African National Parks, Pretoria

Southey, S. (2004) 'Applications of sustainable financing for protected areas', in Quintela, C. E., Thomas, L. and Robin, S. (eds) *Proceedings of the Workshop Stream Building a Secure Financial Future: Finance and Resources*, IUCN, Gland and Cambridge

Spalding, M. (2002) 'The World Heritage List: The best of all worlds?', *Parks*, vol 12, no 3, pp50–57

Specht, R. L. and Specht, A. (1999) *Australian Plant Communities: Dynamics of Structure, Growth and Biodiversity*, Oxford University Press, Melbourne

Spergel, B. (1993) *Trust Funds for Conservation*, WWF-US, Washington, DC

Spergel B. (2001) *Raising Revenue for Protected Areas: A Menu of Options*, Centre for Conservation Finance, WWF, Washington, DC

Staiff, R., Bushell, R. and Kennedy, P. (2002) 'Interpretation in national parks: Some critical questions', *Journal of Sustainable Tourism*, vol 10, no 2, pp97–113

Standards Australia and Standards New Zealand (2004) *AS/NZS 4360: 2004 Risk Management*, Standards Australia International, Sydney

Stankey, G. H., Cole, D. N. and Lucas, R. C. (1995) *The Limits of Acceptable Change (LAC) Systems for Wilderness Planning*, Forest Service, US Department of Agriculture, Ogden

Stanley, M. (2001) 'Editorial', *Geodiversity Update*, vol 1, p1

State of North Carolina (1999) *Executive Order no 156: State Government Environmental Sustainability, Reduction of Solid Waste, and Procurement of Environmentally Preferable Products*, www.p2pays.org/ref/03/02221.pdf

State of Victoria (2004) *Winemakers Environmental Management Kit*, www.epa.vic.gov.au/Businesssustainability/WineEMS/emsiso14001.shtml#envpolicy

Staub, F. and Hatziolos, M. E. (2004) *Scorecard to Assess Progress in Achieving Management Effectiveness Goals in Marine Protected Areas (Revised Version)*, World Bank, Washington, DC

Stedman, R. C. (2003) 'Is it really just a social construction? The contribution of the physical environment to sense of place', *Society and Natural Resources*, vol 16, pp671–685

Steel, B., List, P. and Shindler, B. (1994) 'Conflicting values about federal forests: A comparison of national and Oregon publics', *Society and Natural Resources*, vol 7, no 2, pp137–153

Stevens, S. (1997a) 'The legacy of Yellowstone', in Stevens, S. (ed) *Conservation through Cultural Survival: Indigenous Peoples and Protected Areas*, Island Press, Washington, DC

Stevens, S. (ed) (1997b) *Conservation through Cultural Survival: Indigenous Peoples and Protected Areas*, Island Press, Washington, DC

Stolton, S. and Dudley, N. (2003) 'Threats to the system', in Spalding, M. and Chape, S. (eds) *State of the World's Protected Areas*, Draft for comment, UNEP–WCMC, Cambridge, and IUCN WCPA, Gland

Stolton, S., Hockings, M., Dudley, N., McKinnon, K. and Whitten, T. (2003) *Reporting Progress in Protected Areas – A Site-level Management Effectiveness Tracking Tool*, World Bank/WWF Alliance for Forest Conservation and Sustainable Use, Gland

Stone, R. D. (1991) *Wildlands and Human Needs: Reports from the Field*, WWF-US, Washington, DC

Stoner, J. A. F., Freeman, R. E. and Gilbert, D. R. (2004) *Management*, Prentice Hall, Englewood Cliffs

Strahler, A. N. (1969) *Physical Geography*, 3rd edition, John Wiley and Sons, New York

Strahler, A. H. and Strahler, A. N. (1992) *Modern Physical Geography*, 4th edition, John Wiley and Sons, New York

Strang, H. E. (1962) 'National Parks in Brazil', in Cahalane, V. H. (ed) *National Parks – A World View*, American Committee for International Wildlife Protection, New York

Stunden, G. (2002) *What Is Sustainable Development?* www.jeanlambertmep.org.uk/downloads/briefings/0204sustaindevelopment.doc

Sukotjo, H. W. (2004) *Land and Forest Fire Control Policies and Implementation in Indonesia*, Presented at the regional workshop on strengthening the Asia Forest Partnership, Yogyakarta, Ministry of Forestry, Indonesia

Sullivan, S. (1998) 'Implementation of the World Heritage Convention in Australia', in von Droste, B., Rössler, M. and Titchen, S. (eds) *Linking Nature and Culture*, Report of the Global Strategy Natural and Cultural Heritage Expert Meeting, March, Amsterdam, UNESCO, Paris

Suter, J. (2001a) 'Report on the workshop to review the 1986 Integrated Management and Development Plan for Sapo National Park. Flora and Fauna International', Monrovia, Liberia FFI,

Monrovia

Suter, J. (2001b) *An 18-Month Operational Plan for the Management and Development of Sapo National Park, Sinoe County*, Flora and Fauna International, Monrovia

Sutton, A. and Sutton, M. (1972) *Yellowstone: A Century of the Wilderness Idea*, Collier MacMillan Ltd, London

Swadling, M. (1995) *Paradise on Earth: The Natural World Heritage List*, Jidd Publishers, Columbus

Tache, B. (2000) 'Changing patterns of resource control among the Borana pastoralists of Southern Ethiopia: A lesson for development agencies', in Manger, L., Ghaffar, A. and Ahmed, M. (eds) *Pastoralists and Environment: Experiences from the Greater Horn of Africa*, OSSREA, Addis Ababa, pp51–74

Tafangenyasha, C. (1997) 'Should Benji Dam be dredged? A preliminary impact assessment to dredging a water reservoir in an African national park', *The Environmentalist*, vol 17, no 3, pp191–195

Tasmania Parks and Wildlife Service (2000) *Best Practice in Protected Area Management Planning*, ANZECC Working Group on National Parks and Protected Areas Management Benchmarking and Best Practice Programme, ANZECC, Canberra

Tasmania Parks and Wildlife Service (2004) *State of the Tasmanian Wilderness World Heritage Area: An Evaluation of Management Effectiveness*, Report No 1, TPWS, Hobart

Tawake, A., Meo, S. and Aalbersberg, B. (2005) *Community-based Marine Conservation in Fiji*, Abstract no 47, International Marine Protected Areas Congress (IMPAC1), Geelong, www.impacongress.org/orals%20211005.pdf>

Taylor, D. (2002) 'The Ramsar Convention on Wetlands', *Parks*, vol 12, no 3, pp42–49

Taylor, N. (1998) *Urban Planning Theory Since 1945*, Sage, London

Temple, S. A. (1991) 'The role of dispersal in the maintenance of bird populations in a fragmented landscape', *Acta XX Congressus Internationalis Ornithologici*, vol IV

Terborgh, J. (1999) *Requiem for Nature*, Island Press, Washington, DC

Terborgh, J. (2004) 'Reflections of a scientist at the World Parks Congress', *Conservation Biology*, vol 18, no 3, pp619–620

Thackway, R. and Cresswell, I. D. (eds) (1995a) 'Towards a systematic approach for identifying gaps in the Australian system of protected areas',

in Herman, T. B., Bondrup-Nieslen, S., Wilison, J. H. M. and Munro, N. W. P. (eds) *Ecosystem Monitoring and Protected Areas*, Proceedings 2nd International Conference on the Science and the Management of Protected Areas, Halifax

Thackway, R. and Cresswell, I. D. (eds) (1995b) *An Interim Biogeographic Regionalisation for Australia: A Framework for Establishing the National System of Reserves*, ANCA, Canberra

Thomas, J. (1993) 'The politics of vision and the archaeologies of landscape', in Bender, B. (ed) *Landscape: Politics and Perspectives*, Berg, Oxford

Thomas, L. and Middleton, J. (2003) *Guidelines for Management Planning of Protected Areas*, IUCN, Gland and Cambridge

Thompson, D. (2002) *Tools for Environmental Management: A Practical Introduction and Guide*, New Society Publishers, Gabriola Island

Thompson, L., Jago, B., Fernandes, L. and Day, J. C. (2004) *Barriers to Communication – How These Critical Aspects Were Addressed during the Public Participation for the Rezoning of the Great Barrier Reef Marine Park*, GBRMPA, Townsville

Thorne-Miller, B. and Catena, J. (1991) *The Living Ocean: Understanding and Protecting Marine Biodiversity*, Island Press, Washington, DC

Thorsell, J. W. (1985) *Conserving Asia's Natural Heritage*, IUCN, Gland

Ticktin, T., Nantel, P., Ramirez, F. and Johns, T. (2002) 'Effects of variation on harvest limits for non-timber forest species in Mexico', *Conservation Biology*, vol 16, no 3, pp691–705

Tilbury, D. and Wortman, D. (2004) *Engaging People in Sustainability*, IUCN Commission on Education and Communication, IUCN, Gland and Cambridge

Tilden, F. (1982) *Interpreting our Heritage*, University of North Carolina Press, Chapel Hill

Þingvellir Commission (2004) *Þingvellir National Park Management Plan 2004 to 2024*, Þingvellir Commission, Reykjavík

TNC (The Nature Conservancy) (2002) *The Five–S Framework for Site Conservation: A Practitioner's Handbook for Site Conservation Planning and Measuring Conservation Success*, The Nature Conservancy, Arlington

TNC (2005) *About the Nature Conservancy*, www.nature.org/aboutus

TNC (2006) *Where We Work*, www.nature.org

Tompkins, E. L., Nicholson–Cole S. A., Hurlston, L., Boyd, E., Hodge, G. B., Clarke, J., Gray, G., Trotz, N. and Varlack, L. (2005) *Surviving Climate Change in Small Islands: A Guidebook*,

Tyndall Centre for Climate Change Research, Norwich

TPCG (Technical and Policy Core Group) and Kalpavriksh (2005) *Securing India's Future: Final Technical Report of the National Biodiversity Strategy and Action Plan*, Technical and Policy Core Group and Kalpavriksh, Pune

Transboundary Protected Areas Taskforce (2004) Unpublished meeting notes, IUCN/WCPA Specialist Meting, 17–22 May, Archipelago de La Maddelena, Sardinia

Transboundary Protected Areas Taskforce (2005) *Transboundary Conservation: A New Vision for Protected Areas*, Conservation International, Washington, DC

Trevino, L. K., Weaver, D. G., Toffler, D. G. and Ley, B. (1999) 'Managing ethics and legal compliance: What works and what hurts', *California Management Review*, vol 41, no 2, pp131–151

Trusty, W. (2003) 'Issues in materials selection', *RMI Solutions*, vol 19, no 2, pp26–27

TTF Australia (Tourism and Transport Forum Australia) and STCRC (Sustainable Tourism CRC) (2004) *A Natural Partnership: Making National Parks a Tourism Priority*, TTF Australia, Sydney

Tuan, Yi-Fu (2002) 'Foreword', in Olwig, K. (ed) *Landscape, Nature and the Body Politic: From Britain's Renaissance to America's New World*, University of Wisconsin Press, Madison

Tuler, S. and Webler, T. (1999) 'Voices from the forest: What participants expect of a public participation process', *Society and Natural Resources*, vol 12, pp437–454

Turnage, R. (1980) *Ansel Adams: The Role of the Artist in the Environmental Movement*, Wilderness Society, Washington, DC

Turnbull, C. (1972) *The Mountain People*, Simon and Schuster, New York

Turpie, J., Lange, G., Martin, R., Davies, R. and Barnes, J. (2004) *Strengthening Namibia's System of National Protected Areas: Economic Analysis and Feasibility Study for Financing*, Anchor Environmental Consultants CC, Rhodes Gift

Twidale, C. R. (1968) *Geomorphology*, Nelson, Australia

Udvardy, M. D. F. (1975) *A Classification of the Biogeographical Provinces of the World*, IUCN Occasional Paper no 18, prepared as a contribution to UNESCO's Man and the Biosphere (MAB) programme, Project no 8, IUCN, Morges

Uluṟu–Kata Tjuṯa Board of Management and Parks Australia (2000) *Fourth Uluṟu–Kata Tjuṯa National Park Plan of Management*, Commonwealth of Australia, Canberra

UN (United Nations) (1992) *Framework Convention on Climate Change*, www.unfccc.int/resource/docs/convkp/conveng.pdf

UN (2000) *We, the Peoples: Key Proposals*, www.un.org/millennium/sg/report/key.htm#3

UN (2003) *United Nations Division for Sustainable Development*, www.un.organization/esa/sustdev/index.html

UNDP (United Nations Development Programme) (1988) *Capacity Assessment and Development in a Systems and Strategic Management Context*, Technical Advisory Paper no 3, Management Development and Governance Division, Bureau for Development Policy, New York, www.magnet.undp.org/docs/cap/main.htm

UNDP (1990) *Human Development Report 1990: Concept and Measurement of Human Development*, www.hdr.undp.org/reports/global/1990/en

UNDP (1997) *Governance for Sustainable Human Development: A UNDP Policy Document*, UNDP, New York, www.magnet.undp.org/policy/default.htm

UNDP (1999) *Human Development Report 1999: Globalisation with a Human Face*, UNDP, New York

UNDP (2001) *Human Development Report 2001: Making New Technologies Work for Human Development*, UNDP, New York

UNDP (2002) *Human Development Report: Deepening Democracy in a Fragmented World*, UNDP, New York

UNDP (2004) *Human Development Report 2004: Cultural Liberty in Today's Diverse World*, UNDP, New York

UNDP–GEF (Global Environment Facility) (2003) *Capacity Development Indicators: A UNDP–GEF Resource Kit*, UNDP, New York

UNDP, UNEP (United Nations Environment Programme) and World Bank (2003) *World Resources 2002–2004*, World Resources Institute, Washington, DC

UNEP (United Nations Environment Programme) (1988) *People, Parks and Wildlife: Guidelines for Public Participation in Wildlife Conservation*, UNEP, Nairobi, www.cepf.net/xp/cepf/news/in_focus/2004/may_feature.xml

UNEP (2002) *Global Environmental Outlook 3: Past, Present and Future Perspectives*, Earthscan, London

UNEP (2005a) *GEO Year Book 2004/5: An Overview of Our Changing Environment*, UNEP, Kenya

UNEP (2005b) *United Nations Environment*

Programme, www.unep.org

UNEP–WCMC (World Conservation Monitoring Centre) (2001) *Niger – Air and Ténéré Natural Reserve*, www.unep–wcmc.org/protected_areas/data/wh/atnnr.html

UNEP–WCMC (2003) *Strategic Plan 2003–2004*, www.unep–wcmc.org

UNEP–WCMC (2004) *Australia–Western Australia, Shark Bay*, www.unep-wcmc.org/sites/wh/sharkbay.html

UNEP–WCMC (2005) *UNEP–WCMC*, www.unep–wcmc.org

UNESCO (United Nations Educational, Scientific and Cultural Organization) (1994) *Operational Guidelines for the Implementation of the World Heritage Convention, Intergovernmental Committee for the Protection of the World Cultural and Natural Heritage*, WHC 99/2 Revised, March 1999, UNESCO, Paris

UNESCO (1997) *Operational Guidelines for the Implementation of the World Heritage Convention*, UNESCO, Paris

UNESCO (1999) *World Heritage*, www.unesco.org/whc/index.htm

UNESCO (2000) *The MAB Programme: Recommendations for the Establishment and Functioning of Transboundary Biosphere Reserves*, www.unesco.org/mab/mabicc/2000/eng/TBREng.htm

UNESCO (2002) *Redwood National Park*, www.valhalla.unep-wcmc.org/unesco/sites/4325.htm

UNESCO (2005a) *The Western Caucasus World Heritage Area, Russian Federation*, UNESCO, Paris, www.whc.unesco.org/en/list/900

UNESCO (2005b) *Kinabalu Park World Heritage Area, Malaysia*, UNESCO, Paris, www.whc.unesco.org/en/list/1012

UNESCO (2005c) *Redwood National Park, California, United States of America*, UNESCO, Paris, www.whc.unesco.org/en/list/134

UNESCO (2005d) *Manu National Park, Peru*, UNESCO, Paris, www.whc.unesco.org/en/list/402

UNESCO (2005e) *Cape Floral Region Protected Areas, South Africa*, UNESCO, Paris, www.whc.unesco.org/en/list/1007

UNESCO (2005f) *Air and Ténéré Natural Reserves, Niger*, UNESCO, Paris, www.whc.unesco.org/en/list/573

UNESCO (2005g) *Central Amazon Conservation Complex, Brazil*, UNESCO, Paris, www.whc.unesco.org/en/list/998

UNESCO (2005h) *Belize Barrier–Reef Reserve System*, UNESCO, Paris, www.whc.unesco.org/en/list/764

UNESCO (2005i) *Biosphere Reserves in Focus: Somiedo Biosphere Reserve, Spain*, www.unesco.org/mab/br/focus/Nov01/somiedo.htm

UNESCO (2005j) *Operational Guidelines for the Implementation of the World Heritage Convention, Intergovernmental Committee for the Protection of the World Cultural and Natural Heritage*, WHC02/05, UNESCO, Paris

UNESCO (2005k) *World Heritage*, www.whc.unesco.org/en/about

UNESCO (2005l) *Towards More Responsible Tourism*, www.unesco.org/mab/sustainable/3tourism.htm

UNESCO (2006a) 'Villa d'Este, Tivoli', http://whc.unesco.org/pg.cfm?cid=31&id_site=1025

UNESCO (2006b) 'Palmeral of Elche', http://whc.unesco.org/en/list/930

UNESCO (2006c) 'Vat Phou and associated ancient settlements within the Champasak cultural landscape', http://whc.unesco.org/en/list/481,930,1025

UNFPA (United Nations Population Fund) (2001) *Population Environment and Poverty Linkages: Operational Challenges*, UNFPA, New York

UNHCR (United Nations High Commission on Refugees) (1996) *Environmental Guidelines*, UNHCR, Geneva

United States Fish and Wildlife Service (1999) *South Florida Multi-Species Recovery Plan*, United States Fish and Wildlife Service, Georgia

US Army Corps of Engineers (2006) Why restore the Everglades? www.evergladesplan.org/about/why_restore_pt_01.cfm

US Department of Energy (2004) *Federal Energy Management Program Technologies: Water Efficiency Case Studies, Biscayne National Park – Homestead, Florida*, www.eere.energy.gov/femp/technologies/water_biscayne.cfm

US Department of Homeland Security (2004) *National Incident Management System*, US Department of Homeland Security, Washington, DC

US National Committee of the International Council on Monuments and Sites (1992) *A Preservation Charter for the Historic Towns and Areas of the United States of America*, US/ICOMOS, Washington, DC

Van den Born, R. J. G., Lenders, R. H. J., De Groot, W. T. and Huijsman, E. (2001) 'The new biophilia: An exploration of visions of nature in Western countries', *Environmental Conservation*, vol 28, no 1, pp65–75

van der Linde, H., Oglethorpe, J., Sandwith, T., Snelson, D. and Tessema, Y. (2001) *Beyond Boundaries: Transboundary Natural Resource Management in Sub-Saharan Africa*, Biodiversity Support Programme, Washington, DC

van Schaik, C. P. and Kramer, R. A. (1997) 'Toward a new protection paradigm', in Kramer, R., van Schaik, C. and Johnson, J. (eds) *Last Stand, Protected Areas and the Defence of Tropical Biodiversity*, Oxford University Press, New York

Vandenbeld, J. (1988) *Nature of Australia: A Portrait of the Island Continent*, Collins, Melbourne

Vandergeest, P. (1996) 'Property rights in protected areas: Obstacles to community involvement as a solution in Thailand', *Environmental Conservation*, vol 23, no 3, p259–268

Vanzella-Khouri, A. (2005) 'The protocol on specially protected areas and wildlife in the wider Caribbean', in Pansky, D. (ed) *Governance Stream of the Vth World Parks Congress*, Parks Canada and IUCN/WCPA, Ottawa

Vasu, N. K. (2002) *Periodic Reporting Exercise on the Application of the World Heritage Convention Section II: India, Kaziranga National Park*, www.whc. unesco.org/archive/periodicreporting/cycle01/section2/337.pdf

Vera, W. M. (2002) *Grazing Ecology and Forest History*, CABI Publishing, Wallingford

Vickers-Rich, P. and Rich, T. H. (1993) *Wildlife of Gondwana: The 500 Million Year History of Vertebrate Animals from the Ancient Supercontinent*, Reed, Sydney

Vierros, M. (2004) 'Some considerations on marine and coastal protected areas network design', in *Secretariat of the Convention on Biological Diversity, Biodiversity Issues for Consideration in the Planning, Establishment and Management of Protected Area Sites and Networks*, SCBD, Montreal

Vijayan, V. S. (1991) *Keoladeo National Park Ecology Study 1980–1990*, Bombay Natural History Society, Mumbai

Villa, F., Tunesi, L. and Agardy, T. (20020) 'Zoning marine protected areas through spatial multiple-criteria analysis: The case of the Asinara Island National Marine Reserve of Italy', *Conservation Biology*, vol 16, no 2, pp515–526

Villalón, A. (2005) 'World Heritage inscription and challenges to the survival of community life in Philippine cultural landscapes', in Mitchell, N., Brown, J. and Beresford, M. (eds) *The Protected Landscape Approach: Linking Nature, Culture and Community*, IUCN, Gland and Cambridge

von Droste, B., Plachter, H. and Rössler, M. (eds) (1995) *Cultural Landscapes of Universal Value – Components of a Global Strategy*, Fischer Verlag, Stuttgart, and UNESCO, New York

Wagner, L. (ed) (2003) 'A brief history of the World Parks Congress', *Sustainable Developments*, vol 89, no 9, p1

Wallsten, P. (2003) 'The "inside-out" process: A key approach for establishing Fulufjället National Park in Sweden', *Mountain Research and Development*, vol 23, no 3, pp227–229

Ward, T. J., Heinemann, D. and Evans, N. (2001) 'The role of marine reserves as fisheries management tools: A review of concepts, evidence and international experience', Bureau of Rural Sciences, Canberra

Watson, J. and Sanders, A. (1997) 'Fitzgerald River National Park Biosphere Reserve 1978–1997: The evolution of integrated protected area management', *Parks*, vol 7, no 1, pp9–19

WCED (World Commission on Environment and Development) (1987) *Our Common Future*, WCED, Geneva

WCPA (World Commission on Protected Areas) (2005) *Strategic Plan 2005–2012*, WCPA, Gland

WCPA (2006) *Establishing Networks of Marine Protected Areas – Making It Happen: A Guide for Developing National and Regional Capacity for Building MPA Networks*, Draft manuscript, IUCN, Gland and Cambridge

WDPA (World Database on Protected Areas) Consortium (2005) *World Database on Protected Areas*, IUCN, UNEP WCMC, Cambridge

Wearing, S. and Nelson, H. (2004) *A Natural Partnership: Making National Parks a Tourism Priority – Project Paper 3: Marketing and Promotion*, TTF Australia, Sydney, and Sustainable Tourism CRC, Gold Coast

Webler, T. and Renn, O. (1995) 'A brief primer on participation: Philosophy and practice', in Renn, O., Webler, T. and Wiedemann, P. (eds) *Fairness and Competence in Citizen Participation: Evaluating Models for Environmental Discourse,* Kluwer, Dordrecht

Welch, D. (2005) 'What should protected area managers do in the face of climate change?', *The George Wright Forum*, vol 22, no 1, pp75–93

Wells, M., Brandon, K. and Hannah, L. (1992) *People and Parks: Linking Protected Area Management with Local Communities*, World Bank, Washington, DC

Wells, S. and Day, J. C. (2004) 'Application of the IUCN protected area management categories in the marine environment', *Parks*, vol 14, no 3, pp28–38

West, P. C. and Brechin, S. R. (eds) (1991) *Resident Peoples and National Parks: Social Dilemmas and Strategies in International Conservation*, University of Arizona Press, Tucson

Western, D. and Wright, R. M. (eds) (1994) *Natural Connections: Perspectives in Community-based Conservation*, Island Press, Washington, DC

Westing, A. H. (1998) 'Establishment and management of transfrontier reserves for conflict prevention and confidence building', *Environmental Conservation*, vol 25, no 2, pp91–94

Whande, W., Kepe, T. and Murphree, M. (eds) (2002) *Local Communities, Equity and Conservation in Southern Africa: A Synthesis of Lessons Learnt and Recommendations from a Southern African Technical Workshop*, School of Government, University of the Western Cape, Belville

Wheat, F. (1999) *California Desert Miracle: The Fight for Desert Parks and Wilderness*, Sunbelt Publications, San Diego

White, A., Khare, A. and Molnar, A. (2004) *Who Owns, Who Conserves and Why It Matters*, Forest Trends, Washington, DC

White, M. (1990) *The Nature of Hidden Worlds*, Reed, Sydney

White, M. E. (1994) *After the Greening: The Browning of Australia*, Kangaroo Press, Sydney

White, M. E. (2003) *Earth Alive: From Microbes to a Living Planet*, Rosenburg Publishing, Sydney

Whitehouse, J. F. (1992) 'IVth World Congress on National Parks and Protected Areas, Caracas, Venezuela', *Australian Zoologist*, vol 28, pp39–46

Wieting, R. (EUROPARC Consulting) (2004) *Sustainable Land Use in European Protected Areas*, IUCN Regional Office for Europe, Brussels, www.iucn.org/places/europe/rofe/documents/sustainable_land_use_report.pdf

Wilcove, D. S., McLellan, C. H. and Dobson, A. P. (1986) 'Habitat fragmentation in the temperate zone', in Soulé, M. E. (ed) *Conservation Biology: The Science of Scarcity and Diversity*, Sinauer, Sunderland

Wilderness.net (2005) *Noatak Wilderness*, www.wilderness.net

Wilkinson, C. R. (2002) *Status of Coral Reefs of the World: 2002*, Australian Institute of Marine Science, Townsville

Wilkinson, C. R. (ed) (2004) *Status of Coral Reefs of the World: 2004*, AIMS, Townsville

Wilks, L. C. (1990) *A Survey of the Contingent Valuation Method*, Resource Assessment Commission

research paper no 2, AGPS, Canberra

Williams, M. (2003) *Deforesting the Earth: From Prehistory to Global Crisis*, University of Chicago Press, Chicago

Wilson, A. T. M. (1966) 'Some sociological aspects of systematic management development', *Journal of Management Studies*, vol 3, pp1–18

Wilson, C. (1994) *Earth Heritage Conservation*, Geological Society London and Open University, Milton Keynes

Winter, C., Lockwood, M. and Morrison, M. (2003) 'Value based segmentation of community stakeholders: Applications for natural area management', *Natural Resource Management*, vol 6, no 2, pp33–40

Wolmer, W. (2005) 'Transboundary protected area governance: Tensions and paradoxes', in Pansky, D. (ed) *Governance Stream of the Vth World Parks Congress*, Parks Canada and IUCN/WCPA, Ottawa

Wondolleck, J. M. and Yaffee, S. L. (2000) *Making Collaboration Work: Lessons from Innovation in NRM*, Island Press, Washington, DC

Wood, C. (2003) *Environmental Impact Assessment: A Comparative Review*, 2nd edition, Prentice Hall, Harlow

Wood, H., McDaniel, M. and Warner, K. (eds) (1995) *Community Development and Conservation of Forest Biodiversity through Community Forestry*, Regional Community Forestry Training Centre, Kasetsart University, Bangkok

Wood, L. J., Fish, L., Laughren, J. and Pauly, D. (2005) 'A global review of marine protected areas', Paper presented to the International Marine Protected Areas Congress, Geelong, Australia

Woodford, J. (2000) *The Wollemi Pine*, The Text Publishing Company, Melbourne

Worboys, G. L. (2006) *Requirements for Protected Area Management Evaluation*, PhD thesis, Griffith University, Gold Coast

Worboys, G. L. and De Lacy, T. (2003) 'Tourism and the environment: It's time!', Paper presented at the 11th Ecotourism Australia National Conference, Adelaide

Worboys, G. L., Lockwood, M. and De Lacy, T. (2005) *Protected Area Management: Principles and Practice*, 2nd edition, Oxford University Press, Melbourne

Worboys, G. L., Worboys, P. M., Gare, N. and Snedden, R. (2004) *Protected Area Management: A Chronology of Key Events*, Canberra

World Bank (1995) *Financial Accounting, Reporting and Auditing Handbook (FARAH)*, 1st edition, Central and Operational Accounting Division, World

Bank, Washington, DC

World Bank (1997) *The World Bank Operational Manual*, www.wbln0018.worldbank.org/ Institutional/Manuals/OpManual.nsf/OPolw/ 38797

World Bank (1998) *Audit Manual for World Bank Financed Projects*, Central Operational Services Unit, East Asia and Pacific Region.

World Bank (2003) *Global Economic Prospects: Realizing the Development Promise of the Doha Agenda 2004*, World Bank, Washington, DC

World Bank (2005a) *About Us*, www.worldbank.org/ WBSITE/EXTERNAL/EXTABOUTUS/ 0,,pagePK:50004410~piPK:36602~theSitePK:29 708,00.html

World Bank (2005b) *Biodiversity*, www.worldbank.org/

World Travel and Tourism Council (1997) 'WTTC update – New environmental standard demonstrates compliance with Agenda 21', www.hospitalitynet.org/news/4000904.html

WRI (World Resources Institute) (1989) *Natural Endowments: Financing Resource Conservation for Development*, WRI, Washington, DC

WRI (2005) *The Wealth of the Poor: Managing Ecosystems to Fight Poverty*, WRI, Washington, DC

WRI, IUCN (World Conservation Union) and UNEP (United Nations Environment Programme) (1992) *Global Biodiversity Strategy*, WRI, Washington, DC

WTO (World Tourism Organization) (2004a) *Tourism Highlights: Edition 2004*, WTO, Madrid

WTO (2004b) *Tourism Congestion Management at Natural and Cultural Sites*, WTO, Madrid

WTTC (World Travel and Tourism Council) (2004) *Travel and Tourism Forging Ahead*, WTTC, London

WWF (World Wide Fund for Nature) (1998) *Ecoregion Action Programmes: A Guide for Practitioners*, WWF, Washington, DC

WWF (2004) *Are Protected Areas Working? An Analysis of Forest Protected Areas by WWF*, WWF International, Gland

WWF (2005a) *Conservation Science: Ecoregions*, www.worldwildlife.org/science/ecoregions/.cfm

WWF (2005b) *Conservation Science: Global 200 Ecoregions*, www.worldwildlife.org/science/ ecoregions/g200.cfm

WWF (2005c) *Conservation Science: Terrestrial Ecoregions of the World*, www.worldwildlife.org/ science/ecoregions/terrestrial.cfm

WWF (2005d) *World Wide Fund for Nature Global 200*, www.panda.org/about_wwf/ where_we_work/ecoregions/global200/pages/ home.htm

WWF (2005e) *WWF – The Global Conservation Organization*, www.panda.org/

Yaffee, S. L., Phillips, A. F., Frentz, I. C, Hardy, P. W., Maleki, S. W. and Thorpe, B. E. (1996) *Ecosystem Management in the United States*, Island Press, Washington, DC

Yagoda, B. (1990) 'Cleaning up a dirty image', *Business Month*, April, pp48–51

Yencken, D. and Williamson, D. (2001) *Resetting the Compass: Australia's Journey Towards Sustainability (updated version)*, CSIRO Publishing, Melbourne

Young, A. M. (2005) *A Field Guide to the Fungi of Australia*, UNSW Press, Sydney

Younge, A. (2002) 'An ecoregional approach to biodiversity conservation in the Cape Floral Kingdom, South Africa', in O'Riordan, T. and Stoll-Kleemann, S. (eds) *Biodiversity, Sustainability and Human Communities: Protecting Beyond the Protected*, Cambridge University Press, Cambridge

Zambia National Tourist Board (2005) *South Luangwa National Park*, www.zambiatourism.com/ welcome.htm

Zhuo Rongsheng (2004) *China Determines Panda's Population Using GPS/GIS*, www.chinadaily.com .cn/english/doc/2004–06/10/ content_338386.htm

Zomer, R., Ustin, S. L. and Ives, J. D. (1999) *Remote Sensing for Rapid Ecological Assessment in Mountain Environments: Landscape Analysis of the Makalu Barun National Park and Conservation Area, Nepal*, University of California, Davis

Zuluaga, G. and Giraldo, I. (2002) 'Proceso de creación de un area especial de conservación biocultural', in *Parques con la Gente II*, Unidad Administrativa Especial, Sistema de Parques Nacionales Naturales de Colombia, Min. Medioambiente, Bogotá

Zuluaga, G., Giraldo, J. I. and Larrarte, M. J. (2003) 'Un ejemplo de conservacion bio-cultural – el Parque Nacional Natural Alto Fragua–Indiwasi en Colombia', *Policy Matters*, vol 12, pp171–180

Index